SWEET
WANTS YOU

S0-AVG-721

**NOW DEPLOYING FABULOUS WOMEN FOR
GORGEOUS & MEANINGFUL VACATIONS
ALL OVER THE WORLD.**

ENLIST NOW! CALL 877 793 3830
DISCOVERSWEET.COM

THIS SUMMER,
get away
WITH **curve**

Subscribe to **Around the Curve**,
the eblast for travel lovers,
and read about our hottest travel contests,
including vacations to Sweden,
Las Vegas and the Caribbean!

curve
the best-selling lesbian magazine

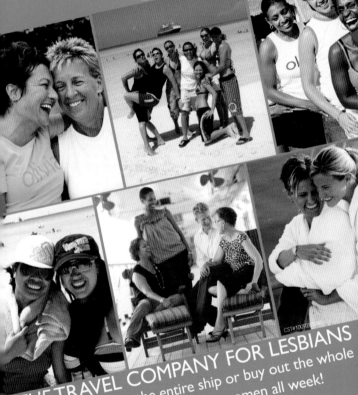

womenfest
2012
gay key west
september 4-9

MEN OVERBOARD.

Actually, between the warm water, endless sunshine and incredible variety of things to eat, drink and do, it's quite easy for everyone to go a little overboard in Key West.

KeyWest

Close To Perfect - Far From Normal

fla-keys.com/gaykeywest ~ 1-888-327-9831

A place for remembrance and renewal

There is a NATIONAL memorial dedicated to all lives touched by AIDS located in San Francisco's Golden Gate Park.

For more information, visit our website at www.AIDSmemorial.org, or call 415 765-0497.

THE NATIONAL AIDS MEMORIAL GROVE

ENSURING THAT THE GLOBAL TRAGEDY OF AIDS WILL NEVER BE FORGOTTEN.

NATIONAL · A I D S · MEMORIAL

Read us online at

LESBIAN NEWS

LN PUBLISHING INC.

JORJA FOX
KRISTEN HOLLY SMITH

Hillary Clinton

LN Magazine
is the longest
running lesbian
periodical in
the world.

of 40,000
with a total
readership
upward of
120,000.

We Got The Beat
THE GO-GO'S

FUSION

GWEN STEFANI

to bookstores including Borders,
Barnes & Noble as well as other
nationwide and local booksellers.

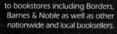

CALIFORNIA
MARRIAGE
VICTORY

The Gymnast
Dena Weber and Addie Yungmee

DO NOT BOX HER IN

are professionals
between the ages
of 18-55, trend setters and brand loyal
supporters of gay-friendly companies.

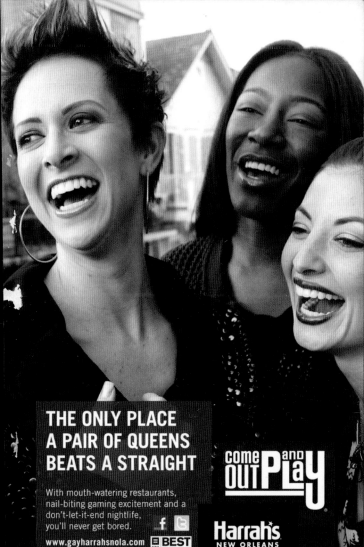

**THE ONLY PLACE
A PAIR OF QUEENS
BEATS A STRAIGHT**

With mouth-watering restaurants,
nail-biting gaming excitement and a
don't-let-it-end nightlife,
you'll never get bored.

www.gayharrahsnola.com

**come and
OUT PLAY**

Harrah's
NEW ORLEANS

BEST
PLACES TO WORK
2011 for LGBT Equality
100% CORPORATE EQUALITY INDEX

[sfpride.org]

SAN FRANCISCO
PRIDE

THE 2012 CELEBRATION AND PARADE TAKES PLACE
JUNE 23-24

"Just Expressing Ourselves."

MIAMI

EXPRESS YOURSELF

Whether it's a splash in a tropical oasis, a stroll in South Beach or an afternoon at one of our pampering spas, Miami's the place to experience together. Miami's the city that inspires you to do the things you couldn't – or wouldn't – do anywhere else.

Explore MiamiLGBT.com for a free LGBT Vacation Guide.
Visit the LGBT Visitor Center on 1130 Washington Ave., Miami Beach.

Winter Party [March] • Miami Beach Gay Pride [April] • Miami Gay & Lesbian Film Festival [April] • Aqua Girl [May] • Sizzle Miami [May] Miami Beach Bruthaz Conference [July] • White Party [November]

frameline36

San Francisco International LGBT Film Festival

June 14-24, 2012   www.frameline.org

Winter PRIDE

FEB. 5-12, 2012
WHISTLER, BC

CELEBRATING

20
YEARS

1992
TO
2012

www.flygirlproductions.com

Girls That Roam

kickin' through continents & bustin' boundaries

wine

dine

buckle up

dance

play

getaway

sleep

groove

Work hard, play rough...relax.

Adventures, journeys, & vacations
about, by, & for you.

**Pack your bags!
SIGN UP TODAY**
@girlsthatroam.com

Catch us in 2012
in a city near you!

COME PLAY WITH pandora events
COAST TO COAST

LAS VEGAS, NV · ORLANDO, FL · MIAMI BEACH, FL · VIEQUES, PUERTO RICO

FOR MORE INFORMATION ON TRAVEL DESTINATIONS, EVENTS AND NEWSLETTER, VISIT WWW.PANDORAEVENTS.COM

DON'T MISS OUR OTHER ANNUAL EVENTS: ATLANTA PRIDE, MIAMI BEACH GAY PRIDE, PENSACOLA WOMEN'S WEEK, NEW YEAR'S IN SOUTH BEACH AND MORE

Traveller Codes

Most of the codes used in this book are self-explanatory. Here are the few, however, that aren't.

▶—This symbol marks an advertiser. Please look for their display ad near this listing, and be sure to tell them you saw their ad in the *Damron Women's Traveller*.

Popular—So we've heard from the business and/or a reader.

Mostly Women—80-90% lesbian crowd.

Mostly Gay Men—Women welcome.

Lesbians/Gay Men—Roughly 50/50 mix of lesbians and gay men.

LGBT—Lesbian, Gay, Bisexual, and Transgendered.

Gay/Straight—A little bit of everything.

Gay-Friendly—LGBT folk are definitely welcome but are rarely the ones hosting the party.

Neighborhood Bar—Regulars and a local flavor, often has a pool table.

Dancing/DJ—Usually has a DJ at least Friday and Saturday nights.

Transgender-Friendly—Transsexuals, cross-dressers, and other transgendered people welcome.

Live Shows—From an open mic to live music.

Multiracial—A good mix of women of color and their friends.

Beer/Wine—Beer and/or wine. No hard liquor.

Nonsmoking—No smoking anywhere inside premises.

Private Club—Found mainly in the US South where it's the only way to keep a liquor license. Call the bar before you go out and tell them you're visiting. They will advise you of their policy regarding membership. Usually have set-ups so you can BYOB.

Wheelchair Access—Includes rest room.

WiFi—Wireless Internet access.

the Damron Women's Traveller

Publisher	**Damron Company**
President	**Gina M. Gatta**
Editor-in-Chief	**Erika O'Connor**
Roving Editor	**Ian Philips**
Editorial Assistant	**David Duckworth**
Director of Art & Advertising	**Kathleen Pratt**
Cover Photo & Design	**Mary Burroughs**

Board of Directors
Gina M. Gatta, Edward Gatta, Jr., Louise Mock

How to Contact Us

Mail:	PO Box 422458,
	San Francisco, CA 94142-2458
Email:	info@damron.com
Web:	www.damron.com
Fax:	415/703-9049
Phone:	415/255-0404 & 800/462-6654

Table of Contents

United States

Table of Contents

International

Tours & Events

ALABAMA

Statewide

PUBLICATIONS

Ambush Mag 504/522–8047 • LGBT newspaper for the Gulf South (TX through FL)

Noise • monthly LGBT publication

Birmingham

ACCOMMODATIONS

The Tutwiler Hotel 2021 Park Pl N (at 21st St N) 205/322–2100 • gay-friendly • also restaurant & lounge • WiFi • wheelchair access • $130+

BARS

The Garage Cafe 2304 10th Terrace S (at 23rd St S) 205/322–3220 • 11am-close, from 3pm Sun-Mon • gay-friendly • great sandwiches • live music

Our Place 205/715–0077 • 4pm-midnight, till 2am Fri-Sat • mostly gay men • neighborhood bar • videos • gay-owned

Wine Loft 2200 1st Ave N 205/323–8228 • 5pm-close, clsd Sun-Mon • gay-friendly • wine bar • light food served

NIGHTCLUBS

Joe's on 7th 2627 7th Ave S (at 27th St) 205/321–2812 • lesbians/ gay men • neighborhood bar • dancing/DJ • drag shows • theme nights • 18+

The Quest Club 416 24th St S (at 5th Ave S) 205/251–4313 • 24hrs • mostly gay men • dancing/DJ • 19+ Wed-Sun • drag shows • private club • patio • wheelchair access • cover charge

Steel Urban Lounge 2300 1st Ave N (at 23rd St) 205/324–0666 • 4pm-close, from 8pm wknds • gay-friendly • upscale lounge • dancing/DJ

Birmingham

LGBT PRIDE:
June. web: www.centralal-abamapride.org.

ANNUAL EVENTS:
March - Birmingham Shout: Gay & Lesbian Film Festival of Alabama 205/324-0888, web: www.bhamshout.com.
April/May - Birmingham International Center 205/252-7652, web: www.bic-al.org.
June - Alabama Shakespeare Festival 800/841-4273, web: www.asf.net.

CITY INFO:
800/458–8085 or 205/458-8000, web: www.birminghamal.org.

BEST VIEW:
Overlook Park.

WEATHER:
Hot and humid in the 80°s and 90°s during the summer, mild in the 50°s to low 40°s during the winter.

ATTRACTIONS:
Alabama Jazz Hall of Fame 205/254-2731, web: www.jazzhall.com.
Birmingham Zoo & Botanical Gardens 205/879-0409, web: www.birminghamzoo.com.
Civil Rights Museum 205/328-9696, web: www.bcri.org.
Sloss Furnaces Nat'l Historic Landmark 205/324-1911, web: www.slossfurnaces.com.
Vulcan Statue at 20th St S & Valley Ave, atop Red Mountain.

TRANSIT:
Yellow Cab 205/328-4444, web:www.birminghamyellow-cab.com.
Birmingham Airport shuttle 205/591-5550, www.birmingham-doortodoor.com.
Birmingham Transit Authority 205/521-0101, web: www.bjcta.org.

CAFES

Chez Lulu 1909 Cahaba Rd **205/870–7011** • lunch & dinner Tue-Sun, Sun brunch, clsd Mon • plenty veggie • also bakery • live shows

RESTAURANTS

Bottega Cafe & Restaurant 2240 Highland Ave S (btwn 22nd & 23rd) **205/939–1000** • 5:30pm-10pm, clsd Sun • some veggie • full bar • wheelchair access

The Bottletree 3719 3rd Ave S (at 37th St S) **205/533–6288** • 11am-close Tue-Sat, till 3pm Sun • vegetarian/ vegan • also bar • also live music venue

Highlands Bar & Grill 2011 11th Ave S (at 20th St) **205/939–1400** • 5:30pm-10pm, clsd Sun-Mon • wheelchair access

John's City Diner 112 21st St N (btwn 1st & 2nd Ave N) **205/322–6014** • lunch weekdays & dinner Mon-Sat, clsd Sun • seafood & steak • full bar • wheelchair access

Rojo 2921 Highland Ave S (at 30th St) **205/328–4733** • 11am-10pm, clsd Mon, wknd brunch • Latin & American cuisine

Silvertron Cafe 3813 Clairmont Ave S (at 39th St S) **205/591–3707** • 7am-10pm, 11am-9pm Sun • also full bar • more gay Mon

Taj India 2226 Highland Ave S **205/939–3805** • lunch & dinner • Indian • plenty veggie

ENTERTAINMENT & RECREATION

Terrific New Theatre 2821 2nd Ave S (in Dr Pepper Design Complex) **205/328–0868**

Tragic City Rollers • Birmingham's female roller derby league • visit www.dixiederbygirls.com for events

PUBLICATIONS

Noise • monthly LGBT publication

EROTICA

Alabama Adult Books 801 3rd Ave N (at 8th) **205/322–7323**

Dothan

NIGHTCLUBS

Club Imagination 4129 Ross Clark Circle NW (off Hwy 431 N) **334/792–6555** • 6pm-4am, clsd Sun-Tue • lesbians/ gay men • dancing/DJ • transgender-friendly • karaoke • drag shows • 18+ • private club

Dothan Dance Club 2563 Ross Clark Circle (at Hwy 52 West) **334/792–5166** • 11pm Fri, from 6pm Sat-Sun, clsd Mon-Th • gay/straight • drag shows • cabaret • private club • gay-owned

Foley

NIGHTCLUBS

Club Evolution 8380 Hwy 59 **251/943–5557** • 9pm-close, from 6pm Fri-Sat, clsd Tue • lesbians/ gay men • dancing/DJ • karaoke • drag shows

Geneva

ACCOMMODATIONS

Spring Creek Campground & Resort 163 Campground Rd (at Hwy 52 & Country Rd 4) **334/684–3891** • mostly gay men • cabins • also tent & RV sites • BYOB • pool • nudity ok • some theme wknds w/ DJ • WiFi • gay-owned • $17-85

Huntsville

BARS

Partners 256/539–0975 • 5pm-2am, from 6pm wknds • lesbians/ gay men • dancing/DJ • food served • live entertainment • karaoke • wheelchair access • lesbian-owned

Vieux Carre 1204 Posey (at Larkin) **256/534–5970** • 6pm-2am • lesbians/ gay men • neighborhood bar • DJ Th-Sun • drag shows Th-Sun • patio • wheelchair access

ENTERTAINMENT & RECREATION

Dixie Derby Girls • Huntsville's female roller derby league • visit www.dixiederbygirls.com for events

Mobile

see also Pensacola, Florida

INFO LINES & SERVICES

Pink Triangle AA Group 251/479–9994 **(AA#),** 251/438–7080 **(CHURCH)** • 7pm Tue, Th & Sat • call for locations

ACCOMMODATIONS

Berney/ Fly B&B 1118 Government St **251/405–0949** • gay-friendly • full brkfst • pool • jacuzzi • nonsmoking • WiFi • wheelchair access • $89-229

BARS

Bacchus 54 S Conception St **251/445–4099** • 8pm-close Wed-Sat • lesbians/ gay men • neighborhood bar • non-smoking

Gabriel's Downtown 55 S Joachim St (off Government) **251/432–4900** • 7pm-close • lesbians/ gay men • videos • karaoke • patio • private club

Midtown Pub 153 S Florida St (at Emogene)
251/450-1555 • noon-2am • lesbians/ gay
men • neighborhood bar • dancing/DJ •
karaoke • food served

NIGHTCLUBS

B–Bob's Downtown 213 Conti St (at
Joachim) **251/433-2262** • 6pm-close, from
7pm Sat • mostly men • dancing/DJ • also gift
shop • wheelchair access

Montgomery

ACCOMMODATIONS

The Lattice Inn 1414 S Hull St (at Clanton)
334/262-3388 • mixed gay/ straight • pool •
nonsmoking • WiFi • wheelchair access • $90-
235

NIGHTCLUBS

Club 322 322 N Lawrence St **334/263-4322**
• 5pm-close, from 9pm Fri-Sat, clsd Mon-Tue •
lesbians/ gay men • dancing/DJ • drag shows

ALASKA

Statewide

ENTERTAINMENT & RECREATION

Out in Alaska PO Box 82096, Fairbanks
99708 **877/374-9958, 907/374-9958** •
adventure travel throughout Alaska for LGBT
travelers

Anchorage

INFO LINES & SERVICES

AA Gay/ Lesbian 336 E 5th Ave (at
Community Center) **907/929-4528** • 6pm
Mon

Gay/ Lesbian Helpline 1300 East St
907/258-4777 • 6pm-11pm, ask about
women's events: usually every Sat except
summers when everyone's outdoors

Identity, Inc 336 E 5th Ave **907/929-4528** •
LGBT community center • newsletter

ACCOMMODATIONS

A Wildflower Inn B&B 1239 I St (at 13th)
907/274-1239, 877/693-1239 • gay/ straight •
close to hiking trails & scenic vistas • fun hosts
• nonsmoking • WiFi • gay-owned • $79-139

Alaska Heavenly Lodge 34950 Blakely Rd
(at Mile 49 Sterling Hwy), Cooper Landing
907/595-2012, 866/595-2012 • gay-friendly •
hot tub • cedar sauna • nonsmoking • $650-
1,000

Alaska's North Country Castle B&B 14600
Joanne Ct **907/345-7296** • gay-friendly •
ocean & mtn views • full brkfst • nonsmoking
• $159-249

Anchorage Jewel Lake B&B 8125 Jewel
Lake Rd **907/245-7321, 877/245-7321** • gay/
straight • full brkfst • kids ok • WiFi •
nonsmoking • gay-owned

Arctic Fox Inn 327 E 2nd Ct **907/272-4818,
877/693-1239** • gay/ straight • also apts
• gay-owned

City Garden B&B 1352 W 10th Ave (at N St)
907/276-8686 • gay-straight • beautiful views
of Mt McKinley • 10-minute walk to downtown
area • nonsmoking • gay-owned • $100-150

Copper Whale Inn 440 L St **907/258-7999,
866/258-7999** • gay/ straight • located
downtown • WiFi • nonsmoking • gay-owned
• wheelchair access • $95-220

Earth B&B & Tours 1001 W 12th Ave
907/279-9907 • gay-friendly • close to
downtown • nonsmoking • WiFi • woman-
owned • $70-130

Gallery B&B 1229 G St (at 12th)
907/274-2567 • gay/ straight • kids/ pets ok •
wheelchair access • lesbian-owned

Inlet Tower Hotel & Suites 1200 L St (at
12th) **907/276-0110, 800/544-0786** • gay/
straight • kids/ pets ok • WiFi • wheelchair
access • also bar & restaurant • $99-319

BARS

Bernie's Bungalow 626 D St (at W 5th Ave)
907/276-8808 • gay-friendly • cocktail lounge
• patio • food served

Kodiak Bar 225 E 5th Ave (btwn Cordova &
Barrow) **907/258-5233, 907/865-8978** • 3pm-
2:30am, till 5am Fri-Sat • lesbians/ gay men •
food served • DJ wknds

Mad Myrna's 530 E 5th Ave (at Fairbanks)
907/276-9762 • 4pm-2:30am, till 3am Fri-Sat
• lesbians/ gay men • neighborhood bar •
dancing/DJ • karaoke • food served • drag
shows

Raven 708 E 4th Ave **907/276-9672** • 1pm-
2:30am, till 3am wknds • lesbians/ gay men •
neighborhood bar • wheelchair access

RESTAURANTS

Bear Tooth Theatre Pub & Grill 1230 W
27th Ave **907/276-4200** • movie theater, pub
& grill all in one

China Lights 12110 Business Blvd, Eagle
River **907/694-8080** • 11:30am-10pm, till
10:30pm wknds

Club Paris 417 W 5th Ave 907/277–6332 • 11am-midnight, from 4pm Sun • perhaps the finest restaurant in town

Garcia's 11901 Business Blvd #104 (next to Safeway), Eagle River 907/694-8600 • 11am-midnight, from noon wknds • Mexican

Ginger 425 W 5th Ave (at D St) 907/929–3680 • lunch Mon-Fri, dinner nightly, bar from 3pm • Pacific Rim/ Asian

Marx Brothers Cafe 627 W 3rd Ave 907/278-2133 • 5:30-10pm, clsd Sun-Mon • great food and views

Simon & Seafort's 420 L St (btwn 4th & 5th) 907/274-3502 • lunch weekdays, dinner nightly • seafood & prime rib • full bar • great views

Snow City Cafe 1034 W 4th Ave (at L St) 907/272–2489 • 7am-3pm, till 4pm wknds

ENTERTAINMENT & RECREATION

Out North 3800 DeBarr Rd 907/279-3800, 907/279-8099 • community-based & visiting-artist exhibits, screenings & performances

BOOKSTORES

Title Wave Books 1360 W Northern Lights Blvd 907/278-9283 • 10am-8pm, till 9pm Fri-Sat, 11am-7pm Sun • largest independent bookstore in Alaska • also at 415 W 5th Ave, 907/258–9283

RETAIL SHOPS

The Sports Shop 570 E Benson Blvd 907/272–7755 • 10am-7pm, till 6pm Sat, noon-5pm Sun • women's outdoor clothing, adventure gear & equipment

Anchorage

LGBT PRIDE:
June. web: alaskapride.org.

ANNUAL EVENTS:
January - Anchorage Folk Festival, web: www.anchoragefolkfestival.org.
February - World Ice Art Championship 907/451-8250, web: www.icealaska.com.
March - Iditarod Sled Dog Race 907/376-5155, web: www.iditarod.com.
June - Mayor's Marathon 907/786-1325, web: www.mayors-marathon.com.
August - Alaska State Fair 907/745-4827, web: www.alaskastatefair.org.
October - Quyana Alaska (native dance celebration) 907/274-3611, web: www.nativefederation.org.

CITY INFO:
907/276-4118, web: www.anchorage.net.

BEST VIEW:
The 11-mile-long paved Tony Knowles Coastal Trail along Cook Inlet offers spectacular views of several mountains, including Denali (Mt McKinley).

ATTRACTIONS:
Alaska Museum of Natural History, 907/274-2400, web: www.alaskamuseum.org.
Alaska Native Heritage Center 907/330-8000, web: www.alaskanative.net.
Alaska Wildlife Conservation Center (in Portage) 907/783-2025, web: www.alaskawildlife.org.
Portage Glacier.
Wolf Song of Alaska Museum 907/622-9653, web: www.wolf-songalaska.org.

WEATHER:
Anchorage's climate is milder than one might think, due to its coastal location. It is cold in the winter (but rarely below 0°F), and it warms up considerably in June, July, and August. Winter sets in around October. Expect more rain in late summer/ early fall.

TRANSIT:
Checker Cab 907/276-1234.
Alaska Shuttle 907/338-8888, 907/694-8888, web: www.alaskashuttle.net.
Rideline (bus) 907/343-6543, www.muni.org/transit1/rideline.cfm.

Anchorage Press 907/561–7737 • alternative paper • arts & entertainment listings

EROTICA

Le Shop 305 W Diamond Blvd (at C St) 907/522–1987 • 8am-1am

Fairbanks

ACCOMMODATIONS

All Seasons B&B Inn 763 7th Ave (at Barnette St) 907/451–6649, 888/451–6649 • gay-friendly • full brkfst • nonsmoking • WiFi • wheelchair access • $99-215

Billie's Backpackers Hostel 2895 Mack Blvd 907/479–2034 • gay-friendly • kids ok • food served • women-owned

CAFES

Hot Licks Ice Cream 3453 College Rd 907/479–7813 • seasonal

Haines

ACCOMMODATIONS

The Guardhouse Boarding House 15 Fort Seward Dr 907/766–2566, 866/290–7445 • lesbians/ gay men • in former jail of Fort William H. Seward • great views of Lynn Canal • bald eagle-watching • nonsmoking • WiFi • lesbian-owned • $85-115

Homer

ACCOMMODATIONS

Sadie Cove Wilderness Lodge Kachemak Bay State Park 907/235–2350, 888/283–7234 • gay-friendly • 5 cabins • tree planted for every guest to offset carbon emissions • built from hand-milled driftwood • uses nonpolluting alternative energy • 3 full meals a day • nonsmoking • $400/person

Spit Sister B&B Homer Spit Rd (at Harbor View Boardwalk #5, at Spit Sister Cafe) 907/235–4921 (SUMMER), 907/299–7748 • gay/ straight • full brkfst • kids/ 1 small pet ok • private deck overlooks Homer Harbor • nonsmoking • WiFi • cafe downstairs • women-owned

CAFES

Spit Sister Cafe Homer Spit Rd (at Harbor View Boardwalk #5) 907/235–4921 (SUMMER), 907/299–6868/ 6767 (WINTER) • 5am-4pm • gay/ straight • WiFi • also B&B • women-owned

ENTERTAINMENT & RECREATION

Alaska Fantastic Fishing Charters 800/478–7777 • deluxe cabin cruiser for big-game fishing (halibut)

Juneau

ACCOMMODATIONS

Pearson's Pond Luxury Suites & Adventure Spa 4541 Sawa Circle 907/789–3772, 888/658–6328 • gay-friendly • B&B resort & spa • hot tub • nonsmoking

The Silverbow 120 Second St 907/586–4146, 800/586–4146 • gay-friendly • full brkfst • also restaurant & bakery • alternative cinema • gallery • kids ok • nonsmoking • WiFi • $89-219

RESTAURANTS

Hangar on the Wharf 2 Marine Way Ste 106 907/586–5018 • lunch & dinner • full bar • great fish & chips

Ketchikan

ACCOMMODATIONS

Anchor Inn by the Sea 4672 S Tongass Hwy 907/247–7117, 800/928–3308 • gay-friendly • nonsmoking • WiFi

ENTERTAINMENT & RECREATION

Southeast Sea Kayak 1621 Tongass Ave, Ste 101B 907/225–1258, 800/287–1607 • trip planning • tours • wilderness kayaking

McCarthy

ACCOMMODATIONS

Ma Johnson's Hotel 907/554–4402 • gay-friendly • full brkfst • also restaurant • kids ok • inside America's largest nat'l park, Wrangell St Elias • nonsmoking • $129-259

Palmer

ACCOMMODATIONS

Alaska Garden Gate B&B 950 S Trunk Rd 907/746–2333 • gay/ straight • full brkfst • hot tub • kids/ pets ok • WiFi • lesbian-owned • $89-169

Seward

ENTERTAINMENT & RECREATION

Puffin Fishing Charters PO Box 606, 99664 907/224–4653, 800/978–3346 • gay/ straight • day fishing trips

Sitka

CAFES

Backdoor Cafe 104 Barracks St (behind Old Harbor Books on Lincoln St, no street sign) 907/747-8856 • 6:30am-5pm, till 2pm Sat, clsd Sun • pleasant & funky hangout

ENTERTAINMENT & RECREATION

Esther G Sea Taxi 215 Shotgun Alley 907/738-6481, 907/747-6481 • marine wildlife tours

ARIZONA

Apache Junction

ACCOMMODATIONS

Susa's Serendipity Ranch 4375 E Superstition Blvd 480/288-9333 • women only • guesthouses on 15-acre ranch • 2 RV hookups • hot tub • nonsmoking • pets ok • lesbian-owned

Bisbee

ACCOMMODATIONS

Casa de San Pedro B&B 8933 S Yell Ln (at Hwy 92 & Palominas Rd), Hereford 520/366-1300, 888/257-2050 • gay-friendly • full brkfst • pool • hot tub • nonsmoking • WiFi • wheelchair access • gay-owned • $169+

Copper Queen Hotel 11 Howell Ave 520/432-2216 • gay-friendly • restored landmark hotel • kids ok • pool • nonsmoking • restaurant • wheelchair access • $89-197

David's Oasis Camping Resort 5311 W Double Adobe Rd, McNeal 520/979-6650 • lesbians/gay men • 21+ • pool • also bar & internet cafe • WiFi • gay-owned • $14-20

Eldorado Suites 55 OK St 520/432-6679 • gay-friendly • territorial architecture •WiFi • kitchens • nonsmoking • $125+

Sleepy Dog Guest House 212A Opera Dr 520/432-3057, 520/234-8166 (CELL) • gay-friendly • reclaimed miner's cabin • patio • great views • very dog-friendly • lots of stairs • WiFi • $115

BARS

Copper Rainbow Bistro 5311 W Double Adobe Rd, McNeal 520/979-6650 • 5pm-10pm Fri-Sat, 2pm-7pm Sun • lesbian/gay men • beer/ wine only

St Elmo's 36 Brewery Ave 520/432-5578 • 10am-2am • gay-friendly • live bands Fri-Sat

Bullhead City

includes Laughlin, Nevada

BARS

The Lariat Saloon 1161 Hancock Rd (at 95) 928/704-1969 • 10am-2am • lesbians/gay men • neighborhood bar • multiracial • patio • wheelchair access • woman-owned

Flagstaff

ACCOMMODATIONS

Abineau Lodge 1080 Mountainaire Rd 928/525-6212, 888/715-6386 • gay/ straight • huskies on premises • cedar sauna • full brkfst • nonsmoking • WiFi • gay-owned • $139-179

The Historic Hotel Monte Vista 100 N San Francisco St (at Aspen) 928/779-6971, 800/545-3068 • gay-friendly • live shows • full bar • nonsmoking

Inn at 410 410 N Leroux St 928/774-0088, 800/774-2008 • gay-friendly • full brkfst • WiFi • wheelchair access • $150-200

Motel in the Pines 80 W Pinewood Blvd (exit 322), Pinewood 928/286-9699, 800/574-5080 • gay-friendly • 20 miles from Flagstaff • wheelchair access • $49-89

Starlight Pines B&B 3380 E Lockett Rd (at Fanning) 928/527-1912, 800/752-1912 • gay/ straight • full gourmet brkfst • kids ok (call for details) • nonsmoking • WiFi • gay-owned • $139-189

BARS

Charly's Pub & Grill 23 N Leroux St (at Weatherford Hotel) 928/779-1919 • 8am-2am • gay-friendly • food served • some veggie • live shows nightly • patio • wheelchair access

Monte Vista Lounge 100 N San Francisco St (at Hotel Monte Vista) 928/774-2403 • noon-2am, from 11am Fri-Sun • gay-friendly • dancing/DJ • live bands • karaoke

CAFES

Macy's European Coffee House 14 S Beaver St 928/774-2243 • 6am-10pm • food served • vegetarian/ vegan bakery

RESTAURANTS

Cafe Olé 119 S San Francisco St (at Butler) 928/774-8272 • lunch & dinner, clsd Sun • Mexican • plenty veggie • beer/ wine • wheelchair access

Granny's Closet 218 S Milton Rd 928/774-8331 • lunch & dinner • also sports bar

Pasto 19 E Aspen (at San Francisco) **928/779-1937** • lunch & dinner, clsd Sun • Italian • beer/ wine • wheelchair access

Golden Valley

EROTICA

Pleasure Palace Adult Bookstore 4150 US Hwy 68 (at Houck Rd) **928/565-5600**

Jerome

ACCOMMODATIONS

The Cottage Inn Jerome **928/634-0701, 928/649-6759** • gay/ straight • full brkfst • kids/ pets ok • gay-owned

Mile High Grill & Inn 309 Main St **928/634-5094** • gay-friendly • cool hotel • also restaurant • lesbian-owned • $85-130

RESTAURANTS

Quince Grill & Cantina 363 S Main St **928/634-7087** • 8am-5pm, 7am-9pm Th-Sun • wheelchair access

Kingman

ACCOMMODATIONS

Kings Inn Best Western 2930 E Andy Devine Ave **928/753-6101, 800/750-6101** • gay-friendly • pool • food served • kids/ pets ok • WiFi • wheelchair access

Lake Havasu City

INFO LINES & SERVICES

Lake Havasu City AA 877/652-9005

ACCOMMODATIONS

Nautical Inn 1000 McCulloch Blvd N **928/855-2141, 800/892-2141** • gay-friendly • beachfront hotel • full restaurant & bar • WiFi • pool • $69-589

Lake Powell

ACCOMMODATIONS

Dreamkatchers Lake Powell B&B **435/675-5828** • gay/ straight • spa on deck • full brkfst • WiFi • gay-owned

Phoenix

see also Scottsdale & Tempe

INFO LINES & SERVICES

1 Voice LGBT Community Center 4442 North 7th Ave **602/712-0111** • noon-7pm, clsd Sun

Lambda Phoenix Center 2622 N 16th St (at Virginia Ave) **602/635-2090** • space for many 12-step programs

ACCOMMODATIONS

Clarendon Hotel & Suites 401 W Clarendon Ave (at 3rd Ave) **602/252-7363** • gay/ straight • boutique hotel in midtown • pool • WiFi • wheelchair access • gay-owned

FireSky Resort & Spa 4925 N Scottsdale Rd, Scottsdale **480/945-7666, 800/528-7867** • gay-friendly • pool • garden courtyard spa • WiFi • wheelchair access

Hotel San Carlos 202 N Central Ave **602/253-4121, 866/253-4121** • gay-friendly • boutique hotel • rooftop pool • restaurant • WiFi • $139

Hotel Theodore 7353 E Indian School Rd, Scottsdale **480/308-1100** • gay-friendly • hip boutique hotel, nightclub & bar & Cielo restaurant • pool • gym • nonsmoking • WiFi

Maricopa Manor B&B Inn 15 W Pasadena Ave **602/274-6302, 800/292-6403** • gay/ straight • pool • hot tub • WiFi • wheelchair access • gay-owned

Orange Blossom Hacienda 3914 E Sunnydale Dr, Gilbert **480/755-4346, 888/575-3484** • gay-friendly • pool • gay-owned

Scottsdale Thunderbird Suites 7515 E Butherus Dr (at Scottsdale Rd), Scottsdale **480/951-4000, 800/951-1288** • gay-friendly • full brkfst • pool • hot tub • nonsmoking • WiFi • kids ok • also full bar • wheelchair access • $139

ZenYard 830 E Maryland Ave **623/252-1002, 866/594-0242** • gay/ straight • private suites w/ kitchens • saltwater pool

BARS

Amsterdam 718 N Central Ave (btwn Roosevelt & Fillmore) **602/258-6122** • 4pm-2am, till 4am wknds • lesbians/ gay men • upscale bar • food served • karaoke • also Club Miami • dancing/DJ

Anvil 2303 E Indian School Rd **602/956-2885** • 1pm-2am • mostly gay men • dancing/DJ • leather • male revue

Apollo's 5749 N 7th St (S of Bethany Home) **602/277-9373** • 8am-2am• mostly gay men • neighborhood bar • karaoke • drag sgows • WiFi • patio

Bar 1 3702 N 16th St (at E Clarendon) **602/266-9001** • 10am-2am • mostly gay men • neighborhood bar • karoke • WiFi

Bar Smith 602/229–1265 • 11am-10pm, till 2am Fri-Sat, from 4pm Sat, clsd Sun • gay/straight • full menu

BS West 7125 E 5th Ave (in pedestrian mall), Scottsdale 480/945–9028 • 2pm-2am • lesbians/gay men • dancing/DJ • videos • karaoke • wheelchair access

Cash Inn Country 2140 E McDowell Rd (at 22nd St) 602/244–9943 • 2pm-close, from noon wknds • mostly women • dancing/DJ • country/western • karaoke • WiFi • wheelchair access

Club Sutra 2424 E Thomas Rd (at 24th St) 602/682–5088 • 5pm-2am Fri & 9pm-4am Sat, clsd Sun-Th • mostly women • dancing/DJ • multiracial clientele • wheelchair access

Cruisin' 7th 3702 N 7th St (near Indian School) 602/212–9888 • 6am-2am, from 10am Sun • mostly gay men • transgender-friendly • drag shows • karaoke • wheelchair access

Friends 1028 E Indian School Rd (at N 10th Pl) 602/277–7729 • mostly gay men • neighborhood bar • bears • food served • karaoke • gay-owned

Ice Pics 3108 E McDowell Rd (at 32nd St) 602/267–8707 • 4pm-2am, from 2pm Sun • mostly men • video bar

Kobalt 3110 N Central Ave 602/264–5307 • 11am-2am • lesbians/gay men • karaoke • live shows

Phoenix

WHERE THE GIRLS ARE:
Everywhere. Phoenix doesn't have one section of town where lesbians hang out, but the area between 5th Ave & 32nd St, and Camelback & Thomas Streets does contain most of the women's bars.

LGBT PRIDE:
April. 602/277-7433, web: www.azpride.org.

ANNUAL EVENTS:
April - Phoenix Film Festival 602/955-6444, web: www.phoenixfilmfestival.com.

April - Phoenix Improv Festival 480/389-4852, web: www.phoeniximprovfestival.com.

October - Rainbows Festival 602/770-8241, web: www.rainbowsfestival.com.

CITY INFO:
Arizona Office of Tourism 866/275-5816, web: www.arizonaguide.com.

Greater Phoenix Convention & Visitors Bureau 877/225-5749, web: www.visitphoenix.com.

BEST VIEW:
South Mountain Park at sunset, watching the city lights come on.

ATTRACTIONS:
Arizona Golf Association 602/944-3035, web: www.azgolf.org.

Castles & Coasters Park on Black Canyon Fwy & Peoria 602/997-7575, web: www.castlesncoasters.com.

Desert Botanical Garden in Papago Park 480/941-1225, web: www.dbg.org.

Heard Museum 602/252-8848, web: www.heardmuseumshop.com.

Hiking trails in Papago Park, Squaw Peak & Camelback Mtns.

Phoenix Zoo 602/273-1341, web: www.phoenixzoo.org.

WEATHER:
Beautifully mild and comfortable (60°s-80°s) October through March or April. Hot (90°s-100°s) in summer. August brings the rainy season (severe monsoon storms) with flash flooding.

TRANSIT:
Yellow Cab 602/252-5252, web: www.aaayellowaz.com.

Super Shuttle 602/244-9000, web: www.supershuttle.com.

Phoenix Transit 602/253-5000, www.valleymetro.org.

Lush Lounge 2050 N Alma School Rd #8, Chandler 480/857–9444 • 11am-2am, from 3pm Mon-Wed • food served • dancing Sat night • karaoke Fri night

Oz 1804 W Bethany Home Rd (at 19th) 602/242–5114 • 6am-2am • lesbians/gay men • neighborhood bar • videos • WiFi • wheelchair access

Plazma 1560 E Osborn Rd (at N 16th St) 602/266–0477 • 4pm-close, from noon wknds • lesbians/gay men • neighborhood bar • karaoke • videos

The Rock/ La Roca 4129 N 7th Ave (at Indian School) 602/248–8559 • 9am-2am, from noon Sun • lesbians/ gay men • neighborhood bar • dancing/DJ • karaoke • live shows

Roscoe's on 7th 4531 N 7th St (at Minnezona) 602/285–0833 • 3pm-1am, from 10am Sun • lesbians/gay men • sports bar • food served

Z Girl Club 4301 N 7th Ave (at Indian School Rd) 602/265–3233 • 5pm-2am, from 10am Th-Sun • mostly women • dancing/DJ • multiracial • karaoke • live /drag shows • wheelchair access • women-owned

NIGHTCLUBS

Hot Flash Phoenix 41 Mill Ave (at School of Rock), Tempe 503/252–9333 • mostly women • dancing/DJ • 2nd Sat of the month

Karamba 1724 E McDowell (at 16th St) 602/254–0231 • 4pm-close, clsd Mon-Wed • mostly gay men • dancing/DJ • drag shows • Latin wknds • wheelchair access

CAFES

Copper Star Coffee 4220 N 7th Ave (at Indian School) 602/266–2136 • 6am-9pm, till 11pm Fri-Sat • coffee in a converted gas station • WiFi

RESTAURANTS

Alexi's 3550 N Central Ave #120 (in Valley Bank Bldg) 602/279–0982 • lunch Mon-Fri, dinner nightly, clsd Sun • full bar • patio • wheelchair access

AZ/88 7553 E Scottsdale Mall, Scottsdale 480/994–5576 • 11:30am-1am (food till 12:30am), from 5pm wknds

Barrio Cafe 2814 N 16th St 602/636–0240 • lunch Tue-Fri, dinner Tue-Sun, Sun brunch, clsd Mon • Mexican • live music • lesbian-owned

Cheuvront Restaurant & Wine Bar 1326 N Central Ave (at McDowell) 602/307–0022 • 11am-10pm, till midnight Fri-Sat, 4pm-9pm Sun • gay/straight

Coronado Cafe 2201 N 7th St 602/258–5149 • lunch Mon-Sat, dinner Tue-Sat, clsd Sun

Durant's 2611 N Central Ave 602/264–5967 • lunch Mon-Fri, dinner nightly • American

Fez 3815 N Central Ave (S of Clarendon) 602/287–8700 • 11am-midnight, from 8:30am wknds • Moroccan influence • full bar • patio

Green 2240 N Scottsdale Rd #8, Tempe 480/941–9003 • 11am-9pm, clsd Sun • new American vegetarian/ vegan

Harley's Bistro 4221 N 7th Ave (N of Indian School) 602/234–0333 • lunch Tue-Fri, dinner nightly, clsd Mon • lesbians/gay men • Italian

Los Dos Molinos 8684 S Central Ave 602/243–9113 • lunch & dinner, clsd Sun-Mon • Mexican homecooking

MacAlpines's Soda Fountain 2303 N 7th St 602/262–5545 • 11am-7pm, till 8pm Fri-Sat, great milkshakes

Malee's 7131 E Main, Scottsdale 480/947–6042 • lunch & dinner • Thai • plenty veggie • full bar

Mi Patio 3347 N 7th Ave 602/277–4831 • 10am-10pm • Mexican

Persian Garden Cafe 1335 W Thomas Rd (at N 15th Ave) 602/263–1915 • lunch & dinner, lunch only Mon, dinner only Sat, clsd Sun • plenty veggie • WiFi

Portland's 105 W Portland St (at Central Ave) 602/795–7480 • lunch Tue-Fri, dinner Mon-Sat, clsd Sun • also wine bar

Restaurant Mexico 423 S Mill Ave, Tempe 480/967–3280 • 11am-9pm, till 10pm Fri-Sat, clsd Sun

Rose & Crown 628 E Adams St 602/256–0223 • 11am-2am • British pub

Switch 2603 N Central Ave 602/264–2295 • 11am-midnight, from 10am wknds • full bar • WiFi

Ticoz 5114 N 7th St (N of Camelback) 602/200–0160 • 11am-midnight • Latin cuisine • full bar • WiFi

Vincent on Camelback 3930 E Camelback Rd (at 40th St) 602/224–0225 • lunch Mon-Fri, dinner Mon-Sat, clsd Sun • Southwestern • wheelchair access

ENTERTAINMENT & RECREATION

Arizona Roller Derby • Arizona's female roller derby league • visit www.azrollerderby.com for events

Lesbian Social Network 480/946–5570 • 7:30pm-10pm Fri • popular informal social evenings of games, videos & discussions • smoke- & alcohol-free • call for location

Soul Invictus 1022 NW Grand Ave (near W Van Buren St) 602/214–4344 • queer-friendly art gallery & cabaret

Stray Cat Theatre 132 E 6th St, Tempe 480/820–8022 • provocative, off-the-beaten-path productions

BOOKSTORES

Changing Hands 6428 S McClintock Dr, Tempe 480/730–0205 • 10am-9pm, from 9am Sat, till 7pm Sun • new & used • LGBT section

RETAIL SHOPS

Off Chute Too 4115 N 7th Ave (at Indian School Rd) 602/274–1429 • 9am-9pm, till 10pm Fri-Sat, 10am-6pm Sun • LGBT gift shop in Melrose District

Root Seller Gallery 4015 N 16th St #H (at Indian School) 602/265–7668 • 10am-7pm, 11am-5pm Sun • LGBT books, music & gifts

PUBLICATIONS

Echo Magazine 602/266–0550, 888/324–6624 • bi-weekly LGBT newsmagazine

Ion Arizona Magazine 602/308–4662 • entertainment guide

'N Touch Magazine 602/373–9490 • LGBT newsmagazine

Women's Community Connection 480/946–5570 • monthly newspaper w/ events & lesbian resources

GYMS & HEALTH CLUBS

Pulse Fitness 18221 N Pima Rd #130, Scottsdale 480/907–5900

EROTICA

Adult Shoppe 111 S 24th St (at Jefferson) 602/306–1130 • 24hrs • also 5021 W Indian School Rd (at 51st Ave), & 2345 W Holly St

Castle Megastore 300 E Camelback (at Central) 602/266–3348 • 24hrs • also 5501 E Washington; 8802 N Black Canyon Fwy; 8315 E Apache Tr

Fascinations 10242 N 19th Ave #1-7 602/943–5859

Tuff Stuff Leatherware 1716 E McDowell Rd (at 17th St) 602/254–9651, 877/875–4167 • 10am-6pm, till 5pm Sat, clsd Sun-Mon • custom leather shop

Zorba's Adult Book Shop 2924 N Scottsdale Rd (N of Thomas), Scottsdale 480/941–9891 • 24hrs • video rentals & arcade

Prescott

INFO LINES & SERVICES

Prescott Pride Center 111 Josephine St (at Gurley St) 928/445–8800 • 2pm-5pm Sat & calendar of events • wheelchair access

ACCOMMODATIONS

The Motor Lodge 503 S Montezuma St (at Leroux) 928/717–0157 • gay-friendly • nonsmoking • WiFi • gay-owned • $89-139

Sedona

ACCOMMODATIONS

A Woman's Way PO Box 127, 86339 928/254–1897 • women only • "healing sanctuary" • retreats

Apple Orchard Inn 656 Jordan Rd 928/282–5328, 800/663–6968 • gay-friendly • full brkfst • hot tub • pool • hiking • scenic views • nonsmoking • wheelchair access

El Portal Sedona 95 Portal Ln 928/203–9405, 800/313–0017 • gay-friendly • suites in a 1910 adobe hacienda • nonsmoking • food served • WiFi • wheelchair acccess

The Lodge at Sedona—A Luxury B&B Inn 125 Kallof Pl 928/204–1942, 800/619–4467 • gay/ straight • full gourmet brkfst • pool • nonsmoking • WiFi • wheelchair access • $189-349

Sedona Rouge Hotel & Spa 2250 W Hwy 89-A 928/203–4111, 866/312–4111 • gay-friendly • pool • nonsmoking • WiFi • restaurant & bar • wheelchair access • $169-299

Southwest Inn at Sedona 3250 W Hwy 89–A 928/282–3344, 800/483–7422 • gay-friendly • pool • spa • workout room • WiFi • nonsmoking

CAFES

Old Town Red Rooster Cafe 901 N Main St, Cottonwood 928/649–8100 • 10am-4pm

RESTAURANTS

Judi's 40 Soldiers Pass Rd 928/282–4449 • lunch & dinner, clsd Sun • some veggie • full bar

Piñon Bistro 1075 S State Rte 260 (Rte 89-A), Cottonwood 928/649–0234 • dinner Th-Sun only • upscale • wheelchair access • lesbian-owned

RETAIL SHOPS

Sedona Green Gallery & Gifts 273 N Hwy 89A #F (btwn Jordan & Mesquite) **928/239–5353** • 10-15% discount to self-identifying gay & lesbian customers

Tucson

INFO LINES & SERVICES

AA Gay/ Lesbian 3269 N Mountain Ave **520/624–4183** • many mtgs

Wingspan, Southern Arizona's LGBT Community Center 430 E 7th St **520/624–1779, 800/553–9387** • 11am-2pm, resources, youth support (3pm-8pm Mon-Fri)

ACCOMMODATIONS

Armory Park Guesthouse 219 S 5th Ave **520/206–9252** • gay-friendly • renovated 1896 residence w/ 2 detached guest units • gay-owned

Catalina Park Inn 309 E 1st St **520/792–4541, 800/792–4885** • gay/ straight • full brkfst • nonsmoking • kids 10+ ok • WiFi • gay-owned

Desert Trails B&B 12851 E Speedway Blvd **520/885–7295, 877/758–3284** • gay-friendly • adobe hacienda on 3 acres bordering Saguaro Nat'l Park • far from the madding crowd • swimming • smoking outside only

Hotel Congress 311 E Congress St **520/622–8848, 800/722–8848** • gay/ straight • historic hotel • WiFi • also cafe, full bar & club

La Casita Del Sol 407 N Meyer Ave (btwn Church Ave & Franklin Ave) **520/623–8882** • gay/ straight • 1880s adobe guesthouse • pets ok w/ permission • nonsmoking • WiFi • gay-owned • $100-115

Natural B&B & Retreat **520/881–4582, 888/295–8500** • gay/ straight • full brkfst • nonsmoking • nontoxic/ nonallergenic • some shared baths • kids ok • WiFi • massage available • gay-owned

Tucson

LGBT PRIDE:
June & Oct 520/622-3200, web: www.tucsonpride.org.

ANNUAL EVENTS:
February - La Fiesta de los Vaqueros (rodeo & parade) 520/741-2233, web: www.tucsonrodeo.com.
April - Int'l Mariachi Music Conference 520/838-3908

CITY INFO:
520/624-1817, web: www.visittucson.org.

BEST VIEW:
From a ski lift heading up to the top of Mount Lemmon.

WEATHER:
350 days of sunshine a year. Need we say more?

TRANSIT:
Yellow Cab Tucson 520/624-6611, web: www.yellowcabtucson.com
Arizona Shuttle 800/888-2749, web: www.arizonashuttle.com.
Sun Tran 520/792-9222, web: www.suntran.com

ATTRACTIONS:
Arizona-Sonora Desert Museum 520/883-1380, web: www.desert-museum.org.
Arizona State Museum 520/621-6302, web: www.statemuseum.arizona.edu.
Biosphere 2 520/838-6200, web: www.b2science.org.
Catalina State Park 520/628-5798.
Colossal Cave 520/647-7275, web: www.colossalcave.com.
Mission San Xavier del Bac, 520/294-2624, web: www.sanxaviermission.org.
Old Tucson.
Saguaro National Park 520/733-5153, web: www.nps.gov/sagu.

Royal Elizabeth B&B Inn 204 S Scott Ave (at Broadway) **520/670-9022, 877/670-9022** • gay/ straight • full brkfst • pool • hot tub • kids ok • nonsmoking • WiFi • gay-owned

BARS

Ain't Nobody's Bizness 2900 E Broadway #118 (at Country Club) **520/318-4838** • 5pm-2am, clsd Mon • mostly women • dancing/DJ • karaoke • Latin Night Sat • wheelchair access

Club Congress/ The Tap Room 311 E Congress (at Hotel Congress) **520/622-8848** • 11am-2am • gay-friendly • neighborhood bar • dance club from 9pm • karaoke • live bands

IBT's (It's About Time) 616 N 4th Ave (at University) **520/882-3053** • noon-2am • lesbians/ gay men • dancing/DJ • live shows • karaoke • wheelchair access

Pulse 915 W Prince Rd **520/293-7339** • 3pm-close, clsd Mon • lesbians/ gay men • dancing/DJ • food served • karaoke • WiFi

Woody's 3710 N Oracle Rd. (at W Thurber Rd) **520/292-6702** • 11am-2am • mostly gay men • karaoke • video/ sports bar • wheelchair access

CAFES

Revolutionary Grounds 606 N 4th Ave (at E 5th St) **520/620-1770** • 8am-8pm, till 11pm Fri-Sat, noon-7pm Sun • plenty veggie • WiFi • also leftist bookstore

RESTAURANTS

Blue Willow 2616 N Campbell Ave (at Grant) **520/327-7577** • 7am-9pm, from 8am wknds • brkfst served all day

Cafe Poca Cosa 110 E Pennington St **520/622-6400** • 11am-9pm, till 10pm Fri-Sat, clsd Sun-Mon • Mexican-influenced bistro • patio

Colors Food & Spirits 5305 E Speedway **520/323-1840** • 4pm-10pm, till midnight Fri, 10am-10pm Sun • also bar from 4pm • lesbians/ gay men • drag shows

The Grill on Congress 100 E Congress St (at Scott) **520/623-7621** • 24hrs • plenty veggie • full bar

ENTERTAINMENT & RECREATION

The Loft Cinema 3233 E Speedway Blvd **520/795-7777** • Tucson's independent art house • pizza, beer & wine

Tucson Roller Derby 520/390-1454 • Tucson's female roller derby league • visit tucsonrollerderby.com for events

BOOKSTORES

Antigone Books 411 N 4th Ave (at 7th St) **520/792-3715** • 10am-7pm, till 9pm Fri-Sat, 11am-5pm Sun • LGBT/ feminist • gifts • wheelchair access

PUBLICATIONS

The Observer 520/622-7176

EROTICA

Hydra 145 E Congress (at 6th) **520/791-3711** • vinyl • leather • toys • shoes • lingerie

White Mountains

ACCOMMODATIONS

Arizona High Country Campground 5064 Sawmill Rd (1 mile off Hwy 260), Clay Springs **928/739-4383** • lesbians/ gay men • 10 campsites & RV hookups • WiFi • lesbian-owned • $30/ night, $2000/ season

ARKANSAS

Crossett

CAFES

Crosses Grocery & Cafe 4223 Hwy 16 (E of Elkins, outside Fayetteville) **479/643-3307** • 6am-8:30pm

Eureka Springs

ACCOMMODATIONS

A Byrds Eye View 36 N Main (at Douglas) **479/253-0200, 888/210-8401** • gay/ straight • in heart of downtown • porch • nonsmoking • WiFi • gay-owned • $99-129

The Grand TreeHouse Resort 350 W Van Buren (at Pivot Rock Rd) **479/253-8733** • gay/ straight • outdoor showers up in trees • WiFi • gay-owned • $149-165

Heart of the Hills Inn 5 Summit St (on Historic Loop) **479/253-7468, 800/253-7468** • gay/ straight • historic inn near downtown • full brkfst • private decks • nonsmoking • gay-owned

Lookout Lodge 3098 E Van Buren **479/253-9335, 877/253-9335** • gay-friendly • private entrances • pets/kids ok • WiFi • nonsmoking • $49-119

Mount Victoria 28 Fairmount St **479/253-7979, 888/408-7979** • gay-friendly • full brkfst & dinner • WiFi • $119-225

Out on Main 269 N Main St (at Magnetic Rd) **479/253-8449** • gay/ straight • 3-room cottage • full kitchen • nonsmoking • WiFi • gay-owned • $89-105

Palace Hotel & Bath House 135 Spring St
479/253-7474, 866/946-0572 • gay-friendly •
historic bathhouse open to all • nonsmoking •
WiFi

Pond Mountain Lodge & Resort
479/253-5877, 800/583-8043 • gay/ straight •
mountaintop inn on 150 acres • cabins • pool
• nonsmoking • jacuzzis • wheelchair access •
lesbian-owned

Red Bud Manor Inn 7 Kingshighway
479/253-9649, 866/253-9649 • gay-friendly •
full brkfst • WiFi • indoor hot tub • women-
owned • $89-149

Roadrunner Inn 3034 Mundell Rd
479/253-8166, 888/253-8166 • gay-friendly •
lake views • reservations advised •
guestrooms & log cabins • $75-275

Texaco Bungalow 77 Mountain St
888/253-8093 • gay/ straight • art deco
service station rentals • gay-owned • $79-139

The Woods Resort 50 Wall St (off Hwy 62)
479/253-8281 • lesbians/ gay men • cottages
• some treehouse cottages • treehouse hot
tub • jacuzzis • kitchens • nonsmoking • gay-
owned

BARS

Chelsea's Corner Cafe 10 Mountain St (at
Center St) **479/253-6723** • 11am-2am, till
10pm Sun • gay-friendly • dancing/DJ • patio •
also restaurant • live shows • WiFi • women-
owned

Eureka Live 35 N Main **479/253-7020** •
4pm-1:30am, clsd Sun-Mon • gay/ straight •
more gay Wed • dancing/DJ • food served •
karaoke

Henri's Just One More 19 1/2 Spring St
479/253-5795 • noon-2am, clsd Tue • gay/
straight • gay night Wed from 5pm • bar menu
• live shows • WiFi

The Lumberyard Saloon & Steakhouse
105 E Van Buren **479/253-0400** • 3pm-2am,
from noon wknds • gay/ straight • live bands •
sports bar • karaoke • WiFi • lesbian-owned

Pied Piper Pub & Inn 82 Armstrong (at
Main St) **479/363-9976, 866/363-9976** •
noon-midnight • gay-friendly • popular
Reuben sandwich, fish & chips • also hotel

CAFES

Mud Street Cafe 22G S Main St
479/253-6732 • 8am-3pm, clsd Wed

RESTAURANTS

Autumn Breeze 190 Huntsville Rd (1/2 mile
off Hwy 62) **479/253-7734** • 5pm-9pm, clsd
Sun, hrs vary in winter • cont'l • nonsmoking

Caribe Restaurant & Cantina 309 W Van
Buren **479/253-8102** • 4pm-9pm, clsd Tue,
from noon wknds • also bar

Cottage Inn 450 Hwy 62 W **479/253-5282** •
5pm-9pm, clsd Mon-Wed • Mediterranean •
full bar

Ermilio's 26 White St **479/253-8806** • 5pm-
9pm • Italian • plenty veggie • full bar

Gaskins Cabin Steak House 2883 Hwy 23
N (Hwy 187) **479/253-5466** • 5pm-9pm, till
8pm Sun, clsd Mon-Tue • full bar •
reservations suggested

ENTERTAINMENT & RECREATION

Diversity Pride Events **479/253-2555** •
produces events during Valentine's & Spring,
Summer, Fall Diversity Wknds & more

Fayetteville

INFO LINES & SERVICES

AA Gay/ Lesbian 568 W Sycamore
479/443-6366 (AA#)

ACCOMMODATIONS

Hilton Garden Inn Bentonville 2204 SE
Walton Blvd (Exit 85, off I-540), Bentonville
479/464-7300, 877/782-9444 • gay-friendly •
pool • kids ok • WiFi • wheelchair access •
$59-169

NIGHTCLUBS

Speakeasy 509 W Spring St (at West St)
479/443-3279 • 5pm-2am, clsd Sun-Tue •
mostly gay men • dancing/DJ • wheelchair
access

CAFES

The Common Grounds 412 W Dickson St
(at West) **479/442-3515** • 7am-midnight • full
bar • also restaurant • lots of veggie

RESTAURANTS

Bordinos 310 W Dickson St. **479/527-6795** •
dinner nightly, lunch Tue-Fri, clsd Sun • full bar

Hugo's 25 1/2 N Block Ave **479/521-7585** •
11am-10pm, clsd Sun

BOOKSTORES

Hastings Bookstore 2999 N College Ave
(Fiesta Square Shopping Center)
479/521-0244 • 9am-11pm

Helena

ACCOMMODATIONS

The Edwardian Inn 317 Biscoe
870/338-9155, 800/598-4749 • gay-friendly •
60 miles from Memphis • full brkfst •
nonsmoking • WiFi • $80-165

Hot Springs

ACCOMMODATIONS

The B Inn 316 Park Ave **501/547-7172** • gay/straight • WiFi • kids/pets ok • gay-owned

Park Hotel of Hot Springs 211 Fountain St (at Central Ave) **501/624-5323, 800/895-7275** • gay/straight • WiFi • $69-225

The Rose Cottage 218 Court St (at Exchange St) **501/623-6449** • gay-friendly • historic Victorian row house • kids/pets ok • jacuzzi • $185

Little Rock

ACCOMMODATIONS

Legacy Hotel & Suites 625 W Capitol Ave (at Gaines) **501/374-0100, 888/456-3669** • gay-friendly • nat'l historic property in downtown area • kids ok • WiFi • wheelchair access • $79-1,299

BARS

Discovery 1021 Jessie Rd (btwn Cantrell & Riverfront) **501/664-4784** • 9pm-5am Sat only • gay/straight • dancing/DJ • drag shows • male dancers • videos • 18+ • private club • wheelchair access

Off Center/ Pulse 307 W 7th St (at Center St) **501/372-3530** • 6pm-2am Tue-Sat • Pulse from 8pm • lesbians/ gay men • drag shows

Sidetracks 415 Main St, North Little Rock **501/244-0444** • 5pm-2am • mostly gay men • neighborhood bar • also restaurant • country/ western • bears • leather • older crowd • WiFi • wheelchair access

Triniti Nightclub 1021 Jessie Rd (btwn Cantrell & Riverfront) **501/664-2744** • 9pm-5am Fri only • lesbians/ gay men • dancing/DJ • drag shows • male dancers • videos • 18+ • private club • wheelchair access

RESTAURANTS

Bossa Nova 2701 Kavanaugh Blvd (at Ash St) **501/614-6682** • lunch & dinner, Sun brunch, clsd Mon • Brazilian • plenty veggie

Little Rock

WHERE THE GIRLS ARE:
Lilly's Dim Sum, Then Some/ B-Side is a lesbian-owned restaurant.

ANNUAL EVENTS:
October - State Fair 501/372-8341, web: www.arkansasstatefair.com.

CITY INFO:
Little Rock Convention & Visitors Bureau 800/844-4781, web: www.littlerock.com.

ATTRACTIONS:
(Check out Bill & Hillary's old digs at 18th & Center Sts.)
Arkansas Arts Center 501/372-4000, web: www.arkarts.com.
Central High Museum & Visitors Center 501/374-1957, web: www.nps.gov/chsc.
Clinton Presidential Library 501/374-4242, web: www.clintonlibrary.gov.
Historical Quapaw Quarter.

BEST VIEW:
Quapaw Quarter (in the heart of the city).

WEATHER:
When it comes to natural precipitation, Arkansas is far from being a dry state. Be prepared for the occasional severe thunderstorm or ice storm. Summers are hot and humid (mid 90°s). Winters can be cold (30°s) with some snow and ice. Spring and fall are the best times to come and be awed by Mother Nature.

TRANSIT:
Greater Little Rock Transportation 501/570-9999, web: www.littlerocktaxi.com.
Suvana Little Rock National Airport Shuttle 267/390-4122, web: www.suvana.com/little-rock-airport-shuttle.html.
Central Arkansas Transit 501/375-6717, web: www.cat.org.

Juanita's 1300 S Main **501/372–1228** • 11am-close, clsd Sun • Mexican • reservations recommended • live music

La Hacienda 3024 Cantrell Rd **501/661–0600** • lunch & dinner • Mexican

Lilly's Dim Sum, Then Some/ B-Side 11121 N Rodney Parham Rd **501/716–2700** • 11am-9pm, till 10pm Fri-Sat, noon-9pm Sun • contemporary Asian • plenty veggie • lesbian-owned

Vino's Pizza 923 W 7th St (at Chester) **501/375–8466** • 11am-close, from 11:30am Sat, from noon Sun • beer/ wine

ENTERTAINMENT & RECREATION

The Weekend Theater 1001 W 7th St (at Chester) **501/374–3761** • plays & musicals on wknds • gay-owned

BOOKSTORES

Wordsworth Books & Co 5920 R St **501/663–9198** • 9am-7pm, till 6pm Fri-Sat, noon-5pm Sun • independent

Texarkana

BARS

The Chute 714 Laurel St **870/772–6900** • 7pm-2am Wed-Sat • lesbians/ gay men • dancing/DJ • karaoke • drag shows

CALIFORNIA

Amador City

ACCOMMODATIONS

Imperial Hotel 14202 Hwy 49 (at Water St) **209/267–9172** • gay-friendly • B&B • brick Victorian hotel • nonsmoking • full brkfst • restaurant & bar (Tue-Sun)

Anaheim

see Orange County

Angels Camp

ACCOMMODATIONS

Cooper House B&B Inn 1184 Church St (at Raspberry Ln) **209/736–2145, 888/330–3764** • gay/ straight • full brkfst • WiFi • gay-owned • $109-239

Antelope Valley

see Lancaster

Arcata

see also Eureka

INFO LINES & SERVICES

Queer Humboldt PO Box 45, 95518-0045 **707/834–4839** • "Humboldt County's online resource for the LGBT community" • includes links & events calendar • check out www.queerhumboldt.org

BARS

The Alibi 744 9th St **707/822–3731** • lesbian/gay men • cocktail lounge w/ live music • neighborhood bar • also restaurant (8am-midnight) • young crowd

CAFES

Cafe Mokka 495 J St (at 5th) **707/822–2228** • from noon • coffee & soups (bread bowls) • live music • also Finnish sauna & hot tubs

North Coast Co-op 811 I St **707/822–5947** • 6am-9pm • co-op store w/ bakery, deli & espresso cafe • WiFi

RESTAURANTS

Wildflower Bakery & Cafe 1604 G St **707/822–0360** • 8am-8pm, till 9pm Th-Sat • popular • vegetarian • organic beer & wine

BOOKSTORES

Northtown Books 957 H St **707/822–2834** • 10am-7pm, till 9pm Fri-Sat, noon-5pm Sun • LGBT section • carries The L Word paper

Arnold

ACCOMMODATIONS

Dorrington Inn at Big Trees 3450 Hwy 4 (at Boards Crossing), Dorrington **209/795–2164, 877/795–2164** • gay/ straight • cottages & suites

Bakersfield

INFO LINES & SERVICES

Gay AA 1001 34th St **661/322–4025 (AA#), 661/324–0371 (ALANO CLUB #)** • 7:30pm Mon

BARS

The Mint 1207 19th St (at M) **661/325–4048** • 6am-2am • gay/ straight • alternative • live music

NIGHTCLUBS

The Casablanca Club 1825 N St (at 19th St) **661/324–0661** • 9pm-2am, clsd Mon-Wed • gay/ straight • neighborhood bar • dancing/DJ • live entertainment • cabaret • drag shows • videos • wheelchair access

BOOKSTORES

Russo's Books 9000 Ming Ave #1-4
661/665–4686 • 10am-8pm • independent

Benicia

see Vallejo

Berkeley

see East Bay

Big Bear Lake

ACCOMMODATIONS

Alpine Retreats 433 Edgemoor (at Big Bear
Blvd) **909/725–4192, 909/878-4155**
(RESERVATIONS) • gay/ straight • 3 cottages •
fireplaces • nonsmoking • kids ok • gay-owned

Knickerbocker Mansion Country Inn 869
Knickerbocker Rd **909/878-9190,**
877/423–1180 • gay/ straight • log mansion
on lake • full brkfst • jacuzzi • hiking •
nonsmoking • WiFi • wheelchair access • gay-
owned • $125-240

Rainbow View Lodge 2726 View Dr (at
Hilltop), Running Springs **909/867–1810,**
888/868–1810 • gay/ straight • cottages w/
themed decor • kids ok • nonsmoking •
women-owned

Switzerland Haus 41829 Switzerland Dr
909/866–3729, 800/335–3729 • gay-friendly •
$125-249

Big Sur

ACCOMMODATIONS

Eagle's Nest Pfeiffer Ridge #10
831/667–2587, 888/742–9321 • gay-friendly •
deck w/ views of Pfeiffer Ridge & ocean • full
kitchen • WiFi • nonsmoking • gay-owned •
$250-350

Lucia Lodge 62400 Hwy 1 **831/688–4884,**
866/424-4787 • gay-friendly • oceanview
cabins • also restaurant & lounge • WiFi

Burlingame

see San Francisco

Cambria

ACCOMMODATIONS

El Colobri 5620 Moonstone Beach Dr
805/924-3003 • gay-friendly • WiFi • pets ok

The J Patrick House B&B 2990 Burton Dr
(1/2 mile off Hwy 1) **805/927–3812,**
800/341–5258 • gay-friendly • full brkfst • WiFi
• fireplaces • nonsmoking • $165-215

Sea Otter Inn 6656 Moonstone Beach Dr
805/927–5888, 800/965–834/ • gay-friendly •
pool • nonsmoking • WiFi • wheelchair access
• $79-299

BARS

Mozzi's Saloon 2262 Main St **805/927–4767**
• 1pm-2am, from 11am Sat-Sun • gay-friendly
cowboy bar • live music

Capistrano Beach

ACCOMMODATIONS

Capistrano Seaside Inn 34862 Pacific
Coast Hwy **949/496–1399, 800/252–3224**
(RESERVATIONS ONLY) • gay-friendly • outdoor
jacuzzi • ocean views • kids/ pets ok •
fireplaces • wheelchair access • packages
available

Carmel

see also Monterey

ACCOMMODATIONS

Best Western Carmel Mission Inn 3665
Rio Rd **831/624–1841, 800/348-9090** • gay-
friendly • near Monterey Bay • pool • pets ok •
also restaurant & lounge • nonsmoking

Carmel Resort Inn Carpenter Ave (btwn 1st
& 2nd Ave) **831/624-3113, 800/454-3700** •
gay-friendly • cottages • kids/ pets ok • WiFi •
nonsmoking • $79-335

Carmel River Inn Hwy 1 at Carmel River
Bridge **831/624–1575, 800/966-6490** • gay-
friendly • kids/ pets ok • pool • nonsmoking •
$79-329

Cypress Inn Lincoln & 7th **831/624–3871,**
800/443–7443 • gay-friendly • pets very
welcome • owned by Doris Day • WiFi • $225-
575

RESTAURANTS

Flaherty's Seafood Grill and Oyster Bar
6th Ave (btwn Dolores and San Carlos)
831/625–1500 • open daily 11am • wheelchair
access

Rio Grill 101 Crossroads Blvd **831/625–5436**
• lunch & dinner daily, Sun brunch • "Creative
American" • full bar

Chico

INFO LINES & SERVICES

Stonewall Alliance Center 358 E 6th St (at
Flume) **530/893-3336** • HIV testing &
counseling • also recorded info • meetings •
events

Chino

RESTAURANTS

Riverside Grill 5258 Riverside Dr (at Central) **909/627-4144** • 8am-9pm

Clearlake

includes major towns of Lake County

ACCOMMODATIONS

Blue Fish Cove Resort 10573 E Hwy 20, Clearlake Oaks **707/998-1769** • gay-friendly • lakeside resort cottages • kitchens • kids ok • pets ok by arrangement • boat launch facilities & rentals

Edgewater Resort 6420 Soda Bay Rd (at Hohape Rd), Kelseyville **707/279-0208, 800/396-6224** • "gay-owned, straight-friendly" • cabin • camping & RV hookups • lake access & pool • boat facilities • WiFi • kids/ pets ok • lesbian-owned

Featherbed Railroad B& B 2870 Lakeshore Blvd, Nice **707/274-8378** • gay-friendly • pool • full brkfst • WiFi • pets ok • $140-220

Sea Breeze Resort 9595 Harbor Dr, Glenhaven **707/998-3327** • gay/ straight • lakefront cottages • swimming • nonsmoking • WiFi • wheelchair access • gay-owned

Cloverdale

see also Healdsburg

ACCOMMODATIONS

Vintage Towers B&B 302 N Main St (at 3rd) **707/894-4535, 888/886-9377** • gay-friendly • Queen Anne mansion • full brkfst • nonsmoking

Concord

see East Bay

Costa Mesa

see Orange County

Cupertino

ACCOMMODATIONS

Cypress Hotel 10050 S De Anza Blvd **408/253-8900, 800/499-1408** • gay-friendly • pool • pets ok • WiFi • nonsmoking • also gym & restaurant

Dana Point

see Orange County

Danville

see East Bay

Davis

see also Sacramento

INFO LINES & SERVICES

LGBT Resource Center University House Annex **530/752-2452** • 9am-5pm, clsd wknds • info • referrals • meetings • library • WiFi • wheelchair access

CAFES

Mishka's Cafe 610 2nd St **530/759-0811** • 7:30am-11pm

BOOKSTORES

The Avid Reader 617 2nd St **530/758-4040** • 10am-10pm • general independent • readings

Desert Hot Springs

see Palm Springs & Joshua Tree Nat'l Park

East Bay

includes major cities of Alameda and Contra Costa Counties: Alameda, Antioch, Berkeley, Concord, Danville, Fremont, Hayward, Lafayette, Newark, Oakland, Pleasant Hill, Richmond, San Leandro, Walnut Creek

INFO LINES & SERVICES

East Bay AA 510/839-8900 (AA#) • variety of LGBT-friendly mtgs

La Peña Cultural Center 3105 Shattuck Ave, Berkeley **510/849-2568** • multicultural center & cafe • hosts meetings, events, performance art • nonsmoking • wheelchair access

Lighthouse Community Center 1217 A St (near 2nd St), Hayward **510/881-8167** • LGBT support groups & social events

Pacific Center for Human Growth 2712 Telegraph Ave (at Derby), Berkeley **510/548-8283** • 4pm-10pm Mon-Fri • wheelchair access

Rainbow Community Center of Contra Costa County 3024 Willow Pass Rd #200 (btwn Parkside & Esperanza), Concord **925/692-0090** • 10am-5pm Mon-Fri

ACCOMMODATIONS

Hotel Durant 2600 Durant Ave, Berkeley **510/845-8981, 800/238-7268** • gay/ straight • nonsmoking • WiFi • restaurant on premises • $95-195

Washington Inn 495 10th St (at Broadway), Oakland **510/452–1776** • gay/ straight • historic boutique hotel • full brkfst • nonsmoking • also restaurant • wheelchair access

Waterfront Hotel 10 Washington St, Oakland **510/836–3800, 888/842–5333** • gay-friendly • pool • bar & restaurant • WiFi • wheelchair access • $95-249

Bars

The Alley 3325 Grand Ave (btwn Lake Park & Elwood Aves), Oakland **510/444–8505** • 4pm-2am • gay/ straight • camptastic sing-along piano bar from 9pm • more gay Th • also restaurant

Bench & Bar 510 17th St, Oakland **510/444–2266** • 4pm-2am • popular • mostly gay men • dancing/DJ • drag shows • theme nights • wheelchair access

East Bay

Where the Girls Are:
Though there's no lesbian ghetto, you'll find many of us shacked up in North Oakland (Rockridge) and North Berkeley, Lake Merritt (Adams Point), around Grand Lake & Piedmont, along MacArthur (from Fruitvale Ave to High St—also known as The Fruit Hills), in the Solano/Albany area, or at a cafe along 4th St in Berkeley.

Annual Events:
October - Community Celebration for the Days of the Dead 510/238-2200, web: www.muse-umca.org.

City Info:
Berkeley Convention & Visitors Bureau 800/847-4823, web: www.visitberkeley.com.
Oakland Convention & Visitors Bureau 510/839-9000, web: www.oaklandcvb.com

Weather:
While San Francisco is fogged in during the summers, the East Bay remains sunny and warm. Some areas even get hot (90°s-100°s). As for the winter, the temperature drops along with rain (upper 30°s-40°s in the winter). Spring is the time to come – the usually brown hills explode with the colors of green grass and wild-flowers.

Attractions:
The Claremont Hotel & Restaurant, Berkeley 510/843-3000, web: www.claremontresort.com.
Emeryville Marina Public Market.
Jack London Square, Oakland, web: www.jacklondonsquare.com.
Oakland Museum of California 510/238-2200, web: www.museumca.org.
The Paramount Theater, Oakland 510/465-6400, web: www.paramounttheatre.com.
UC Berkeley.

Best View:
Claremont Hotel, Tilden Park, various locations in the Berkeley and Oakland Hills. Or from the top of Sather Tower on the UC Berkeley campus.

Transit:
Yellow Cab (Berkeley) 510/524-1999, web: www.yellowcabexpress.com.
Veteran's Cab (Oakland) 510/549-0600.
Bayporter Express 877/467-1800, web: www.bayporter.com.
AC Transit 510/891-4706, web: www.actransit.org.
BART (subway) 510/465-2278, web: www.bart.gov.
Ferry, web: www.eastbayferry.com.

Butta Oakland 510/763-0404 • 3pm-8pm 3rd Sun • mostly women • BBQ & T-dance • dancing/DJ • multiracial • www.butterflyproductions.org for info

Cafe Van Kleef 1621 Telegraph Ave (at Broadway), Oakland 510/763-7711 • 4pm-2am, clsd Sun • gay-friendly • eclectic crowd & live-music scene—from cabaret to blue grass to jazz • cover

Club 21 2111 Franklin St (at 21st St), Oakland 510/268-9425 • mostly gay men • dancing/DJ • mostly Latino/a • theme nights • videos

Easy Lounge 3255 Lakeshore Ave, Oakland 510/338-4911 • 4:30pm-2am, from 2pm Sat • gay-friendly • cool lounge w/ theme nights

Hotbox 510 17th St (at Bench and Bar), Oakland 510/444-2266 • 9pm Fri only • mostly women • dancing/DJ • multiracial clientele • transgender-friendly

Rainbow Room 21859 Mission Blvd (at Sunset), Hayward 510/582-8078 • 2pm-2am, from 11am wknds • lesbians/ gay men • neighborhood bar • dancing/DJ Fri-Sat • wheelchair access • women-owned

White Horse 6551 Telegraph Ave (at 66th), Oakland 510/652-3820 • 3pm-2am, from 1pm wknds (also Sun beer bust) • lesbians/ gay men • dancing/DJ • karaoke • wheelchair access

World Famous Turf Club 22519 Main St (at A St), Hayward 510/881-9877 • 2pm-2am, from noon Sat-Sun • lesbians/ gay men • dancing/DJ • drag shows • huge patio • wheelchair access

NIGHTCLUBS

Club 1220 1220 Pine St (at Civic Dr), Walnut Creek 925/938-4550 • 4pm-2am • lesbians/ gay men • dancing/DJ • theme nights • karaoke • WiFi • wheelchair access

CAFES

Au Coquelet Cafe 2000 University Ave, Berkeley 510/845-0433 • 7am-2am

Bittersweet 5427 College Ave (in Rockridge District), Oakland 510/654-7159 • 9am-7pm, till 9pm Fri-Sat

Caffe Strada 2300 College Ave (btw Way & Durant), Berkeley 510/843-5282 • 6am-midnight • students • great patio • wheelchair access

Cole Coffee 6255 College Ave (btwn 62nd & 63rd Sts), Oakland 510/985-1958 • 7am-7pm • hip hideaway in lovely Rockridge

Raw Energy 2050 Addison St (btwn Shattuck & Milvia), Berkeley 510/665-9464 • 7:30am-7pm, 11am-4pm Sat, clsd Sun • organic juice cafe • gay-owned

World Ground Cafe 3726 MacArthur Blvd (btwn 35th & 38th Aves, in Laurel District), Oakland 510/482-2933 • 6:30am-6pm

RESTAURANTS

Arizmendi Bakery & Pizzeria 4301 San Pablo Ave (at 43rd St), Emeryville 510/547-0550 • 7am-7pm, till 3pm Mon, clsd Sun, excellent pastries, breads & pizzas

Banh Cuon Tay Ho 344-B 12th St (at Webster), Oakland 510/836-6388 • 10am-9pm, till 8pm Sun, clsd Mon

Cactus Taqueria 5642 College Ave (at Shafter, in Rockridge), Oakland 510/658-6180 • 11am-10pm, till 9pm Sun

César 1515 Shattuck Ave (in "Gourmet Ghetto," next door to Chez Panisse), Berkeley 510/883-0222 • noon-11pm • Spanish tapas • full bar • also 4039 Piedmont Ave, Oakland, 510/985-1200

Connie's Cantina 3340 Grand Ave (btwn Lake Park Ave & Mandana Blvd), Oakland 510/839-4986 • 10:30am-9pm, clsd Sun • popular • delicious homemade Mexican food • plenty veggie • patio • woman-owned

Dopo 4293 Piedmont Ave (btwn Glenwood & Echo), Oakland 510/652-3676 • lunch Mon-Th, dinner nightly, clsd Sun • Italian • worth the wait

Le Cheval 1007 Clay St, Oakland 510/763-8495 • 11am-9:30pm, from 5pm Sun • popular • Vietnamese • wheelchair access

Lois the Pie Queen 851 60th St (off Martin Luther King Jr Hwy), Oakland 510/658-5616 • 8am-2pm • popular • Southern homecooking & killer desserts

Mama's Royal Cafe 4012 Broadway (at 40th), Oakland 510/547-7600 • 7am-2:30pm, from 8am wknds • popular • come early for excellent wknd brunch • beer/ wine • wheelchair access

Rockridge Cafe 5492 College Ave (at Forest), Oakland 510/653-1567 • 7:30am-3pm • popular • great brkfsts • plenty veggie

Zachary's Chicago Pizza 5801 College Ave, Oakland 510/655-6385 • 11am-10pm • popular • pizza that is worth the crowds & the long wait!

BOOKSTORES

Black Oak Books 2618 San Pablo Ave, Berkeley 510/486-0698 • 11am-7pm • independent • new & used

Diesel, A Bookstore 5433 College Avenue, Oakland **510/653-9965** • 10am-9pm, till 10pm Fri-Sat, till 6pm Sun • independent

Laurel Book Store 4100 MacArthur Blvd (at 39th Ave, 2 blks from High St), Oakland **510/531-2073** • 10am-7pm, till 6pm Sat, 11am-5pm Sun • general • LGBT section • readings • wheelchair access • lesbian-owned

Pendragon Books 5560 College Ave (at Oceanview), Oakland **510/652-6259** • 9am-10pm, from 10am Sun • used books • magazines • great to browse while waiting for a table in Rockridge

RETAIL SHOPS

Ancient Ways 4075 Telegraph Ave (at 41st), Oakland **510/653-3244** • 11am-7pm • extensive occult supplies • classes • readings • woman-owned

See Jane Run Sports 5817 College Ave, Oakland **510/428-2681** • 11am-7pm, 10am-6pm Sat & Sun • women's athletic apparel

EROTICA

Good Vibrations 2504 San Pablo Ave (at Dwight Wy), Berkeley **510/841-8987** • 11am-8pm, 10am-6pm Fri-Sat • clean, well-lighted sex toy store • workshops & events • wheelchair access

Lingerie Etc 2298 Monument Blvd (at Buskirk), Pleasant Hill **925/676-2962** • 9am-midnight

Elk

RESTAURANTS

Queenie's Roadhouse Cafe 6061 S Hwy 1 **707/877-3285** • 8am-3pm, clsd Tue-Wed • fabulous all-day brkfsts • some veggie • lesbian-owned

Eureka

see also Arcata

ACCOMMODATIONS

Abigail's Elegant Victorian Mansion 1406 C St **707/444-3144** • gay-friendly • sauna • nonsmoking

Carter House Victorians 301 L St **707/444-8062, 800/404-1390** • gay-friendly • enclave of 4 unique inns • full brkfst • nonsmoking • kids ok • restaurant • wine shop • wheelchair access

Trinidad Bay B&B 560 Edwards St (at Trinity), Trinidad **707/677-0840** • gay-friendly • nonsmoking • WiFi • kids ok • full brkfst • gay- & straight-owned • $200-300

Trinidad Escape **707/677-3457** • lesbians/ gay men • WiFi • oceanfront house rental in Tinidad • $200-450 per night

BARS

Lost Coast Brewery 617 4th St (btwn G & H Sts) **707/445-4480** • 11am-1am • gay-friendly • food served till midnight • beer/ wine • WiFi • wheelchair access • women-owned

The Shanty 213 3rd St (at C St) **707/444-2053** • noon-2am • gay/ straight • neighborhood bar • lesbian-owned

NIGHTCLUBS

Where's Queer Bill **707/832-4785** • monthly queer events • check wheresqueerbill.com for info

CAFES

The Boathouse Espresso Bar and Eatery 1125 King Salmon Ave **707/441-1454** • WiFi • wheelchair access • lesbian owned

North Coast Co-op 25 4th St (at B St) **707/443-6027** • 6am-9pm • co-op store w/ bakery, deli & espresso cafe

Ramone's Cafe & Bakery 209 E St (Old Town) **707/445-2923** • 7am-6pm

RESTAURANTS

Chalet House of Omelettes 1935 5th St (at U St) **707/442-0333** • 6am-3pm, brkfst & lunch • wheelchair access

Folie Douce 1551 G St, Arcata **707/822-1042** • dinner only, closed Sun-Mon • bistro • beer/ wine • reservations recommended • wheelchair access

Hurricane Kate's 511 2nd St (Old Town) **707/444-1405** • lunch & dinner, clsd Sun-Mon • World fusion • some veggie • wine

BOOKSTORES

Booklegger 402 2nd St (at E St) **707/445-1344** • 10am-5:30pm, 11am-4pm Sun • mostly used • wheelchair access • women-owned

PUBLICATIONS

The "L" Word PO Box 272, Bayside 95524 • lesbian newsletter for Humboldt County • available at the Co Op & Booklegger in Eureka & North Town Books in Arcata

EROTICA

Good Relations 223 2nd St **707/441-9570, 888/485-5063** • lingerie • toys • books • videos • wheelchair access • queer-owned/ run

Fairfield

see Vacaville

Fort Bragg

see also Mendocino

ACCOMMODATIONS

The Cleone Gardens Inn 24600 N Hwy 1 707/964-2788, 800/400-2189 (N CA ONLY) • gay-friendly • country garden retreat on 2.5 acres • hot tub • WiFi • nonsmoking • wheelchair access

The Weller House Inn 524 Stewart St (at Pine) 707/964-4415, 877/893-5537 • gay-friendly • 1886 Victorian • full brkfst • jacuzzi • nonsmoking • WiFi

RESTAURANTS

Cowlick's 250B N Main St 707/962-9271 • delicious homemade ice cream, including mushroom ice cream (in-season)—it's actually quite good!

Purple Rose 24300 N Hwy 1 707/964-6507 • 5pm-9pm, clsd Mon-Tue • Mexican • wheelchair access

ENTERTAINMENT & RECREATION

Skunk Train California Western foot of Laurel St 707/964-6371, 866/457-5865 • scenic train trips

BOOKSTORES

Windsong Books & Records 324 N Main St (at Redwood Ave) 707/964-2050 • 10am-5:30pm, till 4pm Sun • mostly used • large selection of women's/ lesbian titles

Fountain Valley

see Orange County

Fremont

see East Bay

Fresno

INFO LINES & SERVICES

Community Link 559/266-5465 • info • LGBT support, including LGBT youth group • also publishes Newslink

Fresno AA 559/221-6907 • call or check website (www.fresnoaa.org) for meetings

ACCOMMODATIONS

The San Joaquin Hotel 1309 W Shaw Ave (at Fruit) 559/225-1309, 800/775-1309 • gay-friendly • pool • WiFi • wheelchair access • $149-248

BARS

The Phoenix 4538 E Belmont Ave (at Maple) • 5pm-2am • mostly gay men • country/ western • bears • leather • multiracial • videos • older crowd • popular beer busts • patio • gay-owned

Red Lantern 4618 E Belmont Ave (at Maple) 559/251-5898 • 2pm-2am • mostly gay men • neighborhood bar • country/ western • Latin night Sat very popular • food Sun • patio • WiFi • wheelchair access

NIGHTCLUBS

Club Legends 3075 N Maroa Ave 559/222-2271 • 8pm-2am, from 6pm Fri, from 9pm Sat, from 4pm Sun • lesbians/ gay men • dancing/DJ • drag shows

Express 708 N Blackstone (btwn Olive & Belmont, on Bremer) 559/445-0878 • 9pm-2am, from 6pm Sun, clsd Mon-Wed • mostly gay men • dancing/DJ • theme nights • Latin night Th (drag shows) • videos • gay-owned • cover

North Tower Circle 2777 N Maroa Ave (at E Princeton Ave) 559/229-4188 • 7pm-2am • lesbians/ gay men • dancing/DJ • drag shows

RESTAURANTS

Cafe Rousseau 568 E Olive Ave (in Tower District) 559/445-1536 • lunch Tue-Fri, dinner from 5:30pm, clsd Sun-Mon • cont'l • also wine bar

Don Pepe's 4582 N Blackstone Ave (at Gettysburg) 559/224-1431 • lunch & dinner • Mexican

Irene's Cafe 747 E Olive Ave (in Tower District) 559/237-9919 • 8am-9pm • some veggie • popular hamburgers • beer/ wine

Sequoia Brewing Company 777 E Olive Ave (in Tower District) 559/264-5521 • 11am-10pm, till midnight Fri-Sat, till 9pm Sun • microbrewery w/ restaurant • live music

Veni Vidi Vici 1116 N Fulton (S of Olive Ave, in Tower District) 559/266-5510 • California fine dining • nightclub later

EROTICA

Suzie's Adult Superstores 1267 N Blackstone Ave 559/497-9613 • 24hrs

Garden Grove

see Orange County

Graeagle

ACCOMMODATIONS

Molly's Bed & Breakfast 276 Lower Main St (Hwy 89), Clio **530/836-4436, 866/836-4730** • gay-friendly • near the Feather River • ful brkfst • kids/pets ok • women-owned • $95-120

Grass Valley

see Nevada City

Gualala

ACCOMMODATIONS

Breakers Inn 39300 S Hwy 1 **707/884-3200** • gay/ straight • oceanfront • women-owned

North Coast Country Inn 34591 S Hwy 1 **707/884-4537, 800/959-4537** • gay-friendly • B&B overlooking Mendocino coast • hot tub • nonsmoking

BOOKSTORES

The Four-Eyed Frog 39138 Ocean Dr (in Cypress Village) **707/884-1333** • 10am-6pm, till 5pm Sun • independent

Half Moon Bay

ACCOMMODATIONS

Mill Rose Inn 615 Mill St **650/726-8750, 800/900-7673** • gay-friendly • classic European elegance by the sea • full brkfst • hot tub • nonsmoking • WiFi • kids 10+ ok

RESTAURANTS

Moss Beach Distillery 140 Beach Wy (at Ocean) **650/728-5595** • lunch & dinner, Sun brunch • popular • steak & seafood • some veggie • patio • even own ghost • wheelchair access

Pasta Moon 315 Main St (at Mill) **650/726-5125** • lunch & dinner • Italian • full bar • live shows • wheelchair access

Hayward

see East Bay

Healdsburg

see Russian River & Sonoma County

Huntington Beach

see Orange County

Idyllwild

ACCOMMODATIONS

Alderwood Cabins 25690 Alderwood St **951/659-3571** • gay-friendly • 1920s cabins on 2 wooded acres • full kitchen • satellite TV

The Heritage House Inn 25880 Cedar St **951/659-5150, 877/659-4789** • gay-friendly • inn & cabins • kids/ pets ok in cabins • $80-130

Quiet Creek Inn & Vacation Rentals 26345 Delano Dr (at Toll Gate Rd) **951/659-6110, 800/450-6110** • gay-friendly • vacation rentals • pets ok in certain cabins • WiFi • nonsmoking • $117-500

The Rainbow Inn 54420 S Circle Dr **951/659-0111** • gay/ straight • full brkfst • kids ok • nonsmoking • patio • fireplaces • WiFi • also conference center • gay-owned

Strawberry Creek Inn B&B 26370 Hwy 243 (at S Cir Dr) **951/659-3202, 800/262-8969** • gay-friendly • relaxing getaway w/ sundeck, garden & hammocks • nonsmoking • wheelchair access • gay-owned • $130-240

RESTAURANTS

Cafe Aroma 54750 North Circle **951/659-5212** • 7am-10pm • great ambience & food • live music most nights

Irvine

see Orange County

Joshua Tree Nat'l Park

includes Twentynine Palms

ACCOMMODATIONS

The Desert Lily PO Box 139, 92252-0800 **760/366-4676, 877/887-7370** • gay-friendly • artist-owned adobe-style B&B on 5 acres • also self-catering cabins • seasonal (clsd July-Aug) • woman-owned • $140-155 (B&B) & $275-525 (cabins)

Desert Wonderland & The Tile House **805/452-4898** • gay/ straight • in high desert near Joshua Tree Nat'l Park • gay-owned • $95-700

Joshua Tree Highlands Houses **760/366-3636** • gay/ straight • private modern desert vacation rentals • fully equipped • each home on 5 acres • near Joshua Tree Nat'l Park • nonsmoking • kids/ pets ok • WiFi • wheelchair access • gay-owned • $175-300

Moon Way Lodge **760/835-9369** • gay/ straight • WiFi • swimming • nonsmoking • gay-owned • $120-165

Sacred Sands HC1 Box 1071 A, 63155 Quail Springs Rd (at Desert Shadows), Joshua Tree **760/424-6407** • gay/ straight • private outdoor living • spa • nonsmoking • WiFi • gay-owned • $269-299

Spin & Margie's Desert Hideaway 64491 29 Palms Hwy **760/366-9124** • gay-friendly • hacienda-style B&B • suites w/ private patios • cool trading post on-site • $135-175

Starland Retreat Yucca Valley **760/364-2069** • mostly gay men & radical faeries, but women very welcome • membership-only rustic rural camp • hot tub • nudity permitted

RESTAURANTS

The Crossroads Cafe & Tavern 61715 29 Palms Hwy **760/366-5414** • 7am-8pm, till 9pm Fri-Sat, clsd Wed

Kernville

ACCOMMODATIONS

River View Lodge 2 Sirretta St **760/376-6019** • gay/ straight • riverfront resort • jacuzzi • kids/ pets ok • nonsmoking • gay-owned • $79-199

La Mirada

RESTAURANTS

Mexico 1900 11531 La Mirada blvd **562/941-2016** • lunch & dinner • Mexican

Laguna Beach

see Orange County

Lake Tahoe

see also Lake Tahoe, Nevada

ACCOMMODATIONS

Alpine Inn & Spa 920 Stateline Ave (Lake Ave/ Hwy 50), South Lake Tahoe **530/544-3340, 800/826-8885** • gay/ straight • motel • just steps from casino • swimming • lesbian & gay & straight-owned • $30-45

Black Bear Inn 530/544-4451, **877/232-7466** • gay/ straight • full brkfst • hot tub • fireplaces • nonsmoking • WiFi • gay-owned

The Cedar House Sport Hotel 10918 Brockway Rd, Truckee **530/582-5655, 866/582-5655** • gay-friendly • full bar • WiFi • kids/ pets ok • $150-295

Holly's Place 800/745-7041, 530/544-7040 • gay/ straight • cabins • fireplaces • kitchens • hot tubs • nonsmoking • kids/ dogs ok • WiFi • women-owned • $250-650

Spruce Grove Cabins 3599-3605 Spruce Ave, South Lake Tahoe 530/544-0549, **800/777-0914** • gay-friendly • full kitchens • near Heavenly Ski Resort • hot tub • dog-friendly • nonsmoking • $159-205

Tahoe Valley Lodge 2241 Lake Tahoe Blvd (at Tahoe Keys Blvd), South Lake Tahoe **530/541-0353, 800/669-7544** • gay-friendly • motel • pool • nonsmoking • WiFi • $125-295

RESTAURANTS

Driftwood Cafe 1001 Heavenly Vlg Way #1A **530/544-6545** • 7am-3pm • homecooking • some veggie • wheelchair access

Passaretti's 1181 Emerald Bay Rd/ Hwy 50, South Lake Tahoe 530/541-3433 • 11am-9pm • Italian • beer/ wine

Lancaster

includes Palmdale

Livermore

see East Bay

Long Beach

INFO LINES & SERVICES

AA Gay/ Lesbian 2017 E 4th St (at Cherry, at Gay & Lesbian Center) 562/434-4455 • 7pm Mon • lesbians/ gay men

The Gay & Lesbian Center of Greater Long Beach 2017 E 4th St (at Cherry) **562/434-4455** • 9am-9pm, by appt Sat • activities & support groups • also newsletter

ACCOMMODATIONS

Beachrunners' Inn 231 Kennebec Ave (at Junipero & Broadway) **562/856-0202, 866/221-0001** • gay/ straight • B&B • near beach • hot tub • nonsmoking

Dockside Boat & Bed Dock 5, Rainbow Harbor (at Pine Ave Pier) **562/436-3111** • gay-friendly • spend the night on a yacht • views of the Queen Mary • $210-325

Hotel Current 5325 E Pacific Coast Hwy **562/597-1341, 800/990-9991**

Hotel Maya 700 Queensway Dr **562/435-7676** • gay/ straight • luxury boutique resort hotel w/ waterfront Fuego restaurant • pets ok • $139

The Varden Hotel 335 Pacific Ave (at 3rd St) **562/432-8950, 877/382-7336** • gay/straight • urban boutique hotel • nonsmoking • WiFi • wheelchair access • $109-159

BARS

The Brit 1744 E Broadway (at Cherry) **562/432-9742** • 10am-2am • mostly gay men • neighborhood bar • patio • wheelchair access

The Broadway 1100 E Broadway (at Cerritos) **562/432-3646** • 10am-2am • lesbians/gay men • neighborhood bar • karaoke Fri-Sat • wheelchair access

The Crest 5935 Cherry Ave (at South) **562/423-6650** • 2pm-2am, from noon wknds • mostly gay men

The Falcon 1435 E Broadway (at Falcon) **562/432-4146** • 6am-2am • mostly gay men but women very welcome • neighborhood bar • wheelchair access

Flux 17817 Lakewood Blvd (at Artesia), Bellflower **562/633-6394** • noon-2am • lesbians/gay men • neighborhood bar • patio • theme nights

Liquid Lounge 3522 E Anaheim St **562/494-7564** • gay/straight • neighborhood bar • food served • karaoke Fri-Sat • live music • patio • gay-owned

Mineshaft 1720 E Broadway (btwn Gaviota & Hermosa) **562/436-2433** • 10am-2am • popular • mostly gay men • bears

Paradise Piano Bar & Restaurant 1800 E Broadway Blvd (at Hermosa) **562/590-8773** • 3pm-1am, from 10am Sat-Sun • lesbians/gay men • live entertainment

Pistons 2020 E Artesia (at Cherry) **562/422-1928** • 2pm-2am • mostly gay men • bears • leather • patio

Long Beach

WHERE THE GIRLS ARE:
Schmoozing with the boys on Broadway between Atlantic and Cherry Avenues, or elsewhere between Pacific Coast Hwy and the beach. Or at home snuggling.

LGBT PRIDE:
3rd wknd in May. 562/987-9191, web: www.longbeachpride.com.

ANNUAL EVENTS:
June - AIDS Walk, web: www.aidswalklb.org.
Aug - Long Beach Jazz Festival, web: www.longbeachjazzfestival.com.
September - Q Films LGBT film festival, web: www.qfilmslongbeach.com.

CITY INFO:
800/452-7829, web: www.visitlong-beach.com.

BEST VIEW:
On the deck of the Queen Mary, docked overlooking most of Long Beach. Or Signal Hill, off 405. Take the Cherry exit.

ATTRACTIONS:
Belmont Shores area on 2nd St, south of Pacific Coast Highway—lots of restaurants & shopping, only blocks from the beach.
Long Beach Downtown Marketplace, 10am-4pm Fri.
The Queen Mary 562/435-3511, web: www.queenmary.com.
"Planet Ocean" mural at 300 E Ocean Blvd.

WEATHER:
Quite temperate: highs in the mid-80°s July through September, and cooling down at night. In the winter, January to March, highs are in the upper 60°s, and lows in the upper 40°s.

TRANSIT:
Long Beach Taxi Co-op 562/529-3556, web: www.longbeachyellowcab.com.
Long Beach Transit & Runabout (free downtown shuttle) 562/591-2301, web: www.lbtransit.com.

Que Será 1923 E 7th St (at Cherry) **562/599–6170** • 9pm-2am Tue, from 5pm Wed-Sat, from 3pm Sun, clsd Mon • gay/ straight • dancing/DJ • alternative • live music • cover after 9pm

Silver Fox 411 Redondo (at 4th) **562/439–6343** • 4pm-2am, from noon wknds • popular happy hour • mostly gay men • karaoke Wed & Sun • videos • wheelchair access

Sweetwater Saloon 1201 E Broadway (at Orange) **562/432–7044** • 10am-2am • popular days • mostly gay men • neighborhood bar • wheelchair access

NIGHTCLUBS

The Basement Lounge 149 Linden Ave (at E Broadway) **562/901–9090** • gay/ straight • dancing/DJ • live shows • also restaurant

Club Ripples 5101 E Ocean (at Granada) **562/433–0357** • noon-2am • popular • mostly gay men • more women Fri • dancing/DJ • theme nights • multiracial • food served • karaoke • videos • young crowd • patio

Executive Suite 3428 E Pacific Coast Hwy (at Redondo) **562/597–3884** • 8pm-close Th-Sat • popular • lesbians/ gay men • dancing/DJ • Latin night Th • women's night Sat • 2 levels • wheelchair access

Unzipped 5101 E Ocean (at Granada, at Ripples) **562/433–0357** • 7pm-2am Fri only • popular • mostly women • dancing/DJ • multiracial • food served • videos • live entertainment • karaoke • go-go girls • patio

CAFES

Hot Java 2101 E Broadway Ave **562/433–0688** • 6am-11pm, till midnight Fri-Sat • also soups, sandwiches, salads • WiFi

iCandy Coffee 1708 E Broadway (at Gaviota) **562/437–3785** • 7am-9pm, till midnight wknds • mostly gay men • also sandwiches & desserts • WiFi

The Library 3418 E Broadway **562/433–2393** • 6am-midnight, till 1am Fri-Sat, from 7am wknds

RESTAURANTS

212 Degrees Bistro 2708 E 4th St **562/439–8822** • 8am-2pm Th-Sun only • Mexican-inspired

Cafe Sevilla 140 Pine St **562/495–1111** • dinner only, Sun brunch • Spanish • also music & dancing

Hamburger Mary's 740 E Broadway (at Alamitos) **562/436–7900** • 11am-2am • lesbians/ gay men • full bar • dancing/DJ • theme nights

Omelette Inn 318 Pine Ave **562/437–5625** • 7am-4pm

Open Sesame 5215 E 2nd St **562/621–1698** • lunch & dinner • Middle Eastern

Original Park Pantry 2104 E Broadway (at Junipero) **562/434–0451** • 6am-10pm, till 11pm Fri-Sat • int'l • some veggie • wheelchair access

The Raven's Nest 2941 E Broadway (btwn Temple & Redondo) **562/439–3672** • dinner only • Cuban • wheelchair access

Two Umbrellas Cafe 1538 E Broadway (at Gaviota Ave) **562/495–2323** • 8am-2pm • gay-owned

Utopia 445 E 1st St **562/432–6888** • lunch Mon-Fri, dinner nightly, clsd Sun • seafood, California cuisine • plenty veggie

BOOKSTORES

Open 2226 E 4th St (btwn Cherry & Junipero, in heart of Retro Row) **562/499–6736** • 11am-7pm, till 8pm Sat, till 6pm Sun, clsd Mon • general • also films, art & events

RETAIL SHOPS

Hot Stuff 2121 E Broadway (at Junipero) **562/433–0692** • 11am-7pm, 10am-6pm Sat, noon-5pm Sun • cards • gifts • adult novelties • serving community since 1980 • gay- & lesbian-owned

So Cal Tattoo 339 W 6th St, San Pedro **310/519–8282** • woman-owned tattoo & piercing shop • reservations recommended

PUBLICATIONS

Orange County/ Long Beach Blade **562/314–7674**

EROTICA

The Crypt on Broadway 1712 E Broadway (btwn Cherry & Falcon) **562/983–6560** • 10am-midnight • leather • toys

The RubberTree 5018 E 2nd St (at Granada) **562/434–0027** • 11am-9pm, till 10pm Fri-Sat, noon-7pm Sun • gifts for lovers • women-owned

LOS ANGELES

Los Angeles is divided into 8 geographical areas:
LA—Overview
LA—West Hollywood
LA—Hollywood
LA—West LA & Santa Monica
LA—Silverlake
LA—Midtown
LA—Valley
LA—East LA & South Central

LA—Overview

INFO LINES & SERVICES

Alcoholics Anonymous 323/936–4343 & 735–2089 (EN ESPAÑOL), 800/923–8722 • call or check web (www.lacoaa.org) for meetings

Crystal Meth Anonymous 213/488–4455 • call or check website (www.crystalmeth.org) for meetings in LA County

LA Gay & Lesbian Center 1625 N Schrader Blvd (McDonald/Wright Building) 323/993–7400 • 9am-9pm, till 1pm Sat, clsd Sun • wide variety of services

LA Gay & Lesbian Center's Village at Ed Gould Plaza 1125 N McCadden Pl (at Santa Monica) 323/860–7302 • 9am-9pm, clsd Sun • cybercenter • cafe • theaters

ENTERTAINMENT & RECREATION

The Celebration Theatre 7051 Santa Monica Blvd (at La Brea) 323/957–1884 • LGBT theater • call for more info

The Ellen DeGeneres Show • you know you want to dance w/ Ellen! • check out ellen.warnerbros.com for tickets

The Gay Mafia Comedy Group • lesbians/ gay men • improv/ sketch comedy • gay-owned

The Getty Center 1200 Getty Center Dr, Brentwood 310/440–7300 • 10am-6pm, till 9pm Fri-Sat, clsd Mon • LA's shining city on a hill & world-class museum • of course, it's still in LA so you'll need to make reservations for parking (!)

Griffith Observatory enter on N Vermont St (in Griffith Park) 213/473–0800 • noon-10pm, from 10am wknds, clsd Mon

Highways 1651 18th St (at the 18th Street Arts Center), Santa Monica 310/315–1459 (RESERVATION LINE) • "full-service performance center"

IMRU Gay Radio KPFK LA 90.7 FM • 7pm Mon

LA Sparks 877/447–7275 (LA AREA ONLY), 310/426–6033 • check out the Women's Nat'l Basketball Association while you're in Los Angeles

Outfest 213/480–7088 • LGBT media arts foundation that sponsors the annual LGBT film festival each July • also screens LGBT films Wed at the Egyptian Theater in Hollywood • see listing in Film Festival Calendar

Rainbow Skate/ Moonlight Rollerway Gay Skate 5110 San Fernando Rd (N of W Colorado St, near LA Zoo), Glendale 818/241–3630 • 8pm Wed only • lesbians/ gay men

Vox Femina 310/922–0025 • women's chorus

Women on a Roll 310/578–8888 • "largest lesbian organization in California" • offering sporting, cultural & social events, as well as worldwide travel, for women

PUBLICATIONS

Adelante Magazine 323/256–6639 • bilingual LGBT magazine

Essential Gay & Lesbian Directory 310/841–2800, 866/718–GAYS • business directory serving the LGBT community

Frontiers Business Directory 323/930–3220 • annual survival guide to LGBT Southern CA & Bay Area

➤ **Lesbian News (LN)** 310/548–9888, 800/458–9888 • nat'l w/ strong coverage of Southern CA • see ad front color section

Odyssey Magazine 323/874–8788 • dish on LA's club scene

LA—West Hollywood

ACCOMMODATIONS

Andaz West Hollywood 8401 Sunset Blvd (at Kings Rd) 323/656–1234, 800/233–1234 • gay/ straight • on the Sunset Strip • rooftop pool • nonsmoking • WiFi • wheelchair access

Chamberlain 1000 Westmount Dr (near Holloway) 310/657–7400, 800/201–9652 • gay/ straight • boutique hotel • fitness center • rooftop pool • bistro restaurant & lounge

The Elan Hotel Los Angeles 8435 Beverly Blvd (at Croft) 323/658–6663, 888/611–0398 • gay/ straight • hip & trendy • kids ok • wheelchair access • gay-owned

The Grafton on Sunset 8462 W Sunset Blvd (at La Cienega) 323/654–4600, 800/821–3660 • gay/ straight • pool • sundeck • panoramic views • located in heart of Sunset Strip • wheelchair access

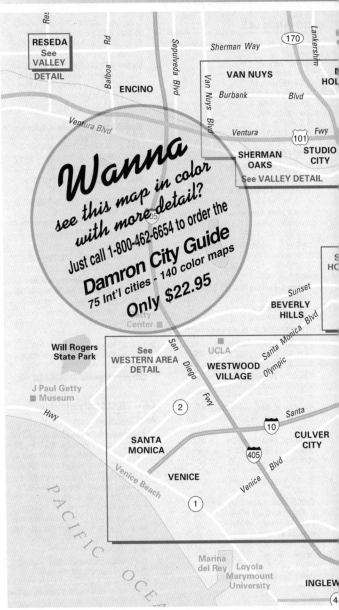

RESEDA
See VALLEY DETAIL

Res...

Rd

Balboa

Sepulveda Blvd

ENCINO

Sherman Way

(170)

Lankershim

VAN NUYS

Van Nuys Blvd

Burbank

Blvd

N... HOL...

Ventura Blvd

Ventura

Fwy

{101}

STUDIO CITY

SHERMAN OAKS

See VALLEY DETAIL

Wanna
see this map in color
with more detail?
Just call 1-800-462-6654 to order the
Damron City Guide
75 Int'l cities - 140 color maps
Only $22.95

...05

...etty Center

Sunset

BEVERLY HILLS

Santa Monica Blvd

S... HO...

Will Rogers State Park

See WESTERN AREA DETAIL

San Diego

UCLA

WESTWOOD VILLAGE

Santa Monica Blvd

Olympic

J Paul Getty Museum

Hwy

Fwy

(2)

SANTA MONICA

10

Santa

CULVER CITY

405

Blvd

Venice Beach

VENICE

Venice

(1)

PACIFIC OCEAN

Marina del Rey

Loyola Marymount University

INGLEW...

(4...

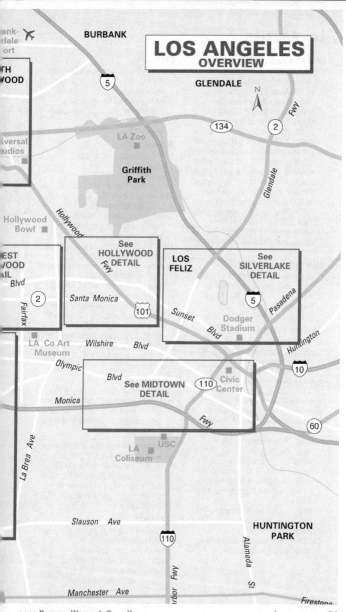

LOS ANGELES
OVERVIEW

BURBANK

GLENDALE

ank-
dale
ort

TH
OOD

5

134

2

N

iversal
udios

LA Zoo

Glendale Fwy

Griffith
Park

Hollywood
Bowl

Hollywood Fwy

EST
OOD
IL

Blvd

See
HOLLYWOOD
DETAIL

LOS
FELIZ

See
SILVERLAKE
DETAIL

Fairfax

2

Santa Monica

101

5

Sunset

Pasadena

Dodger
Stadium

Blvd

Huntington

LA Co Art
Museum

Wilshire

Blvd

Olympic

Blvd

See MIDTOWN
DETAIL

110

Civic
Center

10

Monica

Fwy

60

La Brea Ave

LA
Coliseum

USC

Slauson   Ave

HUNTINGTON
PARK

110

Alameda   St

Manchester   Ave

rbor Fwy

Firestone

Los Angeles

WHERE THE GIRLS ARE:

Hip dykes hang out in West Hollywood, with the boys along Santa Monica Blvd, or cruise funky Venice Beach and Santa Monica. The S&M ("Stand & Model") glamourdykes pose in chichi clubs and posh eateries in West LA and Beverly Hills. There's a scattered community of women in Silverlake. And more suburban lesbians frequent the gay bars in Studio City and North Hollywood. If you're used to makeup-free lesbians, you may be surprised that coiffed and lipsticked lesbian style is the norm in LA. Then again, if you've ever seen an episode of *The L Word*, how could you be?!

LGBT PRIDE:

June. Christopher St West 323/969-8302, web: www.lapride.org.
June-July. Los Angeles Black LGBT Pride 323/285-4225, web: www.atbla.com.

ANNUAL EVENTS:

June - AIDS LifeCycle 323/308-4000, web: www.aidslifecycle.org. AIDS benefit bike ride from San Francisco to LA.
July - Outfest 213/480-7088, web: www.outfest.org. Los Angeles' lesbian/ gay film & video festival.
August - Centre Court, web: www.lataweb.com. LA Tennis Association's int'l tournament.
August - Sunset Junction Fair 323/661-7771, web: www.sunsetjunction.org. Carnival, arts & information fair on Sunset Blvd in Silverlake to benefit Sunset Junction Youth Center.
October - AIDS Walk-a-thon 213/201-9255, web: www.aidswalk.net.
October - Gay Days at Disneyland, web: www.gayday2.com.

CITY INFO:

Los Angeles Convention & Visitors Bureau, 800/228-2452, web: www.discoverlosangeles.com.
West Hollywood Convention & Visitors Bureau, 800/368-6020, web: www.visitwesthollywood.com.

ATTRACTIONS:

3rd St outdoor mall in Santa Monica.
Chinatown, near downtown.
City Walk in Universal Studios.
The Getty Center 310/440-7300, web: www.getty.edu.
Grauman's Chinese Theatre on Hollywood Blvd 323/461-3331, web: www.chinesetheatres.com.
Griffith Observatory 213/473-0800, web: www.griffithobs.org.
Melrose Ave, hip commercial district in West Hollywood.
Theme Parks: Disneyland, Knotts Berry Farm, or Magic Mountain.
Watts Towers (Simon Rodia State Historical Park), 1765 E 107th St (not far from LAX), 213/847-4646, web: www.wattstowers.us.
Westwood Village premiere movie theaters & restaurants.
Venice Beach.

BEST VIEW:

Drive up Mulholland Drive, in the hills between Hollywood and the Valley, for a panoramic view of the city, and the Hollywood sign.

WEATHER:

Summers are hot, dry, and smoggy with temperatures in the 80°s-90°s. LA's weather is at its finest — sunny, blue skies, and moderate temperatures (mid 70°s) — during the months of March, April, and May.

TRANSIT:

LA Yellow Cab 877/733-3305, web: www.layellowcab.com.
LA Express 800/427-7483.
Super Shuttle 310/782-6600.
Metro Transit Authority 323/466-3876, web: www.mta.net. Includes subway.

The Grove Guesthouse 323/876-7770, 888/524-7683 • lesbians/ gay men • 1-bdrm villa • hot tub • pool • kitchens • WiFi • pets ok by arrangement • gay-owned

Holloway Motel 8465 Santa Monica Blvd (at La Cienega) 323/654-2454, 888/654-6400 • gay/ straight • kitchens • nonsmoking • centrally located

Hotel Le Petit 8822 Cynthia St (at Larrabee) 310/854-1114, 800/835-7997 • gay-friendly • all-suite hotel • hot tub • pool • kids ok • wheelchair access

Le Parc Suite Hotel 733 N West Knoll Dr (at Melrose) 310/855-8888, 800/578-4837 • popular • gay-friendly • deluxe-class all-suite hotel • pool • tennis courts • kids/ pets ok • also restaurant • wheelchair access

The London West Hollywood 1020 N San Vicente Blvd 866/282-4560 • gay-friendly • luxury hotel • pool • WiFi • also Gordon Ramsay's restaurant

Mondrian 8440 Sunset Blvd 323/650-8999, 800/697-1791 • gay-friendly • home of trendy Skybar & Asia de Cuba restaurant • $185-425

Ramada Plaza Hotel—West Hollywood 8585 Santa Monica Blvd (at La Cienega) 310/652-6400, 800/845-8585 • gay-friendly • modern art deco hotel & suites • pool & poolside WiFi • kids ok • wheelchair access

Sunset Marquis Hotel & Villas 1200 Alta Loma Rd (1/2 block S of Sunset Blvd) 310/657-1333, 800/858-9758 • gay/ straight • full brkfst • sauna • hot tub • pool • WiFi • kids ok • wheelchair access • $330-3,000

BARS

The Abbey 692 N Robertson Blvd (at Santa Monica) 310/289-8410 • 8am-2am • lesbians/ gay men • popular • also restaurant • patio • wheelchair access

Comedy Store 8433 Sunset Blvd (at La Cienega) 323/650-6268 • 8pm-2am • gay-friendly • legendary stand-up club

East/ West Lounge 8851 Santa Monica Blvd (at San Vicente) 310/360-6186, 877/395-6864 • 4:30pm-2am, clsd Mon • popular • gay/ straight • hip lounge that blends the best of both East & West Coasts • karaoke Tue

Fiesta Cantina 8865 Santa Monica Blvd (at San Vicente) 310/652-8865 • noon-2am • lesbians/ gay men • raucous Mexican restaurant & bar

Here Lounge 696 N Robertson Blvd (at Santa Monica) 310/360-8455 • 4pm-2am • lesbians/ gay men • more women Fri for Truck Stop • swanky & stylish • DJ nightly

Improvisation 8162 Melrose Ave (at Crescent Heights) 323/651-2583 • gay-friendly • stand-up comedy • also restaurant

Micky's 8857 Santa Monica Blvd (at San Vicente) 310/657-1176 • noon-2am, after-hours wknds • mostly gay men • dancing/DJ • videos • younger crowd • food served • patio • gay-owned

The Palms on Las Olas 8572 Santa Monica Blvd (at La Cienega) 310/652-1595 • 8pm-2am, from 4pm wknds, after-hours Fri-Sat • popular • mostly women • multiracial • neighborhood bar • dancing/DJ • theme nights • karaoke • beer bust Sun • patio • wheelchair access • cover some nights

Platinum 8851 Santa Monica Blvd (at San Vicente, at East West) 310/360-6186, 877/395-6864 • 9pm Th only • mostly women • hip lounge

Viper Room 8852 Sunset Blvd (btwn San Vicente & Larrabee) 310/358-1881, 310/358-1881 (TICKETING) • doors open btwn 7pm-8pm nightly • gay-friendly • dancing/DJ • live bands • cover charge

NIGHTCLUBS

Area 643 N La Cienega Blvd 310/652-2012 • 10pm-2am Th-Sat • gay-friendly • dancing/DJ

Eleven Restaurant & Nightclub 8811 Santa Monica Blvd (at Larrabee St) 310/855-0800 • lunch & dinner • more gay for the bar atmosphere till 2am

The Factory 652 N La Peer Dr (at Santa Monica) 310/659-4551 • 9pm-2am Fri-Sat • mostly gay men • dancing/DJ • videos

Girl Bar 310/659-4551, 877/447-5252 • popular • 9pm-2:30am Fri only • women only • dancing/DJ

Rage 8911 Santa Monica Blvd (at San Vicente) 310/652-7055 • noon-2am, lunch Tue-Sun, dinner nightly • popular • mostly gay men • dancing/DJ • live shows • videos • 18+ wknds • wheelchair access

The Ruby 7070 Hollywood Blvd (at Sycamore) 323/467-7070 • 10pm-3am • gay-friendly • dancing/DJ • theme nights: including '70s & '80s night, hip-hop, goth, electronica, house • 18+ • patio • cover charge

Ultra Suede 661 N Robertson Blvd (at Santa Monica) 310/659-4551 • 10pm-2am Wed-Sat • gay/ straight • dancing/DJ • theme nights

CAFES

Champagne French Bakery & Cafe 8917-9 Santa Monica Blvd 310/657-4051 • 6:30am-9pm, till 11pm Fri-Sat • coffees & pastries as well as brkfst, lunch & dinner • some outdoor seating

Grind House Cafe 1051 N Havenhurst Dr 323/650-7717 • 6:30am-10pm • coffeehouse • WiFi • occasional live music

Urth Caffe 8565 Melrose Ave (btwn Robertson & La Cienega) 310/659-0628 • 6:30am-midnight • organic coffees, teas & treats • food served • plenty veggie & vegan • patio

RESTAURANTS

AOC 8022 W Third St (at Crescent Heights Blvd) 323/653-6359 • dinner nightly • wine bar • eclectic • upscale

Basix Cafe 8333 Santa Monica Blvd (at Flores) 323/848-2460 • 7am-11pm • outdoor seating

Bite 8807 Santa Monica Blvd (at San Vicente) 310/659-3663 • 11:30am-11:30pm • plenty veggie • beer/ wine • wheelchair access

Bossa Nova 685 N Robertson Blvd (at Santa Monica) 310/657-5070 • 11am-midnight • Brazilian • beer/ wine • patio • wheelchair access

Cafe La Boheme 8400 Santa Monica Blvd (btwn Benecia Ave & Fox Hills Dr) 323/848-2360 • 5pm-10pm Fri-Sat, till 11pm Sun-Th • American eclectic/ California • full bar • patio w/ fireplace • wheelchair access

Canter's Deli 419 N Fairfax (btwn Melrose & Beverly) 323/651-2030 • 24hrs • hip after-hours • Jewish/ American • some veggie • full bar • wheelchair access

Eat Well 8252 Santa Monica Blvd (at La Jolla) 323/656-1383 • 7am-9:30pm, 8am-3pm wknds • popular • comfort food diner

Falcon 7213 Sunset Blvd (btwn Poinsettia & Formosa) 323/850-5350 • dinner Wed-Sat • gay/ straight • California/ cont'l fusion • full bar & lounge

Hamburger Mary's Bar & Grill 8288 Santa Monica Blvd 323/654-3800 • 11am-1am, till 2am Fri-Sat • lesbians/ gay men • transgender-friendly • karaoke • drag shows

Hedley's 640 N Robertson Blvd 310/659-2009 • lunch & dinner, also wknd brunch, clsd Sun night & Mon

The Hudson 1114 N Crescent Heights Blvd 323/654-6686

Il Piccolino Trattoria 350 N Robertson Blvd (btwn Melrose & Beverly) 310/659-2220 • lunch & dinner, clsd Sun • full bar • patio • wheelchair access

Joey's Cafe 8301 Santa Monica Blvd 323/822-0671 • 8am-10pm • a little bit coffeehouse, a little bit diner • popular at lunch

Kokomo Cafe 7385 Beverly Blvd (between La Brea Ave & Fairfax Ave) 323/933-0773 • 8am-4pm • diner • wheelchair access

Koo Koo Roo 8520 Santa Monica Blvd (at La Cienega Blvd) 310/657-3300 • 11am-11pm, till 10pm Sun • lots of healthy chicken dishes • plenty veggie • beer/ wine • wheelchair access

Lola's 945 N Fairfax Ave (at Santa Monica) 323/654-5652 • 5:30pm-2am • great martinis

Louise's Trattoria 7505 Melrose Ave (at Gardner) 323/651-3880 • 11am-10pm • Italian • great foccacia bread • beer/ wine • patio

Lucques 8474 Melrose Ave (at La Cienega) 323/655-6277 • lunch Tue-Sat, dinner nightly • French • full bar • patio • wheelchair access

Marix Tex Mex 1108 N Flores (btwn La Cienega & Fairfax) 323/656-8800 • 11:30am-11pm, from 11am wknds • lesbians/ gay men • some veggie • great margaritas • patio • wheelchair access

Nyala 1076 S Fairfax (at Whitworth Dr) 323/936-5918 • many Ethiopian, Nigerian & other African restaurants to choose from on this block

O-Bar 8279 Santa Monica Blvd (at Sweetzer) 323/822-3300 • 6pm-2am • gay/ straight • full bar

Real Food Daily 414 N La Cienega (btwn Beverly & Melrose) 310/289-9910 • 11:30am-10pm, till 11pm Fri-Sat, Sun brunch 10am-3pm • organic vegan • beer/ wine • patio • wheelchair access

Sante Libre 345 N La Brea (btwn Melrose & Beverly) 323/857-0412 • 9am-10pm • pastas, salads & wraps • plenty veggie & vegan • cheap

St Felix 8945 Santa Monica Blvd (at Hilldale) 310/275-4428 • 4pm-2am • small plates

Tart 115 S Fairfax Ave (at Farmer's Daughter Hotel) 323/937-3930, 800/334-1658 • 7am-midnight • Southern

Taste 8454 Melrose Ave (at La Cienega) 323/852-6888 • lunch & dinner, wknd brunch • upscale eclectic • full bar

Versailles 1415 S La Cienega (at W Pico) 310/289-0392 • lunch & dinner • Cuban

BOOKSTORES

Book Soup 8818 W Sunset Blvd (at Larrabee) 310/659-3110, 800/764-2665 • 9am-10pm, till 7pm Sun • LGBT section

RETAIL SHOPS

665 Leather 8722 Santa Monica Blvd (at Huntley Dr) 310/854-7276 • noon-8pm, till 10pm Fri-Sat • custom leather & neoprene • also accessories & toys

Marginalized Tattoo 4228 Melrose Ave (at Vermont) 213/422-4801 • featuring Dave Davenport (aka "Dogspunk"), named best gay tattoo artist by *Frontiers* magazine

GYMS & HEALTH CLUBS

24 Hour Fitness 8612 Santa Monica Blvd, West Hollywood 310/652-7440 • recently renovated • tres gay

The Easton Gym 8053 Beverly Blvd (at Crescent Hts) 323/651-3636 • gay-friendly

The Fitness Factory 650 N La Peer Dr (at Santa Monica) 310/358-1838 • 6am-9pm, till 8pm Fri, 7am-5pm Sat, 8am-1pm Sun

EROTICA

Circus of Books 8230 Santa Monica Blvd (at La Jolla) 323/656-6533 • 6am-2am

Hustler Hollywood 8920 Sunset Blvd (at San Vicente) 310/860-9009 • 10am-2am • chic erotic department store • also cafe

Pleasure Chest 7733 Santa Monica Blvd (at Genesee), N Hollywood 323/650-1022 • 10am-midnight, till 1am Th-Sat

LA—Hollywood

ACCOMMODATIONS

Hollywood Heights Hotel 2005 N Highland (at Franklin) 323/876-8600, 866/696-3157 • gay-friendly • also restaurant & lounge • pool • jacuzzi • kids ok • WiFi • wheelchair access

Hollywood Hotel – The Hotel of Hollywood 1160 N Vermont Ave (at Santa Monica) 323/315-1800, 800/800-9733 • gay-friendly • full brkfst • pool • nonsmoking • WiFi • wheelchair access

BARS

Boardner's 1652 N Cherokee Ave 323/462-9621 • 4pm-2am • gay/ straight • "a Hollywood legend & best-kept secret since 1942" • dancing/DJ • food served • theme nights

Faultline 4216 Melrose Ave (at Vermont) 323/660-0889 • 5pm-2am, from 2pm wknds, clsd Mon-Tue • popular • mostly gay men • cruisy • leather • bears • videos • patio

NIGHTCLUBS

Arena/ Circus Disco 6655 Santa Monica Blvd (at Seward, Circus behind Arena) 323/462-1291 • 9pm-2am Tue-Wed & Fri-Sat • popular • gay men • dancing/DJ • theme nights • multiracial • strippers

Avalon 1735 Vine St (at Hollywood Blvd) 323/462-8900 • gay/ straight • one of LAs best dance music clubs • call for events

Booby Trap 1611 N El Centro Ave (at El Centro) • monthly • mostly women • cute girls • dive bar

Mr Black LA 1737 N Vine St (at Hollywood Blvd, at Bardot) 323/462-8900 • Tue only • lesbians/ gay men • dancing/DJ

Sundays 8210 Sunset Blvd (at Havenhurst, at Libertine bar) • Sun only • women's dance party

TigerHeat 1735 Vine St (N of Hollywood Blvd, at Avalon nightclub) 323/467-4571 • 9:30pm-3am Th only • gay/ straight • dancing/DJ • transgender-friendly • live shows • videos • 18+ • cover charge

RESTAURANTS

101 Coffee Shop 6145 Franklin Ave 323/467-1175 • 7am-3am • diner

Hollywood Canteen 1006 N Seward St (at Santa Monica) 323/465-0961 • 5pm-11pm, till 2am Th, 6pm-2am Fri-Sat, clsd Sun • gay-friendly • popular • classic • full bar

La Poubelle 5907 Franklin Ave (at Bronson) 323/465-0807 • 5:30pm-midnight • French/ Italian • some veggie • full bar • wheelchair access

Lucy's Cafe El Adobe 5536 Melrose Ave (near Gower St) 323/462-9421 • 11:30am-11pm, clsd Sun • Mexican • patio

Musso & Frank Grill 6667 Hollywood Blvd (near Las Palmas) 323/467-5123 • 11am-11pm, clsd Sun-Mon • the grand-dame diner/ steak house of Hollywood • great pancakes, potpies & martinis!

Off Vine 6263 Leland Wy (at Vine) 323/962-1900 • lunch & dinner, wknd brunch • beer/ wine

Prado 244 N Larchmont Blvd (at Beverly) 323/467-3871 • lunch & dinner, dinner only Sun • Caribbean • some veggie • wheelchair access

Quality 8030 W 3rd St (at Laurel) 323/658-5959 • 8am-3:30pm • homestyle brkfst • some veggie • wheelchair access

Rockwell VT 1714 N Vermont Ave (at Prospect (enter in alley)) 323/669-1550 • 5pm-2am, brunch wknds

Roscoe's House of Chicken & Waffles 1514 N Gower (at Sunset) 323/466-7453 • 8:30am-midnight, till 4am Fri Sat

Sushi Hiroba 776 N Vine St 323/962-7237 • lunch Mon-Fri, dinner nightly

BOOKSTORES

Skylight Books 1818 N Vermont Ave (at Melbourne Ave) 323/660-1175 • 10am-10pm • way cool independent in Los Feliz • great fiction & alt-lit sections

RETAIL SHOPS

Panpipes Magickal Marketplace 1641 N Cahuenga Blvd 323/462-7078 • noon-7pm, till 9pm Wed & Sat, clsd Mon • "nation's oldest occult store" w/ custom spells & classes

GYMS & HEALTH CLUBS

Gold's Gym 1016 N Cole Ave (near Santa Monica & Vine) 323/462-7012 • 5am-midnight, 7am-9pm Sat-Sun • gay-friendly

LA—West LA & Santa Monica

ACCOMMODATIONS

Casa Malibu 22752 Pacific Coast Hwy, Malibu 310/456-2219 • gay-friendly • on the beach • WiFi • $179-529

The Georgian Hotel 1415 Ocean Ave (btwn Santa Monica & Broadway), Santa Monica 310/395-9945, 800/538-8147 • gay-friendly • food served • wheelchair access

Hotel Angeleno 170 N Church Ln (at Hwy 405) 310/476-6411, 866/264-3536 • gay/ straight • boutique hotel w/ landmark circular shape • pool • gym • nonsmoking • WiFi • $199+

Hotel Erwin 1697 Pacific Ave (at Venice Way), Venice Beach 310/452-1111, 800/786-7789 • gay/ straight • rooftop lounge and restaurant • gym • nonsmoking • WiFi • $169+

Hotel Palomar 310/475-8711, 800/472-8556 • gay/ straight • pool • wheelchair access • $259-2,500

The Inn at Venice Beach 327 Washington Blvd (at Via Dolce), Marina Del Rey 310/821-2557, 800/828-0688 • gay-friendly • 43-room European-style inn • kids ok • WiFi • wheelchair access

The Linnington 310/422-8825 • lesbians/ gay men • B&B • jacuzzi • kids ok • lesbian-owned • $95

Shutters on the Beach 1 Pico Blvd, Santa Monica 310/458-0030, 800/334-9000

W Los Angeles 930 Hilgard Ave (at Le Conte) 310/208-8765, 800/421-2317 • gay-friendly • suites • also restaurant • gym • day spa • pool

BARS

The Dolphin 1995 Artesia Blvd (at Green Ln), Redondo Beach 310/318-3339 • 7pm-2am, more women Mon • lesbians/ gay men • neighborhood bar • dancing/DJ Fri-Sat • karaoke Sun, Tue & Th • patio • wheelchair access

CAFES

The Novel Cafe 212 Pier Ave, Santa Monica 310/396-8566 • 7am-1am, from 8am Sat, 8am-midnight Sun • coffeehouse • used bookstore

RESTAURANTS

12 Washington 12 Washington Blvd (at Pacific), Marina Del Rey 310/822-5566 • 5pm-10pm, till 11pm Fri-Sun • cont'l

Baja Cantina 311 Washington Blvd (at Sanborn), Venice 310/821-2252 • 10:30am-1am, also brunch wknds • full bar

Border Grill 1445 4th St (at Broadway), Santa Monica 310/451-1655 • lunch & dinner from famous "Two Hot Tamales" chefs • Mexican

Cantalini's Salerno Beach Restaurant 193 Culver Blvd (at Vista del Mar), Playa del Rey 310/821-0018 • lunch Mon-Fri, dinner nightly • Italian • homemade pastas • beer/ wine • live music Sun nights

Cora's Coffee Shop 1802 Ocean Ave (N of Pico Blvd), Santa Monica 310/451-9562 • 6:30am-3pm, from 7am wknds, clsd Mon • organic

Drago 2628 Wilshire Blvd (btwn 26th & Princeton), Santa Monica 310/828-1585 • lunch Mon-Sat, dinner nightly • Sicilian Italian • wheelchair access

Gjelina 1429 Abbot Kinney Blvd, Venice 310/450-1429 • pizzas & small plates • beer/ wine only

Golden Bull 170 W Channel Rd (at Pacific Coast Hwy), Santa Monica 310/230-0402 • 4:30pm-10pm, till 11pm wknds, Sun brunch • American • full bar

Hamburger Habit 11223 National Blvd (at Sepulveda) 310/478-5000 • popular • 10am-11pm, till midnight Fri-Sat

Joe's 1023 Abbot Kinney Blvd, Venice 310/399-5811 • lunch Tue-Fri, dinner nightly, wknd brunch, clsd Mon • French/ Californian

Real Food Daily 514 Santa Monica Blvd (btwn 5th & 6th), Santa Monica 310/451-7544 • 11:30am-10pm • organic vegan • beer/ wine • wheelchair access

Wokcano 1413 5th St, Santa Monica 310/458-3080 • 11am-12:30am, till 1:30am Fri-Sat • sushi bar & Chinese cafe

ENTERTAINMENT & RECREATION

Santa Monica Pier Ocean Ave (at Colorado Ave), Santa Monica

Will Rogers State Beach Pacific Coast Hwy (at Temescal Canyon Rd) • gay beach

BOOKSTORES

Diesel, A Bookstore 3890 Cross Creek Rd, Malibu 310/456-9961 • 10am-7pm, till 9pm Fri-Sat, till 6pm Sun • independent

EROTICA

Pleasure Island 18426 Hawthorne Blvd (btwn Artesia & 190th), Torrance 310/793-9477 • 11am-midnight, till 2am Fri-Sat

LA—Silverlake

ACCOMMODATIONS

Sanborn GuestHouse 1005 1/2 Sanborn Ave (near Sunset) 323/666-3947 • gay/ straight • private unit w/ kitchen • nonsmoking • WiFi • gay-owned

BARS

4100 Bar 4100 Sunset Blvd (at Manzanita) 323/666-4460 • 8pm-2am • gay/ straight • neighborhood bar

Cavern Club Theater 1920 Hyperion Ave (at Casita Del Campo) 323/969-2530, 323/662-4255 • wide variety of shows • Wed-Sat nights

Cha Cha Lounge 2375 Glendale Blvd (at Silverlake) 323/660-7595 • 5pm-2am • gay-friendly • hipster lounge • gay-owned

Club Nur 2810 Hyperion Ave (at Rowena, at MJ's) 323/660-1503 • Th only • lesbians/ gay men • Middle Eastern night • dancing/DJ

Eagle LA 4219 Santa Monica Blvd (at Hoover) 323/669-9472 • 4pm-2am, from 2pm wknds • popular • mostly gay men • leather • wheelchair access

Good Luck Bar 1514 Hillhurst Ave (nr Hollywood Blvd) 323/666-3524 • 7pm-2am, from 8pm wknds • gay-friendly • stylish dive bar

Silverlake Lounge 2906 Sunset Blvd (at Silver Lake Blvd) 323/663-9636 • 3pm-2am • gay/ straight • rock 'n' roll club • drag shows wknds

NIGHTCLUBS

A Club Called Rhonda 4212 W Sunset Blvd (at Myra, at El Cid club) 213/995-3969 • gay/ straight • monthly party • "house, disco, and polysexual hard partying"

Club Cafe Con Leche 700 S Almansor St (at The Almansor Court), Alhambra 626/282-0330 (CLUB INFO) • 9pm-2am 2nd Fri only • mostly women • dancing/DJ • Latino/a • live bands

The Echo 1822 W Sunset Blvd (at Glendale Blvd) 213/413-8200 • gay/ straight • dancing/DJ • live shows

Full Frontal Disco 213/626-2285 • last Sun only • gay/ straight • dancing/DJ • transgender-friendly

CAFES

The Coffee Table 2930 Rowena Ave 323/644-8111 • 7am-11pm • patio • fab mosaic magic

RESTAURANTS

Casita Del Campo 1920 Hyperion Ave 323/662-4255 • 11am-midnight, till 2am Fri-Sat • popular • Mexican • patio

Cha Cha Cha 656 N Virgil Ave (at Melrose) 323/664-7723 • lunch & dinner • lesbians/ gay men • Caribbean • plenty veggie • wheelchair access

Cliff's Edge 3626 Sunset Blvd (at Griffith Park Blvd) 323/666-6116 • dinner only, wknd brunch • plenty veggie • romantic • outdoor seating

El Conquistador 3701 W Sunset Blvd (at Lucille) 323/666-5136 • lunch Tue-Sun, dinner nightly • Mexican • beer/ wine • patio

The Flying Leap Cafe 2538 Hyperion Ave (below The Other Side bar) 323/661-0618 • dinner Tue-Sun, Sun brunch • cont'l • full bar • also Mary's Metro Station

The Good Microbrew & Grill 3725 Sunset Blvd (at Lucille) 323/660-3645 • 11am-10pm, till 11pm Fri, 9am-10pm wknds • plenty veggie

Home 1760 Hillhurst Ave, Los Feliz 323/669-0211 • 9am-10pm, patio

The Kitchen 4348 Fountain Ave (at Sunset Blvd) 323/664-3663 • 5pm-1am, from 11am Sat, till 10pm Sun • cozy diner • gay-owned

Michelangelo Pizzeria Ristorante 2742 Rowena 323/660-4843 • lunch & dinner

SiLa Bistro 2630 Hyperion Ave (at Griffith Park Blvd) 323/664-7979 • dinner only, clsd Mon • Sun brunch • beer/ wine • patio • gay-owned

Square One Dining 4854 Fountain Ave (at Vermont Ave) 323/661-1109 • 8am-3pm • great brkfst

Vermont Restaurant & Bar 1714 N Vermont Ave 323/661-6163 • lunch Mon- Fri, dinner nightly, clsd Sun • gay-owned

BOOKSTORES

Serifos 3814 W Sunset Blvd 323/660-7467 • independent bookstore • gifts

RETAIL SHOPS

Syren 2809 1/2 W Sunset Blvd 213/289-0334 • noon-10pm, clsd Mon • leather & latex

GYMS & HEALTH CLUBS

Body Builders 2516 Hyperion Ave (at Tracy) 323/668-0802 • gay-friendly

EROTICA

Romantix Adult Superstore 3147 N San Fernando Rd 323/258-2867 • 24hrs

LA—Midtown

ACCOMMODATIONS

The Standard, Downtown LA 550 S Flower St 213/892-8080 • gay/straight • pool • restaurant • WiFi

BARS

Cafe Club Fais Do-Do 5257 W Adams Blvd (btwn Fairfax & La Brea) 323/931-4636 • 8pm-2am • gay-friendly • live music • also Cajun restaurant

NIGHTCLUBS

Bordello 901 E 1st St (at S Vignes St) 213/687-3766 • gay-friendly • burlesque shows • also restaurant

The Catwalk 801 W Temple St (at N Figueroa, at Vertigos bar) 213/977-0888 • 1st Fri only • mostly women • dancing/DJ

Coco Bongo 3311 S Main St 818/233-5322 • 9pm-2am, clsd Mon-Wed • mostly women • dancing/DJ • Latino/a • drag shows • go-go dancers • 18+

Jewel's Catch One Disco 4067 W Pico Blvd (at Norton) 323/734-8849 (HOTLINE), 323/737-1159 • call for hours, clsd Wed-Th • gay/ straight • dancing/DJ • theme nights • wheelchair access

Mustache Mondays 336 S Hill St (at W 4th St, at La Cita bar) 213/687-7111 • 9pm Mon only • lesbians/ gay men • dancing/DJ • transgender-friendly • queer fashionistas

RESTAURANTS

Border Grill Downtown 445 S Figueroa St (at 5th St) 213/486-5171 • lunch & dinner & late night cocktails • wheelchair access • owned by celebrity chefs Mary Sue Milliken & Susan Feniger

Cassell's 3266 W 6th St (at Vermont) 213/480-5000 • 10:30am-4pm, clsd Sun • great burgers

Doughboys Cafe 8136 W 3rd St 323/852-1020 • 7am-10pm

LA—Valley

includes San Fernando & San Gabriel Valleys

BARS

Cobra 10937 Burbank Blvd (1 block E of Vineland), North Hollywood 818/760-9798 • 4pm-9pm, till 2am Wed-Sun • popular • mostly gay men • dancing/DJ • wheelchair access

The Other Door 10437 Burbank Blvd (2 blocks E of Cahuenga), North Hollywood 818/508-7008 • 3pm-1:30am, from 1pm Fri-Sun • popular • mostly women • neighborhood bar • dancing/DJ • karaoke • live shows • wheelchair access

Oxwood Inn 13713 Oxnard (at Woodman), Van Nuys 818/997-9666 (PAY PHONE) • 3pm-2am, from 2pm Sat, from 1pm Sun, from 5pm Mon-Tue • mostly women • neighborhood bar • dancing/DJ • karaoke • patio • one of the oldest lesbian bars in US • women-owned

Silver Rail 11518 Burbank Blvd (btwn Colfax & Lankershim) 818/980-8310 • 4pm-2am, from noon wknds • lesbians/ gay men • neighborhood bar

NIGHTCLUBS

C Frenz 7026 Reseda Blvd (at Sherman Way), Reseda 818/996-2976 • 3pm-2am, till 3am Sat • popular • lesbians/ gay men • neighborhood bar • dancing/DJ • multiracial • strippers • karaoke • patio • wheelchair access • gay-owned

CAFES

Aroma 4360 Tujunga Ave, Studio City 818/508-0677 • 6am-11pm, from 7am Sun • coffeehouse w/ small bookstore

RESTAURANTS

Du-Par's 12036 Ventura Blvd (at Laurel Canyon), Studio City 818/766-4437 • 24hrs • plush diner schmoozing • also 75 W Thousand Oaks Blvd, Thousand Oaks

Gourmet 88 230 N San Fernando Blvd, Burbank **818/848-8688** • 11:30am-10pm, till 11pm Fri-Sat • Mandarin

GYMS & HEALTH CLUBS

Gold's Gym 6233 N Laurel Canyon Blvd (at Oxnard), North Hollywood **818/506-4600**

EROTICA

Romantix Adult Superstore 21625 Sherman Wy (at Nelson), Canoga Park **818/992-9801**

Manhattan Beach

see also LA—West LA & Santa Monica

ACCOMMODATIONS

Sea View Inn at the Beach 3400 Highland Ave **310/545-1504** • gay-friendly • ocean views • pool • courtyard • nonsmoking • WiFi

RESTAURANTS

The Local Yolk 3414 Highland Ave (at Rosecranz) **310/546-4407** • 6:30am-2pm • WiFi • wheelchair access

Marin County

includes Corte Madera, Mill Valley, San Anselmo, San Rafael, Sausalito, Tiburon

INFO LINES & SERVICES

AA Gay/ Lesbian **415/499-0400** • check website (www.aasf.org) for meeting times

Spectrum LGBT Center of the North Bay 30 N San Pedro Rd # 160, San Rafael **415/472-1945** • drop-in hours: 11am-5pm Mon-Fri • wheelchair access

ACCOMMODATIONS

Acqua Hotel 555 Redwood Hwy, Mill Valley **415/380-0400, 888/662-9555** • gay-friendly • nonsmoking • pets/ kids ok • WiFi • wheelchair access

Casa Madrona Hotel & Spa 801 Bridgeway, Sausalito **415/332-0502, 800/288-0502** • overlooks SF skyline

Larkspur Hotel 160 Shoreline Hwy, Mill Valley **415/332-5700, 866/823-4669** • gay-friendly • pool • nonsmoking • $219

The Lodge at Tiburon 1651 Tiburon Blvd, Tiburon **415/435-3133, 866/823-4669** • gay-friendly • pool • nonsmoking • kids/ pets ok • WiFi • also restaurant & bar

Waters Edge Hotel 25 Main St, Tiburon **415/789-5999, 877/789-5999** • gay/ straight • boutique hotel • kids ok • nonsmoking • WiFi • wheelchair access

RESTAURANTS

Guaymas 5 Main St (at ferry dock), Tiburon **415/435-6300** • gourmet Mexican • great views of the Bay

BOOKSTORES

Book Passage 51 Tamal Vista Blvd, Corte Madera **415/927-0960, 800/999-7909** • 9am-9pm • beloved independent which draws the biggest names to read • also cafe • WiFi

The Depot Bookshop & Cafe 87 Throckmorton, Mill Valley **415/383-2665** • 7am-7pm • independent • also cafe w/ patio

RETAIL SHOPS

Cowgirl Creamery 80 4th St (at Tomales Bay Foods), Pt Reyes Station **415/663-9335** • 10am-6pm Wed-Sun • handmade cheeses • picnic lunches to go • women-owned

Mendocino

see also Fort Bragg

ACCOMMODATIONS

Agate Cove Inn 11201 N Lansing St **707/937-0551, 800/527-3111** • gay-friendly • full brkfst • fireplaces • nonsmoking

The Alegria Quartet & Oceanfront Inn Cottages 44781 Main St **707/937-5150, 800/780-7905** • gay-friendly • located in the village • ocean views • nonsmoking • WiFi • kids ok

Blair House & Cottage 45110 Little Lake St (at Ford St) **707/937-1800, 800/699-9296** • gay-friendly • in former "home" of Jessica Fletcher of Murder, She Wrote • nonsmoking

Brewery Gulch Inn 9401 N Hwy 1 **707/937-4752, 800/578-4454** • gay/ straight • oceanview B&B made of eco-salvaged redwood • full brkfst • jacuzzi • teens welcome • nonsmoking • WiFi • $210-465

Dennen's Victorian Farmhouse 7001 N Hwy 1 (at Hwy 128) **707/937-0697, 800/264-4723** • gay-friendly • nonsmoking • full brkfst • WiFi $135-265

Glendeven Inn 8205 N Hwy 1 (1.7 miles S of Mendocino), Little River **707/937-0083, 800/822-4536** • gay-friendly • charming farmhouse on the coast • full brkfst • nonsmoking

Hill House Inn 10701 Palette Dr **707/937-0554, 800/422-0554** • gay/ straight • New England—style inn • also restaurant

The Inn at Schoolhouse Creek 7051 N Hwy 1, Little River 707/937–5525, 800/731–5525 • gay/ straight • B&B w/ cottages & suites • full brkfst • hot tub • fireplaces • nonsmoking • WiFi • wheelchair access

John Dougherty House 571 Ukiah St (at Kasten St) 707/937–5266, 800/486–2104 • gay-friendly • jacuzzi • gay-owned • $130-275

Little River Inn Resort & Spa 7901 N Hwy 1, Little River 707/937–5942, 888/466–5683 • gay-friendly • resort • ocean views, restaurant & bar • nonsmoking • WiFi • $130-365

MacCallum House Inn 45020 Albion St (at Lansing) 707/937–0289, 800/609–0492 • gay/ straight • nonsmoking • WiFi • wheelchair access • kids ok • also popular restaurant & full bar w/ cafe

Orr Hot Springs 13201 Orr Springs Rd, Ukiah 707/462–6277 • gay-friendly • hostel-style cabins, private cottages & campsites • clothing-optional • kids ok • mineral hot springs • pool • no food provided • reservations required

Packard House 45170 Little Lake St (at Kasten St) 707/937–2677, 888/453–2677 • gay-friendly • full brkfst • jacuzzi • nonsmoking • WiFi • gay-owned • $190-275

Sallie & Eileen's Place 707/937–2028, 888/757–5223 • women only • cabin • hot tub • kitchens • fireplaces • kids/ pets ok • nonsmoking • lesbian-owned

Sea Gull Inn 44960 Albion St 707/937–5204, 888/937–5204 • gay-friendly • in the heart of historic Mendocino • nonsmoking • kids ok • WiFi • wheelchair access

Stanford Inn by the Sea Coast Hwy 1 & Comptche-Ukiah Rd 707/937–5615, 800/331–8884 • gay-friendly • full brkfst • hot tub • pool • organic vegetarian restaurant • nonsmoking • WiFi • kids/ pets ok • wheelchair access

Stevenswood Resort & Spa 8211 N Hwy 1 707/937–2810, 800/421–2810 • gay/ straight • resort w/ forest spas & hot tubs • WiFi • wheelchair access • gay-owned • $225-895

RESTAURANTS

Cafe Beaujolais 961 Ukiah St 707/937–5614 • lunch& dinner • reservations recommended • some veggie • wheelchair access

BOOKSTORES

Gallery Bookshop Main & Kasten St S 707/937–2665 • 9:30am-6pm, till 9pm Fri-Sat • independent • also children's bookstore

Menlo Park

see Palo Alto

Mill Valley

see Marin County

Modesto

see also Stockton

ACCOMMODATIONS

Rodeway Inn 936 McHenry Ave (at Roseburg Ave) 209/523–7701 • gay-friendly • pool • WiFi

BARS

Brave Bull 701 S 9th St 209/529–6712 • 7pm-2am, clsd Mon • lesbians/ gay men • dancing/DJ • Latino/a (Latin Night Th w/ drag show & strippers) • drag shows Sun • karaoke Wed

Tiki Lounge 932 McHenry Ave (at Roseburg Ave) 209/577–9969 • 5:30pm-2am • lesbians/ gay men • neighborhood bar • multiracial • transgender-friendly • karaoke

CAFES

Deva Cafe 1202 J St 209/572–3382 • 7am-3pm, 8am-noon Sun • live music • patio • wheelchair access

Queen Bean 1126 14th St 209/521–8000 • 7am-8pm, till 11pm wknds

RESTAURANTS

Minnie's Restaurant 107 McHenry Ave 209/524–4621 • lunch Tue-Fri, dinner Tue-Sun, clsd Mon • full bar

RETAIL SHOPS

Mystical Body 121 McHenry Ave 209/527–1163 • noon-8pm, clsd Sun-Mon • body piercing

EROTICA

Suzie's Adult Superstores 115 McHenry Ave (at Needham) 209/529–5546 • 8am-midnight

Monterey

ACCOMMODATIONS

Asilomar Conference Grounds 800 Asilomar Blvd, Pacific Grove 831/372–8016, 888/635–5310 • gay-friendly • Arts & Crafts–style buildings designed by Julia Morgan • pool • WiFi • $109+

Gosby House Inn 643 Lighthouse Ave (at 18th), Pacific Grove **831/375-1287, 800/527-8828** • gay-friendly • B&B • full brkfst • some shared baths • nonsmoking • kids ok • wheelchair access

Monterey Fireside Lodge 1131 10th St **831/373-4172, 800/722-2624** • very gay-friendly • hot tub • fireplaces • nonsmoking rooms available • kids ok • WiFi

The Monterey Hotel 406 Alvarado St **831/375-3184, 800/966-6490** • gay-friendly • turn-of-the-century boutique hotel • WiFi • $89-259

NIGHTCLUBS

Franco's Club 10639 Merritt St, Castroville **831/633-2090** • 10pm-2am Sat only • lesbians/gay men • dancing/DJ • Latino/a

RESTAURANTS

Old Fisherman's Grotto 39 Fisherman's Wharf #1 **831/375-4604** • 11am-10pm

Tarpy's Roadhouse 2999 Monterey Salinas Hwy (at Canyon Dr) **831/647-1444** • lunch & dinner, Sun brunch • patios & gardens • full bar

ENTERTAINMENT & RECREATION

Ag Venture Tours PO Box 2634, 93942 **831/761-8463** • customized wine-tasting, agriculture & sight-seeing tours of Monterey Bay area

Monterey Bay Aquarium 886 Cannery Row **831/648-4800** • come for the otters, stay for the day

Morro Bay

see San Luis Obispo

Napa Valley

ACCOMMODATIONS

Beazley House B&B Inn 1910 First St, Napa **707/257-1649, 800/559-1649** • gay-friendly • historic inn • full brkfst • nonsmoking • very pet-friendly • WiFi • wheelchair access

Brannan Cottage Inn 109 Wapoo Ave, Calistoga **707/942-4200** • gay-friendly • B&B in Victorian cottage • full brkfst • 1 block from downtown • nonsmoking • WiFi • $155-280

The Chablis Inn 3360 Solano Ave (Redwood Rd at Hwy 29), Napa **707/257-1944, 800/443-3490** • gay-friendly • motel • pool • hot tub • kids/pets ok • nonsmoking • wheelchair access • $125-265

The Chanric Inn 1805 Foothill Blvd, Calistoga **707/942-4535, 877/281-3671** • gay/straight • pool & spa • nonsmoking • WiFi • gay-owned • $209-329

Chateau de Vie 3250 Hwy 128, Calistoga **707/942-6446, 877/558-2513** • gay/straight • chateau w/ gardens • full brkfst • pool • pets ok • WiFi • gay-owned

Garnett Creek Inn 1139 Lincoln Ave, Calistoga **707/942-9797** • gay-friendly • on historic main street • nonsmoking • wheelchair access • $175-270

The Ink House B&B 1575 St Helena Hwy S, St Helena **707/963-3890** • gay-friendly • full brkfst • nonsmoking • WiFi

The Inn on First 1938 1st St, Napa **707/253-1331, 866/253-1331** • gay/straight • WiFi • pets ok • gay-owned • $205-385

Meadowlark Country House 601 Petrified Forest Rd, Calistoga **707/942-5651, 800/942-5651** • gay-friendly • full brkfst • clothing-optional mineral pool, sauna & hot tub • nonsmoking • WiFi • gay-owned

Napa River Inn 500 Main St (at 5th), Napa **707/251-8500, 877/251-8500** • gay-friendly • luxury boutique hotel w/ spa • located in historic Napa Mill • WiFi • $169-499

Yountville Inn 6462 Washington St, Yountville **707/944-5600, 888/366-8166** • gay-friendly • alongside Hopper Creek • spa • nonsmoking • $175-375

RESTAURANTS

Brannan's 1374 Lincoln Ave (at Washington), Calistoga **707/942-2233** • lunch & dinner, brunch wknds • full bar • live jazz wknds • gay-owned

Cindy's Backstreet Kitchen 1327 Railroad Ave, St Helena **707/963-1200** • 11:30am-9:30pm

Flat Iron Grill 1440 Lincoln Ave (at Washington), Calistoga **707/942-1220** • dinner & seasonal wknd lunches • traditional American classics • gay-owned

Redd 6480 Washington St, Yountville **707/944-2222** • lunch Mon-Sat, dinner nightly, Sun brunch • American • reservations required

SolBar 755 Silverado Trail (at the Solage Hotel), Calistoga **707/226-0850** • soul-food

Tra Vigne 1050 Charter Oak Ave (Hwy 29), St Helena **707/963-4444** • 11:30am-10pm • Northern Italian • also wine bar • reservations recommended

Entertainment & Recreation

Harbin Hot Springs 18424 Harbin Springs Rd, Middletown **707/987-2477, 800/622-2477 (CA ONLY)** • gay-friendly • nonprofit retreat & workshop center • massage • some sundecks clothing-optional

Lavender Hill Spa 1015 Foothill Blvd (at Lincoln Ave), Calistoga **707/942-4495, 800/528-4772** • 9am-9pm

Bookstores

Copperfield's Books 1330 Lincoln Ave, Calistoga **707/942-1616** • 9am-7pm, till 9pm Fri-Sat, 10am- 6pm Sun

Nevada City

Accommodations

The Flume's End B&B 317 S Pine St **530/265-9665** • gay/ straight • creekside Victorian • full brkfst • women-owned • $149-189

Cafes

Java John's 306 Broad St **530/265-3653** • 6:30am-5pm

Restaurants

Friar Tuck's 111 N Pine St (at Commercial) **530/265-9093** • dinner from 5pm • American/ fondue • live shows • full bar • wheelchair access

Newport Beach

see Orange County

Oakland

see East Bay

Orange County

includes Anaheim, Costa Mesa, Garden Grove, Huntington Beach, Irvine, Laguna Beach, Newport Beach, Santa Ana

Info Lines & Services

AA Gay/ Lesbian Laguna Beach **714/556-4555 (AA#)** • call or visit www.oc-aa.org for meeting times

The Center Orange County 1605 N Spurgeon St, Santa Ana **714/953-5428** • 9am-5pm Mon-Fri or by appt or event

Accommodations

Best Western Laguna Brisas Spa Hotel 1600 S Coast Hwy (at Bluebird), Laguna Beach **949/497-7272, 888/296-6834** • gay/ straight • resort hotel • free brkfst • pool • in-room whirlpool spas • nonsmoking • WiFi • wheelchair access

Best Western Raffles Inn & Suites 2040 S Harbor Blvd, Anaheim **714/750-6100, 800/308-5278** • gay-friendly • pool • WiFi • walk to Disneyland

Casa Laguna Inn & Spa 2510 S Coast Hwy, Laguna Beach **949/494-2996, 800/233-0449** • gay-friendly • inn & cottages overlooking the Pacific • pool • kids/ pets ok • nonsmoking • WiFi • gay-owned

Fairfield Inn Placentia 710 W Kimberly Ave, Placentia **714/996-4410, 800/308-5286** • gay-friendly • pool • WiFi • wheelchair access

Holiday Inn & Suites Anaheim 1240 S Walnut, Anaheim **714/535-0300, 800/308-5312** • gay-friendly • walk to Disneyland • pool • restaurant • WiFi • wheelchair access

The Hotel Hanford 3131 S Bristol St (at Baker St), Costa Mesa **714/913-9055, 800/362-1655** • gay-friendly • pool • WiFi • wheelchair access • $129+

Laguna Cliffs Inn 475 N Coast Hwy, Laguna Beach **949/497-6645, 800/297-0007** • gay-friendly • hot tub • pool • kids ok • easy beach access • WiFi • wheelchair access

Laguna Cliffs Marriott Resort & Spa 25135 Park Lantern, Dana Point **949/661-5000, 800/533-9748** • gay-friendly • pool • restaurant • WiFi • wheelchair access • $129-438

The St Regis Monarch Beach One Monarch Beach Resort, Dana Point **949/234-3200** • gay-friendly • restaurant • pool • nonsmoking • wheelchair access • $345-675

Surf & Sand Resort **949/497-4477, 888/869-7569** • gay-friendly • restaurant & spa • WiFi • wheelchair access

Bars

Club Bounce 1460 S Coast Hwy, Laguna Beach **949/494-0056** • 2pm-2am • lesbians/ gay men • dancing/DJ Fri-Sat • karaoke

Frat House 8112 Garden Grove Blvd (at Beach Blvd), Garden Grove **714/373-3728** • 3pm-2am • lesbians/ gay men • dancing/DJ • multiracial • drag shows & strippers • young crowd • wheelchair access

Ibiza Bar & Nightclub 18528 Beach Blvd **714/963-7744** • noon-2am, from 4pm Mon, from 2pm Sun • gay-friendly • neighborhood bar • dancing/DJ • wheelchair access • gay-owned

Metro Q Bar & Grill 19092 Beach Blvd (at Garfield Ave), Huntington Beach **714/968-6677** • 3:30pm-close, from 11:30am wknds, clsd Mon • lesbians/ gay men • food served • WiFi

Tin Lizzie Saloon 752 St Clair (at Bristol), Costa Mesa **714/966-2029** • 11:30am-2am • mostly gay men • neighborhood bar • wheelchair access

NIGHTCLUBS

Bravo 1490 S Anaheim Blvd, Anaheim **714/533-2291** • more gay Th & Sat • gay/ straight • dancing/DJ • goth & electronica Sun • Latin music Wed & Fri-Sat

Club Lucky Presents 949/551-2998 • check www. clubluckypresents.com for weekly parties in OC

El Calor 2916 W Lincoln Ave (at E Beach Blvd), Anaheim **714/527-8873** • 8pm-2am • gay-friendly • dancing/DJ • mostly Latino/a • drag shows

Lions Den 719 W 19th St (at Pomona Ave), Costa Mesa **949/645-3830** • 9pm-2am, clsd Mon • gay/ straight • only lesbian/ gay Fri for Fiesta Latino (Latino/a • drag shows) • dancing/DJ • karaoke Wed • size-acceptance club Sat (www.butterflylounge.com)

CAFES

Avanti Cafe 259 E 17th St (at Westminster), Costa Mesa **949/548-2224** • 11am-10pm, till 8pm Sun • brkfst, lunch & dinner • "hella fierce rockin' world food" • veggie & vegan • beer/ wine

The Koffee Klatch 1440 S Coast Hwy (btwn Mountain & Pacific Coast Hwy), Laguna Beach **949/376-6867** • 7am-11pm, till midnight Fri-Sat • brkfst & lunch • desserts • WiFi

Zinc Cafe 350 Ocean Ave (at Broadway), Laguna Beach **949/494-6302** • 7am-4pm, also market till 6pm • vegetarian • beer/ wine • patio • wheelchair access

RESTAURANTS

Cafe Zoolu 860 Glenneyre St, Laguna Beach **949/494-6825** • 5pm-10pm, clsd Mon • beer/ wine • wheelchair access

The Cottage 308 N Coast Hwy (at Aster), Laguna Beach **949/494-3023** • brkfst, lunch & dinner • homestyle cooking • some veggie

Dizz's As Is 2794 S Coast Hwy (at Nyes Pl), Laguna Beach **949/494-5250** • open 5:30pm, clsd Mon • full bar • patio

Madison Square & Garden Cafe 320 N Coast Hwy, Laguna Beach **949/494-0137** • 8am-3pm, clsd Tue • dog-friendly

Nirvana Grille 303 Broadway St, Laguna Beach **949/497-0027** • dinner nightly • seasonal rooftop deck

Sorrento Grille 370 Glenneyre St, Laguna Beach **949/494-8686** • dinner only • upscale American bistro & martini bar

Sundried Tomato Cafe 361 Forest Ave #103, Laguna Beach **949/494-3312** • lunch & dinner • also full bar • gay-owned

ENTERTAINMENT & RECREATION

San Onofre State Beach on I-5, S of San Clemente (exit at Basilone Rd), Laguna Beach

West St Beach Laguna Beach

PUBLICATIONS

Orange County/ Long Beach Blade 562/314-7674

EROTICA

Pink Kitty 17955 Sky Park Cir, Ste A, Irvine **949/660-4990** • 10am-6pm • gay-owned

Oroville

CAFES

Mug Shots 2040 Montgomery St **530/538-8342** • 6am-6pm, 8am-3pm Sun • WiFi • gay-owned

Palm Springs

INFO LINES & SERVICES

AA Gay/ Lesbian 760/324-4880 (AA#) • call for meeting schedule

ACCOMMODATIONS

Ace Hotel Palm Springs 701 E. Palm Canyon Dr 760/325-9900 • gay/straight • pool • restaurant • WiFi

Caliente Tropics Resort 411 E Palm Canyon Dr 760/327-1391, 888/277-0099 • gay/ straight • hot tub • pool • nonsmoking resort • kids ok • very pet-friendly • wheelchair access • gay-owned

Calla Lily Inn 350 S Belardo Rd (at Baristo) **760/323-3654, 888/888-5787** • gay-friendly • pool • "a tranquil oasis" • nonsmoking • WiFi • $129-398

Casitas Laquita 450 E Palm Canyon Dr (near Camino Real) 760/416-9999, 877/203-3410 • lesbian resort • pool • nonsmoking • small pets ok • WiFi • wheelchair access • lesbian-owned

Desert Hearts Inn Avenida Olancha (across from Queen of Hearts) **760/322-5793, 888/275-9903** • women • pool • hot tub • full kitchens • small pets ok • lesbian-owned • $105-160

Desert Star Hotel 1611 S Calle Palo Fierro **760/778-1047, 800/399-1006** • gay-friendly • boutique hotel of bungalows w/ full kitchens • pool • WiFi • $140-200

The Horizon Hotel 1050 E Palm Canyon Dr **760/323-1858, 800/377-7855** • gay-friendly • pool • jacuzzi • WiFi

Hotel Zoso 150 S Indian Canyon Dr **760/325-9676** • gay-friendly • 4-acre resort • pool • WiFi • also bar & Nick & Stef's restaurant • also spa

Hyatt Regency Suites Palm Springs 285 N Palm Canyon Dr **760/322-9000, 800/554-9288** • gay-friendly • pool • WiFi • also restaurant & bar

Mojave 73721 Shadow Mountain Dr, Palm Desert **800/391-1104** • gay-friendly • boutique hotel • pool • hot tub • spa services • kids ok • nonsmoking • wheelchair access

Queen of Hearts Resort 435 E Avenida Olancha **760/322-5793, 888/275-9903** • women • pool • full kitchens • WiFi • lesbian-owned

Rendezvous 1420 N Indian Canyon Dr **760/320-1178, 800/485-2808** • gay-friendly • '50s chic • pool • WiFi

Ruby Montana's Coral Sands Inn 210 W Stevens Rd (at N Palm Canyon) **760/325-4900, 866/820-8302** • gay/ straight • resort • pool • kitschy 1950s chic • kids/ pets ok • WiFi • wheelchair access • lesbian-owned • $139-189

Villa Mykonos 67-590 Jones Rd (at Cree), Cathedral City **800/471-4753** • lesbians/ gay men • timeshare condos & rental units • pool • WiFi

Villa Royale 1620 Indian Trail **760/327-2314, 800/245-2314** • gay-friendly • pool • jacuzzi • also Europa restaurant • $139-279

BARS

Azul 369 N Palm Canyon Dr **760/325-5533** • 11am-close, from 10am Sun • lesbians/ gay men • neighborhood bar • videos • also restaurant

Digs 36-737 Cathedral Canyon Dr (at Commercial), Cathedral City **760/321-0031** • 10am-2am • lesbians/ gay men • neighborhood bar • karaoke • drag shows & cabaret wknds • country/ western • patio

Georgie's Alibi 369 N Palm Canyon Dr **760/325-5533** • 11am-close, from 10am Sun • mostly gay men • neighborhood bar • food served • patio

Hunter's Video Bar 302 E Arenas Rd (at Calle Encilia) **760/323-0700** • 10am-2am • popular • mostly gay men • dancing/DJ • video bar • go-go boys Fri • theme nights

Pink 302 E Arenas Rd (at Calle Encilia, at Hunter's) **760/323-0700** • 7pm last Sat only • mostly women • dancing/DJ

Toucan's Tiki Lounge 2100 N Palm Canyon Dr (at Via Escuela) **760/416-7584** • noon-2am • lesbians/ gay men • dancing/DJ • live show Mon • drag shows Wed & Sun • male & female go-go dancers wknds

CAFES

Palm Springs Koffi 515 N Palm Canyon Dr (at Alejo) **760/416-2244** • 5:30am-8pm • WiFi

RESTAURANTS

Amici 71380 Hwy 111, Rancho Mirage **760/341-0738** • lunch & dinner, Sun brunch • Italian patio • full bar

Bangkok Five 70-026 Hwy 111, Rancho Mirage **760/770-9508** • dinner nightly • Thai

Billy Reed's 1800 N Palm Canyon Dr (at Vista Chino) **760/325-1946** • 7am-9pm, till 10pm Fri-Sat • some veggie • full bar • also bakery • wheelchair access

Blame It on Midnight 777 E Tahquitz Canyon Wy, Stes 101-109 (at the Courtyard) **760/323-1200** • 5pm-10pm, till 11pm Fri-Sat • mostly gay men • live music Th-Sun • also full bar • patio • gay-owned

Blue Coyote Grill 445 N Palm Canyon Dr **760/327-1196** • 11am-10pm, till 11pm Fri-Sat • Southwestern

Blue Pear Texx Mexx 2249 N Palm Canyon Dr **760/778-5500** • lunch & dinner, Sun brunch from 10am • wheelchair access • gay-owned

Bongo Johnny's 214 E Arenas Rd **760/866-1905** • 8am-10pm, till 11pm Fri-Sat • burgers & sandwiches

Cafe Palette 315 E Arenas **760/322-9264** • 11am-10pm • live shows • also delivers

The Chop House 262 S Palm Canyon Dr **760/320-4500** • from 5pm • steak • reservations recommended

Copley's 621 N Palm Canyon Dr (btwn E Tamarisk Rd & E Granvia Valmonte) **760/327-9555** • 6pm-10pm • contemporary American • full bar

Davey's Hideaway 292 E Palm Canyon Dr 760/320–4480 • from 5pm • steak, seafood & pasta • piano • patio • full bar

Dink's Restaurant & Ultra Lounge 2080 Palm Canyon Dr 760/327–7676 • lunch & dinner • swank lounge

El Gallito 68820 Grove St (at Palm Canyon), Cathedral City 760/328–7794 • 10am-9pm • homemade Mexican • beer/ wine

Grill-A-Burger 166 N Palm Canyon Dr 760/327–8175 • 11am-9pm, till 4pm Tue-Wed & Sun, clsd Mon

Hamburger Mary's 415 N Palm Canyon Dr 760/778–6279 • 11am-close • full bar

Jake's 664 N Palm Canyon Dr 760/327–4400 • lunch & dinner, wknd brunch, clsd Sun night & Mon • American bistro

Las Casuelas 368 N Palm Canyon Dr (btwn Amado & Alejo) 760/325–3213 • 11am-10pm • Mexican

Look 139 E Andreas Rd 760/778–3520 • 11am-10pm • patio bar till 2am

Matchbox 155 S Palm Canyon Dr (in Mercado Plaza, 2nd level) 760/778–6000 • 4pm-11pm, till 1am Fri-Sat • pizza

Ming's Chinese Cuisine 35300 Date Palm Dr, Cathedral City 760/770–3663 • 11:30am-9pm, clsd Sun

Nature's Health Food & Cafe 555 S Sunrise Way #301 760/323–9487 • 8am-7pm, 9am-5pm wknds • vegan/ vegetarian

Pomme Frite 256 S Palm Canyon Dr 760/778–3727 • dinner nightly, lunch wknds, clsd Tue • Belgian beer & French food

Palm Springs

WHERE THE GIRLS ARE:
Vacationers will be staying on East Palm Canyon near Sunrise Way. Women do hang out at the boys' bars too. Try the bar at The Desert Palms Inn, or just about anywhere on Perez Rd.

LGBT PRIDE:
November, web: www.pspride.org.

ANNUAL EVENTS:
Spring - Kraft Nabisco Golf Tournament (aka "Dinah Shore"), web: www.kncgolf.com. One of the biggest gatherings of lesbians on the continent. If you're more interested in the party than the golf, get the info at www.dinahshoreweekend.com.

Spring - White Party, web: www.jeffreysanker.com. Popular circuit party/fundraiser.

CITY INFO:
Palm Springs Visitors Bureau 760/778-8418 or 800/347-7746, web: www.palm-springs.org.

ATTRACTIONS:
Joshua Tree National Park, web: www.nps.gov/jotr.

Palm Springs Aerial Tramway to the top of Mt San Jacinto, on Tramway Rd, web: www.pstramway.com.

Palm Springs Art Museum 760/322-4800, web: www.psmuseum.org.

BEST VIEW:
Top of Mt San Jacinto. Driving through the surrounding desert, you can see great views of the mountains. Be careful in the summer—always carry water in your vehicle, and be sure to check all fluids in your car before you leave and frequently during your trip.

WEATHER:
Palm Springs is sunny and warm in the winter, with temperatures in the 70°s. Summers are scorching (100°+).

TRANSIT:
American Cab 760/416-2594.
Desert Valley Shuttle 800/413-3999.
Sun Line Transit Agency 760/343-3451 or 800/347-8628, web: www.sunline.org.

Red Tomato & House of Lamb 68–784 E Palm Canyon (btwn Date Palm & Cathedral Canyon), Cathedral City **760/328–7518** • 4pm-10pm, clsd Mon • Italian • beer/ wine • wheelchair access

Rick's Restaurant 1973 N Palm Canyon Dr **760/416–0090** • 6am-3pm • Cuban/ American

Rock Garden Cafe 777 S Palm Canyon Dr **760/327–8840** • 7am-9pm • Greek • patio

Shame on the Moon 69–950 Frank Sinatra Dr (at Hwy 111), Rancho Mirage **760/324–5515** • 5pm-9:30pm • cont'l • plenty veggie • full bar • patio • reservations recommended • wheelchair access

Sherman's Deli & Bakery 401 E Tahquitz Canyon Wy **760/325–1199** • 7am-9pm • kosher-style deli

Spencer's Restaurant 701 W Baristo Rd **760/327–3446** • 9am-2:30pm & 5pm-10pm • Sun brunch • upscale contemporary • reservations recommended

Tootie's Texas Barbeque 68-703 Perez Rd, Cathedral City **760/202–6963** • 11am-8pm, clsd Sun • the name says it all

Towne Center Cafe 44491 Town Center Wy, Palm Desert **760/346–2120** • 6am-8pm • Greek diner

Trio 707 N Palm Canyon Dr **760/864–8746** • dinner nightly • also lounge

Wang's in the Desert 424 S Indian Canyon Dr (at E Saturnino Rd) **760/325–9264** • from 5:30pm • Chinese • full bar

Zin American Bistro 198 S Palm Canyon (at Arenas) **760/322–6300** • lunch & dinner

ENTERTAINMENT & RECREATION

Desert Dyners PO Box 5072, 92263-5072 **760/202–6645** • lesbian social club • membership required • hosts mixers, dances, dinners & golf • singles & couples welcome

The Living Desert Zoo & Gardens 47-900 Portola Ave, Palm Desert **760/346–5694** • 9am-5pm (8am-1pm June-Aug) • zoo & endangered species conservation center

Ruddy's 1930s General Store Museum 221 S Palm Canyon Dr **760/327–2156** • 10am-4pm Th-Sun, clsd summers • "the most you can spend is 95¢"

BOOKSTORES

Q Trading Company 606 E Sunny Dunes Rd (at Indian Canyon) **760/416–7150, 800/756–2290** • 10am-6pm • LGBT • also cards, gifts, videos, etc

RETAIL SHOPS

GayMartUSA 305 E Arenas Rd (at Indian Canyon) **760/416–6436** • 10am-midnight

Mischief 210 E Arenas Rd (at Indian Canyon) **760/322–8555** • 11am-7pm, 10am-11pm Fri-Sat

PUBLICATIONS

The Bottom Line/ Pulp **760/323–0552** • the desert's LGBT bar guide & classifieds

Desert Daily Guide **760/320–3237** • LGBT weekly, travel, activity & lodging info for Palm Springs

Odyssey Magazine **323/874–8788** • dish on L.A. & Palm Springs' club scene

GYMS & HEALTH CLUBS

Gold's Gym 4070 Airport Center Dr (at Ramon) **760/322–4653** • gay-friendly

World Gym Palm Springs 1751 N Sunrise Way (at Vista Chino) **760/327–7100** • 5am-10pm, 6am-8pm wknds • mostly gay men • day passes available • steam & sauna • club-quality sound system • wheelchair access • gay-owned

EROTICA

Gear Leather & Fetish 650 E Sunny Dunes #1 (at S Calle Palo Fierro) **760/322–3363** • noon-7pm, till midnight Fri-Sat • leather, fetish & piercing

Palmdale

see Lancaster

Palo Alto

ACCOMMODATIONS

Creekside Inn 3400 El Camino Real (at Page Mill Rd) **650/493–2411, 800/492–7335** • gay/ straight • pool • kids ok • WiFi • nonsmoking • restaurant & lounge • wheelchair access • $179-259

Hotel Avante 860 E El Camino Real, Mountain View **650/940–1000, 800/538–1600** • gay/ straight • in heart of Silicon Valley • pool • WiFi

RESTAURANTS

Junnoon 150 University Ave **650/329–9644** • lunch Mon-Fri, dinner nightly • Indian • reservations recommended

BOOKSTORES

Books Inc 855 El Camino Real **650/321–0600** • 9am-8pm • LGBT section

Pasadena

BARS

The 35er 626/356-9315 • 3pm-1am, from 12:30pm Fri-Sun • gay/ straight • great neighborhood bar • food served

Boulevard/ Club S Karaoke 3199 E Foothill Blvd (at Sierra Madre Villa) 626/356-9304 • 4pm-2am, from 3pm Fri-Sun • mostly gay men • neighborhood bar • karaoke

RESTAURANTS

Chandra 400 S Arroyo Pkwy 626/577-6599 • 11am-10:30pm • Thai • full bar • wheelchair access

Neomeze 20 E Colorado Blvd 626/793-3010 • 4pm-midnight, till 2am wknds • gastropub

ENTERTAINMENT & RECREATION

The Huntington 1151 Oxford Rd, San Marino 626/405-2100 • art collection • botanical gardens

Paso Robles

ACCOMMODATIONS

Asuncion Ridge Vineyards & Inn 805/461-0675 • gay-friendly • WiFi • gay-owned • $249-349

Hotel Cheval 1021 Pine St 805/226-9995, 866/522-6999 • gay-friendly • WiFi

ENTERTAINMENT & RECREATION

River Oaks Hot Springs Spa 800 Clubhouse Dr 805/238-4600 • 9am-9pm, clsd Mon

Petaluma

RESTAURANTS

Brixx 16 Kentucky St (in Lanmart Bldg) 707/766-8162 • dinner from 5pm • popular • handmade pizzas & paninis • live bands Sat

BOOKSTORES

Copperfield's Books 140 Kentucky St (btwn Western & Washington, downtown) 707/762-0563 • 9am-9pm, 10am-6pm Sun

Placerville

ACCOMMODATIONS

Albert Shafsky House B&B 2942 Coloma St (at Spring St/ Hwy 49) 530/642-2776 • gay-friendly • full brkfst • nonsmoking • WiFi • kids ok • lesbian-owned • $135-185

Rancho Cicada Retreat 10001 Bell Rd, Plymouth 209/245-4841, 877/553-9481 • mostly gay men • secluded riverside retreat in the Sierra foothills w/ 2-person tents & cabin • swimming • nudity • gay-owned

RETAIL SHOPS

Tony Matthews 447 Main St (at Bedford) 530/626-9161

Pleasant Hill

see East Bay

Pomona

BARS

Alibi East 225 S San Antonio Ave (at 2nd) 909/623-9422 • noon-2am, till 3am Fri • mostly gay men • dancing/DJ • food served • karaoke

The Hookup 1047 E 2nd St (at Pico) 909/620-2844 • noon-2am • lesbians/ gay men • neighborhood bar • food served • karaoke • beer bust Sun • wheelchair access • gay-owned

Redding

NIGHTCLUBS

Club 501 1244 California St (at Center & Division, enter rear) 530/243-7869 • 6pm-2am, from noon Sun • lesbians/ gay men • dancing/DJ • young crowd

Redondo Beach

see also Los Angeles—West LA & Santa Monica

ACCOMMODATIONS

Best Western Sunrise Hotel 400 N Harbor Dr 310/376-0746, 800/334-7384 • gay-friendly • pool • hot tub • kids ok • WiFi

Palos Verdes Inn 1700 S Pacific Coast Hwy 310/316-4211, 800/421-9241 • gay-friendly • jacuzzi • pool • food served • kids ok • WiFi • wheelchair access

Riverside

see also San Bernardino

NIGHTCLUBS

El Destino 83085 Indio Blvd, Indio 760/775-0686 • 6pm-2am Wed & Fri-Sat • mostly gay men • ladies night Fri • dancing/DJ • Latino clientele

Menagerie 3581 University Ave (at Orange) 951/788-8000 • 4pm-2am • lesbians/gay men • dancing/DJ • karaoke • drag shows Th • wheelchair access

VIP Nightclub & Restaurant 3673 Merrill Ave (at Magnolia) 951/784-2370 • 5pm-2am • lesbians/gay men • dancing/DJ • karaoke • drag shows • food served • 18+

Russian River

includes Cazadero, Forestville, Guerneville & Monte Rio

Info Lines & Services

AA Meetings in Sonoma County 707/544-1300 (AA#), 800/224-1300 • call for meeting times

Russian River Chamber of Commerce & Visitors Center 16209 First St (on the plaza), Guerneville 707/869-9000 • 10am-5pm, till 4pm Sun

Sonoma County Tourism Bureau 800/576-6662

Accommodations

Applewood Inn 13555 Hwy 116 (at Mays Canyon), Guerneville 707/869-9093, 800/555-8509 • gay-friendly • full brkfst • pool • nonsmoking • WiFi • wheelchair access • also restaurant • gay-owned

boon hotel & spa 14711 Armstrong Woods Rd, Guerneville 707/869-2721 • gay/straight • resort w/ full-service spa • kids/pets ok • pool • nonsmoking • jacuzzi • WiFi • gay-owned • $150-325

Fern Grove Cottages 16650 River Rd, Guerneville 888/243-2674 • gay-friendly • pool • kids/pets ok • nonsmoking • WiFi

Guerneville Lodge 15905 River Rd (at Hwy 116), Guerneville 707/869-0102 • gay/straight • WiFi • nonsmoking • gay-owned

Highland Dell Resort 21050 River Blvd (at Bohemian Hwy), Monte Rio 707/865-2300 • gay-friendly • WiFi • full bar & restaurant

Highlands Resort 14000 Woodland Dr, Guerneville 707/869-0333 • lesbians/gay men • country retreat on 4 wooded acres • hot tub • swimming • clothing-optional pool

Inn at Occidental 3657 Church St, Occidental 707/874-1047, 800/522-6324 • gay-friendly • full brkfst • wheelchair access • $199-379

Rio Villa Beach Resort 20292 Hwy 116 (at Bohemian Hwy), Monte Rio 707/865-1143, 877/746-8455 • gay-friendly • kids ok • nonsmoking • WiFi • gay-owned

Village Inn & Restaurant 20822 River Blvd, Monte Rio 707/865-2304, 800/303-2303 • gay/straight • historic inn • nonsmoking • also restaurant & full bar • WiFi • wheelchair access • gay-owned

West Sonoma Inn & Spa 14100 Brookside Ln (at Main St), Guerneville 707/869-2470, 800/551-1881 • gay/straight • 6-acre resort a short walk from Johnson's Beach • pool • spa • some jacuzzis • nonsmoking • WiFi • wheelchair access • $99-299

Westside Lodge Westside Rd (at River Rd), Forestville 707/869-9030, 800/997-3312 • gay/straight • 1936 cabin-style home • sleeps 8 • nonsmoking • WiFi • lesbian-owned • $295-394

The Woods Resort 16484 4th St (at Mill St), Guerneville 707/869-0600, 877/887-9218 • mostly gay men • swimming • WiFi • wheelchair access • gay-owned

Bars

Mc T's Bullpen 16246 1st St (at Church), Guerneville 707/869-3377 • 10am-2am • gay/straight • karaoke • bands • patio • WiFi • wheelchair access

Rainbow Cattle Co 16220 Main St (at Armstrong Woods Rd), Guerneville 707/869-0206 • 6am-2am • gay/straight • neighborhood bar • DJ Bruce Sat

Cafes

Coffee Bazaar 14045 Armstrong Woods Rd (at River Rd), Guerneville 707/869-9706 • 6am-8pm • cafe • soups • salads • sandwiches • WiFi

Coffee Catz 6761 Sebastopol Ave (at Hwy 116), Sebastopol 707/829-6600 • 7am-6pm, till 8pm Th, till 10pm Wed & Fri-Sat • live shows • WiFi • wheelchair access

Roasters Espresso Bar 6656 Front St (Hwy 116), Forestville 707/887-1632 • 6am-6pm, from 7am Sat-Sun • WiFi

Restaurants

Aioli 6536 Front St, Forestville 707/887-2476 • 8am-5pm, from 10am Sat, clsd Sun-Mon • gourmet deli • beer/wine • outdoor seating

boon eat + drink 16248 Main St (at Hwy 116), Guerneville 707/869-0780 • lunch & dinner, clsd Tue-Wed • American

Cape Fear Cafe 25191 Main St, Duncans Mills 707/865-9246 • 9am-2:30pm & 5pm-9pm (clsd Wed & Th off season)

Chef Patrick 16236 Main St (at Hwy 116), Guerneville 707/869-9161 • dinner, clsd Tue-Wed

Farmhouse Inn Restaurant 7871 River Rd, Forestville **707/887–3300, 800/464–6642** • dinner, clsd Tue-Wed

Garden Grill 17132 Hwy 116, Guerneville **707/869–3922** • 8am-8pm, clsd Tue-Wed • great burgers & sandwiches • some veggie • patio

Main Street Station 16280 Main St (at Church St), Guerneville **707/869–0501** • 11am-7pm • Italian restaurant & pizzeria • cabaret dinner shows nightly

Mom's Apple Pie 4550 Gravenstein Hwy N, Sebastopol **707/823–8330** • 10am-6pm • pie worth stopping for on your way to & from Russian River!

River Inn Grill 16141 Main St, Guerneville **707/869–0481** • 8am-2pm • local favorite • wheelchair access

Tahoe Chinese Restaurant 6492 Mirabel Rd, Forestville **707/887–9772** • lunch & dinner Mon-Fri, dinner only Sat, clsd Sun • some veggie

Underwood Bar & Bistro 9113 Graton Rd, Graton **707/823–7023** • lunch & dinner, clsd Mon

Willow Wood Market Cafe 9020 Graton Rd, Graton **707/823–0233** • 8am-9pm, from 9am Sat, brunch 9am-3pm Sun

Russian River

WHERE THE GIRLS ARE:
Guerneville is a small town, so you won't miss the scantily clad, vacationing women walking toward the bars downtown or the beach—especially during Women's Week. The rest of the year, look for gals in tie dye or flannel.

ANNUAL EVENTS:
May - Women's Weekend 707/869-9000 (chamber of commerce #), web: www.russianriverwomensweekend.org.

August - Lazy Bear Weekend, thousands of bears take over the River, web: www.lazybearweekend.com.

September - Jazz & Blues Festival, web: www.omegaevents.com/russianriver.

CITY INFO:
Russian River Chamber of Commerce & Visitors Center 707/869-9000, web: www.russianriver.com.

BEST VIEW:
Anywhere in Armstrong Woods, the Napa Wine Country, and on the ride along the picture-postcard-perfect coast on Highway 1.

ATTRACTIONS:
Armstrong Redwood State Park.
Bodega Bay, web: www.bodegabay.com.
Fort Ross.
Healdsburg.
Jenner & Goat Rock Beach.
Mudbaths of Calistoga.
Wineries of Napa and Sonoma Counties, web: www.napavalley.com & www.sonomacounty.com.

WEATHER:
Summer days are sunny and warm (80°s-90°s) but usually begin with a dense fog. Winter days have the same pattern but are a lot cooler and wetter. Winter nights can be very damp and chilly (low 40°s).

TRANSIT:
Bill's Taxi Service 707/869-2177. As far as public transit goes, this area is easiest to reach by car.

ENTERTAINMENT & RECREATION

Pegasus Theater Co 707/583-2343 • classic to contemporary plays

BOOKSTORES

River Reader 16355 Main St (at Mill), Guerneville **707/869-2240** • 10am-6pm, till 5pm Sun (extended summer hours) • wheelchair access

RETAIL SHOPS

Guerneville 5 &10 16252 Main St, Guerneville **707/869-3404** • 10am-6pm • old-fashioned five & dime • lesbian-owned

Sonoma Nesting Company 16151 Main St, Guerneville **707/869-3434** • antiques & home decorating

Up the River 16212 Main St (at Armstrong Woods Rd), Guerneville **707/869-3167** • cards & gifts • T-shirts

Vine Life 16359 Main St (at Mill St), Guerneville **707/869-1234** • 11am-5pm • wine, cards & gifts

Sacramento

INFO LINES & SERVICES

Gay AA 916/454-1100

Sacramento Gay & Lesbian Center 1927 L St **916/442-0185** • noon-6pm Mon-Fri

ACCOMMODATIONS

Citizen Hotel 926 J Street **916/447-2700** • gay-friendly • bar & restaurant • wheelchair access • $149-249

Governors Inn 210 Richards Blvd (at I-5) **916/448-7224, 800/999-6689** • gay-friendly • pool • hot tub • nonsmoking • WiFi • $92-124

The Greens Hotel 1700 Del Paso Blvd (at Arden) **916/921-1736** • gay/ straight • pool • WiFi • wheelchair access • $119-199

Inn & Spa at Parkside 2116 6th St (at U St) **916/658-1818, 800/995-7275** • gay/ straight • full brkfst • jacuzzi • WiFi • also full-service spa • wheelchair access • gay-owned • $169-259

BARS

The Depot 2001 K St **916/441-6823** • 4pm-2am, till 4am Fri-Sat, from 2pm wknds • mostly gay men • neighborhood bar • transgender-friendly • live shows • videos • wheelchair access

L Wine Lounge 1801 L St (at 19th St) **916/443-6970** • gay-friendly • upscale wine lounge • also restaurant

NIGHTCLUBS

Badlands 2003 K St **916/448-8790** • 6pm-2am • mostly gay men • dancing/DJ • wheelchair access

Club 21 1119 21st St (btwn K & L Sts) **916/443-1537** • Mexican restaurant during the day • gay/straight • more gay Wed & Sun for Bo Jangles (18+) • dancing/DJ • wheelchair access • cover • lesbian-owned

Faces 2000 K St (at 20th St) **916/448-7798** • 4pm-2am • popular • lesbians/ gay men • dancing/DJ • 3 bars w/ various theme nights • karaoke • videos • patio • wheelchair access • cover

Head Hunters Video Lounge & Grill 1930 K St (at 20th St) **916/492-2922** • dinner Tue-Sun, Sun brunch, bar open till 2am • lesbians/gay men • theme nights • more women Sun 2pm-9pm

CAFES

Mondo Bizarro 1827 I St **916/443-6133** • 7am-7pm, from 8am Sun • live music • WiFi

N Street Cafe 2022 N Street **916/491-4008** • 6am-6pm, 8am-3pm Sat-Sun • WiFi • wheelchair access

RESTAURANTS

Chops 1117 11th St (at L St, across from State Capitol Building) **916/447-8900** • lunch Mon-Fri, dinner nightly • steak & seafood • full bar

Hamburger Patty's 1630 J St (at 17th) **916/441-4340** • 11am-10pm, from 10am wknds • full bar • karaoke • drag shows • wheelchair access

Hot Rod's Burgers 2007 K St **916/443-7637** • 11am-2am, till 3am Fri-Sat

Ink Eats & Drinks 2730 N St (at 28th) **916/456-2800** • lunch, dinner, late-night brkfst, wknd brunch • full bar • DJ wknds

Jack's Urban Eats 1230 20th St (at Capitol Ave) **916/444-0307** • 11am-8pm, from 5pm wknds • also 2535 Fair Oaks Blvd, 916/481-5225

Paesanos 1806 Capitol Ave (at 18th) **916/447-8646** • 11:30am-9:30pm, from noon wknds • Italian • funky artwork • patio • full bar • also 8519 Bond Rd, 916/690-8646

Rick's Dessert Diner 2322 K St (btwn 23rd & 24th) **916/444-0969** • 10am-midnight, till 1am wknds, from noon Sun • coffee & dessert

Thai Palace 3262 J St (33rd St) **916/447-5353** • lunch & dinner

Zócalo 1801 Capitol Ave (at 18th St) **916/441–0303** • 11am-10pm • Mexican • full bar

ENTERTAINMENT & RECREATION

Lambda Players 1127 21st St **916/444-8229** • LGBT theater company

Lavender Library, Archives & Cultural Exchange of Sacramento 1414 21st St **916/492-0558** • 4:30pm-8pm Th-Fri, noon-6pm wknds, clsd Mon-Wed

RETAIL SHOPS

Side Show Studios 5635 Freeport Blvd Ste 6 (at Fruitridge) **916/391-6400** • 10am-10pm • tattoo studio • art gallery • reception w/ live music 2nd Sat • lesbian-owned

PUBLICATIONS

Outword Magazine 916/329–9280 • statewide LGBT newspaper w/ Northern & Southern CA editions

EROTICA

G Spot 2009 K St (at 20th) **916/441–3200** • 10am-midnight, till 2am Fri-Sat • gay-owned

Kiss-N-Tell 4201 Sunrise Blvd (at Fair Oaks) **916/966–5477** • clean, well-lighted erotica store • also 2401 Arden Wy, 916/920-5477

San Bernardino

see also Riverside

INFO LINES & SERVICES

AA Gay/ Lesbian 897 Via Lata, Colton **909/825–4700** • call or visit www.inlandempireaa.org for times

NIGHTCLUBS

The Lark 917 Inland Center Dr **909/884-8770** • 3pm-2am, from 7pm Mon, from 2pm Sat-Sun • lesbians/ gay men • DJ Fri-Sat • live & drag shows • karaoke • huge patio • WiFi • wheelchair access • lesbian-owned

EROTICA

Bearfacts Book Store 1434 E Baseline St **909/885–9176**

San Clemente

see Orange County

San Diego

INFO LINES & SERVICES

Live & Let Live Alano Club 1730 Monroe Ave **619/298–8008** • 10:30am-10pm, from 8:30am wknds • various LGBT meetings (see www.lllac.org)

San Diego LGBT Community Center 3909 Centre St (at University) **619/692–2077** • 9am-9pm, till 5pm Fri, clsd wknds

Women's Resource Center (WRC) 3909 Centre St (at University, in SD LGBT Community Center) **619/692–2077** • variety of resources • health care referrals • social services • community activities

ACCOMMODATIONS

Balboa Park Inn 3402 Park Blvd (at Upas) **619/298–0823, 800/938–8181** • gay-friendly • charming guesthouse in the heart of San Diego • theme rooms • nonsmoking

Beach Area B&B/ Elsbree House 5054 Narragansett Ave (at Sunset Cliffs Blvd) **619/226–4133, 800/607–4133** • gay-friendly • near beach • nonsmoking

The Bristol Hotel 1055 First Ave **619/232–6141, 800/662–4477** • gay/ straight • hotel • kids ok • restaurant & bar • great collection of pop art • WiFi • wheelchair access • $119-289

Handlery Hotel & Resort 950 Hotel Circle N **619/298–0511, 800/676–6567** • gay-friendly • pool • hot tub • nonsmoking • kids ok • WiFi • wheelchair access • $89-169

Keating House 2331 2nd Ave (at Juniper) **619/239–8585, 800/995–8644** • gay-friendly • Victorian on Bankers Hill • full brkfst • nonsmoking • kids ok • WiFi

Kings Inn Hotel 1333 Hotel Circle S (Bachman St) **619/297–2231, 800/785–4647** • gay/ straight • pool • WiFi • wheelchair access • $54-139

Lafayette Hotel & Suites 2223 El Cajon Blvd (btwn Louisiana & Mississippi) **619/296–2101, 800/468–3531** • gay-friendly • swimming • kids ok • also restaurant • internet access • nonsmoking • WiFi • wheelchair access

Ocean Inn 1444 N Hwy 101, Encinitas **760/436–1988, 800/546–1598** • gay-friendly • 30 min from downtown San Diego • WiFi • wheelchair access

Park Manor Suites 525 Spruce St (btwn 5th & 6th) **619/291–0999, 800/874–2649** • gay-friendly • 1926 hotel • kids ok

The Sofia Hotel 150 W Broadway **619/234–9200, 800/826–0009** • gay/ straight • kids/ pets ok • wheelchair access • $125-315

Sunburst Court Inn 4086 Alabama St (at Polk) **619/294–9665, 866/217–5490** • gay/ straight • all-suite inn • nonsmoking • WiFi • gay-owned • $99-309

W San Diego 421 W B St 619/398–3100, 888/625–5144 • gay-friendly • restaurant • rooftop bar • pool • WiFi • wheelchair access • $249-379

BARS

Bourbon Street 4612 Park Blvd (at Adams) 619/291–4043 • 4pm-2am • popular • mostly gay men • mostly women Sun • live shows & karaoke in front bar • lounge w/ DJ • patio

The Brass Rail 3796 5th Ave (at Robinson) 619/298–2233 • 7pm-2am, from 2pm Fri-Sun, clsd Tue • lesbians/ gay men • dancing/DJ • Latin night Sat • wheelchair access

El Camino 2400 India St (at Kalmia, in Little Italy) 619/685–3881 • dinner nightly, Sun brunch • kitschy Mexican • live music • full bar

Fiesta Cantina 142 University Ave 619/298–2500 • noon-2am, from 10am wknds • lesbians/ gay men • Mexican restaurant & bar

The Flame 3780 Park Blvd (at University) 619/795–8578 • popular • gay/ straight • lesbian night Fri • goth Sat • dancing/DJ • patio

Gossip Grill 1440 University Ave (at Normal) 619/260–8023 • 2pm-close • mostly women • also restaurant • patio • wheelchair access • gay-owned

Kickers 308 University Ave (at 3rd Ave, at Urban Mo's) 619/491–0400 • Th & Sat only • lesbians/ gay men • dancing/DJ • country/ western • dance lessons • wheelchair access

Ladies Night at Bourbon Street 4612 Park Blvd (at Adams) 619/291–4043 • 8pm Sun • mostly women

No 1 Fifth Ave (no sign) 3845 5th Ave (at University) 619/299–1911 • noon-2am • mostly gay men • neighborhood bar • videos nights • patio

Redwing Bar & Grill 4012 30th St (at Lincoln, North Park) 619/281–8700 • 11am-2am • mostly gay men • neighborhood bar • patio

Soul Kiss 3780 Park Blvd (at University, at the Flame) 619/795–8578 • 9pm Fri only • mostly women • dancing/DJ • patio

SRO Lounge 1807 5th Ave (btwn Elm & Fir) 619/232–1886 • 10am-2am • mostly gay men • cocktail lounge • transgender-friendly

NIGHTCLUBS

Eden 1202 University (at Vermont) 877/255–8812 • gay/ straight • dancing/DJ • also lounge & restaurant

Femme Fatale 3811 Park Blvd (at University, at Numbers) 619/294–7583 • 10pm Sat only • mostly women • dancing/DJ • patio • wheelchair access

Hot Flash San Diego 3112 University Ave (31st St, at U-31) 619/584–4188 (BAR#) • mostly women • dancing/DJ • 1st Sat only

Numbers 3811 Park Blvd (at University) 619/294–7583 • popular • mostly gay men • ladies night Sat • dancing/DJ • karaoke • theme nights • patio • wheelchair access

Repent 1051 University Ave (at Vermont, at Rich's) 619/295–2195 (CLUB #) • 10pm Th only • mostly women • dancing/DJ

Rich's 1051 University Ave (at Vermont) 619/295–2195 • popular • open Wed-Sun • mostly gay men • ladies night Th • dancing/DJ • theme nights

CAFES

Babycakes 3766 5th Ave (at Robinson) 619/296–4173 • 9am-11pm, till midnight Fri-Sat • beer/ wine • patio

The Big Kitchen 3003 Grape St (at 30th) 619/234–5789 • 8am-2pm • wheelchair access • women-owned

Claire de Lune 2906 University Ave 619/688–9845 • 6am-10pm till midnight Fri-Sat

Espresso Roma UCSD Price Center #76 (at Voight), La Jolla 858/450–2141 • 7am-10pm, 8am-4pm wknds

Extraordinary Desserts 2929 5th Ave 619/294–2132 • also store in Little Italy: 1430 Union, 619/249-7001 • the name says it all

Gelato Vero 3753 India St 619/295–9269 • 7am-midnight • great desserts (yes, the gelato is truly delicious) as well as coffee

Twiggs 4590 Park Blvd (at Madison Ave, University Heights) 619/296–0616 • 7am-11pm

Urban Grind 3797 Park Blvd (at University) 619/299–4763 • 7am-10pm • popular • WiFi • gay-owned

RESTAURANTS

Adams Avenue Grill 2201 Adams Ave (at Mississippi) 619/298–8440 • brkfst, lunch & dinner • bistro • plenty veggie • beer/ wine • wheelchair access • gay-owned

Arrivederci 3845 4th Ave 619/299–6282 • lunch & dinner

Bai Yook Thai 1260 University Ave 619/296–2700 • lunch & dinner, dinner only Sun

Baja Betty's 1421 University Ave (at Normal St) **619/269-8510** • 11am-midnight, till 1am Fri-Sat • popular • lesbians/gay men • Mexican • some veggie • patio • wheelchair access

Bamboo Lounge 1475 University Ave (at Herbert St) **619/291-8221** • 4pm-midnight, till 1am wknds • sushi

Bangkok Thai Bistro 540 University Ave **619/269-9209** • 11am-10pm, till 11pm Fri-Sat

Brian's American Eatery 1451 Washington St **619/296-8268** • 6:30am-10pm, 24hrs Fri-Sat • beer/wine

Cafe 222 222 Island Ave **619/236-9902** • 7am-2pm • great brkfst

Celadon 3671 5th Ave (at Pennsylvania) **619/297-8424** • lunch & dinner • upscale Thai

Cody's La Jolla 8030 Girard Ave (at Coast Blvd S), La Jolla **858/459-0040** • brkfst & lunch daily, dinner Th-Sun • contemporary California cuisine • live music

San Diego

WHERE THE GIRLS ARE:
Lesbians tend to live near Normal Heights, in the northwest part of the city. But for partying, women go to the bars near I-5, or to Hillcrest to hang out with the boys.

LGBT PRIDE:
July. 619/297-7683, web: www.sdpride.org.

ANNUAL EVENTS:
February - Hillcrest Mardi Gras, web: www.hillcrestmardigras.com.
April - FilmOut San Diego, web: www.filmoutsandiego.com.
August - Hillcrest CityFest Street Fair, web: www.hillcrestassociation.com.
September - Street Scene, web: www.street-scene.com. Huge, outdoor music festival.

CITY INFO:
San Diego Convention & Visitors Bureau, web: www.sandiego.org. SanDiego.com, web: www.sandiego.com.

BEST VIEW:
Cabrillo National Monument on Point Loma or from a harbor cruise.

WEATHER:
San Diego is sunny and warm (upper 60°s-70°s) year-round, with higher humidity in the summer.

ATTRACTIONS:
Coronado Island (& Hotel Del Coronado), web: www.coronado.ca.us.
Fleet Space Center 619/238-1233, web: www.rhfleet.org.
Hillcrest, web: www.hillquest.com.
Gaslamp Quarter, web: www.gaslamp.org.
Mingei Int'l Museum 619/239-0003, web: www.mingei.org.
La Jolla, web: www.lajollabythesea.com.
The Old Globe Theatre 619/234-5623 (box office), web: www.oldglobe.org.
San Diego Museum of Art 619/232-7931, web: www.sdmart.org.
San Diego Wild Animal Park 760/747-8702, web: www.sandiegozoo.org/wap.
San Diego Zoo 619/231-1515, web: www.sandiegozoo.com.
Sea World 800/257-4268, web: www.seaworld.com.

TRANSIT:
Yellow Cab 619/444-4444.
San Diego Cab 619/226-8294.
Silver Cab/Co-op 619/280-5555.
Super Shuttle 800/974-8885, web: www.supershuttle.com.
San Diego Transit System 619/238-0100, web: www.sdmts.com.
San Diego Trolley (through downtown or to Tijuana).

The Cottage 7702 Fay (at Klein), La Jolla 858/454-8409 • 7:30am-3pm, dinner June-Sept

Crazee Burger 4201 30th St (at Howard) 619/282-6044 • 11am-9pm, till 11pm Fri-Sat • handcrafted burgers

Crest Cafe 425 Robinson (btwn 4th & 5th) 619/295-2510 • 7am-midnight • some veggie • wheelchair access

Gulf Coast Grill 4130 Park Blvd (at Normal) 619/295-2244 • lunch & dinner, also Sun brunch • New Orleans-inspired menu

Hash House A Go Go 3628 5th Ave 619/298-4646 • brkfst, lunch & dinner, clsd Mon • great brkfst

Inn at the Park 525 Spruce St (btwn 5th & 6th, at Park Manor Suites) 619/296-0057 • popular • dinner nightly • piano bar

Jimmy Carter's Mexican Cafe 3172 5th Ave (at Spruce) 619/295-2070 • 7am-9pm

Kous Kous 3940 4th Ave, Ste 110 (beneath Martinis on Fourth) 619/295-5560 • 5pm-11pm • Moroccan

Lei Lounge 4622 Park Blvd (at Madison Ave) 619/813-2272 • 5pm-2am, Sun brunch • also popular lounge • patio

Lips 3036 El Cajon Blvd 619/295-7900 • 5pm-close, Sun gospel brunch, clsd Mon • "the ultimate in drag dining" • Bitchy Bingo Wed • celeb impersonation Th • DJ wknds

Martinis Above Fourth 3940 4th Ave, Ste 200 (btwn Washington & University) 619/400-4500 • 5pm-11pm, 4pm-midnight Fri-Sat, clsd Sun-Mon • also cabaret lounge • outdoor bar • gay-owned

The Mission 3795 Mission Blvd (at San Jose), Mission Beach 858/488-9060 • 7am-3pm

Ono Sushi 1236 University Ave (at Richmond) 619/298-0616 • lunch wknds, dinner nightly

The Prado 1549 El Prado (in Balboa Park) 619/557-9441 • lunch & dinner • Latin/ Italian fusion

Roberto's 3202 Mission Blvd 858/488-1610 • open 24 hrs • the best rolled tacos & guacamole • multiple locations

Rudford's 2900 El Cajon Blvd (at Kansas St) 619/282-8423 • 24hrs • popular homestyle cooking

Saigon on Fifth 3900 5th Ave, Ste 120 619/220-8828 • 11am-3am • Vietnamese

South Park Abbey 1946 Fern St (at Grape St) 619/696-0096 • 3pm-1:30am, from 9am Sat-Sun, till midnight Sun-Mon, clsd Tue

Taste of Szechuan 670 University Ave 619/291-1668 • 11am-11pm

Terra 3900 block of Vermont St (at 10th Ave) 619/293-7088 • lunch & dinner, clsd Mon for dinner

Urban Mo's 308 University Ave (at 3rd) 619/491-0400 • 9am-2am, 10am-midnight Sun • popular • lesbians/ gay men • some veggie • 3 full bars (Club Mo's) • patio • wheelchair access

Veg N Out 3442 30th St (North Park) 619/546-8411 • 11am-9pm, from noon Sun • vegetarian/ vegan

Waffle Spot 1333 Hotel Circle S (at King's Inn) 619/297-2231 • 7am-2pm

West Coast Tavern 2895 University Ave 619/295-1688 • lunch & dinner • upscale • also lounge

ENTERTAINMENT & RECREATION

Diversionary Theatre 4545 Park Blvd #101 (at Madison) 619/220-0097 (BOX OFFICE #), 619/220-6830 • LGBT theater

Ocean Beach I-8 West to Sunset Cliffs Blvd • very dog-friendly

BOOKSTORES

Traveler's Depot 1655 Garnet Ave (btwn Jewell & Ingraham) 858/483-1421 • 10am-6pm, 11am-5pm wknds • guides, maps & more

RETAIL SHOPS

Auntie Helen's 4028 30th St (at Lincoln) 619/584-8438 • 9:30am-5pm, clsd Sun-Mon • thrift shop benefits PWAs • wheelchair access

Babette Schwartz 421 University Ave (at 5th Ave) 619/220-7048 • 11am-9pm, till 5pm Sun • campy novelties & gifts • gay-owned

Flesh Skin Grafix 1155 Palm Ave, Imperial Beach 619/424-8983 • tattoos • piercing

Mankind 3425 5th Ave (at Upas St) 619/497-1970 • 11am-10pm, noon-6pm Sun • books, sex toys and videos

Obelisk the Bookstore 1029 University Ave (at 10th) 619/297-4171 • 10am-9pm, till 10pm wknds • LGBT • wheelchair access

PUBLICATIONS

The Bottomline 3314 4th Ave 619/291-6690 • bi-weekly • news, entertainment & listings • covers San Diego & Palm Springs

The Lavender Lens 619/342-6166 • Southern California's monthly lesbian magazine

LGBT Weekly 1850 5th Ave 619/450-4288

San Diego PIX 1010 University Ave 877/727-5446

GYMS & HEALTH CLUBS

Frog's Athletic Club 901 Hotel Circle S (at Washington), Mission Valley 619/291-3500

EROTICA

The Crypt 3847 Park Blvd (at University) 619/692-9499

Pleasures & Treasures Adult/ Leather Shop 2228 University Ave (at Mississippi St) 619/822-4280 • clsd Tue • gay-owned

Romantix Adult Superstore 1407 University Ave (at Richmond) 619/299-7186

The Rubber Rose 3812 Ray St (at N Park Way) 619/296-7673 • clsd Mon • women-owned sexuality shop

SAN FRANCISCO

San Francisco is divided into 7 geographical areas:
SF—Overview
SF—Castro & Noe Valley
SF—South of Market
SF—Polk Street Area
SF—Downtown & North Beach
SF—Mission District
SF—Haight, Fillmore, Hayes Valley

SF—Overview

INFO LINES & SERVICES

AA Gay/ Lesbian 1821 Sacramento St 415/674-1821 • check www.aasf.org for meeting times

The Center for Sex & Culture 1519 Mission St (at 11th) 415/255-1155 • very queer-friendly classes, workshops, gatherings, events, readings & more

Crystal Meth Anonymous 415/835-4747

GLBT Hotline of San Francisco 415/355-0999 • 5pm-9pm Mon-Fri • peer-counseling • info

LYRIC (Lavender Youth Recreation/ Information Center) 127 Collingwood (btwn 18th & 19th) 415/703-6150 • peer-run support line for LGBT youth under 24

The San Francisco LGBT Community Center 1800 Market St (at Octavia) 415/865-5555 • noon-10pm, from 9am Sat, clsd Sun • cybercenter • cafe • classes • child care & more

Women's Building 3543 18th St (btwn Valencia & Guerrero) 415/431-1180 • 9am-5pm Mon-Fri, till 6pm Sat • social/ support groups • housing & job listings • beautiful murals

BARS

Thursday Ladies Night with "Betty's List" 415/777-1508 • Th only • mostly women • check bettyslist.com for location

NIGHTCLUBS

Hot Flash San Francisco • women's dance parties • check hotflashdances.com for info

Trannyshack 415/863-6623 • occasional drag events, check trannyshack.com for info

RESTAURANTS

Beach Chalet Brewery & Restaurant 1000 Great Hwy (at Fulton St) 415/386-8439

ENTERTAINMENT & RECREATION

Baker Beach Lincoln Blvd at Bowley, in the Presidio • popular nude beach

Bay Area Derby Girls • SF Bay Area's female roller derby league • visit www.bayareaderbygirls.com for events

Betty's List 415/503-1375 • online & email info service for LGBT community • events • check out www.bettyslist.com • lesbian-owned

Brava! 2781 24th St (btwn York & Hampshire) 415/641-7657, 415/647-2822 (**BOX OFFICE**) • theater w/ culturally diverse performances by women • wheelchair access

Castro Theatre 429 Castro (at Market) 415/621-6120 • art house cinema • many LGBT & cult classics • live organ evenings

Cruisin' the Castro Tours tour meets at the rainbow flag at Harvey Milk Plaza (corner of Castro & Market) 415/255-1821 • "a TOP city tour & walking with pride since 1989! Diverse, fun, informative & NO hills"

Femina Potens 415/864-1558 • nonprofit art & performance promoting women & transfolk in the arts

➤**Frameline** 415/703-8650 • LGBT media arts foundation • sponsors annual SF Int'l LGBT Film Festival in June

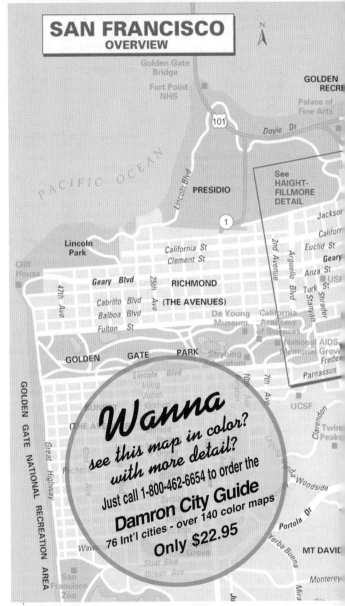

SAN FRANCISCO
OVERVIEW

N

Golden Gate Bridge

Fort Point NHS

GOLDEN RECRE

Palace of Fine Arts

101

Doyle Dr

PACIFIC OCEAN

PRESIDIO

See HAIGHT-FILLMORE DETAIL

Jackson

Californ

Euclid St

Geary

Anza St

USF

Turk St

Shrader

Stanyan

Lincoln Park

Cliff House

California St

Clement St

2nd Avenue

Arguello Blvd

Geary Blvd

25th Ave

RICHMOND

(THE AVENUES)

47th Ave

Cabrillo Blvd

Balboa Blvd

Fulton St

De Young Museum

California Academy of Sciences

National AIDS Memorial Grove

Frede

GOLDEN GATE PARK

Strybing Arboretum

Parnassus

Lincoln Blvd

Irving

Judah

7th Ave

10th Ave

UCSF

Clarendon

Twin Peaks

GOLDEN GATE NATIONAL RECREATION AREA

Great Highway

42nd Ave

Moraga

Kirkham

Quintara

Santiago

Laguna Honda Blvd

Woodside

Pacheco

Portola Dr

Yerba Buena

MT DAVID

Wawona

Sloat Blvd

Ocean Ave

Grove

Monterey

Mira

San Francisco Zoo

Ju

Wanna see this map in color? with more detail?
Just call 1-800-462-6654 to order the
Damron City Guide
76 Int'l cities - over 140 color maps
Only $22.95

San Francisco

Where the Girls Are:

Younger, radical dykes call the Mission or the Lower Haight home, while upwardly mobile couples stake out Bernal Heights and Noe Valley. Hip, moneyed dykes live in the Castro. The East Bay is home to lots of lesbian feminists, older lesbians, lesbians of color, and lesbian moms (see East Bay listings).

Entertainment:

Theatre Rhinoceros 415/861-5079, 2926 16th St.

LGBT Pride:

June. 415/864-0831, web: www.sfpride.org.

Annual Events:

June - San Francisco Int'l Lesbian/Gay Film Festival 415/703-8650, web: www.frameline.org.

July - Up Your Alley Fair 415/861-3247, web: folsomstreetevents.org. Local SM/leather street fair held in Dore Alley, South-of-Market.

September - Folsom Street Fair 415/861-3247, web: folsomstreetevents.org. Huge SM/leather street fair, topping a week of kinky events.

October - Castro Street Fair 415/841-1824, web: www.castrostreetfair.org. Arts and community groups street fair.

City Info:

San Francisco Convention & Visitors Bureau 415/391-2000, web: www.sfvisitor.org.

Weather:

A beautiful summer comes at the end of September and lasts through October. Much of the city is cold and fogged-in June through September, though the Castro and Mission are usually sunny. The cold in winter is damp, so bring lots of layers. When there isn't a drought, it also rains in the winter months of November through February.

Attractions:

Alcatraz 415/981-7625, web: www.nps.gov/alcatraz.

Asian Art Museum 415/ 581-3500, www.asianart.org.

Cablecars.

California Academy of Sciences (adults only on Th eves) 415/379-8000, web: www.calacademy.org.

Chinatown.

Coit Tower.

Exploratorium 415/561-0360, web: www.exploratorium.edu.

Fisherman's Wharf & Pier 39 (take the F Car from the Castro down Market & along the Embarcadero to get there).

Golden Gate Park.

Haight & Ashbury Sts.

Japantown.

North Beach.

Mission San Francisco de Assisi.

SF Museum of Modern Art 415/357-4000, web: www.sfmoma.org.

Twin Peaks.

Best View:

After a great Italian meal in North Beach, go to the top floor of the North Beach parking garage on Vallejo near Stockton, next to the police station. If you're in the Castro or the Mission, head for Dolores Park, at Dolores and 20th St. Other good views: Golden Gate Bridge, Kirby Cove (a park area to the left, just past the Golden Gate Bridge in Marin), Coit Tower, Twin Peaks, Bernal Hill.

Transit:

Yellow Cab 415/333-3333, web: www.yellowcabsf.com.

Luxor Cab 415/282-4141, web: www.luxorcab.com.

Quake City Shuttle 415/255-4899, web: www.quakecityshuttle.com.

511, web: 511.org. Covers all Bay Area transit (also traffic).

Muni 415/673-6864, web: www.sfmuni.org.

Bay Area Rapid Transit (BART) 415/989-2278, subway, web: www.bart.gov.

The Intersection for the Arts 446 Valencia St (btwn 15th & 16th Sts) 415/626–2787, 415/626–3311 (BOX OFFICE) • San Francisco's oldest alternative arts space (since 1965!) w/ plays, art exhibitions, live jazz, literary series, performance art & much more

Local Tastes of the City Tours 415/665–0480, 888/358–8687 • explore the history & culture of local neighborhoods, including Chinatown & North Beach/ Little Italy as "we eat our way through San Francisco"

The Marsh 1062 Valencia (at 22nd St) 415/826–5750 (EVENT INFO) & 641–0235 (OFFICE), 800/838–3006 (BOX OFFICE) • queer-positive theater

➤**National AIDS Memorial Grove** Golden Gate Park (on corner of Middle Drive East & Bowling Green Dr) 415/765–0497, 888/294–7683 • located in a lush, historic dell in Golden Gate Park • guided tours available 9am-noon every 3rd Sat • wheelchair access

QComedy Gay Comedy Showcase 415/533–9133 • see website for locations • popular • lesbians/ gay men • cover charge (sliding scale) • see www.qcomedy.com for location

➤**San Francisco Pride** 1800 Market St, PMB #Q31 94102 415/864–3733 • one of the world's biggest

Steve Silver's Beach Blanket Babylon 678 Beach Blanket Babylon Ave (formerly Green St) (btwn Powell & Columbus, in Club Fugazi) 415/421–4222 • the USA's longest running musical revue & wigs that must be seen to be believed • very popular • 21+ except Sun

Thanks Babs, the Day Tripper 702/370–6961 • tours & getaways • full service concierge for San Francisco & Bay Area • it's like having a lesbian aunt in Northern California!

Theatre Rhinoceros 1360 Mission St #200 800/838–3006, 415/552–4100 • LGBT theater

Victorian Home Walks 415/252–9485 • custom-tailored walking tours w/ San Francisco resident • gay-owned

Yerba Buena Center for the Arts 701 Mission St (at 3rd St) 415/978–2787 (BOX OFFICE) • annual season includes wide variety of contemporary dance, theater & music • also film theater & gallery

PUBLICATIONS

BAR (Bay Area Reporter) 415/861–5019 • the weekly LGBT newspaper

Bay Times 415/626–0260 • popular • good Bay Area resource listings

SF—Castro & Noe Valley

ACCOMMODATIONS

24 Henry & Village House 24 Henry St (btwn Sanchez & Noe) 415/864–5686, 800/900–5686 • B&B • mostly gay men • some shared baths • nonsmoking • WiFi • one-bdrm apt also available • gay-owned

Andrew Whelan House 415/621–7736 • gay/ straight • Victorian home & garden • shared baths • nonsmoking • WiFi • gay-owned • $90-130

➤**Belvedere House** 598 Belvedere St (at 17th St) 415/731–6654, 877/226–3273 • popular • lesbians/ gay men • wall-to-wall books, art & style • WiFi • German spoken • nonsmoking • gay-owned

Casa Buena Vista Corona Heights (near Market & Castro) 916/974–7409, 916/813–3119 (CELL) • gay-friendly • rental apts • nonsmoking • kids ok • WiFi

Castro Suites 927 14th St (at Noe) 415/437–1783 • gay/ straight • furnished apts • kitchen • nonsmoking • WiFi • gay-owned

Edwardian San Francisco 1668 Market St (btwn Franklin & Gough) 415/864–1271, 888/864–8070 • gay-friendly • hot tub • jacuzzi • some shared baths • nonsmoking

Inn on Castro 321 Castro St (btwn 16th & 17th) 415/861–0321 • lesbians/ gay men • B&B known for its hospitality & friendly atmosphere • full brkfst • nonsmoking • WiFi • gay-owned

The Parker Guest House 520 Church St (at 17th) 415/621–3222, 888/520–7275 • popular • mostly gay men • guesthouse complex w/ gardens • steam spa • nonsmoking • WiFi • gay-owned

Travelodge Central 1707 Market St (at Valencia) 415/621–6775, 800/578–7878 (RESERVATIONS) • gay-friendly • nonsmoking rooms available • close to LGBT center • $99-179

The Willows Inn 710 14th St (at Church) 415/431–4770, 800/431–0277 • lesbians/ gay men • "amenities, comfort, great location" • nonsmoking • WiFi • lesbian & gay-owned • $99-190

Bars

13 Licks 456 Castro St (at Q Bar) 415/864-2877 • 9pm-2am Tue only • popular • mostly women • neighborhood bar • dancing/DJ • sidewalk patio • wheelchair access

440 Castro 440 Castro St 415/621-8732 • noon-2am • popular • mostly gay men • neighborhood bar • leather • bears • women genuinely welcome

Blackbird 2124 Market St 415/503-0630 • gay/ straight • neighborhood bar • gay-owned

Buck Tavern 1655 Market St (at Gough) 415/874-9183 • 4:30pm-midnight, till 2:30am wknds, from noon Sun • gay/ straight • neighborhood bar • food served

The Cafe 2369 Market St (at Castro) 415/861-3846 • 4pm-2am, from 3pm Sat, from 2pm Sun • popular • lesbians/ gay men • dancing/DJ • young crowd • deck overlooking Castro & Market

Cafe du Nord 2170 Market St (at Sanchez) 415/861-5016 • gay-friendly • alternative • live music • theme nights • dinner some veggie

Delicious 2369 Market St (at the Cafe) 408/792-3466 (INFO LINE) • 4pm-10pm 3rd Sat only • mostly women • T-dance • go-go girls • smoking patio

Harvey's 500 Castro St 415/431-4278 • 11am-11pm, 9am-2am wknds • popular • lesbians/ gay men • neighborhood bar • occasional drag performers • also restaurant • wheelchair access

The Lookout 3600 16th St (at Market) 415/431-0306 • 11am-2am • mostly gay men

Martuni's 4 Valencia St (at Market) 415/241-0205 • 4pm-2am • gay/ straight • piano bar & lounge • great martinis

The Mint 1942 Market St (at Buchanan) 415/626-4726 • noon-2am • lesbians/ gay men • popular karaoke bar nights • also sushi restaurant • food served till 11pm (till midnight wknds)

The Mix 4086 18th St 415/431-8616 • 3pm-2am, from 8am wknds • mostly gay men • neighborhood bar • heated patio

Moby Dick 4049 18th St (at Hartford) • 2pm-2am, from noon wknds • mostly gay men • neighborhood bar • videos

Pan Dulce 2369 Market St (at the Cafe) 415/861-3846 • 9pm-2am Th only • lesbians/ gay men • dancing/DJ • Latino/a • "The Castro's Biggest Latino Party!"

Pilsner Inn 225 Church St (at Market) 415/621-7058 • 10am-2am • popular • mostly gay men • neighborhood bar • great patio

Q Bar 456 Castro St 415/864-2877 • 4pm-2am, from 2pm wknds • popular • mostly gay men, more women Tue • neighborhood bar • dancing/DJ • sidewalk patio • wheelchair access

Rebel 1760 Market St (at Valencia) 415/431-4202 • 4pm-3am, noon-4am wknds • mostly men • dancing/DJ • drag shows

Swirl 572 Castro St (at 19th) 415/864-2262 • 1pm-8pm, till 9pm Fri-Sat • gay-friendly • wine bar & wine store

Trigger 2344 Market St (at Castro) 415/551-2582 • 4pm-2am • mostly men • dancing/DJ

Cafes

Cafe Flore 2298 Market St (at Noe) 415/621-8579 • 7am-2am • popular • lesbians/ gay men • some veggie • full bar • great patio • WiFi

Caffe Trieste 1667 Market St (at Gough) 415/551-1000 • 7am-8pm • popular • great coffee • live music

Duboce Park Cafe 2 Sanchez St (at Duboce) 415/621-1108 • 7am-8pm • outdoor seating

Jumpin' Java 139 Noe St (at 14th St) 415/431-5282 • 6:30am-7:30pm, 7am-8pm wknds • WiFi

Lovejoy's Tea Room 1351 Church St (at Clipper) 415/648-5895 • 11am-6pm, clsd Mon-Tue • popular • for a tea party fit for a queen

Orbit Room Cafe 1900 Market St (at Laguna) 415/252-9525 • 4pm-2am, till midnight Sun • also bar

Philz Coffee 4023 18th (at Noe) • 6am-8pm

Samovar Tea Lounge 498 Sanchez St (at 18th St) 415/626-4700 • 10am-10pm • tea culture from around the world

Sweet Inspiration 2239 Market St 415/621-8664 • 8am-11pm, till 12:30am Fri-Sat • popular wknd nights • food served • fabulous desserts

Restaurants

2223 Market 2223 Market St 415/431-0692 • dinner, Sun brunch • contemporary American • full bar • wheelchair access

Anchor Oyster Bar 579 Castro St (at 19th) **415/431–3990** • 11:30am-10pm, from 4pm Sun • lesbians/ gay men • beer/ wine • women-owned

Bisou 2367 Market St (at 17th) **415/556–6200** • dinner nightly, Sun brunch, clsd Mon • French

Blue 2337 Market St (btwn Castro & Noe) **415/863–2583** • 11:30am-11pm, wknd brunch from 10:30am • popular • homecooking served w/ style • some veggie • beer/ wine

Catch 2362 Market St **415/431–5000** • lunch & dinner, wknd brunch • seafood • live music

Chloe's 1399 Church St (at 26th St) **415/648–4116** • 8am-4pm • popular • come early for the excellent wknd brunch

Chow 215 Church St (at Market) **415/552–2469** • 8am-11pm, till midnight wknds • popular • patio

Cove Cafe 434 Castro St **415/626–0462** • 8am-9pm, till 10pm Fri-Sat • lesbians/ gay men • some veggie • wheelchair access

Eric's Chinese Restaurant 1500 Church St (at 27th St) **415/282–0919** • 11am-9pm • popular

Eureka Restaurant & Lounge 4063 18th St (at Hartford) **415/431–6000** • dinner nightly • lounge upstairs

Firewood Cafe 4248 18th St (at Diamond St) **415/252–0999** • 11am-11pm • rotisserie chicken, pastas, oven-fired pizzas, salads

Gingerfruit 2029 Market St (at Dolores) **415/252–0700** • 4pm-1am Wed-Sun • popular • ladies night Th • swanky bar • wheelchair access

Hot Cookie 407 Castro St **415/621–2350** • 11am-1am • hot cookies!

Ike's Place 2247 Market St (at Sanchez) **415/553–6888** • 10am-7pm • amazing sandwiches • plenty veggie/ vegan • long wait

It's Tops 1801 Market St (at Octavia) **415/431–6395** • 8am-3pm daily, 8pm-3am Wed-Sat • classic diner • great hotcakes

Kasa Indian Eatery 4001 18th St (at Noe) **415/621–6940** • 11am-10pm, till 11pm Fri-Sat • plenty veggie

La Mediterranée 288 Noe (at Market) **415/431–7210** • 11am-10pm, till 11pm Sat-Sun • beer/ wine

Leticia's 2200 Market St (at 15th) **415/864–5384** • lunch & dinner • Mexican

Nirvana Restaurant & Bar 544 Castro St (btwn 18th & 19th) **415/861–2226** • Southeast Asian • patio

Orphan Andy's 3991 17th St **415/864–9795** • 24hrs • diner • gay-owned

Poesia Osteria Italiana 4072 18th St (at Collingwood) **415/252–9325** • dinner nighly, great food & full bar

The Sausage Factory 517 Castro St **415/626–1250** • 11:30am-midnight • lesbians/ gay men • pizza & pasta • some veggie • beer/ wine

Sparky's 242 Church St (at Market) **415/626–8666** • 24hrs • popular late night • diner • some veggie

Squat & Gobble 3600 16th St **415/552–2125** • 8am-10pm • popular wknds for brkfst • outdoor seating

Takara Sushi 4243 18th St (at Diamond) **415/626–7864** • lunch & dinner, clsd Tue • lesbians/ gay men • cont'l/ Japanese

Thailand Restaurant 438-A Castro St **415/863–6868** • 11am-10pm • plenty veggie

Woodhouse Fish Co 2073 Market St (at 14th) **415/437–2722** • noon-9:30pm • New England clam shack-style seafood

Zuni Cafe 1658 Market St (at Franklin) **415/552–2522** • lunch & dinner • clsd Mon • popular • upscale cont'l/ Mediterranean • full bar

ENTERTAINMENT & RECREATION

Castro Country Club 4058 18th St (at Hartford) **415/552–6102** • alcohol- & drug-free space • cafe

Pink Triangle Park near Market & Castro • "in remembrance of LGBT victims of the Nazi regime"

BOOKSTORES

Aardvark Books 227 Church St **415/552–6733** • 10:30am-10:30pm • mostly used • good LGBT section

Books, Inc 2275 Market St **415/864–6777** • 10am-10pm • LGBT section • readings • wheelchair access

RETAIL SHOPS

Best in Show 545 Castro St (btwn 18th & 19th) **415/864–7387** • 11am-8pm, 11am-7pm Sat, 11am-6pm Sun • pet boutique

De La Sole Footwear 549 Castro St (btwn 18th & 19th) **415/255–3140** • 11am-7pm, till 8pm Sat

HRC Action Center & Store 575 Castro St **415/431–2200** • 10am-9pm, till 10pm wknds • Human Rights Campaign merchandise & info

Kenneth Wingard 2319 Market St (btwn Castro & Noe) 415/431-6900 • modern & affordable home furnishings, decor & clothing

Rolo 2351 Market St 415/431-4545 • 11am-8pm, till 7pm Sun • designer labels

See Jane Run Sports 3910 24th St (at Noe) 415/401-8338 • 11am-7pm, 10am-6pm Sat, till 5pm Sun • women's athletic apparel

Under One Roof 518 Castro 415/503-2300 • 10am-8pm, 11am-7pm Sun • 100% donated to AIDS relief • wheelchair access

GYMS & HEALTH CLUBS

Gold's Gym Castro 2301 Market St 415/626-4488 • lesbians/ gay men • day passes available

SF—South of Market

ACCOMMODATIONS

Americania Hotel 121 7th St (at Mission) 415/626-0200, 800/444-5816 • gay-friendly • pool • bar & restaurant • wheelchair access • $149-249

Budget Hotel 1139 Market St 415/864-9343 • gay-friendly • $66+

Holiday Inn Civic Center 50 8th St (at Market) 415/626-6103, 877/252-1169 • gay-friendly • pool • small pets ok • WiFi • wheelchair access

Hotel Whitcomb 1231 Market St (btwn 8th & 9th) 415/626-8000 • gay-friendly • landmark hotel on Pride route • also restaurant & Starbucks on-site • WiFi • wheelchair access • $89+

The Mosser Hotel 54 4th St (btwn Market & Mission) 415/986-4400, 800/227-3804 • gay/ straight • 1913 landmark hotel • some shared baths • nonsmoking • kids ok • also restaurant • SF cuisine • full bar

Renoir Hotel 45 McAllister St (at Market St) 415/626-5200, 800/576-3388 • gay/ straight • nonsmoking • WiFi • wheelchair access • Damron discount • $89-350

Vagabond Inn San Francisco 385 9th St (at Harrison) 415/431-5131, 800/522-1555 • gay/ straight • motel • close to SOMA bars • limited parking • kids ok • WiFi • wheelchair access • $69-139

W San Francisco 181 Third St 415/777-5300 • gay-friendly • pool • WiFi • wheelchair access • also XYZ restaurant & bar • $229-429

The Westin San Francisco Market Street 50 3rd St 415/974-6400, 888/627-8561 • gay-friendly • hip hotel w/ spectacular views • sauna • kids ok • nonsmoking • $139+

BARS

Dada SF Studio 86 2nd St (btwn Market & Mission) 415/357-1367 • 4pm-midnight, till 2am Th-Sat, from 8pm Sat, clsd Sun • gay/ straight • art gallery • gay-owned

Hole in the Wall Saloon 1369 Folsom (btwn 9th & 10th) 415/431-4695 • noon-2am • mostly gay men • neighborhood bar • leather

NIGHTCLUBS

1015 Folsom 1015 Folsom St (at 6th) 415/431-1200 • 10pm-close Fri-Sat • gay/ straight • popular • dancing/DJ • call for events • cover charge

Asia SF 201 9th St (at Howard) 415/255-2742 • 10pm-close Wed-Sat • popular • gay/ straight • dancing/DJ • mostly Asian American • theme nights • go-go boys • cover charge • also Cal-Asian restaurant w/ en-drag dinner service

Beat Box 314 11th St • gay/ straight • dancing/DJ

Bootie 375 11th St (at Harrison, at DNA Lounge) 415/626-1409 (DNA INFO LINE) • 9pm-close 2nd, 3rd & 4th Sat • gay-friendly • dancing/DJ • mashups, bootlegs, bastard pop • cover charge

Cat Club 1190 Folsom St (at 8th) 415/703-8965 • gay/ straight • dancing/DJ • hosts many one-night clubs & events

The Crib SF 715 Harrison St (at 3rd) • 9:30pm-2am Th only • lesbians/ gay men • dancing/DJ • "all-video pop club" • younger crowd • 18+ • cover

Eight 1151 Folsom St (btwn 7th & 8th St) 415/431-1151 • 9pm-3am • popular • gay/ straight • dancing/DJ • theme nights • smoking patio

Endup 401 6th St (at Harrison) 415/646-0999 (INFO LINE), 415/357-0827 • gay/ straight • dancing/DJ • multiracial • theme nights • popular Sun mornings

Flourish 161 Erie St (at Mission, at Public Works) • quarterly fancy queer party • dancing/DJ • dress to impress!

Ghetto Disco 401 6th St (at Harrison, at Endup) • 11pm Fri-11am Sat only • mostly gay men • dancing/DJ

The Stud 399 9th St (at Harrison) 415/863-6623 • 5pm-2am • popular • lesbians/ gay men • dancing/DJ • theme nights

Tool Box 93 9th St (at Jessie St, at Club 93) 415/522-0200 • Th only • lesbians/ gay men • drag • comedy • dancing/DJ

Cafes

Brain Wash 1122 Folsom St (at 7th St) 415/861–3663, 415/431–9274 • 7am-11pm, 8am-10pm Sun • popular • cafe & laundromat • beer/ wine

Restaurants

Ame 689 Mission St (at 3rd St, in St Regis Hotel) 415/284–4040 • lunch & dinner • full bar • reservations recommended

Ananda Fuara 1298 Market St (at 9th) 415/621–1994 • 8am-8pm, till 3pm Wed, clsd Sun • vegetarian

Anchor & Hope 83 Minna St (at 2nd St) 415/501–9100 • lunch Mon-Fri, dinner nightly • seafood

Butter 354 11th St (btwn Folsom & Harrison) 415/863–5964 • 6pm-2am, clsd Mon • "white trash bistro" • full bar • theme nights

Don Ramon's Mexican Restaurant 225 11th St (btwn Howard & Folsom) 415/864–2700 • lunch Tue-Fri, dinner nightly, clsd Mon • some veggie • full bar

Fringale 570 4th St (btwn Bryant & Brannan) 415/543–0573 • lunch Tue-Fri & dinner nightly • French bistro • wheelchair access

Heaven's Dog 1148 Mission St (at 7th) 415/863–6008 • 5pm-1am, till 9pm Sun • Chinese

Orson 508 4th St • 5pm-11pm, clsd Sun • lesbian-owned

Rocco's Cafe 1131 Folsom St (at 7th) 415/554–0522 • brkfst & lunch daily, dinner Wed-Sat only

The Slanted Door 1 Ferry Building #3 415/861–8032 • popular • Vietnamese • full bar • reservations recommended

Supperclub 657 Harrison St (btwn 2nd & 3rd) 415/348–0900 • 6:30pm-close • live performance art & acrobatics • also full bar & nightclub

Ted's 1530 Howard St (at 11th) 415/552–0309 • 6am-6pm, 8am-5pm wknds • excellent deli sandwiches

Tu Lan 8 6th St (at Market) 415/626–0927 • lunch & dinner, clsd Sun • Vietnamese • some veggie • dicey neighborhood but delicious (& cheap) food

Woodward's Garden 1700 Mission St (at Duboce) 415/621–7122 • dinner from 6pm, clsd Sun-Mon • wheelchair access

Yank Sing 101 Spear St (at Mission, at One Rincon Center) 415/957–9300 • 11am-3pm Mon-Fri, 10am-4pm wknds • popular • dim-sum heaven! • also catering & delivery

Entertainment & Recreation

111 Minna Gallery 111 Minna St (at 2nd St) 415/974–1719 • gay/ straight • also art gallery • call for events

Retail Shops

Dandelion 55 Potrero Ave (at Alameda St) 415/436–9500, 888/548–1968 • 10am-7pm, till 6pm Fri-Sat, noon-5pm Sun • gay-owned

Madame S 385 8th St (at Harrison) 415/863–9447 • 11am-7pm • women's bondage & fetish fashion & equipment

Mr S Leather & Fetters USA San Francisco 385 8th St (at Harrison) 415/863–7764, 800/746–7677 (ORDERS) • 11am-7pm • erotic goods • custom leather • latex

Off Ramp Leathers 342-A 9th St #205 415/255–8117 • custom motorcycle leathers

Stompers 323 10th St (at Folsom) 415/255–6422, 888/BOOTMAN • 11am-6pm, noon-4pm Sun, clsd Mon

Gyms & Health Clubs

Gold's Gym San Francisco 1001 Brannan St (at 9th) 415/552–4653 • popular • day passes available

Erotica

Good Vibrations 899 Mission St (at 5th St) 415/513–1635, 800/289–8423 • 10am-9pm, till 10pm Fri-Sat • popular • clean, well-lighted sex toy store • wheelchair access

SF—Polk Street Area

Accommodations

Inn On Broadway 2201 Van Ness Ave (at Broadway) 415/776–7900, 800/727–6239 • gay-friendly • motel • close to Fisherman's Wharf • kids ok • WiFi • wheelchair access • lesbian, gay & straight-owned • $54-119

The Monarch Hotel 1015 Geary St (at Polk) 415/673–5232, 800/777–3210 • gay-friendly • Edwardian boutique-style hotel • kids ok • nonsmoking rooms available

Nob Hill Motor Inn 1630 Pacific Ave (at Van Ness Ave) 415/775–8160, 800/343–6900 • gay-friendly • hotel • kids ok • nonsmoking • WiFi • wheelchair access • $79-169

The Phoenix Hotel 601 Eddy St (at Larkin) 415/776–1380, 800/248–9466 • gay-friendly • 1950s-style motor lodge • popular • fave of celebrity rockers • pool • kids ok • WiFi • also Bambuddha lounge & restaurant

Radisson Hotel Fisherman's Wharf 250 Beach St (at Hyde) 415/392-6700 • gay-friendly • pool • WiFi • wheelchair access

San Francisco City Center Hostel 685 Ellis St (at Larkin) 415/474-5721 • gay-friendly • shared & private rooms available • free brkfst • kids ok • nonsmoking • WiFi

BARS

The Cinch 1723 Polk St (at Clay) 415/776-4162 • 9am-2am • mostly gay men • neighborhood bar • patio • lots of pool tables & no attitude • DJ Th-Sat • drag shows Fri & Sun • WiFi • wheelchair access

Deco Lounge 510 Larkin (at Turk) 415/346-2025 • 4pm-2am, from 1pm wknds • mostly gay men • neighborhood bar • theme nights • drag shows

Edinburgh Castle 950 Geary St (at Polk) 415/885-4074 • 5pm-2am • mostly straight Scottish pub w/ single malts & authentic fish & chips • live bands

Gangway 841 Larkin St (btwn Geary & O'Farrell) 415/776-6828 • 8am-2am • mostly gay men • dive neighborhood bar

Kimo's 1351 Polk St (at Pine) 415/885-4535 • 8am-2am • gay/ straight • neighborhood bar • live bands upstairs • gay-owned

Lush Lounge 1092 Post (at Polk) 415/771-2022 • 3pm-2am, from noon wknds • popular • gay/ straight • wheelchair access

NIGHTCLUBS

Divas 1081 Post St (at Larkin) 415/474-3482 • 7am-2am • mostly gay men • neighborhood bar • dancing/DJ • multiracial • transsexuals, transvestites & their admirers • drag shows

CAFES

La Boulange de Polk 2310 Polk St (at Green St) 415/345-1107 • 7am-6:30pm, till 6pm Sun, clsd Mon • French bakery & cafe • outdoor seating • Parisian down to the attitude

Quetzal Internet Cafe 1234 Polk St (at Sutter) 415/673-4181 • 6:30am-10pm • popular • beer/ wine • live shows • videos • WiFi

RESTAURANTS

Lemongrass 2348 Polk St (at Union) 415/929-1183, 415/346-1818 • 11am-10pm, till 10:30pm Fri-Sat • Thai • beer served

Rex Cafe 2323 Polk St 415/441-2244, 415/441-9244 • from 5:30pm, dinner, also brunch 10am-3pm wknds • American • full bar

Street 2141 Polk St (btwn Broadway & Vallejo) 415/775-1055 • dinner, clsd Mon • incredible hamburgers

BOOKSTORES

Books Inc Opera Plaza 601 Van Ness Ave (at Turk) 415/776-1111 • 8:30am-9pm • independent • LGBT section • many readings

EROTICA

Glass Kandi 569 Geary St 415/931-2256 • 4pm-9pm, noon-9pm Sat, till 7pm Sun • glass dildos • women-owned

Good Vibrations 1620 Polk St (btwn Sacramento & Clay) 415/345-0400 • 11am-7pm, till 8pm Th, till 9pm Fri-Sat • clean, well-lighted sex toy store

SF—Downtown & North Beach

ACCOMMODATIONS

Adante Hotel 610 Geary St (at Jones) 415/673-9221, 888/423-0083 • gay/ straight • in Union Square/ Theater District • kids ok • nonsmoking • wheelchair access

Andrews Hotel 624 Post St (btwn Taylor & Jones) 415/563-6877, 800/926-3739 • gay-friendly • Victorian hotel • also restaurant • Italian • nonsmoking • WiFi

Argonaut Hotel 495 Jefferson St (at Hyde) 415/563-0800, 866/415-0704 • gay-friendly • boutique hotel in Fisherman's Wharf • pets ok • nonsmoking • wheelchair access • $129+

Dakota Hotel/ Hostel 606 Post St (at Taylor) 415/931-7475 • gay-friendly • near Union Square • kids ok • WiFi

Executive Hotel Vintage Court 650 Bush St (at Powell) 415/392-4666, 888/388-3932 • gay-friendly • nonsmoking • WiFi • also world-famous 5-star Masa's restaurant • French • wheelchair access

Galleria Park Hotel 191 Sutter St (at Kearny) 415/781-3060, 800/792-9639 • gay/ straight • boutique hotel • kids ok • WiFi • nonsmoking • wheelchair access

Grand Hyatt San Francisco 345 Stockton St (at Sutter) 415/398-1234, 800/233-1234 • gay-friendly • restaurant & lounge • gym

Halcyon Hotel 649 Jones St (at Post) 415/929-8033, 800/627-2396 • gay-friendly • kids/ pets ok • nonsmoking • WiFi • gay & straight-owned/ run

Handley Union Square Hotel 351 Geary St 415/781-7800 • gay-friendly • steps from Union Square • pool • WiFi • wheelchair access • $159-309

Harbor Court Hotel 165 Steuart St (btwn Howard & Mission) 415/882-1300, 866/792-6283 • gay-friendly • in the heart of the Financial District • gym • pool • pets ok • WiFi • wheelchair access

Hilton San Francisco Financial District 750 Kearny St (at Clay) 415/433-6600, 800/424-8292

Hotel Adagio 550 Geary St (at Shannon) 415/775-5000, 800/228-8830 • gay-friendly • hotel • kids ok • wheelchair access • $189+

Hotel Bijou 111 Mason St (at Eddy) 415/771-1200, 800/771-1022 • gay/ straight • nonsmoking • kids ok • WiFi • wheelchair access

The Hotel California 580 Geary St (at Jones) 415/441-2700, 800/227-4223 • gay-friendly • also popular Millennium gourmet vegetarian restaurant & bar • nonsmoking • $149-219

Hotel Carlton 1075 Sutter (at Larkin) 415/673-0242, 800/922-7586 • gay-friendly • also Saha restaurant (Arabic-fusion)

Hotel Diva 440 Geary (at Mason) 415/885-0200, 800/553-1900 • gay-friendly • hip hotel • also gym • nonsmoking • WiFi

The Hotel Frank 386 Geary St (at Mason) 415/986-2000, 800/553-1900 • gay/ straight • restored 1908 art deco masterpiece • wheelchair access

Hotel Fusion 140 Ellis St (at Powell St) 415/568-2525, 866/753-4244 • gay/ straight • nonsmoking • kids ok • WiFi • wheelchair access • $79-225

Hotel Griffon 155 Steuart St (at Mission) 415/495-2100, 800/321-2201 • gay/ straight • WiFi • also restaurant • bistro/ cont'l • wheelchair access

Hotel Mark Twain 345 Taylor St (at Ellis) 415/673-2332, 877/854-4106 • gay-friendly • also Fish & Farm restaurant • wheelchair access • $89-250

Hotel Metropolis 25 Mason St (at Eddy) 800/553-1900 • gay-friendly • near Union Square shopping • WiFi

Hotel Monaco 501 Geary St (at Taylor) 415/292-0100, 866/622-5284 • gay-friendly • nonsmoking rooms available • pets ok • also Grand Cafe restaurant (French)

Hotel Nikko San Francisco 222 Mason St (at Ellis) 415/394-1111, 866/645-5673 • gay-friendly • pool • health club & spa • nonsmoking • also restaurant • wheelchair access

Hotel Palomar 12 4th St (at Market) 415/348-1111, 866/373-4941 • gay/ straight • boutique hotel • dogs ok • WiFi

The Hotel Rex 562 Sutter St (at Powell) 415/433-4434, 800/433-4434 • gay-friendly • full bar • wheelchair access

Hotel Triton 342 Grant Ave (at Bush) 415/394-0500, 800/433-6611 • gay/ straight • designer theme rooms • kids/ pets ok • WiFi • wheelchair access

Hotel Union Square 114 Powell St (at Ellis) 800/553-1900 • gay-friendly • 1930s art deco lobby • WiFi

Hotel Vitale 8 Mission St (at Steuart) 415/278-3700, 888/890-8688 • gay-friendly • 4-star, full-service waterfront luxury hotel • rooftop spa • restaurant & bar • nonsmoking • WiFi • wheelchair access • $199-399

Hyatt Regency San Francisco 5 Embarcadero Center (at California) 415/788-1234, 800/233-1234 • gay-friendly • luxury waterfront hotel • WiFi

The Inn at Union Square 440 Post St (at Powell) 415/397-3510, 800/288-4346 • gay-friendly • steps from Union Square • nonsmoking • WiFi • $189-499

JW Marriott Hotel San Francisco 500 Post St (at Mason) 415/771-8600, 800/228-9290 • gay-friendly • hotel • kids ok • nonsmoking • WiFi • wheelchair access • $229-450

Kensington Park Hotel 450 Post St 800/553-1900 • gay-friendly • on Union Square • nonsmoking • WiFi • also Farallon Restaurant

King George Hotel 334 Mason St (at Geary) 415/781-5050, 800/288-6005 • gay/ straight • kids ok • WiFi • wheelchair access

Larkspur Hotel 524 Sutter St (at Powell) 415/421-2865, 800/919-9779 • gay-friendly • B&B-inn on Union Square • afternoon tea • wine hour • WiFi

Luz Hotel 725 Geary St (at Leavenworth) 415/928-1917 • gay/ straight • clothing-optional jacuzzi • gay-owned • $65-85

Nob Hill Hotel 835 Hyde St (btwn Bush & Sutter) 415/885-2987, 877/662-4455 • gay/ straight • European-style hotel • jacuzzi • nonsmoking • kids ok • also restaurant • wheelchair access

Petite Auberge 863 Bush St (at Taylor) 415/928-6000, 800/365-3004 • gay-friendly • B&B • kids ok • nonsmoking • $159+

Prescott Hotel 545 Post St (btwn Taylor & Mason) 415/563-0303, 866/271-3632 • gay-friendly • small luxury hotel • nonsmoking • WiFi

San Francisco Downtown Hostel 312 Mason St (at O'Farrell) 415/788-5604, 800/909-4776 • gay/ straight • hostel • shared baths • kids ok • open kitchen • WiFi • wheelchair access

Sir Francis Drake Hotel 450 Powell St (at Sutter) 415/392-7755, 800/795-7129 • gay-friendly • 1928 landmark • also restaurant & Starlight Room • WiFi

The Stratford Hotel 242 Powell St (at Geary) 415/397-7080, 877/922-5928 • gay-friendly • near Union Square • $69+

The Touchstone Hotel 480 Geary St (btwn Mason & Taylor) 415/771-1600, 800/620-5889 • gay-friendly • in Theater District • full brkfst • kids ok • wheelchair access • $79-169

Union Square Plaza Hotel 432 Geary St (at Mason) 415/776-7585, 800/841-3135 • gay-friendly • 1 block from Union Square • $69-109

Vertigo Hotel 940 Sutter St (at Leavenworth) 415/885-6800, 800/808-9675 • gay/ straight • boutique hotel • nonsmoking • WiFi • wheelchair access • $129+

Bars

Aunt Charlie's Lounge 133 Turk St (at Taylor) 415/441-2922 • 10am-midnight, till 2am Fri- Sat • mostly gay men • neighborhood bar • drag shows wknds

Bourbon & Branch 501 Jones St (at O'Farrell) 415/931-7292 • gay/ straight • in Prohibition-era speakeasy • drinks are worth the price • reservations required

Cafes

Caffe Trieste 601 Vallejo St 415/392-6739 • get a taste of the real North Beach (past & present)

Sugar Cafe 679 Sutter St (at Taylor) 415/441-5678 • 10am-2am, from 8am wknds • cafe by day, cocktails by night • food served • WiFi

Restaurants

Ar Roi 643 Post St (at Jones) 415/771-5146 • lunch & dinner, clsd Sun • Thai

The Buena Vista 2765 Hyde St (at Beach) 415/474-5044 • 9am-2am, from 8am wknds • the restaurant that introduced Irish coffee to America

Cafe Claude 7 Claude Ln (near Bush & Kearny) 415/392-3515 • 11:30am-10:30pm, from 5:30pm Sun • live music Th-Sat • as close to Paris as you can get in SF • beer/ wine

Canteen 415/928-8870 • dinner nightly, brkfst wknds

Le Colonial 20 Cosmo Pl (btwn Taylor & Jones) 415/931-3600 • dinner nightly, wknd brunch • Vietnamese • full bar

Dottie's True Blue Cafe 522 Jones St (at Geary) 415/885-2767 • 7:30am-3pm, clsd Tue • plenty veggie • great brkfst • gay-owned

Golden Era 572 O'Farrell St 415/673-3136 • 11am-9pm, clsd Tue • vegetarian/ vegan

Mario's Bohemian Cigar Store Cafe 566 Columbus Ave (at Union) 415/362-0536 • 10am-close • great foccacia sandwiches • some veggie • beer/ wine • WiFi

Millennium 580 Geary St (at Jones) 415/345-3900 • dinner only • Euro-Mediterranean • upscale vegetarian

Entertainment & Recreation

Rrazz Room 222 Mason (at Nikko Hotel) 415/394-1189, 800/380-3095 • gay/ straight • cabaret w/ world-class performers • wheelchair access

Sunday's A Drag@The Starlight Room 450 Mason St (at Powell) 415/395-8595 • Sun brunch • noon & 2:30pm drag shows

Bookstores

Book Passage 1 Ferry Bldg #42 415/835-1020 • 10am-8pm, from 8am Sat, 10am-7pm Sun-Mon • independent

City Lights Bookstore 261 Columbus Ave (at Pacific) 415/362-8193 • 10am-midnight • historic beatnik bookstore • many progressive titles • LGBT section • whole floor for poetry

Retail Shops

Dragonfly Ink 760 Market St #854 (btw 3rd & 4th St) 415/550-1445 • tattoo studio • woman-owned

Sex Clubs

Power Exchange 220 Jones St 415/487-9944 • play space open to hetero, gay, bi, trans, men & women

SF—Mission District

includes Bernal Heights

Accommodations

Elements 2516 Mission St (at 21st St) 415/647-4100, 866/327-8407 • gay/ straight • hostel w/ private or shared rooms • brkfst included • WiFi • also restaurant & cafe

The Lexington Club

Your friendly neighborhood dyke bar!

Mon - Thur 5 PM to 2 AM
Fri - Sun 3 PM to 2 AM

3464 19th Street
San Francisco
www.lexingtonclub.com

➤The Inn San Francisco 943 S Van Ness Ave (btwn 20th & 21st) 415/641-0188, 800/359-0913 • gay-friendly • Victorian mansion • hot tub • some shared baths • kitchens • fireplaces • patio • nonsmoking • WiFi

Noe's Nest B&B 1257 Guerrero St (btwn 24th & 25th Sts) 415/821-0751 • gay-friendly • WiFi • nonsmoking • kids ok

BARS

Argus Lounge 3187 Mission St, Bernal Heights (at Valencia) 415/824-1447 • 4pm-2am • gay/ straight • pool table

El Rio 3158 Mission St (at Cesar Chavez) 415/282-3325 • 5pm-close Mon-Th, from 3pm wknds • popular • gay/ straight • frequent women's events • neighborhood bar • multiracial • live shows • patio

Esta Noche 3079 16th St (at Mission) 415/861-5757 • 1pm-2am • mostly gay men • dancing/DJ • mostly Latino/a • transgender-friendly • live shows • salsa & disco in a classic Tijuana dive

➤Lexington Club 3464 19th St (btwn Mission & Valencia) 415/863-2052 • 5pm-2am, from 3pm Fri-Sun • popular • mostly women • neighborhood bar • hip young crowd • lesbian-owned

Lone Palm 3394 22nd St (at Guerrero) 415/648-0109 • 4pm-2am • gay/ straight • a bar for grown ups (we know you're out there)

Nihon 1779 Folsom St (at 14th St) 415/552-4400 • 6pm-close, clsd Sun • gay/ straight • whiskey lounge • dancing/DJ • also Japanese restaurant

Phone Booth 1398 S Van Ness Ave (at 25th) 415/648-4683 • 1pm-2am • lesbians/ gay men • neighborhood bar

Pop's Bar 2800 24th St (btwn York & Bryant) 415/401-7677 • 1pm-2am • gay/ straight • neighborhood dive bar • photobooth • wheelchair access

Stray Bar 309 Cortland Ave, Bernal Heights (at Bocana) 415/821-9263 • 4pm-2am, from 2pm wknds • gay/ straight • women's night Wed • neighborhood bar • lesbian-owned

Truck Bar 1900 Folsom St (at 15th) 415/252-0306 • 11pm-2am, from 4pm Sat, from 2pm Sun • lesbians/ gay men • neighborhood bar • food served • gay-owned

Wild Side West 424 Cortland, Bernal Heights (at Wool) 415/647-3099 • 1pm-2am • gay/ straight • neighborhood bar • patio • magic garden • wheelchair access

Zeitgeist 199 Valencia St (at Duboce) 415/255–7505 • 9am-2am • divey biker bar & beer garden • food served

NIGHTCLUBS

Cream 550 Barneveld (at space550, 2 blocks off Bayshore Blvd at Industrial) 408/792–3466 • women's dance party • multiracial • check www.creamsf.com for dates

Hard French 3158 Mission (at El Rio) 3pm-8pm 1st Sat only • lesbians/ gay men • soul dance party • food served

The Make-Out Room 3225 22nd St (at Mission) • 6pm-2am • gay/ straight • dancing/DJ • popular Stay Gold party last Wed of month

Mango 3158 Mission (at El Rio) • 3pm-8:30pm 4th Sat March-Nov • women only • dancing/DJ • multiracial • food served • cover

Mighty 119 Utah St (at 15th St) 415/762–0151 (INFO LINE), 415/626–7001 (OFFICE) • gay-friendly • dancing/DJ • call for events

Stay Gold 3225 22nd St (at Mission, at the Makeout Room) • 10:30pm last Wed only • lesbians/ gay men • dancing/DJ

Sundance Saloon 550 Barneveld Ave (at space550, 2 blocks off Bayshore Blvd at Industrial) 415/820–1403 • 5pm-10:30pm Sun (lessons at 5:30pm) & 6:30pm-10:30pm Th (lessons at 7pm) • mostly gay men • women welcome! • dancing/DJ • country/ western • gay-owned • cover

Thee Parkside 1600 17th St (at Wisconsin, Potrero Hill) 415/252–1330 • gay-friendly • live bands & events

CAFES

Dolores Park Cafe 501 Dolores St (at 18th St) 415/621–2936 • 7am-8pm • outdoor seating overlooking Dolores Park • live music Fri

Farleys 1315 18th St (at Texas St, Potrero Hill) 415/648–1545 • 6:30am-10pm, from 7:30am Sat & 8am Sun • coffeehouse • live music some nights

The Revolution Cafe 3248 22nd St (btwn Mission & Bartlett) 415/642–0474 • 9am-1am • live music

Tartine Bakery 600 Guerrero St (at 18th St) 415/487–2600 • 8am-7pm, from 9am Sun • French bakery w/ a line out the door

RESTAURANTS

Aslam's Rasoi 1037 Valencia St (at 21st) 415/695–0599 • 5pm-11pm • Indian & Pakistani

Boogaloos 3296 22nd St (at Valencia) 415/824–4088 • 8am-3pm • worth the wait

Charanga 2351 Mission St (at 20th St) 415/282–1813 • 5:30pm-close, clsd Sun-Mon • Cuban-Caribbean tapas • beer/ wine/ sangria • plenty veggie • wheelchair access • women-owned

Circolo 500 Florida St (at Mariposa) 415/553–8560 • 5pm-close, clsd Mon • Latin-Asian fusion • full bar

Delfina 3621 18th St (at Dolores) 415/552–4055 • 5:30pm-10pm • popular • excellent Tuscan cuisine • full bar • reservations required • patio (summers)

El Farolito 2779 Mission St (at 24th) 415/824–7877 • popular • 10am-3am • delicious, cheap burritos & more

Farina 3560 18th St (at Guerrero) 415/565–0360 • dinner nightly, Sun brunch • Italian

Just For You 722 22nd St (at 3rd St) 415/647–3033 • 7:30am-3pm • popular • lesbians/ gay men • Southern brkfst • some veggie • women-owned

Luna Park 694 Valencia St (at 18th) 415/553–8584 • lunch & dinner, wknd brunch

Maverick 3316 17th St (btwn Mission & Valencia) 415/863–3061 • dinner nightly, also wknd brunch • upscale American • great wine selection

Medjool 2522 Mission St (at 21st St) 415/550–9055 • 5pm-10pm, till 11pm Fri-Sat, clsd Sun • tapas • plenty veggie • also cafe, lounge & rooftop bar • wheelchair access

Moki's Sushi & Pacific Grill 615 Cortland Ave (at Moultine) 415/970–9336 • dinner nightly

Pauline's Pizza Pie 260 Valencia St (btwn 14th & Duboce) 415/552–2050 • 5pm-10pm, clsd Sun-Mon • popular • lesbians/ gay men • gourmet pizza • beer/ wine

Picaro 3120 16th St (at Valencia) 415/431–4089 • 5pm-10pm, from 9:30am wknds • Spanish tapas bar • beer/ wine • wheelchair access

Pork Store Cafe 3122 16th St (at Valencia) 415/626–5523 • 8am-4pm daily & 7pm-3am Fri-Sat • popular • American/ diner food • great brkfsts • also 1451 Haight St, 415/864-6981

Range 842 Valencia St (btwn 19th & 20th Sts) **415/282-8283** • dinner nightly • popular • California contemporary • full bar

Slow Club 2501 Mariposa (at Hampshire) **415/241-9390** • lunch Mon-Fri, dinner Mon-Sat, wknd brunch • full bar • wheelchair access

ENTERTAINMENT & RECREATION

Dolores "Beach" Church & 19th St (at the top corner of Dolores Park) • popular "beach" in Dolores Park • crowded on sunny days

Metronome Ballroom 1830 17th St (at De Haro) **415/252-9000** • gay/ straight • dance lessons • salsa to swing • dance parties wknds • call for events • cover charge

Women's Building 3543 18th St (btwn Valencia & Guerrero) **415/431-1180** • check out some of the most beautiful murals in the Mission District

BOOKSTORES

Dog Eared Books 900 Valencia St (at 20th) **415/282-1901** • 10am-10pm, till 8pm Sun • new & used • good LGBT section

Modern Times Bookstore 2919 24th St (at Alabama) **415/282-9246**

RETAIL SHOPS

Black & Blue Tattoo 381 Guerrero (at 16th St) **415/626-0770** • noon-7pm • mostly women • women-owned

Body Manipulations 3234 16th St (btwn Guerrero & Dolores) **415/621-0408** • noon-7pm, from 2pm Mon-Th • piercing (walk-in basis) • jewelry

The Scarlet Sage 1173 Valencia St (near 23rd St) **415/821-0997** • 11am-6pm • spiritual & metaphysical emporium • lesbian-owned

EROTICA

Good Vibrations 603 Valencia St (at 17th St) **415/522-5460, 800/289-8423** • 11am-7pm, till 8pm Th, till 9pm Fri-Sat • popular • clean, well-lighted sex toy store • wheelchair access

SF—Haight, Fillmore, Hayes Valley

ACCOMMODATIONS

The Chateau Tivoli 1057 Steiner St (at Golden Gate) **415/776-5462, 800/228-1647** • gay-friendly • historic San Francisco B&B • nonsmoking • WiFi

Francisco Bay Inn 1501 Lombard St (at Franklin) **415/474-3030, 800/410-7007** • gay-friendly • motel • kids ok • nonsmoking • WiFi • $75-169

Hayes Valley Inn 417 Gough St (at Hayes) **415/431-9131, 800/930-7999** • gay/ straight • European-style pension • shared baths • close to opera & symphony • nonsmoking • WiFi

Heritage Marina Hotel 2550 Van Ness Ave **415/776-7500, 866/714-6835** • gay-friendly • vintage '50s hotel • located in the Marina District • pool • $72-169

Hotel Del Sol 3100 Webster St (at Greenwich) **415/921-5520, 877/433-5765** • popular • gay/ straight • pool • nonsmoking • wheelchair access • WiFi

Hotel Drisco 2901 Pacific Ave (at Broderick) **415/346-2880, 800/634-7277** • gay-friendly • 1903 hotel in Pacific Heights • kids ok • nonsmoking • $209+

Hotel Kabuki 1625 Post St (at Laguna) **415/922-3200, 800/533-4567** • gay-friendly • in the heart of Japantown • wheelchair access • $119+

Hotel Majestic 1500 Sutter St (at Gough) **415/441-1100, 800/869-8966** • gay-friendly • one of SF's earliest grand hotels • also restaurant • full bar • kids ok • WiFi • nonsmoking • wheelchair access

Hotel Tomo 1800 Sutter St (at Buchanan) **415/921-4000, 800/738-7477** • gay-friendly • in Japantown • restaurant & bar • nonsmoking • WiFi • $99+

Inn at the Opera 333 Fulton St (at Franklin) **415/863-8400, 800/325-2708** • gay-friendly • nonsmoking • WiFi • wheelchair access

Jackson Court 2198 Jackson St (at Buchanan) **415/929-7670** • gay-friendly • 19th-c brownstone mansion • nonsmoking • kids ok • WiFi

The Laurel Inn 444 Presidio Ave (at Sacramento) **415/567-8467, 800/552-8735** • gay-friendly • hotel • in Pacific Heights • nonsmoking • kids/ pets ok • $139+

Metro Hotel 319 Divisadero St (at Haight) **415/861-5364** • gay-friendly • European-style pension • WiFi

Queen Anne Hotel 1590 Sutter St (at Octavia) **415/441-2828, 800/227-3970** • gay-friendly • wood-burning fireplaces • kids ok • nonsmoking • WiFi • gay-owned • $139-350 (mention Damron for discount)

San Francisco Fisherman's Wharf Hostel Fort Mason, Bldg 240 (at Franklin) **415/771-7277, 800/909-4776** • gay/ straight • hostel • shared baths • kids ok • cafe & kitchen • WiFi • nonsmoking • wheelchair access

Shannon-Kavanaugh Guest House 722 Steiner St (at Hayes) **415/563-2727** • gay-friendly • 1-bdrm garden apt in SF's famous "Postcard Row" • kids/ pets ok • nonsmoking • wheelchair access • gay-owned • $150-300

Stanyan Park Hotel 750 Stanyan St (at Waller) **415/751-1000** • gay-friendly • restored Victorian hotel listed on the Nat'l Register of Historic Places • kids ok • completely nonsmoking • WiFi • wheelchair access • $155-350

BARS

Marlena's 488 Hayes St (at Octavia) **415/864-6672** • noon-2am • mostly gay men • neighborhood bar • drag shows Sat • also piano bar • Cheers for drag queens (a friendly oasis in hip & het Hayes Valley) • wheelchair access

Rickshaw Stop 155 Fell St (btwn Van Ness & Franklin) **415/861-2011** • Wed-Sat only, Cockblock 2nd Sat • popular hipster bar, nightclub (live bands) & restaurant

Trax 1437 Haight St (at Masonic) **415/864-4213** • noon-2am • mostly gay men • neighborhood bar

NIGHTCLUBS

Cockblock 155 Fell St (at Rickshaw Shop) • 10pm-2am 2nd Sat • queer dance party for lezzies, the happy gays, you & your friends • multiracial

Ships in the Night 424 Haight St (at Webster, at Underground SF) **415/864-7386** • 3rd Th only • mostly women • dancing/DJ • alternative

Underground SF 424 Haight St (at Webster) **415/864-7386** • 5:30pm-2am, clsd Mon • gay/straight • dancing/DJ • alternative • theme nights • call for events • more gay Sat

CAFES

Blue Bottle Coffee Company 315 Linden St (at Gough St) **415/252-7535** • 7am-5pm, from 8am wknds • popular • organic coffee & treats from kiosk in front of artists' workshop—wonderful hidden treat

RESTAURANTS

Absinthe Brasserie & Bar 398 Hayes St (at Gough) **415/551-1590** • lunch & dinner, bar till 2am Fri-Sat, clsd Mon

Alamo Square Seafood Grill 803 Fillmore (at Grove) **415/440-2828** • dinner only

Burma Superstar 309 Clement St **415/387-2147** • lunch & dinner • Burmese food that will rock your world

Cheese Steak Shop 1716 Divisadero St (btwn Bush & Sutter) **415/346-3712** • 9am-10pm, from 11am Sun, from 10am Mon • best cheese steak outside Philly • also veggie versions

Citizen Cake 2125 Fillmore St (at California) • 8am-10pm Tue-Fri, from 10am Sat, 10am-5pm Sun, clsd Mon • popular • lesbian chef

Eliza's 2877 California (at Broderick) **415/621-4819** • lunch Mon-Wed, dinner nightly • excellent Chinese food & stylish decor

Ella's 500 Presidio Ave (at California) **415/441-5669** • brkfst & lunch Mon-Fri, popular wknd brunch

Garibaldi's 347 Presidio Ave (at Sacramento) **415/563-8841** • open for lunch weekdays & dinner nightly • Mediterranean • full bar • wheelchair access • gay-owned

Greens Fort Mason, Bldg A (near Van Ness & Bay) **415/771-6222** • lunch Tue-Sat, dinner Mon-Sat, Sun brunch • gourmet vegetarian • spectacular view of the Golden Gate Bridge

Little Star Pizza 846 Divisadero St (btwn Fulton & McAllister Sts) **415/441-1118** • 5pm-10pm, till 11pm Fri-Sat, clsd Mon • Chicago-style deep dish pizza

Memphis Minnie's BBQ 576 Haight St **415/864-7675** • 11am-10pm, till 9pm Sun, clsd Mon

Nopa 560 Divisadero St (at Hayes) **415/864-8643** • dinner 6pm-1am, bar from 5pm • urban rustic

Park Chow 1238 9th Ave (btwn Irving & Lincoln) **415/665-9912** • 11am-10pm, brunch from 10am wknds • popular • eclectic & affordable

Patxi's Chicago Pizza 511 Hayes St (at Octavia) **415/558-9991** • 11am-10pm, clsd Mon • Chicago-style deep dish pizza • also thin crust

Pluto's Fresh Food for a Hungry Universe 627 Irving St (btwn 7th & 8th Aves) **415/753-8867** • 11am-10pm • design your own sandwiches

Suppenküche 601 Hayes (at Laguna) **415/252-9289** • dinner, Sun brunch • German cuisine served at communal tables • beer/wine • gay-owned

Thep-Phanom 400 Waller St (at Fillmore) **415/431-2526** • 5:30pm-10:30pm • popular • excellent Thai food (worth the wait!) • beer/wine

BOOKSTORES

Bibliohead Bookstore 334 Gough St (at Hayes) 415/621–6772 • eclectic used books • queer section

The Booksmith 1644 Haight St 415/863–8688, 800/493–7323 (IN US) • cool independent • big-name author readings

RETAIL SHOPS

Cold Steel America 1783 Haight St 415/621–7233 • noon-8pm • piercing & tattoo studio

Flight 001 525 Hayes St (btwn Octavia & Laguna) 415/487–1001, 877/354–4481 • 11am-7pm, till 6pm Sun • way cool travel gear

Timbuk 2 Store 506 Hayes St 415/252–9860 • 11am-7pm Mon-Sat, noon-6pm Sun, messenger-style bags & backpacks

GYMS & HEALTH CLUBS

Kabuki Springs & Spa 1750 Geary Blvd (at Fillmore) 415/922–6000 • 10am-9.45pm • traditional Japanese bath w/ extensive menu of spa sevices

San Jose

INFO LINES & SERVICES

AA Gay/ Lesbian 274 E Hamilton Ave, Ste D, Campbell 408/374–8511 • 24hr helpline • check www.aasanjose.org for meetings

Billy DeFrank LGBT Community Center 938 The Alameda 408/293–3040 • 3pm-9pm, from 10am Wed, clsd Sat-Mon • wheelchair access

ACCOMMODATIONS

Hotel De Anza 233 W Santa Clara St 408/286–1000, 800/843–3700 • gay-friendly • art deco gem • nonsmoking • Italian restaurant • wheelchair access • $125-329

Moorpark Hotel 4241 Moorpark Ave 408/864–0300, 877/740–6622 • gay-friendly • hotel in heart of Silicon Valley • pool • also bar & restaurant • wheelchair access • $99-149

BARS

Brix 349 s 1st St (at San Salvadore) 408/947–1975 • 6pm-2am, from 4pm Sun • lesbians/ gay men • neighborhood bar • dancing/DJ • multiracial • transgender-friendly • karaoke • videos • wheelchair access

Mac's Club 39 Post St (btwn 1st & Market) 408/288–8221 • noon-2am • mostly men • neighborhood bar • patio

Renegades 501 W Taylor St (at Coleman Ave) 408/275–9902 • noon-2am • mostly gay men • neighborhood bar • leather • patio

NIGHTCLUBS

Afterglow 349 S 1st St (at Brix) • Th only • mostly women • dancing/DJ

Splash 65 Post St (at 1st) 916/441–6823 • 9pm-2am Th-Sat • mostly gay men • dancing/DJ • karaoke • videos • gay-owned

RESTAURANTS

Eulipia Restaurant & Bar 374 S 1st St (at San Carlos) 408/280–6161 • dinner only, clsd Mon • eclectic new American • full bar

Pasta Pomodoro 1205 The Alameda (at Race) 408/292–9929 • Italian

Vin Santo 1346 Lincoln Ave 408/920–2508 • dinner nightly, clsd Mon • Northern Italian • wine bar

ENTERTAINMENT & RECREATION

Tech Museum of Innovation 201 S Market St (at Park Ave) 408/294–8324 • 10am-5pm • IMAX Dome Theater • a must-see for digital junkies

EROTICA

Leather Masters 969 Park Ave (at Race St) 408/293–7660 • noon-8pm, clsd Sun-Mon • handmade leather clothes • rubber/ fetishwear • electrical/ medical gear, etc

Pleasures from the Heart 1565 Winchester Blvd, Campbell 408/871–1826 • 11am-10pm, 1pm-7pm Sun • intimate apparel, toys & gifts • women-owned

San Luis Obispo

INFO LINES & SERVICES

GALA/ Gay and Lesbian Alliance of the Central Coast 1060 Palm St (at Santa Rosa St) 805/541-4252 • 9am-6pm, clsd wknds

Women's Community Center 1124 Nipomo St 805/544-9313 • counseling • support • referrals

ACCOMMODATIONS

The Madonna Inn 100 Madonna Rd 805/543-3000, 800/543-9666 • gay-friendly • one-of-a-kind theme rooms • food served • pool • $168+

The Palomar Inn 1601 Shell Beach Rd, Shell Beach 888/384-4004 • gay/ straight • motel • nonsmoking • WiFi • $80-110

Sycamore Mineral Springs Resort 1215 Avila Beach Dr 805/595-7302, 800/234-5831 • gay-friendly • hot mineral spring spa • integrative retreat center • also award-winning restaurant

Bars

Fuel Dock 900 Main St, Morro Bay
805/772-8478 • gay-friendly • live music on
Sun

Gaslight Lounge 2143 Broad St
805/543-4262 • gay-friendly dive bar

Legends 899 Main St, Morro Bay
805/772-2525 • gay-friendly

The Library 723 Higuera St 805/542-0199 •
gay-friendly • dancing/DJ • wheelchair access

Cafes

Linnaea's Cafe 1110 Garden St (near Marsh)
805/541-5888 • 6:30am-11pm • plenty veggie
• WiFi • live entertainment

Outspoken Cafe 1422 Monterey St (at
California) 805/788-0885 • 7am-5pm, 8am-
4pm Sat, clsd Sun • cafe & juice bar • lesbian-
owned

West End Espresso & Tea 670 Higuera St
#A (at Nipomo) 805/543-4902, 805/544-3581
• 6am-7pm, till 9:30pm Th, till 8pm Fri-Sat •
outdoor seating

Restaurants

Big Sky Cafe 1121 Broad St (btwn Higuera
& Marsh Sts) 805/545-5401 • 7am-10pm,
8am-9pm Sun-Th • plenty veggie/ vegan

High Street deli 350 High St 805/541-4738
• 7am-7pm, 8am-3pm Sun

Novo 726 Higuera St 805/543-3986 • lunch
& dinner • great outdoor seating

Bookstores

Coalesce Bookstore 845 Main St, Morro
Bay 805/772-2880 • 10am-5:30pm, 11am-
4pm Sun • LGBT section • women-owned

Volumes of Pleasure 1016 Los Osos Valley
Rd, Los Osos 805/528-5565 • 10am-6pm,
clsd Sun-Mon • wheelchair access • lesbian-
owned

Publications

GALA News & Reviews 805/541-4252 •
news & events for Central California coast

San Rafael

see Marin County

San Ramon

see East Bay

Santa Ana

see Orange County

Santa Barbara

see also Ventura

Info Lines & Services

Pacific Pride Foundation 126 E Haley St
#A-11 805/963-3636 • 9am-5pm Mon-Fri

Accommodations

Inn of the Spanish Garden 915 Garden St
(at Carrillo) 805/564-4700, 866/564-4700 •
gay/ straight • luxury hotel • pool •
nonsmoking • kids ok • wheelchair access •
$269-519

Old Yacht Club Inn 431 Corona Del Mar Dr
805/962-1277, 800/676-1676 • gay-friendly •
only B&B on beach • full brkfst • nonsmoking
• WiFi • $99-499

The Orchid Inn at Santa Barbara 420 W
Montecito St 805/965-2333, 800/427-2156 •
gay/ straight • 1900s Queen Anne Victorian •
full brkfst • nonsmoking • WiFi • wheelchair
access • gay-owned • $149-295

Bars

Reds Wine Bar 211 Helena Ave
805/966-5906 • 2pm-10pm, till 2am Th-Sat,
clsd Mon • food served • live music • WiFi

Nightclubs

Flavor 15 W Ortega St (at Wildcat Lounge)
805/962-7970 • 9pm-2am Sun only • popular
• lesbians/ gay men • dancing/DJ

Cafes

Our Daily Bread 831 Santa Barbara St
805/966-3894 • 6am-5:30pm, 7am-4pm Sat,
clsd Sun • bakery/ cafe

Restaurants

Joe's Cafe 536 State St 805/966-4638 •
7:30am-11pm

The Natural Cafe 508 State St
805/962-9494 • 11am-9pm

Opal Restaurant & Bar 1325 State St (at
Sola St) 805/966-9676 • lunch (Mon-Sat) &
dinner nightly • full bar

Sojourner Cafe 134 E Canon Perdido (at
Santa Barbara) 805/965-7922 • 11am-11pm •
plenty veggie • beer/ wine • wheelchair access

ENTERTAINMENT & RECREATION

Santa Barbara Mission 2201 Laguna St **805/682–4713** • the "queen of the missions" • take a self-guided tour btwn 9am-4:30pm daily & find out why

BOOKSTORES

Chaucer's Books 3321 State St (at Las Positas Rd, Loreto Plaza) **805/682–6787** • 9am-9pm, till 6pm Sun • popular •

EROTICA

The Riviera Adult Superstore 4135 State St (at Hwy 154 intersection) **805/967–8282** • 10am-midnight • pride items • community resources

Santa Clara

ACCOMMODATIONS

Avatar Hotel 4200 Great America Pkwy **408/235–8900, 800/586–5691** • gay/ straight • nonsmoking • WiFi • wheelchair access • $79-139

Biltmore Hotel & Suites 2151 Laurelwood Rd (at Montague Expwy) **408/988–8411, 866/469–9845** • gay-friendly • pool • also restaurant & gym • nonsmoking • WiFi • $89-359

NIGHTCLUBS

A Tinker's Damn (TD's) 46 N Saratoga Ave (at Stevens Creek) **408/243–4595** • 3pm-2am, from 1pm wknds • mostly gay men • dancing/DJ • drag shows

Santa Cruz

INFO LINES & SERVICES

AA Gay/ Lesbian 5732 Soquel Dr, Soquel **831/475–5782 (AA#)** • call or visit www.aasantacruz.org for meetings

The Diversity Center 1117 Soquel Ave (at Cayuga) **831/425–5422** • open daily • call for events • WiFi

ACCOMMODATIONS

Chaminade Resort & Spa 1 Chaminade Ln (at Soquel Ave) **831/475–5600, 800/283–6569** • gay-friendly • pool • nonsmoking • wheelchair access • $179-399

Dream Inn 175 W Cliff Dr **831/426–4330 ,** **866/774–7735** • gay/ straight • restaurant on-site • pool & hot tub • WiFi • wheelchair access • $150+

Pleasure Point Inn 23655 E Cliff Dr **831/475–4657** • gay-friendly • upscale Mediterranean-style inn • overlooks Monterey Bay • nonsmoking • WiFi • $225-295

BARS

Mad House 529 Seabright Ave (at Murray St) **831/425–2900** • 4pm-2am, clsd Mon • gay-friendly • local bar • drag shows • gay-owned

NIGHTCLUBS

Blue Lagoon 923 Pacific Ave **831/423–7117** • 3:30pm-2am • gay/ straight • dancing/DJ • alternative • transgender-friendly • videos • live bands • wheelchair access

RESTAURANTS

Betty Burgers 505 Seabright Ave (at Murray) **831/423–8190** • 10am-10pm • retro burger joint • outdoor seating • some veggie

Cafe Limelight 1016 Cedar St (at Locust St) **831/425–7873** • lunch & dinner, clsd Mon • European • transgender-friendly • wheelchair access • gay-owned

Cilantros Mexican Restaurant 1934 Main St (in Town Center strip mall), Watsonville **831/761–2161** • lunch & dinner

Crêpe Place 1134 Soquel Ave (at Seabright, across from Rio Theater) **831/429–6994** • 11am-midnight, from 9am Sat-Sun • live music • full bar • garden patio • wheelchair access

Saturn Cafe 145 Laurel St (at Pacific) **831/429–8505** • 10am-3am • vegetarian diner • lesbian-owned

Silver Spur 2650 Soquel Dr **831/475–2725** • 6am-3pm, clsd Sun

BOOKSTORES

Bookshop Santa Cruz 1520 Pacific Ave **831/423–0900** • 9am-10pm • cafe • wheelchair access

GYMS & HEALTH CLUBS

Kiva Retreat House Spa 702 Water St (at Ocean) **831/429–1142** • noon-11pm, till midnight Fri-Sat • check for women-only and men-only hours

EROTICA

Frenchy's Cruzin Books & Video 3960 Portola Dr (at 41st Ave) **831/475–9221** • arcade, adult novelties, lingerie & DVDs

Santa Rosa

see also Sonoma County

INFO LINES & SERVICES

AA Meetings in Sonoma County
707/544–1300 (AA#), 800/224–1300 • call or
visit www.sonomacountyaa.org for meetings

CAFES

A' Roma Roasters 95 5th St (Railroad
Square) 707/576–7765 • 6am-close, from 7am
Sat-Sun • lesbians/ gay men • live music
wknds • wheelchair access • lesbian-owned

RESTAURANTS

Syrah Bistro 205 5th St (at Davis)
707/568–4002 • dinner nightly • California/
French

EROTICA

Santa Rosa Adult Books 3301 Santa Rosa
Ave (at Todd) 707/542–8248

Sausalito

see Marin County

Sebastopol

see Russian River & Sonoma County

Sonoma County

INFO LINES & SERVICES

AA Meetings in Sonoma County
707/544–1300 (AA#), 800/224–1300 • call or
check www.sonomacountyaa.org for meetings

Sonoma County Tourism Bureau
707/522–5800, 800/576–6662

ACCOMMODATIONS

An Inn 2 Remember 171 W Spain St (at
First St W), Sonoma 707/938–2909 • gay-
friendly • located in Wine Country • whirlpool
baths & fireplaces • free use of bikes •
nonsmoking • WiFi • $175-300

Beltane Ranch 11775 Sonoma Hwy (Hwy
12), Glen Ellen 707/996–6501 • gay-friendly •
1892 New Orleans-style ranch house • $140-
220

Best Western Dry Creek Inn 198 Dry Creek
Rd, Healdsburg 707/433–0300, 800/222–5784
• gay/ straight • near wineries • pool, gym
steam & sauna • pets ok • WiFi

Camellia Inn 211 North St, Healdsburg
707/433–8182, 800/727–8182 • gay-friendly •
Italianate Victorian • full brkfst • pool •
nonsmoking • WiFi

The Gaige House 13540 Arnold Dr, Glen
Ellen 707/935–0237, 800/935–0237 • gay-
friendly • boutique hotel in the Wine Country
• pool • WiFi • $225-695

Grape Leaf Inn 539 Johnson St, Healdsburg
707/433–8140, 866/433–8140 • gay-friendly •
Queen Anne Victorian • full brkfst • WiFi •
$200-395

Hyatt Vineyard Creek Hotel 170 Railroad
St (at Third St), Santa Rosa 707/284–1234 •
gay-friendly • resort • pool • kids/ pets ok •
WiFi • seafood restaurant • wheelchair access
• $149-249

Les Petites Maisons 1190 E Napa St (at 8th
St E), Sonoma 707/933–0340, 800/291–8962
• gay-friendly • vacation cottages in a quiet,
private & romantic setting near Sonoma Plaza
• kids/pets ok • WiFi • $150-295

Madrona Manor 707/433–4231,
800/258–4003 • gay-friendly • full brkfst •
pool • nonsmoking • some rooms ok for kids
• also restaurant • wheelchair access

Magliulo's Rose Garden Inn 681 Broadway
(at Andrieux), Sonoma 707/996–1031 • gay-
friendly • WiFi • wheelchair access • $135-175

Sonoma Chalet 18935 5th St W, Sonoma
707/938–3129, 800/938–3129 • gay-friendly •
B&B inn & cottages • hot tub • $125-225

CAFES

Coffee Catz 6761 Sebastopol Ave #300 (in
Gravenstein Station), Sebastopol
707/829–6600 • 7am-6pm, till 10pm Wed
(open mic), till 10pm Fri & Sat (live bands) •
garden • WiFi

Screamin' Mimi's 6902 Sebastopol Ave
(intersection of Hwy 12 & 116), Sebastopol
707/823–5902 • espresso drinks &
homemade ice cream

Sonoma's Best 1190 E Napa St (at 8th St E),
Sonoma 707/996–7600 • 7am-6pm, 8am-
5pm Sun, local products—cheese, wine,
chocolate, olive oils and deli—all under one
roof

RESTAURANTS

Estate 400 W Spain St, Sonoma
707/933–3663 • lunch & dinner, Sun brunch,
clsd Mon • Italian

Fig Cafe & Wine Bar 13690 Arnold Dr, Glen
Ellen 707/938–2130 • dinner nightly, Sun
brunch

Mom's Apple Pie 4550 Gravenstein Hwy N,
Sebastopol 707/823–8330 • pie worth
stopping for on your way to & from Russian
River!

Singletree Inn 165 Healdsburg Ave, Healdsburg **707/433-8263** • 7am-3pm • good brkfsts • famous BBQ sandwiches (including tofu) • some veggie • local wines • outdoor seating • lesbian-owned

Slice of Life 6970 McKinley St, Sebastopol **707/829-6627** • 11am-9pm, from 9am Sat-Sun, clsd Mon • vegan & vegetarian

ENTERTAINMENT & RECREATION

Out In The Vineyard **707/495-9732** • tours of the wine country • gay-owned

River's Edge Kayak & Canoe Company **707/433-7247** • river excursions • lesbian-owned

RETAIL SHOPS

Grower's Collective Tasting Room **707/996-1364** • noon-5:30pm, clsd Tue-Th, open wknds only in winter

Milk & Honey 123 N Main St, Sebastopol **707/824-1155** • 11am-7pm • transgender-friendly • goddess- & woman-oriented crafts • cafe

Springville

ACCOMMODATIONS

Great Energy PO Box 473, 93265 **559/539-2382** • lesbians/gay men • retreat in foothills of Sierra Nevada mtns • pool • hiking • kids ok • woman-owned • $85-125

Stockton

see also Modesto

NIGHTCLUBS

Paradise Club 10100 N Lower Sacramento Rd (near Grider) **209/477-4724** • 6pm-2am, from 3pm Sun • lesbians/gay men • dancing/DJ • live shows • videos • young crowd

EROTICA

Suzie's Adult Superstores 3126 E Hammer Ln **209/952-6900** • 24hrs

Sunnyvale

see also San Jose

ACCOMMODATIONS

Wild Palms Hotel 910 E Fremont Ave (at Wolfe Ave) **408/738-0500, 800/538-1600** • gay-friendly • pool • hot tub • kids ok • WiFi • wheelchair access • $89+

Sutter Creek

ACCOMMODATIONS

The Foxes Inn of Sutter Creek 77 Main St (at Keys St) **209/267-5882, 800/987-3344** • gay-friendly • full brkfst • close to Shenandoah Valley wine region • nonsmoking • WiFi • gay-owned • $160-325

Temecula

NIGHTCLUBS

Club Escape 27497 Ynez Rd (at Aloha J's) **951/506-9889** • 9pm Wed only • lesbians/gay men • dancing/DJ

Tiburon

see Marin County

Twentynine Palms

see Joshua Tree Nat'l Park

Ukiah

BARS

Perkins St Lounge 228 E Perkins St **707/462-0327** • 3pm-2am • gay-friendly • dancing/DJ • live shows • karaoke

Upland

NIGHTCLUBS

Oasis 1386 E Foothill Blvd #H (at Grove) **909/920-9590** • 6pm-2am Wed-Sat, from 8pm Sun • mostly gay men • dinner served Wed-Sun • dancing/DJ • drag shows • wheelchair access

EROTICA

Sensations Love Boutique 1656 W Foothill Blvd (at Mountain) **909/985-1654**

Vacaville

INFO LINES & SERVICES

Solano Pride Center 1125 Missouri St #203-D, Fairfield **707/398-3463** • call for meeting times

Vallejo

includes Benicia

BARS

Town House Cocktail Lounge 401-A Georgia St (at Marin) **707/553-9109** • 1pm-midnight, from 10am Sat-Sun • gay-friendly • neighborhood bar • gay-owned

Bookstores

Bookshop Benicia 856 Southampton Rd, Benicia 707/747–5155 • 10am-7pm, till 6pm wknds • wheelchair access

Ventura

see also Santa Barbara

Info Lines & Services

AA Gay/ Lesbian 805/389–1444 (AA#), 800/990–7750

Ventura County Rainbow Alliance 921 E Main 805/653–5711 • 9am-8pm • LGBT center

Bars

Paddy McDermott's 2 W Main St (at Ventura) 805/652–1071 • 2pm-2am • lesbians/ gay men • dancing/DJ • food served • live shows • karaoke • beer busts

Erotica

Three Star Books 359 E Main St 805/653–9068 • 24hrs

Victorville

Bars

Ricky's 13728 Hesperia Rd #12 760/951–5400 • 6pm-2am, clsd Mon • lesbians/ gay men, more women on Th • dancing/DJ • food served • karaoke

Westside 15 16868 Stoddard Wells Rd (off I-15) 760/243–9600 • 5pm-2am, from 4pm Sat, from 3pm Sun • lesbians/ gay men • neighborhood bar • karaoke

Walnut Creek

see East Bay

Yosemite Nat'l Park

Accommodations

The Ahwahnee Hotel Yosemite Valley Floor 559/252–4848, 866/875–8456 (RESERVATIONS) • gay-friendly • pool • non-smoking • also restaurant

Highland House B&B 3125 Wild Dove Ln (at Jerseydale Rd), Mariposa 209/966–3737 • gay-friendly • B&B near Yosemite & Sierra Nat'l Forest • kids ok • $95-135

The Homestead 41110 Rd 600, Ahwahnee 559/683–0495, 800/483–0495 • gay-friendly • cottages, suite & 2-bdrm house nestled under the oaks on 160 acres • close to restaurants, golf, hiking & biking • kitchens • fireplaces • nonsmoking • WiFi • kids ok • $119-374

June Lake Villager 2640 Hwy 158 (2.5 miles W of Hwy 395), June Lake 760/648–7712, 800/655–6545 • gay-friendly • 20 minutes from Yosemite • jacuzzi • nonsmoking • kids/ pets ok • women-owned • $65-300

Queen's Inn by the River 41139 Hwy 41, Oakhurst 559/683–4354 • gay/ straight • private patios & decks • some fireplaces • garden w/ river view • nonsmoking • WiFi • wheelchair access • lesbian-owned • $150-179

Rivendale Ranch 209/962–7425 • women only • nonsmoking • also RV hookups • women-owned • $95-110 ($25 RV)

Tenaya Lodge at Yosemite 1122 Hwy 41, Fish Camp 559/683–6555, 888/514–2167 • gay-friendly • resort w/ spa services • restaurant • pets ok • pool

The Yosemite Bug Rustic Mountain Resort 6979 Hwy 140, Midpines 209/966–6666, 866/826–7108 • gay-friendly • hostel w/ dorms, cabins, private rooms & tents • some shared baths • kids ok • nonsmoking • WiFi • wheelchair access • $25-155

Yosemite View Lodge 11136 Hwy 140, El Portal 209/379–2681, 888/742–4371 • gay-friendly • 3 pools • lounge & 2 restaurants • wheelchair access

Yosemite's Apple Blossom Inn B&B 559/642–2001, 888/687–4281 • gay-friendly • B&B • 20 minutes from south entrance of Yosemite Nat'l Park • hot tub • kids/ pets ok nonsmoking • wheelchair access • $110-240

COLORADO

Statewide

Publications

➤ **Out Front Colorado** 303/778–7900 • statewide LGBT newspaper

Aspen

Accommodations

Aspen Mountain Lodge 311 W Main St 970/925–7650, 800/362–7736 • gay-friendly • full brkfst • après-ski wine & cheese • kids/ pets ok • hot tub • pool • nonsmoking • $125-329

Hotel Aspen 110 W Main St 970/925–3441, 800/527–7369 • gay-friendly • mountain brkfst • après-ski wine & cheese • hot tub • pool • nonsmoking • kids/ pets ok • $119+

Hotel Lenado 200 S Aspen St 970/925–6246, 800/321–3457 • gay-friendly • full brkfst • hot tub • full bar • $145-345

St Moritz Lodge 334 W Hyman Ave
970/925–3220, 800/817–2069 • gay-friendly •
pool • hot tub/stream • nonsmoking • WiFi •
gay-owned • $22-299

RESTAURANTS

Jimmy's 205 S Mill St (at Hopkins)
970/925–6020 • 5:30pm-11pm, Sun brunch •
also bar from 4pm • patio

Syzygy 308 E. Hopkins Ave 970/925–3700 •
seasonal • 6pm-10pm, bar till 2am • some
veggie • live jazz • wheelchair access

BOOKSTORES

Explore Booksellers & Bistro 221 E Main
St (at Aspen) 970/925–5336, 800/562–7323 •
10am-10pm • also gourmet vegetarian
restaurant • WiFi • wheelchair access

Beaver Creek

ACCOMMODATIONS

Beaver Creek Lodge 26 Avondale Ln (at
Village Rd) 970/845–9800, 800/525–7280 •
gay-friendly • nonsmoking • also restaurant w/
mtn views & fire pits • pool • WiFi •
wheelchair access • $170-899

Boulder

INFO LINES & SERVICES

Out Boulder 2132 14th St (at Pine) 303/499-
5777 • LGBT resource center

ACCOMMODATIONS

The Briar Rose B&B 2151 Arapahoe Ave
(at 22nd St) 303/442–3007, 888/786–8440 •
gay-friendly • full organic brkfst • nonsmoking
• WiFi • $139-204

CAFES

Walnut Cafe 3073 Walnut St (at 30th)
303/447–2315 • 7am-3pm • popular • plenty
veggie • patio • wheelchair access • women-
owned

ENTERTAINMENT & RECREATION

Boulder Area Bicycle Adventures
303/494–7062 • annual LGBT ride in June •
lesbian-owned

BOOKSTORES

Left Hand Books 1200 Pearl St #10 (E of
Broadway) 303/443–8252 • 10am-9pm, noon-
6pm Sun

RETAIL SHOPS

Enchanted Ink 1200 Pearl St #35 (at
Broadway) 303/440–6611 • tattoos, piercing,
henna • RN-owned • lesbian-owned

Breckenridge

ACCOMMODATIONS

Allaire Timbers Inn 9511 Hwy 9, S Main St
970/453–7530, 800/624–4904 • gay-friendly •
full brkfst • hot tub • nonsmoking • WiFi •
wheelchair access • $129-295

Valdoro Mountain Lodge 500 Village Rd
970/453–4880, 800/436–6780 • gay/ straight •
condos w/ access to pool, massage facilities &
outdoor hot tub • nonsmoking • wheelchair
access

Colorado Springs

(includes Manitou Springs)

INFO LINES & SERVICES

Colorado Springs Pride Center
719/471–4429 • noon-5pm • call for events •
WiFi

ACCOMMODATIONS

Blue Skies Inn B&B 402 Manitou Ave (at
Mayfair), Manitou Springs 719/685–3899,
800/398–7949 • gay/ straight • Gothic Revival
built by artist/ innkeeper • full brkfst • gazebo
hot tub • WiFi • kids ok • nonsmoking •
wheelchair access • $145-240

Old Town Guesthouse 115 S 26th St
719/632–9194, 888/375–4210 • gay-friendly •
full brkfst • nonsmoking • WiFi • wheelchair
access • $115-215

Pikes Peak Paradise 236 Pinecrest Rd,
Woodland Park 719/687–6656, 800/728–8282
• gay-friendly • mansion w/ view of Pikes Peak
• surrounded by nat'l forest • full brkfst • hot
tub • fireplaces • nonsmoking • kids ok • WiFi
• gay-owned • $180-240

Two Sisters Inn—A B&B 10 Otoe Pl,
Manitou Springs 719/685–9684,
800/274–7466 • gay-friendly • kids over 10
years ok • full brkfst • women-owned • $79-
155

BARS

Club Q 3430 N Academy Blvd (at N Carefree)
719/570–1429 • 6pm-2am, till 4am Sat, clsd
Mon-Tue • mostly men • ladies night Sun •
neighborhood bar • dancing/DJ • karaoke •
live entertainment • strippers • food served •
18+ • wheelchair access • gay-owned

CAFES

Spice of Life an Ingredients Emporium
727 Manitou Ave, Manitou Springs
719/685–5284 • 7am-6pm • WiFi

Restaurants

Dale Street Bistro Cafe 115 E Dale (at Nevada) **719/578–9898** • lunch & dinner, brunch wknds • some veggie • full bar

Erotica

First Amendment Adult Bookstore 220 E Fillmore St (at Nevada) **719/630–7676**

Denver

Info Lines & Services

Gay/ Lesbian AA 303/322–4440

The GLBT Center of Colorado (The Center) 1301 E Colfax **303/733–7743** • 10am-8pm Mon-Fri, from noon Sat • extensive resources & support groups • wheelchair access

Accommodations

The Brown Palace 321 17th St (at N Broadway) **303/297–3111, 800/321–2599** • gay-friendly • sun in every room • WiFi • restaurant & spa • $149+

Capitol Hill Mansion B&B 1207 Pennsylvania St (at 12th) **303/839–5221, 800/839–9329** • gay-friendly • B&B • full brkfst • hot tub • nonsmoking • kids ok • WiFi • $114-219

Castle Marne 1572 Race St **303/331–0621, 800/926–2763** • gay-friendly • 1889 mansion on Nat'l Register of Historic Places • some jacuzzis • WiFi • $125-270

The Curtis 1405 Curtis St **303/571–0300, 800/525–6651** • gay-friendly • hip hotel • WiFi • also restaurant

The Gregory Inn, LoDo 2500 Arapahoe St (at 25th St) **303/295–6570, 800/925–6570** • gay-friendly • full brkfst • jacuzzis • fireplaces • nonsmoking • WiFi • straight & gay-owned • $139-219

Hotel Monaco 1717 Champa St (at 17th) **303/296–1717, 800/990–1303** • gay-friendly • gym • spa • nonsmoking • WiFi • also Italian restaurant • pets ok • $125+

Lumber Baron Inn 2555 W 37th Ave (at Bryant) **303/477–8205** • gay-friendly • Victorian mansion furnished w/ antiques • full brkfst • hot tub • WiFi • $149+

The Oxford Hotel 1600 17th St **303/628–5400, 800/228–5838** • gay-friendly • hotel • health club & spa • also 2 restaurants, art deco lounge • WiFi • $169-369

Bars

Aqua Lounge 1417 Krameria (btwn 14th & Colfax) **720/287–0584** • 4pm-2am • lesbians/ gay men • piano bar • WiFi

Barker Lounge 255 S Broadway (at Byers Pl) **303/778–0545** • noon-2am • mostly gay men • neighborhood bar • patio w/ bar • dogs welcome

The Beauty Bar 720/542–8024 • gay/ straight • dancing/DJ • shows

Bender's Tavern 314 E 13th Ave (at Grant) **303/861–7070** • 4pm-2am, from 7pm Mon-Wed, clsd Sun • gay-friendly • food served • live bands • karaoke

BJ's Carousel 1380 S Broadway St (at Arkansas) **303/777–9880** • 4pm-2am, from 10am Sat-Mon • popular • lesbians/ gay men • neighborhood bar • karaoke • drag shows • also restaurant, dinner Wed-Sun • transgender-friendly • wheelchair access • gay-owned

Broadways 1027 Broadway (at 11th Ave) **303/623–0700** • 2pm-2am, from noon Sat-Sun • lesbians/gay men • neighborhood bar • cool mix of folk • karaoke • WiFi

Charlie's 900 E Colfax Ave (at Emerson) **303/839–8890** • 11am-2am • popular • mostly gay men • 2 clubs • dancing/DJ • country/ western • wheelchair access • also restaurant

The Compound 145 Broadway (at 2nd Ave) **303/722–7977** • 7am-2am • popular • mostly gay men • neighborhood bar • dancing/DJ Fri-Sat • alternative

Dazzle 930 Lincoln St (btwn 9th & 10th Aves) **303/839–5100** • from 4pm, Sun-Th, from 11am Fri, also Sun brunch (9:30am-1pm) • gay-friendly • jazz club & restaurant • live music

Decatur St Bar 800 Decatur St **303/825–4521** • mostly women • neighborhood bar • live music • food served

Denver Eagle 3600 Blake St (at 36th) **303/291–0250** • 4pm-2am, from 2pm wknds, clsd Mon • mostly men • levi/ leather/ cruise bar • bears • never a cover charge • wheelchair access • gay-owned

El Chapultepec 1962 Market St (at 20th) **303/295–9126** • 9am-2am • popular • gay-friendly • live jazz & blues since 1951 • 1-drink minimum per set • cover

El Potrero 320 S Birch St (at Leetsdale Dr), Glendale **303/388–8889** • gay/ straight • Mexican restaurant early • Latino gay bar late (Wed, Sat-Sun)

JR's Bar 777 E 17th Ave (at Clarkson) **303/831-0459** • 3pm-2am • mostly gay men • neighborhood bar • karaoke • drag shows • videos • gay-owned

Lannie's Clocktower Cabaret 16th St Mall at Arapahoe (in historic D&F Tower) **303/293-0075** • gay-friendly • upscale cabaret w/ variety of acts weekly including drag & burlesque

R&R Denver 4958 E Colfax Ave (at Elm St) **303/320-9337** • 3pm-2am, from 1pm Fri, from 11am wknds • lesbians/ gay men • neighborhood bar

Rock Bar 3015 E Colfax (at Milwaukee) **303/322-4444** • 5pm-2am • gay/ straight • dive bar • theme nights

tHERe Coffee Bar & Lounge 1526 E Colfax (btwn Humboldt & Franklin) **303/830-8437** • 10am-11pm, 10am-8pm Sun • mostly women • transgender-friendly • live music • also cafe • WiFi • wheelchair access • lesbian-owned

Denver

WHERE THE GIRLS ARE:

Many lesbians reside in the Capitol Hill area, near the gay and mixed bars, but hang out in cafes and women's bars scattered around the city.

ENTERTAINMENT:

Denver Women's Chorus 303/274-4177.

LGBT PRIDE:

June. 303/733-7743, web: www.denverpridefest.org.

ANNUAL EVENTS:

July- 2nd weekend, Rocky Mountain Regional Rodeo (gay rodeo), web: cgra.us.

August/September - AIDS Walk, web: coloradoaidsproject.org.

September/October- Great American Beer Festival, web: www.gabf.org.

CITY INFO:

303/892-1112, web: www.denver.org.

BEST VIEW:

Lookout Mountain (at night especially) or from the top of the Capitol rotunda.

WEATHER:

Summer temperatures average in the 90ºs and winter ones in the 40ºs. The sun shines an average of 300 days a year with humidity in the single digits.

ATTRACTIONS:

16th Street Mall (pedestrian mall in Lower Downtown or LoDo).

Black American West Museum 720/242-7428, web: www.black-americanwestmuseum.com.

Cherry Creek Shopping Center 303/388-3900, web: www.shopcherrycreek.com.

Denver Art Museum 720/865-5000, web: denverartmuseum.org.

Denver Botanic Gardens 720/865-3500, web: www.botanicgardens.org.

Denver Center for the Performing Arts 303/893-4100, web: www.denvercenter.org.

Denver Zoo 303/376-4800, web: www.denverzoo.org.

Downtown Aquarium 303/561-4450.

Elitch Gardens 303/595-4386, web: www.elitchgardens.com.

LoDo (Lower Downtown).

Molly Brown House 303/832-4092, web: www.mollybrown.org.

TRANSIT:

Yellow Cab 303/777-7777, web: www.yellowtrans.com.

Metro Taxi 303/333-3333, web: www.metrotaxidenver.com.

Super Shuttle 303/370-1300 or 800/258-3826, web: www.super-shuttledenver.com.

RTD 303/299-6000, web: www.rtd-denver.com.

X Bar 629 E Colfax Ave **303/832-2687** • 2pm-2am, from 10am wknds • lesbians/ gay men • dancing/DJ • brunch wknds

NIGHTCLUBS

Beta Nightclub 1909 Blake St (btwn 19th & 20th) **303/383-1909** • gay/ straight • more gay Th & Sat • cover charge

First Friday/ Babes Around Denver 3500 Walnut St (at 35th, at Tracks) **303/475-4620** • 6pm-2am, 1st Fri only • mostly women • dancing/DJ

Hip Chicks Out • mostly women • roving monthly • check www.hipchicksout.com

La Rumba 99 W 9th Ave (at Broadway) **303/572-8006** • gay-friendly • salsa dancing & lessons Th & Sat • more gay for Lipgloss Fri (Brit-pop & indie music) • cover

Tracks 3500 Walnut St (at 36th) **303/863-7326** • 9pm-2am, clsd Sun-Wed • gay/ straight • women's night 1st Fri • dancing/DJ • drag shows

CAFES

City, O City 206 E 13th Ave (at Sherman) **303/831-6443** • 7am-2am, from 8am wknds, vegetarian/ vegan • also bar

Common Grounds 3484 W 32nd Ave (Lowell) **303/458-5248** • 6:30am-10pm, till 11pm Fri-Sat • WiFi • also 1601 17th St, 303/296-9248 • WiFi

Dazbog 1201 E 9th Ave (at Downing) **303/837-1275** • 6am-10pm, from 7am Sun • popular • gay/ straight • outdoor seating • heated patio • WiFi

Geez Louise 4924 E Colfax Ave (E of Colorado Blvd) **303/322-3833** • 6am-4pm, from 7am wknds, till 2pm Mon • food served • gay-owned

The Market at Larimer Square 1445 Larimer Sq (btwn 14th & 15th) **303/534-5140** • 6am-11pm, till midnight Fri-Sat, till 10pm Sun • food

Paris on the Platte 1553 Platte St (at 15th) **303/455-2451** • 7am-1am, till 3am Fri-Sat, from 8am wknds • soups, salads, sandwiches • WiFi • popular after-hours

RESTAURANTS

Annie's Cafe & Bar 3100 E Colfax (at St Paul) **303/355-8197** • 7am-10pm, from 8am Sat • popular • diner • popular • some veggie

The Avenue Grill 630 E 17th Ave (at Washington) **303/861-2820** • 11am-11pm, till midnight Fri-Sat, till 10pm Sun

Banzai Sushi 6655 Leetsdale Dr (E of Colorado Blvd) **303/329-3366** • lunch Mon-Fri, dinner nightly • sushi

Barracuda's 1076 Ogden St (at E 11th) **303/860-8353** • 10am-2am • also bar

Benny's Restaurante y Tequila Bar 301 E 7th Ave (at Grant St) **303/894-0788** • lunch & dinner • nonsmoking • patio

Devil's Food 1020 S Gaylord St (at E Tennessee) **303/733-7448** • 7am-10pm, till 3pm wknds • yummy desserts

Duo 2413 W 32nd Ave (at Zuni) **303/477-4141** • dinner nightly, wknd brunch • hip, organic, creative American • full bar

Fruition 1313 E 6th Ave **303/831-1962** • 5pm-10pm, till 8pm Sun • contemporary French • seasonal menu

Hamburger Mary's/ Club M 700 E 17th Ave (at Washington St, across from JR's bar) **303/832-1333** • 11am-2am, from 10am Sun • popular • gay/ straight • also Club M • dancing/DJ

Il Vicino 550 Broadway **303/861-0801** • 11am-10pm • pizza • micro-brewed beer

Las Margaritas Uptown 1035 E 17th Ave (at Downing) **303/830-2199** • 11am-1am • popular • Mexican • some veggie • also bar • outdoor dining • gay-owned

Pete's Kitchen 1962 E Colfax Ave **303/321-3139** • 24hrs • diner • very popular after bars close

Racine's 650 Sherman St (at 6th Ave) **303/595-0418** • brkfst, lunch, dinner, late night & Sun brunch • some veggie • full bar

Sexy Pizza 1018 E 11th Ave **303/830-8111**

Steuben's 523 E 17th Ave **303/830-1001** • 11am-11pm, till midnight Fri, 10am-midnight Sat, till 11pm Sun • American comfort food served up hip • patio • full bar

Sunny Gardens 6460 E Yale Avenue **303/691-8830** • Chinese • plenty veggie/ vegan

Thai Pot Cafe 1550 S Colorado Blvd (at E Florida) **303/639-6200** • lunch & dinner • Thai

Tom's Home Cookin' **303/388-8035** • 11am-3pm, clsd Sat-Sun • Southern comfort food • wheelchair access • gay-owned

Vesta Dipping Grill 1822 Blake St (near 18th St) **303/296-1970** • 5pm-10pm Sun-Th, till 11pm Fri-Sat • upscale

WaterCourse Foods 837 E 17th Ave (at Clarkson) **303/832-7313** • 7am-9pm, till 10pm Fri-Sat • vegetarian/ vegan

Wazee Supper Club 1600 15th St (at Wazee) **303/623–9518, 303/825–3199 (PIZZA DELIVERY)** • 11am-2am, noon-midnight Sun • classic comfort food • full bar • wheelchair access

ENTERTAINMENT & RECREATION

Denver Women's Chorus 303/325–3959, 866/862–9382

Mercury Cafe 2199 California St **303/294–9281** • 5:30pm-close • swing, tango, salsa dancing • live shows • also restaurant • dinner only Tue-Sun, wknd brunch • nonsmoking

Rocky Mountain Rainbeaus 303/863–7739 • all-inclusive, all-levels, high-energy square dance club

Rocky Mountain Rollergirls 720/984–3132 • Denver's female roller derby league • visit www.rockymountainrollergirls.com for events

BOOKSTORES

Tattered Cover Book Store 2526 Colfax Ave (at Elizabeth St) **303/322–7727, 800/833–9327** • 9am-9pm, 10am-6pm Sun • independent • cafe • also 1628 16th St, 303/436–1070 • wheelchair access

RETAIL SHOPS

Bound By Design 1332 E Colfax Ave (at Humboldt) **303/830–7272, 303/832–TAT2** • 11am-11pm, noon-10pm Sun • piercing & tattoos

Heaven Sent Me 116 S Broadway (btwn Alameda & Virginia) **303/733–9000** • 11am-7pm • pride items, clothing, gifts • wheelchair access

Rockmount Ranch Wear 1626 Wazee St **303/629–7777, 800/776–2566** • 8am-6pm, from 11am wknds • makers of the shirts worn in *Brokeback Mountain*

PUBLICATIONS

Gayzette 720/435–8914 • LGBT monthly publication

➤ **Out Front Colorado** 303/778–7900 • statewide bi-weekly LGBT newspaper • since 1976

GYMS & HEALTH CLUBS

Pura Vida Fitness & Spa 2955 E 1st Ave #200 **303/321–7872**

EROTICA

The Crypt on Broadway 8 Broadway (at Ellsworth) **303/733–3112** • 11am-11pm, till 7pm Sun • leather, clubwear & more

Smitten Kitten 70 Broadway **303/962–9520** • 11am-9pm, noon-7pm Sun • transgender-friendly • lesbian-owned • something for everyone!

Durango

ACCOMMODATIONS

Leland House B&B 721 E 2nd Ave **970/385–1920, 800/664–1920** • gay-friendly • full brkfst • nonsmoking • WiFi • wheelchair access • $119-359

Mesa Verde Far View Lodge 1 Navajo Hill, Mesa Verde National Park **602/331–5210, 800/449–2288** • gay-friendly • hotel • camping • RV hookups • inside nat'l park at 8250' elevation • views of 4 states • full brkfst • nonsmoking • WiFi • $120-160

Rio Grande Southern B&B 101 S 5th St (at Hwy 145), Dolores **970/882–2125** • gay-friendly • full brkfst • WiFi • kids/ pets ok • $55-120

Rochester Hotel 721 E 2nd Ave **970/385–1920, 800/664–1920** • gay-friendly • popular • newly renovated 1892 house decorated in Old West motif • full brkfst • nonsmoking • kids/ pets ok • wheelchair access • $119-259

Estes Park

ACCOMMODATIONS

Mountain Sage Inn 553 W Elkhorn Ave **970/586–2833, 800/552–2833** • gay-friendly • nonsmoking • $59-129

Stanley Hotel 333 Wonderview Ave **800/976–1377, 970/577–4000** • gay-friendly • pool • restaurant • WiFi • the inspiration for Stephen King's *The Shining*

Fort Collins

INFO LINES & SERVICES

The Lambda Community Center 212 South Mason St **970/221–3247** • 9am-7pm, till 5pm Fri, or by appt

Women's Resource Center 424 Pine St #201 **970/484–1902** • 9am-5pm Mon-Fri • "helping women lead healthy lives"

ACCOMMODATIONS

Archer's Poudre River Resort 33021 Poudre Canyon Hwy, Bellvue **970/881–2139, 888/822–0588** • gay-friendly • cabins, tents, RV hookups • lesbian-owned • $39-430

Bars

Choice City Shots 124 LaPorte Ave (at College) **970/221-4333** • 6:30pm-midnight, till 1:30am Fri-Sat • lesbians/gay men • neighborhood bar • karaoke Th • wheelchair access • lesbian- & gay-owned

Grand Junction

Restaurants

Leon's Taqueria 505 30th Rd **970/242-1388** • 11am-9pm

Hotchkiss

Accommodations

Leroux Creek Inn & Vineyards 12388 3100 Rd **970/872-4746** • gay-friendly • Southwestern-style adobe on 54 acres • full brkfst • $175-195

Restaurants

North Fork Valley Restaurant & Thirsty Parrot Pub 140 W Bridge St **970/872-4215** • 11am-8pm • American/Mexican

Pueblo

Bars

Pirate's Cove 105 Central Plaza (off 1st & Union) **719/543-2683** • 4pm-2am, 2pm-midnight Sun, clsd Mon • lesbians/gay men • neighborhood bar • wheelchair access

Stratton

Accommodations

Claremont Inn 800 Claremont St (off exit 419, I-70) **719/348-5125, 888/291-8910** • gay/straight • 2 hours from Denver • full brkfst • commitment ceremonies • WiFi • gay-owned • $149-279

Vail

Restaurants

Larkspur Restaurant & Market 458 Vail Valley Dr (in the Golden Peak Lodge) **970/754-8050** • lunch & dinner, seasonal hours • fine dining • also bar • patio • ski-in/out • wheelchair access

Sweet Basil 193 E Gore Creek Dr **970/476-0125** • lunch & dinner • some veggie • full bar • wheelchair access

Westcliffe

Restaurants

Westcliffe Wine Mine 109 N 3rd St (at Main St) **719/783-2490** • call for hours • older crowd • wheelchair access • lesbian-owned

CONNECTICUT

Statewide

Publications

Metroline **860/231-8334** • regional newspaper & entertainment guide • covers CT, RI & MA

Bethel

Cafes

Molten Java 102 Greenwood Ave **203/739-0313** • 6am-9pm, till 10pm Fri-Sat, 8am-8pm Sat-Sun • live entertainment • lesbian-owned

Restaurants

Bethel Pizza House 206 Greenwood Ave **203/748-1427** • 11am-11pm, till midnight Fri-Sat

Bridgeport

Restaurants

Bloodroot Restaurant & Bookstore 85 Ferris St (at Harbor Ave) **203/576-9168** • lunch Tue & Th-Sat, dinner Tue-Sat, brunch only Sun, clsd Mon • feminist vegetarian • patio • wheelchair access • women-owned

Erotica

Romantix Adult Superstore 410 North Ave **203/332-7129**

Bristol

Erotica

Amazing Superstore 167 Farmington Ave **860/582-9000**

Danbury

Accommodations

Maron Hotel & Suites 42 Lake Ave Extension (off I-84) **203/791-2200, 866/811-2582** • gay-friendly • kids/pets ok • WiFi • $99-199 • wheelchair access

Bars

Triangles Cafe 66 Sugar Hollow Rd, Rte 7 203/798–6996 • 5pm-1am, till 2am Fri-Sat • popular • lesbians/ gay men • dancing/DJ • live shows • karaoke • patio • gay-owned

Restaurants

Goulash Place 42 Highland Ave (at Davies) 203/744–1971 • lunch & dinner, clsd Mon • Hungarian • beer/ wine

Sesame Seed 68 W Wooster St 203/743–9850 • lunch & dinner, clsd Sun, Mediterranean/ Italian • funky decor • plenty veggie

Thang Long 56 Padanaram Rd (near North Street Shopping Center) 203/743–6049 • lunch & dinner • Vietnamese • bring your own bottle

Enfield

Erotica

Bookends 44 Enfield St/ Rte 5 860/745–3988

Hartford

Info Lines & Services

True Colors 576 Farmington Ave 860/232-0050, 888/565-5551 • support & mentoring for LGBT youth

Accommodations

Butternut Farm 1654 Main St, Glastonbury 860/633–7197 • gay/ straight • 18th-c house furnished w/ antiques • full brkfst • WiFi • $99-125

Inn at Kent Falls 107 Kent Cornwall Rd, Kent 860/927–3197 • gay/ straight • 1 hr from Hartford • pool • kids ok • nonsmoking • WiFi • wheelchair access • gay-owned • $215-350

The Mansion Inn 139 Hartford Rd (at Main St), Manchester 860/646–0453 • gay-friendly • B&B • full brkfst • in-room fireplaces • $95-145

Bars

Chez Est 458 Wethersfield Ave (at Main St) 860/525–3243 • 3pm-1am, till 2am Fri-Sat • popular • lesbians/ gay men • dancing/DJ • food served • karaoke • drag shows • women's night 2nd Sat

Hartford

LGBT Pride:
June, web: www.connecticutpride.org.

Annual Events:
June - Conneticut Gay & Lesbian Film Festival, web: www.outfilmct.org.

City Info:
Greater Hartford Tourism District 800/446-7811, web: www.enjoy-hartford.com.

Weather:
Summer highs are in the low 80°s. But that 50%+ humidity will make it feel like more. Humidity all year round. Winter drops into the low 20°s. January is the coldest and snowiest month. The full four seasons are in effect.

Attractions:
Bushnell Park Carousel & Museum 860/232-6710, web: www.bush-nellpark.org.
Harriet Beecher Stowe Center 860/522-9258, web: www.harri-etbeecherstowecenter.org.
Mark Twain House 860/247-0998, web: www.marktwainhouse.org.
Real Art Ways 860/232-1006, web: www.realartways.org.
Wadsworth Atheneum Museum of Art 860/278-2670, web: www.wadsworthatheneum.org.

Transit:
Yellow Cab 860/666-6666, web: www.theyellowcab.com.
GO Airport Shuttle 800/377-8745, web: www.2theairport.com.
Connecticut Transit 860/525-9181, web: www.cttransit.com.

Polo 678 Maple Ave (btwn Preston & Mapleton) 860/278–3333 • 9pm-1am, till 2am Fri-Sat, clsd Sun-Wed • lesbians/ gay men, Th ladies night • dancing/DJ • karaoke • drag shows

Women After Hours 860/930–8844 • bi-monthly dance/ social • call for schedule & location • cover

NIGHTCLUBS

Club Lucy 458 Wethersfield Ave (at Chez Est) 860/525–3243 • 2nd Sat only • monthly women's party

CAFES

Tisane Tea & Coffee Bar 537 Farmington Ave (at Kenyon) 860/523–5417 • 8am-1am, till 2am Sat • food served • karaoke • WiFi • also bar • women's night 1st Sun

RESTAURANTS

Arugula 953 Farmington Ave, West Hartford 860/561–4888 • lunch and dinner, clsd Mon • Mediterranean • reservations recommended • wheelchair access

Firebox 539 Broad St 860/246–1222 • 11:30am-10:30pm, 4:30pm-8:30pm Sun • contemporary American • also farmers market Th (April-Oct)

Peppercorns Grill 357 Main St 860/547–1714 • lunch Mon-Fri, dinner nightly, clsd Sun • Northern Italian

Pond House Cafe 1555 Asylum Ave, W Hartford 860/231–8823 • lunch & dinner Tue-Sat, wknd brunch • bring your own bottle • patio • wheelchair access

Trumbull Kitchen 150 Trumbull St (at Pearl St) 860/493–7417 • lunch Mon-Sat, dinner nightly • global cuisine/ tapas

ENTERTAINMENT & RECREATION

Real Art Ways 56 Arbor St 860/232–1006 • contemporary art • cinema • performance • also lounge • WiFi

RETAIL SHOPS

MetroStore 493 Farmington Ave (at Sisson Ave) 860/231–8845 • 8:30am-8pm, till 5:30pm Tue, Wed & Sat, clsd Sun • magazines • travel guides • DVD rentals • leather & more

PUBLICATIONS

Metroline 860/233–8334 • regional newspaper & entertainment guide • covers CT, RI & MA

EROTICA

Very Intimate Pleasures 100 Brainard Rd (exit 27, off I-91) 860/246–1875

Mystic

ACCOMMODATIONS

House of 1833 B&B Resort 72 N Stonington Rd 860/536–6325, 800/367–1833 • gay-friendly • full brkfst • pool • kids ok • nonsmoking • WiFi • gay-owned • $139-179

The Mare's Inn B&B 333 Colonel Ledyard Hwy, Ledyard 860/572–7556 • gay-friendly • full brkfst • nonsmoking • wheelchair access • lesbian-owned • $125-220

Mermaid Inn of Mystic 2 Broadway 860/536–6223, 877/692–2632 • lesbians/ gay men (straight-friendly) • B&B w/ village location & river views • full brkfst • kids ok • nonsmoking • WiFi • lesbian-owned • $175-225

The Old Mystic Inn 52 Main St (at Rte 27), Old Mystic 860/572–9422 • gay-friendly • full brkfst • nonsmoking • WiFi • gay-owned • $135-215

New Haven

INFO LINES & SERVICES

New Haven Pride Center 14 Gilbert St, West Haven 203/387–2252 • events • meetings • resources • library • movies • call for info

ACCOMMODATIONS

Linden Point House 30 Linden Point Rd, Stony Creek 203/481–0472 • gay-friendly • WiFi • pets/kids ok • $200-375

Omni New Haven Hotel at Yale 155 Temple St (at Chapel) 203/772–6664, 800/843–6664 • gay-friendly • WiFi • wheelchair access • $129-439

BARS

168 York St Cafe 168 York St 203/789–1915 • 3pm-1am, till 2am Fri-Sat • lesbians/ gay men • also restaurant • dinner Mon-Sat, Sun brunch • patio • gay-owned

The Bar 254 Crown St (at College) 203/495–8924 • 11:30am-1am, from 5pm Mon-Tue • gay/ straight • more gay Tue • dancing/DJ • pizza • wheelchair access

Partners 365 Crown St (at Park St) 203/776–1014 • 5pm-1am, till 2am Fri-Sat • lesbians/ gay men • dancing/DJ • karaoke • leather 1st & 3rd Sat • women's night 4th Sat

NIGHTCLUBS

Gotham Citi Cafe 130 Crown St (at Church) 203/498–2484 • 9pm-4am clsd Sun-Wed • gay/ straight • more gay Sat • 18+ • dancing/DJ • drag shows • wheelchair access

CAFES

Atticus Bookstore/ Cafe 1082 Chapel St (at York St) **203/776-4040** • 7am-9pm

RESTAURANTS

116 Crown 116 Crown St **203/777-3116** • upscale tapas • great mixed drinks

Beachhead 3 Cosey Beach Ave, East Haven **203/469-5450** • 4pm-close, from 1pm Sun • seafood • Italian • patio • live music

Bentara 76 Orange St **203/562-2511** • lunch Mon-Sat, dinner nightly • Malaysian • plenty veggie

Claire's Corner Copia 1000 Chapel St (at College St) **203/562-3888** • 8am-9pm, till 10pm Fri-Sat • vegetarian • WiFi • wheelchair access

Mezcal 14 Mechanic St (at Lawrence) **203/782-4828** • lunch Tue-Sun, dinner nightly • authentic Mexican

Miya Sushi 58 Howe St (at Chapel St) **203/777-9760** • lunch & dinner, clsd Sun-Mon

Soul de Cuba 238 Crown St **203/498-2822** • lunch & dinner • full bar

EROTICA

Very Intimate Pleasures 170 Boston Post Rd, Orange **203/799-7040**

New London

BARS

Frank's Place 9 Tilley St (at Bank) **860/442-2782** • 4pm-1am, till 2am Fri-Sun • mostly gay men • dancing/DJ • live shows • food served • karaoke • patio • wheelchair access

O'Neill's Brass Rail 52 Bank St **860/443-6203** • 11am-1am, till 2am Fri-Sat • mostly gay men • karaoke • drag shows • WiFi

Norwalk

INFO LINES & SERVICES

Triangle Community Center 16 River St (at Wall St) **203/853-0600** • activities • newsletter • call for info

Ridgefield

RESTAURANTS

Caputo's East Ridge Cafe 5 Grove St **203/894-1940** • 11:30am-10pm • also mellow, upscale bar

Uncasville

NIGHTCLUBS

Mohegan SunDayz 1 Mohegan Sun Blvd **888/777-7922** • 8pm Sun only at Mohegan Sun casino and resort • lesbians/gay men • dancing /DJ • live shows

Westport

ENTERTAINMENT & RECREATION

Sherwood Island State Park Beach left to gay area

DELAWARE

Rehoboth Beach

INFO LINES & SERVICES

Camp Rehoboth Community Center 37 Baltimore Ave **302/227-5620** • 9am-5:30pm Mon-Fri, 10am-4pm wknds • drop-in community center • support groups • magazine w/ extensive listings • HIV testing & counseling

Gay & Lesbian AA **302/856-6452** • noon Th

Narcotics Anonymous 37 Baltimore Ave (at Camp Rehoboth center) **302/227-5620** • 5:30pm Sun

ACCOMMODATIONS

At Melissa's B&B 36 Delaware Ave (btwn 1st & 2nd) **302/227-7504, 800/396-8090** • gay/ straight • 1 block from beach • nonsmoking • WiFi • women-owned

Bellmoor Inn 6 Christian St (at Delaware) **866/899-2779, 800/425-2355** • gay-friendly • upscale inn & spa • pool

Breakers Hotel & Suites 105 2nd St (at Olive) **302/227-6688, 800/441-8009** • gay-friendly • pool • kids/ pets ok • wheelchair access

Cabana Gardens B&B 20 Lake Ave (at 3rd St) **302/227-5429** • gay/ straight • lake & ocean views • deck • pool • nonsmoking • gay-owned

Canalside Inn Canal at 6th **302/226-2006, 866/412-2625** • gay/ straight • pool • hot tub • WiFi • nonsmoking • wheelchair access • gay-owned

Delaware Inn B&B 55 Delaware Ave (at Bayard Ave) **302/227-6031, 800/246-5244** • gay-friendly • near beach • lesbian-owned

The Homestead at Rehoboth B&B 35060 Warrington Rd (at John J Williams Hwy) **302/226–7625** • gay-friendly • small dogs ok • pool • nonsmoking • WiFi • wheelchair access • lesbian-owned

Lazy L at Willow Creek 16061 Willow Creek Rd (at Hwy 1), Lewes **302/644–7220** • gay/ straight • full brkfst • pool • hot tub • very pet friendly • WiFi • lesbian-owned

Rehoboth Beach

WHERE THE GIRLS ARE:
If it's summer, on the beach (the North Shores at S end of Cape Henlopen) with all the other women. If it's Sunday during the summer, hanging out at Frogg Pond. Every Friday-Saturday all year, they're dancing at the Ladies Tea at Sky Bar.

LGBT PRIDE:
Every day, but Wilmington has their pride here in September.

ANNUAL EVENTS:
July - Fireworks 302/227-2772, web: www.rehomain.com/fire-works.html.

October - Rehoboth Beach Autumn Jazz Festival, web: www.rehobothjazz.com.

October - Sea Witch Halloween Festival, web: www.beach-fun.com.

November - Rehoboth Beach Independent Film Festival 302/645-9095, web: www.rehobothfilm.com.

CITY INFO:
Rehoboth Beach-Dewey Beach Chamber of Commerce 302/227-2233 & 800/441-1329, web: www.beach-fun.com.

BEST VIEW:
Watching the sun rise over the bay at Dewey Beach or eating a swanky sunset dinner at Victoria's (www.boardwalkplaza.com/ rehoboth-beach-hotel-dining) on the Boardwalk.

ATTRACTIONS:
Anna Hazzard Museum, 302/226-1119. Photos & memorabilia from when Rehoboth was a Christian resort.

DiscoverSea Shipwreck Museum, Fenwick Island, 302/539-9366, web: discoversea.com.

Dolphin- & whale-watching July-Oct. Boat tours leave from Fisherman's Wharf in Lewes, DE. 302/645-8862, web: www.fish-lewes.com/sightseeing.html.

Main Street 302/227-2772, web: www.rehomain.com.

Rehoboth Beach Boardwalk with 2 amusement parks (Funland, web: www.funlandRehoboth.com, & Playland).

Tanger Outlets, web: www.tanger-outlet.com. 130 designer stores with no sales tax.

WEATHER:
You're not far from DC, but you're on the coast. So, yes, it does get hot and muggy in the summers (90ºs for temps and humidity), but you can take a dip in the ocean. In the winter, a lot of businesses close as the temperature drops along with the occasional snow flurries.

TRANSIT:
Seaport Taxi 302/645-6800.

Jolly Trolley 302/227-1197 (seasonal tour & shuttle), web: www.jollytrolley.com.

Cape May-Lewes Ferry (80-minute ferry ride between N Cape May, NJ & Lewes, DE), 800/643-3779, web: www.capemaylewesferry.com.

The Lighthouse Inn B&B 20 Delaware Ave (at 1st St) 302/226-0407 • seasonal • gay/straight • also apt (weekly rental) • nonsmoking • kids/pets ok • gay-owned

Rehoboth Guest House 40 Maryland Ave (btwn 1st & 2nd Sts) 302/227-4117, 800/564-0493 • lesbians/gay men • near boardwalk & beach • nonsmoking • WiFi • gay-owned

Sea Witch Manor Inn & Spa 71 Lake Ave (at Rehoboth Ave) 302/226-9482, 866/732-9482 • gay/straight • hot tub • nonsmoking • WiFi • wheelchair access • gay-owned

Silver Lake Guest House 20388 Silver Lake Dr (at Robinson Dr) 302/226-2115, 800/842-2115 • lesbians/gay men • near Poodle Beach • nonsmoking • lakefront • ocean views • WiFi • gay-owned

Summer Place Hotel 30 Olive Ave (at 1st) 302/226-0766, 800/815-3925 • gay/straight • also apts • near beach

BARS

The Blue Moon 35 Baltimore Ave (btwn 1st & 2nd) 302/227-6515 • 6pm-2am, clsd Jan • popular • lesbians/gay men • live music • drag shows • also restaurant

Dogfish Head Brewings & Eats 320 Rehoboth Ave (at 4th) 302/226-2739 • gay-friendly • micro-brewery • wood-grilled food • live music wknds

Finbar Pub & Grill 316-318 Rehoboth Ave (at 4th) 302/227-1873 • from 3pm, from noon Fri-Sun, clsd Mon-Tue • gay-friendly • popular happy hour

Frogg Pond 3 S 1st St (near Rehoboth Ave) 302/227-2234 • 11am-1am • gay-friendly • popular w/ women in summer • neighborhood bar • food served • karaoke

L Bar 622 Rehoboth Ave (at Church) 302/227-0818 • 4pm-2am • open year round • mostly gay men • dancing/DJ • leather • bears • patio

Rigby's Bar & Grill 404 Rehoboth Ave (at State St) 302/227-6080 • 3pm-1am, from 10am Sun

NIGHTCLUBS

Ladies 2000 856/869-0193 • seasonal parties • call hotline for details

CAFES

The Coffee Mill 127B Rehoboth Ave 302/227-7530, 888/227-7530 • 7am-11pm, till 5pm (off-season) • WiFi • lesbian-owned

Lori's Cafe 39 Baltimore Ave (at 1st) 302/226-3066 • seasonal, call for hours • also sandwiches • courtyard • lesbian-owned

RESTAURANTS

Aqua Grill 57 Baltimore Ave 302/226-9001 • seasonal • deck • full bar

Back Porch Cafe 59 Rehoboth Ave 302/227-3674 • lunch & dinner • Sun brunch • seasonal • live shows • full bar • wheelchair access

Buttery 102 2nd St, Lewes 302/645-7755 • lunch, dinner, Sun brunch • fine dining in elegant Victorian • reservations suggested

Cafe Sole 44 Baltimore Ave 302/227-7107 • lunch daily, dinner Wed-Sun • casual • patio • also full bar

Cloud 9 234 Rehoboth Ave (at 2nd) 302/226-1999 • 4pm-2am • popular bar • fusion bistro • also Sky Bar • wheelchair access

Cosmopolitan Grill 10 Wilmington Ave (on the beach block) 302/227-9752 • 9am-1am • live music • full bar • gay-owned

The Cultured Pearl 301 Rehoboth Ave (2nd flr) 302/227-8493 • dinner only • pan-Asian/sushi • cocktail lounge

Dos Locos 208 Rehoboth Ave (across from Fire Company) 302/227-3353 • 11:30am-10pm, till 11pm Fri-Sat • popular • Mexican • full bar

Eden 23 Baltimore Ave 302/227-3330 • dinner Tue-Sat • seasonal • wine list & martini bar • wheelchair access

Espuma 28 Wilmington Ave 302/227-4199 • 6pm-10pm, clsd Mon • modern Mediterranean • full bar from 5pm

Fins 243 Rehoboth Ave 302/226-3467 • dinner nightly, lunch Sat-Sun • fish house • raw bar

Go Fish! 24 Rehoboth Ave 302/226-1044 • 11:30am-9:30pm (in-season) • authentic British fish & chips

Hobo's Restaurant & Bar 56 Baltimore Ave 302/226-2226 • from 11am (in-season)

Iguana Grill 52 Baltimore Ave 302/227-0948 • lunch & dinner (summers) • Southwestern • full bar • patio

JD's Filling Station 329 Savannah Rd, Lewes 302/644-8400 • 7:30am-9pm

Jerry's Seafood 108 2nd St, Lewes 302/645-6611 • lunch & dinner daily • "home of the crab bomb"

Mariachi 302/227–0115 • 11am–9pm, till 11pm Fri–Sat • Mexican-Latin American • wheelchair access

Planet X Cafe 35 Wilmington Ave 302/226–1928 • seasonal, lunch, dinner, Sun brunch • organic global cuisine • kitschy decor housed in converted Victorian

Purple Parrot Grill 134 Rehoboth Ave 302/226–1139 • lunch & dinner daily, brunch Sun • karaoke & drag shows wknds • wheelchair access

Seafood Shack 42 1/2 Baltimore Ave 302/227–5881 • patio seating • live music wknds

Tijuana Taxi 33401 Tenley Ct 302/644–8294 • lunch & dinner • full bar • wheelchair access

Venus on the Half Shell 136 Dagsworthy St, Dewey Beach 302/227–9292 • seasonal • waterside Asian-inspired restaurant w/ fun Morocco-Meets-the-Far-East setting

ENTERTAINMENT & RECREATION

Cape Henlopen State Park Beach 42 Cape Henlopen Dr, Lewes 302/645–8983 • 8am-sunset

Gordon Pond State Park/ North Shores S end of Cape Henlopen State Park (at jetty S of watch tower) • popular women's beach • 20-minute walk from boardwalk • by car follow the shoreline road to State Park entrance

Poodle Beach S of boardwalk at Queen St • popular gay beach

RETAIL SHOPS

Leather Central 36983 Rehoboth Ave 302/227–0700 • 10am-6pm, till 5pm Sun, clsd Tue-Wed

PUBLICATIONS

Letters from Camp Rehoboth 302/227–5620 • newsmagazine w/ events & entertainment listings

GYMS & HEALTH CLUBS

Body Shop 70 Rehoboth Ave (at Virginia) 302/226–0920 • 8am-7pm, till 6pm Sun • on the beach • $12 day pass

Midway Fitness 34823 Derrickson Dr 302/645–0407 • $12 day pass

Wilmington

NIGHTCLUBS

Crimson Moon Tavern 1909 W 6th St (at Union St) 302/654–9099 • 6pm-2am, from 7pm Sat, clsd Sun-Tue • mostly gay men • dancing/DJ • videos

RESTAURANTS

Eclipse 1020 Union St 302/658–1588 • lunch Mon-Fri, dinner nightly • upscale

The Green Room 11th & Market St (at Hotel Dupont) 302/594–3154 • brkfst, lunch & dinner, Sun brunch • full bar • live music

Mrs Robino's 520 N Union St. (at Pennsylvania) 302/652–9223 • 11am-9pm, till 10pm Fri-Sat • family-style Italian • full bar • wheelchair access

DISTRICT OF COLUMBIA

Washington

INFO LINES & SERVICES

Triangle Club 202/659–8641 • site for various 12-step groups • call for times

ACCOMMODATIONS

Beacon Hotel & Corporate Quarters 1615 Rhode Island Ave NW (at 17th) 202/296-2100

Bloomingdale Inn 2417 1st St NW (at Bryant) 202/319–0801 • gay-friendly • Victorian town house • $90-427

The Carlyle Suites Hotel 1731 New Hampshire Ave NW (btwn R & S Sts) 202/234–3200, 800/964–5377 • gay/ straight • art deco hotel • WiFi • gym • also restaurant & bar • popular gay Sun brunch • wheelchair access • $139-279

Chez Aimee 202/669–7708 • gay-friendly • flat in 1910-era rowhouse in Adams Morgan district • nonsmoking • WiFi • $179-249

Comfort Inn Downtown DC—Convention Center 1201 13th St NW 202/682–5300, 877/424–6423 • gay/ straight • near Dupont Circle • kids ok • WiFi • wheelchair access • $99-279

Creekside B&B 301/261–9438 • mostly women • private home on the shore of the Chesapeake • 40 minutes from DC • hot tub • pool • nonsmoking • lesbian-owned • $100

DC GuestHouse 1337 10th St NW 202/332–2502 • gay/ straight • full brkfst • WiFi • gay-owned • $175-300

The District Hotel 1440 Rhode Island Ave NW (btwn 14th & 15th) 202/232–7800, 800/350–5759 • gay-friendly • conveniently located in Dupont/ Logan Circle Historic District • nonsmoking • kids ok • WiFi • $80+

Donovan House 1155 14th St NW (at Massachusetts Ave NW) 202/737–1200, 800/383–6900 • gay/ straight • stylish hotel • rooftop bar

Doubletree Hotel Washington 1515 Rhode Island Ave NW **202/232-7000** • gay-friendly • boutique hotel • WiFi • $166-399

The Embassy Inn 1627 16th St NW (at R St) **202/234-7800, 877/968-9111** • gay-friendly • small hotel w/ B&B atmosphere • WiFi • $79-179

Embassy Suites Hotel at the Chevy Chase Pavilion 4300 Military Rd NW (at Wisconsin) **202/362-9300** • gay-friendly • pool • gym • wheelchair access • $149-289

Embassy Suites Tysons Corner 8517 Leesburg Pike (at W Park), Vienna, VA **703/883-0707, 800/362-2779** • gay-friendly • full brkfst • kids ok • pool • wheelchair access • $109-329

Washington

WHERE THE GIRLS ARE:
Strolling around DuPont Circle or cruising a bar in the LGBT bar ghetto southeast of The Mall.

ENTERTAINMENT:
Gay Men's Chorus of Washington 202/338-7464, web: www.gmcw.org.

LGBT PRIDE:
June. 202/719-5304, web: www.capitalpride.org.
May. Black Lesbian/ Gay Pride, web: www.dcblackpride.org.

ANNUAL EVENTS:
March - Women's History Month at various Smithsonian Museums 202/633-5330, web: www.smithsonianeducation.org.
October - Reel Affirmations Film Festival, web: www.reelaffirmations.org.

CITY INFO:
DC Convention & Tourism Corporation. 202/789-7000, web: www.washington.org.

BEST VIEW:
From the top of the Washington Monument.

WEATHER:
Summers are hot (90ºs) and MUGGY (the city was built on marshes). In the winter, temperatures drop to the 30ºs and 40ºs with rain and sometimes snow. Spring is the time of cherry blossoms.

ATTRACTIONS:
Ford's Theatre 202/347-4833, web: www.fords.org.
Jefferson Memorial.
JFK Center for the Performing Arts 800/444-1324, web: www.kennedy-center.org.
Lincoln Memorial.
National Gallery 202/737-4215, web: www.nga.gov.
National Museum of Women in the Arts 202/783-5000, web: www.nmwa.org.
National Zoo 202/633-4800, web: nationalzoo.si.edu.
Smithsonian 202/633-5330, web: www.smithsonianeducation.org.
Vietnam Veteran's Memorial.
United States Holocaust Memorial Museum 202/488-0400, web: www.ushmm.org.

TRANSIT:
Yellow Cab 202/544-1212, web: www.dcyellowcab.com.
Washington Flier 703/661-6655 (from Dulles or Ronald Reagan National).
Super Shuttle 800/258-3826.
Metro Transit Authority 202/637-7000, web: www.wmata.com.

Embassy Suites Washington, DC 1250 22nd St NW (btwn M & N) **202/857–3388, 800/362–2779** • gay-friendly • full brkfst • kids ok • pool • WiFi • $119-319

Hotel Helix 1430 Rhode Island Ave NW **202/462–9001, 800/706–1202** • gay-friendly • full-service boutique hotel • also Helix Lounge • nonsmoking • WiFi • wheelchair access • $139-359

Hotel Madera 1310 New Hampshire Ave NW (at N) **202/296–7600, 800/430–1202** • gay-friendly • boutique hotel • kids/ pets ok • Firefly bistro adjacent • WiFi • wheelchair access • $149-429

Hotel Monaco Washington DC 700 F St NW (at 7th) **202/628–7177, 800/649–1202** • gay-friendly • boutique hotel • kids/ pets ok • WiFi • wheelchair access • $129-350

Hotel Palomar 2121 P St NW (at 21st St) **202/448–1800, 866/866–3070** • gay-friendly • in Dupont Circle • gym • WiFi • pool • restaurant • wheelchair access • $175-440

Hotel Rouge 1315 16th St NW (at Rhode Island) **202/232–8000, 800/738–1202** • gay-friendly • ultra-hip, high-tech luxury hotel • kids/ pets ok • also restaurant & bar • WiFi • wheelchair access • $139-399

Kalorama Guest House at Kalorama Park 1854 Mintwood Pl NW (at Columbia Rd) **202/667–6369, 800/974–6450** • gay/ straight • Victorian town house near Dupont Circle • nonsmoking • WiFi • $50-120

Kalorama Guest House at Woodley Park 2700 Cathedral Ave NW (off Connecticut Ave) **202/328–0860, 800/974–9101** • gay/ straight • near Nat'l Zoo & Washington Cathedral • nonsmoking • WiFi • $55-105

Madison Hotel 1177 15th St NW (at M St NW) **202/862–1600, 800/424–8577** • gay-friendly • luxury hotel • WiFi • also restaurant

Morrison-Clark Historic Hotel & Restaurant 1015 L St NW (at Massachusetts Ave NW) **202/898–1200, 800/322–7898** • gay-friendly • hotel in 2 Victorian town houses • very popular restaurant • WiFi • $155-325

Otis Place B&B 1003 Otis Place NW (at 10th St) **202/483–0241, 877/893–3233** • gay/ straight • 1910 Victorian town house • kids ok • WiFi • gay-owned • $75-145

The River Inn 924 25th St NW (at K St) **202/337–7600, 888/874–0100** • gay-friendly • suites w/ kitchen • gym • WiFi • also Dish + Drinks restaurant • wheelchair access • $99-299

Savoy Suites Hotel 2505 Wisconsin Ave NW (at Calvert, in Georgetown) **202/337–9700, 800/944–5377** • gay-friendly • also restaurant • Italian • WiFi • wheelchair access • $129-269

Swann House Historic B&B 1808 New Hampshire Ave NW (at Swann St) **202/265–4414** • gay/ straight • 1883 Victorian mansion in Dupont Circle • pool • roof deck • fireplaces • kids ok • WiFi • $150-365

Topaz Hotel 1733 N St NW (at Massachusetts Ave NW) **202/393–3000, 800/775–1202** • gay-friendly • boutique hotel • kids/ pets ok • also restaurant & bar • no smoking in rooms • WiFi • wheelchair access • $149-429

Washington Plaza 10 Thomas Cir NW (at 14th & Massachusetts) **202/842–1300, 800/424–1140** • gay-friendly • full-service hotel • WiFi • pool • also restaurant • $99-299

The Windsor Inn 1842 16th St NW **202/667–0300, 800/423–9111** • gay-friendly • small hotel w/ B&B atmosphere • WiFi • $119-250

BARS

1409 Playbill Cafe 1409 14th St NW **202/265–3055** • 4pm-2am, till 3am Fri-Sat • lesbians/ gay men • food served • also theater • wheelchair access

The Black Cat 1811 14th St NW (at the Black Cat) **202/667–4490** • gay/ straight • many queer events • live music • dance parties • also cafe

DC Eagle 639 New York Ave NW (btwn 6th & 7th) **202/347–6025** • 4pm-2am, till 3am Fri-Sat, 2pm-2am Sun • popular • mostly gay men • leather • wheelchair access

DIK Bar/ Windows 1637 17th St NW (at R St NW, upstairs) **202/328–0100** • 4pm-2am • mostly gay men • dancing/DJ • karaoke • older crowd

The Fireplace 2161 P St NW (at 22nd St) **202/293–1293** • 1pm-2am, till 3am Fri-Sat • mostly gay men • neighborhood bar • multiracial • videos • wheelchair access

JR's 1519 17th St NW (at Church) **202/328–0090** • 2pm-2am, till 3am Fri, 1pm-3am Sat, 1pm-2am Sun • popular • mostly gay men • neighborhood bar • food served • videos • young crowd

Lace 2214 Rhode Island Ave NE **202/832–3888** • 6pm-3am Fri-Sat, till midnight Sun, clsd Mon-Th • upscale women's bar • mostly African American • also restaurant • lesbian-owned

Larry's Lounge 1840 18th St NW (at T St) **202/483–1483** • 4pm-1am, till 2am Fri-Sat • lesbians/ gay men • neighborhood bar • wheelchair access • gay-owned

Mr Henry's Capitol Hill 601 Pennsylvania Ave SE (at 6th St) **202/546–8412** • 11:30am-11:30pm • popular • gay-friendly • multiracial • live jazz Fri • also restaurant • nonsmoking • wheelchair access

Nellie's Sports Bar 900 U St NW (at 9th) **202/332–6355** • 5pm-midnight, 3pm-2am Fri, from 11am wknds • mostly gay men • gay sports bar

Number Nine 1435 P St NW (at 15th St NW) **202/986–0999** • 5pm-close • lesbians/ gay men • neighborhood bar

Phase One 525 8th St SE (btwn E & G Sts) **202/544–6831** • 7pm-2am, till 3am Fri-Sat (clsd Mon-Wed winter) • mostly women • oldest lesbian bar in the US! • neighborhood bar • dancing/DJ • karaoke • shows • multiracial • wheelchair access

POV Roof Terrace Bar 515 15th Street NW (at Alexander Hamilton Pl) **202/661–2400** • 11am-2am • gay-friendly • pricey cocktails • superior views of the White House & Lincoln Memorial • tapas served

Remington's 639 Pennsylvania Ave SE (btwn 6th & 7th) **202/543–3113** • 4pm-2am, till 3am Fri-Sat, 6pm-2am Sun • popular • mostly gay men • dancing/DJ • 2 flrs • country/ western • dance lessons Mon & Wed • karaoke Wed • T-dance Sun • videos

Rendezvous DC 2226 18th St NW (at Kalorama Rd NW) **202/462–4444** • 6pm-2am, 5pm-3am wknds • lesbians/ gay men • theme nights

NIGHTCLUBS

Bachelors Mill 1104 8th St SE (downstairs at Back Door Pub) **202/546–5979** • 5pm-2am, till 3am wknds • lesbians/ gay men • popular • dancing/DJ • mostly African American • live shows • karaoke • wheelchair access

Bare 1639 R St NW (at 17th, at Cobalt) **202/232–4416** • 10pm 3rd Sat only • mostly women • dancing/DJ

Chief Ike's Mambo Room 1725 Columbia Rd NW (at Ontario Rd) **202/332–2211** • 4pm-2am, till 3am Fri, 6pm-3am Sat, clsd Sun • gay-friendly • dancing/DJ • also restaurant • American • wheelchair access

Club Fuego 1818 New York Ave NE (at Montana Ave, at Aqua) • 10:30pm-3am Sat only • lesbians/ gay men • dancing/DJ • multiracial • salsa, merengue, Latin pop

Cobalt/ 30 Degrees Lounge 1639 R St NW (at 17th) **202/232–4416** • 5pm-2am, till 3am Fri-Sat • mostly gay men • dancing/DJ • live shows • drag shows • videos

Delta Elite 3734 10th St NE (at Perry St NE, in Brookland) **202/529–0626** • midnight-4am Fri & Sat only • ladies night Fri • dancing/DJ • mostly African American

The Fab Lounge 2022 Florida Ave NW (at Connecticut) **202/797–1122** • 5pm-close • lesbians/ gay men • dancing/DJ • multiracial • theme nights

Gloss 1415 22nd St NW (btwn O & P Sts, at Apex) **202/296–0505** • 1st Fri only • mostly women • dancing/DJ • videos • young crowd • wheelchair access • cover

Homo Sonic 1811 14th Street NW (at the Black Cat) • queer dance party • monthly • check local listings for dates

Ladies First 2022 Florida Ave NW (at Connecticut, at Fab Lounge) • 6pm Wed • mostly women • dancing/DJ • multiracial

Mixtape • 3rd Sat only • alternative queer dance party • venue changes, check mixtapedc.com for info

She Rex 1725 Columbia Rd NW (at Ontario Rd, at Chief Ike's) **202/332–2211** • 2nd Fri only • mostly women • dancing/DJ • queer party featuring all music by women • wheelchair access

Town Danceboutique 2009 8th St NW (at U St NW) **202/234–8696** • 9pm-4am Fri-Sat • mostly gay men • dancing/DJ • drag shows • 18+ Fri

CAFES

Cosi 1647 20th St NW **202/332–6364** • 7am-11pm, till midnight Fri-Sat, 8am-10pm Sun • full bar from 4pm • popular • make your own s'mores • WiFi

Hello Cupcake 1361 Connecticut Avenue NW **202/861–2253** • 10am-7pm, till 9pm Fri-Sat, 11am-6pm Sun • cupcakes!

Jolt 'n' Bolt 1918 18th St NW (at Florida) **202/232–0077** • 7am-11pm, till 8:30pm wknds • popular • patio

Soho Tea & Coffee 2150 P St NW (at 21st St) **202/463–7646** • 6:30am-1am, from 7:30am wknds • WiFi • food served • patio • wheelchair access

RESTAURANTS

18th & U Duplex Diner 2004 18th St NW (at Ave U) **202/265–7828** • 6pm-11pm, till 12:30am Tue-Wed, till 1:30am Fri-Sat • American comfort food • full bar

2 Amys Pizza 3715 Macomb St NW **202/885-5700** • lunch & dinner Tue-Sun, dinner only Mon • wheelchair access

Acadiana 901 New York Ave NW **202/408-8848** • lunch Mon-Fri, dinner nightly, brunch Sun • Cajun • great bourbon selection • reservations recommended

Annie's Paramount Steak House 1609 17th St NW (at Corcoran) **202/232-0395** • 10am-11:30pm, till 1am Th & Sun, 24hrs Fri-Sat • popular • full bar • wheelchair access

Armand's Chicago Pizza 4231 Wisconsin Ave NW (at Veazey) **202/363-5500** • 11am-10pm, till 11pm Fri-Sat, noon-10pm Sun • full bar • also 226 Massachusetts Ave NE, Capitol Hill, 202/547-6600

Asylum 2471 18th St NW **202/319-9353** • 5pm-2am, till 3am Fri, from 11am wknds • plenty veggie/ vegan • also bar • live bands

Banana Cafe & Piano Bar 500 8th St SE (at E St) **202/543-5906** • 11am-10:30pm, till 11pm Fri-Sat, till 10pm Sun • Puerto Rican/ Cuban food • some veggie • famous margaritas • piano bar • gay-owned

Bar Pilar 1833 14th St NW (at Swann St) **202/265-1751** • dinner nightly, Sun brunch • new American

Beacon Bar & Grill 1615 Rhode Island Ave NW (at 17th, at Beacon Hotel) **202/872-1126** • brkfst, lunch & dinner • popular Sun brunch • patio

Busboys & Poets 2021 14th St NW (at V St) **202/387-7638** • 8am-midnight, till 2am Fri-Sat, 10am-midnight Sun • also bookstore • live jazz & poetry • WiFi • wheelchair access

Cafe Green 1513 17th St NW **202/234-0505** • 11am-10pm, 10am-4pm Sun, clsd Mon • organic cafe • plenty veggie/ vegan

Cafe Japoné 2032 P St NW (at 21st) **202/223-1573** • 6pm-1:30am, till 2:30am Fri-Sat • mostly Asian American • popular • Japanese food • full bar • live jazz Wed • karaoke

Cafe La Ruche 1039 31st St **202/965-2684** • dinner, Sun brunch • French • patio

Cafe Luna 1633 P St NW (at 17th) **202/387-4005** • 10am-11pm, till midnight wknds • popular • lesbians/ gay men • healthy • plenty veggie

Cafe Saint Ex/ Gate 54 1847 14th St NW **202/265-7839** • lunch, dinner, Sun brunch • modern American • also Gate 54 club downstairs • popular Th dance party • gay-friendly

Chartwell Grill 1914 Connecticut Ave NW (in The Churchill Hotel) **202/797-2000** • 6:30am-10:30pm, also lounge till 12:30am, till 11pm Sun • cont'l • wheelchair access

Dupont Italian Kitchen & Bar 1637 17th St NW (at R St) **202/328-3222, 202/328-0100** • 11am-11pm, bar 4pm-2am • some veggie • wheelchair access

Firefly 1310 New Hampshire Ave NW **202/861-1310** • lunch & dinner, wknd brunch • plenty veggie

Floriana 1602 17th St NW (at Q St NW) **202/667-5937** • dinner nightly • Italian • full bar • patio • gay-owned

Food For Thought 1811 14th St NW (at the Black Cat) **202/667-4490** • 8pm-1am, 7pm-2am Fri-Sat • gay-friendly • mostly vegan/ veggie • nonsmoking • also live music • readings • indie/ punk • young crowd • wheelchair access

Guapo's 4515 Wisconsin Ave NW (at Albemarle) **202/686-3588** • lunch & dinner • Mexican • some veggie • full bar • wheelchair access

Jaleo 480 7th St NW (at E St) **202/628-7949** • lunch & dinner • tapas • full bar • Sevillanas dancers Wed • wheelchair access

Java Green Eco Cafe 1020 19th St NW **202/775-8899** • 8am-8pm, 10am-6pm Sat, clsd Sun • organic cafe • plenty veggie/ vegan

Lauriol Plaza 1835 18th St NW (at S St) **202/387-0035** • 11:30am-11pm, till midnight Fri-Sat • Latin American • wheelchair access

Level One 1639 R St NW (at 17th) **202/745-0025** • dinner nightly, wknd brunch

Logan Tavern 1423 P St NW **202/332-3710** • lunch & dinner, wknd brunch • American comfort food • also bar • gay-owned

Occidental Grill 1475 Pennsylvania Ave NW (btwn 14th & 15th) **202/783-1475** • lunch Mon-Sat, dinner nightly, clsd Sun • upscale • political player hangout

Perry's 1811 Columbia Rd NW (at 18th) **202/234-6218** • 5:30pm-10:30pm, till 11:30pm wknds, popular drag Sun brunch • contemporary American & sushi • full bar • roof deck

Pizza Paradiso 2003 P Street NW **202/223-1245** • 11am-11pm, till midnight wknds

Posto 1515 14th St NW **202/332-8613** • dinner nightly • terrific Italian

Rasika 633 D St NW **202/637-1222** • lunch Mon-Fri, dinner Mon-Sat, clsd Sun • Indian • wheelchair access

Rice 1608 14th St NW (at 'Q') **202/234-2400** • lunch & dinner • Thai

Rocklands 2418 Wisconsin Ave NW (at Calvert) **202/333-2558** • 11am-10pm, till 9pm Sun • BBQ & take-out

Sabores 3435 Connecticut Ave NW (btwn Porter & Ordway) **202/244-7196** • dinner nightly, Sun brunch • tapas • also lounge • live music

Sala Thai 1301 U St NW (at 13th) **202/462-1333** • lunch & dinner • some veggie

Skewers 1633 P St NW (at 17th) **202/387-7400** • 11am-11pm, noon-midnight wknds • popular • Middle-Eastern • belly dancing Sat • full bar

Soul Vegetarian Exodus 2606 Georgia Ave NW **202/328-7685** • 11am-9pm, till 3pm Sun (brunch) • all-vegan menu • no frills

Thaitanic 1326 14th St NW (at Rhode Island Ave) **202/588-1795** • lunch & dinner • Thai • plenty veggie

Trio 1537 17th St NW (at Q St NW) **202/232-6305** • 8am-midnight • American • some veggie • full bar • sidewalk cafe • wheelchair access

Twist Dupont 1731 New Hampshire (at 18th & R Sts, in the Carlyle Suites) **202/518-5011** • lunch & dinner • gay/straight • also art deco bar • internet access • wheelchair access

Zaytinia 701 9th Street NW (at G St) **202/638-0800** • lunch & dinner • Greek/Mediterranean • plenty veggie

ENTERTAINMENT & RECREATION

Anecdotal History Tours 301/294-9514 • gay-friendly • variety of guided tours • by appt only

Bike & Roll Washington DC 1100 Pennsylvania Ave NW (off 12th St, at Old Post Office Pavilion) **202/842-2453** • 9am-6pm • tour the nation's capital on bike!

Capital Bikeshare 877/430-2453 • look for the red bikes at parking stations around the city • join for 24hrs or longer

Hillwood Museum & Gardens 4155 Linnean Ave NW (at Tilden St NW) **202/686-5807** • 10am-5pm Tue-Sat • Fabergé, porcelain, furniture & more • reservations required

National Museum of Women in the Arts 1250 New York Ave **202/783-5000, 800/222-7270**

Phillips Collection 1600 21st St NW (at Q St) **202/387-2151** • clsd Mon • America's first museum of modern art • near Dupont Circle

Washington Mystics **202/266-2277, 877/324-6671** • check out the Women's Nat'l Basketball Association while you're in DC

BOOKSTORES

G Books 1520 U St NW, BSMT (btwn 15th St & U St) **202/986-9697** • 4pm-10pm, till 11pm Fri-Sat, from noon wknds • new & used gay books • pride items • gay-owned

Kramerbooks & Afterwords Cafe & Grill 1517 Connecticut Ave NW (at Q St) **202/387-1400** • 7:30am-1am, 24hrs wknds • general • also cafe & bar • live music • wheelchair access

RETAIL SHOPS

HRC Action Center & Store 1633 Connecticut Avenue NW **202/232-8621** • 10am-9pm, till 10pm wknds • Human Rights Campaign merchandise & info

Leather Rack 1723 Connecticut Ave NW (btwn R & S Sts) **202/797-7401**

Pulp 1803 14th St NW **202/462-7857** • 11am-7pm, till 5pm Sun • cards • gifts • music

Universal Gear 1529 14th St NW (btwn P & Q) **202/319-0136** • 11am-10pm, till midnight Fri-Sat • casual, club, athletic & designer clothing

PUBLICATIONS

Metro Weekly 202/638-6830 • LGBT newsmagazine • extensive club listings

Washington Blade 202/747-2077 • LGBT newspaper

GYMS & HEALTH CLUBS

Washington Sports Club 1835 Connecticut Ave NW (at Columbia & Florida) **202/332-0100**

EROTICA

Pleasure Place 1063 Wisconsin Ave NW, Georgetown (btwn M & K Sts) **800/386-2386** • 10am-10pm, till midnight Wed-Sat, noon-7pm Sun • erotica • clubwear • leather • adult toys • DVDs • clothing & more • wheelchair access

FLORIDA

Statewide

PUBLICATIONS

Ambush Mag 504/522-8047 • LGBT newspaper for the Gulf South (TX through FL)

HOTSPOTS! Magazine 954/928-1862 • "South Florida's largest gay publication"

She Magazine, "The Source for Women" 954/354-9751 • "The hippest & hottest source for women of the rainbow community"

Alligator Point

ACCOMMODATIONS

Mermaid's Tale 703/426-1936, 703/819-5243 • mostly women • beach house • nonsmoking • lesbian-owned • $875-1,275/week

Amelia Island

ACCOMMODATIONS

The Hoyt House 804 Atlantic Ave 904/277-4300, 800/432-2085 • gay-friendly • full brkfst • pool • nonsmoking • WiFi • wheelchair access • lesbian-owned • $190-229

RESTAURANTS

Beech Street Grill 801 Beech St (at 8th St), Fernandina Beach 904/277-3662 • 5:30pm-9pm, also lunch Wed-Fri and Sun brunch • live music

Brett's Waterway Cafe 1 S Front St 904/261-2660 • lunch & dinner • seafood

Boynton Beach

see West Palm Beach

Bradenton

see Sarasota

Clearwater

see also Dunedin, New Port Richey, Port Richey & St Petersburg

ACCOMMODATIONS

Holiday Inn Select 3535 Ulmerton Rd (Rte 688 W) 727/577-9100, 888/465-4329 • gay-friendly • pool • restaurant & lounge • wheelchair access • WiFi • $98-169

BARS

Pro Shop Pub 840 Cleveland St (at Prospect) 727/447-4259 • 1pm-2am • popular • mostly gay men • neighborhood bar • bears • gay-owned

RETAIL SHOPS

Skinz 2027 Gulf to Bay Blvd (aka State Rd 60, at Hercules Rd) 727/441-8789 • 10am-6pm, clsd Sun • men's & women's swimwear, gymwear & clubwear

Cocoa

BARS

The Ultra Lounge 407 Brevard Ave, Cocoa Village 321/690-0096 • 6pm-2am • mostly gay men • neighborhood bar

Daytona Beach

ACCOMMODATIONS

The August Seven Inn 1209 S Peninsula Dr (at Silver Beach) 386/248-8420, 877/797-3836 • gay-friendly • 1 block from ocean • full brkfst • WiFi • $125-185

Mayan Inn 103 S Ocean Ave 386/252-2378, 800/329-8622 • gay-friendly • pool • kids ok • WiFi • wheelchair access

The Villa B&B 801 N Peninsula Dr 386/248-2020, 888/248-7060 • gay-friendly • hot tub • pool • nudity • nonsmoking • gay-owned • $120-200

BARS

Streamline Lounge 140 S Atlantic Ave (at Streamline Hotel) 386/258-6937 • 11am-3am (penthouse lounge) • gay-friendly • dancing/DJ • live entertainment • game room

NIGHTCLUBS

Savoy Daytona 546 Seabreeze Blvd (at Atlantic Ave) 386/226-5600 • 5pm-2:30am, from 3pm Sun • lesbians/ gay men • neighborhood bar • dancing/DJ • videos • wheelchair access • gay-owned

CAFES

Java Joint & Eatery 2201-E N Oceanshore Blvd, Flagler Beach 386/439-1013 • 7am-4pm

RESTAURANTS

Anna's Trattoria 304 Seabreeze Blvd 386/239-9624 • 5pm-10pm, clsd Sun-Mon • Italian • beer/ wine

Barnacles 869 S Atlantic Ave, Ormond Beach 386/673-1070 • 4pm-10pm

The Clubhouse 600 Wilder Blvd (at Daytona Beach Golf & Country Club) **386/257-0727** • 6am-7:30pm

Frappes North 123 W Granada Blvd (at S Yonge St), Ormond Beach **386/615-4888** • lunch Tue-Fri, dinner nightly, clsd Sun • patio • full bar • wheelchair access

Sapporo 501 Seabreeze Ave **386/257-4477** • lunch Mon-Fri, dinner nightly • Japanese steak house & sushi bar • full bar

PUBLICATIONS

Watermark 407/481-2243 (ORLANDO OFFICE), 877/926-8118 • bi-weekly LGBT newspaper for Central FL

Dunedin

see St Petersburg

Fort Lauderdale

INFO LINES & SERVICES

Lambda South Inc 1306 E Las Olas Blvd **954/761-9072** • meeting space for LGBT in recovery • wheelchair access

The Pride Center at Equality Park 2040 N Dixie Hwy, Wilton Manors **954/463-9005** • 10am-10pm, noon-5pm wknds • outreach • wheelchair access

ACCOMMODATIONS

Alhambra Beach Resort 3021 Alhambra St **954/525-7601, 877/309-4014** • gay/ straight • motel • close to gay beach • pool • nonsmoking • WiFi • gay-owned • $99-259

Blue Lagoon Resort 3801 N Ocean Blvd **954/565-6666, 800/663-2985** • gay-friendly • pool • WiFi • gay-owned • $85-169

Fort Lauderdale

WHERE THE GIRLS ARE:
On the beach near the LGBT accommodations, just south of Birch State Recreation Area. Or at one of the cafes or bars in Wilton Manors or Oakland Park.

LGBT PRIDE:
March. www.pridesouthflorida.org. Also Stonewall Street Festival in June.

ANNUAL EVENTS:
March - AIDS Walk, web: www.floridaaidswalk.org.
April - Miami/Fort Lauderdale Gay & Lesbian Film Festival, web: www.mglff.com.
October-November - Int'l Film Fest 954/760-9898, web: www.fliff.com.

CITY INFO:
Greater Fort Lauderdale Convention & Visitors Bureau 954/765-4466 or 800/227-8669 (code 187), web: www.sunny.org.

WEATHER:
The average year-round temperature in this sub-tropical climate is 75-90°.

ATTRACTIONS:
Broward Center for the Performing Arts 954/462-0222, web: www.browardcenter.org.
Butterfly World 954/977-4400, web: www.butterflyworld.com.
Everglades.
Flamingo Gardens 954/473-2955, web: www.flamingogardens.org.
Museum of Art 954/525-5500, web: www.moafl.org.
Museum of Discovery & Science 954/467-6637, web: www.mods.org.
Sawgrass Mills, world's largest outlet mall, web: www.sawgrassmillsmall.com.

TRANSIT:
Yellow Cab 954/777-7777, web: www.taxi9547777777.com.
Super Shuttle 954/764-1700, web: www.supershuttle.com.
Broward County Transit 954/357-8400, web: www.broward.org/bct.

Courtyard Fort Lauderdale 440 Seabreeze Blvd 954/524-8733, 888/821-1366 • gay-friendly • pool • sundeck bar • nonsmoking

The Deauville Hotel 2916 N Ocean Blvd (Oakland Park Blvd & A1A) 954/568-5000 • gay-friendly • pool • non-smoking • wheelchair access • $22-69

Ed Lugo Resort 2404 NE 8th Ave (Wilton Manors) 954/275-8299 • gay-friendly • pool • WiFi • gay-owned • $50-200

Embassy Suites Hotel 1100 SE 17th St 954/527-2700, 800/362-2779 • gay-friendly • full brkfst • kids/ pets ok • WiFi • wheelchair access • $129-369

Manhattan Tower On The Intracoastal 701 Bayshore Dr 754/224-7301 • gay-friendly • apt hotel • pets/kids ok • $120-275

Marriott Harbor Beach Resort 3030 Holiday Dr 954/525-4000, 800/222-6543 • gay-friendly • pool • also restaurant & spa • private beach access

The Royal Palms Resort & Spa 717 Breakers Ave 954/564-6444, 800/237-7256 • mostly gay men • nonsmoking • WiFi • gay-owned

Westin Beach Resort 321 N Fort Lauderdale Beach Blvd (A1A) 954/467-1111, 888/627-7109 • gay-friendly • sports deck, pool & gym • restaurant & lounge • wheelchair access • $230+

Windamar Beach Club 533 Orton Ave 954/563-7062, 888/243-3454 • lesbians/ gay men • pool • WiFi • pets ok • $49-139

BARS

Beach Betty's 625 Dania Beach Blvd (at Fronton Blvd), Dania 954/921-9893 • noon-3am • mostly women • neighborhood bar • dancing/DJ • live music • karaoke • lesbian-owned

Bill's 2209 Wilton Dr (off NE 23rd St) 954/567-5978 • 2pm-2am, till 3am Fri-Sat, from noon Sat-Sun • neighborhood bar • drag shows • karaoke • wheelchair access

Cloud 9 Lounge 7126 Stirling Rd, Davie 954/499-3525 • noon-4am • mostly women • multiracial clientele • live shows • drag shows • live bands

The Depot 2935 N Federal Hwy 954/537-7076 • noon-2am, till 3am Fri-Sat • mostly gay men • neighborhood bar • food served • live shows • karaoke • pool

Georgie's Alibi 2266 Wilton Dr (at NE 4th Ave) 954/565-2526 • 11am-2am, till 3am Fri-Sat • lesbians/ gay men • nonsmoking • food served • videos • WiFi • wheelchair access

J's Bar 2780 Davie Blvd 954/581-8400 • 9am-2am, till 3am Fri-Sat, from noon Sun • lesbians/gay men • neighborhood bar • dancing/DJ

The Manor Complex 2345 Wilton Dr, Wilton Manors 954/626-0082 • 11am-11pm • lesbians/ gay men • also Epic nightclub, Ivy Lounge & Fortitude on Sun • live entertainment • also restaurant & cafe

Matty's on the Drive 2426 Wilton Dr, Wilton Manors 954/564-1799 • 11am-2am, till 3am Fri-Sat • mostly gay men • neighborhood bar • food served • wheelchair access

Mona's 502 E Sunrise Blvd (at 5th Ave) 954/525-6662 • noon-2am, till 3am wknds • mostly gay men • neighborhood bar • karaoke

Monkey Business 2740 N Andrews Ave 954/514-7819 • 9am-2am, till 3am wknds • mostly gay men • neighborhood bar • theme nights • cabaret • drag shows

Naked Grape 2039 Wilton Dr (at NE 20th St), Wilton Manors 954/563-5631 • 4pm-midnight, 2pm-1am Fri-Sat, clsd Sun-Mon • gay-friendly • wine bar

New Moon 2440 Wilton Dr, Wilton Manors 954/563-7660 • 2pm-2am, from noon Fri, from 11am Sat-Sun, from 4pm Mon • mostly women • karaoke Th • dancing/DJ Fri • live music Sat

Noche Latina Saturday 2345 Wilton Dr (at Manor Complex), Wilton Manors 954/626-0082 • 11pm Sat at Ivy nightclub • mostly gay men • dancing/DJ • multiracial

Ramrod 1508 NE 4th Ave (at 16th St) 954/763-8219 • 3pm-2am, till 3am wknds • popular • mostly gay men • leather/ levi cruise bar • patio • also LeatherWerks leather store

Scandals 3073 NE 6th Ave, Wilton Manors 954/567-2432 • noon-2am • mostly men • patio • dancing • country/ western • older crowd • wheelchair access

Sidelines Sports Bar 2031 Wilton Dr, Wilton Manors 954/563-8001 • 2pm-2am, from noon wknds • lesbians/ gay men

Smarty Pants 3038 N Federal Hwy (at Oakland Park Blvd) **954/561–1724** • 9am-2am, till 3am Sat, noon-2am Sun • popular • mostly gay men • neighborhood bar • food served • karaoke • drag shows • wheelchair access

NIGHTCLUBS

Atomic Boom 2232 Wilton Dr, Wilton Manors **954/630–3556** • 3pm-2am, till 3am wknds • popular • mostly gay men • dancing/DJ • live shows • karaoke • drag shows • T-dance Sun • gay-owned

Living Room 300 SW 1st Ave (at Brickell) **888/992–7555** • gay Fri only • mostly men • dancing/DJ

Torpedo 2829 W Broward Blvd (at 28th Ave) **954/587–2500** • 10pm-dawn • mostly men • dancing/DJ • strippers

CAFES

Cafe Emunah 3558 N Ocean Blvd **954/561–6411** • 11am-10pm, clsd Fri, sunset-1am Sat • kosher, kabbalistic cafe & teabar • food served

Gelato Station 2031 Wilton Dr **954/567–5930** • noon-11pm, till 2am Fri-Sat • gay-owned

Java Boys 2230 Wilton Dr, Wilton Manors **954/564–8828** • 7am-11pm • WiFi

Jimmies Chocolates & Cafe 148 N Federal Hwy, Dania Beach **954/921–0688** • bistro w/ fresh fare & wine

Storks 2505 NE 15th Ave (at NE 26th St, Wilton Manors) **954/567–3220** • 6:30am-midnight • Mon ladies night • patio • wheelchair access

RESTAURANTS

La Bonne Crêpe 815 E Las Olas Blvd **954/761–1515** • 7am-9:30pm, till 11:30pm Fri & Sat • patio

Canyon 1818 E Sunrise Blvd **954/765–1950** • Southwestern • full bar

Courtyard Cafe 2211 Wilton Dr **954/563–2499** • 7am-11pm, 24hrs Th-Sat • gay-owned

Diner 24 301 W Oakland Park Blvd, Wilton Manors **954/765–6349** • 7am-midnight, 24hrs Fri-Sat

The Floridian 1410 E Las Olas Blvd **954/463–4041** • 24hr diner • wheelchair access

Galanga 2389 Wilton Dr, Wilton Manors **954/202–0000** • dinner nightly, lunch weekdays • Thai • also sushi

Hi-Life Cafe 3000 N Federal Hwy (at Oakland Park Blvd, in the Plaza 3000) **954/563–1395** • dinner, clsd Mon • reservations recommended

Himmarshee Bar & Grille 210 SW 2nd St **954/524–1818** • lunch & dinner

Humpy's 2244 Wilton Dr, Wilton Manors **954/566–2722** • 11am-10pm, till 2am Th-Sat • pizza & panini

J Marks Restaurant 1245 N Federal Hwy **954/390–0770** • 11am-10pm, till 11pm Fri-Sat • full bar • gay-owned

Kitchenetta 2850 N Federal Hwy **954/567–3333** • dinner nightly, clsd Mon • wheelchair access

La Bamba 4245 N Federal Hwy **954/568–5662** • more gay Mon night

Lester's Diner 250 State Rd 84 **954/525–5641** • 24hrs • popular • more gay late nights • wheelchair access

Lips 1421 E Oakland Park Blvd (at Dixie Hwy) **954/567–0987** • 6pm-close, Sun brunch, clsd Mon • "the ultimate in drag dining" • karaoke

Maracas Mexican Bar & Grill 3001 N Federal Hwy **954/537–2002** • 11:30pm-10:30pm, till 11:30pm Fri-Sat • more gay Mon • patio • wheelchair access

Mason Jar Cafe 2980 N Federal Hwy **954/568–4100** • 11:30am-3pm Mon-Fri, dinner nightly • upscale comfort food • gay-owned

Mojo 4140 N Federal Hwy **954/568–4443** • open 4pm, clsd Sun • live shows • full bar

Le Patio 2401 NE 11th Ave **954/530–4641** • comfort food • lesbian–owned

Rosie's Bar & Grill 2449 Wilton Dr, Wilton Manors **954/563–0123** • 11am-11pm • popular • full bar

Simply Delish Cafe 2287 Wilton Dr, Wilton Manors **954/565–8646** • 8am-2pm, clsd Mon • wheelchair access

Sublime 1431 N Federal Hwy **954/539–9000** • 5:30pm-10pm, clsd Mon • vegan/ vegetarian

Tequila Sunrise Mexican Grill 4711 N Dixie Hwy **954/938–4473** • 11:30am-10pm, till 11pm Th-Sat, 1pm-10pm Sun • live shows

Tropics Cabaret & Restaurant 2000 Wilton Dr (at 20th) **954/537–6000** • lunch & dinner, Sun brunch, till 3am Sat • also piano bar • gay-owned • wheelchair access

Victoria Park Diner 1730 E Sunrise Blvd **954/759–0022** • 6:30am-9pm

The Wine Cellar 199 E Oakland Park Blvd 954/565-9021 • dinner, clsd Mon-Tue • Eastern European • gay-owned

ENTERTAINMENT & RECREATION

Gold Coast Roller Rink 2604 S Federal Hwy 954/547-3419 • 8pm-2am Tue • gay skate • lesbians/gay men • transgender-friendly

Sebastian Beach • more lesbians on the far north end of the beach

BOOKSTORES

Pride Factory 850 NE 13th St 954/463-6600 • 10am-9pm, 11am-7pm Sun

RETAIL SHOPS

GayMartUSA 2240 Wilton Dr (at NE 6th Ave) 954/630-0360 • 10am-11pm

Out of the Closet 2097 Wilton Dr, Wilton Manors 954/358-5580 • 10am-7pm, till 6pm Sun

To The Moon 2205 Wilton Dr (at 6th Ave), Wilton Manors 954/564-2987 • 10am-11pm • pride gifts, cards, & candy candy candy!

PUBLICATIONS

girL) Magazine 954/815-3220 • lesbian news & entertainment for south FL

GYMS & HEALTH CLUBS

Island City Health & Fitness 2270 Wilton Dr, Wilton Manors 954/318-3900 • 5am-11pm, 8am-8pm wknds

EROTICA

Fetish Factory 855 E Oakland Park Blvd 954/563-5777 • 11am-9pm, noon-6pm Sun

Hustler Hollywood 1500 E Sunrise Blvd (at NE 15th Ave) 954/828-9769

Fort Myers

INFO LINES & SERVICES

Gay AA Lambda Drummers 3049 McGregor Blvd (at St John the Apostle MCC) 239/275-5111 (AA#) • 8pm Tue & Sat in social hall • wheelchair access

ACCOMMODATIONS

The Hibiscus House B&B 2135 McGregor Blvd 239/332-2651 • gay-friendly • nonsmoking • WiFi • wheelchair access

Lighthouse Resort Inn & Suites 1051 5th St, Fort Myers Beach 239/463-9392, 800/778-7748 • gay-friendly • pool • kids ok • nonsmoking • WiFi • wheelchair access

The Resort on Carefree Blvd 3000 Carefree Blvd (at Cleveland Ave) 239/731-6366 • mostly women • homes & RV lots • pool • gym • kids/pets ok • older crowd • nonsmoking • woman-owned • $650-800/week

BARS

The Office Pub 3704 Cleveland Ave (at Grove) 239/936-3212 • noon-2am • mostly gay men • neighborhood bar • bears • theme nights

Tubby's 4350 Fowler St (off Colonial Blvd) 239/274-5001 • 2pm-2am • mostly gay men • karaoke • live shows • gay-owned

NIGHTCLUBS

The Bottom Line (TBL) 3090 Evans Ave (at Hanson) 239/337-7292, 800/839-6823 • 2pm-2am • lesbians/gay men • more women wknds • dancing/DJ • live shows • karaoke • videos • wheelchair access

RESTAURANTS

McGregor Food & Spirits Company 15675 McGregor Blvd, Ste 24 239/437-3499 • 11:30am-2am, from 4pm Sun • pub fare • some outdoor dining • also full bar • gay-owned

The Oasis 2260 Dr. Martin Luther King Blvd 239/334-1566 • breakfast, lunch & dinner • beer/wine • wheelchair access • women-owned

Gainesville

INFO LINES & SERVICES

Free to Be AA 3131 NW 13th St (The Pride Center) 352/372-8091 (AA#) • 7:30 Sun LGBT AA group

Pride Community Center 3131 NW 13th St 352/377-8915 • 3pm-7pm, noon-4pm Sat, clsd Sun • also switchboard

BARS

The University Club 18 E University Ave (enter rear) 352/378-6814 • 5pm-2am, from 9pm Sat, till 11pm Sun • lesbians/gay men • 3 levels • young crowd • dancing/DJ • karaoke • live shows • patio • wheelchair access

Wild Angels-Spikes 4130 NW 6th St 352/376-3772 • 5pm-2am, till 11pm Sun • popular • lesbians/gay men • neighborhood bar • wheelchair access

RESTAURANTS

Book Lovers Cafe 505 NW 13th St (at 5th Ave, in Books Inc) 352/352-4241, 888/374-4241 • 11am-9pm • vegetarian cafe & used bookstore

ENTERTAINMENT & RECREATION

Ponte Vedra LGBT Beach • Go N from Gainesville on Waldo Rd to N 301, then E on I-10. I-10 becomes 95. Go S on 95, then take a left. Go E onto Butler Blvd, which ends at A1A. Turn right onto A1A & then drive 5 to 7 minutes looking for Guana Boat Landing parking lot on the right. Park in a parking lot or get ticketed

BOOKSTORES

Wild Iris Books 802 W University Ave (at 8th St) 352/375-7477 • 1pm-9pm, till 5pm Sat, clsd Sun-Mon • feminist/ LGBT

PUBLICATIONS

Kindred Sisters Magazine 352/502-4101 • lesbian/ feminist monthly magazine for N Central FL

Hollywood

EROTICA

Pleasure Emporium 1321 S 30th Ave 954/927-8181

Islamorada

ACCOMMODATIONS

Casa Morada 136 Madeira Rd 305/664-0044, 888/881-3030 • gay-friendly • luxury all-suite hotel w/ private island • pool • pets ok • women-owned • $299+

Lookout Lodge Resort 87770 Overseas Hwy (at Plantation Blvd) 305/852-9915, 800/870-1772 • gay-friendly • waterfront resort • kids/ pets ok • nonsmoking • WiFi • $100-399

Jacksonville

INFO LINES & SERVICES

Free to Be LGBT AA 634 Lomax St 904/399-8535 (AA#) • 6:30pm Mon

Women's Center of Jacksonville 5644 Colcord Ave 904/722-3000

ACCOMMODATIONS

Comfort Inn Oceanfront 1515 N 1st St, Jacksonville Beach 904/241-2311, 800/654-8776 • gay-friendly • pool • fitness center • restaurant & Tiki bar

Hilton Garden Inn Jacksonville JTB/ Deerwood Park 9745 Gate Pkwy (at Southside Blvd) 904/997-6600, 877/782-9444 • gay-friendly • 15 minutes to beach • pool • jacuzzi • kids ok • WiFi • wheelchair access • $89-169

Spring Hill Suites Jacksonville 4385 Southside Blvd (at J Turner Butler Blvd) 904/997-6650, 888/287-9400 • gay-friendly • pool • kids ok • nonsmoking • WiFi • $99-169

BARS

616 Bar 616 Park St (at I-95) 904/358-6969 • 4pm-2am • lesbians/ gay men • neighborhood bar • karaoke • patio

AJ's Bar & Grill 10244 Atlantic Blvd (in Regency Walk Shopping Center) 904/805-9060 • 4pm-2am • mostly women • dancing/DJ • full menu • karaoke • wheelchair access • women-owned

Bo's Coral Reef 201 5th Ave N (at 2nd St), Jacksonville Beach 904/246-9874 • 2pm-2am • lesbians/ gay men • neighborhood bar • dancing/DJ • live shows

Club Sappho 2929 Plum St (upstairs at Metro) 904/388-8719 • 4pm-2am, till 4am Fri-Sat • popular • mostly women • dancing/DJ • multiracial • also Lesbo-a-GoGo 1st Fri

InCahoots 711 Edison Ave (btwn Riverside & Park) 904/353-6316 • 4pm, from 4pm Sun, clsd Mon-Tue • mostly gay men • dancing/DJ • multiracial • karaoke • drag shows • wheelchair access

The Metro 2929 Plum St 904/388-8719 • 2pm-2am, till 4am Fri-Sat • popular • lesbians/ gay men • dancing/DJ • drag shows • 18+ • wheelchair access

The New Boot Rack Saloon 4751 Lenox Ave (at Cassat Ave) 904/384-7090 • 3pm-2am • mostly gay men • country/ western • WiFi • beer/ wine • patio • wheelchair access

The Norm 2952 Roosevelt Blvd (at College) 904/384-9929 • 4pm-close • mostly women but everyone welcome • dancing/DJ • live shows • wheelchair access

Park Place Lounge 931 King St (at Post) 904/389-6616 • noon-2am • lesbians/ gay men • neighborhood bar • dancing/DJ • wheelchair access

NIGHTCLUBS

The Pearl 1101 N Main St (E 1st St) 904/791-4499 • 9pm-2am, clsd Sun-Wed • gay/ straight • dancing/DJ • theme nights

RESTAURANTS

Al's Pizza 1620 Margaret St, Ste 201 904/388-8384 • 11am-10pm, till 11pm Fri-Sat, noon-9pm Sun • in Riverside/ Little 5 Points area

Biscotti's 3556 Saint Johns Ave (Talbot Ave) **904/387-2060** • 10:30am-10pm, till midnight Fri-Sat, from 8am Sat-Sun • popular • killer desserts • women-owned

Bistro Aix 1440 San Marco Blvd **904/398-1949** • 11am-10pm, till 11pm Fri, 5pm-11pm Sat, 5pm-9pm Sun • upscale French bistro

Derby House 1068 Park St **904/356-0227** • 7am-2pm, till 9pm Fri-Sat • very popular wknds for brkfst

European Street Cafe 2753 Park St (at King) **904/384-9999** • 10am-10pm • salads • beer/ wine • patio • wheelchair access • gay-owned

The Grape Wine Bar & Bistro 10281 Midtown Pkwy #119 (at St Johns Town Center) **904/642-7111** • also retail shop & wine bar

Mossfire Grill 1537 Margaret St **904/355-4434** • lunch & dinner • Southwestern • full bar

RETAIL SHOPS

Rainbows & Stars 1046 Park St (in historic 5 Points) **904/356-7702** • 10am-7pm Wed-Fri, noon-7pm Sat, noon-5pm Sun, clsd Mon-Tue

Key West

INFO LINES & SERVICES

Gay & Lesbian Community Center 513 Truman Ave **305/292-3223** • many meetings & groups • WiFi

Keep It Simple (Gay/ Lesbian AA) **305/296-8654 (AA #)** • 8pm

➤ **Key West Business Guild** **305/294-4603, 800/535-7797**

ACCOMMODATIONS

Alexander Palms Court 715 South St (at Vernon) **305/296-6413, 800/858-1943** • gay-friendly • pool • private patios • wheelchair access • gay-owned • $110-320

Alexander's Guest House 1118 Fleming St (at Frances) **305/294-9919, 800/654-9919** • lesbians/ gay men • pool • nudity • WiFi • wheelchair access • gay-owned

Ambrosia House Tropical Lodging 615 & 618-622 Fleming St (at Simonton) **305/296-9838** • gay-friendly • pool • hot tub

Andrews Inn Zero Whalton Ln (at Duval) **305/294-7730, 888/263-7393** • gay-friendly • pool • kids ok • nonsmoking • WiFi • $130-339

The Artist House 534 Eaton St (at Duval) **305/296-3977, 800/582-7882** • gay/ straight • nonsmoking • $99-265

Avalon B&B 1317 Duval St (at United) **305/294-8233, 800/848-1317** • gay-friendly • swimming • near beach • sundeck • WiFi • $89-329

Big Ruby's Guesthouse 409 Appelrouth Ln (at Duval & Whitehead) **305/296-2323, 800/477-7829** • mostly gay men • full brkfst • pool • nudity • nonsmoking • WiFi • wheelchair access • gay-owned • $125-499

Casa de Luces 422 Amelia St (at Whitehead) **305/294-5269, 800/833-0372** • gay-friendly • nonsmoking • WiFi • wheelchair access • $99-229

Cypress House & Guest Studios 601 Caroline (at Simonton) **305/294-6969, 800/525-2488** • gay-friendly • guesthouse • 1888 Grand Conch mansion • pool • sundeck • WiFi • wheelchair access • $165-475

The Grand Guesthouse 1116 Grinnell St **305/294-0590, 888/947-2630** • lesbians/ gay men • in converted rooming house built in 1880s for cigar workers • nonsmoking • WiFi • gay-owned • $98-228

Heartbreak Hotel 716 Duval St (near Petronia) **305/296-5558** • gay/straight • kitchens • lesbian & gay owned • $99-110

Heron House Court 412 Frances St (at Eaton) **800/932-9119** • gay-friendly • full brkfst • swimming • nonsmoking • WiFi • wheelchair access • $149-369

Key West Harbor Inn B&B 219 Elizabeth St (at Greene) **305/296-2978, 800/608-6569** • lesbians/ gay men • pool • hot tub • nonsmoking • WiFi • $155-405

Knowles House B&B 1004 Eaton St (at Grinnell) **305/296-8132, 800/352-4414** • gay/ straight • restored 1880s Conch house • pool • nudity • nonsmoking • gay-owned • $109-229

La Te Da 1125 Duval St (at Catherine) **305/296-6706, 877/528-3320** • popular • lesbians/ gay men • full brkfst • nonsmoking • pool • restaurant & 3 bars • WiFi • gay-owned • $100-350

Marquesa Hotel 600 Fleming St (at Simonton) **305/292-1919, 800/869-4631** • gay-friendly • 2 pools • also restaurant • full bar • nonsmoking • WiFi • wheelchair access • $150-520

The Mermaid & the Alligator—A Key West B&B 729 Truman Ave (at Windsor Ln) **305/294-1894, 800/773-1894** • gay/ straight • full brkfst • pool • nonsmoking • WiFi • gay-owned • $148-318

➤**Pearl's Rainbow** 525 United St (at Duval) **305/292–1450, 800/749-6696** • popular • mostly women • hot tub • pool • sundeck • nudity • nonsmoking • WiFi • also bar & restaurant • wheelchair access • lesbian-owned • $89-389 • see ad in front color section

Pilot House Guest House 414 Simonton St (at Eaton) **305/293–6600, 800/648-3780** • gay/ straight • Victorian mansion in Old Town • pool • nudity • nonsmoking • WiFi • wheelchair access • $115-300

Seascape Inn 420 Olivia St (at Duval) **305/296-7776, 800/765-6438** • gay-friendly • pool • hot tub • WiFi • nonsmoking • $129-224

Simonton Court Historic Inn & Cottages 320 Simonton St (at Caroline) **305/294-6386, 800/944-2687** • gay-friendly • built in 1880s • pool • nonsmoking • WiFi • $160-515

Tropical Inn 812 Duval St (at Petronia) **305/294-9977, 888/611-6510** • gay-friendly • also cottage suites • hot tub • pool • sundeck • WiFi • $158-398

BARS

The 801 Bourbon Bar 801 Duval St (at Petronia) **305/294-4737** • 10am-4am, from noon Sun • lesbians/ gay men • neighborhood bar • dancing/DJ • popular drag shows • Sun bingo

Key West

WHERE THE GIRLS ARE:
You can't miss 'em during WomenFest in September, but other times they're just off Duval St., somewhere between Eaton and South Streets. Or on the beach. Or in the water.

LGBT PRIDE:
June. 305/292–3223, web: www.pridefestkeywest.com.

ANNUAL EVENTS:
February - Kelly McGillis Classic Women's & Girls' Flag Football Tournament 888/464–9332, web: www.iwffa.com.
September - WomenFest, web: www.womenfest.com.
October - Fantasy Fest 305/296-1817, web: www.fantasyfest.net. Weeklong Halloween celebration with parties, masquerade balls & parades.

CITY INFO:
Key West Business Association 800/FLA-KEYS, web: www.fla-keys.com/keywest.

BEST VIEW:
Old Town Trolley Tour (1/2 hour) 888/910-8687, web: www.historictours.com/keywest.

ATTRACTIONS:
Audubon House and Gardens 305/294-2116, web: www.audubonhouse.com.
Dolphin Research Center 305/289–1121, web: www.dolphins.org.
Hemingway House, web: www.hemingwayhome.com.
Red Barn Theatre 305/296-9911, web: www.redbarntheatre.com.
Southernmost Point USA.
Sunset Celebration at Mallory Square.

WEATHER:
The average temperature year-round is 78°, and the sun shines nearly every day. Any time is the right time for a visit.

TRANSIT:
Friendly Cab 305/292-0000.
Key West Express (ferry) 888/539–2628, web: www.seakeywestexpress.com.
Key West Transit Authority, web: www.kwtransit.com.

Bobby's Monkey Bar 900 Simonton St (at Olivia) 305/294-2655 • noon-4am • mostly gay men • neighborhood bar • WiFi • wheelchair access

Bourbon Street Pub 724 Duval St (at Petronia) 305/293-9800 • 11am-4am, from noon Sun • mostly gay men • popular • garden bar w/ pool & hot tub • wheelchair access

Garden of Eden 224 Duval St 305/296-4565 • 10am-4am, from noon Sun • gay/straight • clothing-optional sun bathing • dancing/DJ • live music

Hog's Breath Saloon 400 Front St 305/296-4222 • gay-friendly • food served • live music

La Te Da 1125 Duval St (at Catherine) 305/296-6706 • lesbians/ gay men • 3 bars (piano bar & cabaret) & restaurant • wheelchair access • gay-owned

➤ **Pearl's Patio** 525 United St (at Duval & Simonton, at Pearl's Rainbow) 305/293-9805 x156, 800/749-6696 • noon-10pm, later on wknds, happy hour 5pm-7pm Mon-Sat • women only • sandwiches, burgers, salads & snacks • karaoke • special events

Virgilio's 524 Duval St (at Fleming in La Trattoria) 305/296-8118 • 7pm-4am • gay/ straight • martini bar • garden • food served • live music • late-night DJ

NIGHTCLUBS

Aqua 711 Duval St 305/294-0555 • 3pm-2am, till 4am Th-Sat, also Wet Bar from 9pm Fri-Sat • lesbians/ gay men • dancing/DJ • drag shows • karaoke • wheelchair access

Bottle Cap Lounge 305/296-2807 • noon-4am • gay/straight • dancing/ DJ

CAFES

Croissants de France 816 Duval St 305/294-2624 • bakery 7:30am-6pm, restaurant open till 10pm • beer/ wine • patio

RESTAURANTS

Antonia's Restaurant 615 Duval St (at Southard) 305/294-6565 • lunch & dinner • popular • Italian • full bar

Azur 425 Grinnell St 305/292-2987

Bo's Fish Wagon 801 Caroline (at William) 305/294-9272 • lunch & dinner • popular • "seafood & eat it"

Cafe Sole 1029 Southard St (at Frances) 305/294-0230 • dinner nightly, Sun brunch • romantic • candlelit backyard

Camille's 1202 Simonton (at Catherine) 305/296-4811 • brkfst, lunch & dinner • bistro • hearty brkfst

El Meson de Pepe 410 Wall St (in Mallory Sq) 305/295-2620 • lunch & dinner, Cuban • live music

The Flamingo Buoy Filet Co 1100 Packer St 305/295-7970 • lunch & dinner • wheelchair access

Grand Cafe Key West 314 Duval St 305/292-4740 • lunch & dinner

Half Shell Raw Bar 231 Margaret St 305/294-7496 • 11am-10pm • waterfront

Hurricane Hole 305/294-8025, 305/294-0200 • 10am-10pm • dockside bar

Jack Flats 509 Duval St 305/294-7955 • 11am-2am • wheelchair access

Kelly's Caribbean Bar Grill & Brewery 301 Whitehead St (at Caroline) 305/293-8484 • lunch & dinner • full bar • owned by actress Kelly McGillis

La Trattoria Venezia 524 Duval St (at Fleming) 305/296-1075 • 5pm-10:30pm • full bar

Lobos Mixed Grill 5 Key Lime Sq (south of Southard St) 305/296-5303 • 11am-6pm • sandwiches • plenty veggie • beer/ wine

Louie's Backyard 700 Waddell Ave (at Vernon) 305/294-1061 • 11:30am-1am • popular • fine cont'l dining

Mangia Mangia 900 Southard St (at Margaret St) 305/294-2469 • dinner only • fresh pasta • beer/ wine • patio

Mangoes 700 Duval St (at Angela) 305/292-4606 • lunch & dinner, bar till 1am • "Floribbean" cuisine • full bar • patio • wheelchair access

Michaels 532 Margaret St 305/295-1300 • dinner only, steakhouse

New York Pizza Cafe 1075 Duval St (Duval Square) 305/292-1991 • 11am-10pm

Nine One Five 915 Duval St 305/296-0669 • dinner only, tapas & full bar

Salsa Loca 618 Duval St (in Cowboy Bills) 305/292-1865 • clsd Mon • gay-friendly • tasty, inexpensive Mexican

Sarabeth's 530 Simonton St 305/293-8181

Seven Fish 632 Olivia St (at Elizabeth) 305/296-2777 • 6pm-10pm, clsd Tue • popular

Six Toed Cat 832 Whitehead St 305/294-3318 • brkfst & lunch

Square One 1075 Duval St (at Truman) **305/296-4300** • lunch and dinner, dinner only Mon • full bar • wheelchair access

Sweat Tea 1114 Duval St

Upper Crust 611 Duval St **305/293-8890** • noon-11pm • excellent pizza

ENTERTAINMENT & RECREATION

Fort Zachary Taylor Beach • more gay to the right

Gay & Lesbian Trolley Tour 305/294-4603 • 10:50am Sat • check out all of the gay hotspots & historical points • look for rainbow-decorated trolley

Island Ceremonies 305/304-0806, 305/745-8886 • commitment ceremonies in the Keys with Captain Lynda • woman-owned

Moped Hospital 601 Truman 866/296-1625 • forget the car—mopeds are a must for touring the island

Venus Charters Garrison Bight Marina 305/304-1181 • snorkeling • light-tackle fishing • dolphin-watching • personalized excursions • lesbian-owned

BOOKSTORES

Key West Island Books 513 Fleming St (at Duval) **305/294-2904** • 10am-9pm, till 6pm Sun • new & used rare books • LGBT section

RETAIL SHOPS

Fast Buck Freddie's 500 Duval St (at Fleming) **305/294-2007** • 10am-10pm • wheelchair access

Frank's In Touch 706-A Duval St (at Angela) **305/294-1995** • 9am-9pm • gay gifts

GYMS & HEALTH CLUBS

Body Zone South 2740 N Roosevelt Blvd **305/292-2930**

EROTICA

Fairvilla Megastore 520 Front St **305/292-0448** • 9am-midnight • clean, well-lighted adult store w/ emphasis on couples

Leather Master 418 Appelrouth Ln **305/292-5051** • 11am-10pm, noon-8pm Sun • custom leather, toys & more

Lake Worth

see also West Palm Beach

INFO LINES & SERVICES

Compass LGBT Community Center 201 N Dixie Hwy **561/533-9699** • 9am-9pm, till 7pm Fri, 3pm-7pm Sat, clsd Sun • wheelchair access

BARS

The Bar 2211 N Dixie Hwy **561/370-3954** • 2pm-2am, noon-midnight Sun • lesbians/ gay men • neighborhood bar • dancing/DJ • karaoke • lesbian-owned

The Mad Hatter Bar & Grill 1532 N Dixie Hwy (16th Ave) **561/547-8860** • 1pm-2am, noon-midnight Sun • mostly men • neighborhood bar • older crowd • gay-owned

CAFES

Mother Earth Coffee & Gifts **561/460-8647** • 8am-7pm, till 10pm Fri-Sat • fair trade • organic beans

RESTAURANTS

The Cottage 522 Lucerne Ave **561/586-0080** • dinner only • also bar • wheelchair access

Lakeland

BARS

Pulse 1030 E Main St **863/688-9463** • 6pm-2am, till midnight Sun • mostly gay men • dancing/DJ • transgender-friendly • drag shows • strippers • wheelchair access

Largo

BARS

Christopher Street Bar 13344 66th St N (at Ulmerton Rd) **727/538-0660, 727/520-4111 (INFO LINE)** • 2pm-2am • mostly gay men • dancing/DJ • male dancers • WiFi

Marathon

ACCOMMODATIONS

Tropical Cottages 243 61st St Gulf **305/743-6048** • gay-friendly • outdoor hot tub • pets ok • nonsmoking • $99-129

ENTERTAINMENT & RECREATION

Bahia Honda State Park & Beach 12 miles S of Marathon

Melbourne

ACCOMMODATIONS

Beach Bungalow 312 Wavecrest Ave, Indialantic by the Sea **321/984-1330, 888/414-5314** • gay-friendly • beachfront town homes • nonsmoking • WiFi •$1,400-2,000/wk

Crane Creek Inn B&B 907 E Melbourne Ave **321/768-6416** • gay/ straight • full brkfst • pool • hot tub • dogs ok • WiFi • $139-199

Bars

Cold Keg 4060 W New Haven Ave (1/2 mile E of I-95) **321/724-1510** • 4pm-2am, till Sun • lesbians/ gay men • dancing/DJ • drag shows • 18+ • wheelchair access

MIAMI

Miami is divided into 3 geographical areas:
Miami—Overview
Miami—Greater Miami
Miami—Miami Beach/ South Beach

Miami—Overview

INFO LINES & SERVICES

➤ **Greater Miami CVB** **305/539-3000, 800/933-8448** • plan your Miami vacation! see ad in front color section

Switchboard of Miami **305/646-3600** • 24hrs • gay-friendly info & referrals for Dade County

ENTERTAINMENT & RECREATION

Sailboat Charters of Miami 3400 Pan American Dr (at S Bayshore Dr) **305/772-4221** • lesbians/ gay men • private sailing charters aboard all-teakwood 46-foot clipper to Bahamas & the Keys

PUBLICATIONS

Miami Gay News www.miamigaynews.com

Miami—Greater Miami

NIGHTCLUBS

Club Sugar 2301 SW 32nd Ave (at Coral Wy) **305/443-7657** • 10:30pm-5am Th-Sat, 8pm-3am Sun, clsd Mon-Wed

The Coco Bar 7250 NW 11th St (next to the 836 overpass) **305/262-9500** • 9pm-2am • mostly gay men • dancing/DJ • cabaret • karaoke

Discotekka 950 NE 2nd Ave (at Metropolis Nightclub) **305/371-3773** • after hours Sat only • mostly gay men • dancing/DJ • 18+

Space Miami 34 NE 11th St (at NE 1st Ave) **305/375-0001** • gay-friendly • dancing/DJ • popular club w/ int'l visiting DJs

Vlada Lounge 3215 NE 2nd Ave (at NE 32nd St) **305/381-5015** • 4pm-3am, from 6pm Sat-Sun • mostly gay men • dancing/DJ • drag shows • wheelchair access

CAFES

Gourmet Station 7601 Biscayne Blvd (at NE 71st St) **305/762-7229** • 8am-9pm, till 8pm Fri, clsd Sat-Sun

RESTAURANTS

Area 31 270 Biscayne Blvd Way (at the Epic Hotel) **305/424-5234** • brkfst, lunch & dinner • seafood • amazing view • wheelchair access

Habibi's Grill 93 SE 2nd St (at NE 1st Ave) **786/425-2699** • 11am-8pm, clsd Sun • Lebanese/ Mediterranean • plenty veggie

Jimmy's East Side Diner 7201 Biscayne Blvd **305/754-3692** • 7am-4pm • wheelchair access

The Magnum Lounge & Restaurant 709 NE 79th St **305/757-3368** • 6pm-midnight, bar open 5pm-2am, clsd Mon • neighborhood bar • piano bar • reservations recommended

Michy's 6927 Biscayne Blvd (at NE 69th) **305/759-2001** • dinner only • "luxurious comfort food"

Ortanique on the Mile 278 Miracle Mile (at Salzedo), Coral Gables **305/446-7710** • lunch Mon-Fri, dinner nightly • Caribbean • full bar

Ristorante Fratelli Milano 213 SE 1st St (at 2nd Ave) **305/373-2300** • 11am-10pm • homemade Italian • wheelchair access

Royal Bavarian Schnitzel Haus 1085 NE 79th St **305/754-8002** • 5pm-11pm • German fare

Soyka 5556 NE 4th Ct **305/759-3117** • lunch & dinner, wknd brunch • full bar

UVA 69 6900 Biscayne Blvd (at NE 69th St) **305/754-9022** • 11am-11pm, 8am-midnight wknds • European bistro & lounge • patio

BOOKSTORES

Lambda Passages Bookstore 7545 Biscayne Blvd (at NE 76th) **305/754-6900** • 11am-9pm, noon-6pm Sun • LGBT/ feminist

Miami—Miami Beach/ South Beach

ACCOMMODATIONS

The Angler's 660 Washington Ave **305/534-9600** • gay/straight • luxury boutique resort • restaurant & lounge • pool • WiFi

Aqua Hotel & Lounge 1530 Collins Ave **305/538-4361** • gay/ straight • boutique hotel • $95-395

Beachcomber Hotel 1340 Collins Ave (at 13th St) **305/531-3755, 888/305-4683** • gay-friendly • nonsmoking • WiFi • $65-140

Blue Moon Hotel 944 Collins Ave **305/673-2262, 800/553-7739** • gay-friendly • pool • also bar

Bresaro Suites at the Mantell Plaza 255 W 24th St **305/772-5665** • gay/ straight • pool • kitchens • gay-owned • $129-169

The Cardozo Hotel 1300 Ocean Dr **305/535-6500, 800/782-6500** • gay-friendly • restaurant • Gloria Estefan's plush hotel • kids ok • WiFi • wheelchair access • $170-505

The Century 140 Ocean Dr **305/674-8855, 877/659-8855** • gay-friendly • nonsmoking • WiFi • wheelchair access • $115-200

Chesterfield Hotel, Suites & Day Spa 855 Collins Ave **305/531-5831, 877/762-3477** • gay/ straight • super stylish hotel • $99-450

Miami

WHERE THE GIRLS ARE:

In Miami proper, Coral Gables and the University district, as well as Biscayne Blvd. along the coast, are the lesbian hangouts of choice. You'll see women everywhere in South Beach, but especially along Ocean Dr., Washington, Collins and Lincoln Roads.

LGBT PRIDE:

April, web: www.miamibeach-gaypride.com.

ANNUAL EVENTS:

Feb/March - Winter Party 202/571-1924, web: www.winterparty.com. Beach dance party benefiting the National Gay & Lesbian Task Force.

April/May - Gay & Lesbian Film Festival, web: www.mglff.com.

May - Aqua Girl 305/576.2782, web: www.aquagirl.org. A women's weekend.

November - White Party Vizcaya 305/576-1234, web: www.whiteparty.net. AIDS benefit.

CITY INFO:

Greater Miami Convention & Visitors Bureau 305/539-3000. 701 Brickell Ave, web: www.miamiandbeaches.com.

BEST VIEW:

If you've got money to burn, a helicopter flight over Miami Beach is a great way to see the city. Otherwise, hit the beach.

ATTRACTIONS:

Bayside Marketplace 305/577-3344, web: www.baysidemarketplace.com.

Miami Beach Botanical Garden 305/673-7256, web: www.mbgarden.org.

Miami Design Preservation League 305/672-2014. web: mdpl.org.

Miami Museum of Science & Planetarium 305/646-4200, web: www.miamisci.org.

Monkey Jungle 305/235-1611, web: www.monkeyjungle.com.

Museum of Contempory Art, N Miami 305/893-6211, web: www.mocanomi.org.

Parrot Jungle Island 305/400-7000, web: www.parrotjungle.com.

Jewish Museum of Florida 305/672-5044, web: www.jewishmuseum.com.

WEATHER:

Warm all year. Temperatures stay in the 90°s during the summer and drop into the mid-60°s in the winter. Be prepared for sunshine!

TRANSIT:

USA Taxi 305/525-2455, web: www.taxiservicemiami.com.

Swoop is a slightly pimped up electric golf cart for geting around SOBE 305/409-6636, web: www.swoopmiami.com.

Express Shuttle 305/282-4626, web: www.expressshuttlemiami.com.

Metro Bus Dial 3-1-1 , web: http://miamidade.gov.

Clrca 39 Hotel 3900 Collins Ave (at 39th St) 305/538-4900, 877/824-7223 • gay-friendly • pool • lounge • WiFi • wheelchair access • $99-699

The Colony Hotel 736 Ocean Dr (at 7th St) 305/673-0088 • gay-friendly • bistro • oceanfront • WiFi • wheelchair access • $129-400

Delano Hotel 1685 Collins Ave 305/672-2000, 800/697-1791 • gay-friendly • food served • pool • kids ok • wheelchair access • $350-950

The European Guesthouse 721 Michigan Ave (btwn 7th & 8th) 305/673-6665 • lesbians/ gay men • B&B • full brkfst • pool • WiFi • gay-owned • $99-199

The Hotel 801 Collins Ave 305/531-2222, 877/843-4683 • gay-friendly • restaurant & bar • pool • nonsmoking • WiFi • wheelchair access • $255-525

Hotel Ocean 1230–38 Ocean Dr 305/672-2579, 800/783-1725 • popular • gay/ straight • great location • pets ok • WiFi • wheelchair access • $199-950

Lords of South Beach 1120 Collins Ave 305/674-7800, 877/448-4754 • mostly men • boutique hotel • spa • pool • kids ok • nonsmoking • wheelchair access • $125-600

The National Hotel 1677 Collins Ave 305/532-2311, 800/327-8370 • gay/ straight • pool • kids ok • restaurant & lounge • WiFi • wheelchair access • $400-799

Penguin Hotel 1418 Ocean Dr 305/534-9334, 800/235-3296 • lesbians/ gay men • full restaurant • kids ok • wheelchair access • $145-280

The Raleigh, Miami Beach 1775 Collins Ave (at Ocean Front) 305/534-6300, 800/848-1775 • gay-friendly • pool • restaurant & bars • kids/ pets ok • WiFi • wheelchair access • $225-550

SoBeYou 1018 Jefferson Ave 305/534-5247, 877/599-5247 • gay/ straight • nonsmoking • WiFi • wheelchair access • lesbian-owned • $105-325

Something Special, A Lesbian Venture 305/696-8826 • women only • apt, camping & dining

South Seas 1751 Collins Ave 305/538-1411, 800/345-2678 • gay-friendly • clean & basic • beach access • pool • WiFi • $349-698

The Tides South Beach 1220 Ocean Dr 305/604-5070, 305/503-3268 • gay/ straight • private beach area • pool • WiFi • also La Marea restaurant • $350-5,000

The Winterhaven 1400 Ocean Dr 305/531-5571, 800/553-7739 • gay/ straight • ocean views • also bar • WiFi • wheelchair access • $109-339

BARS

Bar 721 721 N Lincoln Ln 305/532-1342 • 2pm-5am, from 5pm Sat-Sun • gay-friendly • neighborhood bar • karaoke

Buck15 Lounge 707 Lincoln Ln 305/538-3815 • 10pm-5am, clsd Sun-Mon • gay/ straight • more gay Th • gallery

Creme Lounge 725 Lincoln Ln N (upstairs from Score) 305/535-1163 • open Tue & Th-Sat • lesbians/ gay men • Girl party Sat

Jump 1439 Washington Ave (at Lux bar) 786/374-7475 • Sun only • produced by sobesocialclub.com

Palace Bar & Grill 1200 Ocean Dr (at 12th St) 305/531-7234 • 10am-1am, till 2am Fri-Sat • lesbians/ gay men • also restaurant • drag shows

NIGHTCLUBS

Mova 1625 Michigan Ave 305/534-8181 • 3pm-3am, from noon Sun • lesbians/ gay men

➤**Pandora Events** 305/975-6933 • monthly women's parties • locations rotate so check website: www.pandoraevents.com

Score 727 Lincoln Rd (at Meridian) 305/535-1111 • lounge opens 3pm, dance club 10pm-5am Tue & Th-Sat • popular • lesbians/ gay men • drag shows • karaoke • videos

Sweet 1625 Michigan Ave (at Mova) • 8pm Th only • mostly women • dancing/DJ

Twist 1057 Washington Ave (at 11th) 305/538-9478 • 1pm-5am • popular • mostly gay men • 7 bars • dancing/DJ • karaoke • drag shows • go-go boys • wheelchair access

CAFES

News Cafe 800 Ocean Dr (at 8th St) 305/538-6397 • 24hrs • also bookstore & bar

RESTAURANTS

11th Street Diner 1065 Washington (at 11th) 305/534-6373 • 24hrs • full bar

8 Oz Burger Bar 1080 Alton Rd (at 11th St) 305/397-8246 • 11am-3am, till 5am Th-Sat • also bar

B&B: Burger & Beer Joint 1766 Bay Rd (at 18th St) 305/672-3287 • lunch & dinner • the name says it all

Balans 1022 Lincoln Rd (btwn Michigan & Lennox) 305/534-9191 • 8am-midnight

Big Pink 157 Collins (at 2nd St) 305/532-4700 • 8am-midnight, open late wknds • "real food for real people"

David's Cafe II 1654 Meridian Ave 305/672-8707 • 24hrs • Cuban

El Rancho Grande 1626 Pennsylvania Ave (S of Lincoln) 305/673-0480 • 11am-11pm

Juice & Java 1346 Washington Ave (at 14th St) 305/531-6675 • 9am-9pm, 11am-6pm Sun • healthy fast food • wheelchair access

Larios on the Beach 820 Ocean Dr (at 8th) 305/532-9577 • 11:30am-midnight • Cuban • wheelchair access

Nexxt Cafe 700 Lincoln Rd (at Euclid Ave) 305/532-6643 • 11:30am-11pm, till midnight Fri-Sat

Something Special, a Lesbian Venture 305/696-8826 • women only • 6pm-10pm, clsd Mon-Tue • vegetarian • lesbian-owned

Spiga 1228 Collins Ave (at 12th St) 305/534-0079 • dinner only • tasty homemade pastas

Sushi Rock Cafe 1351 Collins Ave (at 14th) 305/532-2133 • noon-midnight • popular

Tiramesu 721 Lincoln Rd 305/532-4538 • lunch & dinner • Italian

ENTERTAINMENT & RECREATION

Beach Scooter Rentals 1341 Washington Ave 305/538-7878

Fritz's Skate & Bike 730 Lincoln Rd 305/532-1954, 877/699-5252

The Gay Beach/ 12th St Beach 12th St & Ocean

Haulover Beach Park A1A S of Sunny Isle Blvd, North Miami Beach • popular nude beach

Lincoln Rd Lincoln Rd (btwn Bay Rd & Collins Aves) • pedestrian mall that embodies the rebirth of South Beach

South Beach Bike Tours 305/673-2002 • half-day bike tour of Art Deco district • gay-owned

RETAIL SHOPS

Pink Palm 723 Lincoln Rd (at Meridian Ave) 305/397-8097 • 10am-11pm • unique gifts

GYMS & HEALTH CLUBS

Crunch 1259 Washington Ave 305/674-8222

David Barton Gym 2323 Collins Ave 305/534-1660

EROTICA

Pleasure Boutique 1019 5th St 305/673-3311

Mt Dora

ACCOMMODATIONS

Adora Inn 352/735-3110 • gay/ straight • full brkfst • kids 6+ ok • nonsmoking • WiFi • gay-owned • $149-250

Naples

see also Fort Myers

ACCOMMODATIONS

Palm Tree Hideaway 239/348-1630 • mostly women • studio • pool • $75

BARS

Bambusa Bar & Grill 600 Goodlette Rd N (at 5th Ave N) 239/649-5657 • 4pm-midnight • gay-friendly • neighborhood bar • karaoke Sat • also restaurant • videos • gay-owned

Snappers Nightclub 2634 Tamiami Trail E (at Bay Shore Dr) 239/775-4114 • 3pm-2am, from 11am Wed-Sat, from noon Sun • lesbians/ gay men • neighborhood bar • dancing/DJ • transgender-friendly • karaoke • drag shows • wheelchair access

CAFES

Sunburst Cafe 2340 Pine Ridge Rd (at Airport Pulling Rd) 239/263-3123 • 7am-3pm • wheelchair access

RESTAURANTS

Caffe dell'Amore 1400 Gulf Shore Blvd N (at Banyan Blvd) 239/261-1389 • open Oct-May only • dinner • Italian • beer/ wine • wheelchair access

Patric's 1485 Pine Ridge Rd #3 239/304-9754 • 11am-10pm • gay/ straight • cont'l • eclectic shabby-chic • jazz piano

New Port Richey

BARS

Chill Chamber 3501 Universal Plaza (at Moog Rd & US 19) 727/844-3474 • 2pm-2am • lesbians/ gay men • dancing/DJ • live music • wheelchair access

Ocala

BARS

Copa/ Tropix 2330 S Pine Ave 352/351-5721 • 2pm-2am • mostly gay men • dancing/DJ • drag shows • food served

Orlando

INFO LINES & SERVICES

GLBT Community Center of Central Florida 946 N Mills Ave 407/228-8272 • 9am-9pm, noon-5pm Sat-Sun

ACCOMMODATIONS

Eo Inn & Spa 227 N Eola Dr (at Robinson) 407/481-8485, 888/481-8488 • gay/ straight • boutique hotel • nonsmoking • sundeck • hot tub • WiFi • cafe on-site • $100-300

Four Points by Sheraton Studio City 5905 International Dr (at Kirkman) 407/351-2100, 866/716-8105 • gay-friendly • bar & restaurant • pool • WiFi • wheelchair access • $89-399

Grand Bohemian Hotel Orlando 325 S Orange Ave 407/313-9000, 888/213-9110 • gay-friendly • luxury hotel • pool • kids ok • nonsmoking • WiFi • wheelchair access • $150-250

Hyatt Residency Grand Cypress 1 Grand Cypress Blvd 407/239-1234 • gay-friendly • 1,500 acre resort • private lake • horseback riding • golf • pool • WiFi • wheelchair access

Parliament House Resort 410 N Orange Blossom Tr 407/425-7571 • lesbians/ gay men • pool • restaurant • wheelchair access • $64-104+tax • also 6 bars • multiracial • live shows • dancing/DJ • young crowd • gay-owned

Rick's B&B PO Box 22318, 32830 407/396-7751, 407/414-7751 (CELL) • mostly gay men • full brkfst • pool • nudity • patio • WiFi • gay-owned • $100-300

Wyndham Orlando Resort 8001 International Dr 407/351-2420, 877/999-3223 • gay-friendly • villa surrounded by gardens • pools • wheelchair access

BARS

Bear's Den 410 N Orange Blossom Tr (at Parliament House) 407/425-7571 • 6pm-2am, from noon wknds • mostly gay men • country/ western • levi/ leather • strippers • piano • also restaurant

Copper Rocket 106 Lake Ave (at 17-92), Maitland 407/645-0069 • 4pm-2am • gay-friendly • also restaurant • wheelchair access

Orlando

WHERE THE GIRLS ARE:
Tourists are—where else?—at the tourist attractions, including Disney World.

LGBT PRIDE:
June. Central Florida Black Pride 407/977-2997, web: orlandoblackpride.com.

ANNUAL EVENTS:
May-June - Gay Days at Disney World 407/896-8431, web: gaydays.com.
May-June - Orlando Fringe Festival 407/648-0077, www.orland-ofringe.org.

CITY INFO:
407/363-5872, web: www.orlandoinfo.com.

WEATHER:
Mild winters, hot summers.

ATTRACTIONS:
Gatorland 407/855-5496, web: www.gatorland.com.
Sea World 888/800-5447, web: www.seaworld.com.
Universal Studios 407/363-8000, web: www.universalorlando.com.
Walt Disney World 407/939-1289, web: www.disneyworld.com.
Wet & Wild Waterpark 407/351-1800, web: www.wetnwildor-lando.com.

TRANSIT:
Mears Taxi 407/422-2222, web: www.mearstaxi.net/CabWeb.
Kelley's Transportation 407/927-2500, web: www.orlandosan-ford.com.
Lynx 407/841-5969, web: www.golynx.com.

Hank's 5026 Edgewater Dr (at Lee Rd) 407/291–2399 • noon-2am • mostly gay men • neighborhood bar • beer/ wine • patio • wheelchair access

Jungle Sundays 26 Wall St Plaza (upstairs) 407/481–1199 • 4pm-2am Sun only (seasonal) • mostly gay men • dancing/DJ • drag shows

The New Phoenix 7124 Aloma Ave (at Forsythe), Winter Park 407/678–9070 • 6pm-2am, from 4pm Th-Sat • lesbians/ gay men • neighborhood bar • dancing/DJ • karaoke • live shows • drag shows

Paradise 1300 N Mills Ave (btwn Virginia & Colonial) 407/898–0090 • 4pm-2am, from noon wknds • mostly gay men, neighborhood bar • WiFi • gay-owned

The Peacock Room 1321 N Mills Ave (at Montana) 407/228–0048 • 4:30pm-2am, from 8pm wknds • gay-friendly • art shows

Sip 724 Virginia Dr (at Dauphin Ln) 407/894–4747 • gay/ straight • neighborhood bar • karaoke • WiFi

Stonewall Bar 741 W Church St (at Glenn Ln) 407/373–0888 • 5pm-2am • mostly gay men • dancing/DJ • karaoke • wheelchair access • gay-owned

Wylde's 3530 S Orange Ave (at Suddath Dr) 407/852–0612 • 5pm-2am • lesbians/ gay men • neighborhood bar • WiFi

NIGHTCLUBS

Mr Sisters 5310 E Colonial Dr (at N Semoran Blvd, on Lake Barton) 407/545–2456, 888/468–7258 • 11am-2am • mostly gay men • dancing/DJ

Parliament House Resort 410 N Orange Blossom Tr (at South St) 407/425–7571 • 10:30am-3am • lesbians/ gay men • 6 bars • dancing/DJ • multiracial • live shows • videos • also restaurant • wheelchair access • gay-owned

Pulse Orlando 1912 S Orange Ave (at Kaley St) 407/649–3888 • 9pm-2am, clsd Sun • mostly gay men • dancing/DJ • theme nights • drag shows • 18+

Revolution 375 S Bumby Ave (at South St) 407/228–9900 • 4pm-close, from 10pm Sun • lesbians/ gay men • 3rd Sat Girl's night • dancing/DJ • multiracial • go-go dancers • videos • drag shows • 18+ • patio • wheelchair access

CAFES

Pom Pom's 67 N Bumby Ave 407/894–0865 • 11am-5am, 24hrs Fri-Sat, tea & sandwiches

White Wolf Cafe & Antique Shop 1829 N Orange Ave (at Princeton) 407/895–9911 • 7am-9pm, till 10pm Fri-Sat, 8am-3pm Sun • beer/ wine • wheelchair access

RESTAURANTS

Brian's 1409 N Orange Ave (at Virginia) 407/896–9912 • 6am-4pm • popular Sun

Dandelion Communitea Cafe 618 N Thornton Ave (at Colonial) 407/362–1864 • 11am-10pm, till 3pm Mon, tilll 5pm Sun • vegetarian/ vegan • beer/wine

Dexter's Thornton Park 808 E Washington St 407/648–2777 • lunch and dinner • also Winter Park & Lake Mary locations

Ethos Vegan Kitchen 1235 N Orange Ave (at Virginia Dr) 407/228–3898 • 11am-10pm, 10am-3pm Sun • WiFi • wheelchair access

Funky Monkey Wine Company 407/427–1447 • 5pm-11pm • sushi • drag shows weekly

Garden Cafe 810 W Colonial Dr (at Westmoreland) 407/999–9799 • 11am-10pm, from noon wknds • clsd Mon • vegetarian Chinese • wheelchair access

Hamburger Mary's Orlando 110 W Church St (at Garland) 321/319–0600 • 11am-midnight, till 1am Th-Sat • full bar • live shows • karaoke • wheelchair access • gay-owned

Houston's 215 South Orlando Ave, Winter Park 407/740–4005 • lunch & dinner • upscale American • wheelchair access

Hue 629 E Central Blvd (at N Summerlin Ave) 407/849–1800 • lunch & dinner • new American • full bar

Lago 4979 New Broad St 407/331–5246 • dinner nightly, clsd Sun • upscale Italian • wheelchair access

Loving Hut 2101 E Colonial Dr (at Palm Dr) 407/894–5673 • 11am-9pm, from 3pm Sun, clsd • vegetarian/ vegan • wheelchair access

The Rainbow Cafe at Parliament House 407/425–7571 • 7am-11pm, till 3am Fri-Sun • lesbians/ gay men

BOOKSTORES

Mojo 930 N Mills Ave (at E Marks St) 407/896–0204 • 1pm-8pm, 3pm-6pm Sun • LGBT

RETAIL SHOPS

A Comic Shop 114 South Semoran Blvd, Winter Park 407/332–9636 • 11am-7pm, till 9pm Wed, till midnight Fri-Sat

Fun Factory 6203 Λ2 W Sand Lake Rd (at Universal Blvd) 407/826–1627 • gifts • adult toys • clothing

Harmony Designs 496 N Orange Blossom Tr 407/481–9850 • 3:30pm-10pm • pride store • wheelchair access • gay-owned

PUBLICATIONS

Hotspots 954/928–1862 • weekly entertainment guide

Watermark PO Box 533655, 32853 407/481–2243, 877/926–8118 • bi-weekly LGBT newspaper for Central FL

EROTICA

Fairvilla Megastore 1740 N Orange Blossom Tr 407/425–6005 • 9am-2am

Palm Beach

ACCOMMODATIONS

The Chesterfield Hotel 363 Coconut Row 561/659–5800 • gay-friendly • pool • jacuzzi

RESTAURANTS

Ta-boo 221 Worth Ave 561/835–3500 • 11:30am-10pm, till 11pm Fri-Sat • cont'l • wheelchair access

Panama City

ACCOMMODATIONS

Casa de Playa 20304 Front Beach Rd, Panama City Beach 850/236–8436 • lesbians/ gay men • guesthouse • steps from Gulf of Mexico • jacuzzi • heated pool • nonsmoking • patios • gay-owned • $150-175

Wisteria Inn 20404 Front Beach Rd, Panama City Beach 850/234–0557 • gay/ straight • tropical inn • hot tub • pool • nonsmoking • $69-149

BARS

La Royale Lounge & Liquor Store 100 Harrison (at Beach Dr) 850/763–1755 • 3pm-3am, till 4am Fri-Sat, from 7pm Sun • lesbians/ gay men • neighborhood bar • courtyard • wheelchair access

Splash Bar 6520 Thomas Dr, Panama City Beach 850/236–3450 • 6pm-2am, till 4am Th-Sat • mostly gay men • 18+ • drag shows • also pride shop • wheelchair access • gay-owned

NIGHTCLUBS

Fiesta Room 110 Harrison Ave (at Beach Dr) 850/763–1755 • 3pm-3am • popular • lesbians/ gay men • dancing/DJ • drag shows • wheelchair access

Pensacola

INFO LINES & SERVICES

GLBT AA Group 317 N Spring St (at Wright) 850/433–4191 (AA#) • 8pm Fri

ACCOMMODATIONS

Gulf-Front Villa Fort Morgan Rd, Gulf Shores, AL 865/522–8547 • gay-friendly • private condo • panoramic views • on golf course on the Gulf of Mexico • pool • nonsmoking • WiFi • wheelchair access • $795-1,295/ week

BARS

The Round-Up 560 E Heinberg St 850/433–8482 • 2pm-3am • popular • mostly gay men • neighborhood bar • videos • patio • wheelchair access

NIGHTCLUBS

Emerald City 406 E Wright St (at Alcaniz) 850/433–9491 • 3pm-3am (happy hour/ video bar), dance club from 9pm, clsd Tue • popular • lesbians/ gay men • dancing/DJ • live shows • 18+ • patio • wheelchair access

CAFES

End of the Line Cafe 610 E Wright St 850/429–0336 • 10am-10pm, 11am-5pm Sun, clsd Mon • vegetarian cafe • live bands • WiFi • wheelchair access

Pompano Beach

RESTAURANTS

J Marks Restaurant 1490 NE 23th St (at Federal Hwy/ US1) 954/782–7000 • 11am-10pm, till 11pm Fri-Sat • live music wknds • full bar • gay-owned

Port St Lucie

NIGHTCLUBS

Rebar 8283 S Federal Hwy (at Prima Vista) 772/340–7777 • 4pm-2am, till midnight Sun • lesbians/ gay men • neighborhood bar • dancing/DJ • videos • wheelchair access • gay-owned

Sarasota

INFO LINES & SERVICES

Gay AA 7225 N Lockwood Ridge Rd (in Pierce Hall, Church of the Trinity MCC) 941/355–0847 (CHURCH #) • 7pm Sun & 7pm Th

ACCOMMODATIONS

The Cypress 621 Gulfstream Ave S
941/955–4683 • gay-friendly • B&B inn • full
brkfst • nonsmoking • WiFi • $150-289

Turtle Beach Resort 9049 Midnight Pass
Rd 941/349–4554 • gay-friendly • pool •
nonsmoking • WiFi • wheelchair access •
$245-430

RESTAURANTS

Caragiulos 69 S Palm Ave 941/951–0866 •
lunch & dinner • Italian-American

South Beach

see Miami Beach/ South Beach

St Augustine

see also Jacksonville

ACCOMMODATIONS

Alexander Homestead 14 Sevilla St
904/826-4147, 888/292-4147 • gay-friendly •
Victorian inn • full brkfst • WiFi • $169-239

Casa Monica 95 Cordova St 904/827–1888,
888/213–8903 • gay-friendly • restaurant &
piano bar • gym • pool • kids ok • wheelchair
access • $150-1,500

The Inn at Camachee Harbor 201 Yacht
Club Dr (at May St) 904/825–0003,
800/688–5379 • gay-friendly • restaurant &
bar • WiFi • $99-159

Our House B&B 7 Cincinnati Ave
904/347-6260 • gay/ straight • full brkfst •
WiFi • gay-owned • $129-189

RESTAURANTS

Collage 60 Hypolita St 904/829-0055 •
dinner nightly • "artful global dining" •
reservations required

St Petersburg

see also Tampa

ACCOMMODATIONS

Bay Palms Waterfront Resort 4237 Gulf
Blvd, St Petersburg Beach 727/360–7642 •
gay-friendly • pool • nonsmoking • WiFi •
kids/ pets ok • $59-189

Boca Ciega B&B 727/381-2755 • women
only • B&B in private home • pool • lesbian-
owned • $40-50

Changing Tides Cottages 225 Boca Ciega
Dr, Madeira Beach 727/397–7706 • lesbians/
gay men • rental cottages • WiFi • lesbian-
owned • $95-175

St Petersburg

LGBT PRIDE:
June.

ANNUAL EVENTS:
April - Tampa Bay Blues Festival
727/502–5000, web:
www.tampabaybluesfest.com.

CITY INFO:
Chamber of Commerce 727/821-
4069, 8am-5pm Mon-Fri, web:
www.stpete.com.

ATTRACTIONS:
Great Explorations, interactive kids'
museum, 727/821-8992, web:
www.greatexplorations.org.
Salvador Dalí Museum 727/823-
3767, web: www.salvadordalimu-
seum.org.

BEST VIEW:
Pass-A-Grille Beach in Tampa.

WEATHER:
Some say it's the Garden of Eden—
winter temperatures occasionally
dip into the 40°s, but for the rest
of the year temperatures stay in
the 70°-80°s.

TRANSIT:
Yellow Cab 727/799-2222, web:
www.yellowcabfla.com.
727/572-1111, web:
www.supershuttle.com/en/
PIEAirportShuttleTampaBay.html
727/540-1900, web: www.psta.net.

Dicken's House B&B 335 8th Ave NE 727/822–8622, 800/381–2022 • gay/ straight • pool • full brkfst • WiFi • gay-owned • $109-235

Flamingo 4601 34th St South 727/321–5000 • lesbians/ gay men • pool • bar & restaurant • live shows • WiFi • wheelchair access • $60-100

The Pier Hotel 253 2nd Ave N (at 2nd St) 727/822–7500, 800/735–6607 • gay/ straight • kids ok • nightly cocktail hour • lesbian & gay-owned • $78-278

Postcard Inn on the Beach 6300 Gulf Blvd 727/367–2711, 800/237–8918 • gay-friendly • pool • restaurant • WiFi

Villa Da Costa 7555 46th Ave N 727/546–1477 • gay/ straight • motel • gay-owned • $185-453

BARS

Detour 2612 Central Ave (at 26th) 727/327–8204 • 2pm-2am • mostly gay men • neighborhood bar • dancing/ DJ • karaoke • patio • WiFi • wheelchair access

The Hideaway 8302 4th St N (at 83rd) 727/570–9025 • 2pm-2am, from 4pm Mon • mostly women • neighborhood bar • live shows • karaoke • wheelchair access

Oar House 4807 22nd Ave S 727/327–1691 • 9am-2am, from 11am Sun • lesbians/ gay men • neighborhood bar • karaoke

Pepperz 4918 Gulfport Blvd S (at 49th), Gulfport 727/623–4837 • 2pm-2am • popular • lesbians/ gay men • dancing/DJ • shows • wheelchair access

A Taste for Wine 241 Central Ave (at 2nd St N) 727/895–1623 • 2pm-9pm, till midnight Fri-Sat, clsd Mon • occasional lesbian events • women-owned

NIGHTCLUBS

Georgie's Alibi 3100 3rd Ave N (at 31st St N) 727/321–2112 • 11am-3am • lesbians/ gay men • neighborhood bar • dancing/DJ • food served • drag shows • videos • WiFi • wheelchair access • patio • gay-owned

Glass 16 2nd St N (at Vintage Ultra Lounge) 727/898–2222 • 10pm Wed only • lesbians/ gay men • dancing/DJ • drag shows • transgender-friendly

RESTAURANTS

Central Avenue Oyster Bar 249 Central Ave 727/897–9728 • 11am-midnight

Sea Porch Cafe 3400 Gulf Blvd (at Don Cesar Beach Resort) 727/360–1884 • beach views

Skyway Jack's 2795 34th St S 727/867–1907 • 5am-3pm • Southern cooking (diner-style)

ENTERTAINMENT & RECREATION

Bedrocks Beach/ Sunset Beach W Gulf Blvd (at S end of Treasure Island, Sunset Beach) • popular park

Fort DeSoto Park Pinellas Bayway S • beautiful gay beach

PUBLICATIONS

Womyn's Words 727/323–5706 • monthly magazine

Tallahassee

INFO LINES & SERVICES

The Family Tree 5126C Woodlane Cir 850/222–8555 • LGBT community center • call for hours

ACCOMMODATIONS

Hampton Inn Quincy 165 Spooner Rd (Pat Thomas Pkwy), Quincy 850/627–7555 • gay-friendly • full brkfst • swimming • WiFi • wheelchair access • $99-129

Tampa

see also St Petersburg

ACCOMMODATIONS

Don Vicente de Ybor Inn 1915 Republica de Cuba 813/241–4545, 866/206–4545 • gay/straight • cafe & bar • $119-129

Gram's Place Hostel 3109 N Ola Ave 813/221–0596 • gay/ straight • nudity • kids ok • nonsmoking • WiFi • $23-60

Hampton Inn & Suites 1301 East 7th Ave 813/247–6700, 800/426–7866 • gay/straight • WiFi • pool • wheelchair access

Hyatt Regency 211 N Tampa St 813/225–1234 • gay/straight • pool • restaurant & bar • WiFi • wheelchair access

Sawmill Camping Resort 21710 US Hwy 98, Dade City 352/583–0664 • mostly gay men • theme wknds w/ entertainment • RV hookups • cabins • tent spots • dancing • karaoke • pool • nudity • gay-owned

BARS

2606 2606 N Armenia Ave (at St Conrad) 813/875–6993 • 3pm-3am • mostly gay men• also leather shop from 9pm • wheelchair access • gay-owned

Baxter's 1519 S Dale Mabry (at W Neptune) 813/258–8830 • noon-3am • mostly gay men • neighborhood bar • karaoke • wheelchair access

Body Shop Bar 14905 N Nebraska **813/971–3576** • 3pm-3am • mostly gay men • neighborhood bar • karaoke • gay-owned

Bradley's on 7th 1510 E 7th Ave, Ybor City **831/241–2723** • 4pm-3am • mostly gay men • dancing/DJ • drag shows

Chelsea Lounge 1502 N Florida Ave (at Hwy 275) **813/228–0139** • 3pm-3am • mostly gay men • neighborhood bar • dancing/DJ • drag shows • karaoke • patio

City Side 3703 Henderson Blvd (at Dale Mabry) **813/350–0600** • 11am-3am • lesbians/ gay men • dancing/DJ • neighborhood bar • karaoke • WiFi • patio

Dive Bar & Grill 3128 Beach Blvd S, Gulfport • 4pm-11pm, till 3am Fri-Sat, from 11am Sat-Sun, clsd Mon • mostly gay men • dancing/DJ • karaoke • rooftop deck • also restaurant

Hamburger Mary's 1600 E 7th Ave (at N 16th St) **813/241–6279** • 11am-11pm, till 3am wknds • lesbians/ gay men • karaoke • drag shows • wheelchair access

Rainbow Room 421 S MacDill Ave (at Azeele St) **813/871–2265** • 3pm-close • mostly women • beer/ wine • live music Fri • karaoke • WiFi

NIGHTCLUBS

The Castle 2004 N 16th St **813/247–7547** • 10:30pm-3am, clsd Tue-Wed • mixed gay/ straight • dancing/DJ

Crowbar 1812 N 17th St **813/241-8600** • 10pm-3am • mixed gay/ straight • dancing/DJ • live shows • karaoke

G Bar 1401 E 7th Ave **813/247–1016** • 4pm-3am, clsd Sun-Mon • lesbians/ gay men • dancing/DJ • drag shows • 18+ • more women Fri • gay-owned

Metro Tampa 2606 N Armenia Ave (at St Conrad) **813/876–4650** • 3pm-3am, from 1pm Sun • mostly gay men • dancing/DJ

Steam Fridays 1507 E 7th Ave (at the Honey Pot) **813/247–4663** • 10pm Fri only • mostly gay men • dancing/DJ • 18+ • 3 flrs

Tease Saturdays 1507 E 7th Ave (at the Honey Pot) **813/247–4663** • 10pm Sat only • mostly women • dancing/DJ • 18+ • 3 flrs

Valentines Nightclub 7522 N Armenia Ave (btwn Sligh & Waters) **813/936–1999** • 3pm-3am • mostly gay men • dancing/DJ • drag shows • male dancers

Tampa

ENTERTAINMENT:
Tampa Bay Gay Men's Chorus 727/580–5517, web: www.tampabayarts.com.
Crescendo, Tampa Bay Womyn's Chorus 813/679-7585, web: www.crescendochorus.org.

LGBT PRIDE:
June. St Pete Pride.

ANNUAL EVENTS:
October- Tampa International Gay & Lesbian Film Festival, web: www.tiglff.com.

CITY INFO:
Greater Tampa Chamber of Commerce 813/228-7777, web: www.tampachamber.com.

ATTRACTIONS:
Busch Gardens/Adventure Island 813/987-5082, web: www.4adventure.com.
Florida Aquarium 813/273-4000, web: www.flaquarium.org.
Harbour Island.
Museum of Science & Industry 813/987-6000, web: www.mosi.org.
Ybor Square.

TRANSIT:
United Cab 813/251-5555, web: thecityoftampa.com/taxis.
Super Shuttle 727/572-1111.
Hartline Transit (bus) 813/254-4278, web: www.hartline.org.

CAFES

Joffrey's Coffee
1600 E 8th Ave **813/247-4600** • 7am-10pm,
till midnight wknds • WiFi

Sacred Grounds Coffeehouse 4819 E
Busch Blvd **813/983-0837** • 6pm-midnight,
till 2am Fri-Sat • lesbians/gay men • live
music • open mic Mon • WiFi

Tre Amici 1907 19th St N **813/247-6964** •
7:30am-6pm, till 10pm Th-Sat, 9am-3pm Sun,
Fri open mic • cafe & wine bar

RESTAURANTS

Bernini 1702 E 7th Ave **813/248-0099** • old
school Italian

Centro Cantina 1600 E 8th Ave
813/241-8588 • Tex Mex • great balcony

Columbia 2117 E 7th Ave **813/248-4961** •
11am-close, from noon Sun • Cuban &
Spanish

Crabby Bill's 401 Gulf Blvd, Indian Rocks
Beach **727/595-4825** • inexpensive seafood
joint

Fresh Mouth 1600 E 8th Ave (plaza level)
813/241-8845 • 11am-9pm, till 2am wknds

Gaspar's Grotto 1805 E 7th Ave **813/248-
5900** • 11am-3am • live shows • karaoke •
WiFi • patio

JJ's Cafe & Bar 1601 E 7th Ave (at N 16th St)
813/247-4125 • 11am-10pm, till 2:30am
wknds

The Laughing Cat 1820 N 15th St
813/241-2998 • Italian • wheelchair access

The Queen's Head 2501 Central Ave, St
Petersburg **727/498-8584** • 4:30pm-2am,
from noon wknds, clsd Mon • European • full
bar

ENTERTAINMENT & RECREATION

Picnic Island Picnic Island Blvd (across from
the military base, on E side) • gay beach at
end of park

RETAIL SHOPS

King Corona Cigars 1523 E 7th Ave
888/248-3812 • local, handmade cigars • also
cafe & bar

The MC Film Festival 1901 N 15th St (at
8th Ave) **813/247-6233** • LGBT pride gift store

PUBLICATIONS

Watermark **813/655-9890, 877/926-8118** •
bi-weekly LGBT newspaper for Central FL

Womyn's Words **727/323-5706** • monthly
magazine

West Palm Beach

ACCOMMODATIONS

Grandview Gardens B&B 1608 Lake Ave
(at Palm) **561/833-9023** • gay-friendly • pool
• nonsmoking • WiFi • wheelchair access •
gay-owned • $119-199

Hibiscus House B&B 501 30th St
561/863-5633, 800/203-4927 • gay/straight •
full brkfst • pet-friendly • pool • nonsmoking •
gay-owned • WiFi • $89-210

Scandia Lodge 625 S Federal Hwy (at 6th
Ave), Lake Worth **561/586-3155** • gay/
straight • pool • pets ok • nonsmoking • $74-
104

BARS

Fort Dix 6205 Georgia Ave (at Colonial)
561/533-5355 • noon-3am, till 4am Fri-Sat •
popular • mostly gay men • neighborhood
dive bar • dancing/DJ wknds • patio •
wheelchair access

HG Rooster's 823 Belvedere Rd (btwn Parker
& Lake) **561/832-9119** • 3pm-3am, till 4am
Fri-Sat • popular • mostly gay men •
neighborhood bar • drag shows • karaoke •
food served • wheelchair access

NIGHTCLUBS

Karma 3097 Forest Hill Blvd • 10pm-5am •
Fri-Sat only • gay/straight • dancing/DJ •

The Lounge 517 Clematis St **561/655-9747**
• 9pm-4am, clsd Sun-Mon • gay/straight •
dancing/DJ • also sushi & sake bar

Monarchy 221 Clematis St **561/835-6661** •
10pm-3am, till 4am Fri-Sat, clsd Sun, Tue & Th
• gay/straight • dancing/DJ

Respectable Street 518 Clematis St
561/832-9999 • 9pm-3am, till 4am Fri-Sat,
clsd Sun-Tue • gay-friendly • dancing/DJ •
alternative • retro & new wave nights • live
music

RESTAURANTS

Rhythm Cafe 3800-A S Dixie Hwy
561/833-3406 • 6pm-10pm, clsd Sun-Mon •
some veggie • beer/wine

Thai Bay 1900 Okeechobee Blvd (in Palm
Beach Market Pl) **561/640-0131** • lunch and
dinner, clsd Sun

ENTERTAINMENT & RECREATION

MacArthur Beach Singer Island, N Palm
Beach

BOOKSTORES

Changing Times Bookstore 911 Village Blvd #806 (at Palm Beach Lakes) **561/640-0496** • 10am-7pm, till 5pm Sat-Sun • community bulletin board • wheelchair access

RETAIL SHOPS

Eurotique 814 Northlake Blvd, Lake Park **561/684-2302** • 10am-8pm, till 6pm Sat, noon-5pm Sun • leather • books • videos

Studio 205 & Java Juice Bar 600 Lake Ave (at L St), Lake Worth **561/533-5272** • 10am-6pm, till 5pm Sun • gay pride items

Wilton Manors

see Fort Lauderdale

Winter Haven

BARS

Old Man Frank's 1005 S Lake Howard Dr (at Central) **863/294-9179** • 11am-2am, from noon-midnight Sun • gay-friendly • on the lake • food served • smoking allowed • wheelchair access

GEORGIA

Athens

ACCOMMODATIONS

Ashford Manor B&B 5 Harden Hill Rd (at Main St), Watkinsville **706/769-2633** • gay-friendly • pool • nonsmoking • WiFi • gay-owned • $99-225

BARS

The Globe 199 N Lumpkin St (at Clayton) **706/353-4721** • 11am-2am, till midnight Sun • gay-friendly • 40 single-malt scotches • also restaurant

NIGHTCLUBS

Forty Watt Club 285 W Washington St (at Pulaski) **706/549-7871** • call for hours • gay-friendly • alternative • live music • wheelchair access

CAFES

Espresso Royale Cafe 297 E Broad St (at Jackson) **706/613-7449** • 7am-11pm, from 8am wknds • best coffee in Athens • gallery • wheelchair access

RESTAURANTS

The Grit 199 Prince Ave **706/543-6592** • 11am-10pm, great wknd brunch 10am-3pm • ethnic vegetarian • wheelchair access

Atlanta

INFO LINES & SERVICES

Galano Club 585 Dutch Valley Rd (at Monroe) **404/881-9188** • meetings throughout the day • LGBT recovery club • call for meeting times

ACCOMMODATIONS

The Gaslight Inn 1001 St Charles Ave NE **404/875-1001** • gay/ straight • 1913 craftsman-style B&B • nonsmoking • WiFi • gay-owned • $115+

The Georgian Terrace Hotel 659 Peachtree St NE (at Ponce de Leon) **404/897-1991, 800/651-2316** • gay-friendly • "Atlanta's only historic luxury hotel" • hosted *Gone with the Wind* world-premier reception in 1939 • pool • kids ok • WiFi • wheelchair access • $119-299

Glenn Hotel 110 Marietta St NW (at Spring) **404/521-2250, 888/717-8851** • gay/ straight • boutique hotel • also restaurant & rooftop lounge • WiFi

Hotel Indigo 683 Peachtree St NE (at 3rd) **404/874-9200, 800/972-2402** • cozy, stylish no-frills hotel • workout room • also restaurant • WiFi

Hotel Palomar Atlanta Midtown 866 W Peachtree St NW (at 7th St NE) **678/412-2400, 866/945-6285** • gay-friendly • hip boutique hotel in midtown

Microtel Inn & Suites 1840 Corporate Blvd (off Buford Hwy) **404/325-4446, 800/337-0044** • gay-friendly • WiFi • wheelchair access • $55-79

Stonehurst Place Bed & Breakfast 923 Piedmont Ave NE (at 8th St) **404/881-0722, 877/285-2246** • gay/ straight • in 1896 shingle-style house furnished w/ antiques • full brkfst • nonsmoking • WiFi • lesbian-owned • $149 - $429

W Atlanta 111 Perimeter Center W (at Ashford Dunwoody Rd) **770/396-6800, 877/WHOTELS (RESERVATIONS ONLY)** • gay-friendly • pool • nonsmoking • WiFi • also restaurant • wheelchair access • $125-399

W Atlanta Midtown 188 14th St NE (at Juniper St NE) **404/892-6000** • gay/ straight • stylish hotel • WiFi • pool • convenient location

BARS

Amsterdam 502 Amsterdam Ave NE **404/892-2227** • 11:30am-close • mostly gay men • dancing/DJ • food served • video & sports bar

Atlanta Eagle 306 Ponce de León Ave NE (at Argonne) **404/873–2453** • 7pm-3am, from 5pm Sat, clsd Sun • popular • mostly gay men • dancing/DJ • bears • leather • also leather store • gay-owned

BJ Roosters 2345 Cheshire Bridge Rd NE (at La Vista) **404/634–5895** • 2:30pm-3am • mostly gay men • neighborhood bar • karaoke • shows • wheelchair access • gay-owned

Blake's on the Park 227 10th St (at Piedmont) **404/892–5786** • 11am-3am, till midnight Sun

Bulldogs 893 Peachtree St NE (btwn 7th & 8th) **404/872–3025** • 2pm-4am Sun-Fri, till 3am Sat

Burkhart's Pub 1492–F Piedmont Ave NE (at Monroe, in Ansley Square) **404/872–4403** • 4pm-2:30am, from 2pm wknds, till midnight Sun • lesbians/ gay men • neighborhood bar • food served • karaoke • live shows • patio • wheelchair access

Eastside Lounge 485-A Flat Shoals Ave (at Glenwood) **404/521–9666** • 9pm-2:30am, from 8pm Fri-Sat, clsd Sun • gay/ straight • dancing/DJ • multiracial • karaoke • theme nights

Eddie's Attic 515–B N McDonough St (at Trinity Place), Decatur **404/377–4976** • 5pm-close Mon-Th, till 2am Fri-Sat, open 1 hr before showtime Sun • gay/ straight • occasional lesbian hangout • live music • open mic & comedy • restaurant • rooftop deck

Felix's on the Square 1510-G Piedmont Ave NE (Ansley Square) **404/249–7899** • 2pm-3am, from 1pm Sat, 1pm-midnight Sun • mostly gay men • food served • wheelchair access

Friends on Ponce 736 Ponce de Leon NE (at Ponce de Leon Pl) **404/817–3820** • 2pm-3am Mon-Fri, from noon Sat, till midnight Sun • rooftop patio • wheelchair access

Halo Lounge 817 W Peachtree St (6th St, btwn W Peachtree & Peachtree) **404/962–7333** • 9pm-3am, from 6pm Sat, clsd Sun • dinner • gay/ straight • DJ

Le Buzz 585 Franklin Rd A-10 (at S Marietta Pkwy, in Longhorn Plaza), Marietta **770/424–1337** • 7pm-3am, clsd Sun • lesbians/ gay men • neighborhood bar • dancing/DJ • drag shows • karaoke • also restaurant • patio • wheelchair access

Mary's 1287B Glenwood Ave (at Flat Shoals) **404/624–4411** • 5pm-3am, clsd Sun • lesbians/ gay men • friendly neighborhood • dancing/DJ • karaoke • videos • wheelchair access

Mixx 1492–B Piedmont Ave NE (at Monroe, in Ansley Square) **404/228–4372** • 4pm-2am, till 3am Fri-Sat, clsd Sun • mostly gay men • neighborhood bar • dancing/DJ wknds • karaoke • bears • food served

My Sister's Room 1271 Glenwood Ave **678/705–4585** • 6pm-close, from 7pm Sat, closed Sun-Mon • popular • mostly women • live music • also restaurant • younger crowd • patio

Opus I 1086 Alco St NE (at Cheshire Bridge) **404/634–6478** • 9am-3am, from 9am Sat, 12:30pm-midnight Sun • mostly gay men • neighborhood bar • wheelchair access

Tripps 1931 Piedmont Circle (at Cheshire Bridge) **404/724–0067** • 2pm-3am, 12:30pm-midnight Sun • mostly gay men • neighborhood bar • food served

NIGHTCLUBS

Bellissima 560-B Amsterdam Ave (at Monroe Dr) **404/917–0220** • 6pm-3am, clsd Mon-Tue • lesbians/ gay men • lounge • dancing/DJ • multiracial clientele • live entertainment • videos • food served • wheelchair access

Chaparral 2715 Buford Hwy (at Lenox Rd) **678/568–9657** • 10pm-4am • more gay Fri & Sun • dancing/DJ • Latino/a

Girls in the Night • women's parties & events around Atlanta • check local listings or girlsinthenight.com

Ladies at Play 79 Poplar St (at Fairlie St) • 9pm 2nd Sat only • mostly women • dancing/DJ • multiracial

Masquerade 695 North Ave NE **404/577–8178** • hours vary • gay-friendly • dancing/DJ • live shows • call for events • food served • 18+ • private club • cover charge

Opera 1150 Peachtree St NE (at 14th St NE, enter on Crescent Ave) **404/874–3006** • gay/ straight • dancing/DJ

Phase One 4933 Memorial Dr (at Delano) Decatur **404/296–4895** • ladies night Wed, Fri & Sun • dancing/DJ • mostly African American

Traxx 1287 Columbia Dr, Decatur **866/602–5553** • Sat only • mostly gay men • dancing/DJ • mostly African American • live shows

Traxx Girls Night 2110 Peachtree Rd (at Vita) **678/368–6435** • 10pm-close Fri only • mostly women • dancing/DJ • mostly African American

Traxx Girls Parties **678/368–6435** • weekly women's dance parties • check traxxgirls.com for info

Traxx Girls Sundays 2425 Wesley Chapel Rd, Decatur **678/368–6435, 678/887–8089** • 11pm-close Sun only • mostly women • dancing/DJ • mostly African American

Wild Mustang/ Jungle 2115 Faulkner Rd NE (off Cheshire Bridge Rd NE) **404/844–8800** • 9pm-close, clsd Sun • lesbians/ gay men • dancing/DJ • also Stars of the Century (drag shows) Mon 11pm • cover charge

CAFES

Apache Cafe 64 3rd St NW **404/876–5436** • food served • poetry readings • events • gallery • multiracial

Australian Bakery Cafe 48 S Park Square, Marietta **678/797–6222** • 7am-5:30pm, 8am-4pm wknds • also 463 Flat Shoals Rd, 404/653–0100

Intermezzo 1845 Peachtree Rd NE **404/355–0411** • 10am-2am • classy cafe • plenty veggie • full bar • great desserts • WiFi till 7pm

Urban Grounds 38 N Avondale Rd, Avondale Estates **404/499–2136** • 6:30am-9pm, till 10pm Fri, 7:30am-10pm Sat, 8am-4pm Sun

RESTAURANTS

Amuse 560 Dutch Valley Rd **404/888–1890** • lunch & dinner, wknd brunch, clsd Mon • full bar • int'l bistro

Apres Diem 931 Monroe Dr #C-103 **404/872–3333** • 11:30am-midnight, till 2am Fri-Sat, from 11am wknds, brunch Sat-Sun • French bistro • live jazz Wed • full bar

Aria 490 E Paces Ferry **404/233–7673** • dinner only, clsd Sun

Aurum 108 8th St (at Peachtree St) **404/815–9426** • 8pm-3am, till 1am Wed • gay/ straight • lounge

Bacchanalia/ Star Provisions/ Quinones 1198 Howell Mill Rd NW **404/365–0410** • lunch & dinner, clsd Sun • upscale • American

Beleza 905 Juniper St (at 8th) **678/904–4582** • 5:30pm-1am, till 2am wknds, clsd Sun-Mon • Brazilian • also cocktails

Buckhead Diner 3073 Piedmont Rd NE **404/262–3336** • lunch Mon-Sun, dinner nightly, Sun brunch • upscale diner fare

Cafe Sunflower 2140 Peachtree Rd NW (at Bennett St NW) **404/352–8859** • lunch & dinner, clsd Sun • vegetarian

The Colonnade 1879 Cheshire Bridge Rd NE **404/874–5642** • dinner nightly, lunch wknds • traditional Southern

Cowtippers 1600 Piedmont Ave NE (at Monroe) **404/874–3751** • 11am-11pm, till midnight Fri-Sat • steak house • transgender-friendly • wheelchair access

Ecco 40 7th St NE **404/347–9555** • 5:30pm-10pm, till 11pm Fri-Sat, till 10pm Sun • Italian • reservations recommended • wheelchair access

Einstein's 1077 Juniper St (at 12th) **404/876–7925** • 11am-11pm, till midnight Fri-Sat, from 10am Sun, wknd brunch • popular • some veggie • full bar • patio • wheelchair access • reservations accepted

The Flying Biscuit Cafe 1655 McLendon Ave (at Clifton) **404/687–8888** • 7am-10pm, till 10:30pm Fri-Sat • popular • healthy brkfst all day • plenty veggie • beer/ wine • wheelchair access • multiple locations

Fresh To Order 860 Peachtree St NE (at 7th St NE) **404/593–2333** • 11am-10pm, brunch Sun from 10am • healthy fast food • patio

Frogs 931 Monroe Dr NE **404/607–9967** • 11am-10pm, till 11pm wknds • Mexican

Gilbert's Cafe & Bar 219 10th St NE (at Piedmont Ave) **404/872–8012** • dinner Tue-Sat, wknd brunch, food till 2am, bar till 3am, till midnight Sun

Hobnob 1551 Piedmont Ave NE (at Monroe) **404/968–2288** • 11am-11pm, 10am-4pm Sun • wheelchair access

Joe's On Juniper 1049 Juniper St NE **404/875–6634** • 11am-2am, till midnight Sun • American

Las Margaritas 1842 Chesire Bridge Rd **404/873–4464** • lunch & dinner • Latin fusion • wheelchair access

The Lobby at Twelve 361 17th St **404/961–7370** • brkfst, lunch & dinner • upscale American • reservations recommended

Majestic Diner 1031 Ponce de Leon Ave (at Highland) **404/875–0276** • 24hrs • popular diner right from the '50s w/ cantankerous waitresses included • at your own risk • some veggie • wheelchair access

Mi Barrio Restaurante Mexicano 571 Memorial Dr SE **404/223–9279** • lunch & dinner, clsd Sun • full bar • wheelchair access

Murphy's 997 Virginia Ave NE (at N Highland Ave) **404/872-0904** • 11am-10pm, till 11pm Fri-Sat, from 8am wknds • popular • plenty veggie • wheelchair access

No Más! Cantina 180 Walker St **404/574-5678** • lunch & dinner daily, wknd brunch • Mexican • also huge furniture & gift store • gay-owned

Atlanta

WHERE THE GIRLS ARE:

Many lesbians live in DeKalb county, in the northeast part of the city of Decatur. For fun, women head to Midtown or Buckhead if they're professionals, Virginia-Highlands if they're funky or 30ish, Little Five Points if they're young and wild, and Castleberry Hill if they're artistic.

LGBT PRIDE:

October. 404/382-7588, web: atlantapride.org.

ANNUAL EVENTS:

July - National Black Arts Festival 404/730-7315, web: www.nbaf.org.
Labor Day weekend - Femmenomen-non (lesbian party), web: www.girlsinthenight.com.
Sept/Oct - Out on Film, lesbian/ gay film festival 404/671-9446, web: www.outonfilm.org.

CITY INFO:

404/521-6600 or 800/285-2682, web: www.atlanta.net.

BEST VIEW:

70th floor of the Peachtree Plaza, in the 3-story revolving Sun Dial restaurant (404/589-7506).
Also from the top of Stone Mountain (only 20 feet taller).

WEATHER:

Summers are warm and humid (upper 80°s to low 90°s) with occasional thunderstorms. Winters are icy with occasional snow. Temperatures can drop into the low 30°s. Spring and fall are temperate – spring brings blossoming dogwoods and magnolias, while fall festoons the trees with awesome fall colors.

ATTRACTIONS:

Atlanta Botanical Garden 404/876-5859, web: www.atlantabotanicalgarden.org.
Centennial Olympic Park
CNN Center 404/827-2300, web: www.cnn.com/StudioTour.
Coca-Cola Museum 404/676-5151, web: www.woccatlanta.com.
Georgia Aquarium (largest aquarium in the US) 404/581-4000, web: www.georgiaaquarium.org.
High Museum of Art 404/733-5000, web: www.high.org.
Margaret Mitchell House 404/814-4000, web: www.gwtw.org.
Martin Luther King Jr. Memorial Center 404/526-8900, web: www.thekingcenter.org
Piedmont Park.
Stone Mountain Park 770/498-5690, web: www.stonemountain-park.com.
Underground Atlanta 404/523-2311, web: underground-atlanta.com.

TRANSIT:

Checker Cab 404/351-1111, web: www.atlantacheckercab.com.
Superior Shuttle 770/457-4794, web: www.atlsuperiorshuttle.com.
Marta 404/848-5000, web: www.itsmarta.com.

Pastries A Go Go 235 Ponce De Leon Place (at Commerce), Decatur 404/373-3423 • 7:30am-4pm, clsd Tue • delicious baked goods • wheelchair access

R Thomas Deluxe Grill 1812 Peachtree Rd NW (btwn 26th & 27th) 404/872-2942 • 24hrs • popular • beer/ wine • healthy Californian/ juice bar • plenty veggie • wheelchair access

Ria's Bluebird Cafe 421 Memorial Dr (at Cherokee) 404/521-3737 • 8am-3pm • very popular • gourmet brunch in quaint old diner in Grant Park • plenty veggie • everything made from scratch • wheelchair access • woman-owned

Roxx Tavern & Diner 1824 Cheshire Bridge Rd NE (at Manchester) 404/892-4541 • lunch & dinner, Sun brunch • patio • wheelchair access

Sauced 753 Edgewood Ave (at Waddell St NE) 404/688-6554 • dinner nightly till 1am, clsd Mon • retro kitsch decor • Southern • plenty veggie • full bar • wheelchair access

Sawicki's 250 W Ponce De Leon Ave, Decatur 404/377-0992 • 11am-7pm, till 8pm Fri-Sat, noon-5pm Sun • deli • great sandwiches

The Shed at Glenwood 475 Bill Kennedy Way 404/835-4363 • dinner nightly, Sun brunch • also bar

Slice 259 Peters St SW 404/588-1820 • 11am-midnight, till 3am Fri, noon-3am Sat, noon-midnight Sun • pizza & martinis • WiFi • wheelchair access • gay-owned • also at 85 Poplar St (917-1820)

Swan Coach House 3130 Slaton Dr NW 404/261-0636 • 11am-2:30pm, clsd Sun • also gift shop & art gallery

Table 1280 1280 Peachtree St NE (at Woodruff Arts Center) 404/897-1280 • 11am-8pm Tue-Sat, till 6pm Sun, Sun brunch, clsd Mon • upscale American & tapas

Thumbs Up Diner 573 Edgewood Ave SE (at Randolph) 404/223-0690 • 7am-3pm, 8am-4pm wknds • brkfst all day

TWO urban licks 820 Ralph McGill Blvd 404/522-4622 • dinner nightly • great grill • full bar • live blues • reservations recommended

Veni Vidi Vici 41 14th St 404/875-8424 • lunch Mon-Fri, dinner nightly • upscale Italian • some veggie • WiFi • wheelchair access

The Vortex 438 Moreland Ave NE (at Euclid) 404/688-1828 • 11am-midnight, till 3am wknds • biker ambiance • great burgers • 18+

Wasabi 180 Walker St SW 404/574-5680 • lunch Th-Fri, dinner nightly, clsd Sun • sushi • wheelchair access

Watershed 406 W Ponce de Leon Ave, Decatur 404/378-4900 • 11am-10pm, Sun brunch • wine bar • also gift shop • owned by Emily Saliers of the Indigo Girls • wheelchair access

ENTERTAINMENT & RECREATION

Actors Express 887 W Marietta St #J-107 404/607-7469, 404/875-1606 • daring, original theater

AIDS Memorial Quilt/ NAMES Project 204 14th St 404/688-5500 • visit The Quilt at the foundation offices

Ansley Park Playhouse 1545 Peachtree St 404/875-1193 • some LGBT-themed productions

Atlanta Gay Men's Chorus 1379 Tullie Rd, Ste 200, 30329-2308 404/320-1030

Atlanta Rollergirls • Atlanta's female roller derby league • visit www.atlantarollergirls.com for events

Joining Hearts Piedmont Park Pool 678/318-1446 • great dance/pool party in July • 100% of every dollar raised in ticket sales & tips is donated to our beneficiaries

Lambda Radio Report WRFG 89.3 FM 404/523-8989 • 6pm Tue • LGBT radio program

Little 5 Points, Moreland & Euclid Ave S of Ponce de Leon Ave • hip & funky area w/ too many restaurants & shops to list

Martin Luther King, Jr Center for Non-Violent Social Change 449 Auburn Ave NE 404/526-8900 • 9am-5pm daily • includes King's birth home, the church where he preached in the '60s & his gravesite

BOOKSTORES

Brushstrokes/ Capulets 1510 Piedmont Ave NE (near Monroe) 404/876-6567 • 10am-10pm, till 11pm Fri-Sat • LGBT variety store • gay-owned

Charis Books & More 1189 Euclid Ave NE (at Moreland) 404/524-0304 • 10:30am-7pm, noon-6pm Sun • feminist • wheelchair access

Outwrite Bookstore & Coffeehouse 991 Piedmont Ave NE (at 10th St) 404/607-0082 • 9am-10pm, till 11pm wknds • popular • LGBT • music • videos • gifts • cafe • wheelchair access

RETAIL SHOPS

The Boy Next Door 1447 Piedmont Ave NE (btwn 14th & Monroe) **404/873-2664** • 10am-8pm, noon-6pm Sun • clothing

The Junkman's Daughter 464 Moreland Ave NE (at Euclid) **404/577-3188** • 11am-7pm, till 8pm Fri, till 9pm Sat, from noon Sun • hip stuff • wheelchair access

Piercing Experience 1654 McLendon Ave NE (at Clifton) **404/378-9100, 800/646-0393** • call for appt

PUBLICATIONS

David Atlanta **404/418-8901** • gay entertainment magazine w/ extensive nightlife calendar, maps & directory

Georgia Voice **404/815-6941** • bi-weekly LGBT publication

GYMS & HEALTH CLUBS

Gravity Fitness 2201 Faulkner Rd (off Cheshire Bridge Rd) **404/486-0506** • day passes available

Urban Body Fitness 500 Amsterdam Ave **404/885-1499**

EROTICA

Inserection 1739 Cheshire Bridge Rd **404/262-9113**

Lollipop Adult Treats 3165 Roswell Rd (at Peachtree St) **404/816-8299** • 24hrs

The Poster Hut, Inc 2175 Cheshire Bridge Rd NE (at Piedmont Rd) **404/633-7491** • 10am-9pm, till 11pm Fri-Sat, from 10pm-7:30pm Sun • clothing • toys • housewares • gifts

Southern Nights Videos 2205 Cheshire Br Rd (at Woodland Ave NE) **404/728-0701** • 24hrs

Starship 2275 Cheshire Bridge Rd **404/320-9101, 800/215-1053** • 24hrs • many locations in Atlanta

CRUISY AREAS

Publix on Ponce 1001 Ponce de Leon Ave • supermarket • dyke cruising territory

Augusta

see also Aiken, South Carolina

BARS

Club Rehab 913 Broad St **706/849-2265** • 9pm-3am, till 2am Sat, clsd Sun • gay/ straight • dancing/DJ

Dahlonega

ACCOMMODATIONS

Mountain Laurel Creek Inn 202 Talmer Grizzle Rd (at Hwy 19 & McDonald Rd) **706/867-8134** • gay-friendly • full brkfst • spa & pub • nonsmoking • gay-owned • $154-195

Swiftwaters Womanspace **706/864-3229** • women only • on scenic river • seasonal • nonsmoking • deck • dogs ok • women-owned • $50-75 (indoors), $15 (camping)

RESTAURANTS

Smith House 84 S Chestatee St **706/867-7000, 800/852-9577** • lunch daily, dinner Fri-Sun, clsd Mon • family-style Southern

Dalton

RESTAURANTS

Dalton Depot 110 Depot St **706/226-3160** • 11am-9pm, till 10pm Th-Sat, from 11:30am Sun • also bar • karaoke

Decatur

see Atlanta

Dewy Rose

ACCOMMODATIONS

The River's Edge 2311 Pulliam Mill Rd **706/213-8081** • mostly gay men • cabins • camping • RV • live shows • pool • nudity • nonsmoking • wheelchair access • $16-130

Lake Lanier

ENTERTAINMENT & RECREATION

Gay Cove btwn Athens Park Rd & Frank Boyd Rd (Channel Marker 21) • a rainbow rendezvous for the pleasure-boating crowd—look for the rainbow flag

Marietta

see Atlanta

Quitman

ACCOMMODATIONS

Bobcat Resort Campground 1877 Hickory Head Rd **229/263-4300** • lesbians/gay men • private membership campground • swimming • clothing-optional • nonsmoking • pets ok • WiFi • wheelchair access • gay-owned • $10-125

Savannah

INFO LINES & SERVICES

First City Network 307 E Harris St
912/236-2489 • complete info & events line •
social group • also newsletter

ACCOMMODATIONS

The Azalea Inn & Gardens 217 E
Huntingdon St (at Abercorn St)
912/236-6080, 800/582-3823 • gay-friendly •
19th-c Italianate • vintage gardens • pool • full
Southern brkfst • nonsmoking • WiFi • $159-
400

Catherine Ward House Inn 118 E
Waldburg St (at Abercorn) 912/234-8564,
800/327-4270 • gay/ straight • Victorian
Italianate • full brkfst • WiFi • $139-229

The Galloway House 107 E 35th St
912/658-4419 • gay/ straight • furnished apts
• cont'l brkfst • $160-330

Kehoe House 123 Habersham St
912/232-1020, 800/820-1020 • gay-friendly •
full brkfst • WiFi

Mansion on Forsyth Park 700 Drayton St
912/238-5158, 888/213-3671 • gay-friendly •
restored Victorian mansion in historic district •
pool • nonsmoking • WiFi • wheelchair access
• $156-600

Park Avenue Manor 107–109 W Park Ave
912/233-0352 • gay-friendly • full brkfst •
nonsmoking • WiFi • $98-159

Statesboro Inn 106 S Main, Statesboro
912/489-8628, 800/846-9466 • gay-friendly •
full brkfst • WiFi • $70-125

Thunderbird Inn 611 W Oglethorpe Ave (at
MLK Blvd) 912/232-2661, 866/324-2661 •
gay-friendly • motel • kids ok • nonsmoking •
WiFi • gay-owned • $99-139

Tybee Vacation Rentals 1010 Hwy 80 E,
Tybee Island 866/935-3861, 877/214-7353 •
gay-friendly • rental homes, cottages & condos
• pool • nonsmoking • WiFi • some gay-
owned • $90-399

BARS

Chuck's Bar 305 W River St 912/232-1005 •
8pm-3am, from 7pm Th-Sat, clsd Sun • gay/
straight • neighborhood bar • young crowd •
student & artist hangout

Rocks on the Roof 102 W Bay St (on the
roof of The Bohemian Hotel) 912/721-3901 •
11am-1am, till midnight Sun • fantastic views
of river & historic district

Venus Di Milo 38 MLK Jr Blvd 912/447-0901
• 5pm-3am, clsd Sun • gay-friendly

NIGHTCLUBS

Club One 1 Jefferson St (at Bay)
912/232-0200 • 5pm-3am, till 2am Sun •
lesbians/ gay men • dancing/DJ • food served •
live shows Th-Sun • karaoke • drag shows
• dancers • videos

CAFES

Cafe Gelatohhh 202 W St Julian St
912/234-2344 • artisanal gelato • also coffee,
sandwiches

The Sentient Bean 13 E Park Ave
912/232-4447 • 7am-10pm • food served •
vegetarian/ vegan • shows at night

RESTAURANTS

B Matthews 325 E Bay St 912/233-1319 •
8am-9pm, till 10pm Fri-Sat, till 3pm Sun •
casual bistro

Bar Food 4523 Habersham St 912/355-5956
• 4pm-1am, clsd Sun • full bar • wheelchair
access • gay-owned

Casbah 118 East Broughton St
912/234-6168 • dinner nightly • Moroccan •
also entertainment

Churchill's Pub 13 W Bay St 912/232-8501 •
5pm-1am

Clary's Cafe 404 Abercorn (at Jones)
912/233-0402 • 7am-4pm, from 8am Sat-Sun
• country cookin'

The Distillery 416 W Liberty St
912/236-1772 • 11am-1am, till 3am Fri-Sat,
noon-9pm Sun • wheelchair access

Fannie's on the Beach 1613 Strand Ave (at
Silver Ave), Tybee Island 912/786-6109 •
noon-11pm, till 2am wknds • dancing/DJ • live
shows

Firefly Cafe 321 Habersham St
912/234-1971 • 10:30am-9pm, till 9:30pm Fri-
Sat, 9am-3pm Sun • wheelchair access

Green Truck Neighborhood Pub 2430
Habersham St 912/234-5885 • 11am-1am,
clsd Sun-Mon • beer/wine • wheelchair access
• gay-owned

Local 11 Ten 1110 Bull St 912/790-9000 •
dinner nightly • upscale dining in a restored
1950s bank • also Perch rooftop bar

Mellow Mushroom 11 W Liberty St
912/495-0705 • 11am-10pm • pizza & beer •
wheelchair access

Olde Pink House/ Planters Tavern 23
Abercorn St 912/232-4286 • upscale
Southern dining upstairs, cozy bar downstairs
• live jazz

Soho South Cafe 12 W Liberty St
912/233-1633 • 11am-4pm daily • eclectic

Wright Square Cafe 21 W York St
912/238-1150 • 7:30am-5pm, from 9am Sat,
clsd Sun • large chocolate selection • patio

ENTERTAINMENT & RECREATION

Savannah Walks, Inc 912/238-9255,
888/728-9255 • gay-friendly • walking tours of
downtown Savannah

Unadilla

ACCOMMODATIONS

Lumberjack's Camping Resort 50 Hwy 230
(at Hwy 41) **478/783-2267, 877/888-1688** •
mostly gay men • campsites, cabins & RV
hookups • pool • live shows • WiFi • pets ok •
gay-owned • also restaurant • $14-139

Washington

ACCOMMODATIONS

Holly Court Inn 301 S Alexander Ave (at
Water St) **706/678-3982, 866/465-5928** • gay-
friendly • 1 hour from Augusta & Athens • full
brkfst • kids ok • dining & bar • WiFi • $90-175

CAFES

Talk of the Town 1 East Public Sq (at
Robert Toombs Ave) **706/678-7661** • 10am-
5pm, clsd Sun • gay-owned & -operated cafe
w/ retail

HAWAII

Please note that cities are grouped by
islands:
Hawaii (Big Island)
Kauai
Maui
Molokai
Oahu (includes Honolulu)

HAWAII (BIG ISLAND)

Captain Cook

ACCOMMODATIONS

Aloha Guest House 84-4780 Mamalahoa
Hwy **808/328-8955, 800/897-3188** • gay/
straight • full organic brkfst • nudity •
nonsmoking • WiFi • wheelchair access • gay-
owned • $120-200

Areca Palms Estate B&B 808/323-2276,
800/545-4390 • gay-friendly • full brkfst •
nonsmoking • $115-145

Horizon Guest House 808/328-2540,
888/328-8301 • gay/ straight • full brkfst •
pool • nonsmoking • WiFi • wheelchair access
• gay-owned • $250-350

Ka'awa Loa Plantation 82-5990 Napoopoo
Rd 96704 **808/323-2686** • gay/ straight •
plantation-style B&B • nonsmoking • WiFi •
wheelchair access • gay-owned • $129-199

Kealakekua Bay B&B 808/328-8150,
800/328-8150 • gay/ straight •
Mediterranean-style villa • nonsmoking • kids
ok • also 2-bdrm guesthouse • $140-300

Hilo

ACCOMMODATIONS

Aloha Healing Women 14-4817 Kapoha Kai
St **808/936-6067** • women only • all-inclusive
holistic healing retreats • full brkfst • pool •
accupuncture • women-owned

The Butterfly Inn for Women
808/966-7936, 800/546-2442 • women only •
hot tub • kitchens • nonsmoking • WiFi •
women-owned • $55-85

Mele Kohola 15-991 Paradise Dr (Paradise
Ala Kai) **808/965-0400** • vacation rental • bay
views • seasonal whale-watching • WiFi •
$150-375

RESTAURANTS

Cafe Pesto 308 Kamehameha Ave
808/969-6640 • lunch & dinner • pizzas,
salads, pastas • on the waterfront • also at
Kawaihae Shopping Center 808/882-1071

ENTERTAINMENT & RECREATION

Best of Hilo Adventures Tours 1477
Kalanianaole Ave **808/987-3905** • lesbian-
owned

Richardson Beach at end of Kalanianaole
Ave (Keaukaha)

Sun and Sea Hawaii 224 Kamehameha Ave
(at Kalakaua Ave) **808/934-0902** • LGBT
snorkel rental & tour company • women's
party producers • lesbian-owned

Honaunau-Kona

ACCOMMODATIONS

Dragonfly Ranch Healing Arts Center
1 1/2 miles down City of Refuge Rd
808/328-2159 • gay/ straight • hot tub •
nonsmoking • $100-250

Kailua-Kona

INFO LINES & SERVICES

Gay AA 808/329–1212 • Sat 7pm • call for location

ACCOMMODATIONS

1st Class B&B Kona Hawaii 77–6504 Kilohana St 808/329–8778, 888/769–1110 • gay-friendly • ocean views • full brkfst • nonsmoking • WiFi • $165-175

KonaLani Hawaiian Inn & Coffee Plantation 76-5917H Mamalahoa Hwy 808/324–0793 • lesbians/ gay men • full brkfst • nonsmoking • gay-owned • $99-155

Royal Kona Resort 75–5852 Ali'i Dr 808/329–3111, 800/222–5642 • gay-friendly • pool • private beach • bar • live shows • WiFi • wheelchair access

BARS

The Mask-querade 75–5660 Kopiko St 808/329–8558 • 10am-2am • lesbians/ gay men • neighborhood bar • dancing/DJ • live shows • karaoke • Mon ladies night • gay-owned

My Bar 74-5606 Luhia St (btwn Kaiwi & Eho St) 808/331–8789 • 10am-2am • gay-friendly

RESTAURANTS

Huggo's 75-5828 Kahakai Rd (on Kailua Bay) 808/329–1493 • dinner only • waterfront dining • also bar • live entertainment • patio

BOOKSTORES

Kona Stories 78-6831 Ali'i Dr #142 (in the Keauhou Shopping Ctr) 808/324–0350 • bookstore that host PFLAG meetings & other LGBT groups

Kamuela

ACCOMMODATIONS

Waimea Views Guest House 65-1546 Kawaihae Rd (at Paki Pl) 808/885–8559 • gay/ straight • peaceful guesthouse on the slopes of Mauna Kea • kids ok • WiFi • wheelchair access • women-owned

Kehena

ACCOMMODATIONS

Kehena Beach Guesthouse 12-7114 Waioleka St 808/965–8625 • gay/ straight • non-smoking • gay-owned • $50

Na'alehu

ACCOMMODATIONS

Margo's Corner near South Point 808/929–9614 • cottage & 4 campsites • full brkfst & dinner • kids ok • sauna • WiFi • lesbian-owned • $90-130

Pahoa

ACCOMMODATIONS

Aloha Inn Hawaii 808/965–2211 • mostly women • cooking & massage available • nonsmoking • wheelchair access • lesbian-owned • $60-120

Coconut Cottage B&B 808/965–0973, 866/204–7444 • gay/ straight • centrally located btwn Hilo & Volcanoes Nat'l Park • gay-owned • $110-140

Dakini Gardens & Retreat Ala 'Ili Rd, Kehena Beach 808/443–3463 • mostly women • cottage • swimming at beach • hot tub • nonsmoking • women-owned

Green Fire Productions 14-4707 Ewa Ln (Kapoho Beach Estates) 808/965–1733 • women only • artesiian ocean pond • nonsmoking • lesbian-owned • $200

Hale 'Ae Kai Guesthouse 13-6768 Kapoho-Kalapana Beach Rd 808/936–8856 • gay/ straight • kids ok • nonsmoking • WiFi • lesbian-owned • $100-125

Hawaiian Retreat 14-234 Papaya Farm Rd 808/640–2157 • gay/ straight • kids/ pets ok • organic farm & orchard • WiFi • $65-110 • also "adventure" cabin (more rustic) $25-125

Kalani Oceanside Retreat 808/965–7828, 800/800-6886 • gay/ straight • coastal wellness retreat & spa • pool • nudity • nonsmoking • WiFi • food served • wheelchair access • $40 (camping), $90-275 (retreat)

Pamalu—Hawaiian Country House 808/965–0830 • gay/ straight • secluded country retreat • pool • kids ok if family rents whole house • nonsmoking • WiFi • gay-owned • $85-150

Rainbow's Inn, Adventures & Retreat Center 808/965–9011 • gay/ straight • large no-chemical pool • hot tub • kids/ pets ok • nonsmoking • limited wheelchair access • lesbian-owned • $65-135/ night, weekly & monthly rates available

ENTERTAINMENT & RECREATION

Kehena Beach off Hwy 137 (trailhead at 19-mile marker phone booth) • lava rock trail to clothing-optional black-sand beach

Volcano Village

ACCOMMODATIONS

The Artist Cottage at Volcano Garden Arts 19-3834 Old Volcano Rd (at Wright Rd) **808/985-8979** • gay-friendly • kids/pets ok • WiFi • $129-863

The Chalet Kilauea Collection 19-4178 Wright Rd **808/967-7786, 800/937-7786** • gay-friendly • full brkfst • hot tub • nonsmoking • WiFi • $60-735

Hale Ohia Cottages **808/967-7986, 800/455-3803** • gay/ straight • WiFi • gay-owned • $109-219

Kulana: The Affordable Artists Sanctuary **808/985-9055** • mostly women • artist retreat • camping, cabins & guest rooms available • no smoking, drugs or alcohol • kids ok • women-owned • $15 (camping), $18-40 (cabin); see website (www.discoverkulana.com) for visitor-to-resident-transition guidelines

CAFES

Ono Cafe 19-3834 Old Volcano Rd (at Wright Rd) **808/985-8979** • 10am-4pm

KAUAI

Anahola

ACCOMMODATIONS

Mahina Kai Ocean Villa 4933 Aliomanu Rd **808/822-9451, 800/337-1134** • gay/ straight • pool • hot tub • nudity • nonsmoking • WiFi • gay-owned • $125-355

Hanalei

NIGHTCLUBS

Tahiti Nui 5-5134 Kuhio Hwy (near Hanalei Center) **808/826-6277** • 11am-2am • gay-friendly • dancing/DJ • live music most nights • karaoke • also restaurant • Italian/ local • wheelchair access

Kapaa

ACCOMMODATIONS

17 Palms Kauai **808/822-5659, 888/725-6799** • gay/ straight • 2 secluded cottages 200 steps from beach • kids ok • nonsmoking • WiFi • wheelchair access • gay-owned

Fern Grotto Inn 4561 Kuamoo Rd (at Kuhio Hwy) **808/821-9836** • gay/ straight • cottages on the banks of the Wailua River • kids ok • nonsmoking • $99-279

Mohala Ke Ola B&B Retreat 5663 Ohelo Rd (at Kuamoo Rd/ Hwy 580) **808/823-6398, 888/465-2824** • gay-friendly • pool • jacuzzi • nonsmoking • WiFi • gay-owned • $100-140

RESTAURANTS

Eggbert's 4-484 Kuhio Hwy (in Coconut Plantation Marketplace) **808/822-4422** • 7am-2pm • also Hula Girl Grill • light fare until 6pm Mon-Sat • wheelchair access

Mema 4-369 Kuhio Hwy (in shopping center) **808/823-0899** • lunch Mon-Fri, dinner nightly • Thai & Chinese • BYOB • wheelchair access

Lihue

ACCOMMODATIONS

Kauai Beach Resort 4331 Kauai Beach Dr **808/245-1955, 866/971-2782** • gay-friendly • pools• also restaurant/ bar • non-smoking • WiFi

Poipu Beach

ACCOMMODATIONS

Poipu Plantation B&B Inn & Vacation Rental Suites 1792 Pe'e Rd **808/742-6757, 800/634-0263** • gay/ straight • full brkfst • near beach • kids ok • WiFi • gay-owned • $125-220

Princeville

ACCOMMODATIONS

Kauai Oceanfront Condo 5300 Ka Haku Rd **610/793-7539** • gay/ straight • pool • nonsmoking • WiFi • $1,390-1,575/ week

Puunene

RESTAURANTS

Roy's Poipu Bar & Grill 2360 Kiahuna Plantation Dr **808/742-5000** • 5:30pm-9:30pm

Wailua

RESTAURANTS

Caffe Coco 4-369 Kuhio Hwy **808/822-7990** • lunch Tue-Fri, dinner nightly, clsd Mon • art gallery • live music • patio • BYOB • wheelchair access

Waimea

ACCOMMODATIONS

Aston Waimea Plantation Cottages **808/338-1625, 877/997-6667** • gay-friendly • swimming • kids ok • WiFi • $198-800

MAUI

INFO LINES & SERVICES

Both Sides Now • all-inclusive LGBT community organization • resources • events

Hana

ACCOMMODATIONS

Hana Accommodations 808/248–7868, 800/228–4262 • gay/ straight • studios & tropical cottages • nonsmoking • kids ok • gay-owned • $68-170

Huelo

ACCOMMODATIONS

Cliff's Edge 808/268–4530, 866/262–6284 • gay-friendly • pool • nonsmoking • WiFi • $185-350

Kaanapali

ACCOMMODATIONS

The Royal Lahaina Resort 2780 Kekaa Dr 808/661–3611, 800/214–5000 • gay-friendly • full-service resort • pool • wheelchair access • $200+

Kihei

ACCOMMODATIONS

Anfora's Dreams 323/467–2991, 800/788–5046 • gay/ straight • rental condo near ocean • hot tub • pool • gay-owned • $89-135

Eva Villa 815 Kumulani Dr 808/874–6407, 800/884–1845 • gay-friendly • B&B • near Wailea beaches • hot tub • pool • WiFi • kids over 12 yrs ok • wheelchair access • $135-175

Koa Lagoon 800 S Kihei Rd 808/879–3002, 800/367–8030 • gay-friendly • oceanfront suites • pool • WiFi • wheelchair access • $140-200

➤ **Maui Sunseeker LGBT Resort** 551 S Kihei Rd (at Wailana Place) 808/879–1261, 800/532–6284 • lesbians/ gay men • ocean views • pool • nudity allowed • nonsmoking • WiFi • gay-owned • $105-395

Tutu Mermaids on Maui B&B 2840 Umalu Pl 808/874–8687, 800/598–9550 • gay/ straight • jacuzzi • pool • near beach • nonsmoking • WiFi • lesbian-owned • $115-140

BARS

Diamond's Ice Bar & Grill 1279 S Kihei Rd 808/874–9299 • 11am-2am, from 7am Sun • gay-friendly local bar • food served • live shows

CAFES

Cafe at La Plage 2395 S Kihei Rd (at Kam Beach I) 808/875–7668 • 7am-5pm, till 3pm Sun • WiFi • wheelchair access

RESTAURANTS

Jawz Tacos 1279 S Kihei Rd 808/874–8226 • 11am-9pm • fresh fish tacos • wheelchair access

Stella Blues Cafe 1279 S Kihei Rd (in Azeka II Shopping Center) 808/874–3779 • 7:30am-11pm • live music • wheelchair access

EROTICA

The Love Shack 1913 S Kihei Rd (in Kalama Vlg) 808/875–0303 • intimate apparel

Kula

ACCOMMODATIONS

The Upcountry B&B 4925 Lower Kula Rd (at Copp St) 808/878–8083 • gay-friendly • nonsmoking • WiFi • wheelchair access • $120

Lahaina

RESTAURANTS

Betty's Beach Cafe 505 Front St 808/662–0300 • 8am-10pm, full bar till midnight

Lahaina Coolers 180 Dickenson St 808/661–7082 • 8am-1am • patio • wheelchair access

RETAIL SHOPS

Skin Deep Tattoo 626 Front St (across from the Banyan Tree) 808/661–8531 • 10am-10pm, till 8pm Sun-Mon

Makawao

ACCOMMODATIONS

Hale Ho'okipa Inn B&B 32 Pakani Pl 808/572–6698, 877/572–6698 • gay-friendly • restored Hawaiian plantation home • nonsmoking • WiFi • wheelchair access • woman-owned • $125-170

RESTAURANTS

Casanova Restaurant & Deli 1188 Makawao Ave **808/572-0220** • lunch & dinner • Italian • full bar till 2am • gay-friendly • ladies night Wed • live music & shows Wed-Sat

Makena

ENTERTAINMENT & RECREATION

Little Beach at Makena • lesbians/ gay men • Pilani Hwy S to Wailea, right at Wailea Ike Dr, left on Wailea Alanui Dr to public beach, then take trail up hill at right end of beach

Wailuku

ACCOMMODATIONS

Maalaea Kai Condo 70 Hauoli St (Maalaea Village) 562/212-3312 • gay-friendly • oceanfront 2-bdrm condo • WiFi • $130-210

MOLOKAI

Kaunakakai

RESTAURANTS

Kanemitsu Bakery & Coffee Shop 79 Ala Malama St **808/553-5855** • 5:30am-5pm, clsd Tue • great sweet bread

OAHU

PUBLICATIONS

Odyssey Magazine Hawaii 808/955-5959 • everything you need to know about gay Hawaii

Aiea

CAFES

Cloud Nine Internet Cafe 99-115 Aiea Heights Dr (Aiea Shopping Center) **808/487-2944**

Haleiwa

ACCOMMODATIONS

Kelea Surf Spa 949/492-7263 • women only • surf spa & yoga on Oahu's North Shore • open during spring only • 18+

Honolulu

INFO LINES & SERVICES

Gay/ Lesbian AA 310 Pa`okalani Ave, Room 203A **808/946-1438** • 8pm Sat

ACCOMMODATIONS

Aqua Palms & Spa 1850 Ala Moana Blvd (at Kalia & Ena) **808/947-7256, 866/406-2782** • gay-friendly • kids ok • nonsmoking • WiFi • wheelchair access • $90+

Aston Waikiki Circle Hotel 2464 Kalakaua Ave (at Uluniu St, Waikiki) **808/923-1571, 877/997-6667** • gay-friendly • kids welcome • nonsmoking • WiFi • $180-220

Hotel Renew 129 Paoakalani Ave (at Lemon Rd, Waikiki) **808/687-7700, 888/485-7639** • gay-friendly • nonsmoking • WiFi • $175-235

Waikiki Grand Hotel 134 Kapahulu Ave **808/923-1814, 808/923-1511** • gay/ straight • rentals above Hula's Bar • pool • nonsmoking • women-owned • $90-299

BARS

In Between 2155 Lau'ula St (off Lewers, across from Planet Hollywood, Waikiki) **808/926-7060** • noon-2am • mostly gay men • neighborhood bar • karaoke

Lo Jax 2256 Kuhio Ave, 2nd flr (at Seaside, Waikiki) **808/922-1422** • noon-2am • lesbians/ gay men • neighborhood/sports bar • food served • WiFi

Tapa's Restaurant & Lanai Bar 407 Seaside, 2nd flr (at Kuhio Ave) **808/921-2288** • 9am-2am • gay/ straight • lanai bar • karaoke • also restaurant • East-West fusion • gay-owned

Wang Chung's 2410 Koa Ave (at Kaiulani) **808/921-9176** • 2pm-2am • lesbians/ gay men • karaoke • wheelchair access

NIGHTCLUBS

Bar 7 1344 Kona St (at Piikoi Rd) **808/955-2640** • 9pm-4am • gay/ straight • dancing/DJ • mostly Asian American • drag shows Sat • wheelchair access

Downe Towne for Women 35 N Hotel St (at Bar 35) **808/537-3535** • 9pm-2am 1st Sat only • mostly women • dancing/DJ

Fusion Waikiki 2260 Kuhio Ave, 2nd flr (at Seaside) **808/924-2422** • 10pm-4am, from 8pm Fri-Sat • mostly gay men • dancing/DJ • transgender-friendly • live shows • karaoke Mon-Tue • drag shows • videos

Hula's Bar & Lei Stand 134 Kapahulu Ave (2nd flr of Waikiki Grand Hotel) **808/923-0669** • 10am-2am • popular • mostly gay men • dancing/DJ • food served • live shows • videos • young crowd • weekly catamaran cruise • WiFi

CAFES

Leonard's Bakery 933 Kapahulu Ave **808/737–5591** • 5:30am-9pm, till 10pm Fri-Sat • irresistible malasadas & doughnuts

Mocha Java Cafe 1200 Ala Moana Blvd (in Ward Center) **808/591–9023** • 8am-9pm, till 6pm Sun • WiFi • outdoor seating • wheelchair access

RESTAURANTS

Alan Wong's 1857 S King St (at Pumehana St) **808/949–2526** • dinner only • upscale, romantic Hawaiian dining

Arancino di Mare 2552 Kalakaua Ave (in Waikiki Beach Marriott) **808/931–6273**

Cafe Che Pasta 1001 Bishop St, Ste 108 (enter off Alakea St) **808/524–0004** • lunch & dinner, clsd Sat-Sun • full bar

Cafe Sistina 1314 S King St **808/596–0061** • lunch Mon-Fri, dinner nightly • northern Italian • some veggie • full bar • wheelchair access

Cha Cha Cha 342 Seaside Ave **808/923–7797** • 11:30am-midnight • Mexican • happy hour

Cheeseburger in Paradise 2500 Kalakaua Blvd **808/923–3731** • 7am-11pm • full bar

Eggs 'n' Things 343 Saratoga Rd (at Kalakaua Ave) **808/923–3447** • 6am-2pm, 5pm-10pm

House Without A Key 2199 Kalia Rd (at Lewers St, at Halekulani Hotel) **808/923–2311** • 7am-9pm • stunning sunset views • Hawaiian music nightly

Hula Grill 2335 Kalakaua Ave (in Outrigger Hotel) **808/923–4852**

Honolulu

WHERE THE GIRLS ARE:
Where else? On the beach. Or cruising Kuhio Ave.

LGBT PRIDE:
June, web: www.honolulupff.org.

ANNUAL EVENTS:
April - Merrie Monarch Festival, hula competition in Hilo, web: www.kalena.com/merriemonarch.

April-May - Golden Week, celebration of Japanese culture.

May - Honolulu Rainbow Film Festival **808/675–8428**, web: www.hglcf.org.

September - Aloha Festivals, web: alohafestivals.com.

CITY INFO:
800/464-2924, web: www.gohawaii.com. Also www.visit-oahu.com.

BEST VIEW:
Helicopter tour.

WEATHER:
Usually paradise perfect, but humid. It rarely gets hotter than the upper 80°s.

ATTRACTIONS:
Bishop Museum 808/847-3511, web: www.bishopmuseum.org.

Foster Botanical Gardens. 808/522-7066, web: www.hawaiimuseums.org/mc/isoahu_foster.htm.

Hanauma Bay.

Honolulu Academy of Arts 808/532-8700, web: www.honoluluacademy.org.

'Iolani Palace 808/522-0822, web: www.iolanipalace.org.

Polynesian Cultural Center 800/367-7060 or 808/293-3333, web: www.polynesia.com.

USS Arizona Memorial, 808/422-3200, web: www.nps.gov/valr.

Waimea Falls Park.

TRANSIT:
Charley's 808/947–0077, web: charleystaxi.com.

Hawaii Super Transit 808/841-2928, web: hawaiisupertransit.com

The Bus 808/848-5555, web: www.thebus.com.

Indigo 1121 Nu'uanu Ave **808/521–2900** • lunch Tue-Fri, dinner Tue-Sat • Eurasian • live music • wheelchair access

Keo's in Waikiki 2028 Kuhio Ave **808/951-9355** • 5pm-10pm • reservations advised • wheelchair access

La Cucaracha 2446 Koa Ave **808/924–3366** • noon-11pm • Mexican • full bar

Liliha Bakery 515 N Kuakini St (at Liliha St) **808/531–1651** • open 24hrs, clsd Mon • diner fare & baked goods • wheelchair access

Lulu's 2586 Kalakaua Ave **808/926–5222** • 7am-4am • full bar • live shows

Rock Island Cafe 131 Kaiulani Ave (off Kalakaua, in King's Village Waikiki) **808/923-8033** • old-fashioned soda fountain

Singha Thai 1910 Ala Moana Blvd **808/941–2898** • 4pm-10pm • Thai dancers

Tiki's Grill & Bar 2570 Kalakaua Ave (in ResortQuest Hotel) **808/923-8454**

ENTERTAINMENT & RECREATION

Diamond Head Beach • gay/ straight • take road from lighthouse to beach • some nude sunbathing

Girls Who Surf 1020 Auahi St, Bldg 4, Ste 4 (Ward Shopping Ctr) **808/772–4583** • surf lessons for all levels • everyone welcome

Honolulu Gay/ Lesbian Cultural Foundation 1670 Makaloa St #204 **808/675–8428** • last wknd of May annual Honolulu Rainbow Film Festival • art exhibits • concerts • plays

Rainbow Sailing Charters **808/347–0235** • lesbians/ gay men • day & overnight sailing adventures • whale-watching • snorkeling • sunset cocktail cruises • lesbian-owned

RETAIL SHOPS

Eighty Percent Straight 134 Kapahulu Ave, Ste B (in Waikiki Grand Hotel) **808/923-9996** • 10am-11pm, till midnight Fri-Sat, noon-11pm Sun • LGBT

PUBLICATIONS

Expression Magazine **808/393–7994** • monthly glossy LGBT magazine

Odyssey Magazine Hawaii **808/955–5959** • everything you need to know about gay Hawaii

EROTICA

Suzie's Secrets 1370 Kapiolani Blvd **808/949–4383** • 24hrs

Windward Coast

ACCOMMODATIONS

Ali'i Bluffs Windward B&B 46–251 Ikiiki St, Kane'ohe **808/235–1124, 800/235–1151** • gay/ straight • pool • nonsmoking • WiFi • gay-owned • $70-85

IDAHO

Statewide

PUBLICATIONS

Diversity Newsmagazine **208/336–3870** • statewide LGBT newspaper • monthly

Boise

INFO LINES & SERVICES

The Community Center 305 E 37th St, Garden City **208/336–3870** • volunteer staff

ACCOMMODATIONS

Hotel 43 981 Grove St **800/243–4622** • gay/straight • restaurant & bar • WiFi

The Modern Hotel & Bar 1314 W Grove St **866/782-6012** • gay-friendly • refurbished 1960's Travelodge with gallery • pets ok WiFi

BARS

The Lucky Dog 2223 W Fairview Ave (at 23rd) **208/333–0074** • 2pm-2am, from noon wknds • mostly gay men • neighborhood bar • patio • WiFi

Neurolux 111 N 11th St (at W Idaho) **208/343-0886** • noon-2am • gay-friendly • dancing/DJ • live music

Pitchers and Pints 1108 W Front St. • 5pm-2am • gay/straight • neighborhood bar • scruffy outside but nice inside • nice patio • gay-owned

NIGHTCLUBS

The Balcony Club 150 N 8th St #226 (at Idaho) **208/336–1313** • 4pm-2am • lesbians/ gay men • popular • dancing/DJ • karaoke • theme nights • wheelchair access • gay-owned

CAFES

Big City Coffee 5517 W State St **208/853–9161** • 6am-5pm, till 4pm Sun

Flying M Coffeehouse 500 W Idaho St (at 5th St) **208/345–4320** • 6:30am-11pm, from 7:30am wknds, till 6pm Sun • WiFi

Tully's 794 Broad St **208/343–2953** • 7am-8pm, till 10pm Fri-Sat, 9am-8pm Sun • WiFi

RESTAURANTS

Lucky 13 Pizza 3662 S Eckert Rd
208/344-6967 • 11am-9pm, till 10pm wknds

ENTERTAINMENT & RECREATION

The Flicks 646 Fulton St 208/342-4222 •
opens 4pm, from noon Fri-Sun • 4 movie
theaters • food served • beer/ wine • patio •
wheelchair access

BOOKSTORES

Crone's Cupboard 712 N Orchard
208/333-0831 • 10am-7pm, clsd Sun-Mon •
Wiccan • New Age • feminist/ lesbian books &
art

RETAIL SHOPS

The Record Exchange 1105 W Idaho St (at
11th) 208/344-8010 • 9am-9pm, till 7pm Sun
• gifts • music • also cafe & live music

See Jane Run Sports 814 W Idaho St
208/338-5263 • 10am-6pm, noon-5pm Sun

EROTICA

The O!Zone 1615 Broadway Ave
208/395-1977, 888/326-3713 • noon-7pm, till
5pm Sun

Pleasure Boutique 5022 Fairview Ave (at
Orchard) 208/433-1161 • toys, videos

Coeur d'Alene

see also Spokane, Washington

ACCOMMODATIONS

The Clark House on Hayden Lake 5250 E
Hayden Lake Rd, Hayden Lake 208/772-3470,
800/765-4593 • gay-friendly • mansion on a
wooded 12-acre estate • full brkfst • also fine
dining • hot tub • nonsmoking • WiFi • gay-
owned • $99-250

Lava Hot Springs

see also Pocatello

ACCOMMODATIONS

Aura Soma Lava 196 E Main St
208/776-5800, 800/757-1233 • gay/straight •
pool • also retail store

Moscow

INFO LINES & SERVICES

Inland Oasis LGBTA Center 412 E 3rd St
(Friendship Hall, 1912 Bldg) 208/352-0456 •
7pm Sun potluck

BOOKSTORES

Bookpeople 521 S Main (btwn 5th & 6th)
208/882-7957 • 9am-8pm • general

Nampa

CAFES

Flying M Coffeegarage 1314 2nd St S
208/467-5533 • 6:30am-11pm, from 7:30am
wknds • entertainment

Pocatello

NIGHTCLUBS

Club Charleys 331 E Center St 208/232-9606
• 5pm-2am, from 8pm Sun • lesbians/ gay
men • dancing/DJ • live shows • karaoke •
drag shows • wheelchair access

CAFES

Main St Coffee & News 234 N Main St
(btwn Lander & Clark) 208/234-9834 •
6:30am-4pm, from 8am Sat, from 9am Sun

EROTICA

The Silver Fox 143 S 2nd St (at Center)
208/234-2477

Twin Falls

CAFES

Annie's Lavender & Coffee Cafe 591
Addison Ave W (at 8th St) 208/736-2003 •
6am-5pm, seasonal wknd hrs • wheelchair
access

RESTAURANTS

Pizza Planet 720 Main St (at 8th St), Buhl
208/543-8560 • 11am-8pm, till 9pm Fri-Sat •
also DVD store

ILLINOIS

Alton

see also St Louis, Missouri

NIGHTCLUBS

Bubby & Sissy's 602 Belle St (at 6th)
618/465-4773 • 3pm-2am, till 3am Fri-Sat,
clsd Mon • lesbians/ gay men • dancing/DJ •
drag shows • karaoke • food served •
wheelchair access

Arlington Heights

see Chicago

Bloomington

BARS

Bistro 316 N Main St (at Jefferson)
309/829-2278 • 8pm-1am, from 4:30pm Fri,
till 2am Fri-Sat • lesbians/ gay men •
dancing/DJ Wed-Sat • WiFi • wheelchair access

CAFES

Coffee Hound 407 N Main St **309/827–7575**
• 6:30am-6pm, 8am-5pm Sun • WiFi

Kelly's Bakery & Cafe 113 N Center St
309/820–1200 • 7am-6pm, till 2pm Sat, clsd
Sun • wheelchair access

Blue Island

see also Chicago

NIGHTCLUBS

Club Krave 13126 S Western Ave (at Grove)
708/597–8379 • 8pm-2am, till 3am Fri-Sat,
from 6pm Mon • lesbians/ gay men •
neighborhood bar • dancing/DJ • transgender-
friendly • karaoke • cabaret • drag shows •
wheelchair access

Bradley

RESTAURANTS

La Villetta 801 W Broadway St **815/939–4960**
• 11am-9pm, till 8pm Sun • Italian

EROTICA

Slightly Sinful 101 N Kinzie Ave (at
Broadway) **815/937–5744**

Carbondale

INFO LINES & SERVICES

AA Lesbian/ Gay 618/549–4633

NIGHTCLUBS

Club Traz 213 E Main St 618/549–4270 •
9pm-2am, clsd Mon-Tue & Th • gay-friendly •
neighborhood bar • dancing/DJ • live shows •
videos • gay-owned

Champaign/ Urbana

ACCOMMODATIONS

Sylvia's Irish Inn 312 W Green St, Urbana
217/384–4800 • gay-friendly • full brkfst •
nonsmoking • WiFi • $85-200

BARS

Emerald City Lounge 118 N First St (at
University Ave), Champaign **217/398–8661** •
5pm-2am, from 10am Sun • lesbians/ gay
men • food served • live music • wheelchair
access • gay-owned

Mike 'N Molly's 105 N Market St (at
University), Champaign **217/355–1236** •
4pm-2am • gay-friendly • live music •
dancing/DJ • beer garden

NIGHTCLUBS

Chester Street 63 Chester St (at Water St),
Champaign **217/356–5607** • 5pm-2am •
lesbians/ gay men • dancing/DJ • drag show
Sun • gay-owned

CAFES

Aroma Cafe 118 N Neil St, Champaign
217/356–3200 • 7am-11pm, from 8am wknds

Cafe Kopi 109 N Walnut, Champaign
217/359–4266 • 7am-midnight • full bar &
menu • nonsmoking • WiFi

Espresso Royale 602 E Daniel St (at 6th St),
Champaign **217/328–1112** • 7am-midnight

Pekara Bakery & Bistro 116 N Neil St,
Champaign **217/359–4500** • 7am-8pm, from
8am Sun

RESTAURANTS

Boltini Lounge 211 N Neil St, Champaign
217/378–8001 • 4pm-2am, till 10pm Mon, clsd
Sun • also full bar • upscale

The Courier Cafe 111 N Race St, Urbana
217/328–1811 • 7am-11pm

Dos Reales 1407 N Prospect Ave,
Champaign **217/351–6879** • 11am-10pm •
Mexican • wheelchair access

Farren's Pub & Eatery 308 N Randolph St,
Champaign **217/359–6977** • 11am-9pm, till
10pm Fri, from noon wknds • full bar

Fiesta Cafe 216 S 1st St (at E Clark),
Champaign **217/352–5902** • 11am-11pm, bar
till 1am • Mexican • gay-owned

The Great Impasta 156C Lincoln Sq,
Urbana **217/359–7377** • 11am-9pm, till 10pm
Fri, 5pm-10pm Sat, clsd Sun • live music •
wheelchair access

Radio Maria 119 N Walnut St, Champaign
217/398–7729 • 5pm-2am, brunch Sun •
eclectic Mexican cuisine

Silvercreek 402 N Race St, Urbana
217/328–3402 • lunch & dinner, brunch Sun •
live music

BOOKSTORES

Jane Addams Book Shop 208 N Neil St (S
of Main), Champaign **217/356–2555** • 10am-
7pm, till 5pm Sat-Sun • full-service antiquarian
bookstore w/ children's room • LGBT &
women's sections

RETAIL SHOPS

Dandelion 9 Taylor St, Champaign
217/355–9333 • 11am-6pm, noon-5pm Sun •
vintage & used clothing

Gyms & Health Clubs

Refinery 2302 W John St, Champaign 217/355-4444 • gay-friendly

Chicago

Chicago is divided into 5 geographical areas:
Chicago—Overview
Chicago—North Side
Chicago—Boystown/ Lakeview
Chicago—Near North
Chicago—South Side

Chicago—Overview

includes some listings for Greater Chicagoland; please check individual cities like Oak Park as well

Info Lines & Services

AA/ New Town Alano Club 909 W Belmont Ave, 2nd flr (btwn Clark & Sheffield) 773/529-0321 • 5pm-11pm, from 8:30am wknds • wheelchair access

Affinity 5650 S Woodlawn Ave (at First Unitarian of Hyde Park) 773/324-0377 • nonprofit "serving Chicago's black lesbian & bisexual women's community" through "education, social & community collaborations"

The Center on Halsted 3656 N Halsted St (at Waveland) 773/472-6469, 773/472-1277 (TTY) • 8am-10pm • LGBT center • organic grocery store • cafe • theater • gym • technology center

Accommodations

Chicago Women's Residence 1957 S Spaulding Ave (at S 21st) 773/542-9126 • women only • furnished rooms in women's residence • WiFi • please call ahead • lesbian-owned • $35-55

Nightclubs

Doll House Entertainment 312/927-1144 • women's parties at clubs around the city • www.myspace.com/lezdollhouse

Entertainment & Recreation

Artemis Singers 773/764-4465 • lesbian feminist chorus

Chicago Neighborhood Tours 77 E Randolph St (at Michigan Ave, at Chicago Cultural Center) 312/742-1190 • gay-friendly • the best way to make the Windy City your kind of town

Heartland Cafe 7000 N Glenwood Ave (in Rogers Park) 773/465-8005 • cafe w/ full bar, theater, radio show • lots of live music including performers popular on women's music circuit

John Hancock Observatory 875 N Michigan Ave (in John Hancock Center) 312/751-3681, 888/875-8439 • 9am-11pm, also Watch the city lights glimmer in the night sky from "The Signature Lounge at the 96th"

Leather Archives & Museum 6418 N Greenview Ave 773/761-9200 • 11am-7pm Th-Fri, till 5pm Sat-Sun • membership required (purchase at door)

Second City 1616 N Wells St (at North) 312/337-3992 • gay-friendly • legendary comedy club • call for reservations

Willis/ Sears Tower Skydeck 233 S Wacker Dr (enter at Jackson Blvd) 312/875-9696 • see the city from the 99th & 103rd floors of North America's tallest building

Publications

Gay Chicago 773/327-7271 • weekly • extensive resource listings

Identity 773/871-7610 • monthly news & features for LGBTs of color

Nightspots 773/871-7610 • weekly LGBT nightlife magazine

Windy City Times 773/871-7610 • weekly LGBT newspaper & calendar guide

Chicago—North Side

Accommodations

House 5863 B&B 5863 N Glenwood (at Admore) 773/944-5555 • gay/ straight • nonsmoking • WiFi • gay-owned • $99-189

Bars

The Anvil 1137 W Granville (E of Broadway) 773/973-0006 • 9am-2am • mostly gay men • neighborhood bar • videos

Big Chicks 5024 N Sheridan (btwn Foster & Argyle) 773/728-5511 • 4pm-2am, from 3pm wknds • lesbians/ gay men • neighborhood bar • dancing/DJ • videos • patio • Sun BBQ • WiFi • wheelchair access

The Call 1547 W Bryn Mawr (at Clark) 773/334-2525 • 4pm-2am • lesbians/ gay men • dancing/DJ • country/ western • drag shows • videos • wheelchair access

Crew 4804 N Broadway St (at Lawrence) 773/784-2739 • 11:30am-midnight, 11am-2am Fri-Sun • lesbians/ gay men • sports bar & grill • videos • patio

The Glenwood 6962 N Glenwood Ave (at Morse) **773/764-7363** • 3pm-2am, from noon Sun • lesbians/gay men • neighborhood sports bar • wheelchair access

Green Mill 4802 N Broadway Ave (at Lawrence) **773/878-5552** • noon-4am • gay/straight • noted jazz venue • hosts the Uptown Poetry Slam

In Fine Spirits 5420 N Clark St (at Rascher Ave) **773/334-9463** • 4pm-midnight, 3pm-2am Fri-Sat • wine bar • patio • food served • also wine store

Jackhammer 6406 N Clark St (at Devon) **773/743-5772** • 5pm-4am, till 5am Sat, from 2pm Sun • mostly gay men • karaoke • videos • patio

Joie de Vine 1744 W Balmoral Ave (at Paulina St) **773/989-6846** • 5pm-midnight, till 2am Fri & 3am Sat • mostly women • wine bar • patio • WiFi • wheelchair access • lesbian-owned

Marty's 1511 W Balmoral Ave (at Clark) **773/561-6425** • 5pm-2am • gay-friendly • upscale wine & martini bar • food served

Parlour on Clark 6341 N Clark St **773/564-9274** • 6pm-2am, from noon Sun, clsd Mon • lesbians/gay men • Th girls night • dancing/DJ • cabaret/drag shows

Scot's 1829 W Montrose Ave (at Damen) **773/528-3253** • 3pm-2am, 1pm-3am Sat, from 11am Sun • mostly gay men • neighborhood bar

Sofo 4923 N Clark St (at W Argyle) **773/784-7636** • 5pm-2am, 3pm-3am Sat • mostly gay men • video bar • backyard beer garden • wheelchair access

Spyner's Pub 4623 N Western Ave (at W Eastwood) **773/784-8719** • mostly women • neighborhood bar • karaoke

T's 5025 N Clark St (at Winnemac) **773/784-6000** • 5pm-2am, 11am-3am, till 2am Sun • mostly women • neighborhood bar • karaoke • also restaurant

Touché 6412 N Clark St (at Devon) **773/465-7400** • 5pm-4am, 3pm-5am Sat, noon-4am Sun • popular • mostly gay men • leather

NIGHTCLUBS

Atmosphere 5355 N Clark St (at W Balmoral Ave) **773/784-1100** • 6pm-2am, till 3am Sat, from 3pm Sat-Sun, clsd Mon • lesbians/gay men • dancing/DJ • male dancers Th-Sat • WiFi • gay-owned

Retro Night 4000 N Sheridan Rd (at Irving Park, at the Holiday Club) **773/348-9600 (HOLIDAY CLUB #)** • 10pm-2am Fri only • gay/straight • dancing/DJ spinning '80s • videos •

CAFES

Charmer's Cafe 1500 W Jarvis (at Greenview) **773/743-2233** • 6am-8pm, from 7am wknds • lesbians/gay men • WiFi • wheelchair access

Coffee Chicago 5256 N Broadway St (btwn Berwyn & Foster) **773/784-1305** • 7:30am-9pm • WiFi • wheelchair access

KOPI: A Traveler's Cafe 5317 N Clark St (at Summerdale) **773/989-5674** • 8am-11pm, till midnight Fri-Sat, from 9am Sat, from 10am Sun • food served • wheelchair access

Metropolis Coffee 1039 W Granville Ave (at Kenmore) **773/764-0400** • 6:30am-8pm, from 7:30am Sat-Sun • popular • WiFi

RESTAURANTS

Andie's 5253 N Clark (btwn Berwyn & Farragut) **773/784-8616** • 10:30am-midnight, till 10:30pm Sun • eastern Mediterranean • full bar • wheelchair access

Anteprima 5316 N Clark St (at Summerdale) **773/506-9990** • dinner nightly • Italian • wheelchair access

Deluxe Diner/ Maria's 6349 N Clark St (at Devon) **773/743-8244 (DELUXE #), 773/743-9900 (MARIA'S #)** • 24hr diner & pizza/Italian restaurant till 11pm • karaoke

Fat Cat 4840 N Broadway (at Lawrence Ave) **773/506-3100** • 4pm-2am, from 11am wknds • full bar

Fireside 5739 N Ravenswood (at Rosehill) **773/561-7433, 877/878-7433** • 11am-4am, till 5am Sat, 10am-4am Sun • Cajun & pizza • patio • full bar

Hamburger Mary's/ Rec Room/ Attic 5400 N Clark St (at Balmoral) **773/784-6969** • opens 11am, from 10am Sun • lesbians/gay men • full bar • karaoke • drag shows • wheelchair access

Hot Woks Cool Sushi 30 S Michigan Ave (at Madison) **312/345-1234** • 11:30am-8:30pm • sushi/Thai

Jin Ju 5203 N Clark St (at Summersdale) **773/334-6377** • dinner only • Korean • also bar • wheelchair access

Pauline's 1754 W Balmoral (at Ravenswood) **773/561-8573** • 7am-3pm • hearty brkfsts • wheelchair access

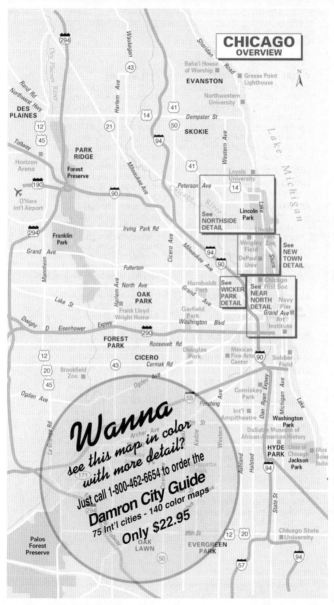

Chicago

WHERE THE GIRLS ARE:

In the Belmont area—on Halsted or Clark streets—with the boys, or hanging out elsewhere in Boystown. Upwardly-mobile lesbians live in Lincoln Park or Wrigleyville, while their working-class sisters live in Andersonville (way north).

LGBT PRIDE:

June. 773/348-8243, web: www.chicagopridecalendar.org.

ANNUAL EVENTS:

May - International Mr. Leather 800/545-6753, web: www.imrl.com.

May - Bear Pride, web: www.bearpride.org.

May-June- Chicago Blues Festival 312/744-3315, web: www.chicagobluesfestival.org.

August - Northalsted Market Days 773/883-0500, web: www.northalsted.com/market_days.php.

November - Chicago Lesbian & Gay Film Festival 773/293-1447, web: www.reelingfilmfestival.org.

CITY INFO:

Chicago Office of Tourism 877/244-2246, web: www.explorechicago.org.

BEST VIEW:

Skydeck of the 110-story Sears Tower, web: www.theskydeck.com or the open-air observation deck at the John Hancock Observatory, web: www.hancockobservatory.com.

WEATHER:

"The Windy City" earned its name. Winter temperatures have been known to be as low as -46°. Summers are humid, normally in the 80°s.

ATTRACTIONS:

900 North Michigan Shops.

Jane Addams Hull-House Museum 312/413-5353, www.hullhouse-museum.org.

The Art Institute of Chicago 312/443-3600, web: www.artic.edu.

DuSable Museum of African American History 773/947-0600, web: www.dusablemuseum.org.

Historic Water Tower.

LaSalle Bank Theatre (formerly Schubert Theatre).

Museum of Contemporary Art 312/280-2660, web: www.mcachicago.org.

Museum of Science & Industry 773/684-1414, web: www.msichicago.org.

National Museum of Mexican Art 312/738-1503, web: www.nationalmuseumofmexica-nart.org.

Steppenwolf Theatre Company, 312/335-1650, web: www.step-penwolf.org.

Terra Foundation for American Art, 312/664-3939, web: www.terraamericanart.org.

Wrigley Field, 773/404-CUBS, web: chicago.cubs.mlb.com.

TRANSIT:

Yellow Cab 312/ 829-4222, web: www.yellowcabchicago.com.

Go Airport Express 888/284-3826. web: www.airportexpress.com.

Chicago Transit Authority 312/836-7000, web: www.transitchicago.com.

Metra Rail 312/322-6777, web: www.metrarail.com.

Reza's Restaurant 5255 N Clark (btwn Berwyn & Farragut) 773/561–1898 • lunch & dinner • Mediterranean/Persian • full bar • wheelchair access

Svea Restaurant 5236 N Clark (btwn Berwyn & Farragut) 773/275–7738 • 7am-2:30pm, till 3:30pm wknds • Swedish/ American comfort food • wheelchair access

Tedino's 5335 N Sheridan Rd (at Broadway) 773/275–8100 • 11am-midnight, from 3pm Mon • popular • pizza • full bar • wheelchair access

Thai Pastry & Restaurant 4925 N Broadway St, Unit E (at Argyle) 773/784–5399 • 11am-10pm, till 11pm Fri-Sat • wheelchair access

Tweet 5020 N Sheridan Rd (at Argyle) 773/728–5576 • 9am-3pm, clsd Tue • brkfst & brunch • cash only • WiFi

ENTERTAINMENT & RECREATION

Hollywood /Osterman Beach at Hollywood & Sheridan Sts • popular • "the" gay beach

BOOKSTORES

Women & Children First 5233 N Clark St (at Foster) 773/769–9299 • 11am-7pm, till 9pm Wed-Fri, 10am-7pm Sat, 11am-6pm Sun • wheelchair access • women-owned

RETAIL SHOPS

Enjoy, An Urban General Store 4727 N Lincoln Ave (Lincoln Square) 773/334–8626 • 10am-7pm, till 6pm Sun • cards & gifts • lesbian-owned

Gaymart 3457 N Halsted St (at Cornelius) 773/929–4272 • 11am-8pm, till 6pm Sun

Leather 6410 6410 N Clark St (at Devon, btwn Jackhammer & Touché) 773/508–0900, 800/910–0666 • noon-midnight, till 4am Th, till 5am Fri, till 6am Sat, from 4pm Sun-Mon • gay-owned

GYMS & HEALTH CLUBS

Cheetah Gym 5248 N Clark St (at Foster) 773/728–7777

EROTICA

Early to Bed 5232 N Sheridan Rd (at Foster) 773/271–1219, 866/585–2233 • clsd Mon • transgender-friendly • 18+ • lesbian-owned

Tulip Sex Toy Gallery 1480 W Berwyn (at Clark) 773/275–6110, 877/708–8547 • noon-10pm, till 7pm Sun • sex toys for women • lesbian-owned

Chicago—Boystown/ Lakeview

ACCOMMODATIONS

Best Western Hawthorne Terrace 3434 N Broadway St (at Hawthorne Pl) 773/244–3435, 888/860–3400 • gay-friendly • in heart of Chicago's gay community • WiFi • wheelchair access • $139-299

City Suites Hotel 933 W Belmont Ave (btwn Clark & Sheffield) 773/404–3400, 800/248–9108 • gay-friendly • European style • nonsmoking rooms available • WiFi • $139-179

Majestic Hotel 528 W Brompton Ave (at Addison) 773/404–3499, 800/727–5108 • gay-friendly • romantic 19th-c atmosphere • nonsmoking • WiFi • $129-389

The Willows 555 W Surf St (at Broadway) 773/528–8400, 800/787–3108 • gay/ straight • nonsmoking • WiFi • $109-379

BARS

3160 3160 N Clark St (at Belmont) 773/327–5969 • 3pm-2am, till 3am Sat • lesbians/ gay men • neighborhood bar • live shows • piano • cabaret • wheelchair access

Beat Kitchen 2100 W Belmont (btwn Hoyne & Damen) 773/281–4444 • 4pm-2am, from 11:30am Sat-Sun, till 3am Sat • gay-friendly • live bands • also grill • some veggie • wheelchair access

Blues 2519 N Halsted St (at Lill Ave) 773/528–1012, 773/549–9436 • 8pm-2am, till 3am Sat • gay-friendly • classic Chicago blues spot

Bobby Love's 3729 N Halsted St (at Waveland) 773/525–1200 • 3pm-2am, from noon wknds, till 3am Sat • lesbians/ gay men • neighborhood bar • karaoke • wheelchair access

Buck's Saloon 3439 N Halsted St (btwn Cornelia & Newport) 773/525–1125 • noon-2am, till 3am Sat, from 11am Sun • mostly gay men • neighborhood bar • great beer garden

Cell Block 3702 N Halsted St (at Waveland) 773/665–8064 • 2pm-3am • mostly gay men • dancing/DJ • leather • also back bar wknds from 10pm • wheelchair access

Charlie's Chicago 3726 N Broadway St (btwn Waveland & Grace) 773/871–8887 • 3pm-4am, till 5am Sat • mostly gay men • dancing/DJ • country/ western • karaoke • club music after 1am

The Closet 3325 N Broadway St (at Buckingham) **773/477-8533** • 4pm-4am, noon-5am Sat, till 4am Sun • popular • lesbians/ gay men • neighborhood video bar • karaoke

Cocktail 3359 N Halsted St (at Roscoe) **773/477-1420** • 4pm-2am, from 2pm wknds, till 3am Sat • lesbians/ gay men • neighborhood bar • food served • dancing/DJ • wheelchair access

D.S. Tequila Company 3352 N Halsted St (at Roscoe) **773/697-9127** • 5pm-2am, from noon Fri-Sun • gay/ straight • good burgers & tacos

Little Jim's 3501 N Halsted St (at Cornelia) **773/871-6116** • noon-4am, till 5am Sat • popular • mostly gay men • neighborhood bar

The Lucky Horseshoe Lounge 3169 N Halsted St (at Briar) **773/404-3169** • 3pm-2am, from 2pm Sat • mostly gay men • neighborhood bar

Minibar 3341 N Halsted St (at Roscoe) **773/871-6227** • 5pm-2am, from 11am wknds • popular • lesbians/ gay men • food served • wheelchair access

The North End 3733 N Halsted St (at Grace) **773/477-7999** • 2pm-2am, from 11am wknds • mostly gay men • neighborhood sports bar • wheelchair access

Roscoe's 3354–56 N Halsted St (at W Roscoe) **773/281-3355** • 4pm-2am, from 3pm Fri, from 2pm Sat • lesbians/ gay men • food served • neighborhood bar • dancing/DJ • live/ drag shows • karaoke • patio

Scarlet 3320 N Halsted St (at Aldine) **773/348-1053** • 4pm-2am, till 3am Sat • mostly gay men • upscale piano bar • cabaret

Sidetrack 3349 N Halsted St (at Roscoe) **773/477-9189** • 3pm-2am, till 3am Sat • popular • lesbians/ gay men • upscale video bar • wheelchair access

Winebar 3341 N Halsted St (at Roscoe) **773/871-6227** • dinner 5pm-11pm, bar till 3am • lesbians/ gay men • Sun brunch 11am-3pm

Nightclubs

Berlin 954 W Belmont (at Sheffield) **773/348-4975** • 5pm-4am, till 5am Sat, from 8pm Sun-Mon • popular • lesbians/ gay men • dancing/DJ • transgender-friendly • live shows • wheelchair access

Boom Boom Room 2200 N Ashland (at Green Dolphin Street bar) • 11pm-4am Mon only • popular • gay/ straight • dancing/DJ • live shows • cover charge

Circuit/Rehab 3641 N Halsted St (at Addison) **773/325-2233** • 9pm-4am, till 5am Sat, clsd Tue-Wed • mostly gay men • dancing/DJ • multiracial • Latin nights Th & Sun (T-dance)

Hydrate 3458 N Halsted St (at Cornelia) **773/975-9244** • 8pm-4am, till 5am Sat, opens earlier in summer • popular • gay/ straight • dancing/DJ • drag shows

Lipstick & Lace 773/779-2399 • checkwww.madmanprod.com for events • mostly women • dancing/DJ • multiracial

Planet Earth 3534 W Belmont (at Late Bar) **773/267-5283** • 10pm-5am Sat • gay/ straight • dancing/DJ • New Wave

Smart Bar 3730 N Clark St (downstairs at the Metro) **773/549-0203** • 10pm-4am, till 5am Sat, clsd Mon-Tue • gay-friendly • dancing/DJ • popular • theme nights

Spin 800 W Belmont (enter on Halsted) **773/327-7711** • 4pm-2am, till 3am Sat, from noon wknds • lesbians/ gay men • dancing/DJ • live shows • karaoke • lounge • young crowd

Stardust Thursdays 954 W Belmont (at Berlin) **773/348-4975** • 10pm-4am Th only • mostly women • dancing/DJ • food served

Cafes

Caribou Coffee 3300 N Broadway St (at Aldine) **773/477-3695** • from 5:30am, from 6:30am Sat, till midnight Fri-Sat • WiFi

The Coffee & Tea Exchange 3311 N Broadway St (at Roscoe) **773/528-2241** • 8am-8pm, 10am-6pm Sun • fair-trade coffee & tea

Restaurants

Angelina Ristorante 3561 N Broadway St (at Addison) **773/935-5933** • 5:30pm-11pm, wknd brunch • Italian • full bar • wheelchair access

Ann Sather's 909 W Belmont Ave (at Sheffield) **773/348-2378** • 7am-3pm, till 4pm Sat-Sun • Swedish diner & Boystown fixture

Cesar's 2924 N Broadway (at Oakdale) **773/296-9097** • 11am-11pm, till 8am Sun • "home of the killer margaritas"

Chicago Diner 3411 N Halsted St (at Roscoe) **773/935-6696** • 11am-10pm, from 10am wknds, till 11pm Fri-Sat • hip & vegan • beer/ wine & organic booze

Firefly 3335 N Halsted St (at Buckingham) **773/525-2505** • 5pm-1:30am, till midnight Sun, clsd Tue • romantic French bistro • wheelchair access

Halsted's Bar & Grill 3441 N Halsted St (btwn Newport & Cornelia) 773/348-9696 • dinner nightly, brunch wknds • neighborhood sports bar • gay-owned

Home Bistro 3404 N Halsted St (at Roscoe, btwn Addison & Belmont) 773/661-0299 • dinner only, clsd Mon • upscale American • bring your own bottle • wheelchair access

Horizon Cafe 3805 N Broadway St (corner w/ Halsted & Grace) 773/883-1565 • 7am-9pm, till 10pm Fri-Sat • diner • brkfst anytime

Joy's Noodles & Rice 3257 N Broadway St (at Melrose) 773/327-8330 • 11am-10pm, till 11pm Fri-Sat • Thai • patio • wheelchair access

Kanok 3422 N Broadway St (at W Hawthorne Pl) 773/529-2525 • 4pm-10:30pm • sushi/ Asian • BYOB • wheelchair access

Kit Kat Lounge & Supper Club 3700 N Halsted St (at W Waveland Ave) 773/525-1111 • 5:30pm-1am, brunch Sun (seasonal) • drag cabaret some nights • gay-owned

Kitsch'n On Roscoe 2005 W Roscoe (at Damen) 773/248-7372 • 8:30am-3pm, dinner served in summer • comfort food for hipsters • full bar

Las Mananitas 3523 N Halsted St (at Cornelia) 773/528-2109 • 11am-11pm, till midnight Fri-Sat • strong margaritas • wheelchair access

Mon Ami Gabi 2300 N Lincoln Park W (at Belden) 773/348-8886 • dinner only • French bistro

Nookie's Tree 3334 N Halsted St (at Roscoe) 773/248-9888 • 7am-midnight, 24hrs wknds • popular • BYOB • wheelchair access

Orange 2413 N Clark St 773/549-7833 • 8am-3pm • popular brunch spot

Panino's Pizzeria 3702 N Halsted St (at Waveland) 773/472-6200 • 11:30am-11pm, till 10pm Sun • full bar • wheelchair access

Pick Me Up Cafe & All Nite Express Lounge 3408 N Clark St (at Roscoe) 773/248-6613 • 11am-3am, 24hrs Fri-Sat • brkfst all day

Pie Hole Pizza 737 W Roscoe St (at Halsted) 773/525-8888 • 5pm-3am, noon-5am wknds

Pingpong 3322 N Broadway St 773/281-7575 • 5pm-midnight • Asian fusion • patio • wheelchair access

The Raw Bar & Grill 3720 N Clark St (at Waveland) 773/348-7291, 773/348-7961 • 11am-2am, till 3am Sat • seafood • lounge • live shows • wheelchair access

Sushisamba Rio 504 N Wells St (at W Illinois) 312/595-2300 • lunch & dinner, popular brunch • glitzy lounge atmosphere • wheelchair access

Tapas Gitana 3445 N Halsted St (btwn Newport & Cornelia) 773/296-6046 • 5pm-11pm, clsd Mon • full bar • patio

Yoshi's Cafe 3257 N Halsted St (at Melrose) 773/248-6160 • dinner Tue-Sun, also Sun brunch • Asian-inspired French • wheelchair access

BOOKSTORES

Unabridged Books 3251 N Broadway St (at Aldine) 773/883-9119 • 10am-9pm, till 7pm wknds • popular • LGBT section

RETAIL SHOPS

Uncle Fun 1338 W Belmont (at Racine) 773/477-8223 • heaven for kitsch lovers

EROTICA

Batteries Not Included 3420 N Halsted St (at Newport) 773/935-9900 • 11am-midnight, till 1am Fri, 10am-2am Sat

The Pleasure Chest 3436 N Lincoln Ave (btwn Roscoe & Addison) 773/525-7152 • 10am-10pm, till midnight Fri-Sat

Tulip Sex Toy Gallery 3448 N Halsted St (btwn Newport & Cornelia) 773/975-1515, 877/708-8547 • 11am-10pm, till midnight Fri-Sat • lesbian-owned

Chicago—Near North

ACCOMMODATIONS

Allegro Chicago 171 W Randolph St (at LaSalle) 312/236-0123, 866/672-6143 • gay-friendly • Kimpton hotel • upscale lounge & restaurant • live shows • kids/ pets ok • WiFi • wheelchair access • $139-399

Chicago Getaway Hostel 616 W Arlington Pl (at Geneva Terr) 773/929-5380 • gay-friendly • in a trendy university area Lincoln Park • nonsmoking • WiFi • $20-295

Comfort Inn & Suites Downtown 15 E Ohio St (at State St) 312/894-0900, 888/775-9223 • gay-friendly • boutique hotel • gym • kids ok • WiFi • wheelchair access • $149-349

Dana Hotel & Spa 660 N State St (at Erie) 312/202-6000, 888/301-7946 • gay-friendly • rooftop lounge & Asian steakhouse • smoke free rooms • wheelchair access • $350-1,180

Flemish House of Chicago 68 E Cedar St (btwn Rush & Lake Shore Dr) **312/664-9981** • gay/ straight • B&B, studios & apts in greystone row house • nonsmoking • WiFi • gay-owned • $175-250

Gold Coast Guest House B&B 113 W Elm St (btwn Clark & LaSalle) **312/337-0361** • gay-friendly • nonsmoking • WiFi • women-owned • $129-229

The Hotel Burnham One W Washington St (at State) **312/782-1111, 877/294-9712** • gay-friendly • Chicago landmark • non-smoking • WiFi • wheelchair access • $149+

Hotel Indigo Chicago 1244 N Dearborn Pkwy (btwn Goethe & Division) **312/787-4980, 800/972-2494** • gay-friendly • gym • WiFi • restaurant & lounge • wheelchair access

Hotel Monaco 225 N Wabash (at S Water & Wacker Pl) **312/960-8500, 800/397-7661** • gay-friendly • 4-star luxury hotel • gym • restaurant • WiFi • $250+

Millennium Knickerbocker Hotel 163 E Walton Pl (Michigan Ave) **312/751-8100, 800/621-8140** • gay-friendly • restaurant • martini bar • gym • right off Magnificent Mile • wheelchair access • $129-269

Old Town Chicago Guest House 1442 N North Park Ave (near Wells & North) **312/440-9268** • gay/ straight • whole house or rent by room • nonsmoking • WiFi

Palmer House Hilton 17 E Monroe St (at State St) **312/726-7500** • gay-friendly • pool • fitness center • shopping arcade • business center

W Chicago—Lakeshore 644 N Lake Shore Dr (at Ontario) **312/943-9200, 877/WHOTELS (RESERVATIONS ONLY)** • gay-friendly • overlooking Lake Michigan • pool • nonsmoking • WiFi • also restaurant & bar • wheelchair access • $229-429

BARS

Club Foot 1824 W Augusta Blvd (in Wicker Park) **773/489-0379** • 8pm-2am, till 3am Sat • gay-friendly • neighborhood bar • dancing/DJ • kitschy • wheelchair access

Davenport's 1383 N Milwaukee (in Wicker Park) **773/278-1830** • 7pm-midnight, till 2am Fri-Sat, till 11pm Sun, clsd Tue • cabaret • piano bar

Downtown 440 N State (at Illinois) **312/464-1400** • 3pm-2am, till 3am Sat • mostly gay men • live shows • cabaret • professional crowd • videos

Martini Bar 401 S LaSalle St **312/922-8025** • noon-9pm, till 11pm Wed, till midnight Th & Fri, clsd Sat-Sun • gay/ straight • karaoke Th • WiFi

NIGHTCLUBS

Baton Show Lounge 436 N Clark St (btwn Illinois & Hubbard) **312/644-5269** • showtimes at 8:30pm, 10:30pm, 12:30am, clsd Mon-Tue • lesbians/ gay men • drag shows • reservations recommended • wheelchair access • since 1969!

Chances Dances 2011 W North Ave (at Damen, at Subterranean) • 3rd Mon 10pm-2am & 2nd Tue at Danny's 1959 W. Dickens Ave • lesbians/ gay men • dancing/DJ • check chancesdances.org for other events

Prop House 1675 N Elston Ave (in Wicker Park) **773/486-2086** • 9pm-4am Fri-Sun only • lesbians/ gay men • great house music • Afrrican-American clientele

The Rails/ The Prop House 2200 N Ashland Ave (at Green Dolphin) **708/543-9114** • 11pm-4am Fri only • popular • mostly gay men • dancing/DJ • live shows • mostly African American & Latino • cover charge

Underground Wonder Bar 610 N Dearborn St (at W Erie) **312/266-7761** • 4pm-close • gay-friendly • live music • multi-racial cliente

CAFES

Earwax Cafe & Film 1561 N Milwaukee Ave (in Wicker Park) **773/772-4019** • 9am-10pm • food served • wheelchair access

RESTAURANTS

Blackbird 619 W Randolph St (at Des Plaines) **312/715-0708** • lunch Mon-Fri, dinner nightly, clsd Sun

Catch 35 35 W Wacker Dr (at Dearborn) **312/346-3500** • lunch Mon-Fri, dinner nightly • steak & seafood

Fireplace Inn 1448 N Wells St (at North Ave) **312/664-5264** • 4:30pm-1am, from 11:30am Fri-Sat • famous for their ribs • patio • full bar

Hot Chocolate 1747 N Damen Ave (in Wicker Park) **773/489-1747** • lunch, dinner & dessert, wknd brunch, clsd Mon • full bar • wheelchair access

Ina's 1235 W Randolph St (at Racine) **312/226-8227** • brkfst, lunch & dinner • full bar • free parking

Kiki's Bistro 900 N Franklin St (at Locust) **312/335-5454** • lunch Mon-Fri, dinner nightly, clsd Sun • French • full bar

Lou Mitchell's 565 W Jackson Blvd 312/939-3111 • great brkfst

Manny's 1141 S Jefferson St (at Roosevelt) 312/939-2855 • 6am-8pm, clsd Sun • killer corned beef

Moonshine 1824 W Division St (at Honore, in Wicker Park) 773/862-8686 • lunch & dinner • American • also bar

Nacional 27 325 W Huron (at N Orleans) 312/664-2727 • 5:30pm-9:30pm, till 1:30pm Fri-Sat, clsd Sun • salsa dancing 11pm-2am Fri

Park Grill 11 N Michigan Ave (in Millennium Park) 312/521-7275 • 11am-10pm • classic American • seasonal outdoor dining

Parthenon Restaurant 314 S Halsted St (near W Jackson) 312/726-2407 • 11am-midnight • full bar • "best gyros in Chicago" • wheelchair access

Shaw's Crab House 21 E Hubbard St (at State St) 312/527-2722 • lunch & dinner • live music • full bar • wheelchair access

Topolobampo/ Frontera Grill 445 N Clark St (btwn Illinois & Hubbard) 312/661-1434 • lunch & dinner, Sat brunch (Frontera only), clsd Sun-Mon • Mexican

Vermilion 10 W Hubbard St (at State) 312/527-4060 • lunch Mon-Fri, dinner nightly • Latin-Indian fusion • full bar • patio • wheelchair access

BOOKSTORES

After-Words New & Used Books 23 E Illinois St (btwn State & Wabash) 312/464-1110 • 10:30am-10pm, till 11pm Fri-Sat, noon-7pm Sun • WiFi • cards • stationery • women-owned

Quimby's Bookstore 1854 W North Ave (at Wolcott, in Wicker Park) 773/342-0910 • noon-9pm, 11am-10pm Sat, noon-6pm Sun • alternative literature & comics • wheelchair access

RETAIL SHOPS

Flight 001 1133 N State St (at Elm) 312/944-1001 • 11am-7pm, till 6pm Sun • way cool travel gear

GYMS & HEALTH CLUBS

Cheetah Gym 1934 W North Ave (at Damen, in Wicker Park) 773/394-5900

Thousand Waves Spa 1212 W Belmont Ave (at Racine) 773/549-0700 • noon-9pm, till 5:30pm Tue, 10am-7pm Fri-Sun, clsd Mon • health spa for women only • women-owned

Chicago—South Side

BARS

Club Escape 1530 E 75th St (at Stoney Island Ave) 773/667-6454 • 4pm-2am, till 3am Sat • lesbians/ gay men • dancing/DJ • drag shows • mostly African American • food served • women's night Th

Inn Exile 5758 W 65th St (at Menard, near Midway Airport; 1 mile W of Midway hotel center at 65th & Cicero) 773/582-3510 • 8pm-2am, till 3am Sat • mostly gay men • dancing/DJ • videos • WiFi • wheelchair access

Jeffery Pub 7041 S Jeffery Blvd (at 71st) 773/363-8555 • noon-4am, till 5am Sat, clsd Mon • popular • lesbians/ gay men • dancing/DJ • mostly African American • drag shows • wheelchair access

BOOKSTORES

57th St Books 1301 E 57th St, Hyde Park (at Kimbark St) 773/684-1300 • 10am-8pm • LGBT section

Barbara's Bookstore 1218 S Halsted St (at W Roosevelt) 312/413-2665 • 9am-10pm, from 10am wknds, till 8pm Sun • popular • wheelchair access • other locations: at Macy's, 111 N State St, 312/781-3033

De Kalb

NIGHTCLUBS

Otto's 118 E Lincoln Hwy 815/758-2715 • 6:30pm-close • gay-friendly • live music venue

Decatur

BARS

The Flashback Lounge 2239 E Wood St (at 22nd) 217/422-3530 • 9am-2am • lesbians/ gay men • neighborhood bar • dancing/DJ • karaoke

RESTAURANTS

Robbie's Grill 122 N Merchant St 217/423-0448 • 11am-9pm, till 2pm Sat, clsd Sun • full bar

EROTICA

Romantix Adult Superstore 2015 N 22nd St 217/362-0105

Du Quoin

ACCOMMODATIONS

The Pit 7403 Persimmon Rd 618/542-9470 • lesbians/ gay men • primitive camping • 18+ • nudity ok • swimming • gay-owned • free except $5 on holiday wknds

Elk Grove Village

see also Chicago

NIGHTCLUBS

Hunter's Night Club 1932 E Higgins Rd (at Busse) **847/439-8840** • 4pm-2am, till 4am Th-Sat • popular • mostly gay men • dancing/DJ • live entertainment • karaoke • videos • patio • wheelchair access

Elkhart

CAFES

Bluestem Bake Shop 107 Governor Oglesby St **217/947-2222** • 9am-4pm, clsd Mon

Forest View

BARS

Forest View Lounge 4519 S Harlem Ave **208/484-9778** • 11am-midnight, till 2am wknds, clsd Sun • mostly women • neighborhood bar • food served • live shows

Franklin Park

NIGHTCLUBS

Temptations 10235 W Grand Ave (at Mannheim) **847/455-0008** • 7pm-2am, till 3am Fri-Sat, clsd Mon-Tue • lesbians/gay men • dancing/DJ • karaoke • wheelchair access

Galesburg

ACCOMMODATIONS

The Fahnestock House 591 N Prairie St (at Losey) **309/344-0270** • gay/ straight • full brkfst • nonsmoking • pool • kids ok • clsd Nov-Jan • gay-owned • $150

EROTICA

Romantix Adult Superstore 595 N Henderson St (at Losey) **309/342-7019**

Joliet

INFO LINES & SERVICES

Community Alliance & Action Network 68 N Chicago St **815/726-7906** • by appointment • LGBT community center

NIGHTCLUBS

Maneuvers & Co 118 E Jefferson (at Chicago) **815/727-7069** • 8pm-2am, till 3am Fri-Sat • lesbians/gay men • more women Tue • dancing/DJ • transgender-friendly • drag shows • frequent events • patio

Lyons

BARS

Stonewall Inn 8143 W 47th St (at Lawndale) **708/442-0234** • 5pm-2am Wed-Sat • lesbians/gay men • dancing/DJ • karaoke • drag shows • theme nights

Monticello

RESTAURANTS

The Brown Bag 212 W Washington St **217/762-9221** • 9am-7pm, till 8pm Tue & Fri, till 4pm Sat, clsd Sun

Normal

CAFES

Coffeehouse & Deli 114 E Beaufort St **309/452-6774** • 7am-10pm • vegetarian/ vegan • WiFi

O'Fallon

RESTAURANTS

Paulo's at the Mansion 1680 Mansion Wy (at Lakepointe Center Dr) **618/624-0629** • 4pm-10pm Tue-Sat • steakhouse • wheelchair access • gay-owned

Oak Park

see also Berwyn & Chicago

BARS

Velvet Rope 728 W Lake St **708/358-8840** • 5pm-1am, till 2am wknds, from 1pm Sun • lesbians/gay men • entertainment • also restaurant • drag shows

Ottawa

EROTICA

Brown Bag Video 3042 N State Rte 71 (at I-80, exit 93) **815/434-0820** • 24hrs

Peoria

ACCOMMODATIONS

Hotel Pere Marquette 501 Main St **309/637-6500, 800/447-1676** • gay-friendly • buffet brkfst • WiFi

BARS

Buddies On Adams 807 SW Adams St (at Oak St) **309/676-7438** • 6pm-1am, till 4am Fri-Sat, clsd Mon • lesbians/gay men • neighborhood bar • karaoke • WiFi

CAFES

One World 1245 W Main St (at University) **309/672–1522** • 7am-11pm, from 8am wknds • WiFi • wheelchair access

RESTAURANTS

Two 25 225 NE Adams St (at Mark Twain Hotel) **309/282–7777** • lunch Mon-Fri, dinner nightly, clsd Sun

PUBLICATIONS

Out & About Illinois 4408 N Rockwood Rd #250 **309/699–6901**

EROTICA

Swingers World 335 SW Adams (at Harrison) **309/676–9275** • 24hrs

Quincy

NIGHTCLUBS

Irene's Cabaret 124 N 5th St (at Washington Park, enter rear) **217/222–6292** • 9pm-2:30am, from 7pm Fri-Sat, till 3:30am Sat, clsd Sun-Tue • lesbians/ gay men • dancing/DJ • multiracial • karaoke • drag shows • wheelchair access • gay-owned

Rockford

NIGHTCLUBS

The Office Niteclub 513 E State St (btwn 2nd & 3rd) **815/965–0344** • 5pm-2am, noon-midnight Sun • popular • lesbians/ gay men • dancing/DJ • live shows • karaoke • drag shows • male & female strippers • videos

RESTAURANTS

Lucerne's Fondue & Spirits 845 N Church St (at Whitman) **815/968–2665** • 5pm-11pm, clsd Mon (also Sun summers) • reservations required • full bar • wheelchair access

Maria's 828 Cunningham St (at Corbin) **815/968–6781** • 4:30pm-9pm, clsd Sun-Mon • Italian • full bar

Springfield

INFO LINES & SERVICES

The Phoenix Center 109 E Lawrence Ave **217/528–5253** • 8:30am-4:30pm, clsd wknds

ACCOMMODATIONS

The State House Inn 101 E Adams St (at First St) **217/528–5100** • gay-friendly • kids/ pets ok • WiFi • wheelchair access • $89-159

BARS

Scandals 126 S E Jefferson St **217/523–4500** • 11am-1am • mostly gay men • dancing/DJ • karaoke • drag shows

The Station House 304–306 E Washington (btwn 3rd & 4th Sts) **217/525–0438** • 2pm-1am, till 3am Th-Sat • lesbians/ gay men • neighborhood bar • karaoke • dancing/DJ • wheelchair access

RESTAURANTS

Caitie Girls 400 E Jefferson (in St Nicholas Hotel) **217/528–1294** • lunch Tue-Fri, dinner nightly, clsd Sun-Mon

RETAIL SHOPS

New Age Tattoos & Body Piercings 2915 S MacArthur Blvd **217/546–5006** • 11am-8pm, till 6pm Sun

INDIANA

Anderson

EROTICA

After Dark 2012 Mounds Rd **765/649–7597** • 10am-11pm, till midnight Fri-Sat, noon-10pm Sun • adult novelties, lingerie, videos, magazines

Bloomington

BARS

Uncle Elizabeth's 1614 W 3rd St **812/331–0060** • 4pm-3am, 7pm-midnight Sun • lesbians/ gay men • neighborhood bar • dance floor • drag shows • patio

CAFES

Soma Coffee House 322 E Kirkwood Ave (below Laughing Planet) **812/331–2770** • 7am-11pm, from 8am Sun • WiFi

RESTAURANTS

Laughing Planet Cafe 322 E Kirkwood Ave (enter on Grant) **812/323–2233** • 11am-9pm • outdoor seating

Village Deli 409 E Kirkwood **812/336–2303** • 7am-8pm, 8am-8pm wknds • lesbians/ gay men • some veggie

ENTERTAINMENT & RECREATION

BloomingOut WFHB 91.3 & 98.1 & 100.7 & 106.3FM **812/325–7870 & 323–1200** • 6pm Th, "your midwest queer connection"

RETAIL SHOPS

Athena Gallery 116 N Walnut **812/339–0734** • 10:30am-7pm, till 8:30pm Fri, noon-5pm Sun • clothing, drums, incense, gifts, etc • wheelchair access

Elkhart

see South Bend

Evansville

NIGHTCLUBS

Someplace Else 930 Main St (at Sycamore) **812/424-3202** • 4pm-3am, 4pm-midnight Sun • lesbians/ gay men • dancing/DJ • drag shows • karaoke • patio

EROTICA

Exotica 4605 Washington Ave **812/401-7399**

Fort Wayne

INFO LINES & SERVICES

Gay/ Lesbian AA 501 W Berry St (at Plymouth church) **260/423-9424** • 6:30pm Tue, 1pm Sun

NIGHTCLUBS

After Dark 1601 S Harrison St (at Grand St) **260/456-6235** • noon-3am, 6pm-12:30am Sun • mostly gay men • dancing/DJ • karaoke • drag shows • male strippers • wheelchair access • gay-owned

Babylon 112 E Masterson Ave **260/247-5092** • 7pm-3am Fri-Sat only • mostly gay men • dancing/DJ • drag shows

CAFES

Firefly 3523 N Anthony Blvd **260/373-0505** • 6:30am-8pm, from 8am wknds • live entertainment • WiFi

RESTAURANTS

The Loving Cafe 7605 Coldwater Rd **260/489-8686** • 10am-8pm, clsd Sun • vegetarian/ vegan • wheelchair access

RETAIL SHOPS

Boudoir Noir 512 W Superior St **260/420-0557** • 10am-midnight, noon-8pm Sun • gifts • sex toys • leather

PUBLICATIONS

Phoenix Magazine **260/433-1916** • LGBT publication

Gary

see also Chicago, Illinois

EROTICA

Romantix Adult Superstore 8801 W Melton Rd/ US 20 (at Ripley Rd) **219/938-2194** • 24hrs

Goshen

see also South Bend

CAFES

The Electric Brew 136 S Main St **574/533-5990** • 6am-10pm, noon-7pm Sun • "Goshen's original coffeehouse" • live music

Hammond

BARS

Dick's R U Crazee? 1221 E 150th St **219/852-0222** • 8pm-3am, from 7pm wknds • mostly gay men • neighborhood bar • karaoke • drag shows

Indiana Dunes

ACCOMMODATIONS

The Gray Goose Inn B&B 350 Indian Boundary Rd (at I-95), Chesterton **219/926-5781, 800/521-5127** • gay/ straight • full brkfst • WiFi • nonsmoking rooms available • $110-195

Indianapolis

INFO LINES & SERVICES

AA Gay/ Lesbian **317/632-7864, 317/631-5099 (EN ESPAÑOL)** • various LGBT meeting • check web (www.indyaa.org) for meeting times & locations

ACCOMMODATIONS

The Fort Harrison State Park Inn 5830 N Post Rd **317/638-6000** • gay-friendly • luxury inn in historic Fort Harrison in NE Indianapolis • nonsmoking • $120-285

Sycamore Knoll B&B 10777 Riverwood Ave, Noblesville **317/776-0570** • gay/ straight • fully restored 1886 estate near the White River • perennial gardens & apple orchard • quiet & casual • full brkfst • nonsmoking • WiFi • lesbian-owned • $110/ night

Wyndham Indianapolis West 2544 Executive Dr (off Airport Expy) **317/248-2481, 800/444-2326** • gay-friendly • seasonal pool • fitness center • WiFi in lobby, restaurant & lounge

BARS

501 Eagle 501 N College (at Michigan St) **317/632-2100** • 5:30pm-3am, from 7:30pm Sat, 4pm-12:30am Sun • popular • mostly gay men • dancing/DJ • bears • leather

Downtown Olly's 822 N Illinois St (at St Clair) **317/636-5597** • 9am-3am Mon-Wed, 24hrs Th-Sun • mostly men • sports & video bar • karaoke • brkfst, lunch, dinner

The Metro Nightclub & Restaurant 707 Massachusetts Ave (at College) 317/639–6022 • 3pm-3am, noon-midnight Sun • popular • lesbians/ gay men • neighborhood bar • piano bar • karaoke • patio • also restaurant • giftshop • wheelchair access

Noah Grant's Grill House & Raw Bar 65 S 1st St (at W Oak St), Zionsville 317/732–2233 • 4pm-close, clsd Mon • gay-friendly • wine bar & bistro • full restaurant serving lunch & dinner, Sun brunch • patio

Varsity Lounge 1517 N Pennsylvania Ave (S of 16th) 317/635–9998 • 10am-3am, till midnight Sun • mostly gay men • neighborhood bar • food served • karaoke • WiFi

Zonie's Closet 1446 E Washington St (at Arsenal) 317/266–0535 • 9am-3am, noon-midnight Sun • gay/ straight • dancing/DJ • karaoke Th & Sat-Sun • drag shows Fri-Sat • wheelchair access

NIGHTCLUBS

Talbott Street 2145 N Talbott St (at 22nd St) 317/931–1343 • 9pm-2am Fri-Sat, 8pm-midnight Mon • gay/ straight • dancing/DJ • drag shows • theme nights

The Ten 1218 N Pennsylvania St (at 12th, enter rear) 317/638–5802 • 6pm-3am, till 1am Wed, till midnight Sun, clsd Mon-Tue • very popular w/ lesbians (gay men welcome) • dancing/DJ • live shows • drag shows • wheelchair access

The Unicorn Club 122 W 13th St (at Illinois) 317/262–9195 • 8pm-3am • popular • mostly gay men • dancing/DJ • male strippers nightly • private club

CAFES

Ah Barista Cafe 201 S Capitol Ave (btwn Maryland & South Sts) 317/638–2233 • 7am-3pm Mon-Fri • brkfst & lunch menu

Bjava 5510 Lafayette Rd (at 56th St) 317/280–1236 • 6am-5pm, 7am-3pm Sat, clsd Sun

Cornerstone Coffeehouse 651 E 54th St (at N College Ave, Broad Ripple) 317/726–1360 • 6am-10pm, 7am-10pm Sat, 7am-9pm Sun • food served • full bar • WiFi

Earth House Collective 237 N East St 317/636–4060 • 11am-9pm, clsd Sun • coffeehouse • also art, music & classes • WiFi

Henry's on East Street 627 N East St 317/951–0335 • 7am-7pm, till 9pm Fri, from 8am wknds • popular • gay-owned

Hubbard & Cravens 4930 N Pennsylvania St (in Broad Ripple) 317/251–5161 • 6am-7pm, 7am-3pm Sun • food served • WiFi

Monon Coffee Company 920 E Westfield Blvd (at Guilford) 317/255–0510 • 6:30am-8pm, till 10pm Fri, from 7am Sat, 8am-8pm Sun

RESTAURANTS

14 West 14 W Maryland St 317/636–1414 • lunch & dinner • seafood & steaks • patio

Adobo Grill 110 E Washington 317/822–9990 • lunch Fri-Sun, dinner nightly • Mexican • full bar • wheelchair access

Aesop's Tables 600 E Massachusetts Ave 317/631–0055 • lunch & dinner, clsd Sun • authentic Mediterranean • some veggie • beer/ wine • wheelchair access

Agio 635 Massachusetts Ave (at East) 317/488–0359 • dinner nightly • cont'l • nonsmoking • wheelchair access

BARcelona 201 N Delaware St 317/638–8272 • 11am-11pm • also full bar • tapas

Bazbeaux Pizza 329 Massachusetts Ave 317/636–7662 • lunch & dinner

Cafe Zuppa 320 N Meridian St (at New York St) 317/634–9877 • 7am-2:30pm, Sun brunch buffet

Creation Cafe & Euphoria 337 W 11th St (in Buggs' Temple) 317/955–2389 • 8am-9pm, clsd Sun • outdoor seating

English Ivy's 944 S Alabama (at 10th) 317/822–5070 • lunch and dinner, till 3am Mon-Sat, 10am-1am Sun • eclectic • also full bar • WiFi • wheelchair access

Hoaglin To Go 448 Massachusetts Ave 317/423–0300 • 8am-2:30pm, market till 6pm • wheelchair access

India Garden 830 Broad Ripple Ave (btwn Carrollton & Guilford) 317/253–6060 • lunch & dinner • Indian • wheelchair access • also 207 N Delaware St, 317/634-6060

King David Dogs 15 N Pennsylvania St • great hot dogs

La Piedad 6524 Cornell Ave 317/475–0988 • lunch & dinner • Mexican

Mama Carolla's 1031 E 54th St (at Winthrop) 317/259–9412 • dinner only, clsd Sun-Mon • traditional Italian

Mikado 148 S Illinois St (at Georgia) 317/972–4180 • lunch & dinner • Japanese • enjoy the saketini

Naked Tchopstix 6253 N College Ave (in Broad Ripple) 317/252–5555 • lunch & dinner • popular • Korean, Japanese, Chinese cuisine • also sushi bar

Oakley's Bistro 1464 W 86th St (at Ditch Rd) 317/824–1231 • lunch & dinner, clsd Sun-Mon • popular • gourmet cont'l • reservations suggested • wheelchair access

Pancho's Taqueria 7023 Michigan Rd (at Westlane) 317/202–9015 • 11am-9pm • popular • authentic Mexican • wheelchair access

Sawasdee 1222 W 86th St (at Ditch Rd) 317/844–9451 • lunch Mon-Sat, dinner nightly • Thai • some veggie • wheelchair access

Shanghai Lil 8505 Keystone Crossing (across from Keystone Mall) 317/205–9335 • lunch & dinner • upscale Chinese & Japanese • full bar • wheelchair access

Three Sisters Cafe 6360 N Guilford Ave (at Main St) 317/257–5556 • 8am-9pm, till 3pm Sun • plenty veggie & vegan • popular Sun brunch

Usual Suspects 6319 Guilford Ave (at Broad Ripple) 317/251–3138 • 5pm-10pm, till 11pm Fri-Sat, till 9pm Sun, clsd Mon • eclectic • full bar • patio

Yats 659 Massachusetts Ave (at Walnut) 317/686–6380 • 11am-9pm, till 10pm Fri-Sat, till 7pm Sun • Cajun • also 5363 N College Ave, 317/ 253-8817 • also 8352 E 96th St, 317/ 585-1792 • wheelchair access

Indianapolis

LGBT Pride:
June, web: www.indyprideinc.com.

Annual Events:
May - Broad Ripple Arts Fair, web: www.indplsartcenter.org.
Memorial Day Weekend - Indy 500 auto race, web: www.indycar.com.
July - Indianapolis International Film Festival, web: indyfilmfest.org.
Aug-Sept - Indianapolis Theatre Fringe Festival, web: www.indyfringe.org.

City Info:
Indianapolis Convention & Visitors Association 317/639-4282, 800/323-INDY, web: visitindy.com.

Weather:
The spring weather is moderate (50°s-60°s) with occasional storms. The summers are typically midwestern: hot (mid-90°s) and humid. The autumns are mild and colorful in southeastern Indiana. As for winter, it's the wind chill that'll get to you.

Attractions:
Benjamin Harrison Home, 317/631-1888, web: www.presidentbenjaminharrison.org.
Eiteljorg Museum of American Indians & Western Art, 317/636-9378, web: www.eiteljorg.org.
Indianapolis Museum of Art 317/923-1331, web: www.ima-art.org.
Morris-Butler Home, 317/639-4534, web: www.historiclandmarks.org.
Speedway 500 317/481-8500, web: www.indianapolismotorspeedway.com.
Zoo 317/630-2001, web: www.indy-zoo.com.

Transit:
Yellow Cab 317/487-7777, web: www.ycindy.com.
Indianapolis Airport shuttle 317/248-0885, web: www.indy-connectionlimousine.com.
IndyGo 317/635-3344, web: www.indygo.net.

ENTERTAINMENT & RECREATION

Indiana Fever 1 Conseco Ct (in Conseco Fieldhouse) 317/917–2500 • check out the Women's Nat'l Basketball Association while you're in Indianapolis

Indianapolis Women's Chorus PO Box 2919, 46206-2919 • various concerts throughout season

Indyindie 7780 Eagle Valley Pass 317/295–9302 • monthly women's music concert series

Theatre on the Square 627 Massachusetts Ave (at East) 317/685–8687 • often presents gay-themed productions

BOOKSTORES

Big Hat Books 6510 Cornell Ave 317/202–0203 • 10am-6pm, noon-5pm Sun • general independent

Bookmamas 9 S Johnson Ave (at E Washington St, in Irvington) 317/375–3715 • open Wed-Sat • call for hours • used bookstore

RETAIL SHOPS

All My Relations 1008 Main St (at 10th), Speedway 317/227–3925 • noon-6pm, till 7pm Wed-Th, 10am-6pm Sat • New Age/ metaphysical store • also classes

The Magic Candle 204 S Audubon St (S of Washington) 317/357–8801 • 10am-7pm, clsd Sun • pagan supplies, books, gifts • also classes

Metamorphosis 828 Broad Ripple Ave (at Carrollton) 317/466–1666 • 1pm-9pm, till 5pm Sun • tattoo & piercing parlor

Metropolis 707 Massachusetts Ave (upstairs at The Metro) 317/639–1029 • 4pm-2am, 1pm-12:30am Sun • also restaurant & nightclub

PUBLICATIONS

Nuvo 317/254–2400 • Indy's alternative weekly

The Word 317/725–8840 • LGBT newspaper

EROTICA

Southern Nights Videos 3760 Commercial Dr (at 38th St) 317/329–5505 • 10am-midnight, clsd Sun • videos • DVDs • toys, etc

Kokomo

BARS

Bar Blue 1400 W Markland Ave (at Park) 765/456–1400 • open Sat only • popular • lesbians/ gay men • dancing/DJ • karaoke • drag shows • patio

Lafayette

INFO LINES & SERVICES

Pride Lafayette, Inc 640 Main St #218 765/423–7579 • community center 6pm-8pm, 5pm-9pm wknds • support/ social activities

NIGHTCLUBS

Zoolegers 644 Main St (at Columbia) 765/742–6321 • 8pm-3am, from 5pm Fri • lesbians/ gay men • dancing/DJ

EROTICA

Fantasy East 2315 Concord Rd (at Teal) 765/474–2417 • open daily, books & videos

Lake Station

NIGHTCLUBS

Encompass Nightclub & Lounge 2415 Rush St (at I-80/94 & Ripley St) 219/962–4640 • 8pm-3am, clsd Sun • popular • lesbians/ gay men • dancing/DJ • cabaret • food served • wheelchair access

Marion

EROTICA

After Dark 1311 W Johnson St 765/662–3688 • 10am-11pm, till midnight Fri-Sat, noon-10pm Sun • adult novelties, lingerie, videos, magazines

Michigan City

ACCOMMODATIONS

Duneland Beach Inn & Restaurant 3311 Pottawattomie Trail (at Duneland Beach Dr) 219/874–7729, 800/423–7729 • gay-friendly • B&B/ restaurant/ bar • 1 block away from Lake Michigan & private beach • 60 miles from Chicago • jacuzzi suites available • $99-239

Tryon Farm Guest House 1400 Tryon Rd (at Hwy 212) 219/879–3618 • gay-friendly • full brkfst • hot tub • kids/ pets ok • nonsmoking • WiFi • women-owned • $108-228

Mishawaka

see also South Bend

ACCOMMODATIONS

The Beiger Mansion 317 Lincolnway E 574/255–6300, 800/437–0131 • gay-friendly • B&B in 4-level neo-classical limestone mansion • pool • nonsmoking • WiFi • gay-owned • $140-225

Muncie

CAFES

The MT Cup 1606 W University Ave (at N Dill St) **765/287–1995** • 7:30am-midnight • sandwiches • baked goods • WiFi • wheelchair access

New Albany

see Louisville, KY

Noblesville

see Indianapolis

South Bend

ACCOMMODATIONS

Innisfree B&B 702 W Colfax **574/283–0740** • gay-friendly • 1892 Queen Anne minutes from Notre Dame • full brkfst • nonsmoking • $95-155

BARS

Jeannie's Tavern 621 S Bendix (at Ford St) **574/288–2962** • 11am-2am • gay-friendly • neighborhood bar • transgender-friendly • gay-owned

Vickies Inc 112 W Monroe St (at S Michigan St) **574/232–4090** • 2pm-midnight • gay/straight • neighborhood bar • transgender-friendly • food served • football party every Sat in season • gay-owned

NIGHTCLUBS

Truman's Nightclub & Lounge/ Little T's 100 N Center St, Mishawaka **574/259–2282, 574/259–7507** • 8pm-3am, from 10pm Fri-Sat • popular • lesbians/ gay men • dancing/DJ • drag shows • Little T's (sports bar, karaoke) open 8pm-2am Fri-Sat, till 12:30am Sun • also John's Grille • also gift shop

ENTERTAINMENT & RECREATION

GLBT Resource Center of Michiana **574/254–1411**

EROTICA

Romantix Adult Superstore 2715 S Main St (at Eckman St) **574/291–1899**

Terre Haute

NIGHTCLUBS

Zim Marss Nightclub 1500 Locust St (at 15th St) **812/232–3026** • 8pm-3am, 7pm-12:30am Sun, clsd Mon-Tue • lesbians/ gay men • dancing/DJ • transgender-friendly • drag shows • strippers

Valparaiso

ACCOMMODATIONS

Inn at Aberdeen 3158 S State Rd 2 **219/465–3753, 866/761–3753** • gay-friendly • 1880s Queen Anne • full brkfst • nonsmoking • WiFi • wheelchair access • $106-201

Vevay

CAFES

Java Bean Cafe & Confectionery 117 W Main St **812/427–2888** • 7am-7pm, clsd Sun • gay-owned

Zionsville

see Indianapolis

IOWA

Statewide

PUBLICATIONS

Accessline **319/550–0957** • LGBT newspaper

Ames

RESTAURANTS

Lucullan's Italian Grill 400 Main St (at Burnett) **515/232–8484** • dinner Tue-Sun • some veggie • full bar

EROTICA

Romantix Adult Superstore 117 Kellogg St. (at Lincoln Wy) **515/232–7717** • 9am-4am

Burlington

ACCOMMODATIONS

Arrowhead Motel, Inc 2520 Mt Pleasant St **319/752–6353** • gay-friendly • kids ok • WiFi • nonsmoking • wheelchair access • gay-owned • $49-119

RESTAURANTS

Steve's Place 852 Washington St (at Central Ave) **319/754–5868** • 9am-2am, clsd Sun • also bar • wheelchair access

Cedar Falls

see Waterloo

Cedar Rapids

BARS

The Piano Lounge 208 2nd Ave SE, Cedar Rapids **319/363–0606** • 4pm-2am, clsd Sun • gay/ straight • live entertainment • game room

NIGHTCLUBS

Club Basix 3916 1st Ave NE (btwn 39th & 40th) **319/363-3194** • 5pm-2am, from noon wknds • lesbians/ gay men • transgender-friendly • dancing/DJ • drag shows • gay/ lesbian-owned

Toxic 616 2nd Ave SE **319/364-1917** • 4pm-2am, from 11am wknds • gay/ straight • dancing/DJ • drag shows • young crowd

CAFES

Blue Strawberry 118 2nd St SE **319/247-2583** • 7am-8pm, till 7pm Sat, 8am-5pm Sun • nonsmoking

ENTERTAINMENT & RECREATION

CSPS Arts Center 1103 3rd St SE **319/364-1580** • galleries • concerts • plays • many LGBT events

Council Bluffs

see also Omaha, Nebraska

ACCOMMODATIONS

Historic Wickham House B&B 616 S 7th Street **712/328-1872** • gay/ straight • full brkfst • WiFi • gay-owned • $100

BARS

Broadway Joe's 3400 W Broadway (at 34th) **712/256-2243** • 4pm-2am • gay/ straight • neighborhood bar

EROTICA

Romantix Adult Superstore 3216 1st Ave (at Broadway) **712/328-2673** • 24hrs

Davenport

see also Rock Island, Illinois

ACCOMMODATIONS

Hotel Blackhawk 200 East 3rd St **563/322 5000, 888/525-4455** • gay-friendly • newly renovated • bowling alley on-site

BARS

Mary's on 2nd 832 W 2nd St (btwn Warren & Brown) **563/884-8014** • 4pm-2am • lesbians/ gay men • neighborhood bar • dancing/DJ • occasional live shows • videos • patio • wheelchair access

NIGHTCLUBS

Connections 822 W 2nd St (at Brown) **563/322-1121** • 5pm-2am • lesbians/ gay men • dancing/ DJ • drag shows • karaoke

Des Moines

INFO LINES & SERVICES

The Center/ Equality Iowa 515/243-0313

ACCOMMODATIONS

Hotel Fort Des Moines 1000 Walnut St (at 10th St) **515/243-1161, 800/532-1466** • gay-friendly • full brkfst • pool • hot tub • kids ok • gym • nonsmoking • WiFi • wheelchair access • $99-400

The Renaissance Savery Hotel 401 Locust St (at 4th) **515/244-2151, 800/514** • gay-friendly • pool • kids ok • restaurant • WiFi • wheelchair access • $109-600

BARS

The Blazing Saddle 416 E 5th St (btwn Grand & Locust) **515/246-1299** • 2pm-2am, from noon wknds • mostly gay men • dancing/DJ • leather • drag shows • WiFi • wheelchair access

Buddy's Corral 418 E 5th St (btwn Grand & Locust) **515/244-7140** • noon-2am, from 10am Sat • gay-friendly • karaoke

NIGHTCLUBS

The Garden 112 SE 4th St **515/243-3965** • 8pm-2am, 5pm-midnight Sun, clsd Mon-Tue • lesbians/ gay men • more women Th • dancing/DJ • live shows • karaoke • videos • patio • young crowd • wheelchair access

Le Boi Bar 508 Indianola Ave (at 7th) **515/284-1074** • 8pm-2am, 3pm-midnight Sun, clsd Mon-Tue • lesbians/ gay men • dancing/DJ • drag shows

CAFES

Baby Boomer's Cafe 303 5th St (at Walnut) **515/244-9107** • 6am-8pm, from 7am Sat, 8am-3pm Sun • great brkfst • wheelchair access • gay-owned

Drake Diner 1111 25th St (btwn University & Cottage Grove) **515/277-1111** • 7am-11pm, from 11am wknds • try the cake shake • full bar • patio • wheelchair access

Java Joe's 214 4th St (at Court Ave) **515/288-5282** • 7am-11pm, till 12:30am Fri-Sat, till 10pm Sun • live shows • WiFi • wheelchair access

Ritual Cafe 1301 E Locust St **515/288-4872** • 7am-7pm, till 11pm Fri-Sat, clsd Sun • live music

Zanzibar's Coffee Adventure 2723 Ingersoll Ave (at 28th St) **515/244-7694** • 6:30am-8pm, till 9pm Fri-Sat, 8am-6pm Sun • wheelchair access

RESTAURANTS

Cafe di Scala 644 18th St (at Woodland) 515/244–1353 • dinner Th-Sat only • Italian • beer/ wine • wheelchair access

Chicago Dog & Deli 523 Euclid Ave (at 6th) 515/243–3085 • 8am-5pm, till 3pm Sat, clsd Sun • gay-owned

Paradise Pizza 2025 Grand Ave, West Des Moines 515/222–9959 • 11am-9pm, till 10pm Fri-Sat

RETAIL SHOPS

Liberty Gifts 333 E Grand Ave, Ste 105 (entrance on E 4th St) 515/508–0825 • 11am-7pm, 10am-8pm Fri-Sat • pride store

EROTICA

Gallery Book Store 1000 Cherry St (at 10th) 515/244–2916

Romantix Adult Superstore 2020 E Euclid Ave (at Delaware) 515/266–7992 • 24hrs

Dubuque

CAFES

Cafe Manna Java 150 John F Kennedy Rd 563/583–5531 • 7am-9pm • WiFi • also at 700 Locust St (full bar) • lesbian-owned

Iowa City

INFO LINES & SERVICES

AA Gay/ Lesbian 500 N Clinton (at church) 319/338-9111 (AA#) • 5pm Sun

Women's Resource & Action Center 130 N Madison St (at Market) 319/335–1486 • 9am-5pm, clsd wknds • community center • support groups • counseling • wheelchair access

BARS

Deadwood Tavern 6 S Dubuque St 319/351–9417 • 11am-2am • popular • gay-friendly • neighborhood bar • college crowd • wheelchair access

The Piano Lounge 347 S Gilbert St, Iowa City 319/351–1797 • 7pm-2am, from 6pm Fri-Sat, clsd Sun-Tue • gay/ straight • live entertainment Wed

Studio 13 13 S Linn St (in the alley btwn Linn & Dubuque Sts) 319/338–7185 • 7pm-2am, clsd Mon lesbians/ gay men • dancing/DJ • drag shows Fri & Sun • 19+ • gay-owned

RESTAURANTS

The Mill 120 E Burlington St 319/351–9529 • lunch & dinner, wknd brunch • popular Americana music venue

ENTERTAINMENT & RECREATION

Old Capitol City Roller Girls • Iowa City's own female roller derby league • facebook.com/oldcapitolcityrollergirls

BOOKSTORES

Prairie Lights Bookstore 15 S Dubuque St (at Washington) 319/337–2681, 800/295–2665 • 9am-9pm, till 6pm Sun • also cafe • wheelchair access

RETAIL SHOPS

New Pioneer Co-op & Bakehouse 22 S Van Buren (at Washington) 319/338–9441 • 7am-11pm • health food store & deli • wheelchair access • also Coralville location at 1101 2nd St, 319/358-5513

EROTICA

Romantix Adult Superstore 315 Kirkwood Ave (at Gilbert) 319/351–9444 • 9am-3am

Marshalltown

EROTICA

Adult Odyssey 907 Iowa Ave E 641/752–6550 • videos • toys • leather

Sioux City

NIGHTCLUBS

Jones Street Station 412 Jones St (at 5th St) 712/258–6338 • 7pm-2am, clsd Sun-Mon • gay/ straight • dancing/DJ • karaoke • wheelchair access • gay-owned

EROTICA

Romantix Adult Superstore 511 Pearl St 712/277-8566 • 9am-3am

Waterloo

ACCOMMODATIONS

Stella's Guesthouse & Gardens 324 Summit Ave (at Chicago) 319/232–2122 • lesbians/ gay men • full brkfst • hot tub • clothing-optional • shared baths • nonsmoking • gay-owned

NIGHTCLUBS

Kings & Queens Knight Club 304 W 4th St (at Jefferson) 319/232–3001 • 6pm-2am, clsd Mon • gay-friendly • dancing/DJ • transgender-friendly • drag shows • videos • young crowd • wheelchair access

KANSAS

Statewide

PUBLICATIONS

The Liberty Press 316/652–7737 • Kansas statewide LGBT newspaper

Junction City

NIGHTCLUBS

Xcalibur Club 384 Grant Ave **785/762–2050** • 6pm-2am, clsd Mon-Tue • gay/ straight • dancing/DJ • live shows • gay-owned

Kansas City

see also Kansas City, Missouri

ENTERTAINMENT & RECREATION

2nd Friday Art Walk downtown 913/371–0024 • 5pm-8pm 2nd Fri • art galleries & food

Lawrence

NIGHTCLUBS

Granada 1020 Massachusetts (at 11th) **785/842–1390** • hours vary • gay/ straight • dancing/DJ • live bands • wheelchair access

Jazzhaus 926–1/2 Massachusetts St 785/749–3320, 785/749–1387 • 8pm-2am • gay-friendly • live music • karaoke

Wilde's Chateau 2412 Iowa St 785/856–1514 • 9pm-2am Wed, Fri & Sat only • gay/ straight • dancing/DJ • theme nights

CAFES

Henry's 11 E 8th St (btwn Massachusetts St & New Hampshire St) 785/331–3511 • 7am-2am • cafe downstairs • bar from 5pm upstairs

Java Break 17 E 7th St (at New Hampshire) 785/749–5282 • 24hrs • sandwiches • desserts • gay-owned

RESTAURANTS

Teller's Restaurant & Bar 746 Massachusetts St (at 8th) 785/843–4111 • 11am-10pm, till 11pm Fri-Sat, from 10am Sun • Italian • some veggie • wheelchair access

BOOKSTORES

The Dusty Bookshelf 708 Massachusetts St 785/749–4643 • 10am-8pm, till 10pm Fri-Sat, noon-6pm Sun • used books • feminist & LGBT section • gay-owned

Manhattan

BOOKSTORES

The Dusty Bookshelf 700 N Manhattan Ave 785/539–2839 • 10am-8pm, till 6pm Sat, noon-5pm Sun • used books • feminist & LGBT section • gay-owned

Overland Park

ACCOMMODATIONS

Holtze Executive Village 11400 College Blvd 913/344–8100, 888/446–5893 • gay-friendly • pool • jacuzzi • WiFi • wheelchair access • $79-189

BARS

The Fox 7520 Shawnee Mission Pkwy (at Metcalf) 913/384–0369 • 1pm-2am, from 6pm Sat-Mon • mostly gay men • neighborhood bar • dancing/DJ • transgender-friendly • karaoke

Topeka

INFO LINES & SERVICES

Freedom Group AA 3916 SW 17th St (at Gage, at church) 785/215–7436 • 8pm Fri

BARS

The Tool Shed Tap 921 S Kansas Ave (near 10th St) 785/234–0482 • 3pm-2am • mostly gay men • neighborhood bar • dancing/DJ • drag shows • country/ western • gay-owned

BOOKSTORES

Barnes & Noble 6130 SW 17th St #101 785/273–9600 • 9am-11pm • LGBT section

Wichita

INFO LINES & SERVICES

One Day at a Time Gay AA 156 S Kansas Ave (at MCC, enter on English) 316/684–3661 • 8pm Tue & Th

ACCOMMODATIONS

Hawthorn Suites 2405 N Ridge Rd 316/729–5700 • gay-friendly • kids/ small pets ok • brkfst buffet • WiFi • wheelchair access • $75-150

BARS

Club 1507 1507 E Pawnee (at Ellis St) 316/260–9070 • 2pm-2am • lesbians/ gay men • dancing/DJ • wheelchair access • gay-owned

J's Lounge 513 E Central Ave (at N Emporia St) 316/262–1363 • 4pm-2am • lesbians/ gay men • cabaret • live shows • karaoke • patio • wheelchair access • "an upscale dive"

Side Street Retro Lounge 1106 S Pattie St (near Lincoln & Hydraulic) 316/267–0324 • 2pm-2am • mostly gay men • dancing/DJ • country/ western • wheelchair access

The Store 3210 E Osie (btw Harry & Hillside) 316/683–9781 • 2pm-2am • mostly women • men welcome • neighborhood bar

NIGHTCLUBS

Fantasy Complex 3201 S Hillside (at 31st) 316/682–5494 • 8pm-2am Th-Sun • lesbians/ gay men • dancing/DJ • karaoke • drag shows • also South Forty country/ western bar • wheelchair access

CAFES

Riverside Perk 1144 N Bitting Ave (at 11th) 316/264-6464 • 7am-10pm, till midnight Fri-Sat, from 10am Sun • WiFi • also Lava Lounge juice bar next door • wheelchair access

The Vagabond 614 W Douglas Ave 316/303–1110 • 7am-2am • theme nights • art gallery • also bar • WiFi

RESTAURANTS

Moe's Sub Shop 2815 S Hydraulic St (at Wassall) 316/524–5511 • 11am-8pm, clsd Sun

Old Mill Tasty Shop 604 E Douglas Ave (at St Francis) 316/264-6500 • 11am-3pm, from 8am Sat, clsd Sun • old-fashioned soda fountain • some veggie

Rain Cafe & Lounge 518 E Douglas (btwn St Francis & Emporia) 316/261–9000 • 11am-2am, from 1pm Sun • full bar & DJ on the wknds

River City Brewing Company 150 N Mosley St 316/263–2739 • 11am-10pm, till 2am wknds • live music

Riverside Cafe 739 W 13th St (at Bitting) 316/262–6703 • 6am-8pm, till 2pm Sun

Uptown Bistro 301 N Mead (at 2nd) 316/262–3232 • lunch & dinner daily, noon-8pm Sun • Mediterranean

Wichita

LGBT PRIDE:
June, web: www.wichitapride.org.

ANNUAL EVENTS:
June - River Festival, web: www.wichitariverfestival.org.
October - Tallgrass Film Festival 316/974–0089, web: www.tallgrassfilmfest.com. Gay-friendly independent film festival w/ some LGBT programming.

CITY INFO:
Kansas Travel & Tourism Dept 785/296-2009, web: www.travelks.com.

ATTRACTIONS:
Botanica 316/264–0448, web: www.botanica.org.
Kansas African American Museum 316/262–7651, web: www.tkaamuseum.org.
Mid-America All-Indian Center 316/350–3340, web: www.theindiancenter.org.
Old Cowtown Museum 316/219-1871, web: www.oldcowtown.org.
Oldtown.
Pyradomes.
Wichita Art Museum 316/268-4921, web: www.wichitaartmuseum.org.

TRANSIT:
American Cab Co. 316/262-7511.
Emu Express 316/734–0100.
Metropolitan Transit Authority 316/265-7221, web: www.wichita.gov/CityOffices/Transit/.

Zen Vegetarian 3101 N Rock Rd 316/425–7700 • 11am-10pm, till 9pm Sun, clsd Mon • wheelchair access

ENTERTAINMENT & RECREATION

Cabaret Oldtown Theatre 412 1/2 E Douglas Ave (at Topeka) 316/265–4400 • edgy, kitschy productions

Mosley Street Melodrama 234 N Mosley St (btwn 1st & 2nd St) 316/263–0222 • melodrama, homestyle buffet & full bar!

Wichita Arts 334 N Mead 316/462–2787 • promotes visual & performing arts • ArtScene publication has extensive cultural calendar

RETAIL SHOPS

East & West Menswear 924 E Douglas 316/440–9210 • 11am-7pm, till 9pm Fri-Sat, clsd Mon

PUBLICATIONS

The Liberty Press 316/652–7737 • statewide LGBT newspaper

EROTICA

Adult Superstore 5858 S Broadway 316/522–9040

Circle Cinema/ Video 2570 S Seneca St (at Crawford St) 316/264–2245 • 24hrs

Fetish Lingerie 2150 S Broadway St (btwn E Clark & E Kinkaid Sts) 316/264–7800 • leather, toys, clubwear • all sizes available

Patricia's 6143 W Kellogg (at Dugan) 316/942–1244

KENTUCKY

Covington

see also Cincinnati, Ohio

BARS

701 Bar and Lounge 701 Bakewell St (at 7th St) 859/431–7011 • 11am-1am • gay-friendly • neighborhood bar • dancing/DJ • live shows • karaoke • food served

Bar Monet 837 Willard St 859/491-2403 • 4pm-1am • lesbians/ gay men • bar food • dancing/DJ • shows

Rosie's Tavern 643 Bakewell St (at 7th St) 859/291–9707 • 3pm-2:30am • gay/ straight • neighborhood bar • lesbian-owned

Yadda Club 404 Pike St (at Main St) 859/491–5600 • 8pm-2:30am Wed-Sun • lesbians/ gay men • neighborhood bar • dancing/DJ • T-dance Sun • multiracial • live shows • karaoke • food served • patio • wheelchair access • lesbian-owned

Lexington

INFO LINES & SERVICES

Gay/ Lesbian AA 472 Rose St (at St Augustine's Chapel) 859/225–1212 (AA#) • 8pm Wed • also 7:30pm Fri at 205 E Short St (church)

GLSO Pride Center of the Bluegrass 389 Waller Ave #100 859/253–3233 • 10am-3pm Mon-Fri

ACCOMMODATIONS

Ramada Limited 2261 Elkhorn Rd (off I-75) 859/294–7375, 800/272–6232 • gay-friendly • pool • WiFi • nonsmoking • wheelchair access • $70-99

Weaver's Rest Cottage 106 Churchill Ct (at Lorraine Ct), Berea 859/582–3475 • rental home • WiFi • lesbian-owned • $85

BARS

The Bar Complex 224 E Main St (at Esplanade) 859/255–1551 • 4pm-midnight, till 2am wknds • popular • lesbians/ gay men • dancing/DJ • drag shows • live shows • WiFi • wheelchair access

Crossings 117 N Limestone St 859/233–7266 • 4pm-2am • mostly gay men • neighborhood bar • live shows • karaoke • leather events • wheelchair access

Soundbar 208 S Limestone 859/523–6338 • 4:30pm-close • gay/ straight • dancing/DJ • karaoke

CAFES

Third Street Stuff 257 N Limestone 859/255–5301 • 6:30am-11pm, from 8am Sun, salads & sandwiches • also funky boutique

RESTAURANTS

Alfalfa Restaurant 141 E Main St 859/253–0014 • lunch & dinner, brunch wknds • healthy multi-ethnic • plenty veggie • folk music wknds

Natasha's Bistro & Bar 112 Esplanade (at Main St) 859/259–2754, 888/901–8412 (SHOP #) • lunch & dinner, clsd Sun • eclectic dining • plenty veggie • also live theater & music

BOOKSTORES

Joseph-Beth 161 Lexington Green Circle (at Nicholasville Rd) 859/273–2911, 800/248–6849 • 9am-10pm, till 11pm Fri-Sat, 11am-9pm Sun • also cafe • WiFi • wheelchair access

Sqecial Media 371 S Limestone St (btwn Pine & Winslow) 859/255–4316 • 10am-8pm, noon-6pm • also pride items

PUBLICATIONS

GLSO (Gay/ Lesbian) News 859/253-3233
• local news & calendar

EROTICA

Romantik Adult Superstore 933
Winchester Rd (at Liberty Rd) **859/252-0357**
• 24hrs

Louisville

INFO LINES & SERVICES

Gay AA 1432 Highland Ave (at MCC)
502/587-6225 • 4:30pm Sun, 6:30pm Mon

ACCOMMODATIONS

21c Museum Hotel 700 W Main
502/217-6300, 877/217-6400 • gay-friendly •
boutique hotel w/ museum • also Proof on
Main restaurant

The Brown Hotel 335 W Broadway (at 4th)
502/583-1234, 888/387-0498 • gay-friendly •
WiFi • nonsmoking • also restaurant & bar

Columbine B&B 1707 S 3rd St (near Lee St)
502/635-5000, 800/635-5010 • gay-friendly •
1896 Greek Revivial mansion • full brkfst •
nonsmoking • WiFi • gay-owned • $119-165

Galt House Hotel & Suites 140 N 4th St (at
W Main) **502/589-5200, 800/843-4258** • gay-
friendly • waterfront hotel

Holiday Inn Southwest 4110 Dixie Hwy (at
I-264) **502/448-2020** • gay-friendly • food
served • swimming • WiFi • lounge •
wheelchair access

Hyatt Regency Louisville 320 W Jefferson
St (at 3rd) **502/581-1234** • gay-friendly • pool
• tennis • WiFi • wheelchair access

Inn at the Park 1332 S 4th St (at Park Ave)
502/638-0045 • gay-friendly • restored
mansion • full brkfst • nonsmoking • WiFi •
$129-229

BARS

Magnolia Bar 1398 S 2nd St (at Magnolia)
502/637-9052 • 2pm-4am • gay-friendly •
neighborhood bar • young crowd

Teddy Bears Bar & Grill 1148 Garvin Pl (at
St Catherine) **502/589-2619** • 11am-4am,
from 1pm Sun • mostly gay men •
neighborhood bar • wheelchair access

Tink's Pub 2235 S Preston St **502/634-8180**
• 4pm-close, from 2pm Sun • lesbians/ gay
men • neighborhood bar • drag shows •
karaoke

Tryangles 209 S Preston St (at Market)
502/583-6395 • 4pm-4am, from 1pm Sun •
mostly gay men • strippers • wheelchair
access

NIGHTCLUBS

The Connection Complex 120 S Floyd St
(at Market) **502/585-5752** • 8pm-4am, till
2am Mon-Tue • popular • lesbians/ gay men •
dancing/DJ • piano bar & cabaret • leather •
videos • wheelchair access

Starbase Q 921 W Main St (at 9th St) •
8pm-close, from 4pm Wed, clsd Mon • mostly
gay men • dancing/DJ • karaoke • industrial
video bar • shows • WiFi

CAFES

Days Espresso & Coffee 1420 Bardstown
Rd (at Edenside) **502/456-1170** • 6:30am-
10pm, till 11pm Fri-Sat • WiFi • wheelchair
access • lesbian-owned

RESTAURANTS

The Bodega at Felice 829 E Market St
502/569-4100 • 7am-7pm, till 11pm Fri, 9am-
4pm Sat, clsd Sun • gourmet market & deli •
coffee bar • WiFi • gay-owned

Cafe Mimosa 1543 Bardstown Rd (at
Stevens Ave) **502/458-2233** • lunch & dinner
• Vietnamese, Chinese & sushi

El Mundo 2345 Frankfort Ave **502/899-9930**
• 11:30am-10pm, full bar till 2am Th-Sat, clsd
Sun-Mon • popular • Mexican • wheelchair
access

Havana Rumba 4115 Oechsli Ave (off State
Hwy 1447) **502/897-1959** • lunch & dinner •
Cuban

Jack Fry's 1007 Bardstown Rd **502/452-9244**
• lunch & dinner • steak/ Southern • live jazz •
wheelchair access

Lynn's Paradise Cafe 984 Barret Ave (at
Baxter) **502/583-3447** • 7am-10pm, from 8am
wknds • popular • lesbians/ gay men •
colorful, funky decor • also bar • WiFi •
lesbian-owned

Mayan Cafe 813 E Market St **502/566-0651**
• lunch Mon-Fri, dinner nightly, clsd Sun •
Mayan/ Mexican

Porcini 2730 Frankfort Ave (at Bayly)
502/894-8686 • dinner nightly, clsd Sun •
Italian

Proof on Main 702 W Main St (at 7th, at 21c
Hotel) **502/217-6360** • brkfst & lunch Mon-
Fri, dinner nightly • upscale • modern
American w/ Tuscan influence

Ramsi's Cafe on the World 1293 Bardstown Rd **502/451–0700** • 11am-1am, till 2am Fri-Sat, Sun brunch • eclectic menu • wheelchair access

Third Avenue Cafe 1164 S 3rd St (at W Oak) **502/585–2233** • 11am-9pm, till 10pm Fri-Sat, clsd Sun • vegan/ vegetarian • patio • wheelchair access

Vietnam Kitchen 5339 Mitscher Ave **502/363–5154** • Vietnamese • plenty veggie • wheelchair access

Windy City Pizzeria 2622 S 4th St (at Winkler) **502/636–3708** • clsd Sun-Mon • gay-owned

Zen Garden 2240 Frankfort Ave **502/895–9114** • lunch & dinner, clsd Sun • Asian • vegetarian • wheelchair access

ENTERTAINMENT & RECREATION

Pandora Productions PO Box 4185, 40204 **502/216–5502** • LGBT-themed productions

Louisville

WHERE THE GIRLS ARE:
On Main or Market Streets near 1st, and generally in the north-central part of town, just west of I-65.

ENTERTAINMENT:
Pandora LGBT-themed Theatre 502/216–5502, web: www.pandoraprods.org.

LGBT PRIDE:
June. 502/649–4851, web: www.kypride.com.

ANNUAL EVENTS:
May - Kentucky Derby 502/584-6383, web: www.kentuckyderby.com.
June-July - Kentucky Shakespeare Festival 502/574-9900, web: www.kyshakes.org.
October - World's Largest Halloween Party, Louisville Zoo, web: www.louisvillezoo.org.
October - St James Court Art Show 502/ 635-1842, web: www.stjamescourtartshow.com.

CITY INFO:
Louisville Visitor Center 800/626-5646.
Convention & Visitors Bureau, web: www.gotolouisville.com.

BEST VIEW:
Aboard the Belle of Louisville steamboat at Waterfront Park.

WEATHER:
Mild winters and long, hot summers!

ATTRACTIONS:
Belle of Louisville steamboat 502/574-2992, web: www.belle-oflouisville.com.
Churchill Downs 502/636-4400, web: www.churchilldowns.com.
Farmington Historic Home 502/452-9920 web: www.historichomes.org/Farmington.
Hadley Pottery 502/584-2171, web: www.hadleypottery.com.
Locust Grove Historic Farm 502/897-9845, web: www.locust-grove.org.
Louisville Slugger Tour 877/775-8443, web: www.sluggermu-seum.org.
St. James Court.
Waterfront Park, web: www.louisvillewaterfront.com.
West Main Street Historic District, web: www.mainstreetassocia-tion.com.

TRANSIT:
Yellow Cab 502/636-5511, web: www.yellowcablouisville.com.
Louisville's Premier Shuttle 502/897-283, web: www.louisvil-letransport.com.
TARC Bus System 502/585-1234, web: www.ridetarc.org.
Louisville Horse Trams 502/581-0100, web: www.louisvillehorse-trams.com.

Rudyard Kipling 422 W Oak St (btwn 4th & Garvin) **502/636–1311** • live music & theater, also restaurant, open wknds

Voices of Kentuckiana 502/583–1013 • LGBT community chorus

BOOKSTORES

Borders 3024 Bardstown Rd (in Gardiner Lane Shopping Center) **502/456–6660, 800/844–7323** • 10am-9pm, 10am-6pm Sun • also 4600 Shelbyville Rd, Shelbyville Plaza, 502/893-0133

Carmichael's 1295 Bardstown Rd (at Longest Ave) **502/456–6950** • 8am-10pm, till 11pm Fri-Sat, from 10am Sun • large LGBT section

PUBLICATIONS

The Letter • LGBT newspaper

Midway

CAFES

Tavern 815 131 E Main St (inside Le Marché boutique mall) **859/846–4688** • 11am-3pm, till 4pm Sat • WiFi

Newport

see also Cincinnati, Ohio

BARS

The Crazy Fox Saloon 901 Washington Ave (at 9th) **859/261–2143** • 3pm-2:30am • gay/ straight • friendly neighborhood bar

Owensboro

BARS

Equals Bar 1006 E 4th St (at Hathaway) **270/313–0820** • 4:30-2am • lesbians/gay men • dancing/DJ • piano bar • karaoke • drag shows

Paducah

EROTICA

Romantix Adult Superstore 243 Brown (at Irvin Cobb Dr) **270/442–5584**

LOUISIANA

Statewide

PUBLICATIONS

Ambush Mag 504/522–8049 • oldest LGBT newspaper for the Gulf South (Texas through Florida)

Baton Rouge

INFO LINES & SERVICES

Freedom of Choice/ Gay AA 7747 Tom Dr (at MCC) **225/930–0026 (AA#)** • 8pm Th & 8pm Sat

BARS

George's Place 860 St Louis **225/387–9798** • 3pm-2am, from 5pm Sat, clsd Sun • popular • lesbians/ gay men • neighborhood bar • videos • karaoke • male strippers Fri • wheelchair access

Hound Dogs 668 Main St (at 7th) **225/344–0807** • 2pm-2am, from 4pm Mon-Tue, clsd Sun • lesbians/ gay men • neighborhood bar • wheelchair access

NIGHTCLUBS

Cajun Cove of Baton Rouge 4550 Concord Ave **225/246–8317** • 6pm-2am, from noon Sat, clsd Sun • lesbians/ gay men • neighborhood bar • dancing/DJ • karaoke • live shows • 18+ • wheelchair access

Splash 2183 Highland Rd **225/242–9491** • 9pm-2am, clsd Sun-Tue • popular • lesbians/ gay men • dancing/DJ • drag shows • 18+ • wheelchair access

RESTAURANTS

Drusilla Seafood 3482 Drusilla Ln (at Jefferson Hwy) **225/923–0896, 800/364–8444** • 11am-10pm

Mestizo 2323 Acadian Thruway (just off I-10) **225/387–2699** • lunch & dinner, clsd Sun • Louisiana-Mexican fusion

Ralph & Kacoo's 6110 Bluebonnet Blvd (off I-10 & Perkins) **225/766–2113** • 11am-9:30pm, till 10:30pm Fri-Sat • Cajun • full bar • wheelchair access

PUBLICATIONS

Ambush Mag 504/522–8049 • LGBT newspaper for the Gulf South (TX through FL)

EROTICA

Grand Cinema Station 10732 Florida Blvd **225/272–2010**

Breaux Bridge

ACCOMMODATIONS

Maison des Amis 111 Washington St (at Bridge St) 337/507–3399 • gay-friendly • charming 1870 residence overlooking legendary Bayou Teche • full brkfst • WiFi • $100-250

Gretna

see New Orleans

Harvey

see New Orleans

Lafayette

INFO LINES & SERVICES

AA Gay/ Lesbian 115 Leonie St 337/991–0830 (AA#) • call for times & locations

NIGHTCLUBS

Jules Downtown 533 Jefferson St 337/264–8000 • 7pm-2am Th-Fri, from 8pm Sat • dancing/DJ • wheelchair access

Tonic 2013 Pinhook Rd 337/269–6011 • 4pm-2am, noon-midnight Sun • mostly gay men • dancing/DJ • karaoke • drag shows • young crowd • gay-owned

Lake Charles

ACCOMMODATIONS

Aunt Ruby's B&B 504 Pujo St (at Hodges) 337/430–0603 • gay/ straight • full brkfst • WiFi • $85-150

NIGHTCLUBS

Crystal's 112 W Broad St 337/433–5457 • 9pm-2am, till 4am Fri • lesbians/ gay men • dancing/DJ • country/ western • drag shows • wheelchair access

RESTAURANTS

Pujo St Cafe 901 Ryan St (at Pujo) 337/439–2054 • 11am-9pm, till 10pm Fri-Sat, clsd Sun • full bar • gay-owned

Metairie

see New Orleans

Monroe

BARS

The Corner Bar 512 N 3rd St (at Pine) 318/329–0046 • 8pm-2am, 3pm-midnight Sun, clsd Mon & Wed, seasonal hrs • lesbians/ gay men • neighborhood bar • multiracial • live shows • karaoke • drag shows • 18+ • gay-owned

Natchitoches

ACCOMMODATIONS

Chez des Amis B&B 910 Washington St (btwn Texas & Pavie) 318/352–2647 • gay/ straight • full brkfst • nonsmoking • WiFi • gay-owned • $110-165

Judge Porter House B&B 321 Second St 318/527–1555, 800/441–8343 • gay/ straight • full brkfst • nonsmoking • WiFi • gay-owned • $145-175

New Orleans

INFO LINES & SERVICES

AA Lambda Center 638 Papworth Ave #A, Metairie 504/838–3399 (GENERAL AA OFFICE #) • daily meetings • call for schedule

LGBT Community Center of New Orleans 2114 Decatur St (btwn Elysian Fields & Frenchmen) 504/945–1103 • 2pm-8pm, noon-6pm Fri-Sat, clsd Sun • call first • wheelchair access

ACCOMMODATIONS

1896 O'Malley House B&B 120 S Pierce St (at Canal St) 504/488–5896, 866/226–1896 • gay/ straight • jacuzzi • nonsmoking • WiFi • gay-owned • $99-250

5 Continents B&B 1731 Esplanade Ave (at Claiborne) 504/324–8594, 800/997–4652 • gay/ straight • B&B • full brkfst • kids/ pets ok • WiFi • gay-owned • $125-200

Aaron Ingram Haus 1012 Elysian Fields Ave (btwn N Rampart & St Claude) 504/949–3110 • gay/ straight • guesthouse • apts • courtyard • WiFi • gay-owned • $68-175

Andrew Jackson Hotel 919 Royal St (btwn St Philip & Dumaine) 504/561–5881, 800/654–0224 • gay-friendly • historic inn • WiFi • nonsmoking • $69-250

Antebellum Guest House 1333 Esplanade Ave (at Marais St) 504/943–1900 • gay/ straight • B&B in 1830s Grand Greek Revival • full brkfst • clothing-optional • nonsmoking • WiFi • gay-owned • $100-175

Ashton's B&B 2023 Esplanade Ave (at Galvez) **504/942–7048, 800/725–4131** • gay-friendly • quiet location • WiFi • $169-269

Auld Sweet Olive B&B 2460 N Rampart St (at Spain) **504/947–4332, 877/470–5323** • gay/straight • popular • kids 13+ ok • nonsmoking • WiFi • $65-150

B&W Courtyards B&B 2425 Chartres St (btwn Mandeville & Spain) **504/324–3396, 800/585–5731** • gay-friendly • three 19th-c bldgs connected by courtyards • hot tub • nonsmoking • WiFi • gay-owned • $99+

Biscuit Palace Guest House 730 Dumaine (btwn Royal & Bourbon) **504/525–9949** • gay-friendly • 1820s Creole mansion • B&B & apts • in the French Quarter • kids ok • WiFi • wheelchair access • $105-150

Block-Keller House 3620 Canal St (at Telemachus) **504/483–3033, 877/588–3033** • gay/straight • nonsmoking • WiFi • gay-owned • $110-165

Bon Maison Guest House 835 Bourbon St (btwn Lafitte's & Bourbon Pub) **504/561–8498** • gay/straight • nonsmoking • gay-owned • $105-400

Bourbon Orleans Hotel 717 Orleans (at Bourbon St) **504/523–2222, 866/513–9744** • popular • gay-friendly • swimming • WiFi • nonsmoking • also restaurant & 2 bars • $99-189

The Burgundy B&B 2513 Burgundy St (at St Roch) **504/942–1463, 800/970–2153** • gay/straight • near French Quarter • clothing-optional hot tub • nonsmoking • WiFi • gay-owned • $80-95

Bywater B&B 1026 Clouet St **504/944–8438** • gay-friendly • fireplace • nonsmoking • kids/pets ok • WiFi • lesbian & gay-owned • $75-175

Chez Palmiers B&B 1744 N Rampart St **877/233–9449** • gay/straight • pool • nonsmoking • kids 12+ ok • WiFi • gay-owned • $80-95

The Cornstalk Hotel 915 Royal St **504/523–1515, 800/759–6112** • gay-friendly • kids ok • WiFi • $95-210

The Degas House 2306 Esplanade Ave (at Tonti St) **504/821–5009, 800/755–6730** • gay-friendly • full brkfst • jacuzzi • WiFi • $149-175

Elysian Guest House 1008 Elysian Fields Ave (at Rampart St) **504/324–4311** • gay-friendly • hot tub • nonsmoking • WiFi • gay-owned • $85-135

Empress Hotel 1317 Ursulines Ave (btwn Treme & Marais) **504/529–4100, 800/311–5192** • gay-friendly • small Euro-style hotel • WiFi • kids/pets ok • $69+

The Frenchmen Hotel 417 Frenchmen St (where Esplanade, Decatur & Frenchmen intersect) **504/948–2166, 800/831–1781** • popular • gay/straight • spa • pool • kids ok • nonsmoking • WiFi • wheelchair access • $59-299

The Green House Inn 1212 Magazine St (at Erato) **504/525–1333, 800/966–1303** • lesbians/gay men • 1840s guesthouse • gym • hot tub • pool • nonsmoking • pets ok • WiFi • gay-owned • $89-199

➤ **Harrah's Casino** 228 Poydras St **504/533–6000, 800/847–5299** • gay-friendly • restaurants & lounges • wheeelchair access • see ad in front color section

Hotel Monteleone 214 Royal St (at Iberville) **504/523–3341, 800/535–9595** • gay-friendly • deluxe historic hotel • rumored to be haunted • pool • WiFi • $139-1,300

Inn The Quarter Reservation Service **888/523–5235, 800/570–3085** • gay-friendly • nonsmoking • WiFi • gay & straight-owned • $79-600

Kerlerec House 928 Kerlerec St (at Dauphine St) **504/944–8544** • gay/straight • 1 block from the French Quarter • hot tub • gardens • kids ok • nonsmoking • WiFi • gay-owned • $75-1,200

La Dauphine, Residence des Artistes 2316 Dauphine St (btwn Elysian Fields & Marigny) **504/948–2217** • gay/straight • B&B • nonsmoking • WiFi • gay-owned • $85-185

La Maison Marigny B&B on Bourbon 1421 Bourbon St (at Esplanade) **504/948–3638, 800/570–2014** • gay-friendly • on the quiet end of Bourbon St • nonsmoking • WiFi • gay-owned • $129+

Lamothe House Hotel 621 Esplanade Ave (btwn Royal & Chartres) **504/947–1161, 800/367–5858** • gay/straight • popular • jacuzzi • pool • kids ok • nonsmoking • WiFi • straight & gay-owned • $69-299

Lions Inn 2517 Chartres St (btwn Spain & Franklin) **504/945–2339, 800/485–6846** • gay/straight • handsome 1850s home • pool • hot tub • WiFi • nonsmoking • semi-tropical patio • gay-owned • $50-175

Maison Dupuy Hotel 1001 Toulouse St **504/586–8000, 800/535–9177** • gay-friendly • luxury boutique hotel • fine dining restaurant • swimming pool • hot tub • WiFi • $99-489

Mentone B&B 1437 Pauger St (at Kerlerec) **504/943-3019** • gay-friendly • suite in Victorian in the Faubourg Marigny district • nonsmoking • WiFi • women-owned • $125-175

New Orleans Guest House 1118 Ursulines Ave (at N Rampart) **504/566-1177, 800/562-1177** • gay-friendly • Creole cottage dated back to 1848 • courtyard • nonsmoking • gay-owned • $79-199

New Orleans

WHERE THE GIRLS ARE:
Wandering the Quarter, or rebuilding the small artsy area known as Mid-City, north of the Quarter up Esplanade St.

LGBT PRIDE:
June. New Orleans Gay Pride. web: www.gaypridenewworleans.com.

ANNUAL EVENTS:
February - Mardi Gras, web: www.mardigras.com. North America's rowdiest block party.
March - Tennesse Williams Festival, web: www.tennesseewilliams.net.
April - Gay Easter Parade 504/522-8049, web: www.gayeasterparade.com.
April/May - New Orleans Jazz & Heritage Festival, web: www.nojazzfest.com.
May - Saints & Sinners, LGBT writers' festival 504/581-1144, web: www.sasfest.org.
August - Southern Decadence 504/522-8047, web: www.southerndecadence.com. Gay mini-Mardi Gras during Labor Day.

CITY INFO:
New Orleans CVB 800/672-6124, web: www.neworleanscvb.com.
Louisiana Office of Tourism 800/994-8620, web: www.louisianatravel.com.

WEATHER:
Summer temperatures hover in the 90°s with subtropical humidity. And on the heels of all that heat and humidity come hurricanes. Hurricane season stretches from June 1 to November 30. Winters can be rainy and chilly. The average temperature in February (Mardi Gras month) is 58°, while the average precipitation is 5.23".

ATTRACTIONS:
Bourbon Street in the French Quarter.
Cabildo (to see the Louisiana Purchase) 504/568-6968.
Cafe du Monde for beignets 504/587-0835, web: www.cafedumonde.com.
Garden District.
Haunted History Tour 504/861-2727, web: www.hauntedhistorytours.com.
Moon Walk.
New Orleans Museum of Art 504/488-2631, web: www.noma.org.
Pat O'Brien's for a hurricane 504/525-4823, web: www.patobriens.com.
Preservation Hall 504/522-2841, web: www.preservationhall.com.
Top of the Market.

TRANSIT:
United Cab 504/522-9771, web: www.unitedcabs.com.
New Orleans Airport Shuttle 504/522-3500. web: www.airportshuttleneworleans.com.
New Orleans Regional Transit Authority 504/248-3900, web: www.norta.com.

The Olivier House 828 Toulouse (at Bourbon) **504/525–8456, 866/525–9748** • gay-friendly • pool • kids/pets ok • WiFi • wheelchair access • $99+

Pierre Coulon Guest House **504/943–6692, 866/328–1497** • gay-friendly • quiet apt patio • nonsmoking • WiFi • $95-150

Royal Barracks Guest House 717 Barracks St (at Bourbon) **504/529–7269, 888/255–7269** • gay-friendly • hot tub • nonsmoking • WiFi • $89-159

Royal Street Courtyard 2438 Royal St (at Spain) **504/943–6818, 888/846–4004** • gay/straight • suites in 1850s guesthouse • hot tub • pets ok • WiFi • gay-owned • $65-249

St Charles Guest House 1748 Prytania St (at Felicity) **504/523–6556** • gay-friendly • some shared baths • pool • patio • WiFi • $50-175

Ursuline Guest House 708 Ursuline Ave (btwn Royal & Bourbon) **504/525–8509, 800/654–2351** • gay/straight • hot tub • nonsmoking • WiFi • wheelchair access • gay-owned • $59-245

W New Orleans—French Quarter 316 Chartres St **504/581–1200, 877/WHOTELS (RESERVATIONS ONLY)** • gay-friendly • pool • WiFi • also restaurant • wheelchair access • $289-489

Bars

700 Club 700 Burgundy (at St Peter) **504/561–1095** • noon- 5am, til midnight Sun • lesbians/gay men • videos • food served • wheelchair access

Big Daddy's 2513 Royal St (at Franklin) **504/948–6288** • 24hrs • lesbians/gay men • neighborhood bar • wheelchair access

Bourbon Pub & Parade 801 Bourbon St (at St Ann) **504/529–2107** • 24hrs • popular • lesbians/gay men • dancing/DJ • theme nights • Sun T-dance • drag shows/strippers • videos • 18+ • WiFi

Cafe Lafitte in Exile/ The Balcony Bar 901 Bourbon St (at Dumaine) **504/522–8397** • 24hrs • popular • mostly gay men • dancing/DJ • live shows • videos • Balcony Bar upstairs w/ cyberbar

Club LAX 2301 N Causeway Blvd (at 34th), Metairie **504/834–7979** • 5pm-close • lesbians/gay men • neighborhood bar • live shows • Sat • karaoke • monthly drag shows • wheelchair access

Club Tribute 3202 N Arnoult Rd (at 18th St), Metairie **504/455–1311** • 9pm-close Fri-Sat only • mostly women

Country Club 634 Louisa St (at Royal) **504/945–0742** • 11am-1am • popular • gay/straight • food served • karaoke • swimming • volleyball • nude sunbathing • WiFi • not your father's country club!

Cutter's 706 Franklin Ave (at Royal) **504/948–4200** • 11am-3am, from 11am wknds • lesbians/gay men • neighborhood bar • live music • WiFi • wheelchair access

The Double Play 439 Dauphine (at St Louis) **504/523–4517** • 24hrs • mostly gay men • neighborhood bar • transgender-friendly

The Four Seasons 3229 N Causeway Blvd (at 18th), Metairie **504/832–0659** • 3pm-close • popular • mostly gay men • neighborhood bar • live music & shows in summer • patio • also the Out Back Bar summers • gay-owned

The Friendly Bar 2301 Chartres St (at Marigny) **504/943–8929** • 11am-close • popular • mostly gay men • neighborhood bar • wheelchair access • women-owned

Good Friends Bar 740 Dauphine (at St Ann) **504/566–7191** • popular • mostly gay men • neighborhood bar • professional crowd • karaoke Tue • wheelchair access • also Queens Head Pub upstairs Sun only • popular piano sing-along 4pm-8pm

Le Roundup 819 St Louis St (at Dauphine) **504/561–8340** • 24hrs • mostly gay men • neighborhood bar • very MTF-friendly crowd

Napoleon's Itch 734 Bourbon (at St Ann, in Bourbon Orleans Hotel) **504/371–5450** • noon-2am, till 4am Fri-Sat • popular • mostly gay men • wine & martini bar • nonsmoking

Rawhide 2010 740 Burgundy St (at St Ann) **504/525–8106** • 1pm-5am • popular • mostly gay men • neighborhood bar • dancing/DJ • alternative, underground sound • leather • videos

Rubyfruit Jungle/ 1135 1135 Decatur St (at Governor Nicholls) **504/571–1863** • gay/straight • dancing/DJ • transgender-friendly • videos • 18+ • goth theme nights & electronica

Spotted Cat 623 Frenchmen St **206/337–3273** • 4pm-2am • gay-friendly • excellent live jazz • dancing • wheelchair access

Tubby's Golden Lantern 1239 Royal St (at Barracks) **504/529–2860** • 8am-4am • mostly gay men • neighborhood bar • drag shows Fri-Sun

NIGHTCLUBS

Girl Bar New Orleans 801 Bourbon St (above the Bourbon Pub) **504/529–2107** • 10pm-3am Tue only • mostly women • dancing/DJ • video • young crowd

Oz 800 Bourbon St (at St Ann) **504/593–9491, 850/433–7499** • 24hrs • popular • mostly gay men • dancing/DJ • drag shows • live shows • videos • young crowd • wheelchair access

CAFES

Cafe Rose Nicaud 632 Frenchmen St (btwn Royal & Chartres) **504/949–3300** • 7am-7pm • WiFi

CC's Coffee House 941 Royal St **504/581–6996** • 7am-9pm • WiFi

Croissants d'Or 617 Ursulines St **504/524–4663** • 7am-2pm, clsd Tue • delicious pastries • wheelchair access

The Orange Couch 2339 Royal St **504/267–7327** • 7am-10pm • ultra mod cafe • food served • live music • WiFi • wheelchair access

Royal Blend Coffee & Tea House 621 Royal St **504/523–2716** • 6am-8pm, till midnight wknds • on a quiet, hidden courtyard • also salads & sandwiches

Z'otz 8210 Oak St **504/861–2224** • 7am-1am • coffee shop & art space • live entertainment

RESTAURANTS

13 Monaghan's 517 Frenchmen St **504/942–1345** • 11am-4am • brkfst, lunch & dinner all the time • some veggie • full bar • wheelchair access

Acme Oyster House 724 Iberville St (at Royal) **504/522–5973** • 11am-10pm, till 11pm wknds • long line moves quickly, worth the wait!

Angeli on Decatur 1141 Decatur St (at Gov Nicholls) **504/566–0077** • 11am-2am, till 4am Fri-Sat • pizza • WiFi • wheelchair access

Brennan's 417 Royal St (at Conti) **504/525–9711** • brkfst, lunch & dinner • upscale • reservations recommended

Bywater Bar-B-Que 3162 Dauphine St (at Louisa) **504/944–4445, 504/947–0000** • 11am-9pm, clsd Wed • also Lorenzo's Pizzeria • gay-owned • wheelchair access

Cafe Amelie 912 Royal St (in Princess of Monaco Courtyard) **504/412–8965** • lunch & dinner, Sun brunch, clsd Mon-Tue • Creole

Cafe Negril 606 Frenchmen St (at Chartres St) **504/944–4744** • dinner, clsd Sun-Mon, Caribbean • live music • dancing/DJ • woman-owned • wheelchair access

Casamento's 4330 Magazine St (at Napoleon Ave) **504/895–9761** • lunch, dinner Th-Sat, clsd Sun-Mon (also clsd June-Aug) • best oyster loaf in city • wheelchair access

Clover Grill 900 Bourbon St (at Dumaine) **504/598–1010** • 24hrs • popular • diner fare

Commander's Palace 1403 Washington Ave (at Coliseum St, in Garden District) **504/899–8221** • lunch Mon-Fri, dinner nightly, jazz brunch wknds • popular • upscale Creole • dress code • reservations required • wheelchair access

Coquette 2800 Magazine St (at Washington Ave) **504/265–0421** • lunch Wed-Sat, dinner Mon-Sat, brunch Sun • wheelchair access

The Court of Two Sisters 613 Royal St **504/522–7261** • daily jazz brunch buffet 9am-3pm, dinner nightly • Creole

Dante's Kitchen 736 Dante St (at River Rd) **504/861–3121** • dinner nightly, wknd brunch, clsd Tue • Cajun • wheelchair access

EAT New Orleans 900 Dumaine St (at Dauphine) **504/522–7222** • lunch & dinner, Sun brunch, clsd Mon • Cajun/ Creole homecooking • some veggie

Elizabeth's 601 Gallier St **504/944–9272** • 7am-10pm, from 8am wknds, clsd Mon • Cajun

Feelings Cafe 2600 Chartres St (at Franklin Ave) **504/945–2222** • dinner Th-Sun, also Sun brunch • Creole • piano bar • courtyard • wheelchair access

Fiorella's Cafe 45 French Market Pl (at Gov Nicholls & Ursulines) **504/553–2155** • noon-midnight, till 2am Fri, 11:30am-2am Sat, 11:30am-midnight Sun • homecooking

Gott Gourmet Cafe 3100 Magazine St (at 8th St) **504/373–6579** • 11am-9pm, 8am-5pm wknds

Gumbo Shop 630 St Peter St (at Chartres) **504/525–1486** • award-winning gumbo

Herbsaint 701 St Charles Ave **504/524–4114** • lunch & dinner, bistro menu afternoons, clsd Sun • French/ Southern

La Peniche 1940 Dauphine St (at Touro St) **504/943–1460** • 24hrs, clsd Tue-Wed • Southern comfort foods • popular for brkfst • some veggie

Marigny Brasserie 640 Frenchmen St **504/945–4472** • lunch Mon-Fri, dinner nightly, wknd brunch • French

Meauxbar Bistro 942 N Rampart St (at St Philip) **504/569–9979** • 6pm-10pm, clsd Sun-Mon

Mike's On The Avenue 628 St Charles Ave (in the Lafayette Hotel) **504/523-7600** • lunch & dinner • great views of St Charles Ave • wheelchair access

Mona Lisa 1212 Royal St (at Barracks) **504/522-6746** • 11am-10pm, from 5pm Tue-Wed • Italian • some veggie • beer/ wine • gay-owned • wheelchair access

Mona's 504 Frenchmen St **504/949-4115** • 11am-10pm, till 11pm Fri-Sat, noon-9pm Sun • cheap Middle Eastern eats • some veggie

Moon Wok 800 Dauphine St **504/523-6910** • 11am-9pm, till 10pm Fri-Sat • Chinese

Napoleon House 500 Chartres St **504/524-9752** • lunch daily, dinner only Mon, clsd Sun • po' boys & muffulettas • wheelchair access

Nola 534 St Louis St (btwn Chartres & Decatur) **504/522-6652** • lunch wknds, dinner nightly • fusion Creole from Emeril Lagasse • wheelchair access

Olivier's 204 Decatur St **504/525-7734** • 5pm-10pm • Creole • wheelchair access

Orleans Grapevine 718-720 Orleans Ave **504/523-1930** • 4pm-10:30pm, till 11:30pm Fri-Sat • wine bar & bistro • wheelchair access

Phillips 733 Cherokee St (at Maple) **504/865-1155** • 4pm-2am • gay/ straight • also tapas restaurant • upscale • wheelchair access • gay-owned

Praline Connection 542 Frenchmen St (at Chartres) **504/943-3934** • 11am-10pm • soul food

Quartermaster 1100 Bourbon St **504/529-1416** • 24hrs • "The Nellie Deli" • sandwiches & more • wheelchair access

Restaurant August 301 Tchoupitoulas St (at Gravier St) **504/299-9777** • lunch Mon-Fri, dinner nightly • upscale French/ Mediterranean • wheelchair access

Sammy's Seafood 627 Bourbon St (across from Pat O' Brien's) **504/525-8442** • 11am-11pm • Cajun/ Creole

Stanley 547 St Ann St (at Chartres) **504/587-0093** • 7am-10pm • upscale diner fare

Stella 1032 Chartres St (at Ursulines Ave) **504/587-0091** • dinner nightly • upscale global fusion cuisine • wheelchair access

The Upperline Restaurant 1413 Upperline St **504/891-9822** • dinner Wed-Sun • Creole • fine dining • full bar • wheelchair access

ENTERTAINMENT & RECREATION

Big Easy Rollergirls • New Orleans' female roller derby league • visit www.bigeasyrollergirls.com for events

Cafe du Monde 800 Decatur St (at St Ann, corner of Jackson Square) **504/525-4544, 800/772-2927** • till you've had a beignet—fried dough, powdered w/ sugar, that melts in your mouth—you haven't been to New Orleans & this is "the" place to have them 24hrs a day • wheelchair access

Haunted History Tour **504/861-2727, 888/644-6787** • guided 2-1/2-hour tours of New Orleans' most famous haunts, including Anne Rice's former home

Mardi Gras World 1380 Port of New Orleans Pl **504/361-7821, 800/362-8213** • tour this year-round Mardi Gras float workshop

Pat O'Brien's 718 St Peter St (btwn Bourbon & Royal) **504/525-4823, 800/597-4823** • gay-friendly • more than just a bar—come for the Hurricane, stay for the kitsch • wheelchair acess

Preservation Hall 726 St Peter St (btwn Bourbon & Royal) **504/522-2841, 888/946-5299** • 8pm-midnight, set begins at 8:30pm • come & hear the music that started jazz: New Orleans-style jazz! • cover charge

St Charles Streetcar St Charles St (at Canal St) **504/248-3900 (RTA RIDELINE #)** • it's not named Desire, but you should still ride it, Blanche, if you want to see the Garden District

BOOKSTORES

Barnes & Noble 1601 Westbank Expwy, Harvey **504/263-1146** • 9am-10pm, till 11pm Fri-Sat, 10am-9pm Sun • wheelchair access

FAB (Faubourg Marigny Art & Books) 600 Frenchmen St (at Chartres) **504/947-3700** • noon-10pm • LGBT

Garden District Book Shop 2727 Prytania St (at Washington) **504/895-2266** • 10am-6pm, till 4pm Sun • independent

Kitchen Witch Cook Books 631 Toulouse St (at Royal St) **504/528-8382** • 10am-7pm, clsd Tue • cook books from rare to campy

RETAIL SHOPS

Angela King Gallery 241 Royal St **504/524-8211** • lesbian-owned

Dutch Alley Artist's Co-Op 912 N Peters St **504/412-9220**

Krazy Katz 909 Bourbon St (at Dumaine) **504/566-1570** • 11am-6pm • LGBT cards • gifts

NOLA Tattoo 1820 Hampson St (Uptown, at Riverbend) **504/524-6147** • tattoos & piercing

Second Skin Leather 521 St Philip St (btwn Decatur & Chartres) **504/561-8167** • noon-8pm, till 10pm wknds

Wicked Orleans 1201 Decatur St (at Gov Nicholls) **504/529-4384, 866/297-9207 (OUTSIDE LA)** • 11am-6pm • leather & goth clothes • wheelchair access

PUBLICATIONS

Ambush Mag **504/522-8049** • LGBT newspaper for the Gulf South (TX through FL)

EROTICA

Bourbon Strip Tease 205 Bourbon St **504/581-6633** • 10am-1am • erotic lingerie, dancewear, adult novelties

Mr Binky's 107 Chartres St (off Canal St) **504/302-2095** • 24hrs

Panda Bear 415 Bourbon St (at St Louis) **504/529-8064** • leather • toys • wheelchair access

Paradise Adult Video 41 W 24th St (at Crestview), Kenner **504/461-0000** • arcade • wheelchair access

Shreveport

ACCOMMODATIONS

Twenty-Four Thirty-Nine Fairfield 2439 Fairfield Ave **318/424-2424, 877/251-2439** • gay-friendly • WiFi • pets ok • $145-225

BARS

Korner Lounge II 800 Louisiana Ave (near Cotton) **318/222-9796** • 3pm-2am • mostly gay men • neighborhood bar • karaoke

NIGHTCLUBS

Central Station 1025 Marshall St (btwn Fairfield & Creswell) **318/222-2216** • 5pm-close, till 4am Fri-Sat • popular • lesbians/gay men • dancing/DJ • country/western wknds • drag shows Fri • transgender-friendly • wheelchair access

EROTICA

Fun Shop Too 9434 Mansfield Rd **318/688-2482** • clsd Sun • adult, novelty & gag gifts • toys

Slidell

see also New Orleans

BARS

Billy's 2600 Hwy 190 W **985/847-1921** • 6pm-1am • lesbians/gay men • neighborhood bar • drag shows • karaoke • WiFi

MAINE

Aroostook County

ACCOMMODATIONS

Magic Pond Wildlife Sanctuary & Guest House Blaine **215/287-4174** • mostly women • nonsmoking • lesbian-owned

Augusta

includes Hallowell

ACCOMMODATIONS

Annabessacook Farm 192 Annabessacook Rd, Winthrop **207/377-3276** • popular • gay/straight • restored 1810 farmhouse • full brkfst • WiFi

The Benjamin Wales House B&B 49 Middle St (at Chestnut St), Hallowell . **207/512-2461, 877/323-4712** • gay/straight • 1820 house is listed on the Nat'l Register of Historic Places • full brkfst • nonsmoking • WiFi • gay-owned

Maple Hill Farm B&B Inn Hallowell **207/622-2708, 800/622-2708** • gay/straight • Victorian farmhouse on 130 acres • full brkfst • swimming pond • nonsmoking • WiFi • wheelchair access • gay-owned • $90-205

RESTAURANTS

Slates 167 Water St (Franklin), Hallowell **207/622-9575, 207/622-4104** • lunch Tue-Fri, dinner Mon-Sat, brunch wknds • also bakery • live shows Mon

Bangor

BOOKSTORES

Pro Libris Bookshop 10 3rd St (at Union) **207/942-3019** • 10am-6pm, clsd Sun-Mon • new & used

Bar Harbor

ACCOMMODATIONS

Aysgarth Station 20 Roberts Ave (at Cottage St) **207/288-9655** • gay-friendly • 10-minute drive from Acadia • cats on premises • nonsmoking • WiFi

The Colonial Inn 321 High St (at US1), Ellsworth **207/667-5548, 888/667-5548** • gay-friendly • pool • WiFi • also restaurant • woman-owned

Manor House Inn 106 West St (near Bridge St) **207/288–3759, 800/437–0088** • open April-Oct • gay-friendly • 1887 Victorian mansion • full brkfst • some rooms w/ whirlpools • nonsmoking • WiFi

RESTAURANTS

Mama DiMatteo's 34 Kennebec Pl (at Firefly Ln) **207/288-3666** • 4:30pm-10pm • upscale casual dining • full bar • gay-owned

ENTERTAINMENT & RECREATION

ImprovAcadia 15 Cottage St (2nd flr) **207/288-2503** • May-Oct • live improvised theater

Bath

ACCOMMODATIONS

The Galen C Moses House 1009 Washington St **207/442-8771, 888/442-8771** • gay/ straight • 1874 Victorian • pets ok • full brkfst • nonsmoking • WiFi • gay-owned

The Inn at Bath 969 Washington St (at North St) **207/443-4294, 800/423-0964** • gay/ straight • 1810 Greek Revival B&B • full brkfst • jacuzzi • nonsmoking • wheelchair access

Bingham

EROTICA

Bingham Village Video 10 Murray St (at Rte 201) **207/672-4900**

Boothbay Harbor

ACCOMMODATIONS

Hodgdon Island Inn PO Box 603, Boothbay 04571 **207/633-7474, 800/314-5160** • gay/ straight • 1810 sea captain's home • full brkfst • pool • nonsmoking • WiFi

Sur La Mer Inn 18 Eames Rd, PO Box 663, 04538 **207/633-7400, 207/380-6400** • gay-friendly • seasonal luxury oceanfront B&B • nonsmoking • kids ok • gay-owned

Brunswick

BOOKSTORES

Gulf of Maine Books 134 Maine St (at Pleasant) **207/729-5083** • 9:30am-5:30pm, clsd Sun • alternative

Camden

ACCOMMODATIONS

Norumbega Inn 63 High St **207/236-4646, 877/363-4646** • gay-friendly • historic castle • nonsmoking • WiFi • gay-owned

Corea

ACCOMMODATIONS

The Black Duck Inn on Corea Harbor **207/963-2689** • gay/ straight • restored farmhouse • also cottages • full brkfst • nonsmoking • WiFi • gay-owned • $140-200

Deer Isle

RESTAURANTS

Fisherman's Friend 5 Atlantic Ave, Stonington **207/367-2442** • seasonal • 11am-9pm, till 10pm Fri-Sat

Dexter

ACCOMMODATIONS

Brewster Inn 37 Zion's Hill Rd (at Dexter St) **207/924-3130** • gay-friendly • historic mansion • full brkfst • kids ok • nonsmoking • WiFi • wheelchair access • $69-149+ tax

Farmington

BOOKSTORES

Devany, Doak & Garrett Booksellers 193 Broadway (at High St) **207/778-3454** • 10am-5pm, till 5:30pm Th, till 6:30pm Fri, 9am-5pm Sat, noon-3pm Sun • LGBT section

Freeport

ACCOMMODATIONS

The Royalsborough Inn 1290 Royalsborough Rd, Durham **207/353-6372, 800/765-1772** • gay-friendly • full brkfst • spa services • massage • also alpaca farm • nonsmoking • kids ok • conference room for 20 • WiFi

RESTAURANTS

Harraseeket Lunch & Lobster Co 36 Main St (at Harraseeket Rd), S Freeport **207/865-4888, 207/865-3535** • lunch & dinner • open May-Oct

Hancock

RESTAURANTS

Le Domaine Restaurant & Inn **207/422-3395, 800/554-8498** • 6pm-9pm, Sun brunch, clsd Mon • open June-Oct

Kennebunkport

ACCOMMODATIONS

The Colony Hotel 140 Ocean Ave (at Kings Hwy) **207/967-3331, 800/552-2363** • May-Oct • gay-friendly • 1914 grand oceanfront property • private beach • pool • nonsmoking • WiFi • also rental cottages • lesbian-run

White Barn Inn & Spa 37 Beach Ave **207/967-2321** • gay-friendly • pool • restaurant • nonsmoking • WiFi • $340-1,500

RESTAURANTS

Bartley's Dockside 4 Western Ave **207/967-6244, 207/233-6037** • lunch & dinner • 11:30am-10pm • seafood • some veggie • full bar • WiFi • wheelchair access

Kittery

see Portsmouth, New Hampshire

Lewiston

ACCOMMODATIONS

Ware Street Inn B&B 52 Ware St (at College St) **207/783-8171, 877/783-8171** • gay-friendly • elegant 1940s colonial • full brkfst • well-behaved kids ok • WiFi • nonsmoking

EROTICA

Paris Adult Book Store 297 Lisbon St (at Chestnut) **207/783-6677, 800/581-6901**

Naples

ACCOMMODATIONS

Lambs Mill Inn **207/693-6253** • gay/ straight • 1890s farmhouse • full brkfst • hot tub • nonsmoking • WiFi • lesbian-owned

RESTAURANTS

Sydney's 377 Roosevelt Tr/ Rte 302 (at Poland Springs Rd) **207/693-3333** • dinner April-Nov only • full bar

Newcastle

ACCOMMODATIONS

The Tipsy Butler B&B 11 High St **207/563-3394** • gay-friendly • on the Damariscotta River • full brkfst • nonsmoking • WiFi

Ogunquit

ACCOMMODATIONS

2 Village Square Inn Ogunquit 14 Village Square Ln (at Main St) **207/646-5779** • open May-Oct • mostly gay men • Victorian w/ ocean views • heated pool • nonsmoking • WiFi • gay-owned

Beauport Inn & Suites on Clay Hill 339 Agamenticus/ Clay Hill Rd **207/361-2400, 800/646-8681** • gay/ straight • English country manor on 11 acres • full brkfst • pool • jacuzzi • nonsmoking • WiFi • wheelchair access

Beaver Dam Campground 551 School St, Rte 9, Berwick **207/698-2267** • gay-friendly • campground on 20-acre spring-fed pond • pool • kids/ pets ok • women-owned • $30-86

Belm House Vacation Units **207/641-2637** • lesbians/ gay men • apt rentals • hot tub • kids/ dogs ok • WiFi • gay-owned

Black Boar Inn 277 Main St (at Ogunquit Rd) **207/646-2112** • lesbians/ gay men • full brkfst • kids ok • nonsmoking • also weekly cottages • gay-owned

Distant Sands B&B **207/646-8686** • gay/ straight • 18th-c farmhouse • full brkfst • nonsmoking • WiFi • also cottage • gay-owned

Leisure Inn 73 School St (at Main St) **207/646-2737** • gay-friendly • nonsmoking • WiFi • seasonal

Meadowmere Resort 74 S Main St (at Rte 1) **207/646-9661, 800/633-8718** • gay-friendly • pool • health club & spa • kids ok • nonsmoking • WiFi • wheelchair access • $79-449

Moon Over Maine B&B Berwick Rd **207/646-6666, 800/851-6837** • lesbians/ gay men • hot tub • nonsmoking • WiFi • gay-owned • $70-150

Morning Dove 13 Bourne Ln (at Main St) **207/646-3891** • lesbians/ gay men • nonsmoking • gay-owned • $100-200

Ogunquit Beach Inn 67 School St **207/646-1112** • mostly men • guesthouse B&B • also cottage • 5 minutes to beach • some shared baths • WiFi • gay-owned • $89-169

The Ogunquit Inn 17 Glen Ave **207/646-3633, 866/999-3633** • clsd Nov-March • lesbians/ gay men • Victorian B&B • nonsmoking • WiFi • gay-owned

Ogunquit-by-the-Sea Lodging 44 School St (at Main St) 207/646-4132 • mostly gay men • self-catering vacation units • nonsmoking • WiFi • gay-owned

OgunquitCottages.com 25 Mill St, N Reading, MA 01864 207/646-3840, 978/664-5813 • lesbians/ gay men • weekly rentals • seasonal (June-Sept) • near bars & beach • nonsmoking • pets/kids ok • gay-owned • $1,350-3,500/week

Old Village Inn 250 Main St (at Berwick Rd) 207/646-7088 • gay-friendly • 1880s B&B • ocean views • kids/ pets ok • nonsmoking • WiFi • also restaurant • seafood • upscale

Rockmere Lodge B&B 150 Stearns Rd 207/646-2985, 800/646-2985 • gay/ straight • Maine shingle cottage • near beach • nonsmoking • gay-owned

Yellow Monkey Guest Houses & Motel 280 Main St 207/646-9056 • gay/ straight • seasonal • roof deck • ocean view • jacuzzi • fitness room • kids/ pets ok • wheelchair access • gay-owned • $90-200

BARS

Front Porch Cafe 9 Shore Rd (at Beach St) 207/646-4005 • lunch & dinner (seasonal) • gay/ straight • piano bar upstairs • full menu

Vine Cafe 478 Main St 207/646-0288, 877/646-0288 • seasonal, 4pm-close • also restaurant • good wine selection

NIGHTCLUBS

Maine Street 195 Main St/ US Rte 1 207/646-5101 • 5pm-1am, T-dance from 3pm wknds • popular • lesbians/ gay men • dancing/DJ • karaoke • cabaret • food served • gay-owned

Women's T Dance 195 Main St/ US Rte 1 (at Maine Street nightclub) 207/646-5101 • monthly, call for dates • popular • mostly women • dancing/DJ

CAFES

Bread & Roses 246 Main St 207/646-4227 • 7am-7pm, seasonal

Fancy That Cafe Main St (at Beach St & Rte 1) 207/646-4118 • 6:30am-11pm • open April-Oct • pastries • sandwiches

RESTAURANTS

Amore Breakfast 309 Shore Rd 207/646-6661, 866/641-6661 • brkfst only • seasonal

Angelina's Ristorante 655 Main St 207/646-0445 • dinner • Italian

Arrows 41 Berwick Rd (2 miles W of Rte 1), Cape Neddick 207/361-1100 • open April-Dec, 6pm-9pm, clsd Mon • popular • eclectic • some veggie • gardens • reservations recommended

Beachfire Bar & Grill 658 Main St 207/646-8998 • dinner nightly, wknd brunch • outdoor fire pit

Bessie's 8 Shore Rd 207/646-0888 • brkfst, lunch & dinner, also bar

Clay Hill Farm 220 Clay Hill Rd (off Logging Rd), Cape Neddick (York) 207/361-2272 • dinner only • seafood • some veggie • also piano bar

Five-0 50 Shore Rd 207/646-5001 • popular • 5pm-midnight • martini bar & restaurant • full bar

Jonathan's 92 Bourne Ln 207/646-4777 • dinner nightly • steak/ seafood • full bar • entertainment • wheelchair access

La Pizzeria 239 Main St 207/646-1143 • lunch & dinner • open April-Dec • some veggie • beer/ wine • gay-owned

Wild Blueberry Cafe & Bistro 82 Shore Rd 207/646-0990 • brkfst, lunch & dinner, jazz brunch 10am-1pm Sun

ENTERTAINMENT & RECREATION

Ogunquit Playhouse 10 Main St 207/646-5511 (BOX OFFICE), 207/646-2402 • summer theater • some LGBT-themed productions

Portland

ACCOMMODATIONS

Auberge by the Sea B&B 103 East Grand Ave (at Old Orchard St), Old Orchard Beach 207/934-2355 • gay-friendly • private pathway to beach • nonsmoking • WiFi

The Chadwick B&B 140 Chadwick St • gay/ straight • full brkfst • WiFi • gay-owned • $99-200

The Inn at St John 939 Congress St 207/773-6481, 800/636-9127 • gay/ straight • kids/ pets ok • nonsmoking • WiFi • gay-owned

The Inn by the Sea 40 Bowery Beach Rd, Cape Elizabeth 207/799-3134, 800/888-4287 • gay-friendly • pool • kids/ pets ok • nonsmoking • wheelchair access • also restaurant

The Percy Inn 15 Pine St (at Longfellow Square) 207/871-7638, 888/417-3729 • gay-friendly • nonsmoking • WiFi

The Pomegranate Inn 49 Neal St (at Carroll St) 207/772–1006, 800/356–0408 • gay-friendly • full brkfst • private garden • nonsmoking • WiFi • $150

Sea View Inn 65 W Grand Ave (at Atlantic Ave), Old Orchard Beach 207/934–4180, 800/541–8439 • gay/ straight • oceanfront motel • pool • patio • kids/ pets ok • gift shop • WiFi • nonsmoking • wheelchair access

West End Inn 146 Pine St (at Neal St) 207/772–1377, 800/338–1377 • gay-friendly • full brkfst • nonsmoking • WiFi

Wild Iris Inn 273 State St (at Grant St) 207/775–0224, 800/600–1557 • gay-friendly • nonsmoking • WiFi • kids ok • women-owned

BARS

Blackstones 6 Pine St (off Longfellow Square) 207/775–2885 • 4pm-1am, from 3pm wknds • mostly gay men • neighborhood bar • leather 3rd Sat • theme nights • wheelchair access

The Wine Bar 38 Wharf St 207/772–6976 • 5pm-close • gay/ straight • food served

NIGHTCLUBS

Styxx 3 Spring St (at Center St) 207/828–0822 • 7pm-1am • popular • lesbians/ gay men • more women Th • dancing/DJ • live shows • theme nights • drag shows • gay-owned

CAFES

Coffee by Design 43 Washington Ave (at Oxford St) 207/879–2233 • 6:30am-5:30pm, from 7:30am Sat, clsd Sun

RESTAURANTS

Becky's 390 Commercial St (at High St) 207/773–7070 • 4am-10pm • great brkfst & chowdah • wheelchair access

Grace 15 Chestnut St 207/828–4422 • fine dining in renovated old church

Katahdin 27 Forest Ave 207/774–1740 • 5pm-11pm, clsd Sun-Mon • American menu • full bar

Norm's Bar & Grill 617 Congress St 207/828–9944 • 11:30am-10pm, from 4pm Sun

Street & Co 33 Wharf St (btwn Dana & Union) 207/775–0887 • 5:30pm-9:30pm, till 10pm Fri-Sat • popular • seafood • beer/ wine • wheelchair access

Walter's Cafe 2 Portland Sq (at Union) 207/871–9258 • lunch & dinner, dinner nightly • seafood/ pasta • some veggie • wheelchair access

BOOKSTORES

Longfellow Books 1 Monument Way 207/772–4045 • 9am-7pm, till 6pm Sat, 9:30am-5pm Sun • LGBT section

Portland

LGBT PRIDE:
June, web: www.southern-mainepride.org.

ANNUAL EVENTS:
August - Portland Chamber Music Festival 800/320-0257, web: www.pcmf.org.

CITY INFO:
207/772-5800, web: www.visitport-land.com.

WEATHER:
Portland has a mild marine climate. Winter temperatures are in the 20°s-40°s, and summers are breezy and mild, with temperatures in the 60°s-80°s.

TRANSIT:
ASAP Taxi 207/791-2727, web: asaptaxi.net.
Metro (bus) 207/774-0351, web: www.gpmetrobus.com.

ATTRACTIONS:
Old Port.
Portland Head Light 207/799-2661, web: www.portlandheadlight.com.
Portland Museum of Art 207/775-6148, web: www.portlandmu-seum.org.
Wadsworth-Longfellow House 207/774-1822, web: www.mainehistory.org/house_overview.shtml.

Retail Shops

The Corner General Store 154 Middle St (at Market) **207/253-5280** • 8am-1am • great wine selection

Emerald City 611 Congress St (at High St) **207/774-8800** • 10am-6pm, First Friday Art Walk • gay-owned

Erotica

Condom Sense 424 Fore St (at Union) **207/871-0356, 877/871-0356** • 10am-8pm, till 9pm Th, till 10pm Fri-Sat, till 6pm Sun • condoms, lube, massage oils, novelties, etc

Richmond

Entertainment & Recreation

Kennebec Tidewater Charters Kennebec River & Casco Bay **207/650-3494, 207/737-4695** • guided fishing & kayak trips • scenic coastal tours • women-owned

Rockland

Accommodations

Captain Lindsey House Inn 5 Lindsey St **207/596-7950, 800/523-2145** • gay-friendly • 19th-c Maine sea captain's home • nonsmoking • WiFi • wheelchair access

The Old Granite Inn 546 Main St **207/594-9036, 800/386-9036** • gay-friendly • 1880s stone guesthouse • full brkfst • nonsmoking • WiFi

Rockport

Restaurants

Chez Michel Rte 1, Lincolnville Beach **207/789-5600** • dinner, Sun brunch, clsd Mon • full bar • some veggie

Lobster Pound Rte 1, Lincolnville Beach **207/789-5550** • 11:30am-8pm • May-Oct • full bar • patio • wheelchair access

Tenants Harbor

Accommodations

Eastwind Inn **207/372-6366, 800/241-8439** • clsd Dec-April • gay-friendly • rooms & apts • full brkfst • pets ok

White Mtns

Accommodations

Mountain Village Farm B&B 164 Main St, Kingfield 04947 **207/265-2030, 866/577-0741** • gay-friendly • rural & sophisticated B&B • full brkfst • nonsmoking • WiFi

York Harbor

Restaurants

York Harbor Inn Rte 1A **207/363-5119, 800/343-3869** • lunch Mon-Sat, dinner nightly, Sun brunch • also the Cellar Pub • also lodging

MARYLAND

Annapolis

Info Lines & Services

AA Gay/ Lesbian 199 Duke of Gloucester St (at St Anne's Parish) **410/268-5441** • 8pm Tue

Accommodations

Two-O-One B&B 201 Prince George St (at Maryland Ave) **410/268-8053** • gay/ straight • English country house • full brkfst • nonsmoking • WiFi • gay-owned • $180-240

Restaurants

Cafe Sado 205 Tackle Cir (at Castle Marina Rd), Chester **410/604-1688** • lunch & dinner • sushi/ Asian fusion

Baltimore

Info Lines & Services

AA Gay/ Lesbian **410/663-1922** • 6:30pm Sat • call for other mtg times

Gay, Lesbian, Bisexual & Transgender Community Center of Baltimore 241 W Chase St (at Read) **410/837-5445** • many groups & services

Accommodations

Abacrombie Fine Food & Accommodations 58 W Biddle St (at Cathedral) **410/244-7227, 888/922-3437** • gay/ straight • 1880s town house • nonsmoking • also restaurant • $98-195

Biltmore Suites 205 W Madison St (at Park) **410/728-6550, 800/868-5064** • gay-friendly • kids/ pets ok • nonsmoking • WiFi • $89

Pier 5 Hotel 711 Eastern Ave (at President) **410/539-2000, 866/283-0951** • gay/ straight • full brkfst • restaurant • WiFi • wheelchair access • $219-1,495

Bars

Baltimore Eagle 2022 N Charles St (enter on 21st) **443/524-3333** • 4pm-2am • mostly gay men • also leather store • patio • wheelchair access

Club Bunns 608 W Lexington St (at Greene St) **410/234–2866** • 3pm-2am, till midnight Mon-Tue • lesbians/ gay men • dancing/DJ • multiracial • live shows • female strippers Sat

The Gallery Bar & Studio Restaurant 1735 Maryland Ave (at Lafayette) **410/539-6965** • 4pm-1:30am • lesbians/ gay men • dinner Mon-Fri • wheelchair access

Grand Central 1001 N Charles St (at Eager) **410/752-7133** • 4pm-close • popular • lesbians/ gay men • Sapphos upstairs for women • dancing/DJ • videos • karaoke • drag shows • 21+

Hippo 1 W Eager St (at Charles) **410/576-0018** • 4pm-2am • popular • lesbians/ gay men • more women 1st Sun for T-dance • dancing/DJ • transgender-friendly • karaoke • drag shows • piano bar • wheelchair access

Jay's on Read 225 W Read St **410/225-0188** • 4pm-1am • mostly gay men • piano bar

Leon's 870 Park Ave (at Chase) **410/539-4993** • 4pm-2am • lesbians/ gay men • neighborhood bar • WiFi • wheelchair access • also Singer's restaurant

Mixers 6037 Belair Rd (at Glenarm Ave) **410/483-6011** • 5pm-2am • lesbians/ gay men • neighborhood bar • dancing/DJ • karaoke • live shows

Port In A Storm 4330 E Lombard St (at Kresson) **410/534-0014** • noon-2am, clsd Mon • mostly women

The Rowan Tree 1633 S Charles St (at E Heath) **410/468-0550** • noon-2am • gay/ straight • karaoke • "where diversity is our name"

Sapphos 1001 N Charles St (upstairs at Central Station) **410/752-7133** • 8pm-2am Fri-Sat only • mostly women • dancing/DJ

Ziascoz 1313 E Pratt St (at Eden) **410/276-5790** • 5pm-2am • gay/ straight • neighborhood bar • karaoke • mostly African American

Baltimore

Where the Girls Are:

The women's bars are in southeast Baltimore, near the intersection of Haven and Lombard. Of course, the boys' playground, downtown around Chase St. and Park Ave., is also a popular hangout.

LGBT Pride:

June. 410/837-5445 x17 (GLCC #), web: www.baltimorepride.org.

City Info:

Maryland Office of Tourism 866/639-3526, web: www.visitmaryland.org.

Best View:

Top of the World Trade Center at the Inner Harbor. 401 E Pratt, 410/837-0845, web: www.viewbaltimore.org.

Transit:

Yellow Cab 410/685-1212, web: yellowcabofbaltimore.com.
MTA Transit 410/539-5000, web: www.mtamaryland.com.

Attractions:

Baltimore Museum of Art 443/573-1700, web: www.artbma.org.
Fort McHenry 410/962-4290, web: www.nps.gov/fomc.
Harborplace 410/332-41941, web: www.harborplace.com.
Lexington Market 410/685-6169, web: www.lexingtonmarket.com.
National Aquarium 410/576-3800, web: www.aqua.org.
Poe House & Museum 410/396-7932, web: eapoe.org.
Walters Art Museum 410/547-9000, web: www.thewalters.org.

Weather:

A temperate and, at times, temperamental climate. Spring brings great temperatures (50°-70°s) and unpredictable rains and heavy winds. In summer, the weather can be hot (90°s) and sticky. Fall cools off with an occasional "Indian Summer" in October. Winter brings cool days and colder nights, along with snow and ice.

NIGHTCLUBS

Club 1722 1722 N Charles St (at Lafayette) **410/547-8423** • afterhours club • Fri & Sat only, 2am-close • gay/ straight • dancing/DJ • multiracial • 18+ • BYOB • dress code

Club Orpheus 1003 E Pratt St **410/276-5599** • gay/ straight • Fri & Sat goth/ fetish party

The Paradox 1310 Russell St (at Ostend) **410/837-9110** • 11pm-5am, midnight-6am Sat • popular • gay/ straight • more gay Sat • dancing/DJ • multiracial • food served • live shows • videos • wheelchair access

Peer Pressure 701 S Bond St (at The Get Down) **443/708-3564** • 2nd Wed • lesbians/ gay men • dancing/DJ • monthly queer dance party

Rehab 1001 N Charles St (at Grand Central) **410/382-7252** • 9pm 2nd Sat only • mostly women • dancing/DJ • multiracial

RESTAURANTS

Aldos 306 S High St **410/727-0700** • Southern-influenced regional Italian

Alonso's 415 W Cold Spring Ln (at Keswick Rd) **410/235-3433** • 4pm-10:30pm, from 11:30am Fri-Sat • pizza & burgers • full bar • wheelchair access

Cafe Hon 1002 W 36th St (at Roland) **410/243-1230** • 7am-9pm, 9am-close wknds • wheelchair access

The Dizz 300 W 30th St **443/869-5864** • 10am-2am, from 8am Fri-Sun • full bar

Golden West Cafe 1105 W 36th St **410/889-8891** • brkfst, lunch & dinner • New Mexican • also bar • live bands

Jerry D's Seafood 7804 Harford Rd, Parkville **410/668-1299**

Loco Hombre 413 W Cold Spring Ln (at Roland) **410/889-2233** • 11:30am-10:30pm, till 11:30pm Fri-Sat • Tex-Mex • burgers

Mount Vernon Stable & Saloon 909 N Charles St (btwn Eager & Read) **410/685-7427** • 11:30am-midnight, from 10am-8pm Sun

Trinidad Gourmet 418 E 31st St **410/243-0072** • 7am-8:30pm, clsd Sun • Caribbean • delicious & inexpensive

Viccino 1317 N Charles St **410/347-0349** • 11am-11pm, till 9pm Sun • New American • full bar

Waterstone Bar & Grille 311 W Madison (at Linden Ave) **410/225-7475** • Mediterranean • also wine bar

Woodberry Kichen 2010 Clipper Park Rd #126 **410/464-8000** • organic meats & sustainable agriculture • full bar • wheelchair access

XS Baltimore 1307 N Charles St **410/468-0002** • 7am-midnight, till 2am Fri-Sat • sushi restaurant, cafe & lounge

ENTERTAINMENT & RECREATION

The Charm City Kitty Club 3134 Eastern Ave (at Creative Alliance) **410/276-1651** • performing arts cabaret for lesbian, dyke, bisexual, trans women & allies

Charm City Roller Girls 722 Dulaney Valley Rd #187, Towson • Baltimore's own female roller derby league • visit www.charmcityrollergirls.com for events

BOOKSTORES

Read Street Books 229 W Read St **410/669-4103** • 10am-6pm, will 8pm wknds • women's bookstore • also cafe

PUBLICATIONS

Baltimore OUTloud **410/244-6780**

Gay Life **410/837-7748** • LGBT newspaper

EROTICA

Chained Desires 136 W Read St **410/528-8441, 888/886-8442** • 11am-8pm, till 9pm Fri-Sat, clsd Mon • custom leather crafts & apparel • adult toys

Sugar 927 W 36th St (at Roland) **410/467-2632** • 11am-close • lesbian-owned sex toy shop • transgender-friendly

Cumberland

ACCOMMODATIONS

Rocky Gap Lodge & Golf Resort 16701 Lakeview Rd NE, Flintstone **301/784-8400, 800/724-0828** • gay-friendly • expansive property w/ forests, lake & elegantly rustic lodge • pool • $120+

RESTAURANTS

Acropolis 45 E Main St, Frostburg **301/689-8277** • 4pm-10pm, clsd Sun-Mon • Greek & American • full bar

Au Petit Paris 86 E Main St, Frostburg **301/689-8946** • 6pm-9:30pm, clsd Sun-Mon • French • also lounge • reservations recommended • wheelchair access

Hagerstown

NIGHTCLUBS

The Lodge 21614 National Pike, Boonsboro **301/591-4434** • 7pm-2am, till midnight Sun, clsd Mon-Wed • mostly gay men • dancing/DJ • drag shows • gay-owned

RETAIL SHOPS

Rainbow Connection LLC 14 1/2 E Washington St (at Potomac St) **301/739-6629** • 10am-7pm, till 6pm Sat, clsd Sun • pride gifts & more

Laurel

BARS

PW's Sports Bar & Grill 9855 N Washington Blvd (at Whiskey Bottom Rd) **301/498-4840, 301/498-4841** • 5am-2am • lesbians/ gay men • sports bar • food served • drag shows • karaoke • WiFi • gay-owned

Princess Anne

ACCOMMODATIONS

The Alexander House Booklovers B&B 30535 Linden Ave (at corner of Beckford) **410/651-5195** • gay-friendly • literary-themed B&B • full brkfst • nonsmoking • $80-150

Rock Hall

ACCOMMODATIONS

Tallulah's on Main 5750 Main St (at Sharp St) **410/639-2596** • gay/ straight • small suite hotel • kids ok • nonsmoking • wheelchair access • gay-owned • $115-150

Rockville

RESTAURANTS

The Vegetable Garden 11618 Rockville Pk **301/468-9301** • lunch Mon-Fri, dinner nightly • vegetarian/ vegan

Snow Hill

ACCOMMODATIONS

River House Inn 201 E Market St (at Green St) **410/632-2722** • gay-friendly • pool • WiFi • gay-owned • $160-300

MASSACHUSETTS

Amherst

see also Northampton

BOOKSTORES

Amherst Books 8 Main St **413/256-1547, 800/503-5865** • 6:30am-9pm, till 5pm Sun • independent • LGBT section

Food For Thought 106 N Pleasant St (at Main) **413/253-5432** • 10am-6pm • progressive bookstore • wheelchair access • collectively run

Barre

ACCOMMODATIONS

Jenkins Inn & Restaurant **978/355-6444, 800/378-7373** • gay-friendly • full brkfst • restaurant • full bar • nonsmoking • English garden • WiFi • gay-owned • $180-215

Berkshires

ACCOMMODATIONS

The B&B at Howden Farm 303 Rannapo Rd, Sheffield **413/229-8481** • gay/ straight • 250-acre working farm • near river • full brkfst • nonsmoking • some shared baths • gay-owned • $99-179

Broken Hill Manor 771 West Rd (at Rte 23), Sheffield **413/528-6159, 877/535-6159** • gay-friendly • B&B • full brkfst • hot tub • kids 12+ ok • WiFi • gay-owned • $185-250

Gateways Inn 51 Walker St (at Church St), Lenox **413/637-2532, 888/492-9466** • gay-friendly • full brkfst • also bar & restaurant • nonsmoking • $150-515

Guest House at Field Farm 554 Sloan Rd, Williamstown **413/458-3135** • gay-friendly • transgender-friendly • nonsmoking • pool • WiFi • $150-295

Hallig Hilltop House 68 West St (at Cross Rd), Mt Washington **413/644-0076** • gay-friendly • surrounded by State Park • near hiking & skiing • pool • nonsmoking • gay-owned • $140-250

Mount Greylock Inn 6 East St, Adams **413/743-2665** • gay/ straight • some views of Mt Greylock • cat on premises • gay-owned • $89-159

River Bend Farm B&B 643 Simonds Rd, Williamstown **413/458-3121** • gay-friendly • restored 1770s home • shared baths • seasonal • well-behaved kids ok • nonsmoking • $120

The Rookwood Inn 11 Old Stockbridge Rd (at Walker St/ Rte 183), Lenox 413/637–9750, 800/223–9750 • gay/ straight • Victorian inn near Tanglewood & skiing • full brkfst • kids ok • nonsmoking • WiFi • women-owned • $175-450

The Thaddeus Clapp House 74 Wendell Ave, Pittsfield 413/499–6840, 888/499–6840 • gay-friendly • full brkfst • nonsmoking • $125-295

Topia Inn 10 Pleasant St (at Rte 8), Adams 413/743–9600, 888/868–6742 • gay-straight • nonsmoking • WiFi • wheelchair access • eco-friendly B&B • organic gourmet brkfst • kids ok • lesbian-owned • $135-260

Windflower Inn 684 S Egremont Rd, Great Barrington 413/528–2720, 800/992–1993 • gay-friendly • gracious country inn • full brkfst • pool • nonsmoking • WiFi • kids ok • $100-225

RESTAURANTS

Allium Restaurant + Bar 42 Railroad St (at Main), Great Barrington 413/528–2118 • 5pm-9pm, till 10pm Fri-Sat • Sun brunch • bar open late

Cafe Lucia 80 Church St (at Tucker), Lenox 413/637–2640 • dinner only, clsd Mon, seasonal

Church Street Cafe 65 Church St (at Franklin), Lenox 413/637–2745 • lunch & dinner, seasonal • American bistro • some veggie

Mezze Bistro + Bar 777 Cold Spring Rd, Williamstown 413/458–0123 • 5pm-9pm, till 10pm Fri-Sat, seasonal hrs

ENTERTAINMENT & RECREATION

Tanglewood 197 Rte 183, Lenox 888/266–1200 • live music venue • summer home of the Boston Symphony/ Pops

Williamstown Theatre Festival just E of Rte 2 & Rte 7 junction, Williamstown 413/597–3400, 413/458–3200 • call for season calendar

Boston

INFO LINES & SERVICES

Gay AA 12 Channel St #604 617/426–9444 (AA#)

GLBT Helpline 617/267–9001, 888/340–4528 • 6pm-11pm

ACCOMMODATIONS

463 Beacon St Guest House 463 Beacon St 617/536–1302 • gay-friendly • nonsmoking • WiFi • gay- & straight-owned • $79-169

Beacon Hill Hotel & Bistro 25 Charles St (at Chestnut St) 617/723-7575 • gay/ straight • food served • WiFi • $215-445

Carolyn's B&B 102 Holworthy St (at Huron Ave), Cambridge 617/864–7042 • gay-friendly • near Harvard Square • nonsmoking • women-owned • $115-150

► **Chandler Inn** 26 Chandler St (at Berkeley) 617/482–3450, 800/842–3450 • gay-friendly • European-style inn • centrally located • nonsmoking • WiFi • $100-180

The Charles Hotel 1 Bennett St (at Eliot), Cambridge 617/864–1200, 800/882–1818 • gay-friendly • in Harvard Square • also restaurants & bar

The Charles Street Inn 94 Charles St (at Mount Vernon, Beacon Hill) 617/314–8900, 877/772–8900 • gay/ straight • kids/ pets ok • nonsmoking • wheelchair access • lesbian-owned • $250-550

Clarendon Square Inn 198 W Brookline St (btwn Tremont & Columbus) 617/536–2229 • gay/ straight • restored Victorian town house • hot tub • kids ok • fireplaces • nonsmoking • WiFi • gay-owned • $155-495

The College Club 44 Commonwealth Ave (at Berkeley St) 617/536–9510 • gay-friendly • B&B in Back Bay • some shared baths • kids ok • nonsmoking • WiFi • wheelchair access • $79-259

Encore B&B 116 W Newton St (at Tremont) 617/247–3425 • gay-friendly • 19th-c town house in Boston's historic South End • nonsmoking • gay-owned • $140-240

Fifteen Beacon Hotel 15 Beacon St (at Somerset) 617/670–1500, 877/982–3226 • gay-friendly • in 1903 Beaux Arts bldg • pets/kids ok

► **Holiday Inn Express & Suites Boston Garden** 280 Friend St (at Causeway) 617/720–5544 • gay-friendly • WiFi • nonsmoking • $109-359 • wheelchair access

Hotel 140 140 Clarendon St (at Stuart St) 617/585–5600 • gay/ straight • boutique hotel • near Copley Square • nonsmoking • wheelchair access • women-owned • $99-399

Hotel Onyx 155 Portland St (at Causeway) 617/557–9955, 866/660–6699 • gay-friendly • kids/ pets ok • WiFi • nonsmoking

The Liberty Hotel 215 Charles St (at Cambridge) 617/224–4000, 866/507–5245 • gay-friendly • in the former Charles St Jail • full brkfst • nonsmoking • WiFi • wheelchair access • $295

Nine Zero Hotel 90 Tremont St (at Bosworth) 617/772–5800, 866/646–3937 • gay-friendly • luxury hotel • full brkfst • jacuzzi • kids/ pets ok • nonsmoking • wheelchair access • $249-3,000

➤ **Oasis Guest House** 22 Edgerly Rd (at Westland) 617/267–2262, 800/230–0105 • popular • gay/ straight • Back Bay location • some shared baths • nonsmoking • WiFi • wheelchair access • gay-owned • $79-179

Victorian B&B 617/536–3285 • women only • full brkfst • nonsmoking • kids ok • WiFi • lesbian-owned • $97

Whitman House Inn 17 Worcester St (at Norfolk St), Cambridge 617/945–5350, 617/913–6189 • gay/straight • nonsmoking • WiFi • gay-owned • $150-195

BARS

Boston Ramrod 1254 Boylston St (at Ipswich, 1 block from Fenway Park) 617/266–2986 • noon-2am • popular • mostly gay men • leather • dress code Fri-Sat • dancing/DJ • game room • wheelchair access

➤ **Club Cafe Bistro, Bar & Nightclub** 209 Columbus (at Berkeley) 617/536–0966 • 4pm-2am, from noon Fri-Sat, Sun brunch from 11am • popular • lesbians/ gay men • upscale • dancing/DJ • karaoke • piano bar • live shows • videos • 3 bars • wheelchair access

Dyke Night 284 Amory St (at Milky Way Lounge), Jamaica Plain 617/524–3740 • 9pm 4th Fri • mostly women • dancing/DJ

Encore 275 Tremont St (at Stuart St, in hotel) 617/728–2162 • 5pm-2am • lounge & cabaret • gay/ straight • live entertainment • wheelchair access

➤ **Fritz** 26 Chandler St (in the Chandler Inn) 617/482–4428 • noon-2am, Sat-Sun brunch • lesbians/ gay men • neighborhood sports bar • wheelchair access

Jacque's 79 Broadway (at Stuart) 617/426–8902 • 11am-midnight, from noon Sun • mostly gay men • popular • drag cabaret • cover charge

Milky Way Lounge & Lanes 284 Amory St, Jamaica Plain 617/524–3740 • 6pm-1am • gay/ straight • food served • theme nights • live music • poetry readings • karaoke • bowling • also restaurant

Ryles 212 Hampshire St (at Cambridge St, in Inman Square), Cambridge **617/876–9330** • gay/ straight • live shows • great wknd jazz brunch

Sexy & Sophisticated 284 Amory St (at Milky Way), Jamaica Plain **617/524–3740** • 9pm 2nd Th only • mostly women • dancing/DJ • multiracial

Sister Sorel/ Tremont 647 647 Tremont (at W Brookline) **617/266–4600** • lesbians/gay men • dinner only, wknd brunch • wheelchair access

NIGHTCLUBS

Blush Boston 105 Canal St (Hideaway at Anthony's), Malden **617/877–1808** • 7pm Sat only, from 8pm winter • mostly women • dancing/DJ • food served • live shows

dbar 1236 Dorchester Ave (at Hancock St), Dorchester **617/265–4490** • 5pm-2am, from 11:30am Sun • gay/ straight • also restaurant • dinner nightly

Dyke Night Productions • special events in various locations • mostly women • dancing/DJ • live shows • younger crowd • wheelchair access • check www.dykenight.com for info

Epic Saturday 15 Lansdowne St **617/338–7699** • 10:30pm Sat only • mostly gay men • dancing/DJ

The Estate 1 Boylston Pl (at The Alley) **617/536–2100** • gay Th only for Glam Life • mostly gay men • dancing/DJ

The Glam Life 1 Boylston Pl (at Estate) **617/351–7000** • Th only • lesbians/ gay men • dancing/DJ • hip-hop • 19+ • cover charge

Hot Mess Sundays 275 Tremont St (at Stuart St, at Underbar) **617/292–0080** • Sun only • mostly gay men • dancing/DJ

Machine 1254 Boylston St (at Park, below Boston Ramrod) **617/536–1950** • 10pm-2am • popular • mostly gay men • women's night 2nd Sat • dancing/DJ • go-go boys • wheelchair access

The Middle East 472 Massachusetts Ave (in Central Square), Cambridge **617/497–0576** • 11am-1am, till 2am wknds • gay-friendly • alternative • live music • young crowd • cover charge • also restaurant

Midway Cafe 3496 Washington St (at William), Jamaica Plain **617/524–9038** • gay/ straight • mostly women Th • dancing/DJ • theme nights • karaoke • live shows

➤**Napoleon Cabaret** 209 Columbus (at Club Cafe) **617/536-0966** • nightly piano & vocals • also restaurant • wheelchair access

CAFES

1369 Cafe 757 Massachusetts Ave (in Central Square), Cambridge **617/576-4600** • 7am-11pm, from 7:30am Sun • also 1369 Cambridge St (Inman Square), 617/576-1369

Berkeley Perk 69 Berkeley St (at Chandler) **617/426-7375** • 6:30am-5pm, from 7:30am Sun • food served • wheelchair access • gay-owned

Diesel Cafe 257 Elm St (in Davis Square), Somerville **617/629-8717** • 6am-11pm, from 7am wknds • pool tables • lesbian-owned • wheelchair access

Fiore's Bakery 55 South St (at Bardwell), Jamaica Plain **617/524-9200** • 7am-7pm, 8am-6pm wknds • some vegan • gay-owned

Francesca's 564 Tremont St (at Clarendon) **617/482-9026** • 8am-11pm • wheelchair access

JP Licks 352 Newbury St (at Massachusetts Ave) **617/236-1666** • "homemade ice cream cafe"—& yes, they serve coffee too • wheelchair access

South End Buttery 314 Shawmut Ave (at Union Park St) **617/482-1015** • cupcakes! also brkfst, lunch & dinner • full bar • wheelchair access

True Grounds 717 Broadway (at Boston Ave), Somerville **617/591-9559** • 7am-9pm, from 8am wknds • brkfst, lunch • live shows • WiFi • wheelchair access

RESTAURANTS

28 Degrees 1 Appleton St (at Tremont St) **617/728-0728** • upscale restaurant & lounge

BarLola 160 Commonwealth Ave (at Dartmouth) **617/266-1122** • 2pm-2am, from 2pm wknds • tapas lounge • flamenco performed Sun • gay-owned

Boston Pita Pit 479 Harvard St (at Commonwealth), Brookline **617/738-7482** • 10:30am-midnight, till 2:30am wknds • lesbian-owned • wheelchair access

Casa Romero 30 Gloucester St (at Commonwealth) **617/536-4341** • dinner • Mexican • also bar

Charlie's Sandwich Shoppe 429 Columbus Ave (at Pembroke St) **617/536-7669** • great brkfst, clsd Sun • wheelchair access

City Girl Cafe 204 Hampshire St (at Inman), Cambridge **617/864-2809** • 11am-10pm, from 10am Sat-Sun, clsd Mon • Italian • great sandwiches • lesbian-owned

➤ **Club Cafe** 209 Columbus (adjacent to Club Cafe) **617/536-0966** • dinner & Sun brunch • popular • some veggie • also 3 bars • piano • videos • wheelchair access

Geoffrey's Cafe 142 Berkeley St (at Columbus Ave) **617/424-6711** • 11am-midnight, from 10am wknds • popular Disco brunch

Johnny D's Restaurant & Music Club 17 Holland St (in Davis Square), Somerville **617/776-2004** • 12:30pm-1am, from 9am wknds • live music • wheelchair access

My Thai Cafe 3 Beach St, 2nd flr (at Washington) **617/451-2395** • 11am-10pm, till 11pm Fri-Sat • Asian • vegetarian/vegan

Rabia's 73 Salem St (at Cross St) **617/227-6637** • 11am-10:30pm • fine Italian • wheelchair access

Ristorante Lucia 415 Hanover St (at Harris) **617/367-2353** • lunch & dinner • great North End pasta • wheelchair access

Boston

WHERE THE GIRLS ARE:
Sipping coffee and reading somewhere in Cambridge or Harvard Square, strolling the South End near Columbus & Mass. Avenues, or hanging out in the Fenway or Jamaica Plain.

ENTERTAINMENT:
Gay Men's Chorus 617/542-7464, web: www.bgmc.org.
The Theatre Offensive 617/621-6090, web: www.thetheateroffensive.org.

LGBT PRIDE:
June. 617/262-9405, web: www.bostonpride.org.

ANNUAL EVENTS:
May - Gay & Lesbian Film/Video Festival 617/369-3300 (Museum of Fine Arts #).

CITY INFO:
Greater Boston Convention & Visitors Bureau 888/733-2678, web: www.bostonusa.com.

WEATHER:
Extreme—from freezing winters to boiling summers with a beautiful spring and fall.

TRANSIT:
Boston Cab 617/536-5010, web: www.bostoncab.us.
Metro Cab, web: www.bostoncab.com.
MBTA (the "T") 800/392-6100, web: www.mbta.com.

ATTRACTIONS:
Beacon Hill, web: www.beaconhillonline.com.
Black Heritage Trail, web: www.afroammuseum.org/trail.htm.
Boston Common.
Faneuil Hall, web: www.faneuilhall.com.
Freedom Trail 617/242-5642, web: www.thefreedomtrail.org.
Harvard University, web: www.harvard.edu.
Isabella Stewart Gardner Museum 617/566-1401, web: www.gardnermuseum.org.
Museum of African American History 617/725-0022, web: www.afroammuseum.org.
Museum of Fine Arts 617/267-9300, web: www.mfa.org.
Museum of Science 617/723-2500, web: www.mos.org.
New England Aquarium 617/973-5200, web: www.neaq.org.
Old North Church 617/523-6676, web: www.oldnorth.com.
Walden Pond, web: www.mass.gov/dcr/parks/northeast/wldn.htm.

Stella 1525 Washington St (at W Brookline) 617/247–7747 • dinner & Sun brunch, full bar till 2am • also cafe 7am-3pm • WiFi • wheelchair access

Trattoria Pulcinella 147 Huron Ave (at Concord), Cambridge 617/491–6336 • 5pm-10pm • fine Italian

Veggie Planet 47 Palmer St (at Club Passim), Cambridge 617/661–1513 • 11:30am-10:30pm • live music venue nights

ENTERTAINMENT & RECREATION

Boston Derby Dames • Boston's female roller derby league • visit www.bostonderbydames.com for events

Freedom Trail 617/357–8300 • start at the Visitor Information Center in Boston Common (at Tremont & West Sts), the most famous cow pasture & oldest public park in the US, then follow the red line to some of Boston's most famous sites

Jamaica Pond • great girl-watching

New Repertory Theatre 321 Arsenal St, Watertown 617/923–8487 (BOX OFFICE), 617/923–7060

Urban AdvenTours 103 Atlantic Ave (at Richmond St) 617/670–0637, 800/979–3370 • guided bike tours of Boston & bike rentals

BOOKSTORES

Calamus Bookstore 92-B South St 617/338–1931, 888/800–7300 • 9am-7pm, noon-6pm • complete GLBT bookstore

The Globe Corner Bookstore 90 Mt Auburn (Harvard Square), Cambridge 617/497–6277, 800/358–6013 • travel books & maps

Trident Booksellers & Cafe 338 Newbury St (off Mass Ave) 617/267–8688 • 8am-midnight • good magazine browsing • also restaurant • beer/ wine • WiFi • wheelchair access

PUBLICATIONS

Bay Windows 617/464–7280 • LGBT newspaper

EROTICA

Good Vibrations 308 Harvard St, Brookline 617/264–4400 • noon-7pm, till 8pm Th-Sat • clean, well-lighted sex toy store • workshops & events • wheelchair access

Hubba Hubba 534 Massachusetts Ave (at Brookline, in Central Square), Cambridge 617/492–9082 • fetish gear

ClubCafe
DINE DRINK DANCE

209 COLUMBUS AVE.
IN BOSTON, MA USA
617 536 0966
CLUBCAFE.COM

Cambridge

see Boston

Cape Cod

see also Provincetown listings

INFO LINES & SERVICES

Gay/ Lesbian AA 508/775-7060 • call for info

ACCOMMODATIONS

The Colonial House Inn & Restaurant 277 Main St, Rte 6A, Yarmouthport **508/362-4348, 800/999-3416** • gay-friendly • dinner & light brkfst included • pool • jacuzzi • also restaurant & lounge • nonsmoking • WiFi • $100-155

Josiah Sampson House 40 Old Kings Rd, Cotuit **508/428-8383** • gay-friendly • 1793 Federal-style house on Nat'l Register of Historic Places • some fireplaces • nonsmoking • WiFi • $129-199

Lamb & Lion Inn 2504 Main St (Rte 6A), Barnstable **508/362-6823, 800/909-6923** • gay-friendly • pool • pets ok • WiFi • $110-349

Night Heron Cottage B&B 35 Lucinda Ct, Eastham **508/255-7063, 845/797-1737** • gay-friendly • near birding, beaches, kayaking & canoeing • nonsmoking • WiFi • lesbian-owned • $130-240

White Swan B&B 146 Manomet Point Rd, Plymouth **508/224-3759** • gay-friendly • in 200-year-old farmhouse • open year-round • at mouth of Cape Cod • nonsmoking • WiFi • $120-165

Woods Hole Passage 186 Woods Hole Rd, Falmouth **508/548-9575, 800/790-8976** • gay-friendly • full brkfst • non-smoking • WiFi • $139-199

Chelsea

see Boston

Greenfield

ACCOMMODATIONS

Brandt House 29 Highland Ave 413/774-3329, 800/235-3329 • gay-friendly • 16-rm estate on hill • full brkfst • kids ok • nonsmoking • WiFi • $95-295

The Charlemont Inn Rte 2, Mohawk Trail, Charlemont 413/339-5391 • gay-friendly • kids/ pets ok • nonsmoking • $75-105 • also restaurant • full bar • live music Sat • lesbian-owned

RESTAURANTS

Hope & Olive 44 Hope St 413/774-3150 • lunch & dinner, clsd Mon

BOOKSTORES

World Eye Bookshop 156 Main St (at Miles St) 413/772-2186 • 9:30am-6:30pm, 9am-5pm Sat, 11am-4pm Sun • general • LGBT section • community bulletin board • women-owned

Haverhill

NIGHTCLUBS

Click Saturdays 717 S Main St (at Club Irge) • mostly women • dancing/DJ

Club Irge 717 S Main St • Th-Sat only • lesbians/ gay men • more women Sat

CAFES

Wicked Big Cafe 19 Essex St (at Wingate) 978/556-5656 • 7am-4pm, 8am-1pm Sat, clsd Sun • coffee house w/ excellent food • WiFi • wheelchair access • lesbian-owned

Lenox

see Berkshires

Lynn

BARS

Fran's Place 776 Washington St (at Sagamore) 781/598-5618 • 3pm-1am • lesbians/ gay men • dancing/DJ • also sports bar • wheelchair access

The Pub at 47 Central 47 Central Ave 781/586-0551 • 2pm-1am • lesbians/ gay men • neighborhood bar • dancing/DJ wknds • leather • karaoke • drag shows • videos • gay-owned

Martha's Vineyard

ACCOMMODATIONS

Arbor Inn 222 Upper Main St, Edgartown 508/627-8137, 888/748-4383 • gay-friendly • B&B • some shared baths • nonsmoking • $125-225

Martha's Vineyard Surfside Motel 7 Oak Bluffs Ave, Oak Bluffs 508/693-2500, 800/537-3007 • gay-friendly • non-smoking • jacuzzis some rooms • pets ok • WiFi • wheelchair access • $85-355

The Shiverick Inn 5 Pease's Pt Wy, Edgartown (at Pent Ln) 508/627-3797, 800/723-4292 • gay/ straight • full brkfst • nonsmoking • WiFi • gay-owned • $135-550

Restaurants

The Black Dog Tavern Beach St Extension #21 (at Water St) **508/693-9223** • brkfst, lunch & dinner, seasonal • wheelchair access

Le Grenier 96 Main St (at Drummer Ln), Vineyard Haven **508/693-4906** • lunch & dinner • French • beer/wine

Bookstores

Bunch of Grapes 44 Main St (at Center St), Vineyard Haven **508/693-2291, 800/693-0221** • 9am-6pm, till 9pm Fri & summers • some LGBT titles & magazines

New Bedford

Bars

Le Place 20 Kenyon St (at Belleville Ave) **508/990-1248** • 2pm-2am • popular • lesbians/gay men • karaoke • dancing/DJ • women-owned

Newton

see Boston

North Adams

see Berkshires

Northampton

see also Amherst

Accommodations

Clarion Hotel & Conference Center 1 Atwood Dr **413/586-1211, 800/582-2929** • gay-friendly • pool • kids ok • nonsmoking • WiFi • also restaurants & bar • wheelchair access • $119+

Corner Porches 82 Baptist Corner Rd (at Main), Ashfield **413/628-4592** • gay/ straight • 1880s farmhouse • 30 minutes from Northampton • shared bath • pets on premises • full brkfst • kids ok • nonsmoking • woman-owned • $70-85

Northampton

Where the Girls Are:
Just off Main St., browsing in the small shops, strolling down an avenue, or sipping a beverage at one of the cafes.

LGBT Pride:
May. 413/586-5602, web: www.northamptonpride.org.

Annual Events:
October - Paradise City Arts Festival 800/511-9725, web: www.paradisecityarts.com.

City Info:
413/584-1900, web: www.explorenorthampton.com.

Best View:
At the top of Skinner Mountain, up Route 47 by bus, car, or bike.

Weather:
Late summer/early fall is the best season, with warm, sunny days. Mid-summer gets to the low 90°s, while winter brings snow from November to March, with temperatures in the 20°s and 30°s.

Attractions:
Academy of Music 413/584-9032, web: www.academyofmusictheatre.com.
The Berkshires.
Emily Dickinson Homestead, Amherst 413/542-8161, web: www.emilydickinsonmuseum.org.
Historic Northampton 413/584-6011, web: www.historic-northampton.org.
Northampton Center for the Arts 413/584-7327, web: www.nohoarts.org.

Transit:
The Taxi 413/585-8259.
Peter Pan Shuttle 413/781-2900, 800/343-9999, web: www.peter-panbus.com.
Pioneer Valley Transit Authority (PVTA) 413/781-7882, web: www.pvta.com.

The Hotel Northampton 36 King St (near Bridge St) **413/584-3100, 800/547-3529** • gay-friendly • gym • cafe & historic tavern • nonsmoking • WiFi • wheelchair access • $180+

NIGHTCLUBS

Diva's 492 Pleasant St (at Conz St) **413/586-8161** • 9pm-2am, clsd Sun-Mon • lesbians/ gay men • dancing/DJ • live music • theme nights • 18+ Tue-Fri

Pearl Street 10 Pearl St (at Main) **413/586-8686** • 7pm-1am • gay/ straight • dancing/DJ • live music • young crowd

CAFES

Haymarket Cafe 185 Main St **413/586-9969** • 7am-10pm, till 11pm Fri-Sat, from 8am Sun • popular • also restaurant • wheelchair access

RESTAURANTS

Bela 68 Masonic St **413/586-8011** • noon-8:30pm, clsd Sun-Mon • vegetarian • wheelchair access • lesbian-owned

Bueno Y Sano 134 Main St (at Center St) **413/586-7311** • 11am-10pm, till 9pm Sun • Mexican

Paul & Elizabeth's 150 Main St (in Thorne's Marketplace) **413/584-4832** • lunch & dinner, Sun brunch • seafood • plenty veggie • beer/ wine • wheelchair access

ENTERTAINMENT & RECREATION

The Iron Horse 20 Center St (at Main) **413/586-8686** • 5:30pm-close • restaurant & bar • live music • all ages • nonsmoking

RETAIL SHOPS

Oh My A Sensuality Shop 122 Main St (at Center) **413/584-9669** • noon-7pm, till 8pm Fri-Sat, noon-5pm Sun • informative, helpful & intimate sex toy store

Pride & Joy 20A Crafts Ave (at Main) **413/585-0683** • open 7 days • LGBT books & gifts • wheelchair access • gay-owned

PUBLICATIONS

Metroline 860/233-8334 • regional newspaper & entertainment guide • covers CT, RI & MA

The Rainbow Times 413/282-8881, 617/444-9618 • bi-weekly LGBT news magazine for MA, northern CT & southern VT

Plymouth

ACCOMMODATIONS

Symphony Hollow B&B at the Round House 82 Mayflower Rd, Plympton **781/640-6936** • gay/ straight • 1859 historic round house • full brkfst • gay-owned • $110-140

Provincetown

see also Cape Cod listings

INFO LINES & SERVICES

Provincetown Business Guild 508/487-2313

ACCOMMODATIONS

Admiral's Landing Guest House 158 Bradford St (btwn Conwell & Pearl) **508/487-9665, 800/934-0925** • mostly gay men • 1860s Greek Revival home & studio efficiencies • WiFi • nonsmoking • $80-205

Aerie House & Beach Club 184 Bradford St (at Miller Hill) **508/487-1197, 800/487-1197** • lesbians/ gay men • hot tub • sundeck • WiFi • gay-owned • $40-330

Anchor Inn Beach House 175 Commercial St (at Winthrop) **508/487-0432, 800/858-2657** • gay/ straight • nonsmoking • private beach • wheelchair access • lesbian & straight-owned/ run • $125-400

Bayberry Accommodations 16 Winthrop St (at Commercial) **508/487-4605, 800/422-4605** • lesbians/ gay men • hot tub • nonsmoking • WiFi • gay-owned • $75-255

Bayshore 493 Commercial St (at Howland) **508/487-9133** • gay/ straight • apts • private beach • kitchens • pets ok • WiFi • nonsmoking • lesbian-owned • $95-299

Beachfront Realty 139 Commercial St **508/487-1397** • vacation rentals

Beaconlight Guest House 12 Winthrop St (at Bradford) **508/487-9603, 800/696-9603** • mostly gay men • WiFi • nonsmoking • parking • gay-owned • $115-385

Benchmark Inn 6-8 Dyer St **508/487-7440, 888/487-7440** • lesbians/ gay men • nonsmoking • WiFi • wheelchair access • gay-owned • $159-395

The Black Pearl Inn 11 & 18 Pearl St (at Bradford) **508/487-0302, 800/761-1016** • lesbians/ gay men • hot tub • nonsmoking • WiFi • "friends of Bill welcome" • $69-250

Boatslip Resort 161 Commercial St 508/487–1669, 877/786–9662 • popular • mostly gay men • resort • pool • seasonal • also several bars • popular T-dance • gay-owned

The Bradford Carver House 70 Bradford St 508/487-0728, 800/826-9083 • lesbians/gay men • restored mid-19th-c home • centrally located • nonsmoking • WiFi • gay-owned • $49-259

Bradford House & Motel 41 Bradford St (at Conant) 508/487-0173 • gay-friendly • near town center • 1 block from the beach • wheelchair access • women-owned • $95-275

Brass Key Guesthouse 67 Bradford St (at Carver) 508/487-9005, 800/842-9858 • popular • mostly gay men • hot tub • pool • nonsmoking • WiFi • wheelchair access • gay-owned • $120-659

Carpe Diem Guesthouse & Spa 12 Johnson St 508/487-4242, 800/487-0132 • lesbians/gay men • also cottage • full German brkfst • hot tub • nonsmoking • WiFi • gay-owned • $75-425

The Carriage House Guesthouse 7 Central St (at Commercial) 508/487-8855, 800/309-0248 • gay/ straight • hot tub • gay-owned • $135-345

Provincetown

WHERE THE GIRLS ARE:
In this small resort town, you can't miss 'em! At the beach, the girls gather on the left side at Herring Cove.

LGBT PRIDE:
August - Provincetown Carnival, web: ptown.org.

ANNUAL EVENTS:
August - Provincetown Carnival 800/637-8696.
October - Fantasia Fair - for trannies & their admirers, web: www.fantasiafair.org.
October - Women's Week 800/637-8696, web: www.womeninnkeepers.com. It's very popular, so make your reservations early!
December - Holly Folly, web: www.ptown.org. Gay & Lesbian Holiday Festival.

CITY INFO:
Provincetown Business Guild 508/487-2313, 800/637-8696, web: www.ptown.org.

BEST VIEW:
People-watching from an outdoor cafe or on the beach.

ATTRACTIONS:
The beach.
Galleries.
Herring Cove Beach.
Pilgrim Monument.
Provincetown Museum 508/487-1310, web: www.pilgrim-monument.org.
Whale-watching.

WEATHER:
New England weather is unpredictable. Be prepared for rain, snow, or extreme heat! Otherwise, the weather during the season consists of warm days and cooler nights.

TRANSIT:
Cape Cab 508/487-2222, web: capecabtaxi.com.
Ferry: Bay State Cruise Company (from Commonwealth/World Trade Center Pier in Boston, during summer) 877/783-3779, web: www.baystatecruisecompany.com.
Air: Cape Air 508/771-6944, 866/227–3247, web: www.flycapeair.com.

Chicago House 6 Winslow St (at Bradford) **508/487–0537, 800/733–7869** • lesbians/ gay men • rooms & apts • hot tub • some shared baths • nonsmoking • WiFi • gay-owned • $60-195

Christopher's by the Bay 8 Johnson St (at Bradford) **508/487–9263, 877/487–9263** • lesbians/ gay men • Victorian guesthouse • some shared baths • patio • nonsmoking • gay-owned

The Clarendon House 118 Bradford St (btwn Ryder & Alden) **508/487–1645, 800/669-8229** • gay/ straight • hot tub • kids ok • nonsmoking • $49-209

Crown & Anchor 247 Commercial St **508/487–1430** • lesbians/ gay men • pool • nonsmoking • WiFi • also bars • cabaret • gay-owned • $85-295

Crowne Pointe Historic Inn & Shui Spa 82 Bradford St **508/487–6767, 877/276–9631** • lesbians/ gay men • full brkfst • heated pool • nonsmoking • WiFi • wheelchair access • gay-owned • $99-627

Designer's Dock 349 Commercial St **508/776–5746, 800/724–9888** • gay/ straight • weekly condos in town & on beach • June-Sept • kitchens • WiFi • gay-owned • $800-3,000/ week

Dexter's Inn 6 Conwell St (at Railroad) **508/487–1911, 888/521–1999** • lesbians/ gay men • B&B • nonsmoking • WiFi • sundeck • gay-owned • $60-155

Enzo 186 Commercial St (at Court) **508/487–7555, 888/873–5001** • gay/ straight • WiFi • Italian restaurant & piano bar on premises • $75-225

➤ **Fairbanks Inn** 90 Bradford St **508/487–0386, 800/324–7265** • popular • lesbians/ gay men • nonsmoking • WiFi • parking • fireplaces • lesbian-owned • $100-275 • see ad

Four Gables 15 Race Rd **508/487–2427, 866/487–2427** • gay/ straight • private cottages • kids/ pets ok • gay-owned • $1,365-2,200/ week in season

Gabriel's at The Ashbrooke Inn 102 Bradford St **508/487–3232** • popular • lesbians/ gay men • full brkfst • nonsmoking • sundecks • kids/pets ok • WiFi • lesbian & gay-owned • $125-380

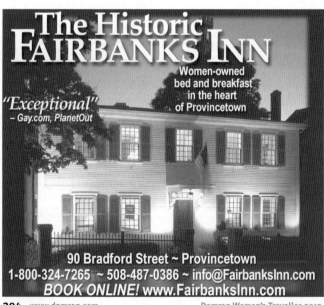

Gifford House Inn 11 Carver St **508/487-0688, 800/434-0130** • lesbians/ gay men • seasonal • WiFi • also several bars & restaurant • dinner only • seafood • gay-owned

Grand View Inn 4 Conant St (at Commercial) **508/487-9193, 888/268-9169** • lesbians/ gay men • nonsmoking • kids/ pets ok • gay-owned • $70-200

Harbor Hill at Provincetown 4 Harbor Hill Rd **508/487-0541** • gay-friendly • condo resort in West End • kids ok • gay-owned • $100-275

Heritage House 7 Center St **508/487-3692** • lesbians/ gay men • shared baths • WiFi • lesbian-owned • $100-150

The Inn at Cook Street 7 Cook St (at Bradford) **508/487-3894, 888/266-5655** • gay-friendly • nonsmoking • women owned • $120-315

➤**Inn at the Moors** 59 Provincelands Rd **508/487-1342, 800/842-6379** • gay-friendly • motel • across from Nat'l Seashore Province Lands • seasonal • nonsmoking • WiFi • pool • lesbian-owned • $109-239

John Randall House 140 Bradford St (at Center) **508/487-3533, 800/573-6700** • lesbians/ gay men • kids ok • nonsmoking • WiFi • gay-owned • $69-199

Land's End Inn 22 Commercial St **508/487-0706, 800/276-7088** • gay/ straight • nonsmoking • WiFi • gay-owned • $170-600

Lotus Guest House 296 Commercial St (at Standish) **508/487-4644, 888/508-4644** • lesbians/ gay men • seasonal • decks • garden • teens ok • WiFi • lesbian & gay-owned • $45-260

Mayflower Apartments & Cottages 6 Bangs St (at Commercial St) **508/487-1916** • gay-friendly • kitchens • $160+ nightly (studio)/ $1,200+ weekly (cottages)

Moffett House 296-A Commercial St (at Ryder) **508/487-6615, 800/990-8865** • lesbians/ gay men • gay-owned • $60-175

Pilgrim House Hotel 336 Commercial St **508/487-6424** • mostly women • seasonal • kids ok • also Vixen bar/ dance club • WiFi • wheelchair access • $129-249

Prince Albert Guest House 164-166 Commercial St (at Central) **508/487-1850** • mostly gay men • Victorian • nonsmoking • WiFi • gay-owned • $80-350

Ravenwood Guest House 462 Commercial St (at Cook) **508/487-3203** • lesbians/ gay men • also apts & cottage • nonsmoking • private beach • wheelchair accessible cottage • lesbian-owned • $85-212

The Red Inn 15 Commercial St (at Point) **508/487-7334, 866/473-3466** • gay-friendly • nonsmoking • wheelchair access • gay-owned • $135-525

Revere Guesthouse 14 Court St (btwn Commercial & Bradford) **508/487-2292, 800/487-2292** • lesbians/ gay men • nonsmoking • gay-owned • $155-375

Rose Acre 5 Center St (at Commercial) **508/487-2347** • women only • suites • also apts & cottage • nonsmoking • decks • gardens • parking • always open • WiFi • women-owned • $125-250

Rose & Crown Guest House 158 Commercial St (at Central) **508/487-3332** • gay/ straight • lesbian-owned • $55-285

Sandbars 570 Shore Rd, Beach Pt, North Truro **508/487-8700** • gay/ straight • private beach • $89-219

Seasons, An Inn for All 160 Bradford St (at Pearl) **508/487-2283, 800/563-0113** • lesbians/ gay men • Victorian B&B • full brkfst • nonsmoking • WiFi • gay-owned • $80-179

The Secret Garden Inn 300-A Commercial St **508/487-9027, 866/786-9646** • lesbians/ gay men • kids ok • nonsmoking • $60-175

Snug Cottage 178 Bradford St **508/487-1616, 800/432-2334** • gay/ straight • nonsmoking • WiFi • gay-owned • $95-259

Somerset House 378 Commercial St (at Pearl) **508/487-0383, 800/575-1850** • lesbians/ gay men • Victorian mansion • nonsmoking • WiFi • gay-owned • $75-299

Sunset Inn 142 Bradford St (at Center) **508/487-9810, 800/965-1801** • lesbians/ gay men • some shared baths • seasonal • clothing-optional sundeck • nonsmoking • WiFi • gay-owned

Surfside Hotel & Suites 543 Commercial (at Kendall Ln) **508/487-1726, 800/421-1726** • gay/ straight • waterfront hotel • lots of amenities • private beach • pool • nonsmoking • WiFi • kids/ pets ok • gay-owned • $139-329

The Tucker Inn 12 Center St (at Bradford) **508/487-0381, 800/477-1867** • lesbians/ gay men • full brkfst • WiFi • also cottage • nonsmoking • gay-owned • $125-245

Victoria House 5 Standish St **508/487-4455, 877/867-8696** • lesbians/ gay men • WiFi • nonsmoking • gay-owned • $95-200

The Waterford 386 Commercial St (at Pearl) **508/487-6400, 800/487-0784** • gay/ straight • deck w/ full bar • also restaurant • $165-275

Watermark Inn 603 Commercial St **508/487-0165** • gay/ straight • kids ok • nonsmoking • WiFi • $85-490

Watership Inn 7 Winthrop St **508/487-0094, 800/330-9413** • mostly gay men • sundeck • WiFi • gay-owned

White Wind Inn 174 Commercial St (at Winthrop) **508/487-1526, 888/449-9463** • lesbians/ gay men • WiFi • gay-owned • $95-275

➤**Women Innkeepers of Provincetown** PO Box 573, 02657 • women-owned accommodations in Provincetown

BARS

The Boatslip Resort 161 Commercial St **508/487-1669, 877/786-9662** • seasonal • popular • lesbians/ gay men • T-dance 4pm daily during season • young crowd • swimming • outdoor/ waterfront grill

Governor Bradford 312 Commercial St (at Standish) **508/487-2781** • 11am-1am, from noon Sun • gay-friendly • "drag karaoke" Sat (nightly in season) • also restaurant in summer

PiedBar 193-A Commercial St (at Court St) **508/487-1527** • seasonal May-Oct, noon-1am • popular • lesbians/ gay men • dancing/DJ • more women Fri-Sat • wheelchair access

Porchside Lounge 11 Carver St (in the Gifford House) **508/487-0688** • 5pm-1am • mostly gay men • neighborhood bar • also restaurant

Shipwreck Lounge 10 Carver St (at Bradford) **508/487-9005** • lesbians/ gay men • upscale lounge • outdoor seating w/ fire pit

Vixen/ Madeira Room 336 Commercial St (at Pilgrim House Inn) **508/487-6424** • noon-1am • mostly women • dancing/DJ • late night food • also wine bar • live shows • videos

Wave Video Bar 247 Commercial St (in the Crown & Anchor) **508/487-1430** • noon-1am, from noon in season • lesbians/ gay men • neighborhood bar • karaoke • T-dance Sun

NIGHTCLUBS

Atlantic House (The "A-House") 6 Masonic Pl **508/487-3169** • 10pm-1am • popular • mostly gay men• neighborhood bar • 3 bars • dancing/DJ • theme parties

Club Purgatory 9-11 Carver St (at Bradford St, in the Gifford House) **508/487-8442** • opens 7pm, from 9pm Sun (in season) • lesbians/ gay men • dancing/DJ

➤ **Girl Power** 193–A Commercial St (at The PiedBar) **508/487-1527** • 9:30pm-close, Fri-Sat only, seasonal • mostly women • dancing/DJ • check www.girlpowerevents.com for events • see ad in front color section

Paramount in the Crown & Anchor **508/487-1430** • 10:30pm-1am (seasonal) • popular • lesbians/ gay men • dancing/DJ • live shows • drag shows • cabaret

CAFES

Post Office Cafe Cabaret 303 Commercial St (upstairs) **508/487-3892** • 8am-11pm, seasonal hours • lesbians/ gay men • some veggie

RESTAURANTS

Bayside Betsy's 177 Commercial St **508/487-6566** • lunch & dinner, brkfst wknds, bar till 10pm • on waterfront • wheelchair access

Big Daddy's Burritos 205 Commercial St **508/487-4432** • 11am-10pm (May-Oct) • Tex-Mex, burritos, veggie wraps, salads & nachos

Bubala's by the Bay 183–185 Commercial **508/487-0773** • brunch & dinner • popular • seasonal • patio

Ciro & Sal's 4 Kiley Ct (btwn Bangs St & Lovett's Ct) **508/487-6444** • dinner from 5:30pm • Northern Italian • reservations recommended

Fanizzi's 539 Commercial St (at Kendall Lane) **508/487-1964** • popular • lunch & dinner • some veggie • full bar • on the water • wheelchair access

Front Street Restaurant 230 Commercial St **508/487-9715** • 6pm-10:30pm, bar till 1am • bistro beer/ wine • seasonal

Lobster Pot harborside (at 321 Commercial St) **508/487-0842** • 11:30am-10pm (April-Nov) • "a Provincetown tradition" • wheelchair access

Lorraine's 133 Commercial St (at Pleasant) **508/487-6074** • dinner, clsd Mon-Th off-season • popular • lesbians/ gay men • Mexican • some veggie • full bar • woman-owned

The Mews Restaurant & Cafe 429 Commercial St (btwn Lovett's & Kiley) **508/487-1500** • dinner • Sun brunch • popular • live shows • wheelchair access • waterfront dining

Napi's Restaurant 7 Freeman St **508/487-1145, 800/571-6274** • dinner • lunch Oct-April • int'l/ seafood • plenty veggie • wheelchair access

The Red Inn 15 Commercial St (at Point) **508/487-7334, 866/473-3466** • dinner nightly, brunch Th-Sun, clsd Jan-April • reservations a must • full bar

Relish 93 Commercial St **508/487-8077** • yummy baked goods • pick up a sandwich on the way to the beach!

Spiritus Pizza 190 Commercial St **508/487-2808** • noon-2am • popular • great espresso shakes & late-night hangout for a slice

ENTERTAINMENT & RECREATION

Art House Theatre & Cafe 214 Commercial St **508/487-9222**

Art's Dune Tours 4 Standish St **508/487-1950, 800/894-1951** • day trips, sunset tours & charters through historic sand dunes & Nat'l Seashore Park • kids ok • gay-owned

Dolphin Fleet Whale Watch 305 Commercial St **508/240-3636, 800/826-9300** • gay-friendly • 3-hr day & evening cruises • full galley & bar on board • wheelchair access

Herring Cove Beach

Ptown Bikes 42 Bradford **508/487-8735** • 9am-6pm • rentals • gay-owned

Spaghetti Strip • nude beach • 1.5 miles south of Race Point Beach

BOOKSTORES

Now, Voyager Bookstore & Gallery 357 Commercial St **508/487-0848** • 10am-10pm (summers) • LGBT & general books • cards

RETAIL SHOPS

HRC Action Center & Store 209-211 Commercial St **508/487-7736** • 10am-9pm, till 10pm wknds • Human Rights Campaign merchandise & info

Piercings by the Bearded Lady 336 Commercial St #4 **508/487-7979** • noon-8pm • seasonal • lesbian-owned

Recovering Hearts 4 Standish St **508/487-4875** • 10am-11pm (in summer), call for off-season hours • recovery • LGBT & New Age books • wheelchair access

➤ **Womencrafts** 376 Commercial St **508/487-2501** • 11am-10pm (in summer), call for off-season hours • women-crafted jewelry, porcelain, pottery, glass, sculpture, mosaics, photographs, books, CDs & DVDs

PUBLICATIONS

Provincetown Banner 167 Commercial St **508/487-7400** • newspaper

Provincetown Magazine **508/487-1000** • seasonal • Provincetown's oldest weekly magazine

GYMS & HEALTH CLUBS

Mussel Beach Health Club 35 Bradford St (btwn Montello & Conant) **508/487-0001** • 6am-9pm, till 8pm in winter • lesbians/ gay men

Provincetown Gym 82 Shank Painter Rd (at Winthrop) **508/487-2776** • 6am-9pm, 7am-7pm wknds (till 9pm in season)

EROTICA

MG Leather Inc 338 Commercial St (at Standish St) **508/487-4036** • leather • fetish • toys • gifts • gay-owned

Quincy

see also Boston

NIGHTCLUBS

My House 609 Washington St (at Cleverly Ct) **617/302-4285** • 6pm-1am • lesbians/ gay men • dancing/DJ • food served • karaoke

Randolph

BARS

Randolph Country Club/ RCC 44 Mazzeo Dr **781/961-2414** • 2pm-2am, from 10am summer • popular • lesbians/ gay men • dancing/DJ • food served • live shows • karaoke • male dancers • videos • volleyball court • pool • wheelchair access

Salisbury

BARS

Hobo's Club & Cafe 5 Broadway **978/465-4626** • lesbians/ gay men • neighborhood bar • food seved • karaoke • gay-owned

Shelburne Falls

RESTAURANTS

Cafe Martin 24 Bridge St (at Water St)
413/625–2795 • 4pm-9pm, brunch Sun, clsd
Mon • full bar • wheelchair access • gay-
owned

Somerville

see Boston

Springfield

BARS

Pure 234 Chestnut St (E of Main)
413/205–1483 • noon-2am • mostly gay men
• neighborhood bar • food served •
wheelchair access

NIGHTCLUBS

Oz Nightclub 397 Dwight St (at Taylor)
413/732–4562 • 7pm-2am, clsd Sun-Mon •
neighborhood bar • dancing/DJ • karaoke

Xstatic 240 Chestnut St (at Liberty)
413/736–2618, 800/710–2618 • 7pm-2am,
from 1pm wknds • mostly gay men •
dancing/DJ • strippers/ nude dancers

Taunton

BARS

Bobby's Place 62 Weir St (at Route 44, 138
& 140, at Taunton Green) **508/824–9997** •
5pm-1am, till 2am Fri-Sat, from 2pm Sun •
lesbians/ gay men • dancing/DJ • food served •
karaoke • drag shows

Williamstown

see Berkshires

Worcester

INFO LINES & SERVICES

AA Gay/ Lesbian 100 Grove St #314 (St
Mark's Episcopal Church) **508/752–9000** •
7pm Sat • nonsmoking

BARS

MB Lounge 40 Grafton St (at Franklin)
508/799–4521 • 5pm-2am from 3pm Fri-Sun •
lesbians/ gay men • neighborhood bar • WiFi
• wheelchair access • gay-owned

NIGHTCLUBS

Blu Ultralounge & Nightclub 105 Water St
(at Harrison) **508/756–2227** • 7:30pm-2am,
from 9pm Sat, clsd Mon-Tue • mostly men
• dancing/DJ • karaoke

Envy Nightclub 63 Jackson St (at
Southbridge) **508/263–0279** • lesbians/ gay
men • dancing/DJ • drag shows

RESTAURANTS

86 Winter Street 65 Water St (at Harrison)
508/459–5400 • lunch Wed-Fri, dinner Wed-
Sun, clsd Mon • wheelchair access • gay-
owned

RETAIL SHOPS

Glamour Boutique 850 Southbridge St,
Auburn **508/721–7800** • noon-8pm, 3pm-
6pm Sun • large-size dresses, wigs, etc

PUBLICATIONS

Central Mass Pride Magazine
centralmasspridemag.com

MICHIGAN

Statewide

PUBLICATIONS

Out Post 313/702–0272 • bi-weekly nightlife
guide for SE Michigan

What Helen Heard PO Box 811, East
Lansing 48826 **517/371–5257** • what's
happening for MI lesbians

Ann Arbor

INFO LINES & SERVICES

Lesbian/ Gay AA 734/482–5700

BARS

\aut\ Bar 315 Braun Ct (at Catherine)
734/994–3677 • 4pm-2am • popular •
lesbians/ gay men • also restaurant (dinner &
wknd brunch) • American/ Mexican • some
veggie • patio • wheelchair access

NIGHTCLUBS

The Necto 516 E Liberty (at Maynard)
734/994–5436 • 9pm-2am • gay/ straight •
dancing/DJ • videos • young crowd • 18+ •
theme nights • gay night Fri

CAFES

Cafe Verde 214 N Fourth Ave (at Catherine
St) **734/994–9174** • 7am-9:30pm, 9am-8pm
Sun • fair trade & organic coffee & tea • also
soups, sandwiches & salads

RESTAURANTS

Dominick's 812 Monroe St (at Tappan Ave)
734/662–5414 • 10am-10pm, clsd Sun •
Italian • beer/ wine • wheelchair access

The Earle 121 W Washington (at Ashley) **734/994-0211** • 5:30pm-10pm, till 11:30pm Fri-Sat, 5pm-9pm Sun • cont'l • some veggie • beer/ wine • wheelchair access

Seva 314 E Liberty (at 5th Ave) **734/662-1111** • 11am-9pm, from 10am wknds • vegetarian • also cafe & wine bar

Zingerman's Delicatessen 422 Detroit St (at Kingsley) **734/663-3354, 888/636-8162** • 7am-10pm • also ship food worldwide

Entertainment & Recreation

The Ark 316 S Main St (btwn William & Liberty) **734/761-1818, 734/761-1800** • gay-friendly • concert house • women's music shows

Bookstores

Common Language 317 Braun Ct (at 4th) **734/663-0036** • 11am-10pm, till midnight Fri-Sat, till 7pm Sun • LGBT • wheelchair access

Crazy Wisdom Books 114 S Main St (btwn Huron & Washington) **734/665-2757** • 10am-10pm, till 11pm Wed-Sat, 11am-6pm Sun • holistic & metaphysical • live music

Nicola's Books 2513 Jackson Ave (at Maple, in Westgate) **734/662-0600** • 9am-9pm, till 6pm Sun

Battle Creek

Nightclubs

Partners 910 North Ave (at Morgan) **269/964-7276** • 7pm-2am, clsd Mon • lesbians/ gay men • dancing/DJ • karaoke • wheelchair access

Erotica

Romantix Adult Superstore 690 W Michigan Ave (at Grand) **269/964-3070**

Bay City

Bars

Malickey's Pub 501 S Madison **989/414-6667** • 11:30am-1:30am • gay/ straight • food served • drag shows

Bellaire

Accommodations

Applesauce Inn B&B 7296 S M-88 **231/533-6448** • gay-friendly • B&B in 100-year-old farmhouse • dog-friendly • WiFi • nonsmoking • $95-150

Bellaire B&B 212 Park St (at Antrim) **231/533-6077, 800/545-0780** • gay/ straight • stately 1879 home • full brkfst • jacuzzi • nonsmoking • WiFi • gay-owned • $68-240

Big Bay

Accommodations

Big Bay Depot Motel **906/345-9350** • gay-friendly • overlooking Lake Independence • kids/ pets ok • lesbian-owned • $75

Coldwater

Erotica

The Lion's Den Adult Superstore 570 Jonesville Rd (exit 16, off I-69) **517/278-9577** • 24hrs

Copemish

Accommodations

Jeralan's Farm B&B 18361 Viaduct Rd (at Simpson Rd) **231/378-2926, 866/250-8444** • gay-friendly • 1872 farmhouse on 80 acres of woods & ponds • full brkfst • nonsmoking • $110-160

Detroit

Info Lines & Services

Affirmations Lesbian/ Gay Community Center 290 W 9 Mile Rd (at Allen), Ferndale **248/398-7105, 800/398-4297** • 11am-close, 10am-10pm, clsd Sun • also cafe

Helpline 800/398-4297 • 4pm-9pm Tue-Sat • support & resources line

Accommodations

The Atheneum Suite Hotel 1000 Brush Ave (at Lafayette) **313/962-2323, 800/772-2323** • gay-friendly • restaurant & lounge • gym • WiFi • wheelchair access

Detroit Marriott at the Renaissance Center 400 Renaissance Center Dr **313/568-8000, 800/228-9290** • gay-friendly • wheelchair access

Milner Hotel 1538 Centre St (at Grand River Ave) **313/963-3950, 877/645-6377** • gay-friendly • downtown

Bars

Centaur Bar 2233 Park Ave (at W Montcalm St) **313/963-4040** • 4pm-2am • gay/straight • sports bar • food served

Club Gold Coast 2971 E 7 Mile Rd (at Conant) **313/366-6135** • 7pm-2am • popular • mostly gay men • dancing/DJ • male dancers nightly • WiFi • wheelchair access

Gigi's 16920 W Warren (at Clayburn, enter rear) **313/584-6525** • noon-2am, from 2pm wknds • mostly gay men • dancing/DJ • transgender-friendly • male dancers Mon & Fri • drag shows • gay-owned

Menjo's 928 W McNichols Rd (at Hamilton) 313/863-3934 • 1pm-2am, popular happy hour • mostly gay men • dancing/DJ • karaoke • live shows • videos • young crowd

Pronto 608 S Washington (at 6th St), Royal Oak 248/544-7900 • 11am-2am Wed-Sat • popular • lesbians/ gay men • patio • also restaurant

Soho 205 W 9 Mile (at Woodward), Ferndale 248/542-7646 • 4pm-close, from 6pm wknds • lesbians/ gay men • karaoke • swank cocktail lounge

Stingers Lounge 19404 Sherwood (at 7 Mile) 313/892-1765 • 10pm-5am • lesbians/ gay men • neighborhood bar • drag shows • grill menu • gay-owned

The Woodward Video Bar & Grill 6426 Woodward Ave (at Milwaukee, rear entrance) 313/872-0166 • 2pm-2am • mostly gay men • DJ Th-Sun • karaoke • videos

NIGHTCLUBS

Leland City Club 400 Bagley St (at Leland Hotel) 313/962-2300 • 10pm-4:30am Fri-Sat • gay-friendly • dancing/DJ • goth/ alternative • 18+

Luna 1815 N Main St (at 12 Mile), Royal Oak 248/589-3344 • from 9pm, clsd Sun-Tue • gay-friendly • dancing/DJ • theme nights

The Rainbow Room 6640 E 8 Mile Rd (at Sherwood) 313/891-1020 • 7pm-2am Wed-Sun • lesbians/ gay men • dancing/DJ • drag shows • karaoke • 18+

Stiletto's 1641 Middlebelt Rd (btwn Michigan Ave & Cherry Hill Rd), Inkster 734/729-8980 • 8pm-2am Th-Sun • lesbians/ gay men • dancing/DJ • drag shows • karaoke

Temple 2906 Cass Ave (btwn Charlotte & Temple) 313/832-2822 • 11am-2am • mostly gay men • dancing/DJ • transgender-friendly • mostly African American • popular wknds • wheelchair access

CAFES

Avalon International Breads 422 W Willis (at Cass) 313/832-0008 • 6am-6pm, clsd Sun-Mon • lesbian-owned

Coffee Beanery Cafe 28557 S Woodward Ave (S of 12 Mile), Berkley 248/336-9930 • 7am-11pm • WiFi

Five 15 515 S Washington St, Royal Oak 248/515-2551 • 11am-9pm, till 7pm Sun • Drag Bingo Sat • performances • art shows • WiFi

Trixie's Cafe 25925 Gratiot Ave, Roseville • noon-1am, from 6pm Sun • live entertainment & open mics

RESTAURANTS

Amici's 3249 12 Mile Rd (at Gardner Ave), Berkley 248/544-4100 • gourmet pizza & martinis

Atlas Global Bistro 3111 Woodward Ave (at Charlotte) 313/831-2241 • lunch & dinner • Sun brunch • American/ int'l • upscale

Cass Cafe 4620 Cass Ave (at Forest) 313/831-1400 • 11am-2am, 5pm-1am Sun • plenty veggie • full bar • WiFi

Coach Insignia 200 Renaissance Ctr, 71st Fl 313/567-2622 • dinner, clsd Sun, steakhouse

Como's 22812 Woodward (at 9 Mile), Ferndale 248/548-5005 • 11am-2am, till 3:30am Th-Sat • Italian • full bar • patio • wheelchair access

Elwood Bar & Grill 300 Adams (at Brush, by Comerica Park) 313/962-2337 • 11am-8pm, till 2pm Mon, clsd Sun (unless there's a Tiger's game) • Art Deco diner

Inn Season 500 E 4th St, Royal Oak 248/547-7916 • lunch & dinner • Sun brunch • clsd Mon • organic vegetarian

La Dolce Vita 17546 Woodward Ave (at McNichols) 313/865-0331 • lunch & dinner, Sun brunch, clsd Mon • lesbians/ gay men • Italian • plenty veggie • full bar • patio • wheelchair access

Laikon Cafe 569 Monroe St 313/963-7058 • 10am-midnight • authentic Greek • full bar • wheelchair access

Pete's Place Broadway Cafe 1225 Woodward Hts (at Hilton Rd), Ferndale 248/544-4215 • 3pm-10pm, brunch wknds • BYOB • WiFi • wheelchair access

Roast 1128 Washington Ave (at State St) 313/961-2500 • dinner nightly, steakhouse

Sweet Lorraine's Cafe & Bar 29101 Greenfield Rd (at 12 Mile), Southfield 248/559-5985 • 11am-10pm, till midnight Fri-Sat • popular • modern American • some veggie • wheelchair access

Traffic Jam & Snug 511 W Canfield St (at SE corner of 2nd Ave) 313/831-9470 • 11am-10:30pm, till midnight Fri-Sat, from noon Sat, till 8pm Sun • eclectic • plenty veggie • also full bar, bakery, dairy & brewery • wheelchair access

Via Nove 344 W 9 Mile Rd, Ferndale 248/336-9936 • Italian • also bar • wheelchair access

Vivio's 2460 Market St (at Napoleon St) **313/**393–1711 • lunch & dinner, clsd Sun • Italian • full bar • wheelchair access

Wolfgang Puck Grille 1777 3rd St (at the MGM Grand Hotel) **313/**465–1648 • 5pm–10pm, 9am–2pm Sat-Sun, clsd Mon-Tue

ENTERTAINMENT & RECREATION

Charles H Wright Museum of African American History 315 E Warren Ave (at Cass) **313/**494–5800

Detroit Derby Girls 37637 Five Mile Rd #311, Livonia • visit www.detroitrollerderby.com for events

Motown Historical Museum 2648 W Grand Blvd **313/**875–2264 • come see where the Motown Sound began • guided tours & gift shop

Detroit

WHERE THE GIRLS ARE:
At the bars on 8-Mile Road between I-75 and Van Dyke Ave., with the boys in Highland Park or Dearborn, or shopping in Royal Oak.

LGBT PRIDE:
June. 313/537-3323 (Triangle Foundation #), web: www.pride-fest.net.

July. Hotter Than July 888/755-9165, web: www.hotterthanjuly.com. "The Midwest's oldest black lesbian, gay, bi-affectionate and transgender pride celebration."

ANNUAL EVENTS:
End of April/early May - London Lesbian Film Festival, web: www.llff.ca. Held in London, Ontario.

August - Detroit International Jazz Festival, web: www.detroitjaz-zfest.com.

Michigan Womyn's Music Festival 231/757-4766, web: www.mich-fest.com. One of the biggest annual gatherings of lesbians on the continent, in Walhalla, in Western Michigan.

CITY INFO:
313/202-1800 or 800/338-7648, web: www.visitdetroit.com.

BEST VIEW:
From the top of the 73-story Marriott Hotel at the Renaissance Center.

WEATHER:
Be prepared for hot, humid

ATTRACTIONS:
Belle Isle Park
Detroit Institute of Arts 313/833-7900, web: www.dia.org.
Greektown.
Motown Historical Museum 313/875-2264, web: www.motownmuseum.com.
Museum of African American History 313/494-5800, web: www.maah-detroit.org.
North American Black Historical Museum in Windsor, Ontario, 800/713–6336, web: www.black-historicalmuseum.com.
Renaissance Center 313/568–5600, web: www.gmrencen.com.
summers and cold, dry winters.

TRANSIT:
Checker Cab 313/963-1000, 800/351–5466, web: www.check-ercab-det.com.
Detroit Cab 313/841–6000.
AA Airport Service 800/720–0797, web: www.metroairportservice.com.
DOT bus service 313/933-1300 & 888/336-8287 (outside 313 area code), web: www.detroittransit.org.
Detroit People Mover 313/224-2160, web: www.thepeoplemover.com.

BOOKSTORES

Just 4 Us 211 W 9 Mile Rd (at Woodward), Ferndale 248/547–5878 • 11am-8pm, till 10pm Th-Fri, till 5pm Sun • also cafe • gay-owned

RETAIL SHOPS

Royal Oak Tattoo 820 S Washington Ave (at Lincoln), Royal Oak 248/398–0052 • tattoo & piercing studio

PUBLICATIONS

Between the Lines 734/293–7200 • statewide LGBT weekly

Metra Magazine PO Box 71844, Madison Heights 48071 248/543–3500 • covers IN, IL, MI, OH, PA, WI & Ontario, Canada

EROTICA

Noir Leather 124 W 4th St (at S Center St), Royal Oak 248/541–3979 • 11am-9pm, till 10pm Fri-Sat, noon-7pm Sun • wheelchair access

Douglas

see Saugatuck

Escanaba

EROTICA

Sensual Arts Adult Bookstore 615 N Lincoln Rd (at 6th Ave N) 906/786–9020 • gay-owned

Flint

BARS

MI 2406 N Franklin Ave (at Belle Ae) 810/234–9481 • 3pm-2am • popular • lesbians/ gay men • dancing/DJ • multiracial • WiFi

Pachyderm Pub G–1408 E Hemphill Rd (btwn I-475 & Saginaw St), Burton 810/744–4960 • 3pm-2am, from 5pm wknds • lesbians/ gay men • also restaurant • dancing/DJ • karaoke • male dancers • multiracial • transgender-friendly • patio • WiFi • gay-owned

State Bar 2512 S Dort Hwy (at Lippincott) 810/767–7050 • 2pm-2am • popular • lesbians/ gay men • dancing/DJ • karaoke • wheelchair access

NIGHTCLUBS

Club Triangle 2101 S Dort (at Lippincott) 810/767–7550 • 9pm-close Wed-Sun • popular • lesbians/ gay men • dancing/DJ • male dancers • 18+

Pride Night at Purple Moon 2525 S Dort Hwy 810/424–9579 • 9pm-2am 1st Mon only • lesbians/ gay men • dancing/DJ

CAFES

The Good Beans Cafe 328 N Grand Traverse (at 1st Ave) 810/237–4663 • 7:30am-4pm, till 9pm Th-Fri, open some wknds • espresso & pastries • live shows • WiFi • gay-owned • wheelchair access

Frankfort

ACCOMMODATIONS

Wayfarer Lodgings 1912 S Scenic Hwy (M-22) 231/352–9264, 800/735–8564 • gay-friendly • cottages • near Frankfort, Lake Michigan & Betsie River • kids/ pets ok • nonsmoking • WiFi • $44/55 - 80/95

Glen Arbor

ACCOMMODATIONS

Duneswood at Sleeping Bear Dunes Nat'l Lakeshore 231/668-6789 • women only • located in northern MI • nonsmoking • lesbian-owned • $60-105

Grand Rapids

ACCOMMODATIONS

Radisson Riverfront Hotel 270 Ann St NW (at Turner Ave) 616/363–9001, 1–800/395–7046 • gay-friendly • nonsmoking • pool • wheelchair access • WiFi • $79-119

BARS

Apartment Lounge 33 Sheldon NE (at Library) 616/451–0815 • 1pm-2am, from noon wknds • mostly gay men • neighborhood bar • sandwiches served • wheelchair access

Diversions 10 Fountain St NW (at Division) 616/451–3800 • 8pm-2am • popular • lesbians/ gay men • dancing/DJ • karaoke • 18+ • videos • also cafe • wheelchair access

Pub 43 43 S Division St (at Weston) 616/458–2205 • 3pm-2am • lesbians/ gay men • neighborhood bar • food served

NIGHTCLUBS

Rumors Nightclub 69 S Division Ave (at Oakes St) 616/454–8720 • 4pm-2am • mostly gay men • women's night Fri • dancing/DJ • karaoke • male strippers • wheelchair access

RESTAURANTS

Brandywine 1345 Lake Dr SE (in East Town) 616/774-8641 • 7am-9pm, 7:30am-9pm Sat, 8am-4pm Sun, 7am-8pm Mon

Cherie Inn 969 Cherry St SE (at Lake Dr) **616/458–0588** • 7am-2pm, till 3pm wknds, clsd Mon • some veggie • wheelchair access

Gaia Cafe 209 Diamond Ave SE (at Cherry St) **616/454–6233** • 8am-8pm, till 3pm wknds, clsd Mon • vegetarian

ENTERTAINMENT & RECREATION

Grand Raggidy Roller Girls 616/752–8475 • Grand Rapids' female roller derby league

Honor

ACCOMMODATIONS

Labrys Wilderness Resort 231/882–5994 • women only • cabins in Sleeping Bear Dunes Nat'l Lakeshore • lesbian-owned • $55-85

Kalamazoo

INFO LINES & SERVICES

Kalamazoo Gay/ Lesbian Resource Center 629 Pioneer St 269/349–4234 • educational/ support groups • youth group • hotline

BARS

Partners Ultra Lounge 7638 S Westnedge, Portage **269/383–1814** • 7pm-2am, clsd Mon • lesbians/ gay men • neighborhood bar • dancing/DJ • theme nights

Lansing

ACCOMMODATIONS

The Leaven Center Lyons 989/855–2606 • gay/ straight • some events women only • spiritual retreat center • nonsmoking • also guesthouse available for individual use

BARS

Esquire 1250 Turner St (at Clinton) **517/487–5338** • 3pm-2am • lesbians/ gay men • neighborhood bar • karaoke

NIGHTCLUBS

Spiral 1247 Center St (at Clinton) **517/371–3221** • 8pm-2am, clsd Mon-Tue • mostly gay men • dancing/DJ • theme nights • shows • videos • 18+ • wheelchair access

X-cel 224 S Washington Square (at Washtenaw St) **517/484–2399, 517/281–9502** • 9pm-2am • popular • gay-friendly • dancing/DJ • live shows • young crowd • cover charge

BOOKSTORES

Everybody Reads 2019 E Michigan Ave **517/346–9900** • 11am-7pm, 10am-4pm Sun • cool general bookstore • also coffeehouse

RETAIL SHOPS

Splash of Color 515 E Grand River Ave, Ste F (at Division), East Lansing **517/333–0990** • open daily • tattoo & piercing studio

Marquette

ACCOMMODATIONS

The Landmark Inn 230 N Front St (at Ridge St) **906/228–2580, 888/752–6362** • gay-friendly • historic boutique hotel overlooking Lake Superior • restaurant & bar • gym • nonsmoking • WiFi • kids ok • $124-269

Owendale

ACCOMMODATIONS

Windover Resort 3596 Blakely Rd **989/375–2586** • women only • seasonal private resort • campsites & RV hookups • pool • $25/ year membership fee • $21-76 camping fee

Petoskey

ACCOMMODATIONS

Coach House Inn 1011 N US 31 (at Mitchell) **231/347–8281, 877/347–8088** • gay-friendly • basic amenities • WiFi • nonsmoking • gay-owned • $39-105

Pontiac

BARS

Liberty Bar 85 N Saginaw 248/758–0771 • 11:30am-2am, from 2pm wknds • lesbians/ gay men • dancing/DJ • food served

Tiki Bob's Cantina 25 S Saginaw 248/335–6100 • 9pm-2am, clsd Sun-Wed • gay/ straight • more gay Th • dancing/DJ

Port Huron

NIGHTCLUBS

Seekers 3301 24th St (btwn Oak & Little) **810/985–9349** • 7pm-2am, from 4pm Fri-Sat, from 2pm Sun • lesbians/ gay men • dancing/DJ • live shows

Saginaw

NIGHTCLUBS

The Mixx Nightclub 115 N Hamilton St (at Court St) **989/498–4022** • 5pm-close Wed-Sun • lesbians/ gay men • dancing/DJ • food served • karaoke • videos • 18+ • wheelchair access

Saugatuck

ACCOMMODATIONS

Beechwood Manor Inn & Cottage 736 Pleasant St (at Allegan) 269/857-1587, 877/857-1587 • gay/ straight • full brkfst • nonsmoking • WiFi • gay-owned • $165-225

Bella Vita Spa & Suites 119 Butler St 269/857-8482 • gay-friendly • upscale, modern suites overlooking downtown Saugatuck • also day spa • WiFi

The Belvedere Inn & Restaurant 3656 63rd St 269/857-5777, 877/858-5777 • gay-friendly • full brkfrst • nonsmoking • gay-owned • $135-325

Bentley Waterfront Suites 326 Water St 269/857-5416, 877/858-5777 • gay-friendly • downtown & on water • nonsmoking • gay-owned • $150-325

Bird Center Resort 584-586 Lake St 269/857-1750 • gay-friendly • cottages across from Saugatuck Harbor • WiFi

The Bunkhouse B&B at Campit 269/543-4335, 877/226-7481 • lesbians/ gay men • cabins • private baths • access to Campit Resort amenities (see listing below) • pool • nonsmoking • WiFi $85-125

Campit Outdoor Resort 6635 118th Ave, Fennville 269/543-4335, 877/226-7481 • lesbians/ gay men • campsites • RV hookups • separate women's area • pool • seasonal • pets ok • WiFi • membership required • lesbian & gay-owned • $20-65

Deerpath Lodge 269/857-3337, 888/333-8827 • women only • studios on 400 waterfront acres • heated pool • hot tub • swimming • kayaks & canoes • lesbian-owned

Douglas House B&B 41 Spring St (at Wall St), Douglas 269/857-1119, 248/478-9392 (WINTER) • gay/ straight • near gay beach • gay-owned • open April-Oct

The Dunes Resort 333 Blue Star Hwy, Douglas 269/857-1401 • lesbians/ gay men • motel & cottages • transgender-friendly • pool • food served • women's wknds in April, June & Oct • dancing/DJ • live shows • pets ok • wheelchair access • gay-owned

Hidden Garden Cottages & Suites 247 Butler St 269/857-8109, 888/857-8109 • gay-friendly • cottages & suites • nonsmoking • WiFi • $135-225

Hillby Thatch Cottages 1438-1440 71st St, Glenn 847/864-3553 • gay/ straight • kitchens • fireplaces • kids ok • nonsmoking • woman-owned

The Hunter's Lodge 2790 68th St (at US 31), Fennville 269/857-5402 • gay/ straight • vintage rustic log cabin • kids ok • nonsmoking • WiFi • gay-owned • $79-199

J Paules Fenn Inn 2254 S 58th St, Fennville 269/561-2836, 877/561-2836 • gay-friendly • B&B • full brkfst • kids/ pets ok • nonsmoking

The Kingsley House B&B 626 West Main St, Fennville 269/561-6425, 866/561-6425 • gay-friendly • full brkfst • nonsmoking • WiFi • gay-owned

Kirby House 294 Center St (at Blue Star Hwy) 269/857-2904, 800/521-6473 • gay/ straight • full brkfst • pool • nonsmoking • WiFi • gay-owned • $110-185

Lake Street Commons 790 Lake St 269/857-1680 • gay-friendly • suites w/ kitchen & private decks • WiFi • kids/ pets ok • gay-owned

Lynn Dee Lea Boat & Breakfast, LLC 868 Holland St, Slip #1 309/360-7498 • gay/ straight • houseboat rental • sleeps 6 • nonsmoking • WiFi

Maple Ridge Cottages 713-719 Maple 269/857-5211 (PINES #) • gay/ straight • quaint cottages • hot tub • nonsmoking • gay-owned • $150-275/ night & $950-1,150/ week

The Newnham SunCatcher Inn 131 Griffith (at Mason) 269/857-4249, 800/587-4249 • gay-friendly • full brkfst • hot tub • pool • nonsmoking • WiFi • $90-160

The Park House Inn B&B 888 Holland St 269/857-4535, 866/321-4535 • gay-friendly • B&B in one of Saugatuck's oldest residences • full brkfst • nonsmoking • WiFi • also cottage

The Pines Motor Lodge & Cottages 56 Blue Star Hwy (at Center St), Douglas 269/857-5211 • gay/ straight • newly renovated boutique retro motel • nonsmoking • also retro gift gallery • WiFi • gay-owned • $69-205

The Spruce Cutter's Cottage 6670 126th Ave (at Blue Star Hwy & M-89), Fennville 269/543-4285, 800/493-5888 • gay/ straight • full brkfst • gay-owned

Timber Bluff 2731 Lakeshore Dr, Fennville 269/857-2586, 616/262-3974 • cottages on Lake Michigan • nonsmoking • kids ok

The Timberline Motel 3353 Blue Star Hwy 269/857-2147, 800/257-2147 • gay-friendly • heated pool • WiFi

Bars

Dunes Disco 333 Blue Star Hwy (at the Dunes Resort) **269/857–1401** • 9am-2am • lesbians/ gay men • dancing/DJ • transgender-friendly • cabaret • patio • gay-owned

Cafes

Uncommon Grounds 127 Hoffman (at Water) **269/857–3333** • 6:30am-10pm • coffee & juice bar • WiFi

The Yum Yum Gourmet Cafe & Gelateria 98 Center St, lower level (at Union St), Douglas **269/857–4567** • gay/ straight • also paninis, soup, salad • gay-owned

Restaurants

Back Alley Pizza Joint 22 Main St (at Center), Douglas **269/857–7277** • 11am-1pm, till 11pm Fri-Sat • fresh grinder bread daily

Chequers 220 Culver St **269/857–1868** • 11:30am-9pm • seasonal • great fish & chips

Everyday People Cafe 11 Center St (at Main), Douglas **269/857–4240** • call for hours • wheelchair access

Kalico Kitchen 312 Ferry St, Douglas **269/857–2678** • 7am-9pm winter, till 10pm summer • wheelchair access

Marro's Italian 147 Water St (at Mason St) **269/857–4248** • dinner only, clsd Mon-Tue • nightclub till 2am Fri-Sat

Monroe's Cafe-Grille 302 Culver St (at Griffith) **269/857–1242** • 8am-9pm, clsd Nov-March • great brkfst

Phil's Bar & Grille 215 Butler St (at Mason) **269/857–1555** • 11:30am-10pm, till 11pm Fri-Sat • patio

Pumpernickel's 202 Butler St (at Mason) **269/857–1196** • 8am-4pm • WiFi

Restaurant Toulouse 248 Culver **269/857–1561** • dinner nightly, lunch wknds (seasonal) • full bar • reservations required • entertainment • wheelchair access

Saugatuck

Where the Girls Are:

Playing in the waves at Oval Beach.

Annual Events:

May - Tulip Time Festival, Holland 800/822–2770, web: www.tulip-time.com.

June - Waterfront Film Festival 269/857-8351, web: www.water-frontfilm.org.

August - Camp Trans, web: www.camp-trans.org.

August - Michigan Womyn's Music Festival 231/757-4766, web: www.michfest.com. One of the biggest annual gatherings of lesbians on the continent, in Walhalla.

City Info:

Saugatuck-Douglas Convention & Visitors Bureau 269/857-1701, web: www.saugatuck.com.

City of the Village of Douglas, web: www.douglasmichigan.com.

Holland Chamber of Commerce 616/392-2389, web: www.holland-chamber.org.

Attractions:

Fenn Valley Wineries 269/561-2396, web: www.fennvalley.com.

Galleries.

Historical Holland (home of the Wooden Shoe Factory), web: www.dutchvillage.com.

Mason Street Warehouse (theatre) 269/857-4898, web: www.masonstreetwarehouse.org.

Saugatuck Center for the Arts 269/857-2399, web: www.sc4a.org.

Saugatuck-Douglas Historical Society Museum 269/857–7900, web: www.sdhistory.com.

Saugatuck Dunes State Park.

Transit:

Saugatuck Douglas Taxi Service 269/543-3355.

Scooters 322 Culver St (at Griffith) **269/857–1041** • noon-9pm, noon-10pm wknds, clsd Tue • great pizza

The White House Bistro 149 Griffith (at Mason) **269/857–3240** • 4pm-10pm, 9am-midnight Sat, 9am-9pm Sun • live music

Wicks Park 449 Water St **269/857–2888** • dinner nightly • live music wknds • wheelchair access

Wild Dog Grill 24 W Center St (at Spring), Douglas **269/857–2519** • dinner nightly, from noon wknds, clsd Mon-Tue

ENTERTAINMENT & RECREATION

Earl's Farm Market 1630 Blue Star Hwy, Fennville **269/227–2074** • 8am-9pm May-Oct only • pick your own berries! • gay-owned

Oval Beach consult local map for driving directions, Douglas • popular beach on Lake Michigan

Tulip Time Festival Holland **800/822–2770**

RETAIL SHOPS

Amaru Leather 322 Griffith St (at Hoffman St) **269/857–3745** • "original & custom creations in leather by two resident designers"

Groovy! Groovy! Retro Gift Gallery 56 Blue Star Hwy (at Center St), Douglas **269/857–5211** • seasonal hours • antiques, funky gifts & goods • gay-owned

Hoopdee Scootee 133 Mason (at Butler) **269/857–4141** • seasonal • clothing • gifts

Saugatuck Drug Store 201 Butler St (at Mason) **269/857–2300** • seasonal • old-fashioned corner drug store, including actual soda fountain!

GYMS & HEALTH CLUBS

Pump House Gym 6492 Blue Star Hwy (at 135th) **269/857–7867** • day passes

South Haven

ACCOMMODATIONS

Yelton Manor B&B 140 North Shore Dr (at Dyckman) **269/637–5220** • gay/ straight • full brkfst • jacuzzi • nonsmoking • WiFi • wheelchair access

St Ignace

ACCOMMODATIONS

Budget Host Inn & Suites 700 N State St **906/643–9666, 800/872–7057** • gay-friendly • pool • facing harbor of Lake Huron & across from ferries to Mackinac Island • WiFi • kids/ pets ok • wheelchair access

Traverse City

ACCOMMODATIONS

Neahtawanta Inn 1308 Neahtawanta Rd (at Peninsula Dr) **231/223–7315, 800/220–1415** • gay-friendly • swimming • sauna • nonsmoking • WiFi • wheelchair access

NIGHTCLUBS

Side Traxx 520 Franklin St (at E 8th) **231/935–1666** • 5pm-2am • lesbians/ gay men • dancing/DJ • videos • gay-owned

BOOKSTORES

The Bookie Joint 124 S Union St (btwn State & Front) **231/946–8862** • noon-6pm, clsd Sun • pride gifts • used books

Union Pier

ACCOMMODATIONS

Blue Fish Guest House & Cottage 10234 Community Hall Rd **269/469–0468 x112** • gay/ straight • cottages & guesthouses available • some shared baths • nonsmoking • kids/ pets ok • gay-owned

Fire Fly Resort 15657 Lakeshore Rd **269/469–0245** • gay/ straight • 1- & 2–bdrm units • kitchens • nonsmoking • gay-owned

Ypsilanti

see Ann Arbor

MINNESOTA

Duluth

see also Superior, Wisconsin

ACCOMMODATIONS

The Olcott House B&B Inn 2316 E 1st St (at 23rd Ave) **218/728–1339, 800/715–1339** • gay-friendly • nonsmoking • WiFi • gay-owned • $145-225

CAFES

Amazing Grace Bakery & Cafe 394 Lake Ave S **218/723–0075** • 7am-10pm, till 11pm Fri-Sat • live shows • more women 2nd Sun for Chick Jam • WiFi

Jitters 102 W Superior St **218/720–6015** • 7am-7pm, clsd Sun • WiFi

BOOKSTORES

At Sara's Table Chester Creek Cafe 1902 E 8th St (at 19th) **218/724–6811** • 7am-8pm • live music • WiFi • wheelchair access • women-owned

Lanesboro

ACCOMMODATIONS

Stone Mill Hotel & Suites 100 E Beacon St (at Parkway Ave) **507/467–8663, 866/897–8663** • gay/ straight • WiFi • non-smoking • wheelchair access • gay-owned • $100-180

Mankato

CAFES

The Coffee Hag 329 N Riverfront Dr **507/387–5533** • 9am-10pm, till 11pm Fri-Sat • veggie menu • live shows • wheelchair access • women-owned

Minneapolis/ St Paul

INFO LINES & SERVICES

AA Intergroup 952/922–0880

OutFront Minnesota 310 E 38th St #204, Minneapolis **612/822–0127, 800/800–0350** • info line w/ 24hr pre-recorded visitor info

Quatrefoil Library 1619 Dayton Ave #105, St Paul **651/641–0969** • 7pm-9pm, 10am-5pm Sat, 1pm-5pm Sun • LGBT library & resource center

ACCOMMODATIONS

Cover Park Manor 15330 58th St N (at Peller), Stillwater **651/430–9292, 877/430–9292** • gay-friendly • full brkfst • nonsmoking • kids ok • $119-199

Graves 601 Hotel 601 1st Ave N (at 6th St N), Minneapolis **612/677–1100, 866/523–1100** • gay-friendly • WiFi • gym

Le Meridien Chambers 901 Hennepin Ave, Minneapolis **612/767–6900, 800/543–4300** • gay-friendly • chic, art-filled hotel • also restaurant & bar • WiFi • kids/ pets ok • wheelchair access • $239-500

Millennium Hotel Minneapolis 1313 Nicollet Mall (btwn W Grant & 13th St), Minneapolis **612/332–6000, 866/866–8086** • gay-friendly • also restaurant & bar • pool • WiFi • wheelchair access • $99-289

BARS

19 Bar 19 W 15th St (at Nicollet Ave), Minneapolis **612/871–5553** • 3pm-2am, from 1pm wknds • mostly gay men • neighborhood bar • wheelchair access

Bev's Wine Bar 250 3rd Ave N #100 (at Washington Ave), Minneapolis **612/337–0102** • 4:30pm-1am • gay-friendly • food served • patio • wheelchair access

Brass Rail 422 Hennepin Ave (at 4th), Minneapolis **612/332–7245** • noon-2am • popular • mostly gay men • karaoke • videos • wheelchair access

Bryant Lake Bowl 810 W Lake St (near Bryant), Minneapolis **612/825–3737** • 8am-2am • gay-friendly • alternative • bowling alley • also theater • restaurant • plenty veggie/ vegan • wheelchair access

Camp Bar 490 N Robert St (at 9th St), St Paul **651/292–1844** • 4pm-2am • mostly gay men • dancing/DJ • karaoke • male dancers • videos • also restaurant • wheelchair access

The Independent 3001 Hennepin Ave (in Calhoun Square, upstairs), Minneapolis **612/378–1905** • gay/ straight • noon-2am • also restaurant, Sun brunch • wheelchair access

Jetset 115 N First St (at 1st Ave N), Minneapolis **612/339–3933** • 5pm-close, from 6pm Sat, clsd Sun-Mon • lesbians/ gay men • dancing/DJ • karaoke • nonsmoking

Lush Food Bar 990 Central Ave (at Spring St), Minneapolis • 4pm-2am, from 11am wknds, clsd Mon-Tue • lesbians/ gay men • dancing/DJ • cabaret • drag shows • food served, brunch Sun

The Town House 1415 University Ave W (at Elbert), St Paul **651/646–7087** • 2pm-2am, from noon wknds • popular • lesbians/ gay men • dancing/DJ • food served • karaoke • drag shows • piano bar • women-owned

NIGHTCLUBS

Coale's 719 N Dale St, St Paul **651/487–5829** • 3pm-2am, from 10am Sun • gay/straight • dancing/DJ • food served • live shows • patio

Gay 90s 408 Hennepin Ave (at 4th St S), Minneapolis **612/333–7755** • 8am-2am (dinner Wed-Sun) • popular • mostly gay men • dancing/DJ • multiracial • karaoke • drag shows Wed-Sun • 18+ • wheelchair access

Ground Zero/ The Front 15 NE 4th St (at Hennepin), Minneapolis **612/378–5115** • 10pm-2am Th-Sat only • also The Front lounge from 4pm • gay/ straight • more gay Sat for Bondage-A-Go-Go • dancing/DJ • live shows • wheelchair access

Kitty Cat Klub 315 14th Ave SE (at SE University Ave) **612/331–9800** • gay-friendly • lounge w/ eclectic decor • food served • live bands

The Saloon 830 Hennepin Ave (at 9th), Minneapolis **612/332–0835** • noon-2am, from 11am Sun • lesbians/ gay men • dancing/DJ • food served • young crowd• wheelchair access • gay-owned

CAFES

Anodyne at 43rd 4301 Nicollet Ave S (at 43rd), Minneapolis **612/824-4300** • 7am-10pm, till 8pm Fri-Sun • food served • open mic/ live music • wheelchair access

Black Dog Coffee & Wine Bar 308 Prince St (at Broadway), St Paul **651/228-9274** • 7am-10pm, till 9pm Sat, 8am-8pm Sun • food served

Blue Moon 3822 E Lake St, Minneapolis **612/721-9230** • 7am-10pm, from 8am wknds • WiFi

Cahoots 1562 Selby Ave (at Snelling), St Paul **651/644-6778** • 6:30am-10:30pm, from 7am wknds • coffee bar • WiFi • wheelchair access

Moose & Sadie's 212 3rd Ave N (at 2nd St), Minneapolis **612/371-0464** • 7am-8pm, 9am-2pm wknds • WiFi • wheelchair access

Uncommon Grounds 2809 Hennepin Ave (at W 28th St), Minneapolis **612/872-4811** • noon-midnight, till 1am Fri-Sat • outdoor seating

The Urban Bean 3255 Bryant Ave S (at 33rd), Minneapolis **612/824-6611** • 6:30am-11pm, from 7:30am Sun • patio • WiFi • wheelchair access

Wilde Roast Cafe 65 Main St SE (at Central Ave NE), Minneapolis **612/331-4544** • 7am-10pm • beer/ wine • wheelchair access • gay-owned

RESTAURANTS

Al's Breakfast 413 14th Ave SE (at 4th), Minneapolis **612/331-9991** • 6am-1pm, from 9am Sun • popular • great hash

Barbette 1600 W Lake St (at Irving), Minneapolis **612/827-5710** • 8am-1am, till 2am Fri-Sat • French/ American • women-owned

Birchwood Cafe 3311 E 25th St, Minneapolis **612/722-4474** • 7am-9pm, from 8am Sat, 9am-8pm Sun • veggie/vegan • WIFI • wheelchair access

Brasa Premium Rotisserie 600 E Hennepin, Minneapolis **612/379-3030** • 11am-9pm, till 10pm Fri-Sat • beer/wine • wheelchair access

French Meadow 2610 Lyndale Ave S, Minneapolis **612/870-7855** • 6:30am-9pm, till 10pm Fri-Sat• organic & local • plenty veggie/ vegan • beer/ wine

Fusion 2919 Hennepin Ave (at Lagoon Ave) **612/824-6300** • 4pm-11pm, till 2am wknds • restaurant & lounge • theme nights

Hard Times Cafe 1821 Riverside Ave, Minneapolis **612/341-9261** • 6am-4am • vegan/ vegetarian • punk rock ambiance • WiFi

Hell's Kitchen 80 9th St S, Minneapolis **612/332-4700** • 7am-9pm, till 2am Fri-Sat • great breakfast and gospel brunch on Sun

Il Gatto 3001 Hennepin Ave S (in Calhoun Square Mall), Minneapolis **612/822-1688** • 4pm-1am

Joe's Garage 1610 Harmon Pl, Minneapolis **612/904-1163** • lunch & dinner, full bar till 1am • rooftop seating

Loring Kitchen & Bar 1359 Willow St, Minneapolis **612/843-0400** • 11am-11pm, till 1am Fri-Sat, from 9am Sat-Sun • delicious food with an enticing bar

Lucia's Restaurant & Wine Bar 1432 W 31st St, Minneapolis **612/825-1572** • lunch & dinner, clsd Mon • wheelchair access

Monte Carlo 219 3rd Ave N, Minneapolis **612/333-5900** • lunch & dinner, bar till 1am • wheelchair access

Murray's 26 S 6th St (at Hennepin), Minneapolis **612/339-0909** • lunch Mon-Fri, dinner nightly • steak & seafood

Nye's Polonaise 112 E Hennepin Ave, Minneapolis **612/379-2021** • 4pm-2am, from 11am Fri-Sat • piano bar • live polka & bands • full bar

Psycho Suzi's Motor Lounge 2519 Marshall St NE, Minneapolis **612/788-9069** • 11am-2am • pu-pu's & pizza • live music • wheelchair access

Punch Neapolitan Pizza 704 Cleveland Ave S, St Paul **651/696-1066** • 11am-9:30pm • wheelchair access • also at 210 E Hennepin Ave

Red Stag Supperclub 509 1st Ave NE (at 5th St), Minneapolis **612/767-7766** • 11am-2am, from 9am Sat-Sun • live music • wheelchair access

Restaurant Alma 528 University Ave SE, Minneapolis **612/379-4909** • dinner nightly, organic New American

Rudolph's Bar-B-Que 1933 Lyndale (at Franklin), Minneapolis **612/871-8969** • 11am-2am, till 1am Sun • full bar • wheelchair access

Seward Cafe 2129 E Franklin Ave, Minneapolis **612/332-1011** • 7am-3pm, 8am-4pm wknds • vegetarian/vegan • wheelchair access

Toast Wine Bar & Cafe 415 N 1st St (in the Heritage Landing Bldg) **612/333-4305** • 5pm-11pm, till midnight Fri-Sat

Trattoria da Vinci 400 Sibley St, St Paul **651/222-4050** • 11am-9pm, 5pm-10pm Sat, clsd Sun-Mon • live music • wheelchair access

ENTERTAINMENT & RECREATION

Calhoun 32nd Beach 3300 E Calhoun Pkwy (33rd & Calhoun Blvd), Minneapolis **612/230-6400**

BOOKSTORES

True Colors 4755 Chicago Ave S, Minneapolis **612/821-9630** • call for hours • feminist bookstore since 1970 • women-owned

RETAIL SHOPS

The Rainbow Road 109 W Grant St (at LaSalle), Minneapolis **612/872-8448** • 10am-10pm • LGBT • wheelchair access

Minneapolis/St Paul

LGBT PRIDE:
June. 612/305-6900, web: www.tcpride.com.

ANNUAL EVENTS:
March - Diva (fashion show benefiting HIV/AIDS service organizations), web: www.divamn.org.
May - Minnesota AIDS Walk 612/341-2060, web: www.mnaidsproject.org.
August - Minnesota Fringe Festival 612/872-1212, web: www.fringefestival.org.
November - Flaming Film Festival, web: www.myspace.com/flamingfilmfest.

CITY INFO:
888/676-6757, web: www.minneapolis.org.

BEST VIEW:
Observation deck of the 32nd story of Foshay Tower, 821 Marquette Ave (closed in winter).

WEATHER:
Winters are harsh. If driving, carry extra blankets and supplies. The average temperature is 19°, and it can easily drop well below 0°, and then there's the wind chill! Summer temperatures are usually in the upper-80°s to mid-90°s and HUMID.

ATTRACTIONS:
American Swedish Institute 612/871-4907, web: www.americanswedishinst.org.
Collection of Questionable Medical Devices at The Science Museum of Minnesota 651/221-9444, web: www.smm.org.
Frederick R Weisman Art Museum 612/625-9494, web: www.weisman.umn.edu.
Mall of America (the largest mall in the US w/indoor theme park) 952/883-8800, web: www.mallofamerica.com.
Minneapolis American Indian Center 612/879-1700, web: www.maic-net.org.
Minneapolis Institute of Arts 888/642-2787, web: www.artsmia.org.
Walker Art Center/Minneapolis Sculpture Garden 612/375-7600, web: www.walkerart.org.

TRANSIT:
Yellow Cab (Minn) 612/824-4444.
Super Shuttle 612/827-7777.
MTC 612/373-3333, web: www.metrotransit.org.

PUBLICATIONS

Lavender Magazine 612/436–4660, **877/515–9969** • LGBT newsmagazine for IA, MN, ND, SD, WI

Minnesota Women's Press 970 Raymond Ave #201, St Paul 651/646–3968 • newspaper

My Scene City 612/886–3151 • LGBTQA Twin Cities publication

EROTICA

Fantasy Gifts 1437 University Ave, St Paul 651/256–7484 • noon-8pm, clsd Sun-Tue

The Smitten Kitten 3010 Lyndale Ave S, Minneapolis 612/721–6088, 888/751–0523 • 11am-9pm, noon-7pm Sun • transgender-friendly • lesbian-owned

Moorhead

see also Fargo, North Dakota

INFO LINES & SERVICES

Pride Collective & Community Center 810 4th Ave S #220 218/287–8034 • 5:30-7pm Tue & 1pm-3pm Sat

NIGHTCLUBS

The I-Beam 1021 Center Ave 218/233–7700 • 9pm-2am Fri-Sat only • lesbians/ gay men • dancing/DJ • karaoke • drag shows

CAFES

Atomic Coffee 16 4th St S (at Main) 218/299–6161 • 6:30am-9pm, from 8am Sun • also gallery • live shows • gay-owned

MISSISSIPPI

Statewide

PUBLICATIONS

Ambush Mag 504/522–8047 • LGBT newspaper for the Gulf South (TX through FL)

Bay Saint Louis

ACCOMMODATIONS

Nella's Park 16145 Hwy 603 (near I-10), Kiln 228/586–0053 • gay/ straight • camping • kids/ pets ok • friendly & clean w/ fishing dock • casino nearby • close to New Orleans

Biloxi

BARS

Just Us Lounge 906 Division St (at Caillavet) 228/374–1007 • 24hrs • lesbians/ gay men • neighborhood bar • live shows • dancing/DJ • drag shows • go-go boys • karaoke

Gulfport

BARS

Salty Dawg Saloon 1105 Broad Ave (at Railroad) 228/864–0463 • 10am-2am • gay-friendly • neighborhood bar • dancing/DJ • karaoke • gay-owned

Jackson

INFO LINES & SERVICES

Lambda AA 4866 N State St (at Unitarian Church) 601/856–5337 • 6:30pm Mon

Natchez

ACCOMMODATIONS

Historic Oak Hill Inn B&B 409 S Rankin St (at Orleans St) 601/446–2500, 601/446–8641 • antebellum mansion near the Mississippi • nonsmoking • WiFi • gay-owned • $115-140

Mark Twain Guesthouse 25 Silver St 601/446–8023 • above Under the Hill Saloon

BARS

King's Tavern Lounge 619 Jefferson St (at N. Rankin St) 601/446–8854 • 4pm-close • gay-friendly • neighborhood bar • food served • 18+

Under the Hill Saloon 25 Silver St 601/446–8023 • 10am-close • gay-friendly • neighborhood bar • live music • WiFi

MISSOURI

Branson

see also Springfield & Eureka Springs, Arkansas

ACCOMMODATIONS

Branson Stagecoach RV Park 5751 State Hwy 165 417/335–8185, 800/446–7110 • gay-friendly • pull-thru & back-in RV sites • cabins • pool • WiFi • gay-owned • $26-90

Cape Girardeau

ACCOMMODATIONS

Rose Bed Inn 611 S Sprigg St 573/332–7673, 866/767–3233 • gay/ straight • B&B • full brkfst • hot tub • gourmet dining by reservation • nonsmoking • WiFi • wheelchair access • gay-owned • $85-200

NIGHTCLUBS

Independence Place 5 S Henderson St (at Independence, at Holiday Happenings) 573/334–2939 • 8:30pm-1:30am Mon-Th, from 7pm Fri-Sat, clsd Sun • lesbians/ gay men • dancing/DJ • transgender-friendly • drag shows

Columbia

BARS

SoCo Club 128 E Nifong Blvd #E (at Providence Rd) 573/499–9483 • 5pm-1:30am, clsd Sun-Mon • lesbians/ gay men • dancing/DJ • food served • karaoke Tue • drag shows • videos • patio • wheelchair access

CAFES

Ernie's Cafe 1005 E Walnut St (at 10th) 573/874–7804 • 6:30am-3pm

RagTag Cinema 10 Hitt St (Broadway) 573/443–4359, 573/441–8504 • 5pm-close, from 2pm wknds • independent & alternative cinema • also theater, music & dance • food served • beer & wine

RESTAURANTS

Main Squeeze 28 S 9th St (at Cherry St) 573/817–5616 • 10am-8pm, till 5pm Sun • local organic ingredients • vegetarian • WiFi • wheelchair access

BOOKSTORES

The Peace Nook 804 C East Broadway (btwn 8th & 9th) 573/875–0539 • 10am-9pm, noon-6pm Sun • LGBT section • books • pride products • women's music

EROTICA

Bocomo Bay 1122–A Wilkes Blvd 573/443–0873

Hannibal

ACCOMMODATIONS

Garden House B&B 301 N 5th St (at Bird) 573/221–7800, 866/423–7800 • gay-friendly • WiFi • nonsmoking • gay-owned • $90-235

Rockcliffe Mansion 1000 Bird St (at 10th St) 573/221–4140, 877/423–4140 • gay-friendly • guilded-age Mansion built in 1898 on a limestone bluff • nonsmoking • WiFi • gay-owned • $139-189

RESTAURANTS

LaBinnah Bistro 207 N 5th St (at Center) 573/221–7800 • dinner only • in a Victorian home • beer/ wine • gay-owned

Joplin

INFO LINES & SERVICES

Gay Lesbian Family & Corporate Center 417/622–7821

BARS

Just Us Bar & Grill 520 S Joplin Ave (at W 5th) 417/782–6666 • 3pm-1am, till midnight Sun • lesbians/ gay men • neighborhood bar • food served • karaoke

Pla Mor Lounge 532 S Joplin Ave 417/624–2722 • 5pm-1am, clsd Sun-Mon • lesbians/ gay men • neighborhood bar • dancing/DJ • karaoke

Kansas City

see also Kansas City & Overland Park, Kansas

INFO LINES & SERVICES

Lesbian & Gay Community Center of Greater Kansas City 4008 Oak St #10 816/931–4420 • call for events

Live & Let Live AA 3901 Main St #211 (at 39th) 816/531–9668 • 6pm daily, noon Sun

ACCOMMODATIONS

Hotel Phillips 816/221–7000, 800/433–1426 • gay-friendly • art deco landmark in downtown KC

The Porch Swing Inn 702 East St, Parkville 816/587–6282, 866/587–6282 • gay-friendly • B&B • full brkfst • kids ok • WiFi • lesbian-owned • $90-140

Q Hotel & Spa 560 Westport Rd (at Mill St) 816/931–0001, 800/942–4233 • gay-friendly • in Westport district • WiFi • wheelchair access • $99-189

The Raphael 325 Ward Pkwy (at Wornall Rd) 816/756–3800, 800/821–5343 • gay-friendly • WiFi • also restaurant • $139+

Southmoreland on the Plaza 116 E 46th St (at Main St) 816/531–7979 • gay-friendly • 1913 B&B • full brkfst • veranda • nonsmoking • $155-250

Su Casa B&B 9004 E 92nd St (off James A Reed Rd) 816/965–5647, 816/916–3444 (CELL) • gay-friendly • Southwest-style home • full brkfst wknds • kids/ dogs/ horses ok • jacuzzi • pool • nonsmoking • WiFi • woman-owned • $120-160

BARS

Balanca's 1809 Grand Blvd (at 18th) 816/474–6369 • 6pm-3am, from 2pm Sat, clsd Sun-Mon • gay/ straight • multiracial • very diverse crowd • dancing/DJ • food served

Danny's 3611 Broadway (at W 36th) **816/569–1878** • 11am-1:30am • mostly men • neighborhood bar • dancing/DJ • bands • patio

Hamburger Mary's KC 101 Southwest Blvd (at Baltimore Ave) **816/842–1919** • 11am-1:30am • lesbians/ gay men • theme nights • karaoke • live entertainment • food served • juicy burgers w/ a side of camp

Missie B's/ Bootleggers 805 W 39th St (at SW Trafficway) **816/561–0625** • noon-3am • lesbians/ gay men • neighborhood bar • dancing/DJ • transgender-friendly • 2 flrs • live shows • karaoke • drag shows

Outa Bounds 3601 Broadway St (W 36th) **816/756–2577** • 11am-1:30am, till midnight Sun • mostly gay men • neighborhood sports bar • food served • wheelchair access

Sidekicks 3707 Main St (at 37th) **816/931–1430** • 2pm-3am, from 4pm Sun, clsd Mon • lesbians/ gay men • dancing/DJ • country/ western • drag shows • wheelchair access

CAFES

Broadway Cafe 4106 Broadway (at Westport) **816/531–2432** • 7am-9pm • food served • nonsmoking • also 412 Washington, 816/931-9955

RESTAURANTS

Beer Kitchen 435 Westport Rd (at Pennsylvania) **816/389–4180** • 11am-3am, from 10am wknds • gastro pub • live music

Bistro 303 303 Westport Rd **816/753–2303** • dinner nightly, brunch wknds • also martini bar • wheelchair access

Blue Bird Bistro 1700 Summit St (at W 17th St) **816/221–7559** • 7am-10pm, 10am-2pm Sun • organic fare • wheelchair access

Cafe Trio/ Starlet Lounge 4558 Main St **816/756–3227** • 5pm-11pm, clsd Sun • piano • gay-owned

Chubby's 3756 Broadway St (at 38th) **816/931–2482** • open 24 hrs • popular late nights • diner fare • wheelchair access

Kansas City

LGBT PRIDE:
June. web: www.gaypridekc.com.

ANNUAL EVENTS:
April - AIDS Walk 816/931-0959, web: www.aidswalkkansascity.org.

CITY INFO:
Convention & Visitors Bureau 816/221-5242, web: www.visitkc.com.

TRANSIT:
Yellow Cab 816/471-5000.
KCI Shuttle 816/ 243-5000.
Metro 816/221-0660, web: www.kcata.org

ATTRACTIONS:
American Jazz Museum 816/474-8463, web: www.american-jazzmuseum.com.
Black Archives of Mid-America 816/701-3590, web: www.blackarchives.org.
Harry S Truman Nat'l Historical Site (in Independence, MO) 816/254-9929, web: www.nps.gov/hstr.
Historic 18th & Vine District (includes Kansas City Jazz Museum & the Negro Leagues Baseball Museum).
Nelson-Atkins Museum of Art 816/751-1278, web: www.nelson-atkins.org.
Thomas Hart Benton Home & Studio 816/931-5722, web: www.mostateparks.com/benton.htm.

Classic Cup Cafe 301 W 47th St (at Central) 816/753–1840 • brkfst, lunch, dinner, Sun brunch • great appetizers • wheelchair access

Grand Street Cafe 4740 Grand St (at 47th St) 816/561–8000 • lunch & dinner, Sun brunch • patio seating • nonsmoking • wheelchair access

Jardine's 4536 Main St 816/561–6480 • dinner nightly • steak/ sea food • live jazz

Le Fou Frog 400 E 5th St (at Oak St) 816/474–6060 • dinner only • French bistro

McCoy's Public House 4057 Pennsylvania Ave 816/960–0866 • 11am-3am, till midnight Sun • huge patio

The Mixx 4855 Main St (at W 48th) 816/756–2300 • lunch & dinner • fast & healthy • huge selection of salads • wheelchair access

Ortega's 2646 Belleview Ave (at W 27th) 816/531–5415 • 10am-6pm, 8am-4pm wknds • real deal Mexican food in the back of a Mom & Pop store

Sharp's 63rd St Grill 128 W 63rd St 816/333–4355 • 7am-10pm, from 8am wknds • full bar • wheelchair access

Tannin Wine Bar 816/842–2660 • 11:30am-1:30am, from 4pm wknds • wine & cheese flights • full dinner menu • patio seating

YJ's Snack Bar 128 W 18th St (at W Baltimore Ave) 816/472–5533 • 8am-10pm, 24hrs Th-Sat • inexpensive • wheelchair access

ENTERTAINMENT & RECREATION

First Fridays Art Walk Crossroads District (Baltimore & 20th) 816/994–9325 • 5pm-10pm 1st Fri • art gallery walk • also live music & vendors

Kansas City Roller Warriors 816/809–8496 • KC's female roller derby league • visit kcrollerwarriors.com for events

Nelson-Atkins Museum 4525 Oak St 816/751–1278 • American Indian galleries

EROTICA

Erotic City 8401 E Truman Rd (off I-435, at Alice Ave) 816/252–3370

Hollywood at Home 9063 Metcalf Ave (at 91st), Overland Park, KS 913/649–9666 • 10am-11pm

Osage Beach

ACCOMMODATIONS

Utopian Inn 1962 Alcorn Hollow Rd, Roach 573/347–3605 • lesbians/ gay men • 3 bdrm rental on a lake • kids/ small pets ok • nonsmoking • gay-owned • $175-225

Overland

EROTICA

Patricia's 10210 Page Ave (E of Ashby) 314/423–8422

Springfield

INFO LINES & SERVICES

AA Gay/ Lesbian 518 E Commercial St 417/823–7125 (AA #) • 6pm Sat • nonsmoking

Gay & Lesbian Community Center of the Ozarks 518 E Commercial St 417/869–3978 • many groups • newsletter • wheelchair access

BARS

The Edge 424 N Boonville 417/831–4700 • 4pm-1:30am, clsd Sun • lesbians/ gay men • dancing/DJ • karaoke • drag shows • wheelchair access • lesbian-owned

Martha's Vineyard 219 W Olive St (at S Patton) 417/864–4572, 417/831–6144 • 5pm-1:30am, clsd Sun • lesbians/ gay men • neighborhood bar • dancing/DJ • drag shows • also martini lounge • patio • wheelchair access • cover charge wknds

Mud Lounge 321 E Walnut 417/865–6964 • 4pm-1:30am, clsd Sun • food served

CAFES

Mudhouse 323 South Ave 417/832–1720 • 7am-midnight, 9am-8pm Sun • food served

BOOKSTORES

Renaissance Books & Gifts 1337 E Montclair St 417/883–5161 • 10am-7pm, noon-5pm Sun • women's/ alternative • wheelchair access

EROTICA

Patricia's 1918 S Glenstone (at E Cherokee) 417/881–8444

St Louis

ACCOMMODATIONS

A St Louis Guesthouse 1032 Allen Ave (at Menard) 314/773–1016 • mostly gay men • located in historic Soulard district • hot tub (nudity ok) • nonsmoking • WiFi • gay-owned • $90-125, cash discount

Brewers House B&B 1829 Lami St (at Lemp) 314/771–1542, 888/767–4665 • lesbians/gay men • 1860s home • jacuzzi • pets ok • nonsmoking • WiFi • gay-owned • $95

Dwell 912 B&B 912 Hickory St (at S 9th St) 314/599–3100 • gay-friendly • nonsmoking • WiFi • gay-owned • $150-175

Grand Center Inn 3716 Grandel Sq (at N Grand Blvd) 314/533–0771 • gay/ straight • WiFi • nonsmoking • gay-owned • $125-275

Millennium Hotel St Louis 200 S 4th St (at Clark Ave) 314/241–9500, 866/866–8086 • gay-friendly • on Mississippi River • view of Gateway Arch • pool • wheelchair access

Napoleon's Retreat B&B 1815 Lafayette Ave (at Mississippi) 314/772–6979, 800/700–9980 • gay/ straight • restored 1880s town house • full brkfst • nonsmoking • WiFi • gay-owned • $109-169

Park Avenue Mansion—A B&B Guesthouse 2007 Park Ave (at Mississippi) 314/588–9004 • gay/ straight • B&B inn • full brkfst • jacuzzi • WiFi • nonsmoking • $89-225

BARS

Absolutli Goosed Martini Bar, Etc 3196 S Grand (at Wyoming) 314/771–9300 • 4pm-midnight, till 1am Fri-Sat, clsd Sun • lesbians/ gay men • neighborhood bar • also desserts • appetizers • patio • wheelchair access • lesbian-owned

Cicero's 6691 Delmar Blvd (at Kingsland Ave), University City 314/862–0009 • 11am-1am, till midnight Sun • gay/ straight • Italian restaurant • tavern • live music venue

Clementine's 2001 Menard St (at Allen) 314/664–7869 • 10am-midnight, from 11am Sun • popular • mostly gay men • neighborhood bar • leather • food served • patio • wheelchair access

Club Escapades 133 W Main St (at 2nd), Belleville, IL 618/222–9597 • 6pm-2am, clsd Sun-Mon • lesbians/gay men • dancing/DJ • drag shows • food served • karaoke • live shows

Erney's 32 Degree 4200 Manchester Ave (at Boyle) 314/652–7195 • 8pm-3am, clsd Sun-Mon & Wed • lesbians/gay men • swank neighborhood bar

Grey Fox Pub 3503 S Spring (at Potomac) 314/772–2150 • 2pm-1:30am, noon-midnight Sun • lesbians/gay men • neighborhood bar • drag shows • transgender-friendly • patio

Hummel's Pub 7101S Broadway (at Blow St) 314/353–5080 • 11am-1am • lesbians/gay men • neighborhood bar • full menu • karaoke • lesbian-owned

Just John 4112 Manchester Ave 314/371–1333 • 3pm-3am, from noon Sun • lesbians/gay men • neighborhood bar • dancing/DJ Fri-Sat • drag shows • karaoke • videos

Keypers Piano Bar 2280 S Jefferson (at Shenandoah) 314/664–6496 • 11am-1:30am, 10am-midnight Sun • lesbians/gay men • piano bar • food served • lunch, dinner & Sun brunch • patio

Korners Bar 7109 S Broadway (at Blow St) 314/352–3088 • 4pm-1:30am, clsd Sun-Mon • lesbians/gay men • dancing/DJ • drag shows

Loading Zone 16 S Euclid Ave (at Forest Park Pkwy) 314/361–4119 • 3:30pm-1:30am • popular • lesbians/gay men • video bar • drag shows • wheelchair access • gay-owned

Novak's Bar & Grill 4121 Manchester (at Sarah) 314/531–3699 • noon-3am • mostly women • dancing/DJ Fri-Sat • live shows • karaoke • Trivia Tue • patio • wheelchair access

Premium Lounge 4199 Manchester Rd (at Boyle) 314/652–8585 • opens 4pm, clsd Sun • gay/ straight • food served

Rehab Lounge 4052 Chouteau Ave (at Boyle) 314/652–3700 • 11:30am-1:30am • gay/ straight • neighborhood bar • also restaurant

Soulard Bastille 1027 Russell Blvd (at Menard) 314/664–4408 • 11am-1:30am • mostly gay men • neighborhood bar

NIGHTCLUBS

Atomic Cowboy 4140 Manchester Ave (btwn Kentucky & Talmadge) 314/775–0775 • 11am-3am, from 5pm Sat-Sun, clsd Mon • gay/ straight • dancing/DJ • live shows • burlesque • also Fresh-Mex Mayan grill • art lounge • WiFi • patio

Attitudes 4100 Manchester Ave (at S Sarah) 314/534–0044 • 7pm-3am, clsd Mon • popular • lesbians/gay men • dancing/DJ • drag shows • karaoke

Bubby & Sissy's 602 Belle St (at 6th St), Alton, IL 618/465–4773 • 3pm-2am, till 3am Fri-Sat • lesbians/gay men • dancing/DJ • live shows • karaoke • drag shows • food served • wheelchair access

The Complex Nightclub & Restaurant
3511 Chouteau Ave (at Grand) **314/772-2645**
• 9pm-3am • popular • lesbians/gay men • 5
bars • dancing/DJ • drag shows • videos •
patio • food served • wheelchair access

Magnolia's 5 S Vandeventer Ave (at Laclede)
314/652-6500 • lesbians/gay men
• dancing/DJ • mostly African American • hip
hop/R&B club

CAFES

Coffee Cartel 2 Maryland Plaza (at Euclid)
314/454-0000 • 24hrs • popular • food served
• WiFi • wheelchair access

MoKaBe's 3606 Arsenal (at S Grand)
314/865-2009 • 8am-midnight, from 9am Sun
• popular • plenty veggie • occasional shows •
wheelchair access

St Louis

WHERE THE GIRLS ARE:
Spread out, but somewhat concentrated in the Central West End near Forest Park. Younger, funkier crowds hang out in the Delmar Loop, west of the city limits, packed with ethnic restaurants.

LGBT PRIDE:
June. PrideFest 314/772-8888, web: www.pridestl.org.

ANNUAL EVENTS:
February - Soulard Mardi Gras 314/771-5110, web: www.mardi-grasinc.com.
July - Fair St Louis & LIVE on the Levee 314/434-3434, web: www.celebratestlouis.org.
September - The Great Forest Park Balloon Race, web: www.great-forestparkballoonrace.com.

CITY INFO:
314/421-1023 or 800/ 325-79621, web: www.explorestlouis.com.

BEST VIEW:
Where else? Top of the Gateway Arch in the Observation Room, web: www.gatewayarch.com.

WEATHER:
100% midwestern. Cold winters — little snow and the temperatures can drop below 0°. Hot, muggy summers raise temperatures back up into the 100°s. Spring and fall bring out the best in Mother Nature.

ATTRACTIONS:
Anheuser-Busch Brewery 800/342-5283 web: www.budweiser-tours.com.
Cathedral Basilica of St Louis (world's largest collection of mosaic art) 314/738-8200, web: www.cathedralstl.org.
Gateway Arch 877/982-1410, web: www.gatewayarch.com.
Grant's Farm 314/843-1700, web: www.grantsfarm.com.
Soulard, the "French Quarter of St Louis."
St Louis Art Museum 314/721-0072, web: www.slam.org.
Stone Hill Winery (in Hermann) 800/909-9463, web: www.stone-hillwinery.com.
The extremely quaint town of St Charles.

TRANSIT:
County Cab 314/993-8294, web: www.countycab.com.
TransExpress 314/428-7799, web: www.transexpress-stl.com.
MetroBus 314/231-2345, web: www.metrostlouis.org.

Soulard Coffee Garden Cafe 910 Geyer Ave (btwn 9th & 10th) 314/241–1464 • 6:30am-4pm, from 8am wknds • food served • WiFi • wheelchair access

RESTAURANTS

Billie's Diner 1802 S Broadway 314/621–0848 • 5am-2:30pm, midnight-1:30pm wknds • wheelchair access

Cafe Osage 4605 Olive St 314/454–6868 • 7am-2pm, till 5pm Th-Sat, from 9am Sun

Chez Leon 7927 Forsyth Blvd (at S Meramec Ave) 314/361–1589 • lunch Tue-Fri, dinner nightly, clsd Mon • French bistro • full bar • gay-owned

City Diner 3139 S Grand Blvd 314/772–6100 • 7am-11pm, 24hrs Fri-Sat, till 10pm Sun • wheelchair access

Dressel's 419 N Euclid (at McPherson) 314/361–1060 • 11am-1am, till midnight Sun • great Welsh pub food • full bar • live shows • wheelchair access

Duff's 392 N Euclid Ave (at McPherson) 314/361–0522 • lunch & dinner, brunch wknds, clsd Mon • fine dining • some veggie • full bar • wheelchair access

Eleven Eleven Mississippi 1111 Mississippi 314/241–9999 • lunch Mon-Fri, dinner nightly, clsd Sun • wine country bistro

Imperial Palace 2543 N Grand Blvd 314/531–1951 • lunch & dinner • soul food • full bar

Joanie's Pizza 2101 Menard St 314/865–1994 • 11am-11pm, till midnight wknds

Majestic Cafe 4900 Laclede Ave (at Euclid) 314/361–2011 • 6am-10pm, bar till 11pm • Greek-American diner fare • wheelchair access

Mango 1101 Lucas Ave 314/621–9993 • 11am-11pm, till 4pm Sun • full bar • Latin American/ Peruvian

Meskerem 3210 S Grand Blvd 314/772–4442 • lunch & dinner • Ethiopian • plenty veggie

Pappy's Smokehouse 3106 Olive St 314/535–4340 • 11am-8pm, till 4pm Sun • excellent BBQ

Rue 13 1311 Washington 314/588–7070 • 5pm-3am, clsd Sun-Mon • sushi • full bar • dancing/DJ • burlesque

Spaghetteria Mamma Mia 904 S Vandeventer Ave 314/531–9100 • lunch & dinner, clsd Sun • Italian

Ted Drewes Frozen Custard 6726 Chippewa (at Jameson) 314/481–2652, 314/481–2124 • 11am-10pm • seasonal • a St Louis landmark • also 4224 S Grand Blvd, 314/352-7376 • wheelchair access

Terrene 33 N Sarah St 314/535–5100 • dinner nightly, clsd Mon • also bar • patio dining in season • wheelchair access

Tony's 410 Market St (at Broadway) 314/231–7007 • dinner only, clsd Sun • Italian fine dining • reservations advised • wheelchair access

Van Goghz 3200 Shenandoah (at Compton) 314/865–3345 • brkfst, lunch & dinner • also bar • WiFi • wheelchair access

Vin de Set 2017 Chouteau Ave (at S 21st St) 314/241–8989 • lunch & dinner, dinner only wknds, clsd Mon • rooftop bar & bistro • wheelchair access

The Wild Flower Restaurant & Bar 4590 Laclede Ave (at Euclid) 314/367–9888 • lunch & dinner, bar till 1:30am, clsd Tue, Sun brunch • wheelchair access

ENTERTAINMENT & RECREATION

Anheuser-Busch Brewery Tours/ Grant's Farm S 12th & Lynch 314/577–2626, 314/843–1700 (GRANT'S FARM) • all-American kitsch: see the Clydesdales in their air-conditioned stables, or visit the Busch family estate that was once the home of Ulysses S Grant

Opera Theatre of Saint Louis 130 Edgar Rd (at Big Bend) 314/961–0644 (BOX OFFICE) • intimate theater w/ operas sung in English • wheelchair access

BOOKSTORES

Left Bank Books 399 N Euclid Ave (at McPherson) 314/367–6731 • 10am-10pm, 11am-6pm Sun • popular • feminist & LGBT titles • also at 321 N 10th St, 314/436-3049

RETAIL SHOPS

CheapTRX 3211 S Grand Blvd (at Wyoming St) 314/664–4011 • alternative shopping • body piercing • tattoos • wheelchair access

PUBLICATIONS

Vital Voice 314/256–1196 • bi-weekly news & features publication

Women's Yellow Pages of Greater St Louis 314/997–6262

GYMS & HEALTH CLUBS

Marbles Yoga Studio 1905 Park Ave 314/621–4744 • 6:30am-8:30pm, drop-in yoga classes • gay-owned

EROTICA

Patricia's 3552 Gravois Ave (at Grand)
314/664-4040 • 10am-10pm, 1pm-10pm Sun
• fetish clothes • toys • videos • dating service

St Peters

EROTICA

Patricia's 1034 Venture Dr (off Veterans
Memorial Pkwy) **636/928-2144**

MONTANA

Billings

BARS

The Loft 1123 1st Ave N (at 12th)
406/259-9074 • 10am-2am • lesbians/ gay
men • dancing/DJ • karaoke • shows •
wheelchair access

EROTICA

Big Sky Books 1203 1st Ave N (at 12th St)
406/259-0051

The Victorian 2019 Minnesota Ave (at 21st)
406/245-4293 • noon-midnight, clsd Sun-
Mon • fireplace & piano • HIV testing

Bozeman

ACCOMMODATIONS

Gallatin Gateway Inn 76405 Gallatin Rd/
Hwy 191 **406/763-4672, 800/676-3522** • gay-
friendly • dinner nightly • hot tub • pool • kids
ok • wheelchair access • $89-245

Lehrkind Mansion Inn 719 N Wallace Ave
406/585-6932 • gay/ straight • full brkfst • hot
tub • nonsmoking • WiFi • gay-owned • $119-
229

CAFES

The Leaf & Bean 35 W Main St
406/587-1580 • 6am-9pm, till 10pm Fri-Sat •
live shows • wheelchair access • women-
owned • also 1500 N 19th Ave, 406/587-2132

The Nova Cafe 312 E Main St (at Rouse
Ave) **406/587-3973** • 7am-2pm

RETAIL SHOPS

Jeannette Rankin Peace Center 519 S
Higgins Ave **406/543-3955** • 10am-6pm, clsd
Sun • fair trade gift store • peace resource
center • events

EROTICA

Erotique 12 N Willson Ave (at Main)
406/586-7825

Butte

RESTAURANTS

Matt's Place 2339 Placer St (btwn Montana
& Rowe) **406/782-8049** • 11:30am-7pm, clsd
Sun-Mon • classic soda-fountain diner

Pekin Noodle Parlor 117 S Main St, 2nd flr
406/782-2217 • 5pm-11pm, till midnight Fri-
Sat, till 10:30pm Sun-Mon, clsd Tue • Chinese
• some veggie

Pork Chop John's 2400 Harrison Ave
406/782-1783 • 10:30am-10:30pm, till 9:30pm
Sun • also 8 W Mercury, 406/782-0812

Uptown Cafe 47 E Broadway **406/723-4735**
• lunch weekdays & dinner nightly • bistro •
full bar • wheelchair access

Kalispell

INFO LINES & SERVICES

Flathead Valley Alliance **406/758-6707** •
LGBT referral service

Missoula

INFO LINES & SERVICES

KISMIF Gay/ Lesbian AA 538 University
Ave (at church) **406/543-0011** • 7pm Mon

**Western Montana Gay/ Lesbian
Community Center** 127 N Higgins Ave #202
406/543-2224 • LGBT resource center • call
for hours

BARS

The Oxford 337 N Higgins Ave (at Pine)
406/549-0117 • popular • gay-friendly • 8am-
2am • 24hr cafe & casino

CAFES

The Catalyst 111 N Higgins **406/542-1337** •
7am-3pm

RESTAURANTS

Montana Club 2620 Brooks **406/543-3200** •
6am-10pm, till 11pm Fri-Sat, casino open till
2am • full bar • wheelchair access

BOOKSTORES

Fact & Fiction 220 N Higgins **406/721-2881**
• 9am-6pm, 10am-5pm Sat, noon-4pm Sun •
many LGBT titles • wheelchair access

PUBLICATIONS

Out Words 127 N Higgins Ave #202
406/543-2224 • Montana's LGBT publication

Swan Valley

ACCOMMODATIONS

Holland Lake Lodge 1947 Holland Lake Rd (at Hwy 83) **406/754-2282, 877/925-6343** • gay-friendly • resort w/ lakefront cabins • full brkfst • hot tub • kids ok • WiFi • restaurant & bar • wheelchair access • gay-owned • $145-290

NEBRASKA

Lincoln

INFO LINES & SERVICES

Rainbow Group Gay/ Lesbian AA 2325 S 24 St (at Sewell, at St Matthew's) **402/438-5214** • 7:30pm Mon & 7pm Fri

BARS

Panic 200 S 18th St (at N St) **402/435-8764** • 4pm-1am, from 1pm wknds • lesbians/ gay men • live shows • WiFi • patio • wheelchair access • gay-owned

NIGHTCLUBS

The Q 226 S 9th St (btwn M & N Sts) **402/475-2269** • 8pm-1am, clsd Mon • lesbians/ gay men • dancing/DJ • live shows • drag shows •

ENTERTAINMENT & RECREATION

No Coast Derby Girls • Lincoln's female roller derby league • visit www.nocoastderbygirls.com for events

Omaha

INFO LINES & SERVICES

AA Gay/ Lesbian 851 N 74th St (at Presbyterian Church) **402/556-1880** • 8:15pm Fri

Rainbow Outreach Center 1719 Leavenworth St **402/341-0330** • call for hrs

ACCOMMODATIONS

Castle Unicorn 57034 Deacon Rd (at Hwy 34 & I-29), Pacific Jct, IA **712/527-5930** • gay/ straight • medieval-style B&B • full brkfst • hot tub • WiFi • nonsmoking • patio • gay-owned • $169-219

The Cornerstone Mansion Inn 140 N 39th St (at Dodge) **402/558-7600, 888/883-7745** • gay-friendly • fireplaces • near downtown • brkfst served • nonsmoking • WiFi • $85-150

BARS

Connections 1901 Leavenworth St (at 19th) **402/933-3033** • 6pm-1:30am, from 4pm Fri-Sun clsd Mon • lesbians/ gay men • dancing/DJ • karaoke • wheelchair access • lesbian-owned

DC's Saloon 610 S 14th St (at Jackson) **402/344-3103** • 4pm-1am, from 2pm wknds • lesbians/ gay men • neighborhood bar • dancing/DJ • country/ western • live shows • wheelchair access

Myth 1105 Howard St (Old Market) **402/884-6985** • 7pm-1am, from 5pm Th-Sat, clsd Sun-Mon • gay/ straight • live music

NIGHTCLUBS

Flixx Lounge 1019 S 10th St **402/408-1020** • 5pm-1am • mostly men • dancing/DJ • cabaret • drag shows

The Max 1417 Jackson St (at 15th St) **402/346-4110** • 11am-9pm, clsd Th-Sat • popular • mostly gay men • dancing/DJ Wed-Sun • drag shows • strippers patio • wheelchair access • cover charge Fri-Sat

RESTAURANTS

The Boiler Room 1110 Jones St **402/916-9274** • dinner only, clsd Sun • full bar • wheelchair access

California Tacos & More 3235 California St **402/342-0212** • 11am-9pm, clsd Sun • beer/wine • wheelchair access

Dixie Quick's 1915 Leavenworth St **402/346-3549** • lunch & dinner, brunch from 9am wkds, clsd Mon • Southern • reservations recommended

The Flatiron Cafe 1722 St Marys Ave **402/345-7477** • dinner only, clsd Sun • full bar • wheelchair access

French Cafe 1017 Howard St (at 10th St) **402/341-3547** • dinner nightly, Sun brunch • full bar

M's Pub 422 S 11th St **402/342-2550** • 11am-1am, from 5pm Sun • full bar • wheelchair access

McFoster's Natural Kind Cafe 302 S 38th St **402/345-7477** • lunch & dinner • vegetarian • full bar • wheelchair access

ENTERTAINMENT & RECREATION

Omaha Rollergirls • Omaha's female roller derby league • visit www.myspace.com/omaharollergirls for events

Bookstores

New Realities 1026 Howard St (in the Old Market) 402/342–1863 • 11am-9pm, noon-6pm Sun • progressive • wheelchair access

NEVADA

Baker

Accommodations

Silver Jack Inn 10 Main St 775/234–7323 • gay-friendly • seasonal motel & restaurant • WiFi • $49-75

Carson City

Accommodations

West Walker Motel 106833 Hwy 395, Walker, CA 530/495–2263 • gay-friendly • WiFi • kids/pets ok • in Toiyabe Nat'l Forest near West Walker River • women-owned • $45-75

Gerlach

Accommodations

F Ranch 775/557–2804 • women only • B&B on remote NW Nevada working horse/cattle ranch • April-Sept • bird-watching • kids ok • nonsmoking

Lake Tahoe

see Lake Tahoe, California

Las Vegas

Info Lines & Services

Alcoholics Together 900 E Karen, 2nd flr #A-202 (at Sahara, in Commercial Center) 702/598–1888 • noon & 8pm daily • call for directions & other meeting times

Betty's Outrageous Adventures 702/991–9929 • Las Vegas' oldest & largest lesbian social organization • lesbian-owned

The Gay/ Lesbian Community Center of Southern Nevada 953 E Sahara Ave #B-31 702/733–9800 • 11am-7pm, clsd wknds

Accommodations

➤ **Paris, Las Vegas Resort & Casino** 3655 Las Vegas Blvd S 702/946–7000, 800/630–7933 • gay-friendly • also restaurants, bars, spas • LGBT honeymoon packages • see ad in front color section

Bars

8 1/2 Ultra Lounge/ Piranha 4633 Paradise Rd (at Naples) 702/791–0100 • lesbians/ gay men • neighborhood bar • videos • dancing/DJ • wheelchair access

Backdoor Lounge 1415 E Charleston (near Maryland Pkwy) 702/385–2018 • 24hrs • mostly gay men • neighborhood bar • dancing/DJ • patio • Latino/a • wheelchair access

Badlands Saloon 953 E Sahara #22 (in Commercial Center) 702/792–9262 • 24hrs • mostly gay men • neighborhood bar • dancing/DJ • country/ western • wheelchair access • gay-owned

The Buffalo 4640 Paradise Rd #11 (at Naples) 702/733–8355 • 24hrs • popular • mostly gay men • leather • videos • wheelchair access

Charlie's Las Vegas 5012 S Arville St (at Tropicana) 702/876–1844 • popular • mostly gay men • dancing/DJ • country/ western • dance lessons 7pm-9pm Mon, Th-Sat • drag shows • wheelchair access

Escape Lounge 4213 W Sahara Ave 702/364–1167 • 24hrs • lesbians/ gay men • neighborhood bar • videos • wheelchair access

Flex 4347 W Charleston (at Arville) 702/385–3539, 702/878–3355 • 24hrs • lesbians/ gay men • dancing/DJ • drag shows • strippers • wheelchair access

Freezone 610 E Naples 702/794–2300 • 24hrs • lesbians/ gay men • women's night Tue • neighborhood bar • dancing/DJ • transgender-friendly • drag shows Fri-Sat • karaoke • young crowd • also restaurant • gay-owned

Goodtimes 1775 E Tropicana Ave (at Spencer, in Liberace Plaza) 702/736–9494 • 24hrs • mostly gay men • neighborhood bar • dancing/DJ Mon & after-hours Fri-Sat • wheelchair access

The Las Vegas Eagle 3430 E Tropicana (at Pecos) 702/458–8662 • 24hrs • mostly gay men • leather • DJ Wed, Fri-Sat

Las Vegas Lounge 900 E Karen Ave (at Maryland Pkwy) 702/737–9350 • 24hrs • gay-friendly • neighborhood bar • mostly transgender • drag shows

Nightclubs

Blush 3131 S Las Vegas Blvd (at Wynn) 702/770–3633 • 9pm-3am, clsd Sun-Mon • ultralounge • dancing/DJ

BootyBar 7700 S Las Vegas Blvd **702/518–4053** • hot monthly women's party • dancing/DJ

Heaven at Bare 3400 S Las Vegas Blvd (at The Mirage) **702/693–8300** • 10pm Sat only • lesbians/ gay men • dancing/DJ • poolside party

House of Blues 3950 Las Vegas Blvd S (at Hacienda Ave, in Mandalay Bay) **702/632–7600** • gay-friendly • dancing/DJ • also restaurant • live shows • cover charge

Kitty Bar 3663 S Las Vegas Blvd (at Harmon St, next to Planet Hollywood, at Krave) **702/836–0830, 800/823–8450** • 9pm-3am Sat only • popular • mostly women • dancing/DJ • multiracial

Krave 3663 S Las Vegas Blvd (at Harmon St, next to Planet Hollywood) **702/836–0830** • 11pm-close, clsd Mon • mostly gay men • dancing/DJ

Mix 3950 Las Vegas Blvd S (at Mandalay Bay) **702/632–9500** • gay-friendly • stylish lounge • DJ • cover charge wknds

Pure Nightclub 3570 S Las Vegas Blvd (at Caesar's Palace) **702/731–7873** • 10pm-4am, clsd Mon & Wed-Th • gay-friendly • upscale • top DJs • cover charge

Restaurants

Bootlegger Bistro 7700 S Las Vegas Blvd (btwn Windmill & Robindale) **702/736–4939** • 24hrs • a Vegas classic • Italian • musical entertainment nightly

Border Grill 3950 Las Vegas Blvd S (at the Mandalay Bay Resort & Casino) **702/632–7403** • 11:30am-close • Mexican • full bar • patio

Carluccio's Tivoli Gardens 1775 E Tropicana (at Spencer St) **702/795–3236** • 4:30pm-10pm, clsd Mon • Italian • formerly owned by Liberace • check out the mirrored, autographed grand piano!

Chicago Joe's 820 S 4th St (at Gass Ave) **702/382–5637** • 11am-10pm, from 5pm Sat, clsd Sun-Mon • old-school Italian • in downtown arts district

Cupcakery 7175 W Lake Mead **702/835–0060**

The Egg & I 4533 W Sahara Ave (near Arville) **702/364–9686** • popular • 6am-3pm • wheelchair access

Firefly 3900 Paradise Rd #A **702/369–3971** • 11am-2am • tapas • also bar • wheelchair access

Go Raw 2381 E Windmill Ln **702/450–9007** • 8am-8pm, till 5pm Sun • organic vegan • also juice bar • also at 2910 Lake East Dr, 702/254-5382

Grand Lux Cafe 3355 Las Vegas Blvd S (at the Venetian) **702/414–3888** • open 24hrs • generous portions

Guy Savoy 3570 Las Vegas Blvd (at Caesar's Palace) **702/731–7110, 877/346–4642** • 5pm-10:30pm, clsd Mon-Tue • French • reservations required

Joël Robuchon 3799 Las Vegas Blvd S (at MGM Grand Hotel) **702/891–7925** • 5:30pm-10pm, till 10:30pm Fri-Sat • French • reservations required

Lindo Michoacan 2655 E Desert Inn Rd (near Eastern) **702/735–6828** • 11am-11pm, till midnight wknds • popular • Mexican

Lotus of Siam 953 E Sahara Ave #A-5 (in Commercial Center) **702/735–3033** • lunch Mon-Fri, dinner nightly • Thai • wheelchair access

Mon Ami Gabi 3655 Las Vegas Blvd S (at Paris Las Vegas) **702/944–4224** • outdoor seating • wheelchair access

Mr Lucky's 4455 Paradise Rd (at Hard Rock Hotel) **702/693–5000** • 24hrs • wheelchair access

Paymon's Mediterranean Cafe & Lounge 4147 S Maryland Pkwy (at E Flamingo Rd) **702/731–6030** • 11am-1am • plenty veggie • wheelchair access • also at 8380 W Sahara Ave, 702/731-6030

Society Cafe Encore 3121 Las Vegas Blvd S (at Encore) **702/248–3463** • 7am-11pm, till 1am wknds • upscale American

Wichcraft at MGM Grand **702/891–1111** • 10am-5pm • creative sandwiches • eat-in or take-out

Entertainment & Recreation

Cupid's Wedding Chapel 827 Las Vegas Blvd S (1 block N of Charleston) **702/598–4444, 800/543–2933** • commitment ceremonies • "Have the Vegas wedding you've always dreamed of!"

Erotic Heritage Museum 3275 Industrial Rd **702/369–6442** • 6pm-10pm Wed-Th, 3pm-midnight Fri, from noon wknds, clsd Mon-Tue

The Forum Shops at Caesars 3570 Las Vegas Blvd S (in Caesars Palace) • you saw it in *Showgirls* & many other movies, now come shop for yourself

Frank Marino's Divas Las Vegas 3535 Las Vegas Blvd S (at the Imperial Palace) **702/794-3261, 888/777-7664** • show at 7:30pm • the biggest drag show in town: Frank Marino & friends impersonate the divas, from Joan Rivers to Tina Turner

Kà by Cirque du Soleil at MGM Grand **702/796-9999, 877/264-1844** • 6:30pm & 9:30pm Tue-Sat • martial arts, puppetry, interactive projections & pyrotechnics

Mystère by Cirque du Soleil at Treasure Island **800/963-9634** • high-energy acrobatics & vivid imagery

O by Cirque du Soleil at the Bellagio **702/796-9999, 888/488-7111** • showstopper in a specially constructed aquatic theater

Red Rock Lanes 11011 W Charleston Blvd **702/797-7777** • 72 lanes • Cosmic Bowling wknds

Sin City Rollergirls • Vegas' female roller derby league • visit www.sincityrollergirls.com for events

Thanks Babs, the Day Tripper **702/370-6961** • tours, shows attractions & getaways • full service concierge for Las Vegas, state of NV, & the Southwest • it's like having a lesbian aunt in Las Vegas!

Las Vegas

LGBT Pride:
May. 866/930-3336, web: www.lasvegaspride.org.

Annual Events:
July - Gay Days & Nights Las Vegas 702/437-3800.
Sept - NGRA (Nevada Gay Rodeo Assn) Bighorn Rodeo, web: www.ngra.com.

City Info:
Convention & Visitors Authority 877/847-4858, web: www.visit-lasvegas.com.

Best View:
Top of the Stratosphere, Top of the Eiffel Tower Experience, or hurtling through the loops of the rollercoaster atop the New York New York Hotel. (*Note: Do not ride immediately after the buffet.*)

Weather:
It's in the desert! Hotter by day, cooler by night.

Attractions:
Bellagio Art Gallery 702/693-7871, web: www.bellagio.com.
Divas Las Vegas, web: www.frankmarinosdivas.com.
Fremont Street Experience, web: www.vegasexperience.com.
Hoover Dam & Museum, 866/730-9097, web: www.usbr.gov/lc/hooverdam.
Imperial Palace Auto Collection 702/794-3174, web: www.imperialpalace.com.
Las Vegas Art Museum 702/360-8000, web: www.lasvegasartmuseum.com.
Liberace Museum 702/798-5595, web: www.liberace.org.
Museum of Natural History 702/384-3466, web: www.lvnhm.org.

Transit:
Western Cab 702/382-7100.
Lucky Cab 702/477-7555.
Various resorts have their own shuttle service.
Las Vegas Monorail 866/466-6672, web: www.lvmonorail.com.
RTC (Regional Transportation Commission) 702/228-7433, web: www.rtcsouthernnevada.com.

Viva Las Vegas Wedding Chapel 1205 Las Vegas Blvd **800/574–4450** • gay-owned

Zumanity at New York–New York Hotel & Casino **702/740–6815, 866/606–7111** • explores human sexuality in an intimate, cabaret-style setting • 18+

BOOKSTORES

Get Booked 4640 S Paradise Rd #15 (at Naples) **702/737–7780** • 10am-midnight, till 2am Fri-Sat • LGBT

RETAIL SHOPS

Glamour Boutique II 714 E Sahara Ave #104 (at S 6th St) **702/697–1800, 866/692–1800** • clsd Sun • large-size dresses, wigs, etc

The Rack 953 E Sahara Ave, Ste 101, Bldg 16 (in Commercial Center) **702/732–7225** • leather • fetish • wheelchair access

PUBLICATIONS

QVegas **702/650–0636** • monthly LGBT news & entertainment magazine

GYMS & HEALTH CLUBS

Hands On Therapeutic Massage & Spa 8335 S Las Vegas Blvd (at Cancun Resort) **702/614–6222** • licensed massage therapists visit home or hotel room • "open to all men & women" • mention Damron for discount

The Las Vegas Athletic Club 2655 S Maryland Pkwy **702/734–5822** • day passes

SEX CLUBS

Power Exchange 3610 S Highland Dr **702/255–4739** • play space open to hetero, gay, bi, trans, men & women • free for women & trans people

EROTICA

Bare Essentials Fantasy Fashions 4029 W Sahara Ave (near Valley View Blvd) **702/247–4711** • exotic/ intimate apparel • toys • gay-owned

Price Video 700 E Naples Dr #102 (at Swenson) **702/734–1342** • 10am-10pm

Rancho Adult Entertainment Center 4820 N Rancho Dr (at Lone Mtn) **702/645–6104** • 24hrs

Romantix Adult Superstore 2923 S Industrial Rd (behind Circus Circus) **702/892–0699** • 24hrs

Sinderella's Adult Superstore 5570 S Valley View (at Russell) **702/736–9700**

Laughlin

see Bullhead City, Arizona

Reno

ACCOMMODATIONS

Ramada Reno Hotel & Casino 1000 E 6th St (at Wells Ave) **775/786–5151** • gay-friendly • seasonal pool • kids/ pets ok • restaurant • WiFi • wheelchair access • $59-139

Terrible's Sands Regency Casino Hotel Downtown Reno 345 N Arlington Ave **775/348–2200, 800/233–4939** • gay-friendly • pool • live shows • also restaurants • $29-119

BARS

Cadillac Lounge 1114 E 4th St (at Sutro) **775/324–7827** • noon-2am • lesbians/ gay men • neighborhood bar

Five Star Saloon 132 West St (at 1st) **775/329–2878** • 24hrs • gay/ straight • neighborhood bar • dancing/DJ • wheelchair access

The Patio 600 W 5th St (btwn Washington & Ralston) **775/323–6565** • 11am-2am • lesbians/ gay men • neighborhood bar • live shows • karaoke

Ten 99 Club 1099 S Virginia St (at Vassar) **775/329–1099** • 10am-2am, 24hrs Fri-Mon • popular • lesbians/ gay men • neighborhood bar • live shows • videos • patio • wheelchair access

NIGHTCLUBS

Neutron 340 Kietzke Ln (btwn Glendale & Mill) **775/786–2121** • 2pm-close • popular • gay/ straight • dancing/DJ • multi-racial • young crowd • patio

Tronix 303 Kietzke Ln (at E 2nd St) **775/333–9696** • 9am-3am, 24hrs wknds • lesbians/ gay men • more women Wed • dancing/DJ • multiracial • transgender-friendly • videos • young crowd • WiFi •wheelchair access • gay-owned

RESTAURANTS

4th Street Bistro 3065 W 4th St **775/323–3200** • dinner nightly, clsd Sun-Mon • upscale • extensive wine list

The Daily Bagel 495 Morrill Ave # 102 **775/786–1611** • 7am-4pm, clsd Mon

Pneumatic Diner 501 W 1st St (in Truckee River Apts, 2nd flr) **775/786–8888 x106** • 11am-10pm, from 8am Sun • vegetarian

ENTERTAINMENT & RECREATION

Brüka Theatre 99 N Virginia St **775/323–3221** • alternative theater & performance space

BOOKSTORES

Sundance Books 1155 W 4th St #106 (at Keystone) **775/786–1188** • 9am-9pm, 10am-6pm wknds • independent

PUBLICATIONS

Reno Gay Page 775/453–4058 • monthly • bar & resource listings • community events • arts & entertainment

EROTICA

Suzie's 195 Kietzke Ln (at E 2nd St) **775/786–8557** • 24hrs

Winnemuca

BARS

Cheers 320 S Bridge St **775/623–2660** • gay-friendly • neighborhood bar

NEW HAMPSHIRE

Concord

ACCOMMODATIONS

Idleday Guest Rooms 180 W Parish Rd **603/520–6886, 603/753–6113** • women only • secluded setting on river • nonsmoking

Keene

ACCOMMODATIONS

The Lane Hotel 30 Main St **603/357–7070, 888/300–5056** • gay/ straight • WiFi • also restaurant • nonsmoking • wheelchair access

Manchester

ACCOMMODATIONS

Radisson Hotel Manchester 700 Elm St **603/625–1000, 800/395–7046** • gay-friendly • food served • pool • pets/kids ok • WiFi • wheelchair access

BARS

The Breezeway 14 Pearl St **603/621–9111** • 4pm-1am, from noon Sun • lesbians/ gay men • neighborhood bar • dancing/DJ • theme nights • cabaret • drag shows • gay-owned

Club 313 93 S Maple St (at S Willow) **603/628–6813** • 6pm-1am, from 7pm Sun • lesbians/gay men • dancing/DJ • live entertainment • karaoke • drag shows • WiFi • wheelchair access

Element Lounge 1055 Elm St **603/627–2922** • 3pm-1:30am, from 6pm Mon • lesbians/ gay men • dancing/DJ • food served • karaoke • drag shows

Nashua

ACCOMMODATIONS

Radisson Hotel 11 Tara Blvd **603/888–9970** • gay-friendly • pool • WiFi • wheelchair access

NIGHTCLUBS

The Amber Room 53 High St **603/881–9060** • 9pm Fri-Sat • gay/ straight • gay night Fri

Newfound Lake

ACCOMMODATIONS

The Inn on Newfound Lake 1030 Mayhew Tpke Rte 3–A, Bridgewater **603/744–9111, 800/745–7990** • gay/ straight • private beach on cleanest lake in NH • also renowned restaurant • full bar • nonsmoking • WiFi • gay-owned

Plaistow

BARS

David's Place 20 Plaistow Rd **603/819–4822** • 7pm-1am • mostly gay men • live shows • drag shows

Portsmouth

ACCOMMODATIONS

Ale House Inn 121 Bow St (at Market St) **603/431–7760** • gay-friendly • WiFi • gay-owned

CAFES

Breaking New Grounds 14 Market Square **603/436–9555** • 6:30am-11pm • espresso shakes • WiFi

RESTAURANTS

The Mombo 66 Marcy St (at State St) **603/433–2340** • dinner only, clsd Sun-Mon • wheelchair access

Surry

ACCOMMODATIONS

The Surry House 50 Village Rd (at Crain Rd) **603/352–2268** • gay/ straight • B&B in private home • full brkfst • pool • kids/ pets ok • nonsmoking • lesbian-owned

White Mtns

ACCOMMODATIONS

Beal House 2 W Main St, Littleton 603/444-2661 • gay-friendly • French country brkfst • WiFi

➤**Highlands Inn** 240 Valley View Lane, Bethlehem 603/869-3978, 877/LES–B–INN (537-2466) • Lesbian Paradise: legal marriage in NH; 19 rms; 100 acres • full brkfst • outdoor & indoor spas • pool • 100 mtn acres • special events • concerts • kids/pets ok • non-smoking • WiFi • wheelchair access • ignore No Vacancy sign • lesbian-owned • see ad on inside front cover

The Horse & Hound Inn 205 Wells Rd, Franconia 603/823-5501, 800/450-5501 • seasonal • gay-friendly • 1830s farmhouse • full brkfst • kids/pets ok • nonsmoking • WiFi • also restaurant • gay-owned

The Inn at Bowman 1174 Rte 2 (Presidential Hwy), Randolph 603/466-5006 • gay/straight • swimming • hot tub • nonsmoking • wheelchair access • gay-owned

Inn at Crystal Lake 2356 Eaton Rd (at Rte 16), Eaton 603/447-2120, 800/343-7336 • gay/straight • full brkfst • also restaurant • kids age 12+ ok • dogs ok • WiFi • gay-owned

The Notchland Inn Rte 302, Hart's Location 603/374-6131, 800/866-6131 • gay/straight • full brkfst • other meals available • nonsmoking • also cottages • gay-owned

Riverbend Inn B&B 273 Chocorua Mtn Hwy (at Rte 113), Chocorua 603/323-7440, 800/628-6944 • gay/straight • B&B • full brkfst • located on the Chocorua River • WiFi • nonsmoking • gay-owned

The Sunny Grange B&B 1354 Rte 175 (Mad River Rd), Campton 603/726-5555, 877/726-5553 • gay-friendly • full brkfst • kids ok • nonsmoking • WiFi

Wildcat Inn & Tavern Rte 16A, Jackson Village 603/356-8700, 800/637-0087 • gay-friendly • full brkfst • also tavern & dining room • nonsmoking

Wyatt House Country Inn 3046 White Mountain Hwy, N Conway 603/356-7977, 800/527-7978 • gay/straight • full brkfst • WiFi • lesbian-owned

BARS

The Up Country Restaurant & Tavern Rte 16, North Conway 603/356-3336 • 11am-1am, from 1pm wknds • more gay on wknds • dancing/DJ • live shows • karaoke • video • WiFi

RESTAURANTS

Polly's Pancake Parlor 672 Rte Sugar Hill Rd (exit 38 off 93 N), Sugar Hill 603/823-5575 • 7am-2pm, till 3pm wknds, clsd winters

The Red Parka Steakhouse & Pub Rte 302, Glen 603/383-4344 • open from 3pm, also bar

ENTERTAINMENT & RECREATION

Reel North Fly Fishing 603/858-4103 • casting lessons • half & full day river trips • custom-tied flies • lesbian-owned/run

NEW JERSEY

Statewide

PUBLICATIONS

Out in Jersey 743 Hamilton Ave, Trenton 08629 609/213-9310 • publication for all of New Jersey's LGBTI community

PM Entertainment Magazine 516/845-0759 • events, listings, classifieds & more for Long Island, NJ & NYC

Asbury Park

ACCOMMODATIONS

Empress Hotel 101 Asbury Ave 732/774-0100 • gay-friendly • swimming • WiFi • also Empress Lobby Lounge on wknds

Sixth Avenue House 305 Sixth Ave (at Berg St) 732/361-6609 • gay/straight • some shared baths • full brkfst • WiFi • gay-owned

BARS

Georgie's 812 5th Ave (at Main) 732/988-1220 • 2pm-2am • lesbians/gay men • neighborhood bar • food served • karaoke • drag shows

NIGHTCLUBS

Ladies 2000 856/869-0193 • seasonal parties • call hotline for details

Paradise 101 Asbury Ave (at Ocean Ave) 732/988-6663 • 4pm-2am, from 2pm Sat, from noon Sun • lesbians/gay men • dancing/DJ • 2 dance flrs • live shows • piano bar • tiki/pool bar in summer

RESTAURANTS

Bistro Olé 230 Main St 732/897-0048 • dinner nightly, clsd Mon • Spanish-Portuguese

The Lazy Dog Saloon 716 Cookman Ave 732/774-2200 • 4pm-close, Sun brunch, clsd Tue

Moonstruck 517 Lake Ave (at Grand) 732/988-0123 • dinner only, clsd Mon-Tue • also bar • live music wknds

Restaurant Plan B 705 Cookman Ave **732/807-4710** • dinner nightly, wknd brunch, clsd Mon • BYOB

Atlantic City

ACCOMMODATIONS

The Carisbrooke Inn 105 S Little Rock Ave, Ventnor **609/822-6392** • gay-friendly • on a beach block • nonsmoking • WiFi • $99-325

Tropicana Casino & Resort 2831 Boardwalk (at Brighton) **609/340-4000, 800/345-8767** • gay-friendly • pool • oceanview rooms

NIGHTCLUBS

Prohibition 1133 Boardwalk (at Resorts Casino) **800/334-6378** • lesbians/ gay men • dancing/DJ • drag shows

RESTAURANTS

Dock's Oyster House 2405 Atlantic Ave **609/345-0092** • 5pm-10pm, till 11pm Fri-Sat • wheelchair access

White House Sub Shop 2301 Arctic Ave (at Mississippi) **609/345-1564** • 10am-10pm, till 11pm Fri-Sat, from 11am Sun

ENTERTAINMENT & RECREATION
➤**RisQue Atlantic City NJ Pride** 603/858-4103

Boonton

NIGHTCLUBS

Switch 202 Myrtle Ave (off Washington) **973/263-4000** • 6pm-2am, from 4pm wknds • lesbians/ gay men • dancing/DJ • country/ western • food served • drag shows • 18+

Camden

see also Philadelphia, Pennsylvania

ENTERTAINMENT & RECREATION

The Walt Whitman House 30 Mickle Blvd (btwn S 3rd & S 4th Sts) **856/964-5383** • the last home of America's great & controversial poet

Cape May

ACCOMMODATIONS

Beauclaires B&B Inn 23 Ocean St (at Columbia Ave) **609/898-1222** • gay/ straight • full brkfst • 1/2 block from ocean • nonsmoking

RISQUE ATLANTIC CITY; NJ PRIDE
RISQUE HER | 07/05/2012 - 07/09/2012 | WWW.RISQUEAC.ORG

Cottage Beside the Point 609/204-0549, **609/898-0658** • gay/straight • studio • kids ok • nonsmoking • lesbian-owned • $135-175

Higher Grounds 479B W Perry St **609/884-1131** • 7am-3pm, clsd Wed • events • music • food served

Highland House 131 N Broadway (at York) **609/898-1198** • gay-friendly • B&B • kids/pets ok • gazebo • nonsmoking • gay & straight-owned • $120-165

The Virginia Hotel 25 Jackson St (btwn Beach Dr & Carpenter's Ln) **609/884-5700, 800/732-4236** • gay-friendly • WiFi • also The Ebbitt Room restaurant • seafood/cont'l

BARS

The King Edward Room 301 Howard St (at The Chalfonte Hotel) **609/884-8409** • 2pm-1am summer only • mostly gay men

Cherry Hill

see Philadelphia, Pennsylvania

Hammonton

NIGHTCLUBS

Club In Or Out 19 N Egg Harbor Rd (at Orchard Ave.) **609/561-2525** • 6pm-3am Fri-Sat, 5pm-1am Sun • lesbians/gay men • dancing/DJ • shows • karaoke • lesbian-owned

Highland Park

INFO LINES & SERVICES

Pride Center of New Jersey 85 Raritan Ave (at S 1st Ave) **732/846-2232** • info line • meeting space for various groups

Hoboken

BARS

The Cage 32 Newark St **201/216-1766** • 5pm-2am, till 3am Fri-Sat • lesbians/gay men • neighborhood bar • dancing/DJ • karaoke • drag shows • theme nights

NIGHTCLUBS

Maxwell's 1039 Washington St **201/653-1703** • popular • gay-friendly • alternative • live music venue • food served

Jamesburg

RESTAURANTS

Fiddleheads 27 E Railroad Ave **732/521-0878** • lunch & dinner, Sun brunch, clsd Mon-Tue • upscale bistro • BYOB

Jersey City

INFO LINES & SERVICES

Hudson Pride Connections 32 Jones St **201/963-4779** • "serving the LGBT communities & all people living w/ HIV, since 1993"

ACCOMMODATIONS

Hyatt Regency Jersey City 2 Exchange Pl (on the Hudson) **201/645-4712, 201/469-1234** • gay-friendly • luxury waterfront hotel • short ride to NYC • pool • nonsmoking • WiFi

BARS

Lamp Post 382 2nd St **201/222-1331** • 11:30am-2am, till 3am Fri-Sat • gay/straight • food served • live bands

LITM 140 Newark Ave (at Grove) **201/536-5557** • 5pm-1am, till 2am Fri-Sat, 11am-midnight Sun • gay/straight • also restaurant & gallery

RESTAURANTS

Baja 117 Montgomery St **201/915-0062** • lunch & dinner • Mexican

Lambertville

see New Hope, Pennsylvania

Lodi

RESTAURANTS

Penang Malaysian & Thai Cuisine 334 N Main St (at Garibaldi Ave) **973/779-1128** • 11am-11pm • full bar • gay-owned

Morristown

INFO LINES & SERVICES

GAAMC (Gay Activist Alliance in Morris County) 21 Normandy Hts Rd (at Columbia Rd, Unitarian Fellowship) **973/285-1595** • info line 7:30pm-9pm, also recorded info • also women's network

New Brunswick

BARS

The Den 700 Hamilton St (at Douglas), Somerset **732/545-7354** • 8pm-2am Wed-Sat only • popular • mostly gay men • more women last Fri • dancing/DJ wknds • multi-racial • shows • restaurant • wheelchair access

RESTAURANTS

The Frog & the Peach 29 Dennis St (at Hiram Square) **732/846-3216** • lunch Mon-Fri, dinner nightly • full bar • upscale • wheelchair access

Stage Left 5 Livingston Ave (at George) **732/828-4444** • popular • lesbians/ gay men • some veggie • full bar • patio • wheelchair access • expensive

Paterson

RESTAURANTS

E&V Ristorante 320 Chamberlain Ave **973/942-8080, 973/942-4664** • lunch & dinner nightly, clsd Mon • Italian • wheelchair access

Plainfield

ACCOMMODATIONS

The Pillars of Plainfield B&B 922 Central Ave (at 9th St) **908/753-0922, 888/745-5277** • gay/ straight • Georgian/ Victorian mansion • full brkfst • nonsmoking • kids/ dogs ok (call first) • WiFi

Red Bank

BOOKSTORES

Earth Spirit 25 Monmouth St **732/842-3855** • 10am-10pm, till 11pm Fri-Sat, noon-5pm Sun • New Age center & bookstore • LGBT sections

River Edge

NIGHTCLUBS

Feathers 77 Kinderkamack Rd (at Grand) **201/342-6410** • 9pm-2am, till 3am Sat, from 7pm Sun • popular • mostly gay men • dancing/DJ • karaoke • live shows • videos • young crowd • wheelchair access

Rosemont

RESTAURANTS

The Cafe 88 Kingwood-Stockton Rd (intersection of CR 519 & 604) **609/397-4097** • lunch Tue-Fri, dinner Wed-Sun, wknd brunch, clsd Mon • BYOB

Sergeantsville

see New Hope, Pennsylvania

Stockton

ACCOMMODATIONS

Woolverton Inn 6 Woolverton Rd **609/397-0802, 888/264-6648** • gay-friendly • full brkfst • jacuzzi • WiFi • wheelchair access

Trenton

BARS

The Mill Hill Saloon 300 S Broad (at Market) **609/394-7222** • 11:30am-2am, from 5pm Sat, clsd Sun, Brew Cellar from 10pm • gay-friendly • live bands from jazz to blues to rock to folk • also restaurant

CAFES

Cafe Ole 126 S Warren St **609/396-2233** • 7am-4pm, 8am-2pm Sat, clsd Sun • bistro • WiFi

Union

RESTAURANTS

Rio Rodizio 2185 Rte 22 West **908/206-0060** • 4pm-10pm, till 1pm Fri-Sat, noon-9pm Sun • Brazilian steakhouse

Westville

see Philadelphia, Pennsylvania

NEW MEXICO

Abiquiu

ACCOMMODATIONS

Casita de Chuparosa **505/685-0823** • gay-friendly • vacation rental in O'Keeffe country • huge views • 2 bdrms • fireplace • gourmet kitchen w/ full brkfst provisions • near hiking trails • nonsmoking • WiFi • $130+

Alamogordo

ACCOMMODATIONS

Best Western Desert Aire Motor Inn 1021 S White Sands Blvd **505/437-2110, 800/637-5956** • gay-friendly • pool • WiFi • wheelchair access • $68+

Albuquerque

includes Bernalillo, Corrales, Placitas & Rio Rancho

INFO LINES & SERVICES

AA Gay/ Lesbian **505/266-1900 (AA#)** • 7pm Mon & Th

Common Bond Info Line **505/891-3647** • 24hrs • covers LGBT community

ACCOMMODATIONS

Adobe Nido 1124 Major Ave NW (at 12th St & Candilaria NW) **505/344-1310, 866/435-6436** • gay-friendly • B&B • also aviary • nonsmoking • WiFi • $119-259

Bottger Mansion of Old Town 110 San Felipe (at Central Ave) 505/243-3639, 800/758-3639 • gay-friendly • transgender-friendly • B&B • WiFi • $104-179

Brittania & W E Mauger Estate B&B 701 Roma NW (at 7th) 505/242-8755, 800/719-9189 • gay-friendly • full brkfst • nonsmoking • WiFi • $99-204

Casa Manzano B&B 103 Forest Rd 321 (at State Rte 55), Tajique 505/384-9767 • gay/ straight • full brkfst • hot tub • nonsmoking • kids/pets ok • wheelchair access • $99-129

Casas de Suenos 310 Rio Grande Blvd SW (btwn Park & Alhambra) 505/247-4560, 800/665-7002 • gay/straight • spacious casitas • patios & beautiful gardens • kids ok • nonsmoking • WiFi • $99-189

La Casita B&B 317 16th St NW (at Lomas Blvd) 505/242-0173 • gay-friendly • adobe guesthouse • nonsmoking • WiFi • $85-145

Golden Guesthouses 2645 Decker NW (at Glenwood) 505/344-9205, 888/513-GOLD • lesbians/gay men • individual & shared units • nonsmoking • lesbian-owned • $125-145

The Nativo Lodge 6000 Pan American Fwy NE 505/798-4300, 888/628-4861

Sandia Courtyard Hotel 10300 Hotel Ave (at Eubank) 505/296-4853, 800/877-4852 • gay-friendly • pool • pets/kids ok • WiFi • also restaurant • $80+

Sheraton Albuquerque Airport Hotel 2910 Yale Blvd SE (at Gibson) 505/843-7000, 800/325-3535 • gay-friendly • 4-star hotel • pool • also restaurant • $99-209

Bars

Albuquerque Social Club 4021 Central Ave NE (at Morningside, enter rear) 505/262-1088 • 3pm-2am, noon-midnight Sun • popular • lesbians/gay men • dancing/DJ • private club

Exhale 6132 4th St NW (near Osuna) 505/342-0049 • 6pm-close, from 4:30pm Sun, clsd Mon-Tue • mostly women • neighborhood bar • dancing/DJ wknds • food served • karaoke • dance lessons

Nightclubs

Effex 420 Central SW (at 5th) • 9pm-2am Th-Sat • lesbians/gay men • dancing/DJ

Fire • monthly dance party • women only • check local listings for location

Cafes

Java Joe's 906 Park Ave SW 505/765-1514 • 6:30am-3:30pm • coffee & pastries • monthly art shows

Restaurants

Artichoke Cafe 424 Central Ave SE (at Arno St) 505/243-0200 • lunch Mon-Fri, dinner nightly • bistro • plenty veggie • wheelchair access

Cafe Cubano at Laru Ni Hati 3413 Central Ave NE (btwn Tulane & Amherst) 505/255-1575 • 9am-9pm, clsd Sun-Mon • cigars • cheap Cuban food • also unisex hair salon • gay-owned

Copper Lounge 1504 Central Ave SE (at Maple) 505/242-7490 • 11am-2am, clsd Sun • pizza, burgers • full bar • wheelchair access

El Patio 142 Harvard St SE (at Central) 505/268-4245 • 11am-9pm, from noon Sun • popular • young crowd • beer/wine • plenty veggie • wheelchair access

El Pinto 10500 4th St NW (at Roy Ave) 505/898-1771 • lunch & dinner, Sun brunch • Mexican

Flying Star Cafe 3416 Central Ave SE (2 blocks W of Carlisle) 505/255-6633 • 6am-11pm, till midnight Fri-Sat • plenty veggie • WiFi • wheelchair access

Frontier 2400 Central Ave SE (at Cornell) 505/266-0550 • 5am-1am • good brkfst burritos

The Original Garcia's Kitchen 1113 4th St NW (at Mountain) 505/247-9149 • 7am-3pm • awesome little down home place • wheelchair access

The Range Cafe 2200 Menaul NE (at University Blvd) 505/888-1660 • 7:30am-9pm • Southwestern

Romano's Macaroni Grill 2100 Louisiana NE (at Winrock Mall) 505/881-3400 • 11am-10pm • Italian • wheelchair access

Sadie's Cocinita 6230 4th St NW (near Osuna) 505/345-5339 • 11am-10pm, 10am-9pm Sun • popular • New Mexican • wheelchair access

Zinc Wine Bar & Bistro 3009 Central Ave NE (at Dartmouth) 505/254-9462 • lunch & dinner, brunch wknds • live music • reservations recommended

Entertainment & Recreation

Bio Park Botanic Garden 2601 Central Ave NW (at New York Ave) 505/768-2000 • an oasis in the desert: native & exotic plants, butterflies

Duke City Derby • Albuquerque's female roller derby league • visit www.dukecityderby.com for events

BOOKSTORES

Bird Song 1708 Central SE (at University) **505/268-7204** • 11am-7pm, clsd Mon • used • wheelchair access

Page One 11018 Montgomery NE (at Juan Tabo Blvd) **505/294-2026, 800/521-4122** • 9am-9pm, till 6pm Sun • "New Mexico's largest independent bookstore"

RETAIL SHOPS

Newsland 2112 Central Ave SE (at Yale) **505/242-0694** • 8am-8pm, till 7pm Sun • some LGBT magazines

EROTICA

Castle Megastore 5110 Central Ave SE (at San Mateo) **505/262-2266**

Self Serve 3904B Central Ave SE (at Morningside) **505/265-5815** • noon-7pm, till 8pm Fri, till 6pm Sun • erotica store & sexuality resource center • lesbian-owned

Chimayo

ACCOMMODATIONS

Casa Escondida B&B **505/351-4805, 800/643-7201** • gay-friendly • full brkfst • hot tub • kids/pets ok w/approval • nonsmoking • WiFi • $105-165

Cloudcroft

RETAIL SHOPS

Off The Beaten Path 100 Glorietta Ave (at 1st) **575/682-7284** • eclectic gifts • original artwork • wheelchair access • lesbian-owned

Farmington

ACCOMMODATIONS

Quality Inn 1901 E Broadway **505/325-3700, 877/424-6423** • gay-friendly • kids/pets ok • WiFi • wheelchair access • $39-99

Albuquerque

ENTERTAINMENT:
New Mexico Gay Rodeo Association www.nmgra.com.

LGBT PRIDE:
June. 505/873-8084, web: www.abqpride.com.

ANNUAL EVENTS:
September - Closet Cinema, LGBT film festival 505/243-1870, web: www.closetcinema.org.
October - Albuquerque Int'l Balloon Fiesta 505/821-1000 or 888/422-7277, web: www.balloonfiesta.com.

CITY INFO:
800/284-2282, web: www.itsatrip.org.

BEST VIEW:
Sandia Peak Tramway (505/856-7325) at sunset.

WEATHER:
Sunny and temperate. Warm days and cool nights in summer, with average temperatures from 65° to 95°. Winter is cooler, from 28° to 57°.

ATTRACTIONS:
Albuquerque Museum 505/842-0111, web: www.albuquerquemuseum.com.
Indian Pueblo Cultural Center 505/843-7270 or 866/855-7902 (outside NM), web: www.indianpueblo.org.
New Mexico Museum of Natural History & Science 505/841-2800, web: www.nmnaturalhistory.org.
Old Town.
Petroglyph National Monument 505/899-0205 x331, web: www.nps.gov/petr/.
Rattlesnake Museum 505/242-6569, web: www.rattlesnakes.com.
Sandia Peak Tramway 505/856-7325, web: www.sandiapeak.com.
Wildlife West Nature Park 505/281-7655, web: www.wildlifewest.org.

Las Cruces

ACCOMMODATIONS

Hotel Encanto de Las Cruces 705 S
Telshor Blvd **575/522-4300, 866/383-0443**

RETAIL SHOPS

Spirit Winds Gifts & Cafe 2260 S Locust St
(at Thomas Dr) **575/521-0222** • 7am-7pm,
9am-6pm Sun • live music some wknds • food
served • patio • WiFi • wheelchair access

Madrid

BARS

Mineshaft Tavern 2846 State Hwy 14
505/473-0743 • 11am-close • gay-friendly •
live shows • also restaurant • some veggie

CAFES

Java Junction 2855 State Hwy 14 **505/438-
2772** • 7am-4pm, till 5pm wknds • WiFi

Ramah

ACCOMMODATIONS

El Morro RV Park, Cabins & Cafe 4018
Hwy 53 **505/783-4612** • gay/ straight • full
brkfst • nonsmoking • WiFi • lesbian-owned

Santa Fe

INFO LINES & SERVICES

AA Gay/ Lesbian 1601 S St Francis Dr
505/982-8932 • 6pm Mon

ACCOMMODATIONS

Bishop's Lodge Resort & Spa 1297
Bishops Lodge Rd **505/983-6377,
800/419-0492** • gay-friendly • kids/ pets ok •
pool • nonsmoking • wheelchair access • WiFi

Dragonfly Canyon Retreat Glorieta
505/757-2991 • gay/ straight • 3-bdrm casita
• near Pecos Wilderness • nonsmoking •
$150+ • also women's retreats • lesbian-
owned

El Farolito B&B 514 Galisteo St (at Paseo
de Peralta) **505/988-1631, 888/634-8782** •
gay/ straight • adobe compound w/ romantic,
private casitas • kids ok • nonsmoking • WiFi •
gay-owned • $160-275

Four Kachinas Inn 512 Webber St
505/982-2550, 800/397-2564 • gay/ straight •
courtyard • kids ok • nonsmoking • WiFi •
wheelchair access • gay-owned

Hacienda Las Barrancas 27 Country Rd 84-D (at Hwy 502) **505/455-2197, 866/455-2197** • gay-friendly • adobe hacienda located in scenic Pojoaque River Valley N of Santa Fe • full brkfst • hot tub • nonsmoking • WiFi • $120-186

Hacienda Nicholas 320 E Marcy St **505/986-1431, 888/284-3170** • gay/ straight • adobe home • full brkfst • teens/ pets ok • nonsmoking • WiFi • wheelchair access • $135-260

➤**Inn of the Turquoise Bear B&B** 342 E Buena Vista St **505/983-0798, 800/396-4104** • lesbians/ gay men • B&B in historic Witter Bynner estate • nonsmoking • WiFi • gay-owned • $99-325

Inn on the Alameda 303 E Alameda (at Canyon Rd) **505/984-2121, 888/984-2121** • gay-friendly • afternoon wine reception • hot tubs • WiFi • wheelchair access • $125-390

Las Palomas 460 W San Francisco St **505/982-5560, 877/982-5560** • gay-friendly • luxury hotel 3 blocks from Plaza • kids ok • nonsmoking • WiFi • wheelchair access • $139-269

The Madeleine Inn 106 Faithway St **505/982-3465, 888/877-7622** • gay/ straight • Queen Anne Victorian • full brkfst • hot tub • kids ok • nonsmoking • WiFi • also spa • $120-265

Marriott Residence Inn 1698 Galisteo St (at St Michaels) **505/988-7300, 800/331-3131** • gay-friendly • hot tub • pool • nonsmoking • kids/ pets ok • WiFi • wheelchair access • $109-279

New Mexico Women's Guesthouse, Retreat & Healing Center PO Box 130, Serafina 87569 **575/421-2533** • women only • two 2-bdrm guesthouses on 1,000-acre wildlife refuge • also healing workshops • hot tub • nonsmoking • lesbian-owned • $60-90/ night; $375-440/ week

Rosewood Inn of the Anasazi 113 Washington Ave **505/988-3030, 888/767-3966** • gay-friendly • luxury hotel 1/2 block from Plaza • kids ok • WiFi • nonsmoking • wheelchair access • also restaurant • $349-1,200

The Triangle Inn—Santa Fe 14 Arroyo Cuyamungue (12 miles N of Santa Fe) **505/455-3375, 877/733-7689** • lesbians/ gay men • secluded rustic adobe compound • hot tub • nonsmoking • casitas available • WiFi • kids/ pets ok • wheelchair access • lesbian-owned • $70-160

The Water Street Inn 427 W Water St **505/984-1193, 800/646-6752** • gay-friendly • historic adobe inn • jacuzzi • nonsmoking • kids/ pets ok • WiFi • wheelchair access • $165-275

BARS

The Matador 116 W San Francisco St (at Galisteo) **505/984-5050** • gay-friendly neighborhood dive bar

SilverStarlight Lounge 500 Rodeo Rd **505/428-7777** • 5pm-midnight Wed-Sun • lesbians/ gay men • cabaret & lounge

RESTAURANTS

Anasazi Restaurant 113 Washington Ave (at Inn of the Anasazi) **505/988-3030** • brkfst, lunch, dinner & wknd brunch • wheelchair access

Bobcat Bite 420 Old Las Vegas Hwy **505/983-5319** • 11am-7:50pm Wed-Sat • award-winning burgers & steaks

Cafe Pasqual's 121 Don Gaspar Ave (at Water St) **505/983-9340, 800/722-7672** • brkfst, lunch, dinner & Sun brunch • popular • Southwestern • some veggie • beer/ wine • wheelchair access

The Compound Restaurant 653 Canyon Rd (at Delgado) **505/982-4353** • lunch Mon-Sat, dinner nightly • upscale • Southwestern • nonsmoking • patio • wheelchair access

Cowgirl BBQ 319 S Guadalupe St (at Aztec) **505/982-2565** • 11am-midnight • great Margaritas • plenty veggie

El Farol 808 Canyon Rd **505/983-9912** • Spanish/ tapas • live music

Garbo's at RainbowVision 500 Rodeo Rd (ar S St Francis) **505/428-7777** • lunch & dinner • full bar • wheelchair access

Geronimo's 724 Canyon Rd (at Camino del Monte Sol) **505/982-1500** • dinner nightly • eclectic gourmet • full bar 11am-11pm • wheelchair access

Harry's Roadhouse 96 Old Las Vegas Hwy **505/989-4629** • 7am-9:30pm • outdoor seating • popular brunch

Koi 135 W Palace Ave, 3rd flr (at Grant) **505/955-0400** • dinner nightly • also Rize nightclub

Pink Adobe 406 Old Santa Fe Trl **505/983-7712** • steak & seafood • also Dragon Room bar

Santacafe 231 Washington Ave **505/984-1788** • lunch & dinner • New American • some veggie • full bar • wheelchair access

Tune Up Cafe 1115 Hickox St (at Cortez) **505/983-7060** • 7am-10pm, from 8am wknds • New Mexican • some veggie • beer/ wine • wheelchair access

Vanessie of Santa Fe 434 W San Francisco St (at Guadalupe) **505/982-9966** • 5pm-9pm (bar 4:30pm-midnight) • popular • lesbians/ gay men • steak house • piano bar

ENTERTAINMENT & RECREATION

Ten Thousand Waves 3451 Hyde Park Rd (4 miles out of town) **505/992-5025 (INFO), 505/982-9304 (RESERVATIONS)** • Japanese health spa & lodging • clothing-optional • kids ok

Wise Fool New Mexico 2778 Agua Fria Unit D (at Siler Rd) **505/992-2588** • women & kids circus art classes, workshops & performances • social justice theatre & puppetry • check local listings for upcoming events & info

BOOKSTORES

Downtown Subscription 376 Garcia St (at Acequia Madre) **505/983-3085** • 7am-6pm • newsstand • coffee shop • wheelchair access

RETAIL SHOPS

The Ark 133 Romero St (at Agua Fria) **505/988-3709** • 10am-6pm, 11am-5pm Sun • spiritual

Silver City

ACCOMMODATIONS

Gila House Hotel & Gallery 400 N Arizona **575/313-7015** • gay-friendly • also Gallery 400

West Street Inn **575/534-2302** • guesthouse • kids/ pets ok (call for details) • $105-125

BARS

Isaac's Bar & Grill 200 N Bullard St **575/388-4090** • 4pm-close, from 10am wknds, clsd Tue • dancing/DJ • live shows

CAFES

Shevek & Co 602 N Bullard St (at 6th St) **575/534-9168** • dinner nightly, clsd Wed • Mediterranean cuisine • espresso • "the best service in town" • beer/ wine • patio • gay-owned

RESTAURANTS

Diane's Restaurant & Bakery 510 N Bullard **575/538-8722** • brkfst, lunch & dinner, clsd Mon • beer/ wine

Taos

ACCOMMODATIONS

Adobe & Stars B&B 584 State Hwy 150 (at Valdez Rim Rd) **575/776-2776, 800/211-7076** • gay/ straight • full brkfst • nonsmoking • WiFi • wheelchair access • woman-owned • $125-189

Casa Benavides B&B 137 Kit Carson Rd (at Paseo del Pueblo Sur) **575/758-1772, 800/552-1772** • fireplaces • hot tubs • extensive gardens • full brkfst • nonsmoking • kids ok • WiFi • wheelchair access • $105-325

Casa Europa Inn & Gallery 840 Upper Ranchitos Rd (at Ranchitos Rd) **575/758-9798, 888/758-9798** • gay/ straight • full brkfst • hot tub • sauna • nonsmoking • WiFi • $115-185

Casa Gallina **575/758-2306** • gay/ straight • charming guesthouse in quiet, pastoral setting • nonsmoking • wheelchair access • gay-owned • $160-200

Dobson House 484 Tune Dr **575/776-5738** • gay-friendly • luxury suites • N of Taos • full brkfst • solar-powered eco-resort • nonsmoking • $118-140

Dreamcatcher B&B 416 La Lomita Rd (at Valverde) **575/758-0613, 888/758-0613** • gay-friendly • near Taos Plaza • full brkfst • hot tub • nonsmoking • WiFi • wheelchair access • $115-175

The Historic Taos Inn 125 Paseo del Pueblo Norte (at Bent St) **575/758–2233, 888/518–8267** • gay-friendly • several adobe houses date from the 1800s • pueblo-style fireplaces • also restaurant & bar • $75-275

Orinda B&B 461 Valverde St (on Valverde Park) **575/758–8581, 800/847–1837** • gay/ straight • full brkfst • nonsmoking • WiFi • $104-169

San Geronimo Lodge 1101 Witt Rd (off Kit Carson) **575/751–3776, 800/894–4119** • popular • gay/ straight • full brkfst • pool • hot tub • massage available • kids/ pets ok • nonsmoking • WiFi • wheelchair access • $95-160

Restaurants

Sabroso 470 State Hwy 150, Arroyo Seco **575/776–3333** • 5pm-10pm • American & Mediterranean • also full bar • patio • wheelchair access

Entertainment & Recreation

Llama Trekking Adventures **800/758–5262** • day hikes & multiday llama treks in Sangre de Cristo Mtns & Rio Grande Gorge

Truth or Consequences

Accommodations

The Belair Inn 705 N Date St (at 7th Ave) **505/740–4100** • gay/ straight • "retro 1950s motel w/ 21st-century amenities" • nonsmoking • WiFi • gay-owned • $45-65

NEW YORK

Adirondack Mtns

Accommodations

The Cornerstone Victorian 3921 Main St (Rte 9), Warrensburg **518/623–3308** • gay-friendly • gourmet brkfst • $98-194

Country Road Lodge B&B 115 Hickory Hill Rd (at State Rte 418), Warrensburg **518/623–2207** • gay-friendly • secluded riverside retreat at the end of a country road • full brkfst • nonsmoking • WiFi • $90-140

The Doctor's Inn 304 Trudeau Rd, Saranac Lake **518/891–3464, 888/518–3464** • gay-friendly • full brkfst • some shared baths • kids/ pets ok (call first) • nonsmoking • $250-500

Falls Brook Yurts in Adirondacks John Brannon Rd, Minerva **518/761–6187** • gay-friendly • access to hiking, fishing & boating • kids/ pets ok • $95

The Griffin House B&B 3 Hudson St (off Rte 9/ Main St), Warrensburg **518/623–2449** • gay-friendly • Victorian country inn • full brkfst • 5 miles from Lake George • nonsmoking • wheelchair access • women-owned • $95-145

Jake's Adirondack Place **609/354–2419** • gay/ straight • 3-bdrm rental home • kids ok • nonsmoking • WiFi • lesbian-owned • $250+

King Hendrick Motel 1602 State Rte 9, Lake George **518/792–0418, 866/521–6883** • gay-friendly • swimming • WiFi • nonsmoking • wheelchair access • $75-125

Secluded Retreat Cabin Lake Luzerne **518/361–2375** • lesbians/ gay men • nonsmoking • secluded, rustic cabin • women-owned • $110-260

Tea Island Resort 3020 Lake Shore Dr, Lake George **518/668–2776** • gay-friendly • chalets, cottages & suites • $115-210

Binghamton

Info Lines & Services

AA Gay/ Lesbian **607/722–5983**

Bars

Merlin's 201 State St **607/722–1022** • 8pm-close, till 3am Fri-Sat • lesbians/ gay men • neighborhood bar • dancing/DJ • live shows • karaoke • 18+ Wed-Fri & Sun

Squiggy's 34 Chenango St (at Court) **607/722–2299** • 6pm-midnight, till 2am Fri-Sat, from 8pm Sat, clsd Sun • lesbians/ gay men • neighborhood bar • dancing/DJ Fri-Sat • karaoke

Cafes

Lost Dog Cafe 222 Water St (at Henry) **607/771–6063** • 11:30am-10pm, till 11pm Fri-Sat, clsd Sun • popular • some veggie • beer/ wine • live shows • wheelchair access

Restaurants

The Whole in the Wall 43 S Washington St **607/722–5138** • 11:30am-9pm, clsd Sun-Mon • plenty veggie/ vegan

Buffalo

Info Lines & Services

Lesbian/ Gay AA 206 S Elmwood Ave, Elmwood **716/852–7743** • 8pm Mon & Wed

Pride Center of Western NY 206 S Elmwood Ave **716/852–7743** • meetings, resources & more

ACCOMMODATIONS

Beau Fleuve B&B 242 Linwood Ave 716/882-6116, 800/278-0245 • gay-friendly • $120-175

The Mansion on Delaware 414 Delaware Ave 716/886-3300 • gay/straight • WiFi • wheelchair access • $195-375

BARS

Adonia's 20 Allen St 716/332-1205 • 3pm-2am, till 4am Fri-Sat, from noon Sun • lesbians/ gay men • dancing/DJ • karaoke

Cathode Ray 26 Allen St (at N Pearl) 716/884-3615 • 1pm-4am, from 7am Sun • mostly gay men • neighborhood bar • wheelchair access

Fugazi 503 Franklin St (near Allen St) 716/881-3588 • 5pm-2am • gay/ straight • intimate cocktail lounge • videos

K Gallagher's 73 Allen St 716/886-6676 • 5pm-10pm, till 11pm Fri-Sat • gay-friendly • neighborhood bar • multiracial clientele • comfort food served • wheelchair access

Q 44 Allen St 716/332-2223 • 3pm-4am, from noon wknds • lesbians/ gay men • neighborhood bar

Roxy 884 Main St (at Carlton) 716/882-9293 • 8pm-4am Wed-Sat • mostly women • dancing/DJ • alternative • live shows • karaoke

The Underground 274 Delaware Ave (at Johnson) 716/853-0092 • noon-4am • mostly gay men • neighborhood bar • dancing/DJ • karaoke

NIGHTCLUBS

Club Marcella 622 Main St 716/847-6850 • 10pm-4am, clsd Mon-Wed • lesbians/ gay men • dancing/DJ • drag shows • wheelchair access

CAFES

Cafe 59 59 Allen St (at Franklin) 716/883-1880 • 8am-6pm, 10am-5pm Sat, clsd Sun • WiFi • gay-owned

RESTAURANTS

Allen Street Hardware Cafe 245 Allen St (at College) 716/882-8843 • from 5pm daily • full bar • live music • art

Anchor Bar 1047 Main St 716/886-8920, 716/884-4083 • 11am-10pm, till midnight Fri-Sat

Atmosphere 62 62 Allen St (at Franklin) 716/881-0062 • from 4pm Wed-Sat • full bar

Mothers 33 Virginia Pl (at Virginia St) 716/882-2989 • 5pm-3am, 2pm-midnight Sun

Rue Franklin 341 Franklin St (at W Tupper) 716/852-4416 • 5:30pm-10pm, clsd Sun-Mon • upscale, contemporary French

Tempo 581 Delaware Ave (at Allen St) 716/885-1594 • upscale Italian/ American

Towne Restaurant 186 Allen St 716/884-5128 • 7am-5am, clsd Sun • Greek

ENTERTAINMENT & RECREATION

Babeville 341 Delaware Ave (at W Tupper) 716/852-3835 • Ani Di Franco's rehabbed church performance space • also Hallwalls Arts Center

Buffalo United Artists 119 Chippewa (btwn Delaware & Elmwood) 716/886-9239 • gay-themed theater company

BOOKSTORES

Talking Leaves 3158 Main St (btwn Winspear & Hertel Aves) 716/837-8554 • 10am-6pm, till 8pm Wed-Th, clsd Sun • also 951 Elmwood Ave, 716/884-9524

PUBLICATIONS

Outcome Buffalo 495 Linwood Ave 716/228-8828 • monthly

EROTICA

Adult Mart 3102 Delaware Ave (at Sheridan), Kenmore 716/877-5027 • 24hrs • women receive 20% off Wed

Video Liquidators 1770 Elmwood Ave 716/874-7223 • 24hrs

Canandaigua

ACCOMMODATIONS

Chalet of Canandaigua Bed & Breakfast 3770 State Rte 21 (at Nott Rd) 585/394-9080 • gay-friendly • log cabin • perfect for romantic getaways • WiFi • lesbian-owned • $235-295

Canton

RESTAURANTS

Spicy Iguana 21 Miner St 315/714-2155 • 4pm-9pm, till 2am Fri-Sat, clsd Sun-Mon • Mexican

Capital District

includes Albany, Cohoes, Salem, Schenectady & Troy

INFO LINES & SERVICES

Capital District Lesbian/ Gay Community Center 332 Hudson Ave, Albany 518/462-6138 • social & human service programs • also Rainbow Cafe 6pm-9pm, clsd Sat

Gay AA 332 Hudson Ave (at L/G Community Center), Albany 518/462–6138 • 7:30pm Sun

Women's Building 373 Central Ave, Albany 518/462–2871 • community center • call for hours

ACCOMMODATIONS

The Morgan State House 393 State St, Albany 518/427–6063, 888/427–6063 • gay-friendly • 1800s town house • nonsmoking • WiFi • $135-260

BARS

Clinton Street Pub 159 Clinton St, Schenectady 518/377–8555 • 11am-close • lesbians/ gay men • neighborhood bar • dancing/DJ • live shows • karaoke

Oh Bar 304 Lark St (at Madison), Albany 518/463–9004 • 2pm-4am • lesbians/ gay men • neighborhood bar • multiracial • karaoke • videos • wheelchair access

Waterworks Pub 76 Central Ave (btwn Lexington & Northern), Albany 518/465–9079 • 1pm-4am • popular • mostly gay men • neighborhood bar • dancing/DJ wknds • garden bar • food served • karaoke • 18+ • wheelchair access

NIGHTCLUBS

Fuze Box 12 Central Ave, Albany 518/432–4472 • 2pm-4am, from 8pm Th-Sat • gay/ straight • dancing/DJ • live shows • swing dancing • gay-owned

RESTAURANTS

Bob's Lunch & Dairy Bar 4139 Rte 22 (Junction Rtes 22 & 29), Salem 518/854–7505 • 11am-9pm April-Oct • great soft serve

Bomber's Burrito Bar 258 Lark St, Albany 518/463–9636 • 11am-2am, till 3am wknds • plenty veggie • gay-owned

Debbie's Kitchen 456 Madison Ave (btwn Lark St & Washington Park), Albany 518/463–3829 • 10am-7pm, 11am-6pm Sat, clsd Sun

El Loco Mexican Cafe 465 Madison Ave (btwn Lark & Willett), Albany 518/436–1855 • lunch Wed-Sat, dinner nightly, clsd Mon • healthy Tex-Mex • full bar

Midtown Tap & Tea Room 289 New Scotland Ave 518/435–0202 • 11am-11pm, till 6pm Sun, clsd Mon • wheelchair access • lesbian-owned

Yono's 25 Chapel St (at Sheridan), Albany 518/436–7747 • 5:30pm-10pm, clsd Sun-Mon • full bar • live music • wheelchair access

ENTERTAINMENT & RECREATION

Albany All Stars Albany • Albany's female roller derby league

RETAIL SHOPS

Romeo's Gifts 299 Lark St (at Madison), Albany 518/434–4014 • noon-9pm, till 5pm Sun

Catskill Mtns

INFO LINES & SERVICES

Wise Woman Center 845/246–8081 • women only • workshops • correspondence courses • newsletter

ACCOMMODATIONS

Beds on Clouds 5320 Main St/ Rte 23 (at CR21), Windham 518/734–4692 • gay/ straight • 1854 mansion features suites & famous artwork • woman-owned • $89-179

Bradstan Country Hotel 1561 Rte 17-B, White Lake 845/583–4114 • gay-friendly • also cottages • piano bar & cabaret from 9pm-1am Fri-Sat • $135-200

Country Suite Rte 23, Windham 518/734–4079 • B&B • Victorian-style farmhouse • full brkfst • some shared baths • nonsmoking • kids ok • wheelchair access • lesbian-owned • $139-179

Cuomo's Cove 33 Cumo's Cove Rd (at South St), Windham 518/734–5903, 800/734–5903 • gay-friendly • nonsmoking • women-owned • $120-350

ECCE B&B 19 Silverfish Rd, Barryville 845/557–8562, 888/557–8562 • gay/ straight • B&B 300 ft above Upper Delaware River • full brkfst • WiFi • nonsmoking • gay-owned • $175-285

Inn at Stone Ridge Rte 209, Stone Ridge 845/687–0736 • gay-friendly • 1700s mansion • full brkfst • also fine dining • full bar • patio • $195-425

Kate's Lazy Meadow Motel 5191 Rte 28, Mt Tremper 845/688–7200 • gay-friendly • love shack owned by Kate Pierson of the B-52s • WiFi • nonsmoking • $230-280

Point Lookout Mountain Inn The Mohican Trail, Rte 23, East Windham 518/734–3381 • gay-friendly • near skiing • hot tub • nonsmoking • kids/ pets ok • also restaurant & cafe • wheelchair access • $90-200

The Roxbury, Contemporary Catskill Lodging 2258 County Hwy 41 (at Bridge St), Roxbury 607/326-7200 • gay/ straight • hip country motel • kids ok • nonsmoking • WiFi • wheelchair access • gay-owned • $90-350

Village Green 845/679-0313 • B&B • gay-owned • $115-150

BARS

Public Restaurant & Lounge 2318 City Hwy 41 (Bridge St), Roxbury 607/326-4026, 607/326-7056 • 5pm-9pm, till midnight Fri-Sat, clsd Mon-Tue • gay-friendly • gay-owned

RESTAURANTS

Catskill Rose 5355 Rte 212, Mt Tremper 845/688-7100 • 5pm-close Th-Sun • some veggie • full bar • patio • also lodging

ENTERTAINMENT & RECREATION

Frog Hollow Farm Old Post Rd, Esopus 845/384-6424 • riding school

BOOKSTORES

Golden Notebook 29 Tinker St, Woodstock 845/679-8000 • 10:30am-7pm, till 6pm Sun • LGBT section • wheelchair access

Cherry Creek

ACCOMMODATIONS

The Cherry Creek Inn 1022 West Rd (CR68) (at Center Rd) 716/296-5105 • gay-friendly • B&B • full brkfst • in wine & Amish country • kids ok • $85-150

Cooperstown

see Sharon Springs

Corning

ACCOMMODATIONS

Black Sheep Inn 8329 Pleasant Valley Rd (Rte 54), Hammondsport 607/569-3767, 877/274-6286 • gay/ straight • full brkfst • nonsmoking • WiFi • $149-269

Hillcrest Manor B&B 227 Cedar St (at Fourth St) 607/936-4548, 607/654-9136 • gay-friendly • 1890 neo-classical mansion • nonsmoking • WiFi • gay-owned • $165-200

Rufus Tanner House B&B 60 Sagetown Rd, Pine City 607/732-0213, 800/360-9259 • gay/ straight • full brkfst • hot tub • nonsmoking • WiFi • wheelchair access • $90-150

Croton-on-Hudson

ACCOMMODATIONS

Alexander Hamilton House 49 Van Wyck St 914/271-6737 • gay/ straight • full brkfst • pool • nonsmoking • kids/pets ok • WiFi • $125-350

Elmira

BARS

Chill 200 W 5th 607/732-1414 • 6pm-1am, clsd Sun-Tue • lesbians/ gay men • neighborhood bar • dancing/DJ • karaoke • drag shows • gay-owned

Findley Lake

ACCOMMODATIONS

Blue Heron Inn 10412 Main St (at Shadyside Rd) 716/769-7852 • gay-friendly • B&B • full brkfst • kids ok • nonsmoking • $129-149

Fire Island

see also Long Island

INFO LINES & SERVICES

AA 631/654-1150 • call for meeting times

ACCOMMODATIONS

Dune Point Guesthouse 631/597-6261, 631/560-2200 (CELL) • lesbians/ gay men • hot tub • kids/ pets ok • nonsmoking • wheelchair access • lesbian & gay & straight-owned/ run • $75-525

Grove Hotel Dock Walk, Cherry Grove 631/597-6600 • mostly gay men • pool • nudity • nonsmoking room available • wheelchair access • gay-owned • $50-550

Hotel Ciel Harbor Walk 631/597-6500 • mostly gay men • swimming • also restaurant • wheelchair access

The Madison Fire Island Pines 631/597-6061 • mostly gay men • guesthouse w/ full amenities • pool • nonsmoking • WiFi • gay-owned • $200-776

BARS

Blue Whale Harbor Walk, The Pines 631/597-6500 • seasonal • lesbians/ gay men • popular • dancing/DJ • popular Low Tea dance • also restaurant • wheelchair access

Cherry's On the Bay 158 Bayview Walk, Cherry Grove **631/597-7859** • seasonal • noon-4am • popular • lesbians/ gay men • dancing/DJ • piano bar • live shows • drag shows • also restaurant • patio

Pines Bistro & Martini Bar 36 Fire Island Blvd, The Pines **631/597-6862** • seasonal, opens 6pm

Sip n' Twirl 36 Fire Island Blvd, The Pines **631/597-3599** • seasonal • noon-4am • mostly gay men • dancing/DJ • also piano bar

NIGHTCLUBS

Ice Palace Bayview Walk, Cherry Grove **631/597-6600** • hours vary • popular • lesbians/ gay men • dancing/DJ • drag shows • wheelchair access

The Pavilion Harbor Walk, The Pines **631/597-6500** • seasonal • noon-8am Fri-Sun only • lesbians/ gay men • popular • dancing/DJ • popular High Tea dance • wheelchair access

CAFES

Canteen Harbor Walk, The Pines **631/597-6500** • coffee, smoothies, cocktails & food

RESTAURANTS

Jumpin' Jack's Seafood Shack Ocean Walk, Cherry Grove **631/597-4174** • seasonal • lunch & dinner • also piano bar

Marina Meat Market Harbor Walk, The Pines **631/597-6588** • great sandwiches

Pines Pizza 36 Fire Island Blvd, The Pines **631/597-3597** • seasonal, 11am-11pm

ENTERTAINMENT & RECREATION

Cherry Grove Beach • lesbians/ gay men • nude beach

Invasion of the Pines The Pines dock (July 4th wknd) • come & enjoy the annual fun as boatloads of drag queens from Cherry Grove arrive to terrorize the posh Pines

GYMS & HEALTH CLUBS

Deck Pool & Gym Harbor Walk, The Pines • 7am-6pm • day passes available

Geneva

ACCOMMODATIONS

Belhurst 4069 Rte 14 S (near Snell Rd) **315/781-0201** • gay-friendly • in historic castle overlooking Seneca Lake • fireplaces • also restaurant • $65-365

Glens Falls

ACCOMMODATIONS

Glens Falls Inn 25 Sherman Ave **646/824-8379** • gay-friendly • B&B in Victorian • full brkfst • WiFi • woman-owned • $130-342

Hamptons

see Long Island—Suffolk/ Hamptons

Hudson Valley

Hudson Valley includes Catskill, High Falls, Highland, Hudson, Hyde Park, Kinderhook, Kingston, New Paltz, Poughkeepsie, Rhinebeck & Saugerties

ACCOMMODATIONS

Barclay Heights B&B 158 Burt St (at Trinity Place), Saugerties **845/246-3788** • gay-friendly • full brkfst • cozy Victorian cottage • nonsmoking • $175-245

The Country Squire B&B 251 Allen St (at 3rd), Hudson **845/822-9229** • gay/ straight • restored Queen Anne • kids ok • nonsmoking • WiFi • $135-195

Harmony House B&B 1659 Route 212, Saugertie **845/679-1277** • gay/straight • full brkfst • WiFi • gay owned

Lefèvre House B&B 14 Southside Ave, New Paltz **845/255-4747** • gay/ straight • full brkfst • hot tub • kids ok • close to outdoor activities • WiFi • gay-owned • $185-265

Van Schaack House 20 Broad St (at Albany Rd), Kinderhook **518/758-6118** • gay-friendly • B&B • full brkfst • nonsmoking • gay-owned • $150-210

BARS

Congress 411 Main St (off Academy), Poughkeepsie **845/486-9068** • 3pm-4am, from 7pm Sat-Sun • lesbians/ gay men • neighborhood bar • wheelchair access

NIGHTCLUBS

Primetime 3353 Rte 9 W, Highland **845/691-7878** • 9pm-4am Fri-Sat only • lesbians/ gay men • dancing/DJ

RESTAURANTS

Armadillo Bar & Grill 97 Abeel St, Kingston **845/339-1550** • lunch wknds, dinner nightly, clsd Mon • full bar • patio

Locust Tree Restaurant 215 Hugcnot St (behind conference center), New Paltz **845/255–7888** • 5pm-close, Sun brunch 11am-3pm, clsd Mon-Tue

Northern Spy Cafe Rte 213, High Falls **845/687–7298** • dinner only, clsd Mon • plenty veggie • full bar • wheelchair access

Quinn's Luncheonette 330 Main St, Beacon **845/831–8065** • 6am-1:30pm • great bread

Terrapin 6426 Montgomery St, Rhinebeck **845/876–3330** • lunch & dinner • bistro & bar • patio

The Would Restaurant 120 North Rd (off Rte 9 W), Highland **845/691–9883** • dinner nightly, clsd Sun • some veggie • full bar • patio • gay-owned

ENTERTAINMENT & RECREATION

Dia:Beacon Riggio Galleries 3 Beekman St (at Rte 9D), Beacon **845/440–0100** • modern art museum

Ithaca

INFO LINES & SERVICES

AA Gay/ Lesbian 607/273–1541

ACCOMMODATIONS

Juniper Hill B&B 16 Elm St (at Main St), Trumansburg 607/387–3044, 888/809–1367 • gay-friendly • full brkfst • nonsmoking • WiFi • gay-owned • $135+

Noble House Farm 215 Connecticut Hill Rd, Newfield 607/277–4798 • gay-friendly • near gorges & wine tours • kids/ pets ok • nonsmoking • wheelchair access • lesbian-owned • $100-135

William Henry Miller Inn 303 N Aurora St (at E Buffalo St) 607/256–4553, 877/256–4553 • gay-friendly • full brkfst • pets ok • kids over 12 ok • WiFi • nonsmoking • $165-250

BARS

Felicia's Atomic Lounge 508 W State St (Meadow St) 607/273–2219 • 4pm-1am • clsd Mon • gay-friendly • food served • live entertainment • piano bar • lesbian-owned

Oasis 1230 Danby Rd/ Rte 96-B (at Comfort) 607/273–1505 • 4pm-1am, clsd Mon • popular • lesbians/ gay men • dancing/DJ • multiracial • live music Fri • also restaurant • wheelchair access

CAFES

Sarah's Patisserie 200 Pleasant Grove Rd (at Hanshaw Rd) 607/257–4257 • 10am-6pm, clsd Sun-Mon • lesbian-owned

ENTERTAINMENT & RECREATION

Out Loud Chorus 607/280–0374

BOOKSTORES

Colophon Books Inc 205 N Aurora St 607/277–5608 • 11am-7pm, clsd Sun-Mon • alternative independent • LGBT section • wheelchair access

Jamestown

ACCOMMODATIONS

Fairmount Motel 138 W Fairmount (Rte 394) 716/763–9550 • gay-friendly • near Chautauqua Institution • kids ok • WiFi • gay-owned • $45+

BARS

Sneakers 100 Harrison (at Institute) 716/484–8816 • 2pm-2am, clsd Mon • lesbians/ gay men • dancing/DJ Fri-Sat • wheelchair access

ENTERTAINMENT & RECREATION

The Lucille Ball Desi Arnaz Center 2 W 3rd St (at Main) 716/484–0800, 877/582–9326 • for those who love Lucy

Little Falls

CAFES

Piccolo Cafe 365 S Ann St 315/823–9856 • lunch Mon-Fri, dinner Wed-Sun

LONG ISLAND

Long Island is divided into 2 geographical areas:
Long Island—Nassau
Long Island—Suffolk/ Hamptons
see also Fire Island

Long Island—Nassau

INFO LINES & SERVICES

Gay/ Lesbian Switchboard of Long Island (GLSB of LI) 631/665–3700 • 7pm-10pm weekdays only

BARS

Franky B's Roadhouse 2955 Merrick Rd, Bellmore 516/765–3892 • 5pm-4am, from noon Sun • gay-friendly • neighborhood bar • dancing/DJ

Roosters 2640 N Jerusalem Rd, Bellmore 516/557–2179 • 8pm-4am, from 5pm wknds • mostly gay men • dancing/DJ • drag shows • karaoke

NIGHTCLUBS

Pure Silk 103 Post Ave (at Chi Lounge), Westbury **516/474-1707** • 4pm-9pm Sun only • monthly party • mostly women • dancing/DJ

Shy Lounge 2686 Hempstead Tpke, Levittown **516/520-1332** • 10pm-4am Wed for Deluxe & Sat for Gation • lesbians/ gay men • dancing/DJ

RESTAURANTS

RS Jones 153 Merrick Ave (off Sunrise), Merrick **516/378-7177** • dinner, clsd Mon • Tex-Mex • women-owned

ENTERTAINMENT & RECREATION

Pride for Youth Coffeehouse 2050 Bellmore Ave, Bellmore **516/679-9000** • 7:30pm-11:30pm Fri • ages 13-20 • live music

PUBLICATIONS

PM Entertainment Magazine 516/845-0759 • covers Long Island, NJ & NYC

Long Island—Suffolk/ Hamptons

ACCOMMODATIONS

East Hampton Village B&B 172 Newtown Ln (at McGuirk St), East Hampton **631/324-1858** • gay/ straight • lovely turn-of-the-century home • nonsmoking • WiFi • $199-699

Hampton Resorts & Hospitality 1655 Country Rd 39, Southampton **631/283-6100** • gay-friendly • pool • jacuzzi • kids/ pets ok • wheelchair access • $120-500

Mill House Inn 31 N Main St (at Newtown Lane), East Hampton **631/324-9766** • gay-friendly • B&B • full brkfst • nonsmoking • kids/ dogs ok • WiFi • wheelchair access • $225-1,950

Stirling House B&B 104 Bay Ave, Greenport **631/477-0654, 800/551-0654** • gay-friendly • full brkfst • jacuzzi • nonsmoking • WiFi • gay-owned • $150-295

Sunset Beach 35 Shore Rd, Shelter Island **631/749-2001** • gay-friendly • seasonal • food served • $345+

NIGHTCLUBS

Bunkhouse 192 N Main St/ Montauk Hwy (at Foster Ave), Sayville **631/319-6808** • 8pm-4am • mostly gay men • dancing/DJ • karaoke • live shows • wheelchair access • gay-owned

RESTAURANTS

Babette's 66 Newtown Ln, East Hampton **631/329-5377** • seasonal • brkfst, lunch & dinner • healthy • plenty veggie • woman-owned

Club Mojo 191 Higbie Ln, W Islip **631/661-2233** • 11:30am-close • karaoke • entertainment

ENTERTAINMENT & RECREATION

Fowler Beach Southampton

Middletown

ACCOMMODATIONS

Best Western Inn at Hunt's Landing 120 Rtes 6 & 209, Matamoras, PA **570/491-2400, 800/528-1234** • gay-friendly • pool • gym • restaurant & bar • WiFi

Montgomery

ACCOMMODATIONS

The Borland House B&B 130 Clinton St **845/457-1513** • gay-friendly • full brkfst • nonsmoking • WiFi • $120-185

NEW YORK CITY

New York City is divided into 9 geographical areas:
  NYC—Overview
  NYC—Soho, Greenwich & Chelsea
  NYC—Downtown
  NYC—Midtown
  NYC—Uptown
  NYC—Brooklyn
  NYC—Queens
  NYC—Bronx
  NYC—Staten Island

NYC—Overview

INFO LINES & SERVICES

AA Gay/ Lesbian Intergroup at Lesbian/ Gay Community Center **212/647-1680**

Lesbian Herstory Archives 718/768-3953 • exists to gather & preserve records of lesbian lives & activities • located in Park Slope, Brooklyn • wheelchair access

LGBT Community Center 208 W 13th (at 7th Ave) **212/620-7310** • 9am-11pm • popular • many group meetings & resources • museum • wheelchair access

ACCOMMODATIONS

Manhattan Getaways 212/956–2010 • gay/straight • B&B rooms & private apts throughout Manhattan • kids over 10 years old ok • woman-owned

NIGHTCLUBS

Kurfew • teen/ twink/ 18+ parties around the city

Sholay Productions/ Desilicious 212/713–5111 • monthly party • lesbians/ gay men • Bollywood, bhangra & house music • multiracial • call for dates

ENTERTAINMENT & RECREATION

Before Stonewall: A Lesbian & Gay History Tour meet: Washington Square Arch (at Big Onion Walking Tours) 212/439–1090

Gotham Girls Roller Derby 888/830–2253 • NYC's female roller derby league

New York Liberty Madison Square Garden, New York 212/465–6766 • check out the Women's Nat'l Basketball Association while you're in New York

PUBLICATIONS

Gay City News 646/229–1890 • LGBT newspaper • weekly

GO Magazine 888/466–9244 • the nation's most widely distributed, free, lesbian publication • "cultural road map for the city girl" • listings, features, entertainment, style, fitness & more

MetroSource 212/691–5127 • LGBT lifestyle magazine & resource directory

Next 212/627–0165 • entertainment & nightlife paper

Odyssey Magazine 323/874–8788 • dish on L.A. & Palm Springs' club scene

PM Entertainment Magazine 516/845–0759 • events, listings, classifieds & more for Long Island, NJ & NYC

Velvetpark Magazine 347/881–1025, 888/616–1989 • quarterly lesbian/ feminist glossy w/ focus on the arts

SEX CLUBS

Submit 718/789–4053 • monthly • women & trans play party • takes place in Park Slope, Brooklyn, call for exact location

New York City

WHERE THE GIRLS ARE:

Upwardly mobile literary types hang in the West Village, hipster dykes cruise the East Village, upper-crusty lesbians have cocktails in Midtown, and working-class dykes live in Brooklyn.

LGBT PRIDE:

Last Sunday in June. 212/807-7433, web: www.hopinc.org.

Brooklyn Pride - June. 718/670-3337, web: www.brooklynpride.org.

ANNUAL EVENTS:

March - Saint-at-Large Black Party, web: www.saintatlarge.com.

May - AIDS Walk 212/807-9255, web: www.aidswalk.net/newyork.

May/June - NewFest: NY LGBT Film Festival 212/571–2170, web: www.newfestival.org.

July - HOT Festival of queer performance, web: hotfestival.org.

July - Siren Music Festival, web: www.villagevoice.com/siren.

September - Howl Festival 212/243–3413, web: www.howlfestival.com. Poetry & cabaret in Tompkins Square Park in the East Village.

November - New York Lesbian/Gay Experimental Film/Video Fest 212/742–8880, web: www.mixnyc.com. Film, videos, installations & media performances.

CITY INFO:

212/484-1200. nycgo.com

BEST VIEW:

Coming over any of the bridges into New York or from the Empire State Building.

WEATHER:

A spectrum of extremes with pleasant moments thrown in. Spring and fall are the best times to visit.

ATTRACTIONS:

American Museum of Natural History 212/769-5100, web: www.amnh.org.

Broadway.

Brooklyn Botanic Garden 718/623-7200, web: www.bbg.org.

Carnegie Hall 212/247-7800, web: www.carnegiehall.org.

Central Park.

Ellis Island, web: www.ellisisland.org.

Elizabeth A. Sackler Center for Feminist Art 718/638-5000, web: www.brooklynmuseum.org/eascfa.

Empire State Building 212/736-3100, web: www.esbnyc.com.

Greenwich Village.

Guggenheim Museum 212/423-3500, web: www.guggenheim.org.

International Center of Photography 212/857-0000, web: www.icp.org.

Lincoln Center 212/875-5000, web: www.lincolncenter.org.

Metropolitan Museum of Art 212/535-7710, web: www.metmuseum.org.

Museum of Modern Art 212/708-9400, web: www.moma.org.

Radio City Music Hall 212/307-7171, web: www.radiocity.com.

Rockefeller Center.

Statue of Liberty 866/782-8834.

Times Square.

United Nations 212/963-8687, web: www.un.org.

Wall Street.

World Trade Center Memorial.

TRANSIT:

Wave an arm on any streetcorner for a taxi.

Public transit MTA 718/330-1234, web: www.mta.info.

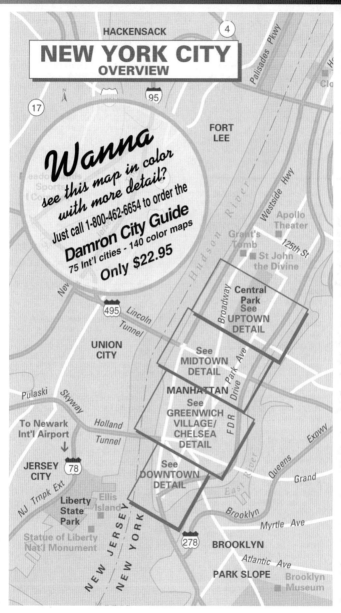

NEW YORK CITY
OVERVIEW

HACKENSACK

Palisades Pkwy

(4)

(17)

(95)

FORT LEE

Wanna see this map in color with more detail?

Just call 1-800-462-6654 to order the

Damron City Guide

75 Int'l cities - 140 color maps

Only $22.95

Hudson River

Westside Hwy

Apollo Theater

Grant's Tomb

125th St

St John the Divine

Broadway

Central Park
See UPTOWN DETAIL

New

(495) Lincoln Tunnel

UNION CITY

See MIDTOWN DETAIL

Park Ave

MANHATTAN

Drive

See GREENWICH VILLAGE/ CHELSEA DETAIL

FDR

Pulaski

Skyway

Holland Tunnel

To Newark Int'l Airport
↓

JERSEY CITY (78)

See DOWNTOWN DETAIL

East River

Queens

Expwy

Grand

Liberty State Park

Ellis Island

Brooklyn

Statue of Liberty Nat'l Monument

NEW YORK

NEW JERSEY

(278)

BROOKLYN

Myrtle Ave

Atlantic Ave

PARK SLOPE

Brooklyn Museum

NYC—Soho, Greenwich & Chelsea

ACCOMMODATIONS

Abingdon Guesthouse 21 8th Ave (at W 12th St) 212/243-5384 • gay/ straight • quiet, mature clientele • nonsmoking • wheelchair access • $179-295

Ace Hotel 20 W 29th St (at Broadway) 212/679-2222 • gay-friendly • hip hotel near Flatiron District

Chelsea Inn 46 W 17th St (btwn 5th & 6th Aves) 212/645-8989, 800/640-6469 • gay/ straight • European-style inn • kids ok • $89-289

Chelsea Pines Inn 317 W 14th St (btwn 8th & 9th Aves) 212/929-1023, 888/546-2700 • gay/ straight • WiFi • gay-owned • $150-275

The Chelsea Savoy Hotel 204 W 23rd St (at 7th Ave) 212/929-9353, 866/929-9353 • gay/ straight • kids ok • WiFi • wheelchair access • $99-425

Chelsea Star Hotel 300 W 30th St (at 8th Ave) 212/ 244-7827, 877/ 827-6969 • gay/ straight • WiFi • $149-499

Crosby Street Hotel 79 Crosby St (at Spring) 212/226-6400 • gay-friendly • chic boutique hotel in Soho • WiFi • $495+

Eventi 851 6th Ave (at 30th St) 212/564-4567, 866/996-8396 • gay-friendly • pets ok • $249+

➤**The GEM Hotel Chelsea** 300 W 22nd St (at 8th Ave) 212/675-1911 • gay/ straight • WiFi • wheelchair access • see ad in front color section

➤**The GEM Hotel SoHo** 135 E Houston St (btwn 1st & 2nd Aves) 212/358-8844 • gay/ straight • WiFi • wheelchair access • see ad in front color section

Gershwin Hotel 7 E 27th St (at 5th Ave) 212/545-8000 • gay-friendly • artsy, seedy hotel w/ model's floor dorms & rooms • art gallery • WiFi • $109+

Holiday Inn SOHO Downtown 138 Lafayette St (btwn Canal & Howard, in Chinatown) 212/966-8898 • gay-friendly • near SoHo, Chinatown & Little Italy • WiFi • $169-349

Hotel 17 225 E 17th St 212/475-2845 • gay-friendly • "East Village chic" budget hotel • shared baths • $100+

Incentra Village House 32 8th Ave (at W 13th St) 212/206-0007 • lesbians/ gay men • nonsmoking • WiFi • gay-owned • $169+

The Jane 113 Jane St (at Hudson River Pk) 212/924-6700 • gay/ straight • inspired by luxury train cabins • some shared baths • $69+

Mercer Hotel 147 Mercer St (at Prince St) 212/966-6060, 888/918-6060 • gay-friendly • food served • nonsmoking • WiFi • wheelchair access • $500+

Soho Grand Hotel 310 W Broadway (at Canal St) 212/965-3000, 800/965-3000 • gay-friendly • big, glossy, over-the-top hotel • WiFi • wheelchair access • $374+

The Standard Hotel 848 Washington St (at W 13th) 212/645-4646, 877/550-4646 • gay-friendly • ultra-modern, luxe hotel straddling the High Line

Tribeca Grand 2 Ave of the Americas 212/519-6600 • gay/ straight • WiFi • pets ok • $259+

W New York—Union Square 201 Park Ave S 212/253-9119 • gay/ straight • also restaurant & bar • WiFi • wheelchair access • $299-569

Washington Square Hotel 103 Waverly Pl (at MacDougal St) 212/777-9515, 800/222-0418 • gay-friendly • renovated 100-year-old hotel • also North Square restaurant & lounge • WiFi • $165+

➤**Wyndham Garden Hotel Chelsea** 37 W 24th St 212/243-0800 • gay-friendly • WiFi • wheelchair access • $149 -399

BARS

Arrow Bar 85 Ave A (btwn 5th & 6th) 212/673-1775 • 4pm-close • gay/ straight • dancing/DJ • theme nights

Barracuda 275 W 22nd St (at 8th Ave) 212/645-8613 • 4pm-4am • popular • mostly gay men • live DJs • drag shows

Beauty Bar 213 E 14th St (at 3rd Ave) 212/539-1389 • 5pm-4am, from 7pm wknds • gay/ straight • dancing/DJ

The Boiler Room 86 E 4th St (at 2nd Ave) 212/254-7536 • 4pm-4am • popular • mostly gay men • neighborhood bar • WiFi

Boots and Saddle 76 Christopher St (at 7th Ave S) 212/633-1986 • noon-4am • mostly gay men • neighborhood bar • bears & leather crowd • multiracial clientele

Cake Shop 152 Ludlow St (btwn Stanton & Rivington) 212/253-0036 • 9am-2am, till 4am wknds • gay-friendly • cafe/ bakery by day, punk bands at night

Cubbyhole 281 W 12th St (at 4th St) 212/243–9041 • 4pm-4am, from 2pm wknds • lesbians/ gay men • neighborhood bar

Desire 45 W 8th St (btwn 5th & 6th Aves) 646/454–9950 • 3pm-close • mostly gay men • neighborhood bar • theme nights

Eastern Bloc 505 E 6th St (at Ave A) 212/777–2555 • 7pm-4am • popular • lesbians/ gay men • trendy lounge w/ DJ • go-go boys Th-Sat • wheelchair access

G Lounge 225 W 19th St (at 7th Ave) 212/929–1085 • 4pm-4am • popular • mostly gay men • lounge • live DJs • gay-owned

Gym Sports Bar 167 8th Ave (btwn 18th & 19th) 212/337–2439 • 4pm-close, from 1pm wknds • mostly gay men • neighborhood sports bar

Henrietta Hudson 438 Hudson (at Morton) 212/924–3347 • 4pm-4am, from 2pm wknds • mostly women • neighborhood bar • dancing/DJ • wheelchair access

Marie's Crisis 59 Grove St (at 7th Ave) 212/243–9323 • 4pm-4am • lesbians/ gay men • piano bar from 9:30pm (from 5pm Fri-Sun)

The Monster 80 Grove St (at W 4th St, Sheridan Square) 212/924–3558 • 4pm-4am, from 2pm wknds • popular • mostly gay men • dancing/DJ • piano bar & cabaret • T-dance Sun • wheelchair access

Nowhere 322 E 14th St (btwn 1st & 2nd) 212/477–4744 • 3pm-4am • lesbians/ gay men • transgender-friendly Th • neighborhood bar

Phoenix 447 E 13th St (at Ave A) 212/477–9979 • 4pm-4am • lesbians/ gay men • neighborhood bar • patio

RF Lounge 531 Hudson St (at Charles St) 917/262–0836 • 4pm-2am, till 4am Th-Sat • mostly women

Stonewall Inn 53 Christopher St (at 7th Ave) 212/488–2705 • 1pm-4am • mostly gay men • neighborhood bar • dancing/DJ • drag shows

Vig 27 119 E 27th St (btwn Park & Lexington) 212/686–5500 • lesbians/ gay men • lounge • theme nights • food served

Nightclubs

Big Apple Ranch 39 W 19th St, 5th flr (btwn 5th & 6th, at Dance Manhattan) 212/358–5752 • 8pm-1am Sat only • lesbians/ gay men • dancing/DJ • country/ western • two-step lessons • beer only • cover charge

The Box 189 Chrystie St (btwn Rivington & Stanton) 212/982–9301 • 11pm-close • gay/ straight • live shows • cabaret • transgender-friendly • cover charge

Creme de la Femme 30 E 16th St (at Union Square Lounge) • 8pm-3am Wed only • lounge around the elliptical stone fireplace at this upscale party for women

Happy Ending 302 Broome St (at Forsyth) 212/334–9676 • 7pm-4am, clsd Sun-Mon • gay/ straight • theme nights

Pyramid 101 Ave A (at 7th St) 212/228–4888 • gay/ straight • dancing/DJ • theme nights

Rush 579 6th Ave (off 16th St) 212/243–6100 • 10pm Fri-Sat • mostly gay men • young crowd • dancing/DJ • 18+

Sea Tea leaves from Pier 40 (West Side Hwy at Houston St) 212/675–2971 • 6pm-10pm Sun (June-Oct) • mostly gay men • dancing/DJ • professional • multiracial • buffet • live shows • gay-owned • cover

Shescape • women only • dance parties held at various locations throughout NYC area • see www.shescape.com for info

Stiletto 363 W 16th St (at 9th Ave, at the Cabanas at Maritime Hotel) • 7pm-2am Sun only (seasonal) • mostly women • dancing/DJ • upscale party

Vandam 150 Varick St (btwn Spring & Vandam, at Greenhouse) 212/807–7000 • gay Sun only • mostly gay men • dancing/DJ • spectacular lighting

Cafes

Brown Cup Cafe 334 8th Ave (at 27th St) 212/675–7765 • 7am-7pm, 8am-6pm Sat, clsd Sun

Restaurants

7A 109 Ave A (at 7th St) 212/673–6583 • 24hrs • popular • American

Agave 140 Seventh Ave (btwn 10th St & Charles) 212/989–2100 • noon-close • popular brunch • Southwestern

Angelica Kitchen 300 E 12th St (at 1st Ave) 212/228–2909 • 11:30am-10:30pm • vegetarian/ vegan

Antica Venezia 396 West St (at W 10th St) 212/229–0606 • dinner nightly • Italian

Awash 338 E 6th (btwn 1st & 2nd Aves) 212/982–9589 • 11am-11pm • Ethiopian

Benny's Burritos 93 Ave A (at 6th St) 212/254–2054 • 11am-midnight, till 1am Fri-Sat • cheap & huge • also 113 Greenwich (at Jane), 212/727-0584

Better Burger 178 Eighth Ave (at 19th St) 212/989-6688 • 11am-midnight • burgers, hot dogs, salads & more • plenty veggie

Blossom 187 9th Ave (at 21st) 212/627-1144 • lunch Fri-Sun, dinner nightly • gourmet vegan

Blue Ribbon 97 Sullivan St (at Spring St) 212/274-0404 • 4pm-4am • chef hangout • wheelchair access

Bone Lick Park 75 Greenwich Ave (at 7th Ave) 212/647-9600 • 11:30am-11pm • real pit BBQ • full bar • wheelchair access

Cola's 148 8th Ave (at 17th St) 212/633-8020 • lunch & dinner • popular • Italian • some veggie

Cowgirl Hall of Fame 519 Hudson St (at W 10th) 212/633-1133 • lunch, dinner, wknd brunch

East of Eighth 254 W 23rd St (at 8th) 212/352-0075 • lunch & dinner, bar open late

Elmo 156 7th Ave (at 20th St) 212/337-8000 • lunch & dinner, also lounge

Les Enfants Terribles 37 Canal St (at Ludlow) 212/777-7518 • 8am-4am • African/Moroccan, Brazilian, French • full bar & DJ

Garage 99 7th Ave S (at Grove St) 212/645-0600 • noon-3am • contemporary American • plenty veggie • live jazz

Gobo 401 Ave of the Americas (at W 8th) 212/255-3242 • 11:30am-11pm • vegetarian/vegan

I Coppi 432 E 9th St (at 1st Ave) 212/254-2263 • 5pm-11pm, 11am-3pm Sat-Sun • Italian

Intermezzo 202 8th Ave (at 21st St) 212/929-3433 • noon-midnight • Italian • great wknd brunch

LaVagna 545 E 5th St (btwn Aves A & B) 212/979-1005 • dinner only • Italian • some veggie

Life Cafe 343 E 10th St (at Ave B) 212/477-8791 • 10am-midnight, till 2am Fri-Sat • full bar • plenty veggie • artist hangout

Lucky Cheng's 24 1st Ave (at 2nd St) 212/995-5500, 212/473-0516 • 5:30pm-midnight • popular • Asian/fusion • full bar • drag shows • karaoke

The Noho Star 330 Lafayette St (at Bleecker) 212/925-0070 • 8am-midnight, from 10:30am wknds • eclectic European & Chinese

Omai 158 9th Ave (at 19th St) 212/633-0550 • dinner nightly • Vietnamese

Philip Marie 569 Hudson St (at 11th St) 212/242-6200 • noon-11pm, clsd Mon • New American dining • outside seating

Red Bamboo 140 W 4th St (at MacDougal) 212/260-1212 • 10am-11pm, till 1am Fri-Sat • vegetarian/vegan

Sacred Chow 227 Sullivan St (btwn W 3rd St & Bleecker) 212/337-0863 • 11am-10pm, till 11pm Fri-Sat • gourmet vegan • juice & smoothie bar • baked goods • kosher • wheelchair access

Sigiri 91 1st Ave (btwn 5th & 6th Sts) 212/614-9333 • lunch & dinner • Sri Lankan

Trattoria Pesce Pasta 262 Bleecker St (at 6th Ave) 212/645-2993 • noon-midnight

Veselka 144 2nd Ave (at 9th St) 212/228-9682 • 24hrs • Ukrainian • great pierogi

ENTERTAINMENT & RECREATION

Chelsea Classics 260 W 23rd St (btwn 7th & 8th, at Clearview Cinema) 212/691-5519 • Th night only • drag diva Hedda Lettuce hosts camp movies

Dixon Place 161 Chrystie St (at Delancey) 212/219-0736 • many gay-themed productions • also HOT Festival of queer performance in July

High Line enter on Gansevoort (at Washington) 212/500-6035 • elevated train track converted to beautiful urban park

La Mama 74 E 4th St 212/475-7710 • experimental theater

Leslie/ Lohman Gay Art Foundation & Gallery 26 Wooster St (btwn Grand & Canal) 212/431-2609 • noon-6pm, clsd Sun-Mon

PS 122 150 1st Ave (at E 9th St) 212/477-5829, 212/352-3101 (TICKETS) • it's rough, it's raw, it's real New York performance art

WOW Cafe Theatre 59-61 E 4th St, 4th flr (btwn 2nd Ave & Bowery) 212/777-4280 • open Th-Sat • women's theater

BOOKSTORES

Bluestockings Women's Bookstore 172 Allen St (btwn Stanton & Rivington) 212/777-6028 • 11am-11pm • also cafe • nightly readings • performances • live music

RETAIL SHOPS

David Samuel Menkes Custom Leather 144 Fifth Ave #3 (at 19th St) 212/989-3706 • custom leather • fetishwear • by appt only

Flight 001 96 Greenwich Ave (btwn Jane & 12th) 212/989-0001, 877/354-4481 • 11am-8pm, noon-6pm Sun • way cool travel gear

Rainbows & Triangles 192 8th Ave (at 19th St) 212/627-2166 • 11am-10pm, noon-9pm Sun • LGBT cards, books, gifts & more

Universal Gear 140 8th Ave (btwn 16th & 17th) 212/206-9119 • casual, club, athletic & designer clothing

Gyms & Health Clubs

New York Sports Club 128 8th Ave (btwn 16th & 17th) 212/627-0065 • popular • mostly gay men • day passes available

Erotica

Babeland 43 Mercer St (btwn Broome & Grande) 212/966-2120 • noon-10pm, till 11pm Wed-Sat

Babeland 94 Rivington (btwn Orchard & Ludlow) 212/375-1701 • noon-10pm, till 6pm Sun • women-owned

Pleasure Chest 156 7th Ave S (at Charles) 212/242-2158

NYC—Downtown

Accommodations

Best Western Seaport Inn 33 Peck Slip (near Front St) 212/766-6600, 800/468-3569 • gay-friendly • nonsmoking • WiFi • wheelchair access • $250+

Embassy Suites Hotel New York City 102 North End Ave 212/945-0100, 877/692-4458 • upscale all-suite hotel • nonsmoking • wheelchair access • $289+

Gild Hall Wall Street 15 Gold St (at Platt) 212/232-7700, 212/232-7800 (RESERVATIONS) • gay/ straight • high-tech boutique hotel • also restaurant & lounge • wheelchair access • $199-569

Millenium Hilton 55 Church St 212/693-2001, 877/692-4458 • pool • nonsmoking • wheelchair access • $189+

Nightclubs

Club Remix (LipStik Productions) Ladies Night 27 Park Pl (at Church & Broadway) 917/363-6907 • 10pm 1st Sat only • mostly women • dancing/DJ • multiracial • dress code

Gekko 15 Gold St (at Platt, at Gild Hall Hotel) 212/232-7700 • 8pm last Wed only • lesbians/ gay men • dancing/DJ

Restaurants

La Flaca 384 Grand St 646/692-9259 • noon-4am • Mexican • full bar

NYC—Midtown

Accommodations

Chambers Hotel 15 W 56th St (at 5th Ave) 212/974-5656, 866/204-5656 • gay-friendly • upscale boutique hotel • fabulous art collection

➤ **Comfort Inn - Midtown West** 442 W 36th St (btwn 9th & 10th) 212/714-6699 • gay-friendly • WiFi • wheelhair access • $129-399

Distrikt Hotel 342 W 40th St (at 9th Ave) 646/831-6780 • gay-friendly • WiFi • upscale boutique hotel • $209+

Doubletree Guest Suites Times Square-New York City 1568 Broadway 212/719-1600, 877/692-4458 • all-suite hotel in heart of Times Square • nonsmoking • WiFi • wheelchair access • $265+

➤ **The GEM Hotel Midtown West** 449 W 36th St (at 10th Ave) 212/967-7206 • gay/ straight • WiFi • wheelchair access • see ad in front color section

Hotel 57 130 E 57th St (at Lexington) 212/753-8841, 800/497-6028 • gay-friendly • upscale • nonsmoking • WiFi • wheelchair access • $295+

Hotel Grace 125 W 45th St (near Sixth Ave) 212/354-2323 • gay-friendly • swimming pool nonsmoking • WiFi • wheelchair access • $229-429

The Hotel Metro 45 W 35th St (at 5th Ave) 212/947-2500, 800/356-3870 • gay-friendly • art deco hotel • 1 block from Empire State Bldg • $175-550

Hudson Hotel 356 W 58th St (at 9th) 512/554-6000, 800/697-1791 • magical hotel w/ trendy bars

Ink48 653 11th Ave (at 48th St) 212/757-0088, 877/843-8869 • gay-friendly • WiFi • lux hotel in former printing house

Ivy Terrace 230 E 58th St 516/662-6862 • private studio rental • terrace • nonsmoking • women-owned • $245-300

The MAve 61 Madison Ave (at 27th St) 212/532-7373 • gay-friendly • $159+

The Pod Hotel 230 E 51st Street (near 2nd Ave) 212/355-0300, 800/742-5945 • gay-friendly • nonsmoking • WiFi • wheelchair access • compact rooms • rooftop lounge • $119+

The Strand 33 W 37th St 212/448-1024 • gay-friendly • WiFi • cont'l brkfst • $239+

Travel Inn 515 W 42nd St (at 10th Ave) 212/695-7171, 800/869-4630 • gay-friendly • outdoor pool • fitness center • wheelchair access • $125-200

The Tuscany 120 E 39th St (at Park Ave) 212/686-1600, 877/WHOTELS (RESERVATIONS ONLY) • gay/ straight • WiFi • also Parisian-style cafe-bar • wheelchair access • $249-569

BARS

9th Avenue Saloon 656 9th Ave (at 46th St) 212/307-1503 • noon-4am • mostly gay men • neighborhood bar

Bar Centrale 324 W 46th St (at 8th Ave) 212/581-3130 • 5pm-close • gay/ straight • neighborhood bar • celebs a-plenty

Bar-tini Ultra Lounge 642 10th Ave (at 45th) 917/388-2897 • 4pm-4am • mostly gay men • theme nights

Don't Tell Mama 343 W 46th St (at 9th Ave) 212/757-0788 • 4pm-4am • popular • gay-friendly • young crowd • piano bar & cabaret • cover + 2 drink minimum for cabaret • call for shows

Evolve 221 E 58th St (at 2nd Ave) 212/355-3395 • 4pm-4am • mostly gay men • theme nights

HK Hell's Kitchen 523 9th Ave (at 39th St) 212/913-9092 • swank lounge • also restaurant • theme nights

Industry 355 W 52nd St (at 9th Ave) 646/476-2747 • 4pm-4am • mostly gay men

The Ritz 369 W 46th St (btwn 8th & 9th Aves) 212/333-2554 • 4pm-4am • dancing/DJ • great place for a drink pre- or post- theater

Therapy 348 W 52nd St (at 9th) 212/397-1700 • 5pm-4am • lesbians/ gay men • live shows • cabaret • food served

Uncle Charlie's 139 E 45th St (btwn 3rd & Lexington) 212/661-9097 • 4pm-4am • mostly gay men • mostly Asian • open mic Fri-Sun • karaoke • piano bar

Vlada 331 W 51st St (btwn 8th & 9th) 212/974-8030 • 4pm-4am • mostly gay men • slick gay lounge

The Web 40 E 58th St (at Madison) 212/308-1546 • 4pm-close, from 8pm wknds • mostly gay men • dancing/DJ • mostly Asian American • go-go boys • theme nights

NIGHTCLUBS

Escuelita 301 W 39th St (at 8th Ave) 212/631-0588 • 10pm-5am Th-Sun • mostly gay men • more women Fri for Secret Fri • dancing/DJ • drag shows • Latino/a • cover • 18+

Girlnation 531 Hudson St (at Charles St, at RF Lounge) 212/391-8053 • 10pm Sat only • mostly women • popular lounge party • dancing/DJ

Jim Caruso's Cast Party 315 W 44th St (btwn 8th & 9th Aves, at Birdland) 212/581-3080 • 9:30pm-1am Mon only • popular • gay/ straight • live music • star-studded Broadway open mic & variety show

LoverGirl NYC 221 W 46th St (at 7th Ave) 212/252-3397 • 10:30pm-4am Sat • mostly women • dancing/DJ • multiracial • live shows • cover charge

RESTAURANTS

44 1/2 626 10th Ave (btwn 44 & 45) 212/399-4450 • 5:30pm-close, brunch wknds • wheelchair access • gay-owned

44 & X Hell's Kitchen 622 10th Ave (at 44th St) 212/977-1170 • lunch & dinner • American comfort food • wheelchair access • gay-owned

A Voce 41 Madison Ave (at 26th) 212/545-8555 • lunch Mon-Fri, dinner nightly • Italian • reservations recommended

Arriba Arriba 762 9th Ave (at 51st) 212/489-0810 • noon-midnight, till 1am wknds • Mexican • great margaritas

Bamboo 52 344 W 52nd St (btwn 8th & 9th Aves) 212/315-2777 • noon-4am, from 4pm Sun • sushi • also sake bar • garden

Bann 350 W 50th St (btwn 8th & 9th Aves) 212/582-4446 • lunch Mon-Fri, dinner nightly • Korean

Beacon 25 W 56th St (btwn 5th & 6th) 212/332-0500 • lunch & dinner, wknd brunch • open-fire cooking • also bar

Cafe Un Deux Trois 123 W 44th St (at Broadway) 212/354-4148 • noon-midnight, brunch wknds • popular • bistro

Lips 227 E 56th St (at 3rd Ave) 212/675-7710 • 6pm-midnight, till 1:30am Fri-Sat, gospel brunch noon-6pm Sun, clsd Mon • "the Hard Rock Cafe of drag" • Italian/ American • served by queens

Market Cafe 496 9th Ave (at 38th St) 212/967-3892 • lunch & dinner, wknd brunch • great food • gay-owned

Rice 'N' Beans 744 9th Ave (at 50th St)
212/265–4444 • 11am-10pm, till 11pm Fri-Sat
• Latin/ Brazilian • plenty veggie • beer/ wine

Vynl 754 9th Ave (at 51st St) **212/974–2003** •
11am-11pm • also bar • also at 102 8th Ave,
212/400-2118

ENTERTAINMENT & RECREATION

Ars Nova 511 W 54th St (at 10th Ave)
212/489–9800 • many gay-themed
productions

Empire State Building 350 5th Ave (btwn
33rd & 34th) • spectacular views of the city •
visit day or night

Sex & the City Tour 5th Ave, in front of the
Pulitzer Fountain (at 58th St) **212/209–3370** •
3 hours • reservations a must!

GYMS & HEALTH CLUBS

Club H Fitness 423 W 55th St (at 9th Ave)
212/245–5802

EROTICA

Come Again 353 E 53rd St (at 2nd Ave)
212/308–9394 • woman-owned erotica store

Eve's Garden 119 W 57th St #1201 (btwn 6th
& 7th) **800/848–3837** • 11am-7pm, clsd Sun-
Mon • women's sexuality boutique

NYC—Uptown

ACCOMMODATIONS

710 Guest Suites 710 St Nicholas Ave (at
145th) **212/491–5622** • gay-friendly • modern,
chic apt suites

BB Lodges 1598 Lexington Ave (btwn 101st
& 102nd) **917/345–7914** • gay/ straight •
private rooms w/ private kitchens •
nonsmoking • WiFi • gay-owned • $120-185

Country Inn the City W 77th St (at
Broadway) **212/580–4183** • gay-friendly •
studio apts in restored 1891 town house •
nonsmoking • $210-375

The Harlem Flophouse **212/662–0678** •
guesthouse • near Apollo Theatre •
nonsmoking • kids ok • WiFi • $100-150

Harlem Renaissance House
212/226–1590 • gay/ straight • in heart of
Harlem's Striver Row District • kids ok •
nonsmoking • WiFi • gay-owned • $220+/
night, $1,250/ week

Hotel Newton 2528 Broadway
212/678–6500, 800/643–5553 • gay/ straight •
hotel on Upper West Side • nearest to
Columbia University • nonsmoking • kids ok •
wheelchair access • $150-350

Mount Morris House B&B 12 Mount
Morris Park W (at 121st St) **917/478–6214** •
gay/straight • private suites and apartments in
1888 historic Manhattan Mansion • WiFi •
gay-owned • $150-295

BARS

Brandy's Piano Bar 235 E 84th St (at 2nd
Ave) **212/650–1944** • 4pm-4am • lesbians/
gay men • piano bar from 9:30pm

Cava Wine Bar 185 W 80th St (at
Amsterdam) **212/724–2282** • 5:30pm-2am,
from 3:30pm Sun • gay-friendly • also tapas

Suite 992 Amsterdam (at 109th St)
212/222–4600 • 5pm-4am • mostly gay men •
friendly neighborhood bar • karaoke • drag
shows

RESTAURANTS

Billie's Black 271 W 119th St (btwn St
Nicholas Ave & Frederick Douglass Blvd)
212/280–2248 • noon-midnight, till 4am Fri-
Sat • soul food • also full bar • live music Th-
Fri • karaoke • gay-owned

NYC—Brooklyn

INFO LINES & SERVICES

Audre Lorde Project 85 S Oxford St
718/596–0342 • noon-6pm Mon & Fri, noon-
9pm Tue-Th, 11:30pm-7pm Sat, clsd Sun •
LGBT center for people of color • transgender
welcoming • events • resources • HIV services

ACCOMMODATIONS

Hotel Le Bleu 370 4th Ave **718/625–1500,
866/427–6073**

Hotel Le Jolie 235 Meeker Ave
718/625–2100, 866/526–4097

The Loralei B&B 667 Argyle Rd (at Foster
Ave) **646/228–4656** • gay/ straight • 3-story
Victorian • nonsmoking • WiFi • gay-owned •
$125-165

South Slope Green B&B 452A 17th St (at
8th Ave) **347/721–6575** • gay/ straight •
nonsmoking • WiFi • lesbian-owned • $115

BARS

The Abbey 536 Driggs Ave (btwn N 7th &
8th), Williamsburg **718/599–4400** • 3pm-4am
• gay/ straight • neighborhood bar •
dancing/DJ

Alligator Lounge 600 Metropolitan Ave (at
Lorimer) **718/599–4440** • 3pm-4am • gay/
straight • free pizza from 6pm • karaoke Th

Bar 4 444 7th Ave (at 15th St, in Park Slope) **718/832–9800** • 6pm-4am • gay/ straight • neighborhood bar • DJ Fri-Sat • live music & performances

Blackout Bar 916 Manhattan Ave (at Kent St, Greenpoint) • gay/ straight • gay night Wed • hipster hangout • dancing/DJ

Branded Saloon 603 Vanderbilt Ave (at Bergen) **718/484–8704** • gay/ straight • more gay Tue • neighborhood bar

Excelsior 390 5th Ave (btwn 6th & 7th) **718/832–1599** • 6pm-4am, from 2pm wknds • lesbians/ gay men • patio

Ginger's Bar 363 5th Ave (btwn 5th & 6th Sts, in Park Slope) **718/788–0924** • 5pm-4am, from 2pm wknds • lesbians/ gay men • neighborhood bar • patio • occasional live shows

Metropolitan 559 Lorimer St (at Metropolitan Ave), Williamsburg **718/599–4444** • 3pm-4am • lesbians/ gay men • comfy neighborhood bar w/ 2 fireplaces • more women Wed

Sugarland 221 N 9th St (at Driggs Ave) **718/599–4044** • 8pm-4am, from 4pm wknds • gay/ lesbian • dancing/DJ • live shows • karaoke

NIGHTCLUBS

Club Langston 1073 Atlantic Ave (btwn Franklin & Classon) **718/622–5183** • 11pm-4am Tue & Th-Sat • mostly gay men • mostly African American • theme nights

Glasslands Gallery 289 Kent Ave, Williamsburg (btwn S 1st & S 2nd) **718/599–1450** • performance, art & dance space

Gumbo 16 Main St (at Water St, at Galapagos Art Space) **718/222–8500** • 10pm 1st & 3rd Fri • lesbians/ gay men • dancing/DJ • gay DUMBO party

CAFES

Jacques Torres 66 Water St **718/875–9772** • 9am-7pm, 10am-6pm Sun • chocolatier

Outpost 1014 Fulton St (at Downing) **718/636–1260** • 8am-10:30pm, from 9am wknds • lesbians/ gay men • art gallery • young, artsy crowd • also beer/ wine • gay-owned

RESTAURANTS

Alma 187 Columbia St (at Degraw) **718/643–5400** • dinner nightly, wknd brunch • upscale Mexican • outdoor rooftop seating w/ view of Manhattan • also B61 Bar downstairs

Aunt Suzie 247 5th Ave (at Garfield Pl) **718/788–2868** • dinner only • Italian

Beast 638 Bergen St (at Vanderbilt Ave) **718/399–6855** • dinner nightly, wknd brunch, also bar from 5pm

Belleville Bistro & Lounge 330 5th St (at 5th Ave) **718/832–9777** • theme nights • also bar • gay-owned

Bogota Latin Bistro 141 5th Ave (at St John's Pl) **718/230–3805** • dinner nightly, wknd brunch, clsd Tue • live music • gay-owned

ChipShop/ The Curry Shop 383 5th Ave (at 6th St) **718/244–7746** • noon-10pm, till 11pm Th-Sat, from 11am wknds • English/ Indian • home of the famous fried Twinkie!

Faan 209 Smith St (at Baltic) **718/694–2277** • lunch & dinner • pan-Asian • also bar downstairs

home made 293 Van Brunt St (btwn Pioneer & King) **347/223–4135** • dinner & wknd brunch • lesbian-owned

Johnny Mack's 1114 8th Ave (btwn 11th & 12th) **718/832–7961** • 4pm-11pm, till midnight Fri-Sat, Sun brunch

Melt 440 Bergen St (btwn 5th & Flatbush) **718/230–5925** • dinner nightly, brunch wknds, clsd Mon • new American

Nita Nita 146 Wythe Ave (at N 8th) **718/388–5328** • 4pm-2am, brunch wknds • also full bar • tapas

Santa Fe Grill 62 7th Ave (at Lincoln) **718/636–0279** • 5pm-close, from noon wknds • also bar

Superfine 126 Front St (at Pearl St) **718/243–9005** • 11:30am-4am, clsd Mon • relaxed atmoephere • live shows • also bar • lesbian-owned

Tandem 236 Troutman St (btwn Wilson & Knickerbocker, in Bushwick) **718/386–2369** • 6pm-4am • also full bar • occasional gay parties

ENTERTAINMENT & RECREATION

The Elizabeth A Sackler Center for Feminist Art 200 Eastern Pkwy (at the Brooklyn Museum, at Washington Ave) **718/638–5000**

Galapagos Art Space 16 Main St (at Water St) **718/222–8500** • performance & art space • gay DUMBO party 1st & 3rd Fri

EROTICA

Babeland 462 Bergen St (at 5th Ave) **718/638–3820** • noon-9pm, till 7pm Sun

NYC—Queens

BARS

Albatross 36-19 24th Ave (at 37th), Astoria **718/204-9045** • 6pm-4am • gay/ straight • neighborhood bar • more gay wknds • gay-owned

Hell Gate Social 12-21 Astoria Blvd (at 14th St) **718/204-8313** • 7pm-4am • gay/ straight • dancing/DJ

Mix Cafe 40-17 30th Ave (at 41st St), Astoria **347/642-4840** • 6pm-2am, noon-4am wknds • lesbians/gay men • dancing/DJ • karaoke • theme nights • brunch wknds

Music Box 40–08 74th St (at Roosevelt Ave), Jackson Hts **718/424-8612** • 4pm-4am • mostly gay men • mostly Latino • drag shows • theme nights

NIGHTCLUBS

Bum Bum Bar 6314 Roosevelt Ave **718/651-4145** • 10pm-4am Th-Sun • mostly women • dancing/DJ • mostly Latina

Club Atlantis 76–19 Roosevelt Ave (at 77th St), Jackson Hts **718/457-3939** • 4pm-4am • lesbians/gay men • dancing/DJ • mostly Latino/a • drag shows

RESTAURANTS

Mezzo Mezzo 31-29 Ditmars Blvd **718/278-0444** • 11am-1am, till 2am Th-Sun • Greek

Mundo Cafe 31-18E Broadway (at 32nd St), Astoria **718/777-2829** • 5pm-11:30pm • Mediterranean/ Turkish • plenty veggie

NYC—Bronx

BARS

Le Boy 104 Dyckman St (at Nagle) **646/692-4630** • 6pm-4am Wed-Sun • mostly gay men • dancing/DJ

No Parking 4168 Broadway (at 177th St) **212/923-8700** • 6pm-3am, from 7pm Sat-Sun • lesbians/ gay men • swank lounge

Nyack

NIGHTCLUBS

Barz 327 Rte 9 W **845/353-4444** • 8pm-4am, from 3pm Sun, clsd Mon • lesbians/ gay men • dancing/DJ • alternative • karaoke

Orange County

RESTAURANTS

Gigi's Folderol 795 Rte 284, Westtown **845/726-3822** • 5pm-close, clsd Tue-Wed • French/ farmhouse • some veggie • piano Fri-Sat • wheelchair access

EROTICA

Exotic Gifts & Videos 658 Rte 211 E (exit 120, off Rte 17), Middletown **845/692-6664**

Rochester

INFO LINES & SERVICES

Gay Alliance of the Genesee Valley (GAGV) 875 E Main St, 5th flr **585/244-8640** • events • education • youth services

ACCOMMODATIONS

Silver Waters Bed & Breakfast 8420 Bay St (at Lummis), Sodus Point **315/483-8098** • gay/ straight • full brkfst • gay-owned

BARS

140 Alex Bar & Grill 140 Alexander St (at Broadway) **585/256-1000** • 4pm-2am, from 2pm Sun • lesbians/gay men • neighborhood bar • also restaurant • dancing/DJ • live shows • karaoke • drag shows • gay-owned

Avenue Pub 522 Monroe Ave (at Goodman) **585/244-4960** • 4pm-2am • popular • mostly gay men • neighborhood bar • dancing/DJ • patio

NIGHTCLUBS

Tilt Nightclub 444 Central Ave **585/232-8440** • 10pm-2am Th-Sat • gay/ straight • dancing/DJ • drag shows

Vertex 169 N Chestnut St **585/232-5498** • 10pm-2am Wed-Sat • gay/ straight • dancing/DJ • goth club

CAFES

Little Theatre Cafe 240 East Ave **585/258-0412** • 5pm-10pm, till 11pm Fri-Sat, till 8pm Sun • popular • beer/ wine • soups • salads • live jazz • wheelchair access • art gallery

RETAIL SHOPS

Equal Grounds 750 South Ave (at Caroline) **585/242-7840** • 7am-midnight, from 10am wknds • LGBT gifts & books • also coffeehouse

Outlandish 274 N Goodman St (in the Village Gate) **585/760-8383** • 11am-9pm, noon-5pm Sun • videos • pride items • books • toys • gay-owned

PUBLICATIONS

Empty Closet 585/244-8640 • LGBT newspaper • resource listings

Saratoga Springs

ACCOMMODATIONS

The Inn at Round Lake 14 Covel Ave (at Burlington), Round Lake 513/289-5018 • gay-friendly • Victorian B&B • pool • nonsmoking • WiFi • gay-owned • $129-359

The Mansion 801 Rte 29, Rock City Falls 518/885-1607, 888/996-9977 • gay-friendly • 1860 Victorian mansion • full brkfst • fireplaces • nonsmoking • wheelchair access • gay-owned • $129-450

Saratoga B&B/ Saratoga Motel 434 Church St 518/584-0920 • gay-friendly • B&B in 1850 farmhouse & motel • full brkfst • fireplaces • nonsmoking • gay-owned • $159-289

BARS

Desperate Annie's 12 Caroline St (off Broadway) 518/587-2455 • 4pm-close • gay-friendly • neighborhood bar

RESTAURANTS

Esperanto 6 1/2 Caroline St (off Broadway) 518/587-4236 • 11am-close • doughboys!

Little India 60 Court St 518/583-4151 • lunch & dinner • tasty & authentic Indian food • beer/ wine only

Seneca Falls

RETAIL SHOPS

WomanMade Products 91 Fall St 315/568-9364 • 10am-6pm, till 4pm wknds • lesbian & feminist T-shirts • crafts

Sharon Springs

ACCOMMODATIONS

American Hotel 192 Main St 518/284-2105 • gay/ straight • 1847 Nat'l Register hotel • kids ok • also restaurant & bar • WiFi • wheelchair access • gay-owned • $150-225

Cobblescote on the Lake 6515 State Hwy 80, Cooperstown 607/437-1146 • gay-friendly • spectacular views at refurbished waterfront resort • food served • gay-owned • $155-245

Edgefield 153 Washington St 518/284-3339 • gay/ straight • full brkfst • nonsmoking • well-appointed English Country house • gay-owned

The TurnAround Spa Lodge 105 Washington St 518/284-9708, 212/628-9008 • lesbians/ gay men • small hotel & health spa • full brkfst • hot tub • food served • nonsmoking • kids ok • clsd Nov-May • lesbian- & gay-owned • $45-85

RETAIL SHOPS

The Finishing Touch 197 Main St (Rte 10) 518/284-2884 • call for hours • gallery & gift shop

Syracuse

INFO LINES & SERVICES

AA Gay/ Lesbian 315/463-5011 (AA#) • call for meeting schedule

ACCOMMODATIONS

B&B Wellington 707 Danforth St (at Carbon) 315/474-3641, 800/724-5006 • gay-friendly • full brkfst wknds • kids ok • nonsmoking • WiFi • $115-160

Yellow Lantern Kampground 1770 Rte 13 N, Cortland 607/756-2959 • gay-friendly • kids/ pets ok • pool campsites & RV hookups • $23-28

BARS

Rain Lounge 218 N Franklin St (at Herald Pl) 315/474-3487 • 4pm-2am • mostly gay men • neighborhood bar • multiracial • transgender-friendly • videos • gay-owned

NIGHTCLUBS

The Mystic 1203 Milton Ave 315/218-5897 • 7pm-2am, clsd Mon • lesbians/gay men • also Mexican food

Trexx 319 N Clinton St (exit 18, off Rte 81) 315/474-6408 • 8pm-2am, till 4am Fri-Sat, clsd Sun-Wed • mostly gay men • dancing/DJ • drag shows Sun • videos • 18+ • wheelchair access

Twist Ultralounge 252 W Genesee (at Franklin) • 4pm-2am, clsd Mon • lesbians/ gay men • theme nights • dancing/DJ • drag shows • piano bar Wed • 18+

RESTAURANTS

Cafe Mira 14 Main St, Adams 315/232-4470 • open 5pm Wed-Sat only • wheelchair access • lesbian owned

Utica

NIGHTCLUBS

That Place 216 Bleecker St (at Genesee) • 9pm-2am Wed-Sat • popular • mostly gay men • dancing/DJ • young crowd • wheelchair access

RESTAURANTS

The Hadley 2008 Genesee St (at Arnold Ave) 315/507–4264 • 5pm-10pm, clsd Sun • also bar • pianist Fri-Sat • wheelchair access • gay-owned

White Plains

INFO LINES & SERVICES

The LOFT 252 Bryant Ave 914/948–2932, 914/948–4922 (HELPLINE) • LGBT community center • call for hours • also newsletter

Westchester Lesbian Connection 914/517–5455, 914/949–3203

NORTH CAROLINA

Statewide

PUBLICATIONS

Q Notes 704/531–9988 • bi-weekly LGBT newspaper for the Carolinas

Asheville

INFO LINES & SERVICES

Lambda AA 9 Swan St 828/254–8539 (AA#), 800/524–0465 • 7pm Mon,Wed & 8pm Fri

ACCOMMODATIONS

1889 WhiteGate Inn & Cottage 173 E Chestnut St 828/253–2553, 800/485–3045 • gay/ straight • 3-course brkfst • nonsmoking • WiFi • gay-owned

The 1900 Inn on Montford 296 Montford Ave 828/254–9569, 800/254–9569 • gay-friendly • full brkfst • kids/ pets ok • nonsmoking • WiFi • $175-650

27 Blake Street 27 Blake St 828/252–7390 • gay/ straight • romantic room w/ private entrance in Victorian home • gardens • nonsmoking • WiFi • woman-owned • $80

Biltmore Village Inn 119 Dodge St (at Irwin) 828/274–8707, 866/274–8779 • gay-friendly • nonsmoking • WiFi • gay-owned • $220-325

Cedar Crest Inn 674 Biltmore Ave 828/252–1389, 877/251–1389 • gay/straight • full brkfst • gay-owned

Compassionate Expressions Mtn Inn & Healing Sanctuary 828/683–6633 • mostly women • cabins & rooms w/ a view of Blue Ridge Mtns • spa services • hot tub • nonsmoking • wheelchair access • women-owned • $90-120

Mountain Laurel B&B 139 Lee Dotson Rd, Fairview 828/628–9903, 828/712–6289 (CELL) • lesbians/ gay men • full brkfst • nonsmoking • kids ok • WiFi • lesbian-owned • $90

North Lodge on Oakland B&B 84 Oakland Rd (at Victoria Rd) 828/252–6433, 800/252–3602 • gay-friendly • nonsmoking • WiFi • gay-owned • $105-180

Rainbows End 23 Deaver St (at Reynolds) 253/732–0458 • mostly women • guest room in private home • shared baths • lesbian-owned • $45-55

The Tree House 190 Tessie Ln, Black Mountain 828/669–3889 • mostly women • transgender-friendly • nonsmoking • lesbian/ trans-owned • $50-90

BARS

Backdoor 237 Haywood St 828/252–1014 • 8pm-2am Wed-Sat only • lesbians/ gay men • neighborhood bar • drag shows • private club

O Henry's/ Straps 237 Haywood St 828/254–1891 • 2pm-2am • gay/ straight • neighborhood bar • also Straps leather bar Fri-Sat

Tressa's 28 Broadway 828/254–7072 • 4pm-2:30am, from 6pm Sat, clsd Sun • gay/ straight • jazz/ cigar bar • dancing/DJ • live shows

NIGHTCLUBS

Club Hairspray 38 N French Broad Ave (at Patton Ave) 828/258–2027 • 8pm-2am • lesbians/ gay men • neighborhood bar • drag shows • game room • patio

Fred's Speakeasy 122 College St 828/281–0920 • 4:30pm-2am, from 6pm Sun • gay-friendly • karaoke • live music venue/ dive bar

Scandals 11 Grove St (at Patton) 828/252–2838 • 10pm-3am Th-Sun • lesbians/ gay men • dancing/DJ • drag shows • videos • 18+ • private club • wheelchair access

CAFES

Laurey's 67 Biltmore Ave 828/252–1500 • 9am-6pm, till 4pm Sat, clsd Sun • popular • lesbian-owned • wheelchair access

RESTAURANTS

Barley's Taproom & Pizzeria 42 Biltmore 828/255–0504 • 11:30am-2am, till midnight Sun

Charlotte Street Grill & Pub 157 Charlotte St 828/253–5348, 828/252–2948 • noon-2am • some veggie • lesbian-owned

Early Girl Eatery 8 Wall St 828/259–9292 • brkfst & lunch daily, dinner Tue-Sat, wknd brunch • Southern • local ingredients

Firestorm Cafe & Books 48 Commerce St **828/255-8115** • 10am-11pm, clsd Sun • vegetarian • WiFi • worker owned

Laughing Seed Cafe 40 Wall St (at Haywood) **828/252-3445** • 11:30am-9pm, till 10pm Fri-Sat, Sun brunch from 10am, clsd Tue • vegetarian/vegan • beer/wine • patio • wheelchair access

Table 48 College St **828/254-8980** • 11am-2:30pm & 5:30pm-11pm, Sun brunch, clsd Tue • moderately priced New American

Tupelo Honey Cafe 12 College St **828/255-4404** • 9am-3pm & 5:30pm-10pm, clsd Sun for dinner • "Southern homecookin' w/ an uptown twist" • woman-owned

ENTERTAINMENT & RECREATION

LaZoom Tours 90 Biltmore Ave **828/225-6932** • city-wide comedy tours of Asheville, afternoons and evenings • BYOB

BOOKSTORES

Malaprop's Bookstore/ Cafe 55 Haywood St (at Walnut) **828/254-6734, 800/441-9829** • 9am-9pm, till 7pm Sun

Montford's Books 31 Montford Ave **828/285-8805** • 10am-7pm, till 8pm Fri-Sat, noon-5pm Sun • used books • WiFi

RETAIL SHOPS

Jewels That Dance: Jewelry Design 63 Haywood St **828/254-5088** • 10:30am-6pm, clsd Sun • gay-owned

EROTICA

BedTyme Stories 2334 Hendersonville Rd, Arden **828/684-8250**

Va Va Voom 36 Battery Park Ave **828/254-6329** • women's lingerie, toys, etc

Atlantic Beach

ACCOMMODATIONS

Palm Suites of Atlantic Beach 602 W Ft Macon Rd **252/247-6400, 800/972-3297** • gay-friendly • rental condos near beach • pool • nonsmoking • kids ok • wheelchair access • $95-199

Asheville

ANNUAL EVENTS:
July - Folkmoot NC International Festival (world cultural heritage celebration) 828/452-2997 or 877/365-5872, web: www.folkmootusa.org.
July - Bele Chere (music & arts festival) 828/259-5800, web: www.belecherefestival.com.

CITY INFO:
828/258-6101, web: www.ashevillechamber.org.

ATTRACTIONS:
Biltmore Estate 800/624-1575, web: www.biltmore.com.
Blue Ridge Parkway.
North Carolina Arboretum 828/665-2492, web: www.ncarboretum.org.

WEATHER:
Gorgeous: temperate summers and mild winters, with a beautiful spring and fall.

TRANSIT:
New Bluebird Taxi 828/258-8331.
Sky Shuttle 828/253-0006, web: www.ashevillelimousine.com.
Asheville Transit System 828/253-5691, web: www.ashevilletransit.com.

Blowing Rock

ACCOMMODATIONS

Blowing Rock Victorian Inn 242 Ransom St (at US 321) **828/295-0034** • gay-friendly • full brkfst • pets ok • nonsmoking • WiFi • gay-owned • $159-289

Maple Lodge 152 Sunset Dr **828/295-3331, 866/795-3331** • gay/ straight • WiFi • pets ok • nonsmoking • lesbian-owned

Brevard

ACCOMMODATIONS

Ash Grove Mountain Cabins & Camping 749 E. Fork Rd **828/885-7216** • gay/ straight • camping & cabins • on 14 wooded acres in Blue Ridge Mtns • hot tub • nonsmoking • WiFi • gay-owned • $100-160 (cabins), $25-40 (camping)

Charlotte

INFO LINES & SERVICES

Acceptance Group Gay/ Lesbian AA 1991 Queens Rd (at church) **704/377-0244, 877/233-6853** • 8pm Fri

The Lesbian/ Gay Community Center 820 Hamilton St #B11 (at Seaboard St) **704/333-0144** • 5pm-8pm Tue-Th, 10am-1pm Fri-Sat, clsd Sun-Mon

ACCOMMODATIONS

Four Points by Sheraton 315 E Woodlawn Rd (at Old Pineville Rd) **704/522-0852** • gay/ straight • fitness center • sundeck • outdoor pool • kids ok • WiFi • $129-229

VanLandingham Estate 2010 The Plaza (at Belvedere) **704/334-8909, 888/524-2020** • gay-friendly • full brkfst • nonsmoking • WiFi • gay-owned • $140-239

BARS

The Bar At 316 316 Rensselaer Ave (at South Blvd) **704/910-1478** • 5pm-2am, from 3pm Sun • popular • lesbians/ gay men • neighborhood bar • private club

Hartigan's Irish Pub 601 S Cedar St (at W Hill St) **704/347-1841** • 11am-10pm, till 2am wknds, clsd Sun • gay/ straight • neighborhood bar • dancing/DJ Fri-Sat • live shows • food served • popular lesbian hangout • gay-owned

Petra's Piano Bar 1917 Commonwealth Ave (at Thomas) **704/332-6608** • 5pm-2am, clsd Mon • gay/ straight • live shows • karaoke • WiFi

Sidelines Sports Bar & Billiards **704/525-2608** • 4pm-2am, from noon Sat-Sun • gay-friendly • neighborhood bar • food served • WiFi • private club • wheelchair access • gay-owned

Wine Up 3306 N Davidson St (at E 36th St) **704/372-2633** • gay/ straight • neighborhood bar • poetry readings, open mic & live music • frequent LGBT events • multiracial

NIGHTCLUBS

Halo 820 Hamilton St (at Seaboard St) **704/332-4256** • 10pm-2am Th-Sat • gay-friendly • dancing/DJ

Marigny Dance Club 1440 S Tryon St #110 **704/910-4444** • 10pm-2am Wed-Sat • mostly gay men • dancing/DJ

The Nickel Bar **704/916-9389** • 9pm-2am, from 5pm Sun, clsd Mon-Wed • lesbians/ gay men • dancing/DJ • mostly African American

Scorpio's 2301 Freedom Dr (at Berryhill Rd) **704/373-9124** • 9pm-3am Wed & Fri-Sun • lesbians/ gay men • dancing/DJ • multiracial • 18+ • private club • wheelchair access

CAFES

Amelie's French Bakery 2424 N Davidson St **704/376-1781** • open 24 hrs • soup & sandwiches, and of course pastries!

Caribou Coffee 1531 East Blvd (near Scott) **704/334-3570** • 6am-11pm • WiFi

Smelly Cat Coffee 514 E 36th St **704/374-9656** • 7am-10pm, till 1am Fri-Sat

RESTAURANTS

300 East 300 East Blvd (at Cleveland) **704/332-6507** • 11am-10pm, till 11pm Fri-Sat, Sun brunch • full bar • wheelchair access

Alexander Michael's 401 W 9th St (at Pine) **704/332-6789** • lunch & dinner, clsd Sun • pub fare • full bar • wheelchair access

Cosmos Cafe 300 N College (at 6th) **704/372-3553** • 11am-2am, clsd Sun • also martini lounge

Dish 1220 Thomas Ave (at Central) **704/344-0343** • 11am-10pm, till 11pm Fri-Sat, clsd Sun • comfort food • patio

Foskoskies Neighborhood Cafe 2121 Shamrock Dr **704/535-2220** • lunch & dinner • full bar • live music • wheelchair access • gay-owned

Lupie's Cafe 2718 Monroe Rd (near 5th St) **704/374-1232** • 11am-10pm, from noon Sat, clsd Sun • homestyle cookin' • some veggie

Penguin Drive-In 1921 Commonwealth Ave (at Thomas) 704/375–1925 • 11am-1am, till 2am wknds • diner extraordinaire • full bar

The Pewter Rose Bistro 1820 South Blvd (near East Blvd) 704/332–8149 • lunch & dinner • live entertainment • outdoor dining

ENTERTAINMENT & RECREATION

One Voice Chorus PO Box 9241 28299 • LGBT chorus

BOOKSTORES

Paper Skyscraper 330 East Blvd (at Euclid Ave) 704/333–7130 • 10am-7pm, till 6pm Sat, noon-5pm Sun • books • funky gifts • wheelchair access

RETAIL SHOPS

The Bag Lady 1710 Kenilworth Ave (at East Blvd) 704/338–9778 • books & gifts • events

PUBLICATIONS

Q Notes 704/531–9988 • bi-weekly LGBT newspaper for the Carolinas

Fayetteville

NIGHTCLUBS

Alias 984 Old McPherson Church Rd (at Raeford Rd) 910/484–7994 • 9pm-2:30am Fri-Sat only • lesbians/ gay men • dancing/DJ • multiracial • transgender-friendly • 18+ • private club • gay-owned

EROTICA

Cupid's Boutique 137 N Reilly Rd (at Morganton) 910/860–7716

Fort Video & News 4431 Bragg Blvd (near 401 overpass) 910/868–9905 • 24hrs

Priscilla McCall's 3800 Sycamore Dairy Rd (at Bragg Blvd) 910/860–1776

Greensboro

INFO LINES & SERVICES

Live & Let Live AA 617 N Elm St (at Presbyterian Church) 336/854–4278 (AA#) • 8pm Tue • also Free Spirit, 8pm Sat, 2105 W Market St (at Episcopal Church)

ACCOMMODATIONS

Biltmore Greensboro Hotel 111 W Washington St (at Elm St) 336/272–3474, 800/332–0303 • gay/ straight • fully restored historic hotel • gym • WiFi • kids/ pets ok • nonsmoking • gay-owned • $109-139

O Henry Hotel 624 Green Valley Rd (at Benjamin Pkwy) 336/854–2000, 800/965–8259 • gay-friendly • pool • full brkfst • afternoon tea • bar/ restaurant popular w/ local gay community • wheelchair access • $249-509

BARS

The Q 708 W Market St 336/272–2587 • 4pm-close, from 9pm Sat, from 7pm Sun • lesbians/ gay men • more women Sun • neighborhood bar • DJ • karaoke • 18+ • WiFi • patio

Time Out Saloon 330 Bellemeade St 336/272–8108 • 8:30pm-2:30am, clsd Sun-Mon • mostly women • neighborhood bar • dancing/DJ • karaoke • private club • lesbian-owned

NIGHTCLUBS

Aldo's After Party 1350 Polar Rd 336/340–5288 • 10pm-2:30am, clsd Sun-Mon • gay/ straight • dancing/DJ • drag shows • Latino • gay-owned

Warehouse 29 1011 Arnold St 336/333–9333 • 9:30pm-2:30am Th-Sun, add'l summer hours • mostly gay men • dancing/DJ • live shows • T-dance Sun (summers) • patio bar • volleyball • 18+ • private club

RESTAURANTS

Much/ Level 2/ Heaven 113 Elm St 336/370–1311 • upscale restaurant & martini lounge • also nightclub

Greenville

NIGHTCLUBS

The Great American Mining Co of New Guinea, Inc 1008 B Dickinson Ave (at 10th St) 252/353–2623 • 10pm-3am • lesbians/ gay men • dancing/DJ • karaoke • drag shows • strippers • videos • private club • gay-owned

EROTICA

Late Show Video 1101 Charles Blvd (at 10th St) 252/758–5883 • gay-owned

Hickory

NIGHTCLUBS

Club Cabaret 101 N Center St (at 1st Ave) 828/322–8103 • 9pm-close, from 5pm Sun, clsd Mon-Tue • lesbians/ gay men • dancing/DJ • live shows • WiFi • private club • wheelchair access

CAFES

Taste Full Beans 29 2nd St NW 828/325–0108 • 7am-5:30pm, till 2:30 Sat, clsd Sun • art exhibits • gay-owned

Little Switzerland

ACCOMMODATIONS

La Petite Chalet 38 Orchard Ln (at Hwy 226A) **888/828–1654** • gay/ straight • located on the Blue Ridge Parkway of North Carolina midway between Asheville & Blowing Rock • gay-owned

Madison

ACCOMMODATIONS

Hunter House B&B 216 W Hunter St **336/445–4730** • gay/ straight • patio • gardens • pool • pets on premises • nonsmoking • WiFi • gay-owned • $115-135

Mooresville

RESTAURANTS

Pomodoro's Italian American Cafe 168 Norman Station Blvd **704/663–6686** • 11am-10pm, till 7pm Sun • beer/ wine • wheelchair access • gay-owned

Raleigh/Durham/Chapel Hill

INFO LINES & SERVICES

Common Solutions Gay/ Lesbian AA 505 Alexander Ave (at Episcopal Student Center), Durham **919/286–9499 (AA#)** • 6:30pm Mon

LGBT Center of Raleigh 411 Hillsborough St, Raleigh **919/832-4484** • social & educational activities, services & groups

ACCOMMODATIONS

Heartfriends Inn Bed and Breakfast 4389 Siler City/Snow Camp Rd (at Ed Clapp Rd), Siler City **919/663–0407** • gay/ straight • WiFi • women-owned • wheelchair access • $80-125

The King's Daughters Inn 204 N Buchanan Blvd, Durham **919/354–7000, 877/534–8534** • gay-friendly • complimentary bikes

Wyndham Raleigh Durham 4620 S Miami Blvd, Durham **919/941–6066 , 877/999–3223**

BARS

Flex 2 S West St (at Hillsborough), Raleigh **919/832-8855** • 5pm-close, from 2pm Sun • popular • mostly gay men • karaoke • private club

Hibernian Restaurant & Pub 311 Glenwood Ave (at W Lane St), Raleigh **919/833–2258** • 11am-2am • gay-friendly • live music

NIGHTCLUBS

313 313 W Hargett St (at Harrington), Raleigh **919/755–9599** • 8pm-close • mostly gay men • dancing/DJ • live shows • also piano bar • private club • wheelchair access

The Bar 711 Rigsbee Ave, Durham **919/956–2929** • lesbians/ gay men • dancing/DJ • deck • drag king shows • karaoke • private club • wheelchair access

Icon Nightclub 320 E Durham Rd, Cary **919/460-4343** • lesbians/ gay men • dancing/DJ • drag shows • karaoke • theme nights • mostly African American

Legends/ View 330 W Hargett St (at S Harrington St), Raleigh **919/831–8888** • 5pm-2:30am • lesbians/ gay men • dancing/DJ • strippers • drag shows • young crowd • private club • wheelchair access

Stir 201 E Franklin St (at East End Martini Bar), Chapel Hill **919/929–0024** • 9pm Sun only • mostly gay men • dancing/DJ

The T 423 W Franklin St (at the Lantern), Chapel Hill **919/969–8846** • 10pm Tue only • chic, eclectic crowd

Tantra 310 S West St (at Martin), Raleigh **919/834–9333** • 7pm-3am Fri-Sun only • gay-friendly • dancing/DJ • young crowd • private club

Unwind 403 W Rosemary St (at the Fuse), Chapel Hill • 10pm Wed only • tranquil night of drinking, socializing & midweek relaxation

CAFES

Bean Traders 105-249 W NC Hwy 54, Durham **919/484-2499** • 6am-8pm, from 8am wknds

Cafe Helios 413 Glenwood Ave (at North St), Raleigh **919/838–5177** • 7am-10pm, till midnight wknds • also beer & wine • patio

Caffe Driade 1215 E Franklin St #A (at Elizabeth St), Chapel Hill **919/942–2333** • live music • also beer & wine served

Reverie: A Coffee Den 2522 Hillsborough St (at Pogue), Raleigh **919/839–2233** • 7am-6pm, 8am-4pm Sat • WiFi • patio

Third Place 1811 Glenwood Ave (at W Whitaker Mill Rd), Raleigh **919/834–6566** • 8am-7pm, till 11pm wknds • also sandwiches & salads

RESTAURANTS

Blu Seafood & Bar 2002 Hillsborough Rd (at 9th St), Durham **919/286–9777** • lunch & dinner, clsd Sun

The Borough 317 W Morgan St, Raleigh **919/832-8433** • 4pm-2am • also bar • WiFi

Crooks Corner 610 Franklin St (at Merritt Mill Rd), Chapel Hill **919/929-7643** • dinner nightly, Sun brunch, clsd Mon • Southern • full bar • patio • wheelchair access

Dain's Place 754 9th St (at Markham), Durham • 11am-2am • great burgers & pub food • also bar • WiFi

Elmo's Diner 776 9th St (in the Carr Mill Mall), Durham **919/416-3823** • 6:30am-10pm

Five Star 511 W Hargett St (at West St), Raleigh **919/833-3311** • 5:30pm-2am • Asian-fusion • sexy ambiance for cocktails & nibbles

Humble Pie 317 S Harrington St, Raleigh **919/829-9222** • 5pm-11pm, bar open late, brunch only Sun • small plates

Irregardless Cafe 901 W Morgan St (at Hillsborough), Raleigh **919/833-8898** • lunch Tue-Fri, dinner Tue-Sat, Sun brunch, clsd Mon • plenty veggie • live music • dancing Sat

Lantern 423 W Franklin St, Chapel Hill **919/969-8846** • dinner nightly, clsd Sun • Asian • also cocktail lounge till 2am

The Mad Hatter's Bakeshop & Cafe 1802 W Main St (at Broad), Durham **919/286-1987** • brkfst, lunch & dinner • awesome cakes & baked goods

Magnolia Grill 1002 9th St (at Knox), Durham **919/286-3609** • dinner, clsd Sun-Mon • upscale Southern • full bar • wheelchair access

The Pit 328 W Davie St (at S Dawson), Raleigh **919/890-4500** • 11am-10pm, till 11pm wknds • upscale BBQ

Raleigh/Durham/Chapel Hill

LGBT Pride:
September, Durham. web: www.ncpride.org.

Annual Events:
August - North Carolina Gay and Lesbian Film Festival, web: www.carolinatheatre.org/screen/film-festivals.

City Info:
919/834-5900 or 800/849-8499, web: www.visitraleigh.com.
Chapel Hill/Orange County Visitors Bureau 888/968-2060, web: www.chocvb.org.

Transit:
Regional Transit Information 919/485-7433, web: www.gotriangle.org.

Attractions:
Ackland Art Museum, Chapel Hill 919/966-5736, web: www.ackland.org.
African-American Dance Ensemble, Durham 919/560-2729, web: www.africanamericandanceensemble.org.

African-American Cultural Complex, Raleigh 919/250-9336, web: www.aaccmuseum.org.
City Market, Raleigh, web: citymarketraleigh.com.
Duke University, Durham.
Exploris (interactive global learning center), Raleigh 919/834-4040, web: www.marbleskidsmuseum.org.
Morehead Planetarium & Science Center 919/962-1236, web: www.moreheadplanetarium.org.
NC Botanical Garden, Chapel Hill 919/962-0522, web: www.ncbg.unc.edu.
NC Museum of Art, Raleigh 919/839-6262, web: www.ncartmuseum.org.
NC Museum of Life & Science, Durham 919/220-5429, web: www.ncmls.org.
Oakwood Historic District, Raleigh.
University of North Carolina, Chapel Hill.
W. Franklin St. in Chapel Hill, south of UNC and into Carrboro— charming and hip shopping area.

Rue Cler 401 E Chapel Hill St (at Mangum St), Durham **919/682-8844** • lunch & dinner, wknd brunch • French

Solas **919/755-0755** • dinner, Sun brunch • upscale dining • dress code • also rooftop lounge & nightclub

Spotted Dog 111 E Main St (at N Greensboro St), Carrboro **919/933-1117** • 11:30am-midnight, clsd Mon • full bar • plenty veggie

Sunrise Biscuit Kitchen 1305 E Franklin St, Chapel Hill **919/933-1324** • great brkfst • drive-thru only

Vivace 4209 Lassiter Mill Rd #115 (at Pamlico Dr), Raleigh **919/787-7747** • lunch & dinner, Sun brunch • Italian • patio seating • full bar

ENTERTAINMENT & RECREATION

Carolina Rollergirls • NC's female roller derby league • visit carolinarollergirls.com for events

BOOKSTORES

Internationalist Books & Community Center 405 W Franklin St (at Kenan St), Chapel Hill **919/942-1740** • 11am-8pm, noon-6pm Sun • progressive/ alternative • cooperatively run • nonprofit • literature readings & events

Quail Ridge Books 3522 Wade Ave (at Ridgewood Center), Raleigh **919/828-1588, 800/672-6789** • 9am-9pm • LGBT section

The Regulator Bookshop 720 9th St (btwn Hillsborough & Perry), Durham **919/286-2700** • 10am-9pm, noon-6pm Sun

EROTICA

Castle Video & News 1210 Capitol Blvd, Raleigh **919/836-9189** • 24hrs

Cherry Pie 1819 Fordham Blvd, Chapel Hill **919/928-0499** • 10am-midnight • adult toys

Frisky Business 1720 New Raleigh Hwy, Durham **919/957-4441** • adult toys • also classes

Rocky Mount

NIGHTCLUBS

Liquid Nightclub 313 Falls Rd **252/266-6464** • 8pm-3am Sat only • mostly gay men • dancing/DJ • go-go dancers • mostly African American

Washington

CAFES

Back Water Jack's Tiki Bar 1052 E Main St (at Havens St) **252/975-1090** • lunch & dinner, clsd Sun-Mon • also bar • wheelchair access

West Jefferson

ACCOMMODATIONS

Blue Ridge Hideaway 115 Arbor Pl (at Skyline) **615/360-7099, 615/484-7171** • gay-friendly • cozy log cabin • private river access • nonsmoking • WiFi • lesbian-owned

Wilmington

ACCOMMODATIONS

Best Western Coastline Inn 503 Nutt St **910/763-2800, 800/617-7732** • gay/ straight • kids ok • nonsmoking • wheelchair access • WiFi • gay-owned • $69-169

Rosehill Inn B&B 114 S 3rd St (at Dock St) **910/815-0250, 800/815-0250** • gay-friendly • WiFi • $119-199

The Taylor House Inn 14 N 7th St **910/763-7581, 800/382-9982** • gay/ straight • romantic 1905 house • full brkfst • nonsmoking • kids ok • $140

BARS

Costello's 211 Princess St (btwn 2nd & 3rd) **910/470-9666** • 7pm-2am • mostly gay men • piano bar • videos • private club • wheelchair access • gay-owned

Tool Box 2325 Burnett Blvd **910/343-6988** • 5pm-2am, from 7pm Tue -Sat • mostly gay men • neighborhood bar • dancing/DJ • karaoke • WiFi • gay-owned

NIGHTCLUBS

Ibiza 118 Market St (rear) **910/251-1301** • 8pm-5am Wed-Sun only • mostly gay men • dancing/DJ • more women Th • karaoke • drag shows • strippers • young crowd • private club • wheelchair access • gay-owned

RESTAURANTS

Caffe Phoenix 9 S Front St **910/343-1395** • 11:30am-10pm, Sun brunch • Mediterranean • some veggie • gay-owned

ENTERTAINMENT & RECREATION

Cinematique 310 Chestnut St (at Thalian Hall) **910/343-1640** • classic, foreign & notable films

Winston-Salem

NIGHTCLUBS

CO2 4019 Country Club Rd (at Hedgecock Ave) **336/602-2720** • 9pm-2:30am, till 3:30am Sat, clsd Mon • popular • lesbians/ gay men • dancing/DJ • live shows • karaoke • multiracial clientele • transgender-friendly • private club • 18+ • wheelchair access • cover charge • gay-owned

NORTH DAKOTA

Fargo

INFO LINES & SERVICES

Pride Collective & Community Center 116 12th St S (at Main Ave), Moorhead, MN **218/287-8034** • 3pm-5pm Sat • referrals • support • social groups • check www.pridecollective.com for events

ACCOMMODATIONS

The Hotel Donaldson 101 Broadway **701/478-1000 , 888/478-8768** • gay/straight • restaurant & bar on site

NIGHTCLUBS

I-Beam 1021 Center Ave (at 11th), Moorhead, MN **218/233-7700** • 9pm-2am Fri-Sat only • lesbians/ gay men • dancing/DJ • drag shows

CAFES

Atomic Coffee **701/478-6160** • 7am-11pm, 8pm-10pm Sun • WiFi

RESTAURANTS

Casa Ramos 1649 38th St S **701/281-1033** • 11am-10pm, full bar

Fargo's Fryn' Pan 300 Main St (at 4th) **701/293-9952** • 24hrs • popular • wheelchair access

Mom's Kitchen 1322 Main St **701/235-4460** • 6am-10pm, full bar

RETAIL SHOPS

One World Imports 614 Main Ave (at Broadway) **701/297-8882** • 10am-7pm, till 6pm Fri-Sat, clsd Sun • gay-owned

Zandbroz Variety 420 N Broadway **701/239-4729** • 9am-8pm, noon-5pm Sun • books & gifts

EROTICA

Romantix Adult Superstore 417 N Pacific Ave **701/235-2640** • 24hrs

Grand Forks

EROTICA

Romantix Adult Superstore 102 S 3rd St (at Kittson) **701/772-9021**

Minot

EROTICA

Risque's 1514 S Broadway **701/838-2837**

OHIO

Statewide

PUBLICATIONS

Gay People's Chronicle 216/916-9338 • Ohio's largest bi-weekly LGBT newspaper w/ extensive listings

Outlook 614/268-8525 • statewide LGBT newsweekly • good resource pages

Akron

INFO LINES & SERVICES

AA Intergroup 330/253-8181 (AA#)

Akron Pride Center 895 N Main St 330/252-1559 • call for meeting schedule

BARS

Adams Street Bar 77 N Adams St (at Upson) **330/434-9794** • 4pm-2am, from 9pm Sun • popular • mostly gay men • piano bar Wed • dancing/DJ Fri-Sat • food served • strippers • WiFi

Cocktails 1009 S Main St (at Crosier) **330/376-2625** • 11am-2:30am, clsd Sun • mostly gay men • videos • drag king show Mon • Daddy's leather bar upstairs wknds

Inferno 1348 S Arlington St (in Arlington Plaza) **330/773-7733** • 4pm-2am, from noon wknds • mostly gay men • dancing/DJ • karaoke • theme nights

The Office Bistro & Lounge 778 N Main St (at Cuyahoga Falls Ave) **330/376–9550** • 11am-2:30am • gay-friendly • bi-sexual friendly • neighborhood bistro & lounge • multiracial • WiFi • wheelchair access

Roseto Club 627 S Arlington St (at Bittaker) **330/724–4228** • 6pm-2:30am, clsd Sun • mostly women • dancing/DJ • karaoke • wheelchair access

Tear-Ez 360 S Main St (near Exchange St) **330/376–0011** • 11am-2:30am, from noon Sun • lesbians/ gay men • neighborhood bar • drag shows Th & Sun • WiFi • wheelchair access

NIGHTCLUBS

Interbelt 70 N Howard St (near Perkins & Main) **330/253–5700** • 9pm-2:30am • lesbians/ gay men • dancing/DJ • live shows • videos • patio

Square 820 W Market St (near Portage Path) **330/374–9661** • 5pm-2:30am, from 8pm Sat, from 7pm Sun • mostly gay men • dancing/DJ • karaoke • wheelchair access • gay-owned

CAFES

Angel Falls Coffee Company 792 W Market St (btwn S Highland & Grand) **330/376–5282** • 7am-10pm • lunch & desserts • patio • WiFi • wheelchair access • gay-owned

RESTAURANTS

Aladdin's Eatery 782 W Market St (at Grand) **330/535–0110** • 11am-10pm • Middle Eastern

Bricco 1 W Exchange St (at S Main St) **330/475–1600** • 11am-midnight, till 1am Fri-Sat, 4pm-9pm Sun • Italian • also bar • gay-owned

Bruegger's Bagels 1821 Merriman Rd **330/867–8394** • 6am-4pm

Athens

ACCOMMODATIONS

SuBAMUH (Susan B Anthony Memorial UnRest Home) Womyn's Land Trust PO Box 5853, 45701 **740/448–6424, 740/448–7285** • women only • cabins & camping • summer workshops • swimming • hot tub • nonsmoking • lesbian-owned • $7 (tent), $12 (cabin) sliding scale • rates per person

Brunswick

see also Akron & Cleveland

RESTAURANTS

Pizza Marcello 67–A Pearl Rd (near Boston Rd) **330/225–1211** • 3pm-close, from noon wknds • Italian

Canton

NIGHTCLUBS

Crew 304 Cherry Ave NE (at 3rd) **330/452–2739** • 6pm-2:30am, from 9pm Sat-Sun • lesbians/ gay men • dancing/DJ • karaoke • cabaret

Cincinnati

INFO LINES & SERVICES

AA Gay/ Lesbian 328 W McMillan St (enter at 445 Herman St), Corryville **513/351–0422 (AA#)** • 8pm Wed • call for locations of wknd meetings

Gay/ Lesbian Community Center of Greater Cincinnati 4119 Hamilton Ave (near Blue Rock) **513/591–0200** • 6pm-9pm, noon-4pm Sat, clsd Sun

ACCOMMODATIONS

Cincinnatian Hotel 601 Vine St (at 6th St) **513/381–3000, 800/942–9000** • gay-friendly • restaurant & lounge • kids ok • nonsmoking • WiFi • wheelchair access

Crowne Plaza 5901 Pfeiffer Rd (at I-71) **513/793–4500, 800/468–3597** • gay-friendly • pool • kids ok • WiFi •wheelchair access

First Farm Inn 2510 Stevens Rd, Petersburg, KY **859/586–0199** • gay-friendly • 20 minutes from Cincinnati • full brkfst • WiFi • nonsmoking • wheelchair access

Millennium Hotel Cincinnati 150 W 5th St **513/352–2100, 800/876–2100** • gay-friendly • outdoor rooftop pool & sundeck • WiFi • wheelchair access • $89-199

Weller Haus B&B 319 Poplar St, Bellevue, KY **859/391–8315, 800/431–4287** • gay-friendly • jacuzzis • nonsmoking • WiFi

BARS

Below Zero Lounge 1122 Walnut St (at E Central Pkwy) **513/421–9376** • 4pm-2:30am, clsd Mon-Tue • dancing/DJ • live music • karaoke • dancing/DJ • food served • WiFi

Junkers Tavern 4158 Langland St (at Chase) **513/541–5470** • 9am-1am • gay-friendly • neighborhood bar

Milton's 301 Milton St (at Sycamore) 513/784–9938 • 4pm-2:30am • gay-friendly • neighborhood bar

Roxy's 909 Vine St (at 9th St) 513/421–6279 • 11am-midnight, bar till 2:30am • lesbians/gay men • drag shows • wheelchair access

Shooters 927 Race St (at Court) 513/381–9900 • 4pm-2:30am • mostly gay men • dancing/DJ • country/western • more women Th • karaoke Wed

Simon Says 428 Walnut St (at 5th) 513/381–7577 • 11am-2:30am, from 1pm Sun • popular • mostly gay men • professional • neighborhood bar • wheelchair access

NIGHTCLUBS

Adonis 4601 Kellogg Ave (at Stites Rd) 513/871–1542 • 9pm-3am Sat only • lesbians/gay men • dancing/DJ • transgender-friendly • drag shows

Bronz 4029 Hamilton Ave (at Blue Rock) 513/591–2100 • 8pm-2:30am, clsd Mon • lesbians/gay men • dancing/DJ • live shows • karaoke • wheelchair access • patio • gay-owned

The Dock 603 W Pete Rose Wy (near Central) 513/241–5623 • 10pm-3am, till 4am Fri-Sat, clsd Mon-Wed • popular • lesbians/gay men • multiracial • dancing/DJ • drag shows • live shows • 19+ • volleyball court • wheelchair access

CAFES

College Hill Coffee Co 6128 Hamilton Ave (at North Bend Rd) 513/542–2739 • 6:30am-6:30pm, till 10pm Fri, 8:30am-10pm Sat, till 4pm Sun, clsd Mon • live music Sat • WiFi • wheelchair access

Zen & Now 4453 Bridgetown Rd 513/598–8999 • 7am-7pm, till 10pm Fri-Sat, clsd Sun • WiFi

RESTAURANTS

Boca 3200 Madison Rd (at Brazee St), Oakley 513/542–2022 • dinner Tue-Sat, clsd Sun-Mon • full bar • patio • wheelchair access

Honey 4034 Hamilton Ave (at Blue Rock) 513/541–4300 • dinner and Sun brunch, clsd Mon, casual fine dining • wheelchair access

The Loving Hut 6227 Montgomery Rd (at Woodmont) 513/731–2233 • 11am-7pm, clsd Sun-Mon • vegetarian/vegan

Melt Eclectic Deli 4165 Hamilton Ave (at Lingo St) 513/681–6358 • 11am-9pm, 10am-3pm Sun

Myra's Dionysus 121 Calhoun St (at Dennis St) 513/961–1578 • 11am-10pm, till 11pm Fri-Sat, from 5pm Sun • diverse menu • plenty veggie

Tucker's 1637 Vine St (at Green) 513/721–7123 • great brkfst hole-in-wall • vegan too • wheelchair access

Cincinnati

LGBT PRIDE:
June. 513/591-0200, web: www.prideisalive.com.

ANNUAL EVENTS:
Oct - OUTReels LGBT film festival 513/591-0200.

CITY INFO:
513/621-2142 or 800/543–2613, web: www.cincyusa.com.

BEST VIEW:
Mt Adams & Eden Park.

TRANSIT:
Yellow Cab 513/821-8294, web: aaataxi.net.
SORTA 513/621-4455, web: www.sorta.com

ATTRACTIONS:
The Beach waterpark (in Mason) 513/398-7946, web: www.thebeachwaterpark.com.
Carew Tower 513/241-3888.
Cincinnati Art Museum 513/639-2995, web: www.cincinnatiartmuseum.org.
Fountain Square.
Krohn Conservatory 513/421-4086.
Museum Center at Union Terminal 513/287-7000, web: www.cincymuseum.org.
Paramount King's Island (24 miles N of Cincinnati) 513/754-5700, web: www.visitkingsisland.com.

Entertainment & Recreation

Ensemble Theatre of Cincinnati 1127 Vine St (at 12th) 513/421–3555

Know Theatre 1120 Jackson St (at Central Pkwy) 513/300–5669 • contemporary multicultural theater

Ohio Lesbian Archives 3416 Clifton Ave (at Clifton United Methodist Church) 513/256–7695 • call first for appt

Retail Shops

Pink Pyramid 907 Race St (btwn 9th & Court) 513/621–7465 • noon-9pm, till 11pm Fri-Sat, 1pm-7pm Sun • pride items • also leather

Publications

Gay People's Chronicle 216/916–9338 • Ohio's largest bi-weekly LGBT newspaper

Cleveland

Info Lines & Services

AA Gay/ Lesbian 6600 Detroit Ave (at LGBT Center) 216/241–7387, 800/835–1935 • 7pm Fri women's meeting

LGBT Community Center 6600 Detroit Ave 216/651–5428, 888/429–8761 • 1pm-8pm, clsd wknds • wheelchair access

Accommodations

Clifford House 1810 W 28th St (at Jay) 216/589–0121 • gay/ straight • 1868 historic brick home • near downtown • fireplaces • nonsmoking • WiFi • gay-owned • $95-135

Radisson Hotel Cleveland—Gateway 651 Huron Rd (at Prospect) 216/377–9000, 888/201–1718 • gay-friendly • also restaurant • kids ok • WiFi • wheelchair access • $94-149 + tax

Stone Gables B&B 3806 Franklin Blvd (at W 38th) 216/961–4654, 877/215–4326 • gay/ straight • full brkfst • jacuzzi • kids/ pets ok • WiFi • wheelchair access • gay-owned

Bars

A Man's World 2909 Detroit Ave (at 29th St) 216/589–9322 • 7am-2:30am, from noon Sun-Mon • mostly gay men • more women Sun for line dancing • dancing/DJ wknds • karaoke • WiFi • patio

ABC The Tavern 1872 W 25th St 216/861–3857 • 4pm-2:30am, from noon wknds • gay-friendly dive bar w/ great food

The Hawk 11217 Detroit Ave (at 112th St) 216/521–5443 • noon-2:30am, from 1pm Sun • lesbians/ gay men • neighborhood bar • wheelchair access

Mean Bull 1313 E 26th St (at St Clair) 216/812–3304 • 7pm-2am • mostly gay men • videos • piano bar

Now That's Class 11213 Detroit Ave (at 112th St) 216/221–8576 • 4pm-close • gay-friendly • punk & metal bands • food served • plenty veggie/ vegan • wheelchair access

Paradise Inn 4488 State Rd (Rte 94, at Rte 480) 216/741–9819 • 11am-2:30am • lesbians/ gay men • neighborhood bar • lesbian-owned

Twist 11633 Clifton (at 117th St) 216/221–2333 • 11:30am-2:30am, from noon Sun • popular • lesbians/ gay men • neighborhood bar • dancing/DJ • professional crowd

Union Station Video Cafe 2814 Detroit Ave (at W 28th) 216/357–2997 • 5pm-2:30am • popular • lesbians/ gay men, more women Sat night • dancing/DJ • drag shows • videos • also Bounce nightclub Fri-Sat • also restaurant • gay-owned

View Ultra Lounge 618 Prospect Ave (at E 4th St) 216/664–1815 • gay/ straight • dancing/DJ • theme nights

Cafes

Gypsy Beans & Baking Co 6425 Detroit Ave (at W 65th St, next to Cleveland Public Theatre) 216/939–9009 • 7am-9pm, till 11pm Fri-Sat • popular • fresh-baked gourmet pastries, soups, sandwiches • WiFi • wheelchair access

Lucky's Cafe 777 Starkweather Ave (at Professor Ave) 216/622–7773 • 7am-5pm, 8am-3pm wknds, popular wknd brunch • cafe & bakery • outdoor seating • WiFi • woman-owned • wheelchair access

Phoenix Coffee 2287 Lee Rd (at Essex), Cleveland Heights 216/932–8227 • 6am-10pm, till 11pm Fri, from 7am Sat, 7am-7pm Sun • great sandwiches • WiFi • patio • wheelchair access

Restaurants

Ali Baba 12021 Lorain Ave (at W 120th St) 216/251–2040 • 4:30pm-10pm Th-Sat • popular • the best Middle Eastern food you'll have outside the Middle East • plenty veggie • BYOB • woman-owned

Bar Cento 1948 W 25th St (at Lorain Ave) 216/274-1010 • 4:30pm-2am, from noon Sat • great pizza • beer/ wine • patio • wheelchair access

Battiste & Dupree Cajun Grill & Bar 1992 Warrensville Ctr Rd (at Wyncote) 216/381-3341 • lunch & dinner, clsd Sun-Mon • wheelchair access

Cafe Tandoor 2096 S Taylor Rd (at Cedar), Cleveland Heights 216/371-8500 • lunch & dinner, 3pm-9pm Sun • Indian • plenty veggie • wheelchair access

The Coffee Pot 12415 Madison Ave (at Robin), Lakewood 216/226-6443 • 6am-4pm, till 3pm Sat, till 2pm Sun, clsd Mon • diner • woman-owned

Crop Bistro 2537 Lorain Ave (at 25th) 216/696-2767 • lunch Tue-Fri, dinner nightly, clsd Mon • innovative American

Diner on Clifton 11637 Clifton Blvd (at W 117th St) 216/521-5003 • 7am-11pm

Flying Fig 2523 Market Ave (at W 25th St) 216/241-4243 • dinner only

Happy Dog 5801 Detroit Ave (at 58th St) 216/651-9474 • 4pm-2am, from 11am Fri • hot dogs w/ 50 toppings • veggie/ vegan choices • live bands • full bar • wheelchair access

Hecks 2927 Bridge Ave (at W 30th) 216/861-5464, 800/677-8592 • lunch & dinner, brunch Sun • popular • gourmet burgers • wheelchair access

The Inn on Coventry 2785 Euclid Heights Blvd (at Coventry), Cleveland Heights 216/371-1811 • 7am-8:30pm, from 8:30am-3pm wknds • homestyle • popular Bloody Marys • some veggie • full bar • wheelchair access • women-owned

Jimmy O'Neill's Tavern 2195 Lee Rd (at Tullamore Rd), Cleveland Heights 216/321-1116 • 5pm-midnight, till 11pm Sun, bar till 2:30am • wheelchair access

Johnny Mango World Cafe & Bar 3120 Bridge Ave (btwn Fulton & W 32nd, in Ohio City) 216/575-1919 • 11am-10pm, till 11pm Fri-Sat • healthy world food • juice bar • also full bar till 1am • nonsmoking

Cleveland

WHERE THE GIRLS ARE:
Dancing downtown near Public Square, hanging out on State Rd below the intersection of Pearl and Broadview/ Memphis.

LGBT PRIDE:
June. 216/226-0004, web: www.clevelandpride.org.

ANNUAL EVENTS:
March - Cleveland International Film Festival 216/623-3456, web: www.clevelandfilm.org.
April - Tri-C JazzFest 216/987-4400, web: www.tricjazzfest.com.
June - Avon Heritage Duct Tape Festival 866/818-1116, web: www.avonducttapefestival.com.

CITY INFO:
216/621-4110 or 800/321-1004, web: www.positivelycleveland.com.

ATTRACTIONS:
Cleveland Metroparks Zoo 216/661-6500, web: www.clemetzoo.com.
Cleveland Museum of Art 216/421-7340, web: www.clemusart.com.
Coventry Road district.
Cuyahoga Valley National Recreation Area 216/524-1497, web: www.nps.gov/cuva.
The Flats.
Rock and Roll Hall of Fame 216/781-7625, web: www.rockhall.com.

TRANSIT:
Yellow Cab 216/623-1500.
AmeriCab 216/881-1111.
Regional Transit Authority (RTA) 216/566-5100, web: www.gcrta.org.
Lolly the Trolley 216/771-4484, web: www.lollytrolley.com.

Latitude 41N 5712 Detroit Ave (at W 58th St, Detroit Shoreway) **216/961-0000** • 8am-9pm, till 10pm Fri, till 3pm Sun • restaurant & cafe • WiFi • wheelchair access • lesbian-owned

Lolita 900 Literary Rd (at Professor Ave, in Tremont) **216/771-5652** • 5pm-11pm, till 1am Fri-Sat, 4pm-9pm Sun • popular • upscale cont'l • full bar

Luchita's 3456 W 117th St (at Governor) **216/252-1169** • lunch & dinner, clsd Mon • popular • Mexican • full bar

Luxe 6605 Detroit Ave (at W 65th St) **216/920-0600** • 5pm-midnight, lounge till 2am • gourmet comfort food • also lounge • live music • wheelchair access

Momocho 1835 Fulton Rd (at Woodbine Ave) **216/694-2122** • 5pm-close, from 4pm Sun • modern Mexican • also bar • wheelchair access

My Friend's Deli & Restaurant 11616 Detroit Ave (at W 117th) **216/221-2575** • 24hrs • beer/ wine • WiFi

Pearl of the Orient 19300 Detroit Rd (in Beachcliff Market Sq), Rocky River **440/333-9902** • lunch & dinner • pan-Asian • some veggie • also restaurant on East Side • wheelchair access

Tommy's **216/321-7757** • 9am-9pm, till 10pm Fri, 7:30am-10pm Sat • plenty veggie • great milkshakes • WiFi • wheelchair access

ENTERTAINMENT & RECREATION

Rock & Roll Hall of Fame 1100 Rock & Roll Blvd (at E 9th & Lake Erie) **216/781-ROCK** • even if you don't like rock, stop by & check out IM Pei's architectural gift to Cleveland

BOOKSTORES

Borders Bookshop & Espresso Bar 2101 Richmond Rd (at Cedar, in LaPlace Mall), Beachwood **216/292-2660** • 10am-10pm, till 9pm Sun • WiFi

Loganberry Books 13015 Larchmere Blvd, Shaker Heights **216/795-9800** • 10am-6pm, till 8pm Th, clsd Sun • used & rare books • woman-owned

Mac's Backs 1820 Coventry Rd (next to Tommy's), Cleveland Heights **216/321-2665** • 10am-9pm, till 10pm Fri-Sat, 11am-8pm Sun • great new & used • 3 floors • reading series • some LGBT titles

RETAIL SHOPS

Big Fun 1814 Coventry Rd (at Hampshire), Cleveland Heights **216/371-4386** • 11am-8pm, till 10pm Fri-Sat, till 6pm Sun • kitschy variety store

Dean Rufus House of Fun 1422 W 29th St (at Detroit) **216/348-1386** • 1pm-midnight, till 2:30am Fri-Sat, clsd Mon • clothing • DVDs

Goddess Blessed 15729 Madison Ave (at Hillard), Lakewood **216/221-8755** • 11am-7pm, clsd Sun-Mon • goddess-focused & occult gifts & supplies • tarot readings • events & classes

PUBLICATIONS

Erie Gay News **814/456-9833**

Gay People's Chronicle **216/916-9338** • Ohio's largest bi-weekly LGBT newspaper w/ extensive listings

EROTICA

Adult Mart 16700 Brookpark Rd (at W 150th) **216/267-9019**

Rocky's Entertainment & Emporium 13330 Brookpark Rd (at W 130th) **216/267-4659**

Columbus

INFO LINES & SERVICES

AA Gay/ Lesbian **614/253-8501, 800/870-3795** (IN OH)

Stonewall Columbus Community Center/ Hotline 1160 N High St (at E 4th Ave) **614/299-7764** • 9am-5pm, clsd wknds • wheelchair access

ACCOMMODATIONS

The Blackwell 2110 Tuttle Park Pl (at Lane Ave) **614/247-4000, 866/247-4000** • gay-friendly • on OSU campus • also restaurant

Garden Manor Bed & Breakfast 108 N 20th St (N of E Broad St) **614/832-4929, 866/925-4929** • gay-friendly • WiFi • wheelchair access • gay-owned

Harrison House B&B 313 W 5th Ave (at Neil Ave) **614/421-2202, 800/827-4203** • gay-friendly • nonsmoking • WiFi • woman-owned

The Lofts 55 E Nationwide Blvd (at High St) **614/461-2663, 800/735-6387** • gay-friendly • boutique hotel

The Westin Columbus 310 S High St (at Main) **614/223-3800, 800/937-8461** • gay-friendly • beautiful old 100+ year old hotel, great location • also restaurant

Bars

Blazer's Pub 1205 N High St (at 5th) **614/299-1800** • 4pm-midnight, till 2am Th-Sat, clsd Sun • lesbians/ gay men • neighborhood bar • karaoke

Cavan Irish Pub 1409 S High St (at Jenkins) **614/725-5502** • 2pm-2:30am, from noon wknds • gay-friendly • shows • karaoke

Club Diversity 863 S High St (at Whittier) **614/224-4050** • 4pm-midnight, till 2:30am Fri, noon-2:30am Sat • lesbians/ gay men • piano bar Fri-Sat

Havana Video Lounge 862 N High (at 1st Ave) **614/421-9697** • 5pm-2:30am • popular • lesbians/ gay men • neighborhood bar • dancing/DJ • drag shows • martini lounge • food served

Inn Rehab 627 Greenlawn Ave (at Harmon) **614/754-7326** • 11am-2:30am • mostly gay men • food served • dancing/DJ • drag shows

Level Dining Lounge 614/754-7111 • 11am-2:30 • gay/straight • restaurant with great bar • dancing/DJ • karaoke • wheelchair access

Score 145 N 5th St (at Spring) **614/849-0099** • 4pm-2:30am • lesbians/ gay men • gay sports bar • karaoke • drag bingo

Slammers 202 E Long St (at N 5th St) **614/221-8880** • 11am-12:30am, till 2:30am Fri-Sat, from 4pm wknds, clsd Mon • mostly women • dancing/DJ • food served • WiFi • wheelchair access

The South Bend Tavern 126 E Moler St (at 4th St) **614/444-3386** • noon-2:30am • lesbians/ gay men • neighborhood bar • drag shows Sat • wheelchair access

Columbus

Where the Girls Are:
Downtown with the boys, north near the University area, or somewhere in-between.

LGBT Pride:
June. 614/299-7764 (Stonewall #), web: www.columbuspride.org.

Annual Events:
June - Columbus Arts Festival 614/224-2606, web: www.gcac.org.
July/August - Ohio State Fair 888/646-3976, web: www.ohio-expocenter.com.
September - Ohio Lesbian Festival, web: www.ohiolba.org.

City Info:
800/282-5393, web: www.ohio-tourism.com.

Weather:
Truly midwestern. Winters are cold, summers are hot.

Attractions:
Brewery District.
Columbus Jazz Orchestra 614/294-5200, web: www.jazzartsgroup.org.
Columbus Museum of Modern Art 614/221-6801, web: www.columbusmuseum.org.
Columbus Zoo 800/666-5397 web: www.columbuszoo.org.
Franklin Park Conservatory 614/645-8733, web: www.fpconservatory.org.
German Village district.
The Short North neighborhood (popular "Gallery Hop" 1st Sat), 614/299-8050 web:www.shortnorth.org.
Wexner Center for the Arts 614/292-0330, web: www.wexarts.org.

Transit:
Yellow Cab 614/444-4444.
Acme Taxi 614/777-7777.
Central Ohio Transit Authority (COTA) 614/228-1776, web: www.cota.com.

Trafik 205 N 5th St (at Spring) **614/222–2401** • 4pm-2am, from 1pm wknds • mostly gay men • dancing/DJ • transgender-friendly • karaoke • patio • gay-owned

Union Cafe 782 N High St (at Hubbard) **614/421–2233** • 11am-2:30am • popular • lesbians/gay men • video bar • also restaurant • plenty veggie • WiFi • wheelchair access

NIGHTCLUBS

Axis 775 N High St (at Hubbard) **614/291–4008** • 10pm-2:30am Fri-Sat only • popular • mostly gay men • dancing/DJ • go-go boys • also Pump cabaret lounge • drag shows • 18+ • wheelchair access • gay-owned

Wall Street 144 N Wall St (at Spring St) **614/464–2800** • 9pm-2:30am, from 10pm Wed, 8pm-midnight Th, clsd Mon-Tue • popular • lesbians/gay men • more women Fri-Sat • dancing/DJ • country/western Th • wheelchair access

CAFES

Cup O Joe Cafe 627 S 3rd St (at Sycamore) **614/221–1563** • 6am-10pm, till 11pm Fri-Sat, from 7am wknds, till 10pm Sun • food served • WiFi • wheelchair access

RESTAURANTS

Alana's Food & Wine 2333 N High St (at Patterson) **614/294–6783** • from 5pm, clsd Sun-Tue

Banana Leaf 816 Bethel Rd (at Olentangy River Rd) **614/459–4101** • 11:30am-9:30pm • vegetarian/vegan Indian • wheelchair access

Betty's 680 N High St **614/228–6191** • 11am-2am • plenty veggie • also bar

Blue Nile 2361 N High St (at W Patterson) **614/421–2323** • lunch & dinner, clsd Mon • Ethiopian

Cap City Diner 1299 Olentangy River Rd (at W 5th) **614/291–3663** • 11am-10pm, till 11pm Fri-Sat, till 9pm Sun

Dragonfly 247 King Ave **614/298–9986** • 5pm-10pm Tue-Sat, Sat brunch, clsd Sun-Mon • upscale vegetarian • patio

L'Antibes 772 N High St #106 (at Warren) **614/291–1666** • dinner from 5pm, clsd Sun-Mon • full bar • wheelchair access • gay-owned

Lemongrass 641 N High (at Russell) **614/224–1414** • lunch & dinner, clsd Sun-Mon • popular • Asian cuisine • reservations advised

Northstar Cafe 951 N High St (at W 2nd Ave) **614/298–9999** • 9am-10pm • popular • plenty veggie

Surly Girl Saloon 1126 N High St (at W 4th Ave) **614/294–4900** • 11am-2am • plenty veggie • also bar • open mic comedy Wed & punk rock aerobics 6:30 Tue

Tip Top Kitchen & Cocktails 73 E Gay St (at 3rd St) **614/221–8300** • 11am-2am

Whole World Bakery & Restaurant 3269 N High St (at W Como Ave) **614/268–5751** • 11am-8pm, Sun brunch, clsd Mon • vegetarian/vegan • wheelchair access

ENTERTAINMENT & RECREATION

Ohio Roller Girls • Columbus' female roller derby league • visit www.ohiorollergirls.com for events

BOOKSTORES

The Book Loft of German Village 631 S 3rd St (at Sycamore) **614/464–1774** • 10am-11pm, till midnight Fri-Sat • LGBT section

RETAIL SHOPS

Hausfrau Haven 769 S 3rd St (at Columbus) **614/443–3680** • 10am-7pm, noon-5pm Sun • greeting cards • wine • gifts

Piercology 190 W 2nd Ave (at Hunter Ave) **614/297–4743** • noon-8pm, 1pm-7pm Sun • body-piercing studio • gay-owned • wheelchair access

Schmidt's Fudge Haus 220 E Kossuth St (in Historic German Village) **614/444–2222** • noon-close • old fashioned fudge & candy • gifts

Torso 772 N High St (at Warren) **614/421–7663** • 11am-10pm, till 5pm Sun-Mon • clothing

PUBLICATIONS

Gay People's Chronicle 216/916–9338

Outlook Weekly 614/268–8525 • statewide LGBT weekly • good resource pages

EROTICA

The Garden 1174 N High St (btwn 4th & 5th Ave) **614/294–2869** • 11am-3am, noon-midnight Sun • adult toys

Dayton

INFO LINES & SERVICES

AA Gay/Lesbian 20 W 1st St (off Main, at Christ Episcopal Church) **937/222–2211** • 8pm Sat

Greater Dayton Lesbian/Gay Center 117 E 3rd St **937/274–1776**

ACCOMMODATIONS

Dayton Marriott 1414 S Patterson Blvd **937/223–1000**

Bars

Argos Bar 301 Mabel Ave (near Linden & I-35) **937/252–2976** • 8pm-2:30am • men only • neighborhood bar • leather • gay-owned

MJ's Cafe 119 E 3rd St (at S Jefferson) **937/223-3259** • 3pm-2:30am • mostly gay men • dancing/DJ • food served • karaoke • male strippers • deck

Stage Door 44 N Jefferson St (at 2nd) **937/223–7418** • noon-2:30am, from 2pm Wed & wknds • mostly gay men • leather • wheelchair access

Nightclubs

Aquarius 135 E 2nd (at St Clair) **937/223–1723** • 9pm-3am Wed-Sun • lesbians/ gay men • dancing/DJ • drag shows • wheelchair access

Masque 34 N Jefferson St (btwn 2nd & 3rd) **937/228–2582** • 8pm-2:30am, till 5am wknds • popular • mostly gay men • dancing/DJ • drag shows • strippers • 18+

Cafes

Expressions Coffee House **937/308–8345** • 7am-9pm, 9am-2pm Sat, clsd Sun • live music • gay-owned

Restaurants

Cold Beer & Cheeseburgers 33 S Jefferson St (at 4th St) **937/222–2337** • 11am-close • grill • full bar • wheelchair access

The Spaghetti Warehouse 36 W 5th St (at Ludlow) **937/461–3913** • 11am-10pm, till 11pm wknds • more gay Tue w/ Friends of the Italian Opera

Bookstores

Books & Co 350 E Stroop Rd (at Far Hills) **937/298–6540** • 9am-11pm, till 8pm Sun

Publications

Gay Dayton **937/623–1590** • monthly LGBT publication

Erotica

Deja Vu Love Boutique 1267 N Keowee St (off I-75) **937/222–1212** • 10am-3am, 24hrs Th-Sat • novelties, toys, DVDs, arcade

Kent

Bars

The Zephyr Pub 106 W Main St (at Water St) **330/678–4848** • 3pm-close • gay-friendly • live shows • wheelchair access

Lima

Nightclubs

Somewhere in Time 804 W North St (at Baxter) **419/227–7288** • 7pm-2:30am, from 8pm wknds • lesbians/ gay men • dancing/DJ • drag shows • male & female strippers

Logan

Accommodations

Glenlaurel—A Scottish Country Inn 14940 Mt Olive Rd (off State Rte I-80), Rockbridge **740/385–4070, 800/809–7378** • gay/ straight • full brkfst & dinner • hot tub • nonsmoking • wheelchair access

Inn & Spa at Cedar Falls 21190 State Rte 374 **740/385–7489, 800/653–2557** • gay/ straight • rooms, log cabins & cottages • fine dining on-site • nonsmoking • WiFi • wheelchair access

Lazy Lane Cabins **740/385–3475, 877/225–6572** • gay-friendly • secluded cabins sleep 2-8 • hot tubs • fireplaces • satellite TV • nonsmoking • kids/ pets ok • $119-229

Lorain

Bars

Tim's Place 2223 Broadway (btwn 22nd & 23rd) **440/218–2223** • 8pm-2:30am, clsd Mon • lesbians/ gay men • neighborhood bar • dancing/DJ • drag shows • patio • wheelchair access

Marietta

Accommodations

Fourth St B&B **614/638–1187** • gay/ straight • kids ok • nonsmoking • gay-owned • $69-149

Monroe

Bars

Old Street Saloon 13 Old St (at Elm St) **513/539–9183** • 8pm-2am Th-Sat, till 1am Wed, clsd Sun-Tue • lesbians/ gay men • neighborhood bar • dancing/DJ • drag shows • karaoke

Niles

Erotica

Niles Books 5970 Youngstown Warren Rd (off Rte 46) **330/544–3755**

Oberlin

ACCOMMODATIONS

Hallauer House B&B 14945 Hallauer Rd 440/774-3400, 877/774-3406 • gay-friendly • eco-friendly historic inn 3 miles S of Oberlin • pool • nonsmoking • WiFi

RESTAURANTS

The Feve 30 S Main St (at College St) 440/774-1978 • 11am-midnight • popular wknd brunch (9:30am-2:30pm) • plenty veggie • full bar (5pm-2am)

Weia Teia 9 S Main St (at College St) 440/774-8880 • lunch & dinner • Thai/ Asian fusion • upscale • full bar • some veggie

BOOKSTORES

MindFair Books 13 W College St (shares storefront w/ Ben Franklin) 440/774-6463 • 10am-6pm, till 8pm Fri, noon-5pm Sun

Sandusky

NIGHTCLUBS

Crowbar 206 W Market St (at Jackson St) 419/624-0109 • 6pm-2:30am • lesbians/ gay men • ladies night Tue • dancing/DJ • karaoke • gay-owned

Xcentricities 306 W Water St (at Jackson St) 419/624-8118 • 6pm-2:30am, from 2pm wknds • lesbians/ gay men • dancing/DJ • drag shows • male & female strippers • patio

RESTAURANTS

Mona Pizza Gourmet 135 Columbus Ave (at Market St) 419/626-8166 • 11am-10pm, till 3am wknds • multiracial • transgender-friendly • gay-owned

Springfield

NIGHTCLUBS

Diesel 1912-14 Edwards Ave (at N Belmont Ave) 937/324-0383 • 8:30pm-2:30am, clsd Mon-Tue • gay-friendly • dancing/DJ • live shows • karaoke • patio

Why Not III 5 N Murray St 937/324-9758 • 9:30pm-2:30am, till 1am Sun-Tue • lesbians/ gay men • dancing/DJ • karaoke • WiFi

Toledo

INFO LINES & SERVICES

AA Gay/ Lesbian 3535 Executive Pkwy (at Unity) 419/380-9862 • 8pm Wed

ACCOMMODATIONS

Mansion View Inn 2035 Collingwood Blvd (at Irving) 419/244-5676 • gay-friendly • 1887 Victorian near downtown in Historic Old West End • nonsmoking • WiFi

BARS

Blush 119 N Erie St 419/255-4010 • 9pm-2:30am Fri-Sat only • mostly men • drag shows

Outskirts 5038 Lewis Ave 419/476-1577 • 3pm-2:30am, till 3:30am Fri-Sat, clsd Sun-Tue • mostly women • dancing/DJ • karaoke

R House 5534 Secor Rd (btwn Laskey & Alexis) 419/474-2929 • 4pm-2:30am • mostly gay men • dancing/DJ • patio

Rip Cord 115 N Erie St (btwn Jefferson & Monroe) 419/243-3412 • 9am-2:30am • mostly gay men • more women Mon • neighborhood bar • Sun brunch • karaoke • strippers • food served

NIGHTCLUBS

Bretz 2012 Adams St 419/243-1900 • 9pm-2:30am, till 4:30am Fri-Sat, clsd Mon-Tue • lesbians/ gay men • dancing/DJ • karaoke • drag shows • strippers • 18+ • wheelchair access

BOOKSTORES

People Called Women 6060 Reinaissance Pl #F 419/469-8983 • 11am-7pm, clsd Sun, clsd Mon • multicultural • feminist

Warren

NIGHTCLUBS

Club 441 441 E Market St (at Vine, enter rear) 330/394-9483 • 4pm-2:30am, from 2pm wknds • lesbians/ gay men • dancing/DJ • live shows • wheelchair access

The Funky Skunk 143 E Market St (at Park Ave) • 9pm-close • mostly gay men • ladies night Sun • dancing/DJ • drag shows • karaoke

West Lafayette

RESTAURANTS

Lava Rock Grill at Unusual Junction 56310 US Hwy 36 740/545-9772 • '50s-style diner in restored railroad station • wheelchair access • gay-owned

Yellow Springs

RESTAURANTS

Winds Cafe & Bakery 215 Xenia Ave (at Cory St) 937/767-1144 • lunch & dinner, Sun brunch, clsd Mon • plenty veggie • full bar • wheelchair access • women-owned

Youngstown

INFO LINES & SERVICES

The Mahoning Valley Pride Center 1523 Poland Ave (at Shirley Rd) • home to many of the local LGBT organizations including: Stonewall Democrats, PFLAG, All Families Matter & Pride Youngstown

NIGHTCLUBS

Split Level/ Pulse 169 S Four Mile Run Rd (at S Mahoning Ave) 330/318–9830 • lesbians/ gay men • dancing/DJ • drag shows • karaoke

Utopia Video Nightclub 876 E Midlothian Blvd (at Zedaker St) 330/781–9000 • 5pm-close, clsd Mon • lesbians/ gay men • dancing/DJ • drag shows

CAFES

The Lemon Grove Cafe 122 W Federal Plaza W (at Hazel St) 330/744–7683 • 7am-4am, from 11am wknds • food served • also bar • events, movies, art & more

OKLAHOMA

Grand Lake

ACCOMMODATIONS

Southern Oaks Resort & Spa 2 miles S of Hwy 28/ 82 Junction, Langley 918/782–9346, 866/452–5307 • gay-friendly • 19 cabins on 30 acres • pool • hot tub • nonsmoking • gay-owned

RESTAURANTS

The Artichoke Restaurant & Bar 35896 S Hwy 82, Langley 918/782–9855 • 5pm-10pm, clsd Sun-Mon

Frosty & Edna's Cafe Highway 28, Langley 918/782–9123 • 6am-9:30pm

Lighthouse Supper Club Highway 85 & Main, Ketchum 918/782–3316 • from 5pm, clsd Sun-Tue

Norman

see also Oklahoma City

RESTAURANTS

La Luna Mexican Cafe 529 Buchanan Ave (on historic Campus Corner) 405/329–9596 • 11am-9pm, 8am-9:30pm Th-Sat, clsd Sun-Mon • full cantina & bar

Oklahoma City

see also Edmond & Norman

INFO LINES & SERVICES

AA Live & Let Live 3405 N Villa 405/947–3834 • 8pm Mon

Herland Sister Resources 2312 NW 39th St 405/521–9696 • 1pm-5pm Sat • women's resource center w/ books, crafts & lending library • also sponsors monthly events • wheelchair access

ACCOMMODATIONS

➤**Habana Inn** 2200 NW 39th St (at Youngs) 405/528–2221, 800/988–2221 (RESERVATIONS ONLY) • popular • lesbians/ gay men • resort • pool • nonsmoking • also 3 bars • restaurant • gift shop • wheelchair access • $40-108

Hawthorn Suites 1600 NW Fxpy (Richmond Square) 405/840–1440, 800/527–1133 (RESERVATIONS) • gay-friendly • full brkfst • pool

Waterford Marriott 6300 Waterford Blvd (at Pennsylvania) 405/848–4782 • gay-friendly • pool • fitness center • also bar & restaurant • nonsmoking • WiFi

BARS

Alibi's 1200 N Pennsylvania (at NW 11th) 405/605–3795 • 3pm-2am, from noon wknds • gay/ straight • neighborhood bar • transgender-friendly • gay-owned

Bearz 3020 3020 N Pennsylvania (at NW 29th St) 405/524–9306 • 2pm-2am • gay/ straight • neighborhood bar

The Boom 2218 NW 39th St (at Pennsylvania) 405/601–7200 • noon-2am, clsd Mon • lesbians/ gay men • neighborhood bar • karaoke Tue • drag shows • WiFi • patio • wheelchair access

Edna's 5137 N Classen Blvd (at NW 51st) 405/840–3339 • 10am-2am • gay-friendly • neighborhood dive bar • food served

➤**The Finishline** at Habana Inn 405/525–2900 • noon-2am • lesbians/ gay men • neighborhood bar • dancing/DJ • country/ western • poolside bar • wheelchair access

Hi-Lo Club 1221 NW 50th St (btwn Western & Classen) 405/843–1722 • noon-2am • lesbians/ gay men • neighborhood bar • live bands weekly • drag shows

➤ **The Ledo** at Habana Inn 405/525–0730 •
4pm-10:30pm, till 2am Fri-Sat • lesbians/ gay
men • martini lounge • food served • karaoke
• nonsmoking • wheelchair access

Partners 4 Club 2805 NW 36th St (at May
Ave) **405/942–2199** • 5pm-close, from 7pm
Fri-Sat, clsd Mon • popular • mostly women •
neighborhood bar • dancing/DJ • karaoke •
live shows • patio • wheelchair access

Oklahoma City

WHERE THE GIRLS ARE:
Scattered all over the largest (in
square miles) city in the US. But
Bricktown is a popular haunt for
many of the city's residents with
all its good eats and good bars.

LGBT PRIDE:
June, web: www.okcpride.com.

ANNUAL EVENTS:
May - Herland Spring Retreat
405/521-9696. Music, workshops, web: www.herlandsis-
ters.org.
May - Paseo Arts Festival 405/525-
2688, web: www.thepaseo.com.
October - Herland Fall Retreat.

CITY INFO:
405/297-8912 & 800/225-5652,
web: www.okccvb.org.

BEST VIEW:
From a water taxi on the Bricktown
Canal (www.brocktownwater-
taxi.com). Or anywhere in Myriad
Gardens.

WEATHER:
Spring brings out the best of
Oklahoma—blue skies for miles
and the dogwood, redbud, and
azaleas in bloom. (It's also the
start of tornado season.) Summer
gets mighty hot (90°s-100°s),
with thunderstorms thrown in for
relief. Fall is the time to head east
to the hills of "Green Country"
and watch the leaves change.
Winters bring cold temps (20°s-
30°s), gray skies, a brown landscape, and the occasional
dusting of snow and the even
rarer but more serious ice storm.

ATTRACTIONS:
Bricktown—renovated nightlife
district with canal.
Historic Paseo Arts District, web:
www.thepaseo.com.
Myriad Gardens' Crystal Bridge
405/297-3995, web: www.myri-
adgardens.com.
National Cowboy and Western
Heritage Museum 405/478-2250,
web: www.nationalcowboymu-
seum.org.
National Softball Hall of Fame
405/424-5266, web: www.soft-
ball.org.
Oklahoma City Museum of Art
405/236-3100, web:
www.okcmoa.com.
Oklahoma City National Memorial
405/235-3313, web: www.okla-
homacitynationalmemorial.org.
Oklahoma City Zoo 405,424-3344,
web: www.okczoo.com.
Science Museum Oklahoma
405/602-6664, web:
www.sciencemuseumok.org.
State Capitol: only one in country
with its own active oil well.
Sylvan Goldman monument (inven-
tor of the shopping cart).
Will Rogers Park.

TRANSIT:
Yellow Cab 405/232-6161.
Airport Express 405/681-3311, web:
www.airportexpressokc.com.
Metro Transit 405/235-7433, web:
www.gometro.org.

Tramps 2201 NW 39th St (at Barnes) **405/521-9888** • noon-2am, from 10am wknds • popular • mostly gay men • dancing/DJ • drag shows • wheelchair access

NIGHTCLUBS

Angles 2117 NW 39th St (at Pennsylvania) **405/524-3431** • Fri-Sat only • lesbians/ gay men • dancing/DJ

➤**The Copa** at Habana Inn **405/525-0730** • 9pm-2am, clsd Mon • popular • lesbians/ gay men • dancing/DJ • drag shows • karaoke • wheelchair access

The Park 2125 NW 39th St (at Pennsylvania) **405/528-4690** • 5pm-2am, from 3pm Sun (free buffet) • mostly gay men • dancing/DJ • patio • wheelchair access

Wreck Room 2127 NW 39th St (at Pennsylvania) **405/525-7610** • 10pm-close Fri-Sat only • lesbians/ gay men • dancing/DJ • live shows • drag shows • young crowd • 18+ after 1am

CAFES

Coffy's Cafe 1739 NW 16th St (at Gatewood) **405/604-8796** • 7am-7pm, till 11pm Fri, 9am-9pm Sat, clsd Sun-Mon • vegetarian/ gluten-free • live music • events

The Red Cup 3122 N Classen Blvd (at NW 30th St) **405/525-3430** • 7am-5pm, till 10pm Th-Fri, 9am-10pm Sat • food served • nonsmoking • WiFi • live music

RESTAURANTS

Bricktown Brewery Restaurant 1 N Oklahoma Ave (at Sheridan) **405/232-2739** • 11am-10pm, till midnight Sat, from noon Sun • full bar

Cheever's Cafe 2409 N Hudson Ave (at NW 23rd) **405/525-7007** • 11am-9:30pm, 5pm-10:30pm Sat, brunch Sun • reservations recommended

Earl's Rib Palace 216 Johnny Bench Dr, Ste BBQ (in Bricktown) **405/272-9898** • 11am-9pm, till 10pm Fri-Sat, noon-8pm Sun

➤**Gusher's** at Habana Inn **405/525-0730** • 11am-10:30pm, from 9am wknds, till 3:30am Fri-Sat for after-hours brkfst • wheelchair access

Iguana Bar & Grill 9 NW 9th St (at N Santa Fe Ave) **405/606-7172** • lunch & dinner • Mexican

Ingrid's Kitchen 3701 N Youngs (btwn Penn & May, on NW 36th) **405/946-8444** • 7am-8pm, 10am-2pm Sun • German/ American bakery & deli

La Luna Mexican Cafe 409 W Reno Ave (at Walker) **405/235-9596** • full bar

Pops 660 W Hwy 66, Arcadia **405/928-7677** • brkfst, lunch & dinner • diner fare • look for the 66-foot tall soda bottle

Rococo Restaurant & Fine Wine 2824 N Pennsylvania (at NW 27th St) **405/528-2824** • lunch Mon-Fri, dinner nightly, Sun jazz brunch • full bar

Someplace Else Deli & Bakery 2310 N Western Ave **405/524-0887** • 7am-6:30pm, 9:30am-4pm Sat, clsd Sun • popular

Sushi Neko 4318 N Western (btwn 42nd & 43rd) **405/528-8862** • 11am-11pm, clsd Sun

Ted's Cafe Escondido 8324 S Western Ave (at 84th St) **405/635-8337** • lunch & dinner • popular • Tex-Mex

ENTERTAINMENT & RECREATION

First Friday Gallery Walk from 28th at N Walker to 30th at N Dewey **405/525-2688** • open tour of Paseo Arts District galleries • first Fri & Sat

BOOKSTORES

Full Circle Bookstore 50 Penn Pl, 1900 NW Expwy (in NE corner of 1st level) **405/842-2900, 800/683-7323** • 10am-9pm, noon-5pm Sun • also cafe & coffee bar

RETAIL SHOPS

23rd St Body Piercing 411 NW 23rd St (btwn Hudson & Walker) **405/524-6824** • noon-9pm, 1pm-6pm Sun

➤**Jungle Red** at Habana Inn **405/524-5733** • 1pm-close • novelties • leather • gifts • wheelchair access

PUBLICATIONS

The Herland Voice **405/521-9696** • monthly newsletter for OKC women's community

Oklahoma Gazette **405/528-6000** • "Metro OKC's independent weekly"

EROTICA

Christie's Toy Box 7914 N MacArthur **405/720-2453** • multiple locations in OKC

Patricia's 615 E Memorial **405/755-8600**

Tulsa

INFO LINES & SERVICES

Dennis R Neill Equality Center 621 E 4th St (at Kenosha) **918/743-4297** • 3pm-9pm, clsd Sun • many activities & Pride store • wheelchair access

Gay/ Lesbian AA 2545 S Yale Ave (at Community of Hope) 918/627-2224 • 7pm Wed & Fri, 5:30pm Sat

ACCOMMODATIONS

Crowne Plaza 100 E Second St (at 2nd St) 918/582-9000, 800/980-6429 • gay-friendly • restaurant • pool • kids/ pets ok • wheelchair access

Tulsa Select 5000 East Skelly Dr (at I-44 & Yale Ave) 918/622-7000, 800/836-9635 • gay-friendly • pool • kids/ pets ok • restaurant/lounge • WiFi • wheelchair access

BARS

Bamboo Lounge 7204 E Pine 918/836-8700 • noon-2am • mostly gay men • neighborhood bar • dancing/DJ • live shows • karaoke • patio • wheelchair access

Club 209 209 N Boulder Ave (at Brady) 918/584-9944 • 7pm-2am, clsd Mon-Wed • gay/ straight • karaoke

New Age Renegade 1649 S Main St (at 17th) 918/585-3405 • 4pm-2am • lesbians/ gay men • neighborhood bar • live shows • karaoke • patio

TNT's 2114 S Memorial Dr 918/660-0856 • 8pm-2am, clsd Mon • popular • mostly women • neighborhood bar • dancing/DJ • karaoke

The Yellow Brick Road 2630 E 15th St (at Harvard) 918/293-0304 • 1pm-2am • lesbians/ gay men • neighborhood bar • wheelchair access

NIGHTCLUBS

Club Majestic 124 N Boston (at Brady) 918/584-9494 • 9pm-2am Th-Sun • dancing/DJ • drag/live shows • transgender-friendly • young crowd • wheelchair access • gay-owned

Club Maverick 822 S Sheridan (at 9th) 918/835-3301 • 4pm-2am • lesbians/ gay men • dancing/DJ • country/ western • karaoke

CAFES

Gypsy's Coffee House 303 N Cincinnati Ave 918/295-2181 • 11am-midnight, till 3am Fri-Sat, noon-10pm Sun, clsd Mon • live shows • WiFi

RESTAURANTS

The Brasserie 3509 S Peoria 918/779-7070 • 4pm-10m, til 11pm Fri-Sat, 10am-9pm Sun

Cancun International 705 S Lewis Ave (at 11th) 918/583-8089 • 11am-9pm, from 10am Sat & Sun, clsd Wed

Eloté 514 S Boston Ave 918/582-1403 • 11am-10pm, till 2pm Mon, clsd Sun, fresh Mexican • full bar

James E McNellie's Public House 409 E 1st St 918/382-7468 • 10am-2am • great burgers • full bar • wheelchair access

White Lion Pub 6927 S Canton Ave (off 71st) 918/491-6533 • 4pm-10pm, clsd Sun-Mon • British-style pub

Wild Fork 1820 Utica Square 918/742-0712 • 7am-10pm, clsd Sun • full bar • wheelchair access • women-owned

ENTERTAINMENT & RECREATION

Gilcrease Museum 1400 N Gilcrease Museum Rd 918/596-2700, 888/655-2278 • one of the best collections of Native American & cowboy art in the US

Green Country Roller Girls 918/269-7228 • Oklahoma's female roller derby league • visit www.tulsarollerderby.com for events

Philbrook Museum of Art 2727 S Rockford Rd (1 block E of Peoria, at end of 27th St) 918/324-7941 • clsd Mon • Italian villa built in the '20s oil boom complete w/ kitschy lighted dance flr • the gardens are a must in spring & summer

RETAIL SHOPS

Brookside Piercing & Tattoo 3314 S Peoria Ave 918/712-1122 • noon-10pm, till midnight Fri-Sat

The Pride Store 621 S E 4th St 918/743-4297 • 3pm-9pm, 3pm-6pm Sun • wheelchair access

PUBLICATIONS

Urban Tulsa Weekly 918/592-5550 • "Tulsa Metro's only independent newsweekly"

OREGON

Statewide

PUBLICATIONS

Just Out 503/236-1252 • LGBT newspaper w/ extensive resource directory

Ashland

INFO LINES & SERVICES

Gay/ Lesbian AA 541/732-1850

Accommodations

The Arden Forest Inn 261 W Hersey St (at N Main) 541/488–1496, 800/460–3912 • gay/ straight • full brkfst • nonsmoking • pool • kids 10+ ok • wheelchair access • WiFi • gay- owned • $149-305

Ashland Creek Inn 70 Water St 541/482–3315 • gay-friendly • secluded forest location minutes to downtown Ashland • kitchens in all suites • multi-course gourmet brkfst • nonsmoking • gay-owned • $110-425

Blue Moon B&B 312 Helman St (at Hersey) 541/482–9228, 800/460-5453 • gay-friendly • full brkfst • kids/ pets ok in cottage • nonsmoking • WiFi • gay-owned • $90-225

Country Willows B&B Inn 1313 Clay St (at Siskiyou Blvd) 541/488–1590, 800/945-5697 • gay-friendly • full brkfst • pool • jacuzzi • nonsmoking • teens ok • WiFi • wheelchair access • gay-owned • $140-275

Lithia Springs Resort 2165 W Jackson Rd (at N Main) 541/482–7128, 800/482-7128 • gay/ straight • full brkfst • natural hot-springs- fed whirlpools in rooms • nonsmoking • teens ok • WiFi • $199-418

Romeo Inn B&B 295 Idaho St 541/488–0884, 800/915-8899 • gay-friendly • full brkfst • jacuzzi • pool • nonsmoking • WiFi • $110-215

Restaurants

The Black Sheep 51 N Main St (on the Plaza) 541/482–6414 • 11:30am-1am • eclectic pub fare • WiFi • woman-owned

Geppetto's 345 E Main St (at 2nd St) 541/482–1138 • 11am-9pm • Italian • full bar • wheelchair access

Greenleaf Restaurant 49 N Main St (on The Plaza) 541/482–2808 • 8am-8pm • creekside dining • beer/ wine

Bookstores

Bloomsbury Books 290 E Main St (btwn 1st & 2nd) 541/488–0029 • 8:30am-9pm, till 10pm Fri-Sat

Retail Shops

Travel Essentials 252 E Main St 541/482–7383, 800/258-0758 • 10am-5:30pm, 11am-5pm Sun • luggage • books • accessories

Bend

Accommodations

Dawson House Lodge 109455 Hwy 97 N, Chemult 541/365–2232, 888/281-8375 • gay- friendly • rustic inn w/ modern amenities • near Crater Lake • nonsmoking • kids/ pets ok • WiFi • gay-owned • $50-110

Restaurants

Blacksmith Restaurant 211 NW Greenwood Ave (at NW Harriman) 541/318–0588 • 4:30pm-close • new American • upscale

Corvallis

Bookstores

Book Bin 215 SW 4th St 541/752–0040 • 8am-9pm, till 10pm Fri-Sat, 9am-7pm Sun

Grass Roots Books & Music 227 SW 2nd St (btwn Jefferson & Madison) 541/754–7668 • 9:30am-6pm, till 7pm Fri, 10am-5:30pm Sat, noon-5pm Sun • wheelchair access

Eugene

Info Lines & Services

Gay/ Lesbian AA 1414 Kincaid (at Koinonia Center) 541/342–4113 • 7pm Mon & Wed, 8pm Fri

Accommodations

C'est La Vie Inn 1006 Taylor St (at W 10th) 541/302–3014, 866/302-3014 • gay-friendly • full brkfst • nonsmoking • WiFi • $140-260

Bars

Hot Flash Eugene 2222 MLK Jr Blvd (at Kowloon's) • 7pm-11pm 2nd Sat only • mostly women • dancing/DJ • "for seasoned lesbians 36+ (& the women who love us!)" • food served • cover charge

Sam's Place Tavern 825 Wilson St (at 11th Ave W) 541/484–4455 • 11am-2:30am, from 9am wknds, till midnight Sun • gay-friendly • neighborhood bar • dancing/DJ • live shows • karaoke • also restaurant

Nightclubs

Club Snafu 64 W 8th Alley (at Willamette Alley) 541/342–3272 • 9pm-2:30am Th-Sat only • lesbians/ gay men • dancing/DJ

Diablo's Downtown Lounge 959 Pearl St 541/343–2346 • gay-friendly • dancing/DJ • karaoke Sun • open mic Tue • theme nights • also restaurant

CAFES

Eugene Coffee Company 1840 Chambers St (at 18th) **541/344-0002** • 7am-6pm • lesbian-owned

RESTAURANTS

Glenwood Restaurant 1340 Alder St (at 13th Ave) **541/687-0355** • 7am-9pm

Keystone Cafe 395 W 5th Ave (at Lawrence) **541/342-2075** • 7am-3pm • popular brkfst • plenty veggie

ENTERTAINMENT & RECREATION

Glassbar Island Nude Beach/ Willamette River Beach on the Coast Fork (Franklin Blvd and I-5) • gay/ straight • nude beach, also hiking & biking • www.glassbarisland.org for details

RETAIL SHOPS

High Priestess Piercing 675 Lincoln St (at 7th Ave) **541/342-6585** • 11am-8pm, till 9pm Wed-Sat

EROTICA

Exclusively Adult 1166 South A St (at 10th St), Springfield **541/726-6969** • 24hrs

Grants Pass

ACCOMMODATIONS

Rainbows on the Fly **541/862-2086** • women's land on 40 acres • cabin, campsites, RV hookups • also guided flyfishing • nonsmoking • WiFi • lesbian-owned • $45-400

WomanShare **541/862-2807** • women only • cabins • shared kitchen • bathhouse • hot tub • girls/pets ok • nonsmoking • lesbian-owned • $25-40

CAFES

Sunshine Natural Foods Cafe 128 SW H St (btwn 5th & 6th Sts) **541/474-5044** • 9am-6pm, 9:30am-5pm Sat • clsd Sun • vegetarian • also market • WiFi • wheelchair access

Idleyld Park

ACCOMMODATIONS

Umpqua's Last Resort Wilderness RV Park & Campground 115 Elk Ridge Ln **541/498-2500** • gay/ straight • WiFi • gay owned

Jacksonville

ACCOMMODATIONS

The TouVelle House 455 N Oregon St (at E St) **541/899-8938, 800/846-8422** • gay-friendly • 1916 Craftsman on 1 1/2 acres • full brkfst • pool • WiFi • nonsmoking • $149-235

Klamath Falls

ACCOMMODATIONS

Crystal Wood Lodge 38625 Westside Road (at Hwy 140) **541/381-2322, 866/381-2322** • gay-friendly • non-smoking • WiFi • lesbian owned

Lincoln City

ACCOMMODATIONS

Ashley Inn 3430 NE Hwy 101 **541/996-7500, 888/427-4539** • gay-friendly • pool • non-smoking • WiFi • wheelchair access • $89-199

Surftides Inn 2945 NW Jetty Ave **800/452-2159** • gay/straight • restaurant & bar • pool • WiFi • nonsmoking • $209+

A Vista d' Mar 1421 NW Harbor Ave (at Hwy 101) **541/994-6300, 866/776-8659** • gay/ straight • kitchens • beach access • nonsmoking

RESTAURANTS

Dory Cove Restaurant 2981 SW Hwy 101 (at 29th) **541/557-4000** • 11:30am-9pm • steak & seafood • beer/ wine • wheelchair access

Mist Restaurant 2945 NW Jetty Ave (at Surftides Inn) **541/994-3877** • 8am-9pm • full bar open later

Newport

ACCOMMODATIONS

Cliff House B&B **541/563-2506** • gay-friendly • oceanfront • great view • full brkfst • hot tub • nonsmoking • WiFi • $125-225

RESTAURANTS

Mo's Annex 657 SW Bay Blvd (at SW Fall) **541/265-7512** • 11am-3pm • great chowder

Portland

see also Vancouver, Washington

INFO LINES & SERVICES

Live & Let Live Club 1210 SE 7th Ave **503/238-6091** • 12-step meetings • call for schedule

Q Center 4115 N Mississippi Ave (at N Mason St) 503/234-7837 • LGBTQ community center • WiFi

Sexual Minority Youth Resource Center (SMYRC) 3024 NE Martin Luther King, Jr Blvd 503/872-9664 • 4pm-9pm Wed, Fri-Sat • drop-in center for LGBTQ youth

ACCOMMODATIONS

The Ace Hotel 1022 SW Stark St (at 11th) 503/228-2277 • gay/ straight • hip hotel for "cultural influencers & opinion leaders on a budget" • nonsmoking • WiFi • kids/ pets ok • wheelchair access • $85-260

Forest Springs B&B 3680 SW Towle Ave, Gresham 503/674-8992 • gay/ straight • full brkfst • kids ok • nonsmoking • gay-owned • $80-185

Hotel deLuxe 729 SW 15th Ave (at SW Morrison) 503/219-2094, 866/895-2094 • gay-friendly • 1940s Hollywood decor • nonsmoking • WiFi • $159-339

Hotel Monaco Portland 506 SW Washington (at 5th Ave) 503/222-0001, 866/861-9514 • gay-friendly • restaurant • gym • kids/ pets ok • WiFi

Hotel Vintage Plaza 422 SW Broadway (at SW Washington) 503/228-1212, 800/263-2305 • popular • gay-friendly • upscale hotel • restaurant & lounge • WiFi • wheelchair access • $143-375

Inn at Northrup Station 2025 NW Northrup St (at NW 21st) 503/224-0543, 800/224-1180 • gay-friendly • cute, colorful boutique hotel

Jupiter Hotel 800 E Burnside 503/230-9200, 877/800-0004 • gay-friendly • boutique hotel • nonsmoking • restaurant & lounge • kids/ pets ok • WiFi • wheelchair access • $89-139

The Kinley Manor Coach House 924 NE Schuyler (at NE Broadway) 503/249-7270 • gay/ straight • rental home • fully equipped kitchen • laundry facilities • nonsmoking • no partiers • WiFi • gay-owned • $99-120

The Lion & the Rose 1810 NE 15th Ave (at NE Schuyler) 503/287-9245, 800/955-1647 • gay/ straight • in 1906 Queen Anne mansion • nonsmoking • WiFi • gay-owned • $134-224

The Mark Spencer Hotel 409 SW Eleventh Ave (near Stark) 503/224-3293, 800/548-3934 • gay-friendly • nonsmoking • kids/ pets ok • WiFi • $99-229

Painted Lady Inn 1927 NE 16th Ave (at NE Hancock St) 503/335-0070 • gay/ straight • nonsmoking • full brkfst • $109-179

Portland's White House B&B 1914 NE 22nd Ave (at NE Hancock St) 503/287-7131, 800/272-7131 • gay/ straight • in 1911 Greek Revival mansion • nonsmoking • WiFi • gay-owned • $125-225

Sheraton Portland Airport Hotel 82335 NE Airport Wy (at 82nd Ave) 503/281-2500, 800/743-7286 • gay-friendly • pool • nonsmoking • WiFi • wheelchair access • $99-199

BARS

Boxxes 1035 SW 11th Ave (at SW 11th) 503/226-4171 • 5pm-close • popular • mostly gay men • karaoke • videos • WiFi • wheelchair access • also Brig • lesbians/ gay men • dancing/DJ • also Red Cap Garage

Candlelight Cafe & Bar 2032 SW 5th (at Lincoln St) 503/222-3378 • 3pm-2:30am • gay-friendly • live blues • food served • wheelchair access

CC Slaughter's 219 NW Davis St (at 3rd) 503/248-9135, 888/348-9135 • 3pm-2am • popular • mostly gay men • dancing/DJ • karaoke • videos • also martini lounge • WiFi • wheelchair access

Chopsticks Express II 2651 E Burnside St (at NE 26th Ave) 503/234-6171 • noon-2am • gay/ straight • karaoke • young crowd • food served • wheelchair access

Crush 1400 SE Morrison (at SE 14th) 503/235-8150 • 4:30pm-2am, from 10am Sat, 9am-midnight Sun, clsd Mon • gay/ straight • wine & martini bar • food served • WiFi • wheelchair access

Darcelle XV 208 NW 3rd Ave (at NW Davis St) 503/222-5338 • 6pm-11pm, till 2am Fri-Sat, clsd Sun-Tue • gay/ straight • cabaret • strippers • drag shows • food served • wheelchair access

Fox & Hounds 217 NW 2nd Ave (btwn Everett & Davis) 503/243-5530 • 11am-2am • popular • mostly gay men • also restaurant • brunch wknds • wheelchair access

Hot Flash Portland 9 NW 2nd Ave (at Barracuda) 503/252-9333 • 6pm-10pm 4th Sat only • "for seasoned lesbians 36+ (& the women who love us!)" • dancing/DJ • cover charge

Northbank 106 W 6th St (btwn Main & Washington), Vancouver, WA 360/695-3862 • 2pm-2am, clsd Mon • lesbians/ gay men • dancing/DJ • food served • karaoke • drag shows • nonsmoking • wheelchair access

Rollure 315 SE 3rd Ave (at SE Pine) **503/234-5683** • 8pm-2:30am • gay-friendly • live music venue • also restaurant

Silverado 318 SW 3rd Ave (at SW Oak St) **503/224-4493** • 9am-2:30am • popular • mostly gay men • dancing/DJ • strippers • karaoke Mon • food served • wheelchair access • gay-owned

Starky's 2913 SE Stark St (at SE 29th Ave) **503/230-7980** • 11am-2am • popular • lesbians/gay men • neighborhood bar • also restaurant • Sun brunch • some veggie • patio • wheelchair access

Vault Martini Bar 226 NW 12th Ave (btwn 12th & Davis Sts) **503/224-4909** • 4pm-1am, till 2am Th-Sat, 1pm-10pm Sun • gay/straight • full menu • wheelchair access

Vino Vixens 2929 SE Powell Blvd (at SE 29th) **503/231-8466** • 1pm-9pm, till 11pm wknds, clsd Mon • gay/straight • "Portland's first rock 'n' roll wine shop" • retail & lounge • nonsmoking • woman-owned

The Weird Bar 3701 SE Division St (at SE 37th Ave) **503/236-8689** • 1pm-close, from 4pm wknds • popular • mostly women • dancing/DJ • karaoke • strippers • food served • transgender-friendly • wheelchair access • lesbian-owned

Portland

WHERE THE GIRLS ARE:
Try along SE Hawthorne & Belmont streets where some of the women's businesses are, or the NW section, 21st & 23rd Aves, for the more upscale lesbians.

LGBT PRIDE:
June. 503/295-9788, web: www.pridenw.org.

ANNUAL EVENTS:
May - QDoc Portland Queer Documentary Film Festival, web: www.queerdocfest.org.
May/June - Rose Festival, web: www.rosefestival.org.
August - Mount Hood Jazz Festival, web: www.mthoodjazz.com.
September - La Femme Magnifique International Pageant, web: www.darcellexv.com.
October - AIDS Walk 503/223-5907, web: www.cascadeaids.org.
October - Portland LGBT Film Festival, web: www.plgff.org.

CITY INFO:
503/275-9750, web: www.travel-portland.com.
Travel Oregon 800/962-3700.

ATTRACTIONS:
The Grotto 503/254-7371, web: www.thegrotto.org.
Microbreweries.
Old Town.
Pioneer Courthouse Square 503/223-1613, web: www.pioneercourthousesquare.org.
Portland Art Museum 503/226-2811, web: www.portlandartmuseum.org.
Washington Park.
World Forestry Center & Discovery Museum 503/228-1367, web: www.worldforestrycenter.org.

BEST VIEW:
International Rose Test Gardens at Washington Park.

WEATHER:
The wet and sometimes chilly winter rains give Portland a lush landscape that bursts into beautiful colors in the spring and fall. Summer brings sunnier days. (Temperatures can be in the 50°s one day and the 90°s the next.)

TRANSIT:
Radio Cab 503/227-1212.
Raz 503/684-3322.
Tri-Met System 503/238-7433.

Nightclubs

Casey's 610 NW Couch St (at 6th) **503/505–9468** • 11am-2:30am • lesbians/ gay men • dancing/DJ • go-go dancers

Chocolate City 1400 SE Morrison (at SE 14th, at Crush) **503/235–8150** • 9pm 3rd Sat only • mostly women • hip hop party • dancing/DJ • multiracial

Embers 110 NW Broadway (at NW Couch St) **503/222–3082** • 11am-3am • popular • mostly gay men • dancing/DJ • drag shows • also restaurant • wheelchair access

Escape 333 SW Park (btwn SW Oak & SW Stark) **503/227–0830** • 10:30pm-close Fri-Sat only • Portland's only all-ages gay club • dancing/DJ • drag shows • videos

Holocene 1001 SE Morrison (at SE 10th) **503/239–7639** • gay/ straight • popular dance club • many LGBT theme nights • live music • check local listings

Maricon at Matador 1967 W Burnside St (at Trinity) **503/222–5822** • 1st & 3rd Sat only • lesbians/ gay men • dancing/DJ • drag shows

Cafes

Blend 2710 N Killingsworth (at Greeley) **503/473–8616** • 7am-6pm, from 8am Sun • WiFi

Cup & Saucer Cafe 3566 SE Hawthorne Blvd (at SE 36th) **503/236–6001** • 7am-9pm • popular w/ lesbians • full menu • vegan-friendly • beer/ wine • nonsmoking • wheelchair access

Elephant's Delicatessen 115 NW 22nd Ave (at NW Davis) **503/299–6304** • 7am-7:30pm, 9:30am-6:30pm Sun • deli, desserts & coffee • wheelchair access

Marco's Cafe & Espresso Bar 7910 SW 35th (at Multnomah Blvd), Multnomah **503/245–0199** • 7am-9pm, from 8am Sat, 8am-2pm Sun • food served • plenty veggie • beer/ wine • wheelchair access

The Pied Cow 3244 SE Belmont St (at 33rd Ave) **503/230–4866** • 4pm-midnight, till 1am Fri, noon-1am Sat, till midnight Sun • funky Victorian • great desserts • patio • wheelchair access

Pix Pâtisserie 3402 SE Division St (at SE 34th) **503/232–4407** • 2pm-midnight, noon-2am Fri-Sat • dessert • beer/ wine • wheelchair access

Three Friends Coffeehouse 201 SE 12th Ave (at Ash) **503/236–6411** • 7am-10pm, from 8am Sun • WiFi • wheelchair access

Voodoo Doughnut 22 SW 3rd Ave **503/241–4704** • 24hrs

Restaurants

The Adobe Rose 1634 SE Bybee Blvd (at SE Milwaukee) **503/235–9114** • lunch & dinner, clsd Sun-Mon • New Mexican • some veggie • beer/ wine • wheelchair access

Andina 1314 NW Glisan St (at 13th Ave) **503/228–9535** • lunch, dinner & tapas • Peruvian • full bar

Aura Restaurant & Lounge 1022 W Burnside St (btwn SW 10th & 11th) **503/597–2872** • 5pm-midnight, till 2:30am Fri-Sat, clsd Sun-Tue • also bar • wheelchair access

Bastas Trattoria 410 NW 21st (at Flanders) **503/274–1572** • dinner nightly • northern Italian • some veggie • full bar till late • wheelchair access

Berbati's Pan 19 SW 2nd Ave (btwn Burnside & Ankeny) **503/226–2122** • 11am-2am, from 3pm Sun-Mon • Greek • full bar • wheelchair access

Besaw's 2301 NW Savier (at NW 23rd) **503/228–2619** • 7am-10pm Tue-Fri, from 8am Sat, 8am-3pm Sun-Mon • American • wheelchair access

Bijou Cafe 132 SW 3rd Ave (at Pine St) **503/222–3187** • 7am-2pm, from 8am wknds • popular • plenty veggie • "farm-fresh brkfst" • WiFi • wheelchair access

Bluehour 250 NW 13th Ave (at NW Everett St) **503/226–3394** • lunch Sun-Fri, dinner nightly, Sun brunch • extensive wine list • upscale • wheelchair access

Bread & Ink Cafe 3610 SE Hawthorne Blvd (at 36th) **503/239–4756** • brkfst, lunch & dinner, packed for brunch on Sun • popular • full bar • WiFi • wheelchair access

Chameleon 2000 NE 40th Ave (at Tillamook) **503/460–2682** • 5:30pm-9:30pm, lounge open later Fri-Sat, clsd Sun-Mon • lesbians/ gay men • Asian fusion • patio • wheelchair access

Daily Cafe in the Pearl 902 NW 13th Ave (at Kearney St) **503/242–1916** • 7am-5pm, till 9pm Wed-Fri, 9am-9pm Sat, 9am-2pm Sun • Northwest cuisine • wheelchair access

Delta 4607 SE Woodstock (at 46th) **503/771–3101** • 5pm-midnight, wknd brunch, bar till 1am Fri-Sat • Southern • plenty veggie • wheelchair access

Dingo's Mexican Grill 4612 SE Hawthorne Blvd (at SE 46th) **503/233–3996** • noon-10pm, till 11pm Th, till 9pm Sun • popular Girls Night Out Th • wheelchair access • lesbian-owned

Dot's Cafe 2521 SE Clinton (at 26th) **503/235–0203** • noon-2am • popular • full bar • eclectic American • plenty veggie • wheelchair access

Equinox 830 N Shaver St (at Mississippi) **503/460–3333** • dinner, brunch wknds, clsd Mon • int'l • patio • wheelchair access

Esparza's Tex-Mex Cafe 2725 SE Ankeny St (at 28th) **503/234–7909** • 11:30am-10pm • popular • funky • wheelchair access

Farm Cafe **503/736–3276** • 5pm-11pm • Northwest cuisine • wheelchair access

Fish Grotto 1035 SW Stark (at SW 11th Ave, at Boxxes) **503/226–4171** • 5pm-10pm, till 9pm Sun-Mon • popular • some veggie • full bar • wheelchair access

Genie's Cafe 1101 SE Division St (at 12th) **503/445–9777** • 8am-3pm • brunch • house-infused vodkas • wheelchair access

Gypsy Restaurant & Lounge 625 NW 21st (btwn Hoyt & Irving) **503/796–1859** • 4pm-2:30am, clsd Sun-Mon • some veggie • full bar • inexpensive • karaoke • wheelchair access

Hamburger Mary's 19 NW 5th Ave **503/688–1200** • 11am-midnight, 10am-3pm Sun • drag shows • karaoke

Hobo's 120 NW 3rd Ave (btwn Davis & Couch) **503/224–3285** • 4pm-2:30am • gay/ straight • piano bar • also restaurant • some veggie • wheelchair access

Le Happy 1011 NW 16th Ave (btwn Lovejoy & Marshall) **503/226–1258** • 5pm-1am, till 2:30am Fri, 6pm-2:30am Sat, clsd Sun • crêpes • wheelchair access

Mama Mia Trattoria 439 W 2nd Ave (at Stark) **503/295–6464** • lunch & dinner • wheelchair access

Masu 406 SW 13th Ave (at Burnside) **503/221–6278** • lunch Mon-Th, dinner nightly • sushi • WiFi • wheelchair access

Mayas Taqueria 1000 SW Morrison (at SW 10th) **503/226–1946** • 11am-10pm, till 8pm Sun • wheelchair access

Melt Bistro & Bar 716 NW 21st Ave (at Johnson) **503/295–4944** • 11am-10pm, clsd Sun • sandwiches & more

Mint 816 N Russell St **503/284–5518** • 5pm-10pm, till 11pm Fri-Sat, clsd Sun-Mon • fusion food • also 820 Lounge • wheelchair access

Montage 301 SE Morrison (at 3rd) **503/234–1324** • lunch Tue-Fri, dinner till 2am, till 4am Fri-Sat • popular • Louisiana-style cookin' • full bar • wheelchair access

Mother's Bistro & Bar 212 SW Stark St (at 2nd Ave) **503/464–1122** • brkfst, lunch & dinner, clsd Mon • American • wheelchair access

Nicholas' 318 SE Grand (btwn Oak & Pine) **503/235–5123** • 11am-9pm, from noon Sun • Middle Eastern • wheelchair access

Noble Rot 1111 E Burnside St (at 11th) **503/233–1999** • 5pm-midnight, clsd Sun • small plates • also wine bar • wheelchair access

Nostrana 1401 SE Morrison **503/234–2427** • lunch Mon-Fri, dinner nightly • fresh, local, wood-fired Italian • wheelchair access

Old Town Pizza 226 NW Davis (at NW 3rd) **503/222–9999** • 11:30am-11pm, till midnight Fri-Sat, clsd Sun • above Shanghai Tunnels • supposedly home to 100-year-old ghost • wheelchair access

Old Wives Tales 1300 E Burnside St (at 13th) **503/238–0470** • 8am-9pm, till 10pm Fri-Sat • popular • multi-ethnic & vegetarian • beer/ wine • live music • wheelchair access

The Original Pancake House 8601 SW 24th Ave (at Barbour) **503/246–9007** • 7am-3pm, clsd Mon-Tue • crowded on wknds • wheelchair access

Paley's Place 1204 NW 21st Ave (at NW Northrup St) **503/243–2403** • dinner nightly • Northwest cuisine

Papa Haydn 701 NW 23rd Ave (at NW Irving) **503/228–7317** • 11am-10pm, till midnight Fri-Sat, 10am-10pm Sun • bistro • some veggie • full bar • reservations recommended • wheelchair access • also at 5829 SE Milwaukie, 503/232-9440

Paradox Cafe 3439 SE Belmont St (at SE 35th) **503/232–7508** • brkfst, lunch & dinner • popular • vegetarian diner • killer Reuben • wheelchair access

Pizzicato 505 NW 23rd (at Glisan) **503/242–0023** • 11:30am-9pm, till 10pm Fri-Sat • popular • plenty veggie • beer/ wine • many locations

Pour 2755 NE Broadway (at NE 28th) **503/288–7687** • 4:30pm-11pm, till close Fri-Sat, clsd Sun • wine bar & bistro • wheelchair access

The Roxy 1121 SW Stark St (btwn 11th & 12th) **503/223-9160** • 24hrs, clsd Mon • popular • lesbians/ gay men • retro American diner • WiFi • wheelchair access

Santa Fe Taqueria 831 NW 23rd (at Kearney) **503/220-0406** • 11am-midnight • live entertainment • wheelchair access

Saucebox 214 SW Broadway (at Burnside) **503/241-3393** • 5pm-close • lesbians/ gay men • pan-Asian • plenty veggie • full bar • DJ • wheelchair access • gay-owned

Under Wonder Lounge 128 NE Russell **503/284-8686** • 5pm-midnight, open show nights only • full bar • transgender-friendly • nonsmoking • gay-owned

Vino Paradiso Wine Bar & Bistro 417 NW 10th Ave (btwn NW Glisan & Flanders) **503/295-9536** • 4pm-10pm, till 11pm Fri-Sat, clsd Sun-Mon • nonsmoking • gay-owned by Timothy Nishimoto of Pink Martini • wheelchair access

Vista Spring Cafe 2440 SW Vista (at Spring) **503/222-2811** • 11am-9:30pm, from noon wknds, till 9pm Sun • pasta & pizza • beer/ wine • wheelchair access

Vita Cafe 3023 NE Alberta St (btwn 30th & 31st) **503/335-8233** • brkfst, lunch & dinner • mostly vegetarian • some free-range meat • wheelchair access

West Cafe 1201 SW Jefferson St (12th Ave) **503/227-8189** • lunch Mon-Fri, dinner nightly, Sun brunch • "comfort food w/ a twist" • live entertainment • WiFi • wheelchair access

Wildwood 1221 NW 21st Ave (at Overton) **503/248-9663** • lunch Mon-Sat, dinner nightly • full bar • upscale • wheelchair access

Yakuza Lounge 5411 NE 30th Ave (at Killingsworth) **503/450-0893** • 5pm-close, clsd Mon-Tue • Japanese • full bar • wheelchair access

ENTERTAINMENT & RECREATION

Brian Marki Fine Art 2236 NE Broadway **503/249-5659** • gallery • gay-owned

Froelick Gallery 714 NW Davis St (at Broadway) **503/222-1142** • gay-owned art gallery

Gay Skate 1 SE Spokane St (at Oaks Park Way, at Oaks Rink) **503/233-5777** • 7pm-9pm 3rd Mon only • lesbians/ gay men

Out Dancing 975 SE Sandy Blvd (at SE Ankeny St & SE 9th Ave) **503/236-5129** • LGBT dance lessons

Portland Lesbian Choir PO Box 8212, 97207 **503/727-3306**

Portland Shockwave • of the Independent Women's Football League • see www.portlandshockwave.com for info

Rose City Rollers • Portland's female roller derby league • visit www.rosecityrollers.com for events

Rose City Softball Association
503/552–4769 • LGBT softball league

Sauvie's Island Beach 25 miles NW (off US 30) • follow Reeder Rd to the Collins beach area, park at the farthest end of the road, then follow path to beach

Wonder Ballroom 128 NE Russell St
503/284–8686 • live music venue

BOOKSTORES

CounterMedia 927 SW Oak (btwn 9th & 10th) 503/226–8141 • 11am-7pm, noon-6pm Sun • alternative comics • vintage gay books/ periodicals/erotica

In Other Words 14 NE Killingsworth St (at Williams) 503/232–6003 • 10am-9pm, noon-6pm wknds • women's books • music • resource center • wheelchair access

Laughing Horse Bookstore 12 NE 10th Ave (near Burnside) 503/236–2893 • 11am-7pm, clsd Sun • alternative/progressive • wheelchair access

Powell's Books 1005 W Burnside St (at 10th) 503/228–4651, 800/878–7323 • 9am-11pm • popular • largest new & used bookstore in the world • cafe • readings • wheelchair access

Reading Frenzy 921 SW Oak St (at 9th) 503/274–1449 • noon-6pm • zines • comics • LGBT selection • wheelchair access

RETAIL SHOPS

Fat Fancy 1013 SW Morrison (btwn 10th & 11th) 503/445–4353 • plus-size clothing boutique • wheelchair access

Hip Chicks Do Wine 4510 SE 23rd Ave (SE Holgate & 26th) 503/234–3790 • 11am-6pm

The Jellybean 721 SW 10th Ave (at Morrison) 503/222–5888 • 10am-6pm, noon-5pm Sun • cards • T-shirts • gifts • wheelchair access

Presents of Mind 3633 SE Hawthorne (at 37th Ave) 503/230–7740 • 10am-7pm • jewelry • clothing • unique gifts • wheelchair access

Robot Piercing & Tattoo 2330 NW Westover Rd (at NW 23rd) 503/224–9916

PUBLICATIONS

Just Out 503/236–1252 • LGBT newspaper w/extensive resource directory

GYMS & HEALTH CLUBS

Common Ground Wellness Center 5010 NE 33rd Ave (at Alberta St) 503/238–1065 • 10am-11pm • gay-friendly • wellness center • call for women's & trans nights • reservations required

EROTICA

Fantasy for Adults 1512 W Burnside (near 15th) 503/295–6969 • 24hrs

It's My Pleasure 3106 NE 64th Ave (at Sandy Blvd) 503/280–8080 • noon-7pm, till 6pm Sun • books • erotica • toys • gifts • workshops

Spartacus Leathers 300 SW 12th Ave (at Burnside) 503/224–2604

Salem

NIGHTCLUBS

Southside Speakeasy 3529 Fairview Industrial Dr SE (at Madrona) 503/362–1139 • 11am-2am, from 3:30pm wknds • gay/ straight • neighborhood bar • dancing/DJ • food served • karaoke • drag shows• WiFi • gay-owned

RESTAURANTS

Davinci's 180 High St SE 504/399–1413 • dinner only, clsd Sun • full bar

Word Of Mouth 503/930–4285 • 7am-3pm

Silverton

ACCOMMODATIONS

The Oregon Garden Resort 895 W Main St 800/966–6490 • gay-friendly • restaurant & lounge • pool • WiFi • $89-199

Yachats

ACCOMMODATIONS

See Vue Motel 95590 Hwy 101
541/547–3227, 866/547–3237 • gay/straight • ocean view • kids/pets ok • nonsmoking • WiFi • lesbian-owned • $90-170

PENNSYLVANIA

Abington

BARS

Kitchen Bar 1482 Old York Rd 215/576-9766
• 7am-2am • gay-friendly • dancing/DJ • food
served • live entertainment

RESTAURANTS

Vintage Bar & Restaurant 1116 Old York
Rd 215/887-8500 • 11am-2am • wheelchair
access

Allentown

see also Bethlehem

BARS

Candida's 247 N 12th St (at Chew)
610/434-3071 • 4pm-2am, from 2pm Fri-Sun
• lesbians/gay men • dancing/DJ •
neighborhood bar • food served • karaoke

Stonewall, Moose Lounge Bar & Grille
28 N 10th St (at Hamilton) 610/432-0215 •
7pm-2am, clsd Mon • popular • mostly gay
men • dancing/DJ • food served • live shows •
karaoke • drag shows • male dancers • videos
• 18+ Th

Altoona

NIGHTCLUBS

Escapade 2523 Union Ave, Rte 36
814/946-8195 • 8pm-2am • lesbians/gay
men • dancing/DJ • gay-owned

Bethlehem

NIGHTCLUBS

Diamonz 1913 W Broad St (at Pennsylvania
Ave) 610/865-1028 • 4pm-2am, from 8pm
Mon-Tue, from 6pm Sun • mostly women •
dancing/DJ • live shows • karaoke • also
restaurant • some veggie • wheelchair access

Bristol

EROTICA

Bristol News World 576 Bristol Pike/ Rte 13
N 215/785-4770

Bryn Mawr

RETAIL SHOPS

TLA Video 761 Lancaster Ave 610/520-1222
• 10am-11pm • extensive LGBT titles

Butler

NIGHTCLUBS

M&J's Lounge 124 Mercer St 724/496-8955
• 9:30pm-3am Fri-Sat only • lesbians/gay men
• neighborhood bar • 18+ •

Vertigo 564 W Cunningham St • 6pm Wed &
Sun, from 9pm Fri-Sat • lesbians/gay/Men •
dancing/DJ •BYOB •

Erie

ACCOMMODATIONS

The Boothby Inn 311 W 6th St
814/456-1888, 866/266-8429 • gay-friendly •
full brkfst • WiFi

NIGHTCLUBS

Craze 1607 Raspberry St 814/456-3027 •
9pm-2am, from 5pm Wed, clsd Tue • gay/
straight • dancing/DJ • karaoke • drag shows •
18+ Wed •

The Zone 133 W 18th St (at Peach)
814/452-0125 • 8pm-2am, from 4pm Wed •
lesbians/gay men • dancing/DJ • food served

RESTAURANTS

La Bella 802 W 18th St 814/456-2244 •
5pm-10pm, clsd Sun-Tue • BYOB • gay-owned

Matthew's Trattoria & Martini Lounge
153 E 13th St (btwn French & Holland)
814/459-6458 • dinner, clsd Sun-Mon •
courtyard

Pie in the Sky Cafe 463 W 8th St (at
Walnut) 814/459-8638 • lunch & dinner, clsd
Sun-Mon • BYOB • reservations
recommended • wheelchair access

RETAIL SHOPS

Ink Assassins Tattoos & Piercings 2601
Peach St 814/455-6752 • noon-10pm, till
6pm Sun

PUBLICATIONS

Erie Gay News 814/456-9833 • covers
news & events in the Erie, Cleveland,
Pittsburgh, Buffalo & Chautauqua County (NY)
region

Gay People's Chronicle 216/916-9338 •
Ohio's largest bi-weekly LGBT newspaper w/
extensive listings

Gettysburg

ACCOMMODATIONS

Battlefield B&B 2264 Emmitsburg Rd (at Ridge Rd) 717/334–8804, 888/766–3897 • gay/ straight • full brkfst • Civil War home • kids ok • WiFi • lesbian-owned • wheelchair access

The Beechmont Inn B & B 315 Broadway, Hanover 717/632–3013, 800/553–7009 • gay-friendly • WiFi • wheelchair access

Sheppard Mansion B&B 117 Frederick St (at High St), Hanover 717/633–8075, 877/762–6746 • gay/ straight • full brkfst • kids 12 years & up ok • nonsmoking • WiFi • also restaurant & bar

Greensburg

NIGHTCLUBS

Longbada Lounge 108 W Pittsburgh St (at Pennsylvania Ave) 724/837–6614 • 9pm-2am, clsd Sun-Mon • lesbians/ gay men • dancing/DJ • karaoke • drag shows • patio • wheelchair access

Harrisburg

INFO LINES & SERVICES

LGBT Community Center Coalition of Central PA 221 N Front St, 3rd flr 717/920–9534

BARS

Bar 704 704 N 3rd St 717/234–4226 • 4pm-2am • mostly gay men • neighborhood bar • older crowd • wheelchair access

The Brownstone Lounge 412 Forster St (btwn 3rd & 6th) 717/234–7009 • 11am-2am, from 5pm wknds • lesbians/ gay men • neighborhood bar • wheelchair access

L Bar & Lounge 881 Eisenhower Blvd 717/939–5573 • 11am-2am • lesbians/gay men • neighborhood bar • food served

The Liquid 891 891 Eisenhower Blvd (near exit 19) 717/939–3590 • 8pm-2am, till 11pm Th, clsd Mon-Wed • lesbians/ gay men • popular • transgender-friendly • dancing/DJ • food served • live shows • drag shows • videos

Neptune's Lounge 268 North St (at 3rd) 717/233–0581 • 5pm-2am • lesbians/ gay men • neighborhood bar •

NIGHTCLUBS

Stallions 706 N 3rd St (enter rear) 717/232–3060 • 7pm-2am • popular • mostly gay men • dancing/DJ • live shows • karaoke • drag shows • strippers • wheelchair access

Irwin

NIGHTCLUBS

The Link 91 Wendel Rd, Herminie 724/446–7717 • 7pm-2am • lesbians/ gay men • dancing/DJ • live shows • drag shows • male dancers • food served

Johnstown

NIGHTCLUBS

Lucille's 520 Washington St (near Central Park) 814/539–4448 • 6pm-2am, clsd Sun-Mon • lesbians/ gay men • dancing/DJ • drag shows • strippers • karaoke

Kutztown

ACCOMMODATIONS

Grim's Manor B&B 10 Kern Rd 610/683–7089 • lesbians/ gay men • 200-yr-old stone farmhouse on 5 acres • full brkfst • nonsmoking • gay-owned • $80

Lancaster

ACCOMMODATIONS

Cameron Estate Inn 1855 Mansion Ln, Mount Joy 717/492–0111, 888/422–6376 • gay/ straight • full brkfst • nonsmoking • restaurant • wheelchair access • gay-owned

Candlelight Inn B&B 2574 Lincoln Hwy E (at Rte 896/ Hartman Bridge Rd), Ronks 717/299–6005, 800/772–2635 • gay-friendly • full brkfst

Lancaster Arts Hotel 300 Harrisburg Ave 717/299–3000, 866/720–2787 • gay-friendly • great restaurant • wheelchair access

BARS

Dad's Bar & Grill 168 S Main St, Manheim 717/665–1960 • 4pm-2am, from 11am Fri • gay/ straight • food served • karaoke

Tally Ho 201 W Orange St (at Water) 717/299–0661 • 8pm-2am • popular • lesbians/ gay men • dancing/DJ • karaoke • drag shows • young crowd

RESTAURANTS

The Loft above Tally Ho bar 717/299–0661 • lunch Mon-Fri, dinner Mon-Sat • contemporary American/ French

Meadville

RESTAURANTS

Peppercorn & Vine 994 Market St 814/337–0005 • steak & seafood • also lounge • non-smoking • gay-owned

Milford

ACCOMMODATIONS

Hotel Fauchere 401 Broad St (at Catharine St) **570/409-1212** • gay-friendly • historic boutique hotel • full brkfst • also restaurant & bar • nonsmoking • kids/pets ok • wheelchair access

Mt Haven Resort RD 1 Log Tavern Rd **570/296-8502, 800/553-1530** • gay-friendly • kids/pets ok • WiFi • also Italian restaurant

New Hope

see also Lambertville & Sergeantsville, New Jersey

ACCOMMODATIONS

Ash Mill Farm B&B 5358 York Rd (at Rte 202), Holicong **215/794-5373** • gay-friendly • full brkfst • nonsmoking • WiFi • gay-owned

The Lexington House 6171 Upper York Rd **215/794-0811** • gay/straight • 1749 country home • pool • nonsmoking • gay-owned

The Mansion Inn 9 S Main St (at Bridge St) **215/862-1231** • lesbians/gay men • pool • nonsmoking • restaurant • gay-owned • $155-275

Silver Maple Organic Farm & B&B 483 Sergeantsville Rd (Rte 523), Flemington, NJ **908/237-2192** • gay/straight • full brkfst • hot tub • pool • nonsmoking • kids/pets ok • WiFi • wheelchair access • gay-owned • $99-175

The Wishing Well Guesthouse 144 Old York Rd **215/862-8819** • gay/straight • nonsmoking • kids ok • gay-owned • $99-150

BARS

Bob Eagans 6426 Lower York Rd (at the Nevermore Hotel) **215/862-5225** • gay/straight • cabaret • dinner served • also hotel

RESTAURANTS

Eagle Diner 6522 Lower York Rd **215/862-5575** • 24hrs • wheelchair access

Havana 105 S Main St **215/862-9897** • noon-midnight, bar till 2am • some veggie • live music • karaoke

Karla's 5 W Mechanic St (at Main) **215/862-2612** • noon-10pm, till midnight Fri-Sat, from 11am Sun • some veggie • full bar

Mother's 34 N Main St **215/862-5857** • 11am-9pm, from 10am Sun

Wildflowers 8 W Mechanic St **215/862-2241** • seasonal, noon-9pm • full bar • outdoor dining

EROTICA

Grownups 2 E Mechanic St (at Main) **215/862-9304** • toys etc • gay-owned

Le Chateau Exotique 27 W Mechanic St **215/862-3810** • fetishwear

New Milford

ACCOMMODATIONS

Oneida Campground & Lodge **570/465-7011** • mostly gay men • seasonal • RV hookups • 1 guest cottage • pool • nudity • WiFi • gay-owned

Norristown

BARS

Beagle Tavern 1003 E Main St **610/272-5133** • 11am-2am • gay/straight • more gay Wed & Fri • dancing/DJ • food served • karaoke

Philadelphia

INFO LINES & SERVICES

William Way LGBT Community Center 1315 Spruce St (at Juniper) **215/732-2220** • 9am-10pm, from 11am Sat, till 7pm Sun

ACCOMMODATIONS

Alexander Inn Spruce (at 12th St) **215/923-3535, 877/253-9466** • gay/straight • gym • nonsmoking • WiFi • gay-owned

The Conwell Inn 1331 Polett Walk (at Montgomery Ave) **215/235-6200, 888/379-9737** • gay/straight • nonsmoking • kids/pets ok • WiFi • wheelchair access

The Gables B&B 4520 Chester Ave **215/662-1918** • gay/straight • nonsmoking • WiFi • gay-owned

Hampton Inn Center City Philadelphia 1301 Race St (13th St) **215/665-9100, 800/426-7866** • gay/straight • pool • WiFi • wheelchair access

The Independent Hotel 1234 Locust St (at 13th) **215/772-1440** • gay/straight • boutique hotel • WiFi • wheelchair access

The Inn at Chester Springs 815 N Pottstown Pike (Exit 312), Exton **610/363-1100, 888/253-6119** • gay-friendly • full-service hotel • pool • kids/pets ok • WiFi • $89-149

Latham Hotel 135 S 17th St (at Walnut) **215/563-7474, 877/528-4261** • gay-friendly • WiFi • wheelchair access

Lippincott House 2023 Locust St **215/523-9251** • gay-friendly • WiFi • exquisite grand mansion

Morris House Hotel 225 S 8th St **215/922-2446** • gay-friendly • nonsmoking • WiFi • also M Restaurant

Palomar Philadelphia 117 S 17th St **215/563-5006, 888/725-1778** • gay-friendly • WiFi • wheelchair access

BARS

Bike Stop 204-206 S Quince St (btwn 11th & 12th, Walnut & Locust) **215/627-1662** • 4pm-2am, from 2pm wknds • mostly gay men • DJ • leather (very leather-women-friendly) • karaoke

L' Etage 624 S 6th St (at Bainbridge) **215/592-0656** • 7:30pm-1am, till 2am Fri-Sat, clsd Mon • gay/straight • dancing/DJ • cabaret 2nd Th • also restaurant downstairs • noon-11pm, from 10am wknds • crêperie

ICandy 254 S 12th St (btwn Locust & Spruce) **267/324-3500** • 4pm-2am • mostly gay men • dancing/DJ • multi-level entertainment complex

Philadelphia

WHERE THE GIRLS ARE:
Partying downtown near 12th St., south of Market.

LGBT PRIDE:
June. 215/875-9288, web: www.phillypride.org.

ANNUAL EVENTS:
April/May - Equality Forum 215/732-3378, web: www.equalityforum.com. Weekend of LGBT film, performances, literature, sports, seminars, parties & more.

June - Womongathering 856/694-2037, web: www.womongathering.com. Women's spirituality fest.

July - QFest Int'l Gay & Lesbian Film Festival 267/765-9800 x701, web: www.qfest.com.

October - OutFest 215/875-9288, web: www.phillypride.org.

CITY INFO:
Philadelphia Convention & Visitors Bureau 215/636-3300, web: www.pcvb.org.

BEST VIEW:
Top of Center Square, 16th & Market.

WEATHER:
Winter temperatures hover in the 20's. Summers are humid with temperatures in the 80's and 90's.

ATTRACTIONS:
Academy of Natural Sciences 215/299-1000, web: www.acnatsci.org.

African American Museum 215/574-0380, web: www.aampmuseum.org.

Betsy Ross House 215/686-1252, web: www.betsyrosshouse.org.

Independence Hall 215/965-2305, web: www.nps.gov/inde.

Liberty Bell Pavilion.

National Museum Of American Jewish History 215/923-3811, web: www.nmajh.org.

Philadelphia Museum of Art 215/763-8100, web: www.philamuseum.org.

Reading Terminal Market, web: www.readingterminalmarket.org.

Rodin Museum 215/568-6026, web: www.rodinmuseum.org.

TRANSIT:
Quaker City Cab 215/728-8000.

Transit Authority (SEPTA) 215/580-7800, web: www.septa.org.

Khyber Pass Pub 56 S 2nd St (btwn Market & Chestnut) 215/238–5888 • 11am-2am • gay-friendly • food served • live bands • wheelchair access

North Third 801 N 3rd (at Brown) 215/413–3666 • 4pm-2am, from 10am wknd brunch • gay/ straight • also restaurant

Q Lounge 1234 Locust St (at 13th) 215/732–1800 • 5pm-2am • lesbians/ gay men • also restaurant • Sun brunch from 11am • dancing/DJ • "Austin-Powers chic"

Stir Lounge 1705 Chancellor St (at Rittenhouse Sq btwn Walnut & Spruce) 215/732–2700 • 4pm-2am • lesbians/gay men • neighborhood bar • dancing/DJ • girl party 1st Sat

Tabu Lounge & Sports Bar 200 S 12th St 215/964 –9675 • 4pm-2am, from noon wknds • gay/straight • food served • karaoke

Tavern on Camac 243 S Camac St (at Spruce) 215/545-0900 • 4pm-2am • lesbians/ gay men • dancing/DJ • piano bar • food served

Venture Inn 255 S Camac (at Spruce) 215/545-8731 • 11am-2am, from noon Sat • lesbians/ gay men • neighborhood bar • food served

The Westbury 261 S 13th (at Spruce) 215/546–5170 • 4pm-2am • lesbians/ gay men • neighborhood bar • food seved • wheelchair access • gay-owned

Woody's 202 S 13th St (at Walnut) 215/545–1893 • 11am-2am • mostly gay men • dancing/DJ • country/ western • karaoke • Latin Th • strippers • WiFi • 18+ Wed • wheelchair access

Nightclubs

Bob & Barbara's Lounge 1509 South St 215/545-4511 • 3pm-2am, from 5pm Sun • gay/ straight • drag shows Th • live jazz Fri-Sat

Fluid 613 S 4th (at Kater) 215/629-3686 • 9pm-2am • gay-friendly • more gay wknds • dancing/DJ • drag shows

Ladies 2000 856/869-0193 • seasonal parties • call hotline for details

Recess Lounge 125 S 2nd St (at Chestnut) 215/351–9026 • 10pm-3am, clsd Sun-Wed • gay/ straight • dancing/DJ • live shows • private club

Shampoo 417 N 8th St (at Willow) 215/922–7500 • 9pm-2am, clsd Mon-Tue & Th • gay/ straight • more gay Fri • dancing/DJ

Sisters 1320 Chancellor St (at Juniper) 215/735–0735 • 5pm-2am, from noon Sun, clsd Mon • mostly women • dancing/DJ • live/drag shows • karaoke • also restaurant • dinner Wed-Sat, Sun brunch • wheelchair access

Voyeur 1221 St James St (off 13th & Locust) 215/735–5772 • 1am-3am, from 9pm wknds • mostly gay men • dancing/DJ • live bands • karaoke • cabaret • private club

Cafes

10th Street Pour House 262 S 10th St (at Spruce) 215/922–5626 • 7:30am-3pm, from 8:30am wknds, popular brunch wknds • wheelchair access

B2 Cafe 1500 E Passyunk Ave 215/271–5520 • great vegan soft serve ice cream • WiFi

Capriccio 110 N 16th St (at Benjamin Franklin Pkwy) 215/735–9797 • 6:30am-7pm, 8am-8pm wknds

Cosi 1128 Walnut St 215/413–1608 • 7am-11pm

Green Line Cafe 4239 Baltimore Ave (at 43rd) 215/222–3431 • 7am-11pm, 8am-8pm Sun • live shows • food served

Restaurants

13th Street Pizza 209 S 13th St (at Chancellor St) 215/546–4453 • 11am-4am • popular late night

Alfa 1709 Walnut St (at 17th) 215/751–0201 • 5pm-2am • also Walnut Room lounge

Bar Ferdinand 1030 N 2nd St • great tapas and wine

The Caboose Grille 2 W Broad St, Souderton 215/721–1001 • lunch & dinner Tue-Sat, brkfst wknds, clsd Mon

Figs 2501 Meredith St 215/978–8440 • lunch Tue-Fri, dinner nightly • wknd brunch • BYOB • wheelchair access

A Full Plate Cafe 1009 N Bodine St (at George St) 215/627–4068 • 11am-9pm, till 10pm Fri-Sat, till 3pm Sun • multiracial • transgender-friendly • BYOB • patio • lesbian-owned

The Happy Rooster 118 S 16th St (at Sansom St) 215/963–9311 • 11:30am-2am, from 4pm Sat • karaoke • full bar

Hinge Cafe 2652 E Somerset St 215/425–6614 • 8am-10pm, till 8pm Sun, till 3pm Mon-Tue

Honey's 800 N 4th St 215/925–1150 • 8am-10pm, till 4pm Sun

Knock 226 S 12th St **215/925–1166** • lunch & dinner, Sun brunch • American • also bar

Liberties 705 N 2nd St (at Fairmount) **215/238–0660** • lunch & dinner • full bar till 2am

Little Pete's 219 S 17th St (at Locust) **215/545–5508** • 24hrs • diner

Lolita 106 S 13th St (at Sansom) **215/546–7100** • 5pm-10pm • upscale Mexican • BYOB

Mercato 1216 Spruce St **215/985–2962** • dinner • Italian • BYOB

Midtown II 122 S 11th St **215/627–6452** • 24 hrs • diner • popular late night • transgender-friendly

Mixto 1141-43 Pine St **215/592–0363** • lunch & dinner, brkfst wknds • Latin American

More Than Just Ice Cream 1119 Locust St (at 12th) **215/574–0586** • 11am-11pm

My Thai 2200 South St (at 22nd) **215/985–1878** • 5pm-10pm, till 11pm Fri-Sat • full bar

New Harmony 135 N 9th St (at Cherry) **215/627–4520** • 11am-11pm • vegan

Paesano's 1017 S 9th St **215/440–0371** • 11am-3pm, till 5pm Fri-Sat • great sandwiches

Sabrina's 910 Christian St **215/574–1599** • 8am-10pm, till 8pm Tue-Th, till 4pm Sun-Mon

Swanky Bubbles 10 S Front St (at Market) **215/928–1200** • 5pm-1am • also bar till 2am • sushi & champagne

El Vez 121 S 13th St (at Sansom) **215/928–9800** • lunch Mon-Sat, dinner nightly, Sun brunch • Latin American/ Mexican • full bar

White Dog Cafe 3420 Sansom St (at Walnut) **215/386–9224** • lunch & dinner, brunch Sun • full bar • cool Mon reading & Sun film series

Zócalo 3600 Lancaster Ave (at 36th) **215/895–0139** • lunch Mon-Fri, dinner nightly • Mexican/ New Southwestern

ENTERTAINMENT & RECREATION

Philly Roller Girls • Philly's female roller derby league • visit www.phillyrollergirls.com for events

The Walt Whitman House 328 Mickle Blvd, Camden, NJ **856/964–5383** • the last home of America's great & controversial poet, just across the Delaware River

BOOKSTORES

Giovanni's Room 345 S 12th St (at Pine) **215/923–2960** • 11:30am-7pm, from 1pm Sun • popular • legendary LGBT bookstore

Robin's Bookstore 108 S 13th St **215/735–9600** • 11am-7pm, till 8pm Sat, clsd Sun

RETAIL SHOPS

Infinite Body Piercing 626 S 4th St (at South) **215/923–7335** • noon-10pm, till 8pm Sun

TLA Video 1520 Locust St (btwn 15th & 16th) **215/735-7887** • 10am-midnight, extensive LGBT titles

PUBLICATIONS

PGN (Philadelphia Gay News) **215/625–8501** • LGBT newspaper w/ extensive listings

Women's Yellow Pages of Greater Philadelphia 610/446-4747

GYMS & HEALTH CLUBS

12th St Gym 204 S 12th St (btwn Locust & Walnut) **215/985–4092** • pool • day passes

EROTICA

The Mood 531 South St **215/413–1930**

Passional Boutique 704 S 5th St (at Bainbridge) **215/829–4986, 877/826–7738** • noon-10pm • corsets • fetishwear • toys • woman-owned

Sexploratorium 620 S 5th St **215/923-1398** • noon-10pm • workshops • gallery

Pittsburgh

INFO LINES & SERVICES

AA Gay/ Lesbian **412/471–7472** • call for times & location

Gay/ Lesbian Community Center 210 Grant St **412/422–0114** • noon-9pm, till 6pm Sun

ACCOMMODATIONS

Camp Davis 311 Red Brush Rd, Boyers **724/637–2402** • April-Oct • lesbians/ gay men • cabins, trailer, & campsites • pool • adults 21+ only • 1 hour from Pittsburgh

The Inn on Negley 703 S Negley Ave (at Elmer St) **412/661–0631** • gay-friendly • full brkfst • nonsmoking • WiFi • wheelchair access • women-owned

The Inn on the Mexican War Streets 604 W North Ave **412/231–6544** • lesbians/ gay men • nonsmoking • WiFi • gay-owned

Morning Glory Inn B&B 2119 Sarah St 412/431–1707 • gay-friendly • WiFi • woman-owned

The Parador Inn 939 Western Ave 412/231–4800, 877/540–1443 • gay-friendly • WiFi • gay-owned

The Priory 614 Pressley St (near Cedar Ave) 412/231–3338, 866/377–4679 • gay-friendly • nonsmoking • kids ok • WiFi • wheelchair access

BARS

5801 5801 Ellsworth Ave (at Maryland) 412/661–5600 • 4pm-2am, from 2pm Sun • lesbians/ gay men • deck • also restaurant • wheelchair access

The Backdraft Bar & Grill 3049 Churchview Ave 412/885–1239 • 11am-2am, till midnight Sun • gay/straight • live bands • karaoke

Blue Moon Bar & Lounge 5115 Butler St (at Stanton) 412/781–1119 • 4pm-2am, till midnight Mon • mostly gay men • neighborhood bar • transgender-friendly • go-go dancers

Brewer's Tavern 3315 Liberty Ave (at Herron Ave) 412/681–7991 • 10am-2am, from 11am Sun • gay-friendly dive bar

Cattivo 146 44th St 412/687–2157 • 4pm-2am Wed-Sun, clsd Mon-Tue • mostly women • dancing/DJ • karaoke • drag shows • food served

Headquarters 2016 Smallman St 412/327–0484 • 4pm-2am • lesbians/gay men • dancing/DJ • karaoke • wheelchair access • gay-owned

Images 965 Liberty Ave (at 10th St) 412/391–9990 • 2pm-2am • mostly gay men • karaoke • videos

Pittsburgh Eagle 1740 Eckert St (off Chateau) 412/766–7222 • 9pm-2am Fri-Sat only • popular • mostly gay men • dancing/DJ • leather • wheelchair access

PTown 4740 Baum Blvd 412/621–0111 • 6pm-2am, clsd Mon • lesbians/ gay men • dancing/DJ • strippers • WiFi

Real Luck Cafe 1519 Penn Ave (at 16th) 412/471–7832 • 4pm-2am • lesbians/ gay men • neighborhood bar • go-go dancers • food served • wheelchair access

Remedy 5121 Butler St, Lawrenceville 412/781–6771 • 4pm-2am, from 12:30pm Sun • gay/ straight • multiracial • neighborhood bar • dancing/DJ • also restaurant upstairs

Spin Bartini/Ultra Lounge 5744 Ellsworth Ave, Shadyside 412/362–7746 • 4pm-2am • gay/ straight • live Jazz Tue • wheelchair access

There Ultra Lounge 931 Liberty Ave (at Smithfield) 412/642–4435 • 3:30pm-2am, from 7pm Sat-Sun • lesbians/ gay men • wheelchair access

NIGHTCLUBS

1226 on Herron 1226 Herron Ave (at Liberty) 412/682–6839 • 6pm-2am, clsd Mon-Wed • mostly men

941 Saloon 941 Liberty Ave (at Smithfield St, 2nd flr) 412/281–5222 • 2pm-2am • lesbians/ gay men • dancing/DJ • karaoke

Pegasus 1740 Eckert St (off Chateau) 412/766–7222 • 10pm-2am Fri-Sat • lesbians/ gay men • dancing/DJ • young crowd

Tilden 941 Liberty Ave (at Smithfield St, upstairs) • mostly gay men • dancing/DJ • after hrs on wknds only • membership required

CAFES

Square Cafe 1137 S Braddock Ave 412/244–8002 • 7am-3pm, from 8am Sun • live shows monthly • lesbian-owned

RESTAURANTS

Abay 130 S Highland Ave (at Baum Blvd) 412/661–9736 • lunch & dinner, clsd Mon • Ethiopian • plenty veggie

Capri 6001 Penn Ave (at Highland Ave) 412/363–1250 • 11am-midnight, 6pm-2am Th-Sat • pizza

Dish 128 S 17th St (at Sarah) 412/390–2012 • 5pm-2am, clsd Sun • Italian • also bar

Double Wide Grill 2339 E Carson St (at S 24th St) 412/390–1111 • lunch & dinner, wknd brunch • BBQ • plenty veggie/ vegan

Eleven 1150 Smallman St (at 11th) 412/201–5656 • lunch & dinner, Sun brunch

Harris Grill 5747 Ellsworth Ave 412/362–5273 • dinner nightly, wknd brunch • full bar

Kaya 2000 Smallman St (at 20th) 412/261–6565 • lunch & dinner • Latin/ Caribbean • plenty veggie

NOLA On the Square 24 Market Sq 412/471–9100 • 11am-11pm, clsd Sun • live music

OTB Bicycle Cafe 2518 East Carson St (at S 26th) 412/381-3698 • 11am-10pm • burgers • plenty veggie • also bar • occasional events

Point Brugge Cafe 401 Hastings (at Reynolds) **412/441–3334** • lunch & dinner, Sun brunch, clsd Mon • Belgian/ European

Quiet Storm 5430 Penn Ave (at Graham St) **412/661–9355** • 9am-9pm, 10am-4pm Sat, clsd Sun & Tue • vegetarian/ vegan • WiFi • wheelchair access

Red Oak Cafe 3610 Forbes Ave (at Lothrop) **412/621–2221** • 7am-7pm, till 5pm Fri, till 3pm wknds • salads & sandwiches • plenty veggie/vegan

Zenith 86 S 26th St **412/481–4833** • 11am-9pm, Sun brunch, clsd Mon-Wed • vegetarian/ vegan • also antiques store • wheelchair access

ENTERTAINMENT & RECREATION

Andy Warhol Museum 117 Sandusky St (at General Robinson) **412/237–8300** • 10am-5pm, till 10pm Fri, clsd Mon • is it soup or is it art? see for yourself

RETAIL SHOPS

Slacker 1321 E Carson St (btwn 13th & 14th) **412/381–3911** • noon-9pm, 11am-6pm Sun • magazines • clothing • leather • wheelchair access

Who New? 5156 Butler St **412/781–0588** • noon-6pm, clsd Mon-Tue, open Sun by chance • vintage modern design • gay-owned

PUBLICATIONS

Cue Pittsburgh 866/638–3822 • monthly LGBT glossy

Erie Gay News 814/456–9833 • covers news & events in the Erie, Cleveland, Pittsburgh, Buffalo & Chautauqua County, NY region

Out 412/381–3350 • LGBT newspaper

EROTICA

Adult Mart 346 Blvd of the Allies 412/261–9119

Pittsburgh

LGBT PRIDE:
June. 412/422-0114 (GLCC #), web: www.glccpgh.org.

ANNUAL EVENTS:
June - Three Rivers Arts Festival 412/471–6070, web: www.arts-festival.net.
October - Pittsburgh International Lesbian & Gay Film Festival 412/422-6776, web: www.plgfs.org.

CITY INFO:
800/359-0758, web: www.visitpittsburgh.com.

TRANSIT:
Yellow Cab 412/665-8100. 888/258-3826.
Port Authority Transit (PAT) 412/442-2000, web: www.portauthority.org.

ATTRACTIONS:
Andy Warhol Museum 412/237-8300, web: www.warhol.org.
Carnegie Museums of Pittsburgh 412/622-3131, web: www.carnegiemuseums.org.
Fallingwater (in Mill Run) 724/329-8501, web: www.paconserve.org.
Frick Art & Historical Center 412/371-0600, web: www.frickart.org.
Golden Triangle District.
Shopping & dining in the Strip District.
National Aviary 412/323-7235, web: www.aviary.org.
Phipps Conservatory 412/622-6914, web: www.phipps.conservatory.org.
Rachel Carson Homestead (in Springdale) 724/274-5459, web: www.rachelcarsonhomestead.org.
Station Square.

Poconos

ACCOMMODATIONS

Frog Hollow 570/595–2814 • lesbians/ gay men • secluded 1920s cottage • kids/ pets ok • lesbian-owned

Rainbow Mountain Resort 570/223–8484 • lesbians/ gay men • transgender-friendly • resort w/ suites • cabins (seasonal) • swimming • hot tub • WiFi • gay-owned • also restaurant & full bar • dancing/DJ Fri-Sat • piano bar • karaoke

Stoney Ridge 570/629–5036 • women only • hot tub • nonsmoking • secluded log home • pets OK • lesbian-owned • $125-175

The Woods Campground 845 Vaughn Acres Ln, Lehighton 610/377–9577 • lesbians/ gay men • 84 campsites • RV spots • also cabins • swimming • 18+ • WiFi

Reading

BARS

The Peanut Bar & Restaurant 332 Penn St 610/376–8500, 800/515–8500 • 11am-11pm, till midnight Fri-Sat, clsd Sun • a Reading landmark! • non-smoking • WiFi

The Red Star 11 S 10th St (at Penn St) 610/375–4116 • 9pm-2am, clsd Sun-Tue • mostly gay men • neighborhood bar • dancing/DJ • leather • multiracial • transgender-friendly • older crowd • gay-owned

RESTAURANTS

Judy's On Cherry 332 Cherry St 610/374–8511 • lunch Tue-Fri, dinner Tue-Sat, clsd Sun-Mon • Mediterranean

The Ugly Oyster 21 S 5th St (at Cherry) 610/373–6791 • 11:30am-10pm, from noon Sat, clsd Sun • traditional Irish pub (bar open till 2am) • live shows

Scranton

BARS

Twelve Penny Saloon 3501 Birney Ave, Moosic 570/941–0444 • 6pm-2pm, from 3pm wknds • lesbians/ gay men • neighborhood bar • dancing/DJ • transgender-friendly • food served • karaoke • drag shows • wheelchair access • gay-owned

State College

INFO LINES & SERVICES

Women's Resource Center 140 W Nittany Ave (at Frasier) 877/234–5050 (24HR HOTLINE), 814/234–5050 • 9am-7pm, clsd wknds

ACCOMMODATIONS

The Atherton Hotel 125 S Atherton St (at College Ave) 814/231–2100, 800/832–0132 • gay-friendly • nonsmoking • WiFi • also restaurant & bar • wheelchair access

BARS

Chumley's 100 W College 814/238–4446 • 5pm-2am, from 6pm Sun • popular • lesbians/ gay men • neighborhood bar • wheelchair access

NIGHTCLUBS

Indigo 112 W College Ave 814/234–1031 • 9pm-2am, clsd Mon-Wed • gay/ straight • "Alternative" night Sun • dancing/DJ • young crowd

Sunbury

BARS

CC's 555 Klinger Rd 570/286–6022 • 7pm-2am Th-Sat, from 5pm Sun • lesbians/ gay men • karaoke • drag shows

Uniontown

BARS

Eddie's Tavern 200 Francis St 724/438–9563 • 11am-midnight • gay-friendly • karaoke • try the wings

NIGHTCLUBS

Club 231 231 Pittsburgh St/ Rte 51 (at Fulton) 724/430–1477 • 9pm-close • mostly men • dancing/DJ • karaoke • drag shows • gay-owned

Wilkes-Barre

INFO LINES & SERVICES

NEPA Rainbow Alliance Resource Center 67 Public Square, 5th Fl, Edwardsville 570/763–9877 • coalition of NE PA's LGBT organizations & businesses • WiFi

NIGHTCLUBS

Twist 1170 Hwy 315 (in Fox Ridge Plaza) 570/970–7503 • 8pm-2am, from 6pm Sun • mostly gay men • dancing/DJ • karaoke • drag shows • patio • wheelchair access

Williamsport

NIGHTCLUBS

Club Z 321 Pine St 570/322–6900 • 8pm-2am, clsd Sun-Mon • lesbians/ gay men • dancing/DJ wknds • karaoke

York

ACCOMMODATIONS

Yorktowne Hotel 48 E Market St
717/848–1111 • gay-friendly • restaurant •
WiFi • wheelchair access

NIGHTCLUBS

Altland's Ranch 8505 Orchard Rd, Spring
Grove **717/225–4479** • 8pm-2am Fri-Sat only
• lesbians/ gay men • dancing/DJ • country
western 3rd Fri • karaoke

Club XS 36 W 11th Ave (at Hwy 30 & N
George St) **717/846-6969** • 4pm-2am •
lesbians/ gay men • dancing/DJ • drag shows •
cabaret • also Underground Lounge

EROTICA

Cupid's Connection Adult Boutique 244 N
George St (at North) **717/846-5029**

RHODE ISLAND

Narragansett

ACCOMMODATIONS

Blueberry Cove Inn 75 Kingstown Rd
401/792–9865, 800/478–1426 • gay/straight •
3 blks from beach • full brkfst • nonsmoking •
WiFi • $150-300

RESTAURANTS

Crazy Burger 144 Boon St **401/783–1810** •
8am-9pm • great brkfst

Newport

INFO LINES & SERVICES

Sobriety First 135 Pelham St (at Channing
Memorial Church) **401/438-8860** • 8pm Fri

ACCOMMODATIONS

Architect's Inn 2 Sunnyside Pl
401/845–2547, 877/466–2547 • gay-friendly •
WiFi • gay-owned • $49-420

Francis Malbone House Inn 392 Thames
St (at Memorial Blvd) **401/846–0392,
800/846-0392** • gay-friendly • nonsmoking •
WiFi • wheelchair access • $175-475

Hilltop Inn 2 Kay St **800/846-0392** • gay-
friendly • craftsman-style inn • full brkfst •
WiFi • gay-owned • $245-425

Hydrangea House Inn 16 Bellevue Ave
401/846-4435, 800/945-4667 • popular • gay/
straight • full brkfst • near beach •
nonsmoking • WiFi • gay-owned • $225-475

The Spring Seasons Inn 86 Spring St (btwn
Mary St & Touro) **401/849–0004,
877/294-0004** • gay-friendly • full brkfst •
jacuzzi baths • nonsmoking • $125-275

RESTAURANTS

Donick's Restaurant and Ice Cream Spa
16 Broadway **401/835–5183** • 6am-2am •
BYOB • gay-owned

Whitehorse Tavern 26 Marlborough St (at
Farewell) **401/849–3600** • lunch & dinner, Sun
brunch • upscale dining • nonsmoking • patio

Pawtucket

INFO LINES & SERVICES

Gay & Lesbian AA 71 Park Place (at Park
Place Congregational Church) **401/438–8860**
• 7:30pm Tue

Providence

ACCOMMODATIONS

Edgewood Manor 232 Norwood Ave (at
Broad) **401/781–0099** • gay-friendly • 1905
Greek Revival mansion • nonsmoking • WiFi •
$129-299

Hotel Dolce Villa 63 De Pasquale Square (at
Atwells) **401/383-7031** • gay/ straight •
boutique hotel • nonsmoking • $179-499

The Hotel Providence 311 Westminister St
(at Mathewson) **401/861–8000, 800/861–8990**
• gay/ straight • Aspire restaurant on-site •
WiFi • nonsmoking • $179-709

Renaissance Providence Hotel 5 Avenue
of the Arts (at Francis) **401/919–5000,
800/468-3571** • gay/ straight • restaurant &
bar • WiFi • nonsmoking • $229-499

BARS

Alleycat 17 Snow St (at Washington)
401/272-6369 • 3pm-1am, till 2am Fri-Sat •
lesbians/ gay men • neighborhood bar •
videos • gay-owned

Club Gallery 150 Point St (at Parsonage)
401/751–7166 • 1pm-1am, till 2am Fri-Sat •
popular • lesbians/ gay men • mostly women
Sat • neighborhood bar • 18+ • dancing/DJ Th-
Sat • wheelchair access

The Providence Eagle 198 Union St (at
Westminster) **401/421–1447** • 3pm-1am, till
2am Fri, from noon wknds

The Stable 125 Washington (at Mathewson)
401/272-6950 • 2pm-1am, till 2am Fri-Sat,
from noon Sat-Sun • lesbians/ gay men •
neighborhood bar • videos • wheelchair
access

NIGHTCLUBS

Girl Spot 681 Valley St (at Club X) 401/751-7166 • Sat only • mostly women • dancing/DJ • live music • 18+ • cover charge

Icon 401/454-4266 • 10pm-1am Tue & Th, till 2am wknds, lesbian night Th • gay/straight • dancing/DJ

Mirabar 35 Richmond St (at Weybosset) 401/331-6761 • 3pm-1am, till 2am Fri-Sat • mostly gay men • dancing/DJ • live shows • male dancers • wheelchair access

Platforms Dance Club 165 Poe St 401/781-3121 • gay/straight • dancing/DJ • gay night Sat • Salsa Sun

State Ultra Lounge 1 Throop Alley (at Canal St) 401/854-6464 • gay/ straight • gay night Sun only • live piano • food served • tapas

Therapy 7 Dike St (at Troy) 401/490-7202 • 9pm-2am, till 6am Fri-Sat, clsd Sun-Mon • gay-friendly • also gallery & cafe from 10am • young crowd • wheelchair access

CAFES

Coffee Exchange 207 Wickenden St 401/273-1198 • 6:30am-11pm • deck

Nicks on Broadway 500 Broadway 401/421-0286 • lunch & dinner Wed-Sat, Sun brunch, clsd Mon-Tue

Pastiche Fine Desserts 92 Spruce St 401/861-5190 • 8:30am-11pm, 10am-10pm Sun

White Electric Coffee 711 Westminster 401/453-3007 • 7am-6:30pm

RESTAURANTS

Al Forno 577 S Main St 401/273-9760 • dinner only, clsd Sun-Mon

Blaze Restaurant 776 Hope St 401/277-2529 • lunch & dinner, clsd Mon • lesbian-owned

Bravo Brasserie 123 Empire St 401/490-5112 • lunch Tue-Sat, dinner nightly, Sun brunch

Caffe Dolce Vita 59 DePasquale Plaza (at Spruce St) 401/331-8240 • 8am-1am, till 2am wknds, wknd brunch • authentic Italian cafe • patio

Camille's 71 Bradford St (at Atwell's Ave) 401/751-4812 • lunch & dinner, clsd Sun • full bar

CAV 14 Imperial Pl 401/751-9164 • 11am-10pm, till 1am Fri, wknd brunch • eclectic menu & decor

DownCity 50 Weybosset St 401/331-9217 • lunch weekdays, dinner nightly • wknd brunch • full bar • wheelchair access

Fellini Pizzeria 166 Wickenden St 401/751-6737 • open late • free delivery • lesbian-owned

Haven Brothers Diner 72 Spruce St (in a truck outside City Hall) 401/861-7777 • 5pm-3am • since the 1930s

Julian's 318 Broadway (at Vinton) 401/861-1770 • lunch & dinner • beer/wine only

Local 121 121 Washington St (at Matthewson St) 401/274-2121 • lunch Tue-Sat, dinner nightly

Providence

LGBT PRIDE:
June. 401/467-2130, web: www.prideri.com.

ANNUAL EVENTS:
Aug - Rhode Island Int'l Film Festival 401/861-4445, web: www.film-festival.org.

CITY INFO:
401/456-0200 or 800/233-1636, web: www.goprovidence.com.

ATTRACTIONS:
Newport.
RISD Museum 401/454-6500, web: www.risd.edu.
Waterfire 401/273-1155, web: www.waterfire.com.

TRANSIT:
Yellow Cab 401/941-1122.
RIPTA Bus Service 401/781-9400, web: www.ripta.com.

ENTERTAINMENT & RECREATION

AS220 115 Empire St (at Washington) 401/831–9327 • nonprofit community arts space • performance, poetry, open mics • also classes • also bar & restaurant

Cable Car Cinema & Cafe 204 S Main St 401/272–3970 • art-house flicks & free popcorn refills

Providence Roller Derby • Providence's female roller derby league • visit www.providencerollerderby.com for events

WaterFire Waterplace Park 401/272–3111 • May-Oct only • bonfire installations along the Providence River at sunset

BOOKSTORES

Books on the Square 471 Angell St (at Wayland) 9am-9pm, 10am-6pm Sun • some LGBT

PUBLICATIONS

Metroline 860/231-8845, 800/233-8334 • regional newspaper & entertainment guide • covers CT, RI & MA

Options 401/724–5428 • LGBT community magazine

EROTICA

Mister Sister 268 Wickenden St 401/421–6969 • women-oriented • fetishwear • sex toys • classes

SOUTH CAROLINA

Statewide

PUBLICATIONS

Q Notes 704/531–9988 • bi-weekly LGBT newspaper for the Carolinas

Aiken

see also **Augusta, Georgia**

NIGHTCLUBS

Marlboro Station 141 Marlboro St 803/644-6485 • 10pm-close Fri-Sun • lesbians/ gay men • dancing /DJ • live shows

Beaufort

RESTAURANTS

Old House Restaurant Hwy 462 (at Hwy 336), Ridgeland 843/258–4444 • 5pm-9pm • wheelchair access • gay-owned

Blacksburg

EROTICA

BedTyme Stories 145 Simper Rd (I-85, exit 100) 864/839-0007

Charleston

INFO LINES & SERVICES

Acceptance Group (Gay AA) 45 Moultrie St (St. Barnabus Lutheran Church) 843/723-9633 (AA#) • 7pm Mon, Th & Sat

ACCOMMODATIONS

A B&B @ 4 Unity Alley 4 Unity Alley 843/577–6660 • gay/ straight • 18th-c warehouse • full brkfst • nonsmoking • parking inside

Aloft Charleston Airport & Convention Center 4875 Tanger Outlet Blvd (at International Blvd), N Charleston 843/566–7300, 877/462–5638 • gay-friendly • gym • pool • WiFi • wheelchair access

Charleston Place 205 Meeting St 843/722-4900 , 888/635-2350 • gay-friendly • restaurant

Phoebe Pember House 26 Society St (at East Bay) 843/722–4186 • gay-friendly • also yoga classes

BARS

Dudley's on Ann 42 Ann St (at King St) 843/577–6779 • 4pm-2am • mostly gay men • neighborhood bar • karaoke • gay-owed/ run

NIGHTCLUBS

Club Pantheon 28 Ann St (at King) 843/577–2582 • 10pm-2am Fri-Sun only • mostly gay men • dancing • multiracial • live shows • drag shows • cabaret • 18+ • gay-owned

Club Patrick's 1377 Ashley River Rd/ Hwy 61 843/571–3435 • 6pm-2am • lesbians/ gay men • transgender-friendly • DJ Fri-Sat • karaoke Th • live shows & music • wheelchair access

Deja Vu II 4628 Spruill Ave 843/554-5959 • 5pm-close Th, from 10pm Fri-Sat • mostly women • dancing/DJ • live shows • food served • karaoke • private club • wheelchair access • lesbian-owned

CAFES

Bear E Patch 1980A Ashley River Rd 843/766-6490 • 7am-9pm, 8am-8pm Sat, clsd Sun • wheelchair access

RESTAURANTS

82 Queen 82 Queen St 843/723-7591, 800/849-0082 • lunch & dinner, Sun brunch • Lowcountry cuisine

Fat Hen 3140 Maybank Hwy, St Johns Island 843/559-9090 • dinner nightly, Sun brunch • French bistro • seafood

Fig 232 Meeting St (near Hasell) 843/805-5900 • 5:30pm-10:30pm, till 11pm Fri-Sat, clsd Sun • local ingredients • full bar • wheelchair access

High Cotton 199 E Bay St 843/724-3815 • dinner nightly, lunch Sat, Sun brunch • Southern cuisine • full bar

Hominy Grill 843/937-0930 • brkfst, lunch & dinner, wknd brunch

Jim 'N Nick's Bar-B-Q 288 King St 843/577-0406 • 10:30am-9pm, till 10pm Fri-Sat

Joe Pasta 428 King St (at John) 843/965-5252 • 11:30am-11pm, till midnight Fri-Sat • also full bar

Mama Q's Kitchen 3157 Maybank Hwy #E, St Johns Island 843/559-0071 • 11:30am-9pm, till 3pm Mon & 4pm Sun • wheelchair access • gay-owned

Melvin's Legendary Bar-B-Que 538 Folly Rd 843/762-0511 • 10:45am-9:30pm, clsd Sun • "the #1 cheeseburger in America"

ENTERTAINMENT & RECREATION

Historic Charleston Foundation 40 E Bay St 843/723-1623 • call for info on city walking tours (March-April only)

PUBLICATIONS

Q Notes 704/531-9988 • bi-weekly LGBT newspaper for the Carolinas

Columbia

INFO LINES & SERVICES

The Harriet Hancock GLBT Community Center 1108 Woodrow St 803/771-7713 • community info • resources & more

Primary Purpose Gay/ Lesbian AA 5220 Clemson (in the house behind St Martin's Church) 803/254-5301(AA#) • 6:30 Tue, 7pm Fri & Sun

ACCOMMODATIONS

Holiday Inn Express 1011 Clemson Frontage Rd 803/419-3558

BARS

Art Bar 1211 Park St 803/929-0198 • 8pm-2am • gay/ straight • dancing/DJ • karaoke

Capital Club 1002 Gervais St 803/256-6464 • 5pm-2am • mostly gay men • neighborhood bar • professional crowd • private club • wheelchair access

NIGHTCLUBS

The "L" Word 625 Frink St (at State St), Cayce 803/794-2111 • 5pm-close • mostly women • dancing/DJ • live shows • karaoke • wheelchair access

PTS 1109 1109 Assembly St (at Gervais St) 803/253-8900 • 5pm-2am, till 6am Fri, till 3am Sat-Sun • lesbians/ gay men • dancing/DJ • live shows • WiFi • multiracial • transgender-friendly • private club • gay-owned

RESTAURANTS

Dianne's On Devine 2400 Devine St 803/254-3535 • dinner only, clsd Sun • upscale Italian

Garibaldi's of Columbia 2013 Greene St 803/771-8888 • dinner nighty, full bar

Salty Nut Cafe 2000 Greene St 803/256-4611 • 11am-midnight, bar open later

Greenville

ACCOMMODATIONS

Walnut Lane Inn 110 Ridge Rd (at Groce Rd), Lyman 864/949-7230, 800/949-4686 • gay-friendly • B&B • full brkfst • kids ok • WiFi • $129-139

BARS

The Twisted Lemon 528 Haywood Rd 864/284-0071 • 3pm-2am • lesbians/gay men • dancing/DJ • drag shows

NIGHTCLUBS

The Castle 8-B Legrande Blvd 864/235-9949 • 9:30pm-3am Wed-Sun • popular • lesbians/ gay men • dancing/DJ • drag shows • videos • young crowd • private club • wheelchair access

BOOKSTORES

Out of Bounds 21 S Pleasanturg Dr 864/239-0106 • 2pm- 8pm, till 6pm Sun, from 11am Fri-Sat • community pride store

Hilton Head

ACCOMMODATIONS

Crowne Plaza Hilton Head Beach Resort
130 Shipyard Dr **843/842–2400, 800/334–1881**

BARS

Club Vibe 32 Palmetto Bay Rd #D-2 (at Sea
Pines Cir) **843/341–6933** • 5pm-3am, from
8pm Sat, clsd Sun • lesbians/ gay men •
neighborhood bar • transgender-friendly •
food served

Lake Wylie

NIGHTCLUBS

The Rainbow In 4376 Charlotte Hwy
803/831–0093 • 4pm-close, 8pm-2am Sat,
clsd Sun-Wed • lesbians/ gay men • dancing/
DJ • drag shows • private club

Myrtle Beach

ACCOMMODATIONS

Aquarius Motel 301 12th Ave N
843/448–7596, 800/244–4386 • gay/ straight •
pool • pets/kids ok • WiFi • $55-200

BARS

Time Out 520 8th Ave N (at Oak)
843/448–1180 • 5pm-close, till 2am Sat •
popular • mostly gay men • neighborhood bar
• dancing/DJ • karaoke • drag shows • live
shows • patio bar • private club • wheelchair
access

NIGHTCLUBS

Rainbow House 815 N Kings Hwy
843/626–7298 • from 3pm Mon-Fri, 1pm
wknds • lesbians/ gay men • dancing/DJ • drag
shows • patio • wheelchair access

RESTAURANTS

Carolina Roadhouse 4617 N Kings Hwy
843/49–9911

Mr Fish 3401 N Kings Hwy **843/839–3474** •
11am-9:30pm • full bar

Sticky Fingers Smokehouse 2461 Coastal
Grand Cir **843/839–7427** • a chain but a good
one

RETAIL SHOPS

Kilgor Trouts Music & More 512 8th Ave N
843/445–2800

Rock Hill

BARS

Hideaway 405 Baskins Rd **803/328–6630** •
9pm-2am Th-Sat• lesbians/ gay men •
neighborhood bar • drag shows • karaoke •
private club

SOUTH DAKOTA

Murdo

ACCOMMODATIONS

Iversen Inn 108 E 5th St (on I-90 Business
Loop) **605/669-2452** • gay-friendly • kids/
pets ok • WiFi • gay-owned

Rapid City

INFO LINES & SERVICES

The Black Hills Center For Equality 1102
West Rapid St (at Omaha St) **605/348-3244** •
call for hours, clsd Sun • LGBT resource center

Salem

ACCOMMODATIONS

Camp America 25495 US 81 **605/425-9085**
• gay-friendly • 35 miles west of Sioux Falls •
camping • RV hookups • pool • kids/ pets ok •
nonsmoking • WiFi • lesbian-owned • $20-35

Sioux Falls

INFO LINES & SERVICES

The Center for Equality 406 S 2nd Ave
#102 **605/331-1153** • support groups •
counseling • library & more

BARS

Toppers 1213 N Cliff Ave **605/339-7686** •
3pm-close, till 2am Th-Sat, clsd Sun •
lesbians/ gay men • more women Wed •
karaoke

NIGHTCLUBS

Club David 214 W 10th St (btwn Main &
Dakota) **605/274-0700** • 4:30pm-2am
• gay/straight • dancing/DJ • karaoke • drag
shows • live music • also restaurant

EROTICA

Romantix Adult Superstore 311 N Dakota
Ave (btwn 6th & 7th) **605/332-9316** • 9am-
2am, from noon Sun

Spearfish

CAFES

The Bay Leaf Cafe 126 W Hudson St 605/642–5462 • lunch & dinner • plenty veggie • espresso bar

TENNESSEE

Chattanooga

BARS

Chuck's II 27–1/2 W Main St (at Market) 423/265–5405 • 6pm-1am, till 3am Fri-Sat • lesbians/ gay men • neighborhood bar • dancing/DJ • patio

NIGHTCLUBS

Alan Gold's 1100 McCallie Ave (at National) 423/629–8080 • 4:30pm-3am • popular • lesbians/ gay men • dancing/DJ • drag shows • food served • young crowd • wheelchair access

Images 6005 Lee Hwy 423/855–8210 • 5pm-3am Th-Sun • lesbians/ gay men • dancing/DJ • drag shows • also restaurant • wheelchair access

Gatlinburg

ACCOMMODATIONS

Big Creek Outdoors 5019 Rag Mtn Rd, Hartford 423/487–5742, 423/487–3490 • gay/ straight • cabins • camping • horseback riding • kids ok • wheelchair access • $25-150

Christopher Place, An Intimate Resort 1500 Pinnacles Wy, Newport 423/623–6555, 800/595–9441 • gay/ straight • full brkfst • pool • nonsmoking • wheelchair access • $165-330

English Mountaintop Villa Cove Rd, Sevierville 865/522–8547 • gay-friendly • private condo in Great Smoky Mtns Nat'l Park • panoramic views • pool • nonsmoking • WiFi • wheelchair access • $695-995/ week

Mountain Vista Cabins 1805 Shady Grove Rd (at Old Birds Creek Rd), Sevierville 865/712–9897 • lesbians/ gay men • hot tub • well-behaved kids/ pets welcome • nonsmoking • WiFi • woman-owned • $89-99

Stonecreek Cabins 865/429–0400 • lesbians/ gay men • 23-acre paradise in Smoky Mtns • hot tub • nonsmoking • lesbian-owned • $135-185

Johnson City

ACCOMMODATIONS

Safe Haven Farm 336 Stanley Hollow Rd, Roan Mountain 423/725–4262 • gay-friendly • cabins • creekside privacy • fireplace & wraparound porch • kids/ pets ok • $100/ night, $550/ week

NIGHTCLUBS

Fuzzy Holes 1410 E Main St (at S Broadway St) 423/929–9800 • 8pm-close • transgender-friendly • sex-positive strip club • food served • 18+ • wheelchair access • lesbian-owned

New Beginnings 2910 N Bristol Hwy 423/282–4446 • 9pm-2am, from 8pm Fri-Sat, clsd Sun-Mon • popular • mostly gay men • dancing/DJ • drag shows • also restaurant • wheelchair access

RETAIL SHOPS

My Secret Closet 2910 N Bristol Hwy (inside New Beginnings) 423/282–4446 • 10pm-3am Fri-Sat only • pride gifts

Knoxville

INFO LINES & SERVICES

AA Gay/ Lesbian 2931 Kingston Pike (at Unitarian Church) 865/522–9667 (AA#) • 7pm Fri

Lesbian Social Group 865/531–7788 • meet 7pm Wed • call for info

BARS

Chrome Pony Saloon 2909 Alcoa Hwy 865/680–1899 • 4pm-3am, clsd Mon-Tue • lesbians/gay men • neighborhood bar • drag shows • great pizza • karaoke

NIGHTCLUBS

Carousel II 1501 White Ave • 9pm-3am Wed-Sat • lesbians/ gay men • dancing/DJ • drag shows

Club XYZ 1215 N Central 865/637–4999 • 5:30pm-3am, from 9pm Sat, from 7pm Sun • lesbians/ gay men • dancing/DJ • drag shows • karaoke

GyrlGroove 865/356–7671 • bi-monthly womens dance parties • check gyrlgroove.com for location

The New Rainbow Club West 7211 Kingston Pike SW (at Cheshire Dr) 865/588–8030 • 5pm-3am • lesbians/ gay men • dancing/DJ • food served • karaoke • drag shows • wheelchair access

Memphis

INFO LINES & SERVICES

AA Intergroup 1835 Union Ave #302 (at McLean) **901/726-6750** • call for times & locations

Memphis Gay/ Lesbian Community Center 892 S Cooper (at Nelson) **901/278-6422** • 2pm-9pm Mon-Fri

ACCOMMODATIONS

Shellcrest Guesthouse 671 Jefferson Ave (at N Orleans St) **901/277-0223** • gay/ straight • suites in downtown Victorian • pool • nonsmoking • WiFi • gay-owned • $175

Talbot Heirs Guesthouse 99 S 2nd St (btwn Union & Peabody Pl) **901/527-9772, 800/955-3956** • gay-friendly • suites w/ kitchens • funky decor • nonsmoking • kids ok • $135-275

BARS

Dru's Place 1474 Madison (at McNeil) **901/275-8082** • 11am-midnight, till 3am Fri-Sat, from noon Sun • mostly women • neighborhood bar • dancing/DJ • karaoke • drag shows • beer & set-ups only

Lorenz/ Aftershock 1528 Madison Ave (at Avalon) **901/274-8272** • 1pm-close • lesbians/ gay men • neighborhood bar • dancing/DJ • drag shows • multi-racial clientele

The Metro 1349 Autumn St (at Cleveland) **901/274-8010** • 4pm-3am • lesbians/ gay men • dancing/DJ • karaoke • food served • patio • wheelchair access

Mollie Fontaine Lounge 679 Adams Ave (at Orleans) **901/524-1886** • 5pm-2am, clsd Sun-Tue • gay/ straight • food served

RP Billiards 525 S Highland St (at Southern Ave) **901/452-6583** • 5pm-3am • gay-friendly

Memphis

WHERE THE GIRLS ARE:
On Madison Ave., of course, just east of US-240.

LGBT PRIDE:
June. Mid-South Pride 901/382-6349, web: www.midsouth-pride.org.

ANNUAL EVENTS:
September - OutFlix International GLBT Film Festival 901/283-5935, web: www.outflixfestival.org.
September - The Cooper-Young Festival (arts, crafts & music) 901/276-7222.

CITY INFO:
901/543-5300, web: www.memphistravel.com.

BEST VIEW:
A cruise on any of the boats that ply the river.

WEATHER:
Suth'n. H-O-T and humid in the summer, cold (30°s-40°s) in the winter, and a relatively nice (but still humid) spring and fall.

ATTRACTIONS:
Beale Street.
Graceland 800/238-2000, web: www.elvis.com/graceland.
Mud Island 800/507-6507, web: www.mudisland.com.
Nat'l Civil Rights Museum 901/521-9699, web: www.civil-rightsmuseum.org.
Rock N Soul Museum 901/205-2533, web: www.memphisrocknsoul.org.
Overton Square.
Stax Museum 901/946-2535, web: www.staxmuseum.com.
Sun Studio 800/441-6249, web: www.sunstudio.com.

TRANSIT:
Yellow Cab 901/577-7777. 877/300-4VAN.
MATA 901/274-6282, web: www.matatransit.com.

The Vault 529 S Highland St (at Southern Ave) **901/452–6583** • 5pm-3am • gay/ straight • dancing/DJ • karaoke

NIGHTCLUBS

901 Complex 136 Webster Ave (at S 2nd St) **901/522–8455** • from 10pm Fri-Sat only • lesbians/ gay men • ladies night Fri • mostly African American • dancing/DJ • drag shows • BYOB

Crossroads 1278 Jefferson Ave (at Claybrook) **901/272–8801** • 4pm-midnight, 3pm-3am Fri-Sun • lesbians/ gay men • neighborhood bar • drag shows Fri-Sat • karaoke

Mary's 405 N Cleveland (at Autumn Ave) **901/725–7334** • lesbians/ gay men • dancing/DJ • WiFi

Senses 2866 Poplar Ave (at Walnut Grove Rd) **901/454–4081** • gay-friendly • dancing/DJ • multiracial • theme nights

CAFES

Java Cabana 2170 Young Ave (at Cooper) **901/272–7210** • 6:30am-10pm, 9am-midnight Fri-Sat, noon-10pm Sun, clsd Mon • poetry readings • live shows • also art gallery • WiFi • wheelchair access

Otherlands Coffee Bar 641 S Cooper (at Central) **901/278–4994** • 7am-8pm • live music till 11pm Fri-Sat • plenty veggie • WiFi • also gift shop • wheelchair access

P&H Cafe 1532 Madison (at Adeline) **901/726–0906** • 3pm-3am, from 5pm Sat, clsd Sun • beer/ wine • food served • live shows • wheelchair access

RESTAURANTS

Automatic Slim's Tonga Club 83 S 2nd St (at Union) **901/525–7948** • lunch & dinner, Sun brunch • Caribbean & Southwestern • plenty veggie • full bar • wheelchair access

Cafe Eclectic 603 N McLean Blvd (at Faxon Ave) **901/725–1718** • 6am-10pm, 9am-3pm Sun

Cafe Society 212 N Evergreen St (at Poplar) **901/722–2177** • lunch Mon-Fri, dinner nightly • full bar • wheelchair access

Circa 6150 Poplar Ave **901/746–9130** • lunch Mon-Fri, dinner nightly, clsd Sun • American

India Palace 1720 Poplar Ave (at Lemaster St) **901/278–1199** • lunch & dinner

Leonard's Pit Barbecue 5465 Fox Plaza Dr (at Mt Moriah Rd) **901/360–1963** • 11am-9pm • Elvis ordered the pork sandwich at the original Leonard's (now closed), but the food is just as good here!

Molly's La Casita 2006 Madison Ave (at N Morrison St) **901/726–1873** • lunch & dinner • Mexican

Restaurant Iris 2146 Monroe Ave (at Cooper) **901/590–2828** • dinner Mon-Sat, brunch 3rd Sun • French/ Creole • upscale • wheelchair access

RP Tracks 3547 Walker Ave (at Brister) **901/327–1471** • lunch & dinner, open till 3am • burgers • some veggie

Saigon Le 51 N Cleveland (at Jefferson) **901/276–5326** • 11am-9pm, clsd Sun • Chinese/ Vietnamese/ Thai

Tsunami 928 S Cooper (at Young) **901/274–2556** • dinner only • Pacific rim cuisine • wheelchair access

ENTERTAINMENT & RECREATION

Center for Southern Folklore 119 S Main St (at Peabody Pl) **901/525–3655** • 11am-5pm, clsd Sun, open later for shows • live music • gallery • cybercafe • food served

Graceland 3734 Elvis Presley Blvd **901/332–3322, 800/238–2000** • no visit to Memphis would be complete w/out a trip to see The King

Memphis Rock 'N Roll Tours **901/359–3102** • historical tour of Memphis music scene

BOOKSTORES

Davis-Kidd Booksellers 387 Perkins Rd Ext (at Poplar & Walnut Grove) **901/683–9801** • 9am-9pm, till 8pm Sun • general • some LGBT titles • also cafe

RETAIL SHOPS

Inz & Outz 553 S Cooper (at Peabody) **901/728–6535** • 10am-8pm, noon-6pm Sun • pride items • books • gifts • wheelchair access

EROTICA

Cherokee Books 2947 Lamar **901/744–7494**

Romantix Adult Superstore 1617 Getwell Rd **901/744–4513**

Romantix Adult Superstore 2220 E Brooks Rd **901/396–9050**

Romantix Adult Superstore 5939 Summer Ave **901/373–5760**

Nashville

INFO LINES & SERVICES

AA Gay/ Lesbian **615/831–1050** • call for info

ACCOMMODATIONS

The Big Bungalow B&B 618 Fatherland St (at 7th) **615/256-8375** • gay-friendly • full brkfst • live music • massage available • nonsmoking • WiFi • woman-owned • $125-185

Doubletree Nashville 315 4th Ave N (at Union St) **615/244-8200** • gay-friendly • also restaurant & lounge • fitness center • WiFi

Hutton Hotel 1808 West End Ave (at 19th Ave) **615/340-9333** • gay-friendly • also restaurant • fitness center • WiFi • $199+

Top O' Woodland Historic B&B Inn 1603 Woodland St (at 16th) **615/228-3868, 888/228-3868** • gay-friendly • full brkfst • also wedding chapel • nonsmoking • WiFi • woman-owned • $160

BARS

Purple Heys 1401 4th Ave S (at Rains) **615/244-4433** • 11am-3am • lesbians/ gay men • neighborhood bar • food served • wheelchair access

Stirrup Nashville 1529 4th Ave S (at Mallory) **615/782-0043** • noon-3am • mostly gay men • multiracial • transgender-friendly • neighborhood bar • food served • patio • wheelchair access

Trax 1501 2nd Ave S (at Carney) **615/742-8856** • noon-3am • mostly gay men • neighborhood bar • karaoke • WiFi

Tribe/ Suzy Wong's House of Yum 1517 Church St (at 15th Ave S) **615/329-2912** • 4pm-midnight, till 2am wknds • lesbians/ gay men • live entertainment • videos • upscale • full restaurant • wheelchair access • gay-owned

Vibe 1713 Church St (at 17th & 18th) **615/329-3838** • 9pm Sat only • lesbians/ gay men • dancing/DJ • drag shows • patio

NIGHTCLUBS

508 508 Lea Ave (at 6th) **615/669-4508** • midnight-7am Fri-Sat night only • gay/ straight • dancing/DJ

Nashville

WHERE THE GIRLS ARE:
Just north of I-65/40 along 2nd Ave. S. on Hermitage Ave.

LGBT PRIDE:
June. 615/650-6736, web: www.nashvillepride.org.
October. Black Pride 800/845-4266 x 269, web: www.brother-sunited.com.

ANNUAL EVENTS:
September - Nashville Film Festival (some gay films), web: nashville-filmfestival.org.
September - AIDS Walk 615/259-4866, web: www.nashvillecares.org.
November - Artrageous 615/259-4866, web: www.nashvillecares.org.

CITY INFO:
800/657-6910, web: www.nashvillecvb.com.

BEST VIEW:
Try a walking tour of the city.

WEATHER:
See Memphis.

TRANSIT:
Yellow Cab 615/256-0101.
Gray Line Airport Shuttle 615/275-1180.
MTA 615/862-5969, web: www.nashvillemta.org.

ATTRACTIONS:
Country Music Hall of Fame 615/416-2001, web: www.countrymusichalloffame.com.
Grand Ole Opry & Opryland USA 615/871-OPRY, web: www.opry.com.
Jack Daniel's Distillery 615/279-4100, web: www.jackdaniels.com.
The Parthenon 615/862-8431, web: www.parthenon.org.
Ryman Auditorium 615/889-3060, web: www.ryman.com.
Tennessee Antebellum Trail 888/852-1860, web: www.antebellum.com.

Bluebird Cafe 4104 Hillsboro Pike (nr Warfield Dr) **615/383-1461** • live country music venue

Lipstick Lounge 1400 Woodland St (at 14th) **615/226-6343** • 4pm-close, from 7pm Fri, from 6pm wknds • mostly women • dancing/DJ • karaoke • live music

Play Dance Bar 1519 Church St (at 16th Ave) **615/322-9627** • 9pm-3am Wed-Sun • mostly gay men • dancing/DJ • multiracial • transgender-friendly • drag shows • 18+ • wheelchair access

CAFES

Bongo Java 2007 Belmont Blvd **615/385-5282** • 7am-11pm, from 8am wknds • coffeehouse • deck • also serves brkfst, lunch & dinner

Fido 1812 21st Ave S **615/777-3436** • 7am-11pm, till midnight Fri-Sat, from 8am wknds • also full menu

Grins Vegetarian Cafe 2421 Vanderbilt Pl (at 25th Ave) **615/22-8571** • 7am-9pm, till 3pm Fri, clsd wknds

RESTAURANTS

Battered & Fried 1008 Woodland St (at S 10th) **615/226-9283** • lunch & dinner • seafood • full bar • also Wave sushi bar • patio • wheelchair access

Beyond the Edge 112 S 11th St **615/226-3343** • 11am-2am • pizza & sandwiches • full bar

Cafe Coco 210 Louise Ave (at State) **615/321-2626** • 24hrs • live music • beer/wine • patio

Couva Calypso Cafe 2424 Elliston Pl **615/321-3878** • 11am-9pm, 11:30am-8:30pm wknds • Caribbean

International Market 2010 Belmont Blvd (at International) **615/297-4453** • 10:30am-9pm • Thai/Chinese • plenty veggie • beer/wine • wheelchair access

Mad Donna's 1313 Woodland St (at 14th) **615/226-1617** • 11am-10pm, till 11pm Sat, clsd Mon • also lounge • drag bingo Tue

The Mad Platter 1239 6th Ave N (at Monroe) **615/242-2563** • lunch Mon-Fri, dinner Wed-Sun • Californian • some veggie • wheelchair access

Nuvo Burrito 1000 Main St (at 10th) **615/866-9713** • 11:30am-9pm • eclectic burrito menu • also bar • theme nights

Pancake Pantry 1796 21st Ave S (at Wedgewood Ave) **615/383-9333** • 6am-3pm, till 4pm wknds • popular for brkfst

Rumba 3009 W End Ave (at 30th) **615/321-1350** • 4pm-close, from 5pm Sun • Latin/Asian • exotic drinks

Rumours Wine & Art Bar 2304 12th Ave S (at Linden) **615/292-9400** • 5pm-midnight, clsd Sun • wheelchair access

Sky Blue Coffeehouse & Bistro 700 Fatherland St (at S 7th St) **615/770-7097** • brkfst & lunch

Sole Mio 311 3rd Ave S **615/256-4013** • 11am-10pm, till midnight Fri-Sat, clsd Mon • Italian • wheelchair access

The Standard at the Smith House 167 Rosa Parks Ave (at Charlotte) **615/254-1277** • dinner Tue-Sat, clsd Sun-Mon • wheelchair access

Watermark 507 12th Ave S (at Division) **615/254-2000** • dinner nightly, clsd Sun • seafood & more • great wine list • wheelchair access

Yellow Porch 734 Thompson Ln (at Bransford Ave) **615/386-0260** • lunch & dinner, clsd Sun • fresh Southern cuisine • wheelchair access

ENTERTAINMENT & RECREATION

NashTrash Tours tours leave from the Farmers Market (900 8th Ave N) **615/226-7300, 800/342-2132** • campy tours of Nashville w/ the Jugg Sisters • ages 13+ • reservations required

Tennessee Repertory Theater 505 Deaderick St (at the Tennessee Performing Arts Center) **615/244-4878**

PUBLICATIONS

Inside Out Nashville **615/831-1806** • LGBT newspaper & bar guide

Out & About Newspaper **615/596-6210** • LGBT newspaper for Nashville, Knoxville, Chattanooga & Atlanta area • monthly

TEXAS

Amarillo

BARS

212 Club 212 SW 6th Ave (at Harrison) **806/372-7997** • 2pm-2am • lesbians/gay men • neighborhood bar • dancing/DJ • drag shows • wheelchair access

Kicked Back 521 SE 10th Ave (at Buchanan St) **806/371-3535** • 3pm-2am, clsd Sun • lesbians/gay men • neighborhood bar • karaoke • lesbian-owned

R&R 701 S Georgia St **806/342–9000** • 4pm-2am • gay-friendly • neighborhood bar • wheelchair access • gay-owned

Sassy's 309 SW 6th Ave **806/374–3029** • 3pm-2am Wed, 6pm-3am Fri-Sat • lesbians/gay men • dancing/DJ • karaoke • drag shows

Whiskers 1219 SW 10th Ave **806/371–8482** • 5pm-2am • lesbians/gay men • neighborhood bar

RESTAURANTS

Furrbie's 210 W 6th Ave **806/220–0841** • 11am-7pm, till 3pm Sat & Mon • gay-owned

EROTICA

Fantasy Gifts & Video 440 N Lakeside **806/372–6500**

Arlington

see also Dallas & Fort Worth

INFO LINES & SERVICES

Tarrant County Lesbian/ Gay Alliance **817/877–5544** • info line • meetings

NIGHTCLUBS

The 1851 Club 1851 W Division (at Fielder) **817/801–9303** • 3pm-2am • lesbians/gay men • dancing/DJ • drag shows • karaoke • videos • wheelchair access

Austin

INFO LINES & SERVICES

Lambda AA (Live & Let Live) 7801 N Lamar Blvd (at W Anderson Ln) **512/444–0071, 512/832–6767 (EN ESPAÑOL)** • 6:30pm & 8pm daily, 10am Sat, 11am Sun

ACCOMMODATIONS

Austin Folk House 506 W 22nd St (at Nueces) **512/472–6700, 866/472–6700** • gay/straight • kids ok • nonsmoking • WiFi • wheelchair access • $95-225

Brava House 1108 Blanco St (at W 12th) **512/478–5034, 866/892–5726** • gay-friendly • close to downtown & 6th Street • nonsmoking • WiFi • lesbian-owned • $139-199

Crowne Plaza Hotel Austin 6121 North IH 35 **512/323–5466**

Hilton Garden Inn Austin Downtown 500 North IH 35 **512/480–8181**

Hotel Saint Cecilia 112 Academy Dr **512/852–2400** • gay-friendly • pool • wheelchair access • $350+

Hotel San Jose 1316 S Congress Ave **512/444–7322, 800/574–8897** • gay/straight • pool • nonsmoking • kids/pets ok • wheelchair access • $95-375

Kimber Modern 110 The Circle **512/912–1046** • gay/straight • WiFi • women owned • $250-295

Mt Gainor Inn B&B 2390 Prochnow Rd (at Mt Gainor Rd), Dripping Springs **512/858–0982, 888/644–0982** • gay/straight • nonsmoking • hot tub • WiFi • $129-195

Omni Austin Hotel Downtown 700 San Jacinto (at 8th) **512/476–3700, 800/843–6664** • gay-friendly • rooftop pool • WiFi • wheelchair access • $179-409

Park Lane Guest House 221 Park Ln (at Drake) **512/447–7460, 800/492–8827** • gay/straight • full brkfst • pool • also cottage • wheelchair access • lesbian-owned • $148-258

riverbarnsuites 30 minutes from Austin airport, Kingsbury **512/488–2175** • women only • river resort w/ lots of outdoor activities • swimming • lesbian-owned • $125

Robin's Nest 1007 Stewart Cove **512/266–3413** • gay-friendly • on Lake Travis • WiFi • $135-375

BARS

'Bout Time 9601 N I H 35 (at Rundberg) **512/832–5339** • 2pm-2am • lesbians/gay men • neighborhood bar • transgender-friendly • karaoke • volleyball court • WiFi • wheelchair access

Casino El Camino 517 E 6th St (at Red River) **512/469–9330** • 4pm-2am • gay-friendly • neighborhood bar • psychedelic punk jazz lounge • great burgers • WiFi • wheelchair access

Cheer Up Charlie's 1104 E 6th St • noon-2am, from 4pm Sun-Mon • lesbians/gay men • live bands/ shows • also vegan restaurant

NIGHTCLUBS

Elysium 705 Red River (7th St) **512/478–2979** • 9:30pm-2am • Tue '90s night • Sun '80s night • dancing/DJ • rest of the week goth, industrial & electronica club

Kiss & Fly 404 Colorado **512/476–7799** • 9pm-close Wed-Sat, from 5pm Sun • mostly gay men • dancing/DJ • drag shows • wheelchair access

Rain 217-B W 4th St (at Colorado St) **512/494–1150** • 4pm-close, from 3pm Fri-Sun • mostly gay men • Girls club 1st Tue • dancing/DJ • go-go dancers • wheelchair access

CAFES

Austin Java Cafe & Coffeehouse 1608 Barton Springs Rd (at Kinney Ave) **512/482–9450** • 7am-11pm, from 8am Sat-Sun • also 1206 Parkway (at 12th & Lamar), 512/476-1829 & 300 W 2nd St, Ste 100, 512/481-9400

Bouldin Creek Coffeehouse 1900 S 1st St **512/416–1601** • 7am-midnight, from 9am wknds • completely vegetarian menu (brkfst all day) • occasional live music

Joe's Bakery & Coffee Shop 2305 E 7th St (at Morelos & Northwestern) **512/472–0017** • 6am-3pm, clsd Mon • Tex-Mex • wheelchair access

Spider House Patio Bar & Cafe 2908 Fruth St (at West Dr) **512/480–9562** • 7am-2am • full bar • art & performance • patio

RESTAURANTS

The Belmont 305 W 6th St **512/457–0300** • 11am-midnight, from 4pm Sat, till 2am Fri-Sat • swank midcentury modern eatery & lounge

Chez Nous 510 Neches St **512/473–2413** • lunch Tue-Fri, dinner nightly, clsd Mon • wheelchair access

Chuy's 1728 Barton Springs Rd **512/474–4452** • 11am-10pm, till 11pm Fri-Sat • Tex-Mex • full bar • wheelchair access

Corazon at Castle Hill 1101 W 5th St (at Baylor) **512/476–0728** • lunch weekdays & dinner nightly, clsd Sun • inspired cuisine • some veggie • wheelchair access

Eastside Cafe 2113 Manor Rd (at Breeze Terrace) **512/476–5858** • 11:30am-9:30pm, 10am-10pm wknds • some veggie • beer/ wine • wheelchair access

El Sol y La Luna 600 E 6th St (at Red River) **512/444–7770** • 10am-10pm, till 1pm Fri-Sat, 9am-4pm Sun • great brkfst • live music Fri-Sat • wheelchair access • lesbian-owned

Fonda San Miguel 2330 W North Loop (at Hancock Rd) **512/459–4121** • dinner only, popular Sun brunch • Mexican • full bar

Galaxy 1000 W Lynn **512/478–3434** • 7am-10pm • quick, stylish & tasty

Guero's 1412 S Congress (at Elizabeth) **512/447–7688** • 11am-11pm, from 8am wknds • great Mexican & people-watching • outdoor seating • live music outdoors on wknds

Imperia 310 Colorado St **512/472–6770** • dinner only • upscale Asian • full bar • wheelchair access

Jo's Hot Coffee & Good Food 1300 S Congress Ave (at James) **512/444–3800** • 7am-9pm, till 10pm Sat • "best lazy day outdoor dining scene" • wheelchair access • also 242 W 2nd St, 512/469-9003 • lesbian-owned

Kenichi 419 Colorado St **512/320–8883** • dinner nightly • Asian/ sushi • wheelchair access

Mother's Cafe & Garden 4215 Duval St (at 43rd) **512/451–3994** • 11:15am-10pm, from 10am wknds • vegetarian • beer/wine • wheelchair access

Polvos 2004 S 1st St (at Johanna) **512/441–5446** • 7am-11pm • Mexican • outdoor seating

Restaurant Jezebel 914 Congress Ave **512/499–3999** • dinner nightly • French/ American

Romeo's 1500 Barton Springs Rd (near Lamar) **512/476–1090** • 11am-10pm, till 11pm Fri-Sat • Italian • full bar • live music wknds • wheelchair access

Santa Rita Cantina 1206 W 38th St **512/419–7482** • lunch & dinner, wknd brunch

Threadgill's 6416 N Lamar **512/451–5440** • 10am-10pm, till 9pm Sun • great chicken-fried steak • live music Wed • also 301 W Riverside Dr, 512/472-9304 • beer garden • live music

Wink 1014 N Lamar Blvd **512/482–8868** • dinner nightly, clsd Sun • upscale • also wine bar • wheelchair access

ENTERTAINMENT & RECREATION

Awthum Empire • avant garde cultural events in Austin • also Awthumfetht each year during SXSW • awthum.com

Barton Springs Barton Springs Rd (in Zilker Park) **512/867–3080** • natural swimming hole

Bat Colony Congress Ave Bridge (at Barton Springs Dr) • everything's bigger in Texas—including the colony of bats that flies out from under this bridge every evening March-Oct

BOOKSTORES

Bookpeople 603 N Lamar Blvd (at 6th) **512/472–5050, 800/853–9757** • 9am-11pm • independent

BookWoman 5501 N Lamar Blvd (at Nelray) **512/472–2785** • 10am-8pm, noon-6pm Sun • books • cards • jewelry • music • DVDs • wheelchair access • woman-owned

RETAIL SHOPS

Milk + Honey Spa 204 Colorado St (at 2nd) **512/236–1115** • 9am-9pm

Tapelenders 1114 W 5th St #501 (at Baylor) **512/472-0844** • 10am-10pm, till midnight Fri-Sat • LGBT videos • novelties • gay-owned

Publications

Austin Chronicle 512/454-5766 • Austin's alternative paper • weekly • has extensive online gay guide (check out www.austinchronicle.com)

Gyms & Health Clubs

Hyde Park Gym 4125 Guadalupe (at 41st St) **512/459-9174** • 5am-10pm, 7am-7pm Sat, 8am-7pm Sun

Beaumont

Info Lines & Services

Lambda AA 1385 Calder Ave **409/832-1107** • 8pm Wed & Sat

Bars

Orleans Street Pub & Patio 650 Orleans St (at Forsythe) **409/835-4243** • 7pm-2am, clsd Mon-Tue • lesbians/ gay men • neighborhood bar • dancing/DJ • karaoke • drag shows

Austin

Where the Girls Are:
Downtown along Red River St., or 4th/5th St. near Lavaca, or at the music clubs and cafes downtown and around the University.

LGBT Pride:
June. www.aglcc.org.

Annual Events:
March - South by Southwest Music Festival, web: www.sxsw.com.

May & Labor Day - Splash Days. Weekend of parties in clothing-optional Hippie Hollow, web: www.houstonsplash.com.

September/October - Austin G/L Int'l Film Festival 512/302-9889, web: www.agliff.org.

City Info:
Austin Convention & Visitors Bureau 800/926-2282, web: www.austintexas.org.

Greater Austin Chamber of Commerce 512/478-9383, web: www.austin-chamber.org.

Best View:
Texas State Capitol or the University of Texas Tower, web: www.utexas.edu/tower.

Weather:
Summers are real scorchers (high 90°s–low 100°s) and last forever. Spring, fall, and winter are welcome reliefs.

Attractions:
Aqua Festival.

Austin Museum of Art at Laguna Gloria 512/458–8191, web: www.amoa.org.

Elisabet Ney Museum 512/458-2255, web: www.ci.austin.tx.us/elisabetney.

George Washington Carver Museum 512/974-4926, web: www.ci.austin.tx.us/carver.

Hamilton Pool 512/264–2740, web: www.texasoutside.com/hamilton-pool.htm.

LBJ Library & Museum 512/721-0200, web: www.lbjlib.utexas.edu.

McKinney Falls State Park 512/243–1643, web: www.tpwd.state.tx.us/park/mckinney.

Mount Bonnell.

Museo del Barrio de Austin 1402 E 1st St.

Zilker Park/Barton Springs, web: www.ci.austin.tx.us/zilker.

Transit:
Yellow Cab 512/452-9999.

Various hotels have their own shuttles.

Capital Metro 512/474-1200, web: www.capmetro.org.

Brownsville

NIGHTCLUBS

Karma 1655 Ruben Torres Blvd # 212
956/544-6800 • 9pm-2am, Th gay night, clsd
Sun-Wed • dancing/DJ

Bryan

BARS

Revolution Cafe & Bar 211 B S Main St (at
27th) **979/823-4044** • 4pm-2am, from 8pm
Sun-Mon, from 6pm Sat • gay-friendly •
neighborhood bar • food served • live music
• WiFi • wheelchair access

NIGHTCLUBS

Halo Bar 121 N Main St (at William J Bryan
Pkwy) **979/823-6174** • 9:30pm-2am Th-Sat •
lesbians/ gay men • dancing/DJ • drag shows •
karaoke • wheelchair access

Corpus Christi

INFO LINES & SERVICES

Clean & Serene AA 3026 S Staples (at MCC
church) **361/992-8911, 866/672-7029** • 8pm
Fri

ACCOMMODATIONS

Anthony's By The Sea 732 S Pearl St,
Rockport **361/729-6100, 800/460-2557** • gay/
straight • quiet retreat 4 blocks from water •
full brkfst • pool • nonsmoking • wheelchair
access • lesbian-owned

Port Aransas Inn 1500 S 11th St (at Ave G),
Port Aransas **361/749-5937** • gay/ straight •
pool • hot tub • WiFi • wheelchair access •
$39-338

BARS

The Hidden Door 802 S Staples St (at
Coleman) **361/882-5002** • noon-2am •
lesbians/ gay men • neighborhood bar •
dancing/DJ • patio • wheelchair access • also
the Loft piano bar Fri-Sun

ENTERTAINMENT & RECREATION

Robert James Provisioners 837 Redmond
361/937-4880 • 8am-10pm • sailboat
charters • classes • transgender-friendly • gay-
owned

Dallas

see also Arlington, Fort Worth

INFO LINES & SERVICES

**John Thomas Gay/ Lesbian Community
Center** 2701 Reagan St (at Brown)
214/528-0144, 214/528-0022 • 9am-9pm, till
5pm Sat, noon-5pm Sun • wheelchair access

Lambda AA 2438 Butler #106 **214/267-0222,
214/887-6699 (CENTRAL OFFICE #)** • call for
meeting details

ACCOMMODATIONS

Bailey's Uptown Inn 2505 Worthington St
(at Hibernia) **214/720-2258** • gay-friendly •
nonsmoking • WiFi • $179-219

Hotel ZaZa 2332 Leonard St (at State)
214/468-8399, 800/597-8399 • gay-friendly •
full spa & restaurant • $249-450

Lumen 6101 Hillcrest Ave **214/219-2400,
800/908-1140**
• gay-friendly • WiFi • wheelchair access

MCM Elegante' Hotel and Suites 2330 W
Northwest Hwy **214/358-7846, 877/351-4477**
• gay-friendly • pool • WiFi • wheelchair
access • $79-179

Melrose Hotel 3015 Oak Lawn Ave (at Cedar
Springs) **214/521-5151** • gay-friendly • also
piano bar & lounge & restaurant • wheelchair
access • $225-350

Palomar Dallas 5300 E Mockingbird Ln
214/520-7969, 888/253-9030
• gay-friendly • pool • WiFi

BARS

Alexandre's 4026 Cedar Springs Rd (at
Knight St) **214/559-0720** • 9am-2pm, from
2pm Sun-Mon • gay/ straight • live music •
karaoke • wheelchair access

Barbara's Pavillion 325 Centre St
214/941-2145 • 4pm-2am, from 2pm Sun •
mostly gay men • neighborhood bar • karaoke
• patio • wheelchair access

Grapevine 3902 Maple Ave (at Shelby)
214/522-8466 • 3pm-2am, from 1pm Sun •
gay/ straight • classic dive bar • WiFi •
wheelchair access

The Hidden Door 5025 Bowser Ave (at
Mahanna) **214/526-0620** • 7am-2am, from
noon Sun • mostly gay men • neighborhood
bar • leather • patio • wheelchair access

Jack's Backyard 2303 Pittman St (at W
Commerce St) **214/741-3131** • 11am-2am •
gay/ straight • food served • live music • WiFi

JR's Bar & Grill 3923 Cedar Springs Rd (at Throckmorton) **214/528-1004** • 11am-2am, from noon Sun • upscale • popular • lesbians/gay men • grill till 4pm • live shows Sun • videos • young crowd • WiFi • wheelchair access

Klub Wet 4100 Maple Ave (at Throckmorton) **214/559-3005** • 4pm-2am, from noon wknds • lesbians/gay men • neighborhood bar • piano bar

Dallas

WHERE THE GIRLS ARE:

Oak Lawn in central Dallas is the gay and lesbian stomping grounds, mostly on Cedar Springs Ave.

LGBT PRIDE:

September. www.dallastavern-guild.org.

ANNUAL EVENTS:

March-April - AFI Dallas Int'l Film Festival, web: dallasfilm.org.

March-April - Dallas Blooms at Dallas Arboretum & Botanical Garden with over 400,000 spring-blooming bulbs.

April – Deep Ellum Arts Festival, web: www.deepellumartsfesti-val.com.

September-October - Texas State Fair, web: www.bigtex.com. Largest in the country.

October - Out Takes Dallas 972/988-6333, web: www.outtakesdallas.org. LGBT film festival.

CITY INFO:

214/571-1000, web: www.visitdal-las.com.

BEST VIEW:

Hyatt Regency Tower.

WEATHER:

Can be unpredictable. Hot summers (90°s – 100°s) with possible severe rain storms. Winter temperatures hover in the 20°s through 40°s range.

TRANSIT:

Yellow Cab 214/426-6262.
Dallas Area Rapid Transit (DART) 214/979-1111, web: www.dart.org.

ATTRACTIONS:

African American Museum 214/565-9026, web: www.aamdallas.org.

Crow Collection of Asian Art 214/979-6430, web: www.crow-collection.com.

Dallas Arboretum & Botanical Garden 214/515-6500, web www.dallasarboretum.org.

Dallas Museum of Art 214/922-1200, web: www.dallasmuseumo-fart.org.

Dallas Theater Center/ Frank Lloyd Wright 214/522-8499, web: www.dallastheatercenter.org.

Dallas World Aquarium 214/720-2224, web: www.dwazoo.com.

Deep Ellum district.

Fair Park, web: www.fairpark.org. 277-acre park since 1880, home to Cotton Bowl, many museums, and Texas State Fair.

Meadows Museum at SMU 214/768-2516, web: smu.edu/meadows/museum/index.htm.

Modern Art Museum, Fort Worth 817/738-9215, web: www.themodern.org.

Nasher Sculpture Center 214/242-5100, web: www.nashersculp-turecenter.org.

Sixth Floor Museum 214/747-6660, web: www.jfk.org.

Texas State Fair & State Fair Park 214/565-9931, web: www.bigtex.com.

The Women's Museum 214/915-0860, web: www.thewomensmuseum.org.

Pekers 2615 Oak Lawn Ave, Ste 101 (btwn Fairmount & Brown) **214/528-3333** • 10am-2am • lesbians/ gay men • neighborhood bar • live music • karaoke • drag shows • wheelchair access

Sue Ellen's 3014 Throckmorton (at Cedar Springs) **214/559-0707** • 5pm-2am, 2pm-close wknds • popular • mostly women • dancing/DJ • live shows/ bands • Sun BBQ (summers) • patio • wheelchair access

Tin Room 2514 Hudnall St (at Maple Ave) **214/526-6365** • 10am-2am, from noon Sun • mostly gay men • neighborhood bar • wheelchair access

Woody's 4011 Cedar Springs Rd (btwn Douglas & Throckmorton) **214/520-6629** • 2pm-2am • lesbians/ gay men • live shows • sports bar • videos • nonsmoking upstairs • karaoke • patio • wheelchair access

NIGHTCLUBS

The Brick/Joe's Dallas 2525 Wycliff Ave (btwn Maple & Tollway) **214/521-3154** • 4pm-2am, till 4am Fri-Sat, from 2pm Sat-Sun • lesbians/ gay men • dancing/DJ • multiracial • drag shows

Elm and Pearl 2204 Elm St (at S Pearl) **214/741-0000** • mostly men Fri • mostly women Sat • dancing/DJ • drag shows Sun • mostly African American

Exklusive 4207 Maple Ave (at Hondo) **469/556-1395** • 9pm-close Th-Sun • lesbians/ gay men • dancing/DJ • drag shows • mostly Latino/a

Havana Bar & Grill 4006 Cedar Springs Rd (at Throckmorton) **214/526-9494** • grill 5pm-10pm, clsd Mon, lounge from 10pm • gay/ straight • dancing/DJ

Kaliente 4350 Maple Ave (at Hondo) **214/520-6676** • 9pm-2am, clsd Tue • mostly gay men • mostly Latino • dancing/DJ • salsa & Tejano • karaoke • drag shows • wheelchair access

Once in a Blue Moon 10675 E Northwest Hwy, Ste 2600B (at DanceMasters Ballroom) **972/662-4706** • 7pm-midnight 2nd Sat • monthly women's dance • dancing/DJ • nonsmoking • BYOB

Round-Up Saloon 3912 Cedar Springs Rd (at Throckmorton) **214/522-9611** • 3pm-2am, from noon wknds • popular • mostly gay men • dancing/DJ • country/ western • karaoke • dance lessons • patio • wheelchair access

Station 4 3911 Cedar Springs Rd (at Throckmorton) **214/526-7171** • 9pm-4am Wed-Sun • popular • lesbians/ gay men • dancing/DJ • drag shows • videos • also Rose Room cabaret • 18+

CAFES

Buli 3908 Cedar Springs Rd **214/528-5410** • 7am-midnight • WiFi • wheelchair access

Opening Bell Coffee 1409 S Lamar St, Ste 012 **214/565-0383** • 7am-10pm, from 9am wknds, till midnight wknds • beer/ wine • live music

RESTAURANTS

Ali Baba Cafe 1901 Abrams Rd (near La Vista Dr) **214/823-8235** • lunch & dinner • Middle Eastern

Bangkok Orchid 331 W Airport Fwy (N Beltline), Irving **972/252-7770** • lunch & dinner, clsd Mon • ask for Danny • BYOB • wheelchair access • gay-owned

Black-Eyed Pea 3857 Cedar Springs Rd (at Reagan) **214/521-4580** • 11am-10pm • wheelchair access

Blue Mesa Grill 5100 Belt Line Rd (at Tollway), Addison **972/934-0165** • 11am-10pm • great fajitas • full bar

Bread Winners 3301 McKinney Ave **214/754-4940** • 7am-10pm • full bar • wheelchair access

Cafe Brazil 3847 Cedar Springs Rd **214/461-8762** • open 24 hrs

Cosmic Cafe 2912 Oak Lawn Ave **214/521-6157** • 11am-10:30pm, till 11pm Fri-Sat, noon-10pm Sun • vegetarian • also yoga & meditation • live events • WiFi

Cremona Bistro 2704 Worthington St (at Howell) **214/871-1115** • lunch weekdays & dinner nightly • Italian • full bar • patio • live music

Dish 4123 Cedar Springs Rd #110 **214/522-3474** • dinner & Sun brunch • full bar • patio • live shows • wheelchair access

Dream Cafe 2800 Routh St (in the Quadrangle) **214/954-0486** • 7am-9pm, till 10pm Fri-Sat • plenty veggie • beer/ wine • WiFi • wheelchair access

Excuses Cafe 3025 Main St (in Deep Ellum) **214/741-1111** • 11am-2am, clsd Sun-Tue

Fitness Essentials 3818 Oak Lawn, Ste 100 (at Reagan St) **214/528-5535** • 9am-7pm, till 6pm Sat, from noon Sun • organic • plenty veggie • wheelchair access • gay-owned

Hattie's 418 N Bishop Ave **214/942-7400** • lunch daily, dinner Tue-Sun • Southern • wheelchair access

Hibiscus 2927 N Henderson Ave **214/827-2927** • dinner only, clsd Sun • steak & seafood • wheelchair access

Hunky's 3940 Cedar Springs Rd (at Reagan) **214/522-1212** • 11am-10pm, till 11pm Sat, from noon Sun • popular • burgers & salads • beer/ wine • patio • wheelchair access • gay-owned

Lucky's Cafe 3531 Oak Lawn **214/522-3500** • 7am-10pm • classic comfort food • great brkfst • wheelchair access

Monica Aca y Alla 2914 Main St (at Malcolm X) **214/748-7140** • lunch Mon-Fri, dinner Tue-Sun, brunch wknds • popular • contemporary Mexican • full bar • live music wknds • Latin jazz/ salsa • transgender-friendly • wheelchair access

Naga Kitchen & Bar 665 High Market St (Victory Park) **214/953-0023** • lunch Mon-Fri, dinner nightly • Authentic Thai

Patio Grill & Bar 3403 McKinney Ave **214/720-3838** • 4pm-2am, from 11am Sat-Sun

Stephan Pyles 1807 Ross Ave, Ste 200 **214/580-7000** • lunch Mon-Fri, dinner Mon-Sat, clsd Sun • Southwestern cuisine

Taco Joint 911 N Peak St **214/826-8226** • 6:30am-2pm, from 8am Sat, clsd Sun • wheelchair access

Thai Soon 101 S Coit, Ste 401 (at Belt Line) **972/234-6111** • lunch & dinner • wheelchair access

Ziziki's 4514 Travis St, #122 (in Travis Walk) **214/521-2233** • 11am-10pm, Sun brunch • Greek & Italian • full bar • wheelchair access

ENTERTAINMENT & RECREATION

Assassination City Derby 1438 Coliseum Dr • Dallas' female roller derby league • visit www.acderby.com for events

The Women's Museum 3800 Parry Ave **214/915-0860, 888/337-1167** • noon-5pm, clsd Mon

RETAIL SHOPS

Obscurities 4008 Cedar Springs **214/559-3706** • 11am-9pm, 2pm-8pm Sun, clsd Mon • tattoo & piercing

Tapelenders 3926 Cedar Springs Rd (at Throckmorton) **214/528-6344** • 9am-midnight • LGBT gifts • gay-owned

PUBLICATIONS

Dallas Voice **214/754-8710** • LGBT newspaper

EROTICA

Alternatives 1720 W Mockingbird Ln (at Hawes) **214/630-7071** • 24hrs

Leather Masters 3000 Main St **214/528-3865** • noon-10pm, clsd Sun-Mon • handmade leather clothes • rubber/ fetishwear

Denison

BARS

Good Time Lounge 2520 Hwy 91 N **903/463-6086** • 7pm-2am Wed-Sun • lesbians/ gay men • karaoke Th & Sun • drag shows • private club

Denton

NIGHTCLUBS

Mable Peabody's Beauty Parlor & Chainsaw Repair 1125 E University Dr **940/566-9910** • 4pm-2am • lesbians/ gay men • dancing/DJ • live shows • karaoke • drag shows • wheelchair access • lesbian-owned

El Paso

see also Ciudad Juárez, Mexico

BARS

Briar Patch 508 N Stanton St (at Missouri) **915/577-9555** • noon-2am • lesbians/ gay men • neighborhood bar • karaoke • patio

Chiquita's Bar 310 E Missouri Ave (at Stanton) **915/351-0095** • 2pm-2am • lesbians/ gay men • neighborhood bar • mostly Latino/a • wheelchair access

Ms Lips Lounge 510 N Stanton St (at Missouri) • mostly women • live bands

The Whatever Lounge 701 E Paisano Dr (at Ochoa) **915/533-0215** • 2pm-2am • lesbians/ gay men • dancing/DJ • karaoke • mostly Latino/a • drag shows • wheelchair access

NIGHTCLUBS

The New Old Plantation 301 S Ochoa St (at Paisano) **915/533-6055** • 9pm-2am, till 4am Fri-Sat • popular • lesbians/ gay men • dancing/DJ • drag shows Sun • videos • wheelchair access • also Generation Q II pride store upstairs

San Antonio Mining Co 800 E San Antonio Ave (at Ochoa) 915/533-9516 • 3pm-2am • popular • lesbians/ gay men • dancing/DJ • drag shows • videos • patio • wheelchair access

RESTAURANTS

The Little Diner 7209 7th St, Canutillo 915/877-2176 • 11am-8pm, clsd Wed • true Texas fare • beer/wine • wheelchair access

Fort Worth

see also Arlington & Dallas

INFO LINES & SERVICES

Tarrant County Lesbian/ Gay Alliance 817/877-5544 • info line • newsletter

ACCOMMODATIONS

Hotel Trinity InnSuites Hotel 2000 Beach St 817/534-4801, 800/989-3556 • gay-friendly • pool • nonsmoking • kids/ pets ok • WiFi • wheelchair access • $80-159

BARS

Best Friends Club 2620 E Lancaster Ave 817/534-2280 • 3pm-2am, clsd Mon • lesbians/ gay men • neighborhood bar • dancing/DJ • food served • karaoke

Crossroads 515 S Jennings Ave (at Pennsylvania) 817/332-0071 • 11am-2am, from noon Sun • mostly gay men • neighborhood bar

NIGHTCLUBS

Rainbow Lounge 651 S Jennings Ave (at Pennsylvania) 817/870-2466 • 9am-2am • mostly gay men • dancing/DJ • drag shows • theme nights • wheelchair access

ENTERTAINMENT & RECREATION

National Cowgirl Museum 1720 Gendy St 817/336-4475, 800/476-3263

Galveston

ACCOMMODATIONS

Cottage by the Gulf 810 Ave L (at Seawall & 8th) 409/770-9332 • gay-friendly • 6 private rental homes • pets ok • wheelchair access • gay-owned • $90-170+

Hotel Galvez 2024 Seawall Blvd 409/765-7721, 877/999-3223 • gay-friendly • nonsmoking • WiFi • kids ok • wheelchair access • $120-300

Lost Bayou Guesthouse B&B 1607 Ave L (at 16th) 409/770-0688 • gay/ straight • 1890 Victorian home survived hurricane of 1900 • nonsmoking • kids ok • WiFi • gay-owned • $130-205

Oasis Beach Cottage 713/256-3000 • gay-friendly • on the Gulf of Mexico • kids ok • nonsmoking • gay-owned • $125-175 & $750-950/ week

BARS

3rd Coast Beach Bar 2416 Post Office St 409/765-6911 • 4pm-2am, from 2pm wknds • mostly gay men • drag shows • male dancers • deck

Pink Dolphin 1706 23rd St (at O Ave) 409/621-1808 • 10am-2am • mostly gay men • drag shows • karaoke • BYOB

Robert's Lafitte 2501 Q Ave (at 25th St) 409/765-9092 • 7am-2am, from 10am Sun • mostly gay men • drag shows wknds • patio • wheelchair access

Stars Beach Club 3102 Seawall Blvd 409/497-4113 • noon-2am • lesbians/gay men, more women Th • dancing/DJ • karaoke • drag shows

CAFES

Mod Coffee & Tea House 2126 Post Office St (at 22nd) 409/765-5659 • 7am-10pm • live shows• also art gallery • beer/wine • WiFi

RESTAURANTS

Eat Cetera 408 25th St 409/762-0803 • 11am-7pm, clsd Sun • beer/wine • wheelchair acccess

Luigi's 2328 The Strand (at Tremont) 409/763-6500 • 11am-9pm, till 4pm Sun

Mosquito Cafe 628 14th St (at Winnie) 409/763-1010 • 11am-9pm, 8am-9pm Sat, till 3pm Sun, clsd Mon • some veggie • wheelchair access

The Spot 3204 Seawall Blvd (at 32nd St) 409/621-5237 • good burgers, great view • also Tiki Bar • wheelchair access

Star Drug Store 510 23rd St 409/766-7719 • 9am-4pm • old-fashioned drug store & soda fountain • wheelchair access

Groesbeck

ACCOMMODATIONS

Rainbow Ranch Campground 1662 LCR 800 254/729-8484, 888/875-7596 • lesbians/ gay men • on Lake Limestone • pool • campsites • cabins • nonsmoking • gay-owned • $20-200

Gun Barrel City

BARS

Friends 410 S Gun Barrel Lane **903/887–2061**
• 4pm-midnight, from 3pm wknds, till 1am Sat
• lesbians/ gay men • neighborhood bar •
food served • private club • wheelchair access

Houston

INFO LINES & SERVICES

Gay & Lesbian Switchboard Houston
713/529–3211 • 24hr crisis hotline

Houston GLBT Community Center 1900
Kane St (in Historic Dow School)
713/524–3818 • noon-9pm

Lambda AA Center 1201 W Clay (btwn
Montrose & Waugh) **713/521–1243** •
wheelchair access

ACCOMMODATIONS

Alden Hotel 1117 Prairie St (at Fannin)
832/200–8800, 877/813–1888 • gay-friendly •
boutique hotel • dogs ok • also • WiFi

Hotel Derek 2525 W Loop S (at
Westheimer) **713/961–3000** • gay-friendly •
modern, chic hotel

Hotel Sorella 800 W Sam Houston Pkwy N
713/973–1600 • gay-friendly • $109+

The Houstonian 111 N Post Oak Ln (near
Woodway Dr) **713/680–2626, 800/231–2759** •
gay-friendly • urban resort

Robin's Nest B&B Inn 4104 Greeley St
713/528–5821, 800/622–8343 • gay-friendly •
Montrose Museum District • WiFi • $89-240

Sycamore Heights B&B 245 W 18th St
713/861–4117 • gay-friendly • circa 1905 •
garden • nonsmoking • WiFi • gay-owned •
$120

BARS

Bayou City Bar & Grill 2409 Grant St (at
Hyde Park Blvd) **713/522–2867** • 4pm-2am,
clsd Mon • lesbians/ gay men • food served •
more women Wed

Beer Island 2631 White Oak Dr (at
Studewood) **713/862–4670** • 3pm-2am • gay-
friendly • beer/wine • dog-friendly • gay-
owned • wheelchair access

Blur 710 Pacific St (at Crocker) **713/529–3447**
• 10pm-2am, clsd Mon-Tue • lesbians/ gay
men • dancing/DJ • 18+

Boom Boom Room 2518 Yale St
713/868–3740 • 4pm-2am, clsd Sun-Mon •
gay-friendly • wine & panini bar

Brazos River Bottom (BRB) 2400 Brazos
(at McIlhenny) **713/528–9192** • noon-2am •
popular • mostly gay men • dancing/DJ •
country/ western • drag shows • WiFi

Club 2020 2020 Leeland **713/227–9667** •
10pm-4am Sat • lesbians/ gay men •
dancing/DJ • mostly African American • hip
hop • 18+

Club Evo 2707 Milam **281/554–3336** • 4pm-
2am, clsd Mon • mostly woman • dancing/DJ

Crocker 2312 Crocker St **713/529–3355** •
11am-2am • mostly gay men • neighborhood
bar • karaoke • WiFi

EJ's 2517 Ralph (at Westheimer)
713/527–9071 • 7am-2am, from 10am Sun •
mostly gay men (women's bar upstairs) •
dancing/DJ • live shows

Guava Lamp 570 Waugh Dr **713/524–3359** •
4pm-2am, from 2pm Sun • lesbians/ gay men
• karaoke • WiFi • wheelchair access

In & Out 1537 N Shepherd (at 16th St)
713/589–9780 • 4pm-2am • lesbians/ gay
men

JR's 808 Pacific (at Grant) **713/521–2519** •
noon-2am • popular • mostly gay men •
karaoke • drag shows • videos • patio •
wheelchair access

Meteor 2306 Genesee St (at Fairview)
713/521–0123 • 4pm-2am • mostly gay men •
professional crowd • wheelchair access • gay-
owned

Michael's Outpost 1419 Richmond (at
Mandell) **713/520–8446** • 3pm-2am, from
noon wknds • mostly gay men •
neighborhood bar • piano • live entertainment
• older crowd

TC's 817 Fairview (at Converse) **713/526–2625**
• 8am-2am, from 10am Sun • lesbians/ gay
men • neighborhood bar • karaoke • drag
shows • transgender-friendly

Tony's Corner Pocket 817 W Dallas (btwn
Arthur & Crosby) **713/571–7870** • noon-2am
• lesbians/ gay men • neighborhood bar •
karaoke • male dancers • large deck • WiFi

The Usual Pub 5519 Allen St **281/501–1478**
• 4pm-2am, from 2pm wknds, from 6pm Mon-
Tue • gay/ straight (more women Wed) •
neighborhood bar • karaoke • live music •
lesbian-owned

Whispers 226 1st St E (off I-59), Humble
281/359–2900 • 4pm-2am, from 6pm Sat, clsd
Mon • lesbians/ gay men • dancing/DJ •
karaoke

NIGHTCLUBS

Crystal 59 Southwest Fwy (at Hillcroft) 713/278–2582 • 5pm-5am, clsd Mon-Tue • lesbians/gay men • Latina/o clientele

Crystal 6680 Southwest Fwy (at Colorado) 713/278–2582 • mostly gay men • dancing/DJ • Latino club • drag shows • theme nights

F Bar Houston 202 Tuam St 713/522–3227 • 5pm-2am, from 8pm Sat, 3pm Sun, clsd Mon • lesbians/ gay men, more women Wed for happy hour • dancing/DJ • karaoke • live shows

Numbers 300 Westheimer (at Taft) 713/526–6551 • gay-friendly • dancing/DJ • 80's Fri • also live music venue • video • young crowd

Ranch Hill Saloon 24704 I-45 N, Spring 281/298–9035 • 1pm-2am • lesbians/ gay men • neighborhood bar • dancing/DJ • country/ western • drag shows • karaoke • wheelchair access • lesbian-owned

Signature Lounge 5959 Richmond Ave 713/636–2087 • 9pm-2am, till 3am Fri-Sun, till 5am Sat, clsd Mon-Wed • lesbians/gay men • dancing/DJ

South Beach Nightclub 810 Pacific 713/521–0107, 713/529–7623 • 9pm-5am, clsd Mon-Wed • mostly gay men • dancing/DJ • live shows

Throb • roving women's dance parties • check www.throbparties.info for details • mostly women • dancing/DJ • live shows

Vue 526 Waugh Dr 713/533–9333 • from 9pm Th-Sat • gay/straight • dancing/DJ

CAFES

Dirk's Coffee 4005 Montrose (btwn Richmond & W Alabama) 713/526–1319 • 6am-11pm, till midnight Fri-Sat, 7am-10pm Sun

Empire Cafe 1732 Westheimer Rd 713/528–5282 • 7:30am-10pm, till 11pm Fri-Sat • WiFi • wheelchair access

Java Java Cafe 911 W 11th (at Shepherd) 713/880–5282 • 7:30am-3pm, from 8:30am wknds • wheelchair access

The Path of Tea 2340 W Alabama St 713/252–4473 • 10am-9pm, till 11pm Fri-Sat, 1pm-6pm Sun • tea house • wheelchair access

RESTAURANTS

Aka 2390 W Alabama St 713/807–7875 • noon-11pm • sushi

Argentina Cafe 3055 Sage Rd (at Hidalgo St) 713/622–8877 • 9am-9pm, till 7pm Sun • wheelchair access

Baba Yega's 2607 Grant (at Pacific) 713/522–0042 • 11am-10pm, till 11pm Fri-Sat, from 10am Sun • plenty veggie • full bar • patio • wheelchair access

Barnaby's Cafe 604 Fairview (btwn Stanford & Hopkins St) 713/522–0106 • 11am-10pm, till 11pm Fri-Sat • popular • beer/ wine • wheelchair access • multiple locations

Beaver's 2310 Decatur (at Sawyer) 713/864–2328 • 11am-10pm, till 9pm Sun, clsd Mon • BBQ

Block 7 Wine Company 720 Shepherd Dr 713 /572–2565 • 11am-11pm, from 4pm Sun

Bocado's 1312 W Alabama 713/523–5230 • lunch & dinner, clsd Sun-Mon • Mexican • gay/ straight • full bar • more women Wed for dancing/DJ

Brasil 2604 Dunlavy (at Westheimer) 713/528–1993 • 7:30am-midnight • plenty veggie • beer/ wine • wheelchair access

Chapultepec 813 Richmond (btwn Montrose & Main) 713/522–2365 • 24hrs • Mexican • full bar • wheelchair access

El Tiempo Cantina 1308 Montrose Blvd 713/807–8996 • 11am-10pm, till 10pm Wed-Th, till 11pm Fri-Sat • Mexican seafood • wheelchair access

House of Pies 3112 Kirby Dr (btwn Richmond & Alabama) 713/528–3816 • 24hrs • popular • wheelchair access

Hugo's 1600 Westheimer Rd (at Mandell) 713/524–7744 • lunch & dinner • Mexican • popular brunch • wheelchair access

Julia's Bistro 3722 Main St (at W Alabama) 713/807–0090 • lunch Mon-Fri, dinner Mon-Sat, clsd Sun • Mexican • wheelchair access

Kelley's Country Cookin' 8015 Park Pl (at Gulf Fwy) 713/645–6428 • 6am-10pm • great brkfst • wheelchair access

Mark's American Cuisine 1658 Westheimer Rd 713/523–3800 • lunch Mon-Fri, dinner nightly • located in renovated 1920s church • wheelchair access

Mo Mong 1201 Westheimer #B (at Montrose) 713/524–5664 • 11am-10pm, clsd Sun • Vietnamese • full bar

Ninfa's 2704 Navigation Blvd (at N Delano St) 713/228–1175 • 11am-11pm • popular • Mexican • some veggie • full bar

Ruggles Green 2311 W Alabama 713/533-0777 • 11am-10pm • organic & all-natural American

Tafia 3701 Travis St 713/524-6922 • dinner Tue-Sat • Mediterranean • also bar • patio • wheelchair access • lesbian-owned

ENTERTAINMENT & RECREATION

After Hours KPFT 90.1 FM (also 89.5 Galveston) 713/526-4000, 713/526-5738 (REQUEST LINE) • 1am-4am Sat • LGBT radio

Beer Can House 222 Malone St 713/926-6368 • noon-5pm Sat-Sun only • 50,000+ beer cans cover the building!

DiverseWorks Art Space 1117 East Fwy (I-10 at N Main) 713/223-8346, 713/335-3443 • gallery noon-6pm, clsd Sun

Houston Roller Derby • Houston's female roller derby league • visit ww.houstonrollerderby.com for events

Orange Show Center for Visionary Art 2402 Munger St 713/926-6368 • performance, music, public art • produces annual Art Car Parade

RETAIL SHOPS

The Chocolate Bar 1835 W Alabama St 713/520-8599 • chocolate gifts & yummy desserts

Hollywood Super Center 2409 Grant St (at Crocker St) 713/527-8510 • 10am-1am, till 3am Fri-Sat • gifts • T-shirts • novelties

PUBLICATIONS

abOUT Magazine PO Box 130948, 713/396-2688

Houston

WHERE THE GIRLS ARE:
Strolling the Montrose district near the intersection of Montrose and Westheimer or out on Buffalo Speedway at the Plaza.

LGBT PRIDE:
June. 713/529-6979, web: www.pridehouston.org.

ANNUAL EVENTS:
March - AIDS Walk 713/403-9255, web: www.aidswalkhouston.org.
Easter weekend - Jungle, web: www.junglehouston.com. Dance party benefiting HIV/AIDS education, research & care.
Sept - Q Fest LGBT Film Festival, web: www.q-fest.org.

CITY INFO:
713/437-5200, web: www.visithoustontexas.com.

BEST VIEW:
JP Morgan Chase Tower, web: www.chasetower.com.

WEATHER:
Humid all year round—you're not that far from the Gulf. Mild winters, although there are a few days when the temperatures drop into the 30°s. Winter also brings occasional rainy days. Summers are very hot.

TRANSIT:
Yellow Cab 713/236-1111.
Metropolitan Transit Authority 713/635-4000, web: www.ridemetro.org.

ATTRACTIONS:
Contemporary Arts Museum 713/284-8250, web: www.camh.org.
The Galleria, 713/622-0663, web: www.galleriahouston.com.
The Menil Collection 713/525-9400, web: www.menil.org.
Museum of Fine Arts 713/639-7300, web: www.mfah.org.
Rothko Chapel 713/524-9839, web: www.rothkochapel.org.
San Jacinto Monument 281/479-2421, web: www.sanjacinto-museum.org.
SplashTown 281/355-3300, web: www.splashtownpark.com.

OutSmart 713/520–7237 • monthly LGBT newsmagazine

GYMS & HEALTH CLUBS

Houston Gym 1501 Durham Rd (at Washington & Eigel) 713/880-9191 • 5am-10pm, 8am-8pm wknds • gay-owned

YMCA Downtown 808 Pease 713/659-8501 • 5am-10pm, till 6pm Sat & 5pm Sun • pool

EROTICA

Eros 1207 1207 Spencer Hwy (at Allen Genoa) 713/910-0220 • gay-owned

Loveworks 25170 I-45 N, Spring 281/292-0070

Laredo

NIGHTCLUBS

Club 311 1310 Iturbide (at Salinas) 956/366-8426 • lesbians/ gay men • dancing/DJ

Lockhart

ACCOMMODATIONS

Lazy J Paradise Campground & Park 270 Hidden Path (CR 303 and FM 2001) 210/863-9314 • campground with RV area catering to the GLBT community • pool • WiFi • $7-30

Longview

BARS

Decisions 2103 E Marshall (2 blocks E of Eastman Rd) 903/757-4884 • 5pm-2am • lesbians/ gay men • dancing/DJ • country/ western • karaoke • drag shows • wheelchair access

Lubbock

INFO LINES & SERVICES

AA Lambda 4501 University Ave (at MCC) 806/792-5562 • 8pm Fri

ACCOMMODATIONS

LaQuinta Inns & Suites North 5006 Auburn St (at Winston) 806/749-1600 • gay-friendly • pool • pets ok • gym • nonsmoking • WiFi • wheelchair access • gay-owned

NIGHTCLUBS

Club Luxor 2211 4th St 806/744-3744 • 9pm-2am Fri-Sun • gay/ straight • more gay Fri & Sun • dancing/DJ • karaoke • drag shows • wheelchair access

Heaven Nightclub 1928 Buddy Holly Ave (at I-27) 806/762-4466 • Th-Sun • gay-friendly • dancing/DJ • multiracial • drag shows • 18+ • young crowd

Marfa

ACCOMMODATIONS

El Cosmico Hwy 67 432/729-1950, 877/822-1950 • gay/straight • vintage trailer, yurt & teepee hotel & campground • WiFi • lesbian-owned • $20-150

McAllen

see Rio Grande Valley

Rio Grande Valley

BARS

PBD's 2908 N Ware Rd (at Daffodil), McAllen 956/682-8019 • 8pm-2am, clsd Mon • mostly gay men • dancing/DJ Th-Sat • drag shows • wheelchair access

NIGHTCLUBS

Club 33 3300 N McColl Rd, McAllen 956/627-3312 • 9pm-3am Fri-Sat only • lesbians/gay men • dancing/DJ • drag shows

San Antonio

INFO LINES & SERVICES

Lambda AA 319 Camden Rm #4 (Madison Square Presbyterian Church) 210/979-5939 • 8:15pm daily

ACCOMMODATIONS

1908 Ayres Inn 124 W Woodlawn Ave (at N Main) 210/736-4232 • gay/ straight • nonsmoking • WiFi • wheelchair access • gay-owned • $125-145

Arbor House Suites B&B 109 Arciniega (btwn S Alamo & S St Mary's) 210/472-2005, 888/272-6700 • gay/ straight • kids/ pets ok • hot tub • nonsmoking • wheelchair access • gay-owned • $110-179

Brackenridge House 230 Madison (at Beauregard) 210/271-3442, 877/271-3442 • gay-friendly • B&B in historic King William district • pool • hot tub • WiFi • $120+

Emily Morgan Hotel 705 E Houston St (at Ave E) 210/225-5100, 800/824-6674 • gay-friendly • gym • pets ok • retaurant & bar • WiFi

The Westin Riverwalk 420 W Market St 210/224-6500, 800/937-8461 • gay-friendly • pool • wheelchair access

Bars

2015 Place 2015 San Pedro (at Woodlawn) 210/733–3365 • 4pm-2am • mostly gay men • neighborhood bar • patio • karaoke Wed

The Annex 330 San Pedro Ave (at Euclid) 210/223–6957 • 2pm-2am • mostly gay men • neighborhood bar • wheelchair access

Bermuda Triangle 10127 Coachlight Dr (at San Pedro) 210/342–2276 • 8pm-3am Wed-Sat • mostly women • neighborhood bar • dancing/DJ • live shows • karaoke • wheelchair access

The Boss 1006 VFW Blvd (Jeffersonville) 210/550–2322 • 8pm-2am • mostly gay men • neighborhood dive bar

Electric Company 820 San Pedro Ave (at W Laurel) 210/212–6635 • 9pm-3am, clsd Mon • lesbians/gay men, more women Wed & Sun • dancing/DJ • live shows • 18+

Essence 1010 N Main Ave (at E Euclid) 210/223–5418 • 2pm-2am • mostly gay men • neighborhood bar • karaoke

The Flying Saucer 11255 Huebner Rd #212 (at I-10) 210/696–5080 • 11am-1am, till 2am Th-Sat, noon-midnight Sun • gay-friendly • large beer selection

Lava Lounge 2702 N St Mary's St (at French Pl) 210/320–1740 • open Wed-Sun • gay/ straight • dancing/DJ • mostly Latino/a • dive bar

Mix 2423 N St Marys St 210/735–1313 • 5pm-2am, from 7:30 Sat-Sun • gay-friendly dive bar • live music

One-Oh-Six Off Broadway 106 Pershing St (at Broadway) 210/820–0906 • noon-2am • lesbians/ gay men • neighborhood bar

Silver Dollar Saloon 1818 N Main Ave (at Dewey) 210/227–2623 • 4pm-2am • lesbians/ gay men • dancing/DJ • country/ western • karaoke

Sparky's Pub 1416 N Main Ave (at Evergreen) 210/320–5111 • 3pm-2am • pub atmosphere

Nightclubs

The Bonham Exchange 411 Bonham St (at 3rd/ Houston) 210/271–3811 • 4pm-2am, 9pm-4am Fri-Sat • popular • in 120-year-old mansion • lesbians/ gay men • dancing/DJ • videos • 18+ • gay-owned

Club Venom 2407 N St Mary's St (at Ashby) 210/738–8180 • 8pm-2am • mostly gay men • dancing/DJ • live music • drag shows • karaoke

San Antonio

Where the Girls Are:
Coupled up in the suburbs.or carousing downtown.

LGBT Pride:
June. web: www.alamopridefest.org.

Annual Events:
Late April - Fiesta San Antonio 877/723–4378, web: www.fiesta-sa.org.

City Info:
800/447-3372, web: www.visit-sanantonio.com.

Best View:
High in the Sky Lounge in the Tower of the Americas.

Weather:
60°s-90°s in the summer, 40°s-60°s in the winter.

Attractions:
The Alamo 210/225-1391, web: www.thealamo.org.
El Mercado.
Hemisfair Park.
The Majestic Theatre 210/226-5700, web: www.majesticempire.com.
McNay Art Museum 210/824-5368, web: www.mcnayart.org.
Plaza de Armas.
River Walk.
San Antonio Museum of Art 210/978-8100, web: www.samuseum.org.

Transit:
Yellow-Checker 210/222-2222.
Via Info 210/362-2020, web: www.viainfo.net.

The Industry 8021 Pinebrook Dr (at Callaghan) **210/366–3229** • 9pm-2am Th-Sat • gay/ straight • dancing/DJ

SA Hot Lezbian **210/777–8127** • mostly women • dancing/DJ • check www.myspace.com/sahotlez for events

The Saint 1430 N Main (at Evergreen) **210/225–7330** • 4pm-3am • mostly gay men • dancing/DJ • drag shows • 18+

Woody's 800 Lexington Ave **210/223–8300** • mostly gay men • drag shows

CAFES

Candlelight Coffeehouse & Wine Bar 3011 N St Mary's (at Rte 281) **210/738–0099** • 2pm-midnight, wknd brunch 10am-2pm, clsd Mon • live music • WiFi • wheelchair access

RESTAURANTS

Chacho's 7870 Callaghan Rd (at I-10) **210/366–2023** • 24hrs • Mexican • live bands • karaoke • wheelchair access

Cool Cafe 12651 Vance Jackson **210/8775/5/20115001** • brkfst, lunch & dinner • Mediterranean

Giovanni's Pizza & Italian Restaurant 913 S Brazos (at Guadalupe) **210/212–6626** • 11am-7pm • some veggie

Guenther House 129 E Guenther (at S Alamo St) **210/227–1061** • 7am-3pm • located in restored Pioneer Flour Mills founding family home

Lulu's Bakery & Cafe 918 N Main (at W Elmira) **210/222–9422** • 24hrs • Tex-Mex • wheelchair access

Luther's Cafe 1425 N Main Ave (at Evergreen) **210/223–7727** • 11am-3am • great burgers • wheelchair access • gay-owned

Madhatter's Tea House 320 Beauregard **210/212–4832** • 8am-9pm, till 3pm Sun • BYOB • patio • WiFi • wheelchair access

El Mirador 722 S St Mary's St (at Durango Blvd) **210/225–9444** • 6:30am-9pm, till 2pm Sun & 3pm Mon • Tex-Mex • plenty veggie • beer/ wine • patio • wheelchair access

San Antone Cafe 1150 S Alamo (at E Johnson St) **210/271–7791** • 11am-11pm, till midnight wknds, clsd Sun -Mon • live music

Taco Taco Cafe 145 E Hildebrand **210/822–9533** • 7am-2pm

WD Deli 3123 Broadway St **210/828–2322** • 10:30am-5pm, till 4pm Sat, clsd Sun

ENTERTAINMENT & RECREATION

Alamo City Rollergirls 223 Recoleta Rd (at the Rollercade) • San Antonio's female flat track roller derby league • visit www.alamocityrollergirls.com for events

First Friday Art Walk S Alamo St (at S St Mary's St) • 6pm-10pm 1st Fri only • stroll the Southtown arts district

RETAIL SHOPS

On Main/ Off Main 120 W Mistletoe Ave **210/737–2323** • 10am-6pm, till 5pm Sat, clsd Sun • gifts • cards • T-shirts

ZEBRAZ.com 1608 N Main Ave (at E Park Ave) **210/472–2800, 800/788–4729** • 9am-midnight, till 10pm Sun-Tue • LGBT dept store

PUBLICATIONS

Ignite SA • LGBT publication for San Antonio • igniteisonline.com

EROTICA

Dreamers 2376 Austin Hwy (at Walzem) **210/653–3538** • 24hrs

Tyler

ACCOMMODATIONS

Cross Timber Ranch B&B 6271 FM 858 (at Hwy 64), Ben Wheeler **903/833–9000, 877/833–9002** • gay/ straight • full brkfst • nonsmoking • WiFi • gay-owned • $105-135

Waco

NIGHTCLUBS

Club Trix 110 S 6th St **254/714–0767** • 10pm-2am Th, 8pm-2am Fri-Sat • lesbians/ gay men • transgender-friendly • dancing/DJ • videos

CAFES

Cafe Vin 208 N Main St, West **254/826–3011** • 8am-10pm, till midnight Fri-Sat • live music • beer/wine • gay-owned

Wichita Falls

BARS

Krank It Karaoke Kafe 1400 N Scott Ave (at Old Iowa Park Rd) **940/761–9099** • 8:30pm-2am, from 7pm Fri-Sat, clsd Mon-Tue • gay-friendly • dancing/DJ • 18+ • wheelchair access

Odds 1205 Lamar St (at 12th) **940/322–2996** • 4pm-2am, from 3pm Sun • lesbians/ gay men • more women Th • neighborhood bar • dancing/DJ • karaoke • drag shows • 18+ • beer/ wine

Wimberley

ACCOMMODATIONS

Bella Vista 2121 Hilltop 512/847–6425 • gay/ straight • pool • nonsmoking • gay-owned • $125

UTAH

Bryce Canyon

ACCOMMODATIONS

Hatch Station 177 S Main, Hatch 435/735–4015 • gay-friendly • also restaurant, laundry & convenience store • safe oasis for LGBT travelers in S UT • WiFi • wheelchair access

The Red Brick Inn of Panguitch B&B 161 N 100 West (at 200 North), Panguitch 435/676–2141, 866/733–2745 • gay-friendly • full brkfst • kids ok • $99-199

CAFES

Scoops from the Past 105 N Main St, Panguitch 435/676–8885 • noon-10pm, till 11pm Fri-Sat, till 6pm Sun • retro ice cream parlor • WiFi

Holladay

RESTAURANTS

Loco Lizard Cantina 1612 Ute Blvd (in Kimball Jct Shopping Ctr) 435/645–7000 • 11am-10pm, till 11pm Fri-Sat, brunch wknds • Mexican • full bar • transgender-friendly • wheelchair access

Moab

ACCOMMODATIONS

Los Vados Canyon House 801/532–2651 • gay/ straight • retreat house in a red rock canyon • pool • kids 10 & over ok • nonsmoking • also tent cabin

Mayor's House B&B 505 Rose Tree Ln (at 400 E) 435/259–6015, 888/791–2345 • gay-friendly • full brkfst • pool • hot tub • kids ok • nonsmoking • WiFi • gay-owned

Mt Peale Resort Inn, Lodge & Cabins 1415 E Hwy 46 (at mile marker 14), Old La Sal 435/686–2284, 888/687–3253 • gay/ straight • B&B & cabins • hot tub • hiking • nonsmoking • WiFi • kids/ pets ok • lesbian-owned

Red Cliffs Lodge Hwy 128 (at mile marker 14) 435/259–2002, 866/812–2002 • gay-friendly • resort • on Colorado River • pool • hot tub • kids ok • nonsmoking • wheelchair access

Park City

ACCOMMODATIONS

ResortQuest Park City 435/649–6606, 877/496–6127 • gay-friendly • vacation rentals • pool • WiFi • nonsmoking

Salt Lake City

INFO LINES & SERVICES

Utah Pride Center 361 N 300 W, 1st flr 801/539–8800, 888/874–2743 • info • resource center • meetings • coffee shop • programs • youth activity center • much more

ACCOMMODATIONS

Anniversary Inn 460 S 1000 E (at 400) 801/363–4900, 800/324–4152 • gay-friendly • elaborate, kitschy theme rms • $139-319

High Aves Modern near 13th Ave & I St 801/355–3521 • gay/ straight • B&B in private home • nonsmoking • WiFi

Hotel Monaco Salt Lake City 15 W 200 S (at S Main) 801/595–0000, 877/294–9710 • gay-friendly • restaurant & bar • gym • kids/ pets ok • wheelchair access • $119-279

Parrish Place 720 E Ashton Ave (at 700 E) 801/832–0970, 855/832–0970 • gay/ straight • Victorian mansion • hot tub • nonsmoking • WiFi

Peery Hotel 110 W 300 S 801/521–4300, 800/331–0073 • popular • gay-friendly • full brkfst • kids ok • $20/ day for pets • also 2 restaurants • full bar • nonsmoking • WiFi • wheelchair access

Under the Lindens 128 S 1000 E (downtown) 801/355–9808 • mostly gay men • studios • hot tub • nonsmoking • WiFi • commitment ceremonies • mention Damron for discount • gay-owned

BARS

Jam 751 North 300 West (at Reed Ave) 801/891–1162 • 5pm-2am, clsd Sun-Mon • lesbians/ gay men • neighborhood bar • dancing/DJ • karaoke • beer only

Paper Moon 3737 S State St (at E 3750 S) 801/713–0678 • 3pm-1am, clsd Mon • mostly women • dancing/DJ • karaoke • live music • private club • food served • wheelchair access

The Tavernacle Social Club 201 E 300 South (at 200 E) 801/519–8900 • 5pm-close, from 8pm Sun-Mon • gay-friendly • food • karaoke • "Duelin' Pianos" • nonsmoking • private club

The Trapp 102 S 600 W (at 100 S) 801/531-8727 • 11am-2am • lesbians/ gay men • dancing/DJ • country/ western • food Sun • private club • wheelchair access

W Lounge 358 SW Temple 801/359-0637 • 8pm-2am • gay/ straight • dancing/DJ • nonsmoking • private club

NIGHTCLUBS

Area 51 451 South 400 West (at 400 S) 801/534-0819 • gay/ straight • dancing/DJ • 80s & goth theme nights Tue, Th & Sat

Pachanga 1051 East 2100 South (at Karamba) 801/637-9197 • 9pm Sun only • mostly gay men • gay Latin night • dancing/DJ

CAFES

Coffee Garden 878 E 900 S 801/355-3425 • 6am-11pm, till midnight Fri-Sat, 7am-11pm Sun • light fare • wheelchair access

RESTAURANTS

Bambara 202 S Main St 801/363-5454 • lunch Mon-Fri, brkfst & dinner daily • upscale American

Blue Plate Diner 2041 S 2100 E 801/463-1151 • 7am-9pm, till 10pm Fri-Sat

Cafe Med 420 E 3300 South 801/493-0100 • lunch & dinner • Mediterranean

Cafe Trio Downtown 680 S 900 E 801/533-8746 • 11am-10pm, Italian

Cedars of Lebanon 152 E 200 South (at State St) 801/364-4096 • lunch & dinner • Lebanese • veggie/ vegan-friendly • belly dancers wknds • WiFi

Citris Grill 2991 E 3300 South 801/466-1202 • 8am-10pm

Finn's 1624 S 1100 East (at Logan) 801/467-4000 • 7:30am-2:30pm

Fresco Italian Cafe 1513 S 1500 East 801/486-1300 • dinner nightly

Lamb's Grill Cafe 169 S Main St 801/364-7166 • 7am-9pm, from 8am Sat, clsd Sun • wheelchair access • live jazz wknds • "oldest restaurant in Utah"

Market St Grill 48 W Market St 801/322-4668 • brkfst & lunch Mon-Sat, dinner nightly, Sun brunch • seafood & steak • full bar • wheelchair access

The Metropolitan 173 W Broadway 801/364-3472 • lunch Mon-Fri, dinner nightly, clsd Sun • upscale New American • reservations recommended

The New Yorker 60 W Market St 801/363-0166 • lunch Mon-Fri, dinner nightly, clsd Sun • fine dining • steak

Salt Lake City

LGBT PRIDE:

June. 801/539-8800, web: www.utahpride.org.

ANNUAL EVENTS:

Jan-Feb - Gay/ Lesbian Ski Week 877/429-6368, web: www.gayskiing.org.

CITY INFO:

801/534-4900, web: www.visitsalt-lake.com.

WEATHER:

Home of "The Greatest Snow on Earth," the Wasatch Mtns get an average of 535 inches of powder, while the valley averages 59 inches. Spring is mild with an average of 62°, while summer temps average 88°, topping out at an average of 92° in July.

ATTRACTIONS:

Family History Library, one of the largest genealogical research databases in the country 801/240-2584, web: www.family-search.org.
Great Salt Lake.
Mormon Tabernacle Choir 801/240-4150, web: www.mormontabernaclechoir.org.
Skiing!
Temple Square.
Trolley Square.

TRANSIT:

Yellow Cab 801/521-2100.
Utah Transit Authority (UTA) 801/743-3882, web: www.utabus.com.

Nick-N-Willy's Pizza 4536 S Highland Dr **801/273-8282** • 11am-8pm, till 9pm wknds

Off Trax 259 W 900 S **801/364-4307** • 7am-7pm, till 3pm Fri, brunch Sun, also from 1am-3am Fri-Sat nights • lesbians/ gay men • WiFi • gay-owned

Omar's Rawtopia 2148 Highland Dr **801/486-0332** • noon-8pm, till 9pm Fri-Sat, clsd Sun • raw food

Red Iguana 736 W North Temple **801/322-1489** • popular • lunch & dinner • Mexican

Rio Grande Cafe 270 S Rio Grande St **801/364-3302** • lunch Mon-Sat & dinner nightly • popular • Mexican • some veggie • full bar • wheelchair access

Sage's Cafe 473 E 300 S **801/322-3790** • lunch & dinner, brkfst wknds • vegan/ vegetarian

Stoneground 249 E 400 South **801/364-1368** • 11am-11pm, 5pm-9pm Sun • pizza & more

Vertical Diner 2280 S West Temple **801/484-8378** • 10am-9pm • vegetarian diner • wheelchair access

ENTERTAINMENT & RECREATION

Lambda Hiking Club • hiking & other activities

Plan B Theatre Company 138 West 300 South (at Rose Wagner Performing Arts Center, btwn W Temple & 200 West) **801/355-2787** • at least one LGBT-themed production each season

Pygmalion Productions Theatre Company 138 W Broadway (at Rose Wagner Performing Arts Center) **801/355-2787, 888/451-2787** • a "feminine perspective" on theatre

Tower Theatre 876 E 900 South **801/321-0310** • alternative films • many LGBT movies

BOOKSTORES

Golden Braid Books 151 S 500 E **801/322-1162, 801/322-0404 (CAFE)** • 10am-9pm, till 6pm Sun • also Oasis Cafe, 8am-9pm, till 10pm wknds • gay/ straight • WiFi

Sam Weller's 254 S Main St **801/328-2586, 800/333-7269** • 10am-7pm Mon-Sat

RETAIL SHOPS

Cahoots 878 E 900 S (at 900 E) **801/538-0606** • 10am-9pm • unique gift shop • wheelchair access • gay-owned

Gypsy Moon Emporium 1011 E 900 S **801/521-9100** • call for hours • Celtic & goddess-oriented gifts

PUBLICATIONS

Q Salt Lake **801/649-6663, 800/806-7357** • bi-weekly LGBT newspaper

EROTICA

All For Love 3072 S Main St (at 33rd St S) **801/487-8358** • clsd Sun • lingerie & S/M boutique • transgender-friendly • wheelchair access

Blue Boutique Sugarhouse 1383 E 2100 South **801/485-2072** • also piercing

Mischievous 559 S 300 W (at 6th St S) **801/530-3100** • clsd Sun

Torrey

ACCOMMODATIONS

Capitol Reef Inn & Cafe 360 W Main St **435/425-3271** • gay-friendly • seasonal • hot tub • gift shop • $48-61 • also restaurant • plenty veggie • beer/ wine

Zion Nat'l Park

ACCOMMODATIONS

Canyon Vista Lodge B&B 2175 Zion Park Blvd (at Hwy 9), Springdale **435/772-3801** • gay-friendly • nonsmoking

Red Rock Inn 998 Zion Park Blvd, Springdale **435/772-3139** • gay/ straight • cottages w/ canyon views • full brkfst • hot tub • nonsmoking • wheelchair access • lesbian-owned

CAFES

Cafe Soleil 205 Zion Nat'l Park Blvd **435/772-0505** • 6am-8pm seasonal • lesbian-owned

VERMONT

Statewide

INFO LINES & SERVICES

Vermont Gay Tourism Association • Vermont's official organization to promote gay & lesbian travel throughout the state • see www.vermontgaytourism.com

Arlington

ACCOMMODATIONS

Arlington Inn 3904 Rte 7-A **802/375-6532, 800/443-9442** • country inn • kids ok • WiFi • nonsmoking • also restaurant & tavern • dinner from 5:30pm, clsd Mon • cont'l

Brattleboro

ACCOMMODATIONS

Nutmeg Inn 153 Rte 9 W, Wilmington
802/464-3907, 855/868-8634 • gay/straight •
WiFi • wheelchair access • gay-owned

RESTAURANTS

Peter Havens 32 Elliot St (at Main)
802/257-3333 • 6pm-10pm, clsd Sun-Mon •
cont'l • gay-owned

BOOKSTORES

Everyone's Books 25 Elliot St 802/254-8160
• 9:30am-6pm, till 8pm Fri, till 7pm Sat, 11am-
5pm Sun • wheelchair access

Bridgewater Corners

RESTAURANTS

Blanche & Bill's Pancake House 586 US
Rte 4 802/422-3816 • 7am-2pm Th-Mon,
dinner Tues • great flapjacks & maple syrup

Brookfield

RESTAURANTS

Ariel's Restaurant & Pond Village Pub 29
Stone Rd (at Rte 65) 802/276-3939 • dinner,
clsd Sun-Tue • eclectic • overlooking Sunset
Lake

Burlington

INFO LINES & SERVICES

R.U.1.2? Community Center The
Champlain Mill, 20 Winooski Falls Way #102,
Winooski 802/860-RU12 (7812) • drop-in &
cybercenter • advocacy & support • events

ACCOMMODATIONS

The Black Bear Inn 4010 Bolton Access Rd,
Bolton Valley 802/434-2126, 800/395-6335 •
gay/ straight • mtn-top inn • full brkfst • hot
tub • pool • kids/ pets ok • nonsmoking • WiFi

Hartwell House B&B Gallery 170
Ferguson Ave 802/658-9242, 888/658-9242 •
gay-friendly • pool • shared bath •
nonsmoking • woman-owned

The Inn at Essex 70 Essex Way, Essex
802/878-1100, 800/727-4295 • gay-friendly •
culinary resort • pool • kids/ pets ok • WiFi •
wheelchair access

One of a Kind B&B 53 Lakeview Terrace
802/862-5576, 877/479-2736 • nonsmoking •
2-rm suite & cottage • WiFi • woman-owned

NIGHTCLUBS

Metronome/ Nectar's 188 Main St
802/658-4771, 802/865-4563 • gay-friendly •
popular 80s night Sat • live bands • also
restaurant

CAFES

Muddy Waters 184 Main St 802/658-0466 •
7:30am-11pm, till midnight Fri-Sat, till 10pm
Sun • coffeehouse • also beer • try the white
hot chocolate

Radio Bean Coffeehouse 8 N Winooski
Ave (at Pearl) 802/660-9346 • 8am-midnight,
till 2am Th-Sat, 10am-11pm Sun • cool
bohemian coffeehouse • live bands & open
mic nights

RESTAURANTS

Bluebird Tavern 317 Riverside Ave
802/540-1786 • 4pm-10pm Th-Sat, 5pm-9pm
Tue-Wed, clsd Sun-Mon • locally grown •
beer/wine • wheelchair access

Daily Planet 15 Center St (at College)
802/862-9647 • 4pm-close, also bar till 2am •
plenty veggie

Loretta's 44 Park St (near 5 Corners), Essex
Junction 802/879-7777 • lunch weekdays,
dinner nightly, clsd Sun-Mon • Italian • plenty
veggie • lesbian-owned

Parima Thai 185 Pearl St (btwn Winooski &
Church) 802/864-7917 • dinner only • full bar
• courtyard garden • entertainment • WiFi

Shanty on the Shore 181 Battery St
802/864-0238 • 11am-10pm • seafood •
views of Lake Champlain

Silver Palace 1216 Williston Rd
802/864-0125 • 11:30am-9pm, till 10pm Fri-
Sat, 3pm-9pm Sun • Chinese • some veggie •
full bar

RETAIL SHOPS

Peace & Justice Store 60 Lake St (at
College St) 802/863-2345 • 9am-7pm, limited
hrs in winter • fair trade retail store

Chester

ACCOMMODATIONS

Chester House Inn 266 Main St
888/875-2205 • gay/ straight • full brkfst •
nonsmoking • kids ok • WiFi • wheelchair
access • gay-owned

Craftsbury Common

ACCOMMODATIONS

Greenhope Farm 2478 Wylie Hill Rd
802/586-7577 • gay/ straight • nonsmoking •
kids ok • WiFi • lesbian-owned

Greensboro

ACCOMMODATIONS

Highland Lodge 1608 Craftsbury Rd
802/533-2647 • gay-friendly • open May-Oct
& Dec-March • includes brkfst & dinner •
nonsmoking • WiFi • wheelchair access •
$138-550

Jay Peak

ACCOMMODATIONS

Four Seasons Apartments 2 10 Elm St (at
Main St), North Troy 802/578-7103 • gay/
straight • kids ok • nonsmoking • WiFi

Grey Gables Mansion 122 River St,
Richford 802/848-3625, 800/299-2117 • gay-
friendly • circa 1888 B&B inn • full brkfst • kids
ok • nonsmoking • WiFi

Phineas Swann B&B 802/326-4306 • gay/
straight • restored Victorian on Trout River •
full brkfst • nonsmoking • WiFi • gay-owned •
$99-289

Jeffersonville

ACCOMMODATIONS

Donomar Inn 916 Rte 108 S 802/644-2937 •
gay/ straight • full brkfst • hot tub • WiFi • gay-
owned • $75-175

Killington

ACCOMMODATIONS

Huntington House Inn 19 Huntington Pl,
Rochester 802/767-9140 • gay-friendly •
located on the park • restaurant & lounge •
WiFi • wheelchair access • gay-owned

Salt Ash Inn 4758 Rte 100A (at Rte 100),
Plymouth 802/672-3224 • gay/ straight •
1830s country inn • full brkfst • hot tub • food
served • pub • near skiing • kids/ small pets ok
• pool • WiFi • wheelchair access

RESTAURANTS

Grist Mill 200 Killington Rd (on Summit
Pond) 802/422-3970 • lunch & dinner • New
England fare • entertainment

Ludlow

ACCOMMODATIONS

Happy Trails Motel 321 Rte 103 S
802/228-8888, 800/228-9984 • gay-friendly •
rooms, suites & cottage • seasonal hot tub •
near skiing • nonsmoking • WiFi

RESTAURANTS

Downtown Grocery 41 Depot St
802/228-7566 • dinner only

Lyndonville

RESTAURANTS

Miss Lyndonville Diner 686 Broad
802/626-9890 • 6am-8pm, till 9pm Fri-Sat

Manchester

ACCOMMODATIONS

Hill Farm Inn 458 Hill Farm Rd (at Historic
Rte 7-A), Arlington 802/375-2269,
800/882-2545 • gay-friendly • full brkfst •
nonsmoking • WiFi

CAFES

Little Rooster Cafe Rte 7-A (at Hillvale Dr),
Manchester Center 802/362-3496 • 7am-
2:30pm, clsd Wed (winters)

RESTAURANTS

Bistro Henry 1942 Depot St (.5 mile E of Rte
7), Manchester Center 802/362-4982 • dinner
only, clsd Mon • Mediterranean • also bar •
reservations advised

Chanteeler Rte 7-A N, E Dorset
802/362-1616 • call for hours • seasonal

BOOKSTORES

Northshire Bookstore 4869 Main St,
Manchester Center 802/362-2200,
800/437-3700 • 10am-7pm, till 9pm Th-Sat

Marshfield

ACCOMMODATIONS

Marshfield Inn & Motel 5630 US Rte 2
802/426-3383 • gay-friendly • full brkfst • WiFi
• lesbian-owned

Montpelier

RESTAURANTS

Julio's 54 State 802/229-9348 • 11:30am-
11pm, till midnight Wed & Fri-Sat • Mexican

Sarducci's 3 Main St 802/223-0229 •
11:30am-9:30pm, from 4:30pm Sun • Italian •
some veggie • full bar • wheelchair access

Wayside Restaurant 1873 Rte 302 **802/223-6611** • 6:30am-9:30pm • wheelchair access

Plainfield

ACCOMMODATIONS

Comstock House 1620 Middle Rd **802/272-2693** • gay-friendly • overlooks Winooski River Valley • full brkfst • WiFi • gay-owned

Richmond

RESTAURANTS

The Kitchen Table Bistro 1840 W Main St **802/434-8686** • 5pm-9pm, clsd Sun-Mon • seasonal menu • local food

Rutland

ACCOMMODATIONS

The Inn of the Six Mountains 2617 Killington Rd, Killington **802/422-4302, 800/228-4676** • gay-friendly • hotel • pool • jacuzzi • WiFi • kids ok • wheelchair access

Lilac Inn 53 Park St, Brandon **802/247-5463, 800/221-0720** • full brkfst • teens/ pets ok • wheelchair access

Maplewood Inn 1108 S Main St (Rte 22-A), Fair Haven **802/265-8039, 800/253-7729** • gay/ straight • 1843 Greek Revival • full brkfst • beautiful antiques • centrally located • nonsmoking

Saxtons River

ACCOMMODATIONS

The Saxtons River Inn 27 Main St (at Academy Ave) **802/869-2110** • gay-friendly • historic Victorian inn • pub & restaurant • nonsmoking • WiFi • pets ok

Shelburne

RESTAURANTS

Barkeaters 97 Falls Rd (at Shelburne Shopping Park) **802/985-2830** • lunch & dinner, clsd Mon • local food

St Albans

RESTAURANTS

Jeff's 65 N Main St **802/524-6135** • lunch Mon, dinner Tue-Sat, clsd Sun • full bar

St Johnsbury

ACCOMMODATIONS

Comfort Inn & Suites 703 US Rte 5 S (at I-91) **802/748-1500, 800/424-6423** • gay-friendly • hotel • pool • hot tub • kids ok • WiFi • wheelchair access

Fairbanks Inn 401 Western Ave **802/748-5666** • gay-friendly • motel • pool • kids & pets ok • WiFi • wheelchair access • $90-190

➤ **Highlands Inn** Bethlehem, NH **603/869-3978, 877/LES-B-INN (537-2466)** • a lesbian paradise • "one of the most romantic lesbian destinations on the planet" (Planet Out) • 19 antique-filled rooms • full brkfst • outdoor & indoor spas • pool • 100 mtn acres • special events • concerts • VT civil union honeymoons • kids/ pets ok • non-smoking • WiFi • wheelchair access • ignore No Vacancy sign • lesbian-owned • $110-220 • see ad on page 1

RESTAURANTS

Elements 98 Mill St **802/748-8400** • dinner, clsd Sun-Mon • local food

Stowe

ACCOMMODATIONS

Arbor Inn 3214 Mountain Rd **802/253-4772, 800/543-1293** • gay/ straight • full brkfst • hot tub • pool • nonsmoking • WiFi

Fitch Hill Inn 258 Fitch Hill Rd, Hyde Park **802/888-3834, 800/639-2903** • gay/ straight • full brkfst • hot tub • older kids ok • WiFi • nonsmoking

The Green Mountain Inn 18 Main St **802/253-7301, 800/253-7302** • gay-friendly • kids ok • heated pool • hot tub • nonsmoking • WiFi • wheelchair access • 2 restaurants

Northern Lights Lodge 4441 Mountain Rd **802/253-8541, 800/448-4554** • gay-friendly • full brkfst • hot tub • pool • sauna • kids/pets ok • WiFi • gay-owned

The Old Stagecoach Inn 18 N Main St (at Stowe St), Waterbury **802/244-5056, 800/262-2206** • gay-friendly • historic village inn • full brkfst • kids/ pets ok • also full bar • nonsmoking

Timberholm Inn 452 Cottage Club Rd **802/253-7603, 800/753-7603** • gay/ straight • B&B • full brkfst • hot tub • nonsmoking

Townshend

ACCOMMODATIONS

Townshend State Park 2755 State Forest Rd 802/365-7500, 888/409-7579 • gay-friendly • campground • great hiking • open Memorial Day wknd to Labor Day wknd

Vergennes

RESTAURANTS

Basin Harbor Club 4800 Basin Harbor Rd 802/475-2311, 800/622-4000 • brkfst & dinner • eclectic New England fare • upscale

Waterbury

ACCOMMODATIONS

Grünberg Haus B&B & Cabins 94 Pine St, Rte 100 S 802/244-7726, 800/800-7760 • gay/straight • Austrian chalet • also cabins May-Oct • full brkfst • fireplace • nonsmoking • WiFi

Moose Meadow Lodge 607 Crossett Hill 802/244-5378 • gay/straight • full brkfst • nonsmoking • WiFi • gay-owned

RESTAURANTS

Cider House BBQ & Pub 1675 US Rte 2 802/244-8400 • lunch Fri-Sat, dinner nightly, clsd Mon • full bar • patio • gay-owned

West Dover

ACCOMMODATIONS

Deerhill Inn 14 Valley View Rd 802/464-3100, 800/993-3379 • gay/straight • inn • pool • teenagers ok • nonsmoking • WiFi • also restaurant

Inn at Mount Snow 401 Rte 100 802/464-8388, 866/587-7669 • gay-friendly • at foot of Mt Snow • near skiing • kids ok • nonsmoking • WiFi • gay-owned

The Inn at Sawmill Farm 7 Crosstown Rd (at Rte 100) 802/464-8131, 800/493-1133 • gay-friendly • kids/pets ok • nonsmoking • WiFi • wheelchair access

Red Oak Inn 45 Rte 100 (at Rte 9) 802/464-8817, 866/573-3625 • gay-friendly • pool • kids/pets ok • also tavern & gameroom • nonsmoking • WiFi

Windham

ACCOMMODATIONS

A Stone Wall Inn 578 Hitchcock Hill Rd 802/875-4238 • gay/straight • hot tub • WiFi • nonsmoking • gay-owned • $125-175

Woodstock

ACCOMMODATIONS

The Ardmore Inn 23 Pleasant St 802/457-3887, 800/497-9652 • gay-friendly • 1880s Greek Revival • full brkfst • jacuzzi • nonsmoking • WiFi • $130-230

Cabin in the Woods 1944 Chateauguay Rd, Bridgewater Corners 802/672-5141 • gay-friendly • hot tub • swimming hole • fireplace • smoking outdoors only • seasonal May-Oct • pets ok • transgender-owned/run • $225

Deer Brook Inn 4548 W Woodstock Rd 802/672-3713 • gay-friendly • B&B • full brkfst • kids ok • WiFi • gay-owned

Village Inn of Woodstock 41 Pleasant St 802/457-1255, 800/722-4571 • gay-friendly • restored Victorian Inn • full brkfst • WiFi • nonsmoking

VIRGINIA

Alexandria

see also Washington, District of Columbia

ACCOMMODATIONS

Crowne Plaza Old Town Alexandria 901 N Fairfax St 703/683-6000

Embassy Suites Alexandria 1900 Diagonal Rd 703/684-5900, 800/362-2779 • gay/straight • full brkfst • kids ok • pool

Holiday Inn Hotel & Suites 625 First St 703/548-6300

Hotel Monaco Alexandria 703/549-6080, 800/368-5047 • gay-friendly • restaurant on-site • kids/pets ok • wheelchair access • $220-679

Lorien Hotel & Spa 1600 King St 703/894-3434, 877/956-7436

Morrison House 116 S Alfred St 703/838-8000, 866/834-6628

Arlington

see also Washington, District of Columbia

INFO LINES & SERVICES

Arlington Gay/Lesbian Alliance • monthly meetings • outreach events • check website for schedule: www.agla.org

ACCOMMODATIONS

Hotel Palomar Arlington 1121 N 19th St 703/351-9170, 866/505-1001

Bars

Freddie's Beach Bar & Restaurant 555 S 23rd St **703/685–0555** • 11am-2am, from 4pm Mon, wknd brunch • lesbians/ gay men • karaoke • drag show • patio • live bands • food served • wheelchair access

Cafes

Java Shack 2507 N Franklin Rd (at Wilson Blvd & N Barton) **703/527–9556** • 7am-8pm, till 10pm Fri-Sat • lesbians/ gay men

Cape Charles

see also Norfolk & Virginia Beach

Accommodations

Cape Charles House B&B 645 Tazewell Ave (at Fig) **757/331–4920** • gay-friendly • 1912 colonial revival home filled w/ antiques • nonsmoking • $140-200

Sea Gate B&B 9 Tazewell Ave **757/331–2206** • gay-friendly • full brkfst • near beach on quiet, tree-lined street • WiFi • gay-owned • $130-140

Charlottesville

Accommodations

CampOut **804/301–3553** • women only • 100-acre rustic campground w/ 50 campsites • nonsmoking • wheelchair access • women-owned • $20-60 membership fee

The Inn at Court Square 410 E Jefferson St **434/295–2800, 866/466–2877** • gay-friendly • restored house w/ period antiques • jacuzzi • lunch served Mon-Fri • kids ok • nonsmoking • women-owned

Nightclubs

Club 216 216 W Water St (enter on South St) **434/296–8783** • 10pm-5am Fri-Sat, some Sun events popular • lesbians/ gay men • dancing/DJ • live shows • private club • wheelchair access

Restaurants

Escafe 227 W Main St (next to the Omni Hotel) **434/295–8668** • 5:30pm-11pm, 4:30pm-9:30pm Sun, clsd Mon • Asian/ American fusion • full bar • live music • gay-owned

Entertainment & Recreation

The Eclectic Woman WTJU 91.1 FM **434/924–3418** • 7pm Th • women's music show

Erotica

Pamela's Secrets 3051 S Main St, Harrisonburg **540/432–6403** • sex toys & videos

Sneak Reviews Video 2244 Ivy Rd **434/979–4420**

Chincoteague Island

Accommodations

1848 Island Manor House 4160 Main St (at Smith St) **757/336–5436, 800/852–1505** • gay/ straight • B&B • full brkfst • nonsmoking • WiFi

Hampton

see also Newport News

Cafes

The Java Junkies 768 Settlers Landing Rd **757/722–6300** • 7am-7pm, from 8am wknds, till 3pm Sun • food served

Harrisonburg

Cafes

Artful Dodger Coffeehouse 47 W Court Square **540/432–1179** • 8am-2am, noon-midnight Sun • DJ • entertainment • also bar • wheelchair access

Herndon

Nightclubs

So Addictive Lounge 733 Elden St (at Spring St) **703/481–0010** • 6pm-2am, from 10:30am Sun • mostly gay men • dancing/DJ • drag shows

Luray

see Shenandoah Valley

Newport News

see also Norfolk & Virginia Beach

Bars

Corner Pocket 6157 Jefferson Ave (at Mercury) **757/825–0440** • 5pm-2am • lesbians/ gay men • neighborhood bar • shows • food served till midnight • wheelchair access

Norfolk

see also Virginia Beach

INFO LINES & SERVICES

Hampton Roads Outreach Center
www.thehroc.org

ACCOMMODATIONS

B&B @ Historic Page House Inn 323 Fairfax Ave 757/625–5033, 800/599–7659 • gay-friendly • B&B in 1899 mansion • nonsmoking • WiFi • $145-230

Tazewell Hotel & Suites 245 Granby St (at Tazewell St) **757/623–6200** • gay-friendly • kids ok • WiFi • wheelchair access

BARS

The Garage 731 Granby St (at Brambleton) **757/623–0303** • 11am-2am, from noon wknds • popular • mostly gay men • neighborhood bar • food served • karaoke • wheelchair access

Hershee Bar 6117 Sewells Pt Rd (at Norview) **757/853–9842** • 4pm-2am • mostly women • dancing/DJ • live shows • food served • some veggie • Sun buffet • wheelchair access • woman-owned

The Wave 4107 Colley Ave (at 41st St) **757/440–5911** • 4pm-2am, from 5pm Sat, clsd Sun • lesbians/ gay men • dancing/DJ • live shows • also restaurant • dinner only • wheelchair access

CAFES

Oasis Cafe 142 W York St #101A (in York Center bldg) **757/627–6161** • 7:30am-3pm Mon-Fri • gay-owned

RESTAURANTS

Charlie's Cafe 1800 Granby St (at 18th) **757/625–0824** • 7am-2pm • some veggie • beer/ wine

Tortilla West 508 Oropax St **757/440–3777** • dinner only, Sun brunch, open till 1am • Mexican • plenty veggie/ vegan

Norfolk

LGBT PRIDE:
September. 757/624-6886, web: www.hamptonroadspride.com.

CITY INFO:
757/441-1852 or 800/368-3097, web: www.norfolkcvb.com.

TRANSIT:
Checker Cab 757/855-3333, web: www.norfolkcheckertaxi.com.
Norfolk Airport Shuttle 877/455-7462, web: www.norfolkairport-express.com.
Hampton Roads Transit 757/222–6100, web: www.hrtran-sit.org.

ATTRACTIONS:
Busch Gardens (in Williamsburg) 800/343-7946, web: www.buschgardens.com.
The Chrysler Museum of Art 757/664-6200, web: www.chrysler.org.
Douglas Macarthur Memorial 757/441-2965, web: www.macarthurmemorial.org.
The Ghent historic district.
Hermitage Foundation Museum 757/423-2052, web: www.hermitagefoundation.org.
Historic Williamsburg.
Norfolk Naval Base 757/322–2337, web: www.cnic.navy.mil/norfolk-sta/index.htm.
St Paul's Episcopal Church 757/627-4353, web: www.saint-paulsnorfolk.org.
Waterside Festival Marketplace 757/627-3300, web: www.water-sidemarketplace.com.

RETAIL SHOPS

Kindred Spirit 7510-C Granby St (at Wards Corner) **757/480-0424** • 10am-7pm, till 5pm Sat, from noon Sun • gifts • books • massage • readings & more

EROTICA

Leather & Lace 149 E Little Creek Rd (at Granby) **757/583-4334**

Petersburg

ACCOMMODATIONS

Walker House B&B 3280 S Crater Rd (at Wagner) **804/861-5822** • gay-friendly • antebellum farmhouse • full brkfst • nonsmoking • WiFi • kids ok • gay-owned

Richmond

INFO LINES & SERVICES

AA Gay/ Lesbian 1205 W Franklin (at St James Episcopal Church) **804/355-1212**

ACCOMMODATIONS

Omni Richmond Hotel 100 S 12th St (at Cary St) **804/344-7000, 800/843-6664** • gay-friendly • pool • views of city & James River • WiFi • wheelchair access

BARS

Babes of Carytown 3166 W Cary St (at Auburn) **804/355-9330** • 11am-2am, from noon Sat, from 9am Sun • lesbians/ gay men • dancing/DJ • country/ western • karaoke • drag shows • live music • food served • wheelchair access • women-owned

Barcode 6 E Grace St (btwn 1st & Foushee Sts) **804/648-2040** • 11am-2am, from 3pm wknds • mostly gay men • neighborhood bar • karaoke • videos • food served • some veggie • wheelchair access

Godfrey's 308 E Grace St (btwn 3rd & 4th) **804/648-3957** • 10pm-close, clsd Mon-Tue, brunch Sun • lesbians/ gay men • dancing/DJ • karaoke • drag shows

NIGHTCLUBS

Club Colours 536 N Harrison St (at Broad) **804/353-9776** • 9pm-3am Sat • lesbians/ gay men • dancing/DJ • multiracial • food served • live shows • wheelchair access

RESTAURANTS

Galaxy Diner 3109 W Cary St **804/213-0510** • 11am-midnight, till 2am wknds • some veggie • full bar

The Village 1001 W Grace **804/353-8204** • 8am-2am • American • plenty veggie

ENTERTAINMENT & RECREATION

Richmond Triangle Players 2033 W Broad St (at Fieldens Cabaret Theater) **804/346-8113** • alternative theater group

Venture Richmond 804/788-6466 • tour the James River • lots of shops, restaurants, etc

BOOKSTORES

Phoenix Rising 19 N Belmont Ave **804/355-7939, 800/719-1690** • 11am-7pm, clsd Tue • LGBT • wheelchair access

Roanoke

BARS

Backstreet Cafe 356 Salem Ave (off Jefferson) **540/345-1542** • 7pm-2am, clsd Sun-Mon • lesbians/ gay men • neighborhood bar • food served

Cuba Pete's 120 Church Ave SW (at First St SW, inside Macado's) **540/342-7231** • 11am-2am • gay-friendly • more gay wknds • also Macado's restaurant • karaoke • wheelchair access

NIGHTCLUBS

The Park 615 Salem Ave **540/342-0946** • 9pm-close Fri-Sun • popular • lesbians/ gay men • dancing/DJ • drag shows • videos • young crowd • wheelchair access

Shenandoah Valley

INFO LINES & SERVICES

SVGLA (Shenandoah Valley Gay/ Lesbian Assoc) 540/574-4636 • 24-hr touchtone info • weekly meetings • also dances & potlucks

ACCOMMODATIONS

Frog Hollow B&B 492 Greenhouse Rd (at Rte 11), Lexington **540/463-5444** • gay/ straight • full brkfst • hot tub • also cottage • gay-owned • $115-155

Mayneview B&B 439 Mechanic St, Luray **540/743-7921** • gay-friendly • full brkfst • Victorian w/ mountain views • near Luray Caverns, wineries & hiking • nonsmoking

The Olde Staunton Inn 260 N Lewis St, Staunton **540/886-0193, 866/653-3786** • gay/ straight • B&B • hot tub • WiFi • nonsmoking

Piney Hill B&B 1048 Piney Hill Rd (at Mill Creek Crossroads), Luray **540/778-5261, 800/644-5261** • gay/ straight • 1750s farmhouse in Shenandoah Valley • full brkfst • hot tub • gay-owned

White Fence B&B 275 Chapel Rd, Stanley **540/778–4680, 800/211–9885** • gay-friendly • 1890 Victorian w/ cottages • full brkfst • jacuzzi • nonsmoking • kids ok

Urbanna

ACCOMMODATIONS

Inn at Urbanna Creek **804/758–4661** • gay-friendly • 1870s home 2 hours from DC • full brkfst • jacuzzi • nonsmoking

Virginia Beach

see also Norfolk

ACCOMMODATIONS

Capes Ocean Resort Hotel 2001 Atlantic Ave (at 20th St) **757/428–5421, 800/456–5421** • gay-friendly • oceanfront rooms • private balconies • some jacuzzis • pool • nonsmoking • WiFi • kids ok • wheelchair access

BARS

Klub Ambush 475 S Lynnhaven Rd (at Lynnhaven Pkwy) **757/498–4301** • 5pm-2am • lesbians/ gay men • neighborhood bar • dancing/DJ • food served • shows • karaoke • gay-owned

Rainbow Cactus 3472 Holland Rd (at Diana Lee) **757/368–0441** • 7pm-2am, clsd Mon-Tue • mostly gay men • dancing/DJ • country/ western • drag shows • food served • wheelchair access

PUBLICATIONS

Lambda Directory **757/486–3546**

EROTICA

Nancy's Nook 1301 Oceana Blvd **757/428–1498** • 24hrs

Washington

ACCOMMODATIONS

Gay Street Inn 160 Gay St **540/316–9220** • gay-friendly • nonsmoking • WiFi • gay-owned

WASHINGTON

Bainbridge Island

BOOKSTORES

Eagle Harbor Book Co 157 Winslow Wy E **206/842–5332** • 9am-7pm, till 9pm Th, till 6pm Sat, 10am-6pm Sun

Bellevue

see Seattle

Bellingham

BARS

Rumors 1119 Railroad Ave (at Chestnut) **360/671–1849** • 4pm-2am • lesbians/ gay men • dancing/DJ • multiracial • wheelchair access

CAFES

Tony's Coffee House 1101 Harris Ave (at 11th), Fairhaven **360/738–4710** • 7am-6pm • plenty veggie • patio • wheelchair access

RESTAURANTS

Bobby Lee's Pub & Eatery 108 W Main St (Washington Ave), Everson **360/966–8838** • 11am-2am, clsd Mon • gay-owned • wheelchair access

Skylark's Hidden Cafe 1308–B 11th St (at McKenzie) **360/715–3642** • 7am-midnight • great soups • full bar • outdoor seating • live jazz wknds

BOOKSTORES

Village Books 1200 11th St (at Harris) **360/671–2626** • 10am-7:30pm, till 7pm Sun • new & used

EROTICA

Great Northern Bookstore 1308 Railroad Ave (at Holly) **360/733–1650**

Bender Creek

ACCOMMODATIONS

Triangle Recreation Camp PO Box 1226, Granite Falls 98252 • lesbians/ gay men • members-only camping on 80-acre nature conservancy • www.camptrc.org

Bremerton

INFO LINES & SERVICES

AA Gay/ Lesbian 700 Callahan Dr (at St Paul's Episcopal) **360/475–0775, 800/562–7455** • 7:30pm Tue

Everett

INFO LINES & SERVICES

AA Gay/ Lesbian 2624 Rockefeller **425/252–2525** • 7pm Sun

NIGHTCLUBS

Twisted at Club Broadway 1611 Everett Ave **425/259–3551** • 6pm-2am, till midnight Sun • lesbians/ gay men • dancing/DJ • karaoke Wed • food served • wheelchair access

Glacier

ACCOMMODATIONS

Mt Baker B&B & Cabins 9434 Cornell Creek Rd **360/599–2299** • gay/ straight • modern chalet • hot tub • kids ok • some shared baths • nonsmoking • WiFi

Kent

BARS

Benchwarmer Bar & Grill 24437 Russell Rd **253/854–2110** • 3pm-2am, from noon wknds • lesbians/ gay men • dancing/DJ • food served • karaoke • patio

Vibe 226 1st Ave S (btwn Meeker & Gowe) **253/852–0815** • noon-2am, till midnight Sun-Mon • lesbians/ gay men • dancing/DJ • karaoke

EROTICA

The Voyeur 604 Central Ave S **253/850–8428** • videos • toys • clothing

La Conner

ACCOMMODATIONS

The Wild Iris 121 Maple Ave **360/466–1400, 800/477–1400** • gay-friendly • inn • nonsmoking • full brkfst • kids ok • WiFi • wheelchair access • gay-owned

Long Beach Peninsula

ACCOMMODATIONS

Anthony's Home Court 1310 Pacific Hwy N, Long Beach **360/642–2802, 888/787–2754** • gay/ straight • cabins & RV hookups • nonsmoking • WiFi • gay-owned

Bloomer Estates 1004 41st Pl (at Oceanfront), Seaview **360/243–9510, 800/747–2096** • gay-friendly • rental homes • nonsmoking • WiFi • hot tub • kids ok • lesbian & gay-owned

The Historic Sou'wester Lodge, Cabins & RV Park Beach Access Rd (38th Pl), Seaview **360/642–2542** • gay-friendly • inexpensive suites • cabins w/ kitchens • vintage trailers • RV hookups • pets ok in cabins & trailers • nonsmoking

Shakti Cove Cottages **360/665–4000** • lesbians/ gay men • cabins on the peninsula • pets ok • nonsmoking • lesbian-owned

Lynnwood

RETAIL SHOPS

Colorbomb Tattoo 15332 Hwy 99 #7 (at 40th Ave W) **425/742–8467** • noon-8pm, by appt only Sun-Mon

Mt Vernon

RESTAURANTS

Deli Next Door 202 S 1st St (at Memorial Hwy) **360/336–3886** • 8am-9pm, 9pm-8pm Sun • healthy American • plenty veggie • WiFi • wheelchair access

Olympia

INFO LINES & SERVICES

Free at Last AA 11th & Washington #106 (at United Church) **360/352–7344** • call for info

ACCOMMODATIONS

Swantown Inn B&B 1431 11th Ave SE (at Central St) **360/753–9123, 877/753–9123** • gay-friendly • nonsmoking • full brkfst • WiFi • $109-179

BARS

Hannah's 123 5th Ave SW (at Columbia) **360/357–9890** • 11am-2am, till midnight Sun-Mon • gay/ straight • neighborhood bar • food served

NIGHTCLUBS

Jakes on 4th 311 E 4th **360/956–3247** • 10am-2am • lesbians/ gay men • dancing/DJ • karaoke

CAFES

Darby's Cafe 211 SE 5th Ave (at Washington) **360/357–6229** • 7am-2pm, 8am-2pm wknds, clsd Mon-Tue • gay/ straight • gay-owned

RESTAURANTS

Saigon Rendez-Vous 117 5th Ave SW (btwn Columbia & Capitol Wy) **360/352–1989** • lunch & dinner • Vietnamese • plenty veggie

Urban Onion 116 Legion Wy SE (at Capitol) **360/943–9242** • 11am-9pm, 9am-2am wknds • plenty veggie • lounge • wheelchair access

RETAIL SHOPS

Dumpster Values 302 4th (at Franklin) **360/705–3772** • 10am-8pm, noon-6pm Sun • new & used clothing • zines • records • toys • women-owned

Erotica

Desire Video 3200 Pacific Ave SE (off I-5, at exit 107) **360/352-0820** • 24hrs • videos • toys • 100-channel video arcade • extensive LGBT section

Pasco

Nightclubs

Out & About Restaurant & Lounge 327 W Lewis **509/543-3796, 877/388-3796** • 6pm-2am, clsd Sun-Mon • lesbians/ gay men • dancing/DJ wknds • karaoke • drag shows • cabaret • 18+ Fri • also restaurant • wheelchair access

Port Townsend

Accommodations

Aunt Jenny's Guest House 1705 Monroe **360/385-2899** • gay/ straight • quiet cottage • kids ok • nonsmoking • wheelchair access • woman-owned

Ravenscroft Inn 533 Quincy St (at Clay St) **360/385-2784, 800/782-2691** • gay-friendly • seaport inn w/ views of Puget Sound • gourmet brkfst • hot tub • nonsmoking

Quinault

Accommodations

Lake Quinault Lodge 345 South Shore Rd (off US 101) **360/288-2900, 800/562-6672** • gay-friendly

San Juan Islands

Accommodations

Inn on Orcas Island **360/376-5227, 888/886-1661** • gay-friendly • luxury • full brkfst • nonsmoking • wheelchair access • gay-owned • $145-285

Lopez Farm Cottages & Tent Camping 555 Fisherman Bay Rd, Lopez Island **360/468-3555, 800/440-3556** • gay/ straight • on 30-acre farm • hot tub • nonsmoking

Spring Bay Cabin on Orcas Island Orcas Island **360/376-5531** • gay/ straight • full brkfst • hot tub • nonsmoking • WiFi • $240

Entertainment & Recreation

Western Prince Whale & Wildlife Tours 2 Spring St (at Front), Friday Harbor **360/378-5315, 800/757-6722** • whale-watching & wildlife tours April-Oct

Seattle

Info Lines & Services

Capitol Hill Alano 1900 E Madison St **206/860-9560 (club), 206/587-2838 (AA#)** • 12-step meetings daily

Accommodations

11th Avenue Inn 121 11th Ave E (at Boren) **206/720-7161, 800/720-7161** • gay-friendly • nonsmoking • WiFi • kids 12+ ok • full brkfst • $79-179

The Ace Hotel 2423 1st Ave (at Wall St) **206/448-4721** • gay/ straight • kids/ pets ok • nonsmoking • WiFi • restaurant & bar • $75-195

Alexis Hotel 1007 1st Ave (at Madison) **206/624-4844, 800/426-7033** • gay-friendly • luxury hotel w/ Aveda spa • kids/ pets ok • WiFi • wheelchair access • $299-595

Artist's Studio Loft B&B 16529 91st Ave SW, Vashon Island **206/463-2583** • gay-friendly • on 5 acres • garden • hot tub • nonsmoking

Bacon Mansion 959 Broadway E (at E Prospect) **206/329-1864, 800/240-1864** • gay/ straight • Edwardian-style Tudor • nonsmoking • WiFi • wheelchair access • $99-234

Bed & Breakfast on Broadway 722 Broadway Ave E (at Aloha) **206/329-8933** • gay/ straight • nonsmoking • WiFi

Gaslight Inn 1727 15th Ave (at E Howell St) **206/325-3654** • popular • gay/ straight • B&B in Arts & Crafts home • pool • WiFi • nonsmoking • gay-owned

Hotel 1000 1000 First Ave **206/957-1000, 877/315-1088** • gay-friendly • WiFi • wheelchair access

MarQueen Hotel 600 Queen Anne Ave N (btwn Roy & Mercer) **206/282-7407, 888/445-3076** • gay/ straight • in Theater District • kitchenettes

Seahurst Garden Studio 13713 16th Ave SW (at Ambaum Ave), Burien **206/551-7721** • women only • nonsmoking • WiFi • wheelchair access • lesbian-owned

Sleeping Bulldog Bed & Breakfast 816 19th Ave S (at S Dearborn St) **206/601-9274** • gay/ straight • nonsmoking • WiFi • gay owned • $116-206

The Sorrento Hotel 900 Madison St **206/622-6400, 800/426-1265** • gay-friendly • restaurant • WiFi

Squire Park Guesthouse 1206 E Barclay Ct (at 12th Ave) 206/329-3914 • gay/ straight • nonsmoking • WiFi • gay-owned

Warwick Seattle Hotel 401 Lenora St (at 4th) 206/443-4300 • gay/ straight • full brkfst • pool • kids ok • wheelchair access • $99-290

Wild Lily Cabins B&B 25 miles W of Stevens Pass, Index 360/793-2103 • gay/ straight • cabins on Skykomish River • 1 hour from Seattle • cedar sauna • hot tub • camping available • nonsmoking • gay-owned • $118-175

BARS

The Baltic Room 1207 Pine St (at Melrose) 206/625-4444 • 9pm-2am, clsd Wed & Sun • gay/ straight • live music

Bar Myx 2810 Western Ave (at Clay) 206/588-1834 • 4pm-midnight, noon-2am wknds • gay/straight • food served • video bar

The Bottleneck Lounge 2328 Madison St (at John St) 206/323-1098 • 4pm-2am • gay/ straight • lesbian-owned

The Can Can 93 Pike St #307 (in the Pike Place Market) 206/652-0832 • 6pm-2am • gay/ straight • food served • cabaret

Canterbury Ale and Eats 534 15th Ave E (at Mercer) 206/322-3130 • 11am-2am • gay-friendly • neighborhood bar • food served • dogs welcome

CC Attle's 1701 E Olive Way 206/323-4017 • noon-2am • popular • mostly gay men • neighborhood bar • videos • also restaurant • wheelchair access

Cha Cha Lounge & Bimbo's Cantina 1013 E Pike St (at 11th Ave) 206/322-0703 • 5pm-2am • gay-friendly • hipster lounge & big burritos • gay-owned

Changes 2103 N 45th St (at Meridian) 206/545-8363 • noon-2am • mostly gay men • neighborhood bar • food served • karaoke • videos • wheelchair access

Chapel 1600 Melrose Ave (at E Pine) 206/447-4180 • 5pm-1am, till 2am Fri-Sat • gay/ straight • DJ • food served

Choice 1010 E Pike St (at Broadway, at Havana Social Club) 206/323-2822 • 10pm Wed only • lesbians/ gay men • dancing/DJ • House music

The Crescent Lounge 1413 E Olive Wy (at Bellevue) • noon-2am • gay/ straight • neighborhood bar • karaoke nightly • wheelchair access

The Cuff 1533 13th Ave (at Pine) 206/323-1525 • 2pm-2am, after-hours wknds, T-dance Sun • popular • mostly gay men • dancing/DJ • country/ western • levi crowd • patio • wheelchair access

Double Header 407 2nd Ave S Extension (at Washington) 206/464-9918 • 10am-11pm, till 1am Fri-Sat • gay/ straight • neighborhood bar

Elite Tavern 1520 E Olive Way (at Denny Way) 206/860-0999 • noon-2am • lesbians/ gay men • neighborhood bar

Hot Flash Seattle 1509 Broadway (at Neighbors) 206/252-9333 • T-dance 5pm-9pm 1st & 3rd Sat only • "for seasoned lesbians 36+ (& the women who love us!)" • cover charge

Hula Hula 106 1st Ave N (at Denny) 206/284-5003 • 4pm-close • gay-friendly • tiki bar • karaoke

The Lobby Bar 916 E Pike St (at Broadway) 206/328-6703 • 3pm-midnight, till 2am Th-Sat • mostly gay men • bar food • live shows

Poco Wine Room 1408 E Pine St (at 14th Ave) 206/322-9463 • 5pm-close • gay/ straight • food served

R Place 619 E Pine St (at Boylston Ave) 206/322-8828 • 4pm-2am, from 2pm wknds • mostly gay men • neighborhood bar • dancing/DJ • food served • karaoke • videos • WiFi • wheelchair access

Rendezvous 2322 2nd Ave (at Battery) 206/441-5823 • 4pm-2am • gay/ straight • live bands • cabaret • theater • also restaurant

The Seattle Eagle 314 E Pike St (at Bellevue) 206/621-7591 • 2pm-2am • mostly gay men • leather • rock 'n' roll • theme nights • patio • wheelchair access

Temple Billiards 126 S Jackson 206/682-3242 • 11am-2am, from 3pm wknds • gay-friendly • more women Wed • food served

Wildrose Bar & Restaurant 1021 E Pike St (at 11th) 206/324-9210 • 3pm-2am, till 1am Sun & Mon • mostly women • neighborhood bar • dancing/DJ • karaoke • live shows • food served • wheelchair access

NIGHTCLUBS

Contour 807 1st Ave (at Columbia) 206/447-7704 • 3pm-2am, till 6am Fri-Sat • gay-friendly • fire performances • dancing/DJ • also bar & restaurant

Dimitriou's Jazz Alley 2033 6th Ave (at Lenora) **206/441-9729** • gay-friendly • call for events & reservations • live music • nonsmoking • cover charge • also restaurant

Girl4Girl Productions • mostly women • dancing/DJ • live shows • go-go dancers • check girl4girlseattle.com for info

Neighbours Dance Club 1509 Broadway (btwn Pike & Pine) **206/324-5358** • 9pm-2am, till 3am Th, till 4am Fri-Sat • popular • lesbians/ gay men • dancing/DJ • 2 flrs • also 18+ room Th-Sat • young crowd • wheelchair access

Purr 1518 11th Ave (at Pike St) **206/325-3112** • 3pm-2am, till midnight Sun • mostly gay men • karaoke • food served

Re-bar 1114 Howell (at Boren Ave) **206/233-9873** • 10pm-2am, clsd Mon • popular • gay/ straight • more women Sat • dancing/DJ Wed-Sun • cabaret/ theater

Showbox 1426 1st Ave (at Pike) **206/628-3151** • gay-friendly • live music venue • no cover charge in Green Room

Seattle

WHERE THE GIRLS ARE:
Living in the Capitol Hill District, south of Lake Union, and working in the Broadway Market, Pike Place Market, or somewhere in between.

ENTERTAINMENT:
Team Seattle 206/322-7769, web: www.teamseattle.org, a 35-team gay network.

LGBT PRIDE:
Last Sunday in June. 206/322-9561, web: www.seattlepride.org.

ANNUAL EVENTS:
September - Bumbershoot music & arts festival 206/281-7788, web: www.bumbershoot.org.
September - AIDS Walk 206/329-6923.
October - Seattle Gay & Lesbian Film Festival 206/323-4274, web: www.seattlequeerfilm.com.

CITY INFO:
206/461-5800, web: www.seattle.com.

BEST VIEW:
Top of the Space Needle, or from Admiral Way Park in West Seattle.

WEATHER:
Winter's average temperature is 50° while summer temperatures can climb up into the 90°s. Be prepared for rain at any time during the year.

ATTRACTIONS:
Experience Music Project 206/367-5483, web: www.empsfm.org.
Fremont, web: www.fremontseattle.com.
International District.
Museum of Flight 206/764-5720, web: www.museumofflight.org.
Pike Place Market, web: www.pikemarketplace.org.
Pioneer Square, web: www.pioneersquaredistrict.org.
Seattle Art Museum 206/654-3100, web: www.seattleartmuseum.org.
Seattle Aquarium 206/386-4300, web: www.seattleaquarium.org.
Seattle Center Monorail 206/905-2620, web: www.seattlemonorail.com.
Seattle Underground 206/682-4646, web: www.undergroundtour.com.
Space Needle 206/905-2100, web: www.spaceneedle.com.
Woodland Park Zoo 206/684-4800, web: www.zoo.org.

TRANSIT:
Farwest 206/622-1717.
Yellow Gray Top 206/282-8222.
Airport Shuttle Express 206/622-1424.
Metropolitan Transit 206/553-3000, web: www.metrokc.gov/tran.htm.

CAFES

The Allegro 4214 University Wy NE (at NE 42nd St) 206/633–3030 • 7am-10:30pm • WiFi

Cafe Besalu 5909 24th Ave NW 206/789–1463 • 7am-3pm, clsd Mon-Tue • great pastries

Espresso Vivace 532 Broadway Ave 206/860–5869 • 6am-11pm • popular • WiFi

Fuel Coffee 610 19th Ave E 206/329–4700 • 6am-9pm • WiFi

Insomniax Coffee & Juice 102 15th Ave E 206/322–6477 • 7am-3pm, clsd Sun • WiFi

Kaladi Brothers Coffee 511 E Pike St (at Summit) 206/388–1700 • 6am-9pm, from 8am wknds • WiFi

Louisa's 2379 Eastlake Ave E 206/325–0081 • 7am-9pm, till 10pm Fri-Sat, 8am-3pm Sun

RESTAURANTS

Al Boccalino 1 Yesler Wy (at Alaskan) 206/622–7688 • lunch Tue-Fri, dinner nightly • classy southern Italian

Bamboo Garden 364 Roy St (at Mercer St) 206/282–6616 • 11am-10pm • Chinese vegetarian & kosher

The Broadway Grill 314 Broadway E (at E Harrison) 206/328–7000 • 11am-11pm, from 8am wknds • popular • full bar

Cafe Flora 2901 E Madison St 206/325–9100 • lunch, dinner, wknd brunch • vegetarian • beer/ wine • nonsmoking • wheelchair accessible

Canlis 2576 Aurora Ave N 206/283–3313 • dinner only • fancy seafood

Capitol Club 414 E Pine St 206/325–2149 • tapas • live entertainment

Dahlia Lounge 2001 4th Ave (at Virginia) 206/682–4142 • lunch Mon-Fri, dinner nightly, wknd brunch • some veggie • full bar

Dick's Drive In 115 Broadway E (at Denny) 206/323–1300 • 10:30am-2am • excellent fries & shakes

Flying Fish 300 Westlake Ave N 206/728–8595 • lunch Mon-Fri, dinner nightly, bar till 2am • lesbian chef

Fresh Bistro 4725 42nd Ave SW (btwn Alaska St & Edmunds) 206/935–3733 • dinner Mon-Sat, lunch Wed-Fri, wknd brunch

Galerias 611 E Broadway (at Mercer) 206/322–5757 • 11am-10pm, brunch wknds • traditional Mexican

Glo's 1621 E Olive Wy (at Summit Ave E) 206/324–2577 • 7am-3pm, till 4pm wknds • brkfst only • popular

Julia's 300 Broadway E (at Thomas) 206/860–1818 • 11am, till midnight Fri-Sat • full bar • drag shows Sat

Kabul 2301 N 45th St 206/545–9000 • 5pm-9:30pm, till 10pm Fri-Sat • Afghan • some veggie

Lola 2000 4th Ave (at Virginia) 206/441–1430 • 6am-midnight, till 2am wknds • popular brunch

Mae's Phinney Ridge Cafe 6412 Phinney Ridge N (at 65th) 206/782–1222 • 8am-2pm, till 3pm wknds • popular • brkfst menu • some veggie • wheelchair access

Mama's Mexican Kitchen 2234 2nd Ave (in Belltown) 206/728–6262 • lunch & dinner • cheap & funky

Paseo 4225 Fremont Ave N (at N 43rd St) 206/545–7440 • 11am-9pm, clsd Sun-Mon • Cuban

Queen City Grill 2201 1st Ave (at Blanchard) 206/443–0975 • dinner only • popular • fresh seafood • some veggie • full bar • wheelchair access

Restaurant Zoe 2137 2nd Ave (at Blanchard) 206/256–2060 • dinner only

Snappy Dragon 8917 Roosevelt Wy NE 206/528–5575 • 11am-9:30pm, 4pm-9pm Sun • Chinese

Sunlight Cafe 6403 Roosevelt Wy NE (at 64th) 206/522–9060 • 8am-9pm • vegetarian • beer/ wine • wheelchair access

Szmania's 3321 W McGraw St (in Magnolia Bluff) 206/284–7305 • dinner nightly, clsd Mon • full bar

Tamarind Tree 1036 S Jackson St 206/860–1404 • 10am-10pm, till midnight Fri-Sat • Vietnamese

Teapot Vegetarian House 345 15th Ave E 206/325–1010 • 11am-10pm • vegan

Thaiger Room 206/632–9299 • 11am-10pm, from noon wknds • Thai

Tidbit Bistro 1401 Broadway (at Union) 206/323–0840 • lunch Tue-Fri, dinner nightly, wknd brunch • tapas • full bar • patio

Verve Wine Bar & Cellar 3820 S Ferdinand St 206/760–0977 • 5pm-10pm, till 11pm Fri-Sat, wknd brunch • women owned

Wild Ginger Asian Restaurant & Triple Bar 1401 3rd Ave (at Union) 206/623–4450 • lunch Mon-Sat, dinner nightly • popular • bar till 1am

Wild Mountain 1408 NW 85th St 206/297–9453 • 8:30am-9pm, clsd Tue • woman-owned

ENTERTAINMENT & RECREATION

Alki Beach Park 1702 Alki Ave SW, West Seattle • popular on warm days

Century Ballroom 915 E Pine, 2nd flr (at Broadway) **206/324-7263** • ballroom dancing • check schedule for gay nights

Garage 1130 Broadway **206/322-2296** • 3pm-2am • popular • way-cool pool hall • food served • full bar • ladies 1/2 price Sun • also bowling alley • 21+

Northwest Lesbian & Gay History Museum Project 206/903-9517 • exhibits & publication

Rat City Roller Girls • Seattle's female roller derby league • visit www.ratcityrollergirls.com for events

Richard Hugo House 1634 11th Ave **206/322-7030** • noon-6pm, till 5pm Sat, clsd Sun • houses the Zine Archive & Publishing Project • open later for events • also cafe & cabaret

The Vera Project corner of Warren Ave N & Republican St (in Seattle Center) **206/956-8372** • gay-friendly • all-ages music arts center

BOOKSTORES

Elliott Bay Book Company 1521 10th Ave N **206/624-6600, 800/962-5311** • 9:30am-10pm, 11am-7pm Sun

Left Bank Books 92 Pike St (at 1st Ave) **206/622-0195** • 10am-7pm, 11am-6pm Sun • worker-owned collective

RETAIL SHOPS

Broadway Market 401 Broadway E (at Harrison & Republican) • popular mall full of funky, hip stores

Lifelong Thrift Store 1002 E Seneca **206/328-8979** • all proceeds to AIDS organization

Metropolis 7321 Greenwood Ave N **206/782-7002** • 10am-7pm, till 6pm Sat, noon-5pm Sun • cards & gifts

PUBLICATIONS

SGN (Seattle Gay News) 206/324-4297 • weekly LGBT newspaper

The Stranger 206/323-7101 • queer-positive alternative weekly

GYMS & HEALTH CLUBS

Hothouse Spa & Sauna 1019 E Pike St (at 11th, 2 blocks E of Broadway) **206/568-3240** • noon-midnight, clsd Tue • women only • baths • hot tub • massage

EROTICA

Babeland 707 E Pike (btwn Harvard & Boylston) **206/328-2914** • 11am-10pm, noon-7pm Sun • wheelchair access • lesbian-owned

The Crypt Off Broadway 1516 11th Ave (at E Pine) **206/325-3882**

Hollywood Erotic Boutique 12706 Lake City Wy NE **206/363-0056** • 24hrs • toys • lingerie

Sequim

ACCOMMODATIONS

Sunset Marine Resort 40 Buzzard Ridge Rd **360/681-4166** • gay-friendly • waterfront cabins • nonsmoking • kids ok • lesbian-owned

Spokane

INFO LINES & SERVICES

AA Gay/ Lesbian 1614 W Riverside **509/624-1442** • call for meeting times

Inland Northwest LGBT Center 1522 N Washington #102 **509/489-1914** • support groups • events • also art gallery

ACCOMMODATIONS

Montvale Hotel 1005 W First Ave (at Monroe) **509/747-1919, 866/668-8253** • gay-friendly • luxury, boutique hotel • transgender-friendly • also bars & restaurant • kids ok • nonsmoking • WiFi • gay-owned

NIGHTCLUBS

Dempsey's Brass Rail 909 W 1st St (btwn Lincoln & Monroe) **509/747-5362** • 3pm-2am, till midnight Sun • popular • lesbians/gay men • dancing/DJ Th-Sat • drag shows Fri-Sat • also restaurant • wheelchair access

RESTAURANTS

Mizuna 214 N Howard **509/747-2004** • lunch Mon-Fri, dinner nightly • seasonal menu • plenty veggie • full bar

BOOKSTORES

Auntie's Bookstore 402 W Main Ave (at Washington) **509/838-0206** • 9am-9pm, 11am-6pm Sun-Mon • wheelchair access

Suquamish

INFO LINES & SERVICES

Kitsap Lesbian/ Gay AA 18732 Division Ave NE (at Congregational Church of Christ) **360/475-0775, 800/562-7455** • 7:30pm Sun

Tacoma

Info Lines & Services

AA Gay/ Lesbian 3640 S Cedar #5 **253/474–8897** • 7:30pm Fri

Rainbow Center 741 St Helens Ave **253/383–2318** • 1pm-5pm Mon-Fri • community center • call for meetings & events

Tacoma Lesbian Concern • social events • resource list • newsletter

Accommodations

Chinaberry Hill 302 Tacoma Ave N **253/272–1282** • gay-friendly • 1889 Victorian inn • also cottage • full brkfst • fireplaces • kids ok • nonsmoking • WiFi

Hotel Murano 1320 Broadway Plaza (at S 15th) **253/238–8000, 888/862–3255** • gay-friendly • restaurants & bars • WiFi • wheelchair access

Bars

Airport Bar & Grill 5406 S Tacoma Wy (at 54th) **253/475–9730** • 2pm-2am • lesbians/ gay men • neighborhood bar

Nightclubs

Club Silverstone 739 1/2 St Helens Ave (at 9th) **253/404–0273** • 11am-2am • lesbians/ gay men • neighboorhood bar • dancing/DJ • karaoke

Cafes

Shakabrah Java Cafe **253/572–2787** • 7am-4pm, clsd Sun • wheelchair access

Erotica

Castle Megastore 6015 Tacoma Mall Blvd **253/471–0391**

Vancouver

see also Portland, Oregon

Bars

Northbank 106 W 6th St (at Main) **360/695–3862** • 2pm-2am • lesbians/ gay men • more women Th • dancing/DJ • food served • karaoke • drag shows • nonsmoking • wheelchair access

Walla Walla

Accommodations

The Boyer House 741 Boyer Ave **888/526–8718** • gay-straight • pool • nonsmoking • full brkfst • gay-owned

Wenatchee

Cafes

The Cellar Cafe 249 N Mission St (at 5th) **509/662–1722** • 9am-3pm Mon-Fri • some veggie • beer/ wine • patio • lesbian-owned

Whidbey Island

Accommodations

Whidwood Inn **360/720–6228** • gay/ straight • near historic Coupeville • nonsmoking • hot tub • gay-owned

Winthrop

Accommodations

Chewuch Inn 223 White Ave **509/996–3107, 800/747–3107** • gay-friendly • inn & cabins • E of N Cascades Mtns • hot tub • kids ok • nonsmoking • WiFi • wheelchair access • $85-200

WEST VIRGINIA

Charleston

Nightclubs

Broadway 210 Leon Sullivan Wy (at Lee) **304/343–2162** • 4pm-3am, from 1pm Sat-Mon • mostly gay men • dancing/DJ • live shows

Entertainment & Recreation

Living AIDS Memorial Garden corner of Washington St E (at Sidney Ave) **304/346–0246**

Bookstores

Taylor Books 226 Capitol St **304/342–1461** • 7:30am-8pm, till 10pm Fri, 9am-10pm Sat, till 3pm Sun • WiFi • also cafe, art gallery & boutique

Follansbee

Bars

Wild Coyote Saloon 869 Main St **304/527–7191** • 6pm-close • lesbians/ gay men • dancing/ DJ Fri-Sat • drag shows

Harpers Ferry

Accommodations

Laurel Lodge 844 Ridge St **304/535–2886** • gay-friendly • bungalow overlooking Potomac River gorge • full brkfst • nonsmoking • WiFi • gay-owned

Huntington

ACCOMMODATIONS

Pullman Plaza Hotel 1001 3rd Ave (at 10th St) 304/525–1001, 866/613–3611 • gay-friendly • full brkfst • pool • nonsmoking • WiFi • wheelchair access

BARS

Polo Club 1037 7th Ave (at 11th St) 304/522–3146 • 5pm-2am, from 2pm wknds • mostly gay men • dancing/DJ • live shows • karaoke • private club • wheelchair access

The Stonewall 820 7th Ave (enter in alley) 304/523–2242 • 8pm-3am, clsd Mon • popular • lesbians/ gay men • dancing/DJ • karaoke • live shows • wheelchair access • gay-owned

RESTAURANTS

Sharkey's 410 10th St 304/523–3200 • 4pm-2:30am, clsd Sun • full bar • karaoke

Lost River

ACCOMMODATIONS

Guest House at Lost River 288 Settlers Valley Wy (at Mill Gap Rd) 304/897–5707 • lesbians/ gay men • full brkfst • also fine-dining restaurant • full bar • pool • hot tub • gym • nonsmoking • WiFi • gay-owned • $145-200

RESTAURANTS

Lost River Grill & Motel St Rd 259 304/897–6482 • 11:45am-9pm, 8am-10pm Sat, till 9pm Sun, 4pm-9pm Mon • full bar • also motel & cabins

Martinsburg

BARS

The Mariner Club 1911 Winchester Ave 304/264–4414 • 5pm-1am, till 2:30am Th-Sat • lesbians/gay men • dancing/DJ • food served • drag shows

EROTICA

Variety Books & Video 255 N Queen St (at Race) 304/263–4334 • 24hrs

Morgantown

NIGHTCLUBS

Vice Versa 335 High St (enter rear) 304/292–2010 • 8pm-3am Th-Sun • lesbians/ gay men • dancing/DJ • karaoke • live shows • private club • 18+ • wheelchair access

Weezie's Pub & Club 3438 University Ave 304/292–3939 • 8pm-close, clsd Sun • lesbians/ gay men • dancing/DJ • live music

Shepherdstown

ACCOMMODATIONS

Thomas Shepherd Inn 300 W German St (at Duke St) 304/876–3715, 888/889–8952 • gay-friendly • B&B • full brkfst • nonsmoking • WiFi • $125-195

Sissonville

RESTAURANTS

Topspot Country Cookin' 7139 Sissonville Rd 304/984–2816 • 7am-8pm, till 7pm Sun, clsd Mon

Teays Valley

BARS

The Phoenix 100 Clubhouse Dr, Hurricane 304/757–5050 • 4pm-2:30, clsd Mon • gay/straight • live/drag shows • karaoke • gay-owned

Wheeling

EROTICA

Market St News 1437 Market St (at 14th St) 304/232–2414 • 24hrs, till midnight Sun-Mon

WISCONSIN

Algoma

RETAIL SHOPS

The Flying Pig N6975 Hwy 42 (at Tenth) 920/487–9902 • 9am-6pm May-Oct, 10am-5pm Fri-Sun only off season • art gallery & coffee bar • lesbian-owned

Appleton

BARS

Rascals Bar & Grill 702 E Wisconsin Ave (at Lawe) 920/954–9262 • 5pm-2am, from noon Sun • lesbians/ gay men, ladies night Wed • fish-fry Fri • patio

Ravens 215 E College Ave 920/364–9599 • 8pm-2am, clsd Sun-Mon • mostly gay men, Th ladies night • dancing/DJ • karaoke • drag shows

CAFES

Harmony Cafe 233 E College Ave 920/734–2233 • 7am-9pm, till 10pm Th-Sat, 8am-6pm Sun • live entertainment • also educational & support groups

EROTICA

Eldorado's 2545 S Memorial Dr (at Hwys 47 & 441) **920/830-0042**

Beloit

BARS

Club Impulse 132 W Grand Ave **608/361-0000** • 4pm-2am, till 2:30am Fri-Sat, from 7pm Sat • lesbians/ gay men • dancing/DJ • karaoke • drag shows

Eau Claire

INFO LINES & SERVICES

LGBT Community Center of the Chippewa Valley 1305 Woodland Ave **715/406-4428** • drop-in 7pm-10pm Fri, call for other hours • library & variety of events

NIGHTCLUBS

Scooters 411 Galloway (at Farwell) **715/835-9959** • 3pm-2am • lesbians/gay men • dancing/DJ • karaoke • drag shows • wheelchair access

Green Bay

INFO LINES & SERVICES

Gay AA **920/432-2600** • call for times & locations

BARS

Ape Hangers 301 S Broadway **920/455-1005** • 10am-close • gay-friendly • karaoke

Napalese Lounge 1351 Cedar St **920/432-9646** • 11am-close • mostly gay men • neighborhood bar • DJ Fri-Sat • food served • drag shows • wheelchair access

Sass 840 S Broadway **920/437-7277** • 6pm-2am Tue, Fri & Sat • lesbians/ gay men • dancing/DJ wknds • karaoke

NIGHTCLUBS

The Shelter 730 N Quincy St (at 54302) **920/432-2662** • lesbians/ gay men • dancing/DJ • country/ western • transgender-friendly • food served • karaoke • drag shows • gay-owned

CAFES

Harmony Cafe 1660 W Mason St **920/569-1593** • 7am-9pm, 10am-6pm Sun • live entertainment • support groups

PUBLICATIONS

Outbound/ Quest **920/655-0611, 800/578-3785** • news & arts reviews for WI's LGBT community

EROTICA

Lion's Den Adult Superstore 836 S Broadway (at 5th) **920/433-9640**

Hayward

ACCOMMODATIONS

The Lake House 5793 Division, Stone Lake **715/865-6803** • lesbians/ gay men • full brkfst • swimming • nonsmoking • kids ok by arrangement • WiFi • wheelchair access • lesbian-owned • $90-160

Kenosha

see also Racine

BARS

Club Icon 6305 120th Ave (on E Frontage road of I-94) **262/857-3240** • 7pm-2am, from 3pm Sun, clsd Mon • lesbians/ gay men • dancing/DJ • drag shows

NIGHTCLUBS

Fierté 5722 3rd Ave **262/764-9713** • 7pm-close, clsd Sun-Tue • lesbians/gay men • dancing/DJ• drag shows

La Crosse

ACCOMMODATIONS

Rainbow Ridge Farms B&B N 5732 Hauser Rd (at County S), Onalaska **608/783-8181, 888/347-2594** • gay-friendly • working hobby farm on 35 acres • WiFi • nonsmoking

BARS

Chances R 417 Jay St (at 4th) **608/782-5105** • 3pm-close • lesbians/ gay men • neighborhood bar

My Place 3201 South Ave (at East Ave) **608/788-9073** • 3pm-close, from noon wknds • lesbians/ gay men • friendly neighborhood bar • games • gay-owned

Players 300 S 4th St (at Jay St) **608/784-4200** • 5pm-2am, from 3pm Fri-Sun, till 2:30am Fri-Sat • popular • lesbians/gay men • dancing/DJ • transgender-friendly • wheelchair access • gay-owned

EROTICA

Pleasures 405 S 3rd **608/784-6350** • DVDs • toys • magazines • lingerie

Madison

INFO LINES & SERVICES

OutReach, Inc 600 Williamson St #P-1
608/255-8582 • 10am-7pm, noon-4pm Sat,
clsd Sun • drop-in center

BARS

Club 5 5 Applegate Ct (btwn Fish Hatchery
Rd & W Beltline Hwy) **608/277-9700,
877/648-9700** • 5pm-2am • popular •
lesbians/ gay men • dancing/DJ • karaoke • live
shows • 18+ Tue

Green Bush 914 Regent St (at Park)
608/257-2874 • 4pm-midnight, clsd Sun •
gay-friendly • also restaurant

Shamrock 117 W Main St (at Fairchild)
608/255-5029 • 4pm-2am, from 11am wknds
• lesbians/ gay men • also grill

Woof's 114 King St **608/204-6222** • 4pm-
2am, from noon Sun • lesbians/ gay men
• neighborhood bar • dancing/DJ • food
served

NIGHTCLUBS

Cardinal 418 E Wilson St (at S Franklin)
608/257-2473 • 7pm-2am, from 4pm Fri, clsd
Tue • gay-friendly • call for gay nights •
dancing/DJ • live shows

IQ/ IndieQueer • weekly & monthly queer
parties in Madison • check local listings for
dates & info

Plan B 924 Williamson St **608/257-5262** •
4pm-2am, from 9pm Sun, clsd Mon •
lesbians/gay men • dancing/DJ • karaoke • 1st
& 3rd Fri women's night • Th 18+

CAFES

Java Cat 3918 Monona Dr (at Cottage Grove
Rd) **608/223-5553** • 5:30am-8pm, till 9pm Fri-
Sat, 7am-7pm Sun • light food served • WiFi

RESTAURANTS

Fromagination 12 S Carroll (on Capital Sq)
608/255-2430 • 9:30am-6pm, 9am-5pm Sat,
clsd Sun

La Hacienda 515 S Park St **608/255-8227** •
9am-3am • popular • Mexican • post–Club 5
spot

Monty's Blue Plate Diner 2089 Atwood Ave
(at Winnebago) **608/244-8505** • 7am-9pm •
some veggie • beer/ wine • wheelchair access

BOOKSTORES

**A Room of One's Own Feminist Books &
Gifts** 307 W Johnson St **608/257-7888** •
10am-8pm, till 6pm Sat, noon-5pm Sun •
wheelchair access

PUBLICATIONS

Our Lives • LGBT publication •
www.ourlivesmadison.com

EROTICA

A Woman's Touch 600 Williamson (at
Gateway Mall) **608/250-1928, 888/621-8880** •
11am-6pm, till 8pm Tue-Th, noon-5pm Sun •
wheelchair access

Red Letter News 2528 E Washington (btwn
North & Milwaukee) **608/241-9958**

Milwaukee

INFO LINES & SERVICES

AA Galano Club 315 W Court #201 (in LGBT
Community Center) **414/276-6936**

Milwaukee LGBT Community Center 252
E Highland Ave **414/271-2656** • 10am-10pm,
from 6pm Sat, till 5pm Mon, clsd Sun

ACCOMMODATIONS

Ambassador Hotel 2308 W Wisconsin Ave
(at N 24th) **414/345-5000, 888/322-3326** •
gay/ straight • nonsmoking • WiFi • wheelchair
access

The Brumder Mansion 3046 W Wisconsin
Ave (at N 31st) **414/342-9767, 866/793-3676**
• gay-friendly • nonsmoking • WiFi

Comfort Inn & Suites 916 E State St (at
Marshall) **414/276-8800, 800/328-7275** • gay-
friendly • also restaurant • WiFi • wheelchair
access

Hotel of the Arts/ Days Inn 1840 N 6th St
(at Reservoir Ave) **414/265-5629** • gay-
friendly • nonsmoking • WiFi

The Iron Horse Hotel 500 W Florida St (at S
5th St) **888/543-4766** • gay-friendly hotel
geared toward motorcycle enthusiasts

The Milwaukee Hilton 509 W Wisconsin
Ave (at 5th St) **414/271-7250, 800/445-8667** •
gay-friendly • also restaurant & pub • pool •
WiFi • wheelchair access

BARS

Art Bar 722 E Burleigh St (at Fratney)
414/372-7880 • 3pm-2am, from 10am wknds
• live entertainment • WiFi • gay-owned

Boom/ The Room 625 S 2nd (at W Bruce)
414/277-5040 • 5pm-2am, from 2pm wknds •
lesbians/ gay men • neighborhood bar • food
served • videos • patio • also martini bar

D.I.X. 739 S 1st St (at National)
414/231-9085 • 4pm-2am, from 11am Sun •
mostly gay men • videos

Fluid 819 S 2nd St (at W National) 414/643-5843 • 5pm-close, from 2pm wknds • mostly gay men • neighborhood bar

Hybrid Lounge 707 E Brady (at Van Buren) 414/810-1809 • 4pm-close, from 10am Sat & Sun • mostly gay men

The Nomad 1401 E Brady St (at Warren) 414/224-8111 • 2pm-2pm, from noon wknds • gay-friendly • soccer pub

Nut Hut 1500 W Scott (at 15th St) 414/647-2673 • 2pm-2am, from noon Fri-Sun • mostly women • neighborhood bar

Taylor's 795 N Jefferson St (at Wells) 414/271-2855 • 4pm-close • gay/ straight • neighborhood bar • patio • wheelchair access • gay-owned

Two 718 E Burleigh St (at Fratney) 414/372-7880 • 7pm-close Wed-Sat • gay/ straight

Walker's Pint 818 S 2nd St (at National Ave) 414/643-7468 • 4:30pm-2am, from noon Sun • mostly women • neighborhood bar • dancing/DJ • live shows • karaoke • patio • WiFi • lesbian-owned

Woody's 1579 S 2nd St (at Lapham St) 414/672-0806 • 4pm-close, from 2pm wknds • mostly men • neighborhood sports bar • WiFi

NIGHTCLUBS

BTW Lounge 231 E Buffalo St 414/273-4289 • 2pm-2am, from 10am Sun brunch

The Circus Club 906 S Barclay 414/301-1424 • 4pm-2am, from 9pm Fri-Sat from 11am Sun, clsd Mon • mostly gay men • dancing/DJ• drag shows • patio

La Cage/ Montage Lounge 801 S 2nd St (at National) 414/383-8330 • 10pm-close Fri-Sat • mostly gay men • dancing/DJ • live shows • videos • wheelchair access

---

Milwaukee

WHERE THE GIRLS ARE:
In East Milwaukee south of downtown, spread out from Lake Michigan to S Layton Blvd.

LGBT PRIDE:
June. 414/272-3378, web: www.pridefest.com.

ANNUAL EVENTS:
June-July - Summerfest, web: www.summerfest.com.
August - Wisconsin State Fair 414/266-7000, 800/884-3247 web: wistatefair.
September - AIDS Walk 800/348–WALK, web: www.aidswalkwis.org.

CITY INFO:
414/273-7222 or 800/554-1448, web: www.visitmilwaukee.org.

WEATHER:
Summer temperatures can get up into 90°s. Spring and fall are pleasantly moderate but too short. Winter brings snow, cold temperatures, and even colder wind chills.

ATTRACTIONS:
Annunciation Greek Orthodox Church 414/461–9400, web: www.annunciationwi.com.
Breweries.
Grand Avenue.
Harley-Davidson Museum, web: www.hdmuseum.com.
Milwaukee Art Museum, web: www.mam.org.
Mitchell Park Horticultural Conservatory, 414/649-9830.
Pabst Theatre 414/286-3663, web: www.pabsttheater.org.

TRANSIT:
Yellow Cab 414/271-1800.
Milwaukee Transit 414/344-6711, web: www.ridemcts.com.

MONA'S 1407 S 1st St (at Greenfield) 414/643–0377 • 4pm-close, from 6pm Sat-Mon • lesbians/ gay men • also restaurant • WiFi • lesbian-owned

CAFES

Alterra Coffee Roasters 2211 N Prospect Ave (at North) 414/273–3753 • 7am-6pm

Bella Caffe 189 N Milwaukee St 414/273–5620 • 6am-9pm, till 11pm Fri-Sat, 8am-6pm Sun

Fuel Cafe 818 E Center St 414/374–3835 • 7am-10pm • WiFi • wheelchair access

RESTAURANTS

Beans & Barley 1901 E North Ave (at Oakland Ave) 414/278–7878 • 8am-9pm • vegetarian cafe & deli

Coquette Cafe 316 N Milwaukee St (btwn Buffalo & St Paul) 414/291–2655 • 11am-10pm, 5pm-11pm Sat, 11am-5pm Sun • bistro fare

Crisp Pizza Bar & Lounge 1323 E Brady St 414/727–4217 • 4pm-2am, from 11:30am wknds • also full bar

Harvey's 1340 W Towne Sq Rd, Mequon 262/241–9589 • dinner nightly • cont'l

Honeypie Cafe 2643 S Kinnickinnic Ave (at Potter) 414/489–7437 • 10am-midnight, 9am-9pm wknds • homemade midwestern classics

The Knick 1030 E Juneau Ave (at Waverly) 414/272–0011 • 11am-midnight, from 9am wknds • popular • some veggie • full bar • wheelchair access

La Perla 734 S 5th St (at National) 414/645–9888 • 11am-10pm, till 11:30pm Fri-Sat • Mexican • also bar

Lulu 2261 & 2265 S Howell Ave 414/294–5858 • 11am-2am • also bar till late • live music wknds

Meritage 5921 W Vliet St 414/479–0620 • 5pm-10pm, till 11pm Fri-Sat, clsd Sun-Mon • American

Range Line Inn 2635 W Mequon Rd, Mequon 262/242–0530 • 4:30pm-10pm, clsd Sun-Mon • reservations recommended

Sanford Restaurant 1547 N Jackson St 414/276–9608 • dinner only, clsd Sun • Milwaukee fine dining Euro-style

ENTERTAINMENT & RECREATION

Boerner Botanical Gardens 9400 Boerner Dr (in Whitnall Park), Hales Corners 414/525–5650 • 8am-dusk • 40-acre garden & arboretum, garden clsd in winter

Harley-Davidson Museum 400 Canal St (at N 6th St) 877/436–8738

Milwaukee Gay Arts Center 703 S 2nd St (at National Ave) 414/383–3727 • art gallery • performance • theater • classes & more

Mitchell Park Domes 524 S Layton Blvd (27th St, at Pierce) 414/257–5611 • 9am-5pm • botanical gardens

BOOKSTORES

OutWords Books, Gifts & Coffee 2710 N Murray Ave (at Park Pl) 414/963–9089 • 11am-7pm, till 8pm Fri-Sat, noon-6pm Sun • pride items • wheelchair access

Peoples' Books 2122 E Locust St (at Maryland) 414/962–0575 • 10am-6pm, clsd Sun

Woodland Pattern 720 E Locust St 414/263–5001 • 11am-8pm, noon-5pm wknds, clsd Mon

RETAIL SHOPS

Miss Groove 1330 E Brady St 414/298–9185 • 11am-7pm, 10am-6pm Sat, noon-5pm Sun • accessories & apparel

PUBLICATIONS

Outbound/ Quest 920/655–0611, 800/578–3785 • news & arts reviews for WI's LGBT community

EROTICA

Booked Solid 7035 Greenfield Ave (at 70th), West Allis 414/774–7210

Norwalk

ACCOMMODATIONS

Daughters of the Earth 18134 Index Ave 608/269–5301 • women only • women's land • camping • retreat space • lesbian-owned

Oshkosh

BARS

Deb's Spare Time 1303 Harrison St (btw main & New York) 920/235–6577 • 11am-2am, from 9am wknds • lesbians/gay men• neighborhood bar • food served • live shows • 18+ • gay owned

EROTICA

Pure Pleasure 1212 Oshkosh Ave (off Hwy 21) 920/235–9727

Racine

NIGHTCLUBS

JoDee's International 2139 Racine St/ S Hwy 32 (at 22nd) **262/634–9804** • 7pm-close • lesbians/ gay men • dancing/DJ • live shows • karaoke • drag shows • park in rear

Sheboygan

BARS

The Blue Lite 1029 N 8th St (off Rte 143) **920/457–1636** • 7pm-close, from 3pm Sun • lesbians/ gay men • neighborhood bar • dancing/DJ Fri-Sat

Stevens Point

EROTICA

Eldorado's 3219 Church St (at Business 51 S) 715/343–9877

Sturgeon Bay

ACCOMMODATIONS

The Chadwick Inn 25 N 8th Ave **920/743–2771** • gay-friendly • 1890 Queen Anne • nonsmoking • lesbian-owned • $100-135

The Chanticleer Guest House 4072 Cherry Rd **920/746–0334, 866/682–0384** • popular • gay-friendly • on 70 acres • pool • WiFi • nonsmoking • wheelchair access • gay-owned

Superior

BARS

The Flame 1612 Tower Ave **715/395–0101** • 3pm-2:30am • lesbians/ gay men • dancing/DJ • live entertainment • karaoke • drag shows • WiFi

JT's Bar & Grill 1506 N 3rd St (at Blatnik Bridge) **715/394–2580** • 11am-10pm, till 11pm Fri-Sat, 7am-10pm Sun • lesbians/ gay men • neighborhood bar • dancing/DJ • food served • karaoke • drag shows • patio • wheelchair access

The Main Club 1217 Tower Ave (at 12th) **715/392–1756** • 3pm-2am • mostly gay men • dancing/DJ • live shows • WiFi • wheelchair access

Wausau

NIGHTCLUBS

Oz 320 Washington **715/842–3225** • 7pm-close • mostly gay men • dancing/DJ • karaoke • drag shows • videos

Wisconsin Dells

BARS

Captain Dix 4124 River Rd (at Rainbow Valley Resort) **608/253–1818, 866/553–1818** • 6pm-close, from 11am wknds • lesbians/ gay men • karaoke • theme nights

WYOMING

Cheyenne

see also Fort Collins, Colorado

INFO LINES & SERVICES

Wyoming Equality/ United Gays & Lesbians of Wyoming 307/778–7645 • 10am-2pm Mon-Fri • info • referrals • newsletter • social activities • also youth services

BARS

Choice City Shots 124 LaPorte Ave (at College), Fort Collins, CO **970/221–4333** • open 6:30pm • lesbians/ gay men • neighborhood bar • dancing/DJ • karaoke • live shows • wheelchair access • lesbian/ gay-owned

Etna

RETAIL SHOPS

Blue Fox Studio & Gallery 107452 N US Hwy 89 **307/883–3310** • open 7 days • hours vary • pottery, jewelry & mask studio • local travel info • gay-owned

Evanston

EROTICA

Romantix Adult Superstore 1939 Harrison Dr **307/789–0800** • 6am-2am

Laramie

ACCOMMODATIONS

Cowgirl Horse Hotel 32 Black Elk Trail **307/745–8794 OR 399–2502** • specializing in women travelers & their horses • men welcome • $85

BOOKSTORES

The Second Story 105 Ivinson Ave **307/745–4423** • 10am-6pm, clsd Sun • independent

Note: In most countries other than the USA and Canada, listings are alphabetical by city rather than by state, province, or region.

Canada

ALBERTA

Provincewide

PUBLICATIONS

Perceptions 306/244–1930 • covers the Canadian prairies

Banff

see also Lake Louise

ACCOMMODATIONS

Fairmont Banff Springs 405 Spray Ave 403/762–2211 • gay-friendly • in Canadian Rockies • also Willow Stream Spa

Simpson's Num-Ti-Jah Lodge 403/522–2167 • gay-friendly • overlooks Bow Lake & Canadian Rockies • 40km N of Lake Louise

Spruce Grove Inn 545 Banff Ave 403/762–3301, 800/879–1991 • gay-friendly • nonsmoking • WiFi • wheelchair access

Calgary

INFO LINES & SERVICES

Calgary Outlink: Centre for Gender & Sexual Diversity 1528 16th Ave SW 403/234–8973, 877/688–4765 (24HR CRISIS & SUPPORT LINE) • 11am-5pm Mon & Wed, 1pm-7pm Tue & Th, by appt Fri, clsd wknds • many groups

Front Runners AA 1227 Kensington Close NW (at Hillhurst United Church) 403/777–1212 • 8:30pm Tue, Th & Sat

Inside Out #4, 1230-A 17th Ave SW 403/234–8973 • 7pm Mon • support group for LGBTQ ages 15-25

ACCOMMODATIONS

11th Street Lodging 403/209–1800 • gay/ straight • kids 10+ ok • "no shoe" policy inside • nonsmoking • gay-owned • Can$65-220

Calgary Westways Guest House 216 25th Ave SW 403/229–1758, 866/846–7038 • gay/ straight • full brkfst • hot tub • nonsmoking • pets ok • WiFi • gay-owned • Can$79-199

Executive Royal Inn 2828 23rd St NE 403/291–2003, 888/388–3932 • gay-friendly • jacuzzi • pets ok • also restaurant

The Westin Calgary 320 4th Ave SW 403/266–1611 • gay-friendly • downtown 4-diamond hotel • pool • nonsmoking • also restaurant • wheelchair access

BARS

The Back Lot 209 10th Ave SW (at 1st St SW) 403/265–5211 • 2pm-2am • mostly gay men • martini lounge • patio • wheelchair access

Club Sapien 1140 10th Ave SW 403/457–4464 • 5pm-2am, till 11pm Sun-Mon • lesbians/ gay men • neighborhood bar • also restaurant

Fab Bar 1742 10th Ave SW (near 14th St) 403/263–7411 • 4pm-11pm Tue-Th, 11am-2am wknds, clsd Mon • lesbians/ gay men • neighborhood bar • food served • karaoke • rooftop patio • wheelchair access

Ming 520 17th Ave SW 403/229–1986 • 4pm-2am • gay-friendly • martini lounge • food served

NIGHTCLUBS

Club Paradiso 1413 9th Ave SE 403/265–5739 • cabaret/ performance club • also restaurant

GirlsGroove • women's dance parties • check local listings for upcoming events

The Twisted Element 1006 11th Ave SW 403/802–0230 • 9pm-close, clsd Mon • mostly men • dancing/DJ • karaoke • drag shows • strippers • WiFi

CAFES

Caffe Beano 1613 9th St SW (at 17th Ave) 403/229–1232 • 6am-midnight, from 7am wknds • some veggie • wheelchair access

RESTAURANTS

Halo 13226 Macleod Trail SE 403/271–4111 • lunch & dinner • steak, seafood & wine bar

Melrose Cafe & Bar 730 17th Ave SW (at 7th St) 403/228–3566 • 11am-2am, from 10am wknds • full bar till 2am • patio

Thai Sa-On 351 10th Ave SW (at 4th) 403/264–3526 • lunch & dinner, clsd Sun • Thai

ENTERTAINMENT & RECREATION

Calgary Men's Chorus PO Box 23217, Connaught RPO T2S 3B1

BOOKSTORES

Daily Globe News Shop 1004 17th Ave SW (at 10th St) 403/244–2060 • 9am-10pm • periodicals

Self Connection Books 4611 Bowness Rd NW **403/284–1486, 866/735–3457** • 10am-6pm, till 8pm Th, till 5pm Sat, clsd Sun • also 10816 Macleod Trail SE, 403/225-8887

RETAIL SHOPS

Priape 1322 17th Ave SW (enter on 16th) **403/215–1800, 800/461–6969 #25** • noon-9pm, till 6pm Sun • clubwear • leather • books • toys & more

PUBLICATIONS

Gay Calgary & Edmonton Magazine 888/543–6960 • monthly LGBT publication

Edmonton

INFO LINES & SERVICES

AA Gay/ Lesbian 11355 Jasper Ave (at church) **780/424–5900** • 7:30pm Mon • also 8pm Fri at 10804 119th St

Pride Centre of Edmonton 9540 - 111 Ave **780/488–3234** • 10am-10pm Tue-Fri, 2pm-6pm Sat, clsd Sun-Mon • youth group 7pm Sat

Womonspace 9540 111 Ave (Pride Centre of Edmonton) **780/482–1794** • social & recreational society • dances & other events • monthly newsletter

ACCOMMODATIONS

Labyrinth Lake Lodge 780/878–3301 • gay/ straight • lodge on private lake • hot tubs • kids/ pets ok • nonsmoking • WiFi

McCracken Country Inn & Tea House 146 Brookhart St, Hinton **780/865–5662, 888/865–5662** • gay-friendly

Northern Lights B&B 780/483–1572 • lesbians/ gay men • full brkfst • pool • nonsmoking • gay-owned

BARS

The Junction 10242 106th St **780/756–5667** • 4pm-close • lesbians/ gay men • dancing/DJ • live music • drag shows • private club

Woody's Pub & Cafe 11723 A Jasper (above Buddy's) **780/488–6557** • 3pm-midnight, till 3am wknds • lesbians/ gay men • neighborhood bar • food served • karaoke

NIGHTCLUBS

Buddy's Nite Club 11725-B Jasper **780/488–6636** • 9pm-3am, from 8pm Fri • lesbians/ gay men • dancing/DJ • drag shows

Flash 10018 105th St **780/969–9965** • lesbians/ gay men • dancing/DJ

RESTAURANTS

Cafe de Ville 10137 124th St **780/488–9188** • 11:30am-10pm, till midnight Fri-Sat, 10am-2pm & 5pm-10pm Sun • nonsmoking • reservations recommended

ENTERTAINMENT & RECREATION

Edmonton Vocal Minority 780/488–1498 • LGBT chorus

Gaywire CJSR FM 88.5 **780/492–2577** • 6pm-7pm Th • LGBT radio

BOOKSTORES

Audrey's Books 10702 Jasper Ave (at 107th St) **780/423–3487** • 9am-9pm, 9:30am-5:30pm Sat, noon-5pm Sun • large LGBT section • wheelchair access

Greenwood's Bookshoppe 7925 104th St (at 80th) **780/439–2005, 800/661–2078** • 9am-9pm, 9:30am-5:30pm Sat, noon-5pm Sun

RETAIL SHOPS

Divine Decadence 10441 82nd Ave (at 105th) **780/439–2977** • hip fashions • accessories

PUBLICATIONS

Gay Calgary & Edmonton Magazine Calgary **888/543–6960** • monthly LGBT publication

Lake Louise

see also Banff

ACCOMMODATIONS

Lake Louise Inn 210 Village Dr **403/522–3791, 800/661–9237** • gay-friendly • mtn resort near Pipestone River • pool • WiFi

Lethbridge

INFO LINES & SERVICES

GALA/LA (Gay/ Lesbian Alliance of Lethbridge & Area) 403/308–2893 • call for events

Westerose

ACCOMMODATIONS

Pine Trails Getaway RR1 **780/586–0002** • gay campground

BRITISH COLUMBIA

Birken

ACCOMMODATIONS

Birken Lakeside Resort 9179 Portage Rd **604/452-3255** • gay-friendly • cabins • campsites • hot tub • swimming • pets ok • lesbian-owned

Chilliwack

RESTAURANTS

Bravo Restaurant & Lounge 46224 Yale Rd (at Nowell St) **604/792-7721** • 5pm-close, clsd Sun-Tue • martinis • wheelchair access • gay-owned

Courtenay

ACCOMMODATIONS

Moonlight Inn Guest House 250/334-0085 • lesbian guesthouse w/ wedding package in a gay-supportive community midway up the east coast of Vancouver Island

Gulf Islands

INFO LINES & SERVICES

Gays & Lesbians of Salt Spring Island (GLOSSI) PO Box 644, Salt Spring Island V8K 2W2 **250/537-7773** • social events • social justice/ community development • info line

ACCOMMODATIONS

Anne's Oceanfront Hideaway B&B 168 Simson Rd, Salt Spring Island **250/537-0851, 888/474-2663** • gay-friendly • full brkfst • ocean views • nonsmoking • WiFi • wheelchair access

Bellhouse Inn 29 Farmhouse Rd, Galiano Island **250/539-5667, 800/970-7464** • gay/ straight • historic waterfront inn • full brkfst • nonsmoking • WiFi

Birdsong B&B 153 Rourke Rd, Salt Spring Island **250/537-4608** • gay/ straight • ocean & harbor views • WiFi

Fulford Dunderry Guest House 2900 Fulford-Ganges Rd, Salt Spring Island **250/653-4860** • gay-friendly • oceanfront guesthouse • nonsmoking • WiFi • gay-owned

Hummingbird Lodge B&B 1597 Starbuck Ln (at Whalebone Dr), Gabriola **250/247-9300, 877/551-9383** • gay-friendly • nonsmoking

Island Farmhouse B&B 185 Horel Rd W, Salt Spring Island **877/537-5912** • gay/ straight • kids/ pets ok • nonsmoking • lesbian-owned • Can$70-155

Salt Spring Inn & Restaurant 132 Lower Ganges Rd (at Hereford Ave), Salt Spring Island **250/537-9339, 877/537-9339** • gay-friendly • full brkfst • WiFi

Kamloops

ACCOMMODATIONS

Mystic Mountain Acres B&B **250/674-2700** • gay- friendly • private home • full brkfst

Watauga Village B&B 250/674-0085 • gay-friendly • cabins w/ kitchenettes

Okanagan Lake

includes Kaleden, Kelowna, Oliver, Penticton & Vernon

ACCOMMODATIONS

Creek View B&B 1520 Pasadena Rd, Kelowna **250/862-3653** • gay/ straight • swimming • lesbian-owned • nonsmoking • WiFi

Eagles Nest B&B 15620 Commonage Rd (at Carrs Landing Rd), Kelowna **250/766-9350, 866/766-9350** • mostly men • overlooking Lake Okanagan • full brkfst • hot tub • nonsmoking • WiFi • gay-owned • Can$80-150

Grapeseed Guesthouse & Gardens 607 Munson Mountain Rd, Penticton **250/809-9998** • lesbians/gay men • WiFi • lesbian owned

Morningside B&B 1645 Carmi Ave (at Government St), Penticton **250/492-5874** • gay/ straight • full brkfst • shared baths • nonsmoking

CAFES

Bean Scene 274 Bernard Ave, Kelowna **250/763-1814** • 6am-9pm, till 11pm Fri-Sat • patio • wheelchair access

RESTAURANTS

Greek House 3159 Woodsdale Rd, Kelowna **250/766-0090** • 4pm-9pm • cont'l

Okanagan Valley

INFO LINES & SERVICES

Okanagan Rainbow Coalition 1476 Water St, Kelowna **250/860-8555** • 24-hr recorded info • support groups • social events • dances

ACCOMMODATIONS

A Kelowna Getaway 2188 Bennett Rd (at McKinley Rd), Kelowna **250/860-5245** • gay/straight • kids ok • WiFi

Powell River

ACCOMMODATIONS

Beacon B&B & Spa 3750 Marine Ave **604/485-5563, 877/485-5563** • gay-friendly • full brkfst • hot tub • massage • nonsmoking • wheelchair access • WiFi

Prince George

INFO LINES & SERVICES

GALA North 250/562-7124 • 24-hr recorded info • social group • call for drop-in hours & location

EROTICA

Doctor Love 1412 Patricia Blvd 250/614-1411

Tofino

ACCOMMODATIONS

Beachwood 1368 Chesterman Beach Rd **250/725-4250** • gay-friendly • private apt • steps to the beach • nonsmoking • gay-owned

BriMar B&B 1375 Thornberg Crescent **250/725-3410, 800/714-9373** • gay/straight • on the beach • full brkfst • teens ok

Eagle Nook Wilderness Resort & Spa Ucluelet **800/760-2777** • gay-friendly • private log cabins • gourmet meals • health spa

RESTAURANTS

Blue Heron 634 Campbell St **250/725-2043** • 7am-10pm • full bar • wheelchair access

Vancouver

INFO LINES & SERVICES

AA Gay/Lesbian 604/434-3933

The Greater Vancouver Pride Line **604/684-6869 x290, 800/566-1170** • 7pm-10pm • info & support

QMUNITY: BC's Resource Centre 1170 Bute St (btwn Davie & Pendrell Sts) **604/684-5307, 800/566-1170** • also Out on the Shelves LGBT lending library

ACCOMMODATIONS

Arbutus Guest House 1904 Arbutus St (at W Third Ave) **604/325-3013** • gay-friendly • lesbian-owned • Can$125-300

Barclay House B&B 1351 Barclay St (at Jervis) **604/605-1351, 800/971-1351** • gay/straight • restored Victorian • full brkfst • nonsmoking • WiFi • gay-owned

The Buchan Hotel 1906 Haro St (btwn Denman & Gilford) **604/685-5354, 800/668-6654** • gay-friendly • built in 1926 • some shared baths • nonsmoking • kids ok

Granville B&B 5050 Granville St (at 34th Ave) **604/739-9002, 866/739-9002** • gay-friendly • B&B in Tudor Revival • nonsmoking • WiFi

Hostelling International—Vancouver Central 1025 Granville St (at Nelson) **604/685-5335, 877/203-4461** • gay/straight • hostel • kids ok • WiFi • also bar • wheelchair access

Hostelling International—Vancouver Jericho Beach 1515 Discovery St **604/224-3208, 888/203-4303** • gay/straight • summer only • beachfront • kids ok • WiFi • wheelchair access

Hotel Indigo Vancouver 500 W 12th Ave (at Cambie St) **604/873-1811, 877/846-3446** • gay-friendly • full brkfst • kids ok • gym • WiFi

L' Hermitage Hotel 788 Richards St (at Robson) **778/327-4100** • gay/straight • pool • nonsmoking • WiFi • wheelchair access

The Langtry 968 Nicola St (at Barclay) **604/687-7892, 800/699-7892** • gay/straight • B&B apts in West End • nonsmoking • gay-owned • WiFi

Moda Hotel 900 Seymour St (at Smithe) **604/683-4251, 877/683-5522** • gay/straight • restaurant • kids ok • WiFi • also 3 bars

Nelson House B&B 977 Broughton St (btwn Nelson & Barclay) **604/684-9793, 866/684-9793** • lesbians/gay men • Edwardian mansion • full brkfst • jacuzzi in suite • sundeck • WiFi • lesbian- & gay-owned

"O Canada" House B&B 1114 Barclay St (at Thurlow) **604/688-0555, 877/688-1114** • gay/straight • restored 1897 Victorian home • full brkfst • WiFi • gay-owned

Opus Hotel 322 Davie St (at Hamilton, Yaletown) **604/642-6787, 866/642-6787** • gay-friendly • hip luxury boutique hotel • also bar & Elixer French brasserie • wheelchair access • Can$299+

Rosedale on Robson 838 Hamilton St (at Robson) **604/689-8033, 800/661-8870** • gay-friendly • all-suite w/ kitchenette • pool • kids/pets ok • WiFi • nonsmoking

Sandman Suites on Davie 1160 Davie St (at Thurlow St) **604/681–7263, 800/726–3626** • gay/ straight • West End suites • pool • nonsmoking • wheelchair access • Can$119+

The Sutton Place Hotel 845 Burrard St (at Smithe) **604/682–5511, 866/378–8866** • gay-friendly • luxurious boutique hotel • nonsmoking • WiFi • pool

Vancouver

WHERE THE GIRLS ARE:

Cruising Commercial Drive, mixing w/ the boys on Davie St, or shopping in Gastown.

ENTERTAINMENT:

Wreck Beach (great gay beach).

LGBT PRIDE:

August. 604/687-0955, web: www.vancouverpride.ca.

ANNUAL EVENTS:

January-February - Gay & Lesbian Ski Week, web: www.gaywhistler.com.

May - Vancouver International Marathon 604/872-2928, web: www.bmovanmarathon.ca.

June - Dragon Boat Festival 604/688-2382, web: www.dragonboatbc.org.

June-July - Vancouver Int'l Jazz Festival 604/872-5200, web: www.coastaljazz.ca.

July - Folk Music Festival 604/602-9798, web: www.thefestival.bc.ca.

August - Queer Film & Video Festival 604/844-1615, web: www.outonscreen.com.

September - BOLD Fest (Bold, Older Lesbians & Dykes), web: www.soundsandfuries.com/BOLD.html.

September/October - International Film Festival 604/685-0260, web: www.viff.org.

CITY INFO:

604/683-2000, web: www.tourism-vancouver.com.

BEST VIEW:

Biking in Stanley Park, or on a ferry between peninsulas and islands. Atop one of the surrounding mountains.

ATTRACTIONS:

Capilano Suspension Bridge, web: www.capbridge.com.

Chinatown.

Dr Sun Yat-Sen Chinese Garden 604/662–3207, web: vancouverchinesegarden.com.

Gastown.

Granville Island, web: www.granvilleisland.com.

Grouse Mountain, web: www.grousemountain.com.

Museum of Anthropology 604/822–5087, web: www.moa.ubc.ca.

Science World 604/443-7443, web: www.scienceworld.ca.

Stanley Park.

Vancouver Aquarium 604/659–3474, web: www.vanaqua.org.

Vancouver Lookout 604/689–0421, web: www.vancouverlookout.com.

Vancouver Museum 604/736–4431 web: www.museumofvancouver.ca.

Van Dusen Botanical Gardens 604/878-9274, web: www.vandusengarden.org.

WEATHER:

It's cold and wet in the winter (32-45°F), but it's absolutely gorgeous in the summer (52-75°F)!

TRANSIT:

Yellow Cab 604/681-1111, web: www.yellowcabonline.com.

TransLink 604/953-3333, web: www.translink.bc.ca.

A Visitors' Map of all bus lines is available through the tourist office.

The West End Guest House 1362 Haro St (at Broughton) 604/681–2889, 888/546–3327 • gay/ straight • full brkfst • nonsmoking • gay-owned • Can$95-275

Bars

1181 1181 Davie St (at Bute) 604/687–3991 • 4pm-close • mostly gay men • upscale cocktail lounge

Avanti's Pub 1601 Commercial Dr (at 1st Ave) 604/254–5466 • 11am-midnight, till 1am Fri-Sat • gay-friendly • sports bar • popular w/ local lesbian ball teams

The Fountainhead Pub 1025 Davie St (at Burrard) 604/687–2222 • 11am-midnight, till 2am Fri-Sat • wknd brunch • lesbians/ gay men • neighborhood bar • transgender-friendly • patio

Gerard Lounge 845 Burrard St (in Sutton Place Hotel) 604/682–5511 • 11:30am-1am, 4:30pm-midnight Sun • gay-friendly • food served • great martinis

The Oasis 1240 Thurlow (at Davie) 604/685–1724 • 5pm-close • lesbians/ gay men • martini bar • dancing/DJ • theme nights

Nightclubs

816 Granville/ The World 816 Granville St • midnight-6am Fri-Sun • mostly gay men • dancing/DJ

Celebrities 1022 Davie St (at Burrard St) 604/681–6180 • 9pm-3am, clsd Sun-Mon • mostly gay men• dancing/DJ • theme nights

Club 23 West 23 W Cordova (at Carrall) 604/200–2923 • 10pm-4am Fri-Sat • gay/ straight • dancing/DJ

Crema 604/875–9907 • women's dance party • check local listings for details

Five Sixty 560 Seymour St (at Pender) 604/678–6322 • gay/ straight • dancing/DJ • live bands • art gallery

Flygirl 604/839–9819 • women's parties • check www.flygirlproductions.com for details

Hershe Bar 604/839–9819 • long wknds only • mega lesbian dance party • check local listings for info

The Junction Public House 1138 Davie St 604/669–2013 • 11am-2am, till 3am Fri-Sat • mostly gay men • dancing/DJ • sports bar • patio

Shine 364 Water St (at Richards) 604/408–4321 • gay-friendly • dancing/DJ

Cafes

Coming Home 753 6th St (at 8th Ave), New Westminster 604/288–9850 • 10am-5pm, 9am-3pm Sat, clsd Sun • gay-owned

Delaney's 1105 Denman St 604/662–3344 • 6am-9pm, from 6:30am wknds • coffee shop

JJ Bean 2206 Commercial Dr 604/254–3723 • 6am-10pm

Rhizome Cafe 317 E Broadway 604/872–3166 • 11am-10pm, till midnight Fri-Sat, till 9pm Sun, clsd Mon • plenty veggie/ vegan • local artists • workshops

Sweet Revenge 4160 Main St (at 26th) 604/879–7933 • 7pm-midnight, till 1am Fri-Sat • patisserie • gay-owned

Turk's Coffee Exchange 1276 Commercial Dr 604/255–5805 • 6:30am-11pm

Restaurants

Bin 941 941 Davie St 604/683–1246 • 5pm-2am, till midnight Sun • tiny tapas parlor • popular • also 1521 W Broadway, 604/734-9421

Brioche 401 W Cordova (at Homer, in Gastown) 604/682–4037 • 7am-7pm, 9am-6pm wknds • Italian restaurant & bakery

Cafe Deux Soleils 2096 Commercial Dr 604/254–1195 • 8am-midnight, till 5pm Sun • lesbians/ gay men • vegetarian • live shows

Cafe Luxy 1235 Davie St (btwn Bute & Jervis) 604/669–5899 • 11am-11pm, wknd brunch 9am-3pm • some veggie • full bar • wheelchair access • live jazz

Cascade Room 2616 Main St (at 10th) 604/709–8650 • 5pm-1am, from noon-2am wknds

Chill Winston 3 Alexander St 604/288–9575 • 11am-1am • in Gastown

Cincin 1154 Robson St (off Bute) 604/688–7338 • dinner nightly • Italian/ Mediterranean • full bar

The Dish 1068 Davie St 604/689–0208 • 7am-10pm, 9am-9pm Sun • veggie fast food • gay-owned

Elbow Room Cafe 560 Davie St (at Seymour) 604/685–3628 • 8am-4pm, till 5pm wknds • great brkfst

Foundation Lounge 2301 Main St 604/708–0881 • noon-1am, till 2am wknds • vegetarian

Glowbal Grill & Satay Bar 1079 Mainland St (Yaletown) 604/602–0835 • lunch, dinner, brunch wknds • also check out Afterglow next door • nightly 6pm-late

Hamburger Mary's 1202 Davie St (at Bute) 604/687–1293 • 8am-3am, till 4am Fri-Sat, till 2am Sun • some veggie • full bar

Havana 1212 Commercial Dr 604/253–9119 • 11am-11pm, from 10am wknds • popular • Cuban fusion • full bar • patio • also gallery & theater

India Gate 616 Robson St (at Granville) 604/684–4617 • lunch Mon-Sat, dinner nightly

J Lounge 1216 Bute St (at Davie St) 604/609–6665 • 5pm-1am, from 11am Sun • live entertainment • DJs • cocktails

Lickerish 903 Davie St (at Hornby) 604/696–0725 • 5:30pm-midnight, till 1am Th-Sun • global cuisine • cocktail lounge

Lift Bar & Grill 333 Menchions Mews 604/689–5438 • 11:30am-midnight

Lolita's 1326 Davie St (at Jervis) 604/696–9996 • 4:30pm till late, wknd brunch • innovative Mexican • tiny space but worth the wait

Maenam 1938 W 4th Ave 604/730–5579 • lunch Tue-Sat, dinner 5pm-midnight • Thai

Martini's Whole Wheat Pizza 151 W Broadway (btwn Cambie & Main) 604/873–0021 • 11am-2am, from 2pm Sat, till 1am Sun • great pizza • full bar

Miura Waffle Milk Bar 829 Davie St 604/687–2909 • 9am-7pm, from 10am Sat, clsd Sun

Naam 2724 W 4th St (at MacDonald) 604/738–7151 • 24hrs • vegetarian • live music • wheelchair access

Score 1262 Davie St (at Jervis St) 604/632–1646 • 10am-late • lesbians/ gay men • sports bar • also popular restaurant

Seasons in the Park Cambie St & W 33rd Ave 604/874–8008 • from 11:30am, 10:30am Sun

Tanpopo Sushi 1122 Denman (at Pendrell) 604/681–7777 • lunch & dinner • excellent, affordable sushi

Entertainment & Recreation

Capilano Suspension Bridge 3735 Capilano Rd, N Vancouver 604/985–7474

Cruisey T leaves from N foot of Denman St (at Harbor Cruises) 604/551–2628 • Sun (seasonal) • 4-hour party cruise around Vancouver Harbour • lesbians/ gay men • dancing/DJ • live shows • food served

Girl Gig Productions • women's performance promoters • popular "Chicks With Picks" series • check girlgigs.com for info

Rockwood Adventures 6578 Acorn Rd, Sechelt 604/741–0802, 888/236–6606 • rain forest walks & city tours for all levels w/ free hotel pickup

Sunset Beach Beach Ave, right in the West End (near Burrard St Bridge) • home of Vancouver AIDS memorial

Vancouver Nature Adventures 1251 Cardero St #2005 604/684–4922, 800/528–3531 • orca-watching safari • guided kayaking day trip & beach BBQ • no experience required • free hotel pickup

Wreck Beach below UBC

Bookstores

Little Sister's 1238 Davie St (btwn Bute & Jervis) 604/669–1753, 800/567–1662 (IN CANADA ONLY) • 10am-11pm • popular • LGBT • wheelchair access

People's Co-op Bookstore 1391 Commercial Dr (btwn Kitchener & Charles) 604/253–6442, 888/511–5556 • LGBT section

Retail Shops

Cupcakes 1116 Denman St (at Pendrell) 604/974–1300 • 10am-9pm, till 10pm Fri-Sat • women-owned cupcake shop • also at 2887 W Broadway

Liquid Amber Tattoo 62 Powell St (at Columbia) 604/738–3667 • women-owned & operated

Mintage 1714 Commercial Dr 604/646–8243 • vintage & future fashions • woman-owned • also Gastown location

Next Body Piercing 1068 Granville St (at Nelson) 604/684–6398 • noon-6pm, 11am-7pm Fri-Sat • also tattooing

Priape 1148 Davie St (btwn Bute & Thurlow) 604/630–2330 • clubwear • leather • books • toys & more

Publications

Xtra! West 604/684–9696 • LGBT newspaper

Gyms & Health Clubs

Fitness World 1214 Howe St (at Davie) 604/681–3232 • gay-friendly • day passes

Spartacus Athletic Club 1522 Commercial Dr 604/254–6267

Erotica

Love's Touch 1069 Davie St 604/681–7024

Womyn's Ware 896 Commercial Dr (at Venables) 604/254–2543, 888/WYM–WARE (ORDERS ONLY) • 11am-6pm, till 7pm Th-Fri, till 5:30pm Sun • toys • fetishwear • lesbian-owned

Victoria

ACCOMMODATIONS

Albion Manor B&B 224 Superior St
250/389-0012, 877/389-0012 • gay/ straight •
full brkfst • jacuzzi • nonsmoking • WiFi •
wheelchair access • gay-owned • Can$109-239

Ambrosia Historic B&B 522 Quadra (at
Humboldt) **250/380-7705, 877/262-7672** •
gay/ straight • 5-star B&B 3 blocks from
Victoria's inner harbor • full brkfst • jacuzzi •
nonsmoking

The Fairmont Empress 721 Government St
250/384-8111, 800/257-7544 • gay-friendly •
Victoria landmark • pool • spa • afternoon tea
• kids/ small pets ok • nonsmoking •
wheelchair access • Can$159-479

Hostelling International—Victoria 516
Yates St **250/385-4511, 888/883-0099** • gay/
straight • hostel in heritage bldg dowtown •
kids ok • WiFi • wheelchair access

Howard Johnson Hotel & Suites Victoria
4670 Elk Lake Dr **250/704-4656,
866/300-4656** • gay-friendly • pool • hot tub
• kids ok • restaurant & lounge • wheelchair
access

Inn at Laurel Point 680 Montreal St (at
Quebec St) **250/386-8721, 800/663-7667** •
gay-friendly • restaurant • pool • WiFi •
nonsmoking • kids/pets OK—wheelchair
access

Oak Bay Guest House 1052 Newport Ave
250/598-3812, 800/575-3812 • gay-friendly •
1912 Tudor-style house in quiet garden setting
• full brkfst • near beaches • kids 10+ ok •
nonsmoking

Prior House 620 St Charles (at Rockland
Ave) **250/592-8847, 877/924-3300** • gay-
friendly • 5-star inn in historic 1912 manor
home • full brkfst • nonsmoking

Sandman Hotel Victoria 1852 Douglas St
250/388-0788, 800/726-3626 • gay-friendly •
pool

BARS

Paparazzi 642 Johnson St (enter on Broad
St) **250/388-0505** • 3pm-2am, from 1pm
wknds • lesbians/ gay men • dancing/DJ •
karaoke • drag shows • videos • wheelchair
access

NIGHTCLUBS

Hush 1325 Government St (in basement)
250/385-0566 • 9pm-2am, clsd Sun-Tue •
gay/ straight • dancing/DJ

RESTAURANTS

Rosie's Diner 253 Cook St **250/384-6090** •
8am-9pm • '50s & '60s music & videos •
wheelchair access • gay-owned

Santiago's Cafe 660 Oswego St
250/388-7376 • 11am-9pm • tapas bar •
patio • gay-owned

ENTERTAINMENT & RECREATION

Butchart Gardens 800 Benvenuto Ave,
Brentwood Bay **250/652-5256, 866/652-4422**

BOOKSTORES

Bolen Books 1644 Hillside Ave #111 (in
shopping center) **250/595-4232** • 8:30am-
10pm • LGBT section

RETAIL SHOPS

Oceanside Gifts 812 Wharf St, Ste 102
(across from Empress Hotel on the lower
causeway) **250/380-1777** • 10am-10pm • gifts
from across Canada • wheelchair access

Whistler

ACCOMMODATIONS

Alpine Vacation Accommodation
604/938-0707, 888/938-0707 • gay-friendly •
ski-in/ ski-out luxury townhouses •
nonsmoking

Best Western Listel Whistler Hotel 4121
Village Green (at Whistler Way)
604/932-1133, 800/663-5472 • gay-friendly •
pool • hot tub • nonsmoking • WiFi •
wheelchair access

Coast Blackcomb Suites at Whistler 4899
Painted Cliff Rd **604/905-3400, 800/716-6199**
• gay-friendly • full-service resort hotel • full
bar & restaurant • hot tub • pool •
nonsmoking • wheelchair access • Can$120+

Fairmont Chateau Whistler 4599 Chateau
Blvd **604/938-8000, 800/606-8244** • gay-
friendly • pool • ski-in/ ski-out hotel & spa •
nonsmoking • wheelchair access

Four Seasons Resort Whistler 4591
Blackcomb Wy **604/935-3400, 800/268-6282**
• gay-friendly • luxury resort & spa • pool •
nonsmoking • wheelchair access

Hostelling International—Whistler 1035
Legacy Way **604/962-0025, 866/762-4122** •
gay/ straight • facility was built for 2010
Olympics • nonsmoking • WiFi • wheelchair
access

Westin Whistler 4090 Whistler Wy
604/905-5000, 800/937-8461 • gay-friendly •
full-service resort hotel • full bar & restaurant •
spa • hot tub • pool • nonsmoking • WiFi •
wheelchair access

RESTAURANTS

Araxi 4222 Village Square **604/932–4540** • lunch & dinner • local ingredients • also seafood bar & lounge

The Bearfoot Bistro 4121 Village Green **604/932–3433** • 6pm-midnight • excellent wine cellar • reservations recommended

Boston Pizza 2011 Innsbruck Dr **604/932–7070** • 11am-11pm, till midnight wknds • full bar

La Rua 4557 Blackcomb Blvd **604/932–5011** • 6pm-close, clsd Tue

Quattro 4319 Main St **604/905–4844** • dinner nightly • Italian

Sachi Sushi 106-4359 Main St **604/935–5649** • lunch & dinner

Southside Diner 2102 Lake Placid Rd (off Hwy 99) **604/966–0668** • 7am-midnight • hosts occasional Gay Social

Trattoria di Umberto 4417 Sundial Pl **604/932–5858** • lunch & dinner • reservations recommended

ENTERTAINMENT & RECREATION

Ziptrek Ecotours PO Box 734 V0N 1B0 **604/935–0001, 866/935–0001** • ziplines crisscross the Fitzsimmons Creek btwn Whistler & Blackcomb

GYMS & HEALTH CLUBS

Solarice 202-4230 Gateway Dr (above Visitor Info Centre) **604/935–1222, 888/935–1222** • spa & wellness center • yoga studio • lesbian-owned

EROTICA

The Love Nest #102-4338 Main St **604/932–6906**

MANITOBA

Provincewide

PUBLICATIONS

Perceptions **306/244–1930** • covers the Canadian prairies

Winnipeg

INFO LINES & SERVICES

Rainbow Resource Centre 170 Scott St (at Wardlaw) **204/474–0212, 204/284–5208** • call for hrs, clsd wknds • also info line • many social/ support groups

BARS

Club 200 190 Garry St (at St Mary Ave) **204/943–6045** • 4pm-2am, 6pm-midnight Sun • lesbians/ gay men • dancing/DJ • karaoke • drag shows • go-go dancers • wheelchair access

Fame 279 Garry St **204/414–9433** • 9pm-2am Fri-Sat only • lesbians/ gay men • dancing/DJ

NIGHTCLUBS

Gio's Club & Bar 155 Smith St (at York Ave) **204/786–1236** • 4pm-11pm, till 2am Wed-Sat, till midnight Sun • lesbians/ gay men • dancing/DJ • live shows • drag shows • screened patio

RESTAURANTS

Buccacino's Cucina Italiana 155 Osborne St **204/452–8251** • 11am-11pm, till 1am Fri, till midnight Sat, 10am-10:30pm Sun • live music • full bar • patio

Step'N Out 157 Provencher Blvd **204/956–7837** • lunch Tue-Fri, dinner Tue-Sat, clsd Sun • fresh dynamic entrees • wheelchair access

ENTERTAINMENT & RECREATION

Queer Power **204/786–9782** • 9pm Mon

BOOKSTORES

McNally Robinson 1120 Grant Ave #4000 (in the mall) **204/475–0483, 800/561–1833** • 9am-10pm, till 11pm Fri-Sat, noon-6pm Sun • some gay titles • wheelchair access

PUBLICATIONS

Outwords **204/942–4599** • LGBT newspaper

EROTICA

Discreet Boutique 340 Donald (at Ellice) **204/947–1307, 800/247–0454** • also Discreet Video next door

Dominion News 262 Portage Ave (btwn Garry & Smith) **204/942–6563** • 8am-9pm, from 9am Sat, noon-6pm Sun • some gay periodicals

Love Nest 172 St Anne's Rd **204/254–0422** • also 1341 Main St, 204/589–4141 • also Portage & Westwood, 204/ 837–6475

NEW BRUNSWICK

Fredericton

ACCOMMODATIONS

River's Edge Campground 19 Cottage Ln, Durham Bridge **506/458-2107, 800/370-1644** • lesbians/ gay men • pool • outdoor activities • gay-owned • camping/ RV hookups • WiFi

NIGHTCLUBS

boom! 474 Queen St **506/463-2666** • 8pm-2am, 4pm-7pm Sun, clsd Mon-Wed • lesbians/ gay men • dancing/DJ

RESTAURANTS

Molly's Cafe 554 Queen St **506/457-9305** • 9am-10pm, noon-midnight Fri-Sun • full bar • garden patio • some veggie

EROTICA

X-Citement 558 Queen St **506/458-2048** • videos • magazines • adult novelties

Lower Sackville

EROTICA

Pleasures & Treasures 295 Sackville Dr **902/864-4159** • videos • magazines • adult novelties

Moncton

ACCOMMODATIONS

Auberge Au Bois Dormant Inn 67 rue John (at Birch) **506/855-6767, 866/855-6767** • gay-friendly • affordable luxury inn • full brkfst • nonsmoking • WiFi • gay-owned

NIGHTCLUBS

Triangles 234 St George St (at Archibald) **506/857-8779** • 8pm-2am • lesbians/ gay men • neighborhood bar • dancing/DJ • karaoke Th

RESTAURANTS

Calactus Cafe 125 Church St (at St George) **506/388-4833** • 11am-10pm • vegetarian

EROTICA

X-Citement 651 Mountain Rd **506/388-2226** • videos, magazines, adult novelties

St Andrews

ACCOMMODATIONS

Fairmont Algonquin 184 Adolphus St **506/529-8823, 866/540-4403** • gay-friendly • swimming • kids/ pets ok

St John

ACCOMMODATIONS

Mahogany Manor 220 Germain St **506/636-8000, 800/796-7755** • gay/ straight • full brkfst • nonsmoking • kids ok • wheelchair access • gay-owned

NIGHTCLUBS

Happinez Wine Bar 42 Princess St **506/634-7340** • 4pm-midnight, till 2am Fri-Sat • gay-friendly

RESTAURANTS

Opera Bistro 60 Prince William St **506/642-2822** • lunch & dinner

NEWFOUNDLAND

Dildo

ACCOMMODATIONS

George House Heritage B&B 80 Front Rd **709/582-3170, 888/339-7829** • gay-friendly • full brkfst • nonsmoking • WiFi

Inn by the Bay 78 Front Rd **709/582-3170, 888/339-7829** • gay-friendly • full brkfst • nonsmoking • WiFi

L'Anse aux Meadows

RESTAURANTS

The Norseman **709/754-3105, 877/623-2018** • 9am-10pm seasonally

St George's

ACCOMMODATIONS

The Palace Inn 2 School Rd (at Main St) **709/647-1377, 877/999-1377** • gay-friendly • 19th-c B&B • bay views • WiFi

St John's

ACCOMMODATIONS

Abba Inn B&B 36 Queen's Rd (at Prescott St) **709/754-0058, 800/754-0058** • gay/ straight • fireplaces • nonsmoking • pets ok • WiFi

Banberry House 116 Military Rd (at Rawlins Cross) **709/579-8006, 877/579-8226** • gay/ straight • full brkfst • kids/ small pets ok • nonsmoking

Bluestone Inn 34 Queen's Rd (at Water St) **709/754-7544, 877/754-9876** • gay-friendly • full brkfst • jacuzzi • gay-owned

Gower House B&B 180 Gower St (at Prescott St) **709/754-0058, 800/563-3959** • gay/ straight • full brkfst • in downtown • some shared baths • nonsmoking • WiFi

NaGeira House 7 Musgrave St (at Water St), Carbonear **709/596-1888, 800/600-7757** • gay-friendly • B&B • jacuzzi • nonsmoking • kids ok • WiFi

RESTAURANTS

Oliver's **709/754-6444** • 11am-10pm, till 11pm Fri, 10am-11pm Sat • building was home to early suffragist Ladies' Reading Room

Zapatas 10 Bates Hill (off Queens Rd) **709/576-6399** • lunch & dinner • full bar • Mexican • some veggie

NOVA SCOTIA

Annapolis

ACCOMMODATIONS

By the Dock of the Bay Cottages 28 Haddock Alley (at Lower Road), Margaretsville **416/588-1500, 800/407-2856** • gay-friendly • lesbian-owned

Annapolis Royal

ACCOMMODATIONS

Bailey House B&B 150 St George St (at Drury Ln) **902/532-1285, 877/532-1285** • gay/ straight • circa 1770 historic waterfront home • full brkfst • nonsmoking • WiFi

King George Inn **902/532-5286, 888/799-5464** • lesbians/ gay men • full brkfst • jacuzzi • nonsmoking • WiFi

Antigonish

INFO LINES & SERVICES

Antigonish Women's Resource Centre 219 Main St, Ste 204 (Kirk Place) **902/863-6221** • 9am-4:30pm Mon-Fri • info • support services & programs

Baddeck

ACCOMMODATIONS

The Dunlop Inn **902/295-1100, 888/290-1988** • gay-friendly • waterfront B&B inn • nonsmoking • WiFi

Cape Breton

ENTERTAINMENT & RECREATION

Rising Tide Expeditions Gabarus Hwy, Gabarus **902/884-2884, 877/844-2884** • Sea kayaking tours

Chester

ACCOMMODATIONS

The Mecklenburgh Inn 78 Queen St **902/275-4638** • gay-friendly • century-old inn constructed by shipwrights • full brkfst • cat on premises • WiFi

ENTERTAINMENT & RECREATION

The Chester Playhouse 22 Pleasant St **902/275-3933, 800/363-7529** • eclectic programming March-Dec

Digby

ACCOMMODATIONS

Harbourview Inn 25 Harbourview Rd (at Hwy 1), Smith's Cove **902/245-5686, 877/449-0705** • gay-friendly • century-old country inn • full brkfst • pool • kids ok • nonsmoking • WiFi • wheelchair access • gay-owned

Seawinds Motel 90 Montague Row **902/245-2573, 877/245-2570** • gay-friendly • views of Annapolis Basin & Digby Harbour • kids/ pets ok • nonsmoking • gay-owned

Guysborough

ACCOMMODATIONS

DesBarres Manor Inn 90 Church St **902/533-2099, 888/933-2099** • gay-friendly • nonsmoking • kids ok • WiFi

Halifax

ACCOMMODATIONS

Forevergreen House B&B 5560 Hwy 1, St Croix **902/792-1692** • gay-friendly • Victorian farmhouse • full brkfst • nonsmoking • women-owned

Fresh Start B&B 2720 Gottingen St (at Black) **902/453-6616, 888/453-6616** • gay-friendly • Victorian mansion • nonsmoking • WiFi • women-owned

BARS

Menz Bar & Mollyz Back Bar 2182 Gottingen St, Level 2 **902/446-6969** • 3pm-2am • lesbians/ gay men • neighborhood bar • dancing/DJ • drag shows • karaoke • piano bar

Reflections Cabaret 5184 Sackville St (at Barrington) 902/422–2957 • 10pm–4am, clsd Tue-Wed • lesbians/ gay men • dancing/DJ • live shows • cabaret • drag shows • wheelchair access

CAFES

Coburg Coffee House 6085 Coburg Rd 902/429–2326 • 7am-9pm • WiFi

The Daily Grind 5686 Spring Garden Rd (near South Park) 902/429–6397 • 7am-9pm, till 10pm Th-Sat, 8am-6pm Sun • also newsstand

The Second Cup 5425 Spring Garden Rd 902/429–0883 • 7am-11pm, till midnight Th-Sat • WiFi

Uncommon Grounds 1030 S Park St 902/404–3124 • 7am-10pm • gay-friendly • WiFi

RESTAURANTS

Chez Tess Creperie 5687 Charles St 902/406–3133 • lunch & dinner, wknd brunch, clsd Mon • gay-owned

Chives Canadian Bistro 1537 Barrington St 902/420–9626 • 5pm-9:30pm

Heartwood 6250 Quinpool Rd 902/425–2808 • 11am-8pm, clsd Sun • vegetarian

Jane's on the Common 2394 Robie St 902/431–5683 • lunch Tue-Sat, dinner nightly, Sun brunch, clsd Mon

Satisfaction Feast 3559 Robie (N of Lady Hammond Rd) 902/422–3540 • 10am-9pm • vegetarian • patio

ENTERTAINMENT & RECREATION

The Khyber 1588 Barrington St 902/422–9668 • visual & performing arts center

BOOKSTORES

Atlantic News 5560 Morris St (at Queen) 902/429–5468 • 8am-10pm, from 9am Sun • periodicals

Coles 5201 Duke St (in Scotia Square) 902/423–6438 • 9:30pm-6pm, till 8pm Th-Fri, clsd Sun

Schooner Used Books 5378 Inglis St (at Victoria Rd) 902/423–8419 • 10am-5:30pm, clsd Sun-Mon • rare & out-of-print books

Trident Booksellers & Cafe 1256 Hollis St (at Morris St) 902/423–7100 • 8am-5:30pm, 8:30am-5pm Sat, 11am-5pm Sun • used • popular cafe • WiFi

RETAIL SHOPS

Venus Envy 1598 Barrington St 902/422–0004, 877/370–9288 • 10am-6pm, till 7pm Th-Fri, noon-5pm Sun • "a store for women & the people who love them" • books • sex toys • alternative health products

PUBLICATIONS

Wayves PO Box 34090 Scotia Square B3J 3S1 902/889–2229 • monthly magazine "for the rainbow community of Atlantic Canada"

EROTICA

Night Magic Fashions 5268 Sackville St 902/420–9309 • clsd Sun • lingerie, toys, videos

X-Citement 6260 Quinpool Rd 902/492–0026 • videos • magazines • adult novelties

Kemptville

ACCOMMODATIONS

Trout Point Lodge 189 Trout Point Rd (off East Branch Rd & Hwy 203) 902/761–2142, 902/761–2142 • gay-friendly • near Tusket River & Tobeatic Wilderness Area • WiFi • nonsmoking • gourmet meal plans • clsd winter

Lunenburg

ACCOMMODATIONS

1880 Kaulbach House Historic Inn 75 Pelham St 902/634–8818, 800/568–8818 • gay-friendly • full brkfst • nonsmoking • WiFi • gay-owned

Atlantic Sojourn B&B 56 Victoria Rd 902/634–3151, 800/550–4824 • gay-friendly • nonsmoking • WiFi • teddy bear museum • women-owned

New Glasgow

INFO LINES & SERVICES

Pictou County Women's Centre 503 S Frederick St 902/755–4647 • 9am-4:30pm Mon-Fri • support, advocacy & information

North Sydney

ACCOMMODATIONS

Chambers Guest House 64 King St 902/794–7301, 866/496–9453 • gay/ straight • full brkfst • kids/pets ok • nonsmoking

Scotsburn

ACCOMMODATIONS

The Mermaid & the Cow West Branch **902/351–2714** • lesbians/ gay men • cabin & 20 campsites • dogs ok on leash • pool • lesbian-owned

Tangier

ACCOMMODATIONS

Spry Bay Campground & Cabins 19867 Highway #7 **902/772–2554, 866/229–8014** • gay/straight • also restaurant & convenience store • lesbian-owned

Windsor

BOOKSTORES

Readers' Haven 40 Water St **902/798–0133** • 9am-5pm, till 3pm Sat, clsd Sun

Wolfville

RESTAURANTS

Tempest 117 Front St **902/542–0588, 866/542–0588** • lunch wknds, dinner nightly, clsd Mon • world cuisine

Yarmouth

ACCOMMODATIONS

MacKinnon-Cann Historic Inn 27 Willow St (at Collins St) **902/742–9900, 866/698–3142** • gay-friendly • nonsmoking • wheelchair access • gay-owned

Murray Manor B&B 225 Main St (at Forest St) **902/742–9625, 877/742–9629** • gay-friendly • full brkfst • shared baths • kids ok • nonsmoking

ONTARIO

Brighton

ACCOMMODATIONS

Apple Manor 96 Main St, Box 11 **613/475–0351** • gay-friendly • 150-year-old Victorian • full brkfst • shared baths • nonsmoking

Burken B&B 14257 County Rd # 2 **613/475–5267** • gay-friendly • nonsmoking • WiFi • gay-owned

BOOKSTORES

Lighthouse Books 65 Main St **613/475–1269** • 9:30am-5:30pm, clsd Sun-Mon

Gananoque

ACCOMMODATIONS

Trinity House Inn 90 Stone St S, 1000 Islands **613/382–8383, 800/265–4871** • gay-friendly • historic country inn • fine dining restaurant • nonsmoking • kids ok; call ahead • sailing charters • gay-owned

Grand Valley

ACCOMMODATIONS

Rainbow Ridge Resort Country Rd 109 (at Hwy 25 S) **519/928–3262** • lesbians/ gay men • trailers & tents • located on 72 acres on Grand River • pool • restaurant • dance hall • day visitors welcome • seasonal • pets ok • gay-owned

Hamilton

ACCOMMODATIONS

BurrBrookHaven 336 8th Concession Rd E (Centre Rd), Carlisle **905/689–7550** • women only • country home, single or groups 8-10 • lesbian-owned

Cedars Campground 1039 5th Concession W Rd, Millgrove **905/659–3655, 905/659–7342** • lesbians/ gay men • private campground • pool • also bar • dancing/DJ • restaurant wknds • gay-owned

BARS

The Embassy Club 54 King St E (at Houston) **905/522–1100** • noon-3am, nightclub from 8pm wknds • lesbians/ gay men • dancing/DJ • transgender-friendly • karaoke • drag shows • videos

Gravity Club 121 Hughson St N (at Canon) **289/389–8568** • 11am-2am • lesbians/ gay men • 3 levels • neighborhood bar • dancing/DJ • gay-owned

EROTICA

Stag Shop 58 Centennial Pkwy N **905/573–4242** • also 980 Upper James St, 905/385-3300

Kitchener

NIGHTCLUBS

Club Renaissance 24 Charles St W **519/570–2406, 877/635–2352** • 9pm-3am, clsd Sun-Tue • lesbians/ gay men • dancing/DJ • food served • drag shows • also billiards lounge

EROTICA

Stag Shop 10 Manitou Dr **519/895–1228**

London

NIGHTCLUBS

Club Lavish 238 Dundas St **519/667–1222** •
9pm-2am clsd Sun-Wed • gay/straight •
dancing/DJ • karaoke

RESTAURANTS

Blackfriars Bistro 46 Blackfriars (2 blocks S
of Oxford) **519/667–4930** • lunch & dinner,
Sun brunch • popular • plenty veggie • full bar

Veranda 546 Dundas St (at William St)
519/434–6790 • dinner nightly, clsd Sun-Mon
• gay-owned

EROTICA

Stag Shop 1548 Dundas St E **519/453–7676**
• also 371 Wellington Rd S, 519/668-3334

Niagara Falls

**see also Niagara Falls & Buffalo, New
York, USA**

ACCOMMODATIONS

Absolute Elegance B&B 6023 Culp St (at
Main & Ferry) **905/353–8522, 877/353–8522** •
gay/straight • full brkfst • nonsmoking • gay-
owned

Angels Hideaway 4360 Simcoe St (at River
Rd) **905/354–1119** • gay-friendly • full brkfst •
nonsmoking

Britaly B&B 57 The Promenade (at Charlotte
& John), Niagara-on-the-Lake **905/468–8778**
• gay-friendly • full brkfst • gay-owned

Kia-Ora B&B 127 Mary St (at Hwy 55/
Mississauga St), Niagara-on-the-Lake
905/468–1328, 888/208–2340 • gay-friendly •
1843 home • full brkfst • WiFi • courtesy bikes
• nonsmoking

Niagara Inn B&B 4300 Simcoe St (at River
Rd) **905/353–8522, 877/353–8522** • gay-
friendly • full brkfst • kids ok • nonsmoking •
WiFi • gay-owned

Stone Boutique Suites 5225 River Rd (at
Otter St) **905/357–2271** • gay-friendly • 2 self-
contained cottage suites • 10 minutes to falls
• nonsmoking

BARS

The Breeze 4776 Bridge St **905/348–5249** •
10pm-2am, from 4pm Sun, clsd Mon-Wed •
lesbians/gay men • also a guest house

Oshawa

NIGHTCLUBS

Club 717 717 Wilson Rd S #7 **905/434–4297**
• 9pm-midnight, till 2am Fri-Sat, from 7pm
Sun, clsd Mon-Wed • lesbians/gay men •
dancing • drag shows

EROTICA

Forbidden Pleasures 1268 Simcoe St N
905/728–0834

Ottawa

see also Hull, Province of Québec

INFO LINES & SERVICES

Pink Triangle Services 251 Bank St #301
613/563–4818 • many groups & services •
library • call for times

ACCOMMODATIONS

Ambiance B&B 330 Nepean St
613/563–0421, 888/366–8772 • gay/straight •
full brkfst • some shared baths • kids ok •
nonsmoking • WiFi • lesbian-owned

Brookstreet 525 Legget Dr **613/271–1800,
888/826–2220** • gay-friendly • pool • golf •
also restaurant

Inn on Somerset 282 Somerset St W (at
Elgin) **613/236–9309, 800/658–3564** • gay/
straight • full brkfst • some shared baths • kids
ok • WiFi • gay-owned

Lord Elgin Hotel 100 Elgin St
613/235–3333, 800/267–4298 • gay-friendly •
pool • also restaurant & bar

Rideau Inn 177 Frank St **613/688–2753,
877/580–5015** • gay-friendly • some shared
baths • nonsmoking • gay-owned

BARS

Centretown Pub 340 Somerset St W (at
Bank) **613/594–0233** • 2pm-3am • lesbians/
gay men • dancing/DJ • leather bar
upstairs • Silhouette Lounge piano bar Fri-Sat

The Lookout 41 York, 2nd flr (in Byward
Market) **613/789–1624** • 2pm-2am, from
noon wknds • lesbians/gay men • more
women Fri • food served • wheelchair access •
lesbian-owned

Swizzles 246 Queen St **613/232–4200** •
11am-2am, from 7pm wknds, clsd Sun •
lesbians/gay men • karaoke • WiFi

NIGHTCLUBS

Flamingo 380 Elgin St **613/288–9243** • 4pm-
2am, from 10am Sun brunch, clsd Mon-Wed •
gay/straight • live shows

Lotus Lounge 129 Bank St 613/216–9661 • 10pm-2am Fri, till 7am Sat

Mercury Lounge 56 Byward Market Sq (side door upstairs) 613/789–5324 • 8pm-3am, clsd Sun-Tue • popular Wed Hump night party • gay/ straight • dancing/DJ • WiFi

Zaphod Beeblebrox 27 York 613/562–1010 • 4pm-2am • gay/ straight • neighborhood bar • dancing/DJ • live music

CAFES

Bridgehead Coffee 366 Bank St (at Gilmour) 613/569–5600 • 7am-9pm • WiFi • gay-owned

Raw Sugar Cafe 692 Somerset W 613/216–2850 • vegan and gluten-free options • aslo occasional Femme Tea parties • live music

RESTAURANTS

Ahora Mexican Cuisine 307 Dalhousie St (below Sweet Art) 613/562–2081 • noon-10pm • gay-owned

The Buzz 374 Bank St 613/565–9595 • dinner nightly, Sun brunch • also bar

Johnny Farina 216 Elgin St 613/565–5155 • Italian • wheelchair access

Kinki 41 York St 613/789–7559 • lunch & dinner • Asian fusion • full bar • DJ • live entertainment • patio

La Dolce Vita 180 Preston Street 613/233–6239 • lunch & dinner, except Mon-Wed dinner only • gluten-free menu available

Savana Cafe 431 Gilmour St (at Bank) 613/233–9159 • lunch wkdays, dinner nightly • Caribbean • popular patio in summer

Shanghai Restaurant 651 Somerset St W (at Bronson Ave) 613/233–4001 • lunch Tue-Fri, dinner nightly, clsd Mon • also bar • DJ • karaoke

BOOKSTORES

After Stonewall 370 Bank St (near Gilmour) 613/567–2221 • 10am-6pm, till 7pm Fri • LGBT

Mags & Fags 254 Elgin St (btwn Somerset & Cooper) 613/233–9651 • till 10pm • gay magazines

mother tongue books/ femmes de parole 1067 Bank St (at Sunnyside Ave) 613/730–2346, 800/366–0514 (CANADA ONLY) • 10am-6pm (clsd Sun summer)

RETAIL SHOPS

Venus Envy 320 Lisgar St (at Bank St) 613/789–4646 • 11am-6pm, till 8pm Fri, till 7pm in winter, noon-5pm Sun • award-winning sex shop & bookstore

Wilde's 367 Bank St (at Gilmour) 613/234–5512 • 11am-7:30pm, clsd Sun • pride items • wheelchair access

PUBLICATIONS

Capital Xtra! 416/925–6665 • LGBT newspaper

To Be Publications 613/236–8888 • LGBT magazine covering Ottawa & Montréal

SEX CLUBS

Breathless 318 Lisgar St (at Bank St, above Venus Envy) • gay/ straight • sexual community center for alternative lifestyles

EROTICA

Wicked Wanda's 382 Bank St 613/820–6032

Stratford

ACCOMMODATIONS

A Hundred Church Street 100 Church St 519/272–8845 • gay/ straight • full brkfst • hot tub • some shared baths • nonsmoking • kids 10+ ok • WiFi • gay-owned

The Maples of Stratford 220 Church St 519/273–0810 • gay-friendly • nonsmoking • some shared baths • WiFi • woman-owned

RESTAURANTS

Down the Street 30 Ontario St 519/273–5886 • 11am-midnight, clsd Mon • popular full bar till 1am

Rundles 9 Cobourg St 519/271–6442 • dinner Tue-Sun, lunch wknds • wheelchair access • gay-owned

Toronto

INFO LINES & SERVICES

519 Church St Community Centre 519 Church St (on Cawthra Park) 416/392–6874 • 9am-10pm, till 5pm wknds • LGBT info center & cafe • wheelchair access

AA Gay/ Lesbian 416/487–5591

Canadian Lesbian/ Gay Archives 34 Isabella 416/777–2755 • 7:30pm-10pm Tue-Th & by appt

ACCOMMODATIONS

1871 Historic House B&B 65 Huntley St (at Selby) 416/923–6950 • gay-friendly • 1871 historic house • full brkfst • nonsmoking • WiFi

213 Carlton—Toronto Townhouse B&B
416/323–8898, 877/500–0466 • gay/ straight •
some shared baths • nonsmoking • WiFi •
gay-owned

312 Seaton 312 Seaton (at Gerrard)
416/968–0775, 866/968–0775 • gay/ straight •
B&B • also rental apt • dog on premises •
nonsmoking • gay-owned

Toronto

WHERE THE GIRLS ARE:

In "The Ghetto"—south of Bloor St., between Yonge and Parliament. The Cabbagetown area (Parliament St.) is more laid-back, while the intersection of Church & Wellesley is queer ground zero. The West Village draws a younger, mixed crowd.

LGBT PRIDE:

June. 416/927-7433, web: www.pridetoronto.com.

ANNUAL EVENTS:

April - International Gay & Lesbian Comedy & Music Festival 416/907-9099, web: www.were-funnythatway.com.

May - Inside Out: Lesbian & Gay Film & Video Festival 416/977–6847, web: insideout.on.ca.

June - Downtown Jazz Festival 416/928-2033, web: www.toron-tojazz.com.

June - International Dragon Boat Race Festival 416/595-1739, web: www.dragonboats.com.

June - Queer West Arts Festival 416/879–7954, web: www.queer-west.org.

September - International Film Festival 416/968-3456, web: www.tiff.net.

November - Mr Leatherman Toronto Competition, web: toron-toleatherpride.ca.

CITY INFO:

800/499–2514, web: www.seetorontonow.com.

BEST VIEW:

The top of one of the world's tallest buildings, of course: the CN Tower. Or try a sight-seeing air tour or a three-masted sailing ship tour.

ATTRACTIONS:

Art Gallery of Ontario 416/979-6648, web: www.ago.net.

Bata Shoe Museum 416/979-7799, web: www.batashoemuseum.ca.

CN Tower 416/868-6937, web: www.cntower.ca.

Dr Flea's International Flea Market 416/745-3532, web: www.drfleas.com.

Gardiner Museum of Ceramic Art, 416/586-8080, web: www.gardinermuseum.on.ca.

Harbourfront Centre 416/973-4000, web: www.harbourfrontcentre.com.

Hockey Hall of Fame 416/360-7765, web: www.hhof.com.

Kensington Market, web: www.kensington-market.ca.

Ontario Place 416/314-9900, web: www.ontarioplace.com.

Rogers Centre 416/341-1707, web: www.rogerscentre.com.

Royal Ontario Museum 416/586-8000, web: www.rom.on.ca.

St Lawrence Market, web: www.stlawrencemarket.com.

Underground City.

WEATHER:

Summers are hot (upper 80°s—90°s) and humid. Spring is gorgeous. Fall brings cool, crisp days. Winters are cold and snowy, just as you'd imagined they would be in Canada!

TRANSIT:

Co-op Taxi 416/504-2667, web: co-opcabs.com.

TTC 416/393-4636, web: www.ttc.ca.

Banting House Inn 73 Homewood Ave (at Maitland) 416/924–1458, 800/823–8856 • lesbians/ gay men • nonsmoking • WiFi • gay-owned

Bonnevue Manor B&B 33 Beaty Ave (at Queen St & Roncesvalles) 416/536–1455 • gay/ straight • full brkfst • kids ok • nonsmoking • WiFi

Drake Hotel 1150 Queen St W (at Beaconsfield) 416/531–5042, 866/372–5386 • gay-friendly • boutique hotel • nonsmoking

Dundonald House 35 Dundonald St (at Church) 416/961–9888, 800/260–7227 • mostly gay men • full brkfst • hot tub • sauna • gym • bicycles • nonsmoking • gay-owned

The Gladstone Hotel 1214 Queen St W (at Gladstone Ave) 416/531–4635 • gay/ straight • artistic • nonsmoking • WiFi • also Melody bar & cafe

The Grange Hotel 165 Grange Ave (at Queen) 416/603–7700, 888/232–0002 • gay-friendly • kitchenettes • kids ok

Hazelton Hotel 118 Yorkville Ave (at Avenue Rd) 416/963–6300, 866/473–6301 • gay-friendly • luxury property • nonsmoking

Hotel Le Germain 30 Mercer St (at Peter St) 416/345–9500, 866/345–9501 • gay-friendly • kids/ pets ok • also restaurant & bar • wheelchair access

House on McGill 110 McGill St (at Church & Carlton) 416/351–1503, 877/580–5015 • gay/ straight • shared baths • nonsmoking • WiFi • gay-owned

Pimblett's Rest B&B 242 Gerrard St E (at Ontario St) 416/929–9525, 416/921–6898 • Victorian • gay/ straight • full brkfst • nonsmoking • gay-owned

BARS

Alto 582 Church St (at Dundonald) 416/929–9108 • 5pm-close, from 11am Sun, clsd Mon • lesbians/ gay men • women's night Fri • dancing/DJ • theme nights

Andy Poolhall 489 College St (at Markham) 416/923–5300 • 7pm-2am, clsd Sun-Mon • gay/ straight • dancing/DJ • also Cherry Bomb party for queer women second-to-last Saturday month

Baby Huey 70 Ossington Ave (at Humbert St) 416/419–3932 • 7pm-2am • gay/ straight

Beaver Cafe 1192 Queen St W (at Northcote Ave) 416/537–2768 • 10am-2am • lesbians/ gay men • DJs • food served • patio • gay-owned

Bistro 422 422 College St (at Bathurst St) 416/963–9416 • 5pm-2am • gay/straight • food served

Boutique Bar 506 Church St 647/705–0006 • 5pm-2am, from 2:30pm wknds • lesbians/gay men • patio

The Cameron House 408 Queen St W (at Cameron St) 416/703–0811 • 4pm-close • gay/ straight • live music • also theater

The Churchmouse & Firkin 475 Church St (at Maitland) 416/927–1735 • 11am-2am • lesbians/ gay men • English pub • neighborhood bar • leather brunch 3rd Sun

Dakota Tavern 249 Ossington Ave (at Dundas) 416/850–4579 • 6pm-2am • gay-friendly • live country music • bluegrass brunch Sun

George's Play 504 Church St (at Alexander) 416/963–8251 • 11am-2pm • mostly men • drag shows • bingo daily

The Hair of the Dog 425 Church St (at Wood) 416/964–2708 • 11am-2am • gay/ straight • neighborhood pub & restaurant • patio

The House on Parliament Pub 456 Parliament St (at Carlton) 416/925–4074 • 11:30am-2am • gay/ straight • neighborhood bar • food served • patio

LeVack Block 88 Ossington Ave (at Humbert) 416/916–0571 • 5pm-close, from 11am wknds, clsd Mon • gay/ straight • dancing/DJ • also restaurant

Lo'la 7 Maitland (at Yonge) 416/920–0946 • 4pm-2am • clsd Sun-Mon • mostly gay men • dancing/DJ • martini lounge

Melody Bar 1214 Queen St W (at Gladstone Hotel) 416/531–4635 • clsd Mon, more days Wed • gay/ straight • karaoke • live music

O'Grady's 518 Church St (at Maitland) 416/323–2822 • 11am-2am, till 3am Fri-Sat • gay/ straight • casual dining • huge patio • also lounge upstairs

Pegasus 489-B Church St (at Wellesley, upstairs) 416/927–8832 • 11am-2am • lesbians/gay men • neighborhood bar

Pic Nic 747 Queen St E 647/435–5298 • 5pm-11pm, till midnight Th-Sat, clsd Sun • gay-friendly • wine bar • food served

The Raq 739 Queen St W, 2nd flr (at Palmerston) 416/504–9120 • 5pm-1am, from 4pm Th-Sun, clsd Mon • gay/ straight • DJs • upscale pool hall

Slack's Restaurant & Bar 562 Church St (at Wellesley) **416/928–2151** • 4pm-2am, clsd Mon • popular • mostly lesbian • dancing/DJ Fri-Sat • live music • also restaurant • lesbian-owned

Smiling Buddha 961 College St (at Dovercourt) **416/516–2531** • 7:30pm-2am • gay/straight • cabaret • younger crowd

Sneaky Dee's 431 College St (at Bathurst) **416/603–3090** • 11am-3am, from 9am Sun • gay-friendly • live bands • kitchen open late • Tex/Mex

Woody's/ Sailor 465–467 Church (at Maitland) **416/972–0887** • 1pm-2am • popular • mostly gay men • neighborhood bar • live shows • drag shows • 18+ • wheelchair access

NIGHTCLUBS

The Annex Wreck Room 794 Bathurst St (at Bloor) **416/536–0346** • 10pm-close • gay/straight • dancing/DJ • bands

Big Primpin' 1279 Queen St W (at Wrongbar) • 10pm 1st Fri • lesbians/ gay men • monthly hip-hop, dancehall, R&B club • check local listings

Cherry Bomb 489 College St (at Andy Poolhall) **416/923–5300 (CLUB#)** • 9pm 3rd Sat • mostly women • transgender-friendly • dancing/DJ

The Comfort Zone 480 Spadina Ave (N of College) **416/763–9139** • after-hours wknds only • gay/straight • dancing/DJ

El Convento Rico 750 College St (at Crawford) **416/588–7800** • 9pm-4am, clsd Mon-Th • gay/straight • dancing/DJ • Latin/ salsa music • mostly Latino • transgender-friendly • drag shows

Fly Nightclub 8 Gloucester St (2 streets N of Yonge & Wellesley) **416/410–5426, 416/925–6222** • open Fri-Sat only • popular • mostly gay men • dancing/DJ • cover charge

Guvernment 132 Queens Quay E (at Lower Jarvis) **416/869–0045** • gay-friendly • dancing/DJ • visiting big-name DJs

Henhouse 1532 Dundas St W (at Dufferin) **416/534–5939** • 6pm-2am, clsd Mon, Sun brunch from 10am • gay/straight • neighborhood bar • food served • lesbian-owned

Lee's Palace/ Dance Cave 529 Bloor St (at Albany) **416/532–1598** • gay/straight • live bands • dance cave Mon, Th-Sat

The Mod Club 722 College (at Crawford) **416/588–4663** • 10pm Fri-Sat • gay/straight • dancing/DJ

Pink Mafia • alternative queer & straight events in hip locations • check www.pinkmafia.ca

Swagger Productions • parties & events for women of color • weaponoftherevolution.com for details

Tattoo Rock Parlour 567 Queen St W (at Denison) **416/703–5488** • 10am-3am Fri-Sun • gay/straight • dancing/DJ • live shows

Wrongbar 1279 Queen St W (at Brock) **415/516–8677** • gay/ straight • dancing/DJ • Big Primpin 1st Fri • check listing for other queer events

CAFES

Alternative Grounds 333 Roncesvalles Ave **416/534–5543** • 7am-7pm

Cafe Diplomatico 594 College (at Clinton, in Little Italy) **416/534–4637** • 8am-2am, clsd Mon • Italian

JetFuel 519 Parliament St **416/968–9982** • 7am-8pm • WiFi

Timothy's 500 Church St (at Alexander) **416/925–8550** • lesbians/ gay men • 7am-midnight, till 3:30am wknds • WiFi

RESTAURANTS

Black Hoof 938 Dundas St W **416/551–8854** • 6pm-midnight, clsd Tue-Wed • charcuterie & cheese • not for vegetarians!

Byzantium 499 Church St (S of Wellesley) **416/922–3859** • 5:30pm-11pm, Sun brunch 11am-3pm • mostly gay men • dancing/DJ• patio • gay-owned

Cafe 668 885 Dundas St W **416/703–0668** • lunch & dinner • vegetarian

Caroline's 554 Parliament St **416/927–1593/7777** • 4:30pm-1am, 11am-midnight Sun • organic & gluten-free menu • occasional women's dance parties

Commensal 655 Bay St (enter on Elm St) **416/596–9364** • brkfst, lunch & dinner • vegetarian

Corner Cafe 1150 Queen St W (at Beaconsfield, Drake Hotel) **416/531–5042** • 8am-11pm, till midnight wknds • popular brkfst spot

Easy Restaurant 1645 Queen St W **416/537–4893** • 9am-5pm

Flo's Diner 70 Yorkville Ave (near Bay St) **416/961–4333** • 7:30am-8pm, till 10pm Th-Sat, from 8am wknds • gay-owned

Fresh 147 Spadina (at Queen St W) **416/599–4442** • lunch & dinner • vegetarian • patio • also at 894 Queen St W& 336 Bloor St W

Fressen 478 Queen St W (at Denison) **416/504–5127** • dinner nightly, wknd brunch • upscale vegan

Fuzion 580 Church St **416/944–9888** • 4pm-2am, Sun brunch • also martini bar

Golden Thai 105 Church St (at Richmond) **416/868–6668** • 11:30am-9pm, from 5pm wknds

Il Fornello 207 Queen's Quay West (at York St, Queen's Quay Terminal Bldg) **416/920–7347** • lunch Mon-Fri, dinner nightly, Sun brunch • Italian • plenty veggie • also 214 King W, 416/977-2855 • also 576 Danforth Ave, 416/466-2931

Joy Bistro 884 Queen St E **416/465–8855** • noon-1am

Kalendar 546 College St **416/923–4138** • 10:30am-1am, patio

La Hacienda 640 Queen St W (near Bathurst) **416/703–3377** • noon-1am, from 11am wknds

Mitzi's Cafe 100 Sorauren Ave (at Pearson) **416/588–1234** • 7:30am-4pm, popular wknd brunch from 9am • gay-owned

Mitzi's Sister 1554 Queen St W **416/532–2570** • 4pm-2am, popular wknd brunch from 10am • upscale pub eats • full bar • live music • gay-owned

Naco Gallery Cafe 1665 Dundas St W **647/347–6499** • 8am-2am, from 9am wknds • Mexican-inspired • also gallery & nightclub

Nota Bene 180 Queen St W **416/977–6400** • lunch Mon-Fri, dinner nightly, clsd Sun • Mediterranean

Saving Grace 907 Dundas St W (at Bellwoods) **416/703–7368** • brkfst & lunch

Smith 553 Church St (at Dundonald) **416/926–2501** • dinner & drinks

Supermarket 268 Augusta Ave (at College) **416/840–0501** • dinner only • Thai • also bar w/ DJs

Urban Herbivore 64 Oxford St (at Augusta) **416/927–1231** • 9am-7pm • vegetarian/vegan

The Village Rainbow 477 Church St (at Maitland) **416/961–0616** • 8am-midnight• full bar • WiFi • big patio • wheelchair acccess

Wine Bar 9 Church St **416/504–9463** • noon-11pm • tapas-style dishes

Zelda's Restaurant & Bar 692 Yonge St **416/922–2526** • noon-10pm, till 1am Fri-Sat from 11am Sat-Sun • popular • lesbians/ gay men • drag shows • full bar • patio

ENTERTAINMENT & RECREATION

AIDS Memorial in Cawthra Square Park

The Bata Shoe Museum 327 Bloor St W **416/979–7799** • 10,000 shoes from over 4,500 years—including the platforms of Elton John & the pumps of Marilyn Monroe

Buddies in Bad Times Theatre 12 Alexander St (at Yonge) **416/975–8555** • LGBT theater • also Tallulah's cabaret Fri-Sat w/ DJ/dancing

Hanlan's Pt Beach Toronto Islands • nude beach • 10 minutes from downtown

BOOKSTORES

Glad Day Bookshop 598–A Yonge St (at Wellesley) **416/961–4161, 877/783–3725** • 10am-6:30pm, till 9pm Th-Fri, noon-9pm Sat, noon-6pm Sun • LGBT books, mags & videos

Toronto Women's Bookstore 73 Harbord St (at Spadina) **416/922–8744, 800/861–8233** • 10am-7pm, 11am-6pm Sat, noon-5pm Sun

RETAIL SHOPS

Flatirons 469 Church St (at Alexander) **416/968–9274** • wonderful kitsch & gay gifts

Out on the Street 551 Church St **416/967–2759, 800/263–5747** • 10am-8pm, 11am-7pm Sun • LGBT

Secrets From Your Sister 560 Bloor St W **416/538–1234, 888/868–8007** • 11am-7pm • "beautiful lingerie in realistic sizes for the modern woman" • wheelchair access

Take a Walk on the Wild Side 161 Gerrard St E (at Jarvis) **416/921–6112, 800/260–0102** • "hotel, boutique & club for crossdressers, transvestites, transexuals & other persons of gender"

PUBLICATIONS

Xtra! **416/925–6665, 800/268–9872** • LGBT newspaper

SEX CLUBS

Pussy Palace Toronto 231 Mutual St (at Carlton, at Club Toronto) • occasional women- & trans-only sex club • check out www.pussypalacetoronto.com for events

EROTICA

Come As You Are 701 Queen St W (at Bathurst) **416/504–7934** • 11am-7pm, till 9pm Th-Fri, noon-5pm Sun • co-op-owned sex store

Good For Her 175 Harbord St (near Bathurst) **416/588-0900, 877/588-0900** • 11am-7pm • women & trans-only hours: noon-5pm Sun • women's sexuality products • wheelchair access

North Bound Leather 586 Yonge (W of Wellesley St) **416/972-1037** • toys and clothing • wheelchair access

Priape 501 Church St () **416/586-9914, 800/461-6969** • clubwear • leather • books • toys & more

Seduction 577 Yonge St **416/966-6969**

Waterloo

ACCOMMODATIONS

Colonial Creekside 485 Bridge St W (at Lexington) **519/886-2726** • gay/ straight• pool • WiFi • • gay-owned

RESTAURANTS

Ethel's Lounge 114 King St N (at Spring) **519/725-2361** • 11:30am-2am • full bar • patio

EROTICA

Stag Shop 7 King St N **519/886-4500**

Windsor

see also Detroit, Michigan

ACCOMMODATIONS

University Place Accommodations 3140 Peter St (btwn Sandwich & Mill) **519/254-1112, 866/618-1112** • gay/ straight • nonsmoking • WiFi • wheelchair access

Windsor Inn on the River 3857 Riverside Dr E (at George Ave) **519/945-2110, 866/635-0055** • gay-friendly • full brkfst • kids ok • nonsmoking

BARS

Club 2012 1056 Wyandotte St E (at Langlois Ave) **519/968-3260** • lesbians/ gay men • dancing/DJ

Club 783 783 Wyandotte St E **519/973-4916** • 5pm-2am • lesbians/ gay men • neighborhood bar • karaoke

Phog 157 University Ave W (at Church St) **519/253-1605** • gay-friendly • food served • art & events

Vermouth 333 Ouellette **519/977-6102** • 4pm-2am, from 6pm Sat, clsd Sun-Mon • gay-friendly • popular martini lounge

NIGHTCLUBS

The Loop 156 Chatham St W (at Ferry St) **519/253-3474** • 9pm-2am • gay-friendly • dancing/DJ • live shows • theme nights • young crowd

Rise 800 Wellington **519/258-7473** • 10pm-2:30am Fri-Sat only • lesbians/ gay men • neighborhood bar • dancing/DJ • karaoke

CAFES

The Coffee Exchange 266 Ouellette **519/971-7424** • 7am-11pm, 8am midnight wknds • WiFi

EROTICA

Stag Shop 2950 Dougall Ave **519/967-8798**

PRINCE EDWARD ISLAND

Charlottetown

INFO LINES & SERVICES

Abegweit Rainbow Collective 375 University Avenue #2 (at Eden St, in AIDS PEI office) **902/894-5776, 877/380-5776** • 24-hour info line • monthly dances & other social activities

ACCOMMODATIONS

Evening Primrose 114 Lord's Pond Rd, Albany **902/437-3134** • gay-friendly • full brkfst • nonsmoking • kids/ pets ok • cottage wheelchair access • seasonal • WiFi • lesbian-owned

The Great George 58 Great George **902/892-0606, 800/361-1118** • gay-friendly • kids ok • nonsmoking • wheelchair access • gay-owned • Can$155-399

The Hotel on Pownal 146 Pownal St **902/892-1217, 800/268-6261** • gay-friendly • WiFi

Rainbow Lodge 7521 Trans Canada Hwy, Vernon Bridge **902/651-2202, 800/268-7005** • lesbians/ gay men • full brkfst • 15 minutes outside of town • nonsmoking • gay-owned

Rodd Charlottetown Hotel 75 Kent St (at Pownall) **902/894-7371, 800/565-7633** • gay-friendly • pool • kids/ pets ok • WiFi • also restaurant & lounge

Shipwright Inn Heritage B&B 51 Fitzroy St **902/368-1905, 888/306-9966** • gay-friendly • full brkfst • nonsmoking

Bars

Baba's Lounge 81 University Ave
902/892–7377 • noon-2am, 5pm-midnight
Sun • gay-friendly • live bands • also Cedars
Lebanese restaurant

Entertainment & Recreation

Blooming Point Blooming Point • nude
beach

Bookstores

Book Mark 172 Queen St (in mall)
902/566–4888 • 9am-8pm, till 9pm Th-Fri, till
5:30pm Sat, clsd Sun

Hermanville

Accommodations

Johnson Shore Inn 9984 Rte 16
902/687–1340, 877/510–9669 • gay/ straight •
full brkfst • kids 10+ ok • wheelchair access •
lesbian-owned

York

Accommodations

Little York B&B 775 Rte 25 **902/569–0271,
800/953–6755** • gay-friendly • full brkfst • WiFi
• gay-owned

Stanhope Beach Resort 3445 Bayshore Rd
902/672–2701, 866/672–2701 • gay-friendly •
restaurant & bar • pool • WiFi • wheelchair
access • gay-owned

PROVINCE OF QUÉBEC

Hull

Restaurants

Le Twist 88 Montcalm St, Gatineau
819/777-8886 • opens 11am daily • full bar

Laurentides (Laurentian Mtns)

Accommodations

Havre du Parc Auberge 2788 Rte 125 N,
St-Donat **819/424–7686** • gay/ straight • quiet
lakeside inn for nature lovers • full brkfst • gay-
owned

Le Septentrion B&B 901 chemin St-
Adolphe, Morin-Heights/ St-Sauveur
450/226–2665, 866/355–2665 • lesbians/ gay
men • full brkfst • pool • hot tub • sauna •
nonsmoking • gay-owned

Magog

Accommodations

À Tout Venant 20 rue Bellevue
819/868–0419, 888/611–5577 • gay-friendly •
full brkfst • on cycling path "La Route Verte" •
WiFi

Au Gîte du Cerf Argenté B&B 2984
chemin Georgeville Rd (off Hwy 10)
819/847–4264 • gay/ straight • renovated
century-old farmhouse • 4 beaches nearby •
kids ok • nonsmoking • gay-owned

Auberge aux Deux Pères 680 chemin des
Pères **819/769–3115, 514/616–3114** • gay-
friendly • pool

Montréal

Note: M°=Metro station

Info Lines & Services

AA Gay/ Lesbian 514/376–9230 • call for
meeting times & locations

**Gay/ Lesbian Community Centre of
Montréal** 2075 rue Plessis, Ste.110 (at
Ontario) 514/528–8424 • 10am-5:30pm, 1pm-
8pm Wed & Fri, clsd wknds • library

Gay Line/ Gai Ecoute
514/866–5090(English) • 7pm-11pm

**The Village Tourism Information Center/
Gay Chamber of Commerce** 1307 rue Ste-
Catherine Est 514/522–1885, 888/595–8110 •
10am-6pm, clsd wknds

Accommodations

Absolument Montréal B&B 1790 Amherst
(at rue Robin) 514/223–0017, 866/360–1351 •
gay/ straight • full brkfst • hot tub •
nonsmoking • WiFi • gay-owned

Alexandre Logan 1631 rue Alexandre
DeSève (at Logan) 514/598–0555,
866/895–0555 • gay-friendly • WiFi

Alexandrie-Montréal 1750 Amherst (at
Robin) **514/525–9420** • gay-friendly • also
bistro • kids/ pets ok • nonsmoking • WiFi •
gay-owned

Auberge le Pomerol 819 boul de
Maisonneuve E (at St-Christophe)
514/526–5511, 800/361–6896 • gay-friendly •
also restaurant • nonsmoking • WiFi

B&B Le Cartier 1219 rue Cartier (at Ste-
Catherine Est) **514/917–1829, 877/524–0495**
• gay/ straight • B&B • private studio • WiFi •
gay-owned

B&B Le Terra Nostra 277 rue Beatty (at Lasalle) **514/762-1223, 866/550-5235** • gay-friendly • full brkfst • nonsmoking • WiFi • woman-owned

Les Bons Matins 1401 Argyle Ave **514/931-9167, 800/588-5280** • lesbians/gay men • apt rental • nonsmoking • WiFi

Le Chasseur B&B 1567 rue St-André (at Maisonneuve) **514/521-2238, 800/451-2238** • gay/straight • Victorian row house • summer terrace • gay-owned

Montréal

WHERE THE GIRLS ARE:

In the popular Plateau Mont-Royal neighborhood or in the bohemian area on Ste-Catherine est.

ENTERTAINMENT:

Info Gay Events Hotline 514/252-4429.

Tourisme Québec www.bonjourquebec.com/gay.

LGBT PRIDE:

July/August. 514/285-4011, web: www.diverscite.org.

ANNUAL EVENTS:

February/March - Festival Montréal en Lumière (Montréal High Lights Festival) 514/288-9955, web: www.montrealenlumiere.com.

June/July - L'International des Feux Loto-Québec (fireworks competition) 514/397-2000, web: www.internationaldesfeux.com.

Festival International de Jazz de Montréal 514/871-1881, 888/515-0515, www.montrealjazzfest.com.

Festival International Montréal en Arts 514/522-4646, web: www.festivaldesarts.org.

July - Just For Laughs Comedy Festival 888/244-3155, web: www.hahaha.com.

August/September - Montréal World Film Festival 514/848-3883, web: www.ffm-montreal.org.

October - Black & Blue Party 514/875-7026, web: www.bbcm.org. AIDS benefit dance & circuit party.

November - International Gay/Lesbian Film Festival, web: www.image-nation.org.

CITY INFO:

514/844-5400, web: www.tourism-montreal.org.

ATTRACTIONS:

Bonsecours Market 514/872-7730, web: www.marchebonsecours.qc.ca.

Latin Quarter.

Montréal Biodome 514/868-3000, web: www2.ville.montreal.qc.ca/biodome.

Montréal Botanical Garden & Insectarium 514/872-1400, web: www2.ville.montreal.qc.ca/jardin

Montréal Museum of Fine Arts 514/285-2000, web: www.mmfa.qc.ca.

Old Montréal & Old Port.

Olympic Park.

Underground City.

BEST VIEW:

From a caleche ride (horse-drawn carriage) or from the top of the Montréal Tower or from the patio of the old hunting lodge atop Mont Royal.

WEATHER:

It's north of New England so winters are for real. Beautiful spring and fall colors. Summers get hot and humid.

TRANSIT:

Diamond Cab 514/273-6331, web: www.taxidiamond.com.

Montréal Urban Transit 514/786-4636, web: www.stcum.qc.ca.

Delta Montréal 475 Ave President Kennedy (at City Councilor) 514/286-1986, 877/286-1986 • gay-friendly • hotel • hot tub • pool • kids/ pets ok • restaurant • bar • WiFi • wheelchair access

Hôtel Dorion 1477 rue Dorion (at Maisonneuve) 514/523-2427, 877/523-5908 • gay/ straight • in the Gay Village • WiFi

Hotel du Fort 1390 rue du Fort (at Ste-Catherine) 514/938-8333, 800/565-6333 • gay/ straight • wheelchair access

Hôtel Gouverneur Montréal Place Dupuis 1415 rue St-Hubert (at Maisonneuve) 888/910-1111 • gay-friendly • pool • also restaurant & bar • WiFi

Hotel L' St-André 1285 rue St-André (at Ste-Catherine) 514/849-7070, 800/265-7071 • gay/ straight • kids ok • WiFi

Hotel La Tour Centreville 400 René-Lévèsque Blvd Ouest (at Bleurry) 514/866-8861, 800/361-2790 • gay-friendly • pool • non-smoking • WiFi

Hotel Lord Berri 1199 rue Berri (at Ste-Catherine) 514/845-9236, 888/363-0363 • gay-friendly • also Italian resto-bar • WiFi • wheelchair access

Hotel Manoir des Alpes 1245 rue St-André (at Ste-Catherine) 514/845-9803, 800/465-2929 • gay-friendly • WiFi • kids ok

Jade Blue B&B 1225 de Bullion St (at Ste-Catherine) 514/878-9843, 800/878-5048 • gay/ straight • theme rooms • full brkfst • nonsmoking • WiFi

L Hotel Montreal 262 rue St-Jacques W (at St Nicolas) 514/985-0019, 877/553-0019 • gay-friendly • also bar and lounge • WiFi

Loews Hotel Vogue 1425 rue de la Montagne (near Ste-Catherine) 514/285-5555, 800/465-6654 • gay-friendly • kids/ pets ok • wheelchair access

La Loggia Art & Breakfast 1637 rue Amherst (at Maisonneuve) 514/524-2493, 866/520-2493 • gay/ straight • nonsmoking • in Gay Village • WiFi • gay-owned

Montréal Boutique Suite Guesthouse 1269 rue de Champlain (at Ste-Catherine) 514/521-9436, 514/521-3523 • lesbians/ gay men • nonsmoking • WiFi • gay-owned

Turquoise B&B 1576 rue Alexandre DeSève (at Maisonneuve) 514/523-9943, 877/707-1576 • mostly gay men • shared baths • gay-owned

BARS

Bar Le Cocktail 1669 Ste-Catherine Est (at Champlain) 514/597-0814 • 11am-3am • lesbians/ gay men • neighborhood bar • karaoke

Bar Rocky 1673 rue Ste-Catherine Est (at Papineau) 514/521-7865 • 10am-close • mostly gay men • drag shows • older crowd

Cabaret Mado 1115 rue Ste-Catherine Est (at Amherst, below Le Campus) 514/525-7566 • 11am-3am • popular • lesbians/ gay men • theme nights • dancing/DJ • karaoke • cabaret • drag shows • owned by the fabulous Mado! • wheelchair access

Citibar 1603 Ontario Est (at Champlain) 514/525-4251 • 11am-3am • gay/ straight • neighborhood bar • live shows

Club Bolo 2093 rue de la Visitation (at Association Sportive) 514/849-4777 • 9:30pm-12:30am Fri, special events Sat, T-dance from 3:30pm Sun • lesbians/ gay men • dancing/DJ • country/ western • also lessons • cover charge

Club Date Piano Bar 1218 rue Ste-Catherine Est (at Beaudry) 514/521-1242 • 8am-3am • lesbians/ gay men • neighborhood bar • karaoke nightly • piano

Le Drugstore 1366 Ste-Catherine Est (at Panêt) 514/524-1960 • 10am-3am • mostly women • 8-bar complex • food served

Foufounes Electriques 87 Ste-Catherine Est (at St-Laurent) 514/844-5539 • 4pm-3am • gay-friendly • dancing/DJ • live bands • patio

Fun Spot 1151 rue Ontario Est (at Wolfe) 514/522-0416 • 11am-3am • lesbians/ gay men • neighborhood bar • dancing/DJ • transgender-friendly • food served • drag shows • karaoke

La Relaxe 1309 rue Ste-Catherine Est, 2nd flr (at Visitation) 514/523-0578 • noon-3am • mostly gay men • neighborhood bar • open to the street • as the name implies, a good place to relax & people-watch

St-Sulpice 1680 rue St-Denis (at Ontario) 514/844-9458 • 11am-3am, till midnight Sun • gay/ straight • karaoke • WiFi • large terrace

NIGHTCLUBS

Circus After Hours 915 rue Ste-Catherine Est 514/844-3626 • 2am-8am Th & Sun, 1am-10pm Fri-Sat • gay/ straight • dancing/DJ

Cirque du Boudoir 514/789-9068 • quarterly • gay/ straight • opulent theme parties • dancing/DJ • performance

Complexe Sky 1474 rue Ste-Catherine Est **514/529–6969, 514/529–8989** • noon-3am • lesbians/ gay men • rooftop pool & spa • cabaret & dance club Fri-Sat

Faggity Ass Fridays 5656 Ave du Parc (at The Playhouse) • last Fri only • lesbians/ gay men • dancing/DJ • performance • benefits Head & Hands sex ed organization

Meow Mix 4848 Boul St-Laurent (at Sala Rossa) • monthly Sat dance party • mostly women • check listings for dates

Parking Night Club 1296 rue Amherst (at Ste-Catherine) **514/282–1199** • 10am-3am, clsd Tue-Wed • popular • mostly gay men • more women Th • dancing/DJ

Pink 28 • monthly events for professional gay women • check www.pink28montreal.com for details

Red Lite (After Hours) 1755 rue de Lierre, Laval **450/967–3057** • Fri-Sun only 2am-10am • popular • gay-friendly

Stéréo 858 rue Ste-Catherine Est (at St-Andre) **514/658–2646** • after-hours Fri-Sun only • gay/ straight • cover • popular

Unity II 1171 rue Ste-Catherine Est (at Montcalm) **514/523–2777** • 9pm-close Fri-Sat only • lesbians/ gay men • dancing/DJ • great rooftop terrace • live shows

Cafes

Cafe Titanic 445 St-Pierre (in Old Montréal) **514/849–0894** • 8am-4:30pm, clsd wknds • popular • salad & soup • WiFi

Kilo 6744 rue Hutchison **514/270–3024, 877/270–3024** • 9am-5pm, clsd wknds • cakes, coffee & light meals

Restaurants

L' Anecdote 801 rue Rachel Est (at St-Hubert) **514/526–7967** • 7:30am-10pm, from 9am wknds • lesbians/ gay men

Après le Jour 901 rue Rachel Est (at St-Andre) **514/527–4141** • 5pm-9pm, clsd Mon • Italian/ French • seafood • BYOB • wheelchair access

Au Pain Perdu 4489 rue de la Roche **514/527–2900** • 7am-3pm • charming brunch spot in renovated garage

Bato Thai 1310 rue Ste-Catherine Est **514/524–6705** • lunch weekdays & dinner nightly • lesbians/ gay men • beer/ wine

Beauty's 93 Mont-Royal Ouest **514/849–8883** • 7am-4pm, till 5pm wknds • diner/ Jewish deli • worth the wait

La Binerie 367 Mt-Royal **514/285–9078** • 6am-8pm, 8am-3pm wknds

Le Cagibi 5490 boul St-Laurent **514/509–1199** • 9am-1am, from 10:30am wknds, 6pm-midnight Mon • vegetarian • also live music & events

Chu Chai 4088 rue St-Denis (at Rachel) **514/843–4194** • lunch & dinner • vegetarian Thai • full bar • wheelchair access

Cluny Art Bar 257 rue Prince (at rue William) **514/866–1213** • 8am-5pm Mon-Fri • Mediterranean

La Colombe 554 Duluth Est **514/849–8844** • 5:30pm-midnight, clsd Sun-Mon • BYOB • French

Commensal 1720 rue St-Denis (at Ontario) **514/845–2627** • 11am-10:30pm, till 11pm Fri-Sat • vegetarian • beer/ wine • wheelchair access

Ella Grill 1237 Amherst **514/523–5553** • upscale Mediterranean/Greek • lesbian-owned

L' Exception 1200 rue St-Hubert (at Réné-Lévesque) **514/282–1282** • 11am-9pm, from 5pm Sat, clsd Sun • terrace

L' Express 3927 rue St-Denis (at Duluth) **514/845–5333** • 8am-2am, from 10am Sat-Sun • full bar • great pâté • reservations recommended • wheelchair access

Fantasie 1355 rue Ste-Catherine Est **514/523–3466** • dinner only • sushi • gay-owned

La Strega 1477 rue Ste-Catherine Est **514/523–6000** • 11am-midnight, from 5pm wknds • inexpensive Italian • some veggie • wheelchair access

La Paryse 302 rue Ontario Est (near Sanguinet) **514/842–2040** • 11am-11pm, clsd Mon • lesbians/ gay men • '50s-style diner • lesbian-owned

Le Planète 1451 rue Ste-Catherine Est (at Plessis) **514/528–6953** • lunch weekdays & dinner nightly, brunch only Sun • global cuisine • young crowd • beer/ wine

Resto du Village 1310 rue Wolfe **514/524–5404** • 24hrs • "cuisine canadienne"

Saloon Cafe 1333 rue Ste-Catherine Est (at Panêt) **514/522–1333** • dinner nightly, lunch wknds only • plenty veggie • big dishes & even bigger drinks

Santropol 3990 St-Urbain (at Duluth) **514/842–3110** • 11:30am-10pm, from 9am during summer • unique sandwiches • wheelchair access

Schwartz's Deli 3895 boul St-Laurent 514/842–4813 • 8am-12:30am, till 1:30am Fri, till 2:30am Sat

Thai Grill 5101 boul St-Laurent (at Laurier) 514/270–5566 • lunch Mon-Fri, dinner nightly • one of Montréal's best Thai eateries

ENTERTAINMENT & RECREATION

Ça Roule 27 rue de la Commune Est 514/866–0633, 877/866–0633 • join the beautiful people skating & biking up & down Ste-Catherine

Prince Arthur Est at boul St-Laurent, not far from Sherbrooke Métro station • closed-off street w/ many outdoor restaurants & cafés • touristy but oh-so-European

RETAIL SHOPS

Cuir Mont-Royal 826-A Mont Royal Est (at St-Hubert) 514/527–0238, 888/333–8283 • leather • fetish

Priape 1311 Ste-Catherine Est (at Visitation) 514 /521–8451, 800/461–6969 • 10am-9pm, till 11pm Fri-Sat, noon-9pm Sun • clubwear • leather • books • toys & more

Screaming Eagle 1424 boul St-Laurent 514/849–2843 • leather shop

PUBLICATIONS

2B 514/521–3873 • English-language LGBT publication covering Québec

Fugues 514/848–1854, 888/848–1854 • glossy LGBT bar/ entertainment guide

The Mirror 514/393–1010 • free queer-positive weekly • reviews, event listings & more in English

EROTICA

Il Bolero 6846 St-Hubert (btwn St-Zotique & Bélanger) 514/270–6065 • fetish & clubwear emporium • ask about monthly fetish party

Québec City

ACCOMMODATIONS

ALT Hotel Québec 1200 av Germain des Prés (at Laurier Blvd), Sainte-Foy 418/658–1224, 800/463–5253 • gay-friendly • non-smoking • WiFi • kids ok • restaurant • wheelchair access • women-owned

---

Québec City

ENTERTAINMENT:
Tourisme Québec web: www.bonjourquebec.com/gay.

LGBT PRIDE:
September. 418/809–3383, web: www.glbtquebec.org.

ANNUAL EVENTS:
January/February - Carnaval (Winter Celebration) 866/422-7628, web: www.carnaval.qc.ca.
July - Summer Festival 888/992–5200, web: www.infofestival.com.

CITY INFO:
877/266–5687 and 514/873–2015, web: www.bonjourquebec.com.

TRANSIT:
Taxi Québec 418/525-8123.
Autobus La Quebecoise 888/872-5525, web: www.autobus.qc.ca
RTC (bus service) 418/627-2511, web: www.rtcquebec.ca.

ATTRACTIONS:
Change of Guards at the Citadel.
Château Frontenac 418/692-3861, web: www.fairmont.com/frontenac.
Grand Allée.
Hôtel du Parlement.
Musée de la Civilisation 418/643-2158, web: www.mcq.org.
Notre-Dame-de-Québec Basilica.
Old Québec.
Quartier du Petit-Champlain 418/692-2613, web: www.quartierpetitchamplain.com

Auberge Place D'Armes 24 rue Ste-Anne (at St-Louis) 418/694-9485, 866/333-9485 • gay-friendly • nonsmoking • WiFi • restaurant

Le Château du Faubourg 429A rue St-Jean (at Claire Fontaine) 418/524-2902 • gay-friendly • B&B in château • nonsmoking • also beauty salon • gay-owned

Le Coureur des Bois Guest House 15 rue Ste-Ursule (at St-Jean, in Old Québec) 418/692-1117, 800/269-6414 • lesbians/ gay men • also apts • shared baths • nonsmoking • gay-owned

Gite TerreCiel 113 rue Sainte Anne, Baie-Saint-Paul 418/435-0149 • gay/straight • WiFi • gay-owned

Hotel Le Clos Saint-Louis 69 St-Louis (at St-Ursule) 418/694-1311, 800/461-1311 • gay/ straight • boutique hotel located in historic district • nonsmoking • WiFi

Hôtel Le Germain Dominion 1912 126 rue St-Pierre (at Marché Finlay) 418/692-2224, 888/833-5253 • gay-friendly • boutique hotel in city's 1st skyscraper • pets ok • wheelchair access

Hôtel-Motel Le Voyageur 2250 boul Ste-Anne (at Estimauville) 418/661-7701, 800/463-5568 • gay/ straight • pool • kids/pets ok • restaurant & bar • WiFi

Le Moulin de St-Laurent Chalets 754 chemin Royal, St Laurent, Ile d' Orleans 418/829-3888, 888/629-3888 • gay/ straight • cottages • pool • kids/ pets ok • also restaurant • nonsmoking

BARS

Bar Le Drague 815 rue St-Augustin (at St-Jean) 418/649-7212 • 10am-3am • popular • mostly gay men • neighborhood bar • dancing/DJ Th-Sun • food served • karaoke • cabaret • drag shows • terrace • wheelchair access

Bar St Matthew's 889 côte Ste-Geneviève (at St-Gabriel) 418/524-5000 • 11am-3am • lesbians/ gay men • neighborhood bar • patio

RESTAURANTS

Le Commensal 860 rue St-Jean 418/647-3733 • 11am-9pm, till 10pm Th-Sat • vegetarian/ vegan

Le Hobbit 700 rue St-Jean (at Ste-Geneviève) 418/647-2677 • 9am-10pm • some veggie

Le Moulin de St-Laurent Restaurant 754 chemin Royal, St Laurent, Ile d' Orleans 418/829-3888 • lunch & dinner, May-Oct only • live music Sun

La Piazzetta 707 rue St-Jean 418/529-7489 • 11am-10:30pm

Le Poisson d'Avril 115 quai St-André (at St-Thomas) 418/692-1010, 877/692-1010 • 5pm-close • name is French for "April Fools"

Vertige 540 Ave Duluth E 514/842-4443 • 5pm-10pm, till 11pm Fri-Sat, clsd Sun

ENTERTAINMENT & RECREATION

Fairmont Le Château Frontenac 1 rue des Carrières 418/692-3861, 800/257-7544 • this hotel disguised as a castle remains the symbol of Québec, come & enjoy the view from outside

Ice Hotel /Hôtel de Glace 75, Montée de l'Auberge, Pavillon Ukiuk, Sainte-Catherine-de-la-Jacques-Cartier 418/875-4522, 877/505-0423 • sometimes getting put on ice isn't a bad thing—check this gay-friendly hotel out before it melts away, 9 km E of Québec City in Montmorency Falls Park (Jan-March only)

PUBLICATIONS

2B 514/521-3873 • English-language LGBT publication covering Québec

EROTICA

Importation André Dubois 46 côte de la Montagne (at Frontenac Castle) 418/692-0264 • transgender-friendly • wheelchair access

Sherbrooke

NIGHTCLUBS

Complex 13-17 13-15-17 Bowen Sud (at rue King) 819/562-2628 • 11am-3am • lesbians/ gay men • dancing/DJ • pub & dance club • strippers Fri-Sun • lesbian bar downstairs • also sauna

St-Georges-de-Beauce

BARS

Le Planet 8450 Blvd Lacroix 418/228-1322 • 2pm-3am, till 10pm Sun, clsd Mon-Wed • gay/straight • neighborhood bar

SASKATCHEWAN

Provincewide

PUBLICATIONS

Perceptions 306/244–1930 • covers the Canadian prairies

Ravenscrag

ACCOMMODATIONS

Spring Valley Guest Ranch 306/295–4124 • gay/ straight • 1913 character home • also cabin • full brkfst • kids/ pets ok • nonsmoking • also restaurant • gay-owned

Regina

INFO LINES & SERVICES

The Gay & Lesbian Community of Regina 2070 Broad St (at Victoria) 306/569–1995 • 7am-3pm

NIGHTCLUBS

The OUTside 2070 Broad St (at Victoria, at Gay Center) 306/569–1995 • 7pm-3am • lesbians/ gay men • dancing/DJ

RESTAURANTS

Abstractions Cafe 2161 Rose St 306/352–5374 • 9am-6pm, from 11am Sat, clsd Sun • live music

The Creek in Cathedral Bistro 3414 13th Ave 306/352–4448 • lunch & dinner, clsd Sun

Saskatoon

INFO LINES & SERVICES

Avenue Community Centre 201-320 21st St W 306/665–1224, 800/358–1833 • 10am-5pm, till 9pm Wed-Fri, clsd wknds • many social/ support groups • queer gift store

Circle of Choice Gay/ Lesbian AA 505 10th St E (at Grace Westminster United Church) 306/665–5626 • 8pm Wed

NIGHTCLUBS

302 Lounge 302 Pacific Ave 306/665–6863 • 7am-2am, till 3am Fri-Sat, clsd Sun-Tue • lesbians/ gay men • dancing/DJ

Diva's 220 3rd Ave S #110 (alley entrance) 306/665–0100 • 8pm-2am, till 3am wknds, clsd Mon-Tue • lesbians/ gay men • dancing/DJ • drag shows • karaoke • WiFi • private club (guests welcome)

RESTAURANTS

2nd Ave Grill 10-123 2nd Ave S 306/244–9899 • 11am-10pm, till 11pm Fri-Sat

The Berry Barn 830 Valley Rd 306/978–9797 • open daily • seasonal • home-style eatery w/ views of river

The Ivy Dining & Lounge 24th St E & Ontario Ave 306/384–4444 • lunch & dinner Mon-Fri, dinner only Sat-Sun

Prairie Ink 3130 8th St E 306/955–3579 • 9am-10pm, till 11pm Fri-Sat, till 6pm Sun • also bookstore

ENTERTAINMENT & RECREATION

AKA Gallery 424 20th St W 306/652–0044 • noon-6pm, till 4pm Sat, clsd Sun-Mon • contemporary art & performance

BOOKSTORES

Turning the Tide 525 11th St E 306/955–3070 • noon-8pm, till 10pm Th-Sat, till 5pm Sun • Saskatoon's alternative bookstore

RETAIL SHOPS

The Trading Post 226 2nd Ave S 306/653–1769 • 10am-5:30pm, clsd Sun • clothing

BAHAMAS
Nassau
NIGHTCLUBS

Club Waterloo E Bay St (1/2 mile E of Paradise Island Bridge) 242/393–7324 • 4pm-close • gay-friendly • more women Th • indoor/ outdoor complex w/ 5 bars • dancing/DJ • live music • restaurant • swimming

BARBADOS
Bridgetown
RESTAURANTS

The Waterfront Cafe The Careenage 246/427–0093 • 10am-midnight, clsd Sun • trendy • also bar • live music • outdoor seating

BRITISH VIRGIN ISLANDS
see also US Virgin Islands
Tortola
ACCOMMODATIONS

Fort Recovery Villa Beach Resort Road Town, Tortola 284/495–4467, 800/367–8455 (WAIT FOR RING) • gay-friendly • grand home on beach & private beachfront villas • pool • kids ok • wheelchair access • women-owned

DOMINICAN REPUBLIC
Boca Chica
ACCOMMODATIONS

Costalunga 3 Av del Sur 809/523–6883 • gay-friendly • closest beach to Santo Domingo

Puerto Plata
ACCOMMODATIONS

Casa de la Luna La Catalina Cabrera (at Calle 5) 809/589–7711 • gay/ straight • villa rental close to La Playa Grande Beach • $550-1100 per week

Tropix Hotel 809/571–2291 • gay-friendly • full brkfst • garden setting near center of town & beach • pool • kids/ pets ok • lesbian & gay-owned

Santiago
BARS

Monaco Bar 40 Av 27 de Febrero, Santo Domingo 809/226–1589 • lesbians/ gay men • dancing/DJ

Santo Domingo
ACCOMMODATIONS

Caribe Colonial Hotel Isabel Catolica 159 809/688–7799 • gay-friendly • boutique hotel

Foreigners Club Hotel 102 Calle Canela (at Estrelleta) 809/689–3017 • lesbians/ gay men • in Zona Colonial • nonsmoking • WiFi • wheelchair access • gay-owned

Hotel Aida Calle El Conde 464 809/685–7692 • gay-friendly

Hotel Venezia Av Independencia 45 (Gazcue) 809/682–5108 • gay-friendly

BARS

Amazonia Dr Delgado 71 • mostly women

Click 3 Vicente Celestino Duarte (Zona Colonial) 829/449–5154 • mostly women • men very welcome • karaoke

Esedeku 809/869–6322 • 8pm-close, from 5pm Sun, clsd Mon • lesbians/gay men • food served

Jay Dee's Jose Reyes 10, Zona Colonial 809/335–5905 • 9pm-4am • mostly gay men • neighborhood bar • strippers • videos

NIGHTCLUBS

Cha Av George Washington 165 (btwn Lincoln & Maximo Gomez) • Fri-Sun only • mostly men • dancing/DJ • drag shows • opened by local gay celebrity Chachita Rubio

RESTAURANTS

El Conuco 152 Casimiro de Moya (behind Jaragua Hotel) 809/686–0129 • touristy local landmark

Green Light Cuisine 20 Heriberto Pieter, Naco 809/732–7719 • sandwiches & salads, fresh & light

Mamajuana 451 Avenida Roberto Pastoriza 809/547–1019 • Nuevo Latino

DUTCH & FRENCH WEST INDIES

Aruba

BARS

Jimmy's Place Windstraat 32, Oranjestad **297/582–2550** • 5pm-2am, till 4am Fri-Sat, from 8pm Sun, clsd Mon • lesbians/ gay men • neighborhood bar • dancing/DJ • food served

The Paddock LG Smith Blvd #13, Oranjestad **297/583–2334, 297/583–2606** • 10am-2am • gay/ straight • neighborhood bar • food served

RESTAURANTS

Cafe the Plaza Seaport Marketplace, Oranjestad **297/583–8826** • 10am-2am • lunch & dinner

Barbados

ACCOMMODATIONS

Gemini House B&B 70 Plover Court, Inch Marlow, Christ Church **246/428–7221** • gay-friendly • WiFi

Inchcape Seaside Villas **246/428–7006** • private villa rentals • WiFi

Bonaire

ACCOMMODATIONS

Coco Palm Garden/ Casa Oleander Kaya Statius van Eps 9 **599/717–2108** • gay/ straight • studios, apts & houses • pool • wheelchair access • $66-86

Ocean View Villas Kaya Statius van Eps 6 **599/717–6105** • gay-friendly • luxury apts w/ secluded patios & outdoor showers • WiFi

Curaçao

INFO LINES & SERVICES

Pink House Charlottestraat 6, Willemstad **5999/462–6616** • LGBT community center, health & rights organization • events

ACCOMMODATIONS

The Avila Beach Hotel 130 Penstraat, Willemstad **800/747–8162** • gay-friendly • $170-275

Floris Suite Hotel Piscadera Bay **800/781–1011 (IN US & CANADA), 5999/462–6111** • gay-friendly

Kura Hulanda Langestraat 8, Willemstad **888/264–3106 (FROM US & CANADA), 5999/434–7700** • gay-friendly • also Jacob's Bar

Lodge Kura Hulanda & Beach Club Langestraat 8 (Willemstad) **5999/434–7700, 877/264–3106** • gay-friendly • pool • diving lessons

Papagayo Beach Resort Willemstad **800/652–2962 (FROM US), 5999/747–4333** • gay-friendly

BARS

Cafe De Heeren Zuikertuintjeweg 1 **599/736–0491** • 9am-1am, till 2:30am Th-Fri, clsd Sun • gay/straight • live shows • also restaurant

Mundo Bizarro Nieuwestraat 12 (in the Pietermaai quarter) **5999/461-6767** • gay-friendly • weird and wonderful eatery and café • live shows

NIGHTCLUBS

Bermuda Disco Scharloweg 72-76 (at the Waaigat, behind the movies), Willemstad **5999/461–4685** • 10pm-4am, popular Fri-Sat • gay-friendly • ladies night Th (mostly straight) • dancing/DJ

Cabana Beach at Seaquarium Beach **599/946–5158** • open Wed-Sat • gay-friendly • dancing/DJ • also restaurant

Tu Tu Tango Plasa Mundo Merced, Punda **5999/465–4633** • 11pm-4am • more gay Fri • also restaurant

RESTAURANTS

Mambo Beach Bapor Kibra, Seaquarium Beach **5999/461-8999** • 9am-midnight, till 4am Sat • full bar • more gay Sat

O Mundo Zuikertuintje Shopping Mall, Willemstad • lunch & dinner • also gay party 2nd Sat

ENTERTAINMENT & RECREATION

Cas Abao Beach • gay-friendly • popular local beach

Dolphin Academy Curaçao Sea Aquarium, Bapor Kibra z/n (east of Willemstad, at Sea Aquarium Park) **5999/465–8900, 5999/465–8300** • swim w/ dolphins!

Jan Thiel Beach • good people-watching

Museum Kura Hulanda Klipstraat 9, Willemstad **5999/434–7765** • African history & culture • Antillean art

Saba

ACCOMMODATIONS

Juliana's Hotel Windwardside **599/416–2269, 888/289–5708** • gay/ straight • pool • hot tub • full brkfst • ocean & garden views • also Saban-style cottages • kids ok • WiFi

Shearwater Resort Cliff Side (Booby Hill) **589/416-2498** • gay-friendly • full brkfst • pool • nonsmoking • WiFi • also restaurant • gay-owned

RESTAURANTS

Rainforest Restaurant Windwardside **599/416-3888, 599/416-5507** • brkfst, lunch & dinner • full bar

Restaurant Eden The Road (Windwardside), Windwardside **599/416-2539** • 5:30pm-9:30pm, clsd Tue

St Barthélemy

ACCOMMODATIONS

Hotel le Village St-Jean St-Jean Hill **590-590/27-61-39, 800/651-8366** • gay-friendly • hotel & cottages • pool

Hotel Normandie Quartier Lorient **590-590/27-61-66** • gay-friendly • WiFi

Hotel St-Barth Isle De France Plage des Flamands **508/528-7727, 800/421-3396** • gay-friendly • ultraluxe hotel

NIGHTCLUBS

Le Sélect Gustavia **590-590/27-86-87** • gay-friendly • more gay after 11pm

RESTAURANTS

Le Grain de Sel Grand Saline Beach **590/524-605** • lunch & dinner, clsd Mon • relaxing & open setting • ideal before & after sunbathing

ENTERTAINMENT & RECREATION

Anse Gouverneur St-Jean Beach • nudity

Anse Grande Saline Beach • nudity • gay section on the left side of Saline

Orient Beach • gay beach

St Maarten

See also St Martin

ACCOMMODATIONS

Blue Ocean Villas 352/505-2805 • private villa rentals

Holland House 43 Front St, Philipsburg **599/542-2572** • gay-friendly • on the beach • restaurant • bar

RESTAURANTS

Cheri's Cafe Rhine Rd #45 (Maho Reef) **599/54-53-361** • 11am-1:30am, clsd Tue • full bar • dancing • live music • touristy • wheelchair access

St Martin

see also St Maarten

BARS

Tantra Rhine Road, Maho Bay, Marigot (at the Marina Royale) **599/545-2861** • 11pm-close Wed, Fri-Sat • gay/ straight

RESTAURANTS

L' Escapade 94 Blvd de Grand Case **590-590/87-75-04** • French • some veggie • reservations recommended

Le Pressoir 30 Blvd de Grand Case **590-590/87-76-62** • dinner nightly, clsd Sun • French

ENTERTAINMENT & RECREATION

Orient Beach on the northeast side of the island • gay-friendly nude beach

JAMAICA

Montego Bay

ACCOMMODATIONS

Half Moon 877/956-625, 866/648-6951 • gay-friendly • upscale resort

Negril

ACCOMMODATIONS

Seagrape Villas The Cliffs, West End Rd **831/625-1255 (US#)** • gay/ straight • 3 seafront villas • excellent sunsets

Ocho Rios

ACCOMMODATIONS

Golden Clouds Villa North Coast Rd, Oracabessa **941/922-9191, 888/625-6007** • gay-friendly • private estate • full brkfst • fully staffed • jacuzzi • pool • kids ok • wheelchair access • gay-owned

Port Antonio

ACCOMMODATIONS

Hotel Mocking Bird Hill 876/993-7267, 876/993-7134 • gay-friendly • eco-friendly inn • fresh local food served • pool • massage • kids ok • wheelchair access • lesbian-owned

Westmoreland

ACCOMMODATIONS

Moun Tambrin Retreat set in the mtns 28 miles from Montego Bay 876/437-4353, 876/357-6363 • gay/ straight • art deco estate • food served • pool

PUERTO RICO

Please Note: For those with rusty or no Spanish, "carretera" means "highway" and "calle" means "street."

Aguada

BARS

Franky's Bar Carr 115 en el Bo Asomante • Wed-Sun • lesbians/ gay men • neighborhood bar • dancing/DJ • drag shows

Baja Sucia

ENTERTAINMENT & RECREATION

Playa Sucia/ La Playuela S of Cabo Rojo Nat'l Wildlife Refuge, Guanica • beautiful, secluded beach

Bayamon

BARS

Start Night 31 Ongay St (behind Clendo lab) 787/536-3579 • open Th-Sat • lesbians/ gay men • drag shows

Boqueron

BARS

El Schamar Bar at corner of Muñoz Rivera & Jose de Diego 787/851-0542 • mostly gay men • drag shows • also hotel • gay-owned

Sunset Sunrise Cabo Rojo 787/255-1478 • 10am-close • gay/ straight

Cabo Rojo

ENTERTAINMENT & RECREATION

Gay Pride • 2nd wknd in June

Camuy

BARS

Distortion Carr 119 Norte, KM 7.6 (Barrio Membrio) 787/614-3404 • 10pm Sat only • lesbians/ gay men • dancing/DJ • swimming

Ceiba

ACCOMMODATIONS

Ceiba Country Inn Carretera 977 787/885-0471, 888/560-2816 • gay-friendly • dramatic ocean views • also bar • 15 minutes to Vieques/Culebra ferry • WiFi • gay-owned

Guanica

ENTERTAINMENT & RECREATION

Gilligan's Island take Rd 333 to Copamarina Resort, then take ferry to island 787/821-5706 (FERRY INFO) • beautiful beach located in a biosphere on Southern coast of PR

Guaynabo

NIGHTCLUBS

Pride Night at Club Eggo Carazo 53 787/708-4982 • gay/ straight • gay night Wed only

Luquillo

NIGHTCLUBS

Undisshi Club Carr 115, Bo Rio Grande, Aguada 787/868-5669 • open Fri-Sat, open Sun on long wknds • mostly gay men • dancing • drag shows

Mayaguez

BARS

Cafe Nova Ley Calle Munoz Rivera 15 • gay/ straight • dancing/DJ • drag shows • live music • karaoke • art gallery

Ponce

BARS

Wejele's Cafe 8 Leon St 787/603-8095 • 9pm-3am Wed-Sat • lesbians/ gay men • neighborhood bar

Rincon

ACCOMMODATIONS

Horned Dorset Primavera Hotel Apartado 1132 800/633-1857 • gay/ straight • swimming pool • kids 12+ ok

Lemontree Oceanfront Cottages Carr 429, km 4.1 (at Carr 115) 787/823-6452, 888/418-8733 • gay/ straight • kids ok • nonsmoking • WiFi • wheelchair access

San Juan

INFO LINES & SERVICES

Centro Communitario LGBTT/ LGBT Community Center 37 Urb Perez Morris, Hato Rey 787/294-9850 • resources, events, AIDS testing • also cyber cafe

Tanama 787/274-8445, 787/751-0856 • HIV prevention & education • very trans-friendly

ACCOMMODATIONS

Acacia Seaside Inn 8 Taft St (at McLeary) 787/727-0668, 787/727-0626 • gay-friendly • hotel • kids ok • pool • WiFi

At Wind Chimes Inn 1750 McLeary Ave, Condado (at Taft) 787/727-4153, 800/946-3244 • gay-friendly • restored Spanish villa • pool • kids/ pets ok • nonsmoking • WiFi • wheelchair access

Casa del Caribe Guest House Calle Caribe 57, Condado (at Magdalena) 787/722-7139, 877/722-7139 • gay-friendly • B&B in heart of Condado • kids ok • nonsmoking • WiFi

La Concha 1077 Ashford Ave, Condado 787/721-7500 • gay/ straight • retro urban showcase & architectural landmark • restaurants & bar

Condado Inn Av Condado 6 (at Av Ashford) 787/724-7145 • mostly men • near beach • also bar • gay-owned

San Juan

LGBT PRIDE:
June.

ANNUAL EVENTS:
January - San Sebastian Street Festival 787/724-4788.

February - Ponce Carnival.

February/ March - Festival Casals, web: www.festcasalspr.gobierno.pr.

June - Heineken Jazz Fest 787/272-8877, web: www.prheinekenjazz.com.

June - San Juan Bautista Day. San Juan celebrates Puerto Rico's own saint w/ week-long music, dance, religious processions, parties. On midnight of the eve before June 24th (the official saint's day), revelers walk/jump backwards into the sea 3 to 7 times to ward off evil spirits & renew good luck for the coming year.

CITY INFO:
Puerto Rico Tourism Company, 800/866-7827, web: www.topuertorico.org.

BEST VIEW:
From El Morro or alternatively, one of the harbor cruises that depart from Pier 2 in Old San Juan.

WEATHER:
Tropical sunshine year-round, with temperatures that average in the mid-80°s from November to May. Expect more rain on the northern coast.

ATTRACTIONS:
Cathedral de San Juan 787/722-0861, web: www.cate-dralsanjuan.com.

Condado Beach.

La Fortaleza 787/ 721-7000, web: www.fortaleza.gobierno.pr.

Historic Old San Juan.

El Morro Fortress & Fort San Cristobal (San Juan National Historic Site) 787/729-6777, web: www.nps.gov/saju.

La Casita weekly festival 787/721-2891.

Pablo Casals Museum 787/723-9185.

Paseo de la Princesa.

Quincentennial Plaza.

San José Church.

San Juan Museum of Art & Histor y 787/724-1875.

Santurce Marketplace.

re rain on the northern coast.

TRANSIT:
TaxiVan, 787/645-8294, web: www.taxivansanjuan.com.

American Taxi, 787/982-3466, web: www.americantaxipr.com.

Santana Taxi Service, 787/562-9836, web: www.taxituristico.com.

Metropolitan Bus Authority (AMA, its Spanish initials, and Metrobus) 787/767-7979, web: www.dtop.gov.pr/mapas/index.asp.

Also look for the free trolley that winds through Old Town.

Coqui del Mar Guesthouse 2218 Calle General del Valle (at General Patton, Ocean Park) **787/220-4204** • gay-friendly • studios & apts • gay-owned

Hotel El Convento Calle Cristo 100, Old San Juan (btwn Caleta de las Monjas & Calle Sol) **787/723-9020, 800/468-2779** • popular • gay-friendly • 17th-c former Carmelite convent • pool • WiFi

Miramar Hotel 606 Ave Ponce de Leon (at Miramar) **787/977-1000** • gay-friendly • WiFi • also restaurant & bar

Numero Uno on the Beach Calle Santa Ana 1, Ocean Park (near Calle Italia) **787/726-5010, 866/726-5010** • gay/ straight • pool • also Pamela's, full bar & grill • kids ok • wheelchair access

Ocean Hostal Playero 1853 McLeary Ave, Condado (at Calle Atlantic Pl) **787/728-8119** • gay/ straight • budget accommodations • great beach location • nonsmoking • vegetarian restaurant

The San Juan Water & Beach Club Hotel 2 Tartak St (Isla Verde), Carolina **787/728-3666, 888/265-6699** • gay-friendly • boutique hotel on the beach • restaurant & lounge • kids ok • rooftop pool • nonsmoking • WiFi • wheelchair access

Sea View Studio by the Sea 1123 Calle Seaview 2B (at Ashford) **787/525-9398** • gay/ straight • full kitchens • WiFi • gay-owned

BARS

Angelu's Cafe Calle Eleanor Roosevelt 239, Hato Rey **787/294-2169** • clsd Sun-Mon • mostly women • neighborhood bar

Cafe Bohemio Calle Cristo 100, Old San Juan (in Gran Hotel El Convento) **787/723-9202** • 11am-2am, clsd Wed • gay-friendly • professional crowd • more gay Tue • live music Th-Sat • also restaurant • food served till 11pm

Esechys 478 Calle Jose Canals (near Calle Rodrigo de Triana, Placita Roosevelt), Hato Rey **787/636-7268** • open Tue-Sun • mostly women • live music Fri

Rabanal Petit Club 1700 Ave Ponce de Leon (at Hotel San Jorge), Santurce **787/390-0336** • 6pm-close Wed-Sun • mostly gay men • neighborhood bar

Tia Maria's 326 Ave Jose de Diego, Parada 22 (at Ponce de León), Santurce **787/724-4011** • 11am-midnight, till 2am Fri-Sat • popular • lesbians/ gay men • neighborhood bar • also liquor shop

NIGHTCLUBS

Circo Bar Calle Condado 650, Parada 18, Santurce **787/725-9676** • 9pm-5am • mostly men • dancing/DJ • karaoke • theme nights

Kali 1407 Ashford Ave, Condado **787/721-5104** • gay-friendly • popular after hrs club • dress code • also lounge & sushi restaurant

Krash Klub Av Ponce de León 1257 (btwn Calles Villamil & Labra), Santurce **787/722-1131** • 10pm-4am, clsd Sun-Mon • popular • lesbians/ gay men • dancing/DJ • drag shows • gay-owned

Metro Lounge Av Roosevelt 1367 (Hato Rey) **787/447-5253** • Th-Sun • lesbians/gay men, more women on Fri • dancing/DJ

CAFES

Cafe Berlin Calle San Francisco 407, Plaza Colón, Old San Juan (btwn Calles Norzagary & O'Donnel) **787/722-5205** • 11am-11pm • popular • espresso bar • plenty veggie

Kasalta Bakery 1966 McLeary Ave (at Teniente Matta) **787/727-7340** • 6am-10pm • bakery & deli

RESTAURANTS

Aguaviva 364 Calle La Fortaleza, Old San Juan **787/722-0665** • dinner nightly • fresh seafood & ceviche • wheelchair access

Ajili Mojili 1052 Ashford Ave, Condado (at Aguadilla) **787/725-9195** • local specialties • live music • great ambiance

Al Dente 309 Calle Recinto S, Old San Juan **787/723-7303** • lunch & dinner, clsd Sun • Italian • also wine bar

Bebo's Cafe 1600 Calle Loiza (at Del Parque) **787/268-5087** • cheap & delicious • cafeteria-style Puerto Rican favorites

La Bombonera Calle San Francisco 259, Old San Juan **787/722-0658** • 7:30am-8pm • popular • come for the strong coffee & pastries • wheelchair access

El Buren 103 Calle Christo, Old San Juan (at Sol) **787/977-5023** • Italian/ Puerto Rican • outdoor seating

Cafe Puerto Rico 208 O'Donnell, Old San Juan **787/724-2281** • noon-11pm • great mofongo • outdoor seating

La Casita Blanca 351 Calle Tapia (off Ave Eduardo Conde, near Laguna Los Corozas) **787/726-5501** • 11am-4pm, till 6pm Th, till 9pm Fri-Sat • amazing local cuisine • best reached by car • no English spoken • beware of neighborhood

Colombo 1024 Ashford Ave (at Aguadilla St) 787/725–1212 • 8am-1am, till 3am wknds • American • also bar • WiFi

Dieguito & Markito's Kiosk 44 in Luquillo 787/355–0875 • 2pm-9pm, open late wknds • also bar • karaoke

Dragonfly 364 S Fortaleza St, Old San Juan (across from Parrot Club) 787/977–3886 • opens 5:30 daily • full bar • Latin/ Asian fusion

Fleria 1754 Calle Loiza, Santurce 787/268–0010 • lunch & dinner, clsd Sun-Mon • Greek • some veggie

El Jibarito Calle Sol 280 787/725–8375 • Puerto Rican/ criolla • also bar

The Parrot Club Calle Fortaleza 363, Old San Juan (btwn Plaza Colón & Callejón de la Capilla) 787/725–7370 • lunch & dinner • chic Nuevo Latino bistro & bar • live music

Perla 1077 Ashford Ave, at La Concha Resort, Condado 787/721–7500 • enjoy an upscale dining experience inside a gigantic conch shell • swank!

Pura Vida 1853 McLeary Ave, Condado (at Calle Atlantic Pl) 787/728–8119 • noon-10pm • vegetarian • WiFi

Sarushe's 1025 Ave Jesus T Piñero 787/948–0548 • 4pm-2:30am, from 8am Sat, clsd Sun-Tue • tapas

Vidy's Cafe Ave Universidad 104 (Rio Piedras) 787/767–3062 • 10am-1am • plenty veggie • karaoke

ENTERTAINMENT & RECREATION

Atlantic Beach in front of Atlantic Beach Hotel • very gay-friendly beach

Nuyorican Cafe San Francisco 312 (by El Callejon) 787/977–1276, 787/366–5074 • live music & arts venue

Ocean Park Beach E of Condado • gay/ straight beach • adult-oriented (less kids)

La Placita/ Plaza del Mercado Santurce • open-air market by day, street-party by night • lots of bars & restaurants

RETAIL SHOPS

The Rainbow Shop Av Ponce de León 1418 #202 (upstairs), Santurce 787/724–9093 • 9am-5pm • gay items

PUBLICATIONS

Conexion G 787/607–3939 • LGBT paper, in Spanish

GYMS & HEALTH CLUBS

International Fitness Av Ashford 1131, Condado (btwn Avs Cervantes & Caribe) 787/721–0717 • 5am-10pm, till 9pm Fri • gay/ straight

Muscle Factory Avenida Ashford (at Vendig, Condado) 787/721–0717

EROTICA

Metro Sexxx Av Roosevelt 1367 (in Plazoleta Julio Garriga), Hato Rey 787/402–0233

Vieques Island

ACCOMMODATIONS

Bravo! North Shore Rd (at Lighthouse) 787/741–1128 • gay/ straight • pool • gay-owned

Casa de Amistad 27 Benitez Castano 787/741–3758 • gay/ straight • guesthouse in heart of Isabel Segunda • WiFi • gay-owned

Crow's Nest Inn 787/741–0033, 877/276–9763 • gay-friendly • small inn • pool • nonsmoking • restaurant

Inn on the Blue Horizon 787/741–3318 • gay-friendly • country inn & cottages • pool • beach access • restaurant • nonsmoking • WiFi • $130-400

TRINIDAD & TOBAGO

Tobago

ACCOMMODATIONS

Grafton Beach Resort 868/639-0191, 888/790-5264 • gay-friendly • pool • food served

Kariwak Village Hotel & Holistic Haven Store Bay Local Rd, Crown Point 868/639-8442, 868/639-8545 • gay-friendly • holistic hotel • kids ok • pool • restaurant • wheelchair access

US VIRGIN ISLANDS

see also British Virgin Islands

St Croix

ACCOMMODATIONS

King Christian Hotel 59 Kings Wharf, Christiansted 340/773–6330, 800/524–2012 • gay-friendly • pool • also restaurant

The Palms at Pelican Cove 4126 La Grande Princesse 340/778–8920, 888/790–5264 • lesbians/ gay men • beachfront resort • food served • pool • gay-owned

Sand Castle on the Beach 127 Smithfield, Frederiksted **340/772-1205, 800/524-2018** • lesbian, gay & straight-friendly • hotel • pool • WiFi • also restaurant & bar • $89-399+tax • lesbian & gay-owned

Sugar Mill Villa 301 Lorraine Ln, Christiansted **340/690-6927** • gay/ straight • villa w/ panoramic views • pool • nonsmoking • gay-run

St John

ACCOMMODATIONS

Gallows Point Suite Resort Cruz Bay **340/776-6434, 800/323-7229** • gay-friendly • beachfront resort • all suites • pool • kitchens • also restaurant • full bar • wheelchair access

Hillcrest Guest House **340/776-6774, 340/998-8388** • gay-friendly • WiFi • nonsmoking • kids ok

RESTAURANTS

Asolare Rte 20, Cruz Bay **340/779-4747** • 5:30pm-9:30pm • Asian/ French fusion • hip & elegant

ENTERTAINMENT & RECREATION

Salomon Bay • 20-minute hike on Salomon Beach Trail

St Thomas

ACCOMMODATIONS

Hotel 1829 Government Hill **340/776-1829, 800/524-2002** • gay-friendly • pool • also full bar & restaurant

Magen's Point Resort 6200 Magen's Bay Rd **340/777-6000, 877/850-4465** • gay-friendly • pool • wheelchair access

Pavilions & Pools Hotel 6400 Estate Smith Bay **340/775-6110, 800/524-2001** • gay-friendly • 1-bdrm villas each w/ own private swimming pool

RESTAURANTS

Oceana Restaurant & Wine Bar Historic Pointe at Villa Olga **340/774-4262** • on the water's edge • owned by renowned chef Patricia LaCorte

ENTERTAINMENT & RECREATION

Beach at Emerald Beach Resort up hill (near airport runway) • walking distance from cruise ship dock

Morning Star Beach • popular gay beach

MEXICO

Please Note: Mexican cities are often divided into districts or "Colonias," which we abbreviate as "Col." Please use these when giving addresses for directions.

Acapulco

ACCOMMODATIONS

Casa Condesa Bella Vista 125 **52-744/484-1616, 800/816-4817 (US & CANADA)** • mostly gay men • full brkfst • near beach • pool

Hotel Boca Chica Punta Caletilla (Fraccionamiento las Playas) **800/337-4685** • gay-friendly • pool • also restaurant

Hotel Encanto Jacques Cousteau 51 (Fraccionamiento Brisas Marques) **52-744/446-7101** • gay-friendly • pool • WiFi • also restaurant

Las Brisas Carretera Escenica 5255 **52-744/469-6900, 866/221-2961 (US#)** • popular • gay-friendly • luxury resort • private pools • kids ok • wheelchair access

NIGHTCLUBS

Baby 'O **52-744/484-7474** • 10:30pm-5am, till midnight Sun • gay/ straight • classic disco for over 30 years

Cabaré-Tito Beach Privada de Piedra Picuda 17 PA (nr Torres Gemelas) **52-744/484-7146** • 9pm-close, clsd Sun-Tue • lesbians/ gay men • dancing/DJ

Relax Calle Lomas de Mar 4 (Zona Dorada) **52-744/482-0421** • 10pm-late, clsd Mon-Wed • popular • lesbians/ gay men • dancing/DJ • drag & strip shows wknds • videos • young crowd

RESTAURANTS

100% Natural Av Costera Miguel Alemán 200 (near Acapulco Plaza) **52-744/485-3982** • 24hrs • fast (healthy) food • plenty veggie

Becco al Mare **52-744/446-7402** • lunch & dinner • Italian • nice views

Beto's Restaurant Av Costera Miguel Alemán 99 (at Condesa Beach) **52-744/484-0473** • 11am-midnight • lesbians/ gay men • full bar • seafood • palapas

El Cabrito Av Costera Miguel Alemán 1480 (near Convention Center) **52-744/484-7711** • 2pm-midnight, till 11pm Sun • local favorite • try the roasted goat

Carlos & Charlie's Blvd de las Naciones #1813 (in La Isla Shopping Village) **52–744/462–2104** • lunch & dinner • entertainment • int'l

Kookaburra 3 Fracc (at Marina Las Brisas) **52–744/446–6039** • lunch & dinner • int'l • expensive

La Cabaña de Caleta Playa Caleta Lado Oriente s/n (Fracc. las Playas) **52–744/469–8553, 52–744/469–7919** • 9am-9pm • seafood • right on Playa Caleta • great magaritas

La Tortuga Calle Lomas del Mar 5 **52–744/484–6985** • noon-midnight, clsd Mon • full bar • good Mexican • seafood • patio • gay-owned

Pampano Carretera Escénica 33-B (past La Vista shopping center) **52–744/446–5636** • 7pm-11pm, bar till 1am • incredible view • reservations recommended

Shu **52–744/462–2001** • Japanese

Su Casa Angel and Shelly Av Anahuac 110 **52–744/484–1261, 52–744/484–4350** • seafood • tasty margaritas • great views

Suntory de Acapulco Costera Miguel Alemán 36 **52–744/484–8088** • 2pm-midnight • Japanese • gardens

El Zorrito's Av Costera Miguel Alemán (at Anton de Alaminos) **52–744/485–3735** • traditional Mexican • several locations along Costera • some all night

Aguascalientes

NIGHTCLUBS

Mandiles Av Lopez Mateos Poniente 730 W (btwn Agucate & Chabacano) **52–449/153–281** • 10pm-3am Fri-Sat only • lesbians/gay men • dancing/DJ

Cabo San Lucas

ACCOMMODATIONS

Cabo Villas Beach Resort Callejon del Pescador s/n (Col. El Medano) **52–624/143–9199** • gay-friendly • resort on Medano Beach • pool

Posada Chabela Calle Tropico y Arcoiris **310/492–5629** • gay/ straight • private hideaway • pool • women-owned

Solmar Suites Av Solmar 1 **800/344–3349, 310/459–9861 (US#)** • gay-friendly • oceanfront suites at southernmost tip • 2 pools • hot tub

NIGHTCLUBS

Las Varitas Calle Vallentin Gomez Farias (at Camino Viejo a San Jose) **52–624/143–9999** • 9pm-3am, clsd Mon • gay-friendly • dancing/DJ • live shows • rock 'n' roll bar • Ladies Night Fri

RESTAURANTS

Mi Casa Av Cabo San Lucas (at Lazarus Cardenas) **52–624/143–1933** • clsd Sun • lunch & dinner • great chicken mole • reservations recommended

Cancún

see also Cozumel & Playa del Carmen

ACCOMMODATIONS

Rancho Sak Ol Puerto Morelos **52–998/871–0181** • gay-friendly • beachfront palapa-style B&B • 30 minutes from Cancún

BARS

Picante Bar Av Tulúm 20, Centro (E of Av Uxmal, next to Plaza Galerías) • 9pm-5am • popular • mostly gay men • dancing/DJ • young crowd • drag shows & strippers Wed-Sat

NIGHTCLUBS

Glow 30 Avenida Tulum (Tulipanes, around the corner from Karamba) **52–998/898–4552** • 11pm-6:30am, clsd Sun-Mon • popular • lesbians/ gay men • women's night every other Fri • dancing/DJ (huge dance flr) • drag shows • strippers • rooftop terrace lounge

Karamba Av Tulúm 9 (Azucenas 2nd flr, SM 22) **52–998/884–0032** • 10:30pm-close, clsd Mon • popular • lesbians/ gay men • dancing/DJ • karaoke • drag shows • go-go boys Fri

RESTAURANTS

100% Natural Sunyaxchen 62 **52–998/884–0102** • healthy fast food

Casa Angelus Av Sayil 10 (Smza 4 Lote 72 y 73 Mza 12) **52–998/887–9444** • upscale int'l • full bar

Modern Art Cafe Kukulcán Blvd, km 12.5 (at La Isla Shopping Center) **52–998/883–4511** • 5pm-3am • full bar • gallery

Perico's Av Yaxhilan 61 **52–998/884–3152** • noon-1am • traditional Mexican served up w/ huge theatrical flare

ENTERTAINMENT & RECREATION

Chichén Itza • the must-see Mayan ruin 125 miles from Cancún

Playa Delfines in the Hotel Zone (next to Hilton's beach) • gay beach

Chihuahua

ACCOMMODATIONS

Hacienda Huiyochi Copper Canyon 51–1/625-121-8101 • first & only hotel in Copper Canyon that caters to the LGBT community • full brkfst • kids/ pets ok

Ciudad Juárez

see also El Paso, Texas, USA

BARS

Club La Escondida Calle Ignacio de la Peña 366 W • gay/ straight • neighborhood bar

Cordoba

BARS

Salon Bar El Metro Av 7 no. 117–C (btwn Calles 1 & 3) • lesbians/ gay men • dancing

Cozumel

see also Cancún & Playa del Carmen

ACCOMMODATIONS

Flamingo Hotel Calle 6 Norte #81 (at Ave 5) 954/351-9236, 800/806-1601 • gay-friendly • WI • pets ok

Cuernavaca

ACCOMMODATIONS

Casa del Angel Calle Clavel 18, Col. Satelite (at Begonia) 52–777/512–6775 • gay/ straight • contemporary guesthouse on hill overlooking Cuernavaca • hot tub • nonsmoking • full brkfst • gay-owned

Las Mañanitas Ricardo Linares 107 52–777/312–8982 & 314–1466, 888/413–9199 (US ONLY) • gay-friendly • gardens • pool • restaurant • peacocks!

La Nuestra Calle Mesalina 18 (at Calle Neptuno) 52–777/315–2272, 404/806–9694 • gay/ straight • B&B • full brkfst • pool • kids ok • WiFi • lesbian-owned

BARS

Barecito Comonfort 17 (at Morrow) 52–777/314–1425 • 10am-1am, clsd Sun-Mon • lesbians/ gay men • food served • lesbian-owned

NIGHTCLUBS

Oxygen Av Vincente Guerrero 1303 (near Sam's Club) 52–777/317–2714 • 10pm-close, Fri-Sat only • mostly gay men • dancing/DJ • food served • live shows • drag shows • videos • 18+ • young crowd

RESTAURANTS

La India Bonita Dwight Morrow 15 (btwn Morelos & Matamoros) 52–777/312–5021 • 9am-9pm, till 5pm Sun-Mon

La Maga Calle Morrow #9 Altos 52–777/310–0432 • clsd Sun, popular lunch buffet • plenty veggie • live music

Marco Polo Calle Hidalgo 30 (in front of cathedral, 2nd flr) 52–777/312–3484, 52-777/318–4032 • 1pm-close • Italian (pasta & pizza) • overlooking cathedral

ENTERTAINMENT & RECREATION

Diego Rivera Murals Plaza de Museo (in Cuauhnáhuac Regional Museum)

Ensenada

NIGHTCLUBS

Sublime Plaza Blanca , 3rd Fl 52–646/128–8798 • 9pm-close • mostly gay men • dancing/DJ

RESTAURANTS

Casamar Blvd Costero 987 52–646/174–0417 • 8am-10:30pm • popular • seafood • also bar • Ensenada landmark for 30 years

Guadalajara

ACCOMMODATIONS

El Aposento Hotel Madero 545 (at 8 de Julio) 52–33/3614–0580, 52–33/3614–1612 • lesbians/ gay men • also restaurant & bar

Casa Alebrijes Hotel Libertad 1016, Zona Centro 52–33/3614–5232 • mostly gay men • boutique hotel in historic center • two blocks from gay nightlife area • WiFi • gay-owned

Casa de las Flores B&B Santos Degollado 175, Tlaquepaque 52–33/3659–3186, 888/582–4896 • gay-friendly • 15 minutes from Guadalajara • great brkfsts & margaritas

Casa Venezuela Calle Venezuela 459 (at Col. Americana) 52–33/3826–6590, 832/519–1904 (US#) • gay/ straight • B&B in 100-year-old colonial house • full brkfst • nonsmoking • WiFi • gay-owned

Hostel Lit Degollado 413 52–33/1200–5505 • gay-friendly • WiFi

Hotel Casa Campos B&B Francisco de Miranda 30-A (Col. Centro), Tlaquepaque **52-33/3838-5296, 52-33/3838-5297** • gay-friendly • 15 minutes SE of Guadalajara • WiFi • also bar & restaurant

Hotel San Francisco Degollado 267 **52-33/3613-3256** • gay-friendly • hotel w/ Old World charm • close to gay bars • also restaurant

Old Guadalajara B&B Belén 236 (Centro Histórico) **52-33/3613-9958** • gay/ straight • nonsmoking • gay-owned

Orchid House B&B Juan de Ojeda 75 (at Ave La Paz) **52-33/3335-19 21** • gay/ straight • gay-owned

La Perla B&B Prado 128, Col. Americana (Vallarta y Lopez Cotilla) **52-33/3825-1948** • gay/ straight • full brkfst • nonsmoking • WiFi • gay-owned

La Villa del Ensueño Florida St 305, Tlaquepaque **52-33/3635-8792** • gay/ straight • full brkfst

BARS

El Botanero Calle Javier Mina 1348 (at Calle 54, Sector Libertad) **52-33/3643-0545** • 6pm-3am, till 1am Sun, clsd Mon-Tue • mostly gay men • dancing/DJ • food served • karaoke • drag shows • T-dance Sun • cover charge

Cactus Beer Bar Galeana 279 (btwn Priscilliano Sanchez & Miguel Blanco) • 5pm-1am • gay/ straight • wide selection of int'l beers • food served • western theme

Caudillos Bar Calle Prisciliano Sánchez 305, Centro (at Ocampo) **52-33/3613-5445** • 5pm-3am • popular • mostly gay men • dancing from 9pm • friendly bar • also restaurant

Club YeYe Prisciliano Sánchez 395 (Zona Centro) **52-33/3337-5253** • 5pm-3am • lesbians/ gay men • chic video lounge • food served

Dona Diabla Colon 530 • 7pm-3am Wed-Sun • gay/ straight • shows

Equilibrio Restaurant & Bar Ocampo 293 (at Miguel Blanco)

Maskaras Calle Maestranza 238 (at Prisciliano Sánchez) **52-33/3614-8103** • noon-3am • lesbians/ gay men • neighborhood bar • colorful atmosphere • live music • food served

NIGHTCLUBS

7 Sins Pedro Moreno 532 (at Donato Guerra, Zona Centro) **52-33/3658-0713** • mostly gay men • dancing/DJ

Black Cherry Grand Popocatepetl 40 (at Adolfo Lopez Mateos Sur) **52-33/3647-9024** • 10pm-5am Sat only • mostly gay men • dancing/DJ

Circus Galeana 277 (at Prisciliano Sánchez, Centro Histórico) **52-33/3613-0299** • 9pm-5am • popular • lesbians/ gay men • dancing • live shows

Duality Vallarta 1488 (Col. La Fayette) **52-33/3615-2308** • lesbians/ gay men • restaurant by day • nightclub from 10pm

Light Kiss Club Av Hidalgo 838 (Zona Centro) **52-33/3563-4332** • 8pm-4am, clsd Mon • lesbians/ gay men • dancing/DJ • transgender-friendly • drag shows • strippers

Lymbo Madero 111 • gay/ straight • dancing/DJ

Mónica's Av Álvaro Obregón 1713 (btwn Calles 68 & 70, Sector Libertad; no sign, look for canopy under a big palm tree) **52-33/3643-9544** • 9pm-5am, clsd Mon-Tue • popular after midnight • mostly gay men • dancing/DJ • drag & strip shows wknds • young crowd • cover charge • take a taxi to & from

Om Club Ocampo 270 **52-33/3121-9547** • 9am-4pm Th-Sat, 5pm-10pm Sun • mostly gay men • dancing/DJ

SOS Club Av La Paz 1413 (Sector Hidalgo, Zona Centro) **52-33/1201-0892** • 9pm-3am, till 5am wknds, clsd Mon • lesbians/ gay men • dancing/DJ • drag shows • strippers Fri-Sat (men only) & Sun (women only) • patio • cover charge

Velvett **52-33/3830-4165** • 9pm-5am • lesbians/ gay men • dancing/DJ

CAFES

Dolce Veele Enrique González Martínez 177 **52-33/1523-9593** • 4pm-1am • lesbians/ gay men • WiFi

Queer Nation López Cotilla 611 • 5pm-midnight, clsd Sun • souvenirs

Vida Caffe Av Hidalgo 907 **52-33/1181-1834** • 4:30pm-close • lesbians/ gay men

RESTAURANTS

Sanborns Av 16 de Septiembre 127 **52-33/3613-6264** • many locations • WiFi

PUBLICATIONS

GAYGDL • online magazine at www.gaygdl.com

Urbana Revista • gay lifestyle magazine w/ bars & clubs for Guadalajara & Puerto Vallarta

Isla Mujeres

ACCOMMODATIONS

Casa de los Amigos Col. La Gloria **52–998/877–1169** • gay/ straight • rental villa on Mayan Riviera • WiFi • gay-owned

Casa Sirena

Jalapa

NIGHTCLUBS

La Mansión take a cab toward Banderillas (20 minutes NW of town, turn right at sign for El Paraíso Campestre & go past RR tracks) • 9pm-4am Fri-Sat only • lesbians/ gay men • dancing/DJ • live shows • cover charge

La Paz

ACCOMMODATIONS

La Casa Mexicana Inn Calle Nicolas Bravo 106 (btwn Madero & Mutualismo) **52–612/125–2748** • open Nov-June • gay/ straight • Spanish/ Moorish retreat • 1 block from La Paz Bay • nonsmoking • WiFi • wheelchair access • woman-owned

Hotel La Casa Jalisco 480 Jalisco (at Ignacio Ramierez) **52–612/128–4311** • gay/ straight • WiFi • nonsmoking • swimming • close to downtown

Hotel Mediterrane Allende 36 (at Malecón) **52–612/125–1195** • gay/ straight • WiFi • nonsmoking • bar & restaurant • sun terrace • gay-owned

BARS

Cafe La Pazta Allende 36 (at Hotel Mediterrane) **52–612/125–1195** • 7am-11pm • gay/ straight • neighborhood bar • also restaurant • young crowd • gay-owned

NIGHTCLUBS

Las Varitas Calle Independencia 111 (at Malecón) **52–612/123–1590** • 9pm-3am, clsd Mon • gay-friendly • dancing/DJ • live shows • rock 'n' roll bar • Ladies Night Fri

León

BARS

G*bar Madero 226 (at Gante, Centro Histórico) **52–477/740–8863** • 6pm-2am • café-bar w/ terrace • young crowd

NIGHTCLUBS

La Madame Blvd A López Mateos 1709 Oriente (in front of Torre Banamex) **52–477/763–3086** • 10pm-3am, clsd Mon-Wed • mostly gay men • dancing/DJ • drag shows • go-go boys

Nation **52–477/716–3695** • gay/straight • dancing/DJ

Manzanillo

ACCOMMODATIONS

Las Hadas Av Vista Hermosa s/n (Fracc. Península de Santiago) **52–314/331–0101, 888/559–4329** • gay-friendly • great resort & location

Mexico's Villa Montaña Adventure Outpost 46 Los Angeles Locos, La Manzanilla **206/937–3882** • gay-friendly • 2-bdrm hilltop villa • ocean views • 1/2 hour N of Manzanillo • kids/ pets ok • nonsmoking • wheelchair access

Red Tree Melaque Inn Primaveras 32 (30 miles N of Manzanillo), Melaque-Villa Obregon **52–315/355–8917** • gay-friendly • bungalows • near ocean • pool • kids/ pets ok • nonsmoking • gay-owned

BARS

OK Independencia 42 (Centro) • Th-Sun only • mostly gay men • dancing/DJ • drag shows • cover charge

Mazatlán

ACCOMMODATIONS

El Cid Resort **866/306–6113, 52–669/913–3333** • gay-friendly

Hotel Los Sábalos Av Playa Gaviotas 100 (Zona Dorada) **52–669/983–5333, 800/528–8760 (US#)** • gay-friendly • upscale resort • swimming • beach • health club • also popular Joe's Oyster Bar

Old Mazatlan Inn **52–520/366–8487, 866/385–2945** • gay-friendly • swimming • WiFi • gay-owned

The Pueblo Bonito Emerald Bay Ave Ernesto Coppel Compaña 201 **52–669/989–0525, 800/990–8250** • gay-friendly • resort on 20 acres • jacuzzi • pool • restaurant • piano bar • gym

BARS

La Alemana Calle Zaragoza 16 (at Benito Juarez & Serdan) • gay/ straight • sports bar

Pepe Toro Av de las Garzas 18 (1 block W of Av Camarón Sábalo, Zona Dorada) **52–669/914–4176** • 9:30pm-4am, clsd Mon-Th • popular • mostly gay men • dancing/DJ • drag & strip shows

Vitrolas Bar Heriberto Frías 1608 (in Centro Historico) **52–669/985–2221** • 6pm-2am, clsd Mon • lesbians/ gay men • lunch menu • karaoke • drag shows & strippers Sun

Restaurants

Panamá Restaurant & Pastelería at Avs de las Garzas & Camarón Sábalo (Zona Dorada) **52–669/913–6977**

Roca Mar Av del Mar (at Calle Isla de Lobos, Zona Costera) **52–669/981–6008** • till 2am • popular • seafood • full bar • lesbian-owned

Mérida

Accommodations

Angeles de Mérida Calle 74-A, #494-A (at Calle 57 & Calle 59) **52–999/923–8163** • gay-friendly • B&B in 18th-c home on quietest streets of Mérida • full brkfst • nonsmoking • pool • spa services available

Los Arcos B&B Calle 66 **52–999/928–0214** • gay-friendly • pool • gay-owned

Casa Ana B&B Calle 52 #469 (btwn 51 & 53) **52–999/924–0005** • gay-friendly • pool • nonsmoking • women-owned

La Casa Lorenzo Calle 41 #516 A (btwn 62 & 64) **52–999/139–0423 , 866/515–4105** • gay-friendly • pool • nonsmoking • WiFi • gay-owned

Casa San Juan B&B 545-A Calle 62 (btwn Calle 69 & Calle 71) **52–999/986–2937, 866/979–6753** • gay/ straight • nonsmoking • kids ok • wheelchair access • gay-owned

Casa Santiago B&B Calle 63 #562 (btwn Calles 70 & 72) **52–999/928–9375** • gay/ straight • colonial restored house • pool • nonsmoking • WiFi • wheelchair access • gay-owned

Gran Hotel Calle 60 #496 (nr Parque Cepeda Peraza) **52–999/924–7730 & 923–6963** • gay-friendly • historic turn-of-the-century hotel • pets ok • also restaurant

Las Arecas Guesthouse Calle 59 #541 (btwn Calle 66 & Calle 68) **52–999/928–3626** • gay-friendly • guesthouse • garden • gay-owned

Posada Santiago Guesthouse Calle 57 No 552 (between Calle 66 & 68, Centro Historico) **52–999/928–4258** • gay/ straight • pool • nonsmoking • WiFi • wheelchair access • gay-owned

Bars

El Establo Calle 60 #482 (btwn Calle 56 & 58) **52–999/924–2289** • gay-friendly • dancing/DJ • food served • popular w/ tourists & locals

Nightclubs

Pride Disco Campeche A (200 meters del Puente de Ulman), Anillo Periferico **52–999/946–4401** • mostly gay men • dancing/DJ • strippers • south of town, all taxi drivers know where it is located

Restaurants

Cafe La Habana Calle 59 #511-A (at Calle 62) **52–999/928–6502** • 24hrs • also bar & café

Cafeteria Pop Calle 57 (btwn Calle 60 & 62) **52–999/928–6163** • brkfst, lunch & "light dinner" • beer & wine

La Bella Época Calle 60 #447 (upstairs in the Hotel del Parque) **52–99/928–1928** • 4pm-1am • Yucatécan cuisine • try to get one of the balcony tables

Villa Maria Hotel & Restaurant **52–999/923–3357**

Mexicali

Bars

El Rey de Copas Av Baja California (at Av Tuxtla Gutierrez, Pueblo Nuevo) • open till 3am • lesbians/ gay men • neighborhood bar

El Taurino Av Juan de Zuazua 480 (near Jose Morelos) • 1pm-2am, clsd Mon • popular • lesbians/ gay men • dancing/DJ

Nightclubs

Mirage Disco Av Lerdo #430 (Zona Centro) **52–686/214–1285** • 6pm-2am Wed-Sun • popular • dancing/DJ

Mexico City

Note: M°=Metro station

Note: Mexico City is divided into "Zonas" (ie, Zona Rosa) & "Colonias" (abbreviated here as "Col."). Remember to use these when giving addresses to taxi drivers.

Info Lines & Services

Cálamo (LGBT AA) Av de Chapultepec 465, desd 202 (Col. Juárez) **52–55/5574–1210** • 8pm Mon-Fri, 7pm Sat, 6pm Sun • LGBT AA group

Centro Cultural de la Diversidad Sexual Colima 267 (Col. Roma Norte) **52–55/5514–2565, 52–55/1450–9511** • Mexico City's LGBT center • also cafe

Jovenes La Villa AA Calle 521 #248 (nr Ave 510) **52–55/2603–7696**

ACCOMMODATIONS

Best Western Majestic Hotel Ave Madero 73, Col. Centro **52-55/5521-8600, 800/528-1234** • gay-friendly • 4-star hotel on the Zócalo Plaza • rooftop restaurant • wheelchair access

Condesa Haus Cuernavaca 142 (at Campeche) **52-55/5256-2494, 310/622-4825 (US#)** • gay-friendly • WiFi • full brkfst • gay-owned

Hostal Central Historico Regina 5 de Febrero #53 (Col. Centro) **52-55/5709-4192** • gay-friendly • also cafe • WiFi

Hotel Casa Blanca Lafragua 7 (Col. Tabacalera) **52-55/5096-4500, 800/905-2905 (US & CANADA #)** • gay-friendly • 5-star hotel • pool • restaurant & bar

Hotel Gillow Isabel la Católica 17 (Col. Centro) **52-55/5518-1440, 52-55/5510-2636** • gay-friendly • also restaurant & bar

Hotel Polanco Edgar Allan Poe 8 (Col. Polanco) **52-55/5280-8082, 800/221-9044** • gay-friendly • steps from Paseo de la Reforma

Hotel Principado Londres 42 (Col Juarez) **52-55/5533-2944** • gay-friendly

El Patio 77 Icazbalceta 77 (Col. San Rafael) **52-55/5455-0332, 52-55/5592-8452** • gay-friendly • eco-friendly B&B

The Red Tree House Culiacan 6 (Col Condesa) **52-55/5584-3829** • gay-friendly • stylish B&B

Valentina Amberes 27, Col. Juárez (Zona Rosa) **52-55/5080-4500** • gay-friendly • small boutique hotel

W Mexico City Campos Eliseos 252 **52-55/9138-1800** • gay-friendly • in trendy Polanco • 2 restaurants & bar • WiFi

BARS

42 Bar Amberes 4 (Zona Rosa) **52-55/5208-0352**

Bar Lili Calle 65 #7 (Col. Puebla) **52-55/4551-0414** • lesbians/ gay men • neighborhood bar

Black Out Amberes 11 (Zona Rosa) **52-55/5511-9247** • gay/ straight • upscale lounge • also restaurant

Cafeína Nuevo Leon 73 (in Condesa) **52-55/5212-0090** • 7pm-4am, 6pm-10pm Sun • gay-friendly • dancing/DJ • co-owned by Diego Luna of Y Tu Mama También fame

Enigma Calle Morelia 111, Col. Roma (4 blocks from Mº Niños Héroes, Zona Rosa) **52-55/5207-7367** • 9pm-3:30am, 6pm-2am Sun, clsd Mon • lesbians/ gay men • dancing/DJ • shows for women Th • live shows • cover charge

La Gayta/ Pussy Bar Amberes 18 (Zona Rosa) **52-551/055-5873** • lesbians/ gay men • neighborhood bar • young crowd

Lipstick Amberes 1 (at Paseo de la Reforma, Zona Rosa) **52-55/5514-4920** • clsd Sun • gay/ straight • more lesbian Th • lounge • videos • live shows

El Marrakech Salón Republica de Cuba 18 (Col. Centro) • lesbians/ gay men • neighborhood bar

Papi Fun Bar Amberes 18 (Zona Rosa) **52-55/5208-3755** • lesbians/ gay men • neighborhood bar • young crowd

Pride Restbar Alfonso Reyes 281 (Col. Condessa) **52-55/5516-2368**

Tom's Leather Bar Av Insurgentes 357 (Col. Condesa) **55-84/5564-0728** • 9pm-4am, clsd Mon

NIGHTCLUBS

Buttergold/ Butterflies Calle Izazaga 9 (at Av Lazaro Cárdenas S, Centro Historico) **52-55/5761-1351 & 1861** • 9pm-3am, till 4:30am Fri-Sat, clsd Mon • popular • lesbians/ gay men • dancing/DJ • 2 flrs • lavish drag shows Fri-Sat • cover charge

Cabaré-Tito Fusion Londres 77 (Zona Rosa) **52-55/5511-1613** • open 4pm, clsd Mon-Tue • lesbians/ gay men • more women Th • 18+

Cabaré-Tito Neón Calle Londres 161, Local 20-A, Plaza del Angel (Zona Rosa) **52-55/5514-9455** • 6pm-close • mostly gay men • dancing/DJ • go-go dancers

Exacto/ The Doors Calle Monterrey 47, Col. Roma (Zona Rosa) **52-55/5533-1691** • 9pm-4am • popular • lesbians/ gay men • 3 flrs • The Doors, 1st floor, is a mixed restaurant/ bar • Exacto, 2nd floor, is for women • food served • live shows • cover charge

Hibrido Calle Londres 161, Plaza del Angel, 2nd flr (Zona Rosa) **52-55/5511-1197** • Th-Sun • lesbians/ gay men • dancing/DJ

Kashbah Disco Bar Insurgentes 234 (Col. Roma) • lesbians/ gay men • dancing/DJ • drag shows

Liverpool 100 Liverpool 100 (Col. Juarez) **52-55/5208-4507** • 9pm-close Wed, Fri & Sat only • mostly gay men • dancing/DJ

Living Bucareli 144 (Col. Juarez) 52–55/5512-7281 • 10pm-close Fri-Sat only • popular • mostly men • popular • theme nights

Romeo Club Niza 19 (Col. Juarez) 52–55/5207-6422 • Fri-Sat only • mostly gay men • dancing/DJ

CAFES

B Gay B Proud Amberes 12-B (Zona Rosa) • food served

Club 24 Santa María La Ribera # 24 Del Cuauhtémoc 52–55/2198-2580 • 9am-4am Fri-Sat only • mostly gay men • dancing/DJ

RESTAURANTS

12:30 Amberes 13 (Zona Rosa) 52–55/5514-5971 • popular before-clubbing hangout

La Antigua Cortesana Chiapas 173-A (Col. Roma) 52–55/5584-4678 • 1pm-11pm, till midnight Fri-Sat, till 7pm Sun • popular Mexican cuisine • also bar

Cafe 22 Montes de Oca 22 (Col. Condesa) 52–55/5212-1533 • 6pm-2am • Mexican & Italian • also shows

El Cardenal Calle de Palma 23 52–55/5521-8815 • incredible pastries

Casa Merlos Victoriano Zepeda 80 (at Observatoria) 52–55/5277-4360 • traditional poblano food • definitely try the molé

Cote Sud Orizaba 87 (Col. Roma) 52–55/5219-2981 • 8am-11pm, till midnight Fri, 10am-6pm Sun • French/ tapas

Fonda San Ángel Plaza San Jacinto 3, Col. San Ángel (across from Bazar San Ángel) 52–55/5550-1641 & 1942 • popular after 7pm Fri-Sat • classic Mexican dishes

Ligaya Nuevo Leon 68 (in Condesa) 52–55/5286-6268 • nouvelle Mexican • dinner nightly • outdoor seating

Mexico City

CITY INFO:
Mexican Tourism 800-446-3942, web: www.visitmexico.com.

ATTRACTIONS:
Ballet Folklorico, web: www.balleta-malia.com.
Frida Kahlo House.
Metropolitan Cathedral.
Diego Rivera Web Museum, web: www.diegorivera.com.
Museo Dolores Olmedo (largest collection of Kahlo's works) 52–55/5555-0891, web: www.museodoloresolmedo.org.mx.
Museum of Anthropology 52–55/4040-5300, web: www.mna.inah.gob.mx.
Museum of the Palace of Fine Arts 800/904-4000, web: www.bellasartes.gob.mx.
Shrine to Our Lady of Guadalupe.
Teotihuacan Pyramids.

WEATHER:
Temperate and dry most of the year, with most of the annual rainfall coming in May-Oct. When the smog gets unbearable, head for a museum or another indoor activity.

TRANSIT:
Official Radio Taxis 52–55/5566-0077 or 52–55/5271-9058, web: www.taxi-mexico.com.
Don't hail a taxi on the street. It costs more to call an official taxi, but it's worth it.
Mexico City Metrobus. Hop on hop off bus 800/702-8000, web: www.turibus.com.mx

La Nueva Opera Ave Cinco de Mayo 10 (Centro Historico) 52–55/5512–8959 • 1pm-midnight, clsd Sun • legendary cantina since Pancho Villa fired a bullet into the ceiling

Sanborns Madera 4 (in Casa de los Azulejos) 52–55/5518–6676 • brkfst, lunch & dinner • superstore

Xel-Ha 52–55/5553–5968 • traditional cuisine of the Yucatan

ENTERTAINMENT & RECREATION

El Hábito Madrid 13 (Coyacán District) 52–55/5659–1139 • avant-garde theater & bar

Museo de Arte Carrillo Gil Av Revolución 1608 (Col San Angel) 52–55/5550–6260, 52–55/5550–3983 • 10am-6pm, clsd Mon • contemporary art

Museo de Frida Kahlo Calle Londres 247 (Coyacán) 52–55/5554–5999 • 10am-5:45pm, clsd Mon • original paintings, furniture, letters & Frida's dresses • also garden & café

Museo Templo Mayor Calle Seminario 8 (at República de Guatemala, enter on plaza, near Cathedral) 52–55/4040–5600 • 9am-5pm, clsd Mon • artifacts from the central Aztec temple at Tenochtitlán

BOOKSTORES

El Armario Abierto Agustín Melgar 25 (Col. Condesa) 52–55/5286–0895 • Mexico's only bookstore specializing in sexuality • some LGBT titles

RETAIL SHOPS

Rainbowland Estrasburgo 31 (Zona Rosa) 52–55/5525–9066

PUBLICATIONS

Homópolis 52–55/2616–0456, 52–55/2616–0457 • twice-weekly LGBT magazine & guide

LeS VOZ Magazine • "The magazine of Mexico's lesbian feminist culture, by & for women"

Rola Gay • nat'l monthly LGBT newspaper • see www.rolaclub.org.mx

Ser Gay 52–55/1450–9511 • quarterly magazine • covers all Mexico nightlife

Monterrey

ACCOMMODATIONS

Holiday Inn Monterrey Centro Av Padre Mier 194 N (at Garibaldi, Centro) 52–81/8228–6000 • gay-friendly • near Zona Rosa • pool • also restaurant

BARS

Akbal Abasolo 870B, 2nd Flr, Casa del Maíz 52–81/1257–2986 • 9pm-2am, clsd Mon • gay/straight • more gay Sun

Casa de Lola 52–81/8343–6210 • Th-Sat only • mostly gay men • dancing/DJ • karaoke

NIGHTCLUBS

Baby Shower Ocampo 433 Puente (btwn Rayon & Aldama Centro) 52–81/8881–5632 • 9pm-close, clsd Mon-Tue • lesbians/ gay men • dancing/DJ • strippers • videos

Parking Allende 120 Ote (btwn Juarez & Guerrero) 52–81/8343–2624 • 10pm-close Wed-Sat • mostly gay men • dancing/DJ

Venneno Club Av de los Héroes 47 (at Av Francisco I Madero) 52–81/8244–5499 • 9pm-close, clsd Mon-Tue • lesbians/ gay men • dancing/DJ • drag shows • strippers

Morelia

ACCOMMODATIONS

Casa Camelinas B&B Jacarandas 172 (Col. Nueva Jacarandas) 52–433/324–5194, 707/942–4822 (US#) • gay-friendly • mostly women • 3 1/2 hours from Mexico City • nonsmoking • also Spanish classes

BARS

Amnesia Happy Bar Gertrudis Bocanegra 905 (Col Ventura Puente) 52–443/312–1578 • 5pm-2am, clsd Sun • lesbians/ gay men • lounge w/ DJ

NIGHTCLUBS

Con la Rojas Calle Aldama 343 (Centro) 52–443/312–1578 • 10pm-2:30am, clsd Sun-Wed • mostly gay men • dancing/DJ • cover charge

RESTAURANTS

La Capilla Ignacio Zaragoza 90 (at Posada de la Soledad Hotel) 52–443/312–1888 • in charming old hotel in converted convent

Fonda Las Mercedes Calle Leon Guzmán 47 52–443/312–6113 & 313–3222 • popular • inside beautiful colonial home

Oaxaca

ACCOMMODATIONS

El Camino Real Oaxaca Calle 5 de Mayo 300 52–951/501–6100, 800/722–6466 • gay-friendly • 5-star hotel in restored 16th-c convent • frescoes & courtyards abound • restaurant • swimming

Casa Adobe B&B Independencia 801 (at Matamoros), Tlalixtac de Cabrera **52-951/517-7268** • gay/ straight • 15 minutes from center of Oaxaca • WiFi • gay-owned

La Casa de Don Pablo Hostel Melchor Ocampo 412, Centro (at Rayon St) **52-951/516-8384** • gay/ straight • nonsmoking

Casa Machaya Oaxaca B&B Sierra Nevada 164, Col. Loma Linda **52/951-1328203** • gay-friendly • kids ok • private level w/ patio & valley views

Casa Sagrada Murguia 403 **310/929-7099** • gay/ straight • 30 minutes from Oaxaca • full brkfst • kids ok • nonsmoking • wheelchair access

Casa Sol Zipolite 6 Arco Iris, Col. Arroyo Tres **52-958/100-0462** • mostly gay men • pool • WiFi • gay-owned • 300 meters from famous Playa Zipolite

Posada Arigalan 52-958/111-5801 • gay/ straight • perched above the Pacific Ocean • women-run

NIGHTCLUBS

Club Privado 502 (aka El Número) Calle Porfirio Díaz 502 (Centro, ring to enter) • 10pm-close, clsd Sun-Tue • gay/ straight • dancing/DJ (wknds) • cover charge

Gavana Dance Club Calzada Porfirio Diaz #216 (Col. Reforma) • 9pm-close Th-Sat • gay/ straight

RESTAURANTS

El Asador Vasco Portal de Flores 10-A (Centro) **52-951/514-4755** • popular • great views • authentic Oaxacan cuisine (can you say ¡mole!)

Sonadores Dreamers 1301 Gardenia (at Palma Real), Huatulco **52-958/105-1592** • 6pm-11pm, till midnight Fri-Sat, clsd Mon • dancing/DJ • live shows • gay-owned

Playa del Carmen

see also Cancún & Cozumel

ACCOMMODATIONS

Acanto Boutique Hotel 16th St N (btwn 5th Ave & the beach) **631/882-1986** • gay-friendly • pool • nonsmoking • full brkfst based on package

Aventura Mexicana Hotel Av 10 (at Calle 24) **52-984/873-1876, 800/455-3417** • gay-friendly • pool • also restaurant & bar

Hotel Copa Cabana 5ta Av Norte (btw 10 & 12) **52-984/873-0218** • gay-friendly • WiFi • wheelchair access

Hotel Playa del Carmen & OM Lounge Calle 12 Norte con 1.ra privada, n.195 **52-984/147-0949** • gay/ straight • WiFi • gay-owned

Luna Blue Hotel & Bar Calle 26 (at 5th Av) **415/839-8541**

NIGHTCLUBS

Playa 69 Av 5 (btwn Calle 4 & Calle 6, ground flr) • wknds 9pm-4am • mostly gay men • dancing/DJ • gay-owned

RESTAURANTS

100% Natural Av 5 (btwn 10th & 12th) **52-984/73-2242** • vegetarian

Puebla

BARS

La Cigarra Ave 5 Poniente 538 (at Calle 7, Centro) **52-222/246-6356** • 6pm-3am • mostly gay men • beer bar • videos

NIGHTCLUBS

Garotos 22 Orient E 602 (close to Blvd 5 de Mayo, Xenenetla) **52-222/242-4232** • 9pm-3am Fri-Sat only • gay-friendly • dancing/DJ • cover charge

Puerto Vallarta

ACCOMMODATIONS

Blue Seas/ Lido Beach Club Malecon 1 Esq Abedul Col Emiliano Zapata **813/855-0190** • gay/straight • all suites • pool

Boana Torre Malibu Condo Hotel Calle Amapas 325 **52-322/222-0999, 52-322/222-6695** • gay/ straight • food served • pool • poolside bar • gay-owned

Bugambilia Blanca Condos Carretera Barra de Navidad 602, Col. Emiliano Zapata (Off Hwy 200) **52-322/222-1152** • gay/ straight • 6-minute walk to gay beach • kids ok • WiFi • gay-owned

Casa Cúpula Callejon de la Igualdad 129, Col. Amapas **52-322/223-2484, 866/352-2511** • lesbians/ gay men • swimming • nonsmoking • WiFi • wheelchair access • gay-owned

Casa de las Flores Calle Santa Barbara #359 **510/763 – 3913** (US#), **52-322/120-5242** • condos and villa compound overlooking Los Muertos Beach • gay-owned

Casa dos Comales Calle Aldama 274 **52–322/223–2042, 52–322/294–9959** • gay-friendly • guesthouse & apts near Old Town • pool • gay-owned

Casa Fantasía Pinot Suarez 203, Col. Emiliano Zapata (near the Rio Cuale) **52–322/223–2444** • gay/ straight • B&B made up of 3 traditional haciendas • full brkfst • terrace • pool • nonsmoking • wheelchair access • gay-owned

Casa Tranquila Morelos #7-A (at Lázaro Cárdenas), Bucerias, Nayarit **52–329/298–1767, 322/728–7519** • gay/ straight • apts • near beach • WiFi • lesbian-owned

Los Cuatro Vientos Matamoros 520 **52–322/222–0161** • gay-friendly • El Nido rooftop bar & restaurant • annual Women's Getaway • pool • WiFi

Hotel Mercurio **52–322/222–4793, 866/388–2689** • popular • lesbians/ gay men • traditional & alternative families welcome • 1 1/2 blocks from beach • pool • WiFi • gay-owned

Hotelito Desconocido Playon de Mismaloya, La Cruz de Loreto, Tomatlán **52–33/3611–3013, 800/851–1143** • gay/ straight • eco-resort on the beach • 60 miles S of Puerto Vallarta • pool • sauna

El Panorama Oceano Atlantico 82, La Penita **52–327/274–3499, 888/246–1369 (US#)** • gay/ straight • pool • WiFi • nonsmoking • gay-owned

Quinta Maria Cortez Calle Sagitario 132, Playa Conchas Chinas **888/640–8100** • gay/ straight • pool

The San Franciscan Resort & Gym Calle Pilitas #213 (at Playa Los Muertos) **52–322/222–6473 x0** • gay/ straight • pool • WiFi

Villa Safari Condo Francisca Rodriguez 203 **269/469–0468 (US #)** • gay/ straight • condos • nonsmoking • gay-owned

Yelapa Casa/ Casa Pericos 51 El Camino Huachanango, Yelapa **52–322/417–4367** • gay/ straight • full brkfst • gay-owned

BARS

Los Amigos Bar Calle Venustiano Carranza 237 (upstairs, next to Paco's Ranch) **52–322/222–7802** • 6pm-4am • lesbians/ gay men • Mexican cantina • patio

Amor Bar Lazaro Cardenas 271 **52–322/222–7427** • 9pm-4am • lesbians/ gay men • martini lounge

Apaches Olas Altas 439 (at Rodriguez) **52–322/222–4004** • 5pm-2am, till 1am Sun-Mon • gay/ straight • classy martini bar • tapas • lesbian-owned

Blue Sunset Rooftop Bar Los Muertos Beach (at Blue Chairs Resort) • 10am-midnight • mostly gay men • karaoke • drag shows • food served

Frida 301-A Insurgentes (at Venustiano Carranza) **52–322/222–3668** • 1pm-2am, from 7pm Mon-Tue • gay/ straight • Mexican cantina • bears • more gay later in evening • food served • gay-owned

Garbo Pulpito 142 (at Olas Altas) **52–322/223–5753** • 6pm-2am • gay/ straight • upscale martini lounge • live music • gay-owned • 18+

Kox Club Ignacio L Vallarta 264 **52–322/223–2175** • lesbians/ gay men • drag shows • karaoke

La Noche Lázaro Cárdenas 257 (Zona Romantica) **52–322/222–3364** • 7pm-2am • lesbians/ gay men • cocktail lounge

The Palm/ Viva Olas Altas 508 (at Rodolfo Gomez) **52–322/223–4818** • 4pm-4am • mostly gay men • dancing/DJ • cabaret

Reinas Lazaro Cardenas 361 **52–322/125–9532** • 5pm-2am • mostly gay men • neighborhood bar

Sama Olas Altas 510 (at Rodolfo Gomez) **52–322/223–3182** • 4:30pm-2am • lesbians/ gay men • small martini bar w/ sidewalk seating

NIGHTCLUBS

Club Manana/ Tease Venustiano Carranza #290 (at Col Emiliano Zapata) **52–322/2222–7772** • 10pm-6am, till 8am Fri-Sun, clsd Mon • popular • lesbians/ gay men • dancing/DJ • drag shows • strippers

No Borders 221 Libertad **52–322/136–8775** • 1pm-2am • lesbians/ gay men • neighborhood bar • rooftop patio

Paco's Ranch 237 Ignacio Vallarta **52–322/222–1899** • 9pm-6am • popular • lesbians/ gay men • dancing/DJ • also rooftop terrace • drag shows • cover charge • gay-owned

CAFES

Cafe San Angel Olas Altas 449 (at Francisco Rodreguez) **52–322/223–1273** • 7am-1am • sidewalk cafe

The Coffee Cup Rodolfo Gómez 146-A (at Olas Altas) **52–322/222–8584** • 7am-10pm, clsd Sun in summer • gay-owned

CyberSmoothie Rodolfo Gómez 111 **52-322/223-4784** • 9am-9:30pm • WiFi • food served

Dee's Coffee Company 52-322/222-1197 • 7am-10pm • homemade pastries

Fuego Calle Amapas 147 (at Calle Pulpito) **52-322/222-2114** • 8am-10pm, clsd Sun • Asian • also bar

Uncommon Grounds Buddha Lounge Lazaro Cardenas 625 **52-322/223-3834** • 5pm-close, clsd Mon-Tue • also aromatherapy & gifts

Xocodiva Rodolfo Gomez 118 **52-322/113-0352** • artisinal chocolate • women-owned

RESTAURANTS

El Arrayan Allende #344 (at El Centro) **52-322/222-7195** • 6pm-11pm, clsd Tue • lesbian-owned

The Blue Shrimp Olas Altas 366 (Zona Romantica) **52-322/222-4246** • 11am-midnight

El Brujo Venustiano Carranza 510 (at Naranjo) **52-322/223-3026** • 1pm-9:30pm, clsd Mon • Mexican/ seafood • worth the wait

Cafe Bohemio Rodolfo Gómez 127 (at Olas Altas) **44-322/134-2436** • 5pm-2am, clsd Sun • lesbians/ gay men • open-air cafe • late-evening happy hour • gay-owned

Cafe des Artistes Calle Guadalupe Sánchez 740 (at Leona Vicario) **52-322/222-3228** • 6pm-11:30pm • popular • upscale French w/ a Mexican twist • reservations required

Chez Elena Matamoros 520, Centro (at Los Quatro Vientos Hotel) **52-322/222-0161** • 6pm-11pm • seasonal • garden restaurant • also rooftop bar • woman-owned

Cilantros Abasolo 169 (at Morelos) **52-322/222-7147** • 5:30pm-1am, clsd Sun • Mexican/ fusion • rooftop deck • also bar

Daiquiri Dick's Olas Altas 314 (on Playa Los Muertos) **310/697-3799** • 8:30am-1:30pm & 5:30pm-11pm, closed Tue & clsd Sept

De Santos 771 Morelos **52-322/221-3090** • 5pm-4am • chic Mediterranean • also dance club

El Dorado Pulpito 102, Playa de los Muertos **52-322/222-4124** • beach club & restaurant • evening shows

Le Bistro Jazz Cafe Isla Rio Cuale 16-A (on the island, at the East Bridge) **52-322/222-0283** • 9am-midnight, clsd Sun • popular • PV's classiest • gay-owned

Memo's Casa de los Hotcakes Calle Basilio Badillo 289 **52-322/222-6272** • 8am-2pm • popular • long lines for cheap & good brkfst • indoor patio

Mezzogiorno Ristorante Italiano Avenida del Pacifico 33 (North Beach Bucerias Nayarit) **52-329/298-0350** • 6pm-11pm (clsd Mon off-season)

La Palapa Pulpito 103, Col Emiliano Zapata **52-322/222-5225** • brkfst, lunch & dinner, beachside dining

La Piazzetta Rodolfo Gomez #143 (at Olas Atlas, Romantic Zone) **52-322/222-0650** • 4pm-11pm • Italian

Planeta Vegetariano Iturbide 270 (Centro) **52-322/222-3073** • 8am-10pm, clsd Sun • buffet-style

Red Cabbage Calle Rivera del Rio 204-A (at Basilio Badillo) **52-322/223-0411** • 5pm-11pm, clsd Sun (Apr-Oct) • on Rio Cuale w/ great kitschy decor • lesbian-owned

The Swedes/ Crows Nest Bar Púlpito 154 (at Olas Altas) **52-322/223-2353** • lesbians/ gay men • Swedish/ European • bar upstairs • gay-owned

Trio Guerrero 264 (Centro) **52-322/222-2196** • 6pm-midnight, clsd Sun • Mediterranean/ Mexican • patio • live music • reservations advised

ENTERTAINMENT & RECREATION

Boana Tours Calle Amapas 325 (at Casa Boana Torre Malibu) **52-322/222-0999, 52-322/222-6695** • horseback tours daily

Diana's Cruise the Bay Tour meet at Los Muertos pier • 9:30am-5pm Th • lesbians/ gay men • cruise on 33-ft trimaran • food served • open bar

Ocean Friendly Paseo del Marlin 510-103, Col. Aralias **52-322/225-3774, 044-322/294-0385 (CELL)** • whale-watching tours • Dec 15-March 31

Playa Los Muertos/ Playa del Sol S of Rio Cuale • popular • the gay beach • now spans "Blue Chairs" & "Green Chairs"

RETAIL SHOPS

La Rosa de Cristal Insurgentes 272 (at Cardenas) **52-322/222-5698** • 10am-8pm • local handicrafts & beautiful blown-glass items • gay-owned

Liquid Men Ignacio L Vallarta 245 (Old Town) **52-322/223-3165** • 10am-10pm • men's clothes & accessories • also tickets to gay events like Latin Fever

PUBLICATIONS

Urbana Revista 52-333/844-6471 • gay lifestyle magazine

GYMS & HEALTH CLUBS

Acqua Day Spa & Gym Calle Constitución 450 (F Rodriguez) 52-322/223-5270 • 7am-9pm, till 5pm Sat, clsd Sun • spa services • also small gym

Total Fitness Gym Calle Timon 1 (Marina Vallarta) 52-322/221-0770 • 6:30am-9:30pm, Sat 8am-2pm, clsd Sun • women only • wide variety of classes

EROTICA

The Closet Lazaro Cardenas 230 52-322/223-3030

Querétaro

NIGHTCLUBS

Con la Rojas Ave Constituyentes Pte 42A (Centro) 52-442/212-4795 • 10pm-2:30am, clsd Sun-Wed • mostly gay men • dancing/DJ • cover charge

San Jose del Cabo

ACCOMMODATIONS

El Encanto Inn 210/858-6649, 52-614/142-0388 • gay-friendly • spa and restaurant • swimming

One & Only Palmilla Apartado Postal 52, 23400 52-624/146-7000, 866/829-2977 (US#) • gay-friendly • upscale resort w/ golf course • swimming

RESTAURANTS

Voila Bistro & Catering 1705 Comonfort (Plaza Paulina) 52-624/130-7569 • noon-10pm, from 4pm Sun • popular • Mexican w/ French twist • full bar • patio

San Miguel de Allende

ACCOMMODATIONS

Casa de Sierra Nevada Calle Hospicio 42 (Centro) 52-415/152-7040, 800/701-1561 • gay-friendly • horseback riding • also spa • swimming • patios • 2,880-4,250 pesos

Casa Schuck Boutique B&B Garita 3, Centro 52-415/152-6618 , 937/684-4092 • gay-friendly • boutique hotel w/ private garden & rooftop deck • full brkfst • pool

Dos Casas Calle Quebrada 101 (Guanajuato) 52-415/154-4073 • gay-friendly • full brkfst

Las Terrazas San Miguel Santo Domingo 3 52-415/152-5028, 707/534-1833 (US#) • gay/ straight • 4 rental homes • nonsmoking • WiFi • gay-owned

Tijuana

BARS

Arco Iris Taberna Av Pacifico 395 52-664/631-8290 • gay/straight • food served • beach bar a with great deck overlooking the new Malacon • gay owned

Noa Noa Av D 150/ Miguel F Martínez (at Calle 1) • 5pm-3am, till 4am Fri, till 5am Sat • lesbians/ gay men • dancing/DJ • drag shows • young crowd

NIGHTCLUBS

Los Equipales Calle 7/ Galeana 2024 (at Av Revolución) 52-664/688-3006 • 9pm-3am, clsd Mon-Tue • popular • lesbians/ gay men • dancing/DJ • drag shows • young crowd

Extasis Larroque 213 (in Plaza Viva Tijuana, next to the border) 52-664/682-8339 • 8pm-late, clsd Mon-Wed • popular • mostly gay men • women's night Th • dancing/DJ • strippers • cover charge

Mike's Disco Av Revolución 1220 (at Calle 6A) 52-664/685-3534 • 8pm-5am, till 3am Th, clsd Wed • popular • lesbians/ gay men • dancing/DJ • drag shows • videos

Terraza 9 Calle 5a (at Av Revolución) 52-664/685-3534 • 5pm-2am, till 5am Fri-Sat, clsd Mon • gay-friendly • dancing/DJ

Todos Santos

ACCOMMODATIONS

The Todos Santos Inn Calle Legaspi #33 (Topete) 52-612/145-0040 • gay/ straight • in historic district • pool • nonsmoking • also bar • gay-owned

Tulúm

ACCOMMODATIONS

EcoTulum Resorts & Spa Carretera Tulum Ruinas Km 5 54-115/5918-6400, 877/301-4666 • gay-friendly • WiFi

Om Tulum Caraterra Ruinas Punta -Allen Km 9.5 521-98/4114-0538 • gay-friendly • WiFi

Posada Luna del Sur Calle Luna Sur 5 52-984/871-2984 • gay-friendly

Veracruz

ACCOMMODATIONS

Casa de la Luz Tropical Guest House Tlacotalpan 52–288/884–2331 • gay-friendly • charming studio apt

Hotel Villa del Mar Blvd Miguel Ávila Camacho 2431 (across street from Playa del Mar beach) **52–229/989–6500** • gay-friendly • hotel w/ separate motel & bungalows • near aquarium

ENTERTAINMENT & RECREATION

San Juan de Ulua Fortress • 9am-4:30pm, clsd Mon • impressive early colonial-era floating fortress

Veracruz Aquarium Blvd Avila Camacho (at Xicolencat) **52–229/932–7984** • 10am-7pm • one of the largest & best in the world • don't miss it!

Zacatecas

ACCOMMODATIONS

Quinta Real Zacatecas Av Ignacio Rayón 434 (Col. Centro) 52–492/1105–1010, 866/621–9288 • gay-friendly • 5-star hotel built into grandstand of bullfighting ring

Zihuatanejo

ACCOMMODATIONS

Casa Bulmaro Calle Adelita 52-755/112–1295, 908/497–7939 • gay/ straight • WiFi • wheelchair access • gay-owned

Hotel Las Palmas Calle de Aeropuerto (at lot 5) 52–755/557–0634 , 888/527–7256 • gay-friendly • full brkfst • pool

NIGHTCLUBS

Tequila Town Cuauhtemoc 3 (Col Centro) **52–755/553–8587** • 8pm-4am • gay-friendly • more gay after 11pm • karaoke • videos

Wilde's Calle La Laja s/n (Col. Centro) 52–755/557–1042 • 8pm-4am • lesbians/ gay men • dancing/DJ • drag shows & strippers Fri-Sun

COSTA RICA

Alajuela

see also San José

BARS

Rick's Bar & Restaurant Rio Segundo de Alajuela **506-2/441-3213** • 6pm-close, from 4pm Sun • lesbians/ gay men

Arenal

ENTERTAINMENT & RECREATION

The Arenal Volcano • currently not very active, but with Mother Nature, you never know...

Escaleras

ACCOMMODATIONS

Paradise Costa Rica 800/708–4552 • gay/ straight • vacation villas • pools • nonsmoking • gay-owned

Guanacaste

ACCOMMODATIONS

Villa Decary Nuevo Arenal, 5717 Tilaran **506–2/694–4330, 800/556–0505 (FROM US & CANADA)** • gay-friendly • former coffee farm overlooking Lake Arenal • gay-owned

Malpais

ACCOMMODATIONS

Kelea Surf Spa 949/492–7263 • women-only • surf spa

Manuel Antonio, Quepos

ACCOMMODATIONS

Casa Antonio Enter at Arboleda Hotel 202/558–6455 • lesbians/ gay men • luxury rental house in the jungle • nonsmoking • gay-owned

Casa Bumerango 213/330–0231 • gay/ straight • kids ok • wheelchair access • gay-owned

Casa de Frutas 506–8/825–3257 (CELL), 800/936–9622 • gay/ straight • luxury villa in Tulemar Gardens

Casa Mono Titi in the hills 506–2/777–5029, 800/282–3680 (US & CANADA) • gay-friendly • luxurious vacation home • pool • near beaches & bars • kids ok • nonsmoking • WiFi • gay-owned

Casa Romano 404/290-6919 • gay/ straight • pool • near gay beach • WiFi • wheelchair access • gay-owned

Casitas Eclipse KM 5 Manuel Antonio Rd 506-2/777-0408 • gay/ straight • detached casitas

Costa Verde 506-2/777-0584, 866/854-7958 (FROM US & CANADA) • gay/ straight • bungalows, studios & apts • pool • gay-owned

Gaia Hotel & Reserve km 2.7 Carretera Quepos a Manuel Antonio 506-2/777-9797, 800/226-2515 • gay-friendly • boutique hotel • surrounded by wildlife refuge • full brkfst • pool • WiFi • gay-owned

Hotel Casa Blanca 506-2/777-0253 • lesbians/ gay men • short hike to gay beach • pool • kids ok • wheelchair access • lesbian & gay-owned

Hotel Parador 506-2/777-1414, 877/506-1414 • gay-friendly • large luxury resort • swimming • also gourmet restaurant • WiFi

Hotel Villa Roca 506-2/777-1349 • mostly gay men • great ocean views • near beaches • pool • nonsmoking • wheelchair access • gay-owned

La Mansion Inn 506-2/777-3489, 800/360-2071 • gay/ straight • luxury hotel • pool • also restaurant • bar • ocean views • gay-owned

La Posada 506-2/777-1446 • gay-friendly • 4 bungalows & 2 guest rooms • pool • full brkfst • gay-owned

Si Como No 506-2/777-0777, 888/742-6667 • gay-friendly • 25-acre wildlife refuge • also spa • pool • wheelchair access

BARS

Tutu/ Gato Negro KM 5 Manuel Antonio Rd (at Casitas Eclipse) 506-2/777-0408 • 4pm-close • popular • gay/ straight • also restaurant • great view

NIGHTCLUBS

Liquid Lounge 506-2/777-5158 • 9pm-3am Wed & Th-Sun • mostly men • dancing/DJ • drag shows

RESTAURANTS

El Barba Roja Carretera al Parque Nacional 506-2/777-0331 • 7am-10pm, from 4pm Mon • American • popular • great sunset location

El Gran Escape & Fish Head Bar Quepos Centro 506-2/777-0395 • brkfst, lunch, dinner, clsd Tue • seafood • full bar

La Hacienda Restaurante Plaza Yara 506-2/777-3473 • 5pm-11pm, clsd Sun • live shows

Jefe's at the Hotel Plinio 506-2/777-0036 • Mexican • full bar

Rico Tico in Hotel Si Como No • brkfst, lunch & dinner • Tex/ Mex • includes use of pool bar • popular • live shows • also Claro Que Sí (seafood restaurant)

Osa Peninsula

ACCOMMODATIONS

Blue Osa Yoga Sanctuary and Spa 506/8704-7006 • gay/ straight • all meals included • kids/ ok • nonsmoking • WiFi • gay-owned

Playa Sámara

ACCOMMODATIONS

Casitas LazDívaz 506/2656-0295 • gay/straight • full brkfst • wheelchair access • lesbian diva-owned

San José

ACCOMMODATIONS

Colours Oasis Resort El Triangulo Noroeste, Blvd Rohrmoser (200 meters before end of blvd) 506-2/296-1880, 866/517-4390 (US & CANADA) • lesbians/gay men • pool • also bar & restaurant • WiFi • gay-owned

Hotel El Mirador Bello Horizonte, Escazú 506/2289-3981

Hotel Kekoldi Av 9 (btwn Calles 5 & 7, Barrio Amón) 506-2/248-0804, 786/221-9011 (FROM US) • gay/ straight • in art deco bldg in downtown • secluded garden • WiFi • gay-owned

Secret Garden B&B 506-2/224-1837 • gay/ straight • in historic Rohrmoser district • private courtyard • WiFi • gay-owned

BARS

Bar Al Despiste in front of Mudanzas Mundiales (W of Universal Zapote) 506-2/234-5956 • 6pm-2am, 5pm-10pm Sun, clsd Mon • gay/ straight • theme nights • karaoke

Buenas Vibraciones Paseo de los Estudiantes 506-2/223-4573 • lesbians/ gay men

NIGHTCLUBS

La Avispa 834 Calle 1 (pink house btwn Avs 8 & 10) **506–2/223–5343** • 8pm-2am, popular T-dance from 5pm Sun, clsd Mon-Wed • lesbians/ gay men • women's night 2nd & 4th Fri • dancing/DJ

Azotea Uruca , de Capris 300 Norte **506–2/220–2506** • gay/ straight • dancing/DJ

El Bochinche Calle 11 (btwn Avs 10 & 12, Paseo de los Etudiantes), San Pedro **506–2/221–0500** • 7pm-2am, till 5pm Fri-Sat, clsd Sun-Tue • also full restaurant • Mexican • dancing/DJ after 10pm • videos

Club Oh! Calle 2 (btwn Avs 14 & 16) **506–22/221–9341** • 9pm-close Fri-Sat • gay/ straight • dancing/DJ • take taxi to avoid bad area

Puchos Calle 11 & Av 8 (knock to enter) **506–2/256–1147, 506–2/222–7967** • 8pm-2:30am, from 4pm Sun • mostly gay men • also restaurant • drag shows

RESTAURANTS

Ankara San José de la Montaña (Heredia, San Antonio de Belén, S of church) **506–2/266–0303, 506–2/293–0089** • clsd Mon-Tue, live music

Cafe Mundo Av 9 & Calle 15 (200 meters E of parking lot for INS, Barrio Amón) **506–2/222–6190** • 11am-11pm, 5pm-midnight Sat, clsd Sun • Italian • garden seating • also cafe/ bar • gay-owned

La Cocina de Leña in El Pueblo complex **506–2/255–1360, 506–2/256–5353** • 11am-11pm • 5 minutes from downtown • reservations recommended

Machu Picchu Calle 32 (btwn Aves 1 & 3) **506–2/222–7384** • Peruvian

Mirador Ram Luna from center of Aserrí, go 4 kilometers on the road toward Tabarca, Aserri **506–2/230–3060** • dinner nightly, lunch & dinner wknds, clsd Mon • hillside restaurant w/ amazing views • special buffet Wed

Olio Escalante, Bario California (N of Baselman's, San Pedro/ Los Yoses) **506–2/281–0541** • lunch & dinner, clsd Sun • Spanish • also full bar

Vishnu Vegetarian Restaurant Av 1 (btwn Calles 3 & 1) **506–2/256–6063** • 8am-9:30pm

ENTERTAINMENT & RECREATION

Gay Tours Costa Rica **506–2/305–8044** • daily events & excursions • Nov-April

Mercado Central/ Central Market Central Avenida (btwn Calles 6 & 8) • bustling market selling food, clothing, souvenirs & more

San Ramon

ACCOMMODATIONS

Angel Valley Farm B&B 200m N & 300m E of Iglesia de Los Angeles (at Autopista to Arenal Volcano) **506–2/456–4084, 506–2/350–7647 (CELL)** • gay/ straight • full brkfst • kids over 5 & small pets ok • nonsmoking • WiFi • wheelchair access

Santa Clara

ACCOMMODATIONS

Tree Houses Hotel Costa Rica **506–2/475–6507** • gay/ straight • private treehouses in canopy of trees on wildlife refuge • full brkfst • nonsmoking • lesbian-owned • kids/ pets ok

Tamarindo

ACCOMMODATIONS

Cala Luna Hotel & Villas Playa Langosta (at Playa Tamarindo) **506–2/653–0214, 800/503–5202** • gay-friendly • pools • kids ok

Hotel Sueño del Mar Playa Langosta **506–2/653–0284** • gay-friendly • private hacienda on the beach • full brkfst • pool • nonsmoking • WiFi

ARGENTINA

Buenos Aires

INFO LINES & SERVICES

La Casa del Encuentro/ Lesbian Feminist Cultural Center Rivadavia 3917 **54–1/4982–2550**

Comunidad Homosexual Argentina Tomas Liberti 1080 **54–11/4361–6382**

La Fulana Callao 339, 5th Fl **54–1/4383–7413**

Pink Point Lavalle 669 (at Florida) **54–1/5353–2046, 54–1/4322–1343** • LGBT tourist info

ACCOMMODATIONS

1555 Malabia House Malabia 1555, Palermo Viejo (at Honduras) **54–11/4833–2410** • gay-friendly • pets ok • WiFi

The Cocker Av Juan de Garay 458 (at Defensa) **54–1/4362–8451** • WiFi • full brkfst • pets ok • gay-owned

Don Sancho Youth Hostel Constitucion 4062 (at Boedo) **54–11/4923–1422** • gay/ straight • hostel • full brkfst • some shared baths • hot tub • kids ok • WiFi

Faena Hotel & Universe 445 Martha Salotti St **54–11/4010–9000** • gay/ straight • luxury hotel • WiFi • live shows at The Universe

Home Hotel Honduras 5860 **54–11/4778–1008** • gay-friendly boutique hotel • pool • loft apts available • WiFi

Hotel Axel Venezuela 649 **54–11/4136–9393** • lesbians/ gay men • luxury gay hotel • WiFi • also restaurant • $173-385

Hotel Intercontinental Buenos Aires Moreno 809 **888/424–6835 (US#), 54–11/4340–7100** • gay-friendly • WiFi • gym • bar • restaurants

Hotel Vitrum 5641 Gorriti **866/986–5844** • gay-friendly • stylish boutique hotel

Palermo Viejo B&B Niceto Vega 4629 (at Av Scalabrini Ortiz) **54–11/4773–6012** • gay/ straight • nonsmoking • WiFi • near shopping & gay nightlife • gay-owned

Solar Soler B&B Soler 5676 (at Bonpland) **54–11/4776–3065** • gay-friendly • kids ok • nonsmoking

Telmho Hotel Boutique 1086 Defensa St (at Humberto Primo) **54–11/4116–5467** • gay-friendly • WiFi

BARS

Bach Bar Antonio Cabrera 4390 **54–11/5184–0137** • 11pm-close, clsd Mon • lesbians/ gay men • live shows Th-Fri • karaoke • videos

Bulnes Class Bulnes 1250 (Palermo) **54–11/4861–7492** • from 7pm Th & 11pm Fri-Sat • lesbians/ gay men • dancing/DJ

Cero Consecuencia Cabrera 3769 • 10pm-close, clsd Mon-Tue • lesbians/ gay men

La Cigale 25 May 597 **54–11/4893–2332** • 6pm-close, from 10pm Sat • gay/ straight • DJs • also restaurant

Flux Bar Marcelo T de Alvear 980 (at 9 de Julio) **54–11/5252–0258** • 7pm-close, from 8pm wknds, clsd Sun • lesbians/ gay men • dancing/DJ • art • English, Portuguese, & Russian spoken

Inside Bartolomé Mitre 1571 **54–11/4372–5439** • 6pm-close • mostly men • also restaurant • live shows • older crowd

KM Zero Av Santa Fe 2516 **54–11/4822–7530** • 7pm-close, clsd Sun • also restaurant • lesbians/ gay men • dancing/DJ • drag shows • strippers • videos

Mundo Bizarro 1222 Serrano **54–11/4773–1967** • gay-friendly • 1950s American-style cocktail lounge • food served

Sitges Córdoba 4119 **54–11/4861–3763** • 10:30pm-4am, till 6am Fri-Sat, clsd Mon-Tue • lesbians/ gay men • women go earlier

NIGHTCLUBS

Ambar La Fox Av Federico Lacroze 3455 (at Alvarez Thomas, at El Teatro) • Sat only • lesbians/ gay men • dancing/ DJ • young, alternative mixed crowd

Amerika Gascón 1040 (at Cordoba) **54–11/4865–4416** • open late • mostly gay men • dancing/DJ • cruisy

Angel's Viamonte 2168 • midnight-7am Th-Sat • lesbians/ gay men • dancing/DJ

Bahrein Lavalle 345 • 6pm-7am Wed & Fri, from 10pm Sat, from midnight Tue • gay/ straight • dancing/DJ • also restaurant

Club 69 Niceto Vega 5510 (btwn Humboldt & Fitzroy, Palermo) **54–1/4779–9396** • 11:30pm Th only • gay/ straight • dancing/DJ • drag shows • performance • over-the-top theme parties

Club Namunkura Niceto Vega 5699 (Palermo, at Club M) • 1st Fri only • lesbians/ gay men • dancing/DJ • transgender-friendly

Cocoliche Rivadavia 878 • gay/ straight • dancing/DJ

Fiesta Eyeliner Sarmiento 1272 (at Salon Real) • monthly queer/ alternative dance party • check www.fiestaeyeliner.tk for dates

Fiesta Plop Av Federico Lacroze 3455 (at Alvarez Thomas, at El Teatro) • Fri only • lesbians/ gay men • dancing/ DJ • young, alternative mixed crowd

Glam Cabrera 3046 **54–11/4963–2521** • midnight-close wknds • mostly gay men • popular • dancing/DJ

Juana 775 Av 44 **54–1/557–6807** • from 11:30pm Fri-Sat only • lesbians/ gay men • dancing/DJ

Pacha Av Costanera y Pampa **54–11/4788–4280** • popular dance club • gay-friendly

Palacio Alsina Alsina 940 (near Plaza de Mayo) **54–11/4334–0097, 54–11/4334–0098** • 2am Fri & 10pm Sun only • lesbians/ gay men

Unna Fiesta at Glam Disco • mostly women • dancing/DJ • check www.fiestaunna.com.ar for dates

CAFES

Gout Cafe Juncal 2124 **54–11/4825–8330** • sandwiches, pastries • gay-owned

Pride Cafe Balcarce 869 (in San Telmo) **54–11/4300–6435** • 10am-10pm • live show Th night

Pure Vida Reconquista 516 (btwn Tucuman & Lavalle) **54–11/4393–0093** • 8:30am-7pm, 10am-5:30pm Sat, clsd Sun • juice bar • food served • plenty veggie

RESTAURANTS

10 Mil y Pico Cabrera 4799 **54–11/4833–2385** • Mediterranean

Arevalito Arevalo 1478 **54–11/4776–4252** • 9am-midnight • vegetarian

Bio Humbolt 2199 (Palermo Viejo) **54–11/4774–3880** • lunch & dinner • vegetarian • organic market

La Cabana Rodriguez Peña 1967 (at Posadas) **54–11/4814–0001** • brkfst, lunch & dinner • popular • upscale 2-flr steak house

Casa Cruz 1658 Uriarte **54–11/4833–1112** • 8:30pm-3am, later Fri-Sat • upscale, trendy restaurant • also bar

Cumana Rodriguez Pena 1149 (at Arenales) **54–11/4813–9207** • popular • regional cuisine

El Palacio de la Papa Frita Lavalle 735 (at Maipu) **54–11/4393–5849** • popular • hearty traditional meals • also Av Corrientes 1612, 11/4374-8063

Filo San Martin 975 **54–11/4311–0312, 54-11/4311–1871** • 8pm-close • Italian • trendy • also art gallery

Lobby Nicaragua 5944 **54–11/4770–9335** • 8am-1am, till 8pm Sun-Mon, wine bar, cafe & restaurant

Mark's Deli & Coffeehouse El Salvador 4107 (in Palermo) **54–11/4832–6244** • 11am-8pm, till 9pm Sun, clsd Mon • popular

Milion Parana 1048 **54–11/4815–9925** • popular • swank lounge/ restaurant spread over 3-flr mansion • garden

Naturaleza Sabia Balcarce 958 (at Carlos Calvo) **54–11/4300–6454** • clsd Mon • vegetarian

Rave Gorriti 5092 **54–11/4833–7832** • lunch Tue-Sun & dinner nightly • popular

Sucre Sucre 676 **54–11/4782–9082** • upscale contemporary

Verde Llama Jorge Newbery 3623 **54–11/4554–7467** • 11am-6pm, till midnight Th-Sat • organic vegetarian cafe

ENTERTAINMENT & RECREATION

Casa Brandon Luis Maria Drago 236 (at Lavalleja) **54–11/4858–0610** • events, dance parties, poetry readings, art & more • also bar/ restaurant

Espanol al Sur Pichincha 1031 #2 (at Carlos Calvo) **54–11/4942–9582, 54–11/6449–5447** • gay-friendly • Spanish language & tango classes • lesbian-owned

La Marshall Maipu 444 **54–11/4912–9043** • 8:30pm Wed • exclusively gay tango lessons

Museo Evita Peron Lafinur 2988 (in Palermo) **54–11/4807–9433** • 2pm-7:30pm, clsd Mon

Out And About Pub Crawl • lesbians/ gay men • make new friends on a tour of the local gay bars

RETAIL SHOPS

Gay Wine Store **54–11/4313–2909, 54–11/4313–7033** • lesbians/ gay men

PUBLICATIONS

AG Magazine **54–11/4304–6357**

G-Maps Buenos Aires Franklin 1463, Florida Oeste **54–11/4730–0729** • free pocket-size gay map of Buenos Aires

La Otra Guía Apartado 78 (Suc Olivos) • free gay monthly guide

The Ronda • gay pocket guide w/ local listings • www.theronda.com.ar

GYMS & HEALTH CLUBS

American Hot Gym Ayacucho 449 (M° Callao, Line B) **54–11/4951–7679** • clsd Sun

BRAZIL

Rio de Janeiro

Note: M°=Metro station

INFO LINES & SERVICES

Grupo Arco-Iris Rio de Janeiro Rua do Senado 230 **55–21/2222–7286** • 1pm-7pm, till 11pm Sat, clsd Sun • LGBT community center

Rainbow Kiosk/ Quiosque Atlantic Av (in front of Copacabana Palace Hotel) **55–21/2275–1641** • popular • 24hrs • lesbians/ gay men • tourist info • drag shows

ACCOMMODATIONS

Casa Dois Gatos Rua Rosalina Terra 6, Cabo Frio **561/282–0023, 55–22/2645–5806** • mostly gay men • free transportation from Rio airport • pool • WiFi • gay-owned

Ipanema Plaza Rua Farme Amoedo (at Rua Prudente de Morais) **55–21/3687–2000** • gay/ straight • near gay beach • rooftop pool • also restaurant

MyRioCondo.com 3150 Avenida Atlantica, Apt 901 (Copacabana) **215/847–2397 (US#)** • gay/ straight • WiFi • kids ok • gay-owned

Pousada Internacional Rua Orlando Carpinelli, Paraty **55–24/3371–7802, 55–24/3371–7806** • gay-friendly • B&B in preserved historic town surrounded by semi-tropical forests • nonsmoking • WiFi • wheelchair access

Rio Penthouse **55–21/2541–3882** • gay-friendly • beachfront apts & penthouse suites

Bars

Melt Rua Rita Ludolf 47 **55–21/2249–9309** • gay-friendly • lounge • also restaurant • live music

TV Bar Av Nossa Senhora de Copacabana 1417 **55–21/2267–1663** • 10pm-5am, 9pm-3am Sun, clsd Mon-Wed • television-themed bar • mostly men • theme nights

Nightclubs

Boite 1140 1140 Rua Capitao Menezes **55–21/7830–8867** • 11pm-5am Th-Sun • lesbians/ gay men • dancing/DJ • drag shows

Casa da Matriz Rua Henrique de Novaes 107 **54–11/2226–9691, 54–11/2266–1014** • 11pm-close, clsd Tue • gay/ straight • dancing/DJ • 18+

Cine Ideal Rua da Carioca 64 **55–21/2252–3460** • gay/ straight • dancing/DJ • huge club w/ visting big-name DJs

Dama de Ferro Rua Vinicius de Moraes 288 (Ipanema) **55–21/2247–2330** • lesbians/ gay men • dancing/DJ

Fosfobox Rua Siqueira Campos 143 **55–21/2548–7498** • open Th-Sun • gay/ straight • underground techno

Galeria Cafe Rua Teixeira de Melo 31 (Ipanema) **55–21/2523–8250** • 10:30pm-close, clsd Sun-Tue • gay/ straight • dancing/DJ • also gallery

La Girl Club Rua Raul Pompeia 102 (Copacabana) **55–21/2247–8342** • 9pm-3am, clsd Mon-Wed • popular • mostly women • dancing/DJ • strippers • young crowd

Papa G 42 Almerinda Freitas **55–21/2450–1253** • lesbians/ gay men • dancing/DJ • drag shows • theme nights

Up Turn 2000 Av das Americas **55–21/3387–7957** • lesbians/ gay men • dancing/DJ • food served • outdoor seating

The Week 154 Rua Sacadura Cabral **55–21/2253–1020** • gay-friendly dance club

Cafes

Cafeína Rua Farme de Amoedo 43 (Ipanema) **55–21/2521–2194** • 8am-11:30pm

Copa Cafe Av Atlantica 3056 **55–21/2235–2947**

Expresso Carioca Rua Farme de Amoedo 76 **55–21/2267–8604**

Restaurants

Bar d'Hotel Av Delfim Moreira 696 (2nd Flr, inside Marina All Suites Hotel, Leblon) **55–21/2172–1112** • food served all day, bar till late • Mediterranean • see & be seen

Boox Rua Br Torre 368 (Ipanema) **55–21/2522–3730** • upscale restaurant & nightclub

Cafe del Mar Av Atlantica 1910 **55–21/7857–8681** • gay-friendly • upscale lounge

Caroline Cafe 10 Rua JJ Seabra **55–21/2540–0705** • sushi • full bar

Gringo Cafe Rua Barao da Torre 240 **55–21/3813–3972** • American classics

Maxim's Av Atlantica 1850 **55–21/2255–7444**

Pizzaria Guanabara 1228 Ave Ataulfo de Paiva, Leblon **55–21/2294–0797**

To Nem Ai Rua Farme de Amoedo 57 **55–21/2247–8403** • lesbians/ gay men • popular bar with outdoor seating

Via Sete **55–21/2512–8100** • noon-midnight • plenty veggie

Zero Zero Av Padre Leonel Franca 240 (inside planetarium) **55–21/2540–8041** • gay/ straight • more gay Sun • dancing/DJ • upscale restaurant & nightclub

Entertainment & Recreation

Copacabana Beach at Rua Rodolfo Dantas • gay across from Copacabana Palace Hotel

Farme de Amoedo/ Farme Gay Beach across from Rua Farme de Amoedo • see & be seen at this popular gay beach

Ipanema Beach • gay E of Rua Farme Amoedo

Publications

Rio For Partiers **55–21/2523–9857** • great guide book

CHILE

Santiago

Note: M°=Metro station

ACCOMMODATIONS

Casa Moro Corte Suprema 177 (Departamento B) **56–2/696–9499** • lesbians/ gay men • full brkfst • gay-owned

BARS

Amor del Bueno Ernesto Pinto Lagarrigue 106 **56–2/737–2790** • 5pm-1am, till 4am Fri-Sat • clsd Sun • mostly women • also restaurant • lesbian-owned

Bar 105 Bombero Nuñez 105 **56–2/403–2990** • 9pm-late Th-Sat • lesbians/ gay men

Bar de Willy Av 11 de Septiembre 2214 (Común Providencia) **56–2/381–1806** • 10pm-4am, till 5am wknds • lesbians/ gay men • live shows

El Closet Santa Filomena 138 (at Bombero Nuñez) • lesbians/ gay men • karaoke

Farinelli Bombero Nuñez 68 (Recoleta) **56–2/732–8966** • 5pm-2am • food served • live shows • drag shows • strippers

Pub Friend's Bombero Nuñez 365 (at Dominica, barrio Bellavista) **56–2/777–3979** • 9:30pm-4am, till 5am Fri-Sat • lesbians/ gay men • drag shows

Vox Populi Ernesto Pinto Lagarrigue 364 (Bellavista) **56–2/671–1267** • 9:30pm-3am, clsd Sun-Mon • mostly gay men • also restaurant • garden patio

NIGHTCLUBS

Blondie Alameda 2879, loc 104 **56–2/681–7793** • gay/ straight • alternative • dancing/DJ • theme nights

Bokhara Discoteque Pio Nono 430 (at Constitución, barrio Bellavista) **56–2/732–1050, 56–2/735–1271** • 10pm-6am, till 7am wknds • popular • mostly gay men • dancing/DJ • food served • strippers • drag shows

Bunker Bombero Nuñez 159 (Bellavista) **56–2/738–2301, 56–2/738–2314** • 11pm-close Fri-Sat • lesbians/ gay men • dancing/DJ • food served • live shows

Club Principe Pio Nono 398 **56–2/777–6381** • mostly gay men • dancing/DJ • drag shows • strippers

Nueva Cero Euclides 1204 par 2 Gran Avenida • mostly gay men • dancing/DJ • drag shows

CAFES

Tavelli Andrés de Fuenzalida 34 (Providencia) **56–2/231–9862** • 8:30am-10pm, from 9:30am Sat • popular

RESTAURANTS

Ali Baba 102 Santa Filomena (Barrio Bellavista, Recoleta) **56–2/732–7036** • Middle Eastern

Capricho Español Purisima 65 (barrio Bellavista) **56–2/777–7674** • dinner only • lesbians/ gay men • Spanish • full bar

La Pizza Nostra Av Providencia 1975 & Pedro de Valdivia **56–2/231–8941** • Italian

Santo Remedio 152 Roman Diaz, Providencia **56–2/235–0984** • 6:30pm-close, from 10:30pm wknds • global cuisine • full bar • live DJs

El Toro Loreto 33 **56–2/737–5937** • noon-midnight

EROTICA

Japi Jane Luis Thayer Ojeda 059, Oficina 11 **56–2/234–4917** • 11am-8pm, till 4pm Sat, clsd Sun

AUSTRIA

Vienna

INFO LINES & SERVICES

Gay & Lesbian AA 43–1/799–5599, 43–665/490–5603 (ENGLISH) • call for info

Hosi Zentrum Heumuhlgasse 14 43–1/216–6604 • LGBT political organization • many groups & events • cafe • news magazine

Rosa Lila Villa Linke Wienzeile 102 (near Hofmühlgasse, U4-Pilgramgasse) 43–1/586–8150 (WOMEN), 43–1/585–4343 (MEN) • LGBT center • staffed 5pm-8pm Mon, Wed, Fri • info • gay city maps • also meeting place for various groups • also cafe-bar

ACCOMMODATIONS

Arcotel Wimberger Neubaugürtel 34–36 (at Goldschlagstr) 43–1/521–650 • gay-friendly • restaurant & bar on premises • also fitness club

Art Hotel Brandmayergasse 7-9 • gay-friendly • modern, art-filled hotel

Boutique Hotel Stadthalle Hackengasse 20 • gay/ straight • eco-friendly boutique hotel

Designapartment Vienna Glockengasse 25/ 9 43–650/592–8941 • gay-friendly • full kitchen • terrace • WiFi • gay-owned

Enjoy B&B 49–30/2362–3610 • lesbians/ gay men • accommodations referral service

Gay At Home 43–1/586–1200 • lesbians/ gay men • rental apts around Vienna • gay-owned

Golden Tulip Art Hotel Vienna Brandmayergasse 7-9 43–1/5445–108 • gay-friendly • stylish hotel • central location

Hotel Urania Obere Weißgerberstr 7 (U-Schwedenplatz) 43–1/713–1711 • gay-friendly • centrally located & inexpensive art hotel • wheelchair access • gay-owned

Le Méridien Wien Opernring 13-15 43–1/588–900, 800/543–4300 • gay-friendly • pool • sauna • hot tub • also restaurant & bar

Pension Wild Lange Gasse 10 (off Lerchenfelder Str) 43–1/406–5174 • mostly gay men • rooms & apts • also restaurant • gay sauna & bar in basement • gay-owned

Das Tyrol Mariahilfer Str 15 43–1/587–5415 • gay-friendly • small luxury hotel

BARS

Cafe Cheri Franzensg 2 43–650/208–1471 • 10pm-4am • mostly gay men • also cafe

Cafe Savoy Linke Wienzeile 36 (at Köstlergasse) 43–1/586–7348 • 8am-2am • popular • lesbians/ gay men • upscale cafe-bar

Felixx Gumpendorferstr 5 43–1/920–4714 • 7pm-3am, from 10am Sat, 7pm-1am Sun • lesbians/ gay men • food • WiFi

Frauencafé Lange Gasse 11 43–1/406–3754 • 7pm-midnight, till 2am Fri-Sat (sometimes clsd Sun-Mon) • mostly women • transgender-friendly • cafe-bar

Frauenzentrum Bar Währingerstr 59 (enter on Prechtlgasse) 43–1/402–8754 • 7pm-midnight Th-Sat • women • dancing/DJ

Marea Alta Gumpendorferstr 28 43–699/1159–7131 • 7pm-2am, till 4am Fri-Sat, clsd Sun-Mon • mostly women • young crowd

Peter's Operncafé Hartauer Riemergasse 9 (at Singer) 43–1/512–8981 • 6pm-2am, clsd Sun-Mon • gay/ straight • food served • terrace

Red Carpet Magdalenenstr 2 43–1/676–782–2966 • lesbians/ gay men • dancing/DJ • younger crowd • theme nights

Schik Schikanedergasse 5 • 7pm-2am, till 4am Fri-Sat, clsd Sun • lesbians/ gay men • WiFi

Studio 67 Gumpendorferstr 67 43–1/966–7182 • 10am-4am Th-Sat • gay/ straight • dancing/DJ • also upscale lounge

Village Bar Stiegengasse 8 (near Naschmarkt) 43–1/676–3848977 • 8pm-3am • mostly men • young crowd

Wiener Freiheit Schönbrunner Str 25 (U4-Kettenbrückengasse) 43–1/931–9111 • 8pm-midnight, till 4am Fri-Sat, clsd Sun-Mon • lesbians/ gay men • transgender-friendly • 3 flrs • disco 10pm-4am Fri-Sat • also cafe

NIGHTCLUBS

BallCanCan Schwarzenberg Platz 10 (at Ost Klub) • lesbians/ gay men • dancing/DJ • monthly queer Balkan club

Bingo! Club Hernalser Gürtel Bogen 72 -73 (at B72 club) • queer techno club • lesbians/ gay men • dancing/DJ • transgender-friendly • check for dates

g.spot Neubaugasse 2 (at Camera Club) 43–1/523–3063 • 9pm 1st Fri • mostly women • dancing/DJ • monthly parties • call for info

Heaven Gay Night 43–1/523–3063 • 10pm-6am Sat • mostly men • dancing/DJ • transgender-friendly • strippers • young crowd

Las Chicas Lederergasse 11 (at Gerard) • check for dates • women only • dancing/DJ

Meat Market • queer electro dance party • check local listings

Queer Beat Landstr Hauptstr 38 (at the Viper Room) • 2nd & 4th Sat only • mostly gay men • dancing/DJ

Up! Mariahilfer Str 3 (at Lutz Club) • 2nd Fri only • mostly gay men • uplifing house music

Why Not? Tiefer Graben 22 (at Wipplinger, U-Schottentor) 43-1/925-3024 • 10pm-close Fri-Sat & before public holidays • mostly gay men • dancing/DJ • live shows • videos

Vienna

LGBT Pride:
Rainbow Parade in June, web: www.regenbogenparade.at.

Annual Events:
January - Regenbogenball (Rainbow Ball), web: www.hosiwien.at/regenbogen-ball/.

January - Resonanzen (classical music festival), web: www.konzerthaus.at.

March/ April - OsterKlang (classical music festival), web: www.theater-wien.at.

May - Life Ball (AIDS benefit), web: www.lifeball.org.

June - Queer Film Festival 43-1/524.62.74, web: www.identities.at.

June/ July - Jazz Fest Wien, web: www.viennajazz.org.

July/ August - ImPulsTanz (dance festival), web: www.impulstanz.com.

October - Vienna In Black, web: www.lmcvienna.at.

October - Viennale Film Festival 43-1/526-5947, web: www.viennale.at.

October - Wien Modern (contemporary music festival) 43-1/242-002, web: www.wienmodern.at.

City Info:
43-1/24-555, web: www.info.wien.at.

Best View:
Overlooking the city from the top of the Giant Ferris Wheel.

Weather:
Mild, rainy summers and chilly winters. September is a good time to visit.

Attractions:
Art Nouveau buildings.

Belvedere Palace/Austrian Gallery 43-1/795-57-0, web: www.belvedere.at.

House of Music 43-1/513-4850 , web: www.hdm.at.

Imperial Palace, web: www.hofburg-wien.at.

Jewish Museum 43-1/535-0431, web: www.jmw.at.

Museum of Fine Arts 43-1/525-24-0, web: www.khm.at.

Schönbrunn Palace 43-1/811-13-239, web: www.schoenbrunn.at.

Sigmund Freud Museum 43-1/319-1596, web: www.freud-museum.at.

St Stephen's Cathedral 43-1/513-7648, web: www.stephansdom.at.

State Opera House 43-1/514-44-2250, web: www.staatsoper.at.

Vienna Boys' Choir, web: www.wsk.at.

Transit:
43-1/60-160, web: www.taxi60160.at.

Vienna Airport Lines, web: postbus.at.

Vienna has an excellent public transit system. Consider purchasing a Vienna Card for 72 hours of unlimited travel by subway, bus, and tram, plus discounts on airport shuttle, at museums, and at many shops and restaurants. 43-1/24-555, web: www.info.wien.at.

Cafes

Bakul Margaretenstr 58 • 9am-2am • also guesthouse

Cafe Berg Berggasse 8 (at Wasagasse, U2-Schottentor) 43–1/319–5720 • 10am-1am • popular • lesbians/ gay men • cafe-bar

Cafe Central Herrengasse 14 (at Strauchgasse) 43–1/533–3763 • 7:30am-10pm, from 10am Sun & public holidays • "world's most famous coffeehouse"

Cafe Standard Margaretenstr 63 43–1/581–0586 • 8am-midnight, from 11am wknds

Cafe Stein Währinger Str 6–8 (near U-Schottentor) 43–1/319–7241 • 7am-1am, from 9am Sun • gay-friendly • cafe-bar • internet access • terrace

Das Möbel Burggasse 10 (Spittelberg) 43–1/524–9497 • 10am-1am • trendy • also art gallery • WiFi

Point of Sale Schleifmuhlgasse 12 43–1/941–6397 • 7am-1am • cafe & deli • also vegan items • WiFi • also bar

Smart Cafe Kostlergasse 9 43–1/585–7165 • 6pm-2am, till 4am Fri-Sat, clsd Sun-Mon • gay/ straight • S/M & fetish cafe

Restaurants

Andino Münzwardeingasse 2 (U4-Pilgramgasse) 43–1/585–6125 • 11am-2am, from 10am Sat, 11am-midnight Sun • Latin American • live music • also full bar

Aux Gazelles Rahlgasse 5 43–1/585–6645 • French/ Moroccan restaurant 6pm-midnight • Arabian-style lounge, cafe & deli 11am-2am • also Turkish steam baths noon-10pm

Bin Im Leo Servitengasse 14 43–1/391–7763 • 4pm-midnight, from noon wknds • beer/ wine • plenty veggie

Cafe-Restaurant Willendorf Linke Wienzeile 102 (near Hofmuhlgasse, U4-Pilgramgasse) 43–1/587–1789 • 6pm-2am, food served till midnight • lesbians/ gay men • plenty veggie • full bar • terrace

Halle Museumsquartier 1 43–1/523–7001 • 10am-2am • modern bistro • artsy crowd

Kantine Porzellangasse 19 43–1/319–5918 • 6pm-2am • Thai

Motto Schönbrunner Str 30 (enter on Rüdigergasse) 43–1/587–0672 • 6pm-2am, till 4am Fri-Sat • popular • trendy • also bar • patio • reservations recommended

Santo Spirito Kumpfgasse 7 43–1/512–9998 • 6pm-11pm, bar till 2am • classical music

Schon Schön Lindengasse 53 (Ecke Andreagasse) • lunch & dinner • fashionable restaurant • also bar • also clothing & hair salon

Sly & Arny Lothringerstrasse 22 43–1/405–0458 • lunch Mon-Fri, dinner nightly, bar till late

Stöger Ramperstorffergasse 63 43–1/544–7596 • 11am-midnight, clsd Sun, from 5pm Mon • Viennese

Zum Roten Elefanten Gumpendorferstrasse 3 43–1/966–8008 • lunch & dinner, open late Fri-Sat, clsd Sun (lunch only in summer)

Entertainment & Recreation

Haus der Musik/ House of Music Seilerstätte 30 43–1/516–4810 • 10am-10pm • interactive museum of sound • also cafe

Kunsthistorisches Museum Maria Theresien-Platz (enter Heldenplatz) 43–1/525–240 • 10am-6pm, till 9pm Th, clsd Mon • not to be missed • works from Ancient Egypt to the Renaissance to Klimt

Bookstores

American Discount Rechte Wienzeile 5 (at Paniglgasse) 43–1/587–5772 • 9:30am-6:30pm, till 5pm Sat, clsd Sun • int'l magazines & books • also Neubaugasse 39, 43–1/523–37–07

Löwenherz Berggasse 8 (next to Cafe Berg, enter on Wasagasse, U2-Schottentor) 43–1/317–2982 • 10am-7pm, till 8pm Fri, till 6pm Sat, clsd Sun • LGBT • large selection of English titles

Publications

Vienna Gay Guide 43–1/789–1000 • city map & guide

Xtra • gay magazine

Erotica

Art-X Percostr 3 43–1/25804–4413 • 10am-8pm, till 9pm Th, till 6pm Sat, clsd Sun • leather, latex, rubber • toys • music • videos • magazines

Sexworld XXL Store Mariahilfer Str 49 43–1/587–6656 • upscale sex shop

Tiberius Lindengasse 2 (at Stiftgasse, U3-Neubaugasse) 43–1/522–0474 • clsd Sun • wheelchair access • designer fetish-wear

CZECH REPUBLIC

PRAGUE (PRAHA)

Note: M°=Metro station

Prague is divided into 10 city districts: Praha—1, Praha—2, etc.

Praha—Overview

ACCOMMODATIONS

Apartments in Prague 420/251–512–502, 303/800-0858 • gay/straight • WiFi • kids/pets ok

Praha—1

ACCOMMODATIONS

Hotel Metropol Narodni 33 (at Na Perstyne) 420/246–022–100 • gay/ straight • design hotel • all-glass facade

The ICON Boutique Hotel V Jame 6 (at Vodickova) 420/221–634–100 • gay/straight • restaurant & bar • WiFi • wheelchair access

The Palace Road Hotel Prague Nerudova 7 (at Malostranske Namesti) 420/257–216–337, 800/860–0571 • gay/straight • located in city center • WiFi

BARS

Café Bar Flirt Martinská 5/419 420/224–248–592 • 10am-2am • mostly gay men • dancing/DJ Fri-Sat • karaoke

Prague (Praha)

LGBT PRIDE:
August, web: www.praguepride.com.

ANNUAL EVENTS:
May/June - Prague Spring International Music Festival, web: www.festival.cz.
October - Mezipatra, Czech Gay & Lesbian Film Festival, web: www.mezipatra.cz.

CITY INFO:
Tourist Info Center Mostecka 4, web: www.prague-information.eu.

BEST VIEW:
For a great view of the whole of Prague, head for the Observation Tower (a mini version of the Eiffel Tower) on Petrin Hill. The Old Town Bridge Tower affords a fabulous view of Old Town, the Charles Bridge, and the Vltava River.

WEATHER:
Continental climate. Late spring or early fall are the best times to visit, especially in June before the tourist season is in full swing. Winters can get very cold with average daytime highs of 34° F.

ATTRACTIONS:
Charles Bridge.
Jewish Museum 420/221-711-511, web: www.jewishmuseum.cz.
Museum of Fine Arts 420/222–220–218, web: www.cmvu.cz.
Old Jewish Quarter.
Prague Castle 420/224-373-368, web: www.hrad.cz/en/prazsky_hrad/navsteva_hradu.shtml.
Wenceslas Square.

TRANSIT:
Taxi AAA 420/222-333-222, web: www.radiotaxiaaa.cz.
Profi Taxi 420/261-314-151, web: www.profitaxi.cz.
CSA shuttle, web: www.cedaz.cz/public-shuttle-bus-from-airport-to-prague-centre.php.
There are 6 Transportation Info Centers throughout city with info on metro, trams, buses & funicular, Ruzyne Airport, web: www.dpp.cz/en/list-of-info-centres/.

Friends Bar Bartolomejská 11 **420/226-211-920** • 7pm-6am • popular • mostly men • dancing/DJ • neighborhood bar • DJ Wed-Sat • videos • WiFi

K.U. Bar Rytirská 13 (at Perlová, near Oldtown Square) **420/221-181-081** • 7pm-4am • gay/ straight • upscale & trendy • dancing/DJ • live shows

Silwer Cafe & Bar **420/222-212-702** • 10am-2am • gay/straight • dancing/DJ • WiFi

Tingl Tangl Karolíny Svetlé 12 (at Konviktska) **420/224-238-278** • 11am-10pm • lesbians/ gay men • dancing/DJ • cabaret 9pm-5am Wed & Fri-Sat • drag shows • also restaurant

CAFES

Cafe Cafe Rytirská 10 (at Perlová, near Oldtown Square) **420/224-210-597** • 10am-11pm • WiFi

Cafe Erra Konviktská 11 **420/222-220-568** • 10am-midnight • salads, sandwiches & entrées

Cafe Louvre Národni 22 (M° Narodni Trida) **420/224-930-949** • 9am-11:30pm • it was the favorite hangout of Albert Einstein & Franz Kafka

Q Cafe Opatovická 166/12 **420/776-856-361** • noon-midnight

Vertigo Havelská 4 (at Perlová) **420/744-744-356** • cafe & restaurant • also nightclub • gay-friendly • theme nights • DJs

RESTAURANTS

Campanulla Cafe Restaurant Velkoprevorske namesti 4 **420/257-217-736** • set in the beautiful garden of The Grand Priory of Bohemia Palace

Casa Andina Dusni 15 **420/224-815-996** • 4pm-midnight, clsd Sun • Peruvian/ Latin American

Maitrea Tynska 6/1064 (nr Old Town Square) **420/221-711-631** • noon-11:30pm • vegetarian

Petrinské Terasy Seminarská Zahrada 13, Petrin **420/257-320-688, 420/602-224-096** • noon-11pm • in a former monastery • great view • gay-owned

Restaurant Dlouhá Dlouhá 23 (basement) **420/222-329-853** • 11am-11pm • good seafood

Staromestska Restaurace Staromestske namesti 19 **420/224-213-015** • 11am-midnight • local Czech specialties

ENTERTAINMENT & RECREATION

Sex Machines Museum Melantrichova 18 **420/ 227-186-260** • 10am-11pm

BOOKSTORES

Globe Patrossova 6 **420/224-934-203** • English-language bookstore • also cafe

Praha—2

ACCOMMODATIONS

Balbin Penzion Balbinova 26 (near Wenceslas Square) **420/222-250-660** • gay/straight • located in city center • full brkfst • WiFi

Prague Saints Polska 32 (office location) (at Trebizkeho, at Saints Bar) **420/775-152-041, 420/775-152-042** • lesbians/ gay men • apts in gay Vinohrady district • gay-owned

BARS

Angels Cafe Vinohradská 30 • 6pm-midnight, from 2pm Sat, 11am-10pm Sun • leabians/gay men • cafe & lounge • stylish interior • WiFi

Charmisma Cafe **420/773-927-774** • 5pm-2am, clsd Sun • lesbians/gay men

Fan Fan Club Dittrichova 5 (at Trojanova) **420/776-360-698** • 5pm-2am • mostly gay men • karaoke

Feno Man Club Blanická 28 (at Vinohradska) **420/603-740-263** • 5pm-5am, till 9am Fri-Sat • mostly gay men • dancing/DJ • food served • WiFi

JampaDampa V Tunich 10 (at Zitna) **420/603-260-678** • 2pm-2am, till 4am Tue, 6pm-6am Fri-Sat, clsd Sun • popular • mostly women • dancing/DJ • karaoke

Klub 21 Rimska 21 (at Balbinova) **420/603-539-475** • 6pm-close, clsd Sun • lesbians/ gay men • cellar bar/ gallery • food • young crowd • mostly Czechs

Klub Strelec Zitna 51 (at Legerova) **420/224-941-446** • 5pm-2am, till midnight Sun • gay-friendly • bear bar on Wed & Sat

Saints Polska 32 (at Trebizkeho) **420/222-250-326** • 7pm-4am • lesbians/ gay men

NIGHTCLUBS

Termix Trebizskeho 4 (at Vinohradska) **420/222-710-462** • 9pm-5am, clsd Mon-Tue • popular • lesbians/ gay men • dancing/DJ • karaoke

Valentino Vinohradska 40 (at Blanicka) **420/222-513-491, 420/776-360-698 (CELL)** • 2pm-5am • lesbians/ gay men • dancing/DJ • video • 3 levels • darkroom

Cafes

Alex Bistro Jecna 4 **420/224–919–125** • 8am-10pm, from 9am Sat & Sun, till 5pm Sun • featuring Italian and Czech specialties

Restaurants

Celebrity Cafe Vinohradska 40 (in Vinohrady) **420/222–511–343** • 8am-2am, noon-3am Sun • also bar

Radost FX Belehradska 120, Vinohrady **420/224–254–776, 420/603–193–711** • fabulous wknd brunch • vegetarian cafe • also straight nightclub w/ popular monthly gay party

Sahara Cafe & Lounge Namesti Miru 6 **420/222–514–987** • 11am-midnight • live music

Praha—3

Bars

Latimerie Club Cafe Slezska 74 (at Nitranska) **420/224–252–049** • 4pm-close • lesbians/ gay men

Piano Bar Milesovská 10 (at Ondrickova) **420/775–727–796** • 5pm-close • lesbians/ gay men • mostly Czech older crowd • food served

Restaurants

Restaurant Mozaika Nitranská 13 **420/224–253–011** • contemporary take on international cuisine

Entertainment & Recreation

TV Tower Mahlerovy sady 1 **420/242–418–778, 420/242–418–766** • get a bird's-eye view of the city from the top of this tower

Praha—4

Gyms & Health Clubs

Plavecky Stadion Podoli Podolská 74 **420/241–433–952** • 6am-9:45pm • gay/ straight • public baths • restaurants • women's sauna Th-Fri & Sun

Praha—5

Accommodations

Andel's Hotel Stroupeznickeho 21 (at Pizenska) **420/296–889–688** • gay-friendly • restaurant & bar

Praha—7

Cafes

Duhova Cajovna Milada Horáková 73 (at Ovenecka) **420/775–269–699** • 3pm-midnight • "Rainbow Tearoom" • food served • WiFi

Praha—10

Accommodations

Ron's Rainbow Guest House Bulharska 4 (at Finská) **420/271–725–664, 420/731–165–022 (CELL)** • gay/ straight • quiet & friendly atmosphere • near city center • gay-owned

DENMARK

Copenhagen

Info Lines & Services

Kafe Knud Skindergade 21 **45/3332–5861** • 4pm-10pm Tue & Th only • HIV resource center • cafe open Tue & Th only

Sabaah Onkel Dannys Plads 1 • community center for LGBT ethnic minorities • events • meetings

Wonderful Copenhagen Convention & Visitors Bureau Vesterbrogade 4A **45/7022–2442 (TOURIST INFO)**

Accommodations

Carstens Guesthouse Christians Brygge 28, 5th flr **45/3314–9107, 45/4050–9107 (CELL)** • lesbians/ gay men • B&B, hostel & apts • shared baths • kids/ pets ok • WiFi • 5 minutes from gay area

Clarion Collection Hotel Twentyseven Løngangstræde 27 **45/7027–56 27**

Copenhagen Admiral Hotel Toldbodgade 24-28 **45/3374–1414**

First Hotel Kong Frederik Vester Voldgade 25 **45/3312–5902**

First Hotel Skt. Petri Krystalgade 22 **45/3345–9100** • hotel embodying the ultra-coolest of Scandinavian design • great bar • WiFi • wheelchair access

Hotel Fox Jarmers Plads 3 **45/3395–7755, 45/3313–3000** • gay/ straight • nonsmoking • artistic rooms • central location • roof terrace • also lounge & restaurant

Hotel Kong Arthur Norre Sogade 11 **45/3311–1212**

Hotel Windsor Frederiksborggade 30, 1360 **45/3311–0830** • mostly gay men • near gay scene • shared baths • gay-owned

Radisson Blu Royal Hotel
Hammerichsgade 1 **45/3342–6000**

The Square Rådhuspladsen 14 **45/3338–1200**

BARS

Cafe Intime Allegade 25, Frederiksberg
45/3834–1958 • 6pm-2am • gay-friendly •
cafe-bar • piano bar

Can-Can Mikkel Bryggers Gade 11
45/3311–5010 • 2pm-2am, till 5am Fri-Sat •
mostly gay men • friendly neighborhood bar

Centralhjørnet Kattesundet 18
45/3311–8549 • noon-2am • mostly gay men
• WiFi

Cosy Bar Studiestræde 24 (in Latin Quarter)
45/3312–7427 • 10pm-6am, till 8am Fri-Sat •
popular • mostly gay men

Dunkel Bar Vester Voldgade 10 • 6pm-5am,
clsd Sun-Mon • gay/ straight • dancing/DJ

Masken Studiestræde 33 **45/3391–0937** •
2pm-3am, till 5am Fri-Sat • popular • lesbians/
gay men • cafe-bar • WiFi

Copenhagen

WHERE THE GIRLS ARE:
Strolling Studiestraede with the
boys, or enjoying a beverage at
Cafe Ziraf.

LGBT PRIDE:
August. www.copenhagenpride.dk.

ANNUAL EVENTS:
July - Queer Festival, web:
www.queerfestival.org.
October - Gay & Lesbian Film
Festival 45/3313-0766, web:
www.cglff.dk.

CITY INFO:
Copenhagen Visitors Bureau
45/7022-2442, web: www.visit-
copenhagen.com.

BEST VIEW:
From the dome of Marble Church, or
from the spiral tower of Our
Savior's Church.

WEATHER:
Winters are cold & wet, with
temperatures in the upper 30ºs.
Early summer is the best time to
visit, when locals enjoy long days
and temperatures around 70º.

TRANSIT:
Kobenhavns Taxa 3535-3535, web:
www.4x35.dk.
Metro 45/3311-1700, www.m.dk.
Ask about the Copenhagen Card,
which offers bargains on museums and public transportation.
Bycyklen 45/3616-4233, web:
www.bycyklen.dk. 110 racks
around the city center offering
free bicycle rental!

ATTRACTIONS:
Botanisk Have (Botanical Garden)
45/3532-2222, web:
www.botanik.snm.ku.dk.
Dansk Design Center
45/3369-3369, web:
www.ddc.dk.
Latin Quarter.
The Little Mermaid.
Marmorkirken (Marble Church)
45/3315-0144, web:
www.marmorkirken.dk.
Nationalmuseet (National Museum)
45/3313-4411, web:
www.natmus.dk.
Statens Museum for Kunst (Royal
Museum of Fine Arts)
45/3374-8494, web:
www.smk.dk.
Strøget shopping district.
Tivoli 45/3515-1001, web:
www.tivoli.dk.
Vor Frelsers Kirke (Our Savior's
Church), web:
www.vorfrelserkirke.dk.
.

Never Mind Nørre Voldgade 2 **45/3311–8886**
• 10pm-6am • mostly gay men

Oscar Bar Cafe Radhuspladsen 77
45/3312–0999 • noon-2am • mostly men •
lesbians welcome • food served • great happy
hour

NIGHTCLUBS

Christopher Club Knabrostræde 3 •
midnight-5am Sat only • lesbians/ gay men •
dancing/DJ

We Love Girls • women's dance parties &
events • check local listings

CAFES

Jernbanecafeen • 7am-2am • WiFi • patio

RESTAURANTS

Jailhouse Restaurant & Bar Studiestraede
12 **45/3315–2255** • 3pm-2am, till 5am Fri-Sat
• popular

ENTERTAINMENT & RECREATION

Amager Strandpark • beach 5 km from
city center

Bellevue Beach **45/32 66 00 00** • mostly
gay beach • left end is nude

PUBLICATIONS

Out & About **45/4093–1977**

EROTICA

Lust Mikkel Bryggersgade 3A **45/3333–0110** •
erotica for women

ENGLAND

London

London is divided into 6 regions:
London—Overview
London—Central
London—West
London—North
London—East
London—South

London—Overview

NIGHTCLUBS

Dyke Bar • 3rd Sat of the month, check
www.facebook.com/dykebar for location

Stiletto • sexy monthly women's party •
check www.stilettoparty.co.ukfor details

Torture Garden **44–020/7700–1441** • the
worlds largest fetish / body art club • check
www.torturegarden.com for venue locations

ENTERTAINMENT & RECREATION

**The Women's Library, London
Metropolitan University** Old Castle St
44–(0)20/7320–2222 • clsd Sun • also cafe •
museum • cultural center • call for events •
nonsmoking

PUBLICATIONS

Diva **44–(0)20/7424–7400** • glorious glossy
magazine for lesbians & bisexual women

g3 **44–(0)20/7724–9898** • free monthly
lesbian glossy

The Pink Paper **44–(0)20/7424–7414** • free
LGBT newspaper

WEBSITES

Fettered Pleasures **44–(0)20/7619–9333** •
11pm-7pm, clsd Sun

London—Central

London—Central includes Soho, Covent
Garden, Bloomsbury, Mayfair,
Westminster, Pimlico & Belgravia

ACCOMMODATIONS

Dover Hotel 42/44 Belgrave Rd
44–(0)20/7821–9085 • gay-friendly • WiFi

Fitz B&B 15 Colville Place (btwn Charlotte &
Whitfield) **44–(0)78/3437–2866** • lesbians/
gay men • 18th-c townhouse • nonsmoking •
WiFi • gay-owned

George Hotel 58–60 Cartwright Gardens (N
of Russell Square) **44–(0)20/7387–8777** • gay-
friendly • full brkfst • some shared baths • kids
ok

Hazlitt's 6 Frith St (Soho Sq)
44–(0)20/7434–1771 • gay-friendly • WiFi

Lincoln House 33 Gloucester Pl, Marble
Arch (at Baker St) **44–20/7486–7630** • gay/
straight • B&B • full brkfst • WiFi • wheelchair
access

Marble Arch Inn 49-50 Upper Berkeley St
44–020/7723–7888 • gay-friendly

BARS

Note: "Pub hours" usually means 11am-
11pm Mon-Sat and noon-3pm & 7pm-
10:30pm Sun

The Admiral Duncan 54 Old Compton St
(Soho) **44–(0)20/7437–5300** • pub hours •
popular • lesbians/ gay men • neighborhood
bar • transgender-friendly

Bar Soho 23-25 Old Compton St (at Frith St)
44–(0)20/7439–0439 • noon-1am, till 3am Fri-
Sat, from 2pm Sun

The Candy Bar 4 Carlisle St, S (at Dean) 44-(0)20/7287-5041 • 5pm-11:30pm, till 2am Fri-Sat • women only (men welcome as guests) • dancing/DJ • food served • karaoke • strippers

Circa 62 Frith St 44-020/7734-6826 • 4pm-1am • mostly gay men • dancing/DJ

Compton's of Soho 51-53 Old Compton St (at Dean St) 44-(0)20/7479-7961 • noon-midnight, till 10:30pm Sun • mostly gay men • leather • food served Sun • wheelchair access

Dog and Duck 18 Bateman St (at Frith St) 44-020/7494-0697 • 10am-11:30pm • gay/straight • neighborhood bar • food served

Duke of Wellington 77 Wardour (Soho) 44-(0)20/7439-1274 • pub hours • gay/straight • snacks

The Edge 11 Soho Square (at Oxford St) 44-(0)20/7439-1313 • noon-1am, till 10:30pm Sun • popular • dancing/DJ • live music • good food • outdoor seating • wheelchair access

The Escape 10-A Brewer St (at Rupert) 44-(0)20/7734-3040 • 5pm-3am, clsd Sun-Mon • popular • mostly gay men • dancing/DJ • videos

Freedom Bar 66 Wardour St (off Old Compton St) 44-(0)20/7734-0071 • 5pm-3am, from 2pm Fri-Sat, 2pm-11:30pm Sun • lesbians/ gay men • dancing/DJ • food served • young crowd

London

LGBT Pride:
June-July. www.pridelondon.org.

Annual Events:
March-April - Lesbian & Gay Film Festival 44-(0)20/7928-3232, web: www.llgff.org.uk.
June-July - Pride Festival Fortnight 44-(0)20-7164-2182, web: www.pridelondon.org.
August - Mr Gay UK Contest, web: www.mrgayuk.co.uk.

City Info:
44-(0)20/7292-2333, web: www.visitlondon.com, www.londoninformation.org.

Best View:
London Eye, 44-(0)87/0990-8883, web: www.londoneye.com.

Weather:
London is warmer and less rainy than you may have heard. Summer temperatures reach the 70°s and the average annual rainfall is about half of that of Atlanta, GA or Hartford, CT.

Transit:
Freedom Cars 44-(0)20-7734-1313.
Ladycabs 44-(0)20/7254-3501.
London Travel Information (Tube & buses) 44-(0)20/7222-1234, 24hr info, web: www.tfl.gov.uk.

Attractions:
British Museum 44-(0)20/7323-8299, web: www.britishmuseum.org.
Buckingham Palace 44-(0)20/7766-7300, web: www.royal.gov.uk.
Globe Theatre 44-(0)20/7902-1400, web: www.shakespeares-globe.org.
Kensington Palace 44-(0)87/0751-5170.
Madame Tussaud's 44-(0)87/0999-0046, web: www.madame-tussauds.co.uk.
National Gallery 44-(0)20/7747-2885, web: www.national-gallery.org.uk.
Oscar Wilde's house (34 Tite Street).
St Paul's Cathedral 44-(0)20/7236-4128, www.stpauls.co.uk.
Tate Gallery 44-(0)20/7887-8008, web: www.tate.org.uk.
Tower of London 44-(0)87/0756-6060.
Westminster Abbey 44-(0)20/7654-4900, www.westminster-abbey.org.

Friendly Society 79 Wardour St (the basement at Old Compton, enter Tisbury Ct) **44–(0)20/7434–3805** • 4pm-11pm, till 10:30pm Sun • lesbians/ gay men • young crowd

G.A.Y Bar 30 Old Compton St (at Frith) **44–(0)20/7494–2756** • noon-midnight • lesbians/ gay men • basement women's bar

G.A.Y Late 5 Goslett Yard • 11pm-3am • lesbians/ gay men • video jukebox

G Spot 10 Adelaide St, at Kudos (off the Strand, Charing Cross) **44–(0)20/7379–4573** • 6pm-midnight Fri-Sat • mostly women • professional crowd • trendy cafe-bar • multiracial • wheelchair access • gay-owned

Girl Friday 52 St Giles High St (btwn Charing Cross & Shaftesbury, at First Out) **44–(0)20/7240–8042** • 7pm-11pm Fri • mostly women

Green Carnation 4-5 Greek St (Soho Sq) **44–(0)20/8123–4267** • 4pm-2am • inspired by the time and life of Oscar Wilde

Ku Bar/ Ku Klub 30 Lisle St (Leicester Sq) **44–(0)20/7437–4303** • noon-3am, till 10:30pm Sun • lesbians/ gay men • karaoke • young crowd • WiFi • also Soho bar at 25 Frith St

Madam JoJo's 8-10 Brewer St (at Rupert) **44–(0)20/7734–3040** • mostly women • live shows • Tranny Shack Wed

The New Bloomsbury Set 76 Marchmont St (at Tavistock Pl) **44–(0)20/7383–3084** • 4pm-11pm, 2pm-10:30pm Sun • gay/straight

The Retro Bar 2 George Ct (at Strand) **44–(0)20/7321–2811** • pub hours • lesbians/ gay men • neighborhood bar • dancing/DJ • karaoke

Rupert Street 50 Rupert St (off Brewer) **44–(0)20/7292–7141** • pub hours • popular • lesbians/ gay men • upscale "fashiony-types" • food served • wheelchair access

Star at Night 22 Great Chapel St (at Hollen St) **44–(0)20/7494–2488** • 6pm -11.30pm, clsd Sun-Mon • lesbians/ gay men • dancing/DJ • relaxed cafe/ bar • live shows

The Village Soho 81 Wardour St (at Old Compton) **44–(0)20/7478–0530** • 4pm-1am, till 11:30pm Sun • popular • mostly gay men • 18+ young crowd • wheelchair access

The Yard 57 Rupert St (off Brewer) **44–(0)20/7437–2652, 871/426–2243** • pub hours • popular • lesbians/ gay men • 2 levels • young crowd • food served • wheelchair access

NIGHTCLUBS

Code 5 Greek St (at Green Carnation, Soho) • last Fri only • mostly women • dancing

The Den & Centro 18 New Central St (at New Oxford St) **44–(0)20/7240–1083** • popular • 10pm-4am • gay/ straight • dancing/DJ • cover charge • theme nights, popular Popstarz party Fri

G.A.Y. Under the Arches, Villers St (at Heaven) **44–(0)20/7734–6963** • 11pm-3am • popular • mostly gay men • dancing/DJ • live shows • young crowd • Camp Attack Fri • cover charge

GAYME Girls 1 Vernon Pl (Holborn) **44–078/705–0051** • 1st Th of the month • mostly women • dancing/DJ

Heaven 9 The Arches (off Villiers St) **44–(0)20/7930-2020** • the mother of all London gay clubs • call for hours/ events • mostly gay men • dancing/DJ

KU Bar Frith St 25 Frith St (at Old Compton St, Soho) **44–(0)20/7287–7986** • noon-11pm, till midnight wknds • mostly men • dancing/DJ

Lounge 1 Leicester Sq (at Vertigo) • women only, men welcome as guests • check www.lounge.uk.net for dates

Popstarz 18 W Central St (at New Oxford St) **44–(0)20/7240–1900** • popular • 10pm-6am Fri • lesbians/ gay men • dancing/DJ • cover charge

Profile/ Lo Profile 84-86 Wardour St (at Peter St) **44–(0)20/7734–3444** • mostly gay men • bar/ restaurant upstairs, hip basement club downstairs wknds • dancing/DJ

The Shadow Lounge 5 Brewer St (Soho) **44–(0)20/7317–9270** • 10pm-3am, from 9pm Th-Sat, clsd Sun • lesbians/ gay men • dancing/DJ • swanky late night club

CAFES

Balans Cafe 34 Old Compton St **44–(0)20/7439–3309** • 24hrs • popular • lesbians/ gay men • all-day brkfst • terrace

Caffe Nero 43 Frith St **44–(0)20/7434–3887** • 7am-2am, till 4am Sat

First Out 52 St Giles High St (btwn Charing Cross & Shaftesbury) **44–(0)20/7240–8042** • 9am-11pm, 10am-10:30pm Sun • popular • gay cafe • full bar • nonsmoking upstairs • WiFi

Flat White 17 Berwick St **44–(0)20/7734–0370** • 8am-7pm, 9am-6pm wknds • Australian-style cafe

LJ Coffee House 3 Winnett St (at Rupert) 44–020/7434–1174 • 7:30am–7pm, 10am–8pm Sat, from 1pm Sun • cozy cafe • street views

Milk Bar 3 Bateman St 44–020/7287–4796 • 8am–7pm, till 5pm wknds • wheelchair access

Restaurants

Cha Cha Moon 15-21 Ganton St 44–(0)20/7297–9800 • noon–11pm, till 10pm Sun • inexpensive Chinese

Food for Thought 31 Neal St, downstairs (Covent Garden) 44–020/7836–0239 • noon-8:30pm, till 5:30pm Sun • vegetarian • inexpensive hole-in-the-wall • BYOB

The Gay Hussar 2 Greek St (on Soho Square) 44–(0)20/7437–0973 • lunch & dinner, clsd Sun • Hungarian • wheelchair access

Mildred's 45 Lexington 44–(0)20/7494–1634 • noon–11pm, clsd Sun • popular • vegetarian • plenty vegan

Mrs Marengo's 53 Lexington 44–(0)20/7287-2544 • vegetarian • plenty vegan

Nusa Dua 11–12 Dean St (Oxford Circus) 44–(0)20/7437–3559, 44–(0)87/1332–7468 • Indonesian

Randall & Aubin 16 Brewer St (at Walkers Court) 44–(0)20/7287–4447 • noon–11pm • casual French • good people-watching

Wagamama Noodle Bar 10-A Lexington St 44–(0)20/7292–0990 • noon–11pm • Japanese • nonsmoking • chain w/ locations throughout city

Entertainment & Recreation

Comedy Camp 3–4 Archer St (at Barcode, btwn Windmill & Rupert, off Shaftesbury, Soho) 44–(0)20/7483–2960, 08–700/600–100 (**TicketWeb**) • 8:30pm Tue & 1st Sat • gay/ straight • amateur & established comedy acts

Bookstores

Gay's the Word 66 Marchmont St (near Russell Square) 44–(0)20/7278–7654 • 10am-6:30pm, 2pm-6pm Sun • LGBT • magazines

Retail Shops

Prowler Soho 5–7 Brewer St (behind Village Soho bar) 44–(0)20/7734–4031 • 11am-10pm, noon-8pm Sun • popular • large gay department store

London—West

London—West includes Earl's Court, Kensington, Chelsea & Bayswater

Accommodations

Cardiff Hotel 5, 7, 9 Norfolk Sq (Hyde Park) 44–(0)20/7723–3513 • gay-friendly • B&B hotel in 3 Victorian townhouses • some shared baths • WiFi

Millennium Bailey's Hotel 140 Gloucester Rd (at Old Brompton Rd, Kensington) 44–(0)20/7373–6000, 44–(0)20/7331–6331 • located in the heart of Kensington • also restaurant & bar •

Myhotel Chelsea 35 Ixworth Place (at Elystan St, Chelsea) 44–020/7225–7500 • gay-friendly • stylish boutique hotel in Chelsea

Parkwood Hotel 4 Stanhope Pl (Marble Arch) 44–(0)20/7402–2241 • gay-friendly • full brkfst • nonsmoking

Bars

West Five (W5) 6 Popes Ln (South Ealing) 44–(0)20/0871–971–4569 • 7pm-close, clsd Mon-Tue • lesbians/ gay men • cabaret • lounge • piano bar • garden

Restaurants

The Churchill Arms 119 Kensington Church St 44–(0)20/7727–4242 • inexpensive, fantastic Thai • also pub

The Gate 51 Queen Caroline St, Hammersmith • lunch & dinner, clsd Sun • vegetarian

Star of India 154 Old Brompton Rd 44–(0)20/737–2901 • lunch & dinner • upscale

Entertainment & Recreation

Walking Tour of Gay SOHO 56 Old Compton St (at Admiral Duncan Pub) 44–(0)20/7437–6063 • 2pm Sun • world-famous historical walking tour covering over 600 years of gay history in London's "square mile of sin"

London—North

London—North includes Paddington, Regents Park, Camden, St Pancras & Islington

Accommodations

Ambassadors Bloomsbury 12 Upper Woburn Pl (at Euston Rd, Bloomsbury) 44–0207/693–5400 • gay-friendly • near Kings Cross St Pancras & Euston Stations • good Italian restaurant on-site • nonsmoking

Ossian Guesthouse 20 Ossian Rd (at Mt Pleasant Villas, Crouch Hill) 44–(0)20/8340–4331 • Victorian house on quiet street in quiet suburb • gay-friendly

Bars

Blush 8 Cazenove Rd (Stoke Newington) **44–(0)20/7923–9202** • 5pm-midnight, 1pm-midnight Sun, clsd Mon • mostly women • friendly cafe-bar • beer garden • live music Sun • karaoke Fri • lesbian-owned

Duke of Wellington 119 Balls Pond Rd **44–(0)20/7275 7640** • 3pm-midnight, till 1am Fri-Sat • gay/straight • popular with lesbians • food served

The George Music Bar 114 Twickenham Rd (Isleworth) **44–(0)20/8560–1456** • 5pm-close, from noon wknds • transgender-friendly • George Cabaret every Fri-Sat • gay-owned

The Green 74 Upper St (Angel tube) **44–020/7226–8895** • 5pm-midnight, till 2am Fri-Sat, from noon-Sat-Sun • lesbians/ gay men • full menu

King William IV (KW) 77 Hampstead High St (Hampstead) **44–(0)20/7435–5747** • pub hours • lesbians/ gay men • food served • beer garden

The Oak Bar 79 Green Lanes (Stoke Newington) **44–(0)20/7354–2791** • 4pm-11pm, 8pm-3am Fri-Sat • mostly women • Chicks Rock last Sat • dancing/DJ • food served • karaoke • dancers • theme nights • women-owned

Nightclubs

Club Kali 1 Dartmouth Park Hill (at The Dome) **44–(0)20/7272–8153 (Dome #)** • 10pm-3am 3rd Fri • popular • lesbians/ gay men • dancing/DJ • mostly Asian • transgender-friendly • South Asian music • cover charge

Dream Bags Jaquar Shoes 34-36 Kingsland Rd **44–020/7729–5830** • noon-1am • jam-packed club in a former shoe shop • also art exhibts

East Bloc/ Disco Fag Bar 217 City Rd (at Shepherdess Walk, Old Street) **44–020/7253–0367** • 10:30pm-6am Fri-Sat only • mostly men • electro dance club in funky basement space

Egg 200 York Way (Kings Cross) **44–(0)20/7871–1111** • 10pm-6am Sat, until late afternoon Sun • gay/ straight • dancing/DJ

Salvation 1A Camden High St (at KOKO) • 1st Sun • gay/ straight • cover charge

Restaurants

Manna 4 Erskine Rd (at Ainger Rd, Camden) **44–(0)20/7722–8028** • lunch Tue-Sun, dinner nightly • vegetarian • reservations recommended

Providores/ Tapa Room 109 Marylebone High St (at New Cavendish St) **44–(0)20/7935–6175** • lunch & dinner • Asian fusion

Entertainment & Recreation

Rosemary Branch Theatre 2 Shepperton Rd **44–020/7704–2730 (bar)**, **44–020/7704–6665 (theatre)** • gay/ straight • also restaurant & bar • many gay-themed plays

London—East

London—East includes City, Tower, Clerkenwell & Shoreditch

Accommodations

Andaz London 40 Liverpool St (near Bishopsgate, at Liverpool Street Station) **44–(0)20/7961–1234** • restaurants, bars, gym

The Hoxton 81 Great Eastern St **44–(0)20/7550–1000** • gay-friendly • also restaurant • nonsmoking • WiFi

Bars

The Angel 21 Church St (at W Ham Ln, Stratford) **44–020/8555–1148** • mostly gay men • dance bar • cabaret

Bar Music Hall 134 Curtain Rd (Shoreditch) **44–(0)20/7729–7216** • 11am-midnight, till 3am Fri-Sat • gay-friendly • great wknd brunch • dancing/DJ • live shows

Bethnal Green Working Men's Club 42-44 Pollard Row (at Squirries St, Bethnal Green) **44–020/7739–7170** • lesbians/ gay men • performance art • cabaret • drag shows • transgender-friendly

Dalston Superstore 117 Kingsland High St (at Sandringham Rd) **44–(0)20/7254 2273** • noon-2am • gay/straight • neighborhood bar • food served • WiFi

The Macbeth 70 Hoxton St (at Crondall St, Old St) **44–020/ 7749–0600** • 8pm-1am • mostly gay men • live shows • terrace

The Old Ship 17 Barnes St (Stepney) **44–(0)20/7790–4082** • from 4pm Mon, from 7pm Wed-Sat, from 6pm Sun, clsd Tue • lesbians/ gay men • neighborhood bar • cabaret • wheelchair access

Royal Oak 73 Columbia Rd (at Hackney Rd, Old St) **44–020/7729–2220** • 4pm-11pm, from noon Fri-Sun • mostly gay men • popular Sun for the Columbia Rd Flower market

Nightclubs

Kaos at Stunners 566 Cable St (at Butcher Row, Cable St Studios, Limehouse) • monthy parties • check www.kaoslondon.com • transgender • dancing/DJ • private club

Rumours 64-73 Minories (at The Minories) 44-(0)79/4947–7804 • last Sat • popular • women only • dancing/DJ

Unskinny Bop 42-44 Pollard Row (Bethnal Green Club) • 9pm 3rd Fri only • mostly women • dancing/DJ • live music

Urban Desi 61 Turnmill St (at Anexo Club, Farmington) 44-(0)79/5568–3144, 44-(0)79/5568–3134 • 11pm-5am 2nd Sat • lesbians/gay men • dancing/DJ • mostly South Asian

Way Out Club 9 Crosswall (at Charlie's) 44-(0)77/7815–7290 • 9pm-4am Sat only • transsexuals & their friends • dancing/DJ • live shows • private club • cover charge

Restaurants

Bistrotheque 23-27 Waderson St 44-(0)20/8983–7300 • expensive & glamorous • also cabaret shows after dinner

Bonds Restaurant & Bar 5 Threadneedle St 44-(0)20/7657–8090 • hours vary, clsd wknds • formerly a bank lobby • tapas served

Cafe Spice Namaste 16 Prescott St 44-(0)20/7488–9242 • lunch Mon-Fri, dinner nightly, clsd Sun • Indian

Cantaloupe 35-42 Charlotte Rd (Shoreditch) 44-(0)20/7729–5566 • 11am-midnight • popular • also bar

Canteen 2 Crispin Pl (Spitalfield) 44-(0)84/5686–1122 • place to be for brkfst

Hoxton Square Bar & Kitchen 2-4 Hoxton Square 44-020/9613–1171 • great dark spot for brkfst • live music

Les Trois Garçons 1 Club Row (at Bethnal, Shoreditch) 44-(0)20/7613–1924 • 6pm-midnight, clsd Sun • eclectic decor • reservations recommended

Lounge Lover 44-020/7012–1234 • fancy Japanese cuisine in a posh lounge • reservations required • wheelchair access

Saf 152-154 Curtain Rd, Shoreditch 44-(0)20/7613–0007 • lunch & dinner, also bar till midnight • upscale vegan/raw food

Erotica

Expectations 75 Great Eastern St (Shoreditch) 44-(0)20/7739–0292 • 11am-7pm, till 8pm Sat, noon-5pm Sun • leather/rubber store • also mail order

Sh! Women's Erotic Emporium 57 Hoxton Sq (off Old St, Shoreditch) 44-(0)20/7613–5458 • noon-8pm • men very welcome when accompanied by a woman

London—South

London—South includes Southwark, Lambeth, Kennington, Vauxhall, Battersea, Lewisham & Greenwich

Accommodations

Griffin House 22 Stockwell Green 44-(0)20/7096–3332 • lesbians/gay men • 2 rental apts near Vauxhall Gay Village & West End • WiFi • gay-owned

Bars

Battersea Barge Riverside Walk Nine Elms Ln (Vauxhall) 44-(0)20/7498–0004 • call for events • gay-friendly • cabaret • comedy • food served • gay-owned

The Bird in Hand 291 Sydenham Rd, Croydon 44-020/8683–3104 • 5pm-midnight, from 2pm Sun • lesbians/gay men • neighborhood bar • karaoke

George & Dragon 2 Blackheath Hill (Greenwich) 44-(0)20/8691–3764 • 6pm-2am, till 4am Fri-Sat • mostly gay men • live shows • cabaret

Kazbar 50 Clapham High St (Clapham) 44-(0)20/7622–0070 • 5pm-midnight, till 1am Fri-Sat, from 1pm Sun • lesbians/gay men

The Little Apple 98 Kennington Ln 44-(0)20/7735–2039 • noon-midnight, till 3am Sat • lesbians/gay men • dancing/DJ • transgender-friendly • food served • terrace • wheelchair access

Rose & Crown 1 Crooms Hill (at Gloucester Circus, Greenwich) 44-020/8293–1898 • pub hrs • lesbians/gay men • 'straight-friendly' pub • sing-alongs • 'Glee' nights

Southbank Surfing BFI Southbank, Belvedere Rd (at Benugo Bar) • 3rd Fri only • women only

The Star & Garter 227 High St (Bromley) 44-(0)20/8466–7733 • pub hours • lesbians/gay men • karaoke • WiFi • wheelchair access

The Two Brewers 114 Clapham High St (Clapham) 44-(0)20/7819–9539 • 4pm-2am, till 4am Fri-Sat, from 2pm Sun • lesbians/gay men • dancing/DJ • karaoke • cabaret

Two8Six 286 Lewisham High St 44-020/8690–7648 • 7pm-2am, till 4am Fri-Sat, clsd Sun • lesbians/gay men • dancing/DJ

Wotever World 372 Kennington Ln (at Royal Vauxhall Tavern) **44–(0)20/7973 797769** • 6pm-midnight Tue (Bar Wotever) • dancing/DJ • genderqueers & their admirers

NIGHTCLUBS

Area Club 67-68 Albert Embankment (Vauxhall) **44–020/3242–0040** • gay/straight • dancing/DJ • Sun morning gay party

Black Sheep Bar 68 High St (at S Norwood Hill, Croydon) **44–(0)20/8680–2233**

Bootylicious 1 Nine Elms (at Club Colosseum) • 11pm 3rd Sat • popular black gay club

Exilio St Thomas St (at Guy's Bar) **44–(0)79/3137–4391** • 9:30pm-2:30am Sat • lesbians/ gay men • dancing/DJ • Latino/a

Fire 47B S Lambeth Rd (Vauxhall) **44–020/3242–0040** • after-hours, Sat mornings & Sun afternoons • dancing/DJ • cover charge

Hard On 65 Goding St (at Factory 65, in Vauxhall) **44–020/7533 402 985** • 3rd Sat only • monthly pansexual fetish dance party • strict dress code • private club

Horse Meat Disco 349 Kennington Ln (at the Eagle) **44–(0)20/7793–0903** • 8pm Sun only • lesbians/ gay men • dancing/DJ • popular queer dance party

Royal Vauxhall Tavern 372 Kennington Ln (Vauxhall) **44–(0)20/7820–1222** • 8pm-late, 9pm-3am Fri-Sat, 2pm-midnight Sun • mostly gay men • popular wknds • more women Sat for Duckie • dancing/DJ • transgender-friendly • food served • wheelchair access

CAFES

Glow Lounge 6 Cavendish Parade (Clapham Common S Side) **44–020/8673–4471** • noon-11pm, 9:30am-1am Fri-Sat, 10am-7pm Sun • WiFi

ENTERTAINMENT & RECREATION

Gay City Rollers at Renaissance Rooms Off Miles Street, opposite Arch #8 (Vauxhall) **44–020/7720–9140** • 7pm-midnight, 1st Wed of the month

Oval Theatre Cafe Bar 52-54 Kennington Oval **44–(0)20/7582–0080** • 6pm-11pm Tue-Sat (cafe) • inquire about current theatre & art

FRANCE

Paris

Note: M°=Métro station

> **Paris is divided by arrondissements (city districts); 01=1st arrondissement, 02=2nd arrondissement, etc**

Paris—Overview

> **Note: When phoning Paris from the US, dial the country code + the city code + the local phone number**

INFO LINES & SERVICES

Centre Gai et Lesbien 63 rue Beaubourg **33–1/4357–2147** • drop-in evenings • call for other events/ groups

Gay AA 7 rue August Vacquerie (at St George's Anglican) **33–1/4634–5965** • 7:30pm Tue

ACCOMMODATIONS

Gay Accommodation Paris 271, rue du Faubourg Saint Antoine **33–1/4348–1382** • studios for rent in central Paris • gay-owned

Marais Flats/ Studios 20 rue Pierre Lescot **33–6/3256–5727 (EUROPEAN DAYTIME ONLY)** • apt rentals in different Paris locations • gay-owned

NIGHTCLUBS

Pinky Boat • huge women's party for gay pride • other lesbian events • pinkyboat.com

Womexx • mostly women • dancing/DJ • lesbian parties in cool spaces • www.womexx.fr

PUBLICATIONS

Têtu 33–1/5680–2080 • stylish & intelligent LGBT monthly (en français)

Paris—01

ACCOMMODATIONS

Hotel Louvre Richelieu 51 rue de Richelieu (M° Palais-Royal) **33–1/4297–4620** • gay/ straight • nonsmoking • WiFi

Hotel Louvre Saint-Honoré 141 rue Saint-Honoré (at rue du Louvre) **33–1/4296–2323** • gay/ straight • full brkfst • kids ok • WiFi • wheelchair access

Bars

Le Banana Cafe 13–15 rue de la Ferronnerie (near rue St-Denis, M° Châtelet) **33–1/4233–3531** • 6pm-dawn • lesbians/gay men • dancing/DJ • tropical decor • theme nights • piano bar • live shows • young crowd • wheelchair access • terrace

Bar du Kent'z 2-4 rue Vauvilliers (M° Chatelet-Les Halles) **33–1/4221–0116** • mostly gay men • 1920s style cocktail lounge

Le Tropic Cafe 66 rue des Lombards (M° Châtelet) **33–1/4013–9262** • 4pm-5am • lesbians/gay men • dancing/DJ Fri-Sat • transgender-friendly • kitschy, fun bar • tapas served • terrace • wheelchair access

Le Vagabond 14 rue Thérèse (at av de l'Opera, M° Pyramides) **33–1/4296–2723** • 6pm-close, clsd Mon • oldest gay bar & restaurant in Paris • older crowd

Paris

LGBT Pride:
June. web: www.gaypride.fr.

Annual Events:
May-June - French Open tennis championship, web: french.open-tennis.com.
July - Tour de France, web: www.letour.fr.
July 14 - Bastille Day.
October - Paris Gay & Lesbian Film Festival, web: www.ffglp.net.

City Info:
Pyramides Welcome Center 3308/9268-3000, 25 rue des Pyramides, web: en.parisinfo.com. Also www.paris-visit.info.

Best View:
Eiffel Tower (but of course!) and Sacre Coeur.

Weather:
Paris really *is* beautiful in the springtime. Chilly in the winter, the temperatures reach the 70°s during the summer.

Best View:
Eiffel Tower (but of course!) and Sacre Coeur.

Attractions:
Arc de Triomphe 33-1/5537-7377, web: www.monuments-nationaux.fr.
Notre Dame Cathedral 33–8/9270-1239, web: www.notredamede-paris.fr.
Eiffel Tower (up in lights for 10 minutes each hour from sunset till past midnight!) 33–1/4411–2323, web: www.tour-eiffel.fr.
Louvre 33–1/4020–5760, web: www.louvre.fr.
Musée d'Orsay 33–1/4049–4814, web: www.musee-orsay.fr.
Picasso Museum 33–1/4271–2521, web: www.musee-picasso.fr.
Rodin Musuem 33–1/4418–6110, web: www.musee-rodin.fr.
Sacre-Coeur Basilica 33–1/5341-8900, web: www.sacre-coeur-montmartre.com.
Sainte-Chapelle 33–1/5340-6096, web: www.monuments-nationaux.fr.

Transit:
Alpha Taxi 33–1/4585–8585, web: www.alphataxis.fr.
Taxi Bleu 33–8/9170-1010, web: www.taxis-bleus.com.
RATP (bus and Métro) web: www.ratp.fr.

RESTAURANTS

L' Amazonial 3 rue Ste-Opportune (at rue Ferronnerie, M° Châtelet) **33–1/4233–5313** • lunch & dinner, brunch wknds • lesbians/ gay men • Brazilian/ int'l • cabaret • drag shows • heated terrace • wheelchair access

Au Diable des Lombards 64 rue des Lombards (at rue St-Denis, M° Châtelet) **33–1/4233–8184** • 8am-1am • American • full bar • terrace

Marc Mitonne 60 rue de l'Arbre-Sec (M° Les Halles) **33–1/4261–5316** • 6pm-2am, clsd Sun-Mon • live shows • cabaret

La Poule au Pot 9 rue Vauvilliers (M° Les Halles) **33–1/4236–3296** • 7pm-5am, clsd Mon • clsd Aug • bistro • traditional French

Velvet Room 43 rue Saint Honore • Thai restaurant and small gay bar

ENTERTAINMENT & RECREATION

Forum des Halles 101 Porte Berger (M° Châtelet-Les Halles) **33–1/4476–9656** • underground sports/ entertainment complex w/ museums, theater, shops, clubs, cafes & more

GYMS & HEALTH CLUBS

Club Med Gym 147 rue St–Honoré (M° Louvre) **33–1/4020–0303** • gay/ straight • day passes available • many locations throughout the city

Paris — 02

BARS

La Champmeslé 4 rue Chabanais (at rue des Petits Champs, M° Pyramides) **33–1/4296–8520** • 4pm-3am, till 7am Fri-Sat, clsd Sun • popular • mostly women • theme nights • older crowd • WiFi • wheelchair access • a lesbian landmark, in business for over 20 years

NIGHTCLUBS

Rex Club 5 blvd Poissonière (M° Bonne Nouvelle) **33–1/4236–1096** • gay-friendly • call for events • clsd August • cover

CAFES

Stuart Friendly 16 rue Marie Stuart • noon-11pm, till midnight Fri-Sat, till 5:30pm Sun • "straight-friendly" cafe • food served

RESTAURANTS

Aux Trois Petits Cochons 31 rue Tiquetonne (at rue St-Denis, M° Etienne-Marcel) **33–1/4233–3969** • 8pm-1am • popular • lesbians/ gay men • gourmet French made w/ fresh seasonal produce • reservations recommended • gay-owned

Le César 4 rue Chabanais (M° Pyramides) **33–1/4296–8113** • 6:30pm-5am • lesbians/ gay men • also bar

Le Lezard Cafe 32 rue Etienne Marcel **33–1/4233–2273** • full bar • terrace year round

Le Loup Blanc 42 rue Tiquetonne (M° Etienne-Marcel) **33–1/4013–0835** • 7:30pm-midnight, till 1am Sat, also brunch 11am-4:30pm Sun • popular • lesbians/ gay men

Paris — 03

ACCOMMODATIONS

Absolu Living 236 rue St Martin **33–1/4454–9700** • lesbians/ gay men • fully furnished apts in central Paris • short & long-term stays • gay-owned

Adorable Apartment in Paris (M° Rambuteau) **415/397–6454 (US#)** • gay-friendly • in heart of Marais • nonsmoking • lesbian & gay-owned

Hôtel du Vieux Saule 6 rue de Picardie **33–1/4272–0114** • gay-friendly

Hotel Jules & Jim 11 rue des Gravilliers • gay/straight • gay-owned

BARS

Le CUD Club 12 rue des Haudriettes **33–1/4277–4412** • 11pm-6am, till 7am wknds • mostly men • dancing/DJ • young crowd

Le Duplex 25 rue Michel-Le-Comte (at rue Beaubourg, M° Rambuteau) **33–1/4272–8086** • 8pm-2am, till 4am Fri-Sat • lesbians/ gay men • neighborhood bar • bohemian types • live shows • WiFi

Le Tango/ La Boite à Frissons 13 rue au Maire (M° Arts-et-Metiers) **33–1/4272–1778** • 10:30pm-5am, clsd Mon • lesbians/ gay men • food served

Unity Bar 176–178 rue St-Martin (near rue Réaumur, M° Rambuteau) **33–1/4272–7059** • 4pm-2am • mostly women • men welcome as guests • neighborhood bar • young crowd • WiFi

RESTAURANTS

La Fontaine Gourmande 11 rue Charlot **33–1/4278–7240** • noon-2pm Tue-Fri & 7:30pm-close Tue-Sun, clsd Mon • women-owned

EROTICA

Rex 42 rue de Poitou (at rue Charlot, M° St-Sébastien-Froissard) **33-1/4277-5857** • 1pm-8pm, clsd Sun • new, custom & secondhand leather & S/M accessories

Paris—04

ACCOMMODATIONS

Chambres D'Hôte Rivoli **33-06/1991-5828** • lesbians/gay men • B&B • WiFi • gay-owned

Hôtel Beaubourg 11 rue Simon le Franc (btwn rue Beaubourg & rue du Temple, M° Hôtel-de-Ville) **33-1/4274-3424** • gay/straight • next to Centre Pompidou • WiFi

Hôtel de la Bretonnerie 22 rue Ste-Croix-de-la-Bretonnerie (M° Hôtel-de-Ville) **33-1/4887-7763** • gay-friendly • 17th-c hotel w/ Louis XIII decor

Hôtel du Vieux Marais 8 rue du Plâtre (M° Hôtel-de-Ville) **33-1/4278-4722** • gay-friendly • centrally located • WiFi

BARS

3W Kafe 8 rue des Ecouffes (M° St Paul) **33-1/4887-3926** • 5pm-2am, till 4am Fri-Sat • mostly women • dancing/DJ • live shows • videos

L' Amnésia Café 42 rue Vieille du Temple (at rue des Blancs-Manteaux, M° Hôtel-de-Ville) **33-1/4272-1694** • 11am-close • popular • lesbians/gay men • dancing • food served

Au Mange Disque 15 rue de la Reynie (at Boule de Sebastopol) **33-1/4804-7817** • 11am-2am, from 5pm Sun-Mon • mostly gay men • theme nights • colorful, modern decor

Le Bar du Palmier 16 rue des Lombards (at bd de Sébastopol, M° Châtelet) **33-1/4278-5353** • 2pm-6am • lesbians/gay men • food served • terrace

Le Carrefour 8 rue des Archives (at rue de la Verrerie) **33-1/4029-9005** • 6am-2am • mostly gay men • neighborhood bar • good location & terrace

Cox 15 rue des Archives (at rue Ste-Croix-de-la-Bretonnerie, M° Hôtel-de-Ville) **33-1/4272-0800** • 5:30pm-2am, from 4:30pm Fri-Sun • mostly gay men • dancing/DJ • huge terrace

Dandy's Cafe 9 rue Nicolas Flamel **33-1/4271-4582** • 2pm-2am • mostly gay men

L' Enchanteur 15 rue Michel Lecomte (M° Rambuteau) **33-1/4804-0238** • 6pm-6am, clsd Mon • lesbians/gay men • karaoke

Les Filles de Paris 57 rue Quincampoix **33-1/4271-7220** • 10pm-5am Wed-Sat, also restaurant from 7pm, clsd Sun-Mon • gay/straight • dancing/DJ • drag shows, burlesque & cabaret

Le Freedj 35 rue Ste-Croix-de-la-Bretonnerie (at rue du Temple, M° Hôtel-de-Ville) **33-1/4029-4440** • 6pm-4am • lesbians/gay men • bar upstairs, club downstairs

L' Imprevu Cafe 9 rue Quincampoix **33-1/4278-2350** • 3pm-2am, from 1pm Sun • mostly gay men • low key neighborhood cafe/bar • food served

Les Jacasses 5 rue des Ecouffes (M° St Paul) **33-1/4271-1551** • 5pm-2am • mostly women • men welcome

Morgan Bar 25 rue du Roi de Sicile **33-1/4277-0666** • lesbians/gay men • dancing/DJ • WiFi

L' Oiseau Bariolé 16 rue Saint-Croix-de-la-Bretonnerie (M° Hotel de Ville) **33-1/4272-3712** • lesbians/gay-men • 5pm-close • quiet

Okawa 40 rue Vieille du Temple (at rue Ste-Croix-de-la-Bretonnerie, M° Hôtel-de-Ville) **33-1/4804-3069** • 10am-2am, till 4am Fri-Sat • gay/straight • trendy cafe-bar in 12th- & 13th-c caves • cabaret • piano bar Tue-Wed • also restaurant from 7pm

L' Open Cafe 17 rue des Archives (at rue Ste-Croix-de-la-Bretonnerie, M° Hôtel-de-Ville) • 11am-2am, till 4am Fri-Sat • popular • lesbians/gay men • sidewalk cafe-bar

Le Pur Bar 12 rue de Plâtre (btwn rue du Temple & rue des Archives, M° Hôtel-de-Ville) **33-1/4887-0259** • 5pm-2am • lesbians/gay men • neighborhood cafe-bar

Le Raidd 23 rue du Temple (M° Hotel de ville) **33-1/4277-0488** • 5pm-5am • mostly men • dancing/ DJ • go-go boys

So What 30 rue du Roi de Sicile (M° Hôtel-de-Ville) • 9:30pm-2am, 10pm-4am Fri-Sat, clsd Sun-Tue • lesbians/gay men • stylish new bar • dancing/DJ • lesbian-owned

Les Souffleurs 7 rue de la Verrerie (M° Hôtel-de-Ville) **33-1/4478-0492** • lesbians/gay men • artsy younger crowd • events in the basement • monthly dyke party Butch is Beautiful

Le Troisieme Lieu 62 rue Quincampoix **33-1/4804-8564** • 6pm-2am, clsd Sun • mostly women • also restaurant & nightclub

Le Voulez-Vous 18 rue du Temple (M°
Hôtel-de-Ville) **33-1/4459-3857** • 11am-2am
• lesbians/ gay men • lounge & restaurant •
terrace

Yono 37 rue Vieille du Temple
33-1/4274-3165 • 6pm-2am, 4:30-11pm Sun,
clsd Mon • lesbians/ gay men • dancing/DJ,
cozy basement bar • Mustache monthy party •
also restaurant

Ze Baar 41 rue des Blancs Manteaux (at rue
du Temple) **33-1/4271-7508** • 5pm-2am •
mostly gay men • neighborhood bar • also
restaurant

NIGHTCLUBS

Le Scarron 3 rue Geoffroy l'Angevin
33-1/4277-4405 • clsd Sun-Mon • lesbians/
gay men • cozy dance club & piano bar

CAFES

Le Kofi du Marais 54 rue Ste-Croix-de-la-
Bretonnerie (M° Hôtel de Ville)
33-1/4887-4871 • 7pm-midnight, clsd Sun •
lesbians/ gay men • coffee & light meals

RESTAURANTS

4 Pat 4 rue St Merri **33-1/4277-2545** • open
24hrs • dancing/DJ • Italian menu

Le Chant des Voyelles 3 rue des Lombards
(M° Châtelet) **33-1/4277-7707** • 11:30am-
3pm & 6:30pm-midnight, open all day in
summer • traditional French • terrace

Curieux Spaghetti Bar 14 rue Saint Merri
(M° Rambuteau) **33-1/4272-7597** • noon-
2am, till 4am Th-Sat, brunch wknds • home of
scented vodka "Chup" shots

Etamine Cafe 13 rue des Ecouffes (at rue
des Rosiers, M° Hotel de Ville)
33-1/4478-0962 • noon-midnight, clsd Mon •
also bar

Le Gai Moulin 10 rue St-Merri (at rue du
Temple, M° Hôtel-de-Ville) **33-1/4887-0600** •
noon-midnight • lesbians/ gay men • French/
int'l

HD Diner 6-8 Square Ste-Croix de la
Bretonnerie **33-1/4277-6934** • 11am-
midnight • 50's style diner

La Pas-Sage-Oblige 29 rue du Bourg-
Tibourg (M° Hôtel-de-Ville) **33-1/4041-9503**
• lunch & dinner • vegetarian

Le Petit Picard 42 rue Ste-Croix-de-la-
Bretonnerie (M° Hôtel-de-Ville)
33-1/4278-5403 • lunch & dinner, clsd Mon •
lesbians/ gay men • reservations
recommended

Les Piétons 8 rue des Lombards (M°
Châtelet) **33-1/4887-8287** • noon-2am •
Spanish/ tapas • also bar

BOOKSTORES

Les Mots à la Bouche 6 rue Ste-Croix-de-
la-Bretonnerie (near rue du Vieille du Temple,
M° Hôtel-de-Ville) **33-1/4278-8830** • 11am-
11pm, 1pm-9pm Sun • LGBT • English titles

RETAIL SHOPS

Abraxas 9 rue St-Merri **33-1/4804-3355** •
tattoos • piercing • large selection of body
jewelry

EROTICA

Dollhouse 24 rue du Roi de Sicile (at
Ferdinand Duval) **33-1/4027-0921** • women's
erotica store

Paris — 05

ACCOMMODATIONS

Historic Rentals 3415 W Cypress St, Tampa,
FL 33607 **800/537-5408 (US#)** • gay-friendly •
1-bdrm apts • full kitchen • steps to Notre
Dame & Luxembourg Gardens • nonsmoking
• WiFi

RESTAURANTS

L' AOC **33-1/4354-2252** • lunch & dinner,
clsd Sun• upscale favorite for fancy lesbians

Le Petit Prince 12 rue de Lanneau (M°
Maubert-Mutualité) **33-1/4354-7726** •
7:30pm-midnight • popular • French

ENTERTAINMENT & RECREATION

Friday Night Fever 16 Bol Saint Germain •
10pm-1am Fri (weather-permitting), meet
9:30pm • rollerblade through the city • gay/
straight

Open-Air Sculpture Museum Quai Saint-
Bernard • along the Seine btwn the Jardin des
Plantes & the Institut du Monde Arabe

Paris — 06

BARS

La Venus Noire 25 rue de l'Hirondelle (M°
St-Michel) • 6pm-1am, till 2am Fri-Sat, clsd
Sun • mostly women • neighborhood bar •
live music

NIGHTCLUBS

Le Rive Gauche 1 rue du Sabot (M° St-
Sulpice) **33-1/4020-4323** • 11pm-dawn Fri-
Sat only • mostly women • dancing/DJ • cover
charge

BOOKSTORES

The Village Voice 6 rue Princesse (M° Mabillon) **33-1/4633-3647** • 10am-7:30pm, from 2pm Mon, noon-6pm Sun • English-language bookshop

Paris—08

ACCOMMODATIONS

François 1er 7 rue Magellan **33-1/4723-4404** • gay-friendly • boutique hotel near les Champs-Elysées • also bar

BARS

Le Day Off 10 rue de l'Isly (M° Gare-St-Lazare) **33-1/4522-8790** • 5pm-3am Mon-Fri only • heavy drinking enjoyed by work-weary lesbians, crowded in the early evening • food served • woman-owned

NIGHTCLUBS

Escualita 128 rue de la boetie (at Club "MadaM") • midnight Sun only • mostly men • transgender-friendly • fab tranny dance party • all are welcome

Le Queen 102 av des Champs-Élysées (btwn rue Washington & rue de Berri, M° Georges-V) **33-8/5389-0890** • midnight-dawn, more gay Sun • popular • gay/ straight • dancing/DJ • drag shows • young crowd • selective door • cover charge

Paris—09

ACCOMMODATIONS

The Grand 2 rue Scribe **33-1/4007-3232, 888/424-6835** • gay-friendly • ultraluxe art deco hotel • WiFi

BARS

Rosa Bonheur 1 rue Botzaris **33-1/4200-0045** • gay-friendly • more gay Sun, arrive before 6pm to avoid the line

NIGHTCLUBS

Folies Pigalle 11 place Pigalle (M° Pigalle) **33-1/4878-5525, 33-1/4280-1203 (BBB INFO LINE)** • midnight-dawn • gay/ straight • dancing/DJ • theme nights • transgender-friendly • multiracial • cover charge

Fox Club 9 rue Frochot **33-1/4281-0923** • 6pm-2am, 7pm-5am Fri-Sat, clsd Sun-Tue • mostly women • dancing/DJ

Paris—10

BARS

Baxo 21 rue Juliette Dodu (M° Colonel Fabien) **33-1/4202-9971** • 9am-2am, from 5pm Sat, clsd Sun • gay/ straight • dancing/DJ • trendy bar/ restaurant • patio

L' Okubi 219 rue St-Maur (M° Goncourt) **33-1/4201-3508** • 6pm-2am, clsd Sun • mostly women • dancing/DJ

Paris—11

ACCOMMODATIONS

Le 20 Prieure Hotel 20 rue du Grand Prieuré **33-1/4700-7414** • gay/straight • WiFi

Le General Hotel 5/7 rue Rampon **33-1/4700-4157** • gay-friendly • WiFi • wheelchair access

Hôtel Beaumarchais 3 rue Oberkampf (btwn bd Beaumarchais & bd Voltaire, M° Filles-du-Calvaire) **33-1/5336-8686** • gay/straight • beautiful hotel • WiFi

BARS

Le Bataclan 50 blvd Voltaire (at Bataclan club, M° Saint Ambroise) **33-1/4314-0030** • gay-friendly • live music venue • more gay for the Follivores & Crazyvores • call for events

L' Escalme 140 Blvd Richard Lenoir **33-1/4805-2955** • 9am-2am • mostly men • also restaurant

Follivores/ Crazyvores 50 blvd Voltaire (M° Saint Ambroise) **33-1/4314-0030** • lesbians/gay men • monthly sing-along dance parties • Follivores is 1960s-1990s French pop • Crazyvores is English-speaking • kitsch factor very high!

In Out 241 rue du Fbg St Antoine **33-9/5241-0037** • 5pm-2am, clsd Sun • gay/straight • dancing/DJ • young crowd

NIGHTCLUBS

Les Disquaires 6 rue des Taillandiers (M° Bastille) **33-1/4021-9460** • gay/ straight • dance bar • live bands

La Scène Bastille 2 bis rue des Taillandiers (M° Bastille) **33-1/4314-0000 (CLUB), 33-1/4806-1213 (RESTAURANT)** • gay-friendly • also restaurant • live music • events

CAFES

Cannibale Café 93 Rue Jean-Pierre Timbaud **33-1/4929-0040** • an old-fashioned Parisian café in Belleville • WiFi

Restaurants

Sans Gêne 122 rue Oberkampf **33-1/4700-7011** • 5pm-2am, Sun brunch, clsd Mon • also bar

Le Tabarin 3 rue Amelot **33-1/4807-1522** • lunch Sun-Fri, dinner Sun-Sat • lesbians/ gay men • full bar • piano bar

Entertainment & Recreation

L' ArtiShow 3 cite Souzy **33-1/4002-1803** • cabaret • also lunch & dinner served

Bookstores

Violette & Co 102 rue de Charonne (at boulevard Voltaire, M° Charonne) **33-1/4372-1607** • 11am-8pm, 2pm-7pm Sun, clsd Mon • LGBT & feminist • English titles • art shows • lesbian-owned

Erotica

Démonia 22 ave Jean Aicard (at rue Oberkampf, M° St-Maur) **33-1/4314-8270** • clsd Sun • BDSM shop • lingerie • videos • toys

Paris—12

Sex Clubs

Atlantide 13 rue Parrot (M° Gare de Lyon) **33-1/4342-2243** • gay/ straight sauna w/ sexual atmosphere • men, women, transgender-friendly • private cabins • also bar

Paris—14

Gyms & Health Clubs

Amphibi 73 rue Hallé (at rue Bézout, M° Alesia) **33-1/4047-5090** • sauna where everyone is welcome: gay, straight, bisexual, transgendered

Paris—16

Accommodations

Keppler 10 rue Keppler **33-1/4720-6505** • gay-friendly • near major tourist stops • also bar • kids/ pets ok • WiFi

Paris—18

Bars

Karambole Cafe 10 rue Hegesippe Moreau (M° Place de Clichy or La Fourche) **33-1/4293-3068** • 9am-2am, from 6pm Sat, clsd Sun • gay/ straight • artsy cafe by day • DJs by night

Le Tagada Bar 40 rue Trois-Frères (M° Abesses) **33-1/4255-9556** • 6pm-2am, clsd Mon • mostly gay men • upscale food

Entertainment & Recreation

Michou 80 rue des Martyrs (at Blvd de Clichy, M° Pigalle) **33-1/4606-1604** • infamous drag cabaret • dinner show

Paris—19

Cafes

Cafe Cherie 44 Blvd de la Villette (M° Belleville) **33-1/4202-0205** • 8am-2am • gay/ straight • live music & DJs starting at 10pm • WiFi

Paris—20

Accommodations

Mama Shelter 109 rue de Bagnolet **33-1/ 4348-4848** • gay/ straight • great location on the Right Bank • kichenettes • also restaurant & cool local bars • WiFi

Entertainment & Recreation

Père Lachaise Cemetery bd de Ménilmontant (M° Père-Lachaise) • perhaps the world's most famous resting place, where lie such notables as Chopin, Gertrude Stein, Oscar Wilde, Sarah Bernhardt, Isadora Duncan, Edith Piaf & Jim Morrison

Germany

Berlin

Berlin is divided into 5 regions:
   Berlin—Overview
   Berlin—Kreuzberg
   Berlin—Prenzlauer Berg–Mitte
   Berlin—Schöneberg-Tiergarten
   Berlin—Outer

Berlin—Overview

Info Lines & Services

Gay AA for English Speakers at Mann-O-Meter **49-30/787-5188** • 5pm Tue, also Gay AA 8pm Th

Lesbenberatung (Lesbian Advice) Kulmer Str 20a (in Kreuzberg) **49-30/215-2000** • switchboard & center • staffed 10am-5pm, till 7pm Tue & Th

Mann-O-Meter Bülowstr 106 (at Nollendorfplatz) **49-30/216-8008** • 5pm-10pm • gay switchboard & center • also cafe • also B&B referral service

Sonntags Club Greifenhagener Str 28 (S/U-Schönhauser Allee) **49–30/449–7590, 49–30/442–3702 (TRANSGENDER LINE)** • info line 10am-6pm daily • LGBT info • also cafe-bar • 5pm-midnight • lesbians/ gay men • women's night Fri 8pm

Spinnboden Lesbian Archive & Library U-Bahn 8, Bernauerstr (in 2nd courtyard, 2nd flr) **49–30/448–5848** • call for hours • also by appt

Berlin

LGBT Pride:

Christopher Street Day, 3rd or 4th Saturday in June, web: www.csd-berlin.de.

Annual Events:

February - Berlinale: Berlin Int'l Film Festival w/ Queer Teddy Award 49-30/259-200, web: www.berlinale.de.

June - Lesbian & Gay City Festival/ Stadtfest, web: www.regenbogenfonds.de.

Sept- Folsom Europe, web: www.folsom-europe.info.

October - Wigstoeckel transgender/ drag festival, web: www.wigstoeckel.com.

November - Jazz Fest Berlin, www.berlinerfestspiele.de.

November/ December - Verzaubert Int'l Queer Film Festival, web: www.verzaubertfilmfest.com.

City Info:

Berlin-Tourism, web: www.visitberlin.de/en.

Europa Center 49–30/2649-7940, web: www.europa-center-berlin.de.

Weather:

Berlin is on the same parallel as Newfoundland, so if you're visiting in the winter, prepare for snow and bitter cold. Summer is balmy while spring and fall are beautiful, if sometimes rainy.

Transit:

Taxifunk Berlin 49–800/443–322, web: www.taxifunkberlin.de.

Jet Express-Bus X9 from Tegel Airport to central Berlin 49–30/19449.

U-Bahn (subway) and bus 49–30/19449, web: www.bvg.de.

S-Bahn (elevated train) 49–30/2974–3333, web: www.s-bahn-berlin.de

Attractions:

Bauhaus Design Museum 49–30/254–0020, web: www.bauhaus.de.

Brandenburg Gate.

Charlottenburg Palace 49–30/2655-7656.

Egyptian Museum 49–30/2090–5544, web: www.egyptian-museum-berlin.com.

Gay Museum 49–30/6959–9050, web: www.schwulesmuseum.de.

Homo Memorial (at Nollendorfplatz station).

The Jewish Museum Berlin 49–30/2599–3300, web: www.juedisches-museum-berlin.de.

Kaiser Wilhelm Memorial Church, web: www.gedaechtniskirche-berlin.de.

Käthe-Kollwitz Museum 49–30/882–5210, web: www.kaethe-kollwitz.de.

Museuminsel (Museum Island) 49–30/266–424-242, web: www.smb.spk-berlin.de.

New National Gallery 49–30/266–424-510, web: www.neue-nationalgalerie.de.

Reichstag 49–30/2273–2152, web: www.bundestag.de.

ACCOMMODATIONS

Enjoy B&B Bülowstr 106 (at M-O-M, gay center) **49–30/2362–3610** • lesbians/ gay men • accommodations referral service

NIGHTCLUBS

MegaDyke Productions **49–30/179 59 12 738** • popular parties & events for lesbians, including L-Tunes at SchwuZ & annual pride events for lesbians in other locations • see www.megadyke.de for more details

RESTAURANTS

Paris Bar Kantstrasse152 **49–30/313–8052** • bistro & bar

ENTERTAINMENT & RECREATION

Fritz Music Tour **49–30/3087–5633** • visit the haunts of David Bowie, Nina Hagen, Iggy Pop & Rammstein, among other popular musical acts

The Jewish Museum Berlin Lindenstr 9-14 **49–30/2599–3300** • 10am-8pm, till 10pm Mon • German-Jewish history & culture

Schwules (Gay) Museum U6/U7 Mehringdamm 61 **49–30/6959–9050** • 2pm-6pm, till 7pm Sat, clsd Tue • guided tours 5pm Sat (in German) • exhibits, archives & library

PUBLICATIONS

Siegessäule **49–30/235–5390, 49–30/2355–3932** • free monthly LGBT city magazine (in German) • awesome maps

Berlin—Kreuzberg

ACCOMMODATIONS

Hotel Transit Hagelberger Straße 53–54 **49–30/789–0470** • gay-friendly • loft-style hotel in 19th-c factory • also bar

The Mövenpick Hotel **49-30/230–060** • gay-friendly • convenient location • also space-agey bar

BARS

Barbie Bar Mehringdamm 77 (at Kreuzbergstr) **49–30/6956–8610** • 3pm-close • lesbians/ gay men • lounge • terrace

Bierhimmel Oranienstr 183 (U-Kottbusser Tor) **49–30/615–3122** • 1pm-3am • gay/ straight • young crowd

Mobel Olfe Reichenbergerstrasse 177 (at Skalitzer) **49–30/2327–4690** • 8pm-close Tue-Sun • popular • lesbians/ gay men

Rauschgold Mehringdamm 62 (U-Mehringdamm) **49–30/7895–2668** • 8pm-close • lesbians/ gay men

Roses Oranienstr 187 (at Kottbusser Tor) **49–30/615–6570** • 10pm-close • popular • lesbians/ gay men • transgender-friendly • young crowd

Sofia • open 9am, from 11am Sat and 8pm Sun • lesbians/gay men

NIGHTCLUBS

L-tunes Mehringdamm 61 (at SchwuZ) **49–30/179 59 12 738** • 10pm last Fri only • mostly women, queer friends welcome • dancing/DJ • events

SchwuZ (SchwulenZentrum) Mehringdamm 61 (enter through Café Sundstroem) **49–30/629–088** • from 11pm Fri-Sat • mostly gay men • more women last Fri • dancing/DJ • live/drag shows • young crowd

Serene Bar Schwiebusser Str 2 **49–30/6904–1580** • lesbians/ gay men • popular Girls Bar Th • Girls Dance 10pm Sat

SO 36 Oranienstr 190 (at Kottbusser Tor) **49–30/6140–1306, 49–30/6140–1307** • popular • gay/ straight • dancing/DJ • transgender-friendly • live shows • videos • young crowd • wheelchair access • theme nights include Café Fatal (ballroom dancing) & Gayhane (Turkish night)

CAFES

Drama Mehringdamm 63 **49–30/6746–9562** • opens 2pm • also bar & terrace

Melitta Sundström Mehringdamm 61 (at Gneisenaustr, U-Mehringdamm) **49–30/692–4414** • 10am-11pm • lesbians/ gay men • terrace • wheelchair access • also LGBT bookstore

Muvuca Gneisenaustr 2a (at Mehringdamm) **49–30/6165–6310** • 4pm-close • radical/ political int'l cafe • Portuguese food

Sudblock Admiralstrasse 1-2 • 10am-7pm • lesbians/gay men • live entertainment

RESTAURANTS

Amrit Oranienstr 202 **49–30/612–5550** • noon-1am • Indian

Locus Marheinekeplatz 4 **49–30/691–5637** • 10am-1:30am • popular • lesbians/ gay men • Mexican • full bar • lesbian-owned

Restaurant Z Friesenstr 12 **49–30/692–2716** • 5pm-1am • Greek/ Mediterranean

SEX CLUBS

Be Cunt Görlitzer Str 71 (at Club Culture Houze) **49–30/6170–9669** • 2nd Tues of the month • trans, dykes, genderfucks, femmes, tomboys & female queers

EROTICA

Altelier Dos Santos Mehringdamm 119 (U Platz der Luftbrucke) **49–30/5059–9919** • noon-6pm, till 4pm Sat • high quality custom leather & fetish wear • lesbian-owned

Playstixx Waldemarstrasse 24 **49–30/6165–9500** • makers & sellers of silicone toys for women & lovers

Sexclusivitäten Fürbringer Str 2 **49–30/693–6666** • lesbian sex shop • Open Salon sex party noon-8pm Fri • also escort service

Berlin—Prenzlauer Berg-Mitte

ACCOMMODATIONS

Andel's Hotel Landsberger Allee 106 **49–30/453–053** • gay-friendly • WiFi • also restaurant • wheelchair access

Arte Luise Kunsthotel Luisenstr 19 (Mitte) **49–30/284–480** • gay-friendly • former palace near River Spree

Intermezzo Hotel for Women Gertrud-Kolmar Str 5 (at Brandenburger Tor) **49–30/2248–9096** • women only • wheelchair access

Schall & Rauch Pension Gleimstr 23 (at Schönhauser Allee) **49–30/339–723** • lesbians/ gay men • also bar & restaurant

BARS

Besenkammer Bar Rathausstr 1 (at Alexanderplatz, under the S-Bahn bridge) **49–30/242–4083** • 24hrs • lesbians/ gay men • tiny "beer bar"

Betty F*** Mulackstrasse 13 (at Gormannstrasse) • from 10pm • lesbians/ gay men • tiny neighborhood bar

Cafe Amsterdam Gleimstr 24 (at Schönhauser Allee) **49–30/448–0792, 49–30/231–6796** • 9am-3am, till 5am Fri-Sat • food served • gay/ straight • transgender-friendly • terrace • wheelchair access • also pension

Marietta Stargarder Str 13 **49–30/4372–0646** • 10am-2am, till 4am Sat-Sun • lesbians/ gay men

Perle Sredzkistrasse 64 • 7pm-close, clsd Sun-Mon • lesbians/ gay men • innovative lighting & electronica

Reingold Novalisstr 11 (U-Oranienburger Str) **49–30/4985–3450** • 9pm-3am, till 5am Fri-Sat • gay/ straight • more gay Th • food served • lesbian-owned cocktail lounge

Sanatorium 23 Frankfurter Allee 23 **49–30/4202–1193** • from 3pm • gay/straight • trendy cafe/bar • also guesthouse

Sharon Stonewall Kleinen Präsidentenstr 3 (at Hackeschen Market) **49–30/2408–5502** • 8pm-2am, till 4:30am Fri-Sat, clsd Mon • lesbians/gay men • WiFi

Zum Schmutzigen Hobby/ Nina's Bar Rykestrasse 45 • 6pm-close • lesbians/ gay men • dancing/DJ • drag shows • transgender-friendly

NIGHTCLUBS

Ackerkeller • 1st Tue 10pm • mostly gay men • dancing/DJ

Berghain Am Wrietzener Bahnhof (off Strasse der Pariser Kommune, near Ostbahnhof station) **49–30/2936–0210** • lesbians/ gay men • converted power station is now popular dance club

Chantals House of Shame • 11pm Th & Bad Girls club monthly parties

Girls Town Karl-Marx-Allee 33 (at Kino International, U-Schillingstr) **49–30/2475–6011** • 2nd Sat every other month • mostly women • dancing/DJ • huge, popular lesbian club

GMF Alexanderstrasse 7 (, at Week End, U-Alexanderplatz) **49–30/2809–5396** • mostly gay men • Sun only 11pm-close

Irrenhouse Am Friedrichshain 33 (at Geburtstagsklub) • 3rd Sat • lesbians/ gay men • dancing/DJ • drag shows • transgender-friendly • Nina Queer's monthly drag party

KitKat Club Kopenickerstrasse 76 (enter on Bruckenstrasse) **49–30/2173–6841** • 8pm-close Th, 11pm-8am Fri-Sat • gay/ straight • also S/M club • cabaret

Klub International Karl-Marx-Allee 33 (at Kino International, U-Schillingstr) **49–30/2475–6011** • 11pm-close, 2nd Sat lesbian night • mostly gay men • dancing/DJ • cover charge

Loreley Karl-Liebknecht-Strasse 11 • mostly gay men • popular Fri • dancing/DJ

Milkshake Warschauer Str 34 (at Monstter Ronson's) • 3rd Sat, every other month • mostly women • dancing/DJ • transgender-friendly

Spy Club Friedrichstr/ Unter den Linden (at Cookies) **49–30/2809–5396** • last Sat only • lesbians/ gay men • dancing/DJ

CAFES

Cafe Seidenfaden Dircksenstr 47 (U-Alexanderplatz) **49–30/283–2783** • 10am-6pm, noon-8pm Sat, clsd Sun • women only • drug- & alcohol-free cafe • info board • nonsmoking

November Husemannstr 15 (at Sredzkistr) **49–30/442–8425** • 10am-2am • lesbians/gay men • cafe-bar • terrace • brkfst buffet wknds

RESTAURANTS

Anda Lucia Savignyplatz 2 **49–30/5471–0271** • 6pm-10pm • tapas bar

Rice Queen Danziger Str 13 (U-Eberswalder Str) **49–30/4404–5800** • 5pm-11pm, from 2pm wknds • Asian fusion

Schall & Rauch Wirtshaus Gleimstr 23 (at Schönhauser Allee) **49–30/443–3970** • 10am-close • lesbians/gay men

Thüringer Stuben Stargarder Str 28 (at Dunckerstr, S/U-Schönhauser Allee) **49–30/4463–3339** • 4pm-1am, from noon wknds • full bar

BOOKSTORES

Ana Koluth Schönhauser Allee 124 **49–30/8733–6980** • 10am-8pm, till 6pm Sat, clsd Sun • lesbian-owned

EROTICA

Blackstyle Seelower Str 5 (S/U-Schönhauser Allee) **49–30/4468–8595** • clsd Sun • latex & rubber wear • also mail order

Berlin–Schöneberg-Tiergarten

ACCOMMODATIONS

Arco Hotel Geisbergstr 30 (at Ansbacherstr, U-Wittenbergplatz) **49–30/235–1480** • gay/straight • centrally located • kids/pets ok • wheelchair access • gay-owned

Axel Hotel Berlin Lietzenburger Str 13/15 **49–30/2100–2893**

Berlin B&B • lesbians/gay men • full brkfst • WiFi • gay-owned

Hotel California Kurfürstendamm 35 (at Knesebeckstr, U-Uhlandstr) **49–30/880–120** • gay-friendly • cafe/bar • nonsmoking flr • kids ok

Hotel Hansablick Flotowstr 6 (at Bachstr, off Str des 17 Juni) **49–30/390–4800** • gay-friendly • full brkfst • kids/pets ok • WiFi

Pension Elegia Niebuhrstr 74 (at Savignyplatz) **49–30/4980–7220** • gay/straight • some shared baths

BARS

Blond Eisenacher Str 3a (at Fuggerstr, U-Nollendorfplatz) **49–30/6640–3947** • 10am-2am, from 2pm wknds • gay/straight • food served • WiFi

Eldorado Motzstr 20 (U-Nollendorfplatz) **49–30/8431–6901** • 24hrs • mostly gay men • food served • music bar • terrace

HarDie's Kneipe Ansbacherstr 29 (in Wittenberplatz) **49–30/2363–9841** • noon-midnight, till 2am wknds • mostly gay men • cafe/pub

Heile Welt Motzstrasse 5 **49–30/2191–7507** • 6pm-4am • popular • lesbians/gay men

Incognito Hohenstauffenstr 53 (off Luther Str, U-Viktoria Luise Platz) **49–30/2191–6300** • 5pm-4am • lesbians/gay men • trangender-friendly

Kumpelnest 3000 Lützowstr 23 (at Potsdamer Str, U-Kurfürstenstr) **49–30/261–6918** • 5pm-5am, till 8am Fri-Sat • popular wknds • gay-friendly • cocktail bar • dancing/DJ • transgender-friendly • young crowd

Nah-Bar Kalkreuthstr 16 **49–30/3150–3062** • opens 2pm, from 5pm Sat • mostly women • games nights & DJ some nights

Neues Ufer Haupstrasse 157 (U-Bahn Kleistpark) **49–30/7895–7900** • 11am-2am, clsd wknds • lesbians/gay men • older crowd

Storks Kleiststrasse 7 **49–30/2362–4700** • 10pm-late, 24hrs wknds • mostly gay men • small bar & bistro

Vielharmonie **49–30/3064–7302** • 6pm-close • mostly gay men • food served

NIGHTCLUBS

Propaganda Nollendorfplatz 5 (at Goya Theater) • 2nd Sat only • mostly gay men • dancing/DJ • drag shows

CAFES

Begine Potsdamer Str 139 (at Bülowstr) **49–30/215–1414** • meeting point for women

Cafe Berio Maaßenstr 7 (at Winterfeldtstr, U-Nollendorfplatz) **49–30/216–1946** • 11am-midnight, from 8am wknds • popular • brkfst all day • also bar • seasonal terrace • wheelchair access

Cafe Savigny Grolmanstr 53–54 (at Savignyplatz) **49–30/4470–8386** • 9am-midnight • artsy crowd • full bar • terrace

Men & Media Nollendorfstr 23 **49–30/2191–7524** • noon-midnight • gay cybercafe

PositHiv Cafe 49–30/216–8654 • 3pm-11pm, from 6pm Sat, clsd Mon • PWA's and their friends • wheelchair access

RESTAURANTS

Diodata Goltzstrasse 51 49–30/2191–7884 • 11am-11pm, 10am-3pm Sun • Viennese

Fritz & Co Wittenbergplatz • organic snack bar • look for the rainbow flags

Gnadenbrot Martin-Luther-Str 20a 49–30/2196–1786 • 3pm-1am • cheap & good

Ma Vie Motzstrasse 28 49–30/2363–1200 • 8am-close • German bistro

More Motzstrasse 28 (at Martin-Lutherstrasse) 49–30/2363–5702 • 9am-midnight • popular

Sissi Motzstr 34 49–30/2101–8101 • great Austrian food, terrace and location

ENTERTAINMENT & RECREATION

Xenon Kino Kolonmenstr 5-6 49–30/7800–1530 • gay & lesbian cinema

Berlin—Outer

ACCOMMODATIONS

Artemisia Women's Hotel Brandenburgischestr 18 (at Konstanzerstr) 49–30/873–8905, 49–30/869–9320 • the only hotel for women in Berlin • a real bargain • quiet rooms • bar • sundeck w/ an impressive view • some shared baths • nonsmoking rooms available

Charlottenburger Hof Stuttgarter Platz 14 (at Wilmersdorfer Str) 49–30/329–070 • gay-friendly • centrally located • also cafe & bar open 24hrs

BARS

Himmelreich Simon Dach Str 36 (off Warschauer Str, in Friedrichshain, U-Frankfurter Tor) 49–30/2936–9292 • from 7pm Mon-Fri, 2pm-close wknds • lesbians/ gay men • women's night Tue

Silver Future Weserstr 206 (Neukölln) 49–30/7563–4987 • 2pm-2am, till 3am Th-Sat

NIGHTCLUBS

Die Busche Warschauer Platz 18 49–30/296–0800 • 10pm-5am, till 7am Fri-Sat, clsd Tue & Th • popular • lesbians/ gay men • dancing/DJ • live shows • terrace • cover charge

Mermaids Falckensteinstr 47 (at Comet Club) • 10pm 3rd Sat, May-Oct only • mostly women • dancing/DJ • also between parties on the 2nd Fri at Hafenbar Marianne Mariannenstr 6

CAFES

Schrader's Malplaquetstr 16b (at Utrechter Str, Wedding) 49–30/4508–2663 • also bar • gay-owned

RESTAURANTS

Cafe Rix Karl-Marx-Str 141 (in Neükolln) 49–30/686–9020 • 9am-midnight • Mediterranean • plenty veggie • also bar

Kurhaus Korsakow Grunbergerstrasse 81 (in Friedrichshain) 49–30/5473–7786 • 5pm-close, from 9am wknds, clsd Mon

IRELAND

Dublin

INFO LINES & SERVICES

AA 105 Capel St (at Outhouse) 353–1/873–4999 • 6pm Tue & 7:45pm Fri

Dublin Lesbian Line 353–1/872–9911 • 7pm-9pm Mon & Th

Gay Switchboard Dublin 353–1/872–1055 • 7pm-9pm, 4pm-8pm wknds

Outhouse 105 Capel St 353–1/873–4999 • LGBT community center, cafe, library, meetings

ACCOMMODATIONS

The Clarence 6-8 Wellington Quay 353–1/407–0800 • gay-friendly • owned by Bono & The Edge of U2 • kids ok • WiFi • wheelchair access

The Dylan Eastmoreland Place 353–1/660–3000 • gay/ straight • restaurant & bar

Fitzwilliam Hotel St Stephen's Green 353–1/478–7000 • gay-friendly • bar & restaurant

The Merchant House 8 Eustace St (Temple Bar Area) 353–1/633–4477 • gay/ straight • WiFi • gay-owned

Waterloo House 8-10 Waterloo Rd 353–1/660–1888 • 5-star hotel • gay/ straight • restaurant & bar

BARS

The Dragon 64-45 S Great Georges St 353–1/478–1590 • 5pm-11:30pm, till 2:30am Th-Sat, till 11pm Sun • lesbians/ gay men • dancing/DJ

Front Lounge 33 Parliament St 353–1/670–4112 • noon-11:30pm, till 2am Sat • popular • lesbians/ gay men • dancing/DJ • transgender-friendly • karaoke

The George aka Bridies 87 S Great George St 353–1/677–6943 • 12:30pm-2:30am, till 11:30pm Mon-Tue • popular • lesbians/ gay men • dancing/DJ • drag shows • karaoke

Panti Bar 7-8 Capel St 353–1/874–0710 • 5pm-close • lesbians/ gay men • dancing/DJ • food • drag shows • wheelchair access

NIGHTCLUBS

Glitz St. Stephen's Green Centre (Dandelion Nightclub) 353–1/727–3874 • 11pm–3am Tue only • lesbians/ gay men • dancing/DJ

Mother Exchange St (at Copper Alley, Arlington Hotel) • 10:30pm Sat only • lesbians/ gay men • dancing/DJ

Nimhneach 41 Middle Abbey St (at The Academy) 353–1/877–9999 • gay/ straight • fetish & BDSM party • strict dress code • call or see www.nimhneach.ie for dates

Prhomo 64-45 S Great Georges St (at Dragon) • 10:30pm Th only • lesbians/ gay men • dancing/DJ

CAFES

Irish Film Institute Bar & Restaurant 6 Eustace St (in Temple Bar) 353–1/679–5744 • lunch & dinner • next to independent cinema • light meals • plenty veggie

Lovinspoon Cafe 13 N Frederick St 353–1/804–7604 • 7am-6pm, clsd Sun (except summers)

RESTAURANTS

Brasserie Sixty6 66 S Great Georges St 353–1/400–5878 • brkfst, lunch, dinner, wknd brunch • meat & seafood • WiFi

La Cave 28 S Anne St 353–1/679–4409 • 12:30pm-close, from 6pm Sun • French

Dublin

LGBT PRIDE:
June. web: www.dublinpride.ie.

ANNUAL EVENTS:
March - St. Patrick's Day 353–1/676–3205, web: www.stpatricksday.ie.
May - Dublin Gay Theatre Festival, web: www.gaytheatre.ie.

CITY INFO:
Dublin Tourism 353–1/605–7700, 353–1/437-0969, web: www.visit-dublin.com.

BEST VIEW:
Crossing the River Liffey on the Ha'Penny Bridge, or on the ferry to Holyhead.

WEATHER:
Wet and mild, with summers averaging in the 60ºs and winters in the 40ºs. Frequent rain keeps the Emerald Isle green.

TRANSIT:
Dublin Bus 353–1/873–4222, web: www.dublinbus.ie.
DART (Dublin Area Rapid Transport) 353–1/703–3504, web: www.irishrail.ie.

ATTRACTIONS:
Book of Kells 353–1/896-1661, web: www.bookofkells.ie.
Guinness Storehouse 353–1/408–4800, web: www.guinness-storehouse.com.
The Hugh Lane Gallery 353–1/222–5550, web: www.hughlane.ie.
James Joyce Centre 353-1/878-8547, web: www.jamesjoyce.ie.
Kilmainham Gaol 353–1/453–5984, web: www.heritageireland.ie.
Malahide Castle 353–1/846–2184, web: www.malahidecastle.com.
National Botanic Gardens 353–1/804-0300, web: www.botanicgardens.ie.
Phoenix Park.
St. Michan's Church (mummies!) 353–1/872–4154.

The Chameleon 1 Lower Fownes St **353–1/671–0362** • 5pm-11pm, from 3pm Sun, clsd Mon • Indonesian

Cornucopia 19 Wicklow **353–1/677–7583** • 8:30am-9pm, till 10:30pm Sat, from noon Sun • affordable vegetarian

L' Ecrivain 109A Lower Baggot St **353–1/661–1919** • lunch Mon-Fri, dinner Mon-Sat, clsd Sun • also piano bar • reservations recommended

Eden Meeting House Square (entrance on Sycamore) **353–1/670–5372** • lunch & dinner, wknd brunch • patio dining

Fire Restaurant Mansion House, Dawson St **353–1/676–7200** • 5:30pm-close, noon-3pm jazz lunch Sat, clsd Sun

FXB Crow St **353–1/671–1248** • 5:30pm-close • steak & seafood

Gruel 68A Dame St **353–1/670–7119** • lunch & dinner

Halo Ormond Quay (in the Morrison Hotel) **353–1/878–2400** • Fri & Sat dinner • creative fusion food • upscale • vegetarian dishes • reservations required

Juice 73-83 S Great Georges St (across from the Globe) **353–1/475–7856** • lunch & dinner, wknd brunch • vegan/vegetarian

Just Off Francis 78 Thomas St **353–1/473–8807** • 11am-11pm, till 9pm Sat-Sun

Odessa 14 Dame Court **353–1/670–7634** • lunch & dinner, wknd brunch • local hot spot • gay/ straight • also nightclub with drag shows

Shack 24 E Essex St **353–1/679–0043** • lunch & dinner

Town Bar & Grill 21 Kildare St **353–1/662–4800** • lunch & dinner, Sun brunch • Italian

Trocadero 4 Saint Andrew St **353–1/677–5545** • 5pm-midnight, clsd Sun

The Winding Stair Restaurant 40 Lower Ormond Quay **353–1/872–7320** • lunch & dinner • Irish • young crowd • also bookshop

ENTERTAINMENT & RECREATION

Irish Queer Archive 2 Kildare St (National Library of Ireland)

BOOKSTORES

Chapters Bookstore Ivy House, Parnell St **353–1/872–3297** • LGBT section

The Winding Stair Bookshop 40 Lower Ormond Quay **353–1/872–7320** • 10am-7pm, til 8pm Th-Sat, from noon Sun • also restaurant • young crowd

PUBLICATIONS

GCN (Gay Community News) Unit 2 Scarlet Row, Essex St W, Temple Bar, 8 **353–1/671–0939, 353–1/671–9076** • monthly LGBT newspaper • many resources

ITALY

Rome

Note: M°=Metro station

INFO LINES & SERVICES

Circolo di Cultura Omosessual Mario Mieli Via Efeso 2a (M° San Paolo) **39–06/541–3985 (HELP LINE)** • 4pm-7pm Mon-Fri • switchboard, meetings & discussion groups

Gay Help Line **800/713–713** • 4pm-8pm, clsd Sun

ACCOMMODATIONS

58 Le Real de Luxe Via Cavour 58, 4th flr (near Colosseum) **39–06/482–3566, 0039/347–182–9387 (CELL)** • gay/ straight • B&B inn • kids ok • nonsmoking • WiFi • wheelchair access

Albergo Del Sole al Pantheon Piazza della Rotonda 63 **39–06/678–0441** • gay-friendly • 4-star hotel • jacuzzi • kids ok

Ares Rooms Via Domenichino 7 **39–06/474–4525, 39–340/278–1248 (CELL)** • gay-friendly • some shared baths

B&B In And Out Rome Via Arco del Monte (at Viale Trastevere) **39–339/784–0653** • gay/ straight • in 18th-c palace • kids/ pets ok • nonsmoking • WiFi • wheelchair access • lesbian-owned

Best Place Via Turati 13 **39–329/213–2320** • lesbians/ gay men • reservations required

Bologna B&B 6 Piazza Bologna (at Via Sambucuccio D'Alando) **39–06/4424–0244, 39/34781–04781 (CELL)** • gay/ straight • central location • some shared baths • kids/ pets ok

Claridge Hotel Via Liegi 62 **39–06/845–441** • gay-friendly • near Borghese park • gym w/ sauna & Turkish bath

Daphne Veneto Via di San Basilio 55 **39–06/8745–0086** • gay-friendly • small, cozy inn in heart of historical Rome • kids ok • nonsmoking • also Daphne Trevi at Via degli Avignonesi 20

Discover Roma Via Castelfidardo 50 **39–06/4470–3154** • lesbians/gay men • woman-owned

Domus International 39–06/6889–2918 • gay/straight • short-term apt rentals in the heart of Rome • kids/pets ok • weekly rates

Domus Valeria B&B Via del Babuino 96, Apt 14 (Spanish Square) **39–339/232–6540** • lesbians/gay men • shared baths • WiFi • gay-owned

Franklin Via Rodi 29 **39–06/3903–0165** • gay-friendly • music-themed hotel w/ CD library

Gaspare B&B Via Balilla 16 **39–06/328–833–3486** • lesbians/gay men • WiFi

Gayopen B&B Via dello Statuto 44, Apt 18 (at Via Merulana, Piazza Vittorio) **39–06/482–0013** • gay/straight • B&B • full brkfst • kids/pets ok • lesbian & gay-owned

Hotel Altavilla Via Principe Amedeo 9 **39–06/474–1186** • gay-friendly • pets ok • also bar

Hotel Derby Via Vigna Pozzi 7 (Largo delle Sette Chiese) **39–06/513–4955, 39–06/513–6978** • gay-friendly • small hotel in heart of Rome • kids/pets ok • wheelchair access

Hotel Edera Via A Poliziano 75 **39–06/7045–3888** • gay-friendly • WiFi

Rome

WHERE THE GIRLS ARE:

Discussing politics at a cafe, or dancing at one of the one-nighters that make up lesbian nightlife in Rome. Visit the bulletin board at the Libreria Babele or the Circolo Mario Mieli center for the latest events.

LGBT PRIDE:

June/July. web: www.romapride.it.

ANNUAL EVENTS:

June-September - Gay Village, web: www.gayvillage.it.

CITY INFO:

Comune di Rome 39-06/060–606, web: www.comune.roma.it.
Enjoy Rome 39–6/445–1843, web: www.enjoyrome.com. Via Marghera 8a.

WEATHER:

Late summer is hot and humid. Winter is mild but rainy. The best times to visit Rome are late spring and early fall.

ATTRACTIONS:

Baths of Caracalla 39–06/3996-7700 or 39-06/574-5748, web: www.operaroma.it.
Campo dei Fiori.
Capitoline Museums 39–06/8205–9127, web: www.museicapitolini.org.
Colosseum 39–06/3996-7700.
Galleria Borghese 39–06/328–10, web: www.galleriaborghese.it.
Pantheon 39–06/6830–0230.
Roman Forum 39–06/3996-7700.
Spanish Steps.
St. Peter's.
Trevi Fountain.
The Vatican and Vatican Museums (includes National Etruscan Museum, Sistine Chapel, and Raphael Rooms) 39–06/6988–4341, web: www.vatican.va.

TRANSIT:

Taxi stands are located in several popular piazzas. Only hire official yellow or white taxis. You can also call 3570 for pick-up service.
ATAC general info: 800/431–784 (in Rome), tourist lines: 39-06/4695–2284, web: www.atac.roma.it.

Hotel Labelle Via Cavour 310 **39-06/679-4750** • lesbians/ gay men • near the Roman Forum

Hotel Malu Via Principe Amedeo 85/a **39-06/9603-1250** • gay-friendly • WiFi • near Termini Station

Hotel Scott House Via Gioberti 30 **39-06/446-5379** • gay-friendly

Hotel Welcome Piram Via Amendola 7 **39-06/4890-1248** • lesbians/ gay men • hot tubs

Nicolas Inn Via Cavour 295 (at Via dei Serpenti) **39-06/9761-8483, 39-338/937-8387** • gay-friendly • elegant rooms located near the Colosseum & Roman Forum • nonsmoking • WiFi • native English speaker

Orsa Maggiore for Women Via San Francesco di Sales 1/a (at Via della Lungara) **39-06/689-3753** • women-only • inside 16th-c former convent • nonsmoking

Pensione Ottaviano Via Ottaviano 6 **39-06/3973-8138** • gay-friendly • in quiet area near St Peter's Square • hostel

The Rainbow B&B Viale Giulio Cesare 151 **39-06/347-507-0344 (CELL), 39-06/348-3343689** • lesbians/ gay men • WiFi

Relais le Clarisse Via Cardinale Merry del Val 20 (at Viale Trastevere) **39-06/5833-4437** • gay/ straight • nonsmoking • WiFi • jacuzzis • Mediterranean garden • on historic site in central Rome • lesbian-owned

Roman Reference Via dei Capocci 94 **39-06/4890-3612** • gay-friendly • apts • kids ok

Sandy Hostel Via Cavour 136 **39-06/4884-4585** • gay-friendly • great location near Colosseum, Roman Forum & Spanish Steps

Scalinata di Spagna Piazza Trinità dei Monti 17 (M° Piazza di Spagna) **39-06/6994-0896, 39-06/679-3006 (BOOKING #)** • gay-friendly • roof garden • kids/ pets ok • nonsmoking • WiFi

Valadier Via della Fontanella 15 **39-06/361-1998** • gay-friendly • 4-star hotel • kids ok • 2 restaurants & piano bar • WiFi

www.romecityapartments.com Via Quintino Sella 23 (at Via Boncompagni) **39-06/4201-6891, 39-34/7440-8267** • gay-friendly • wide range of central apts in Rome from budget to luxury for tourist & business stays • nonsmoking

BARS

Coming Out Via San Giovanni in Laterano 8 (near Colosseum) **39-06/700-9871** • 5pm-2am • popular • lesbians/ gay men • transgender-friendly • food served • live music Th • karaoke • lesbian-owned

Garbo Vicolo di Santa Margherita 1a (in Trastevere, Tram 8) **39-06/581-2766, 39-34/9815-1446** • 10pm-3am, clsd Mon • lesbians/ gay men • cocktail bar • food served • gay-owned

Il Giardino dei Ciliegi Via dei Fienaroli 4 **39-06/580-3423** • 5pm-2am, from 1pm Sun • lesbians/ gay men • tea salon

NIGHTCLUBS

L' Alibi Via di Monte Testaccio 40-44 (M° Piramide) **39-06/574-3448** • 11pm-4am, clsd Mon-Tue • popular • lesbians/ gay men • dancing/DJ • theme nights • live shows • rooftop garden in summer • young crowd

Amigdala Via delle Conce 14 (at Rising Love) • 2nd & 4th Sat only • lesbians/ gay men • dancing/DJ • electronica & queer culture

Black Betty **39-347/244-5810** • lesbians/ gay men • irregular party • dancing/DJ • live shows • call or see www.blackbetty.it for time & location • "the gay side of R 'n' B"

Frutta e Verdura Via Placido Zurla 68-70 (in Casilina) **39-347/244-6721 (ENGLISH), 39-348/879-7063 (ITALIAN)** • 4:30am-10am Sat-Sun & public holiday evenings • lesbians/ gay men • dancing/DJ

Gorgeous Via del Commercio 36 (at Alpheus) **39-06/574-7826** • 10pm-5am Sat • lesbians/ gay men • dancing/DJ

Muccassassina via di Portonaccio 212 (at Qube) **39-06/541-3985** • 10:30pm-5am Fri only (Sept-June) • popular • lesbians/ gay men • dancing/DJ • live shows • young crowd • cover charge

Venus Rising Via Libetta 13 **39-06/574-8277** • last Sun only • special events for women • check www.venusrising.it for upcoming parties

CAFES

Oppio Caffè Via delle Terme di Tito 72 **39-06/474-5262, 39-347/510-8594 (CELL)** • brkfst, lunch & dinner • open 24hrs in Aug • popular • lesbians/ gay men • full bar • live shows • terrace w/ great view

RESTAURANTS

Asino Cotto Ristorante Via dei Vascellari 38 (in Travestere, Tram 8) **39–06/589–8985** • lunch & dinner, clsd Mon • creative gourmet Mediterranean • reservations required • gay-owned

La Carbonara Via Panisperna 214 **39–06/482–5176** • lunch & dinner, clsd Sun • classic Roman cuisine since 1906

Città in Fiore Via Cavour 269 **39–06/482–4874** • lunch Th-Mon, dinner nightly • lesbians/ gay men • Chinese

Ditirambo Piazza della Cancelleria 74-75 (near Campo dei Fiori) **39–06/687–1626**

La Focaccia Via della Pace 11 **39–06/6880–3312** • 11am-2am • pizza

Gelateria San Crispino Via Panettiera 42 (near Trevi Fountain) **39–06/679–3924** • noon-12:30am, till 1:30am Fri-Sat, clsd Tue • gelato!

Mater Matuta Via Milano 47 (basement) **39–06/4782–5746** • lunch Mon-Fri, dinner nightly • also wine bar

Osteria del Pegno Vicolo Montevecchio 8 (Plaza Navona) **39–06/6880–7025** • lunch & dinner, clsd Wed winter • Italian • large pizza selection • wheelchair access

Ristorante da Dino Via dei Mille 10 (at Piazza Indipendenza) **39–06/491–425** • clsd Wed • family run Roman food at reasonable prices • near Termini Station

La Taverna di Edoardo II Vicolo Margana 14 **39–06/6994–2419** • 7:30pm-midnight, clsd Tue • lesbians/ gay men • full bar • wheelchair access

ENTERTAINMENT & RECREATION

Gay Village **39–06/753–8396** • gay summer festival

Through Eternity Via Astura 2/B **39–06/700–9336** • walking tours of Rome • gay-owned

RETAIL SHOPS

Hydra II Via Urbana 139 **39–06/489–7773** • leather, vinyl, clubwear, western, vintage & more

Souvenir via San Giovanni in Laterano 26 **39–06/7720–4593** • 9am-9pm • gay gifts

EROTICA

Alcova Piazza Sforza Cesarini 27 (at Corso Vittorio Emanuele II) **39–06/686–4118** • fetish shop

NETHERLANDS

AMSTERDAM

Amsterdam is divided into 5 regions:
Amsterdam—Overview
Amsterdam—Centrum
Amsterdam—Jordaan
Amsterdam—Rembrandtplein
Amsterdam—Outer

Amsterdam—Overview

INFO LINES & SERVICES

COC-Amsterdam Rozenstraat 14 (at Prinsengracht, in the Jordaan) **31–20/626–3087** • info line 10am-5pm, also cafe 8pm-11:30pm Wed-Fri • also sponsors women's parties at clubs around town • www.cocamsterdam.nl for info

Gay/ Lesbian Switchboard **31–20/623–6565** • noon-10pm, 4pm-8pm wknds • English spoken

Pink Point Westermarkt (Raadhuisstraat & Keizersgracht, in the Jordaan by Homomonument) **31–20/428–1070** • 10am-6pm • info on Homomonument & general LGBT info • friendly volunteers • queer souvenirs & gifts

ACCOMMODATIONS

Simply Amsterdam Apartments **31–20/620–6608** • gay-friendly • apts, studios, canal houses & houseboat • kids/ pets ok • gay-owned

NIGHTCLUBS

Fuckin' Pop Queers/ Ultrasexi/ Multisexi • lesbians/ gay men • monthly queer dance parties at different clubs around the city • check ultrasexi.com for details

Girlesque • mostly women (cool gay guys welcome) • huge quarterly dance parties • check www.girlesque.nl for info

UNK Admiraal de Ruijterweg 56 B (at Club 8) **31–20/685–1703** • 4th Sat only • lesbians/ gay men • electro/ queer dance party

Venus Freaks • "men-friendly women's dance parties" • check www.venusfreaks.nl for info

ENTERTAINMENT & RECREATION

The Anne Frank House Prinsengracht 263-267 (in the Jordaan) **31–20/556-7105 (RECORDED INFO), 31–20/556-7100** • the final hiding place of Amsterdam's most famous resident

Boom Chicago Leidseplein 12 (Leidseplein Theater) **31–20/423-0101 (TICKETS)** • English-language improv comedy • distributes free Boom! guide to Amsterdam

Gay and Lesbian History Walks 31–20/628-689-775 • mention Damron and you get 10% off

Homomonument Westermarkt (in the Jordaan) • moving sculptural tribute to lesbians & gays killed by Nazis

MacBike Stationsplein 12 (next to Centraal Station) **31–20/620-0985** • rental bikes & map for self-guided tour of Amsterdam's gay points of interest

De Pijp near Albert Cuypmarkt • gay-friendly neighborhood teeming w/ lots of interesting shops & restaurants

The van Gogh Museum Paulus Potterstr 7 (on the Museumplein) **31–20/570-5200** • 10am-6pm, till 10pm Fri • a must-see museum dedicated to this Dutch master painter • wheelchair access

PUBLICATIONS

COC Update 31–20/623-4596 • news & events calendar for COC

Amsterdam

LGBT PRIDE:
1st wknd in August, web: www.amsterdampride.nl.

ANNUAL EVENTS:
April 30 - Queen's Birthday/ Roze Wester Festival, web: www.gala-amsterdam.nl.
May - Memorial Day & Liberation Day.
June - Holland Festival, web: www.hollandfestival.nl.
October - Leather Pride, web: www.leatherpride.nl.

CITY INFO:
Amsterdam Tourism & Convention Board 31-20/201-8800, web: www.amsterdamtourist.nl. Visit their office directly opposite Centraal Station. Netherlands Board of Tourism, web: www.holland.com.

WEATHER:
Temperatures hover around freezing in the winter and rise to the mid-60°s in the summer. Rain is possible year-round.

ATTRACTIONS:
Anne Frank House 31–20/556-7105, web: www.annefrank.org.
Hermitage Amsterdam 31-20/530-7488, web: www.hermitage.nl.
Homomonument, web: www.homomonument.nl.
Jewish Historical Museum 31–20/531-0310, web: www.jhm.nl.
Rembrandt House 31–20/520-0400, web: www.rembrandthuis.nl.
Rijksmuseum 31–20/674-7000, web: www.rijksmuseum.nl.
Stedelijk Museum of Modern Art 31–20/573-2911, web: www.stedelijk.nl.
Vincent van Gogh Museum 31–20/570-5200, web: www.vangoghmuseum.nl.
Red District Tour, web: www.amster-damredlightdistricttour.com.

TRANSIT:
31–20/677-7777.
Can also be found at taxi stands on the main squares.
KLM Bus 31–20/653-4975.
GVB 31-20/460-6060, web: www.gvb.nl, or visit their office across from the Centraal Station (Stationsplein 10). Trams, buses & subway.

Gay News Amsterdam 31-20/679-1556 • bilingual paper • extensive listings

Gay & Night 31-20/788-1360 • free monthly bilingual entertainment paper w/ club listings

GK Magazine 31-499/39-10-00 • nat'l LGBT newspaper in Dutch w/ English summaries

Amsterdam—Centrum

ACCOMMODATIONS

Amsterdam B&B Barangay 31-6/2504-5432 • gay/ straight • 1777 town house • near tourist attractions • full brkfst • nonsmoking • WiFi • gay-owned

Amsterdam Central B&B Oudebrugsteeg 6-II (at Warmoesstraat) 31-62/445-7593 • lesbians/ gay men • B&B apts in 16th-c guesthouse • WiFi • full brkfst • gay-owned

Bulldog Oudezijds Voorburgwal 220 (at St Jansstraat) 31-20/620-3822 • gay-friendly • hostel in Red Light District • dorms & private rooms • brkfst included • coffeeshop & lounge/ bar • WiFi • wheelchair access

Cosmos Hostel Nieuwe nieuwstraat 17-1 (at NZ Voorburgwal) 31-20/625-2438 • gay-friendly • hostel in 17th-c bldg formerly a hotel • WiFi • no curfew • ages 18-35 only • nonsmoking

Crowne Plaza Amsterdam City Centre NZ Voorburgwal 5 31-20/620-0500, 877/227-6963 (US#) • gay-friendly • pool • restaurant & bar • wheelchair access

Mauro Mansion Geldersekade 16 (at OZ Kolk)

NH City Centre Hotel Spuistraat 288-292 31-20/420-4545 • gay-friendly • kids/ pets ok • WiFi • wheelchair access

NH Grand Hotel Krasnapolsky Dam 9 (at Warmoesstraat) 31-20/554-9111 • gay-friendly • full-service hotel • in the city center opposite Royal Palace • WiFi • wheelchair access

Palace B&B Spuistraat 224 31-6/3169-3878 • gay/ straight • 1794 bldg w/ indoor garden • nonsmoking • WiFi • gay-owned

Victoria Hotel Amsterdam Damrak 1-5 (opposite Centraal Station) 31-20/623-4255, 800/777-1700 (US#) • gay-friendly • 4-star hotel • pool • gym • restaurants & bar • WiFi • wheelchair access

Winston Hotel Warmoesstraat 129 31-20/623-1380 • gay-friendly • hipster hotel • rockers & artists • popular bar • live DJs • gallery • some shared baths

BARS

De Barderij Zeedijk 14 (at OZ Kolk) 31-20/420-5132 • noon-1am, till 3am Fri-Sat • mostly gay men • large neighborhood bar/ brown café • older crowd

Cafe Mandje Zeedijk 63 (at Stormsteeg) 31-20/622-5375 • gay/ straight • originally opened in 1927 as Amsterdam's first gay bar by dyke-on-bike Bet van Beeren

De Engel Next Door Zeedijk 23-25 (at OZ Kolk) 31-20/427-6381 • 1pm-1am, till 3am Fri-Sat, clsd Mon-Tue • mostly gay men

De Engel van Amsterdam Zeedijk 21 (at OZ Kolk) 31-20/427-6381 • 1pm-1am, till 3am Fri-Sat • mostly gay men • patio

Getto Warmoesstraat 51 (at Niezel) 31-20/421-5151 • 4pm-1am, till 2am Fri-Sat, till midnight Sun, clsd Mon • popular • lesbians/ gay men • live DJs • also restaurant till 11pm • Sun brunch

Prik Spuistraat 109 31-20/320-0002 • 4pm-1am, till 3am Fri-Sat • lesbians/ gay men • food served • patio

NIGHTCLUBS

Club Stereo Jonge Roelensteeg 4 (at Kalvertstraat) 31-20/770-4037 • 7pm-1am, till 3am Fri-Sat • gay/ straight • dancing/DJ • live shows

CAFES

Dampkring Haarlemmerstraat 44 31-20/638-0705 • smoking coffeeshop • great fresh OJ

Gary's Late Night TT Vasumweg 260 31-20/637-3643 • noon-3am, till 4am Fri-Sat • popular • fresh muffins & bagels • organic fair-trade coffee

Puccini Bomboni Staalstraat 17 31-20/626-5474 • If you love chocolate, do we have a cafe for you!

RESTAURANTS

Cafe de Jaren Nieuwe Doelenstraat 20-22 31-20/625-5771 • 10am-1am, till 2am Fri-Sat • some veggie • full bar • terrace • young crowd

Cafe de Schutter Voetboogstraat 13-15 (upstairs) 31-20/622-4608 • noon-1am, till 3am Fri-Sat • popular local hangout • plenty veggie • full bar • terrace

Cafe Latei Zeedijk 143 (in Red Light District) **31–20/625–7485** • 8am-6pm, from 9am Sat, from 11am Sun • Indian food • great coffee hangout • WiFi

Greenwoods Singel 103 (near Dam Square) **31–20/623–7071** • English-style brkfst & tea snacks

Hemelse Modder Oude Waal 11 **31–20/624–3203** • 6pm-10pm • popular • lesbians/ gay men • French/ int'l • also full bar • wheelchair access • gay-owned

Kitsch Utrechtsestraat 42 **31–20/625–9251** • 6pm-close, clsd Sun • kitsch & disco

Krua Thai Staalstraat 22 **31–20/622–9533** • 5pm-10:30pm • terrace • wheelchair access • also at Spuistraat 90a, 620-0623 • full bar

Het Land van Walem Keizersgracht 449 **31–20/625–3544** • lunch & dinner • int'l • inexpensive • local crowd • canalside terrace • wheelchair access • lesbian-owned

Maoz Muntplein 1 **31–20/420–7435** • 11am-1am, till 3am wknds • vegetarian/ falafel

't Sluisje Torensteeg 1 **31–20/624–0813** • 6pm-close, clsd Mon-Wed • popular steak house • lesbians/ gay men • transgender-friendly • full bar (open later) • drag shows nightly

Song Kwae Kloveniersburgwal 14 (near Nieuwmarkt & Chinatown) **31–20/624–2568** • 1pm-10:30pm • Thai • full bar • terrace

Bookstores

The American Book Center Spui 12 **31–20/625–5537** • 10am-8pm, till 9pm Th, 11am-6:30pm Sun • large LGBT section • wheelchair access

Boekhandel Vrolijk Gay & Lesbian Bookshop Paleisstraat 135 (at Spuistraat, near Dam Square) **31–20/623–5142** • 10am-6pm, 11am-6pm Mon, 10am-5pm Sat, from 1pm Sun • LGBT books, videos & gadgets • also mail order

Retail Shops

Gays & Gadgets Spuistraat 44 **31–20/330–1461** • gifts, gadgets, clothing, cards

Magic Mushroom Spuistraat 249 **31–20/427–5765** • 11am-7pm, till 8pm Fri-Sat • "smartshop": magic mushrooms & more • also Singel 524, 31-20/422-7845

Gyms & Health Clubs

The Fitness & Health Garden Jodenbreestraat 158 **31–20/320–0233** • gay/ straight

Splash Looiersgracht 26-30 **31–20/624–8404** • gym & wellness center

Erotica

Absolute Danny Oudezijds Achterburgwal 78 (in the Red Light District) **31–20/421–0915** • 11am-9pm • upscale erotica • woman-owned

Black Body Spuistraat 44 **31–20/626–2553** • clsd Sun • rubber clothing specialists • leather • toys • DVDs • wheelchair access

Christine Le Duc Spui 6 **31–20/624–8265**

DeMask Zeedijk 64 **31–20/423–3090** • 11am-7pm, clsd Sun • rubber & leather clothing

Female & Partners Spuistraat 100 **31–20/620–9152** • 11am-6:30pm, 1pm-6pm Sun • fashions & toys for women

Amsterdam—Jordaan

Accommodations

Budget Hotel Clemens Amsterdam Raadhuisstraat 39 (at Herengracht) **31–20/624–6089** • gay-friendly • small hotel in Amsterdam's center • some shared baths • WiFi • woman-owned

Chic and Basic Amsterdam Herengracht 13-19 (at Brouwersgr) **31–20/522–2345** • gay-friendly • "the quiet hotel"

The Dylan Keizersgracht 384 (at Runstraat) **31–20/530–2010** • gay-friendly • sleep in high style • also restaurant

Hotel Acacia Lindengracht 251 (at Lijnbaansgr) **31–20/622–1460** • gay-friendly • "homey hotel in heart of Jordaan" • also self-catering studios & houseboat • WiFi

Hotel Brian Singel 69 (at Lijnbaanssteeg) **31–20/421–5841** • gay-friendly • bargain rooms • shared baths

Hotel Pulitzer Prinsengracht 315–331 (at Reestraat) **31–20/523–5235** • gay-friendly • occupies 24 17th-c buildings on 2 of Amsterdam's most picturesque canals

Hotel Rembrandt Centrum Herengracht 255 (at Hartenstraat) **31–20/622–1727** • gay/ straight • canalside hotel near Dam Square • nonsmoking rooms available

Maes B&B Herenstraat 26 (at Keizersgr) **31–20/427–5165** • gay/ straight • nonsmoking • WiFi • gay-owned

Marnixkade Canalview Apartments **31–6/1012–1296** • popular • lesbians/ gay men • fully furnished apts in 19th-c canal house on a quiet canal in heart of Jordaan • nonsmoking • WiFi • gay-owned

Sunhead of 1617 Herengracht 152 (at Leliegracht & Raadshuisstraat) **31–20/626–1809** • gay/ straight • B&B • full brkfst • kids/ pets ok • nonsmoking • also several canal apts • WiFi • gay-owned

BARS

Cafe de Gijs Lindengracht 249 (at Lijnbaansgr) **31–20/638–0740, 31–6/2537–3674** • 4pm-1am • 1st Wed of month hosts T&T, social gathering for transvestites & transsexuals, from 10pm

Saarein 2 Elandsstraat 119 (at Hazenstraat) **31–20/623–4901** • 4pm-1am, till 2am Fri-Sat, clsd Mon • mostly women • food served • brown cafe

NIGHTCLUBS

Jet Lounge Groen van Prinstererstraat 41 (3 blks W of Westerpark) **31–20/684–1126** • 6pm-1am, till 3am Fri-Sat, clsd Sun-Mon • gay/straight • dancing/DJ • live music

de Trut Bilderdijkstraat 165 (at Kinkerstraat) **31–20/612–3524** • 11pm-4am Sun only • lesbians/ gay men • hip underground dance party in legalized squat • alternative • young crowd

CAFES

Cafe 't Smalle Egelantiersgracht 12 **31–20/623–9617** • 10am-1am, till 2am wknds • brown cafe • full bar • outdoor seating

Lab111 Arie Biemondstraat 111 **31–20/616–9994** • noon-1am, till 3am Fri-Sat, lab turned cafe • lab turned cafe • live music

Rokerij Singel 8 **31–20/422–6643** • smoking coffeeshop • 3 other locations

RESTAURANTS

Bojo Lange Leidsedwarsstraat 49–51 (near Leidseplein) **31–20/622–7434** • 11am-9pm, from 4:30pm wknds • popular • Indonesian

De Bolhoed Prinsengracht 60 (at Tuinstr) **31–20/626–1803** • noon-10pm, from 11am Sat • vegetarian/ vegan

Burger's Patio 2e Tuindwarsstr 12 **31–20/623–6854** • 6pm-1am • Italian • plenty veggie

Foodism Oude Leliestraat 8 **31–20/627–6464** • noon-10pm, till 6pm wknds • great soups & sandwiches • funky & fun

Freud Spaarndammerstraat 424 **31–20/688–5548** • lunch & dinner, clsd Sun-Mon

Granada Leidsekruisstraat 13 **31–20/625–1073** • 5pm-close • Spanish • tapas • also bar • live music wknds

De Vliegende Schotel Nieuwe Lellestraat 162 **31–20/625–2041** • 4pm-11:30pm, kitchen till 10:45pm, so come early • vegetarian/ vegan • nonsmoking section

ENTERTAINMENT & RECREATION

De Looier Art & Antiques Market Elandsgracht 109 **31–20/624–9038, 31–20/427–4990** • 11am-5pm, clsd Fri

BOOKSTORES

Xantippe Unlimited Prinsengracht 290 **31–20/623–5854** • 1pm-6pm, from 10am Sat, noon-5pm Sun • women's bookstore • lesbian section • English titles • lesbian-owned

RETAIL SHOPS

Dare to Wear Buiten Oranjestraat 15 **31–20/686–8679** • piercing, jewelry & accessories

House of Tattoos Haarlemmerdijk 130c **31–20/330–9046** • 11am-6pm, from 1pm Sun • great tattoos, great people

SEX CLUBS

Sameplace Nassaukade 120 **31–20/475–1981** • gay/ straight • men only Mon • transgender-friendly • dancing/DJ • theme nights • darkroom

Amsterdam—Rembrandtplein

ACCOMMODATIONS

Amsterdam House 's Gravelandseveer 7 (at Kloveniersburgwal) **31–20/626–2577 (OFFICE), 31–20/624–6607 (HOTEL)** • gay-friendly • hotel, apts & houseboats

Dikker & Thijs Fenice Hotel Prinsengracht 444 (at Leidsestraat) **31–20/620–1212** • gay-friendly • 4-star hotel on canal • nonsmoking rooms • bar & restaurant

Eden Hotel Amstel 144 **31–20/530–7878** • gay-friendly • 3-star hotel • nonsmoking rooms • brasserie overlooking River Amstel • WiFi • wheelchair access

Hotel de l'Europe Nieuwe Doelenstraat 2-8 **31–20/531–1777** • gay-friendly • grand hotel on the River Amstel • fitness center • pool

Hotel Monopole Amstel 60 (at Kloveniersburgwal) **31–20/624–6271** • gay-friendly • centrally located • nonsmoking rooms available • kids ok • also Cafe Rouge

Hotel Orlando Prinsengracht 1099 (at Amstel River) **31–20/638–6915** • gay-friendly • beautifully restored 17th-c canal house • gay-owned

Hotel The Golden Bear Kerkstraat 37 (at Leidsestraat) **31–20/624–4785** • lesbians/ gay men • the oldest gay hotel in Amsterdam, since 1948 • WiFi • gay-owned

Hotel Waterfront Singel 458 (at Koningsplein) **31–20/421–6621** • gay-friendly • rooms & studios • brkfst • located in city's center

ITC Hotel Prinsengracht 1051 (at Utrechtsestraat) **31–20/623–0230, 31–20/623–1711** • lesbians/ gay men • 18th-c canal house • great location • also bar & lounge • WiFi • lesbian- & gay-owned

Seven Bridges Reguliersgracht 31 (at KeizersGracht) **31–20/623–1329** • gay-friendly • small & so elegant • canalside w/ view of 7 bridges (surprise!) • brkfst brought to you

Bars

Bump Kerkstraat 23 • 5pm-1am, till 3am wknds, clsd Mon-Tue • lesbians/ gay men • DJs

Cafe Rouge Amstel 60 (at Kloveniersburgwal) **31–20/420–9881** • 4pm-1am, till 3am wknds • mostly gay men • neighborhood bar

Chez Rene Amstel 50 (at Kloveniersburgwal) **31–20/420–3388** • 8pm-3am, till 4am Fri-Sat • lesbians/ gay men • lesbian-owned

Entre Nous Halvemaansteeg 14 (at Reguliersbreestr) **31–20/623–1700** • 9pm-3am, till 4am Fri-Sat • lesbians/ gay men • neighborhood bar

Eve Reguliersdwarsstraat 44 (at Geelvinckssteeg) **31–20/689–7070** • 4pm-1am, till 3am Fri-Sat • gay/ straight • dancing/DJ • hip 20-something crowd • also restaurant

Habibi Ana Lange Leidsedwarsstraat 93 **31–06/2192–1686** • 7pm-1am, till 3am Fri-Sat, clsd Mon-Tue • lesbians/ gay men • Arabian clientele • Arabian & int'l music • bellydancing shows wknds

Havana Reguliersdwarsstraat 17-19 • 2pm-1am, till 3am Fri-Sat • lesbians/ gay men • neighborhood bar

Hot Spot Cafe Amstel 102 (at Bakkersstr) **31–20/622–8335** • 9pm-3am, from 8pm Fri-Sun • mostly gay men • neighborhood bar

Ludwig II Reguliersdwarsstraat 37 (at St Jorisstraat, enter rear) **31–20/616–1181** • 2pm-1am, till 3am Fri-Sat • popular happy hour • mostly gay men • 3 bars • videos

Mankind Weteringstraat 60 (at Weteringschans) **31–20/638–4755** • noon-11pm, clsd Sun • mixed crowd • canalside terrace • food served till 8pm • Dutch/ English • WiFi

Reality Girlz Reguliersdwarsstraat 125 **31–20/639–3012** • 8pm-1am, till 3am Fri-Sat, clsd Mon-Tue • mostly women • neighborhood bar • mixed crowd

Soho Reguliersdwarsstraat 36 (at St Jorisstraat) **31–20/422–3312** • 5pm-3am, till 4am Fri-Sat • popular • lesbians/ gay men • young crowd • British pub 1st flr • lounge upstairs • happy hour 10pm-11pm

Taboo Reguliersdwarsstraat 45 **31–20/775–3963** • 6pm-3am, from 4pm wknds • lesbians/ gay men • neighborhood bar

Vivelavie Amstelstraat 7 (at Rembrandtplein) **31–20/624–0114** • 3pm-3am, till 4am Fri-Sat • mostly women

Nightclubs

Club Roque Amstel 178 (at Wagenstraat) **31–20/421–0900** • 11pm-5am clsd Sun-Tue • lesbians/ gay men • dancing/DJ

Studio 80 Rembrandtplein 17 (at Amstelstraat) **31–20/521–8333** • 9pm-5am Th-Sat • gay/ straight • dancing/DJ

Cafes

Betty, Too Reguliersdwarsstraat 29 (at Leidsestraat) • 10am-1am • occasional gay events

Downtown Coffeeshop Reguliersdwarsstr 31 (at Koningsplein) **31–20/622–9958** • 10am-8pm, till 10pm Fri-Sat • popular • mostly gay men • terrace open in summer

Happy Feelings Kerkstr 51 **31–20/423–1936** • 11am-midnight, till 1am Fri-Sat • smoking coffeeshop • publisher's choice

The Other Side Reguliersdwarsstr 6 (at Koningsplein) **31–72/625–5141** • 11am-1am • mostly gay men • smoking coffeeshop • gay-owned

Restaurants

Garlic Queen Reguliersdwarsstr 27 **31–20/422–6426** • 6pm-close, clsd Mon-Tue • even the desserts are made w/ garlic!

Golden Temple Utrechtsestraat 126 **31–20/626–8560** • brkfst, lunch & dinner • mix of Indian, Mexican & Mediterranean • oldest vegetarian & vegan restaurant in city • nonsmoking

De Huyschkaemer Utrechtsestraat 137 31–20/627–0575 • noon-1am, till 3am wknds

Rose's Cantina Reguliersdwarsstr 40 (near Rembrandtplein) **31–20/625–9797** • 5pm-11pm • popular • Tex-Mex • full bar

Saturnino Reguliersdwarsstr 5 31–20/639–0102 • noon-midnight • lesbians/gay men • Italian • full bar

EROTICA

Mail & Female Nieuwe Vijzelstraat 2, 1017 HT **31–20/623–3916** • erotic fashions & toys for women

Xarina Singel 416 **31–20/624–6383** • latex clothing & accessories

Amsterdam—Outer

ACCOMMODATIONS

Abba Budget Hotel Overtoom 122 (1st Constantijn Huygenstraat) **31–20/618–3058** • gay-friendly • brkfst buffet • free safety deposit boxes • "smoker"-friendly

Amsterdam B&B Roeterstraat 18 (at Nieuwe Achtergracht) **31–20/624–0174** • gay-friendly • full brkfst • powered by green energy • kids ok • nonsmoking • WiFi • gay-owned

Between Art & Kitsch Ruysdaelkade 75-2 (at Daniel Stalpertstraat) **31–20/679–0485** • gay-friendly • near museums • WiFi

Blue Moon B&B Weteringschans 123A (at Weteringstraat) **31–20/428–8800** • gay/straight • WiFi • gay-owned

Chico's Guesthouse Sint Willibrordusstraat 77 (at Van Woustraat & Ceintuurbaan, near Sarphatipark) **31–20/675–4241, 31–61/535–3056** • gay-friendly • in De Pijp

The Collector B&B De Lairessestr 46 hs (in museum area) **31–6/1101–0105 (CELL), 31–20/673–6779** • gay-friendly • B&B • full brkfst • WiFi • kids ok • gay-owned

Freeland Hotel Marnixstraat 386 (at Leidsegracht) **31–20/622–7511** • gay-friendly • 2-star hotel • full brkfst • WiFi • gay-owned

Hemp Hotel Frederiksplein 15 (at Achtergracht) **31–20/625–4425** • only in Amsterdam: sleep on a hemp mattress, eat a hemp roll (THC-free) for brkfst or drink hemp beer in the Hemp Temple bar

Hotel Aadam Wilhelmina Koninginneweg 169 (at Emmalaan) **31–20/662–5467** • gay-friendly • charming • full brkfst buffet • some shared baths

Hotel Arena Gravesandestraat 51 (at Mauritskade) **31–20/850–2400** • gay-friendly • huge hotel in former orphanage • popular nightclub in former chapel • WiFi • also restaurant & cafe-bar

Hotel Fita Jan Luijkenstraat 37 (at Van Baerlestraat) **31–20/679–0976** • small family-owned hotel • WiFi • nonsmoking

Hotel Kap Den Texstraat 5 **31–20/624–5908** • gay/ straight • bikes available to rent • also self-catering apt • gay-owned

Hotel Rembrandt Plantage Middenlaan 17 (at Plantage Parklaan) **31–20/627–2714** • gay-friendly • beautiful brkfst room w/ 17th-c art • near Rembrandtplein • nonsmoking

Hotel Sander Jacob Obrechtstraat 69 (at N Maesstraat) **31–20/662–7574** • gay-friendly • also 24hr bar & coffee lounge

Kerstin's B&B Kwakerstraat 2h (at Bilderdijkkade) **31–20/612–6969** • gay-friendly • B&B & self-catering apt • overlooking new canal • nonsmoking • kids ok

Lilianne's Home Sarphatistraat 119 (at Roeterstraat, at Weesperplein Station) **31–20/627–4006** • women only • brkfst • shared bath • nonsmoking • also apt

Lloyd Hotel Oostelijke Handelskade 34 **31–20/561–3636, 31–20/561–3604** • gay-friendly • hip hotel for all budgets in cool Eastern Harbor area • WiFi

NL Hotel Nassaukade 368 (at B Toussaintstraat) **31–20/689–0030** • gay/straight • WiFi • gay-owned

Prinsen Hotel Vondelstraat 36-38 (near Leidseplein) **31–20/616–2323** • gay-friendly • also bar

Stayokay Amsterdam Vondelpark Zandpad 5 (at Stadhouderskade) **31–20/589–8996** • gay-friendly • inside Vondelpark • bar & restaurant • WiFi • wheelchair access

BARS

Garbo Amsteldijk 223 (at Miranda Paviljoen & Brasseriede Lakey) **31–20/644–5768** • 4pm-midnight 1st Sat only • women only • dancing/DJ • dinner also served

NIGHTCLUBS

Flirtation Oostelijke Handelskade 4 (at Piet Heinkade, at Club Panama) • bi-monthly women's dance party • check local listings for next event

Melkweg Lijnbaansgracht 234 (at Leidseplein) **31–20/531–8181** • gay/ straight • popular live-music venue • restaurant • theater • cinema • gallery

RESTAURANTS

An Weteringschans 76 (in Museum Quarter) **31–20/624–4672** • dinner only, clsd Sun-Mon • Japanese • patio • cash only

De Peper Overtoom 301 **31–20/412–2954** • 7pm-close Sun, Tue & Th-Fri • sliding scale, volunteer-run vegan cafe • also monthly queer & women's parties

De Waaghals Frans Halsstraat 29 **31–20/679–9609** • 5pm-9:30pm, clsd Mon • int'l vegetarian

SCOTLAND

Edinburgh

INFO LINES & SERVICES

LGBT Centre for Health & Wellbeing 9 Howe St **44–0131/523–1100**

ACCOMMODATIONS

94DR 94 Dalkeith Rd **44–131/662–9286** • gay/ straight • guesthouse central location • full brkfst • WiFi • gay-owned

Ardmor House 74 Pilrig St (at Leith Walk) **44–0131/554–4944** • lesbians/ gay men • Victorian • kids/ pets ok • nonsmoking • wheelchair access • gay-owned

Averon Guest House 44 Gilmore Pl **44–0131/229–9932** • gay-friendly • comfortable guesthouse in city center • full brkfst • nonsmoking

Ayden Guest House 70 Pilrig St **44–0131/554–2187** • gay/ straight • guesthouse in quiet, central location • in-house chef cooks fabulous brkfst • WiFi • lesbian-owned

Garlands 48 Pilrig St (off Leith Walk) **44–0131/554–4205** • gay/ straight • Georgian town house • full brkfst • nonsmoking • WiFi • gay-owned

Six Mary's Place Guest House Raeburn Pl (Stockbridge) **44–0131/332–8965** • gay-friendly • B&B • vegetarian brkfst • nonsmoking

The Witchery by the Castle Castlehill (The Royal Mile) **44–0131/225.5613** • gay-friendly • B&B • full brkfst • theatrical suites at the gates of Edinburgh castle • also restaurant

BARS

The Auld Hoose 23-25 St Leonards St **44–0131/668–2934** • 11:30am-1am, from 12:30pm Sun • gay/ straight • neighborhood bar • food served

Cafe Habana 22 Greenside Pl **44–0131/558–1270** • 1pm-1am • lesbians/ gay men • theme nights • popular pre-clubbing • WiFi

Cafe Nom de Plume 60 Broughton St **44–0131/478–1372** • 11am-11pm, till 1am Fri-Sat • food served

CC Bloom's 23 Greenside Pl (at Leith Walk) **44–0131/556–9331** • 6pm-3am, from 7pm Sun • mostly gay men • dancing/DJ • live shows • theme nights

Deep Blue 1 Barony St (below Blue Moon) **44–0131/556–2788** • 4pm-1am • popular • lesbians/ gay men • food served • gay-owned

Frenchies Bar 89 Rose Street Lane N **44–0131/225–6967** • 2pm-1am • lesbians/ gay men • neighborhood bar

Fur Burger Picardy Pl (at GHQ) • 11pm 2nd Fri only • mostly women • dancing/DJ

Newtown Bar 26-B Dublin St **44–0131/538–7775** • noon-1am, till 2am Fri-Sat • lesbians/ gay men • dancing/DJ • food served • WiFi

Planet 6 Baxter's Pl (at Leith Walk) **44–0131/556–5551** • 4pm-1am • lesbians/gay men • popular • food served

Priscilla's 17 Albert Pl (Leith Walk) **44–0798/659–1695** • noon-1am, from 5pm Sat • mostly gay men • karaoke • cabaret • drag shows

The Regent 2 Montrose Terrace **44–0131/661–8198** • 11am-1am, from 12:30pm Sun • mostly gay men • food served • WiFi

The Street 2 Picardy Pl **44–0131/556–4272** • 4pm-1am, from noon wknds • gay/ straight • dancing/DJ • food served • patio

Theatre Royal Bar 25-27 Greenside Pl **44–0131/557–2142** • noon-midnight, clsd Sun • gay-friendly • good ale

NIGHTCLUBS

DV8 Fetish Club 258 Morrison St (in Spiders Web basement) **44–0131/228–1949** • gay/ straight • monthly fetish party • private club

GHQ 4 Picardy Pl **44–0131/550–1780** • 9pm-3am • lesbians/ gay men • dancing/DJ • theme nights

Luvely Faith Nightclub, 207 Cowgate 44-0131/557-4656 • 10:30pm-5am 1st Sat only • gay/ straight • dancing/DJ

Velvet 6 Blair St (at The Speakeasy) 44-0131/558-3758 • 10:30pm-3am 3rd Sat • mostly women • dancing/DJ

CAFES

Blue Moon 1 Barony St 44-0131/556-2788 • 11am-midnight, from 10am wknds • popular • lesbians/ gay men • food served • gay-owned

Cafe Lucia 13-29 Nicolson St (next to Edinburgh Festival Theatre) 44-0131/662-1112 • 10am-10pm

Filmhouse Cafe 88 Lothian Rd 44-0131/229-5932, 44-0131/228-2688 (CINEMA) • 10am-11:30pm, till 12:30am • beer/ wine • also cinema

RESTAURANTS

Black Bo's Vegetarian Restaurant 57/61 Blackfriars St 44-(0)131/557.6136 • 6pm-10pm, also bar till 1am • full bar • vegetarian

Henderson's 94 Hanover St 44-0131/225.2131 • organic vegetarian • also deli & cafe • beer/ wine

Edinburgh

LGBT PRIDE:

June. Alternates between Edinburgh and Glasgow (odd years in Edinburgh), web: www.pride-scotia.org.

ANNUAL EVENTS:

August - Edinburgh Fringe Festival 44-0131/226-0026, web: www.edfringe.com.

October - Glasgay! annual celebration of queer culture (in Glasgow) 44-141/552-7575, web: www.glasgay.co.uk.

CITY INFO:

44-0131/625-8625, web: www.edinburgh.org.

BEST VIEW:

Hike from the Dunsapie Loch parking lot to the top of Arthur's Seat (an extinct volcano). Or take the steps from Waterloo Place, at the E end of Princes St, to Calton Hill. If you're feeling ambitious, continue up the spiral stairs to the top of Nelson Monument.

WEATHER:

60°s-70°s in summer, with nice, long days. Winter brings temps in the 40°s. Be prepared for rain year-round.

ATTRACTIONS:

Camera Obscura, web: www.camera-obscura.co.uk.
Edinburgh Castle, web: www.edinburghcastle.gov.uk.
Mansfield Traquair Centre murals, web: www.mansfieldtraquair.org.uk.
Nat'l Galleries, web: www.national-galleries.org.
Nat'l Museum of Scotland, web: www.nms.ac.uk.
Nelson Monument.
Palace of Holyroodhouse, web: www.royalcollection.org.uk.
Princes St Gardens.
Scotch Whisky Experience, web: www.whisky-heritage.co.uk.

TRANSIT:

Central Taxis 44-0131/229-2468, web: www.taxis-edinburgh.co.uk.
Airlink 44-0131/555-6363, web: www.flybybus.com.
Lothian Buses 44-0131/555-6363, web: www.lothianbuses.com.

Tower Restaurant & Terrace National Museum of Scotland, Chambers St (at George IV Brigde) 44-(0)131/225.3003 • lunch & dinner • panoramic views of Edinburgh's castle & historic skyline • wheelchair access

Valvona & Crolla 19 Elm Row 44-0131/556-6066 • clsd Sun • oldest Italian deli in Scotland

ENTERTAINMENT & RECREATION

The Luvvies • LGBT community theatre company

BOOKSTORES

Bobbie's Bookshop 220 Morrison St 44-0131/538-7069 • 10am-5pm, clsd Sun

Word Power Books 43-45 W Nicolson St 44-0131/662-9112 • 10am-6pm, noon-5pm Sun • independent & radical • events

RETAIL SHOPS

Q Store 5 Barony St 44-0131/477-4756 • 11am-7pm Sat-Wed, till 6pm Sat, 1pm-5pm Sun • pride store

NATIONAL PUBLICATIONS

ScotsGay 44-0131/539-0666 • Scotland's premier magazine for lesbians, gays, bisexuals & friends, published monthly

EROTICA

Leather and Lace 8 Drummond St 44-0131/557-9413 • 10am-9pm, from noon Sun • toys, clothing & videos

SPAIN

Barcelona

Note: M°=Metro station

INFO LINES & SERVICES

Casal Lambda Verdaguer y Callís 10 (M° Drassanes) 34/93-319-5550 • 5pm-9pm • community center • cafe • archives • library • also publish magazine

Col-Lectiu Gai de Barcelona (CGB) 34/934-534-125 • staffed 7pm-9pm Mon-Sat • also publishes Info Gai

Coordinadora Gai Lesbiana Vicant d'Hongria 156, E-08014 34/900-601-601 • 7pm-9pm Mon-Fri, 6pm-8pm Sat • nat'l gay group

ACCOMMODATIONS

Barcelona City Centre 34/653-900-039 • mostly gay men • in Eixample District • kids/pets ok • WiFi • gay-owned

Beauty & the Beach B&B 34/93-266-0562 • exclusively gay, lesbians welcome • full brkfst • right across from gay nude beach • nonsmoking rooms (allowed on terrace) • WiFi • wheelchair access • gay-owned

California Hotel Rauric 14 (at Ferran, M° Liceu) 34/93-317-7766 • gay/ straight

Casa de Billy Barcelona Rambla Catalunya 85, Piso 5, Puerta 1 (at Mallorca) 34/93-426-3048 • gay/ straight • shared baths • full brkfst • nonsmoking • WiFi

Catalonia Albéniz Aragó 591–593 34/93-265-2626 • gay-friendly • WiFi • wheelchair access

Éos Gran Via de los Corts Catalanes 575 (M° Universitat) 34/93-451-8772, 34/617-931-439 • lesbians/ gay men • B&B in gay district • gay-owned

Fashion House Bruc 13 Principal 34/63-790-4044 • lesbians/ gay men • shared baths

GayStay BCN C / Piquer 15, Pral 3 (at Carrer de Mata) 34/676-145-909 • mostly men • WiFi • gay owned

Gran Hotel Catalonia Balmes 142–146 34/93-415-9090 • gay-friendly • kids ok • food served • wheelchair access

HCC Regente Rambla de Catalunya 76 34/93-487-5989 • gay-friendly • in 1913 art nouveau bldg • pool • WiFi • wheelchair access

Hostal Baires 34/93-319-7774 • gay-friendly • in Barrio Gótico

Hostal Que Tal Mallorca 290 (at Bruch) 34/93-459-2366 • mostly gay men

Hotel Axel Aribau 33 (at Consell de Cent) 34/93-323-9393 • lesbians/ gay men • full brkfst • pool • WiFi • also restaurant • also Skybar • wheelchair access

Hotel Colon Avenida Catedral 7 34/93-301-1404 • gay-friendly

Hotel Majestic Barcelona Paseo de Gracia 68 (in city center) 34/93-488-1717 • gay-friendly • 5-star hotel • rooftop pool • wheelchair access

Room Mate Emma Carrer Rosselló 205 34/932-385-606 • gay-friendly • nighclub vibe • WiFi

BARS

Aire/ Sala Diana Valencia 236 (btwn Enriq. Granados & c/ Balmes) 34/93-451-8462 • 11pm-3am, clsd Sun-Wed • seasonal • gay/straight, more women Sun • dancing/DJ • cafe-bar

Al Maximo Assaonadora 25 • lesbians/gay men • neighborhood bar

El Balcon des Aquiles Lleo 9 • 7pm-3am • mostly gay men • neighborhood bar • theme nights

Bar Plata Consejo de Ciento 233 (at Urgell) • 5pm-3am • mostly gay men

BimBamBum Casanova 48 • 11pm-3am, clsd Mon-Tue • mostly gay men • dancing/DJ

El Cangrejo Villarroel 86 • 10:30pm-3am, clsd Mon-Tue • popular • lesbians/gay men • dancing/DJ

La Chapelle Muntaner 65 • mostly gay men • cafe by day

Chiringuito Gay Lorenzo El dulce deseo de Lorenzo, Playa Mar Bella • mostly gay men • beach bar • open during summer

La Cueva Calàbria 91 • open 4pm, clsd Mon • lesbians/gay men

Dacksy Consell de Cent 247 **34/934-519-925** • 5pm-3am • lesbians/gay men • trendy cocktail lounge • dancing/DJ

Deja Vu Aribau 81 (btwn Mallorca & Valencia) • mostly women • dancing/DJ • theme nights

El Dulce Deseo de Lorenzo Playa de la Mar Bella • summer beach bar

Barcelona

LGBT Pride:
July.

Annual Events:
February - Carnival.

July - Grec Summer Festival 34-93/316-1000, web: www.barcelonafestival.com.

July - Gay/Lesbian Film Festival, 34-93/319-5550, web: www.cine-malambda.com.

August - Festa Major de Gràcia (huge street party) 34-93/459-3080, web: www.festamajorde-gracia.ca.

City Info:
34-93/285-3834, web: www.barcelonaturisme.com.

Best View:
Torre de Collserola, 34-93/406-9354, web: www.torre-decollserola.com.

Giant glass elevator takes you to a platform 944 ft into the air.

Weather:
Barcelona boasts a mild Mediterranean climate, with summer temperatures in the 70°s-80°s, and 40°s-50°s in winter. Rain is possible year-round, with July being the driest month.

Attractions:
Barcelona Museum of Contemporary Art 34-93/412-0810, web: www.macba.es.

Barrì Gotic.

Boqueria Market 34-93/318-2584, web: www.boqueria.info.

Catedral de Barcelona 34-93/310-7195, web:catedralbcn.org

Fundació Joan Miró 34-93/443-9470, web: www.bcn.fjmiro.es.

Museu Picasso 34-93/256-3000, web: www.museupicasso.bcn.es.

National Museum of Catalan Art 34-93/622-0376, web: www.mnac.es.

Parc Guëll.

La Sagrada Familia 34-93/207-3031, web: www.sagradafamilia.org.

Transit:
Radio Taxi 34-93/303-3033, web: www.radiotaxio33.com.

Aerobus to Plaza de Cataluña 34-93/223-5151 , web: www.emt-amb.com.

Transports Metropolitans de Barcelona 34-90/207-5027, web: www.tmb.net.

Lust Casanova 75 (at Consell de Cent) • 9pm-2:30am, clsd Mon, pre-clubbing bar • lesbians/ gay men

La Madame Ronda Sant Pere 19-21 (M° Urquinaona) 34/93-426-8444 • from midnight Sun only • gay/ straight • dancing/DJ

Mandarina Diputació 157 (M° Urgell) 34/93-323-3393 • 6pm-3am • lesbians/ gay men • food served • terrace

Mind the Gap Consell de Cent 273 34/931-857-930 • restaurant & cocktail bar

Moeem Muntaner 11 34/659-229-033 • 6pm-3am • lesbians/gay men • cheap drinks

Museum Cafe & Club Sepulveda 178 (at Urgell) • 6:30pm-3am • mostly gay men

New Bahía Carrer de Seneca 12 (in Gràcia) • till 2:30am • mostly women • dancing/DJ

People Lounge Villarroel 71 (M° Urgell) 34/93-451-5986 • 7pm-3am • mostly gay men • food served

Punto BCN Muntaner 63–65 (enter on Consejo de Ciento Yragón, M° Universitat) 34/93-453-6123 • 6pm-2:30am • popular • mostly gay men • upscale cafe-bar • wheelchair access

La Rosa Brusi 39 (btwn Augusta & San Elias, M° Plaza Molina) 34/93-414-6166 • 10pm-3am Th-Sun • mostly women • dancing/DJ • live shows • neighborhood bar

Z:eltas Casanova 75 (M° Gran Vía/ Urgell) 34/93-454-1902 • 11pm-3am • mostly gay men • dancing/DJ • live shows • videos

Zelig 34/93-441-5622 • 7pm-2am, till 3am wknds, clsd Mon • gay/ straight • dancing/DJ • food served

NIGHTCLUBS

Arena Classic Diputació 233 (at Balmes, M° Universitat) 34/93-487-8342 • 12:30am-5am Fri-Sat only • popular • mostly gay men • dancing/DJ • Spanish music • live shows • cover charge

Arena Sala Madre Balmes 32 (at Diputació, M° Universitat) 34/93-487-8342 • 12:30am-5am, clsd Mon (except in Aug) • popular • mostly gay men • dancing/DJ • food served • live shows • cover charge

Les Fatales • mostly women • dancing/DJ • parties around Barcelona • check lesfatales.org for details

Metro Sepúlveda 185 (M° Universitat) 34/93-323-5227 • midnight-5am, from 1am Mon • popular • mostly gay men • dancing/DJ • leather • drag shows • cover charge

Souvenir Barcelona Noi del Sucre 75 (Viladecans) • after-hours club 6am-1pm Sat-Sun & holidays

CAFES

La Concha del Barrio Chino Guardia 14 (M° Liceu) 34/93-302-4118 • 4pm-3am • gay/straight • dancing/DJ • transgender-friendly

RESTAURANTS

7 Portes Passeig d'Isabel II, 14 34/93-319-3033, 34/93-319-2950 • 1pm-1am • Catalan • upscale • over 150 years old!

El Berro Diputació 180 34/933-236-956 • 7am-3am, from 9am wknds • inexpensive diner-style restaurant • also bar

Botafumeiro El Gran de Gràcia 81 34/93-218-4230, 34/93-217-9642 • 1pm-1am • Galician seafood • full bar • reservations recommended

Castro Casanova 85 (M° Urgell) 34/93-323-6784 • 1pm-4pm & 9pm-midnight, clsd Sun • Catalan • full bar • live shows

dDivine Balmes 24 (M° Universitat) 34/93-317-2248 • 9:30pm-1am, clsd Sun-Tue • dinner show hosted by "Divine" • lesbians/ gay men • reservations recommended

Eterna Consell de Cent 127-129 (at Villarroel) 34/93-424-2526 • 1pm-4pm Mon-Fri, 9:30pm-midnight Th-Sat, clsd Sun • lesbians/ gay men • drag shows

La Flauta Magica c/ de Banys Vells 18 (M° Jaume I) 34/93-268-4694 • dinner nightly • vegetarian/ organic • wheelchair access

Iurantia Casanova 42 (M° Urgell) 34/93-454-7887 • lunch Mon-Fri, dinner Mon-Sat, clsd Sun • pizzeria • reservations recommended

Little Italy Carrer del Rec 30 (near Passeig del Born) 34/93-319-7973 • 1pm-4pm & 9pm-midnight • live jazz

Madrid-Barcelona Carrer d'Arago 282 (M° Passeig de Gracia) 34/93-215-7027 • lunch & dinner, clsd Sun • located on old railway line • Catalan

Marquette Diputació 172 (M° Universitat) 34/93-454-6398 • 1pm-4pm & 9:30pm-midnight, dinner only Sat-Sun • Italian food •

Sazzerak 34/93-451-1138 • full bar

Tafino • 1pm-4pm Mon-Fri, 8:30pm-midnight Tue-Sat

Tu Sabes 34/615-999-282 • 7pm-midnight Th, 9pm-3am Fri-Sat

La Veronica Rambla de Raval 2-4
34/93-329-3303 • 1pm-1am, clsd Mon •
popular pizzeria • terrace

ENTERTAINMENT & RECREATION

Chernobyl Beach take the Metro to Sant
Roc • popular gay beach

Mar Bella • popular gay beach

Museu Picasso Montcada 15-23
34/93-256-3000 • early Picasso works

Parc Guell Mount Tibidado • mosaics &
sculpture by Gaudi

Sant Sebastiàn • popular gay beach

BOOKSTORES

Antinous Josep Anselm Clavé 6 (btwn Las
Ramblas & Ample, M° Drassanes)
34/93-301-9070 • clsd Sun • LGBT • books •
gifts • also cafe • wheelchair access

Cómplices Cervantes 2 (at Avinyó, M° Liceu)
34/93-412-7283 • 10:30am-8:30pm, from
noon Sat, clsd Sun • LGBT • Spanish &
English titles

Nosotr@s Casanova 56 (M° Urgell)
34/93-451-5134 • LGBT books • magazines •
gifts • videos • DVDs

PUBLICATIONS

Gay Barcelona Av Roma 152
34/93-454-9100 • monthly gay magazine

EROTICA

Erotic Museum of Barcelona Ramblas 96
34/93-318-9865 • 10am-midnight (seasonal
hours)

Kitsch Muntaner 17-19 (at Gran Vía)
34/93-453-2052 • 10am-10pm, from 5pm
Sun

Madrid

Note: M°=Metro station

INFO LINES & SERVICES

**COGAM (Colectivo de Lesbianas, Gays,
Transexuales, y Bisexuales de Madrid)**
Puebla 9 (Bajo) 34/91-522-4517 • LGBT
center • groups • library • also cafe-bar

ACCOMMODATIONS

Camino de Soto Puente de la Reine 18,
Soto del Real 34-66/744-1351 • gay/ straight
• located 40 minutes from Madrid • full brkfst
• pool • WiFi • gay-owned

Chueca Pension Gravina 4 34/91-523-1473
• mostly gay men • hostel • kids ok • WiFi

Madrid

LGBT PRIDE:
June, web: orgullolgtb.org.

ANNUAL EVENTS:
October/November - International
Gay & Lesbian Film Festival, web:
www.lesgaicinemad.com.

CITY INFO:
Oficina Municipale de Turismo
34/91-308-0400, web:
www.esmadrid.com.

BEST VIEW:
From the funicular in the Parque des
Atracciones.

WEATHER:
Winter temps average in the 40°s
(and maybe even a little snow!).
Summer days in Madrid are hot,
with highs well into the 80°s.

ATTRACTIONS:
Chueca.
El Rastro (flea market).
Museo del Prado 34/91-330-2800,
web: www.museodelprado.es.
Museo Thyssen-Bornemisza
34/91-369-0151, web:
www.museothyssen.org.
Museo de Reina Sofia (home of
Picasso's *Guernica*)
34/91-774-1000, web:
www.museoreinasofia.es.
El Retiro (park).
Royal Palace 34/91-454-8700,
web: patrimonionacional.es.

TRANSIT:
Taxi 34/61-815-8242, web:
taxi24madrid.com.
Aerocity 34/91-747-7570, web:
www.gomadrid.com/aerocity.
Metro 34/90-244-4403, web:
www.metromadrid.es.

Hostal CasaChueca Calle San Bartolomé 4 (at San Marcos) 34/91–523–8127 • mostly gay men • WiFi • gay-owned

Hostal La Fontana Valverde 6, 1° (M° Gran Vía) 34/91–521–8449, 34/91–523–1561 • lesbians/ gay men • WiFi

Hostal la Zona Calle Valverde 7, 1 & 2 (at Gran Vía) 34/91–521–9904 • mostly gay men • full brkfst, • all rooms w/ private baths & balconies • WiFi • gay-owned

Hotel Catalonia Gaudí Gran Vía 7-9 (at Alcalá) 34/91–531–2222 • gay-friendly • WiFi • kids ok • wheelchair access

Hotel Urban Madrid Carrera de San Jerónimo 34 34/91–787–7770 • gay-friendly • upscale hotel w/ 3 restaurants & rooftop pool • WiFi

Pensión Madrid House Barbieri 1 34/651–387 535 • gay/straight • one block from Chueca Square • WiFi • gay-owned

Bars

El 51 Hortaleza 51 (in Chueca) 34/91–521–2564 • 6pm-3am, from 4pm wknds • popular • mostly gay men • upscale cocktail lounge

Ambienta2 22 San Bartolome (at Figueroa) 34/606–939592 • 6pm-2am, till 2:30am wknds, from noon Sun • lesbians/ gay men • dancing/DJ • drag shows • live entertainment • theme nights

Bar Lio Pelayo 58 • 7pm-2am, till 2:30am wknds • lesbians/ gay men • karaoke • drag shows • transgender-friendly

Bar Nike Augusto Figueroa 22 (at Barbieri) 34/915–210–751 • mostly gay men • neighborhood bar • food served • younger crowd • cafeteria-style • popular early evenings

La Bohemia Plaza de Chueca 10 (M° Chueca) • 8pm-close • mostly women • neighborhood cafe-bar

Enfrente Infantas 12 (M° Gran Vía) 34/68–779–1462 • 8pm-3am • mostly gay men • leather • DJs Th & Sun

Fulanita de Tal Calle del Conde de Xiquena 2 (at Prim) • mostly women • stylish & hip • dancing/DJ

Gris • 10pm-3am, from 9pm Th-Sat, clsd Sun-Mon • lesbians/gay men • reduced drink prices until 11:30pm • music bar

LL Pelayo 11 (M° Chueca) 34/91–523–3121 • 5pm-close • popular • mostly gay men • neighborhood bar • dancing • strippers • drag shows • videos

La Lupe de Lavapies Torrecilla del Leal 12 (M° Antón Martín) 34/91–527–5019 • 5pm-2am • lesbians/ gay men • cabaret • flea market Sun

El Mojito Olmo 6 (M° Antón Martin) 34/91–531–1141 • 9pm-3am, till 3:30am Fri-Sat • lesbians/ gay men • cocktail bar • great music

Museo Chicote Calle Gran Via 12 34/915–326–737 • 9pm-3am • gay/ straight • 50s style lounge • food served • live shows

Rick's Calle del Clavel 8 (at Infantas, M° Gran Vía, ring to enter) 34/91–531–9186 • 11pm-6am, open later Fri-Sat, 9pm-2am Sun • popular • mostly gay men • dancing/DJ

Rimmel Calle de Luis de Góngora 2 (M° Chueca) • 7pm-3am • mostly gay men • 2 for 1 drinks till 11:30pm

El Rincón Guay Embajadores 62 (Lavapiés quarter) 34/914–683–769 • lesbians/ gay men • neighborhood bar/cafe

Sacha's Plaza de Chueca 1 (M° Chueca) • 8pm-3am • lesbians/ gay men • dancing/DJ • drag shows • terrace

Sixta Calatrava 15 (M° La Latina) 34/913–663–018 • 10pm-2am, 2pm-10pm Sun, clsd Mon-Tue • packed on Sun afternoon • gay/straight • gay-owned

Soho Plaza de Chueca 6 • mostly women • patio

Studio 54 Madrid Barbieri 7 (btwn San Marcos & Infantas, M° Chueca) 34/615–126–807 • 11:30pm-3:30am, clsd Mon-Tue • lesbians/ gay men • dancing/DJ • live shows

Tántalo Libertad 14 34/915–213–127 • 6pm-2:30am • mostly gay men • WiFi

Truco Calle de Gravina 10 (at Plaza de Chueca) 34/91–532–8921 • 8pm-close, clsd Mon-Tue • popular • mostly women • dance bar • great parties • seasonal terrace

Why Not San Bartolomé 6 (M° Gran Vía) • 9pm-3am, till 5am Fri-Sat • gay/ straight

Nightclubs

Boite Calle Tetuan 27 (Plaza del Carmen) 34/91–522–9620 • gay/ straight • dancing/DJ • check listings for gay club nights

Cool 34/91–542–3439 • midnight-6am • gay/staright ,more gay Sat • dancing/DJ

Escape Gravina 13 (at Plaza de Chueca) 34/91–532–5206 • 10pm-5am Wed-Sun • mostly women • dancing/DJ • live shows

Griffin's Marqués de Valdelglesias 6 (M° Banco de España) **34/91–522–2079** • 11pm-late • mostly gay men • dancing/DJ • drag shows • entertainment

Joy Eslava Arenal 11 (M° Sol) **34/91–366–3733** • 11:30pm-6pm • popular • fabulous crowd • converted theater

Medea Cabeza 33 (M° Antón Martín) **34/91–369–3302** • 11pm-7am, till 10am Sun, clsd Mon • popular wknds • women only • men welcome as guests • dancing/DJ • cabaret • cover charge

Ohm Plaza de Callao 4 (at Sala Bash, M° Callao) **34/91–531–0132** • midnight-close Fri-Sat • popular • gay/straight • dancing/DJ • go-go dancers

Polana Barbieri 10 (M° Chueca) **34/91–532–3305** • 10pm-5am • trendy • lesbians/gay men • dancing/DJ

Space of Sound Sala Macumba (at Estación de Chamartin) **34/90–249–9994** • midnight-close • lesbians/gay men • Sun only • dancing/DJ

Tábata Vergara 12 (next to Teatro Real, M° Opera) **34/91–547–9735** • 11:30pm-late Wed-Sat • lesbians/gay men • dancing/DJ • young crowd • cover charge

Trip Family • gay theme dance parties • check tripfamily.com for events & details

Week-end Plaza de Callao 4 (at Ohm Club) **34/91–541–3500** • midnight-6am Sun • popular • lesbians/gay men • dancing/DJ • alternative • cover charge

CAFES

El Apolo Barco 18 **34/915–210–830** • 8am-3pm & 6pm-2am, 10am-2am Sat, from 5pm Sun

BAires Cafe Gravina 4 (M° Chueca) **34/91–532–9879** • 4pm-2am • lesbians/gay men • also bar • hip crowd

Cafe Acuarela Gravina 10 (M° Chueca) **34/91–522–2143, 34/91–570–6907** • 3pm-3am, from 11am Sat-Sun • lesbians/gay men • bohemian cafe-bar • cocktails

Cafe Figueroa Augusto Figueroa 17 (at Hortaleza, M° Chueca) **34/91–521–1673** • 4pm-midnight, till 2:30am wknds • lesbians/gay men • also bar

Cafe la Troje Pelayo 26 (at Figueroa, M° Chueca) **34/91–531–0535** • 5pm-2am • lesbians/gay men • full bar

D'Mystic Gravina 5 (M° Pelayo) **34/91–308–2460** • 9:30am-close • gay/straight • popular • hot food served • hip cafe-bar in Chueca area

El Jardin Infantas 9 (M° Gran Via) **34/91–521–9045, 34/91–523–1218** • noon-2am, till 3am wknds • lesbians/gay men

Mama Inés Hortaleza 22 (M° Chueca) **34/91–523–2333** • gay/straight • 10am-2am • sandwiches • pies

Star's Marqués de Valdeiglesias 5 (at Infantas, M° Banco) **34/91–522–2712** • 8pm-close, clsd Sun • mostly gay men • cafe-bar • dancing/DJ Th-Sat

XXX Cafe Clavel 2 (M° Gran Vía) **34/91–532–8415** • 1pm-1am • mostly gay men • food served • cabaret wknds

RESTAURANTS

Al Natural Zorrilla 11 (M° Sevilla) **34/91–369–4709** • lunch and dinner, no dinner Sun • vegetarian

El Armario San Bartolomé 7 (btwn Figueroa & San Marcos, M° Chueca) **34/91–532–8377** • lunch & dinner • lesbians/gay men • Mediterranean

Artemisa Ventura de la Vega 4 (at Zorrilla) **34/91–429–5092** • lesbians/gay men • vegetarian • also Tres Cruces 4 location

Botin **34/91–366–4217** • one of the oldest restaurants in the world (open since 1725) & an old Hemingway haunt

Chez Pomme Pelayo 4 (M° Chueca) **34/91–532–1646** • lunch & dinner, clsd Sun • vegetarian

Colby **34/91–521–2554** • 9:30am-close, from 11:30am Sun

Divina La Cocina Colmenares 13 (at San Marcos, M° Chueca) **34/91–531–3765** • lunch & dinner • lesbians/gay men • elegant & trendy

Ecocentro Esquilache 2, 4, y 6 (at Pablo Iglesias, M° Rios Rosas) **34/91–553–5502** • open till midnight • vegetarian • natural foods • also shop • herbalist school

El Chambao Manuel Malasana 16 (at Calle de Monteleon) • tapas restaurant • also bar

Gula Gula Gran Via 1 (M° Gran Via) **34/91–522–8764** • lunch & dinner • popular • lesbians/gay men • buffet/salad bar • drag shows • reservations required

Juntos Libertad 9 • Italian

Marsot Pelayo 6 (M° Chueca) **34/91–531–0726** • lunch & dinner

Momo Calle de la Libertad 8 **34/91–532–7162** • lunch & dinner • nonsmoking • charming staff • gay-owned

Moskada Francisco Silvela 71 (at General Oraa) **34/91–563–0630** • lunch Mon-Fri, dinner Mon-Sat, clsd Sun

Nina Manuel Malasana 10 (M° Bilbao) **34/91–591–0046** • open daily • contemporary Spanish food

Restaurante Miau **34/91–429–2272** • Madrileño cuisine & tapas

El Rincón de Pelayo Pelayo 19 (M° Chueca) **34/91–521–8407** • lunch & dinner • lesbians/ gay men

Sama-Sama San Bartolomé 23 (M° Chueca) **34/91–521–5547** • lunch & dinner, clsd Sun • Balinese decor • also Infante 5 location

Vegaviana Pelayo 35 **34/913–080–381** • lunch & dinner, clsd Sun-Mon • vegetarian

BOOKSTORES

A Different Life Pelayo 30 (M° Chueca) **34/91–532–9652** • 11am-10pm • LGBT • books • magazines • music • videos • sex shop downstairs

Berkana Bookstore Hortaleza 64 **34/91–522–5599** • 10:30am-9pm, from noon Sat-Sun • LGBT • ask for free gay map of Madrid • wheelchair access

RETAIL SHOPS

AKM **34/91–531–1388** • clsd Sun • military-style fashion & fetish store

PUBLICATIONS

Shangay Express **34/91–445–1741** • free bi-weekly gay paper • also publishes Shanguide

GYMS & HEALTH CLUBS

Energy Gym Hortaleza 19 (M° Gran Vía, Chueca) **34/91–531–1029, 34/91–522–3073**

Gimnasio V35 Valverde 35 (M° Gran Via) **34/91–523–9352** • mostly gay men

Holiday Gym Princesa Serrano Jover 3 (M° Argüelles) **34/91–547–4033** • central location • pool

EROTICA

La Jugueteria Travesia de San Mateo 12 **34–91/308–7269** • 11am-2pm & 5pm-9pm, clsd Sun • very lesbian friendly

Los Placeres de Lola Doctor Fourquet, 34 **34/91–468–6178** • noon-10pm, clsd Sun • women & their companions only • toys, leather, books & videos • also cafe

SR Pelayo 7 (M° Chueca) **34/91–523–1964** • clsd Sun • fetish, military, leather • gay-owned

Sitges

ACCOMMODATIONS

Antonio's Guesthouse Passeig Vilanova 58 **34/93–894–9207** • mostly men • WiFi • also apts • gay-owned

B My Guest B&B Ctra Sant Pere de Ribes **34/639–534–979** • women only penthouse apt • WiFi • lesbian-owned

Los Globos Avda Ntra Sra de Montserrat 43 **34/93–894–9374** • lesbians/ gay men • kids/ pets ok • also bar • brkfst buffet • WiFi • wheelchair access • gay-owned

Hotel Antemare Verge de Montserrat 48-50 **34/93–894–7000** • gay-friendly • pool • 1 block from beach

Hotel Liberty Isla de Cuba 45 (at Artur Carbonell) **34/93–811–0872** • lesbians/ gay-men • seasonal • nonsmoking • WiFi • wheelchair access • gay-owned

Hotel Renaixença Illa de Cuba 13 , 08070 **34/93–894–8375** • mostly gay men • some shared baths • hotel bar

Hotel Romàntic Sant Isidre 33 **34/93–894–8375** • gay/ straight • full brkfst • some shared baths • seasonal • kids/ pets ok • also full bar

Hotel Santa Maria Paseo de la Ribera 52 **34/93–894–0999** • gay/straight • clean & modest • great restaurant

Parrot's Hotel Joan Tarrida 16 **34/93–894–1350** • lesbians/ gay men • WiFi • also bar & restaurant

San Sebastian Playa Port Alegre 53 **305/538–9697 (US#), 866/376–7831 (IN US)** • gay-friendly • pool • also bar/ restaurant • nonsmoking • wheelchair access

Sitges Royal Rooms **34/64–998–1148** • mosty gay men • WiFi • gay-owned

BARS

Azul Sant Bonaventura 10 **34/93–894–7634** • 9pm-3am • mostly gay men • neighborhood bar

Dark/ DSB Bonaire 14 • 5pm-3am • mostly men • sleek lounge

Mojito & Co Plaza Industrial 1 • 5pm-3am • mostly men • breezy lounge w/ outdoor seating

Parrot's Pub Plaza Industria 2 (at Primero de Mayo) **34/93–894–7881** • 5pm-close, seasonal • popular • lesbians/ gay men • live shows • patio • also restaurant

Ruby's Terrace Joan Tarrida Ferratges 14 • from 8pm • mostly gay men • drag shows • terrace

XXL Joan Tarrida Ferratges 7 • 11pm-3:30am (wknds only off-season) • popular • mostly gay men • dancing/DJ

NIGHTCLUBS

Bourbon's Sant Bonaventura 13 **34/93–894-3347** • 10:30pm-3:30am (Sat only off-season) • popular • mostly gay men • dancing/DJ • videos • young crowd

Mediterraneo Sant Bonaventura 6 **34/93–894-3347** • 11pm-3:30am • popular • mostly gay men • dance bar • patio

New Port Taco 1-3 **34/93–452-0356** • 10pm-3am, clsd Mon • lesbians/ gay men • dancing/DJ • drag shows • strippers

Orek's Bonaire 13 • 10pm-3am (only Fri-Sat in winter) • mostly gay men • dancing/DJ • strippers • darkroom

Organic Bonaire 15 **34/93–894-2230** • opens 2:30am (wknds only off-season) • mostly gay men • transgender-friendly • dancing/DJ • singles party Th • darkroom • cover charge

El Piano Bonaventura 37 **34/93–814-6245** • 10pm-3am • lesbians/ gay men • piano bar • cabaret

Queenz Bonaire 17 • 10pm-3:30am, seasonal • mostly men • DJs • drag shows • cabaret

Ricky's • midnight-6am, clsd Mon • gay/ straight, more gay Fri

Trailer Angel Vidal 36 • 1am-6am, seasonal • popular • mostly gay men • dancing/DJ

CAFES

Cafe Al Fresco Carrer Major 33 **34/93–811-3307** • 9am-midnight

Cafe Sitges Sant Pau 32 • 11am-3pm, also 6pm-late Wed-Sun, clsd Tue

Cine Cafe Jesus 55 **34/662–560-050** • 10am-midnight, clsd Tue • mostly gay men • Anglo-American • gay-owned

Mont Roig Cafe Marques de Montroig 11-13 **34/93–894-8439** • 9am-3am • patio • WiFi • also full bar

RESTAURANTS

Air Coco Paseo Maritim 2 **34/93–894-2445** • clsd Mon • popular • patio seating • water views • reservations recommended

Alma Tacó 16 **34/93–894-6387** • 8pm-close (clsd Tue-Wed off-season) • lesbians/ gay men • French • terrace

Beach House Sant Pau 34 **34/93–894-9029** • brkfst & dinner • full bar • patio • gay-owned

Can Pagès Sant Pere 24–26 **34/93–894-1195** • 1pm-4pm & 8pm-midnight, clsd Mon

El Celler Vell **34/93–811-1961** • dinner nightly, lunch Fri-Sun, clsd Wed • traditional Catalan

Sitges

ENTERTAINMENT:
Platjes del Mort ("Beach of the Dead") is the gay beach.

ANNUAL EVENTS:
February - Carnival, web: www.sitges.com/carnaval.
October - International Film Festival, web: www.cinemasitges.com.

CITY INFO:
34/93–894-4251, web: www.sitges-tour.com.

TRANSIT:
Taxi Sitgest 34/93-894-1329, web: www.taxisitges.com.
MONBUS 34/93-893-7060, www.monbus.cat.

ATTRACTIONS:
Museu Cau Ferrat 34/93–894-0364, web: www.diba.es/museus/sitges.asp.
Museu Maricel 34/93–894-0364, web: www.diba.es/museus/sitges.asp.

Ma Maison Bonaire 28 **34/93–894–6054** • lunch & dinner • popular • lesbians/ gay men • French • full bar • terrace

Mezzanine Espalter 8 **34/93–894–9940** • dinner only • French

Pic Nic Paseo de la Ribera **34/93–811–0040** • in front of gay beach • also internet cafe

So Ca/ Southern California Sant Gaudenci 9 **34/93–894–3046** • 1pm-close • also bar

Sucré-Salé Sant Pau 39 **34/93–894–2302** • lunch & dinner, clsd Tue off-season • crêpes • terrace

El Trull Mossèn Felix Clará 3 (off Major) **34/93–894–4705** • dinner only, clsd Wed • popular • lesbians/ gay men • French/ int'l

ENTERTAINMENT & RECREATION

Gay Beach Party La Playa De La Bossa Rodona • Tues midnight-6am in season

Gay Beach (Platja de la Bassa Rodona) • in front of Calipolis Hotel & Picnic cafe

Playa De Las Balmins • turn left then pass a long beach strip and then climb a hill past a cemetery

Playa del Muerto • exclusively gay beach 50 minutes walk from the center of Sitges • also beach bar

RETAIL SHOPS

Oscar Marqués de Montroig 2 (at Plaza Industria) **34/93–894–1976** • designer clothing for men & women

EROTICA

The Mask **34/93–811–2214** • 24hr wknds

JAPAN

Tokyo

ACCOMMODATIONS

Capitol Tokyu 10-3 Nagata-cho 2-chome (Chiyoda-ku) **81–3/3581–4511, 800/428–6598** • gay-friendly • near the Diet

Four Seasons Hotel 10-8 Sekiguchi 2-chome (Bunkyo-ku) **81–3/3943–2222** • gay-friendly • wheelchair access • pool • surrounded by historic Japanese garden

HI Tokyo Central Hostel 18F Central Plaza (1-1 Kagurakashi, Shinjuku-ku) **81–3/3235–1107** • gay-friendly • 11pm curfew

Hotel Century Southern Tower 2-2-1 Yoyogi (Shibuya-ku) **81–3/5354–0111** • gay-friendly • near gay district

Hotel Sunroute Plaza Shinjuku 2-3-1 Yoyogi (Shibuya-ku) **81–3/3375–3211** • gay-friendly • near gay district

Keio Plaza Hotel 2-2-1 Nishi Shinjuku **81–3/3344–0111** • gay-friendly • swimming • restaurants & bars

Park Hyatt 3-7-1-2 Nishi Shinjuku **81–3/5322–1234** • gay-friendly • kids ok • restaurant & lounge • luxury hotel featured in Lost in Translation • pool • spa

Shinjuku Prince Hotel 30-1 Kabuki-cho 1-chome (Shinjuku-ku) **81–3/3205–1111, 800/542–8686 (US)** • gay-friendly • WiFi

Shinjuku Washington Hotel 3-2-9 Nishi-Shinjuku (Shinjuku-ku) **81–3/3343–3111** • gay-friendly

Tokyu Stay 5-9-8 Nishi Shinjuku **81–3/3370–1090** • gay-friendly • great location

BARS

Advocates 1-F, Dai-7 Tenka Bldg (Shinjuku 2-18-1) **81–3/3358–3988** • 6pm-4am, till 1am Sun • cafe-bar • lesbians/ gay men • young crowd

Alamas Cafe 1/F Garnet Bldg, Shinjuku 2-12-1 **81–3/6914–9215** • 6pm-2am, till 5am Fri-Sat, 3pm-midnight Sun • lesbians/ gay men • dancie club at night

Arty Farty 2F, #33 Kyutei Bldg (Shinjuku 2-11-7), Shinjuku-ku **81–3/5362–9720** • 6pm-5am, from 7pm Fri, from 5pm wknds, till 3am Sun • mostly gay men • dancing/DJ • young crowd

DNA **81–3/3341–4445** • 3pm-5am • gay/straight • neighborhood bar

GB B1, Shinjuku Plaza Bldg (Shinjuku 2-12-3), Shinjuku-ku **81–3/3352–8972** • 8pm-2am, till 3am Fri-Sat • mostly gay men

Hug Shinjuku 2-15-8 **81–3/5379–5085** • 9pm-5am, clsd Sun • women only • karaoke • cover charge

Keivi 4F Yoshino Bldg, 17-10 Sakuragaoka **81–3/3496–0006** • 6pm-midnight • mostly gay men • neighborhood bar

Kinsmen 2F Shinjuku 2-12-16 (near Shinjuku Sanchome Station) **81–3/3354–4949** • 7pm-1am, till 3am Fri-Sat, clsd Mon • lesbians/ gay men

Kinswomyn 3F, Dai-Ichi Tenka Bldg (Shinjuku 2-15-10) **81–3/3354–8720** • 8pm-4am, clsd Tue • popular • women only

Lamp Post 201 Yamahara Heights (Shinjuku 2-12-15) **81–3/3354–0436** • 7pm-3am • mostly men • piano bar

Mars Bar 2-15-13 Shinjuku-ku (3F Hosono Bldg) 81–3/3354–7923 • 8pm-3am, till 5am Fri-Sun • mostly women • karaoke

Peach 1F (Shinjuku 2-15-8) 81–3/3351–7034 • 11pm-7am, clsd Sun-Mon • women only • in a brick building next to 'Hug' & across from 'Agit • look for the peach mark on the door • cover charge

Sunny 2F Nakabayashi Tenpo (Shinjuku 2-15-8) 81–3/3356–0368 • 8pm-5am • one of the oldest lesbian bars in Tokyo • karaoke • neighborhood bar • piano bar

Tac's Knot 2F, Rm 202 (Shinjuku 3-11-12) 81–3/3341–9404 • 8pm-2am • lesbians/ gay men • also art exhibitions

Town House Ginza 6 Shinbashi, Bldg 1-11-15 (Minato-ku) 81–3/3289-8558 • 6pm-midnight, from 4pm Sat, clsd Sun • mostly gay men • karaoke

Usagi • mostly gay men • great balcony

Wordup Bar 2-10-7 2F TOM Bld Shinjuku 81–3/3353–2466 • mostly gay men • dancing/DJ

NIGHTCLUBS

Agit 81–3/3350–8083 • 8pm-6am • lesbians/gay men • karaoke • lesbian-owned

Arch B1F Hayakawa Bldg (Shinjuku 2-14-6) 81–3/3352–6297 • lesbians/ gay men • dancing/DJ • check www.clubarch.net for info on men-only & women-only nights

Tokyo

LGBT PRIDE:
August.

ANNUAL EVENTS:
July - Tokyo International Lesbian & Gay Film Festival, web: www.tokyo-lgff.org.

CITY INFO:
Japan National Tourist Organization 81–3/3201–3331 or 212/757–5640 (US), web: www.jnto.go.jp.
Tokyo Convention & Visitors Bureau, web: www.tcvb.or.jp.

BEST VIEW:
From any of 3 major observation decks: Tokyo Metropolis Observatories, Bunkyo Civic Center of Edogawa City Office.

WEATHER:
Hot & rainy in the summer, cool (though rarely freezing) in the winter. Spring & fall are clear, mild & gorgeous.

TRANSIT:
Nihon Kotsu 81–3/5755–2151 (English), web: www.nihon-kotsu.co.jp.
Toei, web: www.kotsu.metro.tokyo.jp.
Tokyo Metro, web: www.tokyometro.jp.

ATTRACTIONS:
Edo-Tokyo Museum 81–3/3626–9974, web: www.edo-tokyo-museum.or.jp.
Grand Sumo Tournaments, web: www.sumo.or.jp.
Imperial Palace, web: sankan.kunai-cho.go.jp.
Kabuki-za Theater 81–3/3541–3131, web: www.shochiku.co.jp/play/kabuk-iza/theater.
Meiji Jingu Shrine 81–3/3379–5511, web: www.meijijingu.or.jp.
Roppongi Kingyo 81–3/3478–3000, web: www.kingyo.co.jp.
Sensoji Temple 81–3/3842–0181.
Shinjuku Gyoen National Garden.
Tokyo National Museum 81–3/3822–1111, web: www.tnm.jp.
Tsukiji Market, web: www.tsukiji-market.or.jp.
Ueno Park.

Diamond Cutter B1F Hayakawa Bldg (Shinjuku 2-14-6, at Club Arch) **81-3/3352-6297 (Arch)** • 9pm-5am 1st Fri only • women only • dancing/DJ • cabaret

Motel #203 **81-3/6383-4649** • 8pm-5am, till 2am Sun, clsd Tue • popular happy hour 8pm-9pm • women only • dancing/DJ

Rehab Lounge **81-3/3355-7833** • 7pm-2am, till 3am Fri-Sat • popular happy hour 7pm-9pm • mostly gay men • dancing/DJ

Shangri-La Yume no Shima, Koto ward (at Ageha, Studio Coast) • bi-monthly • mostly men • dancing/DJ

Warehouse Fukao Bldg B 1-4-5 (exit 7 Azabu Juban station) **81-3/6230 0343** • gay/straight • large underground club host Red gay nights

RESTAURANTS

Ban Thai 1-23-14 Kabuki-cho, 3rd flr (Shinjuku) **81-3/3207-0068** • lunch & dinner

Chin-ya 1-3-4 Asukusa **81-3/3841-0010** • lunch & dinner • serving shabu-shabu & sukiyaki since 1880

Edogin 4-5-1 Tsukiji (Chuo-ku) **81-3/3543-4401** • 11am-9:30pm, till 8pm Sun • popular • sushi

Gonpachi 1-13-11 Nishi Azabu, 1F, 2F (Minato-ku) **81-3/5771-0170** • 11:30am-5am • multiple locations

Kakiden 3-37-11 Shinjuku, 8th flr **81-3/3352-5121** • lunch & dinner • upscale Japanese

Kitchen Five 4-2-15 Nishi-Azabu (Minato-ku) **81-3/3409-8835** • 6pm-9:45pm • Mediterranean • woman chef

Las Chicas Jingumae 5-47-6 (off Shibuya), Shibuya-ku **81-3/3407-6865** • 11:30am-11pm • English spoken

Maisen 4-8-5 Jingu-mae (Shibuya-ku) **81-3/3470-0071** • specializes in tonkatsu

Moti 3F Roppongi Hama Bldg (6-2-35 Roppongi) **81-3/3479-1939** • noon-10pm • Indian

New York Grill 3-7-1-2 Nishi Shinjuku (at Park Hyatt Hotel, 52nd flr) **81-3/5322-1234** • lunch & dinner • reservations recommended

The Pink Cow 1-3-18 Shibuya, Shibuya-ku (Villa Modernuna B-1, across from Aoyama Park Tower) **81-3/3406-5597** • 5pm-late, clsd Mon

Sasa-no-yuki 2-15-10 Negishi (Taito-ku) **81-3/3873-1145** • 11am-9pm, clsd Mon • serving homemade tofu for 300 years

Tenmatsu 1-6-1 Dogen-zaka (Shibuya-ku) **81-3/3462-2815** • tempura

RETAIL SHOPS

Isetan Men's 3-14-1 Shinjuku 1-11-15 **81-3/3352-1111** • 6pm-midnight, from 4pm Sat, clsd Sun • mostly gay men • karaoke

THAILAND

Bangkok

INFO LINES & SERVICES

Gay AA 12/3 Silom Rd (at the Coffee Society) **66-2/235-9784** • 7pm Tue

ACCOMMODATIONS

Baan Saladaeng 69/2 Soi Saladaeng 3, Saladaeng Rd (Silom, Bangrak) **66-2/2636-3038** • gay-friendly • upscale • near gay scene

Bangkok Rama Place, City Resort & Hotel 1546 Pattanakarn Rd (in Suan-Luang District) **66-2/722-6602-10** • gay-friendly • full brkfst • pool • kids ok • also restaurant • WiFi • wheelchair access • lesbian-owned

D&D Inn 68-70 Khaosan Rd (Phranakorn) **66-2/629-0526** • gay-friendly • "life's little luxuries at a price you can afford" • central location • pool

Elephantstay Royal Elephant Kraal & Village (74/1 M3 Tumbol Suanpik), Phra Nakhon Si Ayutthaya **66-81/668-7727, 66-87/116-3307** • gay/ straight • live w/, care for & learn about elephants • near Lopburi River • 1 hour to Bangkok • lesbian-owned

Furama Silom 59 Silom Rd **66-2/237-0488** • gay-friendly • pool • sauna • gym • restaurant • bar

Hotel de Moc 78 Prajatipatai Rd, Pra-Nakorn **66-2/282-2831-3, 66-2/629-2100-5** • gay-friendly • pool • WiFi • wheelchair access

Lub d 4 Decho Rd (Silom, Bangrak) **66-2/634-7999** • gay-friendly • hostel with some private rooms • WiFi

Luxx 6/11 Decho Rd **66-2/635-8800** • gay-friendly • style-conscious, minimalist design hotel • full brkfst • WiFi

Old Bangkok Inn 607 Pra Sumen Rd (at Rajdamnern Ave, in Pra Nakhon) **66-2/629-1787** • environmentally-friendly • full brkfst • kids/ pets ok • nonsmoking

Omyim Lodge 72-74 Naratiwat Rd Silom **66-2/635-0169** • gay/ straight • full brkfst • nonsmoking • kids ok • WiFi • lesbian & gay-owned

Pinnacle Hotel 17 Soi Ngam Duphli, Rama 4 Rd, Sathorn 66–2/287–0111 • gay/ straight • fitness center

Regency Park Hotel 12/3 Sukhumvit 22, Soi Sainamthip 66–2/259–7420 • gay-friendly • located in heart of Bangkok • full brkfst • pool

Sheraton Grande Sukhumvit 250 Sukhumvit Rd 66–2/649–8888 • gay-friendly • tropical garden • pool WiFi • wheelchair access • also Thai & Italian restaurant

Tarntawan Place Hotel 119/ 5-10 Surawong Rd 66–2/238–2620 • centrally located • kids ok • discount for gays • WiFi • wheelchair access

White Orchid 409 - 421, Yaowaraj Road 66–2/226–0026 • gay-friendly • also cafe

Bars

70's Bar 231/16 Sarasin (Chitlom) 66–2/253–4433 • lesbians/ gay men • dancing/DJ • retro lounge

The Balcony Pub & Restaurant 86–88 Silom Soi 4 (off Silom Rd) 66–2/235–5891 • 5:30pm-close • popular • mostly gay men • karaoke • terrace

BAS Living Room Silom Soi 4 (opposite Sphinx) 66–2/632–6982 • 6pm-2am • mostly gay men • neighborhood bar • WiFi

Bed Supperclub 26 Soi Sukhumvit 11, Sukhumvit Rd, Klongtoey-nua, Wattana 66–2/651–3537 • 7:30pm-close • gay/ straight • dancing/DJ • dinner served in bed

Club Love Remix Ramkhamhaeng Soi 89/2 66–2/378–4345, 66–1/987–4946 • gay/ straight • dancing/DJ • also restaurant

@Diamond 10/17 Silom Soi 2/1 66–2/234–0459 • 6pm-2am • mostly men • neighborhood bar • food served

Expresso 8/10-11 Silom Rd, Soi 2 (Bang Rak) • mostly gay men • relaxed café-bar

Golden Dome 252/5 Ratchadapisek Rd Soi 18 (Huay Kwang) 66–2/692–8202 • lesbians/ gay men • cabaret • shows nightly at 5pm, 7pm & 9pm

Hamilton's Hideaway Soi Silom 2/1 (Saladaeng BTS Station, Silom) 66–866/143–644 • 6pm-1am • mostly gay men • food served • live jazz • nonsmoking

Bangkok

WHERE THE GIRLS ARE:
Everywhere. Though there are few specifically lesbian establishments in Bangkok, nearly all are welcoming to Toms and Dees (the butch/ femme designations most Thais prefer to the l-word).

ANNUAL EVENTS:
Jan - Chinese New Year Festival.
April - Songkran (Thai New Year or Water Festival).
May - Royal Ploughing Ceremony.
Aug 12 - Queen Sirikit's birthday.

CITY INFO:
Tourism Authority of Thailand 1672, web: www.tourismthailand.org.

BEST VIEW:
Baiyoke Sky Hotel observation deck.

ATTRACTIONS:
The Grand Palace 66–2/224–3328, web: palaces.thai.net.
The Jim Thompson House 66–2/216–7368, web: www.jimthompsonhouse.com.
Lumphini Park.
National Museum 66–2/224–1333.
Wat Arun 66–2/891–1149, web: www.watarun.org.
Wat Benchamabophit 66–2/282–7413.
Wat Pho 66–2/222–5910.
Wat Phra Kaeo 66–2/222–8181.

WEATHER:
Tropical, with heavy rains throughout the summer & drier weather Jan-Feb. Temperatures can dip as low as the 60°s Nov-Dec, and rise as high as the 90°s March-May.

TRANSIT:
SkyTrain 66–2/617-6000, web: www.bts.co.th.

JJ Park 8/3 Silom Rd, Soi 2 (Bang Rak) 66-2/235-1227 • 10:30pm-2am • gay/ straight • food • live music

Maxi's Bar & Restaurant 38/1-2 Soi Pratoochai Suriwong Rd 66-2/2266-4225 • 6pm-2am • mostly gay men

MTV Remix Ramkhamhaeng Soi 24 66-2/319-8340 • gay/ straight • dancing/DJ

Telephone Pub & Restaurant 114/ 11 Silom Rd, Soi 4 66-2/234-3279 • 6pm-1am • lesbians/ gay men • karaoke • WiFi • food served

Nightclubs

DJ Station 8/6-8 Silom Rd, Soi 2 (Bang Rak) 66-02/266-4029 • 10:30pm-2am • lesbians/ gay men • dancing/DJ

E-FUN (Extreme Fun for ladies) • 8pm-2am • 3-story bar popular w/ more mature lesbians • live shows • patio

For Fun 90 Silom Rd, Soi 4 • mostly men • live music venue

Happen 8/14 Silom Soi 2 • 8pm-late, busy after 11pm • mostly gay men • karaoke

Pharaoh's Music Bar 104 Silom Soi 4 (above Sphinx) 66-2/234-7249 • 7pm-2am • gay/ straight • food • karaoke

Zeta 29/67-69 Soi Soonvijai (aka Royal City Ave, or RCA) (Block C, Rama 9) 66-2/203-1043 • 9pm-2am • women only • live music

Cafes

Bug & Bee 18 Silom Rd, Suriyawong (Bang Rak) 66-2/233-8118 • 24hrs

Coffee Society 12/3 Silom Rd (Suriyawong, Bang Rak) 66-2/235-9784 • 24hrs • WiFi • also art gallery

Dick's Cafe Bangkok 894/7-8 Soi Pratuchai (Duangthawee Plaza, off Surawong Rd) 66-2/637-0078 • 11am-2am • European-style cafe in the heart of the action

Restaurants

Cabbages & Condoms 6 Soi 12 Sukhumvit Rd (at Birds & Bees Resort) 66-2/229-4611 • 11am-10pm • Thai food w/ safe-sex education

Coyote on Convent 1/2 Sivadon Bldg Convent (Silom Bangrak) 66-2/631-2325 • 11am-midnight • Mexican • ladies night 6pm-8pm Wed & 10pm-midnight Sat

Crêpes & Co 18/1 Sukhumvit Soi 12 (Klongtoey) 66-2/653-3990 • 9am-midnight, • terrace • lounge • full bar

Eat Me Soi Pipat 2 (off Soi Convent) 66-2/238-0931 • 3pm-1am • upscale • also gallery • live music

Food Loft 1027 Ploenchit Rd, Lumpini, Pathumwan (Central Chisholm, 7th flr) 66-2/655-7777 • upscale int'l food

Full Moon 144/2 Silom Soi 10 66-2/634-0766 • Thai food • gay-owned

Hemlock 56 Phra Arthit Rd, Chanasongkram 66-2/282-7507 • 5pm-midnight, clsd Sun • traditional Thai food • more lesbian wknds

Indigo 6 Convent Rd (off Silom Rd) 66-2/235-3268 • noon-1am, clsd Sun • patio • full bar • French

Loy Nava Dinner Cruises 37 Charoen Nakorn Rd, Klongsan 66-2/437-4932 • traditional Thai cuisine on rice barge on Chao Phraya River • reservations required

Mali 43 Sathorn Soi 1 66-2/679-8693 • 8am-11pm • Thai & int'l • gay-owned

Mango Tree 37 Soi Tantawan (off Suriwong Rd) 66-2/236-2820 • popular • reservations recommended • traditional Thai food • live music nightly

May Kaidee 111 Tanao Rd, Bang-lam-phu (behind Burger King) 66-9/137-3173 • 9am-11pm • innovative vegetarian • also 33 Samen Rd (Soi 1)

O...Ho... 2/8 Soi Sri Bumphen 66-2/286-5292 • 9am-midnight • Thai & Western menu • gay-owned

Once Upon a Time 32 Soi Petchaburi 17, Pratunam 66-2/252-8629 • 11am-11pm • Thai

Sphinx 100 Silom Soi 4 66-2/234-7249 • 6pm-1am • popular • Thai & Western • mostly gay men • full bar • karaoke • terrace

Sweet Basil 86/1 Ramkhamhaeng Rd (at Pure Place Mall) 66-02/729-8527 • 11:30am-9pm • popular • Vietnamese food

Zup Zip 674 Soi 101, Lad Prao Rd 66-081/734-2759 • popular w/ local lesbians • lesbian-owned

Entertainment & Recreation

Calypso Cabaret 296 Phaya Thai Rd, Pathumwan (at Asia Hotel) 66-2/261-6355 • lesbians/ gay men • cabaret • drag shows nightly at 8:15pm & 9:30pm

Mambo 59/28 Sathu-phararam 3 Rd 66-2/294-7381-2 • lesbians/ gay men • cabaret • shows nightly at 7:15pm & 10pm

AUSTRALIA

Sydney

INFO LINES & SERVICES

The Gender Centre 61-2/9569-2366 • free services for transgender/ transsexual people & their partners/ friends/ families • also publishes magazine *Polare*

Lesbian & Gay Counselling Service 61-2/8594-9596, 1-800/18-4527 (OUTSIDE SYDNEY) • 5:30-10:30, info & support

ACCOMMODATIONS

Apartment Hotel East Sydney 150 Liverpool St, E Sydney (at Oxford St) 61/404-793-159 • gay/ straight • 2-bdrm apts • nonsmoking • kids ok terrace & gourmet kitchen

Brickfield Hill B&B Inn 403 Riley St (at Foveaux), Surry Hills 61-2/9211-4886 • gay/ straight • beautifully & carefully restored Victorian terrace-house in the gay Oxford St District • near beaches & downtown • WiFi • gay-owned

Chelsea Guest House 49 Womerah Ave (at Oswald Ln), Darlinghurst 61-2/9380-5994 • gay/ straight • Victorian w/ Italianate courtyard • nonsmoking • gay-owned

Hotel Stellar 4 Wentworth Ave (at Oxford St) 61-2/9264-9754 • lesbians/ gay men • kitchenette in each room • WiFi • cafe & bar

Kirketon Boutique Hotel 229 Darlinghurst Rd (at Farrell Ave) 61-2/9332-2011, 800/332-920 (AUSTRALIA ONLY) • gay-friendly • also restaurant & bars • kids ok • WiFi

Medusa 267 Darlinghurst Rd (at Liverpool), Darlinghurst 61-2/9331-1000 • gay-friendly • modern boutique hotel • WiFi

Nomads Westend 412 Pitt St (at Goulburn St) 61-2/9211-4588, 1800/013-186 • gay-friendly • budget/ backpacker's accommodations • cafe • wheelchair access

Pensione Hotel 631-635 George St (at Goulburn St) 61-2/9265-8888, 800/885-886 • gay-friendly • also restaurant & bar

Victoria Court Hotel Sydney 122 Victoria St (at Orwell, Potts Point) 61-2/9357-3200, 1800/630-505 (IN AUSTRALIA) • gay-friendly • historic B&B-inn in elegant Victorian • full brkfst

BARS

Bar Cleveland/ Hershey Bar 433 Cleveland St (at Bourke), Surry Hills 61-2/9698-1908 • 11am-4am • noon-midnight Sun • gay/ straight • alternative • cocktail lounge • DJ • young crowd

The Beauchamp 265 Oxford St (at S Dowling), Darlinghurst 61-2/9331-2575 • noon-2am popular • gay/ straight • neighborhood bar • food served • pronounced "Bee-chum" • gay-owned

Beresford Sundays 354 Bourke St (at Albion St), Surry Hills 61-2/9357-1111 • from noon Sun • lesbians/ gay men • fun in the sun

The Colombian 117-123 Oxford St (at Crown St), Darlinghurst 61-2/9360-2151 • 9am-6am • lesbians/ gay men • dancing/DJ • theme nights

Green Park Hotel 360 Victoria St (at Liverpool), Darlinghurst 61-2/9380-5311 • 10am-2am, noon-midnight Sun • more gay Sun • stylish bar

The Imperial Hotel 35 Erskineville Rd, Newtown 61-2/9519-9899 • lesbians/ gay men • dancing/DJ • food served • drag shows

Lava Bar 2 Oxford St (top flr of Burdekin Hotel), Darlinghurst 61-2/9331-3066 • 11am-1am, 4pm-4am Sat • gay/ straight • popular w/ lesbians Fri till 4am • live shows

The Oxford 134 Oxford St (at Bourke St, Taylor Square), Darlinghurst 61-2/8324-5200 • 10am-close • popular • lesbians/ gay men • 3 bars include the Polo Lounge, Supper Club & Gilligans

The Palms On Oxford 124 Oxford St (at Bourke St, Taylor Square), Darlinghurst 61-2/9357-4166 • 8pm-late, clsd Mon-Wed • dancing/DJ

Phoenix Bar 34 Oxford St (at Exchange Hotel), Darlinghurst 61-2/9331-2956 • 10am-5am, till 7am Fri-Sun, clsd Mon-Tue • gay/ straight • sweaty downstairs dance den • 5 other bars in complex

The Stonewall 175 Oxford St (at Bourke), Darlinghurst 61-2/9360-1963 • noon-6am, from 9am wknds • popular • mostly gay men • dancing/DJ • drag shows

ZanziBar 323 King St (at Phillips St), Newtown 62-2/9519-1511 • gay-friendly • food served

Nightclubs

ARQ 16 Flinders St (at Taylor Square), Darlinghurst **61–2/9380–8700** • 9pm-late Th-Sun, clsd Mon-Wed • popular • mostly gay men • dancing/DJ • restaurant • drag shows Th • cover charge

Bitch **61–2/439–430–428** • hot weekly women's parties • also big events on long wknds • www.bitchnews.com.au

The Black Boater 16 Wentworth Ave (at Lyons Ln, Surry Hills) **61–2/9267–6440** • check www.theblackboater.com for events • food served

Chicks With Picks 20 Broadway Rd (at Kensington St, at Clare Hotel), Ultimo • 2nd Sun only • women's open mic

Hellfire 16-18 Oxford Square (on corner of Riley, at The Gaff), Darlinghurst • 9:30pm-late 3rd Fri • gay/ straight women-oriented fetish party • dancing/DJ • alternative • leather • burlesque • live shows • cover charge

Home Tenancy 101, Cockle Bay Wharf (at Wheat Rd, Darling Harbour) **61–2/9266–0600** • open Fri-Sun • popular • gay-friendly • hosts Homesexual (www.homesexual.com.au)

The Midnight Shift 85 Oxford St (at Riley), Darlinghurst **61–2/9358–3848** • 10pm-late Fri-Sat • also Saddle Bar • popular • mostly gay men

Moist 16 Flinders St (at Taylor Square, at ARQ), Darlinghurst **61–2/9380–8700** • last Fri only • popular • mostly women • dancing/DJ • drag king shows • cover charge

Nevermind 163 Oxford St, Darlinghurst • Fri-Sun only • gay/ straight • theme nights • cutting edge electronic music

Pussycat Club 134 Oxford St (at Bourke), Darlinghurst **61–2/9331–3467** • 3rd Sat only • mostly women • trans-friendly • dancing/DJ • cabaret & burlesque shows • all queers welcome

Queer Central 199 Enmore Rd (at Sly Fox Hotel), Enmore **61–2/9557–1016** • 9pm Wed only • mostly women • dancing/DJ • live performances

Rising Day Club 34 Oxford St (at Phoenix bar), Darlinghurst • recovery club starts at 4am Sat & Sun • mostly gay men • dancing/DJ

Slide 41 Oxford St (at Pelican) **61–2/8915–1899** • 6pm-3am, 5pm-4am Fri, 7pm-4am Sat-Sun, clsd Mon-Tue • lesbians/ gay men • dancing/DJ • also restaurant • live music • cabaret

Sly Fox 199 Enmore Rd, Enmore **61–2/9557–1016** • lesbians/ gay men • dyke night Wed • karaoke

Tank 3 Bridge Ln (behind Establishment Hotel) **61–2/9240–3000** • 10pm-6am Fri-Sat • check locally for next DTPM gay party at this multi-award wining dance club on Sun nights

Velvet Wednesdays 324 King St (at the Bank Hotel), Newtown • 8pm Wed only • mostly women • dancing/DJ

Cafes

Cafe Sopra 7 Danks St **61–2/9699–3174** • 10am-3pm, from 8am Sat, clsd Mon • Italian vegetarian

Victoire 285 Darling St **61–2/9818–5529** • great bread

Vinyl Lounge Cafe 17 Elizabeth Bay Rd, Elizabeth Bay **61–2/9326–9224** • 7am-4pm, from 8am wknds, clsd Mon • lesbians/ gay men • light menu • plenty veggie • cash only

Restaurants

Bentley Restaurant & Bar 320 Crown St (Surry Hills) **61–2/9332–2344** • noon-late, clsd Sun- Mon • tapas & small plates • excellent wine

Bertoni Casalinga 281 Darling St **61–2/9818–5845** • 6am-6pm, clsd Sat & Sun • Italian

Betty's Soup Kitchen 84 Oxford St, Darlinghurst **61–2/9360–9698** • noon-10pm, till midnight Fri-Sat • lesbians/ gay men • healthy homecooking • plenty veggie

Bills Surry Hills 359 Crown St (Surry Hills) **61–2/9360–4762** • 7am-10pm • great ricotta pancakes

Billy Kwong 3/355 Crown St (Surry Hills) **61–2/9332–3300** • sustainable local and organic Chinese from 6pm daily • reservations recommended • wheelchair access

Bird Cow Fish 500 Crown St (Surry Hills) **61–2/9380–4090** • lunch & dinner • bistro & espresso bar

The Boathouse on Blackwattle Bay End of Ferry Road (Glebe) **61–2/9518–9011** • lunch & dinner Tue-Sun • gourmet seafood • some veggie • great view • reservations required

Bright N Up 77 Oxford St, Darlinghurst **61–2/9361–3379** • 4:30pm-midnight

Chu Bay 312a Bourke St, Darlinghurst **61–2/9331–3386** • 5:30pm-11pm • Vietnamese • some veggie

Danks Street Depot 2 Danks St **61–2/9698–2201** • great brkfst

Fu Manchu 249 Victoria St, Darlinghurst **61–2/9360–9424** • lunch & dinner • chic noodle bar • plenty veggie • nonsmoking • cash only

Iku Wholefood Kitchen 25a Glebe Point Rd, Glebe **61–2/9692–8720, 800/732–962** • lunch & dinner • creative vegan/ macrobiotic fare • nonsmoking • outdoor seating • cash only

Sydney

WHERE THE GIRLS ARE:
In Leichhardt (aka "Dykeheart") and Newtown.

LGBT PRIDE:
June - Sydney Gay & Lesbian Pride. 61–2/9383-0900.

ANNUAL EVENTS:
January - Sydney Festival, web: www.sydneyfestival.org.au.
February/March - Sydney Gay & Lesbian Mardi Gras Festival. Nearly a month of events and parties. 61–2/9383–0900, web: www.mardigras.org.au.
July - Sydney Leather Pride Week, web: www.sydneyleatherpride.org.
September - Manly Jazz Festival 61–2/9976–1430, web: www.manly.nsw.gov.au.
October - Sleaze Ball 61–2/9383–0900, web: www.mardigras.org.au.

CITY INFO:
Sydney Tourist Information, web: www.discoversydney.com.au.
Sydney Visitors Centre, 61–2/9240–8788, web: www.sydneyvisitorcentre.com.

BEST VIEW:
From the AMP Centrepoint Tower or Mrs Macquarie's Chair

WEATHER:
Temperate—in the 50°s-70°s year-round. The summer months (January-March) can get hot and humid. Spring (September-December) sees the least rain. It's sunny most of the year. Bring a hat and lots of sunscreen!

ATTRACTIONS:
Art Gallery of New South Wales 61–2/9225–1700, web: www.artgallery.nsw.gov.au.
Bondi Beach.
Chinatown.
Darling Harbour.
Featherdale Wildlife Park 61–2/9622–1644, web: www.featherdale.com.au.
Manly beaches 61-2/9976-1430, web: www.manlyaustralia.com.au.
Museum of Contemporary Art 61–2/9245–2400, web: www.mca.com.au.
Queen Victoria Building, web: www.qvb.com.au.
The Rocks.
Royal Botanical Gardens 61–2/9231–8111, web: www.rbgsyd.nsw.gov.au.
Sydney Harbour Bridge.
Sydney Jewish Museum 61–2/9360–7999, web: sydney-jewishmuseum.com.au.
Sydney Opera House 61–2/9250–7111, web: www.sydneyoperahouse.com.
The Women's Library 61-2/9557-7060, web: www.thewomensli-brary.org.au.

TRANSIT:
61-2/133-300, web: www.taxiscom-bined.com.au.
Airport Connect 1-300-737-2 12, web: www.airportconnect.com.au.
State Transit Authority 61–2/131–500, web: www.sta.nsw.gov.au.
Monorail 61–2/8584-5288, web: www.metrolightrail.com.au.

Kujin 41b Elizabeth Bay Rd, Elizabeth Bay **61–2/9331–6077** • lunch & dinner, clsd Mon • Japanese

Last Drop Cafe 538 Marrickville Rd (Dulwich Hill) **61–2/9572–9800** • 7:30am-5:30pm, till 4pm Sat, clsd Sun • Greek food • also art gallery

Pink Peppercorn 122 Oxford St (near Taylor Square), Darlinghurst **61–2/9360–9922** • 6pm-11pm • Laotian & Thai • gay-owned

Queen Victoria Hotel/ Razors Bistro 167 Enmore Rd, Enmore **61–2/9517–9685**

Sean's Panorama 270 Campbell Parade, Bondi Beach **61–2/9365–4924** • lunch Fri-Sun, dinner Wed-Sat, clsd Mon-Tue

Thai Kanteen 541 Military Rd, Mosman **61–2/9960–3282** • lunch Th-Sun, dinner nightly • modern Thai • gay-owned

Thai Pothong 294 King St (Newtown) **61–2/9550–6277** • lunch & dinner • Thai • wheelchair access

ENTERTAINMENT & RECREATION

Bondi Beach Bondi Beach • Sydney's most popular beach • more gay at north end

Lady Jane Beach/ Lady Bay Beach Watsons Bay • crowded nude beach • mostly men

McIver Baths/ Coogee Pool Beach St, Grant Reserve, Coogee • pool for women and children only

Obelisk Beach Middle Head Rd (at Chowder Bay Rd) • mostly men • gay beach • nudity permitted

Sydney by Diva departs from Oxford Hotel (in Taylor Square), Darlinghurst **61–2/9310–0200** • tour Sydney w/ drag queen host

Sydney Gay/ Lesbian Mardi Gras 94 Oxford St, Darlinghurst 2010 **61–2/9383–0900** • the wildest party under the rainbow on this planet (see www.mardigras.org.au)

The Women's Library 8-10 Brown St **61–2/9557–7060** • "books, journals, ephemera, & art by, for, & about women"

BOOKSTORES

The Bookshop Darlinghurst 207 Oxford St (near Darlinghurst Rd), Darlinghurst **61–2/9331–1103** • 10am-10pm • Australia's oldest LGBT bookstore • staff happy to help w/ tourist info

The Feminist Bookshop Orange Grove Plaza, Balmain Rd, Shop 9, Lilyfield **61–2/9810–2666** • 10:30am-6pm, till 4pm Sat, clsd Sun

Gertrude & Alice 46 Hall St (Bondi Beach) **61–2/9130–5155** • second-hand books • also coffee shop

RETAIL SHOPS

Bang 4 Flinders St, Darlinghurst **61–2/9357–3362** • designer labels, clubwear

House of Priscilla 47 Oxford St, Darlinghurst **61–2/9286–3023** • wigs, costumes & more

PUBLICATIONS

LOTL Magazine **61–2/9332–2725** • Lesbians on the Loose • monthly magazine

SX Weekly **61–2/9360–8934** • free gay/ lesbian weekly

Sydney Star Observer **61–2/8263–0500** • weekly newspaper w/ club & event listings

GYMS & HEALTH CLUBS

City Gym 107–113 Crown St, E Sydney **61–2/9211–2799** • day passes available

Gold's Gym Sydney 58 Kippax St (level 1), Surry Hills **61–2/9211–2799** • 5:30am-9pm, 8am-8pm Sat, till 6pm Sun

SEX CLUBS

Aarows 17 Bridge St (at Pitt St), Rydalmere **61–2/9638–0553, /1300–062–541** • 24hrs • lesbians/ gay men • transgender-friendly • 18+

EROTICA

House of Fetish 93 Oxford St, Darlinghurst **61–2/9380–9042**

USA

ALABAMA

Geneva

Spring Creek Campground & Resort 163 Campground Rd (at Hwy 52 & Country Rd 4) **334/684–3891** • mostly gay men • cabins • also tent & RV sites • BYOB • pool • nudity ok • some theme wknds w/ DJ • WiFi • gay-owned

ALASKA

Fairbanks

Billie's Backpackers Hostel 2895 Mack Blvd **907/479–2034** • gay-friendly • kids ok • food served • women-owned

ARIZONA

Apache Junction

Susa's Serendipity Ranch 4375 E Superstition Blvd **480/288–9333** • women only • guesthouses on 15-acre ranch • 2 RV hookups • hot tub • non-smoking • pets ok • lesbian-owned

Bisbee

David's Oasis Camping Resort 5311 W Double Adobe Rd, McNeal **520/979–6650** • lesbians/ gay men • 21+ • pool • also bar & internet cafe • WiFi • gay-owned

White Mountains

Arizona High Country Campground 5064 Sawmill Rd (1 mile off Hwy 260), Clay Springs **928/739–4383** • lesbians/ gay men • 10 campsites & RV hookups • WiFi • lesbian-owned

CALIFORNIA

Clearlake

Edgewater Resort 6420 Soda Bay Rd (at Hohape Rd), Kelseyville **707/279–0208, 800/396–6224** • "gay-owned, straight-friendly" • cabin • camping & RV hookups • lake access & pool• boat facilities • WiFi • kids/ pets ok • lesbian-owned

Joshua Tree Nat'l Park

Starland Retreat Yucca Valley **760/364–2069** • mostly gay men & radical faeries, but women very welcome • membership-only rustic rural camp • hot tub • nudity permitted

Mendocino

Orr Hot Springs 13201 Orr Springs Rd, Ukiah **707/462–6277** • gay-friendly • hostel-style cabins, private cottages & campsites • clothing-optional • kids ok • mineral hot springs • pool • no food provided • reservations required

Placerville

Rancho Cicada Retreat 10001 Bell Rd, Plymouth **209/245–4841, 877/553–9481** • mostly gay men • secluded riverside retreat in the Sierra foothills w/ 2-person tents & cabin • swimming • nudity • gay-owned

Russian River

Guerneville Lodge 15905 River Rd (at Hwy 116), Guerneville **707/869–0102** • gay/straight • WiFi • nonsmoking • gay-owned

Highlands Resort 14000 Woodland Dr, Guerneville **707/869–0333** • lesbians/ gay men • country retreat on 4 wooded acres • hot tub • swimming • clothing-optional pool

Yosemite Nat'l Park

Rivendale Ranch 209/962–7425 • women only • nonsmoking • also RV hookups • women-owned

The Yosemite Bug Rustic Mountain Resort 6979 Hwy 140, Midpines **209/966–6666, 866/826–7108** • gay-friendly • hostel w/ dorms, cabins, private rooms & tents • some shared baths • kids ok • nonsmoking • WiFi • wheelchair access

COLORADO

Durango

Mesa Verde Far View Lodge 1 Navajo Hill, Mesa Verde National Park **602/331–5210, 800/449–2288** • gay-friendly • hotel • camping • RV hookups • inside nat'l park at 8250' elevation • views of 4 states • full brkfst • nonsmoking • WiFi

Fort Collins

Archer's Poudre River Resort 33021 Poudre Canyon Hwy, Bellvue **970/881-2139, 888/822-0588** • gay-friendly • cabins, tents, RV hookups • lesbian-owned

FLORIDA

Fort Myers

The Resort on Carefree Blvd 3000 Carefree Blvd (at Cleveland Ave) **239/731-6366** • mostly women • homes & RV lots • pool • gym • kids/pets ok • older crowd • nonsmoking • woman-owned

Miami

Something Special, A Lesbian Venture 305/696-8826 • women only • apt, camping & dining

Tampa

Sawmill Camping Resort 21710 US Hwy 98, Dade City **352/583-0664** • mostly gay men • theme wknds w/ entertainment • RV hookups • cabins • tent spots • dancing • karaoke • pool • nudity • gay-owned

GEORGIA

Dahlonega

Swiftwaters Womanspace 706/864-3229 • women only • on scenic river • seasonal • nonsmoking • deck • dogs ok • women-owned

Dewy Rose

The River's Edge 2311 Pulliam Mill Rd **706/213-8081** • mostly gay men • cabins • camping • RV • live shows • pool • nudity • nonsmoking • wheelchair access

Quitman

Bobcat Resort Campground 1877 Hickory Head Rd **229/263-4300** • lesbians/gay men • private membership campground • swimming • clothing-optional • nonsmoking • pets ok • WiFi • wheelchair access • gay-owned

Unadilla

Lumberjack's Camping Resort 50 Hwy 230 (at Hwy 41) **478/783-2267, 877/888-1688** • mostly gay men • campsites, cabins & RV hookups • pool • live shows • WiFi • pets ok • gay-owned • also restaurant

HAWAII

Hawaii (Big Island)

Margo's Corner near South Point **808/929-9614** • cottage & 4 campsites • full brkfst & dinner • kids ok • sauna • WiFi • lesbian-owned

Kalani Oceanside Retreat **808/965-7828, 800/800-6886** • gay/straight • coastal wellness retreat & spa • pool • nudity • nonsmoking • WiFi • food served • wheelchair access

Kulana: The Affordable Artists Sanctuary 808/985-9055 • mostly women • artist retreat • camping, cabins & guest rooms available • no smoking, drugs or alcohol • kids ok • women-owned

ILLINOIS

Du Quoin

The Pit 7403 Persimmon Rd **618/542-9470** • lesbians/ gay men • primitive camping • 18+ • nudity ok • swimming • gay-owned

MAINE

Augusta

Maple Hill Farm B&B Inn Hallowell **207/622-2708, 800/622-2708** • gay/straight • Victorian farmhouse on 130 acres • full brkfst • swimming pond • nonsmoking • WiFi • wheelchair access • gay-owned

Ogunquit

Beaver Dam Campground 551 School St, Rte 9, Berwick **207/698-2267** • gay-friendly • campground on 20-acre spring-fed pond • pool • kids/ pets ok • women-owned

MICHIGAN

Owendale

Windover Resort 3596 Blakely Rd **989/375-2586** • women only • seasonal private resort • campsites & RV hookups • pool

Saugatuck

The Bunkhouse B&B at Campit 269/543-4335, 877/226-7481 • lesbians/ gay men • cabins • private baths • access to Campit Resort amenities (see listing below) • pool • nonsmoking • WiFi

Campit Outdoor Resort 6635 118th Ave, Fennville **269/543-4335, 877/226-7481** • lesbians/ gay men • campsites • RV hookups • separate women's area • pool • seasonal • pets ok • WiFi • membership required • lesbian & gay-owned

MISSISSIPPI

Bay Saint Louis

Nella's Park 16145 Hwy 603 (near I-10), Kiln **228/586-0053** • gay/ straight • camping • kids/ pets ok • friendly & clean w/ fishing dock • casino nearby • close to New Orleans

MISSOURI

Branson

Branson Stagecoach RV Park 5751 State Hwy 165 **417/335-8185, 800/446-7110** • gay-friendly • pull-thru & back-in RV sites • cabins • pool • WiFi • gay-owned

NEVADA

Gerlach

F Ranch 775/557-2804 • women only • B&B on remote NW Nevada working horse/ cattle ranch • April-Sept • birdwatching • kids ok • nonsmoking

NEW MEXICO

Ramah

El Morro RV Park, Cabins & Cafe 4018 Hwy 53 **505/783-4612** • gay/ straight • in Zuni Mtns • full brkfst • nonsmoking • WiFi • also cafe • lesbian-owned

NEW YORK

Adirondack Mtns

Falls Brook Yurts in Adirondacks John Brannon Rd, Minerva **518/761-6187** • gay-friendly • access to hiking, fishing & boating • kids/ pets ok

Syracuse

Yellow Lantern Kampground 1770 Rte 13 N, Cortland **607/756-2959** • gay-friendly • kids/ pets ok • pool campsites & RV hookups

NORTH CAROLINA

Asheville

Compassionate Expressions Mtn Inn & Healing Sanctuary 828/683-6633 • mostly women • cabins & rooms w/ a view of Blue Ridge Mtns • spa services • hot tub • nonsmoking • wheelchair access • women-owned

Brevard

Ash Grove Mountain Cabins & Camping 749 E Fork Rd **828/885-7216** • gay/ straight • camping & cabins • on 14 wooded acres in Blue Ridge Mtns • hot tub • nonsmoking • WiFi • gay-owned

OHIO

Athens

SuBAMUH (Susan B Anthony Memorial UnRest Home) Womyn's Land Trust PO Box 5853, 45701 **740/448-6424, 740/448-7285** • women only • cabins & camping • summer workshops • swimming • hot tub • nonsmoking • lesbian-owned

OKLAHOMA

Grand Lake

Southern Oaks Resort & Spa 2 miles S of Hwy 28/ 82 Junction, Langley **918/782-9346, 866/452-5307** • gay-friendly • 19 cabins on 30 acres • pool • hot tub • nonsmoking • gay-owned

OREGON

Grants Pass

Rainbows on the Fly 541/862–2086 • women's land on 40 acres • cabin, campsites, RV hookups • also guided flyfishing • nonsmoking • WiFi • lesbian-owned

WomanShare 541/862–2807 • women only • cabins • shared kitchen • bathhouse • hot tub • girls/ pets ok • nonsmoking • lesbian-owned

PENNSYLVANIA

New Milford

Oneida Campground & Lodge 570/465–7011 • mostly gay men • seasonal • RV hookups • 1 guest cottage • pool • nudity • WiFi • gay-owned

Pittsburgh

Camp Davis 311 Red Brush Rd, Boyers 724/637–2402 • April-Oct • lesbians/ gay men • cabins, trailer, & campsites • pool • adults 21+ only • 1 hour from Pittsburgh

Poconos

The Woods Campground 845 Vaughn Acres Ln, Lehighton 610/377–9577 • lesbians/ gay men • 84 campsites • RV spots • also cabins • swimming • 18+ • WiFi

SOUTH DAKOTA

Salem

Camp America 25495 US 81 605/425–9085 • gay-friendly • 35 miles west of Sioux Falls • camping • RV hookups • pool • kids/ pets ok • nonsmoking • WiFi • lesbian-owned

TENNESSEE

Gatlinburg

Big Creek Outdoors 5019 Rag Mtn Rd, Hartford 423/487–5742, 423/487–3490 • gay/ straight • cabins • camping • horseback riding • kids ok • wheelchair access

TEXAS

Groesbeck

Rainbow Ranch Campground 1662 LCR 800 254/729–8484, 888/875–7596 • lesbians/ gay men • on Lake Limestone • pool • campsites • cabins • nonsmoking • gay-owned

Lockhart

Lazy J Paradise Campground & Park 270 Hidden Path (CR 303 and FM 2001) 210/863–9314 • campground with RV area catering to the GLBT community • pool • WiFi

Marfa

El Cosmico Hwy 67 432/729–1950, 877/822–1950 • gay/straight • vintage trailer, yurt & teepee hotel & campground • WiFi • lesbian-owned

UTAH

Moab

Los Vados Canyon House 801/532–2651 • gay/ straight • retreat house in a red rock canyon • pool • kids 10 & over ok • nonsmoking • also tent cabin

VERMONT

Craftsbury Common

Greenhope Farm 2478 Wylie Hill Rd 802/586–7577 • gay/ straight • nonsmoking • kids ok • WiFi • lesbian-owned

Townshend

Townshend State Park 2755 State Forest Rd 802/365–7500, 888/409–7579 • gay-friendly • campground • great hiking • open Memorial Day wknd to Labor Day wknd

VIRGINIA

Charlottesville

CampOut 804/301–3553 • women only • 100-acre rustic campground w/ 50 campsites • nonsmoking • wheelchair access • women-owned

WASHINGTON

Bender Creek

Triangle Recreation Camp PO Box 1226, Granite Falls 98252 • lesbians/ gay men • members-only camping on 80-acre nature conservancy • www.camptrc.org

Long Beach Peninsula

Anthony's Home Court 1310 Pacific Hwy N, Long Beach **360/642–2802, 888/787–2754** • gay/ straight • cabins & RV hookups • nonsmoking • WiFi • gay-owned

The Historic Sou'wester Lodge, Cabins & RV Park Beach Access Rd (38th Pl), Seaview **360/642–2542** • gay-friendly • inexpensive suites • cabins w/ kitchens • vintage trailers • RV hookups • pets ok in cabins & trailers • non-smoking

San Juan Islands

Lopez Farm Cottages & Tent Camping 555 Fisherman Bay Rd, Lopez Island **360/468–3555, 800/440–3556** • gay/ straight • on 30-acre farm • hot tub • nonsmoking

Seattle

Wild Lily Cabins B&B 25 miles W of Stevens Pass, Index **360/793–2103** • gay/ straight • cabins on Skykomish River • 1 hour from Seattle • cedar sauna • hot tub • camping available • nonsmoking • gay-owned

WISCONSIN

Norwalk

Daughters of the Earth 18134 Index Ave **608/269–5301** • women only • women's land • camping • retreat space • lesbian-owned

CANADA

ALBERTA

Westerose

Pine Trails Getaway RR1 **780/586–0002** • gay campground

BRITISH COLUMBIA

Birken

Birken Lakeside Resort 9179 Portage Rd **604/452–3255** • gay-friendly • cabins • campsites • hot tub • swimming • pets ok • lesbian-owned

NEW BRUNSWICK

Fredericton

River's Edge Campground 19 Cottage Ln, Durham Bridge **506/458–2107, 800/370–1644** • lesbians/ gay men • pool • outdoor activities • gay-owned • camping/ RV hookups • WiFi

NOVA SCOTIA

Scotsburn

The Mermaid & the Cow West Branch **902/351–2714** • lesbians/ gay men • cabin & 20 campsites • dogs ok on leash • pool • lesbian-owned

ONTARIO

Grand Valley

Rainbow Ridge Resort Country Rd 109 (at Hwy 25 S) **519/928–3262** • lesbians/ gay men • trailers & tents • located on 72 acres on Grand River • pool • restaurant • dance hall • day visitors welcome • seasonal • pets ok • gay-owned

Hamilton

Cedars Campground 1039 5th Concession W Rd, Millgrove **905/659–3655, 905/659–7342** • lesbians/ gay men • private campground • pool • also bar • dancing/DJ • restaurant wknds • gay-owned

CRUISES

Women Only

Olivia Travel 415/962–5700, 800/631–6277 434 Brannan St, San Francisco, CA 94107 • exclusive cruise, resort & escape vacations for lesbians • www.olivia.com

▶ **Sweet 877/793–3830** PO Box 460862, 94146 San Francisco • "Sweet takes lesbians on fabulous, affordable vacations all over the world where we combine debauchery and do-goodery for loads of meaningful glee" • see ad in front color section • www.discoversweet.com

Gay/Lesbian

Aquafest 800/592–9058 4801 Woodway #400-W, Houston, TX 77056 • LGBT groups mingle w/ mixed clientele on major cruise lines • www.aquafestcruises.com

Gayribbean Cruises 877/560–8318 Dallas, TX • gay & lesbian group cruise organizer • fabulous destinations • annual Halloween cruise from Galveston, TX • www.gayribbeancruises.com

Port Yacht Charters 516/883–0998, 877/DO-A-BOAT 9 Belleview Ave, Port Washington, NY 11050 • custom charters worldwide, specializing in the Caribbean • commitment ceremonies • gourmet cuisine • www.portyachtcharters.com

R Family 866/732–6822 5 Washington Ave, Nyack, NY 10960 • family-friendly vacations designed especially for the LGBT community • www.rfamilyvacations.com

Rainbow Charters 808/347–0235 939 Kawaiki Pl, Honolulu, HI 96825 • gay & lesbian weddings • custom sailing cruises • whale-watching • snorkeling • sunset cruises • www.RainbowChartersHawaii.com

RSVP Vacations 800/328–7787 gay & lesbian cruise vacations • www.rsvpvacations.com

Sailing Affairs 917/453–6425 58 E 1st St #6-B, New York City, NY 10003 • gay sailboat charters, day trips, sunset sails & sailing vacations on 47-foot Beneteau • East Coast, Caribbean, Europe & Mediterranean • www.sailingaffairs.com

LUXURY TOURS

DavidTravel 949/723–0699 310 Dahlia Pl, Ste A, Corona del Mar, CA 92625-2821 • full service travel agency & tour operator • small luxury group departures & customized travel for individuals & groups • milestone events, including honeymoons! • www.DavidTravel.com

Out Traveller 082/826–1552 45 Amarja, Johannesburg, Gauteng 2188, South Africa • guided safaris to South Africa & East Africa • also Thailand, Bali & New Zealand • destination weddings • lesbian-owned • www.out-traveller.com

Steele Luxury Travel 646/688–2274 New York City, NY 10011 • unique travel experiences to exotic destinations worldwide • www.steeletravel.com

GREAT OUTDOORS ADVENTURES

Women Only

Abroad For Adventure 610/667–3300 114 Forrest Ave #210, Narberth, PA 19072 • fun, small groups for unique adventures w/a touch of luxury • Italy, Greece, Belize, Costa Rica, Isla Mujeres, Machu Picchu • travel with just the girls! • www.abroadforadventure.com

Adventure Associates of WA 206/532–8352 PO Box 16304, Seattle, WA 98116 • worldwide eco-adventures for women • cruises, cultural immersion, history & ruins, treks, safaris, hiking, kayaking & biking • www.adventureassociates.net

Adventures in Good Company 410/435–1965, 877/439–4042 5913 Brackenridge Ave, Baltimore, MD 21212 • outdoor & adventure travel for women of all ages & abilities • *www.adventuresingoodcompany.com*

Bushwise Women /61 266840178 PO Box 34, , Mullumbimby, NSW 2482, Australia • international escapes & adventures for women • wilderness & cultural trips in New Zealand, Australia, Egypt & Europe • also hosts
The Women's Accomodation Network • *www.bushwise.co.nz*

Call of the Wild Adventure Travel 650/265–1662, 888/378–1978 (OUTSIDE CA) PO Box 6992, Folsom, CA 95763 • hiking, camping & cultural trips for all levels in Western US, Alaska, Mexico, New Zealand & Peru • longest-running adventure travel company for women • *www.callwild.com*

Chicks with Picks & Chicks Rock 970/626–4424 PO Box 486, Ridgway, CO 81432 • ice climbing & rock climbing for women • all levels welcome • *www.chickswithpicks.net*

Equinox Wilderness Expeditions 206/462–5246 2440 E Tudor Rd, Anchorage, AK 99507 • wilderness trips in Alaska, British Columbia & the Southwest US by raft, canoe, sea kayak & backpack • also ski tours near Whistler, BC • *www.equinoxexpeditions.com*

Grand Canyon Field Institute 928/638–2485, 866/471–4435 PO Box 399, Grand Canyon, AZ 86023 • women's educational backpacking classes in the Grand Canyon • also co-ed trips • *www.grandcanyon.org/fieldinstitute*

Herizen™ Life Adventures Int'l Inc 250/753–4253, 866/399–4253 1-5765 Turner Rd #176, Nanaimo, BC V9T 6M4, Canada • women-only retreats • sailing, yoga, riding & more in Baja, Mexico, Belize, British Columbia & British Virgin Islands • *www.herizenlifeadventures.com*

Mariah Wilderness Expeditions 530/626–6049, 800/462–7424 PO Box 1160, Lotus, CA 95651 • unique vacations for women on roads less traveled • multi-sport adventures • unique cultural & eco-explorations • *www.mariahwe.com*

National Women's Sailing Association 401/682–2064 26 Beach Rd, Hingham, MA 02043 • sailing seminars & workshops • *www.womensailing.org*

Nurture Through Nature 207/452–2929 77 Warren Rd, Denmark, ME 04022 • holistic personal retreats • solar-powered eco-cabin rentals • yoga • custom canoe & kayak tours • hiking & camping • *www.ntnretreats.com*

Octopus Reef Dive Training & Tours 808/875–8759 Maui, HI • experienced instructors teaching & guiding SCUBA divers in Maui • *www.OctopusReef.com*

Sea Sense: The Women's Sailing & Powerboating School 727/289–6917, 800/332–1404 PO Box 1961, St Petersburg, FL 33731 • US & worldwide sailing & powerboating courses • custom courses • also private, "on your own boat" courses • *www.seasenseboating.com*

Skigrlz 206/452–5246 2906 W Broadway #115, Vancouver, BC V6K 2G8, Canada • wilderness hiking & paddling trips in BC • *www.skigrlz.com*

Tethys Offshore Sailing for Women 206/789–5118 2442 NW Market St #498, Seattle, WA 98107 • join Capt Nancy Erley as learning crew for a week in the Pacific Northwest aboard the 38' Tethys • *www.tethysoffshore.com*

WalkingWomen 44 0/1757 249481 York, United Kingdom • women's walking vacations for all levels • England, Scotland, Ireland, Wales, Europe, & as far as Nepal & South Africa! • *www.walkingwomen.com/lesbians.htm*

Wild Women Expeditions 888/993–1222 PO Box 264, Woody Point, NF A0K 1P0, Canada • Canada's outdoor adventure company for women • adventure trips across Canada • decidedly dykey! • *www.wildwomenexp.com*

Wildlotus Adventures 00844/3715–2440 43 Nghi Tam Rd, Tay Ho, Hanoi, Vietnam • tailor made tours & off the beaten path experiences for women in Vietman, Laos, Cambodia & Thailand • *www.wildlotusadventures.com*

Winter Moon Summer Sun 218/848–2442 3388 Petrell, Brimson, MN 55602 • dogsledding trips in winter • kayaking Lake Superior in summer • rustic accommodations w/ meals provided • *www.wintermoonsummersun.com*

Womanship 410/267–6661, 800/342–9295 137 Conduit St, Annapolis, MD 21401 • daily or live-aboard learning cruises for women • sail & "see" adventures in the Greek Isles, Turkey, Florida Keys & more • *www.womanship.com*

WomanTours 585/256–9807, 800/247–1444 2340 Elmwood Ave, Rochester, NY 14618 • fully supported bicycle tours for women • call for a free catalog • *www.womantours.com*

Women On A Roll 310/578–8888 PO Box 5112, Santa Monica, CA 90409-5112 • travel, sporting, cultural & social club for women • wide range of events & trips • largest lesbian organization in Southern California • *www.womenonaroll.com*

Women's Flyfishing® 907/274–7113 PO Box 243963, Anchorage, AK 99524 • women-only fly-fishing schools & guided trips for women & couples in Alaska, Argentina & Mexico • we provide all gear & equipment • beginners welcome! • *www.womensflyfishing.net*

Mostly Women

▶ **Venus Charters 305/304–1181** Garrison Bight Marina, Key West, FL 33040 • snorkeling & dolphin-watching • light-tackle fishing • commitment ceremonies • *www.venuscharters.com*

Gay/Lesbian

▶ **Alyson Adventures, Inc 305/296–9935, 800/825–9766** 923 White St, Key West, FL 33040 • award-winning adventure travel & active vacations • hiking, biking & multi-sport activities • *www.AlysonAdventures.com*

Journeyweavers 607/277–1416 313 Washington St, Ithaca, NY 14850 • group & individual outdoor adventure & birding trips in Costa Rica & beyond • *www.journeyweavers.com*

Out in Alaska 907/347–2214 5063 Heritage Heights Dr, Anchorage, AK 99516 • adventure travel throughout Alaska for LGBT travelers • your best bet for a fun & authentic Alaska vacation! • *www.outinalaska.com*

OutWest Global Adventures 406/446–1533, 800/743–0458 PO Box 2050, Red Lodge, MT 59068 • specializing in gay/ lesbian active & adventure travel • worldwide • *www.outwestadventures.com*

South American Journeys, LLC Cuzco, Peru • yoga, writing workshops, hiking, camping, out-reach programs & more in Peru & South America • women-only & men-only trips available • *www.southamericanjourneys.com*

Undersea Expeditions 858/270–2900, 800/669–0310 758 Kapahulu Ave #100-1188, Honolulu, CA 92816 • gay & lesbian scuba adventures worldwide • *www.UnderseaX.com*

Gay/Straight

Atlantis Yacht Charters 415/332–0800 Schoonmaker Pt Marina, 85 Liberty Ship Way #110-A, Sausalito, CA 94965 • group charters • *www.yachtcharter.com*

GoNorth Alaska Adventure Travel Center 907/479–7271, 855/236–7271 3500 Davis Rd, Fairbanks, AK 99709 • guided tours throughout Alaska & the Arctic • air taxis & transportation • canoe & bike rentals • hostel accommodations & camping • *www.GoNorth-Alaska.com*

Himalayan High Treks 415/551–1005, 800/455–8735 241 Dolores St, San Francisco, CA 94103 • experience indigenous Buddhist & Hindu cultures • *www.hightreks.com*

Natural Habitat Adventures 303/449-3711, 800/543-8917 PO Box 3065, Boulder, CO 80307 • up-close encounters w/ the world's most amazing wildlife in its natural habitat • *www.nathab.com*

Open Eye Tours 808/572-3483 PO Box 324, Makawao, HI 96768 • customized private land tours of Maui & other islands • visit popular spots or places seldom seen, walking or not • sharing Maui's best-kept secrets since 1983 • *www.openeyetours.com*

Pacific Yachting & Sailing 831/423-7245, 800/374-2626 790 Mariner Park Way, Santa Cruz, CA 95062 • international & local yachting vacations for gays, lesbians & mixed groups • also sailing instruction • *www.pacificsail.com*

Paddling South & Saddling South 707/942-4550, 800/398-6200 PO Box 827, Calistoga, CA 94515 • horseback, mountain-biking & sea-kayak trips in Baja • also women-only trips • call for complete calendar • *www.tourbaja.com*

Puffin Fishing Charters 907/224-4653, 800/978-3346 PO Box 606, Seward, AK 99664 • guided charter fishing • almost 30 years of experience • halibut, salmon & rockfish on vessels custom-built for Alaskan waters • *www.puffincharters.com*

Voyageur North Outfitters 218/365-3251, 800/848-5530 1829 E Sheridan, Ely, MN 55731 • canoe outfitting & trips • *www.vnorth.com*

Whitewater Connection 530/622-6446, 800/336-7238 PO Box 270, Coloma, CA 95613 • whitewater rafting adventures • *www.whitewaterconnection.com*

SPIRITUAL/HEALTH VACATIONS

Women Only

Les Be Well 610/966-9668 4840 Beck Rd, Emmaus, PA 18049 • vacation adventures & retreats for mind, body & spirit for lesbians, bisexuals and other women of acceptance • *www.lesbewell.com*

Sounds & Furies 604/253-7189 PO Box 21510, 1424 Commercial Dr, Vancouver, BC V5L 5G2, Canada • economical goddess tours for women • concerts featuring lesbian performers • *www.soundsandfuries.com*

Gay/Lesbian

Spirit Journeys 201/483-3111, 800/754-1875 134 River Rd, New Milford, NJ 97646 • spiritual retreats, workshops & adventure trips throughout the US & abroad • *www.spiritjouneys.com*

THEMATIC TOURS

Women Only

Canyon Calling 928/282-0916 200 Carol Canyon Dr, Sedona, AZ 86336 • worldwide multi-activity adventure trips for moderately fit women, including the premiere trip to New Zealand w/ Kiwi company founder • *www.canyoncalling.com*

Driftwood Dreamers 64-7/315-6627 93 Armstrong Rd, Opotiki, Bay of Plenty 3198, New Zealand • women's adventures in New Zealand • rugged landscapes, gorgeous beaches, fascinating Maori culture • *www.driftwooddreamers.com*

Ela Brasil Tours 203/840-9010 14 Burlington Dr, Norwalk, CT 06851 • custom trips to Brazil • promoting responsible travel & cultural diversity • EcoVolunteer programs • *www.elabrasil.com*

Mouriscastours 351/963-857-776 Faro, Portugal • private tours in Portugal • *www.mouriscastours.com*

Sights & Soul Travels 240/350–5643, 866/737–9602 13610 Chrisbar Ct, Germantown, MD 20874 • small group, upscale, women-only trips to South Africa, New Zealand, Vietnam, the Amazon, Greece, Italy, France, Spain & more • *www.sightsandsoul.com*

Tours of Exploration 604/886–7300, 800/690–7887 PO Box 1503, Gibsons, BC V0N 1V0, Canada • eco-cultural journeys to Ecuador & Bolivia for women • *www.toursexplore.com*

Towanda Women Motorcycle Tours 64–3/314–9097 PO Box 4437, Christchurch, New Zealand • motorcycle tours for women by women in Alaska, Europe, New Zealand & Australia • ride the best motorcycling roads in the world w/ like-minded women • *www.towanda.org*

Women's Motorcyclist Foundation 585/768–6054 7 Lent Ave, LeRoy, NY 14482 • works to improve the sport of motorcycling • also raises money for breast cancer • *www.womensmotorcyclistfoundation.org*

Mostly Women

French Escapade 510/483–5713, 888/483–5713 2389 Blackpool Pl, 94577 San Leandro • discover France, Belgium & Switzerand in small groups • sightseeing, painting, cooking tours • some women-only trips • lesbian owned/run • *www.frenchescapade.com*

Robin Tyler International Tours for Women 818/893–4075 15842 Chase St, North Hills, CA 91343 • upscale int'l five-star lesbian travel founded in 1990 • exotic locations worldwide • also tours for gay men • *www.robintylertours.com*

Gay/Lesbian

Africa Outing 27–21/671–4028 3 Alcyone Rd, Claremont, Capetown 7708, South Africa • gay/lesbian safaris & more • tours customized to your needs • *www.afouting.com*

Brazil Fiesta Tours & Visa Service 415/986–1134, 800/200–0582 268 Bush St #3531, San Francisco, CA 94104 • tours to Brazil • Brazilian visa service • *www.brazilfiesta.net*

CM by Carlos Melia 212/399–6161 (US#), 800/729–7472 x205 630 5th Ave #2207, 10011 New York City • boutique gay travel to Argentina, Uruguay & New York City • all services tested by me • "Been There Done That" • *www.carlosmelia.com*

Gay 2 Afrika 212/385–9770, 866/462–2374 111 John St #1060, 10038 New York City • providing African travel arrangements to the gay & lesbian community • *www.gay2afrika.com*

Gay Bali Tours 62–361/722 483 Jl. Braban No. 67, Seminyak, 80361 Bali, Indonesia • premier & professional tour operator permanently based in Bali • *www.baligay.net*

Gay Travel Brasil 55–21/3415–3126 Rua Sergipe 57 C 201, 20271- 310 Rio de Janeiro, Brazil • gay & lesbian travel in Brazil & South America • *www.gaytravelbrasil.com*

Go Pink China 86/1366–124–6689 Beijing, China • adding queer elements to city tours & national trips in China • *www.gopinkchina.com*

Going Your Way Tours 860/447–9180 123 Ledgewood Rd #509, Groton, CT 06340 • upscale customized group & individual itineraries worldwide • *www.goingyourwaytours.com*

Kuyay Travel 56–65/438–990 Puerto Rosales 46, 5550000 Puerto Varas, Los Lagos, Chile • gay-owned/run travel planner & tour host in Patagonia • *www.gaypatagonia.com*

MexGay Vacations 213/383–9491, 866/639–4299 333 S Grand Ave, Floor 25, Los Angeles, CA 90071 • specializing in gay travel to Mexico • *www.mexgay.com*

National Gay Pilots Association 214/336–0873 PO Box 7271, Dallas, TX 75209 • several annual gatherings • call for more info • *www.ngpa.org*

Pacific Ocean Holidays 808/923–2400 Honolulu, HI • Hawaii vacation packages • *www.gayhawaiivacations.com*

Planetdwellers 61–2/9294–5656 Shop 47 Elizabeth Bay Rd, Elizabeth Bay, NSW 2012, Australia • LGBT tours of Australia • come to OZ! • *www.planetdwellers.com.au*

Venture Out 415/626–5678, 888/431–6789 575 Pierce St #604, San Francisco, CA 94117 • high-end escorted tours for gay & lesbian travelers to countries around the world • *www.venture-out.com*

Winelovertours.com 860/861–2301 123 Ledgewood Rd #509, Groton, CT 06340 • upscale group tours & individual itineraries for foodies & winelovers • *www.winelovertours.com*

Gay/Straight

Alaska Railroad 907/265–2494, 800/544–0552 (RESERVATIONS) 431 W 1st Ave, Anchorage, AK 99501 • rail & tour packages • *www.alaskarailroad.com*

Asian Pacific Adventures 818/881–2745, 800/825–1680 18900 Hatteras St, Tarzana, CA 91356 • custom tours to Asia, including India, Thailand, China, Tibet, Vietnam, Japan & more • festivals, tribes, safaris & art • hiking & biking • *www.asianpacificadventures.com*

Brazil Ecojourneys 55–48/3389–5619 Estrada Rozalia Paulina Ferreira 1132, 88063-555 Armação, Florianopolis, SC, Brazil • incoming tour operator • South Brazil specialists • *www.brazilecojourneys.com*

Ecotour Expeditions, Inc 401/423–3377, 800/688–1822 PO Box 128, Jamestown, RI 02835 • small group boat tours of the Amazon & more • call for color catalog • *www.naturetours.com*

Heritage Tours Private Travel 212/206–8400, 800/378–4555 121 W 27th St #1201, New York, NY 10001 • custom private trips to Morocco, Spain, Portugal, Turkey & Africa • *www.HTprivatetravel.com*

Holbrook Travel 352/377–7111, 800/451–7111 3540 NW 13th St, Gainesville, FL 32609 • natural history tours in Central America, South America & Africa • small groups • *www.holbrooktravel.com*

Lima Tours 51-1/619–6900 Jr De la Union 1040, Lima, Peru • personalized, gay-friendly tours to Peru • *www.limatours.com.pe*

New England Vacation Tours 802/464–2076, 800/742–7669 PO Box 560, West Dover, VT 05356 • gay/ lesbian tours (including fall foliage) conducted by a mainstream tour operator • *www.newenglandvacationtours.com*

Pacha Tours 800/722–4288 295 Madison Ave, 43rd flr, New York City, NY 10017 • trips to Turkey & Greece • *www.pachatours.com*

Shop Around Tours 212/684–3763 305 E 24th St #2-N, New York City, NY 10010 • for people who live to shop & love to travel • *www.shoparoundtours.com*

Sublime Journeys 877/805–7969 progressive, diverse & extraordinary travel experiences in South & Central America • *www.discoversublime.com*

Wild Rainbow African Safaris 707/467–9676 308 Jones St, Ukiah, CA 95482 • unique excursions to Tanzania, South Africa, Zambia, Botswana & more • *www.wildrainbowsafaris.com*

CUSTOM TOURS

Costa Rica Experts 773/935–1009, 800/827–9046 3166 N Lincoln Ave #424, Chicago, IL 60657 • *www.costaricaexperts.com*

Travel & Culture Dubai 971/567–15–90–25 302 Escape Tower Business Bay Sh. Zyed Rd, Dubai, United Arab Emirates • tours, safaris & hotel reservations in Dubai • *www.dubai.travel-culture.com*

Travel & Culture Pakistan 92-321/242–4778 702 Panorama Center Office Plaza, 75530 Karachi, Pakistan • tours, safaris & hotel reservations in Pakistan • *www.travel-culture.com*

Travel & Culture Sri Lanka 94/777-864–479 07-1B, E Tower, World Trade Ctr, Colombo, Sri Lanka • tours, safaris & hotel reservations in Sri Lanka • *www.srilanka.travel-culture.com*

VARIOUS TOURS

Women Only

See Jayne Play 813/263–4003 7321 Canal Blvd, Tampa, FL 33615 • European & Caribbean tours for women • lesbian-owned • *www.seejayneplay.com*

Thanks Babs, the Day Tripper 702/370–6961 Las Vegas, NV • outdoor tours, shows & attractions • Grand Canyon getaways • full service concierge for Las Vegas, state of NV, and the Southwest • it's like having a lesbian aunt in Las Vegas! • also tours in San Francisco, CA • *www.thanksbabs.com*

Gay/Lesbian

Footprints 416/962–8111, 888/962–6211 19 Madison Ave #300, Toronto, ON M5R 2S2, Canada • custom-designed, private tours arranged to worldwide destinations • *www.footprintstravel.com*

Friends of Dorothy Travel® 415/864–1600, 800/640–4918 1177 California St #B, San Francisco, CA 94108 • unique gay & lesbian adventures • individual & group arrangements • *www.fodtravel.com*

Out & About Travel 800/842–4753 161 Federal St, Providence, RI 02903 • full-service travel agency specializing in gay & lesbian tours, cruises, adventure travel, ski trips, honeymoons, customized packages & more • serving the GLBT community since 1999! • *www.gaytravelpros.com*

Postcard Destinations 814/539–4999, 800/484–3250 x2621 188 Crystal St, Johnstown, PA 15906 • purveyors of gay travel worldwide since 1985 • tours, cruises, groups, customized trips, air, hotel • Italy/Germany/Spain specialists • gay-owned • *www.postcarddestinations.com*

Zoom Vacations 773/772–9666, 866/966–6822 2338 N Monticello Ave, Chicago, IL 60647 • takes gay group travel to the next level • experience the best of a destination w/ surprises, insider events & a sense of magic • *www.zoomvacations.com*

LESBIAN/ GAY EVENTS

January

ongoing throughout the year: **Tranny Roadshow**   *TBA, USA*
on-going, touring, performance art extravaganza • check website for shows near you •
617/666-1782 • **www.trannyroadshow.com**

4-8: **Utah Gay & Lesbian Ski Week**   *Salt Lake City, UT*
ski at Alta, Snowbird, Solitude, Brighton, Snow Basin & The Canyons • 877/429-6368 •
www.gayskiing.org

15-22: **Aspen Gay Ski Week**   *Aspen, CO*
LGBT • 3000+ attendees • 970/925-4123, 866/564-8398 • **www.gayskiweek.com**

15-Feb 5: **Midsumma Festival**   *Melbourne, Australia*
arts, culture & community • LGBTQ • 61-3/9415-9819 • **www.midsumma.org.au**

18-22: **Winter Rendezvous**   *Stowe, VT*
annual gay ski week • skiing, winter sports & entertainment • 587/445-7198 • **www.winterrendezvous.com**

February

5-12: **WinterPRIDE: Whistler Gay Ski Week**   *Whistler, BC, Canada*
annual gay/ lesbian ski week • parties for boys & girls! • top-notch DJs & venues • popular destination 75 miles N of Vancouver • LGBT • 3,000+ attendees • 604/288-7218, 866/787-1966 •
www.gaywhistler.com

21: **Mardi Gras**   *New Orleans, LA*
mixed gay/ straight • 800/672-6124 • **www.neworleanscvb.com**

March

4-11: **Lake Tahoe WinterFest Gay & Lesbian Ski Week**   *Lake Tahoe, NV*
world class skiing • gay comedy • Lake Tahoe dinner/dance cruise • LGBT • 800 attendees •
www.LakeTahoeWinterfest.com

26-April 11: **Kraft Nabisco Golf Championship**   *Palm Springs, CA*
previously known as the Dinah Shore Golf Championship • mostly women • 760/324-4546 •
www.nabiscochampionship.com

27-April 1: **OutBoard**   *Steamboat Springs, CO*
annual lesbian/ gay snowboarding festival • 300+ attendees • 877/38-BOARD •
www.outboard.org

TBA: **Chicago Takes Off**   *Chicago, IL*
burlesque show to fight HIV/AIDS in the Chicagoland area • LGBT • 1400 attendees •
773/989-9400 • **www.chicagotakesoff.org**

April

14: **Boybutante Ball**   *Athens, GA*
LGBT • 1000+ attendees • **www.boybutante.org**

22: **AIDS Walk Miami**   *Miami Beach, FL*
5K walk-a-thon fundraiser benefiting Care Resource • LGBT • 305/576-1234 • **www.aidswalkmiami.org**

30: **Queensday**   *Amsterdam, Netherlands*
huge street festival to celebrate what was originally the birthday of the Queen Mother • LGBT •
www.queensdayamsterdam.eu

TBA: **Philadelphia Black Gay Pride**   *Philadelphia, PA*
a weekend of social & cultural activities • films, BBQ, spoken word, parties & more • LGBT •
877/497-7247 • **www.phillyblackpride.org**

May

3-6: **Equality Forum**   *Philadelphia, PA*
largest nat'l & int'l LGBT civil rights forum w/ panels, parties & special events • 215/732-3378 x116
• **www.equalityforum.org**

7-20: **Int'l Dublin Gay Theatre Festival**   *Dublin, Ireland*
353-87/657-3732 • **www.gaytheatre.ie**

20: **AIDS Walk New York**   *New York City, NY*
AIDS benefit • mixed gay/ straight • 212/807-9255 • **www.aidswalk.net**

20: **Minnesota AIDS Walk**   *Minneapolis, MN*
enjoy a 10K walk from Minnehaha Park & raise money for MN AIDS Project • mixed gay/ straight •
10,000 attendees • 612/373-2410 • **www.mnaidsproject.org**

23-28: **Annual Gay Bowling Tournament**   *New York City, NY*
check site for local tournaments throughout the year • **www.igbo.org**

24-27: **Int'l Association of Country Western Dance Clubs**
Annual Convention   *New Orleans, LA*
also semi-annual conventions in March (Fort Lauderdale, FL) & October (San Francisco, CA) • LGBT
• 400-600 attendees • **www.outcountrydance.com**

24-28: **DC Black Pride**   *Washington, DC*
LGBT • **www.dcblackpride.org**

24-28: **Mondo Homo Dirty South**   *Atlanta, GA*
queer-centric festival featuring music, dance, crafts, performance & more • 404/243-3476 •
www.mondohomo.com

24-28: **Pensacola Memorial Day Weekend**   *Pensacola, FL*
many parties on beaches & in bars • LGBT • 35,000+ attendees • 850/433-9491 • **www.memori-
alweekendpensacola.com**

25-June 10: **Spoleto Festival USA**   *Charleston, SC*
one of the continent's premier avant-garde cultural arts festivals • 140+ performances of dance,
theater & music from around the world • mixed gay/ straight • 843/579-3100 (tickets), 843/722-
2764 (office) • **www.spoletousa.org**

29-June 4: **Gay Days Orlando**   *Orlando, FL*
including Gay Day at Disney • 7 days of parties & fun for boys & girls alike! • LGBT • 407/896-
8431 • **www.gaydays.com**

29-June 4: **Girls in Wonderland**   *Orlando, FL*
official women's parties of Gay Days Orlando • 4 days of fun! • tickets available thru www.girlsin-
wonderland.com • mostly women • 305/495-6969 (tickets) • **www.girlsinwonderland.com**

TBA: **Aqua Girl**   *Miami Beach, FL*
a weekend of hot women's parties in Miami • mostly women • 305/576-AQUA •
www.aquagirl.org

TBA: **Splash: Houston Black Gay Pride**   *Houston, TX*
LGBT • 832/443-1016 • **www.houstonsplash.com**

TBA: **We're Funny That Way**   *Toronto, ON, Canada*
comedians from around the world perform at Canada's International Gay/Lesbian Comedy Festival
• LGBT • 416/975-8555 • **www.werefunnythatway.com**

June

ongoing: **LGBT Pride**   *Cross-country, USA*
   celebrate yourself & attend one – or many – of the hundreds of Gay Pride parades & festivities
   happening in cities around the world • www.interpride.org

ongoing: **Music in the Mountains**   *Grass Valley, CA*
   summer music festival • mixed gay/ straight • 530/265-6173 • www.musicinthemountains.org

ongoing: **National Queer Arts Festival**   *San Francisco, CA*
   performances & exhibitions in the San Francisco Bay Area highlighting artists from around the
   country • LGBT • 415/251-9935 • www.QueerCulturalCenter.org

3-9: **AIDS LifeCycle**   *San Francisco to Los Angeles, CA*
   bike from San Francisco to Los Angeles to raise money for HIV/AIDS services • 415/581-7077 •
   www.aidslifecycle.org

8-10: **PrideFest**   *Milwaukee, WI*
   celebrate LGBT pride at Henry W Maier Festival Park • 414/272-3378 • www.pridefest.com

15-17: **Black Gay Pride**   *Memphis, TN*
   LGBT • 901/522-8459 • www.brothersunited.com

17: **Unofficial Gay Day at Cedar Point**   *Sandusky, OH*
   wear red to show your support on the unofficial Gay Day at this popular amusement park • mixed
   gay/ straight •

22-25: **South Carolina Black Pride**   *Columbia, SC*
   • www.southcarolinablackpride.com

23-24: **San Francisco LGBT Pride Parade/ Celebration**   *San Francisco, CA*
   LGBT • 415/864-0831 • www.sfpride.org

23-July 8: **EuroPride 2012**   *London, England*
   parties, politics, performance & more • there is something for everyone at this massive celebration
   of gay pride • www.europride.info

28-July 2: **Windy City Black Pride**   *Chicago, IL*
   a weekend of parties, seminars & more • LGBT • 888/922-7244 • www.windycityblackpride.org

29-July 2: **Int'l Gay Square Dance Clubs Convention**   *Vancouver, BC, Canada*
   303/722-5276 • www.iagsdc.org

30-July 4: **At the Beach/ LA Black Pride Weekend**   *Los Angeles, CA*
   celebrate a weekend of Beach & Diversity gay pride across Los Angeles • LGBT • 323/285-4225 •
   www.atbla.com

TBA: **AIDS Walk Boston & 5K Run**   *Boston, MA*
   mixed gay/ straight • 12,000 attendees • 617/424-9255 • www.aidswalkboston.org

TBA: **Black Gay Pride Boston**   *Boston, MA*
   celebrate Black pride in Boston • www.bostonspyce.com

TBA: **Idapalooza Fruit Jam**   *Dowelltown, TN*
   queer music festival in backwoods TN • camping • vegetarian feasts • 615/597-4409 •
   www.planetida.com

TBA: **Juneteenth Jamboree of New Plays**   *New York City, NY*
   annual theater festival • new works about the African American experience & its legacy • mixed
   gay/ straight • 212/964-1904 • www.juneteenthlegacytheatre.com

TBA: **Paris Circuit Party**   *Paris, France*
   gay culture festival • film • performance • political discussions • dance parties & more • LGBT •
   www.pariscircuitparty.com

TBA: **PDX Black Pride**   *Portland, OR*
   films, workshops, parties & more • LGBT • pridenw.org

July

12-13: Ride for AIDS Chicago   *Chicago, IL*
2-day bike ride to fight HIV/ AIDS in the Chicagoland area • LGBT • 350 attendees •
773/989-9400 • www.rideforaids.org

26-30: Triangle Black Pride   *Raleigh-Durham, Chapel Hill, NC*
celebrate & honor the diversity of the African American LGBTQ community in the Triangle •
919/233-2044, 980/229-9468 • **triangleblackpride.org**

28: Crape Myrtle Festival   *Raleigh-Durham, Chapel Hill, NC*
weeklong festival to raise money for AIDS & LGBT concerns • gala Saturday • also supporting
events throughout the year • mixed gay/ straight • 500+ attendees • 919/656-4205 •
www.crapemyrtlefest.org

TBA: AIDS Walk San Francisco   *San Francisco, CA*
mixed gay/ straight • 27,000+ attendees • 415/615-9255 • **www.aidswalk.net**

TBA: Charlotte Black Gay Pride   *Charlotte, NC*
art & performances, community forums, dance parties & more • 704/953-8813 • www.charlotte-
blackgaypride.com

TBA: Hotter Than July Weekend   *Detroit, MI*
the Midwest's oldest black same-gender-loving pride celebration • LGBT • 888/755-9165 • **black-
pridesociety.org**

TBA: IGLFA World Championship   *Mexico City, Mexico*
Int'l Gay & Lesbian Football Association's annual soccer tournament • **www.iglfa.org**

TBA: Tampa Black Pride   *Tampa, FL*
celebrate African American gay pride in sunny Tampa • LGBT • 813/775-5445

August

3-27: Edinburgh Fringe Festival   *Edinburgh, Scotland*
the largest arts festival in the world • dance, theater, music, comedy, events & more • mixed gay/
straight • 44-131/226-0026 • **www.edfringe.com**

3-6: Blackout: Oakland Black & Brown Pride   *Oakland, CA*
celebrate w/ a weekend of conferences, awards ceremonies & parties • 510/621-3553 • **www.oak-
landblackout.com**

8-12: Rendezvous 2012   *Medicine Bow Nat'l Forest, WY*
5-day camping festival to celebrate LGBT pride • 400+ attendees • 307/778-7645 •
www.wyomingequality.org

10-12: Fire Island Black Out (FIBO)   *Fire Island, NY*
3-day beach event for the LGBT community & friends • all are invited to attend & enjoy, regardless
of race, gender or orientation • LGBT • 215/751-0808 • **www.fireislandblackout.com**

11: AIDS Walk Colorado   *Denver, CO*
303/962-5303 • **www.aidswalkcolorado.org**

18: UK Black Pride   *London, England*
44 020/8257 5358 • **www.ukblackpride.org.uk**

19-26: "Camp" Camp   *Porter, ME*
summer camp for LGBT adults • sports, pottery, theater, yoga & more • LGBT • 347/453-5257 •
www.campcamp.com

29-Sept 3: Atlanta Black Pride Weekend   *Atlanta, GA*
celebrate Black Pride over Labor Day weekend in Atlanta • LGBT • 678/799-8526 • **www.inthe-
lifeatl.com**

30-Sept 3: Inferno Dominican Republic   *Punta Cana, Dominican Republic*
the premier Labor Day pride celebration • deluxe, all-inclusive accommodations • LGBT •
305/891-7536 • **www.infernodr.com**

TBA: **Black Pride NYC** *New York City, NY*
multicultural LGBT festival w/ a wide array of entertainment, forums, workshops & events • LGBT • www.nycblackpride.com

TBA: **Camp Trans** *near Hart, MI*
annual gathering of transgender people & their allies • protest the Michigan Womyn's Music Festival • www.camp-trans.org

TBA: **Gay Ski Week NZ** *Queenstown, New Zealand*
64 21/83-4640 • www.gayskiweeknz.com

TBA: **National Gay Softball World Series** *TBA, USA*
LGBT • 412/362-1247 • www.gaysoftballworldseries.com

TBA: **Northalsted Market Days** *Chicago, IL*
a good ol' summer block party on Main St of Boys' Town, USA • LGBT • 773/883-0500 • www.northalsted.com

TBA: **St Louis Black Pride** *St Louis, MO*
• www.slbp.org

September

4-10: **Gay Days Las Vegas** *Orlando, FL*
including Gay Day at Disney • 7 days of parties & fun for boys & girls alike! • LGBT • 407/896-8431 • www.gaydays.com

18: **Out in the Park** *Springfield, MA*
unofficial gay day at Six Flags New England • wear red to show your support • LGBT • 1000+ attendees • www.outinthepark.com

21-23: **Braking the Cycle** *Boston, MA to New York City, NY*
3-day fully-supported bike ride from Boston to New York • benefiting the HIV/AIDS related services of the LGBT Community Center in NYC • mixed gay/ straight • 212/989-1111 • www.brakingthecycle.org

28: **Out On The Mountain** *Valencia, CA*
gay day at Six Flags Magic Mountain • LGBT • www.outonthemountain.com

28-30: **Get Wet Weekend** *Curaçao, Netherlands Antilles, Caribbean*
discover the Caribbean Dutch Paradise of Curaçao! • gay/ lesbian • 599/9510-6479, 599/9510-6499 • www.gaycuracao.com

TBA: **Black Gay Pride** *Dallas, TX*
LGBT • 214/440-9300 • dfwpridemovement.org

TBA: **Howl Festival** *New York City, NY*
a cabaret from the underworld • outdoor murals • hip hop howl • all in Tompkins Square Park • mixed gay/ straight • 212/243-3413 • www.howlfestival.com

TBA: **Pink Season** *Hong Kong, China*
2 month festival featuring speakers, plays, dance parties, pageants & more • LGBT • www.pinkseason.hk

TBA: **Seattle AIDS Walk** *Seattle, WA*
mixed gay/ straight • 4000+ attendees • 206/328-8979 • www.SeattleAIDSWalk.org

October

ongoing: **October is Breast Cancer Awareness Month**   *Cross-country, USA*
check local listings for fund-raising events in your area to fight breast cancer •

5-7: **Gay Days Anaheim**   *Anaheim, CA*
"join 30,000 GLBT mouseketeers as we turn the happiest place in earth into the gayest!" •
www.GayDaysAnaheim.com

5-7: **Gaylaxicon**   *Minneapolis, MN*
LGBT science fiction, fantasy, horror & gaming convention • **www.gaylaxicon2012.org**

7: **Castro Street Fair**   *San Francisco, CA*
performance, arts & community groups street fair • co-founded by Harvey Milk • 415/841-1824 •
www.castrostreetfair.org

10-Nov 10: **Glasgay!**   *Glasgow, Scotland*
UK's largest lesbian & gay multi-arts festival • 44-141/552-7575 • **www.glasgay.com**

11: **National Coming Out Day**   *Cross-country, USA*
check local listings for events in your area or visit www.hrc.com/ncop • 202/628-4160,
800/777-4723 • **www.hrc.org/comingout**

11-14: **Sundance Stompede**   *San Francisco, CA*
San Francisco's annual country/ western dance weekend • LGBT • 415/820-1403 • **www.stom-pede.com**

14: **AIDS Walk Atlanta & 5k Run**   *Atlanta, GA*
mixed gay/ straight • 10,000+ attendees • 404/876-9255 • **aidswalkatlanta.com**

14: **AIDS Walk LA**   *Los Angeles, CA*
annual AIDS fundraiser in West Hollywood • mixed gay/ straight • 213/201-9255 •
www.aidswalk.net

TBA: **Black Pride**   *Nashville, TN*
gay/ lesbian • 615/974-2832, 800/845-4266x269 • **www.brothersunited.com**

TBA: **Taiwan LGBT Pride**   *Taipei, Taiwan*
• **www.twpride.org**

November

3-4: **Greater Palm Springs Pride**   *Palm Springs, CA*
free entertainment, dance parties, lots of people & a parade on Sunday • 760/416-8711 •
www.PSPride.org

TBA: **Tranny Fest**   *San Francisco, CA*
transgender multi-arts festival • **www.trannyfest.com**

December

12-16: **IAGLBC Annual Bridge Tournament**   *Palm Springs, CA*
Int'l Association of Gay & Lesbian Bridge Clubs • **www.GayBridge.org**

31: **Mummer's Strut**   *Philadelphia, PA*
big New Year's Eve party • followed by New Year's Day Parade • mixed gay/ straight • $40-50 •
215/336-3050 • **www.mummers.com**

TBA: **Holly Folly**   *Provincetown, MA*
lesbian/ gay holiday celebration • fabulous parties • holiday concert • open houses • 1st wknd in
December • **www.ptown.org**

WOMEN'S FESTIVALS, PARTIES & GATHERINGS

January

12-16: **Silver Threads Celebration**   *St Petersburg Beach, FL*
4 day celebration for lesbians over 50 & their younger friends • women only • **www.silverthread-scelebration.org**

February

16-20: **Vallarta Girl**   *Puerto Vallarta, Mexico*
dance parties, booze cruise, lots of fun in the sun • **www.vallartagirl.com**

29-March 5: **Winter Party for Women**   *Miami/South Beach, FL*
mostly women • 305/495-6969 (tickets) • **www.pandoraevents.com**

March

28-April 1: **Club Skirts Dinah Shore Weekend**   *Palm Springs, CA*
women only • 415/596-8730 • **www.thedinah.com**

TBA: **Girl Bar Dinah Shore Weekend**   *Las Vegas, NV*
Girl Bar mega party moves to Vegas • 5,000-8,000 attend • see website for ticket info • also www.girlbar.com • dinahshorevip@aol.com • women only • 310/659-4551 • **www.dinahshore-weekend.com**

April

TBA: **Women's Fun Weekend**   *County Cork, Ireland*
entertainment, sports, dance parties & more! • women only • **www.corkwomensfunweekend.ie**

May

25-28: **Women Outdoors National Gathering**   *Hancock, NH*
camping • hiking • workshops • women only • 110+ attendees • $120-220 • **www.womenout-doors.org**

31-June 3: **Silver Threads North**   *Rehoboth Beach, DE*
4 day celebration for lesbians over 50 & their younger friends • women only • 516/342-6026 • **www.silverthreadsnorth.com**

TBA: **Russian River Women's Wknd**   *Guerneville, CA*
this village is packed w/ dykes for a weekend of pool parties, bumpin' night life, comedy, sports, outdoor activities & more • 75 miles north of San Francisco • mostly women • **www.russian-riverwomensweekend.org**

TBA: **Herland Bi-Annual Retreats**   *Oklahoma City, OK*
music, workshops, campfire events & potluck • girls of all ages & boys under 10 welcome • also in October • women only • 405/521-9696 • **www.herlandsisters.org**

June·

23: **San Francisco Dyke March**   *San Francisco, CA*
join thousands of dykes of all shapes, colors & sizes for music, marching & more through the streets of the Mission & the Castro • women only • 510/533-5489 • **www.thedykemarch.org**

TBA: **Eastern Ontario Womyn's Drum Camp**   *near Sarnia, ON and Port Huron, MI*
all levels welcome • women only • 180 attendees • 613/599-4274 • **www.drumcamps.ca**

July

18-21: **Deaf Lesbian Festival**   *Chicago, IL*
a celebration & global gathering of culturally identified deaf & lesbian women • www.deaflesbianfestival.org

19-22: **OLOC (Old Lesbians Organizing for Change) Nat'l Gathering**   *Tacoma, WA*
lesbians 60+ gather for workshops, guest speakers & entertainment to promote old lesbian pride & fight ageism • women only • 888/706-7506 • www.oloc.org

TBA: **Fabulosa**   *Marin, CA*
women-centered music wknd • healing arts, film & crafts • mostly women • 415/624-9390 • www.fabulosafest.com

TBA: **Girl Splash**   *Provincetown, MA*
4 days of comedy, music, dance parties & more • mostly women • www.womeninnkeepers.com

TBA: **National Women's Music Festival**   *Middleton, WI*
check website for details • mostly women • 317/713-1144 • www.wiaonline.org

August

7-12: **Michigan Womyn's Music Festival**   *near Hart, MI*
theater, music & dance performances • workshops, film festival & craft fair • ASL interpreting & differently-abled resources • child care • camping • women only • 5000-8000 attendees • 231/757-4766 • www.michfest.com

16-19: **Dinah Does San Francisco**   *San Francisco, CA*
presented by Lucy & Gail • the premiere vacation destination for lesbians of color, their partners & friends • women only • 760/416-3545 • www.dinahincolor.com

31-Sept 2: **Festival of Babes**   *Pacific Northwest, USA*
fun, frivolous & flirtatious soccer tournament • Int'l Babes play hard & party harder • rotates btwn Vancouver, Seattle, Portland & San Francisco • women only • www.festivalofthebabes.com

TBA: **Femme 2012**   *Oakland, CA*
femmes from all over the country converge for a hot weekend • www.femmecollective.com

TBA: **Girlie Circuit**   *Barcelona, Spain*
water park events • club nights • pool parties • films, discussions & more • gay/ lesbian • www.circuitfestival.net

TBA: **Women in the Woods**   *Portland, OR*
rustic cabins • natural hot springs • all meals included • women only • 300-400 attendees • 503/284-0722 • www.womeninthewoods.com

TBA: **Womyn's Gathering**   *Louisa, VA*
last wknd in Aug • camping, music & workshops • mixed gay/ straight • $40-140 • 540/894-5126 • www.twinoaks.org/community/women

September

4-9: **WomenFest**   *Key West, FL*
live music • film festival • pool parties • comedy show • dance parties • golf tournament • women only • 800/535-7797 • www.womenfest.com

7-9: **Ohio Lesbian Festival**   *Kirkersville (E of Columbus), OH*
women only • 2000-3000 attendees • 614/578-1764 • www.ohiolba.org

7-9: **Sisterspace Wknd**   *Darlington, MD*
sliding scale • women only • 215/546-4890 • www.sisterspace.org

8-11: **BOLDFest**   *Vancouver, BC, Canada*
Bold Old(er) Lesbians & Dykes meet up for the annual West Coast gathering • 604/253-7189 • www.boldfest.com

29: Houston Women's Music Festival · *Houston, TX*
women from Texas & beyond gather to enjoy music, art, culture & community & a vendor marketplace • produced by the Athena Art Project • mostly women • 1,500 attendees • www.hwfestival.org

TBA: Cambria Women's Weekend · *Cambria, CA*
where the forest meets the ocean and the women come OUT to play! • 310/578-8888 • www.cambriawomensweekend.com

TBA: Iowa Women's Music Festival · *Iowa City, IA*
mostly women • 319/335-1486 • www.prairievoices.net

TBA: Women of the Woods · *Dahlonega, GA*
celebrate the fall solstice with drum circles & fireside jams • women only • 404/502-3539 • www.woodsfest.org

October

5-14: Provincetown Women's Week · *Provincetown, MA*
very popular – make your reservations early! • also Single Women's Weekend in May • mostly women • 5000+ attendees • www.womeninnkeepers.com

TBA: Decibelle · *Chicago, IL*
workshops, panels, cinema & rockin' concerts featuring groundbreaking, fearless women artists • 303/946-9227 • www.decibelle.org

TBA: WomynSpirit Festival · *Orangeville, ON, Canada*
celebrate Samhain at this queer-friendly womyn's pagan weekend • women only • 416/481-7634 • sites.google.com/site/womynspirit/Home

November

16-18: **Nia Gathering** *Petaluma, CA*
   lesbians of African descent gather to reflect on the past & build a postive future • women only • 510/869-4403 • **www.niacollective.org**

21-25: **Women's White Party** *Miami, FL*
   mostly women • 305/495-6969 (tickets) • **www.womenswhiteparty.com**

FILM FESTIVALS

January

23-Feb 4: **Reelout Queer Film & Video Festival** *Kingston, ON, Canada*
   celebrating the best of queer independent film & video • 613/549-7335 • **www.reelout.com**

TBA: **Zinegoak** *Bilbao, Spain*
   LGBT film festival • 34–94/415-6258 • **www.zinegoak.com**

February

TBA: **Mardi Gras Film Festival** *Sydney, Australia*
   Sydney film festival corresponds with massive Mardi Gras event • 61–2/9332-4938 • **www.queer-screen.com.au**

March

15-25: **Melbourne Queer Film Festival** *Melbourne, Australia*
   613/9662-4147 • **www.mqff.com.au**

TBA: **Fusion** *Los Angeles, CA*
   Los Angeles' LGBT people of color film festival • 213/480-7088 • **www.outfest.org/fusion.html**

TBA: **London Lesbian & Gay Film Festival** *London, England*
   grab your tickets for the largest LGBT film fest in Europe • 44 (0)20/7928-3232 • **www.llgff.org.uk**

TBA: **Out at the Movies** *Canton, NY*
   LGBT film festival for Northern New York • **www.outatthemovies.org**

TBA: **Verzaubert Int'l Queer Film Festival** *Berlin, Germany*
   screening in Berlin, Cologne, Frankfurt & Munich • also fall screening in November • LGBT • 49–30/861-4532 • **www.verzaubertfilmfest.com**

April

18-22: **FilmOut San Diego** *San Diego, CA*
   LGBT film festival • 619/512-5157 • **www.filmoutsandiego.com**

20-22: **London Lesbian Film Festival** *London, ON, Canada*
   women only Fri-Sat, open to all on Sunday • **www.llff.ca**

TBA: **Brisbane Queer Film Festival** *Brisbane, Australia*
   61 7/3358 8600 • **www.bqff.com.au**

TBA: **Miami Gay & Lesbian Film Festival** *Miami, FL*
   305/534-9924 • **www.MGLFF.com**

TBA: **Out in Africa** *Cape Town, South Africa*
   the only film festival of its kind on the African continent • three 10-day festivals throughout the year • also August & October • also in Johannesburg • 27 21/461 40 27 • **www.oia.co.za**

TBA: **QFest** *St Louis, MO*
   314/289-4152 • **www.stlqfest.org**

May

3-13: **Boston LGBT Film Festival**   *Boston, MA*
617/369-3300 • www.bostonlgbtfilmfest.org

17-27: **Inside Out: Toronto LGBT Film & Video Festival**   *Toronto, ON, Canada*
416/977-6847 • www.insideout.ca

24-June 2: **Fairy Tales Int'l LGBT Film Festival**   *Calgary, AB, Canada*
403/244-1956 • www.fairytalesfilmfest.com

31-June 3: **Q Cinema**   *Fort Worth, TX*
annual celebration of LGBT-themed movies • 817/723-4358 • www.qcinema.org

TBA: **Honolulu Rainbow Film Festival**   *Honolulu, HI*
808/675-8428 • www.hglcf.org

TBA: **Out Takes LGBT Film Festival**   *Wellington, New Zealand*
week-long festival in Auckland & Wellington • 64-4/972-6775 • www.outtakes.org.nz

TBA: **Translations: Transgender Film Festival**   *Seattle, WA*
206/323-4274 • www.threedollarbillcinema.org

June

1-9: **Connecticut Gay & Lesbian Film Festival**   *Hartford, CT*
gay & lesbian film festival at Cinestudio • 860/586-1136 • www.outfilmct.org

8-10: **Queer Women of Color Film Festival**   *San Francisco, CA*
part of the Nat'l Queer Arts Festival • 415/752-0868 • www.qwocmap.org

9-16: **TLVFest: The Tel Aviv LGBT Film Festival**   *Tel Aviv, Israel*
films will also show in Jerusalem & Haifa • 972-52/875-7955 • www.tlvfest.com

13-17: **Provincetown Int'l Film Festival**   *Provincetown, MA*
mixed gay/ straight • 508/487-3456 • www.ptownfilmfest.org

14-24: **Frameline: San Francisco Int'l LGBT Film Festival**   *San Francisco, CA*
get your tickets early for a slew of films about us • LGBT • 65,000+ attendees • 415/703-8650 •
www.frameline.org

TBA: **Identities Queer Film Festival**   *Vienna, Austria*
43-1/524-6274 • www.identities.at/index/en/

TBA: **Mix Milano Int'l LGBT Film Festival**   *Milan, Italy*
• www.cinemagaylesbico.com

TBA: **NewFest: New York LGBT Film Festival**   *New York City, NY*
646/290-8136 • www.newfest.org

July

12-22: **Outfest**   *Los Angeles, CA*
Los Angeles' lesbian/ gay film & video festival in mid-July • 213/480-7088 • www.outfest.org

TBA: **Fire Island Film & Video Festival**   *Fire Island, NY*
• www.liglff.org

TBA: **Gaze: Dublin Int'l Lesbian & Gay Film Festival**   *Dublin, Ireland*
• www.gaze.ie

TBA: **Mostra Lambda Barcelona**   *Barcelona, Spain*
LGBT film festival • www.cinemalambda.com

TBA: **Philadelphia QFest**   *Philadelphia, PA*
267/765-9800 • www.phillycinema.org

TBA: **Tokyo Int'l Lesbian & Gay Film Festival**   *Tokyo, Japan*
• www.tokyo-lgff.org

August

7-12: **Flickers: Rhode Island Int'l Film Festival**   *Providence, RI*
don't miss the Gay & Lesbian Film Fest • mixed gay/ straight • 401/861-4445 • **www.film-festival.org**

10-19: **North Carolina Gay & Lesbian Film Festival**   *Durham, NC*
919/560-3030 (box office), 919/560-3040 • **festivals.carolinatheatre.org/ncglff**

TBA: **Birmingham Shout**   *Birmingham, AL*
LGBT film festival • 205/324-0888 • **www.bhamshout.com**

TBA: **Vancouver Queer Film & Video Festival**   *Vancouver, BC, Canada*
LGBT • 604/844-1615 • **www.queerfilmfestival.ca**

September

TBA: **Austin Gay & Lesbian International Film Festival**   *Austin, TX*
512/302-9889 • **www.agliff.org**

TBA: **Fresno Reel Pride**   *Fresno, CA*
annual lesbian & gay film festival in central California • 559/999-7971 • **www.reelpride.com**

TBA: **Milwaukee LGBT Film/ Video Festival**   *Milwaukee, WI*
414/229-4758 • **www4.uwm.edu/psoa/programs/film/lgbtfilm**

TBA: **Outflix**   *Memphis, TN*
LGBT film festival • **www.outflixfestival.org**

TBA: **Pikes Peak Lavender Film Festival**   *Colorado Springs, CO*
719/633-5600 • **www.pplff.org**

TBA: **Queer Lisbon**   *Lisbon, Portugal*
Portugal's only LGBT film festival • 351 91/335-8603 • **www.queerlisboa.pt**

October

4-11: **Out on Film**   *Atlanta, GA*
LGBT • 678/671-9446 • **www.outonfilm.org**

5-11: **Southwest Gay & Lesbian Film Festival**   *Albuquerque, NM*
also in Santa Fe, NM • 505/243-1870 • **www.closetcinema.org**

12-21: **Pittsburgh Int'l Lesbian & Gay Film Festival**   *Pittsburgh, PA*
412/422-6776 • **www.plgfs.org**

25-Nov 4: **Barcelona Int'l Gay & Lesbian Film Festival**   *Barcelona, Spain*
gay/ lesbian • 973/664-421 • **www.barcelonafilmfestival.org**

25-Nov 4: **image+nation: Montréal Int'l LGBT Film Festival**   *Montréal, QC, Canada*
LGBT • 514/285-4467 • **www.image-nation.org**

TBA: **Berlin Lesbian Film Festival**   *Berlin, Germany*
49-172/381-2883 • **www.lesbenfilmfestival.de**

TBA: **Cheries-Cheris: Paris Gay, Lesbian & Trans Film Festival**   *Paris, France*
• **www.cheries-cheris.com**

TBA: **Cineffable: Paris Int'l Lesbian & Feminist Film Festival**   *Paris, France*
• **www.cineffable.fr**

TBA: **Copenhagen Gay & Lesbian Film Festival**   *Copenhagen, Denmark*
45/2843-4217 • **www.cglff.dk**

TBA: **Hamburg Int'l Lesbian & Gay Film Festival**   *Hamburg, Germany*
49-40/348-0670 • **www.lsf-hamburg.de**

three
dollar bill
cinema

Coming to Seattle?
We want to show
you a good time.

Keeping audiences entertained since 1996, Three Dollar
Bill Cinema promotes and produces LGBT film events
throughout the year, including free outdoor movies
every summer, our Spring Film Series of vintage queer
classics, the Seattle Lesbian & Gay Film Festival in
October, and other unique events.

*Check out our website or find us on Facebook and Twitter
to see what's happening on your next visit to Seattle.*

three
dollar bill
cinema

TBA: **Madrid LGBT Film Festival** — *Madrid, Spain*
34–91/593–0540 • www.lesgaicinemad.com

TBA: **Portland Lesbian & Gay Film Festival** — *Portland, OR*
• www.plgff.org

TBA: **Q Film Festival** — *Long Beach, CA*
showcasing films of interest to the queer community • 562/434–4455 •
www.qfilmslongbeach.com

TBA: **Reel Affirmations: The Nation's LGBT Film Festival** — *Washington, DC*
lesbian/ gay films • 202/349–7358 • www.reelaffirmations.org

TBA: **Sacramento Int'l Gay & Lesbian Film Festival** — *Sacramento, CA*
916/677–1500 • www.siglff.org

TBA: **Seattle Lesbian & Gay Film Festival** — *Seattle, WA*
206/323–4274 • www.threedollarbillcinema.org

TBA: **St John's International Women's Film Festival** — *St John's, NL, Canada*
mixed gay/ straight • 4500 attendees • 709/754–3141 • www.womensfilmfestival.com

TBA: **Tampa Bay Int'l Gay & Lesbian Film Festival** — *Tampa Bay, FL*
813/879–4220 • www.tiglff.com

November

1-10: **Reeling: Chicago Lesbian & Gay Int'l Film Fest** — *Chicago, IL*
773/293–1447 • www.reelingfilmfestival.org

TBA: **Hong Kong Lesbian/ Gay Film Festival** — *Hong Kong, China*
LGBT • 852/2311 8081 • www.hklgff.hk

TBA: **Long Island Gay & Lesbian Film Festival** — *Huntington, NY*
• www.liglff.org

TBA: **Mezipatra** — *Prague, Czech Republic*
Czech LGBT film festival • www.mezipatra.cz

TBA: **Mix: New York Lesbian & Gay
Experimental Film Fest** — *New York City, NY*
film, videos, installations & media performances • write for info • 212/742–8880 •
www.mixnyc.org

TBA: **OUT TAKES Dallas** — *Dallas, TX*
LGBT film festival • 972/988–6333 • www.outtakesdallas.org

LEATHER & FETISH EVENTS

January

13-16: **Mid-Atlantic Leather Weekend**   *Washington, DC*
LGBT • 202/588–2562 • www.leatherweekend.com

20-22: **Southwest Leather Conference**   *Phoenix, AZ*
workshops, vendors & fetish ball • MASTER/slave, Bootblack & Daddy/boy contests • LGBT •
www.southwestleather.org

March

29-April 1: **International Ms Bootblack Contest**   *San Francisco, CA*
workshops • parties • vending • contest takes place the weekend of International Ms Leather
weekend • mixed gay/ straight • **www.IMsL.org**

29-April 1: **International Ms Leather Contest**   *San Francisco, CA*
contest • workshops • parties • vending • mixed gay/ straight • **www.IMsL.org**

April

5-8: **Rubbout**   *Vancouver, BC, Canada*
don't miss this annual gay rubber weekend • men only • 604/683–8000 • **www.rubbout.com**

13-15: **Leather Leadership Conference**   *Nashville, TN*
join us to develop & strengthen problem-solving & camaraderie in the leather community • LGBT
• **www.leatherleadership.org**

20-22: **Rocky Mountain Olympus Leather**   *Salt Lake City, UT*
leather competition • participants from Utah, Colorado, Wyoming, Idaho & Montana • mixed gay/
straight • 200 attendees • 415/409–9447 • **www.rockymountainolympus.com**

May

18-20: **Northwest Leather Celebration**   *San Jose, CA*
host of the NW regional Master/slave contest • LGBT • **www.northwestleathercelebration.com**

June

7-10: **Southeast Leatherfest**   • *Atlanta, GA*
LGBT • **www.seleatherfest.com**

8-11: **Desire: Leather Women Unleashed**   *Palm Springs, CA*
weekend retreat for leather- & kinky women • women only • 206/963–5844 • **www.desire-
leatherwomen.com**

TBA: **Folsom Street East**   *New York City, NY*
New York City's answer to the famous San Francisco fetish street fair • LGBT • **www.folsom-
streeteast.org**

July

12-15: **International Deaf Leather**   *Baltimore, MD*
weekend of events, including Mr & Ms Deaf Leather Contest •
www.internationaldeafleather.org

13-15: **Thunder in the Mountains**   *Denver, CO*
weekend of pansexual leather events & seminars • kinky comedy revue • talent show • LGBT •
800# attendees • 303/698–1207 • **www.thunderinthemountains.com**

TBA: **CampOUT** *Walton, WV*
games, auctions, a fully equipped outdoor dungeon & swimming • presented by La Garou Leather Club • trans-oriented • everyone welcome to attend regardless of sexual orientation or gender identity • LGBT • 419/376-6724 • **www.transcampout.org**

August

TBA: **Pantheon of Leather** *Los Angeles, CA*
annual leather/ SM/ fetish community service awards & int'l Mr & Ms Olympus Leather • mixed gay/ straight • **www.internationalolympusleather.com**

September

3: **Folsom Europe** *Berlin, Germany*
• **www.folsomeurope.info**

TBA: **Folsom Street Fair** *San Francisco, CA*
huge SM/ leather street fair, topping a week of kinky events • LGBT • thousands of local & visiting kinky men & women attendees • 415/777-3247 • **www.folsomstreetevents.org**

TBA: **Venus' Playground at Folsom Street Fair** *San Francisco, CA*
separate space at Folsom Street Fair for women & genderqueer participants • play, chill, socialize • performances, demos & more • see ad below • 415/777-3247 • **www.folsomstreetevents.org/women**

November

TBA: **Santa Clara County Leather Weekend** *San Jose, CA*
leather fellowship in the San Jose area • LGBT • **www.SCCLeather.org**

CONFERENCES & RETREATS

January

25-29: **Creating Change Conference**   *Baltimore, MD*
for lesbians, gays, bisexuals, transgender people & allies seeking positive & enduring political &
social change • 2500+ attendees • 617/492-6393 • **www.creatingchange.org**

May

TBA: **Lambda Literary Awards**   *New York City, NY*
the Lammies are the Oscars of LGBT writing & publishing • LGBT • 213/458-3570 • **www.lamb-daliterary.org**

TBA: **Saints & Sinners**   *New Orleans, LA*
LGBT writers & readers from around the country gather for a hot weekend of readings, panels &
performance • 300 attendees • $100 • 504/581-1144 • **www.sasfest.com**

June

13-17: **GCLS Annual Literary Convention**   *Minneapolis, MN*
The Golden Crown Literary Society (GCLS) annual gathering for the enjoyment, discussion &
enhancement of lesbian literature • 956/434-6015 • **www.goldencrown.org**

July

TBA: **Transgender Leadership Summit**   *TBA, USA*
join transgender activists to help create a unified voice to advance the movement for transgender
equality • 200+ attendees • 415/865-0176 • **www.transgenderlawcenter.org**

August

2-5: **Gender Odyssey**   *Seattle, WA*
3 days of panels, workshops & meetings • entertainment, art exhibit & vendors • focus on trans-
men, transwomen & families with transgender children & teens • open to all • 206/306-8383 •
www.genderodyssey.org

September

TBA: **Nat'l Lesbian & Gay Journalists Assoc Convention**   *TBA, USA*
workshops • keynote speakers • entertainment • 202/588-9888 x10 • **www.nlgja.org**

TBA: **Southern Comfort Conference**   *Atlanta, GA*
entertainers & leaders from the entire spectrum of the transgender community offering 5 days of
learning, networking & fun • 702/336-1202 • **www.sccatl.org**

October

TBA: **National LGBT MBA Conference**   *TBA, USA*
career fair & discussions of sexual orientation, gender & leadership in the workplace by MBA students & out Fortune 500 company leaders • LGBT • 800+ attendees • **www.reachingoutmba.org**

SPIRITUAL

February

17-20: **PantheaCon**   *San Jose, CA*
pagan convention • mixed gay/ straight • 510/653-3244 • **www.ancientways.com**

May

TBA: **A Gathering of Priestesses & Goddess Women**   *Wisconsin Dells, Southwestern WI*
women's spirituality conference • also Hallows Gathering in October • women only •
608/226-9998 • **www.rcgi.org**

June

17-24: **Pagan Spirit Gathering**   *TBA, USA*
summer solstice celebration • primitive camping • workshops • rituals • advance registration
required • mixed gay/ straight • 608/924-2216 • **www.circlesanctuary.org/psg**

August

9-12: **Elderflower Womenspirit Festival**   *Mendocino, CA*
earth-based spirituality retreat for women and girls • honoring the feminine through the Goddess
• women & girls only • 415/339-8000 • **elderflower.org**

TBA: **BC Witchcamp**   *near Vancouver, BC, Canada*
weeklong Wiccan intensive at Evans Lake • mixed gay/ straight • 250/598-9229 • **www.bcwitch-camp.ca**

BREAST CANCER BENEFITS

March

TBA: **Boarding for Breast Cancer Board-a-thon**   *TBA, USA*
help raise money & awareness for breast cancer • live music & pro exihibitions at ski resorts
around the country • mixed gay/ straight • 323/467-2663 • **www.b4bc.org**

July

27-29: **Susan G Komen 3 Day for the Cure**   *Boston, MA*
walk 60 miles in 3 days to raise money for the Susan G Komen Breast Cancer Foundation • mixed
gay/ straight • 800/996-3329 • **www.the3day.org**

August

10-12: **Susan G Komen 3 Day for the Cure**   *Chicago, IL*
walk 60 miles in 3 days to raise money for the Susan G Komen Breast Cancer Foundation • mixed
gay/ straight • 800/996-3329 • **www.the3day.org**

17-19: **Susan G Komen 3 Day for the Cure**   *Detroit, MI*
walk 60 miles in 3 days to raise money for the Susan G Komen Breast Cancer Foundation • mixed
gay/ straight • 800/996-3329 • **www.the3day.org**

24-26: **Susan G Komen 3 Day for the Cure**   *Minneapolis/ St Paul, MN*
walk 60 miles in 3 days to raise money for the Susan G Komen Breast Cancer Foundation • mixed
gay/ straight • 800/996-3329 • **www.the3day.org**

September

14-16: **Susan G Komen 3 Day for the Cure**   *Seattle, WA*
walk 60 miles in 3 days to raise money for the Susan G Komen Breast Cancer Foundation • mixed
gay/ straight • 800/996-3329 • **www.the3day.org**